Mexico City Metro

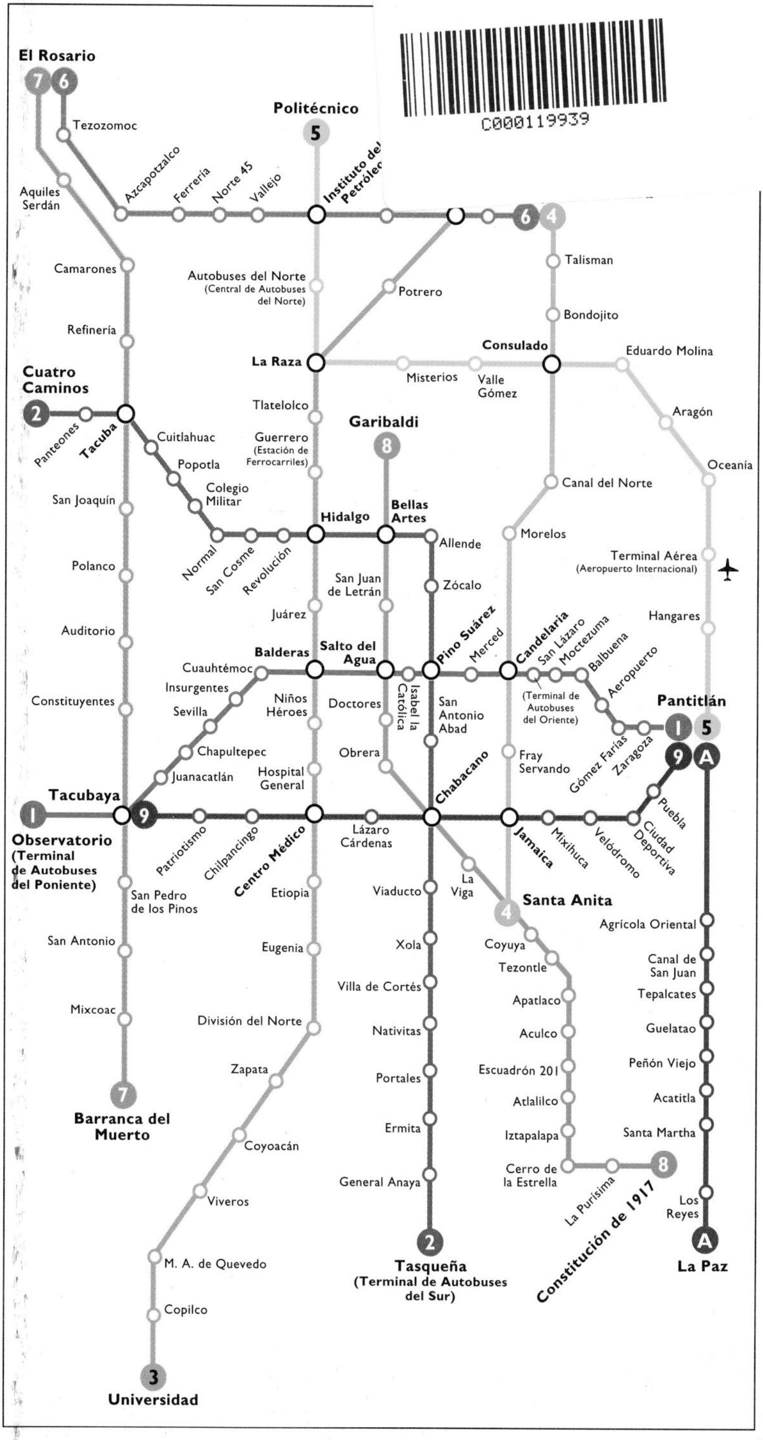

El Rosario
7
6
Tezozomoc
Azcapotzalco
Ferrería
Norte 45
Vallejo
Politécnico
5
Instituto
Aquiles Serdán
Camarones
Autobuses del Norte (Central de Autobuses del Norte)
Potrero
Talisman
Bondojito
Refinería
Consulado
Eduardo Molina
La Raza
Misterios
Valle Gómez
Cuatro Caminos
2
Panteones
Tacuba
Tlatelolco
Garibaldi
8
Aragón
Cuitlahuac
Popotla
Guerrero (Estación de Ferrocarriles)
Oceanía
Colegio Militar
Canal del Norte
San Joaquín
Hidalgo
Bellas Artes
Normal
San Cosme
Revolución
Allende
Morelos
Terminal Aérea (Aeropuerto Internacional)
Polanco
Zócalo
San Juan de Letrán
Juárez
Auditorio
Hangares
Balderas
Salto del Agua
Pino Suárez
Merced
Candelaria
San Lázaro
Moctezuma
Balbuena
Aeropuerto
Cuauhtémoc
Insurgentes
Sevilla
Niños Héroes
Doctores
Isabel la Católica
San Antonio Abad
(Terminal de Autobuses del Oriente)
Pantitlán
Constituyentes
1
5
Chapultepec
Obrera
Fray Servando
Gómez Farías
Zaragoza
9
A
Juanacatlán
Hospital General
Chabacano
Tacubaya
1
9
Observatorio (Terminal de Autobuses del Poniente)
Patriotismo
Chilpancingo
Centro Médico
Lázaro Cárdenas
Jamaica
Mixihuca
Velódromo
Ciudad Deportiva
Puebla
San Pedro de los Pinos
Etiopia
Viaducto
La Viga
Santa Anita
4
Agrícola Oriental
San Antonio
Eugenia
Xola
Coyuya
Tezontle
Canal de San Juan
Villa de Cortés
Apatlaco
Tepalcates
Mixcoac
División del Norte
Nativitas
Aculco
Guelatao
Zapata
Portales
Escuadrón 201
Peñón Viejo
7
Atlalilco
Acatitla
Barranca del Muerto
Ermita
Iztapalapa
Santa Martha
Coyoacán
Cerro de la Estrella
8
General Anaya
Viveros
La Purísima
Los Reyes
Constitución de 1917
2
A
M. A. de Quevedo
Tasqueña (Terminal de Autobuses del Sur)
La Paz
Copilco
3
Universidad

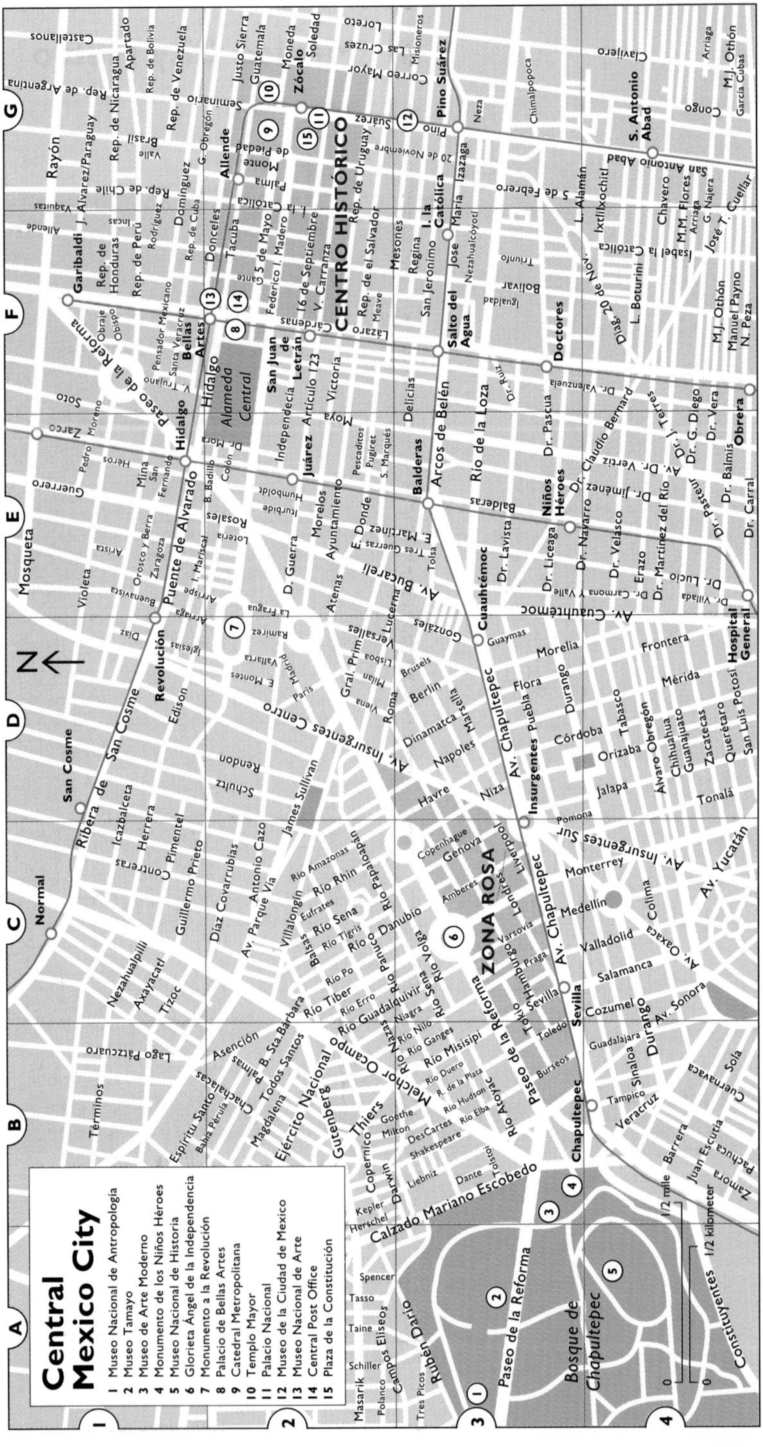
Central Mexico City
1 Museo Nacional de Antropología
2 Museo Tamayo
3 Museo de Arte Moderno
4 Monumento de los Niños Héroes
5 Museo Nacional de Historia
6 Glorieta Ángel de la Independencia
7 Monumento a la Revolución
8 Palacio de Bellas Artes
9 Catedral Metropolitana
10 Templo Mayor
11 Palacio Nacional
12 Museo de la Ciudad de Mexico
13 Museo Nacional de Arte
14 Central Post Office
15 Plaza de la Constitución
CENTRO HISTÓRICO
ZONA ROSA
Bosque de Chapultepec
Alameda Central
Paseo de la Reforma
Av. Insurgentes Sur
Av. Chapultepec
Av. Cuauhtémoc
Av. Bucareli
1/2 mile
1/2 kilometer

LET'S GO
Mexico

■ Let's Go writers travel on your budget.

"Guides that penetrate the veneer of the holiday brochures and mine the grit of real life."

—*The Economist*

"The writers seem to have experienced every rooster-packed bus and lunar-surfaced mattress about which they write."

—*The New York Times*

"All the dirt, dirt cheap."

—*People*

■ Great for independent travelers.

"The guides are aimed not only at young budget travelers but at the independent traveler, a sort of streetwise cookbook for traveling alone."

—*The New York Times*

"Flush with candor and irreverence, chock full of budget travel advice."

—*The Des Moines Register*

"An indispensable resource. *Let's Go*'s practical information can be used by every traveler."

—*The Chattanooga Free Press*

■ Let's Go is completely revised each year.

"Only *Let's Go* has the zeal to annually update every title on its list."

—*The Boston Globe*

"Unbeatable: good sight-seeing advice; up-to-date info on restaurants, hotels, and inns; a commitment to money-saving travel; and a wry style that brightens nearly every page."

—*The Washington Post*

■ All the important information you need.

"*Let's Go* authors provide a comedic element while still providing concise information and thorough coverage of the country. Anything you need to know about budget traveling is detailed in this book."

—*The Chicago Sun-Times*

"Value-packed, unbeatable, accurate, and comprehensive."

—*Los Angeles Times*

Let's Go Publications

Let's Go: Alaska & the Pacific Northwest 1999
Let's Go: Australia 1999
Let's Go: Austria & Switzerland 1999
Let's Go: Britain & Ireland 1999
Let's Go: California 1999
Let's Go: Central America 1999
Let's Go: Eastern Europe 1999
Let's Go: Ecuador & the Galápagos Islands 1999
Let's Go: Europe 1999
Let's Go: France 1999
Let's Go: Germany 1999
Let's Go: Greece 1999 **New title!**
Let's Go: India & Nepal 1999
Let's Go: Ireland 1999
Let's Go: Israel & Egypt 1999
Let's Go: Italy 1999
Let's Go: London 1999
Let's Go: Mexico 1999
Let's Go: New York City 1999
Let's Go: New Zealand 1999
Let's Go: Paris 1999
Let's Go: Rome 1999
Let's Go: South Africa 1999 **New title!**
Let's Go: Southeast Asia 1999
Let's Go: Spain & Portugal 1999
Let's Go: Turkey 1999 **New title!**
Let's Go: USA 1999
Let's Go: Washington, D.C. 1999

Let's Go Map Guides

Amsterdam	*Madrid*
Berlin	*New Orleans*
Boston	*New York City*
Chicago	*Paris*
Florence	*Rome*
London	*San Francisco*
Los Angeles	*Washington, D.C.*

Coming Soon: Prague, Seattle

Let's Go Publications

Let's Go Mexico 1999

Sonesh Chainani
Editor

Anne C. Krendl
Associate Editor

J. Lara Fox
Associate Editor

Researcher-Writers:
Jennifer Gootman
Art Koski-Karell
Maya Sen
Jim Stewart
Paul Torres
Keja Valens

Macmillan

HELPING LET'S GO

If you want to share your discoveries, suggestions, or corrections, please drop us a line. We read every piece of correspondence, whether a postcard, a 10-page email, or a coconut. Please note that mail received after May 1999 may be too late for the 2000 book, but will be kept for future editions. **Address mail to:**

Let's Go: Mexico
67 Mount Auburn Street
Cambridge, MA 02138
USA

Visit Let's Go at **http://www.letsgo.com,** or send email to:

feedback@letsgo.com
Subject: "Let's Go: Mexico"

In addition to the invaluable travel advice our readers share with us, many are kind enough to offer their services as researchers or editors. Unfortunately, our charter enables us to employ only currently enrolled Harvard-Radcliffe students.

Published in Great Britain 1999 by Macmillan, an imprint of Macmillan General Books, 25 Eccleston Place, London, SW1W 9NF and Basingstoke.

Published in the United States of America by St. Martin's Press, Inc.

ISBN: 0 333 74737 2

First edition
10 9 8 7 6 5 4 3 2 1

Let's Go: Mexico is written by Let's Go Publications, 67 Mount Auburn Street, Cambridge, MA 02138, USA.

Printed in the USA on recycled paper with biodegradable soy ink.

ADVERTISING DISCLAIMER

About Let's Go

THIRTY-NINE YEARS OF WISDOM

Back in 1960, a few students at Harvard University banded together to produce a 20-page pamphlet offering a collection of tips on budget travel in Europe. This modest, mimeographed packet, offered as an extra to passengers on student charter flights to Europe, met with instant popularity. The following year, students traveling to Europe researched the first, full-fledged edition of *Let's Go: Europe,* a pocket-sized book featuring honest, irreverent writing and a decidedly youthful outlook on the world. Throughout the 60s, our guides reflected the times; the 1969 guide to America led off by inviting travelers to "dig the scene" at San Francisco's Haight-Ashbury. During the 70s and 80s, we gradually added regional guides and expanded coverage into the Middle East and Central America. With the addition of our in-depth city guides, handy map guides, and extensive coverage of Asia and Australia, the 90s are also proving to be a time of explosive growth for Let's Go, and there's certainly no end in sight. The maiden edition of *Let's Go: South Africa,* our pioneer guide to sub-Saharan Africa, hits the shelves this year, along with the first editions of *Let's Go: Greece* and *Let's Go: Turkey.*

We've seen a lot in 39 years. *Let's Go: Europe* is now the world's bestselling international guide, translated into seven languages. And our new guides bring Let's Go's total number of titles, with their spirit of adventure and their reputation for honesty, accuracy, and editorial integrity, to 44. But some things never change: our guides are still researched, written, and produced entirely by students who know first-hand how to see the world on the cheap.

HOW WE DO IT

Each guide is completely revised and thoroughly updated every year by a well-traveled set of over 200 students. Every winter, we recruit over 160 researchers and 70 editors to write the books anew. After several months of training, researcher-writers hit the road for seven weeks of exploration, from Anchorage to Adelaide, Estonia to El Salvador, Iceland to Indonesia. Hired for their rare combination of budget travel sense, writing ability, stamina, and courage, these adventurous travelers know that train strikes, stolen luggage, food poisoning, and marriage proposals are all part of a day's work. Back at our offices, editors work from spring to fall, massaging copy written on Himalayan bus rides into witty yet informative prose. A student staff of typesetters, cartographers, publicists, and managers keeps our lively team together. In September, the collected efforts of the summer are delivered to our printer, who turns them into books in record time, so that you have the most up-to-date information available for your vacation. Even as you read this, work on next year's editions is well underway.

WHY WE DO IT

We don't think of budget travel as the last recourse of the destitute; we believe that it's the only way to travel. Living cheaply and simply brings you closer to the people and places you've been saving up to visit. Our books will ease your anxieties and answer your questions about the basics—so you can get off the beaten track and explore. Once you learn the ropes, we encourage you to put *Let's Go* down now and then to strike out on your own. You know as well as we that the best discoveries are often those you make yourself. When you find something worth sharing, please drop us a line. We're Let's Go Publications, 67 Mount Auburn St., Cambridge, MA 02138, USA (email: feedback@letsgo.com). For more info, visit our website, http://www.letsgo.com.

HAPPY TRAVELS!

Table of Contents

How to Use This Book

Congratulations: you've just bought yourself a best friend. *Let's Go: Mexico 1999* is written expressly for you, the adventurous, wise-cracking budget traveler. Our six researchers spent the summer of '98 on a shoestring budget with your concerns in mind: how to get from place to place, savor local cuisine, enjoy the evenings, and get some sleep—all in the most economic way possible. Even those not proficient in Spanish will have no problem comfortably meandering through Mexico; the **Glossary** and **Phrasebook** in our **Appendix** (see p. 600) contain not only translations but also essential Spanish words and phrases that cover the spectrum of travel talk.

A few more practicalities are in order. The first chapter of the book, **Essentials,** is bursting at the seams with information you'll want to look at before leaving—among many other things, it deals with passports, packing, mail systems, safety, volunteer opportunities, health, airfare, and Mexican laws. Sub-sections focus on the special needs of specific groups of travelers. Our **Introduction** chapter is a mini-essay on the richness of Mexico's history, politics, culture, and character. And then, there's the heart of the book—10 chapters of all-new, 1999 coverage that will bring you closer to the Mexican millennium. The coverage begins with the world's biggest metropolis, Mexico City; from there, chapters proceed roughly from northwest to southeast, starting with Baja California and ending with the Yucatán peninsula. Following each city's introduction, our **Practical Information** section will give you all the details you need. **Accommodations, Food, Sights,** and **Entertainment** come next; here we describe the very best of the very cheap in each department.

Please take note: **listings are subjectively given in order of value, according to our team's judgement.** This year, we've identified the researchers' favorite establishments in large towns with a , in addition to listing some superlatives toward the beginning of the book (see **Let's Go Picks,** p. xvi). Another addition to the guide is the **Highlights of the Region** box in each chapter, which lists some of the more famous sights; these are a good place to get ideas for regional itineraries.

That said, the best way to use the book is to put it down from time to time. We beg you not to use this book as an excuse not to get out and explore; the best budget gems are the ones you find yourself, and the best memories are the ones that occur when you veer off your itinerary into the unexpected. Remember, this is not a book of rules and regulations—it's your new buddy, your personal traveling companion. Inside, we reveal to you all the treasures we have found, in the hope that—if you don't already—you'll soon love Mexico as much as we do. Hidden within these pages are: a nude Emiliano Zapata, giant cheese balls, the biggest Club Med in the Western Hemisphere, floating *mariachis,* a religious ceremony involving Pepsi, 20th-century ruins, a training site for the Apollo moon mission, a cast-iron church, donkeys painted as zebras, a Viking living on the beach, self-flagellating nuns, the largest tree in the world, thousands of Mennonites, panda bears, a town created by tequila, the site of the most expensive movie ever made, and beaches of black sand.

Check 'em out....and don't forget to call home. Have a wonderful trip.

A NOTE TO OUR READERS

The information for this book was gathered by *Let's Go*'s researchers from May through August. Each listing is derived from the assigned researcher's opinion based upon his or her visit at a particular time. The opinions are expressed in a candid and forthright manner. Other travelers might disagree. Those traveling at a different time may have different experiences since prices, dates, hours, and conditions are always subject to change. You are urged to check beforehand to avoid inconvenience and surprises. Travel always involves a certain degree of risk, especially in low-cost areas. When traveling, especially on a budget, always take particular care to ensure your safety.

Maps

Color Maps

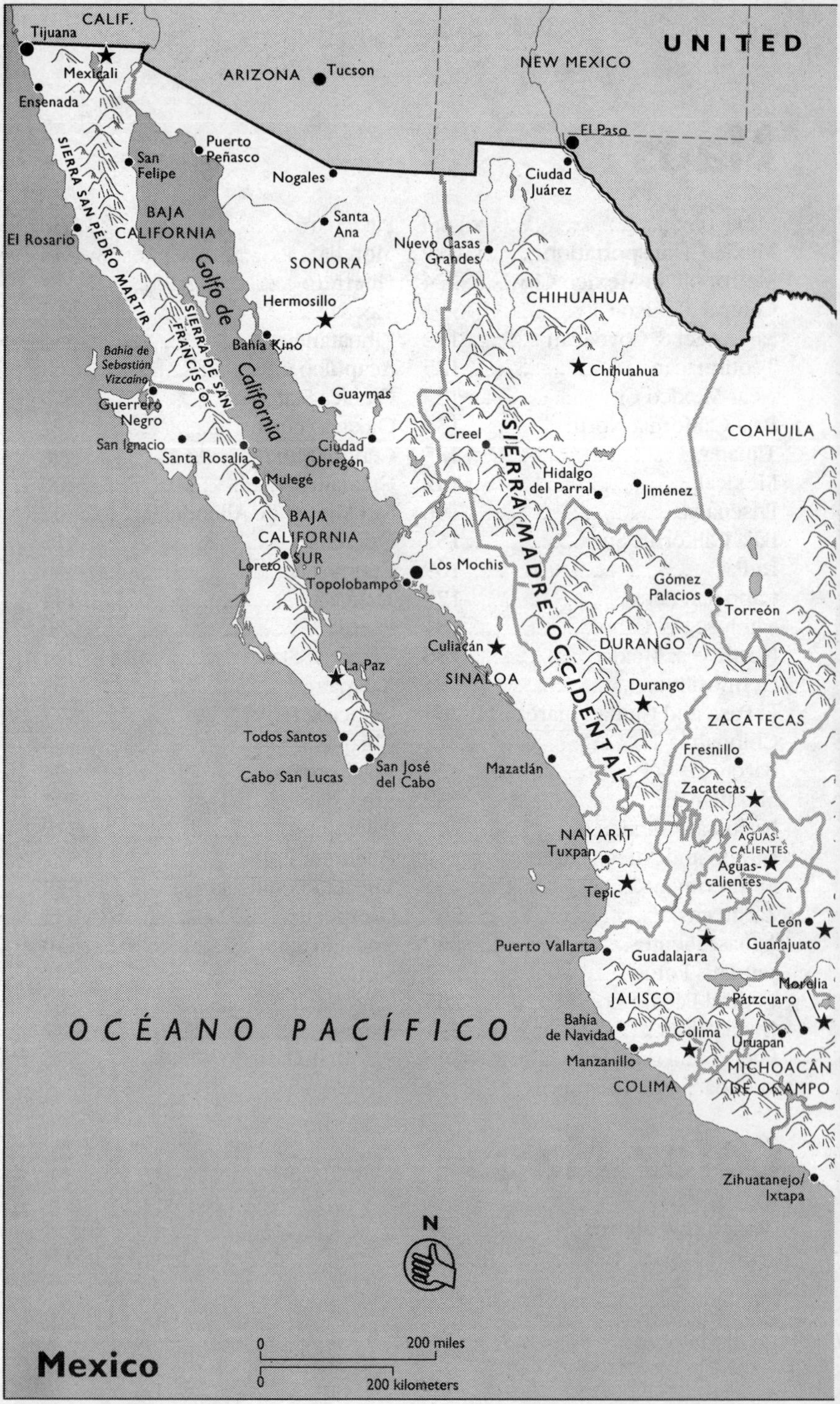
CALIF.
Tijuana
Mexicali
Ensenada
UNITED
NEW MEXICO
ARIZONA
Tucson
El Paso
Puerto Peñasco
San Felipe
Nogales
Ciudad Juárez
SIERRA SAN PEDRO MARTIR
BAJA CALIFORNIA
El Rosario
Santa Ana
Nuevo Casas Grandes
SONORA
Golfo de California
Hermosillo
CHIHUAHUA
SIERRA DE SAN FRANCISCO
Bahía Kino
Bahía de Sebastián Vizcaíno
Chihuahua
Guerrero Negro
Guaymas
San Ignacio
Santa Rosalía
Ciudad Obregón
Creel
COAHUILA
SIERRA MADRE OCCIDENTAL
Hidalgo del Parral
Jiménez
Mulegé
BAJA CALIFORNIA SUR
Loreto
Los Mochis
Topolobampo
Gómez Palacios
Torreón
Culiacán
DURANGO
La Paz
SINALOA
Durango
ZACATECAS
Todos Santos
Fresnillo
Mazatlán
Cabo San Lucas
San José del Cabo
Zacatecas
NAYARIT
Tuxpan
AGUAS-CALIENTES
Aguascalientes
Tepic
León
Puerto Vallarta
Guanajuato
Guadalajara
Morelia
JALISCO
Pátzcuaro
OCÉANO PACÍFICO
Bahía de Navidad
Colima
Uruapan
Manzanillo
MICHOACÁN DE OCAMPO
COLIMA
Zihuatanejo/Ixtapa
N
Mexico
0
200 miles
0
200 kilometers

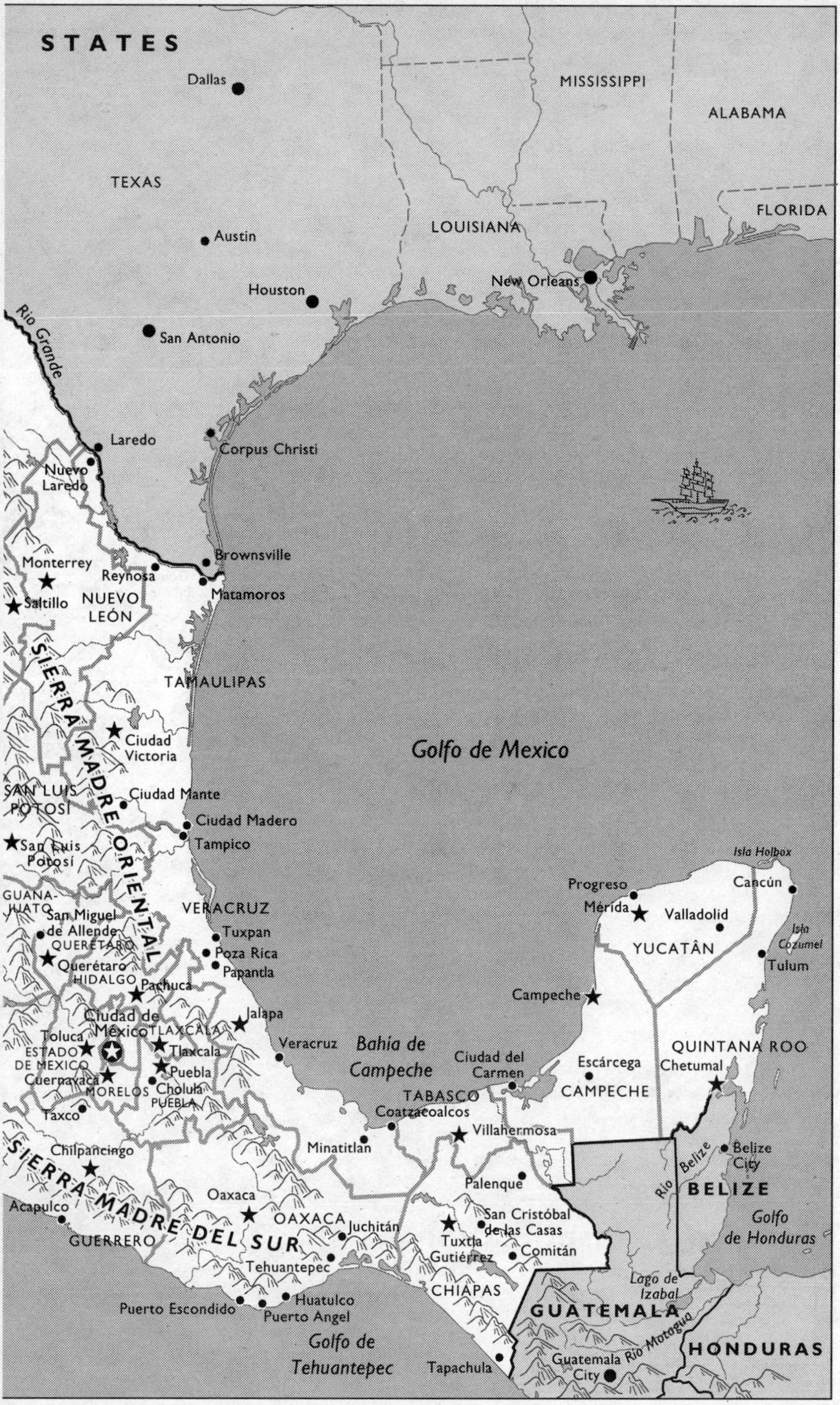
STATES
Dallas
MISSISSIPPI
ALABAMA
TEXAS
FLORIDA
LOUISIANA
Austin
Houston
New Orleans
Rio Grande
San Antonio
Laredo
Corpus Christi
Nuevo Laredo
Monterrey
Brownsville
Reynosa
Matamoros
Saltillo
NUEVO LEÓN
SIERRA MADRE ORIENTAL
TAMAULIPAS
Ciudad Victoria
Golfo de Mexico
SAN LUIS POTOSÍ
Ciudad Mante
Ciudad Madero
Tampico
San Luis Potosí
Isla Holbox
GUANAJUATO
Progreso
Cancún
VERACRUZ
Mérida
San Miguel de Allende
Valladolid
QUERÉTARO
Tuxpan
Isla Cozumel
Poza Rica
YUCATÁN
Querétaro
Papantla
Tulum
HIDALGO
Pachuca
Campeche
Ciudad de México
Jalapa
TLAXCALA
Toluca
Tlaxcala
Veracruz
Bahía de Campeche
Ciudad del Carmen
Escárcega
QUINTANA ROO
ESTADO DE MEXICO
Chetumal
Puebla
Cuernavaca
MORELOS
Cholula
TABASCO
CAMPECHE
PUEBLA
Taxco
Coatzacoalcos
Villahermosa
Minatitlan
Belize City
Rio Belize
SIERRA MADRE DEL SUR
Chilpancingo
Palenque
BELIZE
Oaxaca
Golfo de Honduras
Acapulco
OAXACA
San Cristóbal de las Casas
Juchitán
GUERRERO
Tuxtla Gutiérrez
Comitán
Tehuantepec
Lago de Izabal
CHIAPAS
Huatulco
Puerto Escondido
Puerto Angel
GUATEMALA
Rio Motagua
Golfo de Tehuantepec
HONDURAS
Tapachula
Guatemala City

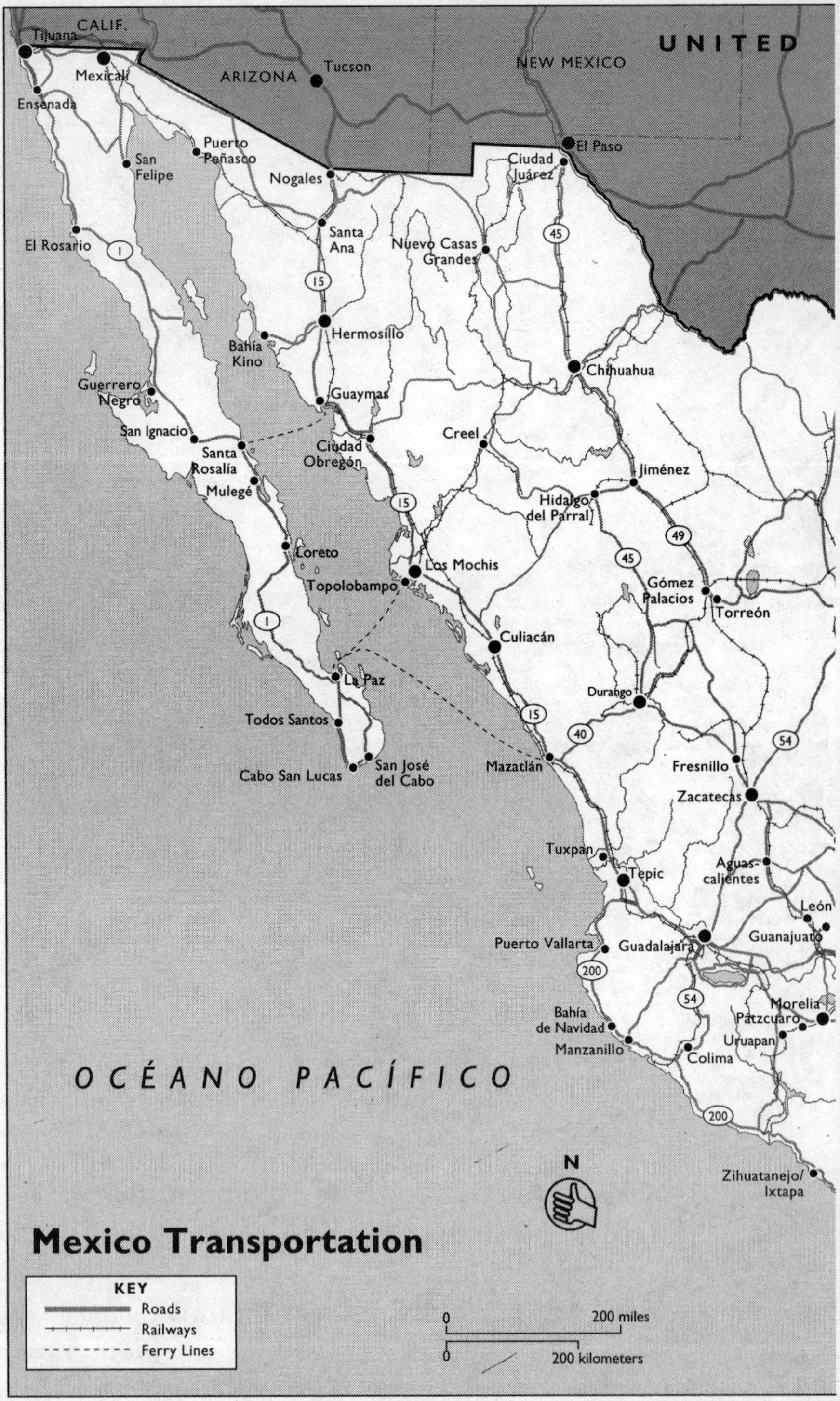
Mexico Transportation
KEY
Roads
Railways
Ferry Lines
0
200 miles
0
200 kilometers
N
UNITED
CALIF.
ARIZONA
NEW MEXICO
Tucson
El Paso
Tijuana
Mexicali
Ensenada
San Felipe
Puerto Peñasco
Nogales
Ciudad Juárez
El Rosario
Santa Ana
Nuevo Casas Grandes
Hermosillo
Bahía Kino
Chihuahua
Guerrero Negro
Guaymas
San Ignacio
Santa Rosalía
Ciudad Obregón
Creel
Mulegé
Jiménez
Hidalgo del Parral
Loreto
Los Mochis
Topolobampo
Gómez Palacios
Torreón
Culiacán
La Paz
Durango
Todos Santos
Mazatlán
Cabo San Lucas
San José del Cabo
Fresnillo
Zacatecas
Tuxpan
Tepic
Aguascalientes
León
Guanajuato
Puerto Vallarta
Guadalajara
Bahía de Navidad
Manzanillo
Colima
Morelia
Pátzcuaro
Uruapan
Zihuatanejo/Ixtapa
OCÉANO PACÍFICO
1
15
45
49
40
54
200

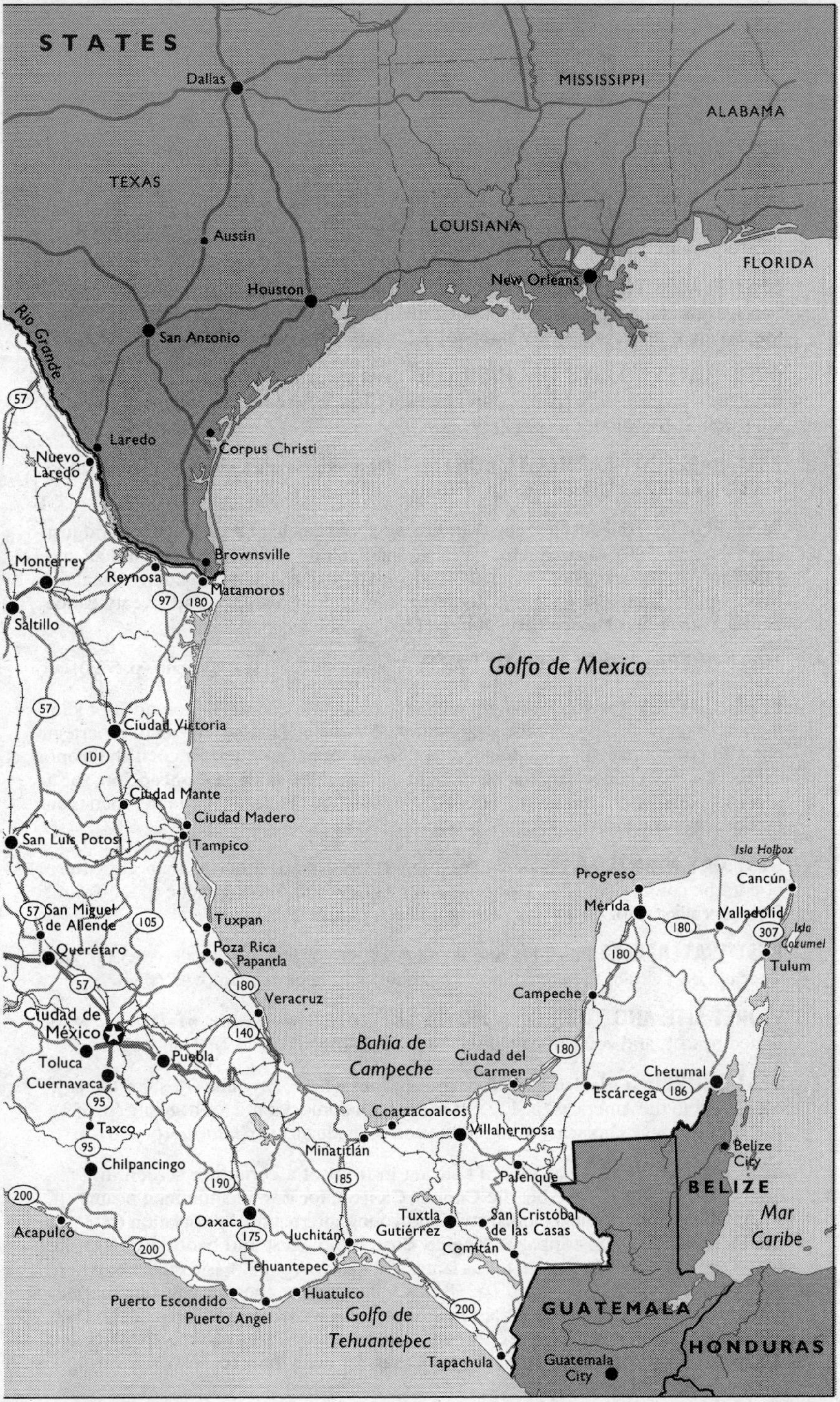
STATES
Dallas
MISSISSIPPI
ALABAMA
TEXAS
Austin
LOUISIANA
FLORIDA
New Orleans
Houston
San Antonio
Rio Grande
57
Laredo
Corpus Christi
Nuevo Laredo
Brownsville
Monterrey
Reynosa
Matamoros
97
180
Saltillo
Golfo de Mexico
57
Ciudad Victoria
101
Ciudad Mante
Ciudad Madero
San Luis Potosí
Tampico
Isla Holbox
Progreso
Cancún
Mérida
Valladolid
57
San Miguel de Allende
105
Tuxpan
180
307
Isla Cozumel
Querétaro
Poza Rica
Papantla
180
Tulum
57
180
Veracruz
Campeche
Ciudad de México
140
Bahía de Campeche
Ciudad del Carmen
180
Toluca
Puebla
Cuernavaca
Chetumal
Escárcega
186
95
Coatzacoalcos
Taxco
Villahermosa
95
Minatitlán
Belize City
Chilpancingo
Palenque
190
185
BELIZE
200
Mar Caribe
Oaxaca
Tuxtla Gutiérrez
San Cristóbal de las Casas
Acapulco
175
Juchitán
200
Comitán
Tehuantepec
Huatulco
Puerto Escondido
GUATEMALA
Puerto Angel
Golfo de Tehuantepec
200
HONDURAS
Tapachula
Guatemala City

Let's Go Picks

BEST RUINS **Chichén Itzá,** especially during the equinox (p. 559); **Las Pozas,** for 20th-century psychedelic madness (p. 283); **Palenque,** for the inscriptions and the dense jungle (p. 518); **Teotihuacán,** for sheer size and stunning views (p. 124); **Tulum,** for beachside ruins (see our cover and p. 591); and **Yaxchilán,** where howler monkeys outnumber people (p. 523).

BEST PLACES TO CHILL **Isla Holbox,** where all you need is a hammock (p. 579); **San Ignacio,** for date palms and stars in the middle of the desert (p. 158); and **Zipolite,** where time passes slowly and people are naked (p. 391).

BEST PLACES TO LIVE THE HIGH LIFE **Cuernavaca,** where posh, international students study language (p. 433); and **Mexico City,** where you can mingle with Mexico's richest and snootiest (p. 72).

BEST BAREFOOT CARMELITE CONVENT **Desierto de los Leones,** self-flagellation just an hour out of Mexico City (p. 430).

BEST PLACES TO PARTY **Cabo San Lucas,** if you graduated high school and just don't care (p. 180); **Guanajuato,** for its young bar/cafe scene (p. 405); **Cholula** and **Puebla,** with thousands of university students (p. 462 and p. 448); **Cuernavaca,** for ritzy nightlife and salsa (p. 439); **Veracruz,** for outdoor marimba and sweaty dance clubs (p. 482); and **Mexico City,** duh (p. 118).

MOST OVERRATED PLACES TO PARTY **Tijuana** (p. 134) and **Cancún** (p. 573).

BEST BEACHES Are you kidding? We can't pick—Mexico's got thousands of kilometers of them. Some off-beat suggestions: **Bahía de Navidad,** for picture-perfect coast and no tourists (p. 316); **Laguna de Chankaab,** in Cozumel, for coral and tropical fish (p. 590); **Cuyutlán,** for black sand (p. 323); **Bahía de la Concepción,** for a piece of paradise pie on the Sea of Cortés (p. 164); **Isla Mujeres,** for better-than-Cancún beaches and less-than-Cancún hustle (p. 581).

BEST GAY NIGHTLIFE **Mexico City,** bigger, brasher, and better than anywhere else in the country (p. 121); **Monterrey,** for its new and thriving scene (p. 260); and **Puerto Vallarta,** for cruises and all-night beach parties (p. 313).

BEST WATERFALLS **Misol-Ha and Agua Azul,** site of 500 jungle falls (p. 523); and **Cascada de Texolo,** the dramatic and beautiful setting of many movies (p. 469).

WORST SITE AND TOUR OF A MOVIE SET **Rosarito**—some of *Titanic* was filmed nearby, and you can pay to see "sets" and "props" (p. 139). 'Nuff said.

BEST SHOPPING **Mexico City,** for anything, anywhere, any time—it's got the largest market in the Americas (p. 122); **Mérida,** for hammocks and for haggling (p. 553); and the area **near Oaxaca,** for incredible and individualized *artesanía* (p. 379).

BEST OF THE BEST If we weren't sitting in front of a computer screen in Cambridge, here's where we'd be: the **Copper Canyon,** for its mind-numbing beauty (p. 222); **Guanajuato,** for its colonial style and young international population (p. 399); the incomparable, unstoppable **Mexico City,** the biggest and baddest city in the world (p. 72); **San Luis Potosí,** for its lantern-lit squares (p. 272); **Isla Mujeres,** where life is like the perfect postcard (p. 581); **La Paz,** where the evening sun sparkles across the harbor (p. 168); **Xilitla,** the closest thing we have to Eden (p. 282); **Oaxaca,** for its stunning *zócalo*, hot chocolate, and amazing nearby markets (p. 370); and the highland city of **San Cristóbal de las Casas,** for everything (p. 504).

Essentials

PLANNING YOUR TRIP

Climate

The Tropic of Cancer bisects Mexico into a temperate north and tropical south, but the climate varies considerably even within these belts. **Northwest Mexico** is the driest area of the country but still offers a unique array of desert flora and fauna, as does arid **Baja California,** which separates the cold, rough Pacific from the tranquil and tepid Sea of Cortés. The **Northeast** is a bit more temperate than the Northwest. The **West Coast,** home to Mexico's famed resorts, boasts warm, tropical weather. Pleasant beaches are also scattered throughout the humid, tranquil **Gulf Coast.** The central region north of Mexico City, known as **El Bajío,** and **South Central Mexico** both experience spring-like weather year-round; the cooler climates of the highlands are tempered by coastal warmth, and natural beauty ranges from world-famous beaches to inland forests. Lush, green jungles obscure the ruins of the ancient civilizations of the **Yucatán Peninsula;** interior jungles are hot and humid, while trade winds keep the beaches along the Gulf and Caribbean coasts cool and pleasant.

There are two seasons in Mexico: rainy and dry. The rainy season lasts from May until November (with a hurricane season in the south Aug.-Oct.), and rainfall can be as high as 15cm per month. The southern half of the country averages over 250cm of rainfall per year (75% of that during the rainy season), so a summer vacation is likely to be on the damp side. Expect an average of two to three hours of rain every afternoon. The best time to hit the beaches is during the dry season (Nov.-May), when afternoons are sunny, evenings balmy, and nights relatively mosquito-free.

The tourist season consists of the month of December, the entire summer, *Semana Santa* (Holy Week, the week before Easter), and Easter. If you travel to Mexico during this time, you can expect to pay slightly higher prices at hotels and restaurants. However, higher prices in Mexico pale in comparison to those in Europe; except during festivals, it is almost never necessary to make advance reservations, even during the summer, at budget hotels. The busy seasons vary regionally; in beach towns and resorts on either coast or Baja, the winter season and U.S. spring break (late March-April) are busy times and the summer is less crowded, while the summer is generally heavily touristed in colonial Mexico.

Average Temp. Low-High	January		May		July		November	
	°C	°F	°C	°F	°C	°F	°C	°F
Acapulco	22-31	72-88	25-32	77-90	25-33	77-91	24-32	75-90
Guadalajara	7-23	45-73	14-31	57-88	15-26	59-79	10-25	50-77
La Paz	13-23	55-73	17-33	63-91	23-36	73-97	17-29	63-84
Mérida	18-28	64-82	21-34	70-93	23-33	73-91	19-29	66-84
Mexico City	6-22	43-72	13-27	55-81	13-24	55-75	9-23	48-73
Monterrey	9-20	48-68	20-31	68-88	22-34	72-93	12-23	54-73
Oaxaca	8-28	46-82	15-32	59-90	15-28	59-82	10-28	50-82
San Cristóbal	5-20	41-68	9-22	48-72	10-22	50-72	7-20	45-68
Tijuana	43-68	6-20	12-23	54-73	16-27	61-81	10-23	50-73
Veracruz	64-77	18-25	25-30	77-86	22-31	75-88	21-28	70-82

Time Zones

Most of Mexico is six hours behind Greenwich Mean Time, as is U.S. Central Standard Time and Central America. It's always one hour earlier in Baja California Sur, Sinaloa, Sonora, and parts of Nayarit, which are on Mountain Standard Time. And you're yet another hour younger in Baja California Norte, which is always on Pacific Standard Time, like California.

Information Resources

GOVERNMENT AGENCIES

Embassy of Mexico: In **Australia,** 14 Perth Ave. Yarralumla, Canberra 2600 ACT (tel. (06) 273 3905; fax 273 1190); in **Canada,** 45 O'Connor St., #1500, K1P 1A4 Ottawa, Ont. (tel. (613) 233-8988 or 233-9272; fax 235-9123); in the **U.K.,** 42 Hertford St., Mayfair, W1Y 7TS, London (tel. (0171) 499 8586; fax 495 4035); in the **U.S.,** 1911 Pennsylvania Ave. NW, Washington, D.C. 20006 (tel. (202) 728-1600; fax 728-1718).

Consulate of Mexico: In **Australia,** Level 1, 135-153 New South Head Rd., Edgecliff, Sydney 2027 NSW (tel. (02) 326 1311 or 326 1292; fax 327 1110); in **Canada,** 199 Bay St., #4440, Commerce Court West, M5L 1E9 Toronto, Ont. (tel. (416) 368-2875; fax 368-3478 or 368-1672); in the **U.K.,** 42 Hertford St., Mayfair, W1Y 7TS, London (tel. (0171) 499 8586; fax 495 4035); in the **U.S.,** 2827 16th St. NW, Washington, D.C. 20036 (tel. (202) 736-1000; fax 797-8458) or 8 E. 41st St., New York, NY 10017 (tel. (212) 689-0456, fax 545-8197).

Fax-Me-Mexico is a fax-on-demand info service run out of Oregon by the national Mexican Government Tourism office (tel. (541) 385-9282). Call first to receive a fax catalog of all available documents, then order by number. Free. Open 24hr.

Mexican Government Tourism Office (Secretaría de Turismo or **SECTUR**), tel. (800) 44-MEXICO (number within Mexico). Offices in **Chicago,** 70 E. Lake St. #1413, Chicago, IL 60601 (tel. (312) 606-9015 or 606-9252; fax 606-9012). In **Houston,** 5075 Westheimer Blvd., #975W, Houston, TX 77056 (tel. (713) 629-1611; fax 629-1837). In **London,** 60/61 Trigonally Sq., 3rd fl., London WC2N 5DS (tel. (0171) 839-3177; fax 930-9202). In **Los Angeles,** 1801 Century Park, #1080, Los Angeles, CA 90067 (tel. (310) 203-8191; fax 203-8316). In **Miami,** 2333 Ponce de Leon Blvd. #710, Coral Gables, FL 33134 (tel. (305) 443-9160; fax 443-1186). In **Montreal,** 1 Place Ville Marie #1526, Montreal, Quebec H3B 2B5 (tel. (514) 871-1052; fax 871-3825). In **New York City,** 405 Park Ave. #1401, New York, NY 10022 (tel. (212) 421-6656 or 755-7261; fax 753-2874). In **Toronto,** 2 Bloor St. W #1801, Toronto, Ontario M4W 3E2 (tel. (416) 925-1876 or 925-2753; fax 925-6061). In **Vancouver** (also for the northwest U.S.), 999 W. Hastings #1610, Vancouver, B.C. V6C 2W2 (tel. (604) 669-2845; fax 669-3498). All have English- and Spanish-speaking representatives and provide maps, information, and tourist cards.

PUBLICATIONS

Guía Oficial de Hospedaje de México, published for the Secretaría de Turismo by Editorial Limusa, Grupo Noriega Editores, Balderas 95, México, D.F., 06040 México (tel. (5) 512 21 05; fax (5) 512 29 03). A thick book with a comprehensive list of all government-registered hotels in Mexico, in all price ranges. Invaluable if you're heading to small towns not covered by *Let's Go: Mexico 1999* and want to know what hotel options are in town. Available for free from some tourist offices—try your luck. In Spanish, but accessible to non-speakers.

John Muir Publications, P.O. Box 613, Sante Fe, NM 87504 (tel. (800) 888-7504; fax (505) 988-1680). Publishes the *People's Guide to Mexico* (US$20).

México Desconocido, Monte Pelvoux 110-104, Lomas de Chapultepec, México, D.F. 11000 (tel. (5) 202 65 85; fax 540 17 71). Monthly travel magazines in Spanish and English describing little-known areas and customs of Mexico. Subscriptions shipped to the U.S. cost US$50 (via phone with a credit card). In Mexico, subscriptions cost 240 pesos.

Rand McNally, 150 S. Wacker Dr., Chicago, IL 60606 (tel. (800) 333-0136; http://www.randmcnally.com), publishes one of the most comprehensive road atlases of Mexico, available in their stores and most other bookstores throughout the U.S. for US$10. Headquarters located at 8255 N. Central Park Ave., Skokie, IL 60076. Phone orders are also available.

Transitions Abroad, P.O. Box 1300, 18 Hulst Rd., Amherst, MA 01004-1300 (tel. (800) 293-0373; fax 256-0373; email trabroad@aol.com; http://transabroad.com). Magazine lists publications and resources for study, work, and volunteering in Mexico (US$25 for 6 issues, single copy $6.25). Also publishes *The Alternative Travel Directory,* a comprehensive guide to living, learning, and working overseas (US$20; postage $4).

Internet Resources

The Internet is now one of the most powerful allies of the budget traveler: it's speedy, easy to use, and rapidly growing in importance in Mexico. With many Mexican businesses, language schools, and individuals now online, the 'Net offers a cheap and accessible alternative to pricey phone calls and the less-than-reliable Mexican mail system. The Web can also open up infinite possibilities for exploring points of interest before you go. It can help you find budget airline tickets, up-to-date information on Mexico and the regions you're planning to visit, and links to literally thousands of sources on Mexico. *NetTravel: How Travelers Use the Internet* (US$25), by Michael Shapiro, is a very thorough and informative guide to all aspects of travel planning through the Internet.

There are a number of ways to access the Internet. Many employers and schools offer gateways to the Internet, often at no cost. Cybercafes are perhaps the most prominent form of Internet access in Mexico. These cafes can be found in even some of the smaller Mexican towns, and they offer the user access to the World Wide Web and the Internet for a nominal fee.

ESSENTIALS

THE WORLD WIDE WEB

Introduction

Increasingly the Internet forum of choice, today's **World Wide Web** allows travelers to consult official sources of information in Mexico and throughout the world, make their own airline, hotel, hostel, or car rental reservations, and browse through a vast library of literature and multimedia material about Mexico's past, present, and future. The Web provides a streamlined interface and standardized format for accessing hyper-linked text, multimedia documents, and compact applications. The Web's lack of hierarchy, however, makes it difficult to distinguish between good information, bad information, and marketing.

The forms of the Internet most useful to budget travelers are the World Wide Web and Usenet newsgroups. **Search engines** (services that search for web pages under specific subjects) can significantly aid the search process. **Lycos** (a2z.lycos.com), **Alta Vista** (www.altavista.digital.com), and **Excite** (www.excite.com) are among the most popular. **Yahoo!** is a slightly more organized search engine; check out its travel links at www.yahoo.com/Recreation/Travel. Check out **Let's Go's web site** (www.letsgo.com) and find our newsletter, information about our books, an always-current list of links, and more.

WWW Links Related to Travel in Mexico

The following is a grab bag of useful Mexico resources on the World Wide Web. All sites are in English unless otherwise noted. *Let's Go* also lists relevant web sites throughout different sections of the **Essentials** chapter. Keep in mind that web sites come and go very rapidly; a good web site one week might disappear the next, and a new one might quickly take its place. Thus, the following should be seen as mere departure points for your own cyber-space adventures.

Consulate General of Mexico (http://www.quicklink.com/mexico). Basic information about the Mexican government branches, economic indicators, and links to other Mexico-related sites. In Spanish or English.

El Mundo Maya (http://www.wotw.com/Mundomaya/). Comprehensive coverage of the Maya region of Mexico, including city and regional descriptions, photos, maps, and restaurant and hotel information.

Foreign Language for Travelers (http://www.travlang.com) can help you brush up on your Spanish. *Te ayuda a practicar tu español.*

Let's Go (http://www.letsgo.com). The mother-page of your favorite series of little, yellow, budget travel guides.

Mexico City Subway System (http://metro.jussieu.fr:10001/bin/select/english/mexico/mexico). An automated route-finder and map of the Mexico City Metro.

Mexico Reference Desk (http://www.lanic.utexas.edu/la/Mexico/). A plethora of hyper-links to sites related to Mexico.

MexWeb (http://mexweb.mty.itesm.mx/). Lots of Mexico-related links by subject. In Spanish.

Microsoft Expedia (http://expedia.msn.com) has everything you'd ever need to make travel plans on the web—compare flight fares, look at maps, make reservations. FareTracker, a free service within Expedia, sends you monthly mails about the cheapest fares to any destination. Travelocity (http://www.travelocity.com) offers similar services.

U.S. State Department Travel Advisory for Mexico (http://travel.state.gov/mexico.html). The word from above on travel safety and recommended precautions.

Yahoo! Mexico links (http://www.yahoo.com/Regional/Countries/Mexico). Well-indexed and searchable database of over 2000 links related to Mexico.

Zapatista Web Page (http://ezln.org) provides up-to-the-minute information in English and Spanish about Mexico's most prominent rebel group.

NEWSGROUPS

Another popular source of information is **newsgroups**—forums for discussion of specific topics. One user posts a written question or thought, to which other users read and respond. There is information available on almost every imaginable topic. In some cases this proliferation has become burdensome; the quality of discussion is often poor, and you have to wade through piles of nonsense to come to useful information. Despite this, a number of newsgroups are useful for travelers. **Usenet,** the name for the family of newsgroups, can be accessed easily from most Internet gateways. In UNIX systems, type "tin" at the prompt. Most commercial providers offer access to Usenet, and often have their own version of Usenet. There are a number of different hierarchies of newsgroups. For issues related to society and culture, try the "soc" hierarchy (such as **soc.culture.mexican**). The "rec" (recreation) hierarchy is also good for travelers, with newsgroups such as **rec.travel.latin-america.** The "alt" (alternative) hierarchy houses a number of different types of discussion. Finally, "Clari-net" posts AP news wires for many different topics (such as **clari.world.americas.mexico**).

Documents and Formalities

When you travel, always carry two or more forms of identification with you, including at least one photo ID. A passport combined with a driver's license or birth certificate usually serves as adequate proof of your identity and citizenship. Many establishments, especially banks, require several types of IDs before cashing traveler's checks. Never carry all of your forms of ID together, however; you risk being left entirely without ID or funds in case of theft or loss. If you plan an extended stay, register your passport with the nearest embassy or consulate.

PASSPORTS

Before you leave, photocopy the page of your **passport** that contains your photograph, passport number, and other identifying information. Carry one photocopy in a safe place apart from your passport, and leave another copy at home. Consulates also recommend that you carry an expired passport or an official copy of your birth certificate separate from other documents. These measures will help prove your citizenship and facilitate the issuing of a new passport.

If you do lose your passport, immediately notify the local police and the nearest embassy or consulate of your home government. A replacement may take weeks to process, and it may be valid only for a limited time. Some consulates can issue new passports within 24 hours if you give them proof of citizenship. Any visas stamped in your old passport will be irretrievably lost. In an emergency, ask for immediate temporary traveling papers that will permit you to reenter your home country.

Your passport is a public document belonging to your nation's government. You may have to surrender it to a Mexican government official, but if you don't get it back in a reasonable amount of time, inform the nearest mission of your home country. Demand for passports is highest between January and August. Try to apply as early as possible.

Australia Citizens must apply for a passport in person. Passport offices are located in Adelaide, Brisbane, Canberra City, Darwin, Hobart, Melbourne, Newcastle, Perth, and Sydney. For more info, call toll-free (in Australia) 13 12 32, or visit http://www.austemb.org.

Canada Citizens may apply in person at any 1 of 28 regional Passport Offices across Canada. For additional info, contact the Canadian Passport Office, Department of Foreign Affairs and International Trade, Ottawa, ON, K1A 0G3 (tel. (613) 994-3500; http://www.dfait-maeci.gc.ca/passport). Travelers may also call (800) 567-6868 (24hr.); in Toronto (416) 973-3251; in Vancouver (604) 775-6250; in Montreal (514) 283-2152.

Ireland Citizens can apply for a passport by mail through either the Department of Foreign Affairs, Passport Office, Setanta Centre, Molesworth St., Dublin 2 (tel. (01) 671 1633; fax (01) 671 1092), or the Passport Office, Irish Life Building, 1A South Mall, Cork (tel. (021) 272 525; fax (021) 275 770).

New Zealand Application forms for passports are available in New Zealand from travel agents and Department of Internal Affairs Link Centres in the main cities and towns. Applications may also be forwarded to the Passport Office, P.O. Box 10526, Wellington, New Zealand. Standard processing time in New Zealand is 10 working days for correct applications. More information is available on the internet (http://www.emb.com/nzemb or http://www.undp.org/missions/newzealand).

South Africa Citizens can apply for a passport at any **Home Affairs Office** or South African Mission. Current passports less than 10 years old (counting from date of issuance) may be renewed until December 31, 1999; every citizen whose passport's validity does not extend far beyond this date is urged to renew it as soon as possible. Renewal is free, and turnaround time is usually 2 weeks. For further information, contact the nearest Department of Home Affairs Office.

United Kingdom British citizens may obtain application forms at passport offices, main post offices, many travel agents, and branches of Lloyds Bank and Artac World Choice. Apply by mail or in person (for an additional UK£10) to one of the offices, located in London, Liverpool, Newport, Peterborough, Glasgow, or Belfast. The U.K. Passport Agency can be reached by phone at (0990) 21 04 10.

United States Citizens may apply for a passport at any federal or state courthouse or post office authorized to accept passport applications, or at a U.S. Passport Agency. Passports may be renewed by mail or in person for US$55. Processing takes 3-4 weeks. Report a passport lost or stolen in the U.S. by writing to Passport Services, 1425 K St., N.W., U.S. Department of State, Washington D.C., 20524 or to the nearest passport agency. For more info, contact the U.S. Passport Information's 24hr. recorded message (tel. (202) 647-0518).

TOURIST CARDS

All persons visiting Mexico for tourism or study for up to 180 days must carry a **tourist card (FMT,** for *Folleto de Migración Turística*) in addition to proof of citizenship. U.S. and Canadian citizens don't need the FMT if they are not staying in the country for more than 72 hours. U.S. and Canadian citizens traveling to Baja California will need a card only if they plan to venture beyond Maneadero on the Pacific Coast, south of Mexicali on Rte. 5.

Tourist cards, like all entry documents, are free of charge. Many people get their cards when they cross the border or when they check in at the airline ticket counter for their flight into Mexico; however, you can avoid delays by obtaining one from a Mexican consulate or tourist office before you leave (see **Government Agencies,** p. 2). You will have to present proof of citizenship, and if your financial condition looks suspect, officials will ask you to flash your return ticket. Travelers from outside North America must present a passport. U.S. and Canadian citizens can obtain a tourist card with an original birth certificate, notarized affidavit of citizenship, or naturalization papers, plus some type of photo ID (with the exception of naturalized Canadians, who must carry a passport). But be forewarned: traveling in Mexico without a passport is asking for trouble. A passport carries much more authority with local officials than does a birth certificate, makes returning home by air a lot easier, and is mandatory for anyone going on to Central America.

On the FMT, you must indicate your intended destination and expected length of stay. Tourist cards are usually valid for 90 days and must be returned to border officials upon leaving the country. However, some border crossings and airport officials have been known to provide 30-day visas by default, and stamp 90-day visas only on request; make sure you get a 90-day stamp if you're staying longer than a month. If you stay in Mexico past your 90-day limit, you will be slapped with a fine. Request a special, 180-day **multiple-entry permit** at your point of entry if you plan to leave and re-enter the country several times within a short time period. Otherwise, you must get a new FMT every time you re-enter the country, even if your old one has not expired. Try to get a card that will be valid longer than your projected stay, since obtaining an extension on a 90-day FMT is a huge hassle: you'll need a physician's authorization stating that you are too ill to travel. If you do need an extension, visit a local office of the **Delegación de Servicios Migratorios** several weeks before your card expires. They also take care of lost cards. While in Mexico, you are required by law to carry your tourist card at all times. Make a photocopy and keep it in a separate place. Although it won't **replace** a lost or stolen tourist card, a copy should facilitate replacement. If you do lose your card, expect hours of delay and bureaucratic inconvenience while immigration verifies your record of entrance.

Special regulations apply if you are entering Mexico on a business trip, or if you expect to study in the country for more than six months (see **Visas**). If you're breezing through Mexico *en route* to Guatemala or Belize, ask for a **transmigrant form,** which will allow you to remain in Mexico for up to 30 days. You'll need a passport or current photo ID, a Guatemalan or Belizean visa, and proof of sufficient funds. The transmigrant form is not required for U.S. or Canadian citizens.

VISAS

A **visa** is an endorsement that a foreign government stamps into a passport which allows the bearer to stay in that country for a specified purpose and period of time. For stays in Mexico up to six months, visas are not necessary for citizens of Australia, Canada, the U.K., the U.S., New Zealand, and most E.U. countries. Businesspeople, missionaries, and students must obtain appropriate visas.

For more information, send for *Foreign Entry Requirements* (US$0.50) from the **Consumer Information Center,** Department 363D, Pueblo, CO 81009 (tel. (719) 948-3334; http://www.pueblo.gsa.gov), or contact the **Center for International Business and Travel (CIBT),** 25 West 43rd St. #1420, New York, NY 10036 (tel. (800) 925-2428 or (212) 575-2811 from NY), which secures visas for travel to and from all countries for a variable service charge (US$145 for a one-year multiple entry visa for business people).

CUSTOMS: ENTERING MEXICO

Crossing into Mexico by land can be as uneventful or as complicated as the border guards want it to be. You might be waved into the country or directed to the immigration office to procure a tourist card (FMT) if you don't have one already. You also need a car permit if you're driving. Customs officials will then inspect luggage and stamp papers. If there is anything amiss when you reach the immigration checkpoint 22km into the interior, you'll have to turn back.

A clean, neat appearance will help upon your arrival. Don't pass out *mordidas* (bribes; literally "bites"). They may do more harm than good. Border officials may still request a tip, but they're not supposed to. Above all, do not attempt to carry drugs across the border (see **Drugs and Alcohol** p. 17).

Entering Mexico by air is easier. Agents process forms and examine luggage, using the press-your-luck traffic light system, right in the airport. Electronics, such as personal computers, might make customs officers uneasy; it is a good idea to write a letter explaining that you need to take your precious laptop into the country for personal use and that it will go back home with you and have the document certified by a Mexican consulate. Because air passengers are rarely penniless, immigration officials are less strict than at the border.

CUSTOMS: LEAVING MEXICO

Getting out of Mexico, especially at the U.S. border, can take five minutes or five hours—the better your paperwork, the shorter your ordeal. Upon returning home, you must declare all articles you acquired abroad and pay a **duty** on the value of those articles that exceed the allowance established by your country's customs service. Goods and gifts purchased at **duty-free** shops abroad are not exempt from duty or sales tax at your point of return; you must declare these items as well. "Duty-free" merely means that you do not have to pay a tax in the country of purchase. To establish value when you return home, keep receipts for items purchased abroad. Since you pay no duty on goods brought from home, record the serial numbers of any expensive items (cameras, computers, radios, etc.) you are taking with you before you begin your travels, and check with your country's customs office to see if it has a special form for registering them.

Most countries object to the importation of firearms, explosives, ammunition, obscene literature and films, fireworks, and lottery tickets. Do not try to take illegal drugs out of Mexico. Label prescription drugs clearly and have the prescription or a doctor's certificate ready to show the customs officer. If you have questions, call the **Mexican Customs office** in the U.S. ((202) 728-1669; fax 728-1664) or contact your specific embassy or consulate for more information (see **Government Agencies,** p. 2).

If you are a resident alien of the United States or simply have a Latino surname you may receive a lot of hassling from immigration upon your return. You must make up your own mind as to how to react to this racist harassment. Pragmatists answer as straightforwardly as possible any questions the border patrol might ask (they have been known to ask "who won the Civil War?" and other "prove-it" puzzles).

YOUTH, STUDENT, AND TEACHER IDENTIFICATION

Although the **International Student Identity Card (ISIC)** (http://www.isic.org) is the most widely accepted form of student identification internationally, it is not particularly useful in Mexico. Information is available on the web at http://www.fiyto.org. A regular **university ID card** usually entitles students to whatever discounts are offered to foreign students; it's definitely worth carrying. Many student discounts in Mexico, however, are only offered to students at Mexican universities.

ESSENTIALS

DRIVER'S LICENSE AND VEHICLE PERMITS

An international driver's license is not necessary for driving in Mexico; any valid driver's license is acceptable. To drive a foreign car into Mexico and beyond the Border Zone or Free Trade Zone (Baja California peninsula and Sonora), you need to obtain a **vehicle permit** when you cross the border. The original and a photocopy of the following documents are needed to obtain a vehicle permit: a state vehicle registration certificate and vehicle title, a valid driver's license accompanied by either a passport or a birth certificate, and a Mexican insurance policy, which can be purchased at the border. If leasing a vehicle, you must provide the contract in your name (also in duplicate). A credit card issued outside Mexico will make your life much easier—simply charge the US$11 fee. Without plastic, you will need to make a cash deposit calculated according to the value of your vehicle. In exchange for all these photocopies, you'll receive two punched stickers bearing the expiration date of your permit. To extend a vehicle permit beyond its original expiration date and to avoid confiscation, contact the temporary importation department of Mexican customs. The maximum permit granted to tourists is six months. Regulations change frequently; for updated information contact a consulate. A vehicle permit is valid only for the person to whom it was issued unless another driver is approved by the federal registry. Violation of this law can result in confiscation of the vehicle or heavy fines. Furthermore, only legitimate drivers may purchase car-ferry tickets.

Resist the temptation to abandon, sell, or give away your car in Mexico. Once you enter the country with a car, your tourist card will be marked such that you will not be allowed to collect the bond or to leave without the vehicle. Even if your car disappears somewhere in Mexico, you must get permission to leave without it; approval can be obtained (for a fee) at either the federal registry of automobiles in Mexico City or a local office of the treasury department.

Money Matters

The Mexican peso is constantly in flux, but for the most up-to-date exchange rate as of August 1998, please see the inside back cover of this book.

CURRENCY AND EXCHANGE

It is cheaper to buy pesos than to buy foreign, so as a rule you should convert money after arriving at your destination. However, converting some money before you go lets you zip through the airport while others wait in exchange lines. You should buy at least US$75 worth of pesos, including the equivalent of US$1 in change, before leaving home, especially if you will arrive in the afternoon or on a weekend. This will save time and help you avoid the predicament of having no cash after banking hours. It's sometimes very difficult to get change for large Mexican bills in rural areas. Therefore, it's wise to obtain (and hoard) change when you're in a big city. The symbol for pesos is the same as for U.S. dollars (although a "$" with two bars is always a dollar-sign); frequently **"N"** or **"N$"** also stand for the peso.

Changing money in Mexico can be inconvenient. Some banks won't exchange until noon, when the daily peso quotes come out, and then stay open only until 1:30pm and extract a flat commission. You can switch U.S. dollars for pesos anywhere, but some banks refuse to deal with other foreign currencies; non-U.S. travelers would be wise to keep some U.S. dollars on hand. The more money you change at one time, the less you will lose in the transaction (but don't exchange more than you need or you'll be stuck with *muchos* pesos when you return home). The lineup of national banks in Mexico includes **Banamex, Bancomer,** and **Serfín.**

Casas de cambio (currency exchange booths) may offer better exchange rates than banks and are usually open as long as the stores near which they do business. In most towns, the exchange rates at hotels, restaurants, and airports are extremely unfavorable; avoid them unless it's an emergency. Withdrawing money directly from an **ATM** is perhaps the best exchange rate you'll find; but remember that most ATM

cards charge a fee for international withdrawals (US$1-6), so take out a large enough sum of money to make the fee worthwhile (see **Cash Cards,** p. 13)

If you use traveler's checks or bills, carry some in small denominations (US$50 or less), especially for times when you are forced to exchange money at disadvantageous rates. However, it is good to carry a range of denominations since, depending on location, charges may be levied per check cashed.

TRAVELER'S CHECKS

Traveler's checks are one of the safest and least troublesome means of carrying funds, as they can be refunded if stolen. Several agencies and many banks sell them, usually for face value plus a small percentage commission. **American Express** is the most widely recognized in Mexico. However, remember that some places (especially in northern Mexico) are accustomed to American dollars and will accept no substitute. Carry traveler's checks in busy towns and cities, but stick to cash, risky though it may be, when traveling through the less touristed spots, particularly small Mexican towns. It's best to buy most of your checks in small denominations (US$20) to minimize your losses at times when you need cash fast and can't avoid a bad exchange rate. If possible, purchase checks in U.S. dollars, since many *casas de cambio* refuse to change other currencies. Each agency provides refunds **if your checks are lost or stolen,** and many provide additional services. (You may need a police report verifying the loss or theft.) To protect your checks, keep your check receipts separate from your checks and store them in a safe place or with a traveling companion. Also, be sure to record check numbers when you cash them. Keep a separate supply of cash or traveler's checks for emergencies. Never countersign your checks until you are ready to cash them, and always bring your passport with you when you plan to use the checks.

American Express: In **Australia** call (800) 25 19 02; in **New Zealand** (0800) 44 10 68; in the U.K. (0800) 52 13 13; in the **U.S.** and **Canada** (800) 221-7282. Elsewhere, call U.S. collect (801) 964-6665. American Express traveler's checks are the most widely recognized traveler's checks in Mexico.

Citicorp: In the **U.S.** and **Canada,** call (800) 645-6556; in **Europe,** the **Middle East,** or **Africa** (44) 171 508 7007; from elsewhere call U.S. collect (813) 623-1709. Call 24hr. per day, 7 days per week.

Visa: In the **U.S.,** call (800) 227-6811; in the **U.K.** (0800) 895 078; from anywhere else in the world call (44) 1733 318 949 and reverse the charges.

CREDIT CARDS AND CASH CARDS

Credit card companies get the wholesale exchange rate, which is generally 5% better than the retail rate used by banks and even better than that used by other currency exchange establishments. However, you will be charged ruinous interest rates if you don't pay the bill quickly, so be careful when using this service. Credit cards also have an added advantage—many of them can be used in **ATMs**. Contact your credit card company for a PIN number before leaving your home country.

Credit cards are also invaluable in an emergency—an unexpected hospital bill, a ticket home, or the loss of traveler's checks—that may leave you temporarily without other resources. Furthermore, credit cards offer an array of other services, from insurance to emergency assistance, that depend entirely on the issuer. **American Express** (tel. (800) 843-2273) has a US$55 annual fee but offers a number of services including a 24-hour hotline with medical and legal assistance in emergencies (tel. (800) 554-2639 in U.S. and Canada; from abroad call U.S. collect (202) 554-2639). **Visa** (Telephone Assistance Center (800) 336-8472) and **MasterCard** are issued in cooperation with individual banks and some other organizations; ask the issuer about services that go along with the cards.

Cash cards—popularly called **ATM (Automated Teller Machine)** cards—are widespread in Mexico because they are convenient and they offer good exchange rates; *Let's Go* notes locations of ATMs in as many cities as possible. Depending on the system that your bank at home uses, you can probably access your own personal bank account whenever you need money. (Be careful, however, and keep all receipts—even if an ATM won't give you your cash, it may register a withdrawal on your next statement). Despite these perks, do some research before relying too heavily on automation. There is often a limit on the amount of money you can withdraw per day (usually about US$500, depending on the type of card and account), you will often be charged a small fee (US$1-US$6) for each withdrawal you make, and computer networks sometimes fail. Memorize your **PIN** code in numeral form since machines in Mexico often don't have letters on their keys. Also, if your PIN is longer than four digits, ask your bank whether the first four digits will work, or whether you need a new number. Many ATMs are outdoors; be cautious and aware of your surroundings when making a withdrawal.

Many major credit cards work in ATMs as well; **Visa** and **MasterCard** are accepted by many Mexican businesses, **American Express** and **Diners Club** to a lesser degree. All major credit card companies have some form of worldwide lost card protection service, and most offer a variety of additional travel services to cardholders—inquire before you leave home. **Cirrus** now has international cash machines in 80 countries, including Mexico; call (800) 4-CIRRUS (424-7787) for the most current ATM availability information. The **Plus** network can also be accessed widely; call (U.S. tel. (800) 843-7587 for the "Voice Response Unit Locator," or http://www.visa.com) to see if there's a machine near you.

GETTING MONEY FROM HOME

If you need to receive emergency money in Mexico, the cheapest thing to do is to have it sent through a large commercial bank that has associated banks within Mexico. The sender must either have an account with the bank or bring in cash or a money order, and some banks cable money only for customers for a fee. Cabled money should arrive in one to three days if the sender can furnish exact information (i.e. recipient's passport number and the Mexican bank's name and address); otherwise, there will be significant delays. To pick up money, you must show some form of positive identification, such as a passport.

Money can also be wired abroad through international money transfer services operated by **Western Union** (tel. (800) 325-6000). In the U.S., call Western Union any time at (800) CALL-CASH (225-5227) to cable money with your Visa, Discover, or MasterCard. If the sender does not have a credit card, he or she must go in person to one of Western Union's offices with cash—no money orders accepted, and cashier's checks are not always accepted. The rates for sending cash are generally US$10 cheaper than with a credit card. If you are in a major city in Mexico, the money should arrive within 24 hours or less. In a smaller town, it could take 48 hours. The money will arrive in pesos and will be held for 30 days.

In emergencies, U.S. citizens can have money sent via the State Department's **Overseas Citizens Service, American Citizens Services,** Consular Affairs, Room 4811, U.S. Department of State, Washington, D.C. 20520 (tel. (202) 647-5225; nights, Sundays, and holidays (202) 647-4000; fax (202) 647-3000; http://travel.state.gov; email ca@his.com). For a fee of US$15, the State Department will forward money within hours to the nearest consular office, which will disperse it according to instructions. The office serves only U.S. citizens abroad in the direst of straits; non-U.S. travelers should contact their embassies for information on wiring cash.

TIPPING AND BARGAINING

In Mexico, it can often be hard to know when to leave a tip and when to just walk away. Play it safe by handing a peso or two to anyone who provides you with some sort of service: this includes the bagboy at the supermarket, the shoeshiner, the old man who offers to carry your luggage half a block to your hotel, the young boys who wash your windshield at the carwash, the eager porters who greet you at the bus station, and the street savvy local who shows you the way to the tourist office. Oddly enough, cab drivers (except in Mexico City) aren't tipped since they don't run on meters. In a Mexican restaurant, *camareros* are tipped based on the quality of service; good service deserves at least 10%, especially since devaluation makes meals so cheap to begin with. And never, ever leave without saying *gracias.*

In Mexico, skillful bargaining separates the experienced budget traveler from the more timid tourist. While you can't bargain everywhere, it is expected in many places, especially outdoor *mercados* (markets). You will also have ample opportunities to refine your bargaining skills in Mexico City and Merida. If you're unsure whether bargaining is appropriate, observe the locals and follow their lead. A working knowledge of Spanish will help convince the seller that you are a serious bargainer, thus awarding you with a better deal. Perhaps the most useful skill is a willingness to walk away from the item you were hoping to purchase if the negotiation isn't going anywhere.

Safety and Security

PERSONAL SAFETY

Mexico is relatively safe, although large cities (especially Mexico City) demand extra caution. After dark, keep away from bus and train stations, subways, and public parks. Shun empty train compartments; many travelers avoid the theft-ridden Mexican train system altogether. When on foot, stay out of trouble by sticking to busy, well-lit streets. Many isolated parks and beaches attract unsavory types as soon as night falls.

NOT the Real Thing

Warnings are out throughout Mexico City about well-dressed, foreign-looking and foreign-sounding Mexicans who approach tourists saying they work for *Let's Go* or *Lonely Planet* travel guides; they ask for your address and phone number so they can contact you at the end of your trip for comments. (Neither guide actually does this.) If they get this info out of you, they will proceed to contact your address and tell your loved ones they have kidnapped you, in the process extorting high ransoms. Their scheme has worked on numerous travelers, whose terrified parents have indeed paid the faux-ransom. Call home regularly and don't give out your vital stats, especially to people who pretend they're from *Let's Go.* They're NOT the real thing.

Tourists are particularly vulnerable to crime for two reasons: they often carry large amounts of cash and are not as street savvy as locals. To prevent easy theft, don't keep all of your valuables (money, important documents) in one place. To avoid unwanted attention, try to **blend in** as much as possible. Respecting local customs (in many cases, dressing more conservatively) may placate would-be hecklers. Familiarize yourself with your surroundings before setting out; if you must check a map on the streets, duck into a cafe or shop. Also, carry yourself with confidence, as an obviously bewildered bodybuilder is more likely to be harassed than a stern and confident 89-pound weakling.

When exploring a new city, extra vigilance is wise but there is no need for panic. Find out about unsafe areas from tourist information, from the manager of your hotel or hostel, or from a local whom you trust. Especially if you are travelling alone, be sure that someone at home knows your itinerary and **never admit that you're traveling alone.** Whenever possible, *Let's Go* warns of unsafe neighborhoods and areas, but you should exercise your own judgment and intuition about the safety of your environment. Buildings in disrepair, vacant lots, and unpopulated areas are all bad signs. The distribution of people can reveal a great deal about the relative safety of the area; look for children playing, women walking in the open alone, and other signs of an active community. Keep in mind that a district can change character drastically between blocks. If you feel uncomfortable, leave as quickly and directly as you can, but don't allow fear of the unknown to turn you into a hermit. Careful, persistent exploration will build confidence and make your stay in an area that much more rewarding.

Exercise extreme caution at pools or beaches without lifeguards. Hidden rocks and shallow depths may cause serious injury and even death. Heed warning signs about dangerous undertows. If you rent scuba diving equipment, make sure that it is up to par before taking the plunge.

If you are using a **car,** learn local driving signals. Motor vehicle crashes are a leading cause of travel deaths in many parts of the world. Wearing a seatbelt is the law in many areas. The convenience or comfort of riding unbelted will count for little if someone you care about is injured or killed in an accident. Children under 40 lbs. should ride only in a specially-designed carseat, available for a small fee from most car rental agencies. Study route maps before you hit the road; some roads have poor (or nonexistent) shoulders, few gas stations, and roaming animals. In many regions, road conditions necessitate driving more slowly and more cautiously than you would at home. Watch out for open manholes and irregular pavement which are prevalent on Mexican roads. If you plan on spending a lot of time on the road, you may want to bring spare parts. Be sure to park your vehicle in a garage or well-traveled area. Certain roads should be avoided altogether (see **Driving,** p. 36).

Sleeping in your car is one of the most dangerous (and often illegal) ways to get your rest. If your car breaks down, wait for the police to assist you. If you must sleep in your car, do so as close to a police station or a 24-hour service station as possible. Sleeping out in the open can be even more dangerous—camping is recommended only in official, supervised campsites or in wilderness backcountry.

In Mexico City, exercise caution when flagging down **taxis.** Although many travelers still use the ubiquitous lime-green taxis as a form of cheap transportation, the U.S. State Department issued a warning against hailing cabs in March 1998. The State Department recommends that tourists get cabs from hotel taxi stands or that they use radio taxis *(sitios)* or airport taxis. *Sitios* tend to cost about twice as much as the lime-green taxis, but travelers should weigh the relative risk against the cost.

There is no sure-fire set of precautions that will protect you from all of the situations you might encounter when you travel. A good self-defense course will give you more concrete ways to react to different types of aggression. **Impact, Prepare, and Model Mugging** can refer you to local self-defense courses in the United States (tel. (800) 345-KICK), Vancouver, Canada (tel. (604) 878-3838), and Zurich, Switzerland (tel. 411 261 2423). Workshop and course prices range from US$50-500. Women's and men's courses offered.

The **Australian Department of Foreign Affairs and Trade** (tel. 2 62 61 91 11) offers travel information and advisories at their website (http://www.dfat.gov.au). The **Canadian Department of Foreign Affairs and International Trade** (DFAIT) provides advisories and travel warnings at its website (http://www.dfait-maeci.gc.ca). Call them at (613) 944-6788 from Ottawa or (800) 267-8376 elsewhere in Canada; to receive extra travel tips, call (613) 944-4000 for their free publication, *Bon Voyage*. Official warnings from the **United Kingdom Foreign and Commonwealth Office** (tel. (0171) 238-4503) are on-line at http://www.fco.gov.uk. For official **United States Department of State** travel advisories, call its 24-hour hotline at (202) 647-5225 or check their website (http://travel.state.gov), which provides travel information and publications. Alternatively, order publications such as *A Safe Trip Abroad* for a small fee by calling the Superintendent of Documents at (202) 512-1800.

FINANCIAL SECURITY

Among the more colorful aspects of large cities are **con artists.** Con artists and hustlers often work in groups, and children are among the most effective. They possess an innumerable range of ruses. Be aware of certain classics: sob stories that require money, rolls of bills "found" on the street, mustard spilled (or saliva spit) onto your shoulder distracting you for enough time to snatch your bag. Do not respond or make eye contact, walk quickly away, and keep a solid grip on your belongings. Contact the police if a hustler is particularly insistent or aggressive.

Don't put a wallet with money in your back pocket. Never count your money in public and carry as little as possible. If you carry a purse, buy a sturdy one with a secure clasp, and carry it crosswise on the side, away from the street with the clasp against you. Secure packs with small combination padlocks which slip through the two zippers. (Even these precautions do not always suffice: moped riders who snatch purses and bags sometimes tote knives to cut the straps). A **money belt** is the best way to carry cash. A nylon, zippered pouch with belt that sits inside the waist of your pants or skirt combines convenience and security. A **neck pouch** is equally safe, although far less accessible. Refrain from pulling out your neck pouch in public; if you must, be very discreet. Avoid keeping anything precious in a fanny-pack (even if it's worn on your stomach): your valuables will be highly visible and easy to steal.

In city crowds and especially on public transportation, pick-pockets are amazingly deft at their craft. Rush hour is no excuse for strangers to press up against you on the metro. If someone stands uncomfortably close, move to another car and hold your bags tightly. Also, be alert in public telephone booths. If you must say your calling-card number, do so very quietly; if you punch it in, make sure no one can look over your shoulder. **Photocopies** of important documents allow you to recover them in case they are lost or filched (see **Documents and Formalities,** p. 5). Keep some money separate from the rest to use in an emergency or in case of theft. Label every piece of luggage both inside and out.

Never leave your belongings unattended; crime occurs in even the most demure-looking hostel or hotel. If you feel unsafe, look for places with either a curfew or a night attendant. *Let's Go* lists locker availability in hostels and train stations, but you'll need your own padlock. Lockers are useful if you plan on sleeping outdoors or don't want to lug everything with you, but don't store valuables in them. When possible, keep anything you couldn't bear to lose at home.

If you travel by **car,** try not to leave valuable possessions—such as radios or luggage—in it while you are away. If your tape deck or radio is removable, hide it in the trunk or take it with you. Similarly, hide baggage in the trunk.

Travel Assistance International by Worldwide Assistance Services, Inc. (http://www.worldwide-assistance.com) provides its members with a 24-hour hotline for travel emergencies and referrals in over 200 countries. Call (800) 821-2828 or (202) 828-5894, fax (202) 828-5896, e-mail wassist@aol.com, or write them at 1133 15th St. NW, Suite 400, Washington, D.C. 20005-2710.

DRUGS AND ALCOHOL

Drinking in Mexico is not for amateurs; bars and *cantinas* are strongholds of Mexican *machismo.* When someone calls you *amigo* and orders you a beer, bow out quickly unless you want to match him glass for glass in a challenge that could last several days. Avoid public drunkenness—it is against the law. Locals are fed up with teen-age (and older) *gringos* who cross the border for nights of debauchery.

Mexico rigorously prosecutes drug cases. Note that a minimum jail sentence awaits anyone found guilty of possessing any drug, and that Mexican law does not distinguish between marijuana and other narcotics. Even if you aren't convicted, arrest and trial will be long, dangerous, and unpleasant. Derived from Roman and Napoleonic law, the Mexican judicial process does not assume that you are innocent until proven guilty but vice versa, and it is not uncommon to be detained for a year before a verdict is reached. Foreigners and suspected drug traffickers are not released on bail. Ignorance of Mexican law is no excuse—"I didn't know it was illegal" won't get you out of jail. Furthermore, there is little your consulate can do other than inform your relatives and bring care packages to you in jail.

Finally, don't even think about bringing drugs back into the U.S. customs agents and their perceptive K-9s won't be amused. On the northern highways, especially along the Pacific coast, expect to be stopped repeatedly by burly, humorless troopers looking for contraband. That innocent-looking hitchhiker you were kind enough to pick up may be a drug peddler with a stash of illegal substances. If the police catch it in your car, the drug possession charges will extend to you, and your car may be confiscated. Under no circumstances should you carry **illegal drugs** in any way, shape, or form. If you carry **prescription drugs** while you travel, it is vital to have a copy of the prescriptions themselves readily accessible at country borders.

Health and Disease Prevention

Before you can say "pass the *jalapeños*," a long-anticipated vacation can turn into an unpleasant study of the wonders of the Mexican health care system. While illness can typically be fended off with preventive measures (see **Before You Go**, p. 18), local pharmacists can give shots and dispense other remedies should mild illness prove inescapable. Wherever possible, *Let's Go* lists a pharmacy open for extended hours. If one is not listed, ask a policeman or cab driver. If you have an emergency and the door is locked, knock loudly; someone is probably sleeping inside.

The main plague of many visitors to Mexico results from their drinking anything made with unpurified water. If it's not purified, don't drink it. When it comes to health, a little preparation goes a long way. For minor problems, bring along a compact **first-aid** kit (see **Before You Go** p. 18).

Those using glasses or contact lens should bring adequate supplies and an extra prescription. Mexican equivalents can be hard to find and could irritate your eyes, although almost all pharmacies will carry saline solution. Also, carry an extra prescription and pair of glasses or arrange to have your doctor or a family member send a replacement pair in an emergency.

Anyone with a chronic condition requiring medication should see a doctor before leaving. Allergy sufferers should find out if their conditions are likely to be aggravated in the regions they plan to visit, and obtain a full supply of any necessary medication before the trip, since matching a prescription to a foreign equivalent is not always easy, safe, or possible. Carry up-to-date, legible prescriptions or a statement from your doctor, especially if you use insulin, a syringe, or a narcotic. While traveling, be sure to keep all medication with you in your carry-on luggage

You can minimize the chances of contracting a disease while traveling by taking a few precautionary measures. Always avoid animals with open wounds; beware of touching any animal at all in developing countries. Often dogs are not given shots, so that sweet-faced pooch at your feet might very well be disease-ridden. If you are bitten, be concerned about **rabies**—be sure to clean your wound thoroughly and seek medical help immediately to find out whether you need treatment. The danger of rabies is greatest in rural areas.

Many diseases are transmitted by insects—mainly mosquitoes, fleas, ticks, and lice. Be aware of insects in wet or forested areas, while hiking, and especially while camping. **Mosquitoes** are most active from dusk to dawn. Wear long pants and long sleeves, and use insect repellent. **Ticks** are responsible for Lyme disease and other ailments and are especially problematic in regions such as the Yucatán. Brush off ticks periodically when walking, using a fine-toothed comb on your neck and scalp. Do not try to remove ticks by burning them or coating them with nail polish remover or petroleum jelly. Topical cortisones may help quell the itching.

Especially in the desert regions of Baja, watch out for **scorpions.** They often like to find shaded places (like inside your shoes) to cool off and will not be very happy if you interrupt their slumber by forcing them to share their cool space with your foot. Although they are rarely fatal (except if you're allergic), they will bite and it will hurt like nothing else. Seek immediate medical attention if a scorpion gets you (right after you kill it for revenge).

BEFORE YOU GO

Though no amount of planning can guarantee an accident-free trip, preparation can help minimize the likelihood of contracting a disease and maximize the chances of receiving effective health-care in the event of an emergency.

For minor health problems, bring a compact first-aid kit, including bandages, aspirin or other pain killer, antibiotic cream, a thermometer, a Swiss Army knife with tweezers, moleskin, a decongestant for colds, motion sickness remedy, medicine for diarrhea or stomach problems, sunscreen, insect repellent, and burn ointment.

In your passport, write the names of any people you wish to be contacted in case of a medical emergency, and also list any allergies or medical conditions of which you would want doctors to be aware.

Visitors to Mexico do not need to carry vaccination certificates (though anyone entering Mexico from South America or Africa may be asked to show proof of vaccination for yellow fever). No vaccinations are required for U.S. citizens entering Mexico; however, a few medical precautions can make your trip a safer one. Try to remember that no matter how bad the needles are, they're better than the diseases they prevent. Travelers should be sure that the following vaccines are up to date: Measles, Mumps, and Rubella (MMR); Diptheria, Tetanus, and Pertussis (DTP or DTap); Polio (OPV); Haemophilus Influenza B (HbCV); and Hepatitis B (HBV). A booster of **Tetanus-diptheria (Td)** is recommended once every 10 years, and adults travelling to Mexico should consider an additional dose of Polio vaccine if they have not already had one during their adult years.

Typhoid fever is common in Mexico, especially in rural areas. Transmitted through contaminated food and water and by direct contact, typhoid produces fever, headaches, fatigue, and constipation in its victims. In recent years **cholera,** caused by bacteria in contaminated food, reached epidemic stages in parts of Mexico. Cholera's symptoms are diarrhea, dehydration, vomiting, and cramps; it can be fatal if untreated. Vaccines are recommended for those planning to travel to rural areas and persons with stomach problems.

Hepatitis A is a high risk in Mexico and Central America. Hep. A is a viral infection of the liver acquired primarily through contaminated water, ice, shellfish, or unpeeled fruits, and vegetables, as well as from sexual contact. Symptoms include fatigue, fever, loss of appetite, nausea, dark urine, jaundice, vomiting, aches and pains, and light stools. Risk is highest in rural areas and the countryside, but it is also present in urban areas. **Hepatitis B** is a viral infection of the liver transmitted by sharing needles, having unprotected sex, or coming into direct contact with an infected person's lesioned skin. If you think you may be sexually active while traveling, working, or living in rural areas, you are typically advised to get the vaccination for Hepatitis B. Vaccination should begin six months before traveling. **Hepatitis C** is like Hepatitis B but is transmitted by intravenous drug users. Those with occupational exposure to blood, hemodialysis patients, or recipients of blood transfusions are at the highest risk. The disease can also be spread through sexual contact and through sharing of items like razors and toothbrushes which may have traces of blood on them, although not through casual contact or saliva. No effective antiviral medication is approved for use in humans.

Malaria, transmitted by mosquitoes, is a risk in many rural regions of Mexico, particularly along the southwest coast (Campeche, Chiapas, Colima, Guerrero, Sinaloa, Michoacan, Nayarit, Oaxaca, Tabasco, and Quintana Roo). Flu-like symptoms can strike up to a year after returning home; visit a doctor if you're in doubt, since untreated malaria can cause anemia, kidney failure, coma, and death. Malaria poses an especially serious threat to pregnant women and their fetuses. The risk is greatest in rural areas. If hiking or staying overnight in certain areas (whether camping or not), you may want to take weekly anti-malarial drugs.

Dengue is just one more reason to arm yourself against dive-bombing mosquitoes. Recent epidemics have been reported in parts of Mexico. Dengue has flu-like symptoms and is often indicated by a rash three to four days after the onset of fever. There is no vaccine; the only prevention is to avoid mosquito bites. If you are experiencing any symptoms associated with dengue fever, see a doctor immediately.

For region-specific health data and up-to-date information about which vaccinations are recommended for your destination, try these resources: The **United States Centers for Disease Control and Prevention** (based in Atlanta, Georgia), an excellent source of information for travelers around the world, maintains an international fax information service for travelers. Call 1-888-232-3299 and select an international travel directory; the requested information will be faxed to you. Similar information is available from the CDC website at http://www.cdc.gov. The **United States State**

Department compiles Consular Information Sheets on health, entry requirements, and other issues for all countries of the world. Particularly helpful is the website at http://travel.state.gov. For quick information on travel warnings, call the **Overseas Citizens' Services** (tel. (202) 647-5225). To receive the same Consular Information Sheets by fax, dial (202) 647-3000 directly from a fax machine and follow the recorded instructions.

Diabetics can contact the **American Diabetes Association**, 1660 Duke St., Alexandria, VA 22314 (tel. (800) 232-3472) to receive copies of the article "Travel and Diabetes" and a diabetic ID card, which carries messages in 18 languages explaining the carrier's diabetic status.

The **International Association for Medical Assistance to Travelers (IAMAT)** offers a membership ID card, a directory of English-speaking doctors around the world who have detailed charts on immunization requirements, various tropical diseases, climate, and sanitation. Membership is free, though donations are appreciated and used for further research. Contact chapters in the **U.S.,** (tel. (716) 754-4883, 8am-4pm/EST; email iamat@sentex.net) or **Canada,** (tel. (519) 836-0102).

WOMEN'S HEALTH

Women traveling in unsanitary conditions are vulnerable to urinary tract and bladder infections, common and severely uncomfortable bacterial diseases which cause a burning sensation, and painful and sometimes frequent urination. Drink tons of vitamin-C-rich juice, plenty of clean water, and urinate frequently, especially right after intercourse. Untreated, these infections can lead to kidney infections, sterility, and even death. If symptoms persist, see a doctor. If you often develop vaginal yeast infections, take along enough over-the-counter medicine, as treatments may not be readily available in Mexico.

Wearing loosely fitting trousers or a skirt and cotton underwear may help. In many smaller Mexican towns, it is next to impossible to find tampons and the pads that are on sale are unlikely to be your preferred brand, so it may be advisable to take supplies along. Refer to the *Handbook for Women Travellers* by Maggie and Gemma Moss (published by Piatkus Books) or to the women's health guide *Our Bodies, Our Selves* (published by the Boston Women's Health Collective) for more extensive information specific to women's health on the road.

BIRTH CONTROL

Reliable contraceptive devices may be difficult to find while traveling. Women on the pill should bring enough to allow for possible loss or extended stays. Bring a prescription, since forms of the pill vary a good deal. The sponge is probably too bulky to be worthwhile on the road. Women who use a diaphragm should have enough contraceptive jelly on hand. Although **condoms** are widely available in Mexico, quality is variable, so buy plenty before you leave.

Abortion is illegal in Mexico; you'll have to cross the border to have one performed legally and safely. Women overseas who want an **abortion** should contact the **National Abortion Federation Hotline** (tel. (800) 772-9100; M-F 9:30am-12:30pm, 1:30-5:30pm), 1775 Massachusetts Ave. NW, Washington, D.C. 20036. The hotline can direct you to organizations which provide information on the availability of and techniques for abortion in other countries. For information on contraception, condoms, and abortion worldwide, contact the **International Planned Parenthood Federation,** European Regional Office, Regent's College Inner Circle, Regent's Park, London NW1 4NS (tel. (0171) 487 7900, fax (0171) 487 7950).

TRAVELER'S DIARRHEA (TURISTA)

One of the biggest health threats in Mexico is the water. **Traveler's diarrhea,** known in Mexico as *turista,* often lasts two or three days (symptoms include cramps, nausea, vomiting, chills, and a fever as high as 103°F (39°C)) and is the dastardly consequence of ignoring the following advice: never drink unbottled water; ask for **agua purificada** in restaurants and hotels. If you must purify your own water, bring it to a rolling boil (simmering isn't enough) and let it boil for about 30 minutes, or treat it with iodine drops or tablets. Don't brush your teeth with tap water, and don't even rinse your toothbrush under the faucet. Keep your mouth closed in the shower. Many a sorry traveler has been fooled by the clever disguise of impure water—the treacherous ice cube. Stay away from those tasty-looking salads: uncooked vegetables (including lettuce and coleslaw) are a great way to get *turista.* Other culprits are raw shellfish, unpasteurized milk, and sauces containing raw eggs. Peel fruits and vegetables before eating them. Beware of food from markets or street vendors that may have been "washed" in dirty water or fried in rancid oil. Juices, peeled fruits, and exposed coconut slices are all risky. Also beware of frozen treats that may have been made with bad water. A golden rule in Mexico: **boil it, peel it, cook it—or forget it.** Otherwise, your stomach will not forgive you.

Virtually everyone gets *turista* on their first trip to Mexico; many get it every time they visit, regardless of how careful they are with food. So don't fret. A common symptomatic diarrhea-only treatment is **Immodium** (the liquid works faster), but to combat all-out *turista,* forget standard remedies like Pepto-Bismol and take **Lomotil,** a miracle drug sold over the counter in Mexican pharmacies. Avoid anti-diarrheals if you suspect you have been exposed to contaminated food or water, which puts you at risk for other diseases. The most dangerous side effect of diarrhea is dehydration; the simplest and most effective anti-dehydration formula is 8 oz. of (clean) water with a ½ tsp. of sugar or honey and a pinch of salt. Also good are soft drinks without caffeine, and salted crackers. Down several of these remedies a day, rest, and wait for the disease to run its course. If you develop a fever or your symptoms don't go away after four or five days, consult a doctor. Also consult a doctor if children develop traveler's diarrhea, since treatment is different.

AIDS, HIV, STDS

Acquired Immune Deficiency Syndrome (AIDS or **SIDA** as it is known in Spanish) is a growing problem around the world. The World Health Organization estimates that there were about 16,000 new HIV infections a day in 1997; more than 90% of those infections occur in developing countries. Mexico does not require HIV testing for travelers entering the country.

The easiest mode of HIV transmission is through direct blood to blood contact with an HIV+ person; never share intravenous drug, tattooing, or other needles. The most common mode of transmission is sexual intercourse. Health professionals recommend the use of latex condoms; follow the instructions on the packet. Since it isn't always easy to buy condoms when traveling, take a supply with you before you depart for your trip. Latex condoms are safer than lambskin ones, which have virus-permeable pores. Avoid oil-based lubricants like Vaseline, which destroy the integrity of the latex, rendering it useless in the prevention of HIV transmission. Casual contact (including drinking from the same glass or using the same eating utensils as an infected person) is not believed to pose a risk.

For more information on AIDS, call the **U.S. Center for Disease Control's** 24-hour Hotline at (800) 342-2437. In Europe, write to the **World Health Organization,** attn: Global Program on AIDS, Avenue Appia 20, 1211 Geneva 27, Switzerland (tel. (41 22) 791-2111; fax. (41 22) 791-0746), for statistical material on AIDS internationally. Or write to the **Bureau of Consular Affairs,** #6831, Department of State, Washington, D.C. 20520. Council's brochure, *Travel Safe: AIDS and International Travel,* is available at all Council Travel offices.

Sexually transmitted diseases (STDs) such as gonorrhea, chlamydia, genital warts, syphilis, and herpes are much easier to catch than HIV. It's wise to look at your partner's genitals before you have sex. Warning signs for STDs include: swelling, sores, bumps, or blisters on sex organs, rectum, or mouth; burning and pain during urination and bowel movements; itching around sex organs; swelling or redness in the throat, flu-like symptoms with fever, chills, and aches. If these symptoms develop, see a doctor immediately. When having sex, condoms may protect you from certain STDs, but oral or even tactile contact can lead to transmission.

Insurance

Travel insurance generally covers four basic areas: medical/health problems, property loss, trip cancellation/interruption, and emergency evacuation. Beware of buying unnecessary travel coverage—your regular insurance policies may well extend to travel-related medical problems and property loss. However, you may consider purchasing travel insurance, especially if the cost of a potential trip cancellation/interruption or emergency medical evacuation is greater than you can absorb. **Medical insurance** (especially university policies) often covers costs incurred abroad; check with your provider. **Medicare's** very limited "foreign travel" coverage is valid in Mexico. Canadians should check with the provincial Ministry of Health or Health Plan Headquarters for details about the extent of coverage. The Commonwealth Department of Health and Family Services can provide more information. Your **homeowners' insurance** (or your family's coverage) often covers theft during travel. Homeowners are generally covered against loss of travel documents (passport, plane ticket, railpass, etc.) up to US$500. Most **American Express** (customer service tel. (800) 528-4800) cardholders receive automatic car rental (collision and theft, but not liability) insurance and ground travel accident coverage of US$100,000 on flight purchases made with the card. Remember that insurance companies usually require a copy of the police report for thefts, or evidence of having paid medical expenses (such as doctor's statements or receipts) before they will honor a claim—they also may have time limits on filing for reimbursement. Always carry policy numbers and proof of insurance. Check with each insurance carrier for specific restrictions and policies. Most of the carriers listed below have 24-hour hotlines:

Access America, 6600 West Broad St., P.O. Box 11188, Richmond, VA 23230 (tel. (800) 284-8300; fax (804) 673-1491). Covers trip cancellation/interruption, on-the-spot hospital admittance costs, emergency medical evacuation, sickness, and baggage loss. 24-hr. hotline (if abroad, call the hotline collect at (804) 673-1159 or (800) 654-1908).

Avi International, 30 Rue de Mogador, 75009 Paris, France (tel. 33 (0) 1 44 63 51 86; fax 33 (0) 1 40 82 90 35). Caters primarily to the international youth traveler, covering emergency travel expenses, medical/accident, dental, liability, and baggage loss. 24-hour hotline.

Travel Assistance International, by Worldwide Assistance Services, Inc., 1133 15th St. NW, Suite 400, Washington, D.C. 20005-2710 (tel. (800) 821-2828 or (202) 828-5894; fax (202) 828-5896; email wassist@aol.com; http://www.worldwide-assistance.com). TAI provides its members with a 24-hr. free hotline for travel emergencies and referrals in over 200 countries. Their Per-Trip (starting at US$21) and Frequent Traveler (starting at US$88) plans include medical (evacuation and repatriation), travel, and communication services.

Alternatives to Tourism

STUDY AND TRAVEL

Popular in Mexico, foreign study programs vary tremendously in expense, academic quality, living conditions, degree of contact with local students, and exposure to local culture and languages. There is a plethora of exchange programs for high school students. Many American undergraduates enroll in programs sponsored by U.S. universities, and most colleges have offices that give advice and information on study abroad. Ask for the names of recent participants in these programs, and get in touch with them in order to judge which program is best for you. Cuernavaca, San Miguel de Allende, Oaxaca, Guanajuato, and Mexico City are all well known for language programs. Smaller local schools are generally cheaper, but international organizations may be better able to arrange academic credit at your home institution.

If you're already fluent in Spanish, consider enrolling in the regular programs of a Mexican university. Applications to Mexican state universities are due in early spring.

However, don't expect to receive credit at your home institution. The only Mexican university accredited in the U.S. is the **Universidad de las Américas,** Ex-Hacienda Santa Catarina Martír, Apartado Postal 100, Cholula, Puebla 72820 (tel. (22) 29 20 00). Some Mexican universities organize programs designed specifically for foreign students. The **Centro de Enseñanza para Extranjeros (CEPE),** part of the **Universidad Nacional Autónoma de México (UNAM),** provides semester, intensive, and summer programs in Spanish, art, history, literature, and Chicano studies. The program is open only to undergraduate and graduate foreign students. The school also has a campus in Taxco. Write to UNAM, Apdo. 70-391, Avenida Universidad, Delegación Coyoacán, México, D.F. 04510 (tel. (5) 622-24-70; fax 616-26-72). Other institutes outside of Mexico that sponsor programs in Mexico include:

American Institute for Foreign Study, College Division, 102 Greenwich Ave., Greenwich, CT 06830 (tel. (800) 727-2437 x6084; http://www.aifs.com). Organizes programs for high school and college study in Mexican universities. Summer, fall, spring, and year-long programs are available. Scholarships available. Contact Yesenia Garcia with questions at email ygarcia@aifs.com.

College Semester Abroad, School for International Training, Admissions, Kipling Rd., P.O. Box 676, Brattleboro, VT 05302 (tel. (800) 336-1616; fax 258-3500). Runs semester-long programs in Oaxaca. Programs cost US$8900, excluding transportation to Mexico, all other expenses included. Financial aid available and U.S. financial aid is transferable.

International Association for the Exchange of Students for Technical Experience (IAESTE), 10400 Little Patuxent Pkwy. #250, Columbia, MD 21044-3510 (tel. (410) 997-3068; fax (410) 997-5186; email iaste@aipt.org; http://www.aipt.orgl). Operates 8- to 12-week programs in Mexico for college students who have completed two years of study in a technical field. Non-refundable US$50 application fee; apply by Dec. 16 for summer placement.

Language Link Incorporated, P.O. Box 3006, Peoria, IL 61612 (tel. (800) 552-2051). Runs the Spanish Language Institute-Center for Latin American Studies in Cuernavaca (US$255 per week) and Mazatlán (US$290 per week). Program offers beginning, intermediate, and advanced level language courses for people of all ages. Students live with Mexican families. To contact the Institute directly, call (800) 552-2051.

WORK AND VOLUNTEER

The Mexican government is wary of giving up precious jobs to foreigners when many of its own people are unemployed. It used to be that only 10% of the employees of foreign firms located in Mexico could have non-Mexican citizenship; now the limit depends on the sector. If you manage to secure a position with a Mexican business, your employer must get you a **work permit.** It is possible, but illegal, to work without a permit and you risk deportation if caught. However, you may be more successful in obtaining a **volunteer** position. Adventurous job-hunters can arm themselves with a battery of books; try *International Jobs: Where They Are, How to Get Them,* published by **Harper Collins** (order 1000 Keystone Industrial Par, Scranton, PA 18512; tel. (800) 242-4090; fax (800) 822-4090; US$16; fifth edition is scheduled for release in early December, available at many bookstores). **Peterson's** publishes a **Vacation Work series** with titles that include *Overseas Summer Jobs 1999*, *Work Your Way Around the World*, *Teaching English Abroad*, and *The International Directory or Volunteer Work* (each is $16.95 each, available in bookstores or call Peterson's Customer Service, 800-338-3282. 20% off list price if you order through their online bookstore, http://boostore.petersons.com.) The following organizations may be able to arrange volunteer opportunities, paid positions, or internships in Mexico:

Global Volunteers, 375 E. Little Canada Rd., St. Paul, MN 55117 (tel. (800) 487-1074; fax (612) 482-0915; email email@globalvolunteers.org; http://www.globalvolunteers.org). Volunteers of all ages spend two weeks in Querétaro, Guanajuato,

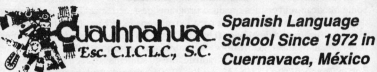

or Dolores Hidalgo teaching English to students in Guanajuato. Participation fee is $995; includes all expenses except transportation to Mexico.

Los Niños, 287 G Street, Chula Vista, CA 91910 (tel. (619) 426-9110; fax 426-6664). Offers groups of 15-22 opportunities to participate in community projects and education programs near the U.S.-Mexico border. Participation fees vary.

Office of Overseas Schools, A/OS Room 245, SA-29, Dept. of State, Washington, D.C. 20522-2902 (tel. (703) 875-7800; fax 875-7979). Keeps a list of schools abroad and agencies that arrange placement for Americans to teach abroad.

Transitions Abroad Publishing, Inc., 18 Hulst Rd., P.O. Box 1300, Amherst, MA 01004-1300 (tel. (800) 293-0373; fax (413) 256-0373; email trabroad@aol.com; http://www.transabroad.com). Publishes a bi-monthly magazine listing of opportunities and printed resources for those seeking to study, work, or travel abroad. The possibilities seem endless. They also publish The *Alternative Travel Directory,* an listing of information for the "active international traveler," and *Work Abroad,* a comprehensive guide to finding and prearing for a job overseas. For subscriptions (U.S. US$20 for 6 issues, Canada US$30, other countries US$42), contact them at Transitions Abroad, P.O. Box 1300, Amherst, MA 01003-1400.

World Teach, Harvard Institute for International Development, 14 Story St., Cambridge, MA 02138 (tel. (617) 495-5527; fax 495-1599; email info@worldteach.org; http://worldteach.org). Volunteers teach English, math, science, and environmental education to students of all ages in Mexico. Bachelor's degree required for six-month and year-long programs. Room and board are provided during the period of service, but volunteers must pay a fee covering health insurance and training.

Specific Concerns

WOMEN TRAVELERS

Women who travel through Mexico are often surprised by the unsolicited attention they receive. If you have two X chromosomes, and especially if you look like an *extranjera* (foreigner), you may find it difficult to shake off unwanted companions. Persistent men will insist on joining you; walking down the street, you will hear whistles and propositions. If you're fair-skinned, *"güera, güera"* will follow you everywhere. Offer no response or eye contact. Attention is usually more annoying than dangerous, but in real emergencies scream for help. Don't consider yourself safe just because people in uniform are around.

Don't hesitate to seek out a police officer or a passerby if you are being harassed. *Let's Go* lists emergency numbers in the **Practical Information** listings of most cities. Memorize the emergency numbers in all of the states you are planning to visit in Mexico. Carry a **whistle** or an **airhorn** on your keychain, and don't hesitate to use it in an emergency. A **Model Mugging** course will not only prepare you for a potential mugging, but it will also raise your level of awareness of your surroundings as well as your confidence (see **Safety and Security**). Women also face additional health concerns when traveling (see **Health**).

Awareness of Mexican social standards can prevent unpleasant and dangerous confrontations. Wearing short shorts or halter tops (or not wearing bras) will result in extra harassment; it's best to wear knee-length shorts. Bring a lightweight long skirt to wear in churches or in conservative regions like Chiapas. Almost without exception, *cantinas* are all-male institutions; the only women who ever enter are working, either as servers or as prostitutes.

If you are traveling with a male friend, it may help to pose as a couple: it will make it easier to share rooms and will also chill the blood of horny Romeos. Wearing a **"wedding ring"** on the left hand might also discourage unwanted attention. Northern Mexico, especially the border towns, is less congenial to women travelers. Oaxaca, Chiapas, and the Yucatán are friendlier, safer places. The following resources may prove useful in finding out more information for women travelers.

More Women Travel: *Adventures, Advice & Experience,* by Miranda Davies and Natania Jansz (Penguin, US$16.95). Essays by women travelers in several foreign countries plus a decent bibliography and resource index. From Rough Guides, 345 Hudson St. 14th fl., New York, NY 10014 (tel. (212) 366 2348; fax 414 3395; email rough@panix.com; www.roughguides.com/women).

Active Women Vacation Guide, by Evelyn Kay (US$17.95; shipping is free for *Let's Go* readers). Includes listings of 1,000 trips worldwide offered by travel companies for active women and true stories of women's traveling adventures. Blue Panda Publications, 3031 Fifth St., Boulder, CO 80304 (tel. (303) 449 8474; fax 449 7525).

Women's Travel in Your Pocket, Ferrari Guides, P.O. Box 37887, Phoenix, AZ 85069 (tel. (602) 863-2408; email ferrari@q-net.com; http://www.q-net.com), an annual guide for women (especially lesbians) traveling worldwide. Hotels, night life, dining, shopping, organizations, group tours, cruises, outdoor adventure and lesbian events (US$14, plus shipping).

OLDER TRAVELERS

Senior citizens are eligible for a wide range of discounts on transportation, museums, movies, theaters, concerts, restaurants, and accommodations. If you don't see a senior citizen price listed, ask, and you may be delightfully surprised. Agencies for senior group travel are growing in enrollment and popularity. Try **ElderTreks** (597 Markham St., Toronto, Ontario, CANADA, M6G 2L7, tel. (800) 741-7956 or (416) 588-5000, fax 588-9839, email passages@inforamp.net; http://www.eldertreks.com) or **Walking the World** (P.O. Box 1186, Fort Collins, CO 80522, tel. (970) 498-0500; fax 498-9100; email walktworld@aol.com), which sends trips to Mexico and Central America.

Elderhostel, 75 Federal St., 3rd fl., Boston, MA 02110-1941 (tel. (617) 426-7788; email Cadyg@elderhostel.org; http://www.elderhostel.org). For those 55 or over (spouse of any age). Programs at colleges, universities, and other learning centers in Mexico on varied subjects lasting 1-4 weeks.

National Council of Senior Citizens, 8403 Colesville Rd., Silver Spring, MD 20910-31200 (tel. (301) 578-8800; fax 578-8999). Memberships cost US$13 per year, US$33 for 3 years, or US$175 for a lifetime. Seniors can receive hotel and auto rental discounts, a senior citizen newspaper, and use of a discount travel agency.

No Problem! Worldwise Tips for Mature Adventurers, by Janice Kenyon. Advice and info on insurance, finances, security, health, packing. Useful appendices. US$16 from Orca Book Publishers, P.O. Box 468, Custer, WA 98240-0468.

Unbelievably Good Deals and Great Adventures That You Absolutely Can't Get Unless You're Over 50, by Joan Rattner Heilman. After you finish reading the title page, check inside for some great tips on senior discounts. US$10 from Contemporary Books or online at http://www.amazon.com.

BISEXUAL, GAY, AND LESBIAN TRAVELERS

Mexican law does not mention homosexuality, and attitudes vary from state to state. While some regions have ongoing campaigns against this "social threat," there is a gay-rights movement in Mexico City and a more rapidly growing movement in Monterrey. Although discreet homosexuality is tolerated in most areas, public displays of gay affection are usually not and might be the quickest way of getting beaten up, especially in smaller Mexican towns. To find cities with **gay and lesbian nightlife** in Mexico, see that index entry. For more information on gay and lesbian travel, check out some of the following resources.

Damron Travel Guides, P.O. Box 422458, San Francisco, CA 94142-2458 (tel. (415) 255-0404 or (800) 462-6654; fax (415) 703-9049 or 703-8308; email damronco@damron.com; http://www.damron.com). Publishers of the Damron Address Book (US$15), which lists bars, restaurants, guest houses, and services in Mexico that cater to gay men. **Damron's Accommodations** lists gay and lesbian hotels around the world (US$19). Mail order is available for an extra US$5

Ferrari Guides, P.O. Box 37887, Phoenix, AZ 85069 (tel. (602) 863-2408; fax 439-3952; email ferrari@q-net.com; http://www.q-net.com). Gay and lesbian travel guides, including the newly released *Gay Mexico* (US$18) as well as *Ferrari Guides' Gay Travel A to Z* (US$16), *Ferrari Guides' Men's Travel in Your Pocket* (US$16), and *Ferrari Guides' Inn Places* (US$16). Available in bookstores or by mail order. (Postage/handling US$5 for the first item, US$1 for each additional item mailed within the U.S. In Canada, first item $10. Overseas, call or write for shipping cost.)

International Gay and Lesbian Travel Association, 4331 N. Federal Hwy., Suite 304, Fort Lauderdale, FL 33308 (tel. (954) 776-2626 or (800) 448-8550; fax (954) 776-3303; email IGLTA@aol.com; http://www.iglta.org). An organization of over 1350 companies serving gay and lesbian travelers worldwide. Call for lists of travel agents, accommodations, and events.

International Lesbian and Gay Association (ILGA), 81 rue Marché-au-Charbon, B-1000 Bruxelles, Belgium (tel./fax 32-2-502-24 71; email ilga@ilga.org; http://www.ilga.org). Not a travel service. Provides political information, such as the most recent homosexuality laws of individual countries.

Spartacus International Gay Guides (US$32.95), published by Bruno Gmunder, Verlag GMBH, Leuschnerdamm 31, 10999 Berlin, Germany (tel. (49) 030 615 0030; fax (49) 030 615 9007; email bgvtravel@aol.com). Lists bars, restaurants, hotels, and bookstores around the world catering to gays. Also lists hotlines for gays in various countries and up-to-date homosexuality laws for each country. Available in bookstores and in the U.S. by mail from Lambda Rising, 1625 Connecticut Ave. NW, Washington D.C., 20009-1013 (tel. (202) 462-6969).

DISABLED TRAVELERS

Mexico is becoming increasingly accessible to travelers with disabilities, especially in popular resorts such as Acapulco and Cancún. Northern cities closer to the U.S. also tend to be more accessible; Saltillo might be the most wheelchair-friendly city in the entire country. Money talks—the more you are willing to spend, the less difficult it is to find accessible facilities. Most public and long-distance modes of transportation and most of the non-luxury hotels don't accommodate wheelchairs. Public bathrooms are almost all inaccessible, as are many ruins, parks, historic buildings, and museums. Still, with some advance planning, an affordable Mexican vacation is not impossible. Those with disabilities should inform airlines and hotels of their disabilities when making arrangements for travel; some time may be needed to prepare special accommodations. The following organizations provide useful information:

Directions Unlimited, 720 N. Bedford Rd., Bedford Hills, NY 10507 (tel. (800) 533-5343; in NY (914) 241-1700; fax (914) 241-0243). Specializes in arranging individual and group vacations, tours, and cruises for the physically disabled. Group tours for blind travelers.

Flying Wheels Travel Service, 143 W. Bridge St., Owatonne, MN 55060 (tel. (800) 535-6790; fax 451-1685). Arranges trips in the U.S. and abroad for groups and individuals in wheelchairs or with other sorts of limited mobility.

Mobility International USA (MIUSA), P.O. Box 10767, Eugene, OR 97440 (tel. (541) 343-1284 voice and TDD; fax 343-6812; email info@miusa.org; http://www.miusa.org). Sells the 3rd Edition of *A World of Options: A Guide to International Educational Exchange, Community Service, and Travel for Persons with Disabilities* (individuals US$35; organizations US$45).

Society for the Advancement of Travel for the Handicapped (SATH), 347 Fifth Av., #610, New York, NY 10016 (tel. (212) 447-1928; fax 725-8253; email sathtravel@aol.com; http://www.sath.org). Advocacy group publishing a quarterly color travel magazine *OPEN WORLD* (free for members or US$13 for nonmembers). Also publishes a wide range of information sheets on disability travel facilitation and accessible destinations. Annual membership US$45, students and seniors US$30.

MINORITY TRAVELERS

Although culturally diverse, Mexico is largely racially homogeneous. Mexicans are indigenous (called *indígenas*), white, or some mixture of the two (called *mestizo)*. The whiter your skin, the better treatment you'll get in larger cities, and the more you'll stand out in rural areas. Speaking English in larger cities may entitle you to royal treatment, whereas in medium to small cities, non-Spanish speakers are immediately viewed as threats. Practically any other ethnicity will mark you as a foreigner in Mexico, and as a result you might receive attention from curious locals, particularly in smaller communities. On most occasions this attention (stares, giggling, questions) is not meant to be hostile; it arises from curiosity rather than racism. Try to be understanding of the excitement produced by difference. In most cases, Mexicans react more strongly to foreignness, particularly Anglophone, than to ethnicity.

A recent **Travel Industry Association of America (TIA)** study was published under the title "Minority Travelers: A Large and Growing Market" (find it at http://www.travelleader.com/tlpr/tia/minority.html) citing general traveling habits of some minority travelers. Another resource is **Go Girl!** The Black Woman's Book of Travel and Adventure., Elaine Lee, editor. The book is published by the Eighth Mountain Press, 624 SE 29th Ave., Portland, OR 97214 (tel. (503) 233-3936 or fax 233-0774). The book includes 52 travelers' tales, advice on how to travel inexpensively and safely, and a discussion of issues of specific concern to black women.

TRAVELERS WITH CHILDREN

Children should not be deprived of the wonders of a Mexican vacation; simply slow your pace and plan ahead to accommodate smaller companions. If you plan on going on walking trips, consider bringing along a papoose for carrying your baby. If you rent a car, make sure the company provides a seat for younger children. When deciding where to stay, find child-friendly accommodations. Restaurants often have children's menus and discounts. Virtually all museums and tourist attractions also have a children's rate. Children under two generally fly for 10% of the adult airfare on international flights (this does not necessarily include a seat). International fares are usually discounted 25% for children between age two and 11. Some of the following publications offer tips for adults traveling with children or distractions for the kids themselves:

Have Kid, Will Travel: 101 Survival Strategies for Vacationing With Babies and Young Children, by Claire Tristram, Lucille Tristram. Published by Andrews & McMeel for US$9; can be ordered at http://www.amazon.com.

How to take Great Trips with Your Kids, by Sanford and Jane Portnoy (US$9.95, shipping US$3). Advice on packing, finding child-friendly accommodations, and planning trips geared toward the age of your children. The Harvard Common Press, 535 Albany St., Boston, MA. 02118 (tel. (888) 657-3755; fax 695-9794).

DIETARY CONCERNS

It's not easy for **vegetarians** in Mexico: most meals include meat or are prepared with animal fat. Always find out if your *frijoles* were prepared using *manteca* (lard). Wherever possible, *Let's Go* includes vegetarian dining options, but if you have any doubts, check with your *camarero* to make sure that your food is completely meat-free. For more ideas, contact the **North American Vegetarian Society,** P.O. Box 72, Dolgeville, NY 13329 (tel. (518) 568-7970), which publishes *Transformative Adventures,* a guide to vacations and retreats (US$15). Membership in the Society costs US$20; family membership is US$26 and members receive a 10% discount on all publications. *The International Vegetarian Travel Guide* (UK£2) was last published in 1991. Order back copies from the Vegetarian Society of the UK (VSUK), Parkdale, Dunham Rd., Altringham, Cheshire WA14 4QG (tel. (0161) 928 0793; fax (0161) 926 9182; email veg@minxnet.co.uk; http://www.vegsoc.org). VSUK also publishes other titles, including *The European Vegetarian Guide to Hotels and Restaurants.* Call or send a self-addressed, stamped envelope for a listing.

Travelers who keep **kosher** should contact synagogues in larger cities for information on kosher restaurants; your own synagogue or Hillel should have access to lists of Jewish institutions across the nation. If you are strict in your observance, consider preparing your own food on the road. The **Jewish Travel Guide** lists synagogues, kosher restaurants, and Jewish institutions in over 80 countries. The book is available from Vallentine Mitchell Publishers, Newbury House 890-900, Eastern Ave., Newbury Park, Ilford, Essex, U.K. IG2 7HH (tel. (0181) 599 88 66; fax 599 09 84).

TRAVELING ALONE

Traveling alone results in greater freedom: you choose which museums to visit and which to avoid, whether to take the early bus or the midnight train. When you get sick of yourself, it annihilates shyness and pushes you to meet people. On the other hand, it makes you a more vulnerable target for robbery and harassment. Lone travelers need to be well organized and look confident at all times. Do not wander around back alleys looking confused, and try to regularly contact someone at home who knows your itinerary. Resources for the solo traveler include:

Connecting: Solo Traveler Network, P.O. Box 29088, 1996 W. Broadway, Vancouver, BC V6J 5C2, Canada (tel. (604) 737-7791 or (800) 557-1757; http://www.travel-wise.com/solo). Bi-monthly newsletter features member reports, going solo tips, single-friendly tips and travel companion ads. Annual directory lists holiday suppliers that avoid single supplement charges. Advice and lodging exchanges facilitated between members. Membership US$25.

A Foxy Old Woman's Guide to Traveling Alone, by Jay Ben-Lesser encompasses practically every specific concern, offering anecdotes and tips for anyone interested in solitary adventure. Available in bookstores and from Crossing Press in Freedom, CA (tel. (800) 777-1048), US$11.

Traveling On Your Own, by Eleanor Berman (US$13). Lists information resources for "singles" (old and young) and single parents. Crown Publishers, Inc., 201 East 50th St., New York, NY 10022 (tel. (212) 751-2600).

Traveling Solo: Advice and Ideas for More Than 250 Great Vacations, by Eleanor Berman. Published by Globe-Pequot Press, 6 Business Park Rd., Old Saybrook, CT 06475 (tel. (800) 285-4078; fax (860) 395-1418). Vacation ideas and how to translate them into the perfect solo vacation. Chapters for women traveling alone, single parents, and older travelers (US$17).

Packing

Two words: Pack light. The more things you have, the more you have to lose or get stolen, though having someone lighten your load may not seem like such a bad deal after a few days of back-breaking travel. Before you leave, pack your bag, strap it on, and imagine yourself walking uphill on hot asphalt for the next three hours. A good rule is to lay out only what you absolutely need, then take half the clothes and twice the money. One *New York Times* correspondent recommends that you "take no more than you can carry for half a mile at a dead run." You should also plan your packing according to the type of travel you'll be doing (multi-city backpacking tour, week-long stay in one place, etc.) and the area's high and low temperatures (see p. 1).

LUGGAGE

Backpack: If you plan to cover most of your itinerary by foot, a sturdy backpack is unbeatable. Many packs (mostly internal frame) are designed specifically for travelers, while others are for hikers; consider how you will use the pack before purchasing one or the other. In any case, get a quality pack with a strong, padded hip belt to transfer weight from your shoulders to your hips. Good packs cost anywhere from US$150-420. Bringing a smaller bag in addition to your pack allows you to leave your belongings behind while you go sight-seeing and to carry essentials onto the plane.

Duffel bag: If you are not backpacking, an empty, lightweight duffel bag packed inside your luggage will be useful: once abroad you can fill your luggage with purchases and keep your dirty clothes in the duffel.

Moneybelt or neck pouch: Guard your money, passport, railpass, and other important articles in either one of these, available at any good camping store, and keep it with you *at all times*. The moneybelt should tuck inside the waist of your pants or skirt; you want to hide your valuables, not announce them with a colorful fanny- or butt-pack. See **Safety and Security** for more information on protecting you and your valuables.

CLOTHING AND FOOTWEAR

Clothing: When choosing your travel wardrobe, aim for versatility and comfort, and avoid fabrics that wrinkle easily (to test a fabric, hold it tightly in your fist for 20 seconds). Solid colors mix and match best. At certain sights and in smaller towns, stricter dress codes (especially for women) call for something besides the basic shorts, t-shirts, and jeans. Always bring a jacket or wool sweater.

Walking shoes: Well-cushioned **sneakers** are good for walking, though you may want to consider a good waterproof pair of **hiking boots.** A double pair of socks—light silk or polypropylene inside and thick wool outside—will cushion feet, keep them dry, and help prevent blisters. Bring a pair of flip-flops for protection in the shower. Talcum powder in your shoes and on your feet can prevent sores, and moleskin is great for blisters. Break in your shoes before you leave.

Rain gear: A waterproof jacket and a backpack cover will take care of you and your stuff at a moment's notice. Gore-Tex and Gore-Tex imitation knockoffs are miracle fabrics that are both waterproof and breathable—a must if you plan on hiking. Avoid cotton as outer-wear, especially if you will be outdoors a lot.

MISCELLANEOUS

Washing clothes: Although laundromats are often available, at times it is easier to use a sink. Bring a small bar or tube of detergent soap such as **Woolite**, a rubber squash ball to stop up the sink, and a travel clothes line.

Film is expensive just about everywhere. Bring film from home and, if you will be seriously upset if the pictures are ruined, develop it at home. If you're not a serious photographer, you might want to consider bringing a **disposable camera** or two rather than an expensive, permanent one. Despite disclaimers, airport security X-rays *can* fog film, so either buy a lead-lined pouch, sold at camera stores, or ask the security to hand-inspect it. Always pack it in your carry-on luggage, since higher-intensity X-rays are used on checked luggage.

Other useful items: first-aid kit; umbrella; sealable plastic bags (for damp clothes, soap, food, shampoo, and other spillables); alarm clock; waterproof matches; sun hat; moleskin (for blisters); needle and thread; safety pins; sunglasses; a personal stereo (Walkman) with headphones; pocketknife; plastic water bottle; compass; string (makeshift clothesline and lashing material); towel; padlock; whistle; rubber bands; toilet paper; flashlight; cold-water soap; earplugs; insect repellent; electrical tape (for patching tears); clothespins; maps and phrasebooks; tweezers; garbage bags; sunscreen; vitamins. Some items not always readily available or affordable on the road: deodorant; razors; condoms; tampons.

GETTING THERE

Budget Travel Agencies

For help finding budget tickets, try some of the following travel agencies:

Council Travel (tel. 800-2-COUNCIL (226-8624); http://www.ciee.org/travel/index.htm), the travel division of Council, is a full-service travel agency specializing in youth and budget travel. They offer discount airfares on scheduled airlines, low-cost accommodations, guidebooks, and budget tours.

STA Travel, 6560 Scottsdale Rd. #F100, Scottsdale, AZ 85253 (tel. (800) 777-0112 nationwide; fax (602) 922-0793; http://sta-travel.com). A student and youth travel organization with over 150 offices worldwide offering discount airfares for young travelers, accommodations, tours, and insurance.

Travel CUTS (Canadian Universities Travel Services Limited), 187 College St., Toronto, Ont. M5T 1P7 (tel. (416) 979-2406; fax 979-8167; email mail@travelcuts). Canada's national student travel bureau and equivalent of Council, with 40 offices across Canada. Also in the U.K., 295-A Regent St., **London** W1R 7YA (tel. (0171) 637 31 61). Discounted domestic and international airfares open to all; special student fares to all destinations with valid ISIC. Issues ISIC, FIYTO, GO25, and HI hostel cards, as well as railpasses. Offers free *Student Traveller* magazine, as well as information on the Student Work Abroad Program (SWAP).

Let's Go Travel, Harvard Student Agencies, 17 Holyoke St., Cambridge, MA 02138 (tel. (617) 495-9649; fax 495-7956; email travel@hsa.net; http://hsa.net/travel). Railpasses, HI-AYH memberships, ISICs, ITICs, FIYTO cards, guidebooks (including every *Let's Go* at a substantial discount), maps, bargain flights, and a complete line of budget travel gear. All items available by mail; call or write for a catalogue (or see the catalogue in center of this publication).

Journeys International, Inc., 4011 Jackson Rd., Ann Arbor, MI 48103 (tel. (800) 255-8735; fax (313) 665-2945; email info@journeys-intl.com; http://www.journeys-intl.com). Offers small-group, guided explorations of 45 different countries in Asia, Africa, the Americas, and the Pacific. Call or email to obtain their free 74-page color catalogue, *The Global Expedition Catalogue.*

By Plane

The price you pay for airfare varies widely depending from whom you purchase your ticket and how flexible your travel plans are. Understanding the airline industry's byzantine pricing system is the best way of finding a cheap fare. Very generally, courier fares (if you can deal with restrictions) are the cheapest, followed by tickets bought from consolidators and stand-by seating. However, last-minute specials, airfare wars, and charter flights can often beat these fares. Always get quotes from different sources; an hour or two of research can save you hundreds of dollars. Call every toll-free number and don't be afraid to ask about discounts, as it's unlikely they'll be volunteered. Knowledgeable **travel agents,** particularly those specializing in the region(s) you will be traveling to, can provide excellent guidance. An agent whose clients fly mostly to Denver or Boise will not be the best person to hunt down a bargain flight to Mexico City. Travel agents may not want to spend time finding the cheapest fares (for which they receive the lowest commissions), but if you travel often you should definitely find an agent who will cater to you and your needs and track down deals in exchange for your frequent business.

Students and others under 26 should never need to pay full price for a ticket. Seniors can also get great deals; many airlines will also offer them airline passes with few restrictions and discounts for their companions as well. Sunday newspapers often have travel sections that list bargain fares from the local airport. Outsmart airline reps with the phone-book-sized *Official Airline Guide* (check your local library; at US$359 per year, the tome costs as much as some flights), a monthly guide listing nearly every scheduled flight in the world (with fares, US$479) and toll-free phone numbers for all the airlines that allow you to call in reservations directly. More accessible is Michael McColl's *The Worldwide Guide to Cheap Airfare* (US$15).

There is also a wealth of travel information to be found on the Internet. The **Air Traveler's Handbook** (http://www.cs.cmu.edu/afs/cs.cmu.edu/user/mkant/Public/Travel/airfare.html) is an excellent source of general information on air travel. **TravelHUB** (http://www.travelhub.com) provides a directory of travel agents that includes a searchable database of fares from over 500 consolidators (see **Ticket Consolidators**, below). Edward Hasbrouck maintains a **Consolidators FAQ** (http://www.travel-library.com/air-travel/consolidators.html) that provides great background on finding cheap international flights. Groups such as the **Air Courier Association** (http://www.aircourier.org) offer information about traveling as a courier and provide up-to-date listings of last minute opportunities.

Most airfares peak between mid-June and early September. Midweek (M-Th morning) round-trip flights run about US$40-50 cheaper than on weekends; weekend flights, however, are generally less crowded. Traveling from hub to hub will win a more competitive fare than from smaller cities. Return-date flexibility is usually not an option for the budget traveler; traveling with an "open return" ticket can be pricier than fixing a return date and paying to change it. Whenever flying internationally, pick up your ticket well in advance of the departure date, have the flight confirmed within 72 hours of departure, and arrive at the airport at least three hours before your flight.

COMMERCIAL AIRLINES

The airlines' published airfares should be just the beginning of your search. Even if you pay an airline's lowest published fare, you may waste hundreds of dollars. For the adventurous or the bargain-hungry, there are other options. But before shopping around it is a good idea to find out the average commercial price in order to measure just how great a "bargain" you are being offered.

Many airlines are now offering ticketing and reservations over the Internet, and some award discounts to web servers. The *Official Airline Guide* has a website (http://www.oag.com) that allows access to flight schedules. (One-time hook-up fee $25 and a user's fee of $.17-47 per minute). The **Air Traveler's Handbook** (http://www.cis.ohio-state.edu/hypertext/faq/usenet/travel/air/handbook/top.html) is an excellent source of general information on air travel. **Airlines of the Web** (http://www.itn.net/airlines) provides links to pages for most of the world's airlines.

American: (tel. 800-433-7300; http://www.americanair.com).
Continental: (tel. 800-525-0280; http://www.flycontinental.com).
United: P.O. Box 66100, Chicago, IL 60666 (tel. 800-241-6522; http://www.ual.com).
Cheap Tickets: (tel. 800-377-1000 or 310-645-5054).
NOW Voyager: Sells tickets over the Internet at its web page (http://www.nowvoyagertravel.com).

For flights in Mexico, contact the two major carriers to find the best bargain: **Mexicana** (tel. (800) 531-7921) or **Aeroméxico** (tel. (800) 237-6639).

By Bus or Train

Greyhound (800-231-2222; http://www.greyhound.com) serves many border towns, including El Paso and Brownsville, Texas. Schedule information is available at any Greyhound terminal, on the web page, or by calling the 800 number. Smaller lines serve other destinations. Buses tend not to cross the border, but at each of these stops you can pick up Mexican bus lines (among them **Tres Estrellas de Oro, Estrella Blanca, ADO,** and **Transportes Del Norte**) on the other side.

By train, you can take **Amtrak** (tel. 1-800-USA-TRAK) to El Paso, walk across the border to Ciudad Juárez and use other forms of transportation to travel within Mexico. Amtrak also serves San Diego and San Antonio, where you can catch a bus to the border towns (US$285-433 one-way from New York to El Paso, San Diego, or San Antonio). For more information, contact **Amtrak Vacations,** 2211 Butterfield Rd. Downers Grove, IL 60515 (tel. 800-321-8684).

By Car

Driving entails no bureaucratic complications within the *Zona Libre* (Free Zone). The *Zona Libre* extends from the U.S. border 22km into Mexico; it also includes all of Baja California. You will encounter checkpoints as soon as you reach the end of the Zona Libre (see **Driver's Licenses and Vehicle Permits,** p. 11). On the U.S. side of the border, several **auto clubs** provide routing services and protection against break-downs. Members of the **American Automobile Association (AAA),** Travel Agency Services Dept., 1000 AAA Dr., Heathrow, FL 32746 (tel. (800) 222-4357, (407) 444-4300, or (407) 894-3333; http://www.aaa.com) can receive free road maps and the excellent Mexico guide; members can also buy traveler's checks commission-free and are eligible for Mexican auto insurance. (AAA members needing road assistance while in Mexico should call (5) 588 70 55). o

Make sure you arrange to have your car insured in Mexico if you plan to drive it there. You can buy insurance at the border from one of the many small insurance offices located next door to the Mexico immigration offices. **Sanborn's,** Home Office, 2009 South 10th St., McAllen, TX 78503 (tel. (210) 686-0711; fax 686-0732), offers Mexican and Central American insurance through each of its 21 U.S. agencies located at major border cities in California, Texas, and Arizona. Along with insurance, you get all of the trimmings, including road maps, newsletters, a ride board and mile-by-mile guide to all the highways in Mexico called the Travelog. If you do not purchase a separate Legal Aid policy, and you are involved in an accident, the police might hold you in jail until everything is sorted out and all claims are settled.

ONCE THERE

Embassies and Consulates

Embassies and **consulates** provide a plethora of services for citizens away from home. They can refer you to an English-speaking doctor or lawyer, help replace a lost tourist card, and wire family or friends if you need money and have no other means of obtaining it. They cannot, however, cash checks, act as a postal service, get you out of trouble, supply counsel, or interfere in any way with the legal process in Mexico. Once in jail, you're on your own.

Procuradura General de Justicia has an office in Mexico City, Florencia 20 (tel. 625 76 92 or 625 76 96) and caters especially to tourists. If you need to file a complaint or police reports or seek legal advice, the *Procuradura* can assist you.

Getting Around

BY BUS

Mexico's extensive, astoundingly cheap bus service never ceases to amaze. Travel luxury class, often called **servicio ejecutivo** (executive service), and you'll get the royal treatment: reclining seats, sandwiches and soda, air-conditioning, and movies galore. Only slightly less fancy is **primera clase** (first-class). Buses are relatively comfortable and efficient; they occasionally even have videos, bathrooms, and functioning air-conditioners (ask at the ticket window). **Segunda clase** (second-class) buses, which are only slightly cheaper than *primera clase,* are sometimes overcrowded, hot, and uncomfortable. To maximize your comfort at night, choose a seat on the right side of the bus (to avoid the constant glare of oncoming headlights); during the day try to get the shady side of the bus. Even on non-air-conditioned buses, drivers or passengers often refuse to drive with the windows open. Don't make a scene. Air-conditioning can be refreshing...until the icicles start forming; bring a sweater or prepare to sniffle.

Buses are either *local* or *de paso* (passing by; you can't buy advance tickets). *Locales* originate at the station from which you leave. If few *locales* leave each day, try to buy your ticket in advance. Once you get on the bus, keep your ticket stub in case you're asked to show it later. *De paso* buses originate elsewhere and pass through your station. First-class *de pasos* sell only as many tickets as there are available seats—when the bus arrives, the driver disembarks to give this information to the ticket seller. When these tickets go on sale, forget civility, chivalry, and anything which might possibly stand between you and a ticket, or plan to spend the greater portion of your vacation in bus stations. You may end up sitting on the floor of a second-class *de paso* bus; ticket sales are based on the number of people with assigned seats who have gotten off the bus. This system does not, unfortunately, take into account the people and packages jammed into the aisle. In any case, if you know when boarding the bus that no seats are available, it's best to wait and board last. That way, while all other passengers without seats have to stand in the aisle, you are able to sit semi-comfortably on the step between the driver's compartment and the aisle.

BY TAXI

Taxis in Mexico are ubiquitous in big cities. Prices are reasonable (by U.S. standards), but since public buses are so frequent and cover so much ground, you shouldn't have to resort to a cab unless it's late at night or you're in a remote part of town. Be careful to avoid getting overcharged by always negotiating a price beforehand (bargaining is the norm) and not agreeing to go by *taxímetro* (metered fare)—it's often more expensive even if legit, but, most importantly, taxi drivers often tamper with the machine to make it charge exorbitant amounts to unsuspecting tourists. Also, the U.S. Department of State (http://www.state.gov) has warned of a rash of reported taxi robberies at gunpoint, particularly in the lime green cabs in Mexico City, but also elsewhere; the best way to avoid this is to only get *sitio* cabs at authorized stands or at hotels instead of flagging them down along the street.

BY CAR

Driving in Mexico is as exciting as swimming in shark-infested waters, and it's much more dangerous. The maximum speed on Mexican highways is 100km per hour (62mph) unless otherwise posted, but it is often ignored. Be especially careful driving during the rainy season (May-Oct.), when roads are often in poor condition, potholes become craters, and landslides are common. When driving on roads near the capital, watch out for fog. A sign warning *Maneje despacio* (drive slowly) should be taken seriously. Dirt roads can mean serious damage for your car if you don't have four-wheel drive. Watch for rocks and gravel and always have a spare tire available.

At night, pedestrians and livestock pop up on the roadway at the most unlikely times. If you can help it, don't drive at night. If you must, beware of oncoming cars without headlights. Whatever you do, never spend the night on the side of the road. When approaching a one-lane bridge, labeled *puente angosto* or *solo carril,* the first driver to flash headlights has the right of way. Lanes are narrow, so if a truck tries to pass your car on a two-lane road, you might need to pull off onto the gravel or graded dirt in order to give the vehicle enough room. (But be careful: the shoulder is often nonexistent or covered with vegetation.)

Exercise particular caution when driving along potentially dangerous Rte. 15 in the state of Sinaloa; Rte. 2 in the vicinity of Carborca, Sonora; Rte. 57 between Matehuala and San Luis Potosí; the highway between Palomares and Tuxtepec, Oaxaca; Rte. 3 in Baja (full of pot holes); and Rte. 40 between the city of Durango and the Pacific Coast. If possible, avoid Rte. 1 in Sinaloa. Check with local authorities or the nearest U.S. consulate for updates on bandit activity and areas of potential danger.

In Baja California, if you want to leave your car and go somewhere by public transportation for a few days, you must pay to park in an authorized lot; otherwise, the car will be towed or confiscated. The Motor Vehicle Office will tell you where to leave your car legally. To help reduce the heinous pollution in Mexico City, traffic in the metropolitan area is restricted (see p. 85)

PEMEX (Petroleos Mexicanos) sells two types of gas: Magna (regular) and Premium (unleaded). Unleaded gas is now almost universally available in Mexico; you will find it throughout Baja as well as in Guadalajara, Monterrey, Mexico City, most border towns, and all major metropolitan areas. Both Magna and Premium are extremely cheap by all but Saudi Arabian standards. Don't get overcharged: know how much gas you'll need before you pull in and make sure the register is rung back to zero before pumping begins. PEMEX accepts cash and checks only. When checking the tires, remember that pumps in Mexico are calibrated in kilograms.

The heat, bumpy roads, and fair-to-middling gas may well take a toll on your car. No matter what kind of car you sport, bring spare oil, spark plugs, fan belts and air, a spare tire, and fuel filters—these should take care of all but the biggest problems. If you break down on one of the major toll highways between 8am and 8pm, pull completely off the road, raise the hood, stay with your car, and wait for the **Angeles Verdes** (Green Angels) to come to the rescue. Green Angels are green-and-white emergency trucks dispatched by radio, staffed by almost a thousand mechanics, and equipped for performing common repair jobs, towing, changing tires, and addressing minor medical problems. Your green saviors may take a while to show up, but the service (except for parts, gas, and oil) is free. Tipping is optional but polite. These guardian angels will assist you anywhere but in the *Distrito Federal,* where you can contact the **Asociación Nacional Automovilística (ANA)** (tel. (5) 597 42 83).

While on the road in Mexico, you'll probably be stopped more than once by agents of the Federal Public Ministry and the Federal Judicial Police for a search of your car and its contents. To avoid being detained or arrested, be as cooperative as possible; they will usually just open your trunk and look around your car, it's fairly painless if you give them no reason to make it painful. Do *not* carry drugs, firearms, or shoulder-fired missiles in your car.

BY PLANE

Flying within Mexico is more expensive than taking a bus or train, but it is considerably cheaper than comparable flights between U.S. cities. It can be an excellent way of avoiding a 40-hour (or longer) bus ride; many budget travelers rule out the possibility, only to learn later that it would have been much cheaper than they had thought. Check with Mexican airlines (see p. 34) for special rates.

BY TRAIN

The Mexican railroads are all government-owned, with most lines operating under the name of **Ferrocarriles Nacionales de México** (National Railways of Mexico, FFNN). The train system is not as extensive, punctual, cheap, comfortable, or efficient as the bus system. Even when they are on time, trains (yes, even the "fast" ones) can take twice as long as buses to reach their destination. Other than the spectacular ride through the **Copper Canyon (Los Mochis-Creel;** see p. 222) you probably won't want to rely on trains unless you're nearly broke or crave a leisurely crawl through the country. Don't be surprised if the rail system is privatized and the majority of it axed completely in the next few years—it is already disappearing in most regions.

BY THUMB

> *Let's Go* urges you to use common sense if you decide to hitch, and to seriously consider all possible risks before you make that decision. The information listed below and throughout the book is not intended to recommend hitchhiking.

The Mexicans who pick up tourists are often friendly, offering meals, tours, or other extras. More often than not, they are generous and well-meaning; in fact, people who *don't* pick you up will often give you an apologetic look or a gesture of explanation. However, always be careful. Women should never hitchhike alone. Hitchhikers should size up the driver and find out where the car is going before getting in. Think twice if a driver opens the door quickly and offers to drive anywhere. Some bandit-ridden highways are particularly dangerous for hitchhikers (see **By Car,** p. 36).

Before getting in, make sure the passenger window or door opens from inside. If there are several people in the car, do not sit in the middle. Assume a quick-exit position, which rules out the back seat of a two-door car. Keep backpacks and other baggage where they are easily accessible—don't let the driver store them in the trunk. If you have trouble getting out for any reason, affecting the pose of someone about to vomit works wonders.

Accommodations

HOTELS

Bargain-seekers will not be disappointed with Mexico's selection of hotels. Although some (particularly in resort towns) are among the world's most overpriced, the majority of Mexican accommodations are shockingly affordable. Usually located within a block or two of the *zócalo,* the cheapest hotels rarely provide private bathrooms or air conditioning, though they do often have hot water and/or fans. Slightly higher-priced hotels usually reside in the same district but are much better equipped, including rooms with private bathrooms (often some with and some without). Before accepting any room, ask to see it, and always find out before paying whether the price includes any meals and if there are any extra taxes or surcharges.

All hotels, ranging from luxury resorts in Cancún to dumps in Monterrey, are controlled by the government's **Secretaria de Turismo (SECTUR).** This ensures that hotels of similar quality charge similar prices; you should always ask to see an up-to-date **official tariff sheet** if you doubt the quoted price. Although hotel prices are regulated, proprietors are not prohibited from charging *less* than the official rate. If the hotel looks like it hasn't seen a customer in several weeks, a little bargaining may work wonders, especially if you offer to stay a number of days. For a room with one bed, request *una habitación (un cuarto) con una cama.* If bedding down with a fellow wayfarer, ask for one *con dos camas* (with two beds).

For the bare-bones budget traveler, the hammock is the way to go, particularly on the coast: if you plan to travel on a shoestring, buy one. Most beach towns in Mexico are dotted with *palapas* (palm-tree huts). For a small fee, open-air restaurants double as places to hang your hat and hammock when the sun goes down. In small *yucateco* towns, locals often let travelers use hammock hooks for a pittance.

Hotels in Mexico often lock their doors at night, and small-town establishments may do so surprisingly early. A locked door doesn't necessarily mean "closed for the night," as someone is usually on duty. By arriving early in small towns or calling ahead if you can't avoid arriving late, and by checking with the hotel desk before going out for a late night on the town, you'll be able to stay out as late as you want to, and help dispel the Mexican myth of the obnoxious foreigner.

Reservations are absolutely necessary during Christmas, Semana Santa (Easter), and local festivals. *Semana Santa* is the week before Easter; in 1999, Easter is on April 4. However, at most other times, even during the summer season, you need not worry too much about reserving *budget* hotels ahead.

HOSTELS

With a few exceptions, Mexican hostels tend to be run-down and far from town. Their ban on alcohol, smoking restrictions, and limited hours (most are open daily 7-9am and 5-10pm) also deter many budget travelers. Although a bit cheaper than hotels, the couple of dollars you save don't usually make up for the inconvenience. Therefore, **Hostelling International** cards are not as useful in Mexico as they are in other countries. Most hostels will give you a bed even if you don't have a hostel card. They may, however, charge you more for it.

CAMPING

For the budget travel experience par excellence, try camping in Mexico. Campers accustomed to prim and proper campgrounds will be taken aback, however. Mexican national parks often exist only in theory; many are indistinguishable from the surrounding cities. Trails, campgrounds, and rangers are strictly *gringo* concepts.

Privately owned **trailer parks** are relatively common on major highways—look for signs with a picture of a trailer, or the words *parque de trailer, campamento,* or *remolques.* These places may or may not allow campers to pitch tents. Don't sleep in

a vehicle parked next to a well-traveled road, or screeching brakes and the shattering glass of your car may shake you from that peaceful slumber.

Purchase **equipment** before you leave. This way you'll know exactly what you have and how much it weighs. Spend some time examining catalogs and talking to knowledgeable salespeople.

Keeping In Touch

MAIL

Mexican mail service is slow. Although mail usually arrives, it can take anywhere from one to three weeks for **correo aéreo** (airmail) to reach the U.S., and at the very least two weeks to reach Europe and other destinations. Official estimates average 40 days by boat, but in reality sea-mail will take months. In Mexico, never deposit anything important in the black holes called mailboxes; take it straight to the **oficina de correos** (post office) instead. There you can buy all the *estampillas* or *timbres* (stamps) that your *carta* (letter) needs. Anything important should be sent *registrado* (registered mail) or in duplicate. For the speediest service possible, **MexPost** works in collaboration with Express Mail International in the U.S. and similar express mail services in other countries to deliver mail quickly and reliably. Three days is the official MexPost delivery time to the U.S., but allow up to a week; in any case, it's *much* faster than regular or registered mail (and much more expensive). MexPost offices are usually found next to regular post offices, but sometimes they're located kilometers away—in either case, post office staff can direct you to the right place.

It's wise to use the Spanish abbreviations or names for countries (EE.UU. or EUA for the U.S.). Write *Por Avión* on all postcards and letters not otherwise marked. There is no size limitation for packages, but parcels cannot weigh more than 25kg. Regulations for mailing parcels may vary from state to state. While it is often possible to send packages from smaller towns, post offices in large cities provide more reliable service. Before attempting to send anything, go to the post office and note the weight limitations, necessary documentation, addresses and hours of the customs and trade offices in the city, and whether the box should be brought open or sealed. All packages are reopened and inspected by customs at the border, so closing the box with string, not tape, is recommended. In general, in order to send packages you must provide the following: tourist card data (number, duration of validity, date of issue, place of issue), list of contents including estimated value and nature of the package ("Gift" works best), address and return address. It is customary for those mailing parcels to use their home address, or at least some address in the same country as the parcel's destination, as a return address to ensure eventual delivery. In a trade office, you may need to show receipts for each item purchased in Mexico. Postal officials usually record the information from the customs form on the front of the package as well.

You can have letters sent to you in Mexico through **Lista de Correos,** a letter-holding service available at any post office. When picking up mail sent to you via *Lista de Correos,* look for the list posted, and check it carefully for any possible misspellings. If there is no list posted, ask the attendant, *"¿Está la lista de hoy?"* (Is today's list here?). If it is, give your name. Letters should be marked *Favor de retener hasta la llegada* ("Please hold until arrival"); they will be held up to 15 days. If you know people in Mexico, using their addresses may be better.

Mail sent to *Lista de Correos* should be addressed to a first and last name only, capitalizing and underlining the name under which the item should be filed alphabetically. A letter could be filed under any misspelled permutation of the recipient's names. If possible, go through the *Lista de Correos* yourself. If not, watch the person who does and ask for the mail under both your first and your last name, just to make sure. Address letters as follows:

Carrie GLIDDEN
Lista de Correos
Calle 65 (street address for post office, if known—otherwise leave it out)
Mérida (city), Yucatán (state)
79000 (postal code)
MEXICO

Packages sent via **Express Mail International, FedEx,** or other express services might be retained at a different office (often the **MexPost** office). Be sure to make it clear to officials exactly what type of package you're expecting, and if it is express, ideally come armed with the tracking number. Also, Express Mail International has lately encountered problems with bandits near Mexico City; some packages are robbed and never arrive. In any case, it would be foolish to send anything particularly valuable via any sort of mail to Mexico.

Hotels where you have reserved a room will usually hold mail for you, but let them know ahead of time. **American Express** travel offices throughout the world will act as a mail service for cardholders if you contact them in advance. Under this free **"Client Letter Service,"** they will hold mail for no more than 30 days, forward upon request, and accept telegrams. Once again, the last name of the person to whom the mail is addressed should be capitalized and underlined. Some offices will offer these services to non-cardholders (especially those who have purchased AmEx Travellers' Cheques), but you must call ahead to make sure. Check the **Practical Information** section of the countries you plan to visit; *Let's Go* lists AmEx office locations for most large cities. A complete list is available free from AmEx (tel. (800) 528-4800) in the booklet **Traveler's Companion** or online at http://www.americanexpress.com. Connect from there to world-wide sites.

TELEPHONES

When trying to reach Mexico from another country, patience is the key to success. Dial your country's **international long-distance access number** (011 from the U.S. and Canada; 0011 from Australia; 00 from U.K., Ireland, and New Zealand; 09 from South Africa), then **52** (Mexico's country code), then the **city code** (listed in this guide at the end of each city's practical information section), and then the **phone number.**

Once you are in Mexico, getting lines to foreign countries can be very difficult. Many public phones don't access international lines. Dial 09 for an English-speaking international long-distance operator. If you speak Spanish fluently and can't reach the international operator, dial 07 for the national operator, who will connect you (sometimes even a local operator can help). The term for a collect call is a *llamada por cobrar* or *llamada con cobro revertido.* Calling from hotels is usually faster.

Taxes and surcharges make it extremely expensive to call abroad from Mexico. Call with a card or collect if you can; not only is it cheaper (about half the price of direct), but you will also avoid enormous surcharges from hotels. Remember, however, that there can be a fee of 1-5 pesos for collect calls that are not accepted.

International calls using **LADATEL** touch-tone payphones are cheaper and involve less waiting than any of the alternatives. You can buy LADATEL phone cards at most *papelerías* (stationers) or *abarrotes* (grocers). Without the cards, the challenge is finding enough coins of large denominations: these phones take no more than 10 coins at a time, and some calls require an initial deposit. **When dialing, use the station-to-station prefixes.** The blue push-button phones do direct dial; the orange old-fashioned ones do not. To reach an **AT&T** operator from a LADATEL phone, call 95 800 462 4240; for **MCI** call 95 800 674 7000; for **Sprint** call 95 800 877 8000.

To reach the English-speaking international operator on a plain old phone, dial 09 and wait until the operator answers (be prepared to wait 30min. or more). For direct calls, dial 01; for a national operator 02; directory assistance 04; for bilingual **emergency operators 06.** To make long-distance phone calls within Mexico, dial 91 plus the telephone code and number (station to station), or 92 plus the telephone code and number (person to person). The prefix for calling the U.S. or Canada is 95 for station-to-station; for all other countries the prefix is 98.

If, for example, you want to place a **long distance call within** Mexico to Erin Billings's Taco Heaven in Chihuahua, you would dial the long distance code (92), the telephone code for Chihuahua (14), then the number: (tel. 92 14 65 29 00). If, however, you want to call Erin's Taco Heaven **from another country** before you leave, you must dial the long-distance code (011 from the U.S.), the Mexican country code (52), the telephone code for the city (14) and the number (65 29 00). Therefore, the number you would have to dial to call Ms. Billings's Taco Heaven from the U.S. is: (tel. 011 52 14 65 29 00).

MEXICO

A Brief History

PRE-HISPANIC SOCIETIES

The Beginnings of a History

The **Olmecs** of the Gulf Coast Lowlands are known to be the first large-scale society that developed in Mesoamerica. Although they are no longer thought of as the "mother culture" of the region, they were able to exert an influence on the art and culture of contemporaneous and later civilizations through networks with nearby regions. The Olmecs inhabited the cities now known as **La Venta** (see p. 497), **San Lorenzo,** and **Tres Zapotes** (see p. 491), spanning the period from 2200 BC to AD 400. However, their existence was not recognized as a distinct civilization until the early 1940s, when an archaeologist stumbled upon an immense basalt head standing several meters tall in the jungles of southern Mexico. In the following years, several more **colossal heads** were found, all with thick eyelids, big lips, broad noses, and helmet-like head covers. However, each clearly depicted a unique individual, and were, in fact, portraits of royal figures. These monumental carvings (each weighing up to 20 tons) are indicative of the highly developed artistic culture for which the Olmecs are now known. The heads are also indicative of the socially stratified communities founded by the Olmecs, which were concentrated in present-day Tabasco and southern Veracruz and whose cultural influence can be traced as far south as Costa Rica.

Another hallmark of Olmec influence is the **were-jaguar,** a symbol of great importance in Olmec cosmology. These sculpted figures combining the human and jaguar forms reflect the Olmec belief that their lineage was originated by the mating of a jaguar and a human being (the jaguar being one of the most revered animals in Mesoamerican thought). Among the most notable Olmec developments were a system of **glyphic writing** and recorded dates. Indeed, it is thought that they may have been the inventors of the Mesoamerican dating system known as the **Long Count.** The Olmec civilization and all its achievements, though lasting for over a millennium, eventually came to an end, probably as the result of either internal revolt or invasion from outside. San Lorenzo was violently destroyed around 900 BC, and La Venta suffered a similar fate some five or six centuries later. Although the Olmecs perished, many of their cultural achievements were transmitted to other Mesoamerican peoples, including the Maya.

The Maya Dominion

The genius of the **Maya** can be seen in the remains of their ancient cities—most notably **Palenque** (see p. 518), **Chichén Itzá** (see p. 559), **Uxmal** (see p. 543), and **Tulum** (see p. 591)—scattered throughout the Yucatán Peninsula and modern-day Chiapas. These and other, smaller sites reflect the high level of cultural and political achievement the Maya reached while also exemplifying the lack of centralized power in the Maya realm. Although no empire ever succeeded in controlling any large region of Maya settlement, larger sites were connected by upraised roads known as *sacbeob* (singular *sacbe)* and by trade networks that resulted in continuous contact between polities.

The time frame for Maya habitation in Mexico and Central America begins during the period known as the **PreClassic** (2000 BC to AD 250). Large cities were being founded in nearby Guatemala during this period, and sites in Mexico such as Palenque were also beginning to be constructed. By the time of the Classic Period (300-900) in Mexico, the Maya had become proficient in engineering, mathematics, art, architecture, calendrical calculations, and astronomy. Having mastered these skills, they were able to devise a method to predict the movement of celestial bodies with total precision.

One of the hallmarks of the Classic Period was the inscription on numerous stone surfaces of dates in one of the two Maya calendars. Around 900, changes began to take place in the Maya area which led to a transition into what is now called the **Post-Classic** (900-1500). This period saw the end of inscribed dates and writing, and it also witnessed the dissolution of a substantial number of Maya polities. While this change used to be referred to as the "Maya Collapse," it is now thought of not so much as the end of Maya civilization but rather as the end of a certain type of Maya culture. As the Maya polities—located in modern-day Chiapas, Guatemala, Honduras, and Belize—began to disperse in the early 9th century, new settlements popped up in northern Yucatán. A new style of architectural design, known as the **Puuc** style, emerged at sites such as Uxmal and lasted until around 1000. After this time, most Maya activity took place in northern Yucatán. Here, **Chichén Itzá** was the reigning state until falling in 1221. Chichén was followed by the historical site of **Mayapan,** which was abandoned just half a century before the Spanish arrived.

The Development of Central Mexico

While the Maya were the dominant people of southern Mexico and the Yucatán, other groups were developing societies in **central Mexico.** One of the grandest hallmarks of civilization in this region is the ruined city of **Teotihuacán** (see p. 124), which may have been inhabited by up to 200,000 people. Although there are neither written records nor oral accounts of the inhabitants of this city, the ruins themselves illustrate the power the rulers of this site commanded. Built atop a cave (a sacred spot in Mesoamerican cosmology), this pyramid's location was believed by the later Aztec to be the place where the gods met to create the fifth sun under which the Aztecs lived (they believed that each cyclical era was recreated with the rebirth of the sun).

An end seems to have come to the city in the 8th century, when it was abandoned. Evidence of fire in the site's core raises the question of whether it was burned by outside conquerors or perhaps by restless inhabitants hoping to overthrow the power structure. Whatever did happen, various traditions had lasted for hundreds of years in the eight centuries that Teotihuacán dominated the landscape. Images of deities such as **Tlaloc,** the god of rain and lightning, and the **feathered serpent** are plentiful at this site, and they show up repeatedly through time at sites constructed by later peoples. Additionally, the site itself was reused later by the **Toltecs,** who conducted ceremonies in its ruins and buried their leaders in the surroundings, believing it to be a sacred spot.

The Toltecs had established their presence in central Mexico by about 800. They settled cities such as **Xochicalco, Cholula,** and **Tula** during the **PostClassic Period.** Known both archaeologically and historically (in the form of legends), names of leaders and deities are often confused, since leaders commonly took on the names of deities. The most famous of the Toltec leaders is **Ce Acatl Topiltzin** (renamed **Topiltzin Quetzalcóatl**) who, after much infighting between Toltec groups, regained the previously lost seat of authority at Tula. Finding himself immediately confronted by opposition forces led by **Huemac** (renamed **Tezcatlipoca**), he left Tula with a promise to return one day. His legend lived on into the time of the Aztecs, whose emperor at the time of Spanish invasion is said to have believed that Cortés was the returning Quetzalcóatl. More than just this legend followed the Toltecs after their demise, however. Their influence can be seen at sites in Yucatán state, most notably **Chichén Itzá,** where Puuc architecture is mixed with a distinctly Toltec style.

By the mid 12th century, Toltec civilization had faded from prominence, and the **Aztecs,** next in line for central Mexican fame, wandered nomadically from that time until 1345. In that year, legend has it, the Aztec peoples (including the Mexica, later called "Mexicans") arrived at **Lake Texcoco,** an unappealing swamp that no other group had claimed. They had been forewarned by their patron deity, **Huitzilopochtli,** that they would come across an eagle perched upon a cactus with a serpent in its talons; when they did, they were to settle in that very spot. Having seen this vision by the side of Lake Texcoco, they succeeded in building a city there called **Tenochtitlán**—a city so prominent that modern-day Mexico City was built atop the ruins of the former capital. Additionally, the legend was important enough that the foretold image now appears as a symbol of the nation of Mexico, placed centrally on its flag.

The Aztecs practiced a religion derived from their Toltec predecessors; they worshipped a supreme being, the aggregate force of numerous deities. **Quetzalcóatl,** the feathered serpent and god of wisdom, remained a crucial element of religious iconography. The Aztec religion differed, however, in its central legend of the sun-related warrior-deity **Huitzilopochtli.** His mother, **Coatlicue,** was said to have been a chaste woman. One day, however, she found a **ball of feathers** which she placed in her pocket; it proceeded to impregnate her. Coatlicue already had some 400 sons and a daughter, all of whom were enraged at their mother's pregnancy. They began plotting to kill her to prevent her from giving birth, but while they planned this, Huitzilopochtli spoke to his mother from the womb and promised to protect her once he was born. Soon she gave birth to him, fully armed, atop **Coatepec** (serpent mountain) where, immediately after birth, he saved his mother from the jealous half-siblings by cutting them all into small pieces. Aztec imperialism and violent ascendancy over all other Mesoamerican tribes was justified by the story of Huitzilopochtli, who is memorialized at the principal Aztec temple, **Templo Mayor; Coyolxauhqui,** the half-sister, is depicted with dismembered body parts at the base of the Templo.

The Aztec civilization was as bloody and hierarchical as any that followed it in Mexican history. At the height of their power, Aztec priests practiced **human sacrifice** on a large scale. Rival warriors were regularly dismembered and thrown down the Templo Mayor stairs to honor Huitzilopochtli. Also, in the Aztec view of creation, the **fifth sun** (historical cycle) in which they lived was begun by an act of large-scale sacrifice; the gods **Tecuciztecotl** and **Nanahuitzin** sacrificed themselves to become the moon and sun, and the other gods were sacrificed by Quetzalcóatl in order to set the sun moving through the sky. The Aztec believed they had to replicate the behavior of their creators, and thus they supplied human hearts and blood to the gods in symbolic efforts to keep the sun in its path

The Aztecs built Mexico's largest pre-Hispanic empire and one of the larger cities in the world. About five million people inhabited a territory that stretched from the Atlantic to the Pacific and all the way to Guatemala and Nicaragua. Aztec hegemony consisted of indirect rule over towns that were required to recognize Aztec sovereignty and contribute goods, land, and sacrificial victims to the Aztec rulership. By fulfilling these requirements, they would be allowed to maintain their own leadership, culture, and religion, although inevitably there was some cultural influence exerted in both directions. Within the capital city, the Aztecs also exerted dominance over their natural environment. **Chinampas** (floating gardens) enabled the Aztecs to cultivate the swamp efficiently, extracting seven rounds of crops a year from each garden. Additionally, the beauty and architectural sophistication of the island city Tenochtitlán, connected to the mainland by a network of canals and causeways, led Western chroniclers to dub it the Venice of the New World. The city and the empire were thriving in the early 16th century; the Aztecs had reached the top of the Central Mexican hierarchy of power.

CONQUEST AND COLONIZATION

The Arrival of Cortés

The growth of the Aztec empire came to an abrupt end in the 16th century with the arrival of the Europeans. After **Christopher Columbus** inadvertently discovered the islands of the Caribbean in 1492, a wave of explorers flocked to Mesoamerica and began to explore and exploit the new territories. In the early decades of the 1500s, Governor of Cuba **Diego Velázquez** launched numerous expeditions to the so-called New World to search for slaves and gold. The natives responded to these new explorers with confusion, awe, and fear. **Hernán Cortés**, who was commissioned by Velázquez to lead an expedition to Cozumel in 1519, bewildered the natives with his large ships and shiny armor. The Spaniards carried "fire-breathing" guns, sat atop armored horses (which the *indígenas* believed to be immortal) and spoke a language they had never heard before. Some communities capitulated instantly and their *caciques* (leaders) showered the Spaniards with fruit, flowers, gold, and women; other towns fought tooth and nail to resist the impending conquest. But Cortés, who was heavily in debt, was not deterred by the resistance he met and pressed ahead. He sabotaged his own ships to prevent his men from turning back, cut off the feet of those who attempted mutiny, and marched on toward the great Aztec capital of Tenochtitlán with the assistance of **Jerónimo de Aguilar,** a Spaniard who had been held captive by the Maya for eight years and spoke their native language. As the Europeans moved westward through Tabasco and toward the capital, they acquired a second interpreter, **La Malinche**—an Aztec princess who became Cortés's mistress and adviser. She translated Aztec speech into Maya, which Aguilar in turn translated into Spanish. La Malinche is generally considered to be a traitor who sold out the thousands of people who died at Cortés's hand. One of the bloodiest slaughters for which Cortés was responsible was the **Cholula Massacre.** Cortés recruited 6000 warriors from the **Totonacs** and **Tlaxcalans**—enemies of the Aztecs—and massacred 6000 of the Aztecs' allies in this deadly assault.

But despite the bloodshed Cortés left in his wake, the *indígenas* were not willing to bow to his demands. When the Aztec emperor **Moctezuma II** (1502-1520) received word of Cortés's approach to Tenochtitlán, he had negotiators work with Cortés to discourage his marching on to the capital. Moctezuma, however, also supposedly grappled with rumors that Cortés was the light-skinned, bearded ruler **Quetzalcóatl,** who had sailed east after being defeated by his adversary **Tezcatlipoca.** According to the legend, after being banished, Quetzalcóatl declared that he would return in the Maya year "1 Reed." Year-names recur every 52 years in the Maya calendar; the year in which Cortés happened to arrive was also "1 Reed" (see p. 45). In the end, Moctezuma decided to welcome the Spaniards into the city. The initial period of peaceful, though tense, relations quickly soured when Moctezuma was kidnapped by the Spanish, and Cortés was driven from the city. An incredible string of lucky coincidences let Cortés regroup quickly and the Aztecs—who had been weakened by plagues and famine and were overwhelmed by the Spaniards' superior military technology—were unable to continue holding off the Spaniards. Finally, on August 13, 1521, the Aztecs, led by their new emperor **Cuauhtémoc,** were soundly defeated at **Tlatelolco.** The empire had fallen.

The Plagues of Mesoamerica

As the Spaniards pushed their way through the New World, they left in their wake horrific plagues that killed millions of *indígenas*. Unlike the Spaniards, the *indígenas* of the Americas were not naturally resistant to the European diseases—such as smallpox, typhoid, and dysentery—that swept through Mesoamerica. The mild childhood diseases of Europe—measles, mumps, and influenza—proved fatal to *indígenas.* Within 100 years of Cortés's landing, these European diseases had wiped out as much as 96% of the indigenous population—about 24 million people. **Smallpox,** which caused an eruption of sores on its victims, leading to high fevers and rashes, was by far the biggest killer. Those who lived were sometimes left blind or hideously scarred. Entire villages disappeared from the map, and Spaniards simply moved onto the empty lands, called *tierras baldías,* or bought deserted acreage at bargain prices. Settlers quickly grabbed huge estates; by 1618, one family had acquired over 11 million acres on the northern frontier.

Land and Power

From the Spaniards' point of view, the epidemics meant that more land was available for them, but it also meant that there were chronic labor shortages. For a time, *conquistadores* enslaved prisoners captured in battle, but due to rampant disease and maltreatment, *indígena* **slavery** was abolished in 1542. Instead, royal officials—including Cortés—gave Spanish settlers **encomiendas** (labor grants): *indígena* villages had to send a quota of workers to labor on the Spaniards' farms, and in return, the *encomendero* was supposed to Christianize them and then educate and defend the village. The practice of *encomiendas* was first employed in the Caribbean, and it ended in disaster for the *indígenas* who were overworked, abused, cheated, and segregated from their families. In Mesoamerica, *encomiendas* were replaced by the *repartimiento* system, which required each village to provide a weekly supply of labor—usually Indian workers—to work on projects that included building churches, constructing roads, and producing food. This system also led to widespread abuses, but lasted for most of the colonial era.

Out of fear that maverick *encomenderos* would challenge royal authority, the crown tried to restrict the usage of the faraway *encomiendas,* but regulations protecting *indígenas* were rarely enforced. After the Church and Crown began imposing taxes on villagers, *encomenderos* had an easier time recruiting and exploiting *indígena* labor because *indígenas* needed the once-useless colonial currency to pay taxes, and they would work any job to get it.

Abuses were the most extreme where wealth was greatest—in the mines. Rich veins of **silver** were discovered in central Mexico in the 1540s, and mining camps proliferated overnight, fueling the growth of colonial boom towns. Miners climbed out of the shafts on ladders made of notched logs, and at night they slept on the same pieces of cloth they used to haul their loads of ore. *Indígenas* forced to work in the mines died in the pits by the thousands, killed by floods, explosions, and noxious gases.

The Church

Christianization was central to the Conquest; even Cortés took every opportunity to lecture indigenous villages on their salvation. When the Spaniards took Tenochtitlán, they razed the Aztecs' central temple and built a cathedral atop the rubble. Such bombastic tactics often backfired, and some communities, like the tenacious **Lacandóns,** fiercely defended their native religions all the way up until the late 20th century.

Later missionaries were more successful, especially those with a notable gimmick. Many *indígenas* were particularly impressed by the arrival of the first 12 **Franciscan friars,** who walked barefoot all the way from Veracruz to the capital. Upon their arrival, Cortés bent down at their feet and kissed their robes, making a fantastic impression on the awestruck *indígenas* who witnessed the exchange. While the Franciscans concentrated their efforts in the center of the country, the **Jesuits** pushed north, and the **Dominicans** moved into the southern regions. Religious services and holidays were the only sanctioned days of rest for many villagers, and by the mid-1500s, missionaries had won millions of converts. But Roman Catholic ritual and belief were mixed with traditional practices, creating the religious **syncretism** that persists today in many rural areas.

Many clergymen tried to protect *indígenas* against exploitation, often locking horns with local *encomenderos* and crown officials. The Dominican friar **Bartolomé de Las Casas,** a vocal critic of the *encomienda* system, was largely responsible for early crown laws protecting *indígenas.* The Franciscan **Juan de Zumárraga,** Mexico's first bishop, personified the best and worst of colonial Catholicism. Zumárraga condemned corrupt judges and lobbied for *indígena* rights—yet he burned native nobles at the stake on charges of heresy and regularly boasted that he had razed 500 temples and crushed 20,000 idols.

Race and Class

When the Spanish built a new city on the ruins of Tenochtitlán, they tried to establish clear racial boundaries. Only whites could live in the city's core; **peninsulares,** whites born in Spain, were at the top of the social hierarchy. **Criollos** (creoles), Spaniards born in Mexico, were considered "second-class" citizens and were overlooked for high positions in the Church and government. **Indígenas** were confined to the fringes and had to commute into the city each day, rowing through narrow canals in dugout canoes. But complete segregation was impossible, and, within a few generations, a huge new racial group had emerged—**mes-**

tizos, children of mixed Spanish and *indígena* parentage. This group would eventually form the entire racial fabric of Mexican civilization. Today, an overwhelming majority of Mexicans are products of this *mestizo* heritage.

INDEPENDENCE AND REFORM

The First Calls for Freedom

Enter **Miguel Hidalgo y Costilla,** an iconoclastic priest in the small parish of Dolores. Always rebellious, Hidalgo had been tried by the Inquisition on charges of gambling, dancing, reading forbidden books, fornicating, questioning the immaculate conception, and denouncing the king of Spain (he was acquitted because there was insufficient evidence). Hidalgo spent little time proselytizing; instead, he tried to improve his parishioners' economic lot by introducing new trades and crafts to the village of Dolores. He also stockpiled guns. When Spanish officials discovered his hidden reserve, Hidalgo ran to Dolores' church and rang the bells to summon the parishioners. On September 16, 1810, Hidalgo delivered a ringing call to arms—**El Grito de Dolores** (The Cry of Dolores)—to end the rule by Spanish *peninsulares*, to promote equality of races, and to demand a redistribution of the land. **Mexican Independence Day** commemorates these initial rebellious stirrings. Hidalgo was able to whip his congregation into an instant army because *indígena* resentment toward the Spanish was enormously high, especially since the Mexican economy was withering away. The summer of 1809 had been so dry that corn wilted in the fields, and shortages had sparked 400% inflation in some regions. Hidalgo's army quickly swelled, capturing several major cities before Hidalgo was killed in an ambush by Spanish troops in March 1811.

Another parish priest, **José María Morelos y Pavón**—a former student of Hidalgo's—rose to lead the Independence movement after Hidalgo's death. Morelos was unable to rally the support of the *criollos* because they were opposed to the radical turn the revolution it had taken. Morelos thus turned to *mestizos* and *indígenas* to rally against the Spanish, and he trained them in guerrilla warfare tactics. Under his command, the rebels captured Oaxaca, Orizaba, and Acapulco in attempts to cut off the capital from both coasts. Once he isolated the capital, Morelos centered his focus on political reform. In September 1813, Morelos convened a meeting of an Athenae Congress to serve as the revolutionary movement's government. On November 6, 1813, the Congress issued Mexico's first formal **Declaration of Independence,** and a year later published a constitution that, in only 242 articles, declared Mexico a republic, abolished slavery, and eliminated all class distinctions. Although the constitution was never put into effect, it lent an aspect of legality to Mexico's cause and served as a model for reformers in years to come.

During these years, Spain was undergoing a profound political change. Napoleon's troops finally withdrew from Spain, and in 1814 Ferdinand VII returned from involuntary exile. A few years later, constitutionalists led a rebellion in Spain that, in 1820, forced Ferdinand VII to reinstate the liberal constitution of 1812, which provided for a constitutional monarchy, sovereignty of the people, and freedom of the press. Additionally, its anticlerical provisions led to attacks on the privileges and property of the Catholic Church. Mexican conservatives and clerical leaders, alarmed by radicalism in Spain, saw that one way to preserve their ideals was to establish an independent Mexico. The movement was spearheaded by **Agustín de Iturbide,** a *criollo* loyalist who had led Spanish troops in battle against Hidalgo. In 1820, he joined forces with rebel leader **Vicente Guerrero.** Reassuringly conservative, Iturbide and Guerrero drafted the **Plan de Iguala,** which is most remembered for its "three guarantees"—independence, religion, and equality. Under the plan, Mexico was to be declared an independent constitutional monarchy, Roman Catholicism was to be the state religion and the only one tolerated, and there was to be racial equality for all inhabitants of New Spain, thus making all Europeans, Africans, and *indígenas* equal in the eyes of the law. The compromise received widespread support, and, on August 24, 1821, the **Treaty of Córdoba** formalized Mexico's independence forever.

The First Empire

"He is prompt, bold, and decisive, and not scrupulous about the means he employs to obtain his ends," wrote a U.S. visitor about Iturbide. Iturbide controlled the first Mexican Empire, which only lasted two years during the short transitional period from colony to republic. During this period, Mexico was ruled by a provisional governing *junta* (council) that was presided over by Iturbide. The *junta* arranged for the election of an official Congress to write a constitution for Mexico. The Congress was made up of conservatives, professionals, elites, and members of the aristocracy; no seats were available to the lower class. In 1822, Iturbide began vying for control of the throne. Congress was reluctant grant him such power. The liberals and conservatives within Congress were torn by the argument over who should rule Mexico. On May 18, 1822, a coup was launched in support of Iturbide's bid for the emperor of Mexico; Congress then voted to name Iturbide constitutional emperor of Mexico.

The first Mexican Empire collapsed within 10 months. After the turbulent previous decade of war, the economy was in shambles, the mining industry was in disarray, commerce was at a standstill—because trade with Spain had ended—and the country was unable to secure a large loan. Iturbide was faced early on with numerous economic barriers and a discontented nation. The conflicts became more prevalent during Iturbide's short rule, as antagonism arose between him and Congress. On October 31, 1822, Iturbide dismissed Congress and ruled through an appointed 45-man *junta.* This act provided the discontented military men with a pretext to revolt. Anticlericalists, *indígenas,* and *criollos* of modest means rebelled against Iturbide, led by the *criollo* military commander **Antonio López de Santa Anna.** On March 19, 1823, Iturbide finally resigned, but his legacy of despotism endured. Iturbide left Mexico for Europe but returned the next year, claiming to have come back to defend his country against a supposed Spanish plan to reconquer Mexico. When he returned, he was seemingly unaware of a congressional decree that called for his death should he ever return to Mexico. Iturbide landed near Tampico where he was apprehended and shot by a firing squad on July 19, 1824.

After the fall of the first empire, Mexico was left in shambles. In the fighting between 1810 and 1823, half a million people—one in 12 Mexicans—had died, and the fledgling government was flat broke. The political instability that ensued made borrowing abroad an expensive endeavor. But as the national debt increased, so did the nation's problems. Whenever public funds were insufficient to pay the army, its officers revolted, captured the government, and negotiated international loans. In 1824, a new constitution provided for a federal republic, consisting of 19 states, four territories, and a federal district.

The Era of Santa Anna

Although the presidency of Mexico officially changed hands 36 times between May 1833 and August 1855, Santa Anna dominated the political scene. Initially elected on a liberal, mildly anticlerical platform, Santa Anna quickly abandoned his duties and retired to his personal estate. When his vice president implemented promised reforms, Santa Anna led an uprising and recaptured the presidency, this time as a conservative supporter of the Church. Throughout his lifetime, Santa Anna occupied the presidency no fewer than 11 times.

As his cronies grew rich on graft and bribery, Santa Anna drained the state treasuries, desperately levying taxes on everything and everyone to build a huge standing army. Sure enough, Mexico was soon at war again. In 1838, France attacked Veracruz, demanding reparations for property damaged during the war a decade earlier. The conflict was dubbed **"The Pastry War"** in honor of a French pastry cook whose wares had been gobbled by marauding Mexican troops. The attacking French ships were driven back to sea, but Santa Anna lost part of his left leg in the bombardment. Four years later, Santa Anna had his severed leg removed from its grave, carried to the capital in a huge procession, and entombed in an urn atop a towering pillar as the Congress, cabinet, diplomatic corps, and army serenaded the decayed limb.

Meanwhile, the Mexican army was fighting a losing battle on its northern frontier. Conflict between Texas and Mexico was perpetuated by Anglo settlers in Texas who were resistant to adapting Mexican culture and laws. Angered by Mexico's **abolition of slavery** in 1829 and under-represented in the legislature, Texan settlers demanded independence. In an effort to quell the rebellion, Santa Anna gathered an army of 6000 men and marched north. In February of 1836, his troops overwhelmed Texan rebels holed up in an old Franciscan monastery called the **Alamo.** Santa Anna and his troops triumphed, killing all 150 defenders of the fortress. The bloody battle only made the Texans rally together harder; "Remember the Alamo!" became a universal battle cry. The Texans made a notable comeback and defeated and captured Santa Anna in April 1836. Santa Anna was freed shortly after his capture, but Mexico made no further attempt to reconquer Texas, though it refused to recognize Texas's newly won independence.

Mexico's territorial problems however, were far from over, and when the U.S. annexed Texas in 1845 as part of its doctrine of **Manifest Destiny,** Mexico became entrenched in a drawn-out battle over land with the U.S. The U.S. government tried to negotiate a purchase of some of Mexico's territory, but Mexico refused to compromise. U.S. and Mexican troops clashed in the disputed territory. In April 1846, the U.S. formally declared war. U.S. troops captured present-day New Mexico and California. The U.S. army then decided that the only way to defeat Mexico was to capture Mexico City. U.S. forces closed in on the capital from the north and east. Young cadets, known as the **Niños Héroes** (Boy Heroes), valiantly fought off U.S. troops from their military school in Chapultepec Castle and then, according to legend, wrapped themselves in the Mexican flag and leapt off the tower when all hope was lost. Things only got worse for the Mexicans when, on April 18, 1847, Santa Anna was defeated in a critical battle at **Cerro Gordo;** Mexico City was captured on September 14th of the same year. Santa Anna went into voluntary exile while the new government negotiated a peace agreement. Under the terms of the **Treaty of Guadalupe Hidalgo,** on February 2, 1848, Mexico sold Texas, New Mexico, and California to the U.S. for a paltry sum. Five years later, Santa Anna returned to Mexico and was made dictator. To raise funds for an extended army, he sold off what today is Arizona and southern New Mexico in the **Gadsden Purchase.** Two thousand Mexicans had died in the battle for Mexico City—only to lose half the nation's territory.

While the international turmoil had settled with the Gadsden Purchase, the social and economic conditions for most Mexicans did not. Most Mexicans lived as they had for centuries—poor and isolated. Over one-third of the population lived in remote *indígena* villages. Although *pueblos* were largely self-governed, most villagers lived in grinding poverty. Education was a luxury enjoyed only by the *criollo* elite; only 1% of the total population was enrolled in school.

Juárez and Reform

Eventually, the facade of Santa Anna's regime cracked under enormous opposition. The emerging leader of the reform movement was **Benito Juárez,** who rose from humble roots in a tiny Zapotec *pueblo* in Oaxaca to become one of the more revered presidents in Mexican history. He was exiled to New Orleans by Santa Anna because of his radically egalitarian policies as governor of Oaxaca, but Juárez joined other liberal politicians and journalists in stirring up opposition to Santa Anna abroad while dissidents in Mexico raised **rebel armies.** In 1855, Santa Anna was forced to resign.

The Juárez administration's policies reflected the ideology of 19th-century liberalism. As the Minister of Justice, Juárez passed the *Ley Juárez,* which abolished the old *fueros* and special regulations protecting the military and Church from prosecution under civil laws. Juárez also pushed through a new law prohibiting any institution from owning property not directly used in its day-to-day operations. Intended to weaken the Church, which owned vast rural and urban properties, the new law ended up stripping *indígenas* of their lands and livelihoods, since *ejidos* (indigenous communal lands) had to be auctioned off as well.

In 1857 a new constitution was drafted to appease the reformers. The constitution prohibited slavery and abridgments of freedom of speech or press; abolished special courts and prohibited civil and ecclesiastical corporations from owning property; eliminated monopolies; decreed that Mexico was to be a representative, democratic, and republican nation; and defined the states and their responsibilities. This constitution, which remained in force until it was modified in 1917 after the Revolution, increased the power of the central executive and became the longest-lasting constitution in the Mexican republic's history.

Conservatives, especially high-ranking army officers, were ardently opposed to the new constitution. In opposition, they supported a revolt in 1858 that became known as the **War of the Reform,** Mexico's bloodiest civil war to date. The conservatives marched to the capital, dissolved Congress, arrested Juárez, and tried to win the president to their side. Juárez escaped to Guanajuato, where he assumed the presidency and declared that constitutional government had been reestablished. The Church joined the military and dispossessed *pueblos* in fighting the liberal government. Meanwhile, the liberals were aided by *mestizo* reformers and many *indígenas* who supported Juárez. Both sides committed atrocities; conservatives shot doctors who treated liberal casualties, while liberals defaced churches and executed priests who refused to give the sacrament to their troops. Juárez eventually won the presidential elections in 1861 and the fighting ended, but the country was far from unified. The liberal triumph in the civil war provided only temporary peace, as an international crisis soon erupted.

French Intervention

After the liberals finally regained the upper hand in 1861, Juárez faced a massive federal budget deficit. He declared a moratorium on the payment of Mexico's foreign debts, prompting Spain, Britain, and France to attack Veracruz once again. Spain and Britain soon pulled out, but Napoleon III sent his troops inland. On May 5, 1862, outnumbered Mexican troops successfully repelled French soldiers from the city of Puebla. **Cinco de Mayo** is now a huge national holiday that commemorates this triumph—but the invaders captured the capital a year later.

When Napoleon selected Austrian archduke **Ferdinand Maximilian of Hapsburg** as emperor of Mexico, he made a poor choice. Maximilian was extremely naive; he insisted that the Mexican people approve his ascension in a national plebiscite (Napoleon saw to it that Maximilian "won" overwhelmingly), then immediately hired a Spanish tutor for his wife **Carlota.** Maximilian and Carlota landed in Veracruz expecting a grand welcome, but the *veracruzanos* refused to leave their houses. The royal couple drove through silent streets in a delicate Viennese carriage, which soon became mired in the muddy roads leading to Mexico City. Carlota cried.

Weirdly idealistic, Maximilian did not realize that he was the puppet of European imperialism. The new emperor was moderately liberal and anti-Catholic; instead of rescinding Juárez's anticlerical laws, Maximilian imposed forced loans on the Church to shore up the collapsing treasury. In 1864, he decreed that republicans were to be considered bandits and brigands, subject to extreme penalties. Mexican conservatives were predictably infuriated, and Maximilian's modest popularity evaporated. Meanwhile, liberals stockpiled weapons and hired thousands of U.S. Civil War veterans to fight against the French. Napoleon belatedly withdrew his troops in 1867, abandoning Maximilian despite Carlota's wild pleas. Carlota traveled to Paris to try to put a stop to the hostilities and then went to Rome to plead with the Pope, where she eventually went mad. Maximilian surrendered himself to Juárez and was promptly shot. The human toll of the war was far higher on the Mexican side—50,000 had died fighting the French.

Struggling to Rebuild

Juárez returned to the capital in a solemn black carriage—a stark contrast to Maximilian's flimsy Viennese vehicle. Juárez's characteristically dour appearance seemed appropriate, since the Mexican economy was once again in tatters. Unemployment was rampant; to assert the executive's control over the military, Juárez had slashed the size of the Mexican army by two-thirds, so thousands of decommissioned soldiers wandered through the countryside, raiding haciendas and rural villages for food. *Léperos* (beggars) roamed the streets of Mexico City. Even the small middle class—merchants, bureaucrats, prosperous shopkeepers—lived in modest homes without running water. There were only enough schools for 10% of Mexican children to attend classes; of these students, just 22% were girls. In his remaining years, Juárez helped Mexico modernize its economy and some of its social institutions by expanding the rail, road, and telegraph systems, and developing secular education. But despite these innovations, the nation was left in shambles. When Juárez died in office in July of 1872, Mexico enjoyed peace but not prosperity.

The Porfiriato

The regime of José de la Cruz **Porfirio Díaz,** which lasted from 1876 to 1911, was one of the more colorful and brutal chapters in Mexican history. In the 55 years since Independence, the Mexican presidency had changed hands 75 times; now stability was vital. Díaz's official motto was "Liberty, Order, and Progress"—but for the dictator, the price of order and progress was liberty itself. Elections were rigged, dissident journalists were jailed (one more than 30 times), and Díaz's strident critics were assassinated in Díaz's *pan o palo* (bread or stick) policy. The provinces were controlled by **jefes políticos** (political bosses). When uprisings occurred, they were swiftly smothered by bands of **rurales** (rural police).

Díaz's wealthy, European-trained, *criollo* advisors believed that the nation's problems could be solved with scientific techniques. Under Díaz, Mexico was mechanized, paved, and electrified. Ironically, the regime that brought prosperity to Mexico harbored deeply anti-Mexican prejudices. The Positivist *científicos*—as Díaz's advisors were called—believed that *indígenas* were weak, immoral, and ineducable. Few of the new schools built during the Porfiriato were located in indigenous *pueblos.* When the **Fifth Pan-American Congress** was held in Mexico City just after the turn of the century, *indígenas* and *mestizos* were prohibited from serving foreign dignitaries; only whites could work as waiters and porters during the Congress. French—not Mexican—furniture, food, dance, opera, and fashion were popular among the *criollo* elite.

During Díaz's regime, the Church enjoyed a comeback. The national population increased by 62% while the growth of the Church and land holdings grew by a much larger percentage. The priesthood more than doubled, and the number of Catholic schools increased sixfold. Additionally, the Porfiriato focused on making drastic improvements in the economy. Under Díaz, the value of exports and imports increased fivefold and the government paid off its past foreign debts, simplified its system of taxation, and increased foreign investment in Mexico. Foreign investors such as the U.S. and Europe took over the railroad and petroleum industries, which would create problems for Mexico down the road.

Díaz brought in French and British firms to build a vast infrastructure of railroads linking agricultural areas to urban factories. As a result, industry prospered and land values skyrocketed. But few poor Mexicans profited from the economic boom. Under a new law, indigenous *ejidos* could be forced to sell their public lands if they couldn't show a legal title to the plots they farmed. By the turn of the century, most villages saw their *ejidos* taken by wealthy individuals and private companies. In one case, a town was so entirely stripped of its communal lands that it no longer had space to bury its dead. Meanwhile, *científicos* made millions speculating in the volatile land market, manipulating railroad contracts to their own advantage.

Vast haciendas sprung up in the north, some as large as seven million acres, fed by cheap land prices. Half of Mexico's rural population worked as **peones,** legally bound to the hacienda owners. But as criticism of the regime increased, so did repression. By 1895, Díaz's popularity began to decline. The hostilities of the people toward the Porfiriato culminated in revolution.

REVOLUTION

Challenges from All Sides

Unlike the war for independence, which was ignited by *criollo* discontent, the Revolution began smoldering in the lower levels of Mexican society. In 1906, copper miners in Sonora went on strike, citing low wages and the discriminatory policies of the mine's U.S. owners. The protest was quashed when Díaz permitted U.S. mercenaries to cross the border and kill strikers in order to protect the interests of U.S. investors. But similar strikes elsewhere fueled a growing sense of instability.

In the 1910 presidential election, Díaz faced a vocal opponent. **Francisco I. Madero,** a wealthy hacienda owner from Coahuila, was no social revolutionary, but his calls for liberty and democracy were enough for Díaz to throw him into jail. Escaping to the U.S., Madero orchestrated a series of grass-roots rebellions in northern states from his base in San Antonio. Meanwhile, **Emiliano Zapata** led the revolt against Díaz in the southern state of Morelos. Unlike Madero, Zapata believed that the rebels' first priority was to restore communal lands to the indigenous *pueblos.* Traveling to remote *pueblos* and addressing villagers in their native language, Náhuatl, when necessary, Zapata quickly raised an army of angry *indígenas.* After Madero's troops captured Ciudad Juárez, the 81-year-old Díaz fled to Paris. But once in power, the cautious Madero hesitated to restore any land to the Zapatistas, and he ordered the rebels in the south to disband. Zapata resisted the order, and the Zapatistas tangled with General **Victoriano Huerta's** troops. A pattern for the Revolution had been set.

The Coalition Collapses

After fending off rebellions from radical factions, Madero's government finally fell to a conservative uprising led by Huerta and Díaz's nephew. **Venustiano Carranza,** the governor of Coahuila, urged state governors to revolt against the federal government. **Guerrilla armies** sprung up in the north, led by **Pancho Villa** in Chihuahua and **Alvaro Obregón** in Sonora. Villa worked with **Pascual Orozco** in leading guerrilla forces; by the end of 1910, the two had used the bands to attack federal forces, cut railroad connections, and capture towns and territory in Chihuahua. Villa was especially beneficial to the rebellion because he was able to recruit cowboys and roustabouts to fight. According to legend, he had made these contacts after living in the mountains for years and joining a gang of bandits. (He had supposedly fled to the mountains after shooting a *hacendado* who had raped his sister.)

In 1911, the Zapata-led and Villa-led revolts flourished. The group of armed peasants (mostly *indígenas*) that Zapata led took over ancestral lands, destroyed sugar haciendas, and seized several towns, including Cuernavaca and Villa. On May 21, 1911, Madero and Díaz signed the **Treaty of Ciudad Juárez,** which provided for the removal of the president and vice president and called for new elections. It left the federal army intact but called for the disbanding of rebel forces. Although Zapata followed the new leaders in the beginning, he grew increasingly frustrated with the Madero government. Finally, on November 25, 1911, Zapata proclaimed his own agrarian program, the **Plan of Ayala,** which disavowed Madero as president. Zapata and his revolutionaries rallied together again to fight for "*Tierra y Libertad!*" (Land and Liberty). Provisional governments proliferated; by late 1913, there were more than 25 different types of paper money in circulation. After U.S. troops bombed Veracruz in 1914, Huerta resigned.

Next, Obregón seized the capital; Carranza controlled Veracruz; Villa ruled the north; Zapata held the south. When Villa's troops attacked Obregón's forces at the bloody **Battle of Celaya,** 4000 Villistas were shredded on barbed-wire entrenchments, and 5000 more were wounded. As Villistas wreaked havoc on Texas border towns, Carranza's own government found itself hopelessly divided between old-style liberals and radical land reformers. The fighting in the south was the most vicious: thousands of civilians were executed as alleged Zapatista sympathizers; Zapata retaliated by blowing up a train and killing about 400 innocent passengers. In 1919, Carranza's men assassinated Zapata in an ambush, and Carranza assumed the presidency, inaugurating a period of relative calm. But one in eight Mexicans had died in the wars of 1910-1920. Since all of the rebel governments had printed their own money, the economy was in ruin. Inflation slashed the real wages of urban laborers; flooding and sabotage put miners out of work, and many Mexicans were on the brink of starvation.

Institutionalized Revolution

In 1917, Carranza gathered delegates to draft a **new constitution;** the document they produced still governs the Republic today. Zapatistas, Villistas, and Huertistas were barred from the convention, yet delegates outlined a thoroughly radical agenda for the nation. Present was the familiar liberal anticlericalism of the 19th century; more startling were the socialistic articles of the new constitution. Private ownership of land was declared to be a privilege, not a right, and the state was supposed to redistribute lands seized from *pueblos* during the Porfiriato. Workers were guaranteed better work conditions and the right to strike. But the moderate Carranza failed to implement most of the radical document, and the Revolution drifted to the right as successive presidents reversed modest gains in land reform and workers' rights.

The **Constitution of 1917** codified the Revolution; the government of the 1920s institutionalized it. **Plutarco Elías Calles,** elected president in 1924, ruled the country for a decade through a series of puppet presidents. Calles, known as the "Jefe Máximo," consolidated the government's support in the new **Partido Nacional Revolucionario (PNR),** which in other forms has run Mexico virtually unopposed since its creation in 1929. In 1934 **Lázaro Cárdenas** took the office and became the first President since the revolution to enforce the Constitution of 1917. His rule marked the beginning of a new era in Mexico.

MODERN MEXICO

Carrying Out the Revolution

The Great Depression hit Mexico in the gut: as the value of the peso plummeted, wages dropped by 10%, and many Mexicans began to question the direction of the Revolution. Reacting to the mood of the times, Mexico's new president **Lázaro Cárdenas** seized the reins from his PNR handlers and steered the Revolution sharply to the left. Cárdenas redistributed 44 million acres—twice as many as all of his predecessors combined—to thousands of indigenous *ejidos,* systems in which lands were owned communally and farmed either as common land or by individuals given rights to particular tracts. Economically, most *ejidos* were a failure, and agricultural productivity dropped drastically. But the *ejido* program achieved an enormous symbolic goal: worried peasants were given reassurance that the new government intended to meet the goals of the Mexican Revolution.

New Directions

In addition to drastically increasing the rate of land redistribution, Cárdenas also altered the nature of the government party. Incorporating the peasant, labor, popular, and military sectors into the party, he succeeded in establishing a means by which these groups could be organized *under the control of the government*. By so doing, Cárdenas immeasurably strengthened the ruling party, which he renamed the **Partido de la Revolución Mexicana (PRM).** To top off Cárdenas's radicalization of Mexico, he took hold of the oil industry in an effort to boost Mexican nationalism. The companies had previously been supported financially by foreign investors, but Cárdenas expropriated them, turning the industry to the hands of Mexican investors. Additionally, he established **Petróleos Mexicanos (PEMEX)** as a means of regulating the oil industry. Unfortunately, due to developing economic woes, PEMEX failed to have the strong impact he had hoped for.

In 1940 **Avila Camacho** was elected president of Mexico. His rule, combined with the onset of World War II, altered any new order Cárdenas had set in motion in Mexico. Camacho's main goal was to modernize the country through industrialization; the war sped up the pace of Mexican development, accelerating the shift from socialism to industrial capitalism. However, the working class didn't share proportionately in the new prosperity. Policy-makers believed that some measure of inequity was necessary in order to increase the size of the economic pie. Mexican industrialists were urged to keep costs down and, by implication, to keep wages low. Inevitably, oil workers responded to the shift in economic distribution by going on strike in the early 1950s; the army was called in and dozens of union leaders were fired.

The Legacy of the Official Government Party

At the end of WWII, the official political party in Mexico, the **Partido Revolucionario Institucional (PRI),** was derived from its PRM predecessor. Under the direction of President **Miguel Alemán,** the PRI integrated the labor, peasant, and popular sectors—a structure it has maintained to this day. The PRI has been likened to a floating log: if you want to stay afloat, you have to grab on. Lured by the promise of cushy government jobs, union officials and peasant leaders joined the PRI's swelling political machine. Enjoying wide institutional support, the PRI has not yet lost a presidential election since its inception in 1929.

However, the stability of single-party rule (which is fading in the late 1990s) has come at the price of liberty. Even under president **Adolfo López Mateos**—who between 1958 and 1964 expanded social security coverage and redoubled efforts at land reform—Mexicans were not free to speak their minds. López Mateos removed the Communist leadership of the teachers' and railroad unions and sent in the army to break a railroad-workers' strike in 1959. When the head of the PRI tried to reform the party's nomination process, he was fired by the president under pressure from state political bosses. **Student unrest** and worker dissatisfaction culminated in 1968 at Mexico City's **Tlatelolco Plaza,** where police killed an estimated 400 peaceful demonstrators and jailed another 2000 protesters just 10 days before the Olympics were to open (see p. 109). Recently, the preferential treatment practiced by the PRI has been scrutinized as the result of a massacre in Chiapas in the last days of 1997 (see **Acteal Massacre** p. 59).

Salinas: Toward Democracy

"The era of one-party rule in Mexico is over," declared PRI presidential candidate **Carlos Salinas de Gortari** during the tense week following the 1988 presidential elections. Salinas officially (and conveniently) received 50.4% of the vote when the final contested results were announced, but many interpreted his remarks and the election itself as a fresh start for Mexican politics.

Mexico's ruling party did not lose a single presidential, senatorial, or gubernatorial race from 1929 to 1988; in the few local elections that it did lose, the PRI often installed its own candidates anyway. Through a combination of patronage, fraud, and ineffectual opposition, the party stayed in power and ran Mexico uncontested. But in the 1982 election, the murmurs of dissent were heard, and the right-of-center **Partido de Acción Nacional (PAN)** won 14% of the vote, most of it in the northern states. In 1983, when the PRI experimented with fraud-free elections, the PAN picked up three mayorships in the state of Chihuahua alone.

When the Harvard-educated Salinas began his six-year term as president on December 1, 1988, the country was faced with numerous problems including high unemployment, a US$105 billion foreign debt, a drug crisis, and a skeptical nation. Salinas instituted wage and price controls to keep inflation down. He then proceeded to boost his popularity with the arrests of a union boss, a fraudulent businessman, and a drug trafficker.

On February 4, 1990, representatives of the Mexican government and its 450 foreign commercial creditors signed a debt reduction agreement designed to ease the U.S. banking crisis and to deflect outlandishly high interest payments. This reprieve, along with Salinas's austerity program, led to growing foreign investment and steady growth (3% per year) in Mexico's gross domestic product. Unemployment, however, remains near 20%. Reduced or not, foreign debt has continued to suck capital out of the country, and a blossoming trade deficit is squeezing out small and medium businesses as foreign franchises muscle their way in.

The fate of these smaller firms was at the center of the controversial **North American Free Trade Agreement (NAFTA).** The treaty eliminated the tariffs, quotas, and subsidies that had protected Mexican industry and agriculture since the 1940s, by driving up the prices of foreign goods, thus allowing national and local companies to corner certain markets. The implementation of NAFTA meant that smaller Mexican-owned businesses were often driven out of business by *maquiladores,* U.S.-owned assembly and automotive-sector factories. On the other hand, freer trade means cheaper consumer goods for financially strapped Mexicans—a blessing in a nation plagued by constant inflation. Increased competition may eventually reap profits for the Mexican economy, but development is now exacting high human and environmental costs.

In 1992, PRI technocrats dismantled the *ejido* system, which had ostensibly guaranteed communal land rights for rural *campesinos.* Salinas asserted that while redistributing land had served to implement justice in the decades following the Revolution, that program had become unproductive and even detrimental to economic growth by the 1990s. With this constitutional reform and other changes, including rapid **privatization,** an agrarian culture thousands of years old is being phased out to pave the way for **industrialization.** Traditional support systems are often lost in urbanization while government safety nets are eliminated; this is all part of an economic streamlining backed by the U.S. and international lenders. The costs of this structural adjustment program (centered around NAFTA) have yet to be determined, but in the meantime they fall squarely on the shoulders of the lower classes, while benefits still loom on the long-term horizon.

MEXICO

The Ejército Zapatista de Liberación Nacional (EZLN)

On January 1, 1994, Mexico's government officials were celebrating the beginning of NAFTA, which was put into effect that day. In the southern state of Chiapas, however, Mexicans were rallying for a different kind of progress. In the day's early hours, a force of rebels captured the capital city of **San Cristóbal de las Casas** and other strategically chosen cities in the region. Named the **Ejército Zapatista de Liberación Nacional (EZLN),** or **Zapatista National Liberation Army,** this army of over 9000 peasants (mainly Mayas) stepped forward to demand a voice in Mexican politics. Twelve days of fighting ensued, leaving about 150 dead. Months of negotiations followed, and mediator and **Bishop of San Cristóbal Samuel Ruiz** eventually forged a delicate relationship between the government and the rebels. The rebels rejected the government's peace plan and threatened to shatter the fragile cease-fire unless upcoming presidential elections were free and fair.

In an election year that was supposed to express Mexico's material progress and fledgling democracy, the rebels from Chiapas drew attention to the vast inequities that still existed within the Republic. From the first day that the EZLN arrived on the international stage, their spokesman **Subcomandante Marcos** has aired demands for a change in the definition of the Mexican nation. Although many observers have taken the rebellion to be an assertion of indigenous rights, numerous other issues have been brought to the table by the Zapatista rebels (named after revolutionary war hero Emiliano Zapata). Chiapas is Mexico's poorest state, and President Salinas had poured more anti-poverty money into the state than any other—but to little avail. Furthermore, *indígena* rebels clearly harbored deep resentments that no amount of PRI money could assuage. The EZLN not only brought social change to the table—it also demanded a political restructuring of the national system. Rather than continuing to live in Maya communities whose governments are dominated by the federal bureaucracy, the directorate of the movement (the **Clandestine Committee**) designed a system in which Mexico would be divided into **autonomous regions,** defined by existing political alliances. In fact, **autonomy** has been one of the main demands of the **Zapatistas,** as has **self-determination.** These terms emphasize Zapatistas' concern with achieving a political structure in which people are guaranteed representation nationally and individual decision-making locally.

While the EZLN's goal has been to establish a new structure for the Mexican nation, much of the commentary on the group has focused on the witty, poetic Marcos. Green-eyed and white-skinned, the ski-mask he wears serves only symbolically to hide his identity. Indeed, he has said himself that the mask acts not to protect him but to transform him—to erase the man behind the mask (revealed by President Zedillo on Feb. 9, 1995, to be **Rafael Sebastián Guillén Vicente**, a university-educated Marxist) and to establish, instead, the Marcos who has come to be the voice of the movement. He calls himself a poet; he writes—in addition to lengthy letters to Zedillo, the Mexican nation, and foreign observers—fiction and short stories. In his soft voice, he intertwines Maya oral styles with cunning analyses of his nation. It is no wonder, given his charm and astute speech, that observers are drawn in by him; however, the extent to which discussion of the Zapatistas has focused on Marcos has created a superhero-like aura around him which some observers think diverts important from the movement itself.

Bringing a movement for justice and equality to national and international attention, the Zapatistas have taken advantage of the modern setting in which they find themselves. Writing communiqués to the world on the Internet (**www.ezln.org**; see **Sources,** p. 69), Marcos and the Clandestine Committee have succeeded in reeling in numerous supporters world-wide while keeping them abreast of events and changes.

Death and Transfiguration

"Oh, this fearful, vibrant vale of shadows that is our country."

-Efraín Huerta

The Zapatista uprising foreshadowed turmoil to come. On March 23, 1994, the likeable and reform-minded PRI presidential candidate **Luis Donaldo Colosio** of Mexicali was assassinated as he left a rally in Tijuana. Many believe that the leaders of hard-line faction of the PRI killed their own candidate when they found him too radical and conciliatory for their taste; the subsequent murders of the chief investigator of Colosio's assassination and several other officials connected with the investigation fueled these rumors. After three years of conflicting investigations by five different prosecutors, Colosio's case remains officially unsolved, but official versions don't satisfy most Mexicans.

Meanwhile, the PRI picked Budget and Planning Minister and free-market man **Ernesto Zedillo** to replace the slain candidate and to rebuild the campaign from scratch. The party relied on more than 800,000 grass-roots organizers to comb the country door-to-door, building on an old network of patronage and old-school politics. Sure enough, the PRI won hands-down in a relatively fair election, receiving remarkable support from Mexico's poorer voters.

Just months into his presidency, on December 20, 1994, the Ivy-League educated Zedillo was faced with a precipitous drop in the value of the peso. Spooked by the assassination of Colosio and the unsettling events in Chiapas, foreign investors dumped US$25 billion of Mexican government peso bonds, heralding the imminent monetary **devaluation.** Aided by the International Monetary Fund (IMF) and the U.S. government, Mexico was salvaged from the depths of economic crisis. Still, severe financial difficulties persisted: in March 1995, interest rates skyrocketed to more than 90%, bringing the banking system to a near collapse. The growing legions of middle-class professionals and entrepreneurs that relied on foreign dollars were left frustrated and frightened. Mexicans have laid the blame squarely on Zedillo's shoulders, citing his delay in appointing key cabinet posts and in instituting promised economic reforms.

Although the prospect of successfully taming the economy seems distant, Zedillo has sought to pacify the anxious masses with further political reforms. The president has committed himself to **decentralizing power** and **exposing corruption** in an attempt to restore the nation's faith in the government. In addition to slowly defrauding elections, Zedillo has arrested several high-level officials on charges of conspiracy and murder, earning respect and U.S. endorsement as a "partner in the war on drugs."

However, no end to the war is in sight: narcotics and their devastating effects have eaten away at Mexico in recent years. Most disheartening has been the large overlap, only beginning to be exposed, between high-level anti-drug enforcement officials, politicians, and drug lords. In May of 1998, an American undercover operation resulted in the indictment of 26 Mexican bankers who were charged with laundering more than US$110 million in drug profits. Zedillo decried the investigation as a violation of Mexican law. U.S. President Bill Clinton and Zedillo met after a drug summit conference in June to try to find a solution to the increasingly problematic relationship between U.S. drug demand and Mexican drug supply. Whatever happens, there is no easy solution: more than half of the cocaine smuggled to the United States still travels through Mexico.

Mexico at a Crossroads

Fortunately, the consolidation of large drug cartels has not been the only Mexican news item fit to print in recent years. Equally newsworthy has been the country's dramatic shift away from one-party rule toward democracy. Under Zedillo's leadership, Mexico has moved toward fair elections that have actually begun to undermine his own party's domination. The PRI once controlled all state governorships; now, several state governors, including that of Jalisco, belong to an opposition party, the right-leaning PAN. Furthermore, the liberal **Partido de la Revolución Democrática (PRD)** party poses a threat from the other side.

On July 6, 1997, Mexico's elections took an unprecedented turn. The PRI, increasingly linked with instability rather than stability, lost its majority in the lower house of Congress for the first time since it took control of the house 68 years ago. PAN, the right-center, and PRD, the burgeoning left, each took nearly 30% of the Congressional vote, leaving only 41% for the PRI—far from one-party rule. Without a PRI majority supporting Zedillo in Congress, much of the president's power has now passed to that body. But Congress was not the only institution shaken up by the turn of events in the summer of 1997: in the first direct Mexico City mayoral vote since 1928, leftist Cuauhtémoc Cárdenas of the PRD won a landslide victory. Cárdenas is an outspoken opponent of Zedillo's free-market policies. Like his father Lázaro (the famous 1930s president; see p. 55), Cárdenas is said to have his eye on the top job (Zedillo will be replaced after one term, as are all Mexican presidents, in the year 2000). For the first time, the prospect of a non-PRI president is not entirely inconceivable.

But while a victory may have been achieved for liberal democracy, the situation in the southern part of the country is deteriorating rapidly. The long-awaited peace talks between the Zapatista rebels and the government have been stalled since late 1996, while thousands of federal troops are posted (as of August 1998) throughout the state of Chiapas. The precarious peace has given way to more bloodshed and tragedy. On December 22, 1997, 45 people (including 20 women and 18 children), most of them Zapatista rebel sympathizers, were massacred in the small village of Acteal in Chiapas. Although the government has blamed the massacre on a family feud, there is evidence that state officials had advance knowledge of the **Acteal massacre** and did nothing to prevent it. In the aftermath of the massacre, the governor of Chiapas, **Julio César Ruiz Ferro,** a member of the PRI, resigned. Ferro stepped down under pressure from the Roman Catholic Church and opposition leaders as well as from President Zedillo himself. Although federal prosecutors arrested state officials (including the mayor of Chenhalhó), Zapatista rebels accuse the government of agreeing to peace, while secretly arming paramilitary units. Inquiries are still being made into the role played by the police and high officials of the ruling party in the Acteal massacre.

In the meantime, however, peace is still far from becoming a reality. Less than a month after the Acteal massacre, a police force in Chiapas fired on a crowd of Indians protesting the massacre, killing a defenseless woman and wounding others. In June of 1998, **Bishop Samuel Ruiz,** a public critic of the government, resigned from his position as the mediator of peace talks between the federal government and the Zapatista rebels. Accused of siding with the Zapatistas and of condoning violence, Ruiz has been the main negotiator between the opposing factions since the initial uprising of January 1994.

June of '98 also saw seven people dead in a bloody clash in Chiapas, in which the Mexican Army tried to retake control of **El Bosque,** a small town near San Cristóbal that was sympathetic to the Zapatista rebels. The relationship between the government and the rebels is continually tense and exemplifies the problems and paradoxes of current Mexico. Carlos Fuentes, one of Mexico's premier writers and intellectuals, expresses eloquently that "it is impossible for the drama of Chiapas and its democratic solution not to affect the drama of Mexico and the entire's country's democratic solution...if the problems of democracy are not resolved in Chiapas, they will not be resolved in Mexico; if they are not resolved in Mexico, there will be one, two, three Chiapas in Hidalgo, Oaxaca, Michoacán, Guerrero."

Culture and Character

ART AND ARCHITECTURE

Art historians classify Mexican art into three periods: the **Indigenous** (6000 BC-AD 1525), the **Colonial** (1525-1810), and the **Modern** (1810-present). The study of the creations that came before the Spanish invasion is based on the work of archaeologists, since our understanding comes from the actual pieces themselves. For the most part, no written commentary on artistic expression exists from the time before the Conquest. Once the Spanish came onto the scene, they drastically influenced the styles used and provided their own interpretations of their art, trends that have continued into the Modern period.

The Pre-Hispanic Era

Much of the art and architecture from this period has provided the basis for understanding its history (see **Pre-Hispanic Societies,** p. 44). Some general trends in pre-Hispanic style can be seen over time and across Mexico. The use of **stone** is perhaps one of the most noticeable continuities. It is also the most easily uncovered by archaeologists, since stone is relatively durable and often used in large quantities. The Olmecs shaped basalt into the colossal heads for which they are famous. The Maya used limestone and sandstone all over their cities, as building blocks for palaces and temples, stelae (upright stone monuments often inscribed with glyphs and reliefs), and altars. Cities such as Teotihuacán, Tula, and Tenochtitlán show the continued use of monumental stone architecture in their buildings, carved reliefs, and statuary.

On a smaller scale, some of the most impressive pieces of pre-Hispanic art would fit in your hand. **Carved jade** and **ceramic figurines** are plentiful from the very beginnings of Mexican culture through to the Colonial period. Maya gods and nobility are often depicted adorned with massive headdresses replete with lengthy feathers, necklaces with beads the size of eggs, and gold and copper bracelets to match the enormous bangles hanging from their earlobes. Much of the information gained from art such as stone monuments or small carved objects pertains only to the elite members of those societies; unfortunately, much less material has been recovered from the non-elite segments of these cultures.

While archaeologists have found all kinds of objects and monuments, a final form of creative expression used by pre-Hispanic peoples is **narrative depiction. Murals** such as those covering the walls at the Maya site of Bonampak reveal scenes of warfare, sacrifice, and celebration. **Frescoes** on interior walls of buildings at Teotihuacán depict, among other subjects, paradise scenes, floral arrangements, religious rituals, and athletic events. Scenes painted onto the **pottery** of all of these cultures depict mythological stories. Other reliefs and objects reveal calendrical events and dates—the famous **Aztec Stone of the Sun** is a prime example. Measuring nearly four meters in diameter, this calendar's narrative is a tragic one: within its concentric rings are contained the four symbols of previous suns—rain, jaguars, wind, and fire, the plagues responsible for the destruction of earlier populations. The Aztecs believed that they were living in the period of the fifth sun, and they expected to be obliterated by an earthquake—the symbol for which also ominously appears on the stone.

The Architecture of New Spain

Not surprisingly, the first examples of **colonial art** were created specifically to facilitate religious indoctrination of the *indígenas* as quickly as possible. Churches were often constructed on top of pre-existing temples and pyramids, causing serious and irreparable damage to the ancient sites. Volcanic stone, plentiful in most areas, was the main building material. Colonial architecture, much of it recalling **Romanesque** and **Gothic** stylistic elements, is characterized by the use of huge buttresses, arches, and crenulations (indented or embattled moldings). An early architectural phenomenon that developed early on was the open chapel *(capilla abierta)*, a group of arches enclosing an atrium.

The monasteries and churches under the direction of **Franciscan, Dominican,** and **Augustinian** missionaries were built according to climatic and geographic limitations. The Franciscan style tended to be functional and economic, while the Dominican style was more ascetic and harsh, due to earthquake danger and warm weather. The Augustinian style was the most free-spirited and grandiose, and architects indulged in gratuitous and excessive decoration whenever possible. Remarkable Augustinian buildings include the **Monastery of St. Augustín of Acolman** near Mexico City and the **Monastery of Actopán** in Hidalgo.

A Blossoming of the Baroque

The steady growth and spread of the Catholic Church throughout the 17th and 18th centuries necessitated the construction of cathedrals, parochial chapels, and convents; moreover, this period brought the Baroque style to New Spain. Elegant and garish—but always luxurious—**Baroque** facades, teeming with dynamic images of angels and saints, aimed to produce a feeling of awe and respect in the hearts of the recently converted *indígenas.* The narratives set in stone could be understood even by *los analfabetos* (the illiterate people) and easily committed to memory. A look at the cathedrals of Zacatecas and Chihuahua reveals the degree of artistry Baroque ideals encouraged. Baroque painting found its quintessential expression in the works of **Alonso López de Herrera** and **Baltazar de Echave Orio** (the elder).

Sumptuousness, frivolity, and ornamentation became more prevalent in the works of the late 18th-century artists and builders who couldn't get too much of a good thing. During this time, the **Churrigueresque** style was born and **Mexican High Baroque** was carried to the extreme. The hallmarks of this style are excessively and intricately decorated *estípites* (pilasters), often installed merely for looks, not support.

20th Century Murals and Beyond: The Political Aesthetic

As the Revolution reduced their land to shambles, Mexican painters developed an unapologetic national style. This success was made possible by **José Vasconcelos's** Ministry of Education program, which commissioned *muralistas* to create their art on the walls of hospitals, colleges, schools, and ministries. Vasconcelos also sent the artists into the countryside to teach and participate in rural life.

The Mexican **mural,** unequivocally nationalistic in its current form, dates back to the early days of the Conquest when Catholic evangelists, who could not communicate with the *indígenas,* used allegorical murals to teach them the rudiments of Christian iconography. **Diego Rivera,** the most renowned of the *muralistas,* based his artwork on political themes—land reform, Marxism, and the marginalization of *indígena* life. Rivera used stylized realism to portray the dress, action, and expression of the Mexican people, and natural realism (complete with ugly faces, knotted brows, and angry stances) to represent Spaniards and other oppressors of the *indígenas.* His innovative of combinations of Mexican history and culture reached a wide audience and embroiled him in international controversy.

Though Rivera is credited as the first to forge the path for *muralistas,* many other artists have contributed to the definition of the art form and have thus achieved national recognition. Some of the best-known *muralistas* include: **David Álfaro Siqueiros,** who brought new materials and dramatic revolutionary themes to his murals; the Cubism-influenced **Rufino Tamayo,** arguably the most abstract of the *muralistas*; and **José Clemente Orozco,** whose murals in Mexico City and lifelike plaster-of-paris skeleton characters have won him a great deal of fame.

Not all 20th-century Mexican artists have exchanged the traditional canvas for walls. **Juan Soriano** forged a name for himself as a painter and sculptor. Under the tutelage of painter **Juan Reyes Ferreira,** Soriano was introduced to international art as well as Mexican popular art. Soriano is renowned for combining vanguard and traditional Mexican art. His award-winning paintings often include his friends, the women of his family, or himself.

Frida Kahlo and the Woman Artist

And where are the **women artists?** In a culture anchored by misogyny and machismo, within an art world unabashedly biased toward the U.S. and Western Europe, it is not surprising that the art of Mexican women wasn't dealt with seriously until the latter half of this century. Celebrated 20th-century Mexican women artists include the painters **María Izquierdo** and **Lilia Carrillo,** and the photographer **Lola Alvarez Bravo.** Due in part to her incredible talent and **Hayden Herrera's** landmark biography, **Frida Kahlo** (1907-54) surpasses all other Mexican artists—men included—in terms of current worldwide recognition. Kahlo's paintings and self-portraits are icons of pain: the viewer is forced to confront the artist's self-obsession in its most violent and extreme manifestations.

LITERATURE

Pre-Hispanic Writing: A Multi-Media Affair

As far as linguists and archaeologists have been able to tell, three languages were dominant in Mexico before the arrival of the Spanish: **Náhuatl, Mayan,** and **Cakchiquel.** The earliest examples of writing are thought to be the glyphs inscribed at **San José Mogote** and **Monte Albán,** Oaxaca—two sites containing reliefs perhaps dating back to 600 BC. The Spaniards' destructive rampage, particularly in the initial years of the Conquest, and the imposition of the Spanish language resulted in the loss of valuable information relating to *indígena* language. Considered a dangerous affront to Christian teachings, Maya and Aztec **codices** (unbound "books" or manuscripts) were fed to the flames. But due to the grace of God or to less-than-scrupulous destruction, a number of Maya codices did survive. Other historical works such as the **Books of Chilam Balam** (Books of the Jaguar Priest) and the **Annals of the Cakchiquel** cover a range of topics. They are not exclusively historical works, but are instead narrative and poetic, laden with symbolism and lofty metaphor. The **Rabinal Achi** (Knight of Achi), the story of a sacrificed warrior, is considered to be the only surviving example of pre-Hispanic drama.

Colonial Literature

Like astronauts on a new planet, the Spanish were eager to send news home about the land they had conquered and the way of life of Mexico's *indígenas*. These letters home, among them Cortés's **Cartas de relación** (Letters of Relation), were mainly Crown- and Church-flattering documents detailing the exhaustive ongoing efforts being undertaken to educate and Christianize *indígenas.* Other chronicles, such as the *Nuevo Mundo y Conquista* (New World and Conquest), by **Francisco de Terrazas,** and *Grandeza Mexicana* (Mexican Grandeur), by **Bernardo de Balbuena,** were written in rhyme in order to take the edge off the monotonous melange of factoid stew.

In the harsh and brutal society of New Spain, only religious orders enjoyed the luxury of genuine intellectual freedom. Many members of the clergy worked to preserve the languages and texts of the *indígenas,* and a handful of universities sprung up. The **Jesuits'** 23 colleges were the best in the colony—until the Crown expelled the Jesuits from the Americas in 1767 because of their growing influence.

Although historical texts dominated Mexico's literary output throughout much of the 16th and 17th centuries, poets made substantial achievements. **Sor Juana Inés de la Cruz** (1648-1695) became a master lyricist known for her razor-sharp wit. A *criolla* of illegitimate birth, Sor Juana turned to the cloistered life and married God, instead of the numerous suitors she undoubtedly had—her beauty was legendary. In the Church she found a moral and physical haven where she produced her most famous works, **Respuesta a Sor Filotea** (Response to Sor Filotea) and **Hombres Necios** (Injudicious Men). Her love poems display a passionate outlook, and many verses display a feminist sensibility ahead of their time.

Struggling for a Literary Identity

During the 18th century, the Inquisition vied with the French Enlightenment to distract Mexican writers from anything that could be described as innovative. The establishment of the **Academia de la Lengua Española** (Academy of the Spanish Language) in 1713 grew out of a desire to regulate Spanish where it was spoken, including colonies. An explosion of science writing occurred about this time. Studies of Mexican geography, weather, flora, and fauna swept away scientists and writers on a wave of rational and analytical thought.

The literary impetus of philosophical movements eventually gave way to political ones. By the end of the 18th century, the struggle for independence became the singular social fact from which many Mexican texts grew. In 1816, **José Fernández de Lizardi,** a prominent Mexican journalist, wrote the first Latin American novel: **El Periquillo Sarniento** (The Itching Parrot), a picaresque tale that revealed Mexican society's displeasure with the status quo. His ideological, moralizing fiction was very influential. With the Spanish-American modernists of the 19th century, poetry reached a level it had not achieved since Sor Juana. At the same time, **Manuel Gutierrez Nájera** composed the poem *De Blanco* (On Whiteness), a linguistic representation at its most distilled and self-contained.

Many romantic novels of the period used historical themes to introduce sweeping indictments of the military and clergy. Novelists sought to define Mexico's national identity, glorifying strength, secularism, progress, and education. Artists were didactic, producing works with such inspirational titles as *Triumph and Study Over Ignorance.* Whereas European Romanticism was an aesthetic challenge to Neoclassicism, Mexican Romanticism was an artistic response to the country's political and social realities. Shortly after the heyday of the Romantic novel came the popular novel of manners, most notably *El Fistol del Diablo* by **Manuel Payno,** and *Juanita Sousa* and *Antón Pérez* by **Manuel Sánchez Mármol.**

Literature during the **Porfiriato** (1876-1911) abandoned Romanticism for realism, and most writers expressed little sympathy for the poor. Others adopted a Modernist style, emphasizing language and imagery, and replacing didactic social themes with psychological topics. Visual artists, by contrast, began to reject the creed of the *científicos.* Many favored experimental techniques and chose to depict **slums, brothels,** and **scenes from indigenous life.** Their iconoclasm foreshadowed a growing dissatisfaction with the Díaz regime.

20th-Century Global Perspectives

Mexican literature in the post-Revolutionary era is marked by a frustrated desire to forge a national tradition from the vestiges of pre-colonial culture. Nobel prize winner **Octavio Paz,** in such works as **El Laberinto de la Soledad** (The Labyrinth of Solitude), draws on Marxism, Romanticism, and post-Modernism to explore the making and unmaking of a national archetype. Paz, like his equally famous successor **Carlos Fuentes,** concerns himself with myths and legends in an effort to come to terms with Spanish cultural dominance. Fuentes published his first novel, *La region más transparente,* in 1958. **Juan Rulfo's** novel **Pedro Páramo,** set in rural Jalisco, blurs the line between life and death, past and present, as it relates one man's search for his father. **Juan José Arreola,** a leading fiction writer whose prose paints a picture of Mexican society, published *Confabulario Total* and *La Feria* in the 1960s. **Emilio Carballido** is best-known for his *obras de teatro* (plays). In 1978, he published *D.F. 26 obras en un acto*, which showed the chages in Mexico City over the past century through a series of short scenes.

The wildly popular works of **Gustavo Sainz** and **José Agustín,** the instigators of *literatura de la onda* ("hip" literature), address universal vices such as sex and drugs. Of late, the work of female writers, such as Hollywood darling **Laura Esquivel** *(Like Water for Chocolate,* see p. 66), has been well received both nationally and internationally. Elena Poniatowska, the author of *Tinisma*—a novel about the life of Tina Modotti who was a secret agent for the Soviet Union during the Spanish Civil War—is making a name for herself in the world of Latin American writers.

A New Movement Is Born

In the past two decades, a new literary movement has emerged from Mexico—the Chicano movement. Chicano literature describes the experiences of Latinos who come to the United States and must overcome numerous barriers to adapt to the new culture. Many Chicano authors are rapidly gaining respect in the international community. **Sandra Cisneros's** *House on Mango Street*—a novel narrated by an eleven-year-old girl who talks about her life on both sides of the Mexican border—has made Cisneros one of the most recognized Chicana authors today. **Ana Castillo** (*The Mixquialhuala Letters*—a story about an Indian-Mexican woman and an Anglo woman who meet in Mexico and build a lasting friendship through letters over the ensuing decade) and **Helena Maria Viramontes** *(Under the Feet of Jesus*—a story about Mexican migrants in the U.S.) are also prominent figures in the Chicana community.

Rudulfo Anaya *(The Anaya Reader)* and **Richard Rodriguez** (*Days of Obligation: An Argument With My Mexican Father* and the controversial autobiography *Hunger of Memory)* have become intricately connected with the Chicano movement. Other Chicano writers such as **Américo Paredes** have used their status as Chicano authors to put traditional Mexican folklore into written form. In *With His Pistol in His Hands,* Paredes put into written form the story of **Gregorio Cortez**, a Mexican who was persecuted by the U.S. judicial system for shooting a sheriff in self-defense. The ballad of Gregorio Cortez has since become an inspirational story to Mexicans.

POPULAR CULTURE

Music

Mexico City has become one of the major recording centers for the Americas. Like most other components of its culture, Mexican music is an eclectic stew of styles and flavors borrowed from across the continent and overseas. Mexico's traditional music is mostly regional, making for a rich and varied collage of styles and artists. Up north, one will hear groups such as **Los Bukis, Bronco,** and **Los Tigres del Norte** sing in the style aptly labeled *norteño.* One of the most popular and well-known styles of traditional Mexican music is **mariachi.** Mariachi songs, commonly called *rancheras,* are usually played live by a sombreroed, gregarious brass-and-string band. The world-famous tradition of women being serenaded by a group of *mariachis* in traditional Mexican garb is seen as an almost obligatory supplement to a romantic evening—foreplay, if you will. Traditional *rancheras* tend to deal with one or several of the following topics: being very drunk, being abandoned by a woman, being cheated on by a woman, getting drunk, leaving a woman, pondering the fidelity of one's horse, loving one's gun, and wanting to get drunk. While male singers like **José Alfredo Jiménez** and **Vicente Fernández** continue to sing popular tunes in this tradition, **Lupita D'Alessio** provides the angry-woman response. Although she gets betrayed or left on almost every one of her songs, the culprit men often get their due.

The Mexican music scene is adorned with both Spanish and American influences. The former is apparent with young artists such as the pop group **Garibaldi,** whose scantily clad bods perennially grace music and teen fanzines. Travelers from up north will feel at home, as American music in all forms is ubiquitous on the radio and in bars and *discotecas.* Always striving to Mexicanize imports in some way,

Mexican artists will often take an American piece and make it their "own" with altered lyrics or a slightly more Latin beat. Cotton-candy pop is sung by such artists as **Luis Miguel** (sigh), **Lucero, Alejandra Guzmán** (dubbed the Reina del Rock, Queen of Rock, in the early 90s) and **Christian Castro.** In 1989, **Gloria Trevi** burst onto the pop music scene with her first album "*¿Que Hago Aquí?*" ("What am I Doing Here?"). She made her film debut in 1992 with *Pelo Suelto,* the biggest moneymaker in Mexican film history. Trevi's immense popularity peaked in the early 90s, but her calendars can still be found around the country. **Selena,** the "Latin Madonna" and most beloved of Tejano singers, was born American, but in typical Tejano style, she fused polka, country, Mexican, and R&B. Her bouncy Spanish album *Amor Prohibido* was wildly popular in both Mexico and the U.S., but it didn't hit #1 on the Billboard charts until Selena was murdered—shot in the back by **Yolanda Saldivar,** the president of her fan club, on March 31, 1995. After her death, she became even more of an icon for Mexican youth.

Television

Mexican television can, for the most part, be broken down into four categories: *telenovelas* (soap operas), weekly dramas, sitcoms, and imported American shows. **Telenovelas** are by far the most popular and widely aired of the bunch. Occupying a huge block of midday air time, these addictive hour-long examples of dramaturgy tend to run for two to four months before being ousted for a fresh group of characters and conflicts. *Preciosa* and *Vivo por Elena* are two of the current favorite *telenovelas* in Mexico. The half-hour **sitcoms** that are central to American TV are not as popular in Mexico, though there are a few. Popular shows include *Sabado Gigante, Papá Soltero, Chespirito,* and just about anything on the **Canal de las Estrellas** (Channel of the Stars). When the World Cup is raging, the *fútbol* (soccer) talk shows such as *Los Protagonistas* dominate the airwaves. American shows are often dubbed; as in the U.S., shows such as *Melrose Place* and *Baywatch* are very popular. Cartoons are imported from both the U.S. and Japan. One cannot claim to have *lived* without having watched at least one episode of **Los Simpson.**

There are about a dozen major national and regional networks that are the most likely to appear on television sets throughout Mexico. The national networks include: **XEW 2,** which broadcasts its own *telenovelas* and old Mexican movies; **XHGC 5,** *Televisa,* which airs children's programming, late-night movies, and police, suspense, and horror shows; **Canal 7,** which broadcasts children's American shows dubbed into Spanish and some movies; **Canal 9,** which broadcasts mainly syndicated shows including old Mexican comedy shows, old *telenovelas*, and Mexican movies; **Canal 11,** *Instituto Politécnico Nacional,* which airs mainly culturally oriented shows and movies; and **Canal 13,** *Television Azteca*, which airs mainly *telenovelas,* particularly from Brazil, Colombia, Venezuela, and Argentina. In many regions, **Canal 22,** a cultural channel that airs movies and interviews with artists; and **Canal 40,** which airs news and music shows, have gained immense popularity.

Film

"Popular cinema is still alive and well in Mexico," wrote one disgruntled director, "mainly as sex comedies and cop dramas." The recent recession has led to an influx of subtitled Hollywood imports and a paucity of quality films. Mexico's golden age of cinema *(cine de oro)* was kicked off in the 1940s and 50s with **Emilio "El Indio" Fernández's** *Maria Candelaría* (1943), an honoree at the first Cannes Film Festival in 1946, and **Luis Buñuel's** *Los Olvidados* (1950), a grisly portrait of *barrio* life in Mexico City. During the 1950s, Buñuel went through what were later referred to as his "Mexican years." During this decade, he produced a series of satirical Latin American films, many of which were filmed in Mexico. The films took off with *The Great Madcap* in 1949. In 1952, he directed *Una Mujer Sin Amor*, a film about a married woman who has a passionate affair that later comes back to haunt her. In 1956, Buñuel collaborated on a French and Mexican co-production and filmed *La Muerte de este Jardín* and in 1959, he filmed a political film about fascism in a mythical South

American country called *Fever Mounts in El Pao.* In 1960, Mexican cinema reached a new plateau when **Roberto Gavalin's** *Macario*—a film about a starving woodcutter who cuts a deal with Death and gets the gift of healing—was the first Mexican film to receive an Oscar nomination.

The past decade has seen the rise of such luminaries as **Arturo Ripstein** *(La Mujer del Puerto; Reina de la Noche),* **Jorge Fons** *(Rojo Amancecer),* and **Paul Leduc.** Known for his experiments without dialogue, Leduc's *Frida* provides an unsettling look at one of Mexico's controversial cultural icons. The 1983 Mexican film *Eréndira*, by director **Roy Guerra,** made its mark as the first film to be adapted from a work by the famous Colombian writer Gabriel García Márquez. The film portrays the disturbing story of a young woman who is forced into prostitution. The success of *Eréndira* prompted García Márquez to allow movie adaptations to be made of many of his other works throughout the 1980s.

Throughout the 1990s, many Mexican films have achieved international fame and recognition. One of the more famous films from the 90s was **Maria Novaro's** *Danzón*—a critically acclaimed film in 1991 about a Mexican City telephone operator who journeys to Veracruz to find her ballroom dance partner and love. Other Mexican films such as **Robert Rodriguez's** *El Mariachi* have been readily accepted by the international film community, though more for their bloody appeal than for their cultural significance. But the one Mexican film that has enjoyed perhaps the most crossover success is the delicious romance *Como Agua para Chocolate (Like Water for Chocolate),* based on the best-selling **Laura Esquivel** novel and directed by **Alfonso Arau,** now Esquivel's ex-husband. The film has the distinction of being the highest-grossing foreign film in U.S. history.

FOOD AND DRINK

Mexican food and drinks aren't just good; they're **orgasmic.** Leave your preconceived notions of what constitutes "real Mexican food" behind and prepare your tastebuds for a culinary treat.

Mexicans usually have their big meal of the day—**la comida**—between 2 and 4pm. Restaurants often offer **comida corrida**—sometimes called *la comida* or *el menú*—a fixed price meal including soup, salad, tea or *agua fresca,* a *plato fuerte* (main dish), and sometimes a dessert. The main dish is often a **guisado**—a soup or stew with meat—although a **caldo** (broth-like soup) and a regular plate of meat are also common; *arroz* (rice, sometimes *con huevo,* with chopped egg), beans, and tortillas are always included. Breakfasts *(desayunos)* range from continental to grandiose. Dinner *(cena)* is usually a light meal served around 8pm.

The Staples

From tacos slapped together at a roadside *taquería* to magnificent plates full of garlic shrimp or chicken with *mole* sauce (see p. 67), Mexican food invariably maintains one common link: the **tortilla.** This most ubiquitous staple of Mexican cuisine is a flat, round, thin pancake made from either wheat flour *(harina)* or corn flour *(maíz).* You will surely develop a preference for one or the other early on, and most restaurants will let you choose which kind you want with your *antojito* or full meal.

The other two staples of Mexican food make a cheap, filling, and remarkably nutritious pair—rice and beans. **Rice** *(arroz)* is usually standard fare; yellow Spanish or Mexican rice—prepared with oil and tomato sauce and often flavored with onions and garlic—is a special treat. **Beans** *(frijoles)* are soft and range from soupy to pasty *(refritos).* These three foods will be served in various forms with just about every full plate of food you order, be it breakfast, lunch, or dinner.

Good Morning

Aside from the standard **café con leche** or **pan dulce** (sweetened bread), almost any breakfast in Mexico will include **eggs** in some shape or form. **Huevos al gusto** (eggs any style) provide people with a choice of *jamón* (ham), *tocino* (bacon), or *machaca* (dried, shredded beef). **Tortillas, frijoles,** and sometimes **rice** or **papas fri-**

tas (french fries) are served on the side. The eggs themselves are usually *revueltos* (scrambled) with the meat mixed in, but you can ask for the meat fried on the side or the eggs *estrellados* (fried) instead. Other popular styles of preparing *huevos* include *rancheros* (fried eggs served on corn tortillas and covered with a spicy red salsa), *albañil* (scrambled eggs cooked in green sauce), *a la mexicana* (scrambled with onion, tomato, and chopped green chile), *motuleños* (fried eggs served on a fried corn tortilla, topped with sauteed green peas and ham, Sam I Am), *ahogados* (eggs cooked in boiling red sauce), and *borrachos* (fried eggs served with beans cooked in beer). More expensive Mexican breakfasts include **omelettes** with any of the above meats or **seafood** such as *camarones* (shrimp) or **langosta** (lobster).

Ah, Antojitos

Antojito comes from the Spanish word *antojo* (craving). An *antojito* (little craving) is a small meal or big snack found on almost any Mexican menu. Popular legend says that if a pregnant woman is refused an *antojo* she will lose the baby. Although anything could be an *antojito,* the term is often, but not always, restricted to nine categories. **Tacos** are small, grilled chunks of meat (sometimes chicken, fried fish, or fried shellfish) placed on an open, warm tortilla—top it with a row of condiments ranging from lettuce and tomato to guacamole and hot sauce. As always, be sure to watch for anything that may have been cleaned with impure water, such as lettuce. **Burritos** are thin, rolled flour tortillas filled with meat (often *machaca,* chicken, or beans) and a few cooked vegetables such as green peppers and onions. Occasionally you will see Tex-Mex style *súper burritos* filled with everything but the kitchen sink. Burritos are not very common in the southern parts of Mexico. **Enchiladas** are corn tortillas filled with meat or chicken, topped with a special red or green sauce and shredded cheese, and then baked or fried, though some variations do exist. **Quesadillas** are filled with melted cheddar cheese. Sometimes other things are added: *quesadillas sincronizadas* are filled with ham, and regular quesadillas served with *pastor* (gyro style) pork meat are called **gringas. Tostadas** consist of a deep-fried tortilla garnished with vegetables, cheese, and some kind of meat—ranging from beef or chicken to exotic seafood like *pulpo* (octopus). Tostadas are the only *antojito* to which raw vegetables are always added (be wary of raw vegetables unless you are sure they have been cleaned in purified water). A **chile relleno,** a unique and wonderful Mexican creation, consists of a large, green chile pepper stuffed with cheese (and occasionally meat), dipped in a batter, fried, and topped with red *salsa.* They are not particularly *picante* (spicy-hot)—the frying process rids the chile of most of its potency. **Tamales,** also unique to the country, are ground-corn dough packed with meat or chicken in corn husks; they have the consistency of thick dumplings. Finally, **chimichangas** are essentially the same as burritos but deep fried to produce a rich, crunchy, artery-hardening shell; **flautas** are like chimichangas but small and finger-thin.

Meats, Poultry, Seafood, and Soup

Meat platters usually feature either **bistek** (derived from the little-used English term "beefsteak"), which is a standard fried cut of beef; **carne asada,** thin slices of beef fried until crispy; or **pricier cuts of steak** such as T-bone, filet mignon, or New York steak (English names are used). The meat can be prepared normally (it's usually served fairly well-done), *empanizada* or *milanesa* (breaded or fried), or *a la mexicana* (charred up and topped with a Mexican red salsa). *Encebollado* means served with grilled onions. In any case, meat dishes are accompanied by *arroz, frijoles,* tortillas, and sometimes *papas fritas.* **Pollo** (chicken) is ubiquitous and (usually) quite tasty. Whether by itself or included in a platter, it is generally either *rostizado* (spit-roasted over an open fire, "rotisserie"-style) or *asado* (grilled), served with the same side dishes mentioned above. **Mole,** which is arguably Mexico's national dish, is a delectable sauce composed of chiles, chocolate, and other spices that is usually served over chicken. **Mole poblano** is named after its home, the city of Puebla. A common recipe for *mole poblano* includes turkey, dried chiles, nuts, seeds, vegetables, spices, and melted chocolate (Ibarra Mexican chocolate is usually used). Seafood dishes include **pescado** (generic fish fillet, usually a local catch), **camarones** (shrimp), **langosta** (lobster), **calamar** (fillet of squid), scrumptious **jaiba** (crab), and **huachinango** (the exceedingly tasty red snapper, with a name that's as fun to pronounce—wa-chee-NAAN-go—as the fish to eat). Seafood is usually served either *empanizado* (breaded and fried) or in garlic, as in the delicious **al mojo de ajo**. Many regions have their own special ways of preparing seafood. One of the most famous of these is **a la veracruzana**—a special preparation native to Veracruz in which the fish is decked out in olives, capers, and olive oil.

Soups in Mexico can also be delicious; among others, **sopa de tortilla** is made with bits of softened tortilla, and **sopa de lima** is flavored with lime.

When You Get Thirsty

Cerveza (beer) ranks only slightly below tortillas and beans on the list of Mexican staples. It is impossible to drive through any Mexican town without coming across a double-digit number of Tecate and Corona billboards, painted buildings, and cheap beer stores proudly selling their products. **Tecate** is Mexico's version of Budweiser—it's cheap and widespread. Popular beers in Mexico (listed roughly in order of quality) are **Bohemia** (a world-class lager), **Negra Modelo** (a fine dark beer), **Dos Equis** (a light, smooth lager), **Pacífico, Modelo, Carta Blanca, Superior, Corona Extra,** and **Sol** (watery and light). **Tecate** is an integral part of Mexican culture; any honest and authentic traveler will drink as much of it as possible. The Mexicans share their love for bargain beer with the world, as demonstrated by the fact that the Mexican-made Corona Extra is the leading export in Mexico and tops many international charts—including Canada, Australia, New Zealand, France, Italy, Spain, and most European markets—as one of the most popular beers.

Tequila is king when it comes to Mexican liquor. It is the quintessential Mexican drink, a more refined version of *mezcal* (distilled from the *maguey* cactus). **Herradura, Tres Generaciones,** and **Cuervo 1800** are among the more famous, more expensive, and altogether better brands of tequila. Cheap tequila can be bought for prices you wouldn't believe: one Hermosillo supermarket frequently advertises a liter for under US$1! While many hard-core tequila lovers will drink the liquor straight, others may prefer a **margarita** (tequila, triple sec, lime juice, and ice) or **tequila sunrise** (tequila, orange juice, and blackberry brandy) to doing shots. **Mezcal,** coarser than tequila, is sometimes served with the worm native to the plant—upon downing the shot, you are expected to ingest the worm. Some say it induces hallucination; however evidence is to the contrary. If you get a chance to sample **pulque,** the fermented juice of the *maguey,* don't hesitate—it was the sacred drink of the Aztec nobility.

Clean and Sober

"Waiter," you say, "I ordered a Bloody Mary, not a Shirley Temple." He smirks and points to the pink fizzy drink in front of you. *"Ley seca,"* he says. "Makealikeawhat?" you ask. But before you get too confused (and annoyed), realize this is a recent tradition. On the day before elections, the national government applies the *ley seca* (dry law). No alcohol may be bought, sold, or consumed the Saturday before elections or election day itself. Need a smoke? Fat chance. Cigarettes are not sold, and shops close early. No movies are shown on public TV. The reason? Explanations vary. One explanation is that the government wants people sober, alert, and completely sane when they vote, hence the prohibitions on "distractions." Another common explanation is that the government is trying to reduce corrupt party practices. In the past, it was not uncommon for party leaders to set up free liquor stands outside election booths and do some "campaigning." Well, whatever the reason, Mexicans take this law (and their politics) very seriously. So even if it's Saturday night, the day before elections, and you want to rock n' roll, remember two words: *ley seca.* Hit the bottled water and save the beer for early Monday morning.

Mexican mixed drinks enjoy at least as much recognition worldwide as its beers. Coffee-flavored **Kahlúa,** Mexico's most-exported liqueur, deserves its lofty reputation. Enjoy it with cream, with milk, or as part of a **White Russian** or **Black Russian.** Bottles are ridiculously cheap below the border. Frozen drinks aren't too shabby, either; unfortunately, because of tainted ice from the low-quality water, only daredevils or Cancún-goers indulge in a margarita, a **piña colada** (pineapple juice, cream of coconut—or, if you're lucky, fresh pineapple and coconut—and light rum), or a **coco loco** (coconut milk and tequila served in a hollowed-out coconut).

There are also plenty of popular beverage options that don't include alcohol. **Coca-Cola** ("Coca") is at least as prevalent as Corona Extra in restaurants, bars, and grocery stores. Pepsi, Sprite, 7-Up, and orange sodas are also available, as are some unique Mexican **refrescos** (sodas). *Soda de fresa* (strawberry soda) is delicious; also try *soda de piña* (pineapple soda), *toronja* (grapefruit soda—try Kas brand), *manzanita* (apple soda—try Sol), and Boing! (mango soda). Soda rarely costs more than 5 pesos, even at fancy restaurants, and usually costs between 3 and 4 pesos for a bottle or can. **Aguas frescas,** including *limonada* (lemonade), are noncarbonated fruit-based drinks.

Recommended Reading

One of the best ways to learn about a place is to delve headfirst into its culture. Mexico has a history rich in self-representation: from the ancient texts of **The Books of Chilam Balam** to the poetry of Octavio Paz. Outsiders, as well as the people of Mexico, have continually explored, envisioned, and re-envisioned Mexico: though it is a wasteland at times, and a wonderland at others, it is always a land fertile with possibility. The complexities and excitement of Mexican history have tempted innumerable scholars; there is no dearth of sources on Mexico. Here are some reading suggestions before you venture out on your own and explore.

SOURCES

Mexican Literature in Translation

Where the Air is Clear, by Carlos Fuentes, trans. Peden (1976). A monumental book that attempts to capture the vast, constantly changing panorama of Mexico City. Fuentes is Mexico's most eminent novelist and one of the world's most celebrated writers. Also be sure to check out **The Death of Artemio Cruz** (1964) and **Terra Nostra** (1976). Anything he has written is guaranteed to be insightful.

Pedro Páramo, by Juan Rulfo, trans. Peden (1994). The new translation of this 1955 classic is faithful to the stark, concise language of the original. This oft-studied paragon of Mexican novels deals with a young man's search for his roots in the barren town of Comala in the wake of the Revolution.

Selected Poems of Octavio Paz, trans. Aroul (1984). Paz's grandiose poetry is the stuff of which myths are made. His poetry, replete with phalluses and earth-mothers, is about nothing less than...the cosmic soul of Mexico. The Nobel didn't hurt either.

The Underdogs, by Mariano Azuela, trans. Fornoff (1992). One of the earliest novels (1938) and definitely one of the best about the Revolution. Azuela's experiments with form and style (and his clean, unsentimental prose) initiated a mini-revolution within Latin American literature.

Meditation on the Threshold: a Bilingual Anthology of Poetry, by Rosario Castellanos, trans. Palley (1988). Until her death in 1974, Castellanos was one of Mexico's leading feminist voices. Her poetry combines lyricism and acerbic social commentary on what it means to be a woman in Mexico.

Literature about Mexico

Under the Volcano, by Malcolm Lowry (1947). Set in Cuernavaca on the Day of the Dead, Lowry's meditative, moody novel about an alcoholic consulate has been compared to Joyce's *Ulysses*.

Stones for Ibarra, by Harriet Doerr (1984). A tender, atmospheric novel about a couple who move from their home in San Francisco to a deserted mining town in Mexico only to confront tragedy. Winner of the United States National Book Award.

Aztec, by Gary Jennings (1980). What *Shogun* did for ancient Japan, this almost-1000-page mass-market paperback does for ancient Mexico. Tons of violence, sex, and sensationalism. And, of course, there's human sacrifice.

The Power and the Glory, by Graham Greene (1940). Greene's famous novel about the fate of a martyred whiskey priest in Mexico. His book explores the fate of a weak-willed but well-intentioned clergyman struggling with God—a tale charged with meaning for modern Mexico.

History

Mexico: A History, by Robert Miller (1985). One of the best general histories available, this comprehensive and engaging account of Mexican history starts with the ancient Indian civilizations and passes through the centuries to modern day. Its big print will help ease sore eyes.

Mexico: From the Olmecs to the Aztecs, by Michael Coe (1994). This is a first-rate account of the habitation of Mexico from the first hunter-gatherers up through the Spanish Conquest. Beautiful photographs of sites and artifacts help guide the reader through the thousands of years covered.

The Ancient Maya, by Robert Sharer (1994). With over 800 pages dedicated to every site in the Maya region from the early PreClassic to the PostClassic periods, you can't find a more comprehensive or precise account of the Maya past.

The Aztecs, by Richard Townsend (1992). This well-researched, well-organized account of Aztec life is fun to read, containing information not just on history and art but also about daily life and culture. It also has lots of pictures.

Zapata and the Mexican Revolution, by John Womack Jr. (1970). This book goes where few historians have gone before; it beautifully recounts the events and people behind the Mexican Revolution. Although it is loaded with precise history, it reads like a novel. You'll cry when Zapata dies.

Mexico Since Independence, by Leslie Bethell (1991). This historical book details the major events in Mexican history from 1821 to the present day. The book is divided into chapters written by different scholars.

Mexico: A Biography of Power, by Enrique Krauze (1998), trans. Krauze. A thorough and entertaining account of Mexican history from 1810 to 1996. This indispensable book takes a "great man" approach—it looks at the pattern of Mexican history by focusing on its leaders.

Current Events and Contemporary History

A New Time for Mexico, by Carlos Fuentes, trans. Castañeda and author (1996). Although the book touches on history from pre-Hispanic times to the '94 peso crisis, Fuentes here concerns himself primarily with Mexico's future. Political commentary, history, poetry in prose, economic prescriptions—a great introduction to modern Mexico.

EZLN web page: www.ezln.org. An absolute must for anyone remotely interested in the EZLN. The best resource available anywhere. Timelines, links, articles, essays, direct quotes from Subcomandante Marcos, and even bilingual translations of EZLN communiques. A cyberspace gem.

First World, Ha Ha Ha! The Zapatista Challenge, by Elaine Katzenberger (1995). This compilation of journals, poems, articles, and essays by Mexican and U.S. writers is a sensitive introduction to the plight of the residents of Chiapas.

Culture and Society

The Labyrinth of Solitude, by Octavio Paz, trans by Kemp, Milos, and Belash (1990). Although Paz's alpha-male, instant myth-making can grate, he was Mexico's artistic emissary to the world until his death in 1998. Insanely famous, this book of philosophical reflections on Mexican society and character is a literary landmark.

Across the Wire: Life and Hard Times on the Mexican Border, by Luis A. Urrea (1993). A harrowing, true account of life south of the border. His chronicle of poverty and tragedy in modern-day Tijuana is a result of first-hand experience.

Massacre in Mexico, by Elena Poniatowska, trans. Lane (1975). Perhaps the best chronicle of the 1968 Tlatleloco massacre; one of Mexico's greatest writers uses eyewitness accounts and different voices to recreate this important historical event.

Mexico City

When the war god Huitzilopochtli commanded the Aztec people to build their great capital wherever they witnessed an eagle gripping a snake in its beak while roosting upon a *nopal* cactus, he could never have imagined what he was about to set in motion. The wandering Aztec tribe is said to have encountered this vision on an island in a murky lake nestled in the highland Valley of Mexico; they dutifully founded the island city of Tenochtitlán, which became the nucleus of the most systematic and dominating empire on the continent. Almost seven centuries and 25 million inhabitants later, the Valley of Mexico now cradles the largest city in the world.

To fathom the size of the city, it helps to see the heart of Mexico from the air. As soon as your jet descends beneath the clouds, urban settlement fills every neck-craning angle of your window view. It will soon become clear that the word "city" hardly does justice to the 1480 square kilometers of sprawling urban settlement shrouded in a stagnant yellow haze: there appear to be no boundaries, no suburbs, no beginning, no end; buildings tall and short are kneaded into the cupped, drained, saline lake-land as far as the eye can see.

Mexicans call this cosmopolitan conglomeration of neighborhoods **el D.F.** (deh-EFF-ay), short for **Distrito Federal** (Federal District), or simply **México.** The *defectuoso* (defective), as local *chilangos* (Mexico City inhabitants) teasingly call their city, is a breeding ground for staggering statistics. Depending on how you view it, it is home to between 17 and 30 million people and has over 220 *colonias* (neighborhoods). Virtually the entire federal bureaucracy inhabits the D.F., including the Ministry of the Navy—2240m above sea level. One-quarter of Mexico's population lives in the D.F. From the enormous central square to a blocks-long governmental palace to downtown's 40-story skyscrapers to Parque Chapultepec, the biggest city park in the Americas, everything here is larger than life. First-time visitors stop dead in their tracks when they realize that the gorgeous three-story art-nouveau edifice across from El Palacio de Bellas Artes is...just the post office. No one buries the ruins of the past nor apologizes for the excesses of the present.

If you give it a chance, though, México will treat you to sublime moments amid the overwhelming bustle. Sniff the orchids while gliding down the floating gardens of Xochimilco. Meander inconspicuously through the throngs of devout *chilangos* at the Basílica de Guadalupe. Lie in the shade of the Alameda listening to water rush through the stone fountains. Try to get into some of the most exclusive discos in the world. Be dazzled by the grandeur of the ancient Templo Mayor (see p. 46), center of the Aztec religious, political, and cultural world. Everywhere you look in the city today, from subway stations to the *zócalo,* such ruins peek out through the centuries for a breath of fresh smog.

Indeed, nowhere else in the world does a country's history breathe so heavily down the back of day-to-day life. After an epic siege and the ultimate defeat of Aztec Emperor Moctezuma II (see p. 47), Cortés and his men purposefully founded the crux of their colonial endeavors directly atop the floating city of Tenochtitlán and its pantheistic stone monuments to symbolize the crushing of Aztec religion. His hubris came back to haunt the colonists when, having destroyed the hydraulic infrastructure, they discovered that their newly won valley, slouching in a huge highland puddle of standing water blocked by mountains, presented a logistical nightmare. After colonization, floods tore through the city again and again, and buildings began to sink into the mud. The *Desagüe General,* a project to drain all of the stagnant water out of the valley, began in 1629 but was not completed until the draining of Lake Texcoco in 1900. When all the water was finally gone, Mexico City—10.33m lower than it was at the time of Conquest and no longer an island—found itself surrounded by infertile salt flats which, as the 20th century progressed, were soon filled in by miles of sprawling shantytowns settled by newcomers from surrounding central Mexico. Landlocked and ringed by mountains, the city lets neither water in nor sewage out.

To make things worse, Aztec legend predicted that the modern world would be destroyed by earthquakes; this almost came true in 1985, when Mexico City was shaken by a quake measuring 8.1 on the Richter scale. Tens of thousands of people died, and entire neighborhoods were reduced to rubble. In 1997, Armageddon stepped closer when the majestic, snow-capped volcano Popocatépetl awakened to spew ash over the city in late June. Mexico City has truly been subjected to its own version of the plagues; among them are huge-scale water shortage (a problem that will soon blossom to epic proportions), volcanic eruptions, massive earthquakes, poverty, the proliferation of petty crime, and the worst air-pollution problem anywhere on earth. The pollution reached new heights of wheezing horror in the summer of 1998; smoke from the fires in Chiapas billowed in, and late rains refused to offer any respite. The eye-reddening air is kept in place by the bowl formed by surrounding mountains—some say that just breathing for a day in Mexico City is equivalent to smoking 20 cigarettes. As people from all around the country continue to arrive in hopes of finding scarce jobs, Mexico City's infamous demographic crisis becomes more difficult to ignore, and the prospect of feeding everyone becomes increasingly unrealistic.

In the summer of 1998, just one year after the mayoral victory of the PRD (Partido Revolucionario Democrático) ended years of one-party rule (see p. 59), frustration at the lack of any rapid remedy to the city's illnesses is mixed with continued hope. What will this resplendent, rubbish-ridden city accomplish now? Millions each day strut down Paseo de la Reforma, contemplating their sinking city's future under the watchful eye of El Angel. Most see the city not as an enemy but as a brother gone astray. The *chilangos'* laments are grounded in unconditional love for this apocalyptic metropolis. They are proud of its past, preoccupied with its present, and hopeful about leading their capital to a new and glorious future.

HIGHLIGHTS OF MEXICO CITY

- Don't miss Mexico City's **zócalo** (see p. 92), the center of the country's capital, home to ruins, cathedrals, and government buildings lovingly covered with murals by Rivera, Siquieros, and Orozco—all right next to each other.
- The **Bosque de Chapultepec** (see p. 106) is the biggest urban park in the Americas—it's got everything from panda bears to free concerts to the **Museo Nacional de Antropología** (see p. 106), Mexico's biggest and best museum.
- Wear your fanciest duds to party in the perennially packed bars and discos of the glamorous **Zona Rosa** (see p. 93).
- Flock with the devout to the **Basilica de Guadalupe** (see p. 110).
- Take a nap on the park benches of the gloriously green **Alameda** (see p. 101) across from the beautiful, French-inspired **Palacio de Bellas Artes** (see p. 102).
- Some of Mexico City's most fabulous attractions aren't actually in the city—check out our suggestions for **daytrips** (see p. 127), especially the nearby pyramids of **Teotihuacán** (see p. 124), the most visited ruins in all of Mexico.

Getting There and Away

All roads lead to Mexico City. Buses, trains, and planes haul passengers from every town in the Republic into the smoggy hyperactivity of the city's many temples of transport—the expanding Benito Juárez International Airport, four crowded bus stations, a desolate train station, and a network of freeways. Fortuitously, airports and stations in Mexico City usually have information booths for frazzled tourists equipped with quasi-English-speaking personnel, free (or cheap) maps, official zone-rated taxi service, and a connected or very nearby Metro station. Except for the typically terrible train service, getting around can even be fun. *Buena suerte* (good luck).

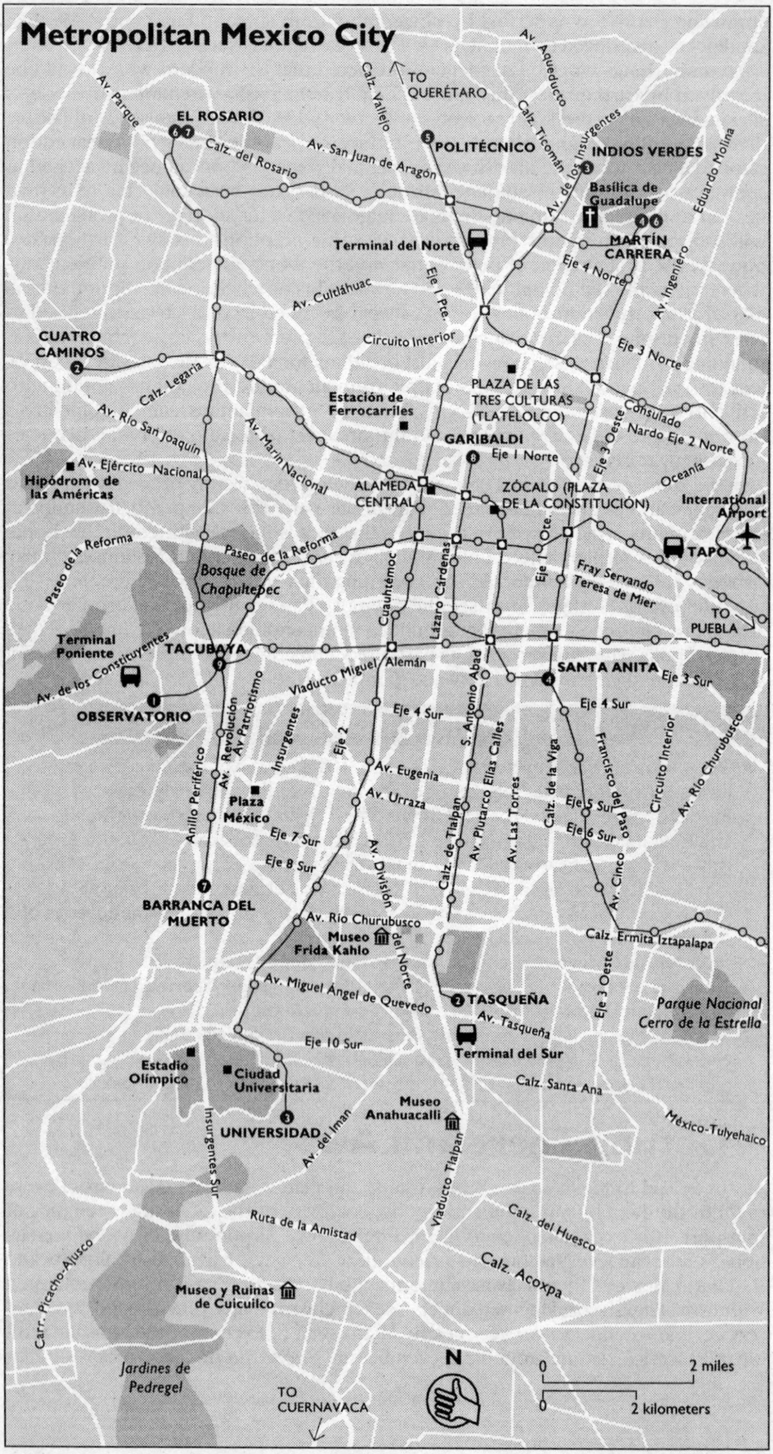
Metropolitan Mexico City
TO QUERÉTARO
EL ROSARIO
POLITÉCNICO
INDIOS VERDES
Basílica de Guadalupe
Terminal del Norte
MARTÍN CARRERA
CUATRO CAMINOS
PLAZA DE LAS TRES CULTURAS (TLATELOLCO)
Estación de Ferrocarriles
GARIBALDI
Hipódromo de las Américas
ALAMEDA CENTRAL
ZÓCALO (PLAZA DE LA CONSTITUCIÓN)
International Airport
TAPO
Bosque de Chapultepec
TO PUEBLA
Terminal Poniente
TACUBAYA
SANTA ANITA
OBSERVATORIO
Plaza México
BARRANCA DEL MUERTO
Museo Frida Kahlo
TASQUEÑA
Terminal del Sur
Parque Nacional Cerro de la Estrella
Estadio Olímpico
Ciudad Universitaria
UNIVERSIDAD
Museo Anahuacalli
Museo y Ruinas de Cuicuilco
Jardines de Pedregel
TO CUERNAVACA
N
0 2 miles
0 2 kilometers
Av. Parque
Calz. del Rosario
Av. San Juan de Aragón
Calz. Vallejo
Av. Aqueducto
Calz. Ticomán
Av. de los Insurgentes
Eduardo Molina
Eje 4 Norte
Eje 1 Pte.
Av. Cultláhuac
Av. Ingeniero
Circuito Interior
Eje 3 Norte
Calz. Legaria
Av. Río San Joaquín
Av. Marín Nacional
Eje 3 Oeste
Consulado
Nardo Eje 2 Norte
Eje 1 Norte
Av. Ejército Nacional
Oceanía
Paseo de la Reforma
Cuauhtémoc
Lázaro Cárdenas
Eje 1 Ote.
Fray Servando Teresa de Mier
Av. de los Constituyentes
Viaducto Miguel Alemán
S. Antonio Abad
Eje 3 Sur
Eje 4 Sur
Av. Revolución
Av. Patriotismo
Insurgentes
Eje 2
Av. Eugenia
Av. Plutarco Elías Calles
Calz. de la Viga
Francisco del Paso
Circuito Interior
Av. Río Churubusco
Anillo Periférico
Av. Urraza
Calz. de Tlalpan
Av. Las Torres
Eje 5 Sur
Eje 6 Sur
Eje 7 Sur
Eje 8 Sur
Av. División del Norte
Av. Cinco
Av. Río Churubusco
Calz. Ermita Iztapalapa
Av. Miguel Ángel de Quevedo
Av. Tasqueña
Eje 10 Sur
Calz. Santa Ana
México-Tulyehaico
Insurgentes Sur
Av. del Iman
Viaducto Tlalpan
Ruta de la Amistad
Calz. del Huesco
Calz. Acoxpa
Carr. Picacho-Ajusco

BY AIR

Flying into Mexico City from abroad entails the usual customs and immigration procedures. **Tourist cards (FMTs)** are distributed on the plane and stamped at the airport. Although many border officials are lax about enforcement, the "stoplight" customs system at the airport ensures that a certain percentage of random passengers is inspected—those unlucky enough to get a red light. Be prepared to allow an agent to sift through your silky intimates.

The **Benito Juárez International Airport** (tel. 571 32 95) lies 6.5km east of the *zócalo,* the formal center of the city. Blvd. Capitán Juan Sarabio heads northeast to the airport from Blvd. Puerto Aéreo, one of the major roads circling the city. The surprisingly small airport is expanding at an exponential rate and is jam-packed with facilities, including **24-hour restaurants** and **cafeterias.**

Getting To and From the Airport

Transportation into the city is uncomplicated. Buy a *transporte terrestre* ticket from the *venta de boletos* desk in *Sala A* and *Sala E,* and present it to any of the white and yellow authorized taxis waiting outside. The price is set by the zone of the city to which you're traveling (53 pesos to the *centro,* 66 pesos to El Monumento de la Revolución; 20% more after hours). Ask to see the map—just because it's an official-looking booth does not mean you won't be overcharged. Avoid people wearing uniforms trying to direct you to a taxi booth or to the taxi stand. They will try to charge large tips for small services. Avoid unauthorized taxis, especially those with bags over the meters. **Taxis** (tel. 784 48 11 or 571 36 00; both numbers available 24hr.) will also take you to the airport from the city. For more taxi etiquette and warnings, see p. 84.

The Metro is by far the cheapest (1.50 pesos) route to the city. The airport **subway** station, **Terminal Aérea** (Line 5), located at the junction of Capitán Juan Sarabio and Blvd. Puerto Aéreo, is only a 10-minute walk from *Sala E.* Signs will point you in the right direction (see p. 82 for the scoop on the Metro). Large bags are officially prohibited, but provided you avoid rush hours and can maneuver through the turnstile, a typical pack should not pose much of a problem. For the comfort of others, and mainly for your own safety, remove the pack from your back when you're on the subway. Also, try to ride in the less crowded cars at the end. If a train appears frighteningly jam-packed, simply let it pass; another will arrive within minutes, and you'll be at the front of the pack. **If you return to the airport by Metro, do not get off at the Aeropuerto stop. The correct stop is Terminal Aérea.**

Flight Information

Flight Info Hotline: (tel. 571 36 00 or 571 44 00). Specify domestic or international.

Carriers: Sala A: All **Aeroméxico,** baby. The most complete air transportation throughout the Republic. **Sala B: Mexicana** plays a strong second fiddle, also giving a tiny bit of space to **Aeromar** and **Aerocalifornia**, which really does go to California (Los Angeles) via a variety of Mexican cities (including Tijuana). One of the few airlines with significantly lower prices. **Sala C:** Really tiny, with only **Aerolineas Internacionales** (don't be fooled by the name: they only offer domestic service) and **AVIACSA**. **Sala D: ALLEGRO, TAESA,** and charter flights. **Sala E:** International arrivals. **Sala F_1: Aeroméxico** (international flights), **America West, Avianca, Continental, Delta, Lan Chile,** and **LAB. Sala F_2:** The big one! **Air France, Aviateca, British Airways, Canadian, Copa, Cubana, ETA, JAL, KLM, Lufthansa, Malaysia, Miami Air, Northwest,** and **Taca. Sala F_3: American Airlines, Argentinian Airlines, Iberia,** and **United Airlines.**

Domestic Flights: Flight schedules and prices change frequently. Prices are roughly the same from airline to airline. **Aerocalifornia** (tel. 207 13 92), at *Sala B,* tends to be the most competitive. Open daily 7am-10pm. Usually no student discounts, but always ask about *tarifas promocionales,* which can save you up to 50%. Aeroméxico and Mexicana airlines can take you anywhere in the country, provided there's an airport: **Aeroméxico,** Paseo de la Reforma 445 at Mississippi (tel. 327 40 00), and Reforma 80 (tel. 566 10 78). Both locations open M-Sa 9am-6:15pm. At the airport, *Sala A* (tel. 13 34 00). Open daily 4:30am-2am. **Mexicana,** Reforma 312 at

Amberes in the *Zona Rosa* (tel. 511 04 24), and Reforma 51 at Lafragua (tel. 592 17 71). Both open M-F 9am-6pm. At the airport, *Sala B* (tel. 448 09 04). Open 24hr.

International Flights: Aeroméxico and **Mexicana** fly to Central America and the U.S. **Air Canada,** Hamburgo 108, 5th fl. (tel. 280 34 34 or 281 45 81). **Air France,** Reforma 404, 15th fl. (tel. 627 60 00 or 627 60 60). At the airport (tel. 627 60 60) on the 3rd floor above *Sala F.* Open M 10am-2pm, Tu-Sa 10am-10pm, Su 1:30-10pm. **American,** Reforma 314, 1st fl. (tel. 209 14 00). Also at the airport in *Sala F.* Open daily 6am-10pm. **British Airways,** Reforma 10, 14th fl. (tel. 628 05 00, toll-free 91 800 00 657). **Canadian Airlines,** Reforma 390 (tel. 208 18 83). **Continental,** Andrés Bello 45 (tel. 280 34 34). At the airport (tel. 283 55 00) between *Salas D* and *E.* Open daily 8am-7pm. **Delta,** Reforma 381 (tel. 202 16 08 or 207 34 11, toll-free 91 800 90 221). At the airport (tel. 202 18 06 or 395 23 00) in *Sala F.* Open daily 6am-6pm. **Northwest/KLM,** Paseo de las Palmas 735, 7th fl. (tel. 202 44 44, toll-free 91 800 90 747). At the airport (tel. 571 32 46 or 24hr. 202 44 44) in *Sala F.* Open daily 9am-5pm. **Lufthansa,** Las Palmas 239 (tel. 230 00 00), at Col. Lomas de Chapultepec. Open M-F 9am-6pm. **Swissair,** Hamburgo 66, 3rd fl. (tel. 207 24 55), between Niza and Havre in the *Zona Rosa.* Open M-F 9am-6pm. **United,** Hamburgo 213, ground fl. (tel. 627 02 22, toll-free 91 800 00 307). At the airport (tel. 627 02 22 for flight information) in *Sala F.* Open daily 6am-9pm.

MEXICO CITY

Airport Services

Tourist Office: INFOTUR, *Sala A* (tel. 76 27 73). The wonderful staff in this small office has maps and guides of the city, can give you basic info, and can direct you to other resources. There's also a small touch-screen computer replete with info. Open daily 9am-9pm. Other "information" kiosks in *Salas A* and *F* have flight info.

Currency Exchange: Banks exchange currency and traveler's checks in almost all of the *salas.* **ATMs** take both **Cirrus** and **Plus** (including **Visa, MasterCard, AmEx**) in *Sala A,* directly under *Sala B,* and throughout *Salas E* and *F.* **Casas de cambio,** every foot or so, are open 6am-8pm, sometimes later. Not the best rates in the city.

Hotel Reservations: In *Sala E.* Name an area and they'll make the reservation for you. No charge, but be prepared to pay for the first night on the spot. English spoken. Open daily 7am-midnight.

Car Rental: In *Sala E* (see p. 85).

Storage Lockers: Next to the snack bar, to the left of the arrival gate in *Sala A* and in *Sala E.* Storage 25 pesos per 24hr., 35-65 pesos for larger bags.

Lost and Found: Bags overflow in a small room next to Aeropost in *Sala D.* International carriers have lost luggage offices on the third floor, above *Sala F.*

Bookstore: In *Sala C.* Novels, art books, and history books in Spanish and English. Maps available. Open M-Sa 7am-9pm, Su 8am-8pm.

Cultural Information: Instituto Nacional de Antropología e Historia, *Sala A* (tel. 571 02 67). Essentially a bookstore but with free (and not free) information about archaeological sites and museums throughout the country. Open daily 9am-9pm.

Airport Emergency and Communications

Telephones: LADATELs around the airport accept phone cards sold at nearby magazine stands. Some phones take international credit cards. Phone center with **fax** as well as local and international calls between *Salas* D and E. Open 24hr.

Police: (tel. 625 70 07), outside the airport in front of *Sala C.* Open 24hr.

Pharmacy: In *Sala C,* open daily 6am-midnight; in *Sala F,* open daily 6am-11pm.

Post Office: In *Sala A.* Open M-F 8am-7pm, Sa 9am-5pm.

BY TRAIN

Mexican trains tend to be **excruciatingly slow** (for more on that, see p. 37). The fastest route—to Veracruz (11hr., 8:45am and 8:15pm daily plus 8:20am M,W, and F, 65 pesos)—is barely bearable. Buy tickets for morning trains when the ticket booth (tel. 547 10 84 or 547 10 97) opens at 7am. Buy tickets for evening trains by 9am. No advance ticket sales or phone purchases. (Booths open daily 7am-last train.)

Estación Buenavista of the **Ferrocarriles Nacionales de México** (tel. 547 10 97) is located north of the **Monumento de la Revolución** at the corner of Insurgentes and

Mosqueta (Eje 1 Alzate), five long blocks from the nearest Metro station, Revolución (Line 2; open M-F 6am-12:30am, Sa 6am-1:30am). **Taxis** leave from the parking lot on the Mosqueta side of the main building.

BY BUS

Mexico City's four main bus stations correspond to the cardinal directions. **Central de Autobuses del Norte** (North Station) serves the Bajío, northern Veracruz, Jalisco, and most of northern Mexico; **Terminal Central de Autobuses del Sur** (South Station) launches buses to Guerrero, Morelos, and Oaxaca; **Terminal de Autobuses de Pasajeros de Oriente (TAPO;** East Station) sends buses to Puebla, southern Veracruz, Oaxaca, Chiapas, and the Yucatán Peninsula; and the **Terminal de Autobuses del Poniente** (West Station) serves Mexico state and Michoacán. First-class, Plus (an intermediate between first- and second-class), and second-class service are available.

All stations are served by the Metro and offer an official 24-hour taxi service that charges fixed rates (set by zones) for a ride to any point in the city or adjacent parts of Mexico state. Buy your ticket inside to avoid being ripped off, but be wary of being charged for an extra zone—if you can find it, consult the zone map. *Peseros* (a.k.a. *colectivos*) also serve the four stations. Quality budget hotels near the bus stations are virtually nil (see p. 92). It's a much safer bet to head toward the city center. The following bus prices change almost weekly, and listings are by no means comprehensive. Given the extensive network, it is possible to go almost anywhere at any time.

Central de Autobuses del Norte

The Central de Autobuses del Norte (tel. 587 15 52) is on Cien Metros. Metro: Autobuses del Norte (Line 5). **Banamex ATM, restaurant,** a **luggage storage** (10-20 pesos per 24hr.), **phone** and **fax** offices, and a **pharmacy** are all open around the clock. A **casa de cambio** near the main entrance offers poor rates (open daily 11am-6pm daily). There's also a **post office** (open M-F 8am-8pm and Sa 9am-1pm) and a **telegram office** (open M-F 9am-8pm, Sa 9am-4:30pm). A hotel **reservations** service booth is occasionally open near the main entrance (supposedly open 8am-9pm). From the **taxi stand,** rides to the *zócalo* or Revolución should be 27 pesos. A plethora of bus companies populate the *Central;* prices are often suspiciously similar, and it's not uncommon for "competing" bus companies to share phone numbers. You've got an infinite but unvaried selection in this terminal/zoo. A few of the perennial faves:

Autobuses de Oriente (ADO; tel. 133 24 24). First-class to Oaxaca (6hr., 4 per day 7am-11:30pm, 160 pesos), Papantla (5hr., 5 per day 9am-12:30am, 85 pesos), Puebla (2hr., every 30min. 4am-9:30pm, 45 pesos), Tuxpan (6hr., 15 per day, 95 pesos), Veracruz (7hr., 5 per day 8am-12:15am, 137 pesos), and Xalapa (5hr., 2:15pm and 12:30am, 95 pesos). **ADO GL,** run by the same company, offers *ejecutivo* service to Oaxaca (6hr., 11:30pm, 160 pesos), Tampico (9hr., 10 and 11pm, 193 pesos), Veracruz (6hr., midnight, 187 pesos), and Villahermosa (10hr., 10pm, 321 pesos). **UNO,** also run by ADO, goes super-deluxe to Tampico (9hr., 9 and 9:45pm, 276 pesos).

Elite (tel. 729 07 81). The name says it all. Posh service to places like Hermosillo (30hr., every hr. 5:30am-1:15pm, 818 pesos), Puerto Vallarta (14hr., 4 per day 5-11:45pm, 385 pesos), and Tijuana (42hr., every hr. 7:15am-10:30pm, 877 pesos),

Estrella Blanca (tel. 729 07 07). To Chihuahua (20hr., 10:30pm, 465 pesos), Durango (12hr., 1:15 and 5:30am, 288 pesos), Torreón (13hr., 8:30, 10, and 11:40pm, 326 pesos), and Zacatecas (7hr., 1:15am and 8:30pm, 199 pesos).

Flecha Amarilla (tel. 576 78 87). First-class service to Guadalajara (9hr., every hr. 5:45am-1:20am, 195 pesos), Guanajuato (6½hr., 4 per day 1:45am-7:40pm, 121 pesos), León (6½hr., 8 per day 1am-3pm, 130 pesos), Manzanillo (16hr., 12:40, 4:25, and 10:40pm, 269 pesos), Morelia (5hr., every 20min. 6am-12:30am, 100 pesos), Querétaro (3½hr., every 15min. 4:45am-1:15am, 70 pesos), San Luis Potosí (7hr., every hr. 7:05am-11pm, 139 pesos), and San Miguel de Allende (4½hr., every 40min. 5:20am-12:45am, 86 pesos).

Futura (tel. 729 07 07). To Acapulco (5hr., every 2hr. 6am-1am, 177 pesos), Aguascalientes (6hr., every hr. 7:30am-12:30am, 200 pesos), Chihuahua (18hr., 5 per day 8:50am-11:30pm, 539 pesos), Ciudad Valles (9½hr., every hr., 126 pesos), Matamoros (14hr., 5 per day 2:15-10:30pm, 383 pesos), Monterrey (12hr., every hr. 7am-11:55pm, 343 pesos), and Tampico (9½hr., every hr., 163 pesos).

Transportes del Norte (tel. 729 07 07). To Matamoros (14hrs., 2:15 and 7:15pm, 383 pesos), Matehuala (8hr., 4 per day 1am-9:15pm, 223 pesos), Monterrey (12hr., 4 per day, 343 pesos), Nuevo Laredo (15hr., 5, 6, and 9pm, 439 pesos), Reynosa (14hr., 4 and 7pm, 385 pesos), and Saltillo (10hr., 7 per day 12:45pm-1am, 310 pesos).

Terminal de Autobuses de Pasajeros de Oriente (TAPO)

The TAPO, General Ignacio Zaragoza 200 (tel. 762 59 77), is behind Metro station San Lázaro (Line 1). To get to the bus station from the Metro, follow the red railings. Ticket counters await in a rotunda at the end of a long, store-lined passageway. Helpful **police** booths are scattered throughout the station. Taxi ticket booths are near the entrance to the Metro. Don't try following the signs to the tourist information booth; it no longer exists. The station also contains a **24-hour ATM, currency exchange** services (open daily 7am-11pm), a **travel agency** (tel. 542 90 92; open M-F 9:30am-2pm and 3-7pm, Sa 10am-1pm.), **food stands,** and a **pharmacy. Luggage storage** is available (tel. 542 23 23; 25 pesos per 24hr.; open daily 24hr.).

ADO (tel. 542 71 92). First-class to Campeche (18hr., 4 per day 10am-10pm, 392 pesos), Cancún (24hr., 8:30am, 1, and 4:45pm, 499 pesos), Córdoba (4½hr., 21 per day 6:45am-12:30am, 105 pesos), Mérida (20hr., 4 per day 10am-8pm, 443 pesos), Oaxaca (6hr., 17 per day 7am-12:30am, 180 pesos), Palenque (12hr., 4 and 6:10pm, 311 pesos), Veracruz (5hr., 15 per day 7am-12:30am, 160 pesos), Villahermosa (10½hr., 19 per day 7am-11pm, 272 pesos), and Xalapa (4½hr., 22 per day 7:30am-12:45am, 95 pesos). **ADO GL** offers *ejecutivo* service to all of the above locations, less frequently and at slightly higher prices.

Autobuses Cristóbal Colón (tel. 133 24 33). First-class to Oaxaca (6hr., 9 per day 6:45am-11:50pm, 172-201 pesos), San Cristóbal de las Casas (18hr., 2:30, 5:30, and 7:30pm, 375 pesos), Tonalá (13hr., 5, 7:45, and 10pm, 313 pesos), and Tuxtla Gutiérrez (15hr., 4 per day 2-9:30pm, 326 pesos).

Autobuses Unidos (AU; tel. 133 24 44). To Córdoba (5hr., every hr. 6:30am-12:40am, 94 pesos), Oaxaca (6-9hr., 13 per day 7am-midnight, 127-143 pesos), San Andrés Tuxtla (8hr., noon and 9pm, 160 pesos), and Xalapa (5hr., 19 per day 7am-1am, 85 pesos).

Estrella Roja (tel. 542 92 00). To Puebla (2hr., every 12min. 5am-11pm, 38 pesos).

UNO (tel. 522 11 11). To Oaxaca, Tampico, Veracruz, Villahermosa, Xalapa, and other cities. Only if you must travel in the lap of luxury.

Terminal de Autobuses del Poniente

The Terminal de Autobuses del Poniente is on Av. Sur 122 (tel. 535 24 52). Metro: Observatorio (Line 1). Follow signs to **Buses Forraneos** and then to **Central Camionero Poniente** as you exit the Metro—a vendor-lined bridge leads to the terminal. Many of these are second-class routes; brace yourself for slow, indirect service. The station is built in the shape of a "V" with the most important services clustered at the vertex. Round-the-clock services include a **restaurant,** long-distance **caseta,** and **luggage storage** (small bags 2.5o pesos for up to 4hr., 5 pesos for 4-8hr., and 7.5o pesos for 8-24hr.; 10 pesos for subjectively determined "larger" bags). There is also a **pharmacy** (open daily 7am-10pm), a **post office** (open M-F 8am-7pm, Sa 9am-1pm), a **phone & fax** office (office open daily 6am-10pm), **food stands, shops, newspaper stands,** and a **Western Union.**

Autobuses del Occidente (tel. 271 00 49). Second-class to Guadalajara (12hr., 8 per day 10am-10pm, 195 pesos), Manzanillo (16hr., 7:20pm, 269 pesos), Morelia (6hr., every 20min., 94 pesos), and Tuxpan (4hr., every 20min., 65 pesos).

Caminante. First-class service to Toluca (1hr., every 5min. 6am-10:30pm, 21 pesos).

Elite (tel. 729 07 07 or 729 07 93). Travels in style to Guadalajara (8hr., 2pm, 220 pesos) and Morelia (4hr., 3:30 and 6:30pm, 105 pesos).

ETN (tel. 273 71 55). Plush luxury service to Guadalajara (7hr., 5 per day, 310 pesos), Morelia (4hr., every hr., 165 pesos), Toluca (1hr., every 30min., 30 pesos), Uruapan (5½hr., 6 per day, 230 pesos), and many other cities.

Pegasso Plus (tel. 277 77 61) gallops in a first-class way to Morelia (4hr., 15 per day 6am-1am, 120 pesos) and Pátzcuaro (5hr., 10 per day 6:30am-midnight, 135 pesos).

Servicios Coordinados has first- and second-class service to León (8hr., 7 and 10:45pm, 130 pesos), Morelia (5½hr., 8 per day 9:30am-10:30pm, 94 pesos), and Querétaro (6hr., 10:45pm, 66 pesos), among other destinations.

Terminal de Autobuses del Sur (Tasqueña)

The Tasqueña terminal, Tasqueña 1320 (tel. 689 97 45), is served by Metro: Tasqueña (Line 2)—exit to the right, through the market. The station has a **post office** (open M-F 8am-7pm, Sa 9am-1pm), long-distance **caseta** with **fax** service (open 24hr.), and **LADATELs** scattered about. There is also a mini-travel agency for **hotel reservations** in select cities (open S-F 9am-9pm, Sa 9am-3pm), a 24-hour **pharmacy** (tel. 689 08 83) and a round-the-clock **cafeteria. Luggage lockers** (small 10 pesos, large 20 pesos for 24hr.) are near exit 3. From the **taxi stand,** a trip to the *zócalo* should be 35 pesos and one to the area near Revolución 40 pesos.

ADO, Cristóbal Colón, and **Estrella Roja** to Cuáutla (1½hr., every 15min. 6:10am-10:20pm., 33 pesos), Oaxaca (6hr., 7:30am, 4pm, and midnight, 160 pesos), Oaxtepec (1½hr., every 15min. 6:10am-10pm, 32 pesos), Yacutepec (1½hr., every hr. 6:10am-10:20pm, 32 pesos), and some places in the Gulf Coast and Yucatán.

Estrella de Oro (tel. 549 85 20). Plus-class to Acapulco (5hr., every hr. 6:30am-12:30am, 170 pesos), and first-class to Chilpancingo (3hr., 10 per hr. 5:40am-12:50am, 95 pesos), Cuernavaca (1½hr., 5 per day, 28 pesos), Iguala (3hr., 7 per day 7:20am-12:10am, 50 pesos), Ixtapa/Zihuatanejo (9hr., 8:40, 9:30, and 10pm, 200-250 pesos), and Taxco (2hr., 4 per day 7:40am-7:50pm, 50 pesos).

Futura and **Turistar** (tel. 628 57 71). First-class and *ejecutivo* to Acapulco (first-class 5hr., 19 per day 5am-2am, 177-250 pesos) and Ixtapa/Zihuatanejo (first-class 9hr., 10:15am, 7:40pm, 9pm, and 11pm, 260-325 pesos).

Pullman de Morelos (tel. 549 35 05). First-class to Cuautla (1½hr., every 20min. 6am-11pm, 33 pesos), Cuernavaca (1¼hr., every 15min. 5:30am-midnight, 29 pesos), Oaxtepec (1½hr., every 25min. 6am-11pm, 33 pesos), and Tepotzlán (1¼hr., every 15min. 6:30am-8:30pm, 32 pesos).

BY CAR

No other vehicular endeavor matches the experience of driving into Mexico City. Serene mountain roads slowly metamorphose into blaring, bumper-to-bumper, multilane highways. Don't expect anyone to drive defensively—welcome to a city where stoplights are only suggestions (see **Getting Around,** p. 82). Remember that because of a desperate attempt to control congestion and contamination, one day of each week your car is not allowed to be driven in the city during the day. This is determined by the last number on your license plate; no one is exempt (see p. 85). Several major highways lead into the city and intersect with the **Circuito Interior,** the highway that rings the city, at which point they change names. **Rte. 57,** from Querétaro and Tepotzlán, becomes **Manuel Avila Camacho** just outside the Circuito. **Rte. 15,** from Toluca, turns into **Av. Reforma** as it enters the city. **Rte. 95,** from Cuernavaca and Acapulco, becomes **Av. Insurgentes,** which plugs into the Circuito on the south side. **Rte. 150,** from Puebla and Texcoco, becomes **Ignacio Zaragoza,** which connects to the Circuito on the east side. **Rte. 85,** from Pachuca, Teotihuacán, and Texcoco, also becomes **Av. Insurgentes** in the city.

Orientation

The city is difficult to know well; even most *chilangos* don't have it all down pat. It's not uncommon for *taxistas* to ask passengers how to get to their destinations. What's more, many different neighborhoods use the same street name; the 300 Benito Juárez streets in the city attest to this redundant and repetitive tradition. Still, it is only a matter of cardinal directions and good ol' trial and error before you've mastered this megalopolis. The most important thing is to know the name of the **colonia** (neighborhood) to which you're going (common examples are the *centro*, Col. Polanco, *Zona Rosa*, Col. Roma, Col. Juárez). Since street numbers are often useless, cross streets and landmarks are *muy importantes*. Try to locate nearby monuments, museums, *glorietas* (traffic circles), cathedrals, and skyscrapers. It shouldn't be hard—there are loads of them.

More good news: street names tend to be clustered systematically. Streets in the *Zona Rosa* are named after European cities, those directly across Reforma are named after large rivers of the world, and the ones in Polanco are named after famous philosophers. The **Guía Roji Ciudad de México** (75 pesos), a comprehensive street atlas, is a valuable aid for anyone planning to stay in the city for some time. It's available at the airport, most large and English-language bookstores, Sanborn's, museum shops, and at many newspaper stands. Or try the abridged **mini-Guía Roji** (25 pesos).

Mexico City extends outward from the *centro* roughly 20km to the south, 10km to the north, 10km to the west, and 8km to the east. Year after year, the city's boundaries extend hungrily into neighboring communities. There is much debate about where the city actually begins and where it ends. Because of the central location of most sights, few travelers venture past the Bosque de Chapultepec to the west, La Basílica de Guadalupe to the north, the airport to the east, or San Angel and the UNAM to the south. While the best way to navigate the city is by foot, its vast size does not always make it amenable to strolling. A rectangular series of highways **(Circuito Interior)** and a thorough thoroughfare system **(Ejes Viales)** help to make inter-neighborhood travel manageable.

CIRCUITO INTERIOR AND EJES VIALES

The **Circuito Interior** is a roughly rectangular artery made up of several smaller, connected highways. **Blvd. Puerto Aéreo** forms the upper east side of the box, running north from the airport. As it bends left at the northeast corner of the box and heads west, it becomes **Av. Río Consulado.** Río Consulado turns south and becomes **Calzada Melchor Ocampo.** Ocampo heads south until it intersects **Paseo de la Reforma** at Bosque de Chapultepec, after which it continues as **Av. Vasconcelos.** From Vasconcelos, two roads run to the southwest corner of the Circuito, **Av. Patriotismo** and **Av. Revolución,** either of which could be considered the Circuito at this point. They turn into **Av. Río Mixcoac,** which becomes **Av. Río Churubusco,** running east-west. Río Churubusco is the longest and sneakiest of the highways that constitute the Circuito. It continues east, turns north for a while, heads east again, then turns north once more to connect with Blvd. Puerto Aéreo south of the airport to complete the Circuito.

Aside from the large thoroughfares—Insurgentes, Reforma, Chapultepec, and Miguel Alemán—a system of **Ejes Viales** (axis roads) conducts the majority of traffic within the Circuito. *Ejes* run one way. Running east-west, Eje 1 Nte. and Eje 2 Nte. are north of the *zócalo,* while Ejes 2 through 8 Sur run south of it. The numbers increase heading away from the *zócalo.* **Eje Central Lázaro Cárdenas** runs north-south and bisects the box formed by the Circuito. East of it and parallel lie Ejes 1 through 3 Ote., which veer off to the northwest; west of it are Ejes 1 through 3 Pte. Theoretically, using the Ejes together with the Circuito, you can reach any general area of the city without much delay. Unfortunately, because of heavy traffic and frequent processions (and hence barricades), zipping around gleefully is not the norm. The up side is that most travelers' needs are located within the **city center.**

CITY CENTER

As huge as Mexico City is, almost everything of interest to visitors lies within the northern half of the area circumscribed by the Circuito Interior. Moreover, many attractions are within easy reach of **Paseo de la Reforma,** the broad thoroughfare that runs southwest-northeast, or **Av. Insurgentes,** the boulevard running north-south through the city. These two main arteries intersect at the **Glorieta Cuauhtémoc.** The **Bosque de Chapultepec,** home to the principal museums of the city, is served by Metro stops Chapultepec (Line 1) and Auditorio (Line 7). From Chapultepec, Reforma proceeds northeast, punctuated by **glorietas** (traffic circles), each with a monument in the center. Some of the more famous ones, in southwest-to-northeast order, include: **Glorieta Angel de la Independencia, Glorieta Cuauhtémoc,** and the **Glorieta Cristóbal Colón.** Slightly north of the city center lie the **Plaza de Tres Culturas (Tlatelolco)** and the **Basílica de Guadalupe.**

The accommodations and food listings for Mexico City are divided according to the four areas of most interest to tourists. In terms of *barrios,* moving up Reforma from Chapultepec, the **Zona Rosa** is followed by **Buenavista (near the Monumento a la Revolucíon), the Alameda,** and, to the east of the Alameda, the **centro.**

MEXICO CITY

Centro

The *centro* contains most of the historic sights and museums, extensive budget accommodations, and lively inexpensive restaurants. Metro stops Allende (closer to the accommodations and Alameda) and Zócalo (literally the center of México) serve the *centro* (Line 2). This area is bounded by Cárdenas to the west, El Salvador to the south, Pino Suárez to the east, and Rep. de Perú to the north.

Alameda

The Alameda, the central city park, contains budget accommodations and many restaurants. It is accessible by Metro at Hidalgo (Lines 2 and 3), Bellas Artes (Lines 2 and 8; closer to the park, the Palacio de Bellas Artes, and the post office), and San Juan de Letran (Line 8; closer to most food and accommodations listings). The area is bounded by Eje 1 Pte. (known as Rosales, Guerrero, and Bucareli) to the west, Arcos de Belén to the south, Cárdenas to the east, and Pensador Mexicano to the north.

Near the Monumento a la Revolución/Buenavista

The Monumento a la Revolución/Buenavista area contains perhaps the most copious and inexpensive hotels and eateries. It is bounded by Insurgentes Norte to the west, Reforma to the south and east, and Mosqueta to the north.

Zona Rosa

The *Zona Rosa* (Pink Zone) is the capital's most touristy, commercial district, home to some of the country's most exciting nightlife. This neighborhood is accessible by Metro stops Insurgentes (primary location) and Sevilla (both on Line 1). The *Zona Rosa* is bounded by Reforma to the north and west, Av. Chapultepec to the south, and Insurgentes to the east. A few of the area's listings lie just east of Insurgentes, and a string of bars and clubs spill south past Chapultepec along Insurgentes Sur.

SOUTHERN DISTRICTS

The major southern thoroughfare is **Insurgentes Sur.** Most sights to the south, including the suburbs of **San Angel** and **Coyoacán,** as well as **Ciudad Universitaria** and the **Pyramid of Cuicuilco,** lie near or along Insurgentes. Metro Line 3 parallels Insurgentes on Cuauhtémoc and then Universidad, ending at Ciudad Universitaria (Metro: Universidad, Line 3). Two other important avenues are **Av. Revolución,** which runs parallel to Insurgentes, and **Av. Miguel Angel de Quevedo,** which runs parallel to **Francisco Sosa** in Coyoacán. Metro Line 2 runs east of Line 3 and is closer to **Xochimilco,** one of the few southern sights not along Insurgentes.

Getting Around

While most neighborhoods are easily traversed by foot, public transportation is necessary to travel between different areas. The Metro is the fastest, cleanest, and quickest mode of transportation. Unfortunately it becomes inhumanly crowded during rush hour (7:30-9:30am and 6-9pm) and doesn't reach all parts of the city. More extensive are the thousands of white and green mini-buses known as *peseros, micros,* or *colectivos* (1-3 pesos depending on the distance), with stickers (hopefully) marking the route on front. Within the heart of the city, *peseros* are particularly fast and easy to catch along Insurgentes. Taxis, while more expensive, are especially handy for traversing the city late at night and for women traveling alone. However, if you love life, do not ever hail cabs on the street. **Sitio cabs** can be found at official stands or reached by phone. **Use them and them only.** The ancient *tren ligero* (trolley) still travels some routes, mainly at the city's edge and in some suburbs.

BY METRO

The Metro never ceases to amaze visitors—trains come quickly and regularly, the fare is insanely cheap, the crowds are enormous and bizarre, the ride is smooth, the service is extensive, and the stations are immaculate and monumental. Built in the late 1960s, the Metro transports five million people and makes the equivalent of two and a half trips around the earth every day. On top of this, new tracks are laid daily. México's Metro system knows no bounds.

Metro tickets are sold in *taquillas* (booths) at every station. Lines can stretch for huge distances, so buy in bulk. Sets of 25 tickets, called **planillas,** also get you a discount (31 pesos for the *planilla*). Come prepared with exact change, since the *taquillas* are often short of small denominations. **The 1.50 peso fare includes transfers.** It's simple—you insert a magnetically coded ticket and pass through turnstiles. Transfer gates are marked **correspondencia** and exits are marked **salida.** Most transfer stations have information booths to help clueless travelers. If they are not staffed, you can ask the guards standing by the turnstiles to help orient you. A vital resource for all travelers is a color-coded subway guide, available at the tourist office or at Metro Information booths. If you are lost, wander off to a corner and discreetly check your guide. Directions are stated in terms of the station at either end of a given line. Each of the two *andenes* (platforms) has signs indicating the terminus toward which trains are heading. For example, if you are on Line 3 between Indios Verdes and Universidad, you can go either "Dirección Indios Verdes" or "Dirección Universidad." If you realize you are headed in the wrong direction, fear not; simply get off and walk under (or sometimes over) to the other side.

The first train on all lines runs Monday through Friday at 5am, Saturday at 6am, and Sunday at 7am. The last train runs at midnight from Sunday through Friday, and on Saturday as late as 1am. Try to avoid the Metro from 7:30am to 9:30am and 6 to 9pm on weekdays. Lunch break (2-4pm) during weekdays is also crowded. During these times, huge crowds attract pickpockets. Cars at either end of the train tend to be slightly less crowded, and therefore safer and more comfortable.

Safety is a big concern in the Metro. As in many parts of Mexico, being single and having two X chromosomes just isn't a convenient combination. Lewd remarks and stares are a given, and the horrible experience of being groped is a very distinct possibility when the train is crowded or if it stops mid-tunnel between stations. Do not be afraid to call attention to the offender. A loud "*¿No tiene vergüenza?*" (Don't you have any shame?) tends to be effective. During rush hours, many lines have cars reserved for women and children. If you qualify, use them. They are usually located at the front of the train and designated by a partition labeled *Mujeres y Niños.* Often you will see women and children gathering on a separate part of the platform for the reserved car.

Theft is a chronic problem on the Metro. Carry bags in front of you or on your lap; simply closing the bag does little good because thieves use razors to slit the bag open

Metropolitan

Some Metro stops are sights in their own right. Pino Suárez (Lines 1 and 2) houses a small Aztec building located at mid-transfer. The **Tunel de la Ciencia** (science tunnel) in the marathon transfer at **La Raza** (Lines 3 and 5) is an educational experience: marvel at the nifty fractals, or wear your whites and glow in the dark under a map of the constellations. The stop even has a small **science museum** (open M-Sa10am-6pm). The **Zócalo** stop (Line 2) has scale models of the plaza as it has appeared throughout its history, the *andenes* at **Copilco** (Line 3) are lined with **murals,** and the **Bellas Artes** stop (Lines 2 and 8) houses **Aztec statuettes.** In fact, nearly every Metro transfer stop has some kind of exhibit, from elementary school drawings of the subway system to a re-creation of a London theater.

from the bottom. Subway thieves often work in pairs—one will distract you while the other pulls your wallet. Rear pockets are easy to pick, front pockets are safer; empty pockets are best. If you ride with a backpack on your back, the small pocket is likely to be violated. The safest place in a crowded car is with your back against the wall and your backpack (if you have one) in front of you. Because of overcrowding, large bags or suitcases are not allowed on the Metro. Some travelers have slipped bags past the gate, but on a crowded train, luggage will make fellow passengers uncomfortable and attract thieves. If you are intent on making it on the Metro with that overstuffed pack, come very early or after 10:30pm, when the Metro is fairly empty and guards are more likely to look the other way.

For Metro and bus information, ask at any information booth or contact **COVITUR (Comisión de Vialidad y Transporte Urbano del D.F.;** Public Relations), Felicia 67 (tel. 709 80 36 or 709 11 33), outside the Salto de Agua Metro station (Lines 1 and 8). Nearly all stations have guards and security offices, and all are required to have a *jefe de la estación* (chief of station) in a marked office. These people are valuable resources, ready to deal with questions, complaints, panic attacks, and just about anything else. Further, each train has a red emergency handle, to be pulled in the event of severe harrassment or any emergency. If you lose something on the Metro, call the **Oficina de Objetos Extraviados** (tel. 542 53 97 or 627 46 43), located in the Candelaria station (Lines 1 and 4), but don't hold your breath (open M-F 9am-8pm).

BY PESERO

Peseros, a.k.a. **colectivos, combis,** or **micros,** are white and green minibuses. The name *pesero* comes from the time when they used to cost one old peso, equivalent to US$0.01 today. Although not quite the steal they used to be, these easily affordable *peseros* cruise the streets on set routes. No printed information is available, though destinations are either painted or posted on the front window. In 1997, a great effort was made to establish set *pesero* stops. Look for the traditional bus stand or a little blue sign with a picture of the front of a *pesero*. Most *peseros* now only let you on and off at these stops, but some will still slow down at any corner, and any red light is an excuse for a "stop." Even when you're at a designated stop, you still need to hail the passing *peseros.* To do so, wave your hand or hold out as many fingers as there are people in your group. To get off, ring the bell (if there is one) or simply shout loudly *¡Bajan!* (coming down). To prevent a missed stop, pay when you get on and tell the driver your destination. Drivers will honk horns (often rigged to play such perennial faves as "It's a Small World" and the love theme from *The Godfather*) to signal availability during rush hour.

Expect to fork over 1.50-2.50 pesos for cross-city rides, 5 pesos for long-distance trips over 17km (10% more 10pm-6am). Tell the driver your destination as you get on, and he'll tell you the price. Some *peseros* only run until midnight, but the major routes—on Reforma, between Chapultepec and San Angel, and along Insurgentes—run 24 hours. Other well-traveled *pesero* routes travel from Metro: Hidalgo (Lines 2 and 3) to Ciudad Universitaria (via Reforma, Bucareli, and Av. Cuauhtémoc); La Villa to Chapultepec (via Reforma); Reforma to Auditorio (via Reforma and Juárez); the *zócalo* to Chapultepec (via 5 de Mayo and Reforma); San Angel to Izazaga (via 5 de Mayo and Reforma); Bolívar to Ciudad Universitaria/Coyoacán (via Bolívar in the *centro*); and San Angel to Metro: Insurgentes (Line 1; via Av. de la Paz and Insurgentes Sur). Many depart from the Chapultepec Metro station (Line 1) to San Angel, La Merced, and the airport. In heavy rush-hour traffic (7-10am and 6-9pm), even a circuitous Metro ride will often be faster than a *pesero,* but for short, direct trips *peseros* are useful. Check the routes posted on the windshield, but don't be shy about asking the driver personally: *"¿Se va a (La Merced)?"*.

BY BUS

The red, gray, and white school buses that make up the *autobuses metropolitanos* are among the least desirable ways to travel. There is no published information about routes and schedules for the extensive bus system. Always check with the driver before you board; getting on a crowded bus going in the opposite direction is the quickest way to get lost and to ruin a perfectly good day. Moreover, buses are usually slower than the Metro, particularly during rush hours. Buses cost 0.50 to 2 pesos—have change ready when you board. They run daily from 5am to midnight but are scarce after 10pm. Keep in mind that each one-way Eje has a single bus lane running in the **opposite** direction to traffic. Flag down a bus anywhere by holding out your arm and pointing at the street in front of you. Like the Metro, buses are crowded and seats are hot items. The popular routes along Paseo de la Reforma are notorious for robbery. Leave your valuables at the hotel, don't keep money in your pockets, put your bag in front of you, and keep your fingers crossed.

BY TAXI

The U.S. State Department issued a warning about taxis in May 1998 (see p. 36). Heed it. Robberies and rapes in street-hailed taxis are on a rapid rise.

Cabs constantly cruise the major avenues. If you want to be safe, don't hail them, especially not at night. If you have absolutely no other option, make sure that the meter is working and immediately threaten a driver with non-payment if the meter jumps and prices skyrocket. Some taxis have meters that display reference numbers for the driver's price conversion table instead of direct prices. Ask to see the chart before you pay to ensure that the price you're given matches the meter number. Carry small denominations, as drivers will often cite a lack of change as a reason to pocket some extra pesos. Base fares typically begin at 5 pesos, and at night, drivers will add 20% to the meter rate. If a meter is out of order, insist on setting the price before the driver goes anywhere.

The best taxi options, by far, are the official **sitio cabs.** There are several *sitios* (taxi bases) in every neighborhood. *Sitios* will respond to your phone call by sending a car to pick you up. If you're near the *sitio,* walk up to the first cab in line. All restaurants and hotels, as well as most locals, will know the number. Since *sitio* taxis don't use meters, ask the operator what the trip will cost. Prices are set by the zone. Operators will always give you the right price, and drivers very rarely overcharge. Official *sitio* cabs do cost up to twice as much, but it's well worth it. The great advantage of *sitio* taxis, in addition to home pick-up, is that they are much safer than anonymous cabs. Hotel cabs and *turismo* taxis are equally safe but charge more than the *sitio* taxis.

Try to consult a zone map before buying your tickets, and always count your change. If you can't locate a *sitio* number or a hotel cab, try **Servi-taxi** (tel. 271 25 60) or **Taxi Radio Mexicana** (tel. 519 76 90). They offer safe service at *sitio* prices. To get to the airport in a pinch, try calling **Transportación Terrestre al Aeropuerto** (tel. 571 41 93). While tips are technically unnecessary, an extra peso or two (nothing fancy), especially to cabbies who help with your bags, is a kind gesture.

BY CAR

You must like pain and be insane. Driving is the most complicated and least economical way to get around the city, not to mention the easiest way to get lost. Mexico City's drivers are notoriously reckless; they became that way in large measure because highway engineers did not think about them at all when designing city roads. Highway dividers are often absent, and stop signs are planted midstream. Is it any wonder that red lights are routinely defied? Even the fast and free *Angeles Verdes* (see p. 37) do not serve the D.F. If your car should break down within city boundaries, call the **Asociación Nacional Automovilística (ANA;** tel. 597 42 83) and request assistance. Wait for them beside your car, with the hood raised. If you leave your car alone, give it a good-bye kiss before you go.

Parking within the city is seldom a problem; parking lots are everywhere (4-8 pesos per hr., depending on the location and condition of the lot). Street parking is difficult to find, and vandalism is extremely common. Never leave anything valuable inside your car. Police will put an *inmobilizador* on your wheels if you park illegally; they will often tow your car. If you return to an empty space, try to locate the nearest police depot (not station) to figure out if your auto has been towed—if it's not there, it was stolen. If anything is missing from your car and you suspect that the police tampered with it, call the English-speaking **LOCATEL** (tel. 658 11 11).

All vehicles, even those of non-Mexican registration, must follow Mexico City's anti-smog regulations. Depending on the last digit of the license plate, cars may not be driven one day per week, according to this schedule: Monday final digits: 5 or 6; Tuesday: 7 or 8; Wednesday: 3 or 4; Thursday: 1 or 2; Friday: 9 or 0. Restrictions apply from 5am to 10pm, and penalties for violations are very stiff. There are no limitations on weekdays between 10pm and 5am or on weekends.

Car rental rates are exorbitant, driving is a hassle, and the entire process is draining. Still interested? Then you must have a valid driver's license (from any country), a passport or tourist card, and be at least 25 years old. Prices for rentals at different agencies tend to be similar: a small VW or Nissan with free mileage, insurance, and tax (which is known as IVA) costs about 330-430 pesos per day or 3000-3300 pesos per week. Most agencies have offices at the airport and in the *Zona Rosa.* **Avis** (general tel. 588 88 88) is at the airport (tel. 786 94 52; open daily 7am-11pm) and at Reforma 308 (tel. 533 13 36, open M-F 7am-10:30pm); **Budget** (tel. 784 30 11) is at the airport (open daily 24hr.) and at Hamburgo 68 (tel. 533 04 50); **Dollar** is at the airport (tel. 207 38 38) and at Av. Chapultepec 322 (open daily 7am-8pm); **Economovil** is at the airport (tel. 726 05 90) and at Universidad 749 (tel. 604 59 60), in Colonia de Valle (open daily 7am-11pm); **Hertz** is at the airport (tel. 762 83 72; open 7am-10:30pm).

■ Safety

Like all large cities, Mexico City presents safety problems to the traveler. Misery-induced crime, corruption, authority abuse, and a lax justice system don't help a bit. A volatile political situation only aggravates problems in the world's largest city. In general, the downtown area, where most sights and accommodations are located, tends to be safer, although the back streets near Buenavista and the Alameda are significantly less so. Try to avoid carrying large amounts of cash, and use a money belt or a similar security device that carries valuables inside your clothing, next to your body. Never use a fanny pack. Ignore strangers who seem even slightly suspicious, no matter how friendly their chatter or smiles may seem.

Speaking in Spanish makes would-be attackers far less likely to bother you. Never follow a vendor or shoeshiner out of public view. Don't wear cameras, expensive watches, or flashy jewelry if you want to be left alone. Sunglasses for men convey don't-mess-with-me *machismo;* for women, they may be less advisable.

Women are, unfortunately, at higher risk of attack. Women in Mexico receive attention that they may not be used to; insistent stares, provocative smiles, whistling, cat-calling, and even extremely vulgar propositions are all part of everyday life. Light hair and skin, revealing or tight clothing, or any sign of foreignness will result in even more attention. Although horribly annoying, most such displays are harmless, provided you take good care of yourself. Stick with other people, especially at night or in isolated areas. A loud clear *¡Déjame!* (DEH-ha-meh; leave me alone) will make your intentions clear. If in trouble, don't be shy about screaming *¡Ayúdame!* (ah-YOO-dah-may; help me). For extensive information on safety, see p. 15.

The city that used to be known as *la región más transparente del aire* (the most transparent region of air) is now the most polluted in the world. The city's smoggy air may cause problems for contact-lens wearers and people with allergies. Pollution is particularly bad during the winter, due to thermal inversion; the summer rainy season does wonders for air cleanliness. For more information on health, see p. 18.

Practical Information

Navigating the city will be easier if you pick up a few current publications. The **Mexico City Daily Bulletin,** which includes news, information on tourist sights, and a helpful map of Mexico City, is available free at the City Tourism Office and all over the *Zona Rosa.* The best resource for truly getting down and dirty in this city is the phenomenal **Tiempo Libre** (Free Time), a weekly paper on sale at most corner newsstands: it covers movies, galleries, restaurants, dances, museums, and most cultural events (comes out Thursdays, 7 pesos). **The Mexico City News** (5 pesos; an English-language daily) and **La Jornada** (5 pesos; a top national newspaper) have film and theater listings as well as extensive international news, in case you miss gossip from the homefront. **Ser Gay,** available at newsstands and many gay bars, is less widely distributed but has a more complete listing of gay and lesbian nightlife options (for more information, see **Gay and Lesbian Entertainment,** p. 121). Of course, the best way for anyone to find his or her way around and to discover new and exciting bars, restaurants, theaters, and museums is to get out and talk to people.

If you come during the summer, keep a light rain poncho or umbrella handy. The rainy season (May-Oct.) features daily one- or two-hour-long rain storms anywhere from 4-6pm. Otherwise, sunny and moderate weather prevails year-round.

TOURIST AND FINANCIAL SERVICES

City Tourist Office: Infotur, Amberes 54 (tel. 525 93 80), at Londres in the *Zona Rosa.* Metro: Insurgentes (Line 1). Helpful and friendly. Some officials speak English. The best free maps of the city and Metro upon request. Lists hotels, grouped by region and price range. Open daily 9am-9pm. The office operates information booths at the airport and Terminal Central del Norte bus stations.

Ministry of Tourism: Presidente Masaryk 172 (tel. 250 85 55 ext. 111), at Hegel in Col. Polanco. From Metro: Polanco (Line 7), walk 1 block down Arquímedes, take a left on Masaryk, and walk 3½ blocks—the building is to your right and easy to miss. The tourist information desk gives out copies of *El Mirón,* a free but awful weekly guide with a few poor maps of the downtown area and the Metro. Strangely enough, the staff knows much more about sites outside of Mexico City. At the **reservations desk** (tel. 25 51 06 or 255 31 12), friendly staff makes hotel reservations and offers copious brochures, information, and advice. Office open M-F 8am-9pm, Sa 10am-1pm; 24hr. phone lines.

Tourist Card (FMT) Info: Secretaría de Gobernación, Dirección General de Servicios Migratorios, Homero 1832 (tel. 626 72 00 or 206 05 06), in Col. Palanco. Take the Metro to Polanco, then catch a "Migración" *pesero.* The last stop is at the office. Come here to extend the date on your FMT or to clear up any immigration problems. Arrive early to avoid the long lines and to prepare yourself for Mexican bureaucracy. Open M-F 8am-2pm.

Accommodations Service: Hoteles Asociados, Airport *Sala A* (tel. 571 59 02 or 571 6382) and the Central de Autobuses del Norte. Up-to-date information on prices and locations of Mexico City hotels. Give 'em a price range and an area; they'll get you a reservation free of charge. For budget lodgings, be sure to ask for rock-bottom prices. English spoken.

Embassies: Will replace lost passports, issue visas, and provide legal assistance. Visa processing can take up to 24hr.; bring plenty of forms of ID. If you find yourself in an emergency after hours, try contacting the embassy anyway—you could be in luck. **Australia,** 9255 Rubén Darío 55 (tel. 531 52 25; emergency after-hours tel. 905 407 16 98), at Campos Eliseos in Col. Polanco. Open M-Th 8:30am-2pm and 3-5:15pm, F 8:30am-2:15pm. **Belize,** Bernardo de Galvez 215 (tel. 520 12 74), in Col. Lomas de Chapultepec. Metro: Observatorio (Line 1). Open M-F 9am-1:30pm. **Canada,** Schiller 529 (tel. 724 79 00), in Col. Polanco. Metro: Polanco or Auditorio (Line 7). Open M-F 9am-1pm and 2-5pm. **Costa Rica,** Río Po 113 (tel. 525 77 64, 65, or 66), between Río Lerma and Río Panuco, behind the U.S. Embassy. Open M-F 9am-5pm. **Guatemala,** 1025 Av. Explanada (tel. 540 75 20). Metro: Auditorio (Line 7). Open M-F 9am-1:30pm. **Honduras,** Alfonso Reyes 220 (tel. 211 57 47), between Saltillo and Ometusco in Col. Condesa. Open M-F 10am-2pm. **New Zealand,** José Luis Lagrange, 103 10th fl. (tel. 281 54 86). Metro: Polanco (Line 7). Open M-Th 9am-5pm, and F 9am-1:30pm. **Nicaragua,** Payo de Rivera 120 (tel. 540 56 1), between Virreyes and Monte Atos. Open M-F 9:30am-3pm. **U.K.** (tel. 207 21 49, emergency tel. 207 20 89), at Río Lerma Riosena. Open M-F 8:30am-3:30pm. **U.S.,** Reforma 305 (tel. 533 56 93; emergency after-hours tel. 211 00 42), at Glorieta Angel de la Independencia. Open M-F 9am-5pm.

Currency Exchange: *Casas de cambio* keep longer hours than banks, give better exchange rates, and typically stay open on Saturdays and sometimes even on Sundays. There are many in the *centro,* along Reforma, and in the *Zona Rosa.* Most can change other currencies in addition to U.S. dollars. Call the **Asociación Mexicana de Casas de Cambio** (tel. 264 08 84 or 264 08 41) to locate the exchange bureau nearest you. **Casa de Cambio Tíber** (tel. 722 08 02 or 722 08 00), is on Río Tíber at Papaloapan, one block from the Angel. Open M-F 8:30am-5pm, Sa 8:30am-2pm. On the south side of the Alameda: **Casa de Cambio Plus,** Juárez 38 (tel. 510 89 53). Open M-F 9am-4pm, Sa 10am-2pm. Near the Monumento a la Revolución/ Buenavista: **Casa de Cambio Catorce,** Reforma 51, 4th fl. (tel. 705 24 60), near the Glorieta de Colón. Open M-F 9am-4pm. All banks offer one exchange rate and usually charge commissions.

ATM: The nation-wide ATM network, **Red Cajeros Compartidos,** takes Visa for cash advances, and all ATMs work with U.S. system cards with Plus or Cirrus. Scores of ATMs are located throughout all major districts. Lost or stolen cards can be reported 24hr. to 227 27 77. **Citibank,** Reforma 390 (tel. 258 32 00 or 227 27 27; open 24hr.), and **Bank of America,** Reforma 265, 22nd floor (tel. 230 64 00; open M-F 8:30am-5:30pm), can also help in an emergency.

American Express: Reforma 234 (tel. 207 72 82 or 208 60 04), at Havre in the *Zona Rosa.* Cashes personal and traveler's checks and accepts customers' mail and money wires. Report lost credit cards to the main office at Patriotismo 635 (tel. 326 26 66) and lost traveler's checks to either office. Open M-F 9am-6pm, Sa 9am-1pm.

LOCAL SERVICES

English Bookstores: American Bookstore, Madero 25 (tel. 512 03 06), in the *centro,* has an extensive selection of fiction, guidebooks, and a great Latin American history and politics section. Also a branch at Insurgentes Sur 1188 (tel. 575 23 72), in San Angel. Both branches open M-Sa 9:30am-8pm; *centro* store also open Su 10am-3pm. **Pórtico de la Ciudad de México,** Central 124 (tel. 510 96 83), at Carranza. English and Spanish books on Mexican history and guides to archaeological sites. Check out the frescoes while you browse. Open M-F 10am-7pm, Sa 10am-5pm. Also popular is the **Librería Gandhi** (tel. 510 42 31), on Juárez along the Alameda. Open M-Sa 10am-8:45pm, Su 11am-8pm. Another location at M.A. de Quevedo 128 in San Angel.

English Library: Biblioteca Benjamin Franklin, Londres 16 (tel. 209 91 00), at Berlín, 2 blocks southeast of the Cuauhtémoc monument. Books, newspapers, and periodicals. Council and Fulbright fellowships on the 1st floor. Open M and F 3-7:30pm, Tu-Th 10am-3pm.

Cultural and Arts Info: Palacio Nacional de Bellas Artes (tel. 521 92 51 ext. 132 and 217), Juárez and Eje Central, for info and reservations for Bellas Artes events. Open M-Sa 11am-7pm, Su 9am-7pm. Check *Tiempo Libre* for city-wide listings.

Gay, Lesbian, and Bisexual Information: Colectivo Sol, write to Apdo. 13-320 Av. México 13, D.F. 03500. Has info on upcoming political and social events. Events publicized at gay bars and clubs and in *Tiempo Libre* and *Ser Gay.* Lesbians and bisexual women can contact **LesVoz** (tel. 399 60 19; email lesvoz@laneta.apc.org), the lesbian journal at Apartado Postal 33-091 Mexico, D.F. 15900. Open M-Th 9am-1pm. Another resource is **El Closet de Sor Juana,** Xola 181, 2nd fl. (tel. 590 24 46), in Col. Alamos, a lesbian and bisexual group that organizes daily activities.

LOCATEL: (tel. 658 11 11). Officially the city's lost-and-found hotline. Call if your car (or friend) is missing. Limited English spoken.

Legal Advice: Organización Nacional Pro-Derechos Humanos de las Mujeres y las Lesbianos (tel. 399 60 19; email proml@laneta.apc.org), gives free legal advice and support to women in cases of sexual discrimination or harassment. Open M-Th 9am-1pm.

Supermarket: Most supermarkets are far from the *centro,* at residential Metro stops. Supermarket prices are higher than *mercados* but lower than corner stores and have it all-in-one. **Mega,** on the way to Tlatelolco from Metro: Tlatelolco (Line 3). Take the González *salida,* turn right on González and walk 3 blocks; it's at the intersection with Cárdenas. Open daily 8am-10pm. **Aurrerá,** 5 blocks north of Puente de Alvarado, on Insurgentes. Metro: M.A. Quevedo. Open daily 7:30am-11pm. **Superama,** Río Sena and Balsas, in the *Zona Rosa,* directly outside the Polanco Metro station (Line 7). Open daily 8am-9pm.

Laundromats: Near the Monumento a la Revolución: **Lavandería Automática Edison,** Edison 91. Wash or dry 13 pesos per 3kg. Full-service 42 pesos. Soap 3 pesos. Open M-Sa 10am-7pm, Su 10am-6pm. In the *Zona Rosa,* most hotels have laundry service. Near Metro: Chilpancingo is **Lavandería Automática,** José Martí 224C (tel. 515 07 44). 33 pesos per load full-service or 10 pesos per load self-service. Open M-F 8am-6pm, Sa 8am-4pm.

EMERGENCY AND COMMUNICATIONS

Police: Secretaría General de Protección y Vialidad (tel. 588 51 00). Open 24hr. In case of an **emergency,** dial 08 for the Policía Judicial. Call to report assaults, robberies, crashes, or abandoned vehicles. Beware abuses of power. No English.

Police Aid for Tourists: Patrullas de Auxilio Turistico (tel. 250 82 21), in marked vans in the *Zona Rosa* near el Angel and in the *zócalo*. The police in the vans speak English and are available for any and all help 9am-9pm. Those who answer the phone speak little English and deal primarily with automobile issues (accidents, break-downs, thefts). Phone staffed 24hr. **Procuradura General de Justicia,** Florencia 20 (tel. 625 76 92 or 625 76 96), in the *Zona Rosa*. A department of justice catering especially to tourists. Go here to file police reports on anything—a minor robbery, a major abuse of power, or a lost or stolen tourist card. Some English spoken. Staffed 24hr.

Emergency Shelter: Casa de Asistencia Social (tel. 744 81 28 for women, 530 47 62 for men), on Calle Santanita in Col. Viaducto Pietá, near the treasury building.

Rape Crisis: Hospital de Traumatología de Balbuena, Cecilio Robelo 103 (tel. 552 16 02 or 764 03 39). Metro: Moctezuma (Line 1). Also call 06 or LOCATEL.

Legal Advice Hotline: Supervisión General de Servicios a la Comunidad, Fray Servando 32 (tel. 625 72 08 or 625 71 84), south of the *centro*. Metro: Isabel la Catolica (Line 1). On José Maria Izagaza, 2 blocks south of the Metro stop. Call the hotline if you are the victim of a robbery or accident and need legal advice. Little to no English spoken. Open daily 9am-9pm.

Sexually Transmitted Disease Info and Innoculation Info: Secretaría de Salud, Benjamin Gil 14 (tel. 277 63 11), in Col. Condensa. Metro: Juanacatlán (Line 1). Open M-F 8am-7pm, Sa 9am-2pm.

AIDS Hotline: TELSIDA/CONASIDA, Florencia 8 Calzada de Tlalpan, 2nd fl. (tel. 207 41 43 or 207 40 77) Col. Torielo Guerra. From Metro: General Anaya (Line 2), take a *micro* headed for *Zona de Hospitales*. Runs AIDS tests, provides prevention information, and serves as a general help center. Open M-F 9am-9:30pm.

Red Cross: Ejército Nacional 1032 (tel. 395 11 11), in Polanco. Open 24hr.

Pharmacies: Small *farmacias* abound on almost every street corner and are great for most purchases; many drugs requiring prescriptions in the U.S. can be bought over the counter. Rarer drugs and more important, specialized medications should be bought at large, international-looking (and more expensive) pharmacies such as **Farmacia El Fénix,** Isabel La Católica 15 (tel. 585 04 55), at 5 de Mayo, open M-Sa 9am-10pm; or **VYR,** San Jerónimo 630 (tel. 595 59 83 or 595 59 98), near Perisur shopping center and at other locations, open 24hr. All **Sanborns** and big supermarkets have well-stocked pharmacies.

Medical Care: The **U.S. Embassy** (see p. 87) has a list of doctors with their specialties, addresses, telephone numbers, and languages spoken. **Dirección General de Servicios Médicos** (tel. 518 51 00) has information on all city hospitals. Open M-F 9am-5pm. **American British Cowdray (ABC) Hospital,** Calle Sur 136 (tel. 227 50 00), at Observatorio Col. Las Américas. Expensive but generally trustworthy and excellent. No foreign health plans valid, but major credit cards accepted. Open 24hr. **Torre Médica,** José Maria Iglesias 21 (tel. 705 25 77 or 705 18 20), at Metro station Revolución (Line 2), has a few doctors who speak English.

Central Post Office: (tel. 521 73 94), on Lázaro Cárdenas at Tacuba, across from the Palacio de Bellas Artes. Open for stamps and *Lista de Correos* (window 3) M-F 8am-8pm, Sa 9am-5pm, Su 9am-1pm; for registered mail M-F 8am-6pm. Postal museum upstairs with turn-of-the-century mailboxes and other old-school gear. Museum open M-F 8am-10pm, Sa 8am-8pm, Su 8am-4pm. **Postal Code:** 06002.

Courier Services: UPS, Reforma 404 (tel. 228 79 00), and various smaller offices, provides international shipping services and express mail. Open M-F 8am-8pm. **Federal Express,** Reforma 308 (tel. 51 09 96), in Colonia Juárez near the Glorieta Angel de Independencia. Send before 4:30pm M-F, 1:30pm Sa, for overnight service. Open M-F 8am-7pm, Sa 9am-1:30pm.

Fax, Telegrams, and Western Union: Tacuba 8 (tel. 21 20 49; fax 512 18 94), at the Museo Nacional de Arte in the right wing of the building, behind the central post office. Open M-F 9am-11:30pm, Sa 9am-10:30pm, Su 9am-4:30pm. Domestic and international service. Many *papelerías* also offer fax services.

Internet Access: El Universal-Internet Sala, Bucareli 12, across the street from the giant yellow horse sculpture in an unmarked entrance, right next to the main entrance of *El Universal* newspaper office. This service provides absolutely free Internet usage. All you have to do is sign in and leave ID, and then enjoy up to 2hr. of computer escapades—they even have people to help you. Open M-F 10am-7pm. Access runs 25-50 pesos per hr. at other spots, including **Java Chat,** Genova 44K (tel. 514 68 56 or 525 68 53), in the *Zona Rosa.* Enjoy free coffee and soda as you type. Telnet connections available and lots of friendly help. 30 pesos per hr. Open M-F 9am-9pm, Sa-Su 10am-9pm. **Cyberspace Cafe,** Mazatlán 148 (tel. 211 68 77), in Col. Condesa. From Metro station: Patriotismo (Line 9), walk down 4 blocks in the direction of traffic, then turn right on Mazatlán—it's 2 blocks down. 30 pesos per hr., 20 pesos per 30min. **Multiservicios de Computo,** Universidad 2079 (tel. 54 64 08 or 54 87 24), Pl. Manzana 18, a very long 3 blocks down Universidad from Metro: M.A. Quevedo. Theoretically open M-F 9-5 and Sa 10-3, but call to double-check before you make the trek.

Telephones: LADATELs and **Telmexes** are everywhere and can be used for international collect and credit card calls, as well as with a LADATEL card. You need to insert a LADATEL card into the phone in order to make collect and credit card calls, but no money will be deducted from the phone card. For those who miss the golden days of the Mexican phone system, long-distance **casetas** are at the airport between *Salas D* and *E* (open 24hr.) and at Central Camionera del Norte (open daily 8am-9pm).

Phone Code: 5.

Accommodations

Rooms abound in the *centro* (between Alameda and the *zócalo*) and near the Alameda Central. Perhaps the best budget bargains (and the best places to meet eclectic and wacky locals and tourists) are found near El Monumento a la Revolución on the Pl. de la República. Rooms priced at 60 to 80 pesos for one bed and 85 to 100 pesos for two beds should be clean and have carpeting, a TV, and a telephone with free local calls. Some budget hotels charge according to the number of beds needed and not per person; beds tend to be large enough for two people. If you don't mind, snuggling is a potential source of substantial savings.

Avoid the filthier sections of the Alameda and any area that makes you feel uncomfortable—there are plenty more from which to choose. In an attempt to cut down on problems with prostitution, many budget establishments have adopted "No Guests Allowed" policies. Beware of any place where the hotel itself (and not the parking lot) is marked "Hotel Garage." These rooms are frequented by businessfolk "working late at the office" and are designed to allow entry directly from the garage to the room. Figure it out. Always ask to look at a room before you accept it; this is easier to do after check-out time (between noon and 2pm).

For the little hostel information available, call **Villa Deportiva Juvenil** (tel. 525 26 99), the city's lone hostel on Pl. de la Independencia, near the *Zona Rosa* (30 pesos a night). Don't get your hopes up; it's often full with visiting sports teams.

CENTRO

Situated between the *zócalo* and Alameda Central, this neighborhood is the historic colonial heart of Mexico City. Its hotels are reasonably priced and feel fairly safe, although the streets become empty once locals head home for the night. Still, the *centro* remains an exciting and convenient place to stay. With action inevitably come noise and congestion. If you crave quieter surroundings, consider moving west to the Alameda or Revolución areas. Many of the hotels listed below are north of Madero and 5 de Mayo, the parallel east-west streets that connect the Alameda with the *zócalo;* and east of Lázaro Cárdenas, the north-south Eje Central that runs one block east of Alameda. Metro stations Bellas Artes (Lines 2 and 8) and Allende (Line 2) are nearby. Hotels on 5 de Mayo, Isabel la Católica, and Uruguay are better served by Metro stations Zócalo (Line 2) and Isabel la Católica (Line 1). Street names change north of Tacuba: Isabel la Católica becomes República de Chile, and Bolívar turns into Allende. Even in the *centro,* **most budget hotels do not accept credit cards.**

Hotel Principal, Bolívar 29 (tel. 518 25 05), by the Parilla Leonesa restaurant. Helpful staff bustles down the pale yellow, plant-filled hallways under the enormous skylight. Gorgeous high ceilings and little balconies make the simple yellow rooms feel like palatial suites. TV, telephone, bottled water, and a safe are also provided in your room. Singles 110-125 pesos; doubles 140-170 pesos; specific prices depend on the number of people.

Hotel Antillas, Belisario Domínguez 34 (tel. 526 56 74 through 79), between Allende and República de Chile. The colonial exterior promises history-drenched grandeur: the interior does not disappoint. A winding marble staircase leads up to newly renovated (read: extra-clean) modern rooms. Full amenities (TVs, bottled water, and phones) and an eager staff will assure a relaxing stay. Singles 120 pesos; doubles 130 pesos.

Hotel La Marina, Allende 30 (tel. 518 24 45). Although they're fake, the plants at every corner give a light and airy feel to this pretty little hotel. The orange furniture clashes a little with red rugs, but the comfortable king-sized beds, prime location, and low prices should override color concerns. 1 person 90 pesos; 2 people 95 pesos; doubles 130 pesos; triples 150 pesos; quads 180 pesos.

Hotel Buenos Aires, Motolina 21 (tel. 518 21 04 or 518 21 37). A little fountain in the courtyard adds character to this simple, clean hotel. Each room comes complete with a TV and drinking water. Ask for a window that faces the outside. Singles 70-80 pesos; doubles 90-120 pesos; specific prices depend on the number of people.

Hotel Monte Carlo, Uruguay 69 (tel. 521 25 59), between Metro stops Isabel la Católica (Line 1) and Allende (Line 2). Relaxing lounge and top-floor skylight. Rooms have balconies, red carpets, and yellow satin furniture—lots of large, lovingly mismatched bedrooms. Clean, tiled bathrooms without shower curtains. Singles 80 pesos with shared bath, 100 pesos with private bath; doubles (all with private baths) 120 pesos.

Hotel Atlanta (tel. 518 12 00), on the corner of Allende and República de Cuba. Offers bright rooms with small, spic-'n'-span bathrooms, TVs, and phones. 1-person singles 90 pesos, 2-person singles 95 pesos; doubles 130-170 pesos.

ALAMEDA CENTRAL

The expansive Alameda is always throbbing with activity. But the greenery fades over the course of a few blocks, making way for dirt and danger in some of the surrounding streets. Use caution. Use a *sitio* cab.

Hotel Manolo Primero, Luis Moya 111 (tel. 521 37 39 or 521 31 49), near Arcos de Belén, halfway between Metros Balderas and Salto del Agua (Lines 1 and 8). Spacious blue hallways and cavernous lobby with LADATEL phone lead to spanking new rooms with king-sized beds, TVs, and lounge chairs. Clean, large bathrooms with gigantic mirrors. Singles and doubles a steal for 100 pesos.

Hotel Hidalgo, Santa Veracruz 37 (tel. 521 37 39), just north of the Alameda. Metro: Bellas Artes (Lines 2 and 8). Up the 2 de Abril walkway to the left of Teatro Hidalgo, in a somewhat dingy area, Hidalgo is a resplendent vision in peach. Ultra-modern decorations include elegant wood paneling, beautiful carpeting, tasteful decorations, and enormous closets and mirrors. Large singles and pleasant courtyard views make it worth the price. TV, bottled water, and phone, of course. Singles 150 pesos; doubles 160 pesos; triples 180 pesos; quads 200 pesos.

Hotel Sevillano, Ayuntamiento 78 (tel. 512 67 15), between Revillagigedo and Moya, 4 blocks from the Alameda. Small, clean rooms with cute TVs perched up near the ceiling and tiny, tidy bathrooms with space for a bidet but not a shower curtain. Central courtyard lets in a lot of light. Singles and doubles 50 pesos.

MEXICO CITY

NEAR THE MONUMENTO A LA REVOLUCIÓN/ BUENAVISTA

Hotels near the Monumento a la Revolución are cheaper and quieter than their counterparts in the *centro* or the Alameda. Backpackers and bargain-scouting travelers tend to congregate here, particularly in the hotels on Mariscal and Edison. Metro: Revolución (Line 2) serves hotels south of Puente de Alvarado/Hidalgo, while Metro: Guerrero (Line 3) serves those to the north, near the train station.

Casa de Los Amigos, Ignacio Mariscal 132 (tel. 705 05 21 or 705 06 46), across from Gran Hotel Texas. Metro: Revolución (Line 2). Originally the home and studio of painter José Clemente Orozco, now a Quaker-run guest house for tourists and social activists. Fascinating, amazing place with dynamic, youthful, international atmosphere. Visitors required to respect the cooperative atmosphere in order to stay (rules are few), and it's worth it. Backpackers, grad students, eco-warriors—people from all over the world come here. You're bound to go home with many international addresses and fond memories of your new-found *amigos.* Weekly cultural exchanges, ample library offerings, and a lively lounge. Kitchen and laundry facilities. Dorm rooms 50 pesos; private rooms 65-70 pesos; doubles 110-150 pesos. Breakfast 15 pesos. 2-day min. stay, 15-day max. stay. Key deposit 20 pesos.

Hotel Oxford, Ignacio Mariscal 67 (tel. 566 05 00), at Alcázar, next to the small park. Metro: Revolución. Large, colorful rooms, many with TV, telephone, and great views of the park. Inviting bathrooms with huge sinks (ideal for laundry). Adjoining bar with swinging doors. Singles 60-90 pesos; doubles 100 pesos; triples 135 pesos; quads 160 pesos.

Hotel Yale, Mosqueta 200 (tel. 591 15 45), between Zaragoza and Guerrero, to the left as you exit the train station. Metro: Guerrero. Recently remodeled rooms and bathrooms, full-length mirrors, TVs, phones, and colorful furniture that doesn't quite match. An endearing hotel, for those who can't get into a better place. 1-2 people 80 pesos; 3-4 people 130 pesos.

Hotel Edison, Edison 106 (tel. 566 09 33), at Iglesias, offers luxury at prices that are comparatively high for the area but worth the splurge. Enormous rooms with full amenities surround the beautiful, flower-filled courtyard. Singles 130 pesos; doubles 150 pesos.

Hotel Buena Vista, Bernal Díaz del Castillo 34. These are some of the cheapest rooms in the area. Rooms are a little small and simple, but they offer all you need at great prices. Singles 41 pesos, with bath 47 pesos; doubles for 1-2 people 56 pesos; doubles for 3-4 people 64 pesos.

NEAR THE BUS STATIONS

There are few good budget accommodations in the vicinity of any of the four bus stations. The areas around these stations generally offer expensive rooms in shabby *barrios.* Even if you arrive late at night, it is not safe to walk a few blocks—you'd do best to catch a cab (and once in a cab, why not head to the center of town?). For travelers just passing through who arrive at the **Central de Autobuses del Norte,** the pricey but comfy **Hotel Brasilia,** Av. de los 100 Mts. 4823 (tel. 587 85 77), is three blocks to the left along the main thoroughfare as you exit the bus station. Rooms are carpeted and clean, with TV, phone, and private safe. (Singles 140 pesos; doubles 200 pesos.) Both the TAPO and Poniente station are in exceedingly dubious neighborhoods. If you arrive at the **TAPO,** take the Metro to the *centro,* and if you are at the **Terminal de Autobuses del Poniente,** swing over to the Tacubaya Metro stop (Lines 1, 7, and 9) for the nearest hotels.

Food

Options for meals fall into six basic categories: the very cheap (and sometimes risky) vendor stalls scattered about the streets; fast, inexpensive, and generally safe *taquerías;* slightly more formal *cafeterías;* more pricey and decorous Mexican restaurants; locally popular North-Americanized eateries; and expensive international fare. In addition, U.S. fast-food chains mass-produce predictable fare for the timid palate. **VIPS** offers 60 commercialized, Denny's-like eateries throughout the D.F. that are very popular with rich Mexicans (and correspondingly priced); some are open 24 hours. If you're preparing your own food, local neighborhood markets and supermarkets stock almost anything you could need. For a good time, try **La Merced** market (see p. 123), the mother of them all. As always, avoid unpurified water, including ice, uncooked or unpeeled vegetables, and meat that is not fully cooked (see p. 20).

Soda is sold at every corner. *Agua mineral* means mineral water, *sidral* is a great carbonated apple drink, and *refrescos* are your standard soda. Perhaps the best way to combat thirst is through the delicious *aguas* sold everywhere, made with fresh fruit and sugar—just make sure the ice is purified. Bottles are recycled, and patrons pay extra for the privilege of keeping them. If you want your soda to go, try getting it *en una bolsa* (in a plastic bag with a straw).

CENTRO

The historic downtown area of Mexico City offers a wide selection of food at super-low prices. Slick U.S. fast-food establishments, enormous *cafeterías,* and countless small eateries offer inexpensive *comida corrida,* tacos, *tortas,* and other staples. Motolina and Gante host a high concentration of little eateries. There's plenty of good fare for vegetarians.

Café Tacuba, Tacuba 28 (tel. 512 84 82). Metro: Allende (Line 2). A bastion of excellent food and engaging conversation in the heart of downtown since 1912. Everyone who's anyone has been here; this place is perennially "in." An amazing combo of camp and class—pure artisanship, brass pitchers, murals, and, if you're lucky, men outside in colonial garb eager to greet you. *Antojitos* 15-42 pesos, entrees 30-70 pesos. Full bar. Be patient: all dishes are made from scratch, and they're well worth the wait. Open daily 8am-11:30pm.

Restaurantes Vegetarianos del Centro, Mata 13 (tel. 510 01 13), between 5 de Mayo and Madero. Shiny, happy, healthy, sunshine-yellow eatery filled with an eclectic group of veggie lovers. *Comida corrida* for 29 pesos. Open daily 8am-8pm.

X-Can-Kin, Motolina 15c (tel. 512 40 68). A lovely Yucatec eatery with *antojitos* (all 4 pesos each) that will leave you groveling for more. Tasty *comida corrida* runs 30 pesos. Open M-Sa 9am-9pm.

Restaurant Rincón Mexicano, Uruguay 27 (tel. 512 03 60). From the street you can see only the tiled stove heating fresh tortillas, but the hand-carved wooden chairs and blue tablecloths extend back. Serving only 1 meal, this place produces a scrumptiously home-cooked, 15-peso *comida corrida.* Open M-Sa 1-6pm.

Café Dayi, Isabela la Católica 9-11 (tel. 521 62 03), near Tacuba. Watermelon-ish cafeteria decor is kitschy, but the food—both Chinese and Mexican—is excellent. Chicken and duck dishes 28 pesos; *comida corrida china y mexicana* 36 pesos. Don't be afraid to crane your neck to check out *fútbol* on TV as aproned waitresses refill your *agua de sandía* (watermelon juice). Open daily 8am-11pm.

Restaurant Danubio, Uruguay 3 (tel. 512 09 12), just east of Lázaro Cárdenas. Stately seafood joint boasts its own coat-of-arms and hefty price tags. Perennially packed, but the good food and drink ain't no laughing matter. Famous artsy types have left their scribblings framed on the walls. Entrees (around 70 pesos) and specials (65-88 pesos) are big enough for 2. Open daily 1-10pm.

Súper Soya, Tacuba 40 (tel. 510 29 80), and several locations throughout the *centro.* A wildly colorful grocery store/cafe/diner/yogurt stand. Salads 10-23 pesos, vegetarian pizzas 7 pesos, *tacos de guisado* 5 pesos, and an incredible variety of *licuados* for 10 pesos each. Open daily 9am-9pm.

ALAMEDA CENTRAL

The convivial atmosphere that permeates the Alameda carries over to the various restaurants that pepper the area. Gone is the stuffy elitism of the *Zona Rosa* and the frenetic pace of the *centro.* Instead, you'll find good, back-to-basics food. Prices are on the high side, but portions are large. For something a bit different, try one of the Chinese restaurants on Dolores, two blocks west of Cárdenas and one block south of the Alameda. Cheap, small eateries line Independencia, one block south of the Alameda.

Fonda Santa Anita, Humboldt 48 (tel. 518 46 09). Metro: Juárez (Line 3). Go a block west on Artículo 120, turn right on Humboldt, and continue half a block more. A classic restaurant that has represented Mexico in 5 World's Fairs, this friendly eatery feels no need to dispel stereotypes—the tablecloths are bright pink, and colorful depictions of bullfights and busty women cover the walls. More importantly, it serves incredible versions of old standards and regional specialties from all over the country. *Comida corrida* 32 pesos. Open M-F 1-10pm, Sa-Su 1-8pm.

Oriental (tel. 521 30 99), on a pedestrian walkway at the corner of Dolores and Independencia, on a block of Chinese restaurants. The prices here are slightly lower (38-peso *comida corrida*), and there's an enormous bronze Buddha at the entrance whose belly is sure to bring you good luck. Open daily 10am-11pm.

Energía Natural (tel. 521 20 15), at the corner of 16 de Septiembre and Dolores, is the brightest and most beautiful of the bunch, with no walls and little healthy touches such as whole wheat bread. Sandwiches and burgers 9-20 pesos. Open daily 8am-7pm.

NEAR THE MONUMENTO A LA REVOLUCIÓN

Without many affluent residents or big tourist draws, this area lacks the snazzy international cuisine of other areas. Instead, homey cafes, *torterías,* and *taquerías* dominate the scene. For hearty portions and low prices, this is your spot.

La Especial de París, Insurgentes Centro 117 (tel. 703 23 16). Yes! Yes! This *nevería* has been scooping up ecstasy since 1921. Lots of 100%-natural treats, ranging from *malteadas* (milkshakes, 16 pesos) to *frutas glacé* (fruit ices). It's hopeless to order a single scoop—you'll claw your way back to the front of the line for more. Doubles 12 pesos, triples 15 pesos, 4 scoops 20 pesos. Open daily noon-9pm.

La Taberna (tel. 591 11 00), Arriaga at Ignacio Mariscal, below street level. Next to Hotel Pennsylvania. The service is fast and the *ambiente* awesome. The 4-course Italian *comida corrida* (20 pesos) is sure to please. Open M-Sa 8am-6pm.

Super Cocina Los Arcos, Ignacio Mariscal at Iglesias. Homey, cozy atmosphere amid bright orange clean furnishings. Service is a little slow, but it's worth it—their chicken soups (12-14 pesos) and *alambres con queso* (17 pesos) are the best around. *Comida corrida* 12 pesos. Many dishes 9-19 pesos. Open M-Sa 8am-11pm.

Restaurant El Paraiso, Orozco y Berra at Enrique Gonzales Martinez, across the street from Museo del Chopo. Offers a vegetarian *comida corrida* (15 pesos) in a friendly family atmosphere. Open daily 8am-2am.

ZONA ROSA

The myth: only loaded tourists eat in the *Zona Rosa.* The reality: although the area has some of the city's more expensive restaurants, serving everything from international cuisine to traditional Mexican cooking, many eateries cater chiefly to clerks from the scores of surrounding office buildings. The *Zona Rosa* also has more fast-food joints than any other area of the city. If you're more interested in the *Zona Rosa*'s slick party atmosphere than in filling your stomach, skip dinner and settle for a drawn-out evening appetizer.

Ricocina, Londres 168 (tel. 514 06 48), east of Florencia. Once the *Zona Rosa*'s best-kept secret, this wonderful family-owned restaurant is quickly becoming the joint *du jour.* Still, the food is the best around. Soft peach surroundings help you enjoy your delicious *menú del día* (23 pesos). Open daily 9am-6pm.

Saint Moritz, Genova 44, next to Java Chat. This tiny, lively restaurant offers the *Zona Rosa*'s best prices for great eats (*menú del dia* 12 pesos). Open daily 1-6pm.

La Luna, Oslo 11, on the narrow walkway between Niza and Copenhagen. Beautiful sketches of *indígenas* grace the walls of this cozy restaurant. The *comida corrida* (18 pesos) includes soup, a small entree and a large one, and a beverage—a great budget value. Very popular; avoid the 2-3pm lunch rush. Open M-Sa 7am-9pm.

Vegetariano Yug, Varsovia 3 (tel. 526 53 30 or 533 32 96), near Reforma. Dig the classy Indian furnishings, plants, and erotic (¡ay-yay-yay!) Hindu sculpture. Then sample the *carnitas vegetarianas* (vegetarian pork bits, 26 pesos). The fab buffet starting at 1pm features bits of Indian, French, and other cuisines (32 pesos). Open M-F 7am-10pm, Sa 8:30am-8pm, Su 1-8pm.

Coffee House, Londres 102 (tel. 525 40 34), is a great place to sip a cappuccino (11 pesos), munch on a salad, sandwich, or crepe (15 pesos), and gawk at/fantasize about Mexico's most fashionable couples strolling the street. Open daily 8am-9pm.

Kai Lam, Londres 114 (tel. 514 58 37). This cute, homey restaurant serves both *comida mexicana* (*menú del día* 36 pesos) and *comida china* (24-38 pesos). Open doors and location make it a good place to chill. Open daily 8am-10:30pm.

Teriyaki San, Niza 22 (tel. 207 24 07), makes trendy but affordable Japanese food, now the rage in Mexico City (dishes 18-38 pesos). This quiet restaurant serves your meal fast-food style. While the eco-minded may flinch at the styrofoam containers, most savor their sushi while watching Mexican TV. Open daily 11am-8pm.

NEAR CHAPULTEPEC

Inside the Bosque de Chapultepec, sidewalk stands offer an enormous variety of snacks. Should you want a sit-down eatery, the immediate vicinity of the Chapultepec Metro station, just outside the park, is cluttered with vendors and small restaurants offering popular and mundane *tortas* and *super-tortas* (not for the weak of stomach). A bit farther east, however, lie a few more adventurous options easily accessible from Metro: Sevilla (Line 1). A ritzier alternative might be *antojitos* in beautiful Colonia Polanco, north of the Anthropology Museum, which is also accessible by Metro station Polanco (Line 7).

Los Sauces, Av. Chapultepec 530 (tel. 28 67 05), at Acapulco Roma, 1½ blocks east of the Chapultepec Metro stop (Line 1). Uniquely tiled bar and grill cluttered with pictures of Mexican politicians and stars. Lots of choices regarding entertainment:

zone out to *telenovelas* on TV, listen to the blaring radio, or watch chefs chop onions and peppers to make your 15-20 peso meal. Open daily 9am-9pm.

El Kioskito (tel. 553 30 55), on Chapultepec, at the corner with Sonora, serves succulent specimens (*antojitos* 12-20 pesos, specialties 30-35 pesos) in a classy, but relaxed atmosphere with a tiled fountain and old photos of the city. The guacamole (7.50 pesos) has pizazz. Open daily 8am-9pm.

COYOACÁN

The southern suburb of Coyoacán attracts students, young couples, and literati to its restaurants. If you crave brie, cheesecake, or pesto, spend an afternoon here. Outdoor cafes and ice cream shops fill the colonial buildings that line the cobbled streets. For some great ice cream, try **Santa Clara,** at Allende and Cuauhtémoc (9 pesos per scoop), and **La Siberia,** on the northeast corner of Jardín Centenario (8 pesos per scoop, floats 11 pesos). For a cheap, excellent meal, try the **food court** on Hijuera, just south of Plaza Hidalgo. Populated almost exclusively by locals, these tiny restaurants offer home-cooked food at un-Coyoacán-like prices. (Open M-Sa 9am-9pm.)

MEXICO CITY

Café El Parnaso, Carrillo Puerto 2 (tel. 554 22 25 or 658 3195), on Jardín Centenario, across from the cathedral. A celebrated book and record store with an outdoor cafe in a prime locale on the plaza's edge. Although the food is a bit pricey, the people-watching and eavesdropping here are unbeatable. Have coffee and cheesecake with strawberries (16-20 pesos). Open daily 8:30am-10:30pm.

El Guarache (tel. 554 45 06), on the south side of Jardín Centernario, offers *jardín* sitting and Mexican tasties at wonderfully reasonable prices (*antojitos* 13-25 pesos, meals 29-34 pesos). Open daily 10am-10pm.

Café Kowloon (tel. 554 78 90 or 554 62 65), on the southeast side of Jardín Centenario, is a Chinese joint with pastel decor, bubbling fish tanks, and startlingly good *menús del día* (25-36 pesos). Open Su-Th 7:30am-11pm, F-Sa 7:30am-1am.

El Jarocho (tel. 568 50 29), on Allende, 1 block north of Pl. Hidalgo. The aroma of freshly ground coffee and the long line will lead you to this legendary corner stand. The Jarocho has been serving some of the best java in the city since 1953. Cappuccino, mocha, and hot chocolate for under 5 pesos each. Open daily 7am-midnight.

SAN ANGEL

The chic restaurants and *típico* taco stands of San Angel pack 'em in, especially on Saturdays, when crowds of well-to-do tourists and Mexicans flock to the booths of overpriced art in the Bazaar Sábado. If you want to dine in style, Plaza San Jacinto is the place to be. Many places will empty out your wallet in five seconds flat, but a few budget gems can be easily discovered.

La Mora, Madro 2 (tel. 616 20 80), offers a great view of the plaza from its spiffy upstairs patio. The brick walls are hung with flowering gardenias and cacti for atmosphere, and the food is finger-lickin' good. *Comida corrida* during the week is only 18 pesos—it includes a jar of *agua purificada* and dessert. Prices rise on the weekends to 25 pesos. Open daily 10am-8pm.

Chucho el Roto, Madero 8 (tel. 616 20 41). A simple, deliciously inexpensive spot situated just steps from the action. This daytime diner serves up *menú del día* of soup, rice, an entree, and dessert for 17 pesos. Breakfast specials 16 pesos. Open daily 9am-5:30pm.

Restaurante Hasti Bhawan: La Casona del Elefante, Pl. San Jacinto 9 (tel. 616 16 01). An unbelievable restaurant: it even has a colon in its name. Indian ambience and scrumptious fare. Indo-Thai chicken 37 pesos, vegetarian platter 35 pesos, *pakoras* or *samosas* 9 pesos. Treat yourself to a *lassi,* a thick yogurt drink (10 pesos). Live jazz Friday and Saturday nights. Open Tu-Th 2-11pm, F-Sa 2pm-midnight, Su 1-6:30pm.

El Rincón de La Lechuza, Miguel Angel de Quevedo 34 (tel. 661 00 50), straight down from Metro: M. A. Quevedo (Line 3), just past La Paz. Joyfully crowded and decorated in yellow and white with wood tables. Tasty tacos 14-20 pesos; specials 29-38 pesos. Open daily 10am-1am.

Central Mexico City

SIGHTS

Casa de los Azulejos, **35**
Catedral Metropolitana, **44**
Centro Cultural José Martí, **23**
Fonart, **26**
Glorieta Ángel de la Independencia, **8**
Glorieta Cristóbal Colón, **16**
Glorieta Cuauhtémoc, **14**
Iglesia de San Francisco, **37**
La Lagunilla, **46**
Mercado de Artesanías de la Ciudadela, **27**
Mercado San Juan Artesanías, **28**
Monumento a la Revolución, **17**
Monumento de los Niños Héroes, **7**
Museo de Arte Moderno, **6**
Museo del Chopo, **18**
Museo del Claustro de Sor Juana, **40**
Museo Diego Rivera, **24**
Museo de la Ciudad de México, **41**
Museo de la Charrería, **39**
Museo del Ejército, **33**
Museo Franz Mayer, **29**
Museo Nacional de Antropología, **3**
Museo Nacional de Arte, **34**
Museo Nacional de Historia, **5**
Museo Nacional de la Estampa, **30**
Museo San Carlos, **20**
Museo Siqueiros, **2**
Museo Tamayo, **4**
Palacio de Bellas Artes, **31**
Palacio Iturbide, **38**
Palacio Nacional, **43**
Pinacoteca Virreinal de San Diego, **2**

Suprema Corte de Justicia, **42**
Templo Mayor, **45**
Tianguis del Chopo, **22**
Torre Latinoamericana, **36**

SERVICES
American Express, **13**
Biblioteca Ben Franklin, **15**
Central Post Office, **32**
Federal Tourist Office, **10**
Ministry of Tourism, **1**
Procedura General de Justicia, **9**
Torre Medica, **19**
Train Station, **21**
U.S. Embassy, **11**
U.K. Embassy, **12**

HOTELS
Casa de los Amigos, **B**
Hotel Antillas, **I**
Hotel Atlanta, **H**
Hotel Buena Vista, **D**
Hotel Buenos Aires, **K**
Hotel Edison, **A**
Hotel Hidalgo, **F**
Hotel la Marina, **G**
Hotel Manolo Primero, **N**
Hotel Monte Carlo, **J**
Hotel Oxford, **C**
Hotel Principal, **L**
Hotel Sevillano, **M**
Hotel Yale, **E**

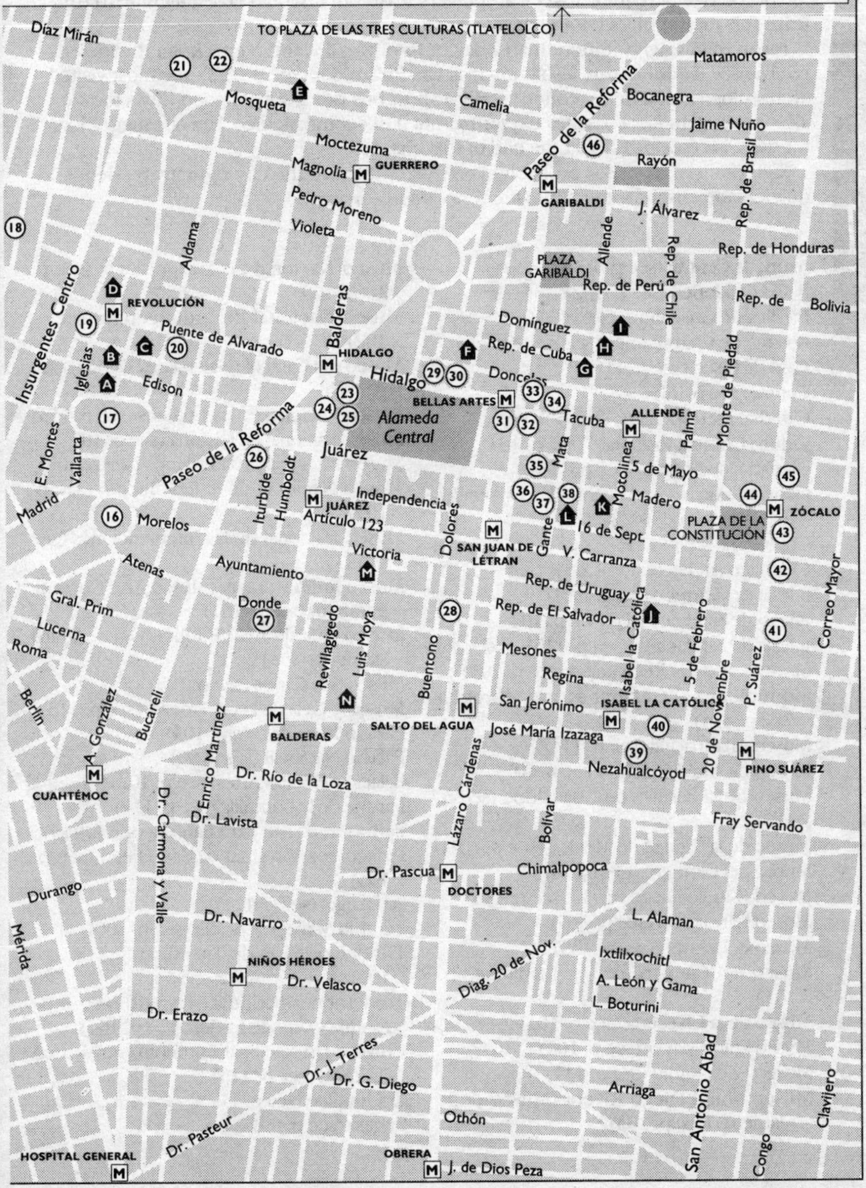

La Finca Café de Dios (tel. 550 94 82), on Madero right off the Pl. de San Jacinto. This hole-in-the-wall coffee stand only serves coffee that is 100% Mexican grown...and it kicks Colombia's butt. All mocha, espresso, and other pipin' hot treats under 5 pesos. If you're truly hard-core, check out the kilos of coffee beans (48-70 pesos) grown in Chiapas. Open daily 8am-8pm.

Sights

It would be impossible to find an appetite that couldn't be satiated by Mexico City's incredibly diverse range of sights and attractions. Getting a well-rounded picture of Mexico City will require a week at the very least, but it would take a lifetime to truly learn this metropolis's ins and outs.

If you're in town for more than a day or two, you'll want to check out the incredible ruins at **Teotihuacán,** also known as **Las Pirámides** (see p. 127), the most visited archaeological site in the country, only a short bus ride away. Mexico City's location also makes it an ideal base for exploring much of central Mexico. See our suggestions for **daytrips** (see p. 127), at the end of this chapter.

Still, the typical visitor probably won't want to leave the city right away. Here's a quick, handy list of some of the metropolis's major sights:'

CENTRO

Mexico City spans hundreds of kilometers and thousands of years, but it is all drawn together in the *centro.* On the city's main plaza, known as the **zócalo,** the Aztec **Templo Mayor,** the gargantuan **Catedral Metropolitana,** and the **Palacio Nacional,** decorated with the work of Mexico's great Leftist muralists, sit serenely side by side. It's not just the architecture that's eclectic; the space is shared by street vendors hawking everything from handwoven bags to used-looking razors, Uzi-sporting soldiers reading comic-strip *novelas,* permanent political protestors, and endless lines of unemployed men advertising their skills on cardboard scraps. The crowds of tourists who come here daily don't even begin to compare to the numbers of Mexicans who pass through or work in this center of the center. If you have time for only one area in Mexico City, make it here. To reach the *zócalo* by Metro, take Line 2 to Metro: Zócalo. The station's entrance sits on the east side of the square, in front of the Palacio Nacional. The Catedral Metropolitana lies to the north, the Federal District offices to the south, and the Suprema Corte de Justicia (Supreme Court) to the southeast.

The Zócalo

Officially known as the **Plaza de la Constitución,** the *zócalo* is the principal square of Mexico City. Now surrounded by imposing colonial monuments, the plaza was once the nucleus of **Tenochtitlán,** the Aztec island-capital and later the center of the entire Aztec empire. Cortés's men razed the city and, atop the ruins, built the power center from which they would rule New Spain (see p. 46 and p. 72). To the southwest of the **Templo Mayor**—the Aztecs' principal place of worship, which they called Teocalli—was the Aztec marketplace and major square. The space was rebuilt and renamed several times, becoming the Plaza de la Constitución in 1812. In 1843, the dictator Santa Anna ordered that a monument to independence be constructed in the center of the square. Only the monument's *zócalo* (pedestal) was in place when the project was abandoned. The citizens of Mexico City began to refer to the square as the *zócalo,* which has become the generic name for the central plazas that mark most of the cities and towns in Mexico. Modern-day urban life has emerged out of this past. Now, indigenous drummers vie with *chicle* (gum) sellers to be heard. The *zócalo* gets hectic and confusing during the day; it becomes deserted and dreamlike at night.

Palacio Nacional

On the east side of the zócalo. If you can't see it, get your eyes checked. ***Open*** *daily 9am-5pm.* ***Free,*** *but you must trade a piece of ID for a big red "turista" badge at the entrance. Ask local officials and tour guides about prices; you should be able to get a guided tour (M-F 10am-4pm) for 60-70 pesos. Then again, joining a tour that has already begun is free. Museum open M-F 9am-8pm, Sa 9am-5:30pm; free.*

Stretching the entire length of the enormous *zócalo,* the **Palacio Nacional** is a sight to behold. Over 200m long, this regal mammoth of a government palace is as over-the-top as Mexico City itself. It's hard to believe the *palacio* could have ever been anything else. Its history, however, is more fantastic and fairy tale-ish than the armed guards standing outside would make you think. Completely demolished during the riots of 1692, the *palacio* had been the site of an Aztec ruler's (Moctezuma II) palace, Hernán Cortés's house, and the palace of the king of Spain's viceroys. Now the chief executive center of the Republic, the *palacio* houses monumental murals and a museum honoring Benito Juárez.

It took Diego Rivera from 1929 to 1951 to sketch and paint the **frescoes** on the *palacio*'s western and northern walls. **Mexico Through the Centuries,** one of his most famous works, is on the west wall of the *palacio,* at the top of the grand staircase. The mural is divided into eight smaller scenes, each of which depicts an event in the social history of Mexico. Each of the five arches at the top of the mural deals with the Mexican nation—from the beginning of the fight for independence in 1810 to the start of the Mexican Revolution in 1910. These colorful, larger-than-life murals tackle such varied themes as the horror of the slave trade, the early-20th-century class struggle, and the legendary Aztec priest-king Quetzalcóatl. At times, his murals look like an illustrated *Who's Who?* of famous people. Look for his famous wife, Frida Kahlo, hidden in the frescoes. Guides to the murals wait at the central staircase trying to charge exorbitant fees.

The *palacio* also contains the **Bell of Dolores,** which was brought to the capital in 1896 from Dolores Hidalgo (see p. 413). It can be seen from outside, at the top of the *palacio's* Baroque facade. Miguel Hidalgo rang this bell on September 16, 1810, summoning Mexicans to fight for their independence. Every year on that date it rings in memory of the occasion, and the Mexican president repeats the words once shouted by the father of independence. On the east side of the *palacio's* second floor is the **Museo del Recinto del Parliamento,** dedicated to the one and only Benito Juárez.

Catedral Metropolitana

Tel. 521 76 37. On the north side of the zócalo. ***Open*** *daily 10am-6pm. Exact schedules posted on the westernmost door.*

In the wake of Cortés's military triumphs, a land devoted to Quetzalcóatl, Tlaloc, and Huitzilopochtli became a stronghold of Christianity. The third cathedral built in New Spain was the **Catedral Metropolitana**, a mishmash of architectural styles from three different centuries that somehow turned out beautifully. Construction started in 1562 but wasn't completed until 1813. Modeled after the cathedral in Sevilla, Spain, its scalloped walls and high arches give it a Moorish feel. Overwhelmingly gold altars maintain the Baroque influence. Unfortunately, the splendor of the cathedral is occluded by the green support structures placed to combat the ongoing floor damage—the temple, along with the rest of the city, is sinking into the murky ground. Ongoing renovations mean scaffolding and partitions occasionally obscure parts of both the exterior and the interior. If you use your imagination and block out the ugly green and yellow supports, the cathedral still glows. Attached to it are several annexes. The main one, with its door to the left of the cathedral, holds the **Altar de Perdón** (Forgiveness), a replica of a Churrigueresque altarpiece built by Jerónimo de Balbás between 1731 and 1736, and destroyed by fire in 1967. The cedar interior of the choir gallery, constructed in 1695 by Juan de Rojas, boasts an elegant grille of gold, silver, and bronze, and Juan Correa's murals of dragon-slaying and prophet-hailing cover the sacristy walls. Perhaps the most magnificent part of the cathedral is the **Altar de los Reyes,** dedicated to those kings who were also saints—not a common occurrence. Two chapels near the entrance honor Mexico's patron, the Virgin of Guadalupe (also honored in the **Basilica de Guadalupe,** see p. 110). Mass takes place almost hourly on weekends; visitors should take extra care to show respect and be silent during these times.

Templo Mayor (Teocalli)

Tel. 542 47 84 or 542 06 06. On the corner of Seminario and República de Guatemala. Just east of the cathedral and north of the Palacio Nacional. ***Museum and ruins open*** *Tu-Su 9am-5pm.* ***Guided tours*** *in Spanish free, in English 10 pesos per person.* ***Admission*** *16 pesos, free for children under 13, for Mexican students, and for all on Sundays. 10 pesos for camera permit, 30 pesos for video permit.*

According to myth, Tenochtitlán was the first place that the Aztecs, having wandered for hundreds of years, could call home; when they arrived at this spot, they saw, as the war god Huitzilopochtli had predicted, an eagle perched on a cactus eating a snake (see the Mexican flag and p. 45). **Teocalli** is now an astonishingly huge excavated archaeological site in the middle of the world's largest city. Although work was initiated at the beginning of this century, the excavation was completed only in 1982. At first, the site appears to be little more than the foundation of a demolished modern complex. Before making any judgments, however, have a look inside. The excavated ruins reveal five layers of pyramids, each one built on top of the others as the Aztec empire grew, topped off by structures added by the conquistadors to mark their domination. Over 7000 artifacts, including sculpture, jewelry, and pottery, have been found in the ruins. Highlights include the enormous flat, round sculpture of **Coyolxauhqui,** the moon goddess.

The extraordinary **Museo del Templo Mayor,** now part of the archaeological complex, houses this unique collection. A must-see stop even for visitors on a whirlwind tour of Mexico City, the museum is divided into eight *salas* that are meant to imitate the layout of the original temple, and the artifacts found in the excavation are accompanied not only by dry museum inscriptions (in Spanish) but also by excerpts from the ancient Aztec texts which describe them (also in Spanish).

South of the Zócalo

Built in 1929, the **Suprema Corte de Justicia** (tel. 522 15 00) stands on the corner of Pino Suárez and Corregidora, on the spot where the southern half of Moctezuma's royal palace once stood. *(Officially, murals can be viewed only 9am-noon or by appointment. Call M-F 10am-2pm to schedule a free visit; however, lucky visitors should be able to wheel and deal their way in any time of the day, provided a really big case is not being tried. Bring an ID to leave at the entrance.)* Aside from the spectacle of manacled foreigners pleading that they don't know who planted cannabis in their socks, the Supreme Court draws tourists because of its murals. Four frightening murals by José Clemente Orozco cover the second-floor walls of the present-day Supreme Court. Filled with roaring tigers, masked evildoers, bolts of hellish flame, and a thuggish Mr. Justice himself wielding a huge axe, the murals are not to be missed. If nothing else, they'll make you think twice about breaking the law.

The **Museo de la Ciudad de México,** Pino Suárez 30 (tel. 542 00 83), at República del Salvador, three blocks south of the *zócalo's* southeast corner, features a random assortment of modern Mexican art and temporary exhibits focusing on the city's colonial history. *(Museum and store open Tu-Su 10am-6pm; free. Free guided tours are also available by appointment.)* The spacious courtyard is a good place to rest, and the store has excellent information not only on the city, but on all of Mexico.

Southwest of the *zócalo*, near the Isabel la Católica Metro stop, two wonderfully quirky museums await. The **Museo del Claustro de Sor Juana** (tel. 709 59 89), on José Maria Izagaza, between Isabel la Católica and 5 de Febrero, is located at the very spot where, as a plaque states, this "most illustrious poetess, literate, and philosopher of Hispano-American thought" actually lived and worked. *(Open Tu-Su 10am-5pm; free.)* The buildings are used today primarily as a private university, but the small chapel holding Sor Juana's remains can be visited, as can several rooms inside the Gran Claustro. No plaques in the museum tell the story of this outstanding 17th-century woman who dressed as a man for several years in order to attend university classes. Sor Juana entered the convent in order to escape marriage. There, she produced some of Latin America's most famous and most beautiful literature. Just across the street from the Claustro, at the corner of Izagaza and Isabel la Católica, is the **Museo de la Charreria.** *(Open M-F 10:30am-7pm; free.)* Amid a wild collection of saddles, spurs, and ropes, a series of out-of-order panels proudly explain in Spanish, English, and French, the development of *charreria* (being-a-cowboy; rodeoing) and its ultimate incarnation as Mexico's national sport. Learn how quintessentially Mexican the cowboy, his clothes, and his sport are as you marvel at tons of artifacts.

ALAMEDA

The area around the Alameda Central is doubly blessed, filled with must-see sights and easily accessible by public transportation. It's within walking distance of the *centro* and the Monumento a la Revolución, and—bonus—it has the best crafts market in the city, **La Ciudadela** (see p. 123). Near the park are three Metro stations: Hidalgo (Lines 2 and 3), at the intersection of Hidalgo and Paseo de la Reforma, one block west from the park; Bellas Artes (Lines 2 and 8), one block east of the park's northeast corner, between the park and Bellas Artes itself; and San Juan de Letrán (Line 8), one block south of the **Torre Latinoamericana.**

Alameda Central

Amid the howling sprawl that is downtown Mexico City, the Alameda is an oasis of sanity and photosynthesis. But while the Alameda can feel like an island, it is not impervious to the urban life that bustles around it—three major thoroughfares (Avenidas Hidalgo, Juárez, and Lázaro Cárdenas) flank the Alameda, and the park is packed with mimes, young lovers, protesters, and *comerciantes* selling their trinkets. The Alameda was originally an Aztec marketplace and then the site at which heretics were burnt at the stake under the Inquisition; it was finally turned into a park in 1592 by Don Luis de Velasco II, who intended it to be a place where the city's elite could meander peacefully. Enlarged in 1769 to its actual size, the park was repaired after the 1985 earthquake, and in 1997 the sidewalks were restored by the city government. The park takes its name from the rows of shady *alamos* (poplars) that flood it. Since it was opened to the public in this century, Mexico City has fallen in love with the park; Mexicans of all sorts enjoy the Alameda, and even in a city with soaring real-estate prices and over-crowding, no one ever considers paving over the park.

At the center of the Alameda's southern side is the **Monumento a Juárez,** a semicircular marble monument constructed in 1910 to honor the revered former president on the 100th anniversary of Mexican Independence. A somber-faced Benito Juárez sits on a central pedestal among 12 doric columns. On July 19 of each year, a civic ceremony commemorates the anniversary of Juárez's death.

Palacio de Bellas Artes

Located at Juárez and Eje Central, at the northeast corner of Alameda Central complex. **Open** *Tu-Su 10am-6pm.* **Admission** *15 pesos to see the murals and art exhibits on the upper floors, free for students and teachers with ID. Temporary exhibits on the first floor are generally free for all.*

This impressive Art Nouveau palace is perhaps one of the most obvious (and one of the only) beautiful things to come out of Porfirio Díaz's dictatorship (1876-1911; see **The Porfiriato,** p. 53). Soon after construction began in 1900, the theater started to sink into the city's soft ground—it now sits many meters lower than when it was built. Most tourists, however, come to the palace to see the second and third floors, where the walls have been painted by the most celebrated Mexican muralists of the 20th century. If you have time for only one mural, see Diego Rivera's, on the west wall of the third floor. John D. Rockefeller commissioned Rivera to paint a mural depicting the topic "Man at Crossroads Looking with Hope and High Vision to the Choosing of a New and Better Future" in New York City's Rockefeller Center. Rivera, however, was dismissed from the project when Rockefeller discovered Lenin's portrait in the foreground. The Mexican government allowed Rivera to duplicate the work in the *palacio.* The result, **El Hombre, Controlador del Universo, 1934,** includes an unflattering portrayal of John D. Rockefeller looking like a mad scientist, his hands on various technological instruments designed to rule the world. The second floor also has a permanent collection of less-well-known pieces by Rivera, Kahlo, Tamayo, and others, as well as space for temporary exhibits by well-known artists.

On the east wall of the third floor, murals by the leftist José Clemente Orozco depict the supposed tension between natural human characteristics and industrialization. In addition to Orozco's work, the *palacio* displays the frescoes of David Alfaro Siqueiros, the 20th-century Mexican muralist, Stalinist, nationalist, and would-be assassin of Leon Trotsky. Look for his work on the third floor. Like his contemporary Diego Rivera, Siqueiros favored overt themes of class struggle and social injustice; he flaunted a cavalier disregard for topical subtlety. His *Tormento de Cuauhtémoc* describes Cortés's attack on the last vestiges of the Aztec nation.

On the fourth floor of the palace is the **Museo Nacional de Arquitectura** (tel. 709 31 11). It exhibits early sketches and blueprints for the most architecturally distinctive buildings in the city, including the Teatro Nacional, and the *palacio* itself.

The **Ballet Folklórico de México** performs regional dances in the Palacio de Bellas Artes and in the **Teatro Ferrocarrilero** (tel. 529 17 01), near the Revolución Metro station. *(Dance performances W 8:30pm, Su 9:30am and 8:30pm. Tickets 140-250 pesos.*

Sold 3 or 4 days in advance at Bellas Artes.) Their two companies, one resident and one traveling, are world-renowned for their choreographic and theatrical skill. Their program combines folk and *indígena* dancing with the formal aspects of traditional ballet. Bellas Artes performances are the only way to see the crystal curtain designed by Gerardo Murelli, made up of almost one million pieces of multicolored crystal which, when illuminated from behind, represent the Valley of Mexico at twilight. The Bellas Artes **ticket office** sells tickets for these and other artistic performances throughout the city (open daily 11am-7pm). An **information booth** (tel. 521 92 51 ext. 132 and 217), up the first set of stairs next to the ticket booth, has information on all performances in Mexico City, and the staff speaks some English (open daily 11am-7pm). Travel agencies snatch up a lot of tickets during Christmas, *Semana Santa,* and summer; check first at Bellas Artes, then try along Reforma or in the *Zona Rosa*.

Museo Nacional de Arte

Tacuba 8. Tel. 512 32 24. Half a block east of the palacio's north side. ***Open*** *Tu-Su 10am-5:30pm.* ***Admission*** *15 pesos, free for students and teachers with ID, adults over 60, children under 13, and for all on Sundays. Camera permits 5 pesos.*

The **Museo Nacional de Arte,** half a block east of the *palacio*'s north side, was built during the Porfiriato to house the Secretary of Communications. In 1982, it was inaugurated as a museum. The building's architect, Silvio Conti, paid particular attention to the central staircase—its sculpted Baroque handrails were crafted by artists in Florence. The museum is not as frequented as the *palacio* or other nearby *museos,* despite its enormity. Because of this and its spacious design, the museum has an empty feel; footsteps echo through the galleries. The museum contains works from the stylistic and ideological schools of every era in Mexican history. Look for Guerra's *Monumento a José Martí,* a celebration not only of the young revolutionary's life, but also of color and space. Check the list of *salas* downstairs for current exhibits. With everything from *arte deco* (art deco) to *retrato popular del siglo XIX* (popular portraits of the 19th century), there's at least one *sala* that's right for you.

NEAR ALAMEDA CENTRAL

Museo Mural Diego Rivera

Tel. 510 23 29; fax 512 07 54. On Calzada Colón and Balderas, facing the small park at the west end of the Alameda. ***Open*** *daily 10am-6pm.* ***Admission*** *10 pesos; free on Sundays and for Mexican national students and teachers with ID.*

Also known as **Museo de la Alameda,** this fascinating building holds Diego Rivera's masterpiece, **Sueño de un Tarde Dominical en la Alameda Central** (Sunday Afternoon Dream at the Alameda Central). The work was originally commissioned by the Hotel del Prado in 1946, but when the hotel proudly hung the just-finished work in 1948, a national controversy ensued over the figure of Ignacio Ramírez, who is shown holding up a pad of paper that reads "God does not exist," an excerpt from a speech he gave in 1836. The archbishop of Mexico refused to bless the hotel, and on June 4th at dawn, more than 100 angry students broke into the hotel, erased the "does not exist" fragment from the original phrase, and damaged the face of the young Diego Rivera in the center of the mural. After the 1985 quake, the mural was moved to the museum, which was constructed solely to showcase this piece. The key in front of the mural points out the portrayal of historical figures woven into the crowd: Frida Kahlo, José Martí, and a chubby young Rivera, among others. José Guadalupe Posada's *La Calavera Catrina,* the central figure in the mural (the smiling skeleton wearing the boa), mocks the aristocratic pretentions under the Díaz presidency. Along with the mural, the museum displays original clippings of 1948 describing the vandalism. It also has Rivera's original notes regarding plans for the reconstruction, as well as extensive information (in Spanish) on Rivera's life and the cultural scene of the time. Changing exhibits upstairs also relate to Rivera's life and work.

West of the Alameda

The poet José Martí was a leader of the Cuban independence movement in the late 19th century. He dreamed of a united and free Latin America, led by Mexico, and he repeatedly warned of the dangers of North American imperialism. Martí's visionary poetry figures prominently at the **Centro Cultural José Martí,** Dr. Mora 2 (tel. 518 14 96), at Hidalgo, on the Alameda's west end. *(Open M-F 9am-9pm, Sa 9am-3pm; free.)* Covering three walls of the building is a rainbow-colored mural depicting Martí's poetry as well as Martí himself and the people of Latin America. A tally sheet in the corner of the mural records Spanish, British, French, and U.S. interventions in Latin America from 1800 to 1969; the grand total is a staggering 784. Temporary exhibits on Cuba share the space. Movies and other cultural events take place in the adjoining theater. Stop by or call the Centro Cultural to see what's on the program.

The **Pinacoteca Virreinal de San Diego,** Dr. Mora 7 (tel. 510 27 93), next door to Centro Cultural José Martí, was constructed between 1591 and 1621. *(Open Tu-Su 9am-5pm. Admission 10 pesos, students with ID 5 pesos; free for all on Sundays.)* Once a church-cum-convent, the huge rooms with high, decorated ceilings and wooden floors now contain an extensive collection of Baroque and Mannerist paintings that are almost exclusively religious. Don't miss the almost endless spiral staircase leading up to a second floor balcony to the left of the entrance.

East of the Alameda

The second-tallest building in the city, the **Torre Latinoamericana,** 181m and 44 stories high, touches the sky over the corner of Lázaro Cárdenas and Madero (the continuation of Juárez), one block east of Alameda Central's southeast corner. *(Top-floor observatory open daily 9:30am-10:30pm. Admission 26 pesos, 20 pesos for children under 12. Telescope fee 5 pesos.)* Its 44th-floor observatory, 2422m above sea level, commands a startling view of the sprawling city on a clear day: all you can see in any direction is city, city, and more city. At night, the *torre* is positively sexy, with city lights sparkling for miles in every direction. The 38th floor holds the gimmicky and depressing **"highest aquarium in the world"** (open daily 10am-10pm; admission 18 pesos, children 15 pesos).

The first and largest Franciscan convent in Mexico City, **La Iglesia de San Francisco,** rests in the shadow of the Torre Latinoamericana, just to the east on Madero. *(Open M-F 9am-1pm and 5-7pm, Sa 9am-1pm.)* It was once a vast Franciscan complex that included several churches, a school, and a hospital built in the early 1500s and visited by Hernán Cortés. Two fragments of the original cloisters can be seen at Gante 5, on the east side of the church, and at Lázaro Cárdenas 8, behind a vacant lot. Holy water runs freely from a tap inside and is quickly put into bottles by locals.

Across the street from San Francisco shimmers the delicate **Casa de los Azulejos,** an early 17th-century building covered with *azulejos* (blue and white tiles) from Puebla. *(Both the Casa and Sanborn's open daily 7:30am-10pm.)* To be able to afford even a token few of these tiles was a mark of considerable status. This mansion was festooned by an insulted son who set out to prove his worth to his father. An Orozco mural is on the staircase wall; check out the great view of the building from the second-floor balcony. Go through **Sanborn's** (tel. 512 13 31) to view them.

Palacio Iturbide, Madero 17 (tel. 225 24 71), between Bolívar and Gante, one-and-a-half blocks east of Lázaro Cárdenas, near the Iglesia de San Francisco, is a grand 18th-century palace with an impressive colonnaded courtyard. *(Open daily 10am-7pm.)* A great place to chill, the *palacio,* in recent years, has been taken over by Banamex (Banco de México); before that it was the residence of Mexico's old Emperor, the despotic Agustín Iturbide. Symbolism, anyone? There is a gallery on the ground floor with exhibitions that change every three months.

North of the Alameda

In the small, sunken Plaza de Santa Veracruz, flanked by the beautifully aging facades of the churches of San Juan de Dios and Santa Veracruz, lies one of the loveliest sights in this area. The **Museo Franz Mayer,** Hidalgo 45 (tel. 518 22 65), was formerly the

Hospital de San Juan de Dios. *(Open Tu-Su 10am-5pm. Admission 15 pesos to the museum, 10 pesos to the cloister, 10 and 5 pesos for students with ID, free for all on Tuesdays. Guided tours Tu-F 10am-2pm, 10 pesos.)* The building has been expertly restored and now houses an extensive collection of ceramics, colonial furniture, and religious paintings. Plush red velvet, gleaming display cases, and an ultra-professional staff make wandering through the lavish display cases a joy. The old cloister of San Juan de Dios lies inside the first entrance to the left; its courtyard holds benches, trees, and a fountain, and its upper level holds more exhibits.

The **Museo Nacional de la Estampa,** Hidalgo 39 (tel. 521 22 44 or 510 49 05), is next door to the Franz Mayer museum, in the pretty pink building. *(Open Tu-Su 10am-6pm. Admission 10 pesos, free on Sundays and for students with ID.)* Here lies the National Institute of Fine Arts's graphic arts and engraving collection, tracing the art of printmaking from pre-Hispanic seals to contemporary engravings. The highlight of the museum is the work of the acclaimed José Guadalupe Posada, Mexico's foremost engraver and print-maker. His woodcuts depict skeletons dancing, singing, and cavorting in ridiculous costumes—a truly graphic indictment of the Porfiriato's excesses. Catch an excellent view of the Alameda from the second floor.

NEAR THE MONUMENTO A LA REVOLUCIÓN

Monumento a la Revolución and Museo Nacional de la Revolución

Tel. 546 21 15. At the Plaza de la República; you can't miss it. The museum is just northeast of the monument, in a blackstone park. ***Museum open*** *Tu-Sa 9am-5pm, Su 9am-3pm.* ***Admission*** *5 pesos, 2.50 pesos for students and teachers with ID. Call to arrange a tour.*

Díaz originally planned the site as the seat of Congress, but progress halted as revolutionary fighting entered the city streets, and the dome was left only half-completed. It wasn't until the 1930s that the monument and the space below were finally dedicated to the memory of the Revolution. Today, 32 flag poles representing the Mexican states line the pathway to this marmoreal dome. The entrance to the subterranean exhibition is just northeast of the monument. Inside the doors, a thorough chronology of the Revolution unfolds. Although everything is in Spanish, great collections of Revolutionary artifacts (cars, clothing, guns) will interest all. Temporary exhibits reach beyond the Revolution; they comment on and connect contemporary artistic expression and politics.

Other Museums

The relatively tourist-free **Museo del Chopo,** Dr. Enrique Gonzalez Marine 10, resides in a beautiful glass and steel building. *(Open Tu-Su 10am-2pm and 3-7pm. Admission 6 pesos, 2 pesos for students with ID, free on Tuesdays. Free guided visits Tu-F 10:30am, noon, 4:30, and 6pm.)* Just after Puente de Alvarado turns into San Cosme, turn right on Dr. Enrique Gonzalez Martinez—it's one block up on the left. The modern, friendly Chopo (as it's commonly called) displays the works of up-and-coming modern Mexican artists in every medium. Every mid-June to mid-July, for 12 years running, they have proudly hosted a show of uncensored gay and lesbian photography, sculpture, and painting—passionate pictures of pain and love.

The **Museo San Carlos** (tel. 566 85 22), at the corner of Puente de Alvarado and Ramos Arizpe, three blocks north of the Monumento a la Revolución, lets you feel as though you've gone to Spain instead of Mexico. *(Open M and W-Su 10am-6pm. Admission 10 pesos, students and teachers 5 pesos, free on Sundays.)* Housing an old art school and an impressive collection of European paintings spanning the 16th to 19th centuries, the eclectic museum features excellent work by minor artists, as well as standards by artists like Rubens and Goya. Temporary exhibits often highlight certain themes in post-Renaissance European art.

BOSQUE DE CHAPULTEPEC

Mexico City has to do everything a little bigger and better than everywhere else, and this, the D.F.'s major park and recreational area, is no exception. Literally "Forest of Grasshoppers," this 1000-acre green expanse on the western side of the *centro* is the biggest urban-situated park in all the Americas and one of the older natural parks in the New World. With its manifold museums, hiking paths, zoos, bikes, amusement parks, castles, balloon vendors, and modern sports facilities, one could easily spend several days in the Bosque. Mexico's most famous museum, the **Museo Nacional de Antropología,** sits among the hills of the park.

The area that is officially the Bosque is open only 5am to 5pm daily. During this time, it is fairly safe (as safe as anywhere in the city). Hordes of cleanup crews emerge at 5pm to ensure the Bosque will be bright and beautiful each morning. The areas north of Reforma near the Museo Nacional de Antropología are open 24 hours. They tend to be a little dirtier and, while full of happy families during the day, should be avoided after nightfall, especially by women. Helpful signs point you toward major sites, but the Bosque's myriad paths wind and curve without warning; keep a close watch on your bearings. Try to visit on Sunday, when families flock here for the cheap entertainment. Musical spectacles and open-air concerts enliven the park. Best of all, the zoo and all of the museums in the area are **free on Sundays.**

All the museums and sights listed are in Old Chapultepec, the eastern half of the park, which fans out to the west of the *Zona Rosa.* To reach the park, take the Metro to Auditorio (Line 7, closer to the **zoo**), to the more convenient Chapultepec (Line 1, closer to the **Niños Héroes** monument and the museums), or take any *pesero* going down Reforma to Auditorio or Chapultepec.

Museo Nacional de Antropología

Tel. 553 62 66. Paseo de la Reforma and Gandhi—you can't miss it. Take an auditorio pesero (2 pesos) southwest on Reforma and signal the driver to let you off at the second stop after entering the park. By Metro, take Line 7 to the Auditorio station; the museum is just east down Reforma. Take the first left on Gandhi for the main entrance. ***Museum open*** *Tu-Su 9am-7pm.* ***Admission*** *16 pesos, free for national students and teachers (try your luck with international student or teacher's card; they sometimes work), free for all on Sundays. Audio guides in Spanish 30 pesos, in English 36 pesos. Camera permits 10 pesos, video camera permits 30 pesos.*

Some journey to Mexico just to consult this magnificent and massive mega-museum, considered by many to be the best of its kind in the world. This mini-universe houses 4km of Mexico's most exquisite archaeological and ethnographic treasures; it's the yardstick by which all other Mexican museums are measured. Constructed of volcanic rock, wood, and marble, the museum opened in 1964. A huge stone image of the goggle-eyed rain god Tlaloc hails you outside, and 23 exhibition halls await within. Poems from ancient texts and epics grace the entrances from the main courtyard. In the center of the courtyard, a stout column covered with symbolic carvings supports a vast, water-spouting aluminum pavilion. Although guards may give you menacing looks, it is quite all right to run through this refreshing inverted fountain—as long as you don't look like you're going to stay and bathe.

You would need about three days to pay homage to the entire museum, though some visitors are afflicted with pottery overload after a few hours. As you enter on the right side of the ground floor, a general introduction to anthropology precedes a series of chronologically arranged galleries moving from the right to the left wings of the building. These trace the histories of many central Mexican groups, from the first migrations to the Americas up to the Spanish Conquest. Among the highlights not to be missed: the **Sala Teotihuacana,** with detailed models of the amazing city of Teotihuacán; the **Sala Toltec,** with huge statues of Quetzalcóatl; the museum's crown jewel, the **Sala Mexica,** with the dazzling and famous **Aztec Calendar Stone (Sun Stone),** featuring Tonatiuh, the Aztec god of the sun, tongue stuck out, and an enormous statue of Coatlicue ("the one with the skirt of snakes"), goddess of life and death; the **Sala Golfo de Mexico,** with colossal stone Olmec heads; and the **Sala Maya,** where you can descend into a model of the tomb of King Pacal. The museum also contains a **restaurant** (open Tu-Su 9am-6pm) and a large **bookshop** that sells English guides to archaeological sites around the country, as well as histories and ethnographies of Mexico's indigenous populations. Some of these guides are not available at the sites themselves, so plan ahead.

Museo Rufino Tamayo (Museo Arte Contemporáneo)

Tel. 286 65 19. Just to the east of the Museo Nacional de Antropología, on the corner of Reforma and Gandhi. Take the first right on Gandhi from the Chapultepec Metro stop (Line 1). After a five-minute walk on Gandhi, the museum lies to the left down a small, semi-hidden path through the trees. Alternatively, walk due east (straight ahead as you exit) from the entrance of the anthropology museum into the woods; Tamayo is 100m straight ahead. ***Open*** *Tu-Su 10am-5:45pm.* ***Admission*** *15 pesos, free on Sundays and for students and teachers with ID. Call to arrange guided tours.*

The Mexican government created the nine halls of the museum after Rufino and Olga Tamayo donated their international collection to the Mexican people. The murals of Rufino Tamayo were much criticized in the wake of the Revolution of 1910 for not being sufficiently nationalistic. Since the museum's opening in 1981, however, his reputation has been rehabilitated, and he has taken his place with Rivera, Siqueiros, and Orozco as one of the omnipresent bad boys of modern Mexican art. The museum, opened in 1981, houses a large permanent collection of Tamayo's work, as well as important works by Willem de Kooning and Surrealists Joan Miró and Max Ernst. Although some of the *salas* are currently closed for renovation, the museum is still stellar; featuring excellent exhibits by top international artists and filmmakers.

MEXICO CITY

Museo de Arte Moderno

Tel. 553 62 33. On Reforma and Gandhi, north of the Monumento a los Niños Héroes and on the opposite side of Reforma from the anthropology museum. ***Open*** *Tu-Su 10am-6pm.* ***Admission*** *15 pesos, free on Sundays and for students and teachers with ID.*

This wonderful museum houses a fine collection of contemporary paintings by Kahlo, including perhaps her most famous work: the exquisite **Las Dos Fridas.** Works by Siqueiros, José Luis Cuevas, Rivera, Orozco, Velasco, Angelina Beloff (supposedly a lover of Rivera's), and Remedios Varo (the only well-known female Spanish surrealist painter) are also on display. Temporary exhibits feature other up-and-coming, extremely talented Mexican artists. The museum is linked to **Galería Fernando Camboa,** a remarkable outdoor sculpture garden with pieces by Moore, Giacometti, and others.

Museo Nacional de Historia

Tel. 286 99 20. Inside the Castillo de Chapultepec, on top of the hill behind the Monumento a los Niños Héroes. To get to the top, walk up (way up) the road directly behind the Niños Héroes monument and be prepared to open your bag for the guard. ***Open*** *Tu-Su 9am-5pm; tickets sold until 4pm.* ***Admission*** *14 pesos, free on Sundays, but all second-floor salas are closed Sundays. Camera permit 5 pesos; video permit 15 pesos.*

This fascinating museum lives up to its name; it exhaustively narrates the history of Mexico from before the time of the Conquest. An immense portrait of King Ferdinand and Queen Isabella of Spain greets visitors in the first *sala* before they meander through the excellent exhibits on the not-so-distant past. Galleries contain displays on Mexican economic and social structure during the war for independence, the Porfiriato, and the Revolution. The particularly interesting upper level exhibits Mexican art and dress from the viceroyalty through the 20th century. The walls of *Sala 13* are completely covered by Siqueiros's *Del Porfirismo a la Revolución,* a pictoral cheatsheet to modern Mexican history. Admission to the museum also allows you a peek at some of the castle's interior.

Museo del Caracol (Galeria de Historia)

Tel. 553 62 85. On the southern side of Chapultepec hill. On the road up to the castle, turn right just before the castle itself, at the sign. ***Open*** *daily 9am-5:30pm.* ***Admission*** *14 pesos, free on Sundays and for students and teachers with ID.*

The official name for this museum is **Museo Galería de la Lucha del Pueblo Mexicano por su Libertad** (Museum of the Struggle of the Mexican People for Liberty), but it's more commonly known as **Museo del Caracol (Snail Museum)** because of its spiral design. The gallery consists of 12 halls dedicated to the greatest hits of Mexican history from the early 19th to the early 20th century. A quotation at the entrance urges visiting Mexicans to live up to the legacy embodied in the museum. From the start of your downward spiral, the gist of the museum's message is clear: foreign intervention has made Mexico's fight for liberty an uphill battle. There are especially interesting exhibitions on the executions of Hidalgo and Morelos, the execution of Maximilian, and the battles of Villa, Zapata, and Obregón. A whole room is dedicated to "remembering the Alamo." The museum's exhibitions consist of amazingly life-like mini-dioramas, documentary videos, paintings, and various other historical artifacts. The staircase leads to a beautiful, round, skylit hall that holds a copy of the Constitution of 1917 handwritten by Venustiano Carranza himself. Visitors less familiar with the contours of Mexican history, however, will be bewildered by the Spanish-only explanations written next to each piece. Spanish also blares from speakers in each room; visitors are treated to an annoying audio tour complete with mini-dramatizations.

Elsewhere in Chapultepec

At the end of the long walkway just inside the park on the east side stands the **Monumento a los Niños Héroes,** six white pillars capped with monoliths and teased by small fountains. The monument is dedicated to the young cadets of the 19th-century military academy, now known as the **Castillo de Chapultepec.** In 1847, during the last major battle of the war with the U.S., the Niños Héroes fought the invading army of General Winfield Scott. Refusing to surrender, the last five boys and their lieutenant are said to have wrapped themselves in the Mexican flag before throwing themselves from the castle wall. To the side of the monument is the **Tree of Moctezuma,** boasting a circumference of 13m and reputed to have been around since the time of the Aztecs. Behind the monument, Av. Gran cuts through the park. Walk west on this street and take the second right on Gandhi. A five-minute stroll north takes you to Reforma and the Museo Nacional de Antropología. On weekends, indigenous groups perform traditional dances in front of the museum and welcome donations.

Twenty-five days before his death in January 1974, famed fanatic, muralist, and would-be Trotsky assassin David Álfaro Siqueiros donated his house and studio to the people of Mexico. In compliance with his will, the government created the **Museo Sala de Arte Público David Alfaro Siquieros,** Tres Picos 29 (tel. 531 33 94), at Hegel, just outside the park. *(Open Tu-F 10am-2pm, Sa-Su 10am-2pm. Admission 10 pesos, free for students with ID and free on Sundays. Call to arrange a guided tour.)* Walk north from the Museo Nacional de Antropología to Rubén Darío. The street Tres Picos forks off to the northwest on the left; follow it for one block. The quirky little museum is on the right. Siqueiros was not only an artist, but also a revolutionary soldier, propagandist, communist, republican, Stalinist, and anti-fascist. Fifteen thousand murals, lithographs, photographs, drawings, and documents recount his fascinating life.

West of the Siqueiros museum, up Reforma past the Auditorio metro station, is the **Jardín de la Tercera Edad,** reserved for visitors over age 50. It contains the **Jardín Escultórico,** a sculpture park full of realist and symbolist statues, as well as the **Jardín Botánico,** a botanical garden with a little lake (botanical garden open daily 9am-5pm; free). The big lake is the **Lago de Chapultepec,** situated at the heart of the park; it has rowboats for rent that fit up to five people (rowboat rentals open daily 7:30am-4:30pm; 6 pesos per hr.). The **Parque Zoológico de Chapultepec** (tel. 553 62 63) is accessible from the entrance on Reforma, east of Calzado Chivatitio. *(Open Tu-Su 9am-4:30pm; free.)* When you exit the Auditorio Metro Station, it is in the opposite direction from the National Auditorium. Signs throughout the *parque* also point you in the right direction. Although animal lovers might shed a tear or two over some of the humbler habitats, the zoo is surprisingly excellent, mostly shunning the small-cage approach for larger, more amenable tracts of land. Everyone's favorites—those huggable **panda bears**—have survived quite well here.

TLATELOLCO

Tlatelolco lies north of the *centro.* To get to Tlatelolco, take the Metro to the Tlatelolco stop (Line 3) and exit through the Gonzalez *salida.* From the exit, turn right on Gonzalez, walk three blocks east until you reach Cárdenas (Eje 2 Norte), cross the street here and then turn right to follow it one long block up. The plaza will be on your left. Archaeological work has shown that the city of **Tlatelolço** ("Mound of Sand" in Náhuatl) existed long before the great Aztec capital of Tenochtitlán. By 1463, the Tlatelolco king, Moquíhuix, had built his city into a busy trading center coveted by the Aztec ruler, Axayácatl. Tension mounted over territorial and fishing boundaries, and soon Moquíhuix learned that the Aztecs were preparing to attack his city. Even forewarned, Moquíhuix couldn't handle the Aztec war machine, and Tlatelolco was absorbed into the huge empire.

Today, a monstrous state low-income housing project looms over the 17th-century church that stands on the grounds of Tlatelolco's ancient temple. Three cultures—ancient Aztec, colonial Spanish, and modern Mexican—have left their mark on this square, giving rise to the name **Plaza de las Tres Culturas,** at the corner of Lázaro Cárdenas and Ricardo Flores Magón, 13 blocks north of the Palacio de Bellas Artes. Today the three "cultures" are emblematized by ancient ruins, a mammoth church, and the nearby ultra-modern Ministry of Foreign Affairs, also known as the **Relaciones Exteriores** building. With stoic optimism, a plaque in the southwest corner of the plaza asserts: "On August 13, 1521, heroically defended by Cuauhtémoc, Tlatelolco fell to Hernán Cortés. It was neither a triumph nor a defeat, but the birth of the *mestizo* city that is the México of today." That battle marked the last serious armed resistance to the *conquista.*

More than 400 years later, the plaza witnessed another gruesome and bloody event, for which it is, sadly enough, most famous: the **Tlatelolco Massacre** of October 2, 1968. An adolescent rivalry between two secondary schools led to fighting in the streets; with the Mexico City Olympic games just a few months away, the government thought it necessary to quell all disturbances forcefully. Fueled by anger at the government's violence and at President Díaz Ordaz's militant anti-protest laws (as well as the city's debt incursion for the upcoming summer Olympics), the street fighting gave way to protests, which were answered with even more violence—in September the national university was occupied by soldiers. On October 2, a silent pro-peace sit-in was held at the Plaza de Las Tres Culturas. Toward the end of the day, government troops descended on the plaza, shooting and killing hundreds of protesters; prisoners were taken and tortured to death. In memory of the victims of the massacre, a **simple sandstone monument** was erected in the plaza and dedicated in 1993, on the 25th anniversary of the incident—before then, the government had repressed any mention of the event, going so far as to remove related newspaper articles from all national archives. The humble monument lists the names of the dead, and a small plaque on the back of the monolith explains that the present monument, already dirtied and defaced, is just temporary construction—a more fitting memorial will be built when more funds are collected. This may finally be about to happen; in the summer of 1998, PRD members of Congress proposed a reopening of the investigation of the army's actions on that fateful day.

In the plaza, parts of the **Pyramid of Tlatelolco** (also known as the **Templo Mayor**) and its ceremonial square remain dutifully well kept. Enter from the southwest corner, in front of the Iglesia de Santiago, and walk alongside the ruins, down a steel and concrete path that overlooks the eight building stages of the main pyramid. At the time of the Conquest, the base of the pyramid extended from Insurgentes to the Iglesia de Santiago. The pyramid was second in importance to the great Teocalli of the

Aztec capital, and its summit reached nearly as high as the skyscraper just to the south (the Relaciones Exteriores building). During the Spanish blockade of Tenochtitlán, the Aztecs heaved the freshly sacrificed bodies of Cortés's forces down the temple steps, within sight of the *conquistadores* camped to the west at Tacuba. Aztec priests collected the leftover body parts at the foot of the steps; food was scarce during the siege and all meat was valuable. Another notable structure is the **Templo Calendárico "M,"** an M-shaped building used by the Aztecs to keep time. Scores of skeletons were discovered near its base. A male and female pair that were found facing each other upon excavation have been dubbed "The Lovers of Tlatelolco."

On the east side of the plaza is the simple **Iglesia de Santiago,** an enormous, fortress-like church erected in 1609 to replace a structure built in 1543. *(Open daily 8am-1pm and 4-7pm.)* This church was designed to fit in with the surrounding ruins, and with its stonework and solid, plain masonry, it does.

LA BASÍLICA DE GUADALUPE

To get to the Villa de Guadalupe, take the Metro to La Villa Basílica (Line 6), go past the vendor stands, and take a right on Calzada de Guadalupe. A small raised walkway between the two lanes of traffic leads directly to the Basílica.

Ever since the legend of Juan Diego and his mantle (see above), Our Lady of Guadalupe has since been the patron of Mexico, an icon of the nation's religious culture. Diego's mantle can be seen in **La Basílica de Guadalupe,** north of the city center. *(Open daily 5am-9pm.)* Designed by the venerated Pedro Ramírez Vásquez in the 1970s, the new basilica is an immense, aggressively modern structure. Although the flags from different cultures inside of the basilica make it feel more like the United Nations than a church, crowds of thousands flock daily to the Virgin's miraculous likeness. The devout and the curious alike throng around the central altar and impressive organ to step onto the **basilica's moving sidewalk**—it allows for easier (and faster) viewing of Diego's holy cloak. On December 12th, the Virgin's name day, pilgrims from throughout the country march on their knees up to the altar. Perhaps the most striking feature of the basilica is the set of huge, haunting words written in gold Byzantine script across the top of the edifice: *"¿Aqui no estoy yo que soy tu madre?"* ("Am I not here, I who am your mother?").

Next to the new basilica is the **old basilica,** built at the end of the 17th century. These days, the old basilica houses the **Museo de la Basílica de Guadalupe,** Plaza Hidalgo 1 (tel. 781 68 10), in the Villa de Guadalupe. *(Open Tu-Su 10am-6pm. Admission*

The Dark Virgin

Probably the most important figure in Mexican Catholicism is the **Virgen de Guadalupe.** She first appeared as a vision on a hill to the *indígena* peasant Juan Diego in December 1531. When Juan Diego informed the bishop of his vision, the clergyman was dubious. Juan Diego returned to the hill and had another vision of the Virgin; she told him that on the hill he would find a great variety of roses (in December!) that he should gather and bring to the bishop as proof. The Virgin also instructed Juan Diego to build her a shrine at that very spot. Juan Diego gathered the roses in his cloak, and when he let them fall at the feet of the bishop, an **image of the Virgin** remained emblazoned on the cloak. The bishop was convinced, and the shrine was built.

The image was of a woman with brown skin, an *indígena.* She quickly became a symbol of religious fusion between the *indígenas* and Christians for the people of Mexico. Depictions of La Virgen of Guadalupe have maintained her dark skin and indigenous features, and she is often referred to proudly as the **Dark Virgin.** A plaque on the Old Basílica of Guadalupe in Mexico City commemorating her words to Juan Diego sums up her enormous importance. It reads: "I am the eternal Virgin Mary, mother of the true God, author of life, creator of all...I ardently desire that here a temple to me be raised...I will show you my clemency and the compassion I have for all natural things and for those who love and seek me."

3 pesos.) This gorgeous, lavish museum makes you wonder why they built the new, ungainly basilica. The colonial paintings dedicated to the Virgin pale beside the intensely emotional collection of *ex votos* (small paintings made by the devout to express their thanks to the Virgin of Guadalupe for coming to their assistance) in the entryway. A room at the base of the staircase contains a pair of golden *fútbol* shoes offered to the Virgin before the 1994 World Cup by the Mexican star Hugo Sánchez.

Behind the basilica, winding steps lead up the side of a small hill, past lush gardens, crowds of the faithful, and cascading waterfalls. A small chapel dedicated to the Virgin of Guadalupe, the **Panteón del Tepeyac,** sits on top of the hill. The bronze and polished wood interior of the chapel depicts the apparitions witnessed by Juan Diego. Upon entering, one can stop in front of a priest to be blessed with holy water. From the steps beside the church, one can absorb a breathtaking panoramic view of the city framed by the hillsides and distant mountains. Descending the other side of the hill, past the spouting gargoyles, statues of Juan Diego and a group of *indígenas* kneel before a gleaming Virgin doused with the spray from a rushing waterfall. Vendors, both in and around the basilica's grounds, hawk religious paraphernalia: holy water, holy shoes, holy T-shirts, holy jeans, and more.

COYOACÁN

To reach Coyoacán from downtown, take the Metro directly to the Coyoacán station (Line 3). Taxis cost about 10 pesos. It's also a pleasant walk.

The Toltecs founded **Coyoacán** (Place of the Skinny Coyotes, in Náhuatl) between the 10th and 12th centuries. Cortés later established the seat of the colonial government here, and, after the fall of Tlatelolco, had Cuauhtémoc tortured; he hoped the Aztec leader would reveal the hiding place of the legendary Aztec treasure. Although no longer a refuge for the aforementioned "skinny coyotes," it is a haven for "English-speaking tourists." South of the center, wealthy Coyoacán today is the city's most attractive suburb. Well-maintained and peaceful, it is worth visiting for its museums or simply for a stroll in beautiful **Plaza Hidalgo,** neighboring **Jardín Centenario,** or nearby **Placita de la Conchita.** Come to Coyoacán for a respite from the hurried *centro;* the pace is slower and life a little easier here. Coyoacán is centered around the Plaza Hidalgo, which is bounded by the cathedral and the Casa de Cortés. The two parks are split by Calle Carrillo Puerto, which runs north-south just west of the church.

Coyoacán's center of **tourist info** (tel. 659 22 56 ext. 181) is found in the **Casa de Cortés,** the big red building on the north side of Plaza Hidalgo. *(Open daily 8am-8pm.)* From here, **free guided tours of Coyoacán** leave whenever a few people gather. On Saturday mornings from 8am to noon, **free tours** of various other areas also leave from here. Originally Cortés's administrative building, the *casa* now houses the municipal government. Inside are murals by local artist Diego Rosales, a student of Diego Rivera's, showing scenes from the Conquest.

Museo Frida Kahlo

Londres 247. Tel. 554 59 99. On Allende, five blocks north of Plaza Hidalgo's northeast corner, in the colorful indigo and red building at the northeast corner of the intersection. ***Open*** *Tu-Su 10am-6pm.* ***Admission*** *10 pesos, Mexican students and teachers with ID 5 pesos.*

Perhaps Coyoacán's most wonderful and moving sight is the **Museo Frida Kahlo.** Works by Rivera, Orozco, Duchamp, and Klee hang in this restored colonial house, the birthplace and home of Frida Kahlo (1907-1954). Kahlo's disturbingly exquisite work and traumatic life story have been growing in international renown since Andre Breton proclaimed her a surrealist during one of his visits to Mexico. She was impaled by a post during a trolley accident when she was a teenager, suffered innumerable complications, and was confined to a wheelchair and bed for most of her life. She married Diego Rivera twice, and became a celebrated artist in her own right. Kahlo was notorious for her numerous affairs, most famously with Leon Trotsky. Those looking for loads of her work will be disappointed (only a few paintings and early

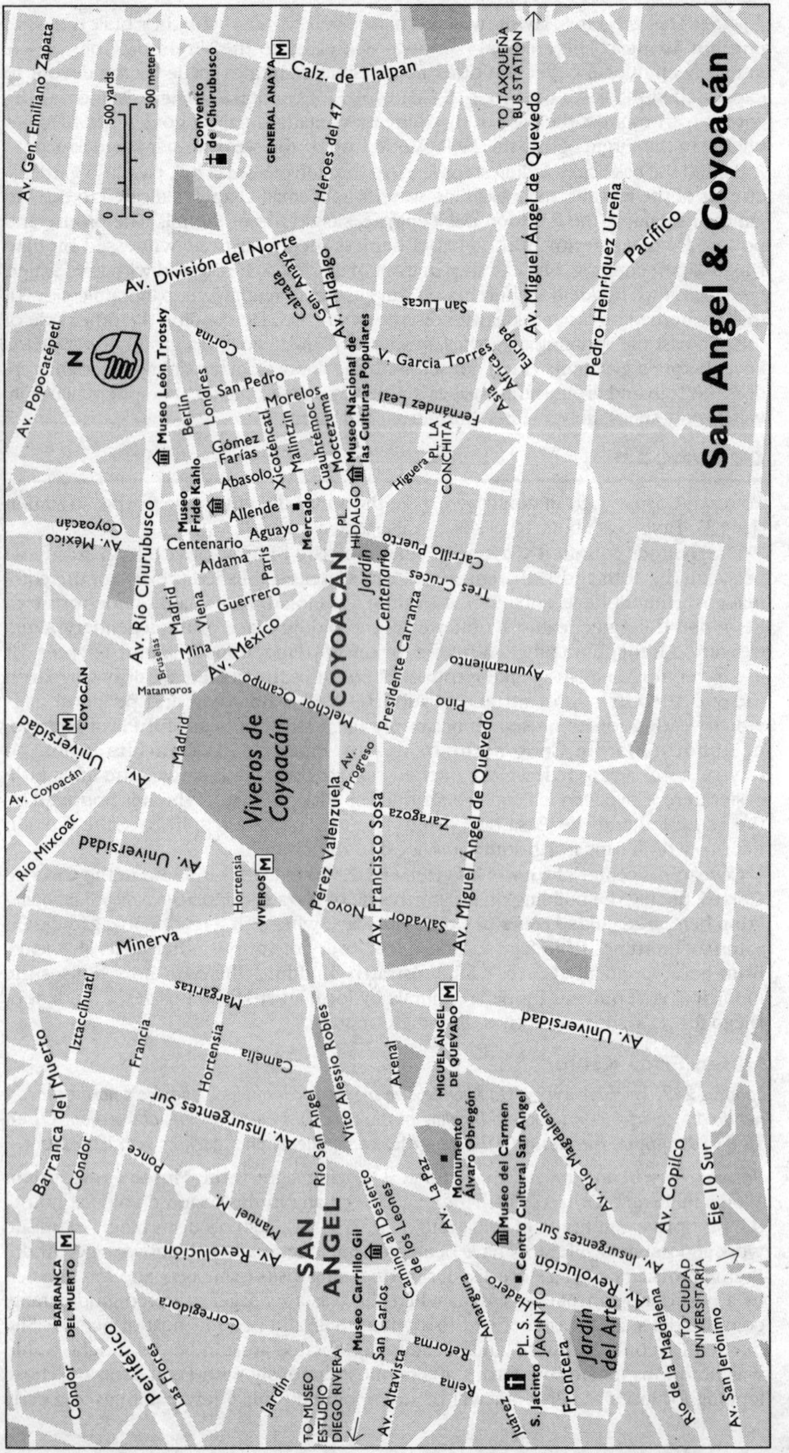
San Angel & Coyoacán
500 yards
500 meters
0
0
N
Av. Gen. Emiliano Zapata
Convento de Churubusco
GENERAL ANAYA
Calz. de Tlalpan
Héroes del 47
TO TAXQUEÑA BUS STATION
Av. Miguel Ángel de Quevedo
Pedro Henríquez Ureña
Pacífico
Av. División del Norte
Calzada
Gen. Anaya
Av. Hidalgo
San Lucas
Av. Popocatépetl
Corina
Museo León Trotsky
Berlín
Londres
San Pedro
V. Garcia Torres
Europa
Africa
Asia
Fernández Leal
Morelos
Gómez Farías
Malintzin
Xicoténcatl
Cuauhtémoc
Moctezuma
Museo Nacional de las Culturas Populares
PL. LA CONCHITA
Higuera
Abasolo
Museo Fride Kahlo
Allende
Mercado
PL. HIDALGO
Av. México Coyoacán
Av. Río Churubusco
Centenario
Aguayo
Aldama
París
Jardín Centenario
Carrillo Puerto
Tres Cruces
Madrid
Viena
Guerrero
COYOACÁN
Presidente Carranza
Bruselas
Mina
Av. México
Ayuntamiento
Matamoros
Melchor Ocampo
Pino
COYOCÁN
Av. Universidad
Viveros de Coyoacán
Av. Coyoacán
Av. Progreso
Pérez Valenzuela
Zaragoza
Río Mixcoac
Av. Universidad
Hortensia
VIVEROS
Novo
Av. Francisco Sosa
Salvador
Av. Miguel Ángel de Quevedo
Minerva
Margaritas
MIGUEL ANGEL DE QUEVEDO
Av. Universidad
Iztaccíhuatl
Francia
Hortensia
Camelia
Vito Alessio Robles
Arenal
Barranca del Muerto
Cóndor
Av. Insurgentes Sur
Río San Angel
Monumento Álvaro Obregón
Museo del Carmen
Centro Cultural San Angel
Av. Río Magdalena
Ponce
Manuel M.
SAN ANGEL
Camino al Desierto de los Leones
Av. La Paz
Av. Insurgentes Sur
Av. Copilco
Eje 10 Sur
BARRANCA DEL MUERTO
Av. Revolución
Museo Carrillo Gil
Amargura
Hadero
Av. Revolución
Av. Insurgentes Sur
TO CIUDAD UNIVERSITARIA
Corregidora
Periférico
Las Flores
Cóndor
Jardín
TO MUSEO ESTUDIO DIEGO RIVERA
San Carlos
Av. Altavista
Reforma
Reina
PL. S. JACINTO
S. Jacinto
Juárez
Frontera
Jardín del Arte
Río de la Magdalena
Av. San Jerónimo

sketches are around), but the museum still has much to offer. Wandering through the house is an emotionally wrenching experience: witness the bed on which Frida suffered, the words "Diego" and "Frida" lovingly scrawled on the kitchen wall, and Diego's painting of his "little girl" Frida hanging next to sultry portraits of various women (many of whom were his lovers). Those looking for insight into Kahlo's morbid work will find it in this house, full of reminders about her chronic health problems and her obsession with adultery. Read (or have someone translate) the excerpts of her diary and her letters hanging on the walls. They eloquently and intimately explain her childhood dreams and the inspiration for some of her work. The house also hides a gorgeous garden full of flowering lilies and hidden pre-Hispanic artifacts.

Museo y Casa de Leon Trotsky

Río Churubusco 410. Tel. 658 87 32. Continue north on Allende toward the highway and make a right on Viena. The entrance is around back. **Open** *Tu-Su 10am-5pm.* **Admission** *10 pesos, students with ID 5 pesos.*

After Leon Trotsky was expelled from the USSR by Stalin in 1927, he wandered in exile until Mexico's president Lázaro Cárdenas granted him political asylum at the suggestion of Trotsky's friends, muralist Diego Rivera and his wife Frida Kahlo. Trotsky arrived in 1937 with his wife and first lived in the "Casa Hazel," now the Museo Frida Kahlo (see above). A falling out with Rivera in 1939 led the Trotskys to relocate to the house on Curubusco. Bunny rabbits nibble peacefully in the gardens while bullet holes riddle the interior walls—relics of an attack on Trotsky's life led by the Stalinist muralist David Alfaro Siqueiros on May 24, 1940. Perhaps because this self-proclaimed "man of the people" living in a posh house in a posh suburb feared Stalinist wrath, Trotsky had **bullet-proof bathroom doors** created. Apparently, this paranoia wasn't enough; Trotsky was eventually assassinated by a Spanish Communist posing as a Belgian journalist-in-search-of-a-mentor who buried an axe in his skull. For more juicy details on Trotsky's life and work, Jesús the English-speaking goth tour guide and the kitty he saved from the street will be happy to accommodate you.

Other Sights

South of the plaza is the 16th-century **Parroquia de San Juan Bautista,** bordered by Plaza Hidalgo on the north and Jardín Centenario on the west. *(Open Tu-Sa 5:30am-8:30pm, M 5:30am-7:30pm.)* The church interior is elaborately decorated with gold and bronze. Enter south of the church's main door.

A few blocks southeast of Plaza Hidalgo, facing the Placita de la Conchita and marked by the gardened plaza at the end of Higuera, is the **Casa Colorada,** Higuera 57, which Cortés built for La Malinche, his Aztec lover. When Cortés's wife arrived from Spain, she stayed here briefly with her husband, but soon disappeared without a trace. It is believed that Cortés murdered his spouse because of his passion for La Malinche (see p. 46), although he later gave her away as loot to another *conquistador.* The *casa* is now a private residence and cannot be visited.

Highly developed technology facilitates a visit to the **Museo Nacional de las Culturas Populares** (tel. 554 86 10), on Hidalgo between Allende and Abasolo, two blocks east of Plaza Hidalgo. *(Open Tu-Th 10am-6pm, F-Su 10am-8pm; free.)* Listen to hundreds of tunes, watch videos of dances, and, if you read Spanish, learn an overwhelming amount about instruments and rhythms from all over the country; the permanent exhibit deals with indigenous music. Temporary exhibits usually feature specific regions of the country or specific mediums of artistic expression.

The **Convento de Nuestra Señora de Los Angeles de Churubusco,** 20 de Agosto and General Anaya, was built in 1524 over the ruins of a pyramid dedicated to the Aztec war god Huitzilopochtli. To get to the convent and museum from Coyoacán, walk four blocks down Hidalgo and then follow Anaya as it branches left; it's four blocks farther to the convent grounds. The General Anaya Metro stop (Line 2) is only two blocks east of the convent along 20 de Agosto. The Gen. Anaya *pesero* goes from Plaza Hidalgo to the museum (2 pesos); the Sto. Domingo goes back. The present structure was built in 1668. The walls near the main gate are riddled with bullet holes from the U.S. invasion of Mexico in 1917. Commemorating Mexico's valiant defense and the many before is the **Museo Nacional de las Intervenciones** (tel. 604 06 99), inside the ex-convent. *(Museum open Tu-Su 9am-6pm. Admission 14 pesos, free on Sundays and for students and teachers with ID.)* This tremendous nationalistic homage to the Mexican military is set in one of the most serene and peaceful buildings in the D.F. The museum's halls cover four eras, from the late 18th century to 1917. A few rooms are also dedicated to exhibitions on North American expansionism and cruelty to *indígenas,* U.S. slavery and its significance for Mexico, and European imperialism. This excellent museum really makes its point: international "interference" (whether in peace or war) has done Mexico more harm than help.

The **Museo Anahuacalli** (tel. 617 43 10 or 617 37 97) is on Calle Museo. Designed by Diego Rivera with Aztec and Maya architectural motifs, the building is an exhibit in and of itself. *(Open Tu-Su 10am-2pm and 3-6pm; free.)* To reach the museum from Plaza Hidalgo or Churubusco, take a "Huipulco" or "Huayamilpa" *pesero* going south on Av. División del Nte. and get off at Calle Museo. You might want to ask the driver to point out the stop; it is not visible immediately. Turn right onto Museo, and soon you'll reach the place. It houses Rivera's huge collection of pre-Hispanic art. Built atop a hill, Anahuacalli commands one of the best views in Mexico, comparable to those of the Torre Latinoamericana and Castillo de Chapultepec.

SAN ANGEL

South of Mexico City near Coyoacán is the wealthy community of San Angel. Neither as artsy or bohemian as Coyoacán, San Angel's main appeal is that, quite simply, it's beautiful. Dotted with churches and exquisite colonial homes, this mecca of Mexican suburbia is a great place for a stroll. To reach the area, 10km south of the *centro* along Insurgentes, take the Metro to the M.A. Quevedo station (Line 3). Head west on Quevedo (away from the big Santo Domingo bakery) for three blocks; when it forks, take a left onto Av. La Paz, and continue along the very green (but sometimes trash-laden) **Parque de la Bombilla.** The centerpiece of this park is the concrete **Monumento al General Álvaro Obregón.** *(Open daily 7am-4:30pm; free.)* Obregón was one of the Revolution leaders who united against Huerta, the usurper who executed President Madero and seized power in 1913. During the Revolution, Obregón lost an arm. The statue in the monument shows him thus, while a separate statue of the severed limb can be viewed on the lower level of the monument. In 1920, Obregón became the first president of the post-revolutionary era. The inscription in the sunken lower level reads, "I die blessing the Revolution."

One block past the monument, you'll arrive at the intersection with Insurgentes. Cross, and walk up La Paz one block until you come to the intersection with Av. Revolución. One block to the south (left) are the three tiled domes of **Iglesia del Carmen,** at Revolución and Monasterio. *(Open daily 7am-1pm and 5-9pm.)* Designed and built between 1615 and 1626 by Fray Andrés de San Miguel of the Carmelite order, the church and adjacent ex-convent are decorated with tiles and paintings. An outstanding statue of Christ the Nazarene is located in the Capilla del Señor Contreras. The **Museo del Carmen** (tel. 550 48 96) is located in the converted ex-convent next to the church. *(Open Tu-Su 10am-5pm. Admission 14 pesos, free for Mexican students and for all on Sundays.)* The museum tells the history of the barefoot Carmelites in the New World—they were the first order to renounce missionary work—and displays colonial art, crucifixes galore, and portraits of various holy figures. Also exhibited are typical convent rooms—look out for the flat wooden bed and oh-so-comfy log pillow. Most tourists come to see the **mummies,** located in an underground crypt; the grotesque cadavers were originally found in 1916 when the Zapatistas arrived in search of treasure.

Across the street from this complex is the **Centro Cultural** (tel. 616 12 54 or 616 20 97), which borders the lovely **Plaza del Carmen.** *(Open Tu-Sa 10am-8pm, Su 10am-7pm.)* Besides hosting changing art exhibits and plays, this building displays billboards that explain what's hip and hot in the Mexican art world. One block up Madero, which runs along the left side of the Casa de Cultura (as you face the Casa), is the

Plaza de San Jacinto, at San Francisco and Benito Juárez. Every Saturday, the plaza fills up with ritzy shoppers scoping out pricey arts and crafts at the **Bazaar Sábado** (see p. 123). A kiosk in the center frequently hosts orchestras and big bands, and plastic chairs and peanut vendors span the plaza.

On the north side of the plaza is the **Casa de Risco,** Plaza San Jacinto 15 (tel. 550 92 86), a well-preserved 17th-century house holding an important collection of 14th- through 18th-century European art. *(Open Tu-Su 10am-5pm; free.)* The whitewashed inner courtyard contains an exquisitely tiled fountain made of pieces of bowls and plates (called *riscos*) that were collected from around the world. Also look out for *Crisol de las Razas,* a painted colonial chart that lists racial combinations with names like *lobo* (wolf) and *salto atrás* (a step backwards). One block farther up Juárez lies the beautiful **Iglesia de San Jacinto,** a 16th-century church with an ancient orange facade, beautifully carved wooden doors, and a peaceful courtyard (open daily 8am-8pm). This neighborhood, the oldest in San Angel, contains some obscenely swank and impressive modern mansions. Come see how the *ricos* (rich) live, Mexican style.

Three blocks north on Revolución from the intersection with La Paz, to the right if coming from the Parque de la Bombilla, is the small **Museo Carrillo Gil,** Revolución 1608 (tel. 550 39 83), a modern building housing the contemporary art collection of the late Carillo Gil, including works by Siqueiros, Orozco, and the young Rivera. *(Open Tu-Su 10am-6pm. Admission 10 pesos, students with ID 6 pesos; free for all on Sundays.)* Siqueiros's famous *Caín en los Estados Unidos* (Cain in the United States) is on the third floor, revealing the potential whereabouts of this biblical bad boy. The top two floors house temporary exhibits.

Follow the signs five blocks up Altavista, which crosses Revolución, to the **Museo Estudio Diego Rivera** (tel. 550 15 18), just before the Museo Carillo Gil. *(Open Tu-Su 10am-6pm. Admission 10 pesos; free for students and for all on Sundays.)* This wild and windy studio-turned-museum houses a tiny but phenomenal collection of Rivera's *Niños Indígenas* with a beautiful commentary by Rigoberta Menchú. On the top floors, you can see where this great artist worked and comment on his taste in furniture. Even his left-over paints are lying around untouched.

CIUDAD UNIVERSITARIA

Metro: Universidad (Line 3) lets you off (via *Salidas D* and *E*) in front of the free shuttle service. The shuttles are limited and irregular when classes are not in session (July 5-Aug. 15), but still available to all campus areas.

Universidad Nacional Autónoma de Mexico (UNAM)

The **Universidad Nacional Autónoma de México** (National Autonomous University of Mexico), or **UNAM,** is the largest university in Latin America, boasting a staggering enrollment of over 100,000. Immediately after the new colonial regime was established, the religious orders that arrived in Mexico built elementary and secondary schools to indoctrinate new converts and to educate young men who had come over from Spain. After petitioning the king of Spain, the first university was established in 1553 in the building at the corner of Moneda and Seminario, just off the *zócalo.* As the university grew, classes were moved to the building that now houses the Monte de Piedad, on the west side of the *zócalo,* and then to a building at the east end of the Plaza del Volador, where the Suprema Corte now stands. In 1954, the **Ciudad Universitaria (C.U.)** reached its present size of **7.3 million square meters.** This veritable "city" boasts 26km of paved roads, 430,000 square meters of greenery, and 4 million planted trees—and it's not even residential. With all of the modern architecture around, it's easy to forget that UNAM is **one of the three oldest universities in the Americas.**

Its size makes UNAM a little difficult to navigate on foot unless you have plenty of time to wander. Luckily, a continuous flow of free buses circulate throughout the C.U.'s many streets from the Universidad Metro stop. Follow the students. Routes do not always overlap—your best bet to get from one campus location to the next is usually to ride back to the Metro station and catch a new bus from there. Pick up a map of the C.U. (16 pesos) at the photocopy store across the greenery from the library (store open M-F 8am-7pm). Should you have any serious problems, call **university security** (tel. 55 from a university phone, tel. 616 09 14 from an outside phone).

Despite the rock-bottom tuition (something like US$5 per semester), the university is still able to support an amazingly varied collection of student groups, activities, and social and cultural events. Films, shows, and club meetings abound. You name it, it's here—from a Tae Kwon Do club to a film about young gay Mexicans to local bands playing Mexican alternative rock to tribal dances that explore the country's indigenous heritage. **Tiempo Libre** magazine and the leaflets **Cartelera** and **Los Universitarios** provide comprehensive schedules; hundreds of other events are posted on kiosks around campus. The most notable bulletin board is in the **Centro Cultural Universitario (CCU).** This large, modern complex houses the **Teatro Juan Ruiz de Alarcón,** the **Foro Sor Juana Inés de la Cruz** (tel. 665 65 83; ticket booth open Tu and F 10am-2pm and 5-9pm; tickets 50 pesos, students 25 pesos), the **Sala Netzahualcóyotl** (tel. 622 71 11; shows Saturdays 8pm and Sundays noon; tickets 50-100 pesos, students 50% off), several other concert halls, and two movie theaters, **Salas José Revueltas** and **Julio Bracho** (tel. 665 28 50; tickets 20 pesos, students 10 pesos). The CCU is accessible by Line 3 of the UNAM shuttle which leaves from the Universidad Metro station.

Just outside the CCU is the impressive **Espacio Escultórico.** Out of a huge lava bed and surrounding cave formations rises a pan-chromatic collection of metal, cement, and wood sculptures constructed in the early 1980s. The artists strove to revive the architectural traditions of pre-Hispanic ceremonial centers through modern techniques. The Espacio Escultórico should only be visited during the day; its secluded location makes it dangerous after nightfall.

Hop on another yellow and blue UNAM shuttle to get to the heart of the campus. The **Estadio Olímpico 1968** is located on the opposite side of Insurgentes Sur from the Jardín Central; cross via the pedestrian underpass. The stadium, built in the 1950s, was appropriately designed to resemble a volcano with a huge crater—lava coats the ground on which it is built. The impressive mosaic that covers the stadium was made by the incomparable and unstoppable Rivera using large colored rocks; it depicts a man and a woman holding two torches, a symbol of the 1968 Olympics, which were held in the stadium.

Although the university's architecture is impressive, most visitors come to see the mosaic murals that cover its larger buildings. From the stadium, cross Insurgentes (use the pedestrian tunnel), and continue east (straight ahead) to the Jardín Central. West of the Jardín Central's southern half, the university's administrative building is distinguished by a 3-D Siqueiros mosaic on the south wall, which shows students studying at desks supported by society. One of the world's larger mosaics, the work of Juan O'Gorman, wraps around the university **library** (tel. 622 16 13), a breathtaking, nearly windowless box next to the rectory tower ahead and to your left as you come out from under Insurgentes. *(Library open daily 8:30am-7pm.)* A pre-Hispanic eagle and Aztec warriors peer out from the side facing the philosophy department. The side facing the esplanade shows the Spaniards' first encounter with the natives; the opposite side depicts a huge atom and its whirling components. Across the *jardín* from the library, the **Museo Universitario de Arte Contemporáneo** has single-artist exhibits that change every three months. *(Open Tu-F 10am-noon for guided visits and noon-2pm for regular visits, Sa-Sun 10am-6pm. Admission 6 pesos, students 3 pesos. Museum closes during school break, July 5-Aug. 15.)* Guided tours by art students are available in the mornings for only 5 pesos. Most speak English.

A beautiful and pleasantly secluded attraction is the **Jardín Botánico,** a stop on the free UNAM shuttle leaving from the Metro station. *(Open M-F 9am-4:30pm; free.)* From the endless species of cactus to the shady arboretum to the tropical plants pavilion, the *jardín* is a welcome change from the city's urban sprawl; it offers a peek into the Valley of Mexico as it was hundreds of years ago. The trails of red volcanic sediment that wander past lagoons and glens and a helpful map at the entrance provide guidance. You must leave your bags with the guard at the entrance.

Cuicuilco Archaeological Zone

Tel. 553 22 63. On the southeast corner at the intersection of Insurgentes Sur and Anillo Periférico. Take the "Huipulco" pesero (1 peso) from Metro: Universidad to the entrance on the west side of Insurgentes Sur, south of the Periférico. Most peseros will let you off on the other side of Insurgentes. Cross over on one of the yellow pedestrian bridges and head right (away from the Escuela Nacional de Arqueología) to the entrance. ***Open*** *daily 9am-4pm; free.*

Near the end of the pre-Classic Period, the tiny volcano **Xitle** erupted, leaving eight square kilometers covered with several meters of hardened lava. The lava flow preserved one of the first pyramids constructed in the Valley of Mexico and formed what is now the archaeological zone. The **Pyramid of Cuicuilco,** which means "Place of the Many-Colored Jasper," was built between 600 and 200 BC by the early inhabitants of the Valley of Mexico, when ceremonial centers first began to spring up in Mesoamerica, and their priests gained extraordinary powers. Measuring 125m across at its base and 20m in height, Cuicuilco consists of five layers, with an altar to the god of fire at its summit. The lava rock around the base has been removed, allowing visitors to walk along it up to the altar. However, very little other restoration has taken place. On a clear day, you can faintly see Xitle to the south and Popocatépetl to the east from the pyramid. These volcanoes are far from "dead." One night in late June 1997, Popocatépetl threw a temper tantrum that sent ash and debris over 100km. *Chilangos* were distressed to find their white party clothes soiled and their roofs covered in silt.

XOCHIMILCO

To get to Xochimilco, take the Metro to Tasqueña (Line 2) and then ride the *tren ligero* (trolley, 1.50 pesos; follow the *correspondencia* signs) in the *Embarcadero* direction and get off at that stop. Numerous signs labeled "Embarcadero" and white-shirted bike-riding boat owners will direct you to the boats. *Peseros* below the station will also take you there; ask to be let off at *las canoas* (the canoes).

The **floating gardens** were not designed by nautical engineers—they are remnants of the Aztec agricultural system. In fact, this tourist trap was once an important center of Aztec life. In the Aztec's brilliantly conceived system, *chinampas* (artificial islands) were made by piling soil and mud onto floating rafts. These rafts were held firm by wooden stakes until the crops planted on top eventually sprouted roots, reaching through the base of the canals. They became fertile breeding grounds, supporting several crops a year. Although polluted today, the canals still bear the bright colors and waterborne commerce they did centuries ago.

Multicolored *chalupa* boats crowd the maze of fairly filthy canals, ferrying passengers past a **floating market** offering food, flowers, and music. The market is especially popular on Sundays, when hordes of city dwellers and tourists pack the hand-poled *chalupas.* Visitors lounge and listen to the waterborne *mariachis* and marimba players, and celebrate Mexico City's aquatic past as they munch goodies from the floating taco bars that tie up pirate-style to the passenger boats. Although nothing of great quality or value is sold (no crafts, *artesanías,* cultural relics, or clothes), you can buy delicate orchids and bubbly beer, and the festive mood is more than enough to make Xochimilco a popular Sunday afternoon spot.

The key word for almost anything you do in Xochimilco is **bargaining.** From markets to boats, this is the only way to get around in this overly popular tourist spot. Be aware that if you come earlier, you'll find a much emptier Xochimilco, with far fewer boats and much higher prices. For a private boat for two people, expect to pay about 50 pesos per hour with bargaining; consult the official diagram for prices, as boat owners will try to charge eight or 10 times as much. On weekend afternoons, *colectivo* boats are cheaper (5 pesos) and more fun than the private boats. The standard price for *mariachis* is 35 pesos per song.

Xochimilco also offers two enormous land-bound markets, one with the usual food and household items, the other lusciously filled with live plants and animals. To reach the marketplace from the *tren ligero,* turn left on any street within three blocks of the station as you walk away from it, and then walk until you hit the market just beyond the **Iglesia de San Bernandino de Cera.**

Nightlife

As the sun sets, storefronts pull their shutters closed and a new street scene begins to emerge. The city doesn't stop hopping until 6 or 7am on weekends, when the last pooped partiers stumble out of tired taxis. Be it the Ballet Folklórico at Bellas Artes, an old film at an art cinema, a bullfight, someone playing the blues in a smoke-filled bar, or some down-and-dirty techno in a three-story warehouse, Mexico City has something for everyone; this crazy chameleon of a city shows it true colors in the entertainment department.

Different areas of the city boast different entertainment specialties. As a general rule, the best *discotecas* are found along Insurgentes Sur and in the *Zona Rosa.* Rock clubs with young, hip crowds abound in the *Zona Rosa,* and a few exist around the Alameda. More posh bars and discos in the *centro* cater to an older, business-oriented crowd. *Mariachi* bands teem in Garibaldi Plaza, while merengue and salsa clubs cluster near the *zócalo* and in San Angel and Coyoacán. Jazz bands, salsa, and traditional Mexican music can also be found in the city's southern suburbs. Topless bars disguised as traditional bars abound in the *Zona Rosa*—double-check at the door if you don't see enough women entering.

Tourists and Mexicans alike flood the streets in the evenings, dressed to kill, and determined to have a good time. Bars and discos clog the streets, each attempting to outdo the others in flashiness and decibel output. Although the Alameda and other areas also have some places to dance, discos in more run-down parts of town can get seedy.Women venturing out alone should be aware that they will most likely be approached by men offering drinks, dances, and much, much more.

At many large nightclubs, in the *centro* and *Zona Rosa,* men are unofficially required to have a female date for admission. If you're pushy enough, foreign, and appropriately attired, this unwritten rule shouldn't apply to you. Cover charges range anywhere from 10 to 150 pesos, but women are often admitted free or at reduced prices. A very steep cover charge may signify an open bar; be sure to ask. Places with no cover often have minimum consumption requirements and high drink prices. Covers magically drop during the week when business is scarce, especially for *norteamericanos,* reputed to have hearty appetites and deep pockets. If prices are not listed, be sure to ask before ordering, lest you be charged exorbitant gringo prices. Be aware that *bebidas nacionales* (Mexican-made drinks, from Kahlúa to *sangría*) are considerably cheaper than imported ones. In fact, *barra libre* (open bar) often means *barra libre nacional* (open bar including only nationally made drinks). No biggie, though. Settling for Mexican beer or tequila is hardly settling for second-best. Watch out for ice cubes—unpurified water in disguise. **Cantinas,** bars with dimly lit interiors, no windows, or swinging doors reminiscent of Wild West saloons are often not safe for unaccompanied women. For safety, the *Zona Rosa* offers the best lighting and least lonely streets, which are problems in other areas. Taxis run all night and are the safest way of getting from bar to disco to breakfast to hotel, but—especially after dark—do not flag a cab on the street. Ask any bartender, bouncer, or waiter to call or give you the number for a local *sitio* taxi company.

Mexico City also has more clubs, bars, and discos that cater to gay and lesbian travelers than anywhere else in the country (see **Gay and Lesbian Entertainment,** p. 121).

ZONA ROSA

Bars

While cover charges get steeper and steeper (and drinks weaker and weaker) as the 90s progress, the *Zona Rosa* is still a bar-hopper's dream come true. The high price tags often mean live performers and tasty *botanas* (appetizers). *Zona Rosa* bars cater to all ages and tastes, from teenybopper to elderly intellectual. Many feature live music or, at the very least, beamed-in video entertainment. Women will probably feel safer in this area than elsewhere in the city, but men still aggressively try to pick up any female who comes along. Catch a ride home in a *pesero* running all night along Reforma or Insurgentes Sur (1-1.50 pesos). Or better yet, call a *sitio* cab.

Luna Bar, Insurgentes Sur 123 (tel. 208 87 21), at the corner of Liverpool, has two floors of intimate tables lit with glowing black light. The blaring music may not facilitate deep conversation, but it creates a great atmosphere for relaxing, drinking, and people-watching—this place draws a snazzy crowd of all ages. Beers are a hefty 30 pesos, but no cover. Open daily 5pm-4am.

Bar Osiris, Niza 22 (tel. 525 66 84). Suffers from mid-week attendance problems, but on weekends, this small, dark second-floor bar turns into a throbbing dance pit. Live rock bands perform after 8pm, 3 per night F and Sa, 1 on W and Th. 1 beer 15 pesos, a pitcher 70 pesos. Cover F-Sa 25 pesos. Open W-Su 7pm-4am.

El Chato, Londres 117 (tel. 511 17 58), with a stained-glass doorway. This splendid faux old-Euro bar has a dark smokey rear piano bar with fitting "bohemian" tunes. No glitz, no booming beat, but the somewhat older crowd likes it that way. Beer 15 pesos, tequila 20 pesos. Occasionally visited by musicians from the Yucatán, when a 30-peso cover charge takes effect. Open M-Sa 6pm-2am.

El Tlacoache, Londres 142 (tel. 514 31 68), at Ambres. Step upstairs into this brand-new, cool, classy restaurant/bar where chairs are pushed aside to make room for dancing as the night progresses. All ages and all types of music. Starts to fill up by 8pm and closes only after you leave—don't rush.

Melodika, Florencia 52 (tel. 208 01 98). This 3-part bar is host to everything from rave music to karaoke. Make lots of young local friends as you all huddle together and croon everybody's favorite ballads. Karaoke every night to your favorite Mexican, American, or even French hits. Cover 15 pesos. Open Th-Sa 7pm-2am.

Discos

The *Zona Rosa* has some of the Republic's flashiest discos and highest cover charges—on weekend nights, the *Zona* can seem like the center of the entire universe. Club-hopping, however, is becoming more difficult, as many discos are moving over to the high cover charge and open bar system. Long lines around the block mean a club is *de moda* (in)—expect tons of trendy teens and Armani-clad young couples eager to pay *muchos pesos* in order to get down. If being seen in the hippest nighttime hangouts isn't terribly important to you, try hitting a less populated, slightly *de paso* (out) club and hold out for a deal. Even in the *Zona Rosa,* some clubs offer entrance and open bar for under 40 pesos. Sidewalk recruiters will likely try to lure in groups, especially those with high female-to-male ratios; hold out and you just might be offered a deal. Dress codes of sorts apply: if you look particularly foreign, it is unlikely that you'll be turned away by the fashion police, but it still does happen. If you can't find something to your liking here, keep on truckin' south on Insurgentes Sur and then along the thoroughfare—you'll run across the whole gamut of clubs.

Rock Stock Bar & Disco, Reforma 260 (tel. 533 09 07), at Niza. Clubs come and go, but *el estok* remains packed and fun year after year. Follow the street signs through the rotating darkroom-style doors upstairs into a huge open-attic room in which railings, scaffolding, and metal cages are doused in fluorescent paint. Lively action, with everything from rave to underground rhythms. Two shifts of music and shows. 3-9pm is cheaper and less crowded (40-50 pesos; women free 3-4pm). Come early if you want to be part of the 10pm-to-late crowd—later, swarms of people wait outside, hoping to be let in. Being foreign and/or being a young female (especially in tight clothes) helps. Marvel at Mexico City's teens, who mix grunge with body piercing. Cover includes open bar: 120 pesos for men, women free. Open M-Sa 3pm-late.

Mecano (tel. 208 96 11), on Genova, near the corner with Hamburg, up the spiral staircase. Blasting dance music reverberates off the metal floor and walls of this enormous industrial-themed disco. Crowds fill up two floors worth of dance space while they shake and shimmy. Cover (including *barra libre*) for men 130 pesos; women free until 11pm, after 11pm 50 pesos. Open Th-Sa 9pm-3am.

Urano, Hamburgo 115 (tel. 514 74 18). At the end of a long metal hallway, a deep high-ceilinged dance floor features caged dancers (ahem...they are clothed) at one end and on the upper balcony. Get into their groove and let the music move you and hundreds of beautiful, hip young Mexicans to the bar. *Barra libre* comes with the 14 pesos cover for men, 30 pesos cover for women. Open Th-Su 9pm-2am.

Celebration, Florencia 56 (tel. 541 64 15). Rigged with speakers heard 'round the world. A combination of disco, techno, salsa, merengue, and house accompanies a stylish set and varied theme nights. Scattered tables provide an oasis from the active dance action. A slightly older, more dressy crowd celebrates here. Cover (including *barra libre*) 130 pesos. Women often get in for free, and covers drop during the less crowded weeknights. Don't be afraid to bargain (this is Mexico—you even haggle for nightlife) with the men outside. Open daily 7pm-3am.

Yarda's, Niza 42, is a restaurant/bar during the day and a booming disco after 8pm. With an enormous dance floor and disco, house, and techno music, everyone from young adults to 40-somethings keep this place packed with dancers. Cover 30 pesos.

CENTRO

A hop, skip, and a jump away from the *zócalo,* a testament to the proud and complex history of the Mexican people, lies a slew of nightclubs, testaments to something even grander: people here sure know how to party. The clubs in the *centro* are elegant and upscale (most have valet parking), but this doesn't stop 1600 corporate executives from cramming into a three-story disco and "workin' it." Most of the clubs have terraces with fully stocked bars and smashing skyline views.

Opulencia, Católica 26 (tel. 512 04 17), on the corner of Madero. What's in a name? A heck of a lot, in this case. Spic-and-span elevator and velvet curtains are just the beginning. The enormous dance floor features big bouncers, black lights, video screens, headsets, and the best of 1980s dance music. Check out the zany living room on the 3rd floor with plush couches and silly furnishings a la Lewis Carroll. Totally decadent. Totally cool. Cover (including open bar) for men 130 pesos Th, 170 pesos F-Sa, includes open bar. No cover for women. Open Th-Sa 10pm-4:30am.

La Ópera, 5 de Mayo 10 (tel. 355 34 36), just west of Filomeno Mata. A restaurant and bar since 1807 with Baroque ceilings, mirrored walls, a grandfather clock, and dark wooden booths. While it's relatively low-key today, government alliances were made and betrayed within these walls. A great place to grab a whiskey and soda and talk politics. Drinks 15-23 pesos. Open M-Sa 1pm-midnight, Su 1-6pm.

El Bar Mata (tel. 518 02 37), Filomeno Mata at 5 de Mayo. For the *centro,* it packs in a youthful crowd ready to party. Take the elevator or walk up 5 flights to check out the sophisticated design with mood lighting and hip architecture. Equals nearly everything the *Zona Rosa* has to offer mid-week, although on non-band nights (no cover) the clientele noticeably thins out. Live bands Wednesdays and Saturdays. Mixed drinks 20-25 pesos. Cover 30 pesos Wednesday. Open Tu-Sa 8pm-3am.

ALAMEDA CENTRAL

While bars and discos near the Alameda can't compare in luster to those in the *Zona Rosa,* prices are refreshingly low. Unfortunately, surrounding neighborhoods may be dangerous, especially late at night. Although Metro stops are abundant, taxis are somewhat less so, so you'll want to ask for the phone number of a nearby *sitio* (it's safer, anyway).

Especially noteworthy is the **Hostería del Bohemio,** Hidalgo 107 (tel. 512 83 28), just west of Reforma. Leave the Hidalgo Metro stop (Lines 2 and 3) from the Ave. Hidalgo/Calle de Héroes exit and turn left. Situated in the cloister of the ex-convent of San Hipólito, this romantic cafe is saturated with music, singing, and poetry in the evenings. Seating is on the outdoor terraces of both levels and on all four sides of a lush, two-tiered courtyard with a gurgling central fountain. At night, thousands of Christmas lights only add to the already unparalleled ambiance. The slice-of-a-tree tables and chairs are lit by old-fashioned lanterns, making it the perfect spot for intimate conversations. Guitars strum in the background. You're guaranteed to fall in love here, if not with the attractive, googly-eyed *joven* sitting next to you, then with the amazing assortment of coffee, cake, and ice cream. (Every single gosh-darn thing on the menu is exactly 16 pesos, except for cigarettes at a whopping 12 pesos; no cover; open daily 5-11pm.)

GARIBALDI PLAZA

Garibaldi Plaza hosts some of Mexico City's gaudiest, seediest, and funniest nightlife. The plaza is at the intersection of Lázaro Cárdenas and República de Honduras, north of Reforma. Take the Metro to the Bellas Artes stop (Lines 2 and 8), and walk three blocks north along Cárdenas; Garibaldi is the plaza on your right. Metro: Garibaldi (Line 8) takes you three blocks north of the plaza. Exit to your left from the stop and walk south. By 5pm, wandering *mariachis* fill the plaza, striking up as it gets dark to compete with each other while roving *ranchero* groups play your favorite tune for 30-40 pesos (foreigners often get the privilege of paying more). Tourists, locals, prostitutes, musicians, vendors, transvestites, young kids—just about anybody and everybody mingles here, many reeling, dancing, and screaming in the street because of the copious amounts of liquor they've just downed. Big nightclubs surrounding the plaza, each with its own *mariachi*, do their best to lure the crowds. Although they advertise no cover, per-drink prices are staggeringly high. Don't wander too far away from the plaza looking for cheaper options; you'll find only strip joints and dangerous *cantinas*. Beware of pickpockets, purse-snatchers, and prostitutes (or some combination of the three); it's best to leave your credit card, wallet, and purse at home. The best time to visit Garibaldi is from 8pm to 2am on weekends, but it's also the least safe then. Prostitutes turn tricks here, and the neighboring streets, strip joints, and *cantinas* can be dangerous. Women should be particularly cautious.

COYOACÁN AND SAN ANGEL

While generally very safe sections of town, these two southern suburbs fall just outside many of Mexico City's public transportation axes. The Metro serves both until midnight, after which a taxi is the best option. Most moderately- to high-priced restaurants have live jazz at night. Coyoacán and San Angel are infamous for their slews of moody gringos getting drunk and wistful to blues and rock. For a good time, hang out in Coyoacán's main plaza and soak up all the noise from comedians and musicians as you think deep thoughts. An option is **El Hijo del Cuervo** (tel. 658 78 24), on the north side of the Jardín Centenario, in Coyoacán. A mötley international crue of people-watching, liquor-downing folks crowd here weekend nights for live rock and Latin music. Beers run 15 pesos. (Open daily 1pm-2am.)

Gay and Lesbian Entertainment

Mexico City offers the full range of social and cultural activities for gays and lesbians. There is an active gay rights movement in Mexico City, even though the general tolerance of public homosexual activity is still very low. Although not illegal, public displays of affection by gay and lesbian couples on the Metro and in other public places often results in harrassment, especially by the police. Gay men will have a much easier time finding bars and discos, although more and more venues integrate lesbians. For exclusively lesbian activities, contact the lesbian groups (see p. 88). Pick up a copy of the free pamphlet *Ser Gay*. All of the clubs below carry this excellent, information-laden resource: it details gay entertainment and art events in the city and provides a complete listing of all the gay bars in town and many throughout the country. Once you get your hand on one of these puppies, a whole new world of alternative opportunity arises. Often, clubs will waive cover provided you show a copy of *Ser Gay*. In June, Mexico's gay pride month, an inordinate number of parties, rallies, art exhibits, marches, and fun *fiesta*-type events occur throughout the city.

El Antro, Londres 77 (tel. 511 16 13), near the intersection with Insurgentes. This enormous, tasteful new club occupies a prime spot in the *Zona Rosa.* Only men are allowed to enjoy the multiple bars, pianos, dance floors, private rooms, video screens, and just about anything (and everything) else. Men of all ages come here to check out the acclaimed stripper shows or get down to hard-core disco. Check *Ser Gay* for schedules that include play-money casino night, social/cocktail night, and "all fun" night (Saturdays). Cover Wednesday 20 pesos, Th-Sa 35 pesos with 1 drink, Sunday 20 pesos. Open Tu-Sa 7pm-late, Su 6pm-2am.

Anyway, Exacto, and the Doors, Monterrey 47 (tel. 533 16 19), half a block from Durango in Col. Roma, just south of the *Zona Rosa*. A 3-part party. Food and drink are offered at The Doors, while dancing, more drinks, and dancing are offered at the other two. On Thursdays, Exacto offers the only all-women's disco in the city, and on other days, it caters to a high concentration of lesbians. 20-peso cover on Wednesday and Thursday includes 1 drink, 40-peso cover on Friday and Saturday includes 2 drinks. Open daily 8pm-late

El Celo, Londres 104 (tel. 514 43 09), in the *Zona Rosa.* A gay-friendly restaurant during the day, this candle-lit restaurant/bar is filled by an exclusively gay and lesbian clientele after 7pm. The 15-peso beers are 2-for-1 from 9-11pm, and there's no cover. Later in the evening, tables are pushed aside and the boogeying begins.

Butterfly, Izazaga 9 (tel. 761 18 61), near Metro Salto del Agua (Lines 1 and 8), half a block east of Lázaro Cárdenas, just south of the cathedral. Although no signs point out this club, don't be afraid to ask. This big, brash gay nightspot is worth the searching. Although lesbians are beginning to come out, men, men, and more men make the huge dance floor a crowded tangle of humanity. Video screens and a superb lighting system. Male revue late on weekend nights. Tu-Th no cover, F-Sa cover 40 pesos with 2 drinks. Gay events throughout the city are advertised from here. Open Tu-Su 9pm-3:30am.

El Almacen, Florencia 37 (tel. 207 69 56). A bar that serves Mediterranean food and plays 1980s pop. A growing number of lesbians are joining the men kicking back beers on their way to the high-octane gay male dance club in the basement, **El Taller** (open daily noon-late).

El Taller, Florencia 37A (tel. 533 49 84), in the *Zona Rosa.* Underground; watch carefully or you'll miss the entrance. Well-known hangout for blue-collar gay men. Wednesdays and Sundays attract a twentyish crowd; private barroom attracts an older crowd. Throbbing dance music, faux construction-site decorations and dark, private alcoves make for an intense men-only pickup scene. Check *Ser Gay* for schedules; Saturday is usually theme night (i.e., cowboy, boxer, businessman). Th-Su cover 30 pesos including 1 drink. Open Tu-Su 8pm-5am.

La Estación, Hamburgo 234 (tel. 514 47 07), in the *Zona Rosa.* A brand new all-men leather bar—wear your leather or latex to get into this enormous 2 floor bar. Open daily 4pm-2am.

La Cantina de Vaquero, Algeciras 26, Col. Insurgentes, near el Parque Hundido, between Metro: Mixcoáo and Metro: Zapata. This was the first openly gay *cantina* in Mexico—it just celebrated its 24th anniversary. Working-class gay men still flock to "El Vaquero," a low-profile bar in a commercial center, to watch XXX videos, sample the "darkroom," or, simply grab a beer and *parlar* (chat). Videos screened daily 5-11pm. 2 beers included with the 25-peso cover. Open daily 5pm-late.

Shopping

While most Mexican cities have a single central market, Mexico City has one specializing in every retail good. These markets are relatively cheap. Each *colonia* has its own market, but the major marketplaces are all in the center of town. Shopping throughout the *centro* and the Alameda proceeds thematically: there is a wedding dress street, a lighting fixtures street, a lingerie street, a windowpanes street, a power tools street, a military paraphernalia street, and so on.

San Juan Artesanías, Pl. El Buen Tono, 4 blocks south of Alameda Central, 2 blocks west of Lázaro Cárdenas. Bounded by Ayuntamiento, Aranda, Pugibet, and Dolores. From Metro: Salto de Agua, walk up López 4 blocks and make a left on Ayuntamiento; 3 floors of artisanry from all over Mexico will greet you. The typical mix of mold-made cheesy tourist items and handmade treasures. Prices are similar to La Ciudadela (see below), but comparison shopping always helps. Fewer tourists wander around here. Open M-Sa 9am-7pm, Su 9am-4pm.

Mercado de La Ciudadela, 2 blocks north of Metro station Balderas (Lines 1 and 3) off Av. Balderas. An incredible array of *artesanías,* crafts, and traditional clothing at low prices. Its reputation as the biggest and best *artesanía* market in the city makes tourist traffic rampant. Open daily 8am-7pm.

La Merced, Circunvalación at Anaya, east of the *zócalo.* Metro: Merced (Line 1). Not just a market but a way of life. The **largest market in the Americas,** it has a ridiculously wide selection of fresh produce from all over the country at rock-bottom prices. You'll find every kind of fruit imaginable, and crayfish abound. Check out the **Mercado de Dulces** (candy market) and watch candy-lovers' sweet teeth quiver in ecstasy. Between the two lies the **Mercado de Flore**s (flower market). All three markets open daily 8am-7pm.

FONART, Patriotismo 691 (tel. 563 40 60), Juárez 89 (tel. 521 01 71), and Carranza 115 (tel. 554 62 70) in Coyoacán. A national project to protect and market traditional crafts. *Artesanías* from all over the country: giant tapestries, Oaxacan rugs, silver jewelry, pottery, and colorful embroidery. Regulated prices are not quite as low as the markets, but if you're not in the mood for crowds and haggling, come here and pay only a little more. Open M-Sa 10am-7pm.

Sonora, Teresa de Mier and Cabaña, 2 blocks south of La Merced. Specializes in witchcraft, medicinal teas and spices, figurines, and ceremonial images. Search no further for lucky cows' feet, shrunken heads, eagle claws, black salt (for nosy neighbors), powdered skull (for the domination of one's enemies), and dead butterflies, among other useful things. Cures are prescribed for almost any illness—bee venom cream supposedly works wonders on arthritis. Open daily 8am-7pm.

La Lagunilla, Comonfort at Rayón, east of the intersection of Lázaro Cárdenas and Reforma. Two large yellow buildings on either side of the street with stands spilling outside. Although now a daily vending site, this market really gets going on Sundays when it turns into a gargantuan flea market, most notable for its antique books. Feel completely authentic as you browse and get battered by the throngs of wise locals looking for the real deal. The rest of the week, their specialty is communion and party dresses. Taffeta, anyone? Open daily 8am-7pm.

Bazaar del Sabado, Plaza San Jacinto, in the center of San Angel. Saturdays only, this market opens up and spills onto the plaza with arts and crafts. It tends to be pricey and touristy, but it's one of the few markets to which contemporary artists bring their work. This posh market is the equivalent of a nightclub to which "everyone who's anyone" goes. Open Saturday 9am-6pm

Jamaica, Congreso and Morelos (Eje 3 Sur). Metro: Jamaica (Lines 4 and 9). Immediately as you exit the subway station, there is a clump of vendor stalls selling cheap eats and some of the juiciest mangos and *piñas* in town. The real pride and joy of the market is the assortment of fragrant and brightly colored flowers, including, of course, the deep-red Jamaica flower, source of the lip-smacking *agua de Jamaica* sold at many stands. Also be sure to check out live animals and exotic birds (all for sale) squawking and screaming in their confining cages. Open M-Sa 8am-6pm.

Sports

Whether consumed by their passion for bullfighting, soccer *(fútbol),* jai alai, or horse racing, Mexican fans share an almost religious devotion to *deportes.* If sweaty discos and cavernous museums have you craving a change of pace, follow the crowds to an athletic event and prepare yourself for a rip-roarin' rowdy good time. *Andale!*

The famous **Frontón Mexico,** facing the north side of the Revolution monument, as well as the **Hipódromo de las Américas,** beyond the Tacuba Metro station, were both still on strike as of July 1998. The Frontón is usually the site of the popular **jai alai** matches, while the Hipódromo houses a **racetrack.** Check to see if there have been any new developments.

Angels and Insects

One kilometer east of Chapultepec Park is the **Angel de la Independencia.** Situated at the fourth traffic circle on the Paseo de la Reforma, the Angel soars 50m above passing cars. Designed by Antonio Rivas Mercado, the monument is a stone column capped by a golden angel; its round-terraced base holds the remains of Hidalgo, Allende, and other national heroes. The original angel fell during an earthquake in 1957, and the head was so mangled that a new one had to be cast. Solid ever since, the Angel stands erect as a symbol of Mexican victory, and crowds often converge here after major *fútbol* triumphs. The view at night, when the angel is embraced by the surrounding lights and skyline of the city, is magnificent. There are also a lot of Volkswagen **bugs** driving around.

Aztec Stadium, Calz. de Tlalpan 3465 (tel. 617 80 80 or 617 20 88). Take a *pesero* or *tren ligero* (trolley) directly from the Tasqueña Metro station (Line 2). The Azteca is the greatest of many Mexican stadiums where professional *fútbol* is played and one of the largest in the world. In the 1998 World Cup, Mexico proved itself to be a formidable rising star, losing to Germany in a very close game. Read the sports pages of any newspaper for information on games, and keep your eye out for any **Mexico-Brazil** matches. These teams are fierce rivals and any match at the Azteca promises to be frighteningly exciting and overpopulated; good luck trying to get tickets. Many bars, though, have 2-for-1 *fútbol* specials with the game on TV. The only better thing than *fútbol* is *fútbol* with beer. Season runs Oct.-July.

Plaza México (tel. 563 39 59), on Insurgentes Sur. Accessible by Metro: San Antonio (Line 7). Mexico's principal bullring, seating 40,000 fans. Bullfights on Sundays. Professionals fight only late July-Nov.; *novilladas* (young *toreros* and bulls) Nov.-Feb. Tickets run 25-150 pesos. Prices depend on the seats' proximity to the ring and whether they fall on the *sombra* (shady) or *sol* (sunny) side. If you're going cheap, bring sunglasses, a hat, and a pair of binoculars.

NEAR MEXICO CITY

Teotihuacán

For about 1000 years, a consummately organized, theocratic society thrived in the Valley of Mexico, then disappeared as mysteriously as it had arisen. The cultural and commercial center of this society was Teotihuacán (teh-oh-tee-wah-KAN), founded in 200 BC. An important holy city, Teotihuacán drew hundreds of pilgrims and became something of a market town in order to accommodate their needs. Its influence on architecture and art was so great that many of the styles developed here can be found in Maya civilizations' ruins as far south as Guatemala.

Much about Teotihuacán is a mystery. Probably built by the Olmeca-Xicalanca, a Mixtec-speaking group, the city eventually became an international cosmopolitan center, inhabited by a diversity of geographical and linguistic groups. Little can be said for certain, however, about the inhabitants of Teotihuacán or its rise to prosperity and sudden decline. Some scholars speculate that the city eventually collapsed under its own weight, having grown so unwieldy that it could no longer produce enough food to keep its inhabitants properly fed. Evidence of a tremendous fire around 800 can be found in layers of blackened stone, but the city had experienced significant decline before that time. At its heyday between 150 and 250, Teotihuacán covered nearly 22.5 sq. km and accommodated a population of nearly 200,000. Overcrowding resulted in construction on older buildings during the twilight of the city.

By 850, only a trickle of people was left in the enormous urban complex. When the Aztecs founded Tenochtitlán in 1325, Teotihuacán, 50km northeast of their capital, lay in ruins. The Aztecs adopted the area as ceremonial grounds and believed its huge structures had been built by gods who sacrificed themselves here so that the sun

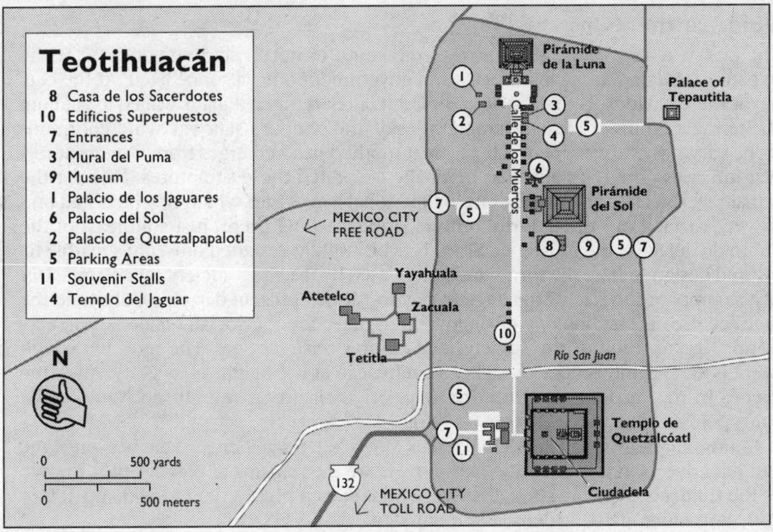

would shine on the Aztec world. Believing that those buried in this hallowed place were of some superhuman order, the Aztecs called the area Teotihuacán, meaning "Place Where Men Become Gods."

THE ARCHAEOLOGICAL SITE OF TEOTIHUACÁN

Teotihuacán (tel. 6 01 88 or 6 00 52; from Mexico City add the prefix 91 595) has some of the most enormous ruins in the country. *(Site open daily 7am-6pm. Admission 20 pesos, free on Sundays for national students and children under 13. Free parking.)* There are five entrances to the site. Buses drop visitors off by *Puerta 1,* the main entrance, surrounded by souvenir stalls. *Puerta 5,* the easternmost entrance, is by the Pirámide del Sol. Free guided tours for groups of five or more can be arranged at the administration building by *Puerta 1* (southwest corner). The museum and souvenir stalls sell guidebooks for about 40 pesos. Expect to spend about 30 minutes at the museum and another three to four hours exploring the ruins. Be sure to bring plenty of water, a hat, and sunglasses. Rapacious vendors descend upon the slew of international tourists offering water, as well as hats, silver, and *"piezas originales"* (original pieces). A firm *"¡No, gracias!"* will sometimes help keep vendors away; if it doesn't suffice, try to avoid eye contact. If you want to eat more than peanuts, splurge on a rare fancy meal just outside *Puerta 5*—**La Gruta** (tel. 9 15 95) is located inside a real natural cave, with tables lining the sides and floor. *(Open daily 10am-10pm.)* La Gruta offers tourists traditional dance shows and truly delicious gourmet Mexican dishes. It does, however, come with a price tag. Meals run 54-70 pesos.

The ceremonial center, a 13 sq. km expanse, was built along a 2km stretch now called **Calle de los Muertos** (Avenue of the Dead) for the countless human skeletons that were discovered alongside it. Since the Teotihuacanos planned their community around the four cardinal points, this main road runs in what is almost a perfectly straight north-south line from the **Pirámide de la Luna** (Pyramid of the Moon) to the **Templo de Quetzalcóatl**. The main structure, the **Pirámide del Sol** (Pyramid of the Sun), is on the east side and is squared with the point on the horizon where the sun sets at the summer solstice.

Las Pirámides, as the place is commonly called, is the **most visited archaeological site** in the Republic for a reason. The pyramids themselves loom over a vast expanse of traipsing tourists (both Mexican and international) and vying vendors; off in the distance, wildflowers and rolling hills metamorphose into majestic mountains. Don't turn the scaling of the pyramids into a chore or a race. Take some time, savor the view, and hang out.

Guide to the Ruins

The best way to explore the ruins is from south to north, starting your visit at the expansive **Ciudadela,** where priests and government officials once lived. At the center of the Ciudadela is the **Templo de Quetzalcóatl,** once a giant walled-in stadium sheltering a group of ancient temples. Beside the temple's stairway wind enormous stone carvings of the serpent whose great toothed head emerges from flowers at regular intervals. The red paint that originally decorated these sculptures (look for the remaining traces) was made by cutting off nopal leaves into which tiny bugs had burrowed, carving out the colorful critters, and smashing them. Just southeast of the Pirámide del Sol is the **Museo de Sitio.** This beautifully designed museum's marble tiling and design imitate the forms and colors used by the site's ancient inhabitants. Displays compare the size of the ancient city to various present-day cities, illustrate the architecture and technology of the pyramids, describe the social, religious, and economic organization of the society, and exhibit *indígena* art. The museum's high point is an enormous floor model of Teotihuacán at the height of its glory. All of the pieces in the museum are replicas. The originals are at the Museo Nacional de Antropología in Mexico City (see p. 106).

Continuing north along the Calle de los Muertos, you will cross what was once the San Juan river. On the west side of the street are the remains of two temples, known as the **Edificios Superpuestos,** that were built in two phases, 200 to 400 and 400 to 750, atop older, partially demolished temples.

Farther to the north and east is the **Pirámide del Sol,** the most massive single structure in the ceremonial area. Second in size only to the pyramid at Cholula, its base measures 222m by 225m—dimensions comparable to those of Cheops in Egypt. The pyramid rises 63m, but the grand temple that once crowned its summit is missing. Smokers and slowpokes: don't quit. Although the climb to the top may leave you out of breath, a rope rail runs the length of the pyramid, and the platforms of the multitiered pyramid make convenient rest stops. Unfortunately, the ubiquitous vendors are everywhere, even on the peak of this mammoth pyramid. As soon as you reach the top, weary and awe-struck, be prepared to say, "No, I don't need any more obsidian turtles, thank you." (In Spanish: *"No me faltan tortugas de obsidiana, gracias.")* For quieter contemplation, walk around a terrace to the back side.

Between the Pyramid of the Sun and the Pyramid of the Moon on the west side of the street is the **Palacio de Quetzalpapalotl** (Palace of the Quetzal Butterfly). This columned structure was the residence of nobles who staked out an area next to the ceremonial space, far from the residential complexes of the common folk. The inner patio is one of the most beautiful sights of the ancient city; the colored frescoes and bird glyphs have survived years of decay and retain much of their intricate detail.

Behind the first palace is the **Palacio de los Jaguares** (Palace of the Jaguars) and the now-subterranean **Palacio de las Conchas Emplumadas** (Palace of the Feathered Seashells). This palace dedicated to jaguars is entirely restored, complete with fluorescent lights and plastic handrails, and some of the original frescoes remain, adorned with red, green, yellow, and white symbols representing birds, corn, and water. This palace is a prime example of multi-level construction; it was built over another temple in which patterns of plumed seashells adorn the walls.

At the northern end of the Calle de los Muertos is the stunning **Pirámide de la Luna.** A sculpture of **Chalchiutlicue,** a water goddess and important Aztec deity, was found here during excavations. Although the climb is not as steep as the one up the Pyramid of the Sun, there are fewer vendors here to greet you and the view is even more magnificent. You will have a stunning view of the Calle de los Muertos and Teotihuacán in all its glory.

If you still have the energy, on the northeast side of the Pyramid of the Sun near *Puerta 4* is the **Palacio de Tepantitla,** which has some of the best-preserved frescoes on the site complete with a full range of colors. You can still see priests with elaborate headdresses and representations of Tlaloc. His goggle-eyes and snaky hair identify him as the god of water, important stuff. The lower part of the mural displays the Teotihuacano ideal of paradise where butterflies abound.

Getting There: Direct bus service from Mexico City to the pyramids is available from **Autobuses Teotihuacán** (1hr., every 30min. 5am-6pm, 13 pesos), located in the Terminal de Autobuses del Norte (tel. 781 18 12 or 587 05 01) at *Sala* 8. Alternatively, buses marked "Teotihuacán" (13 pesos) leave from outside the Indios Verdes Metro station (Line 3) every 20 minutes or so from opening until closing. The last bus back from the pyramids to Mexico City leaves the main entrance at 6pm. A few kilometers before reaching Teotihuacán, the bus passes just to the right of the town of **Acolmán,** founded shortly after the Conquest by Franciscans. The majestic lines of the ex-monastery of Acolmán rise to the sky, breaking the monotony of the corn fields. If you want to stop at the ex-monastery on your way back to Mexico City, take the "Indios Verdes" bus from the main entrance and get off at Acolmán.

Daytrips

Even those who've fallen in love with Mexico City need some time away. Fortunately, its great location makes it easy to escape (but who can escape it for long?). From small towns to not-so-small towns and from posh getaways to volcanoes, all of these places make cool and convenient daytrips.

YET MORE FUN

Cuernavaca, Morelos

This lovely-colonial-town-turned-chic-upperclass-getaway still hits the mark every time. The large number of expats and language school students testify to the fact that people can't stay away. Despite its gaggle of gringos and high prices, it's worth saving up for this one. Come check out lush greenery, luxurious living, and trendy nightlife *a la mexicana* (distance: 85km; see p. 433).

Desierto de los Leones, Estado de Mexico

Don't worry—this isn't a desert. It's a pine forest (go figure). Just outside of Mexico City, this "desierto" offers gorgeous hiking and fresh, pine-scented air; it's the perfect antidote to the smog and congestion of the city. The 2000-hectare park is also host to a Carmelite convent with lovely gardens. Free music and theater events take place on Sundays, when the park is filled with picnickers (distance: 25km; see p. 430).

Grutas de Cacahuamilpa, Guerrero

Have you ever wanted to see rock formations shaped like people making out? Well, these enormous, impressive caverns provide the opportunity for much merriment. Let your imagination run wild here through stalagmites, stalactites, and caves, some over 85m high. Raucous tour guides lead you through the underground wonderland (distance: 130km; see p. 356).

Ixtapan de la Sal, Estado de México

Despite the presence of nearby Disneyland-ish waterparks and resorts, Ixtapan couldn't be lovelier or more good-natured if it tried. The Mediterranean-style plaza and church are one of a kind. This is a good place to check out rustic life and take long mid-afternoon siestas (distance: 117km; see p. 426)

MEXICO CITY

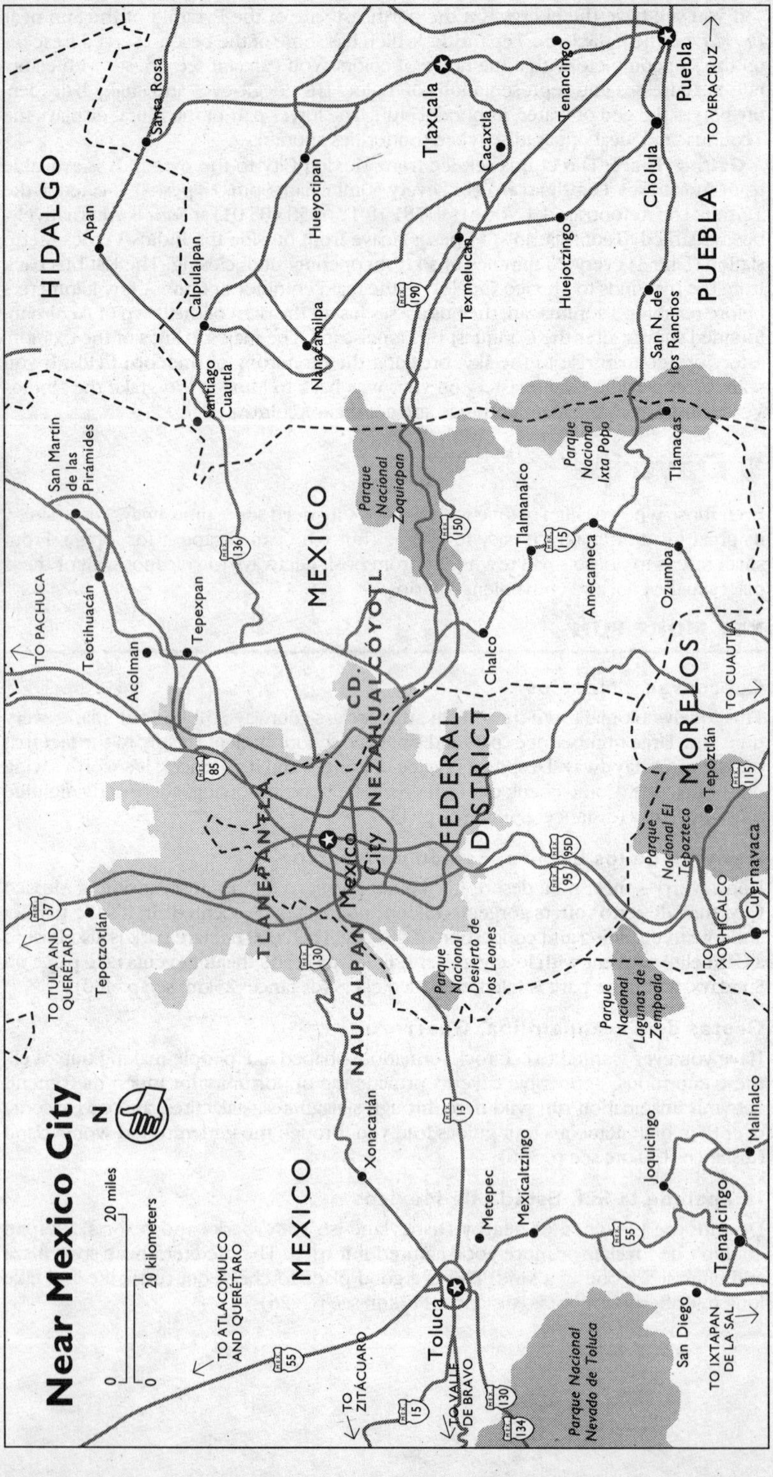
Near Mexico City
N
0
20 miles
0
20 kilometers
TO ATLACOMULCO AND QUERÉTARO
TO ZITÁCUARO
TO VALLE DE BRAVO
TO TULA AND QUERÉTARO
TO PACHUCA
TO IXTAPAN DE LA SAL
TO XOCHICALCO
TO CUAUTLA
TO VERACRUZ
HIDALGO
MEXICO
MEXICO
PUEBLA
MORELOS
FEDERAL DISTRICT
TLANEPANTLA
NAUCALPAN
CD. NEZAHUALCÓYOTL
Mexico City
Toluca
Metepec
Mexicaltzingo
Xonacatlán
Tepotzotlán
Teotihuacán
San Martín de las Pirámides
Acolman
Tepexpan
Santiago Cuautla
Calpulalpan
Apan
Santa Rosa
Hueyotipan
Nanacamilpa
Texmelucan
Tlaxcala
Cacaxtla
Tenancingo
Huejotzingo
Cholula
Puebla
San N. de los Ranchos
Tlamacas
Tlalmanalco
Amecameca
Ozumba
Chalco
Tepoztlán
Cuernavaca
Malinalco
Joquicingo
Tenancingo
San Diego
Parque Nacional Nevado de Toluca
Parque Nacional Desierto de los Leones
Parque Nacional Lagunas de Zempoala
Parque Nacional El Tepozteco
Parque Nacional Zoquiapan
Parque Nacional Ixta Popo
55
15
130
134
57
85
136
190
150
115
95
95D
15
55
115

Pachuca, Estado de México

An important center for silver mining and processing since the 16th century, Pachuca offers several lovely plazas, a few worthwhile museums, extremely friendly inhabitants, and invigoratingly crisp mountain air. The city exudes a sense of prosperity and contentment that is infectious, and the delightful streets are mostly free of tourists, making Pachuca a refreshing daytrip from the D.F. (distance: 90km; see p. 421).

Popocatépetl and Ixtaccíhuatl Volcanoes, Estado de Mexico

Veiled in Aztec mythology, the snow-capped Popocatépetl (Smoking Mountain) and Ixtaccíhuatl (Sleeping Woman) volcanoes overlook the state of Morelos and nearby Puebla. The volcanoes look like calmly majestic mountains when you see them from Mexico City (on a clear day), but they are really just slumbering beasts. In June 1997, Popocatépetl "smoked" more than it had in decades, dumping tons of ash and debris on nearby areas, including Mexico City. Although Popo is closed to hikers, some of Ixta can be climbed on well-marked tourist trails, or higher up in organized tour groups (distance: 60km; see p. 432).

Taxco, Guerrero

You've heard about the silver. Have you heard about the cable cars, stunning vistas, and fab church? Taxco boasts more than tourist treasures—it is a picturesque white pearl of a town way up in the hills. Its pink stone Catedral de Santa Prisca ranks among the loveliest in Mexico (distance: 180km; see p. 352).

Tepotzotlán, Estado de México

On the highway from Mexico City to Tula and Querétaro, Tepotzotlán offers a glimpse of small-town life, and its church and monastery house some of the country's most exquisite religious art. The beautiful *zócalo* and religious museum can be comfortably enjoyed in a couple of hours, and the comparatively smog-free air might make you crave even more of this town (distance: 36km, see p. 431).

Tepoztlán, Morelos

Surrounded by towering cliffs, this quiet *pueblo* occupies one of Morelos' more scenic sites. The cobbled *indígena* village preserves a colonial feel amid growing modernization, and many indigenous people still speak Náhuatl. Bring plenty of spirit (and bottled water and sunscreen) if you plan to scale Tepoztlán's "mother" hill. On Sundays, the *zócalo* comes alive with vibrant market activity. Quetzalcóatl, however, who was supposedly born in this sacred place, would be disturbed by the tons of *turistas* and gradual gringo-ization (distance: 70km; see p. 442).

Tula, Hidalgo

Tula itself offers not much more than a cute plaza, a good meal, and a bed, which may be why the fascinating ruins a 10-peso taxi ride away are relatively tourist free. The archaeological site at Tula houses the ruins of what was the capital city of the Toltec civilization. A great combination of desert-like and hilly terrain makes for picturesque ruins. Particularly interesting are the famous **Atlantes,** 10-meter tall massive stone statues of warriors with bad attitudes (distance: 65km; see p. 440).

Valle De Bravo, Estado de Mexico

Wealthy Mexico City residents go to play in the beautiful town of Valle de Bravo and the surrounding area are where. The lake may be man-made, but the beautiful red-roofed white stucco houses, cobblestone streets, and blossoming bougainvillea are irresistible. You don't have to jet-ski or golf to enjoy Valle; grab a picnic basket and loll around on the grassy hills (distance: 140km; see p. 425).

Xochicalco, Morelos

Ceremonial center, fortress, and trading post rolled into one, Xochicalco (Náhuatl for Place of the Flowers) is the most impressive archaeological site in the state. Because it has not gotten as much hype as other places, Xochicalco's beauty lies quiet and deserted in the rolling green hills. Aside from the occasional busload of screaming children, only swarms of dragonflies can be heard for miles. Photographers will writhe in ecstasy here, as will museum-lovers—the site's museum is truly phenomenal (distance: 120km; see p. 440).

Baja California

The peninsula of Baja California is cradled by the warm, tranquil Sea of Cortés on the east and the cold, raging Pacific Ocean on the west. Baja claims one of the most spectacular and diverse landscapes in the world—sparse expanses of sandy deserts give way to barren mountains jutting into Baja's traditionally azure, cloudless sky at incredible angles. The high-altitude national parks of northern Baja are home to seemingly out-of-place evergreens and snow during the winter months. And then, of course, there's the bizarrely blue-green water slapping at Baja's miles of uninhabited shore. This Crayola-aqua liquid flows past coral reefs, bats around in rocky storybook coves, and laps at the white sandy shores of thousands of miles of paradisiacal beaches lining both coasts. Meanwhile, the sands and outcrops of areas such as the bucolic Bahía de Concepción are watched over from above by many thousands of species of cacti that thrive on Baja's otherwise barren hillsides.

Called "el otro Mexico" (the other Mexico), Baja is neither here nor there, not at all California, yet nothing like mainland Mexico. Even its history is different—it was permanently settled by the Franciscans and Jesuits in the 1600s. Mainland Mexico has massive Aztec and Maya temples; Baja has serene little Jesuit missions. The peninsula's tradition of carefully blending wildness and tranquility, domesticity and simplicity, are emblematized by the Jesuit legacy in sleepy towns like San Ignacio.

Until relatively recently, Baja was an unknown frontier of sorts; the only way to reach its rugged desert terrain was by plane or boat. With the completion of the Transpeninsular Highway (Rte. 1) in 1973, and the addition of better toll roads and ferry service, Baja has become a popular vacation spot among Californians, Arizonans, Mexicans, and others. Vacationers range in type from hardy campers setting out to tame the savage deserts of central Baja to families living in one of Baja's many RV parks to the ubiquitous U.S. tourists who prefer a day on the beach, an evening when they can drown their inhibitions in many a *cerveza* and *margarita,* and a night of posh resort life, all without the inconvenience of changing currency.

Large resort hotels and condominium complexes are sprouting like grass to house these human torrents in the south. The heavily Americanized Los Cabos on the southern tip now have almost as little integrity and authenticity as Tijuana, the bawdy border wasteland of the **Baja California** state, wedged in the hilly crevices of the peninsula's northern extreme. The honest Mexican city of La Paz, the capital of **Baja California Sur,** is a southern beacon of beauty for resort-weary port-seekers. But it is Baja's southern midsection—from the tranquility of Mulegé to the palm-laden oasis town of San Ignacio to the thousands of undisturbed beaches beneath sheer cliffs—that is most pristine and mysterious. Most of Baja is still somewhat of an undiscovered country, prime for the hearty budget traveler to explore.

HIGHLIGHTS OF BAJA CALIFORNIA

- Explore the secluded and beautiful beaches of **Bahía de La Concepción** (p. 164), 48km of turquoise water, coves, powdery sand, bubbly springs, and abundant marine life.
- Sleep under a million stars in **San Ignacio** (see p. 158), a tiny leafy Northern Baja town/oasis with a remarkable **mission** (see see p. 159).
- Hike through the amazing **Parque Sierra Nacional San Pedro Mártir** (see p. 152), home to mountains, valleys, waterfalls, and Mexico's **National Observatory** (see p. 152).
- Despite over-development, **Los Cabos** (see p. 176) still draws curious U.S. travelers: lie on the peaceful beaches of **San José del Cabo** (see p. 182) by day, party with reckless abandon in **Cabo San Lucas** (see p. 177) by night.
- Stroll down the gulfside boardwalk of breezy, beautiful **La Paz** (see p. 168), the good-natured capital of Baja Sur, and a favorite Mexican vacation destination.

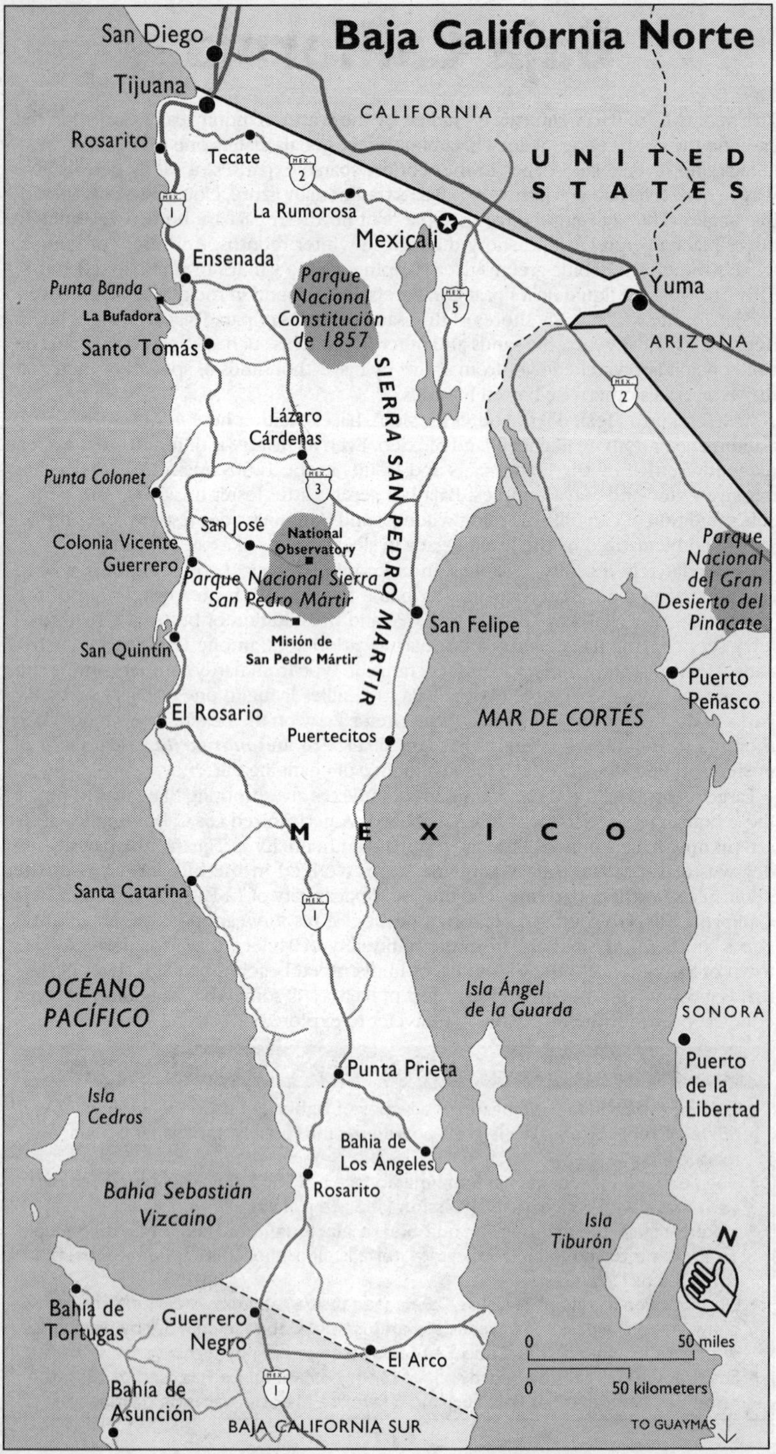
Baja California Norte
San Diego
Tijuana
CALIFORNIA
UNITED STATES
Rosarito
Tecate
MEX. 2
MEX. 1
La Rumorosa
Mexicali
Ensenada
Punta Banda
La Bufadora
Parque Nacional Constitución de 1857
MEX. 5
Yuma
ARIZONA
MEX. 2
Santo Tomás
SIERRA SAN PEDRO MARTIR
Lázaro Cárdenas
MEX. 3
Punta Colonet
San José
National Observatory
Colonia Vicente Guerrero
Parque Nacional Sierra San Pedro Mártir
Misión de San Pedro Mártir
San Felipe
Parque Nacional del Gran Desierto del Pinacate
San Quintín
Puerto Peñasco
El Rosario
MAR DE CORTÉS
Puertecitos
MEXICO
Santa Catarina
MEX. 1
OCÉANO PACÍFICO
Isla Ángel de la Guarda
SONORA
Puerto de la Libertad
Punta Prieta
Isla Cedros
Bahia de Los Ángeles
Rosarito
Bahía Sebastián Vizcaíno
Isla Tiburón
N
Bahía de Tortugas
Guerrero Negro
El Arco
0
50 miles
0
50 kilometers
MEX. 1
Bahía de Asunción
BAJA CALIFORNIA SUR
TO GUAYMAS

Getting Around

BY LAND

Driving through Baja is far from easy. The road was not designed for high-speed driving; often you'll be safely cruising along at 60mph and suddenly careen into a hidden, poorly banked, rutted curve that can only be taken at 30mph. Beware of potholes—some of the biggest and baddest in Mexico lurk on the roads leading off the transpeninsular highway. They will rock your world and eat your tires for breakfast; always be sure to have a good spare tire.

Still, a car (especially if it's four-wheel drive) is the only way to get close to the more beautiful and secluded areas of Baja, opening up an entire world of hiking and camping opportunities. The ride through Baja is probably one of the more beautiful in Mexico. During the journey, you will see vast deserts filled with cacti, gigantic mountains with ominous peaks, and stupendous cliffs that will make you hold on to your seat. If you need roadside assistance, the Angeles Verdes (Green Angels) pass along Rte. 1 twice per day. Unleaded gas may be in short supply along this highway, so don't pass a PEMEX station without filling your tank. All of Baja is in the *Zona Libre* (Free Zone), so strict vehicle permits are not required. If you will be driving in Baja for more than 72 hours, you only need to get a free permit at the border; to do this, show the vehicle's title and proof of registration. For more information on driving in Mexico, see p. 36.

If you plan to navigate the peninsula by bus, be forewarned that almost all *camiones* between Ensenada and La Paz are *de paso.* This means you have to leave at inconvenient times, fight to procure a ticket, and then probably stand the whole way. A much better idea is to buy a reserved seat in Tijuana, Ensenada, La Paz, or Los Cabos, and traverse the peninsula in one shot while seated. Unfortunately, you'll miss the fantastic Mulegé-Loreto beaches (for more info on buses, see p. 35).

Anyway you cut it, Baja's beaches and other points of interest off the main highway are often inaccessible via public transportation. Some swear by hitching—PEMEX stations are thick with rides (for more info on hitchhiking, see p. 39). *Let's Go* does not recommend hitchhiking; it is unpredictable and potentially hazardous.

BY SEA

Ferry service was instituted in the mid-1960s as a means of supplying Baja with food and supplies, not as a way for tourists to get from here to there—passenger vehicles may take up only the ferry space left over by the top-priority commercial vehicles. There are three different ferry routes: Santa Rosalía to Guaymas (8hr.), La Paz to Topolobampo/Los Mochis (9hr.), and La Paz to Mazatlán (17hr.). The La Paz to Topolobampo/Los Mochis route provides direct access to the train from Los Mochis through the Barrancas del Cobre (Copper Canyon).

Ferry tickets are generally expensive, even for *turista*-class berths, which cram two travelers into a cabin outfitted with a sink; bathrooms and showers are down the hall. It's extremely difficult to find tickets for *turista* and *cabina* class, and snagging an *especial* berth (a real hotel room) is as likely as stumbling upon a snowball in the central Baja desert—there are only two such suites on each ferry. This leaves the bottom-of-the-line *salón* ticket, which entitles you to a bus-style seat in a large room with few communal baths. If, as is likely, you find yourself traveling *salón*-class at night, ditch your seat early on and stake out a spot on the floor, or outside on the deck—simply spread out your sleeping bag and snooze. A small room is available to store your belongings, but once they're secured there is no way of retrieving any items, so make sure you take what you'll need during the trip. A doctor or nurse is always on board in the (rare) event that someone gets seasick. For those who plan to take their car aboard a ferry, it's a good idea to make reservations a month in advance; consult a travel agent or contact the ferry office directly. For further ferry information, contact a **Sematur** office, listed in the **Practical Information** sections of the cities from which the ferry departs.

BAJA CALIFORNIA NORTE

Tijuana

In the shadow of swollen, sulphur-spewing factories smeared across a topographical nightmare of gorges and promontories lies the most notorious specimen of the peculiar border subculture: Tijuana (pop. 2,000,000)—the most visited border town in the world. By day, swarms of tourists cross the border to explore the curio-filled alleys, haggle with street vendors, gulp cheap margaritas, and get their picture taken with donkeys painted as zebras. By night, Av. Revolución, the city's wide main drag, becomes a big, bad party. *Mariachi* bands triumph over the thumping dance beats blaring from the city's many clubs as bottle rockets explode in the near distance. This three-ringed, duty-free extravaganza comes complete with English-speaking, patronizing club promoters and every decadent way of blowing money, from *jai-alai* to dark, dingy strip joints, from mega-curio shops to Las Vegas-style hotels. And this is exactly how most of its 30 million yearly tourists would have it. A short distance from where U.S. dollars are exchanged for shots of tequila poured down tourists' throats, thousands of undocumented emigrants leave their tin shacks and make a midnight run for the U.S. in a perpetual and deadly game of tag. But with the fastest growth rate (13.6%) of all the world's major cities, Mexico's fourth-largest metropolis (founded in 1829 when Don Santiago Argüello received the title to Tía Juana—Aunt Jane's—ranch) continues to proliferate at an alarming rate. Beyond the gaudy neon lights and curio shops of Av. Revolución, Tijuana does offer some more refined attractions such as cultural museums, palm-shaded *parques,* and a winery. However, it's hard to say whether it's the city's strange charm, its cheap booze, or its sprawling, unapologetic hedonism that attracts tourists to Tijuana like flies.

ORIENTATION

From San Diego to Tijuana, take the red **Mexicoach** bus (tel. 85 14 70 or 619 428-9517 in the U.S.) from its terminal at the border (every 30min., 9am-9pm, US$1). It passes **Plaza Pueblo Amigo** on the Mexican side and leaves you beside the **Frontón Palacio** on Revolución between Calles 7 and 8 in the heart of the *centro*. Alternatively, grab a **trolley** to San Ysidro, at Kettner and Broadway in downtown San Diego (US$1.75), and walk across the border. Transfers from airport buses are also available.

If you arrive at the central bus station, avoid the cab drivers' high rates (80 pesos to downtown) and head for the public bus (30min., every 5min. 5am-10pm, 3 pesos). When you exit the terminal, turn left, walk to the end of the building, and hop on a bus marked "Centro Línea." It will let you off on Calle 3 and Constitución one block from Revolución. In Tijuana, *calles* run east-west; *avenidas* run north-south. The avenidas in the *centro* area are (from east to west) **Mutualismo, Martínez, Niños Héroes, Constitución, Revolución** (the main tourist drag), **Madero, Negrete,** and **Ocampo.** *Calles* in the *centro* area are both named and numbered. Beginning at the north, they are **Artículo 123** (Calle 1), **Benito Juárez** (Calle 2), **Carrillo Puerto** (Calle 3), **Díaz Mirón** (Calle 4), **Zapata** (Calle 5), **Magón** (Calle 6), **Galeana** (Calle 7), **Hidalgo** (Calle 8), and **Zaragoza** (Calle 9).

Driving across the border is fairly hassle-free, though traffic can be heavy at times, especially on weekends. A quick wave of the hand will usually notify you that you are no longer in the United States. However, driving in Tijuana can be harrowing: many traffic lights function merely as stop signs, four-way stop signs act as traffic lights, and the crowded streets can leave you ready to turn around (for more info on driving into Mexico, see p. 34). If you're only in Tijuana for a day, it's a better idea to leave your car in a lot on the U.S. side and join the throngs of people walking across the border. Parking rates start at US$3 per day and

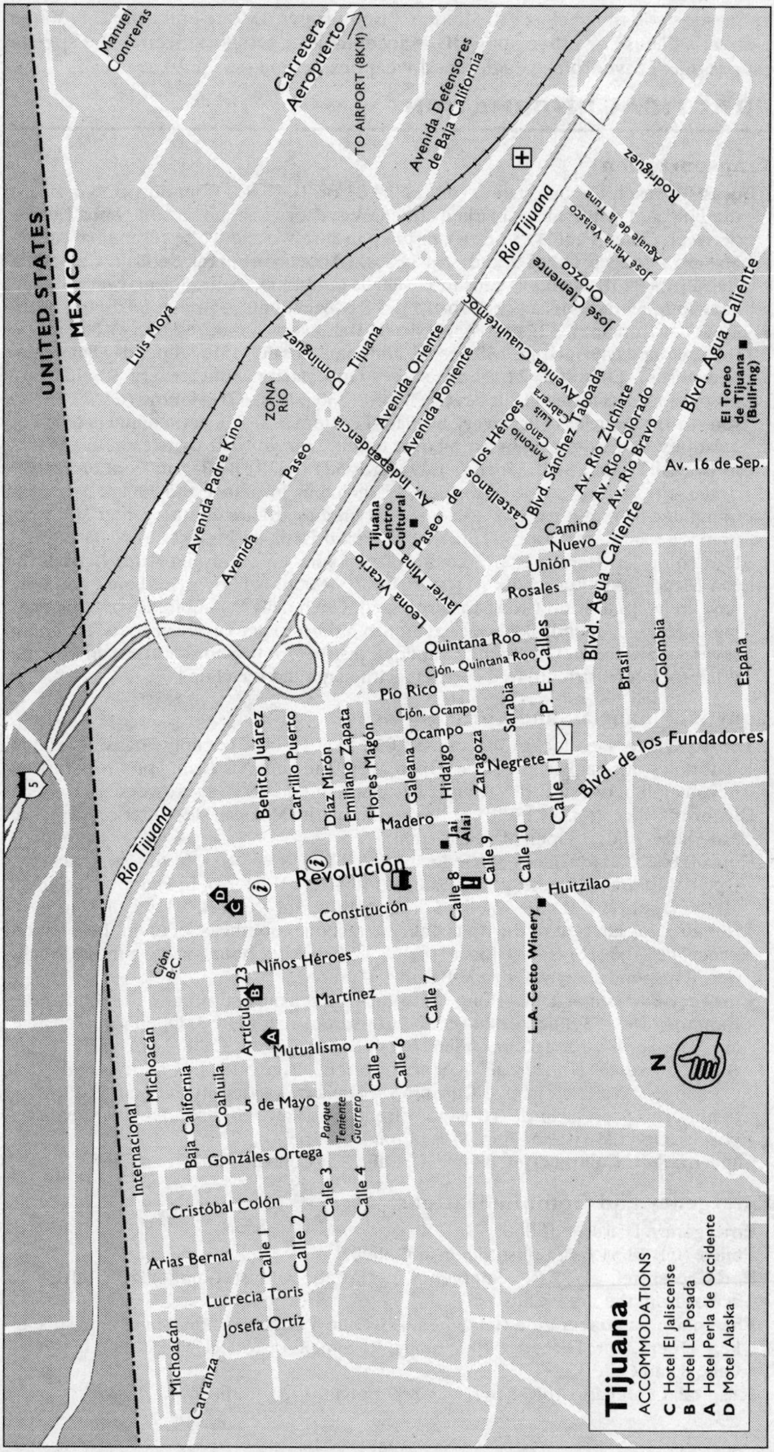
Tijuana
ACCOMMODATIONS
C Hotel El Jaliscense
B Hotel La Posada
A Hotel Perla de Occidente
D Motel Alaska
UNITED STATES
MEXICO
N
Manuel Contreras
Carretera Aeropuerto
TO AIRPORT (8KM)
Avenida Defensores de Baja California
Luis Moya
Avenida Padre Kino
Avenida
Paseo
ZONA RÍO
Domínguez
Tijuana
Avenida Oriente
Avenida Poniente
Av. Independencia
Río Tijuana
Avenida Cuauhtémoc
José Clemente Orozco
José María Velasco
Aguaje de la Tuna
Rodríguez
Paseo de los Héroes
Antonio Cano
Luis Cabrera
Avenida Taboada
Blvd. Sánchez Taboada
Av. Río Zuchiate
Av. Río Colorado
Av. Río Bravo
Blvd. Agua Caliente
El Toreo de Tijuana (Bullring)
Av. 16 de Sep.
Tijuana Centro Cultural
Javier Mina
Leona Vicario
Camino Nuevo
Unión
Rosales
Quintana Roo
Cjón. Quintana Roo
Pío Rico
Cjón. Ocampo
Ocampo
P. E. Calles
Sarabia
Negrete
Blvd. de los Fundadores
Brasil
Colombia
España
Benito Juárez
Carrillo Puerto
Díaz Mirón
Emiliano Zapata
Flores Magón
Galeana
Hidalgo
Zaragoza
Madero
Jai Alai
Revolución
Constitución
Calle 8
Calle 9
Calle 10
Calle 11
Huitzilao
L.A. Cetto Winery
Río Tijuana
Cjón. B.C.
Niños Héroes
Artículo 123
Martínez
Mutualismo
Calle 7
Calle 5
Calle 6
5 de Mayo
Parque Teniente Guerrero
Michoacán
Baja California
Coahuila
Internacional
Gonzáles Ortega
Calle 3
Calle 4
Cristóbal Colón
Arias Bernal
Calle 1
Calle 2
Lucrecia Toris
Josefa Ortíz
Michoacán
Carranza
5

increase as you move closer to Mexico. Bring proper ID to re-enter the U.S. While a driver's license or other photo ID is acceptable, a passport ensures the speediest passage. Leave fruits, veggies, and weapons behind (see p. 9).

PRACTICAL INFORMATION

Transportation

Buses: To reach the bus station (tel. 21 29 83 or 21 29 84) from downtown, board the blue and white buses marked "Buena Vista" or "Camionera" on Niños Héroes between Calles 3 and 4 (3 pesos), or jump in a brown-and-white communal cab on Madero between Calles 2 and 3 (4 pesos). **Autotransportes de Baja California** (tel. 21 29 82 through 87) runs to Ensenada (1½hr., every hr. 5-9am, every 30min. 9am-9pm, 55 pesos), La Paz (24hr., 4 per day 8am-9pm, 495 pesos), Loreto (18hr., 4 per day 8am-9pm, 377 pesos), Mexicali (3hr., every 30min., 84 pesos), San Felipe (5hr., 4 per day 5am-4pm, 158 pesos), and Santa Rosalía (15hr., 4 per day 8am-9pm, 306 pesos). **Elite** (tel. 21 29 48) serves Guadalajara (36hr., every 30min., 887 pesos) and Hermosillo (12hr., every 30min., 330 pesos). **Greyhound** (tel. 21 29 82) runs to Los Angeles (3hr., every hr. 5am-11:30pm, US$18), and connects to other locations. **Communal cabs** are all over town; some go to Rosarito (30min.).

Car Rental: Dollar, Blvd. Sánchez Taboada 10521 (tel. 81 84 84), in front of the VW dealership. Starting at 248 pesos per day, including insurance and 200km free. Minimum age to rent a car is 25; license and credit card are a must. Open M-F 9am-6pm, Sa 9am-2pm. Also in Tijuana is **Central Rent de Mexicali** (tel. 84 28 52), located on Los Héroes 104, Zona Río. Open 9am-3pm. **Bargain Auto Rentals,** in San Diego, 3860 Rosecrans St. (tel. (619) 299-0009) is fairly priced, and you only have to be 18 to rent. Credit card required. Open daily 8am-6pm. If you'll be driving in Mexico, spend US$5 per day in San Ysidro to get **car insurance.** There are several drive-through insurance vendors, just before the border at Sycamore and Primero, who distribute free booklets with maps and travel tips.

Tourist, Financial, and Local Services

Tourist Office: Revolución 711 (tel. 88 05 55) at Calle 1. Friendly English-speaking staff doles out maps and advice. Open M-Sa 9am-7pm, Su 10am-5pm. A booth on Revolución between Calles 3 and 4 has maps and may be less crowded.

Customs Office: (tel. 83 13 90), at the border on the Mexican side, after crossing the San Ysidro bridge. Open M-F 8am-3pm.

Consulates: Canada, German Gedovius 5-202 (tel. 84 04 61), in the Zona del Río. Open M-F 9am-1pm. **U.K.,** Blvd. Salinas 1500 (tel. 81 73 23), in Fracc. Aviacón, La Mesa. Open M-F 8am-3pm. **U.S.,** Tapachula Sur 96 (tel. 81 74 00), in Col. Hipódromo, adjacent to the Agua Caliente racetrack southeast of town. In an emergency, call the U.S. Duty Officer (tel. 28 17 62). After hours, leave a message and they'll respond shortly. Open M-F 8am-4:30pm.

Currency Exchange: Banks along Constitución exchange currency at the same rate. **Banamex** (tel. 88 00 21 or 88 00 22), Constitución at Calle 4. Open for exchange M-F 9am-5pm. with a 24hr. **ATM. Bital,** Revolución at Calle 2 also has a 24hr. **ATM.** *Casas de cambio* all over town offer better rates but generally do not exchange traveler's checks. **Cambio de Divisas,** located in the market directly behind the Secretario de Turismo, offers good rates. It also changes traveler's checks. Open M-Tu 9am-7pm, W-F 1-7pm, Sa 1-5pm.

Supermarket: Calimax (tel. 88 08 94), Calle 2 at Constitución. Open 24hr.

Emergency and Communications

Emergency: Dial 134 or 060.

Police: (tel. 38 51 68), Constitución at Calle 8.

Red Cross: (tel. 21 77 87, emergency 132), Calle Alfonso Gamboa at E. Silvestre, across from the Price Club.

Pharmacy: Farmacia Vida (tel. 85 14 61), Calle 3 at Revolución. Some English spoken. Open 24hr. **Discount Pharmacy,** Revolución 615 (tel. 88 31 31), between Calle 2 and Calle 3.

Hospital: Centenario 10851 (tel. 84 02 37 or 84 00 78), in the *Zona del Río.*

Post Office: (tel. 84 79 50), on Negrete at Calle 11. Open M-F 8am-7pm, Sa-Su 9am-1pm. **Postal Code:** 22001.

Fax: Telecomm (tel. 84 79 02; fax 84 77 50). To the right of the post office, in the same building. Open M-F 8am-7pm, Sa-Su 8am-1pm.

Telephones: Tijuana's streets are paved with **LADATELs.** There is a reasonably priced **caseta** at **Motel Díaz,** Av. Revolución 650 at Calle 1 (open daily 24hr.), and at **Hotel San Jorge,** Calle 1 at Constitución. Calls within Mexico 4 pesos per min., to the U.S. 10 pesos per min. Open daily 8am-9pm.

Phone Code: 66.

ACCOMMODATIONS

There's no shortage of budget hotels in Tijuana. You'll find plenty on Calle 1 between Revolución and Mutualismo, and they tend toward the roachy side. Ask to see rooms before paying. The area teems with people during the day and is relatively safe. Come nightfall, it becomes something of a red-light district, especially on Calle 1 between Revolución and Constitución. Women should be extra cautious when walking in this area at night; to return to your hotel, head down Calles 2 or 3, or take a taxi (US$2) from anywhere on Revolución.

Hotel El Jaliscense, Calle 1 #7925 (tel. 85 34 91), between Niños Héroes and Martínez. A great deal. Clean, small rooms with high, resilient beds, private baths, fans, and phones. Singles and doubles 100 pesos; each additional person 20 pesos.

Hotel Perla de Occidente, Mutualismo 758 (tel. 85 13 58), between Calles 1 and 2. 4 blocks from the bedlam of Revolución. Multicolored translucent roofing over the central hallway casts beautiful rays of light along the tiled floor. An odd picture of a chimp smoking a joint hangs two doors down from a tile mosaic of Jesus. Large, soft beds, roomy bathrooms, and fans on request. Singles 100 pesos; spacious doubles 180 pesos.

Hotel La Posada, Calle 1 #8190 (tel. 85 41 54 or 85 83 91), at Revolución. Just seconds away from all the action. Select your room carefully—the good ones have fans, comfy beds, and bathrooms even your mother would approve of. Singles 50 pesos, with bath 100 pesos; doubles 105 pesos; rooms for 3 or more 120 pesos.

Motel Alaska, Revolución 1950 (tel. 85 36 81), at Calle 1, smack in the middle of things. Simple clean rooms with comfy beds and small showers. Parking lot. Singles 150 pesos; doubles 160 pesos.

FOOD

Tijuana's touristy eats are essentially Tex-Mex, but some cheap *típico* restaurants line Constitución and the streets leading from Revolución to Constitución. Even cheaper are the mom-and-pop mini-restaurants all over town. If you choose the ubiquitous taco stands, select carefully. Slightly more expensive tourist restaurants and U.S. fast-food chains crowd Revolución. To save money, pay in pesos, even if the menu quotes prices in dollars.

El Pipirín Antojitos, Constitución 878 (tel. 88 16 02), between Calles 2 and 3. Sit at orange tables under orange brick arches and enjoy great food with friendly service. *Burritos de pollo con arroz y frijoles* (chicken burritos with rice and beans) all for 20 pesos. Open daily 7am-9pm.

Los Panchos Taco Shop (tel. 85 72 77), Revolución at Calle 3. Orange plastic booths are packed with hungry locals munching on ultra-fresh tortillas. Since it's open late during the summer months, this is a good place to satisfy those nighttime munchies. Steak taco US$1, bean burritos US$2. Open Su-Th 8am-midnight, F-Sa 8am-2am (8am-4am during the summer).

Hotel Nelson Restaurant (tel. 85 77 50), Revolución at Calle 1, under the hotel. Good, cheap food in a clean, fan-cooled, coffee-shop atmosphere. Jukebox blares Mexican oldies. Gringo breakfast (eggs, hotcakes, ham) 15 pesos; 3 enchiladas 18 pesos. Open daily 7am-11pm.

Lonchería Tico-Tico, Madero 688 (tel. 85 06 16), on the corner of Calle 1. Provides homey service. Both the cooks and the clients enjoy themselves. *Batido de platano* (banana milkshake) 15 pesos; breakfast tacos 12 pesos, 17 pesos with coffee. Open daily 6am-5pm.

SIGHTS

In the 1920s, when prohibition laws were enacted in the U.S., many of its citizens crossed the border to revel in the forbidden nectars of cacti (tequila), grapes (wine), and hops (beer). Ever since, Tijuana has had a reputation for being the venue for nights of debauchery. Although Tijuana still has the ability to satiate the wildest of party animals, it has a great deal to offer the sober tourist as well. Try **people-watching** while strolling down **Revolución;** you'll see plenty of surprising sights, including tourists having their pictures taken while wearing gaudy sombreros. Be serenaded by mariachis as you explore the **artisan's market** on Calle 1. When you get tired, relax in the beautiful and shady **Parque Teniente Guerrero,** Calle 3 and 5 de Mayo; it's one of the safer, more pleasant parts of town. The **cathedral,** with its massive chandelier, is nearby at Niños Héroes and Calle 2. **Morelos State Park,** Blvd. de los Insurgentes 26000 (tel. 25 24 70), features an exotic bird exhibition and picnic area. *(Open Tu-Su 9am-5pm. Admission 4 pesos, children 1.50 pesos.)* To get to the park, board the green and white bus on Calle 5 and Constitución.

The Cetto family has been making **wine** from grapes grown in the Valle de Guadalupe, northeast of Ensenada, since 1926. Visit the family-owned **L.A. Cetto Winery,** Cañón Johnson 2108 (tel. 85 30 31), at Calle 10, just off Constitución. *(Tours M-Sa every 30min. 10am-5pm. US$1, with wine-tasting US$2, with wine-tasting and souvenir goblet US$3. Reservations recommended for large groups.)* Tours are available; just don't try to remove a bottle from the storeroom—one American woman recently tried it and caused a wine avalanche that destroyed 30 cases of bottles. A harvest festival is held in the Cetto vineyards every August. Make reservations from January to June.

Walk off your wine buzz with a visit to one of Tijuana's museums. The **Museo de Cera** (tel. 88 24 78), on Calle 1 between Revolución and Madero, is home to a motley crew of wax figures, including such strange bedfellows as Tía Juana, Gandhi, Michael Jackson, and Marilyn Monroe (open daily 10am-7pm; admission US$1, children under 6 free). Nearby, **Mexitlán,** Benito Juárez 8901 (tel. 38 41 01), at Calle 2 and Ocampo, is home to over 200 intricate miniatures depicting famous Mexican historical, religious, and cultural monuments. *(Open W-Su 9am-7pm, closed M and Tu. Admission US$1.25.)* Absorb Maya architecture, Mexico City's Paseo de la Reforma, and Teotihuacán without having to consult a single bus schedule. Mexican folk art is also sold.

SPORTS

Jai alai is played in the majestic **Frontón Palacio** (tel. 85 78 33), Revolución at Calle 7. *(Open M-Sa 9am-11pm, Su 8am-11pm. Admission US$20; free admission coupons are often distributed outside.)* Two to four players take to the three-sided court at once, using arm-baskets to catch and throw a Brazilian ball of rubber and yarn encased in goatskin. The ball travels at speeds reaching 180mph; jai alai is reputedly the world's fastest game. After each point, the winning one- or two-player team stays on the court, while the losing team rotates out in king-of-the-hill style. The first team to score seven points wins; after the first rotation through the entire eight team lineup, rallies are worth two points, not one. If you can, try to catch a doubles match—the points are longer and require more finesse. Players are treated like horses, with betting and odds. All employees are bilingual, and the gambling is carried out in greenbacks.

If you're in town on the right Sunday, you can watch the graceful and savage dance of a bullfight in one of Tijuana's two bullrings. **El Toreo de Tijuana** (tel. 80 18 08), downtown to the east of Agua Caliente and Cuauhtémoc, hosts *corridas* (bullfights) on chosen Sundays at 4:30pm from early May to July. The more modern **Plaza Monumental,** northwest of the city near Las Playas de Tijuana (follow Calle 2 west), employs famous *matadores* and hosts fights from August to mid-September. Tickets to both rings are sold at the gate and at the ticket window at Mexicoac, on Revolución between Calle 6 and 7. To get to the Plaza Monumental, catch a blue and white bus on Calle 3 between Constitución and Niños Héroes.

ENTERTAINMENT

If bullfighting turns your stomach, stroll over to the **Tijuana Centro Cultural** (tel. 84 11 11), on Paseo de los Héroes at Mina (open daily 10am-9pm); the monumental sphere in the plaza houses the **Space Theater,** an auditorium with a giant 180° screen that shows U.S. OmniMax movies dubbed in Spanish (shows Tu-F every hr. 3-9pm; Sa-Su every 2hr. 11am-9pm; admission 25 pesos, children 13 pesos). A **performance center** (Sala de Espectáculos) and **open-air theater** (Caracol al Aire Libre) host visiting cultural attractions, including the **Ballet Folklórico.** The **Sala de Video** screens free documentaries, and the **Ciclo de Cine Extranjero** shows foreign films (W-F 6 and 8pm, Sa-Su 4, 6, and 8pm; 15 pesos). Children's films are shown on weekends (Sa and Su 10am, noon, 2pm; parents and kids free). The *Centro Cultural* also serves as a gallery for local and visiting art exhibits. Pick up a monthly calendar at the information booth in the *Centro's* art gallery.

While all of this is just swell, if you've come to party, brace yourself for a raucous good time. Strolling down Revolución after dusk, you'll be bombarded by thumping music, neon lights, and abrasive club promoters hawking "two-for-one" margaritas (most places listed below charge US$4 for 2). All clubs check ID (18-plus), with varying criteria of what's acceptable, and many frisk for firearms. If you'd like to check out a more local scene, peek into the small clubs on Calle 6 off Revolución.

Iguanas-Ranas (tel. 85 14 22), Revolución at Calle 3. Drink your beers (US$2.25) in the schoolbus or raise hell on the omnipresent dance floor. Lively on weeknights; packed on weekends. Myriads of margarita-drinking iguanas and *ranas* (frogs) adorn the walls. A twentyish crowd of both *norteños* and *norteamericanos* breaks it down. Open daily 10am-4am.

Tilly's 5th Avenue (tel. 85 90 15), at Revolución and Calle 5. The tiny wooden dance floor in the center of this upscale, balloon-filled restaurant/bar resembles a boxing ring, but rest assured—there's only room for dancing. The reflections from the disco ball are enhanced by the mirrored walls and the dance-happy staff. Tilly's is packed on weekends. Beer US$2. Wednesday night is "Student Night"—all drinks US$0.49. Open M-Th 10:30am-2am, F-Sa 10:30am-5am.

Caves (tel. 88 06 09), Revolución and Calle 5. Dinosaurs and prehistoric beasts perched on a rock facade lead to a dark but airy bar and disco with orange decor, stalactites, and black lights. Drink 2 beers (US$3) with the blond clientele. No cover. Open Su-Th 11am-2am, F-Sa 11am-2am.

The Vibe, Revolución by Calle 6. Prepare yourself for this 3-tiered party palace. Miami-esque neon decor and pool tables bring in the masses. Drink down those US$2 margaritas. Cover only on weekends.

El Ranchero Bar (tel. 85 28 00), in front of the fountain in Plaza Santa Cecilia on Calle 1 and Revolución. Red, white, and green paper hang from the ceiling of this dimly-lit gay bar. Beers US$1. Open M-W 10am-2am, Th-Su 10am-6am.

Rosarito

Once a little-known playground for the rich and famous, the beach haven of Rosarito (pop. 100,000) has expanded at breakneck speed to accommodate the throngs of northern sunseekers who have discovered its hotels, restaurants, shops, and beaches. Hollywood has also discovered Rosarito. The largest grossing movie of all time, **Titanic,** was filmed here. Giant 10-story hotels and posh resorts cater to the tastes of American tourists. Most of the visitors are from the north or are semi-permanent U.S. expats. English is ubiquitous and prices are quoted in dollars. On weekends, the sands and surf overflow with people, volleyball games, and horses; finding a place for your towel may be a struggle.

ORIENTATION AND PRACTICAL INFORMATION Rosarito lies about 27km south of Tijuana and stretches along the shore. Virtually everything in town is on the main street, **Blvd. Juárez,** upon which street numbers are non-sequential. Most of the action can be found on the southern half of Juárez. You can pick up a map at the tourist office. Most of what is listed below is near the purple Ortega's Restaurant in Oceana Plaza. To get to Rosarito from Tijuana, grab a yellow and white *taxi de ruta* (30min., 6.50 pesos) that leaves from Madero, between Calles 5 and 6. To return to Tijuana, flag down a *taxi de ruta* along Juárez or at its starting point in front of the Rosarito Beach Hotel. Getting to Ensenada is more of an adventure. Take a blue-and-white striped cab marked "Primo Tapia" from Festival Plaza, north of the Rosarito Beach Hotel, to the toll booth *(caseta de cobro)* on Rte. 1 (3 pesos). From there, buses leave for Ensenada (every 30min. until about 9pm, 18 pesos).

The **tourist office** (tel. 2 02 00), on Juárez at Centro Comercio Villa Floreta at the beginning of Juárez, has tons of brochures. The friendly staff will orient you. Some English is spoken. (Open M-F 9am-7pm, Sa-Su 10am-5pm.) **Banamex** (tel. 2 15 56 or 2 24 48) is on Juárez at Ortiz (open for exchange M-F 9am-5pm). On weekends, you'll have to go to one of the *casa de cambios* scattered along Juárez, which charge a commission. **Calimax** (tel. 2 15 69), at Lázaro Cárdenas and Juárez, just before Quinta del Mar heading south on Juárez, has plenty of foodstuffs (open 24hr.). **Lavamática Moderna** is on Juárez at Acacias (wash and dry 10 pesos; open M-Sa 8am-8pm, Su 8am-6pm). In an **emergency,** dial 134. The **police** (tel. 2 11 10) are at Juárez and Acacias. The **Red Cross** (tel. 132) is on Juárez at Ortiz, just around the corner from the police. **Farmacia Hidalgo** (tel. 2 05 57; open M-Sa 8am-10pm, Su 8am-9pm), **IMSS Hospital** (tel. 2 10 21; open 24hr.), and the **post office** (tel. 2 13 55; open M-F 8am-3pm, Sa 9am-1pm) are on Juárez, near its intersection with Acacias. The **postal code** is 22710. The **phone code** is 661.

ACCOMMODATIONS AND FOOD Budget hotels in Rosarito are either inconvenient or cramped, with the exception of the outstanding **Hotel Palmas Quintero** (tel. 2 13 59), on Lázaro Cárdenas near the Hotel Quinta del Mar, three blocks inland from north Juárez. A helpful staff and a dog welcome tourists to giant rooms with double beds and clean, private baths with hot water. Chill in the patio under the palm trees. (Singles 120 pesos; doubles 240 pesos.) **Rosarito Beach Rental Cabins** (tel. 2 09 68), on Lázaro Cárdenas two blocks toward the water, are the cheapest housing in Rosarito. You get what you pay for—each small cabin contains bunk beds, a toilet, and a sink. Disney-castle spires make the cabins hard to miss. (Singles US$5, with shower US$10; doubles US$10, with shower US$15; key deposit US$5; erratic reception 8am-2pm and 4-7pm.)

Fresh produce and seafood abound in the restaurants that line Juárez. For an economic seafood dinner, head to **Vince's Restaurant** (tel. 2 12 53), on Juárez between Acacias and Robie, across from the police station. Enjoy a feast of soup, salad, rice, potatoes, tortillas, and an entree—*filete especial* (fillet of halibut, 28 pesos), jumbo shrimp (40 pesos), or a veritable seafood extravaganza of fish, shrimp, octopus, and lobster (46 pesos; open daily 8am-10pm). **La Flor de Michoacán,** Juárez 306 (tel. 3 02 78), serves up fresh tacos filled with the meat of your choice (5.50 pesos, 10 pesos with beans; open daily 10am-8pm). Get your morning grub at **Ortega's Ocean Plaza,** Juárez 200 (tel. 2 27 91), in a gaudy purple building. Prick your appetite with a cactus omelette (US$2), or catch the all-you-can-eat Mexican buffet (open Su-Th 8am-10pm, F-Sa 8am-11pm).

SIGHTS AND ENTERTAINMENT Rosarito attracts tourists with its fancy resorts, beautiful shores, and rollicking nightlife. **Rosarito Beach** boasts soft sand and gently rolling surf. The **Museo de Historia Wa Kutay,** on Juárez just south of the Rosarito Beach Hotel, showcases folk art and history of the area. **Fox Studios Baja** (tel. 4 01 10), 2km south of Rosarito on the Tijuana-Ensenada road, offers a short film and tour (US$5) of some of the set and props used in the movie **Titanic** (open daily 10am-6pm). Once the sun goes down, travelers live the dream at **Papas and Beer,** Calle de

Coronales 400 (tel. 2 04 44), one block north of the Rosarito Beach Hotel and two blocks toward the sea. Reminiscent of a giant wooden jungle gym, the open-air dance floor, bar, and sandy volleyball courts are packed with revelers on the weekends. Beer is 15 pesos, and mixed drinks run 17-25 pesos. Don't forget the ID; they take carding very seriously. (Cover US$15-20 on Saturdays and holidays; open daily 11am-3am.) Or follow the striped sidewalk outside **Festival Plaza,** on South Juárez at Nogal, to **ChaChaCha's,** where you can dance the night away. (Beers 18 pesos, mixed drinks 24 pesos; open daily 6pm-3am.)

SWM: Seeking Petite, Dangerous Scorpio

"Scorpions? But this isn't the jungle," you gasp, "this is Baja." Tough break. These nasty little pests (known in Spanish as *alacranes)* frequent Baja, especially around Mulegé and the mid-peninsula. Unless you are allergic to them, don't worry about a slow, painful death—these aren't the fatal black scorpions that are found in Asia and Africa. These are beige, desert-and-beach-camouflaged scorpions. The smaller (and lighter-colored) the scorpion, the bigger the bite. Most scorpion-bite victims experience intense pain for a day or two. These critters like dark, warm, damp places, so be sure to shake your shoes and clothing before you put 'em on. Ice packs help to alleviate the pain, though locals swear that garlic is the best relief. If you wake up in the middle of the night and a scorpion is crawling up your chest, don't try to flatten or squash it; it will just get angry and sting your hand. Because of their hard protective armor, scorpions are hard to crush. The best thing to do is to give it a hard flick from the side and watch it fly far, far away.

Mexicali

The highly industrialized capital of Baja California, Mexicali (pop. 1 million) straddles both the U.S. and the Mexican mainland. From the cheap, duty-free stands on the border to the 11 industrial plants that ring the city, Mexicali is large, loud, and rapidly growing. As a result, the city is heavily polluted—there's not much tourism here. Some portions of Mexicali, including the mall and surrounding plaza, wear the U.S. facade so well that if not for the language, they could be across the border. Still, Mexicali is a good place to stock up on supplies and to check out the local Chinese cuisine before heading south. Because of turn-of-the-century immigration, thousands of Chinese live in Mexicali; Chinese food is more popular than Mexican food, and a Chinese-influenced dialect has emerged in the city center.

ORIENTATION

Although far from the beaten path between the U.S. and Mexico, Mexicali can still serve as a starting point for travelers heading south. The city lies on the California border 189km inland from Tijuana, with Calexico and the Imperial Valley immediately to the north. Its valley location subjects Mexicali to chilly winters and hot summers. Mexicali is one of the more difficult cities in Mexico to navigate. Run directly to the **tourist office** and pick up a deluxe **map.** Mexicali is plagued with haphazardly numbered, zigzagging streets. The main boulevard leading away from the border is **López Mateos,** which heads southeast, cutting through the downtown area. North-south *calles* and east-west *avenidas* both intersect Mateos, causing even more confusion. **Cristóbal Colón** (also known as Blvd. Internacional), **Madero, Reforma, Obregón, Lerdo, and Zaragoza** (in that order from the border) run east-west. **Azueta, Altamirano, Morelos, México, Bravo, Del Comercio,** and streets **A-L** (in that order from west to east) run north-south, starting from where Mateos meets the border (a gigantic green canopy marks the spot). Although the border area can be confusing, a few well-directed questions will set you on the right path. To reach the border from the bus station, take the local bus marked "Centro" (every 10min. 5am-11pm, 3 pesos)

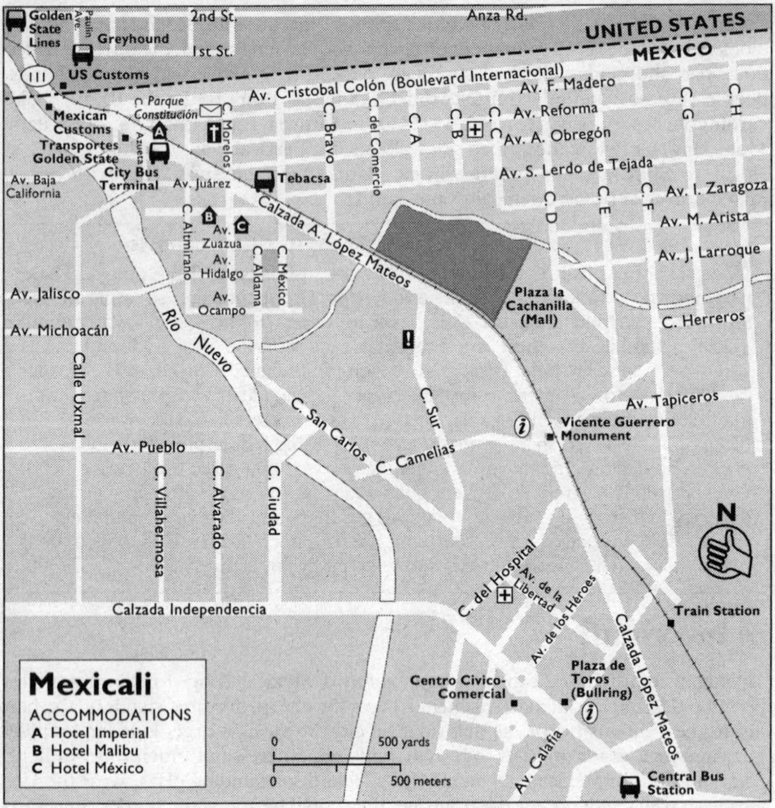

from outside the bus terminal, just across the footbridge. Ride past the Vicente Guerrero monument and the enormous new mall, get off at López Mateos, and walk until the border crossing.

PRACTICAL INFORMATION

Buses: The station (tel. 57 24 10 or 57 24 15) is near the intersection of Mateos and Independencia, about 4km south of the border. A blue and white bus will take you to the station from the border (3 pesos). **Autotransportes de Baja California** (tel. 57 24 51) sends buses to Ensenada (14hr., 4 per day, 122 pesos), La Paz (27½hr., 5:30pm, 396 pesos), Puerto Peñasco (5hr., 9am, 2, and 8pm, 113 pesos), San Felipe (2½hr., 5 per day 8am-8pm, 67 pesos), and Tijuana (3½hr., every hr., 84 pesos). **Elite** (tel. 56 01 10) sends buses to most of the above locations at higher prices, plus Chihuahua (17hr., 11am and 2:45pm, 423 pesos), Juárez (14-16hr., 3:20pm, 418 pesos), and Nogales (9hr., 11:15pm, 226 pesos). **Golden State** (tel. 53 61 69) sends buses to Californian cities, including Los Angeles (4½hr., 8am, 2:30, and 10pm, US$28), Palm Springs (2½hr., 8am, 2:30, and 10pm, US$18), and Pomona (4hr., 8am, 2:30, and 10pm, US$26). **Transportes del Pacífico** (tel. 57 24 61) offers *de paso* service to most of the above locations for slightly higher fares than Norte de Sonora, as well as second-class buses for around 15% less that take 2-6hr. longer. Service to Guaymas (250 pesos), Tijuana (*primera clase* 68 pesos, *segunda clase* 60 pesos), and more. **Transportes Norte de Sonora** (tel. 57 24 10) sends buses to Guadalajara (33hr., every hr., 616 pesos), Guaymas (11hr., every hr., 251 pesos), Hermosillo (9hr., every hr., 209 pesos), Los Mochis (17hr., every hr., 372 pesos), Mazatlán (24hr., every hr., 494 pesos), and Tepic (30hr., every hr., 583 pesos).

Tourist Office: Comité de Turismo y Convenciones (tel. 57 23 76; fax 52 58 77), a white building at Mateos and Compresora facing the Vicente Guerrero monument and park, 3km from the border. Lots of brochures, huge (thank goodness!) maps, and a friendly English-speaking staff. Open Aug. 8am-4:30pm; Sept.-July M-F 8am-6pm. **Tourist cards** are available at the Federal Immigration office at the border.

Currency Exchange: Exchange currency at any *casa de cambio* along Madero, or try **Banamex** (tel. 54 28 00), at Altamirano and Lerdo, where you can exchange traveler's checks. 24hr. **ATM**. Bank open M-F 9am-5pm. The **Bital** across the street from the post office also has a 24hr. **ATM.** Open M-F 8am-7pm, Sa 8am-5:30pm.

Emergency: Dial 060.

Police: (tel. 58 17 00 or 58 27 00) at Calle Sur and Mateos. English spoken.

Pharmacy: Farmacia Genéricos (tel. 52 90 88) at López Mateos and Morelos. Open daily 8am-10pm.

Hospital: IMSS Centro de Salud (tel. 51 51 50), Lerdo at Calle F, has an English-speaking staff. Otherwise, try the **Hospital Civil** (tel. 53 11 23).

Post Office: Madero 491 (tel. 52 25 08), at Morelos. Open M-F 9am-5pm, Sa 9am-1pm. **Postal Code:** 21000.

Fax: Telecomm (tel. 52 20 02) is in the same building as the post office. Service to the U.S. (10 pesos per page) and within Mexico (7 pesos per page). Open M-F 8am-5pm, Sa 9am-1pm.

Telephones: LATADELs can be found all over the city. There is a *caseta* at the **Farma Genéricos.** Local calls 1 peso; long-distance within Mexico 3 pesos per min.; calls to U.S. 7 pesos per min.

Phone Code: 65.

ACCOMMODATIONS

Budget hotels crowd the noisy bar strip on Altamirano between Reforma and Lerdo and line Morelos south of Mateos. Hotels on Madero close to Mateos will dig deeper into your wallet but tend to be cleaner.

Hotel Málibu, on Morelos near Lerdo. Look out for the big sign. Although the hotel doesn't quite live up to its name, the worn rooms are clean and come with the basics. Windows and light-colored rooms help a bit. One of the cheapest joints in town, it's ideal for the hard-core budget traveler. Singles 65 pesos, with bath 90 pesos, with bath and TV 100 pesos; doubles with bath 130 pesos; 40 pesos for each additional person.

Hotel México, Av. Lerdo 476 (tel. 54 06 69), at Morelos. This hotel offers clean, pink rooms that not only have color TV and super-cold A/C but also overlook a central patio. Bathrooms are small but clean. The office doubles as a grocery store, and the staff is *muy simpático.* Singles 170 pesos; doubles 190 pesos.

Hotel Kennedy, Morelos 415 (tel. 54 90 62), between Lerdo and Zoazua. Color TV, A/C, and a phone grace the sparkling rooms of this hotel. Singles (1-2 people) 170 pesos, with carpet 190 pesos.

FOOD

Some of the best and cheapest food in town is at the food court in Mexicali's huge mall on Lopez Mateos. Here, yummy, cheap Chinese cuisine is bountiful, but the constant crowds make it a challenge to find a seat. Most places have combination plates that offer three entrees for 17 pesos, four entrees for 20 pesos.

Restaurant Hollis (tel. 52 66 96), Morelos and Mateos opposite Farma Genéricos. Select your meal from the choices of Chinese, Mexican, or American cuisine. Lots of locals converse casually as they enjoy home-cooked meals. Chinese combo plates 32 pesos. Filling steak sandwiches 20 pesos. Open daily 8am-10pm.

Restaurant Buendía, Altamirano 263 (tel. 52 69 25). Despite sharing a name with the illustrious family of Gabriel García Márquez's epic, Buendía specializes in Chinese cuisine—but chefs are always happy to whip up some *antojitos.* Try a heaping plate of beef with broccoli, fried rice, egg roll, and fried chicken (30 pesos). Three burritos are 30 pesos. Vegetarians can delight in a veggie combo for only 24 pesos. Open daily 7am-9pm.

Tortas El Chavo, Reforma 414 at Altamirano, off Mateos, 3 blocks from the border. A fast-food joint with mirrored walls that reflect its bright green and yellow booths.

Tortas, any style, are 14.5 pesos; *tacos de machaca* (tacos filled with strips of beef) go for a mere 4.5 pesos. Open daily 8:30am-8pm.

SIGHTS AND ENTERTAINMENT

Mexicali's **park, forest, lake,** and **zoo** (tel. 55 28 33) are located on Alvarado between San Marcos and Lázaro Cárdenas in the southwestern part of town. *(Zoo open Tu-Sa 9am-5pm, Su 9am-5pm. Admission 3 pesos, children 2 pesos.)* Wink at the birds in the aviary, pedal a paddleboat on the lake, or admire lions and tigers from the train that circles the park and nature reserve. The grounds contain carousels, bumper cars, a pool, and a **science museum.** To reach the park area, board a black and white *colectivo* marked "Calle 3" downtown. If you've got wheels, drive south on Azueta over the Río Nuevo. The road becomes Uxmal south of the river; turn left on Independencia, then right on Victoria. The city's **Parque Vicente Guerrero** (tel. 54 55 63), off Calle López Mateos and next door to the mall, has jungle gyms as well as picnic spots and party space rentals (open daily 9am-9pm).

Plaza de Toros Calafia (tel. 56 11 96), on Calafia at Independencia in the *centro* is host to regularly scheduled bullfights in the fall. Take a 10-minute ride on the blue and white bus (2.50 pesos) from the *centro* to the plaza, which holds up to 11,500 people (11,499 if the bull's having a good day). Wild and crazy rodeos rampage in the winter and spring at **Lienzo Charro del Cetys,** at Cetys and Ordente. Check with the tourist office for schedules. Good, clean fun awaits at **Mundo Divertido,** an amusement park at Mateos 850 (tel. 52 56 75), across from the mall. To get to the park, board a blue and white bus marked "Centro Cívico" departing from Madero and Altamirano (every 10min. 5am-11pm, 2.50 pesos; park open M-F noon-9pm, Sa-Su 11am-10pm). A trip that's fun for all is to Mexicali's huge, centrally located mall, the **Centro Comercial Gigante,** also known as **La Cachanilla.** Inside this air-conditioned behemoth are cheap food stands, video arcades, clothing stores, and crowds of people seeking refuge from the heat. The mall is quite definitely one of Mexicali's best people-watching spots. For a film, check out **Cinema Gemelos** in the mall (20 pesos).

Tecate

Any one who has spent any time in Mexico will recognize the name of this small border town. Indeed, the ubiquitous brand of Mexican beer is named after this town and is brewed here at Cervecería Cuauhtémoc Moctezuma. However, Tecate's alcoholic creations are not its only claim to fame—it also serves as one of the quickest border crossings in Baja California, especially for those headed to Ensenada. Unlike its industrialized neighbors, Tijuana and Mexicali, Tecate's air is refreshingly clean and the town's central park is among the more pleasant in Baja California. Street vendors and curio shops are absent here, making it the ideal destination for a daytrip from the frenzied streets of Tijuana.

ORIENTATION AND PRACTICAL INFORMATION Tecate lies 49km east of Tijuana on Rte. 2. If you drive in from Tijuana, you'll be on Av. Benito Juárez (the main street); from the U.S. you'll drive in on the palm-tree lined **Calle Lázaro Cárdenas.** These two streets intersect at the northwest corner of **Parque Hidalgo,** the hub of activity. The entire town slants north (uphill is north; downhill is south). *Avenidas* and *callejones* run east-to-west parallel to the border and *calles* run north to south. Starting from the north, the streets are **Callejón Madero, Av. Revolución, Callejón Reforma, Av. Benito Juárez, Callejón Libertad,** and **Av. Hidalgo.** Starting from the east, the *calles* are **Portes Gil, Rodriguez, Ortiz Rubio, Lázaro Cárdenas, Elias Calles, Obregón, De la Huerta, Carranza,** and **Aldrete.** Simple maps of the town are available at the **tourist office,** Libertad Alley 1305 (tel. 4 10 95), located on the south side of Parque Hidalgo (open daily 9am-5pm).

The **bus station** is two blocks east of the park on Av. Juárez. **Autotransportes de Baja California** (tel. 4 12 21) sends buses to Ensenada (5 per day 8am-7pm, 30 pesos), Mexicali (every hr. 6:30am-10pm, 58 pesos), and Tijuana (every 30min. 5am-9pm, 15 pesos). **Elite** and **Transportes Norte De Sonora** (tel. 4 23 43) share a ticket window and jointly send buses to Guaymas (13hr., 300 pesos), Hermosillo (12hr., 259 pesos), Mazatlán (24hr., 539 pesos), Mexicali (2hr., 50 pesos), and Sonoita (6hr., 132 pesos). All buses are *de paso* and leave every hour beginning at 7am. **Bancomer** (tel. 4 14 50 or 4 13 49), on the corner of Cárdenas and Av. Juárez, exchanges traveler's checks and has a 24hr. **ATM** (bank open M-F 8:30am-4pm, Sa 10am-2pm). A **Banamex** at Av. Juárez and Obregón, across from the PEMEX station, with 24hr. **ATM** (open M-F 9am-4pm, Sa 9am-2pm). **Calimax** (tel. 4 00 39), on Av. Juárez between Carranza and Aldrete, sells groceries and more (open daily 6am-11pm). In an **emergency,** dial 134. The local **police** (tel. 4 11 76) can be reached 24 hours. **Red Cross** can be reached in an emergency by dialing 132. **Farmacia Santa Lucia,** Av. Juárez 45 (tel. 4 32 00), next to the Calimax, is open every day for your convenience (open M-Sa 9am-9pm, Su 9am-7pm). The **post office,** Ortiz Rubio 147 (tel. 4 12 45) is two blocks north off Av. Juárez (open M-F 8am-3pm, Sa 8am-noon). The **postal code** is 21400. **Faxes** can be sent from **Telecomm** (tel. 4 13 75), next door to the post office (open M-F 8am-6pm, Sa 8am-11am). There is a long distance **caseta** in the bus station and **LADATELS** line Av. Juárez. The **phone code** is 665.

ACCOMMODATIONS AND FOOD Although most visitors to Tecate do not spend the night, there are a few places for budget travelers to rest. **Hotel Tecate** (tel. 4 11 16), on Libertad at Cárdenas around the corner from the tourist office, is centrally located and offers simple, clean rooms with bathrooms and fans (singles and doubles 140 pesos, with TV 180 pesos, with A/C 250 pesos). Farther from the center of activity is **Motel Paraíso,** Aldrete 83 (tel. 4 17 16), one block north of Av. Juárez, with clean, but worn, rooms. (1-2 people 85 pesos; 2-3 people 110 pesos; 35 pesos each additional person.) **Hotel Juárez,** Juárez 230 (tel. 4 16 17), about two blocks east of the park, offers small, clean rooms with tile floors. An open air hallway lets in cool breezes and glittering daylight. (Singles 80 pesos; doubles 100 pesos; 10 peso towel deposit.) As always, the cheapest eats in town are in *taquerías*, which line Av. Juárez between the park and the bus station.

Cafe de Pollo, Juárez 170 (tel. 4 07 46), one block west of the park, serves *tortas* of many varieties (13-18 pesos) in a turquoise environment. At the **Restaurant Jardín Tecate** (tel. 4 34 53), on the south side of the park next to the tourist office, you can enjoy your meal under the shade of park trees as you watch the world go by (quesadillas 21 pesos, Mexican combo 32 pesos).

SIGHTS Undoubtedly, the **Tecate Brewery** is the biggest attraction in town, on Av. Hidalgo two blocks west of Cárdenas. *(Open M-F 10am-5:30pm, Sa-Su 10am-4pm. Free tours are offered for groups of 5 or more M-F 11am and 3pm, Sa 11am.)* The brewery was started in 1944 and was the first *maquiladora* in Baja California. Today it pumps out 20 million liters of amber-colored beer per month. The **Jardín Cerveza Tecate** (tel. 4 20 11), in front of the brewery, offers a free beer to anyone who wants one (18 years of age and older, of course). The garden was opened in 1994 to commemorate the company's 50th anniversary. Besides Tecate, the company also produces Bohemia, Carta Blanca, Superior, Sol, Dos Equis and Dos Equis, Lager. After your beer, check out the art galleries that line the south side of the park, or just sidle up to a bench and relax under the shade of palm trees.

Ensenada

The secret is out—beachless Ensenada (pop. 72,000) is fast becoming a weekend hot spot. The masses of Californians that arrive every Friday evening have gringo-ized the town to an incredible degree; everyone speaks some English and store clerks turn to their calculators if you try to buy something with pesos. Street vendors wander up and down the main drag, Av. Lopez Mateos, dressed in bright colors and quoting prices. Stores in all sizes and shapes populate the streets. Fear not, Ensenada is nothing like its brash and raucous cousin to the north, the infamous Tijuana. Ensenada's

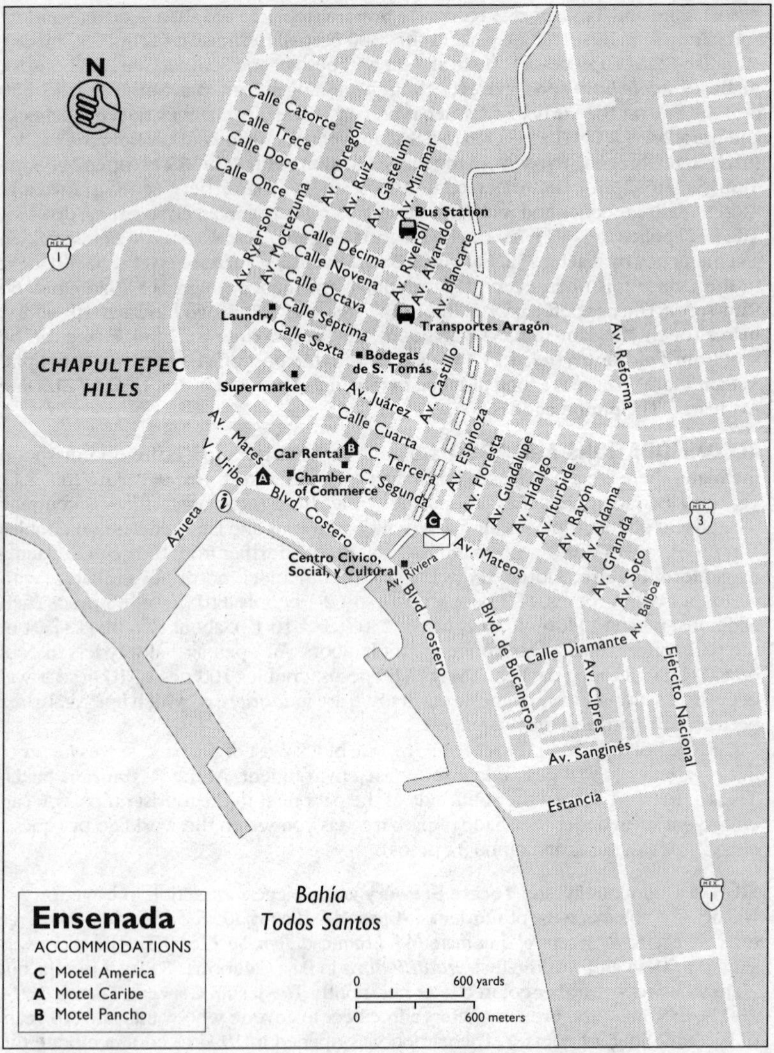

cool sea breezes, warm hospitality, and vast assortment of activities all contribute to its allure. However, the city is more pleasant during the week when fewer tourist-consumers populate the city.

The 90-minute ride from Tijuana to Ensenada offers continuous views of the Pacific, and its last 20 minutes are breathtaking if you take the Ensenada *cuota* (toll road), as the buses do. Three toll gates along the way each charge 16 pesos. Don't begrudge the money, though; you'll enjoy a smashing view of the ocean, large sand dunes, stark cliffs, and broad mesas—if busing it, be sure to grab a seat on the right-hand side. The *cuota* is also the safer of the two roads, with a breakdown lane and emergency phones about every 10 miles. The less scenic *libre* (free road) is a poorly maintained two-lane highway that parallels the toll road to La Misión, then cuts inland for the remaining 40km to Ensenada. If you're coming by car, drive during the day—there are no streetlights and many tight curves. Be sure to drive in the right lane; the left is for passing only. Keep an eye out for rest spots along the road; they provide the perfect chance to enjoy a fantastic view or take a short hike along the lonely cliffs.

ORIENTATION Ensenada is 108km south of Tijuana on Rte 1. If you're driving, follow signs on Rte. 1 to the centro. You'll come into town on **Azueta,** which later becomes **Gastelum.** Buses from Tijuana arrive at the main terminal, at Calle 11 and Riveroll. Turn right as you come out of the station, walk 10 blocks, and you'll be at **Mateos** (also called **Primera**), the main tourist drag. **Juárez (Calle 5)** runs parallel to Mateos, while from north to south, **Avs. Ryerson, Moctezuma, Obregón, Ruíz, Gastelum, Miramar, Riveroll, Alvarado, Blancarte,** and **Castillo** are perpendicular to it north of the arroyo, a grassy trench crossed by small bridges; below the arroyo, **Avs. Espinoza, Floresta, Guadalupe, Hidalgo, Iturbide,** and (later) **Balboa** also run perpendicular to Mateos. **Blvd. Costero** traces the shoreline, parallel to (and west of) Mateos. Calles are numbered, avenidas are named; together they form a grid. Calles run northwest-southeast, while most avenidas run northeast-southwest (Juárez and Mateos are exceptions). After sundown, avoid the area near the shoreline, and use caution while navigating the regions bounded by Avenidas Miramar and Macheros, and Mateos and Cuarta. While orienting yourself, keep in mind that the large residential Chapultepec Hills lie to the north and the water to the west.

PRACTICAL INFORMATION **Transportes Norte de Sonora** (tel. 78 67 70) sends buses to Guaymas (16hr., 361 pesos) and Los Mochis (20hr., 6 per day 7am-9:30pm, 482 pesos). **Autotransportes de Baja California** (tel. 78 66 80) runs to several destinations: Guerrero Negro (10hr., 6 per day 10am-11pm, 90 pesos), La Paz (22hr., 4 per day 10am-11pm, 438 pesos), Loreto (16hr., 6 per day 10am-11pm, 322 pesos), Mexicali (4hr., 4 per day 5:30am-8pm, 107 pesos), San Felipe (3hr., 8am and 6pm, 103 pesos), Santa Rosalía (13hr., 7 and 9:30pm, 251 pesos), and Tijuana (1½hr., every 30min., 55 pesos). **Transportes Aragón** (tel. 74 07 17), on Riveroll between Calles 8 and 9, runs to Tijuana (every hr. 5am-9pm, 48 pesos). Local **urbano** buses (tel. 78 25 94) leave from Juárez at Calle 6, and from Calle 2 at Macheros (every 8-15min., 3 pesos). **Hertz** (tel. 61 78 29 82), Calle 2 at Riveroll, rents cars, but they ain't cheap (US$51 per day with unlimited kilometers; open M-F 9am-6pm, Sa 9am-4pm). **Luggage storage** is available at the main bus terminal (7 pesos for the first 5hr., 0.50 pesos each additional hr.).

The **tourist office,** Blvd. Costero 540 (tel. 78 24 11; fax 78 36 75), at Azueta, has friendly, English-speaking staff members who dole out plenty of helpful information about Ensenada and the surrounding area as well as maps and pamphlets in English (open M-F 9am-7pm, Sa-Su 10am-2pm). The **Chamber of Commerce,** Mateos 693, 2nd floor (tel. 78 37 70, 78 23 22, or 74 09 96), at Macheros, is closer to the center of town and provides brochures and city maps (open M-F 8:30am-2pm and 4-6:30pm). **Banks** cluster along Juárez at Av. Ruíz. **Bancomer** (tel. 78 18 01; fax 78 11 08), on Juárez at Av. Ruíz, exchanges dollars and traveler's checks (open M-F 8:30am-4pm, Sa 10am-2pm). **ATMs** are along Juárez in the bank district, including one at **Serfin, on** Juárez at Gastelum. **Supermarket Calimax** (tel. 78 33 97), Gastelum at Calle 4, has just about everything (open daily 6am-midnight). A laundromat, **Lavandería Lavadero** (tel. 78 27 37), is on Obregón between Calles 6 and 7, across from Parque Revolución (open M-Sa 8am-7pm, Su 8am-4pm).

In an **emergency,** dial 060. **Police** (tel. 76 24 21) are at Calle 9 at Espinoza. The **Red Cross** (tel. 74 45 85, **emergency** 066) is on Blvd. de Jesús Clark at Flores. **Farmacia del Sol,** Av. Ruíz 447 (tel. 74 05 26), between Calle 4 and Juárez, is open 8am to 11pm. **Farmacia San Martín** (tel. 78 35 30), at Av. Ruíz and Calle 8, is open 24 hours. The **Hospital General** (tel. 76 78 00 or 76 77 00) is on the Transpeninsular Highway at the 111km mark (open 24hr.). The **post office** (tel. 76 10 88) is on Mateos and Espinoza (open M-F 8am-7pm, Sa 8am-noon). The **postal code** is 22800. **Faxes** can be sent from **Telecomm** (tel. 77 05 45), Av. Floresta at Calle 3 (open M-F 8am-6pm, Sa 8am-11am). The **Internet** can be accessed at **Cafe Internet** (tel. 76 13 31; fax 76 29 23) at Juárez and Floresta (30 pesos per hr.; open M-F 9am-6:30pm, Sa 9:30am-2pm). The **phone code** is 61.

ACCOMMODATIONS Budget hotels line Mateos between Espinoza and Riveroll and at Miramar. Most rooms are a 15-minute stroll from the beachfront "boardwalk" and the popular clubs. Although many owners quote prices in greenback, pay in pesos to save cash. **Motel Caribe,** Av. López Mateos 627 (tel. 78 34 81), offers great rooms and a superb location: it's right on the main drag and one block from some of Ensenada's popular dance clubs and bars. Comfortably firm beds and carpeted floors deck out the rooms. (Singles 160 pesos; doubles 225 pesos; 20 peso key deposit; rates go up on weekends.) Cheaper, more modest rooms are available across the street if you ask for them. **Motel America** (tel. 76 13 33), on López Mateos at Espinoza, is a little farther from all the action, but its rooms have kitchens! Besides a place to cook, the rooms have fans and TVs. (Singles for 1-2 people 170 pesos; doubles 260 pesos.) **Motel Pancho** (tel. 78 23 44), on Alvarado at Calle 2, one block off Mateos (in line with the giant flagpole) has large rooms and clean baths with tiny showers. The hospitable staff will direct you to neighborhood bars. (Singles 110 pesos; doubles 170 pesos.) The beach between Tijuana and Ensenada is lined with RV parks; one near Ensenada is **Ramona RV Park** (tel. 74 60 45), on km 104 of the Transpeninsular Highway (US$9 for full hookup).

FOOD The cheaper restaurants in town line Juárez and Espinoza; those on Mateos jack up their prices. The eateries along the waterfront near the fish market compete fiercely for their customers and offer good, cheap, fresh seafood. Fresh fruit, seafood, and taco stands abound, but be wary of how the food is handled. If you have a kitchen, the best bargains are at the **supermarkets** on Gastelum. **Mary's Restaurant,** Av. Miramar 609 between Costero and Mateos, serves scrumptious seaside fare, with good old down-home hospitality. Fish filets start at 30 pesos, and a whopping portion of huevos rancheros with an ice-cold Coke goes for just 20 pesos. Snack on homemade tortilla chips and check out the wall of foreign money or the various knick knacks caught in the fish nets on the walls. The friendly atmosphere at **Cafetería Monique Colonial** (tel. 76 40 41), Calle 9 at Espinoza, makes it a local favorite. Diners sit in anxious anticipation of their breaded steak with salad and fries (42 pesos). Check out the Galeria Infantil over the kitchen, which displays the masterful artwork of local school children. No alcoholic drinks are served. (Open M-Sa 6am-10pm, Su 6am-5pm.) Chefs at **Las Parrillas** (tel. 76 17 28), Espinoza at Calle 6, grill up fresh meat cutlets on the flaming pit as customers make like Pavlov's dog. Squeeze onto a counter stool and scarf down burritos (28 pesos) and súper hamburgesas with veggies, avocado, and chile (28.50 pesos; open daily 7:30am-10:30pm).

SIGHTS Seeing Ensenada requires more than a quick cruise down Mateos. For a spectacular view of the entire city, climb the **Chapultepec Hills.** The steep road to the top begins at the foot of Calle 2; expect a 10- to 15-minute hike. Or take a stroll down **Av. López Mateos,** where herds of curio shops allow for endless shopping. Many of the outdoor cafes are perfect for people-watching.

The mild, dry climate of northern Baja's Pacific coast has made it Mexico's prime grape-growing area. **Bodegas de Santo Tomás,** Miramar 666 (tel. 78 33 33) at Calle 7, devilishly located in a less-visited part of town, has produced wine since 1888. Today, the *bodegas* distill over 500,000 cases of wine and champagne per year. Tours include free wine tasting and an assortment of breads and cheeses (daily 11am, 1, and 3pm; US$2).

The larger-than-life golden busts of Venustiano Carranza, Miguel Hidalgo, and Benito Juárez stare seriously onto **Plaza Civica.** Grab an ice cream cone, strut over to the *Ventana al Mar* (window to the sea) next to the Plaza Civica, and marvel at the **largest flag** in Mexico. The nearby gardens of the **Centro Cívico, Social, y Cultural de Ensenada** (tel. 76 43 10 or 76 42 33) are one block from Costero (US$1 entrance fee). Once a world-famous casino (the Riviera) built in 1930, the Centro is now a shrine to Ensenada's archaeological and social history. The architecture and gardens alone make a visit worthwhile. The **Instituto Nacional de Antropología e Historia,** Ryerson 99 (tel. 78 25 31) at Virgilio Uribe, is the oldest building in town. *(Open M-F*

9am-4pm; free.) There are numerous artifacts and images of the earliest missionary settlements in Baja including several mission church bells. Nearby, the **Museo Histórico Regional** (tel. 78 25 31), on Gastelum between Virgillo Uribe and Mateos, houses artifacts from all over Baja, include a charming photograph of two elderly Cucapa men standing next to their shared young wife, whom they acquired during a robbery in a nearby town. *(Open T-Su 10am-5pm. Admission US$1.)* Originally built in 1886 as barracks, it is the **oldest public building** in the state. The building was converted to a jail in 1914 and served as such until 1986. A 15-minute walk from Mateos is the **Museo de Ciencias,** Obregón 1463 (tel. 78 71 92) at Catorce. *(Open M-F 9am-5pm, Sa noon-5pm. Admission 12 pesos, children 10 pesos.)* Housed in an old wooden boat, the museum displays photographs of and information about the endangered species of Baja.

ENTERTAINMENT Most of the popular hangouts along Mateos are members of the hybrid species known as the restaurant/bar/disco. Food and drinks are served only until 8pm or so, when the eateries metamorphose into full-fledged dance club monsters. On weekends, almost every place is packed with festive tourists. Better known than Ensenada itself is **Hussong's Cantina** (tel. 78 32 10), on Ruíz between Mateos and Calle 2. Now 106 years old, Hussong's is the prototypical Mexican watering hole: with dark, wood-paneled walls adorned with deer heads and sawdust on the floor, you get the true *cantina* flavor with your Tecate. Gulp down beer (12 pesos) or a margarita (16 pesos) at the long, shiny bar. (Open daily 10am-2am.) When you tire of the continuous stream of *mariachis,* cross the street to **Papas and Beer** (tel. 74 01 45), a frenetic high-tech music emporium popular with a young crowd that swigs large margaritas (21 pesos) and spends horse-choking wads of cash. Escape the congestion and whistle-blowing staff by stepping onto the terrace, where hockey-rink-like plexiglass boards prevent carousers from cross-checking each other off the balcony to the street below. Thursday night is theme night (birthday, pajamas, whatever) and Friday is ladies' night, when men aren't let in until 10pm (cover US$3-5; open F-Sa 10am-4am, Su-Th noon-3am).

If you're looking for a less alcohol-centered evening, join the gyrating mass of teens whirling to late-80s pop hits at **Roller Ensenada** (tel. 76 11 59), a roller rink on Mateos at Hidalgo (open Tu-Th 2-10pm, F-Su noon-10pm; admission 13 pesos with or without skates). If you just want to zone out in front of a big screen, **Cinema Gemelos** (tel. 76 36 16 or 76 36 13), on Balboa and Mateos, at the southern end of town, screens subtitled U.S. features (shows daily 4-10pm; admission 20 pesos).

Near Ensenada

Ensenada is an excellent base from which to explore Baja's natural wonders. Unfortunately, to reach most of them, you'll need some wheels, particularly a four-wheel-drive or all-terrain vehicle. Try Hertz in Ensenada, or, better yet (if you're driving down from Cali), Bargain Auto Rentals in San Diego (see **Tijuana: Car Rental,** p. 136).

Near Ensenada: Beaches

Good sand to accompany your swim in the bucolic Bahía de Todos Santos can only be found outside of the city. To the north, **Playa San Miguel,** with its rocky coastlines and large waves, is great for surfers but might not be ideal for others. To get there, drive north up Calle 10 to the toll gate; turn left at the sign marked "Playa San Miguel." Buses also run to this beach—catch a bus marked "San Miguel" departing from Gastelum at Costero (3 pesos). Buses back must be flagged down.

Somewhat more frequented beaches lie 8km south of Ensenada off the Transpeninsular Highway. Probably the nicest beach around is **Playa Estero,** dominated by the Estero Beach Resort. Volleyball courts fill the beach's clean but hard and unforgiving sand. You can rent water skis, banana boats, or bicycles (US$5 per hr.). Sea lions can be spotted off the coast during low tide. The **Estero Beach Museum** (tel. 6 62 35), located in the Estero Beach Resort, has an impressive display of Mexican folk art (open daily except Tu 9am-6pm; free). To get there, take a right at the "Estero Beach" sign on Rte. 1 heading south. Free parking is available in the first lot of the hotel. Alternatively, catch a bus marked "Aeropuerto," "Zorrillo," "Maneadero," or "Chapultepec" from Pl. Cívica. **Playa El Faro** (tel. 77 46 30) is similarly rife with volleyball courts and Americans but has slightly better sand and offers camping on the beach (camp space, parking, and bathroom privileges US$7 for 4 people; full RV hookup US$12; rooms with bath US$30 for 2 people). Another nearby beach is **Playa Santa María,** where you can rent a horse (US$9 per hr.) and ride around the bay.

Heading onto the Punta Banda peninsula (continuing south from Ensenada, take the paved road BCN 23, which splits west off Rte. 1 north of Maneadero), you'll find lonelier beaches along the stretch known as **Baja Beach.** Horses are available for rent, and you can swim anywhere along the clean, soft, white sand (remember, all beaches are public) in front of a quiet scattering of Americans in semi-permanent RV parks. The rolling hills and marshes provide a pleasant backdrop. The Baja Beach Resort also runs a pool of hot springs, located on Hwy. 1 on the left, 2km before turning off onto the Punta Banda peninsula. To get to Baja Beach, walk down a dirt road after the sign, on the right hand side. By car, bear right at the first fork in the road after turning onto the peninsula. Proceed with caution; this road is very poorly maintained. Look for "Horses for Rent" and "Aguacaliente" signs. Beautiful hiking spots are nearby (see **Hiking** below). You can also take a bus to La Bufadora (below) and ask the driver to let you off, but don't count on a ride back.

■ Near Ensenada: Hiking

The area's most beautiful spots remain essentially undiscovered by most tourists. Breathtaking hikes on well-kept trails can be completed around the mountains of the **Punta Banda** peninsula near La Bufadora. Bring a snack, as there are some good spots with spectacular view of cliffs and never-ending blue sea to stop and picnic. Don't forget a bathing suit—when you reach the bottom, you can relieve your sweaty body with a dip amid the rocks in the chilly Pacific. Most of the trails consist of unmarked footpaths and dirt roads. Be sure to stay on a path once you've chosen it; trail blazing will damage the surrounding flora.

The best spot to enter the trails is **Cerro de la Punta,** on the road to La Bufadora near the end of the Punta Banda peninsula. Turn right up a long driveway at the "Cerro de la Punta" sign (parking 10 pesos). You'll see a small clearing and a large house on the cliffs; here, you can hike up among the cacti to the top of the mountains for views of the surrounding area or down beautiful trails on the oceanside.

Other stops earlier along the road to La Bufadora are equally scenic. The bus to La Bufadora (see below) will drop you off anywhere along this road, including Cerro de la Punta, but you may wait quite a while for the bus back. **Punta Banda** itself has a roadside **grocery market** and **post office** (open M-F 8am-3pm; but, honestly, go to Ensenada) on the main road after the turn-off for Baja Beach. You can camp or park an RV in Punta Banda at **Villarino** (tel. 54 20 45; fax 54 20 44), adjacent to the plaza, which has modern shower and bathroom facilities and full hookups (US$5 per person per night; call for reservations).

Hiking farther inland offers completely different terrain, ranging from deep lagoons to cactus forests to ponderosa pine. The rugged mountain range east of Ensenada is the solitary **Sierra de Juárez,** where **Parque Nacional Constitución de 1857** is located. Be forewarned that you'll need an **all-terrain vehicle** or **pickup truck** to make the trek. If you can afford it, find a guide who can show you the correct paths to take once off the main roads. Dirt roads and brush make these paths difficult to navigate. To get there, follow **Highway 3** east from Av. Juárez in Ensenada all the way past **Ojos Negros.** At about km 58, turn left onto the dirt road leading into the park. Follow signs (or, better, ask a guide for help); after about one hour and 20 minutes, you will find yourself at **Laguna Hanson,** a little lake surrounded by basic camping spots. If you aren't wheeled, **Ecotur** (tel. 76 44 15; fax 74 67 78), Calle 9 and Espinoza 1251, offers excursions. The owner, Francisco Detrell, also leads tours in Ensenada and parts of Baja. Call or fax at least three days in advance to book a tour.

■ Near Ensenada: La Bufadora

La Bufadora, the largest geyser on the Pacific coast, is 30km south of Ensenada. On a good day, the "Blowhole" shoots water 40m into the air out of a water-carved cave. On a bad day, visitors will have to be satisfied with the beautiful view from the Bufadora peak. The area is crowded with droves of visitors, cheesy curio shops, and food vendors. Be sure to try the *churros*. In spite of the bustling buzz of the area, the geyser makes the trip worthwhile. To get there, drive south on the Transpeninsular Highway (take a right onto the highway off López Mateos at the southern end of town), head straight past exits for the airport, military base, and Playa Estero, and take a right after about 20 minutes at the sign marked "La Bufadora." Continue on that road until its end. You'll know you're there when you've finished a brain-numbing series of road loops and you find yourself on a small street with multi-colored vending stalls (parking US$1 or 8 pesos). Alternatively, you can take a yellow *microbús* from Ensenada to **Maneadero** (3 pesos) and a connecting bus to La Bufadora (2 pesos).

Valle de San Quintín

Occupying the lonely mid-Pacific coast of northern Baja, San Quintín Valley (pop. 30,000) is the lifeblood of the peninsula's agricultural production. Driving south from Ensenada on Rte. 1 (the transpeninsular highway) for 180km, you'll encounter a series of small, bland towns bordered by the ocean on the west and the mountains on the east—farmland lies everywhere in between. The valley's settlement is made up of numerous ranches belonging to gallant *vaqueros* (cowboys) and three tiny towns (listed north to south): **San Quintín, Lázaro Cárdenas** (not to be confused with its same-named neighbor only about 100km to the northeast), and **El Eje del Papaloto.** What brings most people here, however, is the superb fishing off the small *bahía.* Americans and other foreigners are hard to find in the area's main strip (as is virtually everything). The summer morning fogs and the cool bay breezes of the old port area give way to hot afternoon sun and vistas of desert and cacti. Above all, the town makes a good rest stop on the way to points further south, or a convenient place to stock up on supplies for a camping excursion to the nearby **Parque Nacional Sierra San Pedro Mártir** (see p. 152).

ORIENTATION AND PRACTICAL INFORMATION All three towns border **Rte. 1,** Mexico's **Transpeninsular Highway.** Small streets off the highway have neither street signs nor common-use names. Addresses are designated by highway location. The beaches are all west of the highway, off small dirt and sand roads. Coming from the north, San Quintín is the first town, Cárdenas (as it is known in the region) is second, and little Eje comes last. The Valle de San Quintín **tourist office** (tel. 6 27 28) actually comes before the towns themselves at km 178.3 in Col. Vicente Guerrero—look for signs. The friendly staff will provide plenty of info about the valley and the surrounding area (open daily 8am-3pm and 4-7pm). To **exchange currency,** head to BITAL, the Valle's bank, located in Lázaro Cárdenas behind the PEMEX station. **BITAL** has an **ATM** and exchanges traveler's checks. (Bank open M-F 8am-7pm, Sa 9am-2:30pm.) In an **emergency,** dial 134. The **police** are in Cárdenas, east of the highway. In Cárdenas, try **Farmacia Baja California** (tel. 5 24 38), Rte.1 at km 195 (open daily 8am-10pm). In case of a health emergency, call **Clínica Santa María** (tel. 75 22 63 or 75 22 12) in San Quintín, located on a dirt road off Rte. 1 at km 190. The **post office** is a gray building next to the Farmacia Baja California in Cárdenas (open M-F 8am-5pm). The **postal code** is 22930. **LADATELs** are in all three towns and a **caseta** is in Cárdenas. The **phone code** is 616.

ACCOMMODATIONS AND FOOD Sleeping arrangements in the Valle are minimal but, for the most part, comfortable. In San Quintín, **Hotel Chavez** (tel. 5 20 05), on Rte. 1 at km 194 just before the bridge, offers large, airy rooms, soft beds, and cable TV in the main lobby. Call early for reservations. (Singles 155 pesos; doubles 205 pesos.) In Lázaro Cárdenas, **Motel Romo** (tel. 5 23 96), at km 196 on the west side of

Rte. 1, has almost-new carpeted rooms. Clean bathrooms border on art deco and large windows let in the sunlight. (Singles 90 pesos; doubles 110 pesos.) About 3km down a dirt road just south of Lázaro Cárdenas lies **Motel San Carlos** (follow signs for the Old Mill). Situated near the old pier on San Quintín Bay, its carpeted rooms with baths offer guests a nightly serenade of wind and waves lapping at the shore. (Singles US$20; doubles US$25.) Cheap eats aren't tough to find in San Quintín. Small **loncherías** along both sides of Rte. 1 serve tacos for 9 pesos. Enjoy a *bistec milanesa* (49 pesos) among framed portraits of John Wayne, Clint Eastwood, and other *vaqueros* in the air-conditioned **Asadero El Alazán** in San Quintín, at km 190 on Rte. 1.

SIGHTS AND ENTERTAINMENT San Quintín is best known for fishing off the San Quintín bay. You can drive out to the **Molino Viejo** (Old Pier) and to the **Old Mill Hotel** (U.S. tel. (619) 428-2779 or (800) 479-7962), where you can get a fishing permit, hire a boat for the day, and catch a glimpse of some original mill machinery of the failed 19th-century English colony. The surrounding mountains and peaceful bay waters will soothe the worn traveler. The Old Mill itself is a semi-permanent American expat community. To get there, turn west on a sand and dirt road on km 198 and head down about 4km (signs will point you in the right direction). Or, if you'd like something a little different, check out the salt lakes formed on the edge of the sea, west of Cárdenas. To get there, turn left at the corner of the military base. Head down a dirt and sand road for approximately 8.2km miles. You don't need an ATV, but follow the sand paths very carefully. Although San Quintín's nightlife is hardly hoppin', those in search of spirits can wet their whistle at **Bar Romo** (tel. 5 23 96), on Rte. 1 in Cárdenas, where *mariachis* and local singers are cheered on by catcalls until the late hours. In San Quintín, grab a chilly *cerveza* (about 12 pesos) or margarita (20 pesos) at the friendly tourist-oriented **Restaurant Bar San Quintín** (tel. 5 23 76) on Rte. 1 next to Hotel Chavez. The well-stocked bar and weekend *mariachis* will help you strum a buzz in no time. (Open daily 7am-2am.)

■ Near Valle de San Quintín: Parque Nacional Sierra San Pedro Mártir

Although the trippy towns of the Valle de San Quintín appeal mostly to anglers, the nearby **Parque Nacional Sierra San Pedro Mártir** has enough canyons, peaks, and waterfalls to satisfy the urges of the most zealous land lover. Founded in 1947, the park occupies the highest zone on the peninsula and is home to **Picacio del Diablo** (also known as **Cerro de la Encantada** or **La Providencia**), the highest peak in Baja at 3086m above sea level. From its peak on a clear day, you can admire the aquamarine waters of the Sea of Cortés, turn around, and check out the vast Pacific Ocean. The climb to the peak is rated three to five and is said to be one of the most challenging climbs in Mexico. For those uninterested in scaling mountains, the park has three canyons to explore as well as the San Pedro Mártir Falls, an 800m fall accessible only with an authorized guide. Check out the tourist office in San Quintín or contact **Ecotur** (see **Hiking** in Ensenada, p. 150). The park is situated on a plateau, and because of its elevation, it has considerably more rainfall than its lowland desert surroundings—it even snows in the winter here. As a result, the park is beautifully shaded by evergreens (pines and junipers abound) and is host to a vast array of wildlife including deer, puma, eagles, not-so-wild cows, and the Nelson rainbow trout (a species endemic to the region). The park's isolated location makes it one of the least-visited parks in Mexico and a prime destination for backpackers and hikers who wish to be alone to commune with nature. There are several tent site locations, but none for trailer or car camping. A few trails leading to viewpoints and wilderness campsites are nominally maintained and can be accessed off the park's only road. See a ranger at the entrance to the park for information and help with orientation.

The park is also home to Mexico's **National Observatory.** Founded in 1967, the observatory is one of the most important in all of Latin America; it houses both reflecting telescopes and a new state-of-the-art telescope that utilizes infrared technology.

The observatory lies at the end of the road leading into the park and tours are given on Saturdays from 11am to 1pm upon arrangement with the administration.

Getting There: The road leading to the park and observatory lies approximately 51km north of San Quintín and runs east of the highway for 100km. Be forewarned—this road is not for the faint of heart. The ride to the park is approximately 2½ hours on a poorly maintained dirt road (due to heavy rainfall, the road may be temporarily closed). You can make the trek in a passenger vehicle, but it is highly recommended to go with four-wheel drive. Be careful of oncoming traffic as the road is narrow and the cliffs steep. Also watch out for cattle; local *vaqueros* use the road to herd their cows to greener pastures. In spite of the dangerous curves, the views from the road are unparalleled—breathtaking vistas of canyons and hills tinted yellow and red by wildflowers are some of the best in all of Baja. The trails in the park are not well marked, and it is advisable to bring a compass and, for some trails, mandatory to bring along an authorized guide. If you plan on backpacking or spending the night in the park, be sure to bring plenty of safe drinking water.

Bahía de los Angeles

The village of Bahía de los Angeles is quiet, peaceful, and the perfect place to sip a margarita while watching the sun set. Wedged between steep rocky hills to the west and the Sea of Cortés to the east, the Bahía is home to a rich variety of marine life. Hunchback and finback whales can be spotted during the summer, while whale sharks cruise the bays around October. Dolphins, both common and bottlenose, as well as sea lions, are present all year. Several small rock islands guard the entrance to the bay and provide beautiful scenery. You won't find any dance clubs or *mariachis* in this little Baja town; most visitors come to fish or just relax—modern amenities are not yet universal here.

Bahía de los Angeles is very small and easily navigable by foot. The road that leads from the transpeninsular highway to the bay becomes the town's main road. None of the streets are named, but everything is right off the main strip. The owner of **Guillermo's,** a *mercado*/restaurant/RV park/motel serves as the official **tourist** liaison. There are no banks; exchange your traveler's checks before you drive into town (you will be driving—there is no bus service). A **public phone** can be found in the office of Hotel Costa Azul on the main road (12 pesos per minute). The **police** are behind the park across from Guillermos. The cheapest way to stay in the Bahía is to camp, and the best place to do that is at **Daggett's Campground.** Follow the signs from the main road just before entering town. Situated right on the beach, each space comes with a small *palapa* and barbecue pit. The campground has bathrooms, hot showers, and a great view. (US$6 per couple; US$2 each additional person.) The owner, Ruben, is a great source of information. He also leads fishing and diving tours (US$85 for a half day). **Hotel las Hamacas** in town off the main road has very clean rooms with concrete floors, air-conditioning, and fans (singles 150 pesos; doubles 200 pesos). Park your RV at **Guillermos,** off the main road (an unbeatable US$3 per person per night for a full hookup). Because of its isolated location, food in town is not so cheap. Your best bet is to grill up your catch of the day. If the fish just aren't biting, try **Restaurante las Hamacas,** in front of the hotel. The simple, trophy-adorned dining room is cooled by fans and ice-cold *cerveza.* Try the Mexican combo for 30 pesos. (Open 8am-8pm.) **Restaurante Isla** has a great view of the bay from its second floor *palapa*-roofed patio. Inside, the immaculate white-tiled floor and walls create a refreshingly cool effect. Silk flowers peeking out of tinfoiled beer bottles grace the tables along with delicious *tacos de pescado* (35 pesos; open 7am-9pm).

Although Bahía de los Angeles is small and relatively undeveloped, it has a rich history. The area was originally inhabited by the **Cochimi,** a group of Native Americans that was prevalent in this area of Baja. A Jesuit mission built in 1697 introduced ranching to the area. More information about the town, its history, and its natural surroundings can be found at the small but exquisite **Museo de Historia y Cultura,** located directly behind the police office; look for the large white skeleton in front. The well-maintained wooden museum holds detailed exhibits on the Cochimi and local wildlife, fossils, stuffed animal specimens, and a collection of old photographs of the town in its previous incarnations as mining town and fishery. It's well worth the visit. (Open in summer daily 9am-noon and 3-5pm; in winter daily 9am-noon and 2-4pm; free, but donations accepted.)

Most visitors to Bahía de los Angeles come to catch fish and many come with their own boats. If you plan to fish, be sure to bring (or borrow) your own supplies—there is no place to pick up fishing supplies in town. **Ruben Daggett** of Daggett's Campground will take you fishing on his diving boat (US$85 per half day). Fill your dive tank or rent your dive gear at the only dive shop in town, **Larry and Raquel's,** next to Daggett's Campground. They also rent kayaks for the day (US$15). The best beaches lie north of town along Ensenada la Gringa. Permanent RVs park along the coast, but you can access the beach via dirt paths off the unpaved road leading to **Punta la Gringa,** the northern lip of the Bahia. The road to la Gringa can be accessed by following signs to Daggett's Campground. Once on the dirt road outlined by white stones, follow it north for about two miles until it ends.

San Felipe

San Felipe may put on Mexican airs, but it's a tourist-oriented beach town at heart, complete with high prices, sandy volleyball courts, and vendors selling shell sculptures. From October to April, San Felipe's 200 RV parks are packed with northerners. Right next door at **Larry and Raquel's** (tel. (619) 429-7935), a fully furnished house for rent accommodates five to seven people easily and has its own video library (starting at US$80 per day). Northerners claimed the area as a regular hangout in the 50s, bringing with them handfuls of greenbacks and a new industry—tourism. Cashiers look positively perplexed if you try to pay in pesos. However, San Felipe offers a stellar selection of seafood and a beautiful stretch of beach teased by the warm, shallow waters of the Gulf. The town is laid-back and scenic, and provides the perfect place to relax for a day or 10, and grab a drink or 20. As one local bar has written on the wall, "No worries—be happy."

ORIENTATION San Felipe is 198km south of Mexicali at the end of sizzling-hot Rte. 5. The town is also accessible via Rte. 3 from Ensenada, a poorly maintained pothole-infested paved road. If coming from Tijuana, the latter makes for a more pleasant ride. A dirt and gravel road connects San Felipe to points farther south (attempt with four-wheel drive only). **Los Arcos** (a tall arched structure) is immediately recognizable when entering the village; **Chetumal** is the street continuing straight from the arch toward the sea. Hotels and restaurants cluster on **Mar de Cortés,** one block from the beach. The **Malecón,** lined with seafood stands, is right on the beach. Almost all of the "action" (restaurants, hotels, services) is on these two streets. All cross-streets named "Mar" run parallel to the beach; from west to east they are **Malecón, Mar de Cortés, Mar Baltico, Mar Tasmania, Man Cantabrico, Mar Negro,** and **Mar Blanca.** From south to north, **Manzanillo, Topolobampo, Ensenada, Chetumal,** and **Acapulco** run perpendicular to the beach. To get downtown from the **bus station,** walk north on Mar Caribe to Manzanillo and turn right toward the water. Hike until you see the Hotel Costa Azul, and you're on Mar del Caribe, one block from the beach.

PRACTICAL INFORMATION Catch **buses** at the terminal on Mar del Caribe (tel. 7 15 16), a 15-minute walk from the center of action. **Autotransportes de Baja California** runs buses to Ensenada (3½hr., 8am and 6pm, 103 pesos), Mexicali (2½hr., 5 per day 6am-8pm, 66 pesos), and Tijuana (5 per day 6am-4pm, 150 pesos). Tickets are on sale daily from 5:30am to 10:30pm. **Luggage storage** is available at the bus station (5 pesos). The air-conditioned **tourist office,** Mar de Cortés 300 (tel. 7 18 65) at Manzanillo, has English-speaking staffers and handy maps and brochures (open M-F 8am-7pm, Sa 9am-3pm, Su 10am-1pm). The only bank in town, **Bancomer** (tel./fax 7

10 90), Mar de Cortés Nte. at Acapulco, near Rockodile Bar, exchanges currency (open M-F 8:30am-4pm, Sa 10am-2pm) and has a 24-hour **ATM.**

In an **emergency,** dial 134. The **police** (tel. 7 13 50 or 7 11 34) are on Mar Blanco Sur, just south of Chetumal. The **Red Cross** (tel. 7 15 44) at Mar Bermejo and Peñasco, has English-speaking staff (open 24hr.). **Farmacia San José,** Pto. Mazatlán 523 (tel. 7 13 87), is open 24 hours. The **Centro de Salud** (tel. 7 15 21) is on Chetumal, near the fire and police station (English spoken; open 24hr.). The **post office** (tel. 7 13 30) is on Mar Blanco across from the police station, five blocks inland from Cortés (open M-F 8am-3pm, Sa 9am-noon). The **postal code** is 21850. **Faxes** can be sent from **Telecomm** (tel. 7 10 43) on Mar Bermejo between Puerto Peñasco and Zihuatanejo (open M-F 8am-2pm, Sa 9am-1pm). Some **LATADELs** line Mar del Caribe. The **phone code** is 657.

ACCOMMODATIONS There are two kinds of accommodations in San Felipe: those with air-conditioning and those without. Travelers who prefer the former will end up paying *mucho dinero* for mediocre rooms (although during summer it might be worth it). Sadly enough, San Felipe is one of the most expensive cities in one of the most expensive parts of the country; serious penny-pinchers will not find any cheap lodging. Those who plan on staying in this expensive little town should consider camping. A cheaper option is to rent a room in a private residence; check with the tourist office for a list. **Carmelita** (tel. 7 18 31), across from the Chapala Motel, is one of the private residences renting out rooms with air-conditioning and private bath. Four rooms are available, housing single people or married couples only (US$25 per room). Crammed between curio shops and administered from the liquor store next door, **Motel El Pescador** (tel. 7 11 83 or 7 13 28), on Mar de Cortés at Chetumal, offers spacious and nicely furnished rooms overlooking the beach with air-conditioning, color TV, and private baths. It's a real bargain, at least by San Felipe standards. (Singles 200 pesos; doubles 240 pesos; check-out noon.) RV parks abound in San Felipe and are the most economical way (besides camping) to spend the night. The best known is **Ruben's** (tel. 7 20 21), toward the end of Av. Golfo de California in Playa Norte. To reach Ruben's, turn left from Chetumal onto Mar de Cortés, and follow the signs on the short drive up. Individual beachfront parking spaces are topped with two-story, open-air bungalows that look like palapa tree-forts. Each spot easily accommodates carloads of folks with sleeping bags. RVs can hook up to electricity, hot water, and sewer connections. (2 people in summer US$15, in winter US$12; US$2 per extra person; office open daily 7am-7pm.) **Campo San Felipe** (tel. 7 10 12), on Mar de Cortés just south of Chetumal, lures campers with a fabulous beachfront location. A thatched roof shelters each fully loaded trailer spot. (Most spots US$17-27, a few US$9-10, depending on location and proximity to the beach; US$2 per extra person, children under 6 free; hookups US$1 extra; tent space US$10.)

FOOD Mar de Cortés is crammed with restaurants advertising air-conditioned relief. The beach, Malecón, is lined with fish taquerías serving up inexpensive fresh seafood under shady thatched roofs. Shrimp tacos are US$1, while full shrimp dinners run US$5-6. **Los Gemelos** (tel. 7 10 63), on Mar de Cortés at Acapulco, near Bancomer, serves tasty huevos rancheros for US$2.50 (open daily 6am-10am). Enjoy beef, chicken, or shrimp enchiladas (23 pesos) and a calming view of the sea at **Restaurant El Club** (tel. 7 11 75) on the Malecón at Acapulco. Shark fins and plastic turtles hang over bright multicolored table cloths. The camarones al mojo de ajo (garlic shrimp; 55 pesos) is one of the world's most perfect meals. Ice-cold agua purificada available free. (Open daily 7am-11pm.)

SIGHTS AND SAND People come to San Felipe to swim in the warm, tranquil, and invitingly blue Gulf waters. The beach in town follows along the Malecón and gets crowded on weekends. Try the beaches farther south for scuba and snorkeling—the water's clearer. A booth that rents **jet skis** and **beach buggies** is located right next to Motel El Pescador (US$25 per hr., open 8am-6pm). **Banana boats** wait along the beach in front of Bar Miramar, ready to take you for a 20-minute spin (boats run 9am-6pm, 20 pesos per person, min. 5 people).

The whole Bahía is generally clean, safe, and appealing; beaches outside of town are more isolated, but might require a long walk or a drive. Every beach is accompanied by a commercialized RV trailer park, but, as always, beaches are free—you only need to pay if you're parking.

Take time to visit the **Altar de la Virgen de Guadalupe,** a shrine to the virgin at the top of the hill near the lighthouse. After a short hike, you'll be rewarded with a spectacular view of San Felipe and the blue bay. Sixty-four kilometers south of San Felipe is the **Valle de los Gigantes National Park.** With cacti up to 15m tall, the park was the original home of the giant cactus that represented Mexico at the 1992 World's Fair in Seville, Spain. Fossil hunters will be elated to find a vast array of petrified sea life. Ask at the tourist office about guided dune buggy tours of the park.

ENTERTAINMENT San Felipe merrily courts throngs of migrant snowbirds and tourists with its picturesque beaches and a variety of venues to get tipsy or blasted. The high-priced, high-profile bar **Rockodile** (tel. 7 12 19), on Malecón at Acapulco, caters to a younger crowd and has a full line of Rockodile beachwear at its souvenir store on Mar de Cortés. Drunk customers write their names with magic marker on dollar bills and paste them up. Check out the volleyball court, pool table, and outdoor terrace. It's mellow during the day, but on weekend nights, it's a sweaty dance party. To begin inducing amnesia, try the electric-blue king-sized beverage, the "Adios motherfucker" (US$4). Cover $3-4 on Friday and Saturday nights (half-price happy hour Su-F 11am-7pm; open daily 11am-3am). Seasoned veterans nurse drinks at **Bar Miramar,** Mar de Cortés 486 (tel. 7 11 92). The oldest bar in San Felipe may look like a *cantina* from the 60s, but the patrons come for company, not glitz. Push a few cues over green felt on the pool tables out front (beer US$1.50, margaritas US$2.50; open daily 10am-2am). **Beachcomber** (tel. 7 21 22), on Malecón and Chetumal, always has sports on TV and tourists tranquilly nursing a buzz. A well-stocked bar, long wooden counter, and jukebox makes this a quiet, understated place to get trashed—and one of the cheapest (beer US$1.50, margaritas US$1.50, flavored drinks US$2.50; open daily 10am-2am).

BAJA CALIFORNIA SUR

Guerrero Negro

Twenty degrees cooler than the bleak Desierto de Vizcaíno to the southeast, Guerrero Negro (pop. 10,000), though dusty and painfully industrial, might earn a soft spot in the hearts of heat-weary northbound travelers. There's always a cool breeze here, and even late summer nights can be positively chilly. The town is named for a whaling boat, "Black Warrior," that wrecked in the town's lagoon in 1858. In Guerrero Negro, salt is God, king, and country. So saline-ridden is Guerrero Negro that even a deep breath of the town's air can send the hypochondriac's blood pressure soaring. The salt plant is now the **world's largest,** dominating the town's economy and attracting job-seekers from throughout the region. Although the locals are friendly and the cool breezes cathartic, Guerrero Negro's most attractive feature is its **gas station,** a beautiful **PEMEX** wonder. Be prepared for lots of wind and gray—Guerrero Negro resembles a beach town without the beach. Fill up that tank, and burn, baby, burn.

Guerrero Negro sprawls along a 3km strip west of the transpeninsular highway. Its two main roads, **Blvd. Zapata** and **Av. Baja California,** are home to basically all of the town's industrial and commercial centers. The **ABC Autotransportes de Baja California** terminal (tel. 7 06 11) is one of the first buildings from the highway on Blvd. Zapata as you come from the highway. ABC sends **buses** north (6 per day 7:30pm-

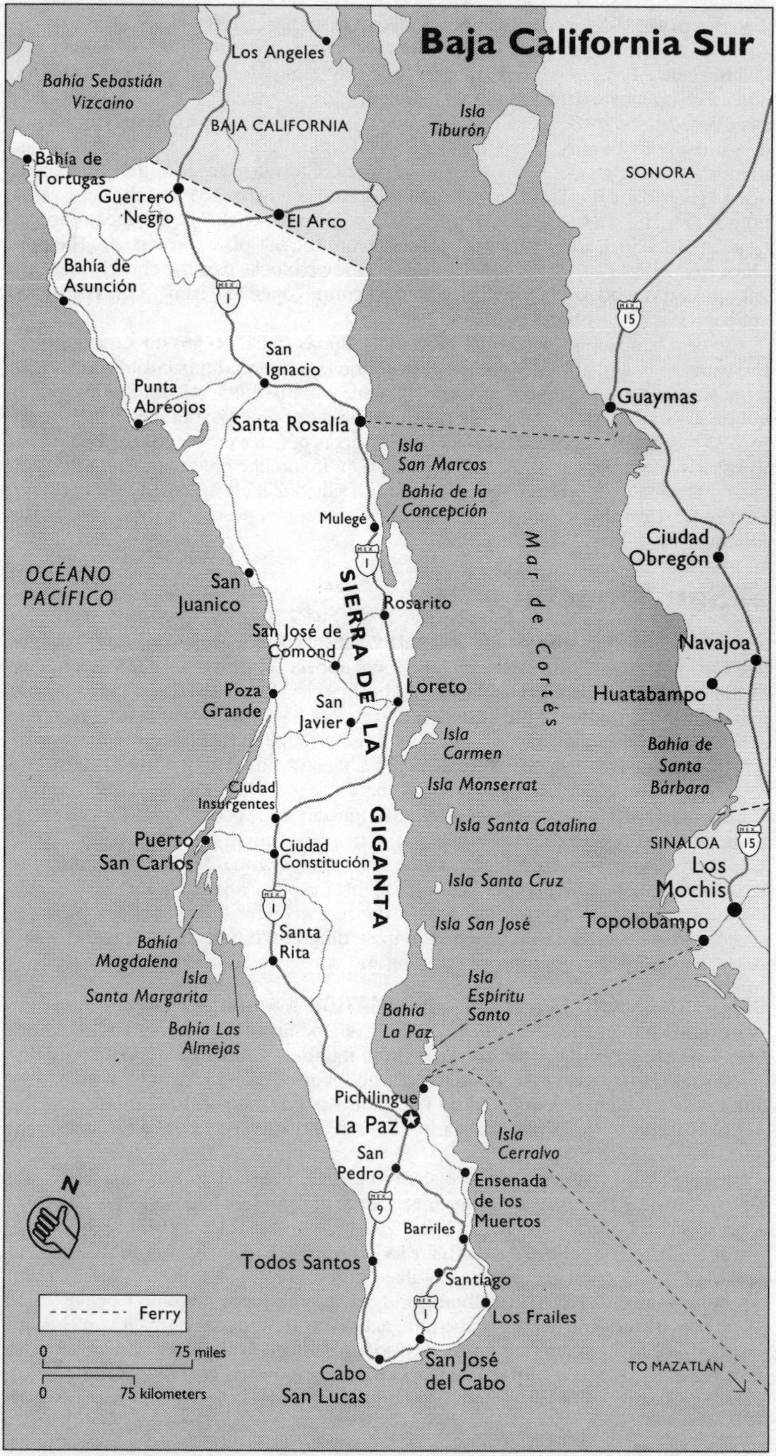
Baja California Sur
Los Angeles
Bahía Sebastián Vizcaíno
Isla Tiburón
BAJA CALIFORNIA
SONORA
Bahía de Tortugas
Guerrero Negro
El Arco
Bahía de Asunción
MEX 1
MEX 15
San Ignacio
Punta Abreojos
Santa Rosalía
Guaymas
Isla San Marcos
Bahía de la Concepción
Mulegé
Mar de Cortés
Ciudad Obregón
OCÉANO PACÍFICO
San Juanico
SIERRA DE LA GIGANTA
Rosarito
San José de Comond
Navajoa
Poza Grande
Loreto
Huatabampo
San Javier
Isla Carmen
Bahía de Santa Bárbara
Ciudad Insurgentes
Isla Monserrat
Isla Santa Catalina
SINALOA
Puerto San Carlos
Ciudad Constitución
Los Mochis
Isla Santa Cruz
Isla San José
Topolobampo
Santa Rita
Bahía Magdalena
Isla Santa Margarita
Bahía Las Almejas
Isla Espíritu Santo
Bahía La Paz
Pichilingue
La Paz
Isla Cerralvo
San Pedro
Ensenada de los Muertos
MEX 9
N
Barriles
Todos Santos
Santiago
Los Frailes
Ferry
0
75 miles
0
75 kilometers
Cabo San Lucas
San José del Cabo
TO MAZATLÁN

BAJA CALIFORNIA

8:30am) to El Rosario (6hr., 122 pesos), Ensenada (10hr., 218 pesos), Lázaro Cárdenas (7hr., 142 pesos), Punta Prieta (4hr., 55 pesos), Rosarito (2hr., 37 pesos), San Quintín (8hr., 149 pesos), and Tijuana (11hr., 264 pesos); and south to La Paz (11hr., 5 per day 4:30pm-8:30am, 288 pesos), Mulegé (4hr., 5 per day, 115 pesos), Santa Rosalía (3hr., 7 per day, 86 pesos), and points in between. Yellow **minivans** run up and down the transpeninsular highway (every 15min. 7am-10pm, 6 pesos). Change money at **Banamex** (tel. 7 05 55), on Av. Baja California in front of the plant (bank open M-F 9:30am-3pm). Travelers heading south should change currency here, as 24-hour **ATMs** and bank services become sparse. The **police** (tel. 7 00 22) are in the Delegación Municipal, a few hundred meters before the salt plant, on the left. The **post office** (tel. 7 03 44) is off Av. Baja California. Go two blocks past the church, and turn left onto a dirt road just before the basketball courts (open M-F 8am-3pm). The **postal code** is 23940. The **phone code** is 115.

The best bargain in town is the **Motel Las Dunas** (tel. 7 00 55) on Zapata, below the water tank and a short walk north from the bus station. Immaculate rooms with large showers are as worthy as those at more expensive spots, and the extremely courteous staff helps in every way possible. (Singles 66 pesos; doubles 77 pesos; triples 81 pesos; key deposit 10 pesos.) Many aspects of Guerrero Negro are a little hard to swallow, and the city's food is no exception. If you like entertainment while you eat, try **Cocina Económica Letty,** on the south side of Zapata before the water tower. Diners feast on the scrumptious *bistec milanesa* (35 pesos) as they gaze at the mounted TV. (Open M-Sa 8am-8pm.)

San Ignacio

More than any other stop on the arid Baja Peninsula, San Ignacio (pop. 2000) seems like a tropical oasis. From a distance, the town appears to be a cruel illusion, a mirage of the mind—leafy date palms, flowering bushes, and broad swaths of green appear magically in the middle of the blistering desert. Pinch yourself—you're not dreaming. The area around San Ignacio is blessed with the most plentiful underground freshwater supply in all Baja California Sur; of late, it's been dammed up to form a murky lake used for swimming and irrigating local orchards.

Although it's hot during summer days, San Ignacio earns points for just about everything else. Locals are extremely amiable, and the whole town is one big, happy, close-knit family that is super-hospitable to the few gringos who disrupt the solitude. San Ignacio's intimate atmosphere, beautiful nighttime starscapes, and historic mission overlooking the *zócalo* are just a few of the reasons why so many of the pleasure-seekers who set eyes on the town end up settling down here. San Ignacio is also a prime point of departure for cave painting and whale-watching tours.

ORIENTATION AND PRACTICAL INFORMATION A winding road canopied by swaying date palms leads south from the Transpeninsular Highway and becomes **Juan Bautista Luyando** at the *zócalo*. Within minutes of pulling in, you'll know tiny San Ignacio better than your hometown. Life revolves around the wonderfully tranquil *zócalo*, which is delineated by Juan Bautista Luyando and the mission to the north, **Morelos** to the south, **Juárez** to the east, and **Hidalgo** to the west. Locals are more than happy to give directions.

Buses pick up passengers at the sheltered bench 2km from San Ignacio on the Transpeninsular Highway. *De paso* buses leave at 7pm heading north for Guerrero Negro (3hr., 51 pesos), Ensenada (13hr., 252 pesos), and Tijuana (14hr., 309 pesos); and at 10am and 6pm heading south for La Paz (8hr., 237 pesos), Mulegé, Loreto, and Rosarita (1hr., 35 pesos) via Santa Rosalía. There's no official **tourist office** in town, but to hear informative chatter about San Ignacio, visit **Jorge Antonio Fischer** (tel. 4 01 50 or 4 01 60), the owner of the mini-mart next to Restaurant Chalita on Hidalgo (open M-Sa 7am-6pm, Su 7am-1pm); he also leads whale expeditions and tours to the cave paintings. **Nuevos Almacenes Meza S.A.,** a good-sized **grocery store** (tel. 4 01 22), is on the corner of Juárez and Juan Bautista Luyando, facing the *zócalo* (open M-

Sa 8am-noon and 2-7pm, Su 8am-noon). The **police** are in the Delegación Municipal on Ocampo and Zaragoza (open daily 8am-3pm). The **pharmacy, Boticas Ceseña,** Madero 24A (tel. 4 00 76, after hours 4 00 75), parallel to and east of Juárez and Hidalgo, is unmarked (open daily 8:30am-1pm and 2-9pm; available 24hr. in case of emergency). To reach the **Centro de Salud,** walk away from the highway down Hidalgo. Turn right on Cipris, a tiny dirt road; when you reach the auto parts shop, turn right and take a quick left just after the tin-roofed warehouse. Continue straight for two blocks; it's the white building with the white flag on the right-hand side. (Open daily 8am-3pm.) If you have a **medical emergency** after hours, call **Fischer Lucero** (tel. 4 01 90), the local doctor. The **post office** is in the gray stone building on Juárez next to the *zócalo* (open M-F 8am-3pm). The **postal code** is 23930. **LADATELs** can be found at all four corners of the *zócalo* and in front of Restaurant-Bar Rene's. You can place calls and send **faxes** at a pricier **caseta,** at Hidalgo 24 (tel. 4 02 50; open M-F 8am-1pm and 3-6pm). The **phone code** is 115.

ACCOMMODATIONS San Ignacio has few accommodations, and they don't come cheap. Make reservations or call early if you're going to be in town during *Semana Santa* or the week-long celebration of El Día de San Ignacio (July 31). The town is converted into a giant *fiesta* complete with horse races, dances, fireworks, and lots of merriment. The family living in **Restaurant Chalita,** Hidalgo 9 (tel. 4 00 82), rents bedrooms that ooze with local culture and have fans and black and white TVs. (Singles 120 pesos.) **Hotel Posada** (tel. 4 03 13), on Ocampo and Independencia, a three-minute walk down Ciprés from Hidalgo, has remarkably clean rooms with standing fans, private baths, and a family-type atmosphere (singles and doubles 160 pesos). **El Padrino RV Park** (tel. 4 00 89) is 500m from the *zócalo* on the road connecting San Ignacio to the highway. A full trailer hookup costs US$10; a hookup without electricity runs US$7. Motorcycles cost US$3 to park. El Padrino also offers four new rooms with private baths. (Singles 70 pesos or US$10; doubles 140 pesos or US$20.)

FOOD There are few places to dine in San Ignacio, but not to worry. All of the restaurants are within a stone's throw of the *zócalo* and serve delectable and affordable cuisine. Seafood dishes receive top billing on restaurant menus. Eat outdoors under the starry sky at **Restaurant-Bar Rene's** (tel. 4 02 56), just outside the *zócalo,* off Hidalgo. If you'd rather eat under a roof, head into their round stone-floored thatched hut. Inside you can enjoy your meal under the cooling breeze of a ceiling fan and listen to the soothing sounds of the 80s while staring out at the small adjoining pond. Wash down the house special, the *calamar empanizado* (breaded squid, 45 pesos) with a beer (10 pesos), or try the delicious *filete pescado* for 34 pesos. (Open daily 7am-10pm.) **Restaurant Chalita,** Hidalgo 9 (tel. 4 00 82), is housed in an old-fashioned Mexican kitchen. Listen to the caged birds sing, and find salvation in a warm plate of *pescado al mojo de ajo* (35 pesos), enchiladas (18 pesos), or *chiles rellenos* (20 pesos; open daily 7:30am-10pm). **Flojo's Restaurant/Bar** (tel. 4 00 89) is part of El Padrino RV Park (see above) and a five-minute walk from town. You'll be full for days when you overstuff yourself with three chicken burritos with rice and beans (25 pesos) or breaded Italian meat (34 pesos). Lean back, watch the stars shine between the reeds of the enormous palapa, listen to the crickets chirp, and marvel at how small the pet chihuahua is. (Open daily 7am-10:30pm.)

SIGHTS A colonial colossus towering over wild, leafy vegetation, the **Mission of San Ignacio,** on the northern side of the *zócalo,* was founded in 1728 by Jesuit missionary Juan Bautista Luyando. The construction of the mission proved a logistic nightmare: wood had to be hauled in from the Guadalupe mission in the Sierras, furniture was brought from Mulegé after a scorching four-day mule ride through the unpaved desert, and the paintings were carried by boat from the mainland. Its walls, over 1m thick, are made from blocks of volcanic rock. Despite the problems its construction imposed, the mission is a beautiful achievement—magnificent on the outside, cool on the inside, and heavenly at night when illuminated by outdoor spotlights. The majestic stone exterior has aged well; it is one of the most fantastic of the Baja missions. When you are inside, look up to see a a flying gold angel seemingly suspended in the dome. From halfway between the *zócalo* and Hotel Posada, on Cipris, the evening view of the mission poking above palms and huts is particularly striking. The newly opened **Mission Museum** (tel. 4 02 22), on Loyando, 30m west of the mission, tells the story of the nearby cave paintings and even has its own huge faux cave painting (open Tu-Sa 8am-3pm; free).

The main tourist draw near San Ignacio is the **painted caves,** 75km away in the **Sierra de San Francisco.** Five hundred paintings, probably more than 10,000 years old, reside within a 12 sq. km area. **Oscar Fischer** of Hotel Posada and his son, **Dagoberto** (tel. 4 03 13 or 4 01 56) offer various tours to the caves. During the tourist season, US$25 gets you a nine-hour trip to one cave and two petroglyphic zones. The tour leaves at around 8am and makes as many stops as requested. A two-day tour will take you to the impressive **La Pintada** and the minor **El Ratón** caves. For 65 pesos, you'll get transportation, a guide, and a mule. Some adventurous travelers make the trip between caves on foot (about 8km each way), saving all mule costs but leaving their bodies worn. US$80 plus the cost of a tent and a mule gets you the grandest tour of all: a three-day, eight-cave extravaganza that will show you more indigenous paintings than you probably ever wanted to see—all but the most resilient travelers will feel battle-worn. All trips must be cleared with the Mexican government, so call well in advance. The managers also run trips to the Laguna San Ignacio to spy on **gray whales.** The trips leave before 7am and cost US$45 per person. Note that prices for all tours (caves and whales) assume groups of six or more; smaller parties can expect to pay more. Tours of the painted caves and whale-watching expeditions are also led by the owner of **Flojos Restaurant/Bar** and **El Padrino RV Park** (tel. 4 00 89).

BAJA CALIFORNIA

Santa Rosalía

Santa Rosalía is not only a convenient transportation hub for buses and ferries but also the heir to a rich and colorful history. After enormously rich copper ore was discovered here in 1868, a French-owned mining company settled Santa Rosalía. The French built the town on the sides of the mountain in an orderly fashion according to rank; the wealthier, higher-ranking officials lived at the top of the mountain, overlooking the "lower" classes below. Santa Rosalía is not nearly as picturesque as its history might suggest—today, mountains of abandoned machinery and railroad cars bristle with rust, returning their metals to the ground. Even the public beaches are somewhat dirty and deserted. If you're planning to visit, keep in mind that the town is unbearably hot and humid in the summer and that the entire town shuts down by 9pm. Still, Santa Rosalía isn't a bad stopover—you'll get a chance to see jarring European architecture in the middle of Baja; the town's cast-iron church, **Iglesia Santa Bárbara,** was designed by **Gustave Eiffel** (of Tower fame). The town is often used as a departure or arrival point for the cross-Gulf ferry to and from Guaymas, Sonora.

ORIENTATION AND PRACTICAL INFORMATION To get from the **ferry** to **Obregón,** Santa Rosalía's main strip, turn right as you leave the ferry compound (from the bus station, take a left); walk along the water toward town until you come to the old train engine in front of the town's two main streets—the one on the left is Constitución, and the one on the right is Obregón.

Most **buses** depart from the **ABC station** (tel. 2 01 50), across the street from the ferry office. Buses travel north (7 per day, 3pm-5am) to San Ignacio (1hr., 35 pesos), Guerrero Negro (3½hr., 86 pesos), Punta Prieta (7hr., 125 pesos), El Rosario (9hr., 195 pesos), San Quintín (9½hr., 212 pesos), Ensenada (13½hr., 287 pesos), Tijuana (15hr., 334 pesos), and Mexicali (18½hr., 415 pesos). Heading south (7 per day 9:30am-3am), all buses go to San Ignacio (1hr., 35 pesos), Loreto (3hr., 77 pesos), Ej. Insurgentes (4hr., 116 pesos), Ciudad Constitución (4½hr., 128 pesos), and La Paz (7hr., 180 pesos). From Santa Rosalía, you can catch the **ferry** connecting Baja to Guaymas on the mainland (8hr., Tu and F 11pm, *salón* 123 pesos, *turista* 243 pesos, *cabina* 363 pesos, *especial* 483 pesos). The boat leaves from the modern, blue and green **Sematur** office (tel. 2 00 13) on Rte. 1 (the Transpeninsular Highway), just south of town. To reach the docks, catch a bus from the **ABC Autotransportes** station, about 200m south of the ferry. Those with **cars** must purchase tickets in advance and show a tourist card, registration, and proof of their Mexican insurance (cars up to 5m long 1254 pesos, motorcycles 316 pesos; office open M, W-Th, and Sa 8am-3pm, Tu and F 8am-1pm and 3-6pm). Departure days and times, prices, and office hours are constantly in flux, so be sure to call the office or talk to a travel agent to confirm the schedule. **Banamex** (tel. 2 01 60), on Obregón and Calle 5, changes traveler's checks, has a 24-hour **ATM,** and, most importantly, sports ice-cold air-conditioning. Find some excuse to go in. (Open M-F 8:30am-2:30pm.) **Farmacia Central** (tel. 2 20 70; fax 2 22 70), on Obregón at Plaza, is owned by the English-speaking Dr. Chang Tam (open M-Sa 9am-10pm, Su 9am-1pm and 7-10pm). The **Centro de Salud** (tel. 2 13 37 or 2 13 36) is at Juan Michel Costeau. Send letters home from the **post office** (tel. 2 03 45), on Constitución, between Calles 2 and Altamirano (open M-F 8am-3pm). The **postal code** is 23920. The **phone code** is 115.

ACCOMMODATIONS AND FOOD f you're going to stay in sweltering Santa Rosalía, consider popping the few extra pesos for air-conditioning. The budget standout is **Hotel Olvera,** Calle Plaza 14 (tel. 2 00 57 or 2 02 67), about three blocks from the shore on Constitución, just right of the foot bridge. Enjoy spacious bathrooms, large double beds, and free lukewarm *agua purificada.* Rooms come with color TV and naturally hot water, but then again, you'll have trouble finding cold water during a Baja summer. (Singles 100 pesos, with A/C 130 pesos; doubles 120 pesos, with A/C 150 pesos.) Perhaps the cheapest room in town can be found at the **Hotel Playa,** between Calles 1 and 2 on Constitución, behind the Hotel Olvera. There are only 12 rooms, and though they're run down, the mattresses are soft. (Singles 50 pesos; doubles 80 pesos; triples 110 pesos.) **RV Park Las Palmas,** 3.5km south of town, has 32 spots with full hookups, a laundromat, and a restaurant (US$10 for 2 people, US$2 per additional person).

Constitución is lined with cheap and good *taquerías* and several *comida corrida* joints. Santa Rosalía's best-known establishment, **El Boleo Bakery** (tel. 2 03 10), on Obregón at Calle 4, renowned for its French architecture, deserves a visit for its excellent baked goods as well. Otherwordly French bread (1.50 pesos), *pan dulce* (1.70 pesos), and turnovers (2.50 pesos) thrill customers. (Open M-Sa 8am-10pm.)

SIGHTS Travelers looking for fun in the sun and abundant water sports would do better to make tracks south for the heavenly beaches in Bahía de la Concepción. The wooden houses, general stores, and saloons along Santa Rosalía's streets recall the town's mining-boom days. Startling specimens of 19th-century French architecture include the long and many-windowed **Palacio Municipal,** the **Hotel Francés,** and **El Boleo Bakery** with their pure colors, simplicity of form, and modern use of glass and steel. The most serendipitous of artifacts is the pre-fabricated, white, cast-iron **Iglesia Santa Bárbara,** at Obregón and Calle 1. Designed by Gustave Eiffel for a mission in Africa, the church was never picked up by the company that had commissioned it. French mining *concessionaires* spotted the church at the 1889 Exhibition Universale de Paris and decided Santa Rosalía couldn't do without it. Observers either love it or hate it; its outside panels look like they fell off an industrial washing machine. The purple stained-glass windows are "interesting." For a great view of the church and all of Santa Rosalía, climb the decrepit stone steps just off the beginning of Obregón. The steps lead to the new **Museo Histórico Minero de Santa Rosalía.** *(Open M-F 9am-3pm. Admission 10 pesos.)* The museum, housed in the old office building of the Compagnie du Boleo, exhibits journals, photographs, and mining equipment.

Mulegé

Although many are inclined to keep driving when they reach the Mulegé, a small town dominated by desert, palm trees, and a winding river, it actually as much more to offer visitors than may meet the eye. Mulegé is one of Baja's best-kept secrets, boasting good food and amiable people. Best of all, Mulegé, located 136km north of Loreto and 300km south of Guerrero Negro, is the ideal place from which to explore the glistening beaches and storybook-blue sea of **Bahía de la Concepción** to the south (see p. 164). By day, most of the town's visitors—and many of its expats—abandon the little parcel of preciousness that is Mulegé proper and head for the heavenly sands of the Bahía.

ORIENTATION AND PRACTICAL INFORMATION Soon after bearing left off the Transpeninsular Highway, the road into Mulegé forks. To the left is **Moctezuma;** to the right is **Martínez.** Both are soon crossed by **Zaragoza;** take a right onto Zaragoza to get to the zócalo, which is one block away. **Madero** heads east from the zócalo (away from the highway) and, after following the Mulegé River for about 3km, hits the water at the town beach, **Playa de Mulegé.** You can pick up a simple map of the town from Cortez Explorers on Moctezuma (see p. 163).

El Candil restaurant serves as the unofficial **tourist office.** English-speaking **Kerry "El Vikingo" Otterstrom** has written and published a 160-page book on Mulegé (50 pesos). Look for him at El Candil after 2:30pm. The **Hotel Las Casitas,** Madero 50 (tel. 3 00 19), also has tourist info. Ask for Javier—besides leading tours, he also has info on beaches, camping, and fishing.The **"Igriega" bus station** is simply a sheltered blue bench at the turnoff to Mulegé from Rte. 1. All buses are *de paso,* a phrase that might roughly be translated as "inevitably arrives late and full." Northbound buses stop by daily at 4:30, 10:30am, 4, 7, and 10:30pm and head to Mexicali (19½hr., 469 pesos) via Santa Rosalía (1hr., 35 pesos), San Ignacio (2hr., 70 pesos), Rosarito (6hr., 152 pesos), Punta Prieta (8hr., 170 pesos), El Rosario (10hr., 237 pesos), San Quintín (10½hr., 264 pesos), Lázaro Cárdenas (11hr., 257 pesos), Ensenada (14½hr., 333 pesos), Tijuana (16hr., 379 pesos), and Tecate (17hr., 363 pesos). Southbound buses stop by daily at 10 and 11:30am and go to La Paz (6hr., 167 pesos) via Loreto (2hr., 51 pesos), Insurgentes (3hr., 66 pesos), and Ciudad Constitución (3½hr., 85 pesos). The **police** (tel. 3 00 49) are in the old Pinatel de Educacion building on Martínez, across from the PEMEX station. The **Red Cross** (tel. 3 01 10), is on Madero, on the Transpeninsular Highway 20m past the turnoff into town. **Farmacia Moderna** (tel. 3 00 42) is on Madero, on the plaza (open daily 8am-1pm and 4-10pm). **Centro de Salud B (ISSTE),** Madero 28 (tel. 3 02 98), treats **medical emergencies** (open 8am-2:30pm). The **post office** (tel. 3 02 05) is in the same building that houses the police (see above; open M-F 8am-3pm). The **postal code** is 23900. **Minisúper Padilla** (tel./fax 3 01 90), on Zaragoza at Martínez, one block north of plaza, has many **phones** for international calls and now offers fax service. The **phone code** is 115.

ACCOMMODATIONS Although Mulegé has plenty of cheap rooms, those with sleeping bags find the best deals, as always, on the shore. Unfortunately, all accommodations in town are far from the beaches. **Scorpions** sometimes stalk unsuspecting tourists in Mulegé; they like warm, moist places (like shoes), so look before you slip your feet in. Scorpions will attack even if unprovoked; if you cross paths with one, give it plenty of room. The most economical hotels crowd the center of town. **Casa de Huéspedes Manuelita** (tel. 3 01 75), on Moctezuma, next to Los Equipales, around the corner from Zaragoza, has clean rooms with soft beds, table fans, and private showers. Campers who simply need to use the bathroom and shower pay 10 pesos. (Singles 50 pesos; doubles 70 pesos; all prices negotiable.) The brand new **Hotel Mulegé** (tel. 3 00 90) is right near the bus station, on your left as you head into town. Live in luxury—all of the big, white-tiled rooms with spotless bathrooms come with TVs and remote controls. The frigid air-conditioning is a blessing. (Singles 186 pesos; doubles 245 pesos.) **Orchard RV Park** and **María Isabel RV Park,** both just south of town and accessible from the Transpeninsular Highway, are on the Mulegé River (US$15 per night; space for tents US$4; US$1.50 per extra person).

FOOD For something informal and delicious, try **Taquería Doney,** known more commonly as **Doney's,** near the bus station, across the street from Hotel Mulegé. Locals cram both the indoor tables and outdoor stools, wolfing down delicious tacos (6 pesos) or huge steak tortas (13 pesos; open daily 9am-10pm). **Restaurant La Almeja,** at the end of Madero near the lighthouse, about 3km from the center of town, is right on the beach. It offers a great view and outstanding seafood, including the tasty and filling *sopa de siete mares* (soup of the seven seas, which includes just about every creature that ever swam in the sea, 45 pesos; open daily 8am-11pm). The newly renovated **El Candil Restaurant,** on Zaragoza near Martínez north of the plaza, serves an enormous Mexican combination platter with rice, beans, *chiles rellenos,* and tacos (45 pesos) and an excellent fish fillet (37 pesos). Dine under the stars out back, or enjoy the chatter of local expats inside next to the bar. (Open daily 7am-10pm.)

SIGHTS AND SAND Mulegé's lovely **Misión Santa Rosalía de Mulegé** sits on a hill to the west. To get there, walk down Zaragoza away from the *zócalo,* go under the bridge, and turn right on the shaded lane with all the palms. Although not quite as impressive as the Mission of San Ignacio, the church's massive stone facade is imposing and its interior beautiful and quiet. The small hill behind the missionary affords a great view of the whole town, river, and palms. Despite the fact that the paths are not lit at night, the mission is a perfect place for a meditative stroll; walk where you will be immediately visible to cars. Mass is still held every Sunday at the mission.

Over 700 14,000-year-old pre-Hispanic cave paintings are located at **La Trinidad** and the **Cuevas de San Borjita.** Kerry Otterstrom of El Candil Restaurant leads hiking trips to La Trinidad that include a 200m swim in a narrow canyon (US$40 per person). The trip to San Borjita has a milder hike, no swimming, and more spectacular caves (US$50 per person). Longer trips can be arranged (up to 7 days, US$50 per person per day including hotel, food, and drink). If you plan to bring a camera you must have a permit. Permits are issued at the INAH office in town—Kerry will direct you. Tours are given in English, Spanish, German, Thai, or Korean. Other tours are available from **Salvador Castro Tours,** at Hotel Las Casitas (tel. 3 00 19).

Although they are conveniently located—3km from the center of town—Mulegé's two beaches can't hold a candle to those 18km south in Bahía de la Concepción (see p. 164). **El Faro** is at the end of Madero, which becomes a dirt road long before you reach the beach. Alternatively, reach the **public beach** by following the Mulegé River to the Sea of Cortés, where it drains. For a more isolated beach, walk to the PEMEX station about 4km south on the highway, continue about 20m south, and take the dirt road leading to the left until you reach a lonely beach with sand dunes and desert hills overlooking somewhat rocky sand. Locals say this area is quite safe, but watch out for **jellyfish,** especially in June and July.

Mulegé's abundance of sea life makes for great **sport-fishing** and **clamming.** Alejandro Bukobek can usually be found at the **Hotel Serenidad** on the Mulegé River—he leads tours to do both. Fishing usually runs US$110 for three to four people. If you just want to look at all the marine life, head over to **Cortez Explorers,** Moctezuma 75-A (tel. 3 05 00), just past the entrance to town. This newly opened dive shop is the only one in Mulegé; it's owned by a charming Swiss couple who speak Spanish, German, English, French, and Italian. They **rent snorkel and scuba equipment,** lead boat excursions into Bahía de la Concepción, and rent mountain bikes (US$15 per day, US$10 per day for 4 days). If you already know how to scuba dive and brought your own equipment, try the five-hour trip (US$40, min. 2 people); otherwise, an instruction course helps you get your feet wet (US$70). They also organize five-hour **snorkeling** excursions (US$25 including equipment, min. 2 people). All excursions leave at 8am. Make reservations at least one day in advance. (Open M-Sa 10am-1pm and 4-7pm.) The best snorkeling is at nearby **Islas Pitahaya, San Ramón, Liebre, Blanca, Coyote,** and **Guapa.** Ask at the tourist office or the dive shop for maps.

The **Museo Comunitario Mulegé** just opened and is still in its developmental stages. *(Open daily 9am-1pm. Admission 10 pesos.)* To get to the museum, walk down Moctezuma away from the highway until you reach a steep set of stairs on your left. Look up. If you see a big prison-looking building peering down at you, you're there. There's also a great view of the town from the top of the stairs. The museum is housed in the town's old prison, once known as the "prison without doors." Each day, the inmates were allowed to leave their cells to work in town on the condition that they would return at the end of the workday. The exhibit includes artifacts of the Cohimi and displays of local marine life.

Bahía de la Concepción

Heaven on earth may just be the 48km arc of rocky outcrops, shimmering beaches, and bright blue sea known as the Bahía de la Concepción. Cactus-studded hills and stark cliffs drop straight down to white sand, translucent waters, and coves, creating the most breathtaking beaches in Baja. Grown sport fishers and shell collectors weep for joy at the variety and sheer size of the specimens caught here, and divers fall under the spell of underwater sights. As if this isn't enough, the Bahía remains relatively quiet and virginal, still untouched by running water and permanent electricity. While the Bahía is generally blissfully noiseless, Christmas holidays and *Semana Santa* bring strewn beer cans and noisy rows of RVs stretching from the highway to the beach. Although the beer cans and bottles have accumulated into unsightly meter-high mounds of refuse along the access roads to some of the beaches, the *playas* are still some of the most beautiful in all Baja. During the high season, come early to find some peace and a place to put your towel. At other times, Bahía de la Concepción might just be Mexico's most secret treasure.

To get there from Mulegé (or from anywhere north of Mulegé), check at the bus station for the next *de paso* bus south (10 and 11:30am). Wait to pay the fare until the bus arrives; check with the bus driver to ensure that he will stop at one of the beaches. But don't count on a bus to take you back; service to the beaches is infrequent, and bus drivers may not stop along the busy highway. Beach-hoppers might consider renting a car for the day, as access to and from the beaches farther south is limited. Many nomadic travelers hitch (known in Americanized Spanish as "*pedir* ride") from Mulegé to the beaches, catching one of the RVs or produce trucks barreling down the Transpeninsular Highway toward the bay. While *Let's Go* does not recommend hitching, those who hitch are most successful getting rides right across the island from the bus stop, and telling the driver exactly where they are heading. Hitching back to Mulegé is reputedly even easier, since many people go in that direction.

THE BEACHES

The beaches of Bahía are otherworldly after dark, illuminated by millions of stars, but only come at night if you plan to camp out or if you're equipped with wheels—it's impossible to hitch back, no buses run, and oncoming cars spell disaster for would-be pedestrians.

Playa Punta Arena, 16km south of Mulegé, is far enough from the road that the roar of the waves drowns out the noise from muffler-less trucks. From the highway, travel 2km down a rocky dirt road. Bear right at all forks in the road. A dozen palm-frond *palapas* line the beach with sand-flush toilets in back (cabanas US$5; parking US$3). The waters near the shore are great for **clam fishing,** but beware of the manta rays that lurk under the water's surface. If you walk down the dirt road to Playa Punta Arena, take a left instead of a right at the second fork, and you'll end up at **Playa San Pedro** and **Los Naranjos RV Park,** where payments for your space may be made with freshly caught fish.

Playa Santispac, the most popular beach on the Bahía, is connected to Playa Punta Arena by a dirt path that winds through mountains for a grueling 1km. The beach is most easily accessible by the highway (about 20km south of Mulegé), from where it is visible and clearly marked. During the winter, Santispac is the liveliest beach on the bay. In the summer, however, the sands are sparsely populated by laid-back sunbathers. If you drive in a vehicle, it will cost you 40 pesos to park it on the beach for the day. On Playa Santispac, **Las Palapas Trailer Park** rents *palapas* and tent space (both US$5 per night; use of bathrooms and showers US$1). At **Ana's Restaurant,** guests enjoy fried fish (30 pesos) and shrimp omelettes (32 pesos) while marveling at the exotic shells on sale to the right of the counter (2 for US$1). The restaurant doubles as a bakery and sells cakes, huge loaves of bread (13 pesos), and *pan dulce* (15 pesos; open in summer daily 7am-7pm, high season 7am-10pm). Ray and Diane Lima from Rosarito have just opened **Restaurant Santispac,** a *palapa*-roofed place for eats with a TV-equipped bar. Their fish tacos (6 pesos) are the best around. (Open daily 2-7pm.) Watch out in the water—there are mating sting rays in the spring and manta rays in the summer. In case of a sting, locals recommend treating the affected area with hot, salty water. Such a treatment can be found in the warm, bubbly (though somewhat dirty) **hot springs** on the south end of Playa Santispac.

Playa La Posada, which looks essentially like a minuscule village, is covered by permanent homes, but large *palapas* house temporary visitors (US$10 with electricity, US$7 without; both include access to bathrooms). Two distant rocky islands and an overgrown islet are popular destinations for jet-skiers. **Kayak Concepción Bay** (tel. 3 04 09; fax 3 01 90), on the south side of the beach, rents **kayaks** (both sit-on-tops and sea kayaks), mask-snorkel-fin sets, and wet suits. They offer a special all-day package that includes a kayak trip, snorkeling, diving for shellfish, and a cookout of the day's catch. (Minimum 4 people, US$39 per person.) They also rent *palapas,* with fans and two hammocks, plus access to bathrooms (US$12 per night). **Playa Escondida** (Hidden Beach) is at the end of a 500m dirt path winding through the valley between two hills; look for a white sign with black letters at the southern end of Playa Concepción. True to its name, the short, facility-less Escondida is refreshingly secluded from civilization. **Playa Los Cocos** is identified by its white garbage cans adorned with palm trees. Access to the beaches is free, but use of the facilities is not. Still, the cabanas that line the shallow beach can be rented for a pittance—10 pesos or so. A grove of trees and shrubs separates the strip from the highway. At **Playa El Burro,** you can rent a *palapa* next to hordes of RVs for 32 pesos per day.

Playa El Coyote is perhaps the most populated beach after Santispac. Shelter and camping space can be rented for reasonable, completely negotiable prices; the better sands and *palapas* are down on the southern end. Down the road 15km is the exquisite (and even less populated) **Playa Resquesón.** Park your car and rent a *palapa* for the day for US$4, or just park and enjoy the beach for US$3. Even farther south, two more spots—**La Ramada** and **Santa Bárbara**—are currently undergoing development and are closed to the public, though *palapas* have been built. Another nearly deserted stretch of sand separating Mulegé from Loreto is the last before Rte. 1 climbs into the mountains. All of these beaches are marked from the highway. Enjoy the more secluded beaches before they start to look like Miami Beach.

Loreto

Founded by Jesuit missionaries in 1697, Loreto (pop. 10,000) deserves homage for its history and beauty. It was the first capital of the Californias, and its mission was the first in a chain of Jesuit missions along the west coast of Baja. Although the town was wiped out by a freakish combination of hurricanes and earthquakes in the late 19th century, Loreto's loveliness didn't languor for long. The Jesuits were no aesthetic dummies—300 years after settlement, the town is quiet, restful, and a great place to adore nature. Sandwiched between the calm blue waters of the Sea of Cortés and golden mountains, Loreto remains an unassuming, simple town with a long, tranquil *malecón* (pier, beach-side road) shaded by rows of palm trees and sprinkled with stone benches overlooking the rocky shore. You won't find any raucous dance clubs here; the few visitors are mostly laid-back *norteamericanos* who come to fish and enjoy happy hour at small local bars.

ORIENTATION AND PRACTICAL INFORMATION The town is easy to navigate; almost everything of interest is on the main road. The principal street in Loreto is **Salvatierra,** which connects the Carretera Transpeninsular to the Gulf. When Salvatierra becomes a pedestrian walkway, **Hidalgo** roughly becomes its continuation. **Allende,**

León, and **Ayuntamiento** run north-south (roughly) and intersect Salvatierra. **Independencia** intersects Salvatierra just as it turns into Hidalgo, and **Madero** intersects Hidalgo closer to the water. **Malecón,** which leads north to the beach and outlines the entire width of the city at the coast, runs perpendicular to Hidalgo where Hidalgo ends. **Juárez** runs parallel to, and north of, Salvatierra and Hidalgo. The **zócalo** is at Hidalgo and Madero. To get to the *centro* from the **bus station,** walk down Salvatierra toward the distant cathedral (10min.) or indulge in a taxi (14 pesos).

Aguila buses stop by Terminal E (tel. 5 07 67), on Salvatierra two blocks west of Allende near the highway, about 2km from Madero (ticket office open daily 7-10:30am, noon-5pm, and 6:30pm-1am). Northbound buses leave at 3, 9, 11pm, and 2:30am, heading to San Ignacio (5hr., 122 pesos) and Guerrero Negro (7½hr., 170 pesos) and at 2 and 5pm heading to Mulegé (2½hr., 51 pesos) and Santa Rosalía (4hr., 77 pesos); southbound buses go to La Paz (2, 8am, 1, 2:30, 11pm, 5hr., 116 pesos). **Thrifty** (tel. 5 08 15) rents cars for US$50 per day including insurance, tax, and mileage. The Palacio Municipal, on Madero, between Salvatierra and Comercio, facing the *zócalo,* houses the air-conditioned **tourist info center** (tel. 5 03 17). English is spoken (open M-F 8am-3pm). An informal tourist info center (tel. 5 02 59) is on Salvatierra, between Independencia and Ayuntamiento, in a jewelry shop. The only bank in town, **Bancomer** (tel. 5 00 14 or 5 09 10), on Madero, across from the *zócalo,* exchanges dollars (open M-F 8:30am-2:30pm). Stock up for the day at **Supermarket El Pescador** (tel. 5 00 60), on Salvatierra and Independencia (open daily 7:30am-10:30pm). The **Red Cross** (tel. 5 11 11) is on Salvatierra at Deportiva (open daily 9am-1pm and 3-8pm). **Farmacia Flores** (tel. 5 03 21), on Salvatierra, between Ayuntamiento and Independencia, is open daily from 8am to 10pm. The **Centro de Salud** (tel. 5 00 39) is on Salvatierra, one block from the bus terminal (open 24hr.). The medical **emergency numbers** are 5 03 97 and 5 09 06. The **post office** (tel. 5 06 47) is on Salvatierra and Deportiva, near the bus station, behind the Red Cross (open M-F 8am-3pm). The **postal code** is 23880. **Fax** Mom a picture of the marlin you caught from **Telecom** (tel. 5 03 87), next to the post office (open M-F 8am-2pm, Sa 8-11am). **LADATELs** can be found along Salvatierra. The **phone code** is 113.

ACCOMMODATIONS AND FOOD **Motel Salvatierra** (tel. 5 00 21), on Salvatierra, across from the PEMEX and close to the bus station, has clean, air-conditioned rooms that are a bit small but mercifully cold (singles 110 pesos, with cable TV 130 pesos; doubles 150 pesos, with TV 170 pesos). The most economical hotel in town is the **Motel Davis** on Calle Davis, about four blocks north of the *zócalo.* Both the unmarked motel and street are difficult to find, so don't be afraid to ask. If you can put up with the muddy courtyard and slightly worn-down rooms, it's a real deal. Rooms are small and clean, with beds, baths, and not much else. (All rooms 70 pesos.) **El Moro RV Park,** Robles 8 (tel. 5 05 42), though not on the water, allows you to hook up a trailer (US$10) or just camp out (US$4). Showers are a two-dollar luxury. If no one is there, you can park on the honor system—leave your payment under the door. (Office open 7am-8pm.)

Decent, cheap meals are served in establishments up and down Salvatierra, and a number of restaurants cluster conveniently near the bus terminal, offering roast chicken and the like for good prices. *Palapa*-roofed **Café Olé,** Madero 14 (tel. 5 04 96), south of the *zócalo,* offers huge portions, great food, excellent prices, and amazing gossip. Both tourists and locals chatter salaciously over their jumbo burritos (24 pesos) or fresh fish fillet with fries and *frijoles* (37 pesos). Huge omelettes with sides of beans and fries (20-25 pesos) will make breakfast buffs roar like the morning tigers they are. (Open M-Sa 7am-10pm, Su 7am-2pm.) The popular **Restaurant-Bar La Palapa** (tel. 5 11 01), on Hidalgo between Madero and López Mateos, fills the bellies of hungry diners with enormous Mexican combination platters (enchiladas or quesadillas, rice, and beans for 60 pesos). Lots of totally tranquil tourists eat and hang out here. (Open M-Sa 1-10pm.)

SIGHTS With shaded benches along the water and the sidewalk, the **Malecón** is a popular place for an evening stroll. Loreto's **public beach,** a few blocks north of Hidalgo, is nice enough. Although the beach is often crowded, the gray sand and the yellow and black fish that practically swim to shore can amuse you for hours as you soak up the sun. Equally enjoyable is the **Museo de las Misiones** (tel. 5 04 41), next to the reconstructed mission, one block west of the plaza. *(Open Tu-Su 9am-1pm and 1:45-6pm. Admission 14 pesos.)* The museum recounts the complete history of the European conquest of Baja California. Here you can also receive information on Loreto's mission, built in 1697, and on other missions scattered throughout the peninsula. The **Misión de Nuestra Señora de Loreto** is home to eerie, yet beautiful, life-sized statues of Jesus, Mary, and other saints.

If you're angling for a fresh seafood meal, rent a fishing boat and a guide (US$100 for 1 or 2 people, US$110 for 3 people; both 7hr.), or go at it alone with some fishing equipment (US$7 per day) from **Alfredo's** (tel. 5 01 32). **Arturo's Sports Fishing Fleet** (tel. 5 04 09 or 5 07 66), on Hidalgo, half a block from the beach, offers five-hour snorkeling trips (US$80, min. 2 people; equipment US$90 extra). **Tony,** owner of the **Happy Hour Bar,** off Salvatierra between the bus station and the *centro,* also offers sport-fishing excursions for US$85-95; prices are negotiable. Any of the above options may take you on a trip to **Isla Coronado,** where wide, sandy beaches and herds of sea lions await. **Isla Carmen,** another popular destination, contains an eerie ghost town and abandoned salt mines. North of Loreto the road passes the beautiful **Bahía de la Concepción** (see p. 164), with its incredible expanse of coves, blue-green water, and barren, cacti-dotted mountains. South of Loreto, the road winds away from the coast into rugged mountains and the **Planicie Magdalena,** an intensively irrigated and cultivated plain. The striking white stripes on the first hillside beyond town are formed by millions of clams, conch, oyster, and scallop shells—refuse left by the region's Paleolithic inhabitants. Some caves on the hillside, inhabited as recently as 300 years ago, contain shells and polished stone.

Loreto celebrates the **festival** of its patron saint from September 5-8 with a great regional fair. From October 19-25, people come to celebrate the founding of the town with cultural and sporting events (boxing, wrestling, etc.).

Puerto San Carlos

Puerto San Carlos (pop. 4000) is a strange little town. Completely seasonal, it hosts pods of tourists from around the world during whale-watching season and then settles down for an insanely quiet summer featuring boarded-up restaurants, vacant dirt roads, and the town's two policemen playing dominoes in the heat. There is little of anything to do here during the summer months. Visit Puerto San Carlos from November to March, when an estimated 18,000 gray whales migrate yearly from the Bering Sea southward through the Pacific to **Bahías Magdalena and Almejas,** just south of town and easily accessible by boat. During mating season (mid-January to mid-March), the lovestruck creatures wow crowds with aquatic acrobatics. Few travelers have discovered Puerto San Carlos, and locals observe *extranjeros* with the same bemused fascination with which tourists view whales.

To get to San Carlos, take a transfer bus from **Ciudad Constitución** (1hr., 16 pesos), a nondescript tumbleweed town that has connections on **Autotransportes Águila** south to La Paz (3hr., every hr. 5am-11pm) and points in between, and north to Tijuana (19hr., every hr. 5am-11pm) and points in between. In Ciudad Constitución, basic hotels and restaurants abound; try the **Hotel Conchita** and the 24hr. **Ricos Tacos,** both on Olachea at Hidalgo, if you're stuck in town.

In Puerto San Carlos, most services are on the two main streets, **La Paz** and **Morelos,** which are perpendicular to each other. Both of these major roads are made of sand and marked by illegible street signs. Don't fret if the bus drops you off in what seems like the middle of nowhere—you're actually smack in the middle of town. If you have a car, drive carefully, as it is easy to become stuck in the sand roads. **Autotransportes Aguila buses** leave from the small white terminal on La Paz and Morelos. Buses are few and far between, heading to Constitución (45min., 7:30am and 1:45pm, 16 pesos), La Paz (3½hr., 7:30am and 1:45pm, 80 pesos), and Cabo San Lucas (7hr., 1:45pm, 150 pesos). The **tourist office** is on La Paz (tel. 6 02 53), in a house next to the IMSS Hospital, marked by a cardboard sign. The extremely helpful English-speaking staff also leads **whale-watching tours** (open 24hr.; just don't ring late at night and wake them). The pink **information booth** at the edge of town near the PEMEX station provides maps of the bay and islands (closed in summer).

Finding budget rooms in San Carlos isn't easy. This town has few hotels, and they're pricey; come whale-watching season, the town becomes a tourist trap. Possibly the best deal in town is the **Motel Las Brisas** (tel. 113 6 01 52 or 113 6 01 59). To get there from the bus station, turn right on La Paz, then left on Madero; the hotel will be on your left. Clean, yellow rooms with large fans surround a somewhat stark courtyard. If, for some very strange reason, you're here when the whales aren't, console yourself by studying the fading courtyard mural dedicated to these gentle giants. (Singles 100 pesos; doubles 120 pesos.) A **trailer park** at Playa la Curva outside of town offers full hookups for US$10. Dining in San Carlos is homey—literally. A string of combination restaurant-living rooms along La Paz and Morelos allows you to meet locals, their kids, and their pets while you enjoy remarkably fresh delicacies from the sea. **El Patio Restaurant-Bar** (tel. 113 6 00 17; fax 113 6 00 86), in front of Hotel Alcatraz on La Paz, welcomes you into white plastic Corona chairs under open skies. They also offer tourist info to anyone desperately in need of something to do. Enjoy an oyster cocktail (50 pesos) or chicken with *mole* (35 pesos) while you watch the palm trees sway. (Open daily 7am-10pm.)

The islands and bays surrounding Puerto San Carlos teem with life. The cheapest way to explore the islands is to make an ad-hoc deal with one of the fishermen departing from Playa la Curva in front of the PEMEX station. Unless you plan to camp out on the islands, make definite pick-up plans before you disembark. Both **Bahía Magdalena** and **Bahía Almeja** lie just south of Puerto San Carlos. These bays are home to some of the best **whale-watching** in the world. From January to March, enormous numbers of whales have sex with each other. In a peculiar maneuver called "spy hopping," a huge hormonal whale pops its head out of the water, fixes an enormous eye on whatever strikes its fancy, and remains transfixed for minutes on end, staring hypnotically like a submarine periscope.

Feisty Pacific waves at **Cabo San Lázaro** and **Point Hughes,** both on the western tip of **Isla Magdalena,** will keep even veteran surfers on their toes. Reed huts scattered along the beach offer protection from the oppressive midday sun. Fifteen species of clams and starfish inhabit the waters of these immaculate beaches. Farther south, the island narrows to less than 50m in width, tapering off into perfectly white sand tufted with occasional bits of foliage, unusual flowers, and cacti. An enormous colony of *lobos marinos* (sea lions) lives near the island's southern tip.

La Paz

The eclectic and beautiful capital of Baja California Sur, La Paz (pop. 140,000) is part port, part party town, and part peaceful paradise. Home to 10 tranquil beaches along the Sea of Cortés, this is where Mexicans vacation, leaving the honky-tonk Cabos to U.S. tourists. In a past life, La Paz was a quiet fishing village, frequently harassed by pirates for the iridescent white spheres concealed in the oysters off its coast; John Steinbeck's *The Pearl* depicted the town as a tiny, unworldly treasure chest. La Paz's hour of reckoning came in the 1940s, when the oysters got sick and died, wiping out the town's pearl industry. Within two decades after the completion of the Transpeninsular Highway in the late 1960s and the institution of Baja ferries, La Paz was reborn. Now, the row of nightclubs along the beach may make La Paz (The Peace)

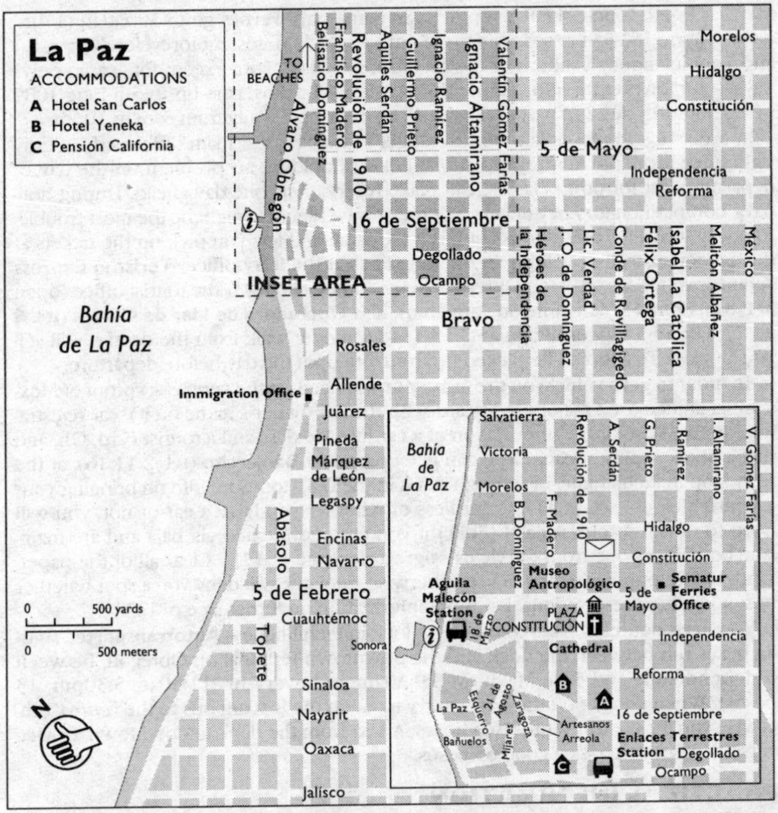

BAJA CALIFORNIA

feel sheepish about its name. No worries, though: the days are still hot and nonchalant and the fishermen are still friendly. At night, despite the big bass beats issuing from semi-gringoized dance clubs, pelicans still skip along the lamp-lit water, and a merciful breeze ruffles the hair of couples strolling along the rocky beach and the serene boardwalk pier at sunset.

ORIENTATION

La Paz lies 222km north of Cabo San Lucas and 1496km southeast of Tijuana, on the Transpeninsular Highway (Rte. 1), and overlooks the **Bahía de la Paz** on Baja's east coast. The city's main street and loveliest lane for a stroll is **Av. Obregón,** more commonly known as the **Malecón,** which runs along alternately sandy and rocky shore. Activity centers around the area delineated by **Constitución, Ocampo, Serdán,** and the shore. The **municipal bus system** in La Paz serves the city sporadically (approximately every 30min. 6am-10pm, 3-3.50 pesos). Flag buses down anywhere, or wait by the stop on Revolución and Degollado, next to the market. From the station, try to convince your driver to drop you off in the *centro.* If you're in the center of activity, you need not worry about the buses; it's all easily navigable on foot.

CROSSING THE GULF

Ferries leave from the suburb of **Pichilingue;** they're the best way to get from La Paz to the mainland. Buy tickets at the **Sematur Company office** (tel. 5 46 66), on 5 de

Mayo at Prieto (open M-F 8am-6pm, Sa-Su 8am-4pm). Ferries go to Mazatlán (17hr., daily at 3pm, 183-544 pesos, cars up to 5m long 1783 pesos, motorcycles 396 pesos) and Topolobampo, a suburb of Los Mochis (8hr., daily 1pm except for "cargo only" days—call for precise info, *salón* (third-class) 123 pesos, cars up to 5m long 1089 pesos, motorcycles 242 pesos). The dock office is open daily from 8am to 10pm.

In order to secure a ticket, be sure to get to the Sematur main office early, ideally right after it opens. Acquiring a *salón* ticket should be no problem on the day of departure, but for other classes, call make reservations one day ahead. During holidays, competition for ferry tickets is fierce. A travel agency might be the most trouble-free way to make reservations—it costs the same and lets you pick up the tickets at the agency instead of waiting in the long lines at the ferry office. **Turismo Express Aventuras** (tel. 5 63 10), on Obregón, in the same building as the tourist office (open M-F 8am-8pm, Sa 9am-8pm, Su 9am-2pm), and **Operadora de Mar de Cortés** (tel. 5 22 77; fax 5 85 99), on Bravo at Ortega, a 15-minute walk from the center, will sell you a ticket. Tickets can be picked up from 4 to 6pm the day before departure.

In order to get a vehicle on the ferry, you will need (at the very least) proof of Mexican insurance (or a major credit card with the car owner's name on it), car registration, permission for the importation of a car into Mexico, and a tourist card. Oh, and **three photocopies** of each. You can get a permit at **Banjército** (tel. 2 11 16), at the ferry stop in Pichilingue, or through **AAA** in the U.S. (for more info on bringing your car into Mexico, see p. 11). Regardless of whether you have a car or not, you will need to obtain a **tourist card (FMT)** if you entered Mexico via Baja and are mainland-bound; get one from **Servicios Migratorios** (see p. 171). Clear all of the paperwork before purchasing the ticket; otherwise, Sematur will deny you a spot whether or not you hold reservations. For more information on ferries, see p. 133.

You need not hike 17km to the ferry dock in Pichilingue—**Autotransportes Aguila** buses run between the dock and the downtown terminal on Obregón, between Independencia and 5 de Mayo (M-F 9:30am and every hr. 11:30am-5:30pm, 13 pesos). When you get off the ferry, hurry to catch the 9:30am bus to the *centro;* otherwise you'll have to wait for two hours. A taxi from the dock to downtown, or vice versa, will set you back a good 65 pesos.

PRACTICAL INFORMATION

Transportation

Airplanes: West of La Paz, accessible only by taxi (80 pesos). If heading from the airport to the center, buy taxi tickets inside to avoid being swindled. Served by **Aeroméxico** (tel. 4 62 88; central phone 1 20 09), at Obregón, between Hidalgo and Morelos (open M-F 8:30am-7pm, Sa 8:30am-5pm) and **Aerocalifornia** (tel. 4 62 88).

Buses: There are 3 stations. The **main station** is on Jalisco and Independencia, about 25 blocks southeast of downtown. Two municipal buses, "Central Camionera" and "Urbano," head to the terminal; catch them near the public market at Degollado and Revolución. Taxis cost 10 pesos. **Aguila** and **ABC** (tel. 2 42 70) provide service to points north, including Loreto (5hr., 8 per day 9am-10pm, 116 pesos), Mulegé (7hr., 8 per day 9am-10pm, 167 pesos), Santa Rosalía (8hr., 8 per day 9am-10pm, 180 pesos), San Ignacio (9hr., 5 per day 10am-10pm, 237 pesos), Ensenada (19½hr., 4 per day 10am-10pm, 504 pesos), Tijuana (21hr., 4 per day 10am-10pm, 552 pesos), and Mexicali (24½hr., 4pm, 636 pesos). A bus from the **Aguila Malecón station** (tel. 2 78 98), on Independencia at Obregón, is the best way to get to nearby beaches. Buses run to El Carmancito, El Coramuel, Playas Palmira, Tesoro, and Pichilingue (up to 30min., 11 per day 7am-7pm, 5-10 pesos) and to Playas Balandras and Tecolote (45min., Sa-Su only, every hr. 8am-6pm, 10 pesos). The last bus back to La Paz leaves Tecolote 7pm weekdays only and Pichilingue at 6pm weekdays, 7pm weekends. But be sure to ask the driver before you get off the bus. The new **Enlaces Terrestres station** (tel. 3 31 80), on Degollado at Serdán, is more convenient for heading south. Buses run to Todos Santos (2hr., 9 per day 7am-8pm, 22 pesos), Cabo San Lucas (3hr., 7 per day 6:30am-7pm, 51 pesos), and San José del Cabo (3½hr., 7 per day 6:30am-7pm, 58 pesos).

Tourist and Financial Services

Tourist Office: (tel. 2 59 39), Obregón at 16 de Septiembre, in a pavilion on the water. Excellent city maps and information about Baja Sur, especially Los Cabos. English-speaking staff. Open M-F 8am-8pm.

Tourist Police: Fabulous folks recognizable by their starched white uniforms and big grins. Their job is "protection and orientation," but they'll do so much more.

Immigration Office: Servicios Migratorios, Obregón 2140 (tel. 5 34 93; fax 2 04 29), between Juárez and Allende. You must stop here to obtain a tourist card if you entered Mexico via Baja and are mainland-bound. Open M-F 8am-3pm. After hours, head to their outpost in the airport outside of town (tel. 4 63 49). Outpost open daily 8am-10pm.

Local Services

Currency Exchange: Bancomer (tel. 5 42 48), on 16 de Septiembre, half a block from the waterfront. Open for exchange M-F 8:30am-2:30pm, Sa 9am-2:30pm. Has 24hr. **ATM. BITAL,** 5 de Mayo (tel. 2 22 89), at Madero, has a 24hr. **ATM** and talking doors. Open for exchange M-Sa 8am-7pm.

American Express: Esquerro 1679 (tel. 2 83 00; fax 5 52 72), at La Paz off 16 de Septiember, 1 block north of the sea. Open M-F 9am-2pm and 4-6pm, Sa 9am-2pm.

Laundromat: Lavandería Yoli (tel. 2 10 01), 5 de Mayo at Rubio, across the street from the stadium. Wash and dry a hefty load for 18 pesos. Open M-Sa 7am-9pm, Su 8am-3pm.

Emergency and Communications

Emergency: Dial 06.

Police: (tel. 2 07 81), on Colima at México. Open 24hr.

Red Cross: Reforma 1091 (tel. 2 11 11), between Isabel la Católica and Félix Ortega. Open 24hr.

Pharmacy: Farmacia Bravo (tel. 2 69 33), next to the hospital. Open 24hr.

Hospital: Salvatierra (tel. 2 14 96 or 2 14 97), on Bravo at Verdad, between Domínguez and the Oncological Institute.

Post Office: (tel. 2 03 88 or 5 23 58), on Revolución at Constitución. Open M-F 8am-7pm, Sa 9am-1pm. **Postal Code:** 23000.

Fax: TELECOM (tel. 2 67 07; fax 5 08 09). Upstairs from the post office. Open M-F 8am-7pm, Sa 8am-3pm, Su 8:30-11:30am.

Internet: Baja Net Cafe Internet, Madero 430 (tel. 5 93 80), between Hidalgo and Constitución. Email all your friends in a comfortable air-conditioned environment. 20-30 pesos per 30min. Open M-Sa 8am-8pm.

Telephones: Sexy young **LADATELs,** as well as older, more mature payphones, pepper the downtown area and *zócalo.*

Phone Code: 112.

ACCOMMODATIONS

The city is full of inexpensive establishments bound to satisfy even the most finicky of travelers. The cluttered artistic look, however, seems to be making a resurgence in the budget hotels of La Paz. A student of Mexican folk art could skip the Museo Antropológico and tour the lobbies of these hotels instead. Many economical lodgings cluster in the downtown area.

Hotel Yeneka, Madero 1520 (tel. 5 46 88), between 16 de Septiembre and Independencia. Quite possibly the most unique hotel in all of Baja. Doubles as a museum of eccentric items, including a 1916 Model-T Ford, a pet hawk, and a stuffed monkey. Each Tarzan-hut room has been remodeled in matching twig furniture and painted with rainbow colors. You can see the painted handprints of the owner's little son on the walls, and the green hallways are a labor of love. All rooms come with fans and foam mattresses laid on concrete frames. Laundry, fax, bike rentals, and a restaurant are but a few of the services this budget bunkhouse offers. Singles 105 pesos; doubles 162 pesos; triples 215 pesos.

Pensión California Casa de Huéspedes (tel. 2 28 96), on Degollado at Madero. Bungalow rooms have concrete floors and concrete-slab beds. You have to admire the plastic turtle sculpture, sea shells, washing machine, picture mural of past guests, and unique shower-toilet-sink combo. Prices include use of the communal kitchen and TV. Bring your own blanket. Padlocks on the doors provide security. Singles 70 pesos; doubles 100 pesos; triples 130 pesos. **Hostería del Convento** (tel. 2 35 08), across the street, has the same owner and an identical setup.

Hotel Posada San Miguel, B. Domínguez 1510 (tel. 5 88 88), just off 16 de Septiembre. Step back in time as you enter the beautiful fountained courtyard. Oversized framed black-and-white photographs of La Paz in its early days, tiled arches, and wrought-iron scrollwork on windows and railings help to create a feeling of an earlier, simpler time. Cubical rooms with sinks and large, comfortable beds. Singles 80 pesos; doubles 100 pesos; triples 120 pesos.

Hotel San Carlos (tel. 2 04 44), on 16 de Septiembre between Revolución and Serdán, is worn, with pink, peach, and oh-so-clean rooms. The staff is prompt and helpful. Singles and doubles 80 pesos, 100 pesos for a room with a view.

FOOD

On the waterfront you'll find decor, menus, and prices geared toward peso-spewing tourists. Move inland a few blocks and watch the prices plunge. Seafood meals are generally fresh. The **public market,** at Degollado and Revolución, offers a cheap selection of fruits, veggies, and fresh fish.

Restaurante El Quinto Sol (tel. 2 16 92), on B. Domínguez at Independencia. One of the few vegetarian joints in Baja. Menu includes sausage à la soybean, as well as an assortment of juices. Yummy yogurt smoothie with fruit 21 pesos; vegetarian steak 35 pesos; tasty pastries 12 pesos. Open M-Sa 7am-10pm.

Restaurant Palapa Adriana (tel. 2 83 29), on the beach, off Obregón at Constitución. Not just on the water, but practically in the water. *Huachinango* (red snapper) 40 pesos; *pollo con mole* 28 pesos; *pulpo al ajo* 50 pesos. Great view and sea breeze *gratis.* Open daily 10am-10pm.

La Luna Bruja, on Playa Pichilingue, the second cabana on shore, farthest from the ferry dock. Defying the stereotype of the overpriced beachfront *palapa,* this quiet restaurant offers amazing seafood at good prices. *Tostados de ceviche* 30 pesos; fish about 50 pesos. Ice-cold beer 10 pesos (or buy 40 oz. for 20 pesos)—a real deal when it's hand-delivered to you on the beach. Open daily 11am-8pm.

La Fuente, on Obregón at Bañuelos, across from the big arch. What better way to battle the heat than with a few scoops of ice cream? This local *nevería* is always buzzing—at day with little kids, at night with eager clubgoers and families. Open daily 8am-midnight.

SAND AND SIGHTS

Instead of curving around long expanses of wave-washed sand, the beaches of La Paz snuggle into small coves sandwiched between cactus-studded hills and calm, transparent water. This is prime windsurfing territory. But be careful—La Paz lifeguards make appearances only on weekends and at popular beaches.

The best beach near La Paz is **Playa Tecolote** (Owl Beach), 25km northeast of town. A quiet extension of the Sea of Cortés laps against this gorgeous stretch of gleaming white sand near tall, craggy mountains. Even though there are no bathrooms, Tecolote is terrific for **camping.** Several spots on the eastern side of the beach along the road to the more secluded **Playa El Coyote** come equipped with a stone barbecue pit. **Actividades Aquatica,** on Tecolote, rents **snorkeling** gear (50 pesos per day), sit-on-top kayaks, and paddle boats and organizes trips to **Isla Espiritu Santo** (250 pesos per person, min. 4 people). The **snorkeling** off **Playa Balandra,** just south of Tecolote, is excellent. Balandra is actually a cove with almost no view of the sea; it resembles a big blue swimming pool with rocky hills instead of cement walls. Because facilities are sparse and sporadically open, it is best to rent equipment either in the city or at nearby Pichilingue or Tecolote. You may not be able to reach Tecolote or Balandra weekdays without a car; **Autotransportes Aguila** buses get you there from the mini-station on Obregón and Independencia (spring break and July-Aug. daily, in the low season Sa-Su only; 10 pesos).

Plenty of other beaches are easily accessible by taking the "Pichilingue" bus up the coast (10 pesos). Be forewarned that neither of these buses run back to La Paz after 6:30 or 7pm. The "Pichilingue" bus goes as far as the ferry dock, at which point you need to walk 1km farther on the paved road to **Playa de Pichilingue.** This beach is the most crowded and a favorite among the teen set, who splash in the shallow waters and ride **paddleboats** in the winter (12 pesos per hr.). Unfortunately, the view from Pichilingue is corrupted by the ferry docks and the nearby power plant. Along the same bus route lies **Playa El Coromuel,** near La Concha Hotel, where visitors and locals congregate on weekends. All of the above beaches are out of walking distance from the city center, though a short ride away. The farther you venture from La Paz, the prettier and more secluded the beaches get.

The aquatic fun in this city doesn't stop at the shoreline; many popular dive spots are located around La Paz. North of La Paz is **Salvatierra Wreck,** a dive spot where a 100m boat sank in 1976. Also popular is the huge **Cerraluo Island,** east of La Paz. This popular destination promises reefs, huge fish, and untouched wilderness. Both of these destinations (and many others) require guides because of strong currents, fluctuating weather conditions, and inaccessibility.

For some of the lowest rates in town, try the newly opened **La Paz Dive Center** (tel. 5 70 48; email divelap@lapaz.cromwell.com.mx), on Esquerro, off 16 de Septiembre near the coast. The center runs tours to various points around the coast. (Dives around US$70, snorkeling tours US$30, snorkel sets US$5 per day. Open 8am-6pm.) **Baja Diving and Service,** Obregón 1665 (tel. 2 18 26; fax 2 86 44), between 16 de Septiembre and Callejón La Paz, organizes daily scuba and snorkeling trips to nearby reefs, wrecks, and islands, where you can mingle with hammerheads, manta rays, giant turtles, and other exotica (scuba trips US$77 per day without equipment, US$15 extra for equipment, snorkeling US$40 per day). Trips leave at 7am and return between 3 and 5pm. Nearby, **Sea & Scuba** (tel./fax 3 52 33), at the corner of Obregón and Ocampo, offers similar activities and rates. Forty-five kilometers south of La Paz along the transpeninsular highway is **El Triunfo,** an abandoned mining town. Marked by a huge tower/chimney, this lonely desert town offers lovely views, solitude, and a chance to see some local artwork done in shell or stone.

ENTERTAINMENT

Structure (tel. 2 45 44), Obregón and Ocampo, three blocks east of the center, is a new, hoppin' disco with a dim interior and loud, terrific techno. The dance floor looks like a boxing ring. Many Thursdays feature live karate and sporting events while young couples drink beer (12 pesos) and watch Mexico's version of MTV on scattered TV screens. The cover includes an open bar. (Cover Tuesday men 50 pesos, women 30 pesos; Friday men 70 pesos, women 30 pesos; Saturday 2-for-1 specials; open in summer daily 10pm-late, in winter Tu-Sa.) For something more mature, **La Cabaña,** Obregón 1570, on the second floor in the Hotel Perla, is a gem. Every night, live music and bands crooning favorite Mexican ballads entertain a dressy, scotch-sipping, over-35 crowd. This joint is bizarre, kitschy, and rockin'. Wednesday nights you can catch a boxing match, and on Sunday nights you can two-step to good ol' country tunes. Grab a tall cool *cerveza* from the long dark bar and knock yourself out. (Cover F-Sa 30 pesos; open W-Su 10pm-5am.) **Carlos 'n' Charlie's/La Paz-Lapa,** Obregón and 16 de Septiembre, is the most central and noticeable structure in town. You can savor huge margaritas (22 pesos) at C 'n' C, a staple of gringo nightlife, or go buck-wild at the La Paz-Lapa, an outdoor booze and rockfest. U.S. and Mexican teens get down and sing along to Aerosmith amid giant palm trees and an imposing bar. Funny signs like "Do not dive from balcony" turn into real warnings after about 3am. Cover and drink prices vary. Women usually pay much less; sometimes before 10pm they can enter and drink free. The cover includes open bar. (Cover Thursday men 90 pesos, women 50 pesos; open W-Su 10pm-late.)

Todos Santos

Dick and Jane have moved to Todos Santos. She runs an outdoor fish market and has started surfing—at age 47. He got his ear pierced (three times), and now makes sculptures out of chrome and cactus flowers. And yes, of course, they've never been happier. Todos Santos (pop. 3500) is paradise for the frugal surfer/painter/zoned-out vacationer/nature-lover/Deadhead/elderly expat set. Halfway between La Paz and Cabo San Lucas, this serene and sophisticated town is one of the few on the southern Baja coast that oozes culture, is easily accessible by bus, offers budget accommodations, and is largely unmutilated by resort development.

John Steinbeck used to hang his hat here; a number of lesser-known (but more ecologically concerned) U.S. expats have recently fallen in love with Todos Santos's rolling cactus hills, huge surfing waves, dusty roads, and laid-back demeanor. Their presence is revealed by the myriad gourmet shops, classy restaurants, and art galleries that now inhabit the buildings whose large brick chimneys are all that remain of the town's sugar-cane-producing past. Still, expats and locals seem to coexist in harmony; the result is a hospitable and lively environment. It's OK to ogle art, but don't think too hard; follow Dick and Jane's example and rediscover yourself—slowly.

ORIENTATION AND PRACTICAL INFORMATION Todos Santos's two main streets, running parallel and north-south, are **Colegio Militar** and **Benito Juárez.** Juárez is just west of Militar; west of and parallel to Juárez run **Centenario** and **Legaspi.** East of Militar and parallel runs **Rangel** and **Cuauhtérloc.** From north to south, **Ocampo, Obregón, Topete, Hidalgo, Márquez de León, Morelos, Zaragoza,** and **Degollado** run east-west. Activity centers around the area between **Legaspi, Militar, Zaragoza, and Topete;** León crosses Legaspi and Centenario at the church and main plaza. You may be dropped off near Degollado and Militar, as this is where the **Transpeninsular Highway** (from La Paz) turns to head toward Los Cabos.

The **bus** stop (tel. 5 01 70) is at Pilar's taco stand, on the corner of Zaragoza and Colegio Militar. If you have any questions about bus times or anything else, Pilar is an excellent person to talk to. *De paso* **buses** run north to La Paz (1hr., 8 per day 7am-11:30pm, 30 pesos), and south to Cabo San Lucas (1½hr., 8 per day 8am-10pm, 35 pesos) and San José del Cabo (2hr., 8 per day 8am-10pm, 35 pesos). Todos Santos has no tourist office, but the American-owned **El Tecolote Libros,** on Juárez and Hidalgo, sells English-language newspapers, maps, and a comprehensive book on the town (100 pesos; open July-Oct. M-Sa 9am-5pm, Nov.-June daily 9am-5pm). To exchange currency, try the **Bancrecer,** the only bank in town, on the corner of Obregón and Juárez (open M-F 9am-2pm). **Faxes** (tel./fax 5 03 60) can be sent at the Delegación Municipal, on Centenario and Hidalgo (open M-F 8am-2pm). Meet your recommended daily nutritional allowances at **Mercado Guluarte** (tel. 5 00 06), on Morelos, between Colegio Militar and Juárez (open M-Sa 7:30am-9pm, Su 7:30am-2pm). Other markets are on Degollado and Juárez. The **police** are in the Delegación Municipal complex on Legaspi, between León and Hidalgo. For standard pharmaceutical fare, try **Farmacia de Guadalupe** (tel. 5 00 06), on Juárez at Zaragoza (open Su-Th 8am-11pm, F-Sa 8am-2am). In case of an **emergency,** call the **hospital** (tel. 5 00 95), on Juárez at Degollado (open 24hr.). The **post office** (tel. 5 03 30) is on Colegio Militar at León (open M-F 8am-3pm). The **postal code** is 23300. The **phone code** is 114.

ACCOMMODATIONS AND CAMPING The town has four main hotels; two are in the center of town, and the other two are a 15-minute jaunt away. Beware: red ants are everywhere. The best deal in town is the centrally located **Motel Guluarte** (tel. 5 00 06), on Juárez at Morelos. This tiny motel is run out of a grocery store in the Mercado Guluarte (see above). The pool is well-suited to those who enjoy bathing in full view of the street. Clean, cozy rooms have TVs, fans, and refrigerators. (Singles 100 pesos; doubles 130 pesos; triples 200 pesos.) The **Hotel Miramar** (tel. 5 03 41), on Pedrajo at Mutualismo, is far from all the action but offers quality rooms at affordable prices. From the center, head to the south end of town and turn left onto Degollado.

Walk five minutes down Degollado, past PEMEX and a supermarket, until you see a sign for "Hotel Miramar." Take the following right, and it's four blocks down on your left. Clean rooms with fans, large tiled bathrooms, color TVs, and a pool will reward you at the end of your hike. (Singles 110 pesos; doubles 150 pesos; triples 190 pesos.)

The best deals in town are the campgrounds. If you have the equipment, Todos Santos is an excellent place to camp, with plenty of gorgeous beaches, scenic views of rolling hills, and pot-smoking, Kerouac-reading, surfing-hard bodies. Two RV parks hide along the coast, south of town, both with great beaches and facilities. To reach the closer one, **San Pedrito Trailer Park** (tel. 2 45 20; fax 112 3 46 43), turn right off the Transpeninsular Highway, 6km south of town—you can't miss the giant welcome sign and arch. Pass under the arch, drive 3km, bear left at the fork, and you're there. The beach here is beautiful and has prime surfing waves. (RV hookups US$15; simple, semi-sheltered cabanas where you can pitch your tent US$3.50; full-size, indoor cabanas with amenities US$25-35; gates to the park open 7am-9pm.)

FOOD Good budget eats aren't hard to find in Todos Santos. Several **loncherías** line Colegio Militar near the bus station, offering triple tacos for 10-12 pesos. **Pilar's Taco Stand** (tel. 5 03 52), on the corner of Zaragoza and Colegio Militar, is not only the town's de facto bus station but also an excellent place to indulge in glorious fish tacos (12 pesos) or fries (8 pesos; open M 8am-8pm, Tu-Su 8am-midnight). **Restaurant Santa Monica** (tel. 5 02 04), on Degollado and Colegio Militar, has been open for 23 years—try their *pescado a la veracruzana* (35 pesos) and you'll know why. Simple yet elegant decorations, giant potted cacti, and tiny birds playing in the next room create an enjoyable dining experience. (Open daily 7am-10pm.) Locals love **Carnitas y Chicharrones,** an outdoor stand on Degollado near Colegio Militar, with excellent meat tacos (6 pesos).

Stealing Home

If you're feeling energetic at night, you might want to take in a **baseball game** at the local stadium, off Degollado to the south. Follow the light towers—any local will show you the way. Admission is only 5 pesos, though a cold Tecate is another 5 pesos. Root, root, root for the home team—**Los Tiburones** (the Sharks)—while analyzing the odder aspects of Mexican League professional baseball: you'll see an all-sand playing field, umpires in bright blue pants, baserunners without batting helmets, players trading gloves between batters, lots of submarine-ball pitchers, players on the same team in different uniforms, and huge crowds dancing between innings to popular dance music. Oh, and if, by chance, you catch a ball, don't even think about keeping it as a souvenir—you will first be swarmed by young children paid by commission for every ball (and crushed beer can) they recover, and eventually you'll even be bothered by the police. Games are at 7pm some weeknights and 1 or 2pm on weekends.

SIGHTS AND SAND Todos Santos is home to strange and cool combination of offbeat art galleries and beautiful beaches.

Art Galleries

Modern art lovers are sure to be wowed by the plethora and high quality of galleries. Todos Santos's new pride and joy (among art fans, at least) is the **Todos Santos Gallery** (tel. 5 00 40), on Legaspi and Topete, opened in 1995 by artist Michael Cope. *(Open M and W-Sa 10am-5pm.)* The gallery is devoted strictly to the work of artists who reside in Baja California—exactly half of them Mexican, the other half from the U.S. and other countries. Cutting-edge bronze and clay sculptures, off-the-wall wall clocks, and ornate mirrors are on parade at the **Santa Fe Art Gallery,** Centario 4, between Hidalgo and Márquez de León (open daily Nov.-Aug. 11am-4pm, Oct. 10am-5pm, Sept. closed). **Casa Franco Gallery** (tel./fax 5 03 56), on Juárez at Morelos, has furniture, bowls, and pipes from Todos Santos, Guadalajara, and all over Mexico; the staff will be happy to tell you more (open M-Sa 9am-5pm). It's worth peeking into the

Charles Stewart Gallery & Studio (tel. 5 02 65), on Obregón at Centenario, which is both Mr. Stewart's home and his studio (open 10am-4pm).

Beaches

If you overdose on art, don't forget that Todos Santos is surrounded by some of the region's most unspoiled (and unexplored) beaches. **La Posa,** only 2km from town, is perfect for that romantic stroll or uplifting solitary walk. To get there, go up Juárez and turn left on Topete. Follow the road as it winds across the valley and past a white building, and....voilà! Unfortunately, vicious undercurrents and powerful waves make this beach unequivocally unsuitable for swimming. To reach **Punta Lobos,** the stomping ground of the local sea lion population and a beach popular with locals, turn left onto Degollado as you walk away from the town center. Roughly six blocks later, the city limits end. To catch a spectacular aerial view of the sea, turn right 1.5km south on the highway at the first possible fork in the road. Follow the main dirt path east for 2.5km; the path will bear left past an old fish plant and continue up a hill, with steep drop-offs to the seashore. Most other beaches are accessible via the Transpeninsular Highway south of town. These sights are isolated, and therefore both attractive and hazardous. Bring a friend, and plan to return before nightfall.

The only beaches considered suitable for swimming are **Playa de las Palmas** and **Playa los Cerritos.** Los Cerritos, a popular picnic spot and family beach, lies approximately 14km south of Todos Santos. Look for a turn-off on the right side of the Transpeninsular Highway. Head south about 3km past the signs for Gypsy's Bed and Breakfast. The current is tamer here than elsewhere, but the waves are just as big, and there's always some sort of party going on. To reach the appropriately named **Playa de las Palmas** (Beach of the Palm Trees), travel 5.1km south from town on the highway, and turn right when you see the white Campo Experimental buildings on the left. Travel another 2.6km and you'll be bowled over by palm trees; just past these is the beach. The serene and deserted shore here is excellent for swimming.

A quiet and lovely beach by the highway is **San Pedrito,** 8.2km south of town. Lots of surfing and hangin' loose goes on here. It's easy to find a sunbathing spot, and on these Bohemian beaches, nobody cares if you bare all. Just be careful in the water—the current is not as friendly as the big, inviting waves are. To get there, just turn off at the sign for San Pedrito RV Park.

Sierra de la Laguna, a beautiful lake atop a mountain, is accessible only by car (it's a 90-minute drive). One kilometer south down the highway, past the Punta Lobos turnoff, turn left at the fenced-off cattle ranch. A 45-minute drive brings you to **Rancho La Burera,** which serves as the trailhead for the *laguna.* Be social and make friends in town, then invite them to show you the way.

Los Cabos

The towns of **Cabo San Lucas** and **San José del Cabo** comprise the southwestern part of the Los Cabos district (pop. 70,000), which includes most of the coastline of Baja California's southern end. Los Cabos (the capes) is the most tourist-oriented area in all of Baja outside of Tijuana. Million-dollar resorts and golf courses infest the otherwise heavenly natural elements of the tip of Baja—otherworldly rock formations, surf that is said to compare with the waves in Hawaii, and vast expanses of fine white-sand beaches. Visitors are drawn here by the stretch of beach leading from San José del Cabo to Cabo San Lucas, where luxury hotels form a glittering strip between the desert and the ocean. Don't expect wilderness or hidden pirate plunder, though: Bud-guzzling, sunbathing, sightseeing, gift-buying, jet-skiing *norteamericanos* congregate by the thousands. The *vía corta* bus from La Paz heads first to Cabo San Lucas, then to San José del Cabo, then back to La Paz.

Los Cabos: Cabo San Lucas

Perched on the southern tip of Baja, **Cabo San Lucas** (a.k.a. Land's End) is a reflection of the heavy U.S. influence on the resort industry of Mexico. Although small (pop. 8000), the town has surpassed such classic resorts as Acapulco in popularity among honeymooners and U.S. college spring-breakers due to its peaceful waters and ultra-modern pleasure domes. A favorite vacation spot among families looking for an easy, pampered escape from stress, Cabo is best suited to those who desire neither a peek into real Mexican culture nor the "inconvenience" of changing their dollars into pesos—or even of learning what a peso is. Cabo San Lucas now has one of the country's highest costs of living, and it is quickly turning into a city dominated by endless neon-lit, fog-machined discotheques, cigar shops, and U.S. fast-food joints.

If all this sounds like it's not for you, then Cabo can be depressing. Tensions between maltreated Mexicans, elderly resident U.S. expats, and carefree tourists run

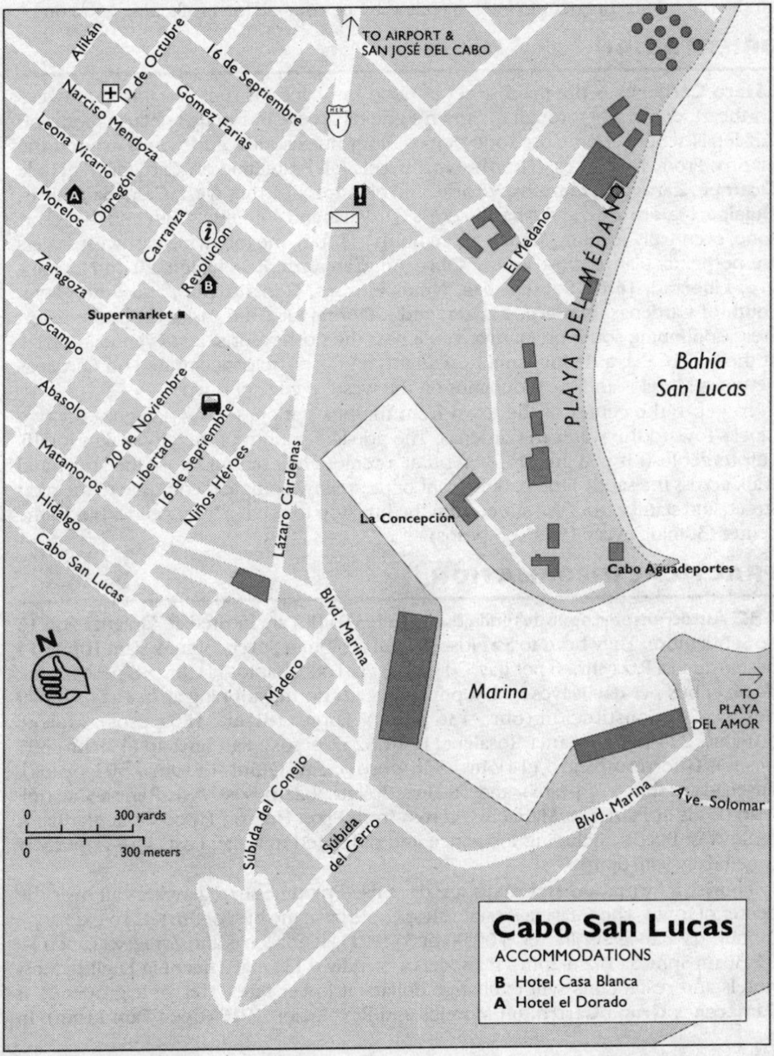

BAJA CALIFORNIA

high. Local fishermen are finding it increasingly hard to survive, and the dolphins and whales that once flourished near the coast have all but disappeared. Recent legislation to reduce pollution may be just a little too late. Outside of the natural beauty that surrounds Cabo San Lucas, the town itself is nothing to write home about. The crowning architectural achievement is the spiraling globe that sits on top of the Planet Hollywood restaurant. The many resort hotels try hard to distinguish themselves from one another. The result: bizarrely shaped buildings and a gimmicky faux lighthouse that gives the town the feel of a giant mini-golf course.

Despite its influx of dollar-rich, culture-poor tourists, Cabo San Lucas holds some appeal for the budget traveler, mostly due to its superb beaches and picturesque rock formations: **El Arco** is the famous arch rock that marks the very tip of the Californias. Cabo San Lucas has yet to develop extensive facilities for budget travelers. If you don't plan to spend a lot of money, then stay in town only for the day and camp on the beach, or simply treat the town as a big supermarket—buy your sunscreen and make tracks for cheaper San José del Cabo. If you've come to party, you're knocking on the right door. Break out your wallet and brace yourself for a rollicking good time.

ORIENTATION

Lázaro Cárdenas is the main street in Cabo San Lucas. It runs roughly southwest-northeast, diagonally through the town's grid of streets. **Paseo de la Marina** forks off Cárdenas where the resort zone begins, continues south, and winds around the marina. From west to east, north-south streets (all branching off Cárdenas) include **Ocampo, Zaragoza, Morelos, Vicario,** and **Mendoza.** Farther west, **Cabo San Lucas, Hidalgo, Matamoros,** and **Abasolo** cross Cárdenas and continue south into the resort zone, eventually meeting Marina. From north to south, the following east-west streets are perpendicular to those above: **Obregón, Carranza, Revolución, 20 de Noviembre, Libertad, 16 de Septiembre, Niños Héroes, Constitución,** and **5 de Mayo.** South of Cárdenas, **Madero, Zapata,** and **J. Domínguez** run east-west in the resort area. Continuing south on Marina, you'll pass the posh resorts, and eventually arrive at the beach, **Playa de Médano.** Restaurants and bars are concentrated on Cárdenas between Morelos and the mountains on the western edge of town.

To get to the center of the town from the bus station, follow Zaragoza for two blocks toward the water to Cárdenas. The grid-like pattern of the city makes it difficult to get lost. If you are dropped off at a remote bus station, cross the street and walk across the sandy little park in front of the yellow complex; continue to the next street, and stand across the street from the bus stop to catch a local yellow bus to the center (30min., every 15min., 3 pesos).

PRACTICAL INFORMATION

ABC Autotransportes and **Aguila buses** (tel. 3 04 00) are located at Zaragoza and 16 de Septiembre. They head to San José del Cabo (30min., every 30min. 7am-10pm, 14 pesos) and La Paz (3hr., 6 per day, 70 pesos) via Todos Santos (1½hr., 38 pesos). One *de paso* bus per day leaves at 4:30pm and heads north, stopping at La Paz (3hr., 70 pesos), Cd. Constitución (6hr., 136 pesos), Loreto (8½hr., 186 pesos), Mulegé (10½hr., 224 pesos), Santa Rosalía (11½hr., 252 pesos), San Ignacio (12½hr., 307 pesos), Guerrero Negro (14½hr., 358 pesos), San Quintín (19hr., 501 pesos), Ensenada (23hr., 574 pesos), and Tijuana (26½hr., 622 pesos). **Avis Rent-a-Car** (tel. 3 46 07) is at Plaza Los Mariachis, across from Pizza Hut, on Paseo de la Marina. A funky VW Beetle, including insurance and unlimited mileage, costs US$44 per day (open daily 9am-6pm).

Tourist information and **maps** are dispensed by time-share hawkers all over the center of town. The "Marina Fiesta" salespeople have the best of the lot. To exchange money, try **Banca Serfín** (tel. 3 09 90 or 3 09 91), at Cárdenas and Zaragoza (open M-F 8:30am-5pm, Sa 10am-2pm). It also has a friendly **ATM** that's fluent in English. Most hotels and restaurants will exchange dollars at lower rates. Get your groceries at **Almacenes Grupo Castro,** on Morelos and Revolución 1910 (open 7am-11pm). In an **emergency,** dial the **police** (tel. 3 39 77) on Cárdenas, two blocks north of Morelos. **Farmacia Aramburo** (tel. 3 14 89) is on Zaragoza and Cárdenas, at Plaza Aramburo (open 7am-10pm). The **Red Cross** (tel. 3 33 02) is on Delegación, on the outskirts of town toward San José del Cabo, 200m from the gas station. The **post office** (tel. 3 00 48) is next to the police station (open M-F 9am-5pm, Sa 9am-noon). The **postal code** is 23410. You can access the **Internet** at **Cabonet** (tel. 3 01 20), on Blvd. Lázaro Cárdenas at 16 de Septiembre, across from the PEMEX station (40 pesos per hr.; open M-F 9am-2pm and 4-7pm, Sa 9am-2pm). The **phone code** is 114.

ACCOMMODATIONS

Multi-million-dollar resorts with every service imaginable dominate San Lucas's coast; as a result, simple, cheap beds are seriously lacking. During the winter high season, make reservations early and be prepared to shell out more *pesos* than you would during the slower summer months. The only legitimate budget accommodation remaining may be the **Hotel Casa Blanca** (tel. 3 53 60), on Revolución at Morelos. Slightly less luxurious than its namesake, the hotel provides clean and simple rooms with fans and functional private bathrooms (singles 140 pesos; doubles 160 pesos). The next best deal in town is **Hotel El Dorado** (tel. 3 28 10), on Morelos about two blocks north of Casa Blanca. The spotless gigantic tiled rooms are almost luxurious. (Singles or doubles with TV and fan 200 pesos, with TV and A/C 295 pesos.)

FOOD

Restaurant-bars along the water gang up on tourists; the cheap spots line Morelos, a safe distance from the million-dollar yachts. King of taquerías, **Asadero 3 Hermanos,** Morelos at 20 de Noviembre, serves up scrumptious, cheap, and safe tacos and quesadillas (5-6 pesos; open 24hr.). Growling stomachs gravitate toward the enormous rotating chickens at **El Pollo de Oro** (tel. 3 03 10), Cárdenas at Morelos. Enjoy a half-chicken for 32 pesos or a quarter bird for 20 pesos. (Open daily 6am-11pm.) Although it's not a bargain eatery (70-90 pesos per entree), you will not find better seafood in all of San Lucas than at **Mariscos Mocambo** (tel. 3 21 22), on Morelos at 20 de Noviembre. The atmosphere and decor are simple, and ceiling fans cool the hungry masses who crowd the wooden tables every night. If you plan to eat with a big group, it would be wise to call ahead. (Open 11am-11pm.)

SIGHTS AND SAND

All major activity in Cabo San Lucas revolves around the pristine waters off the coast. **Playa del Médano,** one of the area's better beaches, stretches east along the bay around the corner from the marina. Escape the blazing sun in one of the beach's many restaurants or *palapas.* The waters of the Playa de Médano are alive with para-sailers and motorboats full of lobster-red, beer-guzzling vacationers. **Cabo Acuadeportes** (tel. 3 01 17), in front of the Hotel Hacienda, rents **water equipment** (open 9am-5pm), as does **JT Watersports** (tel. 7 56 08), adjacent to Hotel Plaza Las Glorias (snorkeling gear US$10 per day, wave runners US$40 per 30min.; open 9am-6pm).

The famous **Arch Rock** (El Arco) of Cabo San Lucas is only a short boat ride from the marina. The rocks around the arch are home to about 40 sea lions who can usually be seen hanging out, sunning themselves, or swimming alongside the taxis checking out the funny-looking passengers. To get there, walk through the Plaza Las Glorias hotel or the big Mexican crafts market farther down Paseo Marina to the docks. Eager, English-speaking boat captains will be happy to take you on a 45-minute glass-bottom **boat ride** to El Arco and back (US$7). In addition to the picturesque Arch and the creatures that visit it, you may catch a glimpse of the summer dwellings of Sly Stallone, Michael Jackson, Madonna, Van Halen, and others. The boat also stops at **La Playa del Amor** (yes, that's the Beach of Loooove) right near El Arco and allows you to get out and head back later on a different boat for no additional charge. At high tide, the light, tranquil Sea of Cortés meets the rough, deep blue Pacific, and the two bodies of water kiss. Swimming is good on the gulf side, but beware of the Pacific's

> **The Player**
>
> Timeshare vendors disguised as "tourist officials" roam the streets of Cabo San Lucas. If you want to take advantage of what they have to offer for free, you must be 25 years old and possess a major credit card. If you have both, and a free afternoon, it's quite possible to go on the Arco boat ride for free and order anything you want at an expensive restaurant in exchange for an hour and a half of "listening," ears closed but eyes open, mouth pleasantly grinning, and head nodding to the English-speaking con man's pitch. He will try to convince you to dump US$15,000 into his hands in exchange for yearly time at an exclusive, American-oriented resort in Cabo. Don't admit until after dinner that you're not prepared to spend $15,000 (unless you want a struggle). Other lures include a free car rental for a day and a free day at a resort.

currents; two unlucky swimmers died recently after being dragged out to sea on this side. To get to the Love Beach and back, you can also take a water taxi (US$7). A beautiful and more secluded Pacific beach where you shouldn't swim is **Playa del Divorcio** (Divorce Beach). To get there, hop on a yellow bus (1.50 pesos) or walk out on Marina and turn right across from the Mexican crafts market. Slip out to the beach between massive condo complexes right after you pass the Terra Sol Hotel.

Snorkeling is popular on La Playa del Amor and around the rocks between the marina and the beach, where tropical fish abound. Bring your own gear or pay the pesos for rented equipment from one of the vendors in the marina area (see above). Although pricey, the snorkeling here is some of the best you'll find in Mexico; once you've seen the incredible array of angelfish, rays, and octopus, you'll be glad you did it. The best snorkeling beach is said to be **Playa Santa María,** 13km from Cabo San Lucas, on the highway between San Lucas and San José del Cabo (see p. 181).

ENTERTAINMENT

If you want to go buck-wild, you couldn't pick a better place. At night, the couple of streets near the sea turn into a huge laser-lit party ground, and everyone stumbles down the street smoking Cuban cigars and shrieking. You too can join rich Americans and hip Mexican teens in the nightly ritual of alcohol-induced gastrointestinal reversal. Typical Cabo San Lucas bar decor is in the same booze-can-punish vein—signs like "Sorry, We're Open" and "Wrong Way—Do Not Exit" vie for space with assorted driver's licenses. Cabo is a great place to cut loose; just don't expect cheap booze—this ain't Tijuana. Here, those who play hard pay hard.

La Concepción (tel. 3 49 63), north of the Marina, next to Hotel Marina Fiesta. Probably Los Cabos's best-kept secret. The ambiance is amazing—sit outside in old hanging boats, listen to the latest in Mexican reggae, or sample one of 105 different tequilas. They'll give you a 20-page history of the drink (in Spanish) and explain tequila from A (agave) to W (worm). Laid-back atmosphere, Mexican clientele. Check out the ceiling, which is a rendition of an old pirate's map, while you nibble on delicious *botanas* or down tequila shots (20-400 pesos). The house drink, La Concepción, contains cranberry and pineapple juice, tequila, and *creme de cacao* (38 pesos). Open daily noon-2am.

Squid Roe (tel. 3 06 55), Cárdenas at Zaragoza. The undisputed heavyweight champion of the loud, beer-guzzling, dance clubs in Los Cabos—the most popular spot in town, especially around 12:30am, when tourists from other clubs flock here to end their night (hopefully not alone). The pick-up scene is frantic. Conga lines, tequila everywhere, and short-skirted, cigar-peddling salesgirls dancing on any and all surfaces. When things get too hot, the MC sprays the crowd with ice-cold water. Beer 24 pesos. Mixed drinks 22 pesos. Open daily noon-3am.

Kokomo's (tel. 3 52 52), on Blvd. Marina, across the street from Squid Roe. Although tamer than its rowdier neighbor, things get pumping at 10:30pm, when this new club starts spouting fog from all corners, and the lights really start acting up. The music is "contemporary"—late 80s top-40 abounds, and there's plenty of room to dance on the mosaic tile dance floor. Beer 24 pesos, margaritas 30 pesos. Open daily 11am-3am.

Carlos 'n' Charlie's, Marina Blvd. 20 (tel. 3 12 80 or 3 21 80), near Zaragoza. This club (owned by the same franchise as Squid Roe) is hip, loud, and happening. Young crowd drinks and dances to U.S. pop tunes from the 80s and 90s. Choreographed "waiter show" at 9 and 11pm. Beer 24 pesos, huge margaritas 45 pesos. Wednesday is ladies night—women drink free 9pm-midnight. Open daily 10am-1am; kitchen closes at midnight.

Cool Hippo's/Sorry Charlie's, on Marina, in the Plaza de los Mariachis. Both outdoor and indoor bar and dining area. Casual and fun: impromptu dancing occurs whenever the urge (or the beer rush) hits you. Not as taxing as some of the other nightspots. Specials include 4 tacos and a beer for US$5 or 3 chicken enchiladas, rice, beans, and a beer for US$5. Comparatively inexpensive drinks (beer 10 pesos, margaritas 15-20 pesos) and glorious 80s background music make this a great place to chill. Open daily 8am-3am; kitchen closes at 1am.

■ Los Cabos: Between Cabo San Lucas and San José del Cabo

The 30km stretch of coast between Cabo San Lucas and San Jose del Cabo is dotted with many beautiful beaches. Unfortunately, development is creeping over the small strip of land from both sides. The only pristine beaches are those that lie in the middle; you have to maneuver around condos and resorts to access the beaches closer to the two towns. Despite the expansion of touristy resorts, the beaches in between San Jose and San Lucas are far less crowded than those in Cabo San Lucas.

All of the following beaches are accessible from the Transpeninsular Highway. Many lie at the end of winding, sandy access bars, and all are easily maneuverable in passenger vehicles. Access roads to some beaches are identified by blue and white palm tree signs—the Los Cabos symbol for *playa.* Others are marked by an entrance to a dirt road and little else. Although the easiest way to get to the private little oasis is to drive there, the bus running in between the two towns will leave you at any of the marked beaches. Getting a bus ride back into town is slightly more difficult.

Starting from San Jose del Cabo, the first beach of note is **Playa Barco Varada** (Shipwreck Beach) at the 9km marker. Ideal for scuba diving, this beach is home to a sunken tuna boat that lies just 2-7m below the water's surface. There's no beach sign; look for the access road around the 9km marker. The access road to **Playa Twin Dolphin** lies just south of the entrance to the eponymous resort. The rough sandy road

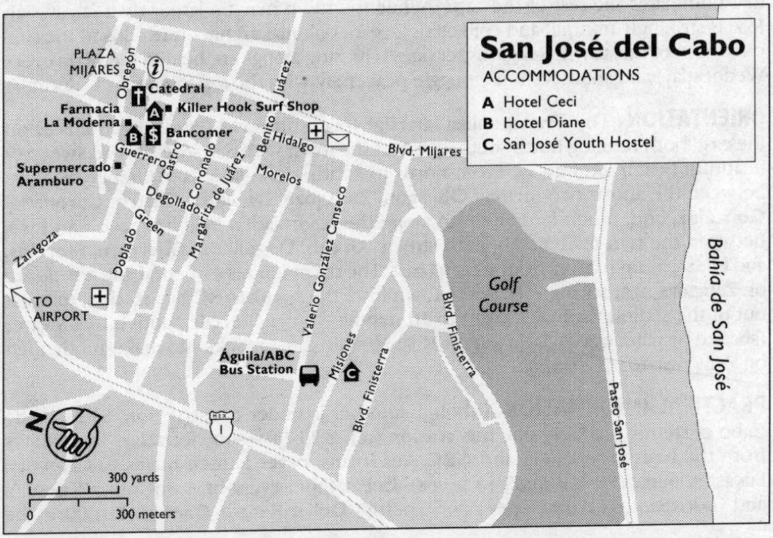

leads to a small secluded rocky beach. Unfortunately, the rough break and rocky shore make it unsuitable for swimming.

Playa Santa María is just past the Twin Dolphin Resort at km 12. This small clear water beach is protected from harsh waves by a slight cove; it's the perfect place to spend the day in solitude swimming and **snorkeling.** The snorkeling here is said to be the best in Los Cabos. You can rent gear for 80 pesos or bring your own. Next is **Playa Ponta Chievo,** at the 14km marker, a popular swimming spot. Chievo comes complete with public baths and showers, as well as a small dock. **Kayaks** and **snorkel** gear are available for rent from **Cabo Acuadeportes** (open daily 9am-5pm).

Although there are no signs pointing the way to **Playa del Tule,** it is easy to find. Just past the entrance to Hotel Cabo San Lucas (around km 15), you'll see signs for Punta del Tule. When the road drops level with the sand and there's a bridge on your left, pull off to the right—you're there. The shore is rocky and not suitable for swimming. Surfers, however, abound. From km 16 to km 20 are Playas **Canta Mar, Costa Brava, El Zalate, San Carlos,** and **El Mirador.** Unfortunately, these areas are under heavy construction, and access is obscured by bulldozers and concrete walls. **Playa Buenos Aires** comes next, at km 22. It too is under development but is accessible by a crude sand and dirt road. The waves are rough but the beach is long and desolate.

Under the shadow of Hotel Palmilia, the first resort hotel in Los Cabos, **Playa Punta Palmilia** offers smooth, gentle waves and great swimming. There are plenty of fishing *pangas* for hire, and if you get thirsty, you can pop in to Restaurant/Bar Pepes. **Playa Acapulquito,** km 27, is easy to miss. Look for cars parked on the side of the highway just before the Acapulquito Scenic Overlook. Walk down the steep dirt path and slip through the condos; great waves make this a popular surfers' beach. The last beach before San Jose del Cabo is **Costa Azul,** the best **surfing beach** in all of Los Cabos. Swim if you dare, but this beach belongs to surfers. You can rent a board for the day (US$12), or, for virgin surfers, get a lesson for US$20 from **Playa Costa Azul Rentals** (tel. 7 15 96) on the beach, located around km 29—keep your eye out for a posse of surfers and a small beachside restaurant called Zippers.

Los Cabos: San José del Cabo

If Los Cabos were two brothers, then José would be the more sedate of the two: unlike his ill-fated, party-animal, bad-boy younger brother Lucas, José would be better-looking, charming, sincere, and polite, yet still lots of fun. San José del Cabo remains relatively untouristed and peacefully Mexican, a haven from the Resortville that dominates the rest of the cape. While the town may be larger than Lucas, San José is strikingly tranquil and collected. Elegant colonial architecture adds to the simple charm of this town. Religious services with sing-alongs are held in the plaza every Wednesday, and snorkel shops snuggle peacefully with the *loncherías* next door.

ORIENTATION The **Transpeninsular Highway** on the west and **Blvd. Mijares** on the east, both running north-south, connect the town with San José's broad sweep of beautiful beach 2km away. From north to south, cross-streets, running east-west between the above two include **Obregón, Zaragoza, Doblado, Castro, Coronado, González,** and, much farther south along the resort-laden beach, **Paseo San José.** Between the two main north-south streets, **Green, Degollado, Guerrero, Morelos,** and **Hidalgo** run parallel from west to east. The conspicuous cathedral and *zócalo* are on Zaragoza near Hidalgo. To get to town from the **Aguila/ABC bus station,** turn left out of the station, and walk eight to 10 minutes down González until it hits Mijares (shaded by palm trees). Turn left on Mijares, walk three blocks and make another left on Zaragoza, to the *zócalo.*

PRACTICAL INFORMATION Although another is under construction, San José de Cabo currently has only one **bus station** (tel. 2 11 00)—on González, two blocks from the highway. **Aguila** and **ABC Autotransportes** launch **buses** to Cabo San Lucas (30min., every 30min., 14 pesos), La Paz (3hr., every hr. 6am-7pm, 81 pesos), and Todos Santos (1½hr., 8 per day, 50 pesos). **Dollar Rent-A-Car** (tel. 2 01 00; at the airport 2 06 71), across from the supermarket on Zaragoza and Guerrero, will set you on the road for US$55 per day plus US$11 per day for insurance with free mileage. You need a credit card and at least 25 candles on your last birthday cake. The **tourist center** (tel. 2 29 60 ext. 150), on Zaragoza and Mijares, in the beige building next to the *zócalo,* offers a valuable map as well as plenty of brochures and info (open M-F 8am-3pm). Change money at **Bancomer** (tel. 2 00 30 or 2 00 40), on Zaragoza and Morelos (open M-F 8:30am-4pm, Sa 10am-2pm); traveler's checks can be cashed at most of the **casas de cambio** that line Mijares. **ATMs** can be found in many banks, including **Banamex** on Mijares, two blocks south of the *zócalo*. The **police** (tel. 2 30 61) are in the City Hall at Zaragoza and Mijares. The ever-ready **Red Cross** (tel. 2 03 16) is on Mijares in the same complex as the post office and offers 24-hour ambulance service. The **hospital** (tel. 2 37 13 or 2 38 13) is on Retorno Atunero, in Col. Clamizal; the **Centro de Salud** is at Manuel Doblado 39 (tel. 2 02 41). **Farmacia La Moderna** (tel. 2 00 50) is on Zaragoza and Degollado (open daily 8am-9pm). The **post office** (tel. 2 09 11) is on Mijares and González, several blocks toward the beach on the right-hand side (open M-F 9am-5pm, Sa 9am-1pm). The **postal code** is 23400. For **Internet access,** try **CafeNet** (http://www.cafe.net.mx). To get there, follow Zaragoza north out of town past the PEMEX station. As you approach the Transpeninsular Highway, you'll see a sign for a big pharmacy on the left; CafeNet is in that complex. The **phone code** is 114.

ACCOMMODATIONS With the approach of the mega-resorts, room prices in the center of town look have been slowly increasing. However, compared to Cabo San Lucas, San Jose is a virtual heaven for the seeker of budget accommodations. Several economical hotels can be found along Zaragoza. You can enjoy multi-colored bedspreads and ancient paint jobs at **Hotel Ceci,** Zaragoza 22 (tel. 2 00 51), a block and a half up from Mijares. Clean, cold rooms put guests in a positive mood, ready to appreciate the pastel curtains and matching lampshades. Bathrooms have colored glass windows—take a shower while admiring the lovely cathedral. (Singles 85 pesos, with A/C 105 pesos; triples with A/C 130 pesos.) **The Hotel Diana** (tel. 2 04 90), on Zaragoza, near the *centro,* has big, clean rooms with TVs and air-conditioning. All rooms have one king-sized bed and one single bed. An upbeat staff maintains this good location. (All rooms 150 pesos.) **San José Youth Hostel** (tel./fax 2 24 64), on Obregón and Guerrero, has relatively clean and spacious pink rooms with fans, thick mattresses, and warm water. Although the hotel offers mail service, bike rentals, and long-distance phone calls, it can be a little desolate at times. (Singles 80 pesos; spacious doubles with TV 140 pesos.) **Trailer Park Brisa del Mar,** just off the highway to San Lucas when it reaches the coast, provides beach campers, communal bathrooms, and a bar with TV (full hookup US$7 plus tax; US$5 for tent).

FOOD Budget restaurants in San José del Cabo are being pushed out by real estate offices and fancy tourist eateries, leaving few options between taco stands and filet mignon. A healthy suspicion of anglophone restaurants will save you money: if the menus are printed in flawless English, the food is probably more expensive than it ought to be. Good, moderately priced meals hide on Doblado and along Zaragoza, between the cathedral and the banks. The food at **Cafetería Rosy,** on Zaragoza and Green, will have you riveted. Seafood dishes like *sopa de camarones* (shrimp soup, 30 pesos), *pescado en mantequilla* or *al mojo de ajo* (fish in butter or garlic sauce, 40 pesos), and *pollo a la naranja* (chicken in orange sauce, 38 pesos) will knock your socks off. (Open Oct.-May daily 8am-10pm; June-Sept. 8am-5pm.) Follow locals to **El Nuevo Imperial,** Zaragoza and Green, a Chinese restaurant with great food and low prices. Entrees are usually below 30 pesos, and even the frighteningly named *paquete turistico* (tourist package) offers egg rolls, fried rice, and an entree for 35 pesos. People-watch on the outdoor patio, but if you must catch some sun, grab take-out (open daily 8am-9:30pm). For a delicious and cheap lunch, try **Super Tortas,** on Mijares, half a block south of Banamex. This tiny booth serves a variety of tasty *tortas* staring at 14 pesos. (Open daily 8:30am-6pm.)

SIGHTS The most popular beach in town (for surfing, if not swimming) is **Costa Azul,** on Palmilla Pt., 1km south of the Brisa del Mar trailer park. To get there, take a bus headed for San Lucas (every 30min.) and ask the driver to drop you off at Costa Azul; or take a bus from Valerio González (US$3). A 15-minute walk down Mijares leads to good beaches much closer to town. The newer luxury hotels mar the sand in spots, but there's plenty of natural, clean coastline in the stretches between the artificial structures. Folks at the **Killer Hook Surf Shop** (tel. 2 24 30), on Hidalgo between Doblado and Zaragoza, rent **snorkel** gear (US$7), **fishing poles** (US$8), and **surfboards** (US$12); they also repair surfboards and provide tips. (Open M-Sa 8am-9pm).

If you've got time between trips to the beach, stop by the **Huichol Gallery** (tel. 2 37 99), on Zaragoza and Mijares; it features beautiful handicrafts by local Huichols, who have lived centuries without much outside influence (open daily 8am-10pm).

ENTERTAINMENT San José del Cabo can't compete with its noisy neighbor, but it's still possible to have a good time here—just kick back, relax, and don't expect conga lines and table dancing. **Eclipse** (tel. 2 16 94), on Mijares and Guerro, one block down from Doblado, is very upscale, pumping soft rock into tasteful decor. Dress "nicely" and make sure you have your wallet—beers will cost you 20 pesos each. Saturday sees live bands, and Wednesday and Thursday are **karaoke** nights. (Cover Saturday 20 pesos; open M-Tu 8pm-3am, W-Sa 10pm-5am.) **Piso #2,** Zaragoza 71, two blocks from the church, is even mellower. Red chairs, palm trees, and neon lights help you digest your Dos Equis (20 pesos). Huge mixed drinks are 20 pesos—don't try hitting the bar's pool tables after you've had one (open bar on Wednesday). Downstairs, **Piso #1** offers the same prices and a similar atmosphere. (Friday 9-11pm free open bar for women; Wednesday 9pm-2am men pay 120 pesos and women drink for free; open in summer daily 6pm-3am; in winter noon-3am.)

Northwest Mexico

Northwest Mexico is home to raucous border towns, calm fishing villages, vast expanses of desert, and warm water beaches along the alluring Sea of Cortés. For many, the first taste of life south of the border consists of nights of debauchery, rounds of tequila shots, oversized straw sombreros, and blistering heat. But in the midst of all this madness, many tourists overlook the rows of shantytowns, border-patrol battles, and miles of industrial wasteland that consume a large part of the cities. Things calm down considerably as you venture farther south. The grime and frenetic madness of Ciudad Juárez and Nogales, Mexico's brawny border towns, give way to bustling markets, colonial mansions, iconoclastic museums, and a surreal cactus-studded landscape. In some towns, things slow to a virtual standstill—you can hear the flies buzz and the wind whistle through the desert. The condominiums, time-shares, and resort hotels that cast their shadows over the *palapas* gracing the light-colored sands mark the presence of the U.S. citizens and Canadians who have discovered the elegant beaches of Sonora. Despite the gentrification of some of its beach towns, swaggering *vaqueros* clad in tight jeans can still be spotted in Sonora's smaller towns (like Kino Viejo). You may want to bring along a pair of cowboy boots and a wide-brimmed sombrero of your own—the rugged terrain requires a lot of stamina, and the *noroeste* sun is merciless.

The Sierra Madre Occidental rips through the heart of Northwest Mexico. To the east of the mountains, the parched desert gives even the larger cities in Chihuahua the feel of dusty frontier; frequent sandstorms enhance the mood. Along the coast, in the states of **Sonora** and **Sinaloa,** a melange of commercial ports, quiet fishing villages, and sprawling beaches overlook the warm waters of the Sea of Cortés. Landlocked **Durango,** traversed by the Sierra Madres, thrives on mining and is known for its Old-West ruggedness. But the most stunning sight in the *noroeste* is the **Barrancas del Cobre (Copper Canyon),** a spectacular series of deep gorges and unusual rock formations in **Chihuahua** brimming with tropical vegetation, all cut through by the Río Urique far below. The caves in the area are home to the reclusive Tarahumara Indians. The Northwest's diverse landscape and natural wonders are overlooked by most tourists, but those who look past the border towns and into the region's heartland and coast will reap the rewards.

HIGHLIGHTS OF NORTHWEST MEXICO

- Mexico's best-kept secret is the **Barrancas del Cobre** (**Copper Canyon;** see p. 222), which provide some of the most awe-inspiring vistas in the world—these canyons are four times the size of Arizona's Grand Canyon. Most travelers use the gorgeous town of **Creel** (p. 219) as a base from which to explore.
- Take long, placid naps on the beaches of **Bahía Kino** (p. 195), a pair of tiny laid-back fishing towns.
- **El Pinocate** (see p. 190) is a four million-acre volcanic preserve and one of the most spectacular biospheres in the world. NASA trained astronauts for the Apollo moon mission here because the terrain is so similar.

SONORA

Nogales

Pushed up against the border and straddled by steep hills covered with tin houses and block-long Corona signs, Nogales (pop. 250,000) is an archetypal border town with cheap curio shops and cheesy bars. The streets are crowded with street vendors actively promoting their merchandise to anyone who appears interested. On shack-

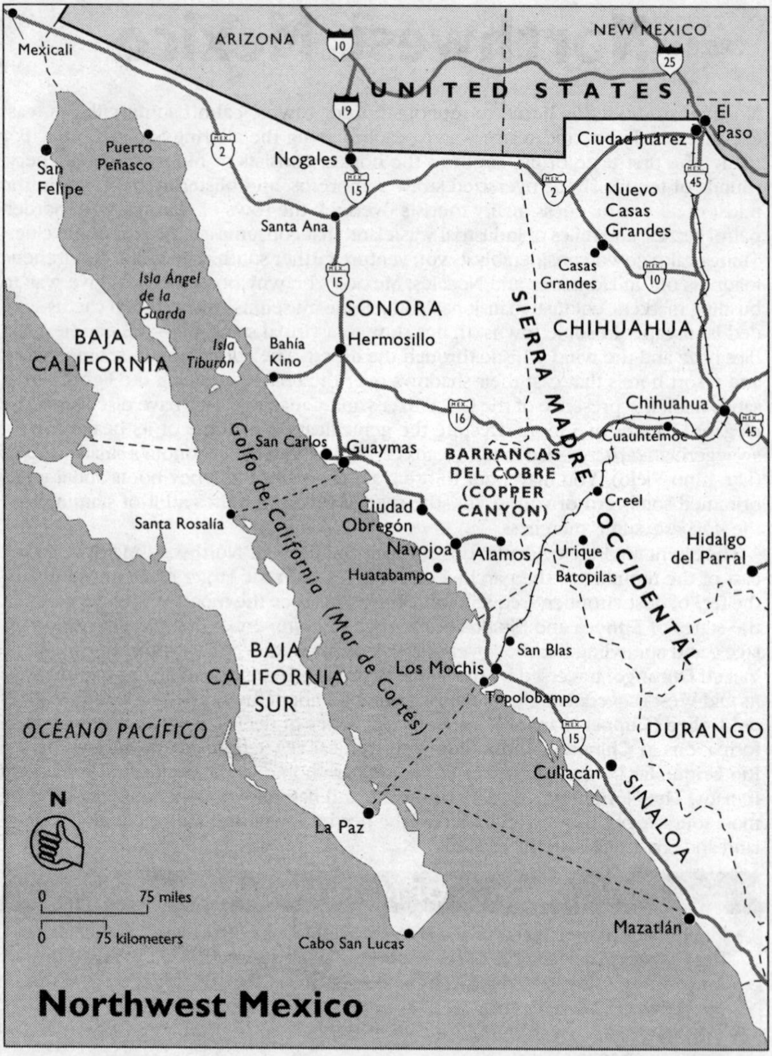

Northwest Mexico

lined, candle-lit dirt roads far above the border bustle, entire blocks of families watch TV and cook together each evening. Born out of the 1848 Mexican-American War as something of an unarmed fortress, Nogales is rapidly growing as a result of the influx of U.S.-owned *maquiladoras*. More than 100 U.S. companies have established production centers in the hills outside the downtown area, attracting Mexicans from all 31 states and Mexico City. However, in spite of its swelling population, Nogales remains a friendly place to get a good meal and to enjoy the thrill of good old-fashioned bargaining.

ORIENTATION If you plan to venture beyond Nogales, obtain a **tourist card** (see **Tourist Cards,** p. 7) at the border (have your passport on hand). It's much simpler to get the card here than farther south. When you cross the border through the arched crossing complex, turn right into the first building you encounter; it's the immigration and **tourist office.**

The **bus terminal** and **train station** are directly across from each other on **Carretera Internacional,** 4.5km from town. A taxi from the bus station to the center of town will cost an exorbitant 40 pesos; instead cross the street and walk north to the end of the block, where you can catch one of the local white buses (2.50 pesos) marked "Parque Industrial" or "Villa Sonora." Downtown Nogales is the last stop. To get from downtown to the bus terminal and train station, wait at the bus stop on Juárez and Lopez Mateos, one block south of the tourist office. Take the "Parque Industrial" bus and ask the driver to let you off before the bus terminal. A large supermarket should be to your right when you reach the correct stop.

The downtown area is relatively small, making Nogales fairly easy to navigate. If you're crossing the border by foot, you'll be on **Pesqueira;** by car, you'll drive in on **López Mateos.** From east to west, **Pesqueira, Juárez** (which becomes **López Mateos** several blocks south), **Morelos** (a walkway), **Obregón** (the main tourist drag), **Hidalgo,** and **Ingenieros** run parallel to each other and perpendicular to the border. **Internacional** runs parallel to the tall picket fence that marks the border. Proceeding south, away from the border, **Campillo, Ochoa, Pierson, Aguirre, Vázquez, Díaz,** and **González** all run parallel.

PRACTICAL INFORMATION **Elite** (tel. 3 16 03) sends posh buses to Guadalajara (666 pesos), Hermosillo (75 pesos), Los Mochis (207 pesos), Mazatlán (463 pesos), and Mexico City (859 pesos). Call for schedules. **Greyhound** buses (tel. in Tuscon, USA (520) 287-5628) leave for Tucson (every hr. 7am-7pm and 9pm, US$7) from their station half a block from the U.S. side of the border. **Transportes del Pacífico** (tel. 3 16 06) has buses *de paso* that leave every two hours from 8am to 8:30pm and go to Guaymas (5hr., 100 pesos), Hermosillo (3hr., 70 pesos), Puerto Vallarta (26hr., 570 pesos), Querétaro (32hr., 700 pesos), and Tepic (22hr., 500 pesos). Prices listed are for 1st-class fares. **Transportes Norte de Sonora** (tel. 3 16 03) runs **buses** to Guadalajara (26hr., 578 pesos), Hermosillo (3hr., every hr. 8:30am-6:30pm, 60 pesos), Los Mochis (11hr., 7:30am-11:30pm, 182 pesos), Mazatlán (16hr., 423 pesos), and Mexico City (32hr., 3 per day, 739 pesos). Check schedules for changes.

The **tourist office** (tel. 2 06 66) is to the left of the border from the Mexican side, in the Edificio Puerta de México, room #1. The friendly, English-speaking staff is best at directing visitors to curio shops or bars—the two main attractions for many Americans—but they will also hand out a map of the downtown area. (Open M-F 8am-3pm). **Banks** line Obregón near the border. **Banamex** has two locations: one at Obregón and Ochoa (tel. 2 07 80 or 2 55 05; open M-Th 8:30am-4:30pm, F 8:30am-6:30pm); the other a 10-minute walk farther south on Obregon (tel. 2 12 51 or 2 10 65; open M-F 8:30am-4:30pm, Sa 9am-3:30pm). Both exchange dollars and traveler's checks and feature 24-hour **ATMs. Luggage storage** is available from 6am to 10pm at the bus terminal (1 peso per hr.). Buy goodies at **VH Supermarket,** Obregón 475 (tel. 2 48 00), between Ramos and Rodríguez, and 10 minutes from Av. Juárez (open daily 8am-10pm).

The **police** (tel. 2 01 16 or 2 01 14) are at González and Leal with English speakers on hand in the afternoon (open 24hr.). For **Highway Patrol,** dial 4 18 30 or 4 18 33. The **Red Cross** (tel. 3 58 00) is on Elías Calles and Providencia (open 24hr). For **medical assistance,** try **Seguro Social,** Escobedo 756 (tel. 3 59 65), at Obregón (take the "Parque Industrial" bus). English is spoken (open 24hr.). Some English is spoken at the **Hospital Básico,** Doctor Francisco Arriola 1277 (tel. 3 07 94 or 3 08 59; open 24hr.). There's no shortage of pharmacies here, but most close early. If it's late at night and you're feelin' sicker than a dog, try **Farmacia San Xavier,** Campillo 73 (tel. 2 55 03), between Juárez and Morelos (open 24hr.). The **post office** is on Juárez 52 (tel. 2 12 47), at Campillo. The **postal code** is 84000. The **bus terminal caseta** (above) has fax machines. Downtown Nogales has a high concentration of **LADATELs.** Look for them at Obregón and Campillo, Obregón and Flores Guerra, and at the border in front of the tourist office. The **caseta** in the bus terminal (tel. 3 50 81; fax 3 50 82) offers overpriced international calls, but collect calls are free from the marked phone next to the *caseta* (open 24hr.). The **phone code** is 631.

ACCOMMODATIONS AND FOOD Relative to towns farther south in Mexico, rates in Nogales are steep. Fortunately, a couple of (sort of) budget hotels can be found on the block behind the tourist office on Av. Juárez. The **Hotel San Carlos,** Juárez 22 (tel. 2 13 46 or 2 14 09; fax 2 15 57), between Internacional and Campillo, features a lobby with an ever-replenished ice-cold purified water dispenser and a mural of San Carlos. Large, clean rooms have A/C, color TVs with U.S. cable, massage-showers, and phones (singles 158.50 pesos; doubles 220 pesos). Right next door is the **Hotel Regis** (tel. 2 51 81 or 2 55 35). Clean, peach-colored rooms have A/C, phones, and TV. If you're afraid you'll oversleep, don't worry—*norteño* tunes are piped in through the speakers in each room's ceiling. To adjust the volume, look for the black dial. (Singles 185 pesos; doubles 200 pesos).

The are oodles of overpriced restaurants that cater to daytrippers from the U.S. Ditch the tourist traps and head straight for **La Posada Restaurant,** Pierson 116 (tel. 2 04 39), off Obregón, where you can mingle with the town's *petit-bourgeoisie.* Tiny birds chirp quietly in the cool breeze provided by the ceiling fans. Painted tiles and miniature clay pots adorn the walls, while *burritos de machaca* (dried beef, 12 pesos) and *chimichangas* (10 pesos) grace the tables. (Open daily 7:45am-10pm.) If it's late and you're in need of some tacos, try **Restaurant Olga,** Juárez 43 (tel. 2 16 41), off Obregón. Open 24 hours, Olga offers decent portions of *tacos de carne* and enchiladas (both for US$3.20). To enjoy a cup of coffee and the soothing weather, visit **Café Ajijic,** Obregón 182 (tel. 2 30 31). The restaurant features a picturesque fountain in the middle of its red-tiled patio. Relax under the shade of a table umbrella with an espresso or cappuccino (both US$1; open 9am-midnight).

SIGHTS AND ENTERTAINMENT Most of the curio and craft shops line Obregón. You may get good deals if you bargain and know something about quality. In fact, vendors expect shoppers to haggle. Often, you can obtain low prices by pretending to walk away uninterested. Before buying, ask turquoise vendors to put the rocks to "the lighter test." Plastic or synthetic material will quickly melt under a flame. Likewise, when buying silver, look for a ".925" stamp on the piece; if it's not there, the goods are (oxymoronically) bad.

At night, the bars on Obregón are filled with a mix of locals and tourists. **Bora Bora,** Obregón 38, between Campilio and Internacional, offers live music at night and drinks from 15 to 30 pesos (open W-Su noon-3am). Across the street, giant metal palm trees greet you at the entrance to **Kookaracha's,** Obregón 1 (tel. 2 47 73; fax 2 44 20). Dance the night away and down US$1 tequila shots or relax with a *cerveza* by the fountain in the "roach's" multi-colored courtyard (open W, F, Sa 10pm-3am). There is a US$5 minimum on Saturdays at **Catoche Cafe Bar** (tel. 2 31 10), on López Mateos but with it comes three beers and...**karaoke!** (happy hour M-F 6-8pm; open M-Sa 1pm-2:30am).

Not in the mood to get intoxicated? Head for **Cinemas Gemelos,** Obregón 368 (tel. 2 50 02) between Gonzales and Torres, which shows first- and second-run American films (open M-F 3:30pm-midnight, Sa-Su 1:30pm-midnight; M, Tu, Th 25 pesos; W 15 pesos; Sa-Su 30 pesos; either dubbed or subtitled in Spanish). For those looking for more culture, the new **Teatro Auditorio de Nogales** on Obregón between Vasquez and Gonzalez brings live performances from Mexico City (check the box office for showtimes and prices). Finally, there's always the option of gambling your fortune away: off-track betting on dog or horse races can be done at the **Nogales Turf Club,** Campillo 85 (tel. 2 33 02), between Obregón and Juárez underneath the tall, pink building (open daily 9:30am-midnight). Or try your luck at the **Casino de Nogales,** on Campillo between López Mateos and Elias Calles.

Puerto Peñasco

Once a launching pad for shrimp boats, Puerto Peñasco dried up when overfishing decimated the shrimp population of the Sea of Cortés. Economically widowed, the town now courts investors with a dowry of tax breaks and other incentives. Just

105km from the border, the town with the English nickname "Rocky Point" attracts a fair share of weekenders, much like neighboring northern Baja. Despite the throngs of gringos, somewhat tranquil beaches and clean streets make this dusty port worth a trip. Budget travelers, however, should beware of the special "tourist pricing." For the better bargain, always ask for prices in pesos instead of in dollars, even if the seller is reluctant. Fifty kilometers north on the road to Sonoita lies the fascinating **El Pinacate** volcanic area.

ORIENTATION AND PRACTICAL INFORMATION To reach the *centro* from the bus station, take a left past PEMEX and walk nine blocks down Puerto Peñasco's main road, **Blvd. Juárez;** continue south on Juárez past the **Dársena**—the port area—and eventually to **Malecón** (or Old Port), Peñasco's old section, on the western edge of town. **Playa Hermosa** (Beautiful Beach) lies to the northwest, **Playa Miramar** to the south. Town activity centers around two intersections: **Fremont** and **Juárez** and **Constitución** and **Juárez.** Numbered *calles* run east-west and start with 1 at **Playa Miramar** (southernmost); boulevards run north-south.

Buses depart from Juárez and Calle 24. **Autotransportes de Baja California** (tel. 3 20 19) sends buses to Ensenada (10hr., 209 pesos), Mexicali (5hr., 113 pesos), San Luis (3hr., 80 pesos), Sonoita (1hr., 30 pesos), Tecate (6hr., 161 pesos), and Tijuana (8hr., 177 pesos). All buses are *de paso;* buses leave for Mexicali at 8:30am and 5pm while those headed for Tijuana and farther leave at 8:30am and 1am. **Transportes Norte de Sonora** (tel. 3 36 40) sends buses to Guaymas (9hr., 4 per day, 209 pesos) and Hermosillo (7hr., 3 per day, 169 pesos). Puerto Peñasco's **tourist office** (tel. 3 41 29) is on N. Bravo CP, Calle 18, off Blvd. Juárez and next to a travel agency. Little English is spoken (open daily 9am-mid-afternoon). **Bancomer** (tel. 3 24 30), just past Jim Bur Plaza heading south on Juárez exchanges currency and traveler's checks (open M-F 8:30am-4pm, Sa 10am-2pm). **Banamex** on Freemont and Juárez provides the same services (open M-F 8:30am-4:30pm). Both have 24hr. **ATMs.**

Stock up at **Supermarket Jim Bur** (tel. 3 25 61), on Juárez at the Jim Bur Plaza (open M-Sa 8am-9pm, Su 9am-4pm). At **Lavamática Peñasco** on Constitución at Morúa across from Hotel Paraíso del Desierto, a wash costs six pesos; a dry costs five (open M-Sa 8am-7pm). **Police** (tel. 3 26 26) wait at Fremont and Juárez but speak little English (open 24hr.). The **Red Cross** (tel. 3 22 66), on Fremont at Chiapas, is open 24hr. Little English is spoken. **Farmacia Botica Lux,** Ocampo 146 (tel. 3 28 81), two blocks east of Blvd. Juárez, lives up to its name—it can medicate you (open daily 7:30am-midnight). **Farmacia 24 Horas** (tel. 3 54 45), on Calle 13 between Francisco Villa and Pino Suarez, can meet your need for drugs around the clock. **Hospital Municipal** (tel. 3 21 10) is at Morúa and Juárez; little English is spoken (open 24hr.). The **post office** (tel. 3 27 82) is at Chiapas, two blocks east of Juárez on Fremont (open M-F 8am-3pm). The **postal code** is 83550. The **fax** and **telegram office** (tel. 3 27 82), is in the same building (open M-F 8am-6pm, Sa 9am-noon). **Internet access** can be found at **Infotec** (tel. 3 64 60; fax 3 37 84), at Juárez and Ocampo for US$3 per hour (open daily 9am-9pm). The **phone code** is 638.

ACCOMMODATIONS AND FOOD Budget rooms in Puerto Peñasco are a rare commodity, since cheap accommodations are being torn down left and right to clear space for expensive resorts, condos, and time-shares. The most economical way to spend the night is to camp in your tent or RV. Trailer parks abound in the south around Playa Miramar. **Playa Miramar RV Park** (tel./fax 3 25 87), on Playa Miramar (go figure), rents scenic spots year-round with cable TV, full hookup, and hot water. Washers, dryers, and showers available. (US$13 per day for 1-2 people; US$2 per day each additional person; US$80 per week with beachfront spaces slightly higher; check-out noon.) Otherwise, one of the last remaining quasi-budget hotels is the **Motel Playa Azul** (tel. 3 62 96), Calle 13 and Pino Suárez, about two blocks from Playa Hermosa. It offers nicely furnished rooms with ancient TVs that receive a single channel, generous A/C, and yes, private bathrooms with hot water. Bargain with the manager. (Singles 200 pesos, doubles 280 pesos.)

As always, *taquerías* are the spot for budget grub; find some at Juárez between Constitución and Calle 24, near the bus station and the Old Port area. Most beachside restaurants cater to gringos, with their (high) prices quoted in U.S. dollars; insist on paying in good ol' *moneda nacional.* For traditional Mexican cuisine, head east on Calle 13 and turn left onto Blvd. Kino to **La Curua** (tel. 3 34 70). This family owned restaurant will treat you right and satiate your appetite. The *combinación grande* includes chips-'n-salsa, rice, beans, and your choice of entree for only 34 pesos. (Open M-Th 8am-10:30pm, F-Su 8am-11pm.) **Gamma's** (tel. 3 56 80), on Calle 13, directly in front of Plaza Las Glorias Hotel, specializes in fried fish. Dine at picnic tables under an open air *palapa* and gaze at the sunbathers on Playa Hermosa. A small plate of fried shrimp goes for US$3. (Open 8am-11pm.)

SIGHTS AND ENTERTAINMENT Puerto Peñasco's clean and rarely crowded beaches are blessed with clear, warm waters. Shallow tide pools cradle clams, small fish, and colorful shells. **Sandy Beach** and **Playa Hermosa** are the best choices for swimming; both have curio shops, restaurants, and hotels galore. The beaches around **Rocky Point** and **Playa Miramar,** at the southern end of town, are less crowded but also rockier and rougher. Playa Miramar also brims with RV parks and condominiums. For those interested in sand-and-sea research and conservation, the **Intercultural Center for the Study of Deserts and Oceans** (**CEDO;** tel. 2 01 13), at Playa Las Concaas, 9km from town (taxi 30 pesos), gives free tours of its wet lab and museum Tuesdays at 2pm and Saturdays at 4pm (open M-Sa 9am-5pm, Su 10am-2pm). **Excursions Paraiso,** Victor Estrella 14 (tel. 3 62 09), across from Thrifty Ice Cream in the Old Port, rents bikes for US$20 per day. Half-day rates are also available. The friendly folks at **Sun 'n Fun** (tel. 3 54 50), on Juárez at the entrance to the Old Port, will teach you how to go clamming and give you tips on how to prepare your catch, all for US$10 (open M-F 10am-7pm, Sa-Su 9am-8pm).

To get to Playa Hermosa, turn right on Calle 13 when heading south on Juárez; the beach is straight ahead five or six blocks down. To reach Playa Miramar, head south on Juárez, and turn left onto Campeche near the Benito Juárez monument. Continue uphill for three blocks; Playa Miramar will be on your left. To reach Playa Las Conchas, head south on Juárez, turn left on Fremont near the Plaza del Camaronero, take a right onto Camino a las Conchas, and follow the rock-slab road for 3 or 4km. To reach Sandy Beach, head north on Encinas or Juárez until the intersection with Camino a Bahía Choya. Take a left and follow the road; turn left on the road labeled "To Sandy Beach."

■ Near Puerto Peñasco: El Pinacate

Forty-eight kilometers north of Puerto Peñasco on Rte. 8 to Sonora is the **El Pinacate** volcanic preserve, one of the largest and most spectacular biospheres in the world. Encompassing more than four million acres, and extending to upper reaches of the Sea of Cortés, the biosphere was created in June 1992 to limit volcanic rock excavation and protect endangered species. Pockmarked by over 600 craters and 400 cinder cones, the Pinacate lava fields form 30,000-year-old islands in a vast sea of sand. From inside the park, the only thing visible for kilometers around are fields of igneous rock and monochromatic moonscape (NASA trained astronauts here for the Apollo moon mission because the terrain is so similar). The people of the Tohono O'odham nation have lived in this region for tens of thousands of years, crossing the desert on foot from Arizona to bathe in the waters they consider to be sacred and healing. They also extract fresh water from *saguaro* cacti.

Ecoturismo Peñasco (tel. 3 32 09) lead tours into the area; ask at the tourist office for details or talk to Peggy at **CEDO** (see above). Prices: $50 per person (1-2 people), $40 per person (3-4 people), $35 per person (5 or more people). The vast, isolated, climatically harsh region makes a guide necessary. If you do decide to tough it out alone, four-wheel-drive high-clearance vehicles with partially deflated tires are a must. Bring tons of water, a shovel, a spare tire, and firewood. Camping is permitted, but don't leave anything behind and don't remove any souvenirs. The ideal time to visit is from November to March, when temperatures range from approximately 15 to 32°C, as opposed to summer months, when temperatures can exceed 47°C.

Hermosillo

This capital city of Sonora, named after the famous Mexican general, is an expansive metropolis and a center for commerce and education. With glorious cathedrals, majestic government palaces, stylish open-air malls, a remarkably endearing *zócalo*, and an incredible ecological research center/zoo, areas of Hermosillo (pop. 700,000) are certainly worth exploring. Daytrippers to the beaches of Kino will find hopping university-spurred nightlife in Hermosillo (if they seek it out). Not all of this huge city, however, boasts such allure. The crowded, dusty thoroughfares of the *centro* which scream during the day with the frenzied activity of urban life are left by sundown without much more than garbage on the streets. The low-level architecture of the

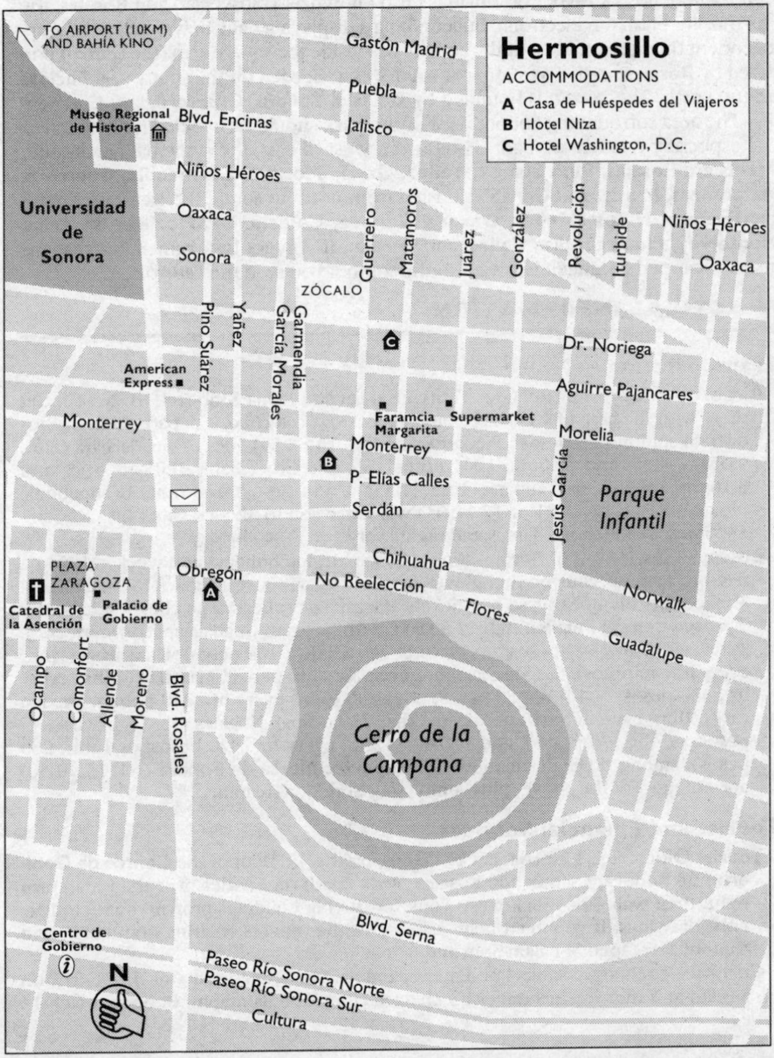

centro affords a clear view of the distracting *Cerro de la Campana* (a tall mountain cluttered with radio towers and satellite dishes) from practically every street corner, and much of Hermosillo is unsavory and unsafe at night. If you get an early start and the buses run on time, you can breeze from Tucson to the beaches of Guaymas or Mazatlán in a single day (or vice versa), and skip the lonelier parts of Sonora entirely. But a layover in lively Hermosillo can add a pleasant surprise to your trip.

ORIENTATION

Hermosillo lies 271km south of the border on Rte. 15, the main north-south highway connecting the western U.S. and central Mexico. **Buses** depart from the main terminal on Blvd. Encinas, 2km east of the city center. To get from the bus station to the center of town, cross the street and catch a bus marked "Circuito Norte-Mendoza" or "Centro" (every 10min. 5am-10:30pm, 2.5 pesos). Taxis will ask 35 pesos for a trip to the *centro;* haggle, and don't get in until settling a price. To get to the bus station from town, wait for a bus at Elías Calles and Matamoros, across from Óptica Morfín.

At the junction of **Blvd. Luis Encinas** (also known as Transversal) and **Rosales,** the **Hermosillo Flash** (an electronic bulletin board displaying daily news) helps the mapless orient themselves. Most of the activity lies inside the square area (the *centro*) bordered by **Rosales** on the west, **Juárez** on the east, **Serdán** on the south, and **Encinas** on the north. The *zócalo* is bounded by **Colosio, Sonora, Guerrero,** and **Garmendia.** The area surrounding Sonora west of the park should be avoided by lone travelers, especially women, at night. Listed from west to east, the principal north-south streets are **Rosales, Pino Suárez, Yañez, García Morales, Garmendia, Guerrero, Matamoros, Juárez,** and **González.** Listed from north to south, the east-west streets are **Encinas, Niños Héroes, Oaxaca, Sonora, Colosio, Dr. Noriega, Morelia, Monterrey, Plutarco Elías Calles,** and **Serdán.** If you get lost, remember that the antenna-capped mountain is always to the south if you're in the *centro.*

PRACTICAL INFORMATION

Transportation

Airport: 10km west of town on Transversal toward Bahía Kino (tel. 61 00 08). Get there with the help of a small red bus called a *taxi colectivo;* it departs from the bus or train station (2.5 pesos). **Aeroméxico** (tel. 16 82 59) goes to Guadalajara (2hr., 9:05am, 4:35, and 4:50pm, 1201 pesos), Mexico City (2½hr., 9:05am, 4:35, and 8:10pm, 1306 pesos), Tijuana (1hr., 11:45am, 514 pesos), and other destinations. **Mexicana** (tel. 17 11 01 or 17 11 03) will carry you to Mexico City (4hr., 8:25am, 1306 pesos) and more. Times and flights vary.

Buses: All service out of Hermosillo is *de paso;* during holidays and weekends you'll need to lace up your boxing gloves in order to win a seat. Buses to Tijuana and Mexico City fill up early, so buy tickets at least a day ahead. The cheapest carrier is **Transportes del Pacífico** (tel. 12 50 91), with buses to Guadalajara (*primera clase* 22hr., every hr., 567 pesos; or *segunda clase* 24hr., 408 pesos), Guaymas (1½hr., every hr., 36 pesos), Los Mochis (7hr., every hr., 130 pesos), Mazatlán (13hr., every hr., 330 pesos; or 14hr., 280 pesos), Mexicali (9hr., every hr., 240 pesos), Mexico City (30hr., every hr., 818 pesos; or 32hr., 710 pesos), Nogales (4hr., 3 per day, 75 pesos; or 4hr., 70 pesos), and Tijuana (12hr., every hr., 320 pesos; or 12hr., 280 pesos), among other destinations. **Transportes Norte de Sonora** (tel. 13 40 50) goes to most of the above, plus sunny, tourist-ridden Acapulco.

Tourist and Financial Services

Tourist Office: (tel. 17 29 64; fax 17 00 60), on the 3rd floor of the **Centro de Gobierno de Sonora,** Cultura and Rosales. Walk south on Rosales over the canal, turn right, then walk one block west. Look for the big buildings crowned with indigenous drawings. If you need help, ask one of the officers wearing gray-and-brown camouflage. Open M-F 8am-3pm and 6-9pm.

Currency Exchange: Banks line Encinas and Serdán. **Bancomer** (tel. 17 36 81), on Serdán at Yañez, cashes traveler's checks. Open M-F 8am-5pm. **Banamex** (tel. 14

76 15), on Serdán at Matamoros, is closer to the center. Open M-F 8:30am-4:30pm. You'll see 24hr. **ATMs** at both. There's also **Bital** on the first floor of the Centro de Gobierno (see above), open M-F 8:30am-5pm.

American Express: Hermex Travel (tel. 17 17 18), Rosales at Monterrey. Open M-F 8:30am-1pm and 3-6:30pm, Sa 9am-1pm.

Local Services

Supermarket: Ley Centro (tel. 17 32 94), Juárez at Morelia. Absolutely huge. Bigger than big—check out the public toilets and the hundreds of young clerks decked out in red aprons. Takes U.S. dollars at a good exchange rate. Open daily 6:30am-10pm.

Laundromat: La Burbuja, corner of Guerrero and Niños Heroes. Open daily 8am-1pm and 3-7pm.

Emergency and Communications

Emergency: Dial 08.

Ambulance: Dial 76 75 27.

Police: (tel. 18 55 64), at Periférico Nte. and Solidaridad. Little English spoken. Open 24hr.

Transit Police: (tel. 16 08 77).

Red Cross: (tel. 14 07 69), on Encina at 14 de Abril. Open 24hr. (Barely) English-speaking staff on hand daily 9am-5pm.

Pharmacy: Farmacia Margarita, Morelia 93 (tel. 13 15 90), at Guerrero. Open 24hr.

Hospital: (tel. 13 25 56), on Transversal at Reyes. Open 24hr. English spoken.

Post Office: (tel. 12 00 11), on Elias Calles at Rosales. Open M-F 8am-7pm, Sa-Su 8am-noon. **Postal Code:** 83000.

Fax: Telecomm (tel. 17 21 50 or 12 03 56), in the same building as the post office. Also **telegram** service. Open M-F 8am-7pm, Sa 8:30am-4:30pm, Su 9am-12:30pm.

Phone Code: 62.

ACCOMMODATIONS

Hermosillo has its fair share of budget hotels, allowing those who must watch every peso they spend to sleep comfortably and safely. Air conditioning is costly but sometimes indispensable, especially in the blistering summer heat.

Hotel Washington, D.C., Dr. Noriega 68 Pte. (tel. 13 11 83) between Matamoros and Guerrero. This place has nothing to do with the capital of the U.S., but it does have helpful management and everything you would want in a good budget hotel—good-sized rooms with A/C and clean bathrooms. The gated entrance provides solid security, and the open air hallways and red clay tiles are reminiscent of a Spanish villa. The only drawback is that the "D.C." can get a little loud sometimes. LADATEL in the lobby. Singles 90 pesos; doubles 100 pesos; each additional person 25 pesos.

Hotel Niza, Elías Calles 66 (tel. 17 20 28 or 17 20 35) between Guerrero and Garmendia. A grandiose Art Deco hotel, its pink atrium is graced with murals and a colossal stained glass globe. Rooms branching off this centerpiece have A/C, color TV, and comfy beds. Singles 120 pesos; doubles 160 pesos.

Casa de Huéspedes del Viajero, Sufragio Efectivo 90, between Pino Suárez and Yañez. Walk south on Suárez; as you pass Extasis Nite Club, turn left onto S. Efectivo. Unbelievably large rooms in an 84-year-old building. Adobe construction and fans keep the rooms cool. Aging outdoor bathroom. Lock your bags, since there's only someone at the entrance 7am-7pm. Singles 50 pesos; doubles 100 pesos.

FOOD

For a cheap and quick refueling, head for the **taco** and **torta** places around Serdán and Guerrero, where *taquitos* and quesadillas cost 7 or 8 pesos and *comida corrida* goes for around 15 pesos. Alternatively, try the counters lining the inside of the **public market** at Matamoros, Guerrero, and Elías Calles. Although busy and smelly, some are sufficiently sanitary. Choose wisely: look out for flies and dirty pans and tabletops. Most offer tacos for a paltry sum, but both *Let's Go* and your mother do not recommend eating foods containing uncooked vegetables in these establishments. Locals, however, do recommend that you eat two bananas a day for an extra boost of potassium to help combat the blistering Sonora sun. Stick to enchiladas, burritos, and the like—these wonderfully cheap and cooked goodies cost about 5 pesos apiece.

Mi Cocina, Obregón 84 (tel. 17 55 88) between Pino Suárez and Yañez. Omar opens his *cocina* (kitchen) to budget travelers, serving up a mean 2-course home-cooked meal for only 21 pesos and making great conversation all the while. Open M-F 7:30am-6pm.

Restaurant "My Friend," Elías Calles at Yañez (tel. 13 10 44). This restaurant is definitely trying to make some American *amigos.* A framed photo of a cheeseburger (18 pesos), fries, and a soft drink beckons to starved and homesick gringos. Otherwise, enjoy delicious *huevos al gusto* (15 pesos) or a platter of 3 *tacos de cabeza y barbacoa* (15 pesos). Open M-Sa 7am-7pm, Su 8am-1pm.

Restaurant Jung, Niños Héroes 75 (tel. 13 28 81) at Encinas. A new-age vegetarian restaurant a mere 6 blocks from the center of town? Yes indeed. Relax to soothing music and the faint smell of incense as you savor the rejuvenating *comida corrida,* which comes with wheat rolls, soup, fruit juice, an entree, *frijoles,* whole-grain rice, and dessert (whew!...45 pesos). Jung also offers a breakfast buffet starting at 8am (25 pesos). The adjoining herbal medicine, Eastern philosophy, and pseudo-psychology store has a wide assortment of natural products from ginseng to sesame candy (plus *agua purificada).* Happy hour M-F 5-7pm (30 pesos). Open M-Sa 8am-8pm, Su 9am-5pm.

Restaurant Chapala (tel. 12 39 92), on Guerrero between Sonora and Oaxaca. Mexican golden oldies blare from the jukebox while throngs of middle-aged men drown their sorrows in 40s of Tecate. Chicken, fish, or meat dishes come fried to crispy perfection and served with french fries, *frijoles,* tortillas, side salad, and a drink (30-35 pesos). The tipsy men aside, you might as well be in your Mexican aunt's house—if you're Mexican and if you have an aunt, that is. Open daily 7am-10pm.

SIGHTS AND ENTERTAINMENT

The architecturally eclectic and beautifully adorned **Catedral de la Asunción** (tel. 12 05 01) is on Hidalgo and Ocampo. *(Office and gift shop open M-F 9am-7pm, Sa 9am-4pm.)* Look for its cross-capped spires as you walk south on Rosales past the post office. Fugitives from the blistering sun can find refuge in the bee-yoo–tiful and refreshingly shady **Plaza Zaragoza,** where looming trees surround an open-air bandstand. Other shady parks line the streets near the plaza, making this one of the more peaceful areas of Hermosillo and a welcome change from the dusty, filth-ridden streets of the *centro.* This area is well lit at night, making it safer than the lonely *centro.* For the kids, a **playground** (also very well lit), complete with basketball courts, dwells on the corner of Pino Suárez and Elías Calles, adjacent to the post office.

Further north on Rosales, at Encinas by the University of Sonora, is the **Museo Regional de Historia,** which contains exhibits on pre-Hispanic and colonial history (open M-F 9am-1pm and 4-6pm, Sa 9am-1pm; free). **Cuartel Catorce** (tel. 17 12 41, for Sec. de Intercambios try ext. 122), on Guerrero and Colosio, is a rough structure with formidable walls of brown brick. *(Open M-F 8am-3pm.)* The colonnaded inner courtyard is an oasis; the room in the back of the courtyard was once home to the army's cavalry.

Across the street from the Plaza Zaragoza and facing the cathedral is the majestic, gray-and-white **Palacio de Gobierno.** The *palacio,* from which the state of Sonora is governed, should not be confused with the pink brick **Palacio Municipal** nearby, where city government functions are carried out. Both are worth investigating for their architecture. The Palacio de Gobierno contains four fascinating and detailed murals surrounding its beautiful, tree-laden inner courtyard, where statues immortalize Sonoran patriots and senators. Those in need of a bit more levity can head to **Multicinemas,** Blvd. Encinas 227 (tel. 14 09 70), on Transversal at Reforma, to absorb U.S. movies with Spanish subtitles (a 5min. bus ride from the center of town; open daily 3-9pm; admission 17 pesos). There is not a great deal of nightlife in Hermosillo. However, if you're in the mood for a drink or two, a couple of watering holes can be found on Rosales south of Colosio. Go with caution, though; many of the bars are situated in less than desirable areas.

Bars in this area include **La Fogata** at **Dr. Noriega, La Bella Epoca** at Morelia, and **Fook Lam Moon** (tel. 12 17 17), a Chinese restaurant and bar also at Morelia (FLM open noon-11:30pm). For a tougher bar-going experience, try **La Verbena** or **El Grito del Callejón** (literally, "the Scream of the Alley"), both at Obregón and Pino Suárez—La Verbena to the south and El Grito to the north. Adjacent to La Verbena is **Extasis Night Club,** located in what would be a beautiful colonial building if it weren't for the neon green glow.

■ Near Hermosillo: Centro Ecológico de Sonora

Lions and tigers and bears and emus...oh my! Hermosillo's **Centro Ecológico de Sonora** (tel. 50 12 25), 3km south of downtown off Vildosola, is more than just your token neighborhood zoo: it is host to an impressive array of animal life, a mini-aquarium (complete with outdoor sea lions), and hundreds of plant species from Sonora and elsewhere. *(Open summers W-Su 8am-7pm; winters W-Su 8am-5pm. Admission 10 pesos, students 5 pesos, children 7 pesos.)* Founded in 1985, the Centro is also home to groundbreaking biological research. A clean and clearly marked walkway guides visitors through the exhibits and aviaries and often affords a spectacular view of Hermosillo and its surrounding mountains.

Among the animal exhibits, the sea lions, desert owls, and noisy wild boars stand out. The most spectacular feature of the Centro Ecológico, however, is its incredible collection of cacti—over 340 species are labeled and displayed throughout the animal exhibits or just outside the main pavilion. Keep your eyes peeled for the rare and beautiful *cina* and *biznaga,* from which fruit and candy are made, and the *maguey bacanora,* the fanned-out, spiked cactus that is the source of all those tequilas you've been downing.

The Centro is an excellent place for children; they delight in the clowns and Disney or Disney-esque flicks shown every Saturday and Sunday in the air-conditioned movie theater (noon-6pm; free). The enthusiastic and knowledgeable student staff is happy to answer any questions about the Centro and its flora and fauna. Cafeterias and *agua purificada* can be found throughout the park, and there is a LADATEL at the entrance.

Getting There: To get to the Centro, grab the orange-and-green-striped bus marked "Luis Orci" from the corner of Guerrero and Dr. Noriega (20min., 2 pesos). Ask the driver to let you off at the Centro Ecológico since there is no sign—it actually lies about a quarter of a mile from the bus stop.

■ Bahía Kino

Bahía Kino, a 20km stretch of glistening sand, blue water, and radiant sun, is comprised of a pair of beach towns on the beautiful Sea of Cortés (or Golfo de California). **Kino Viejo,** a dusty, quiet fishing village, lies down the road from **Kino Nuevo,** a 4km-long strip of posh, secluded homes and condos where the satellite dishes are as abundant as the pelicans overhead. This is a place to kick back with your favorite book, your favorite watercolors, or your favorite fishing pole for the day. As the residents of Hermosillo who flock there on weekends will tell you, Kino (as the two towns are collectively known) is an ideal destination for a daytrip and escape from dusty urbanity to the beach. The soothing breezes, warm waters, and vast expanses of sand make the hot, rickety ride from the city worthwhile.

ORIENTATION AND PRACTICAL INFORMATION Bahía Kino is located 107km west of Hermosillo. **Buses** in Hermosillo leave from the old blue-and-red-striped **Transportes Norte de Sonora** station on Sonora between Jesús García and González, near the *zócalo* (2hr., 10 per day 5:40am-5:30pm, 23 pesos one way). The bus stops in Kino Viejo before going on to Kino Nuevo. Look for water on your left and get off wherever you'd like. Early birds catch the daytrip-to-Kino worms—get an early bus from Hermosillo and sleep (if you can) during the ride. Missing the 5:30pm bus back to Hermosillo means spending the night in Kino.

To get from one Kino to the other or back to Hermosillo, flag down the bus (every hr., 2 pesos between Kinos) on Nuevo's main (and only) road, **Av. Mar de Cortés,** or on **Blvd. Kino** in Kino Viejo. If you choose to walk (4km), be sure to keep plenty of water or other hydrants on hand as well as adequate sun protection. Some travelers have been able to hitch rides between the two towns.

Public bathrooms are on the beach in Kino Nuevo, at the end closer to Kino Viejo. In Kino Viejo itself, some downright pleasant potties are available at the **Centro de Salud** at Tampico and Kino. Bring your own toilet paper. In any type of **emergency,** your best bet might be to look for the American-run **Club Deportivo** (tel. 2 03 21) and knock on the door; the friendly expatriate community takes good care of foreign visitors. Another option is to dial the **emergency phone number:** 08. The **police** (tel. 2 00 67) are available at Santa Catalina and Av. Mar de Cortés in Kino Viejo or at Kino and Cruz (tel. 2 00 32) in Kino Viejo. Near the post office and the police in Kino Viejo is the **Red Cross,** at Kino and Manzanillo, which has no phone but can be contacted via the Hermosillo emergency number. For medical services, call **Dr. José Luís** (tel. 2 03 95), who speaks English. Next to the police in Nuevo is the **post office** (open M-F 8am-3pm). Small markets dot the road through Kino Nuevo under inviting "Tecate" signs. **Long-distance phones** are available at the clothing shop at Kino and Tampico in Kino Viejo. LADATELS dot Mar de Cortés in Kino Nuevo. The **phone code** is 624.

ACCOMMODATIONS AND FOOD If you plan to spend the night in Kino, bring your tent or RV; most of the hotel prices are geared toward wealthy northerners. Nearby Hermosillo provides more choices for the budget traveler. If you miss the bus, **Islanda Marina** (tel. 2 00 81), on Guaymas at Puerto Peñasco just off Blvd. Kino, charges 40 pesos per day for a spot (90 pesos with electricity). It is run by two Arizona women who own a purified water plant—you'll never be short on that precious commodity. You can also rent cabins there (150 pesos for 4 people; 30 pesos for each additional person). In Kino Nuevo, **Hotel Posada del Mar** (tel. 2 01 55), Mar de Cortés at the beginning of Kino Nuevo, is the cheapest you'll find (singles 250 pesos with A/C, private bath, TV, and use of the pool; doubles 300 pesos). Call ahead to reserve a room. **Caverna del Seri,** at the end of Mar de Cortés, offers full RV hookups for US$14 a day and rents tent space for US$10 a day. The more adventurous traveler can camp for free under one of the many *palapas* (thatched umbrella structures) one the Kina Nuevo beach. Locals claim the area is fairly safe.

For a meal that's as economical as you want it to be, do as the *hermosillanos* do and pack a lunch to enjoy under a beach *palapa.* Otherwise, a decent budget meal can be found in Kino Viejo. Try the nice 'n' spicy **Dorita,** Av. Eusebio Kino and Sabina Cruz (tel. 2 03 49), decorated with Spice Girls paraphernalia; they have relatively inexpensive breakfasts (20-22 pesos) and delicious *carne asada* (35 pesos). Fill up on free purified water. (Open daily 7am-8pm). If you're looking for a taste of Acapulco, the **Acapulco Restaurant** (tel. 2 03 22) at Acapulco and Puerto Vallarta won't provide it. However, it will provide you with a fine meal (breakfast 12 pesos; lunch 15 pesos; dinner 15-28 pesos; open daily 7:30am-9pm), and that's what matters, isn't it? In Kino Nuevo, **Restaurante la Palapa** serves up decent *hamburguesas* (20 pesos) and *mariscos* (starting at 30 pesos).

SAND AND SIGHTS The **beaches** of Kino are peacefully deserted early in the week, but as the weekend approaches, so do the masses. Fortunately, the masses of Kino are nothing compared to the masses at many other beach towns. Americans with homes in Kino tend to populate the beaches during the winter, making for some long, lonely stretches of sand during the summer months. In general, the beaches are better in Kino Nuevo.

For water fun in Kino Nuevo, ask at **Hotel La Posada** on Av. Mar de Cortés toward Kino Viejo, just before Kino Nuevo's main strip begins, for the names of people renting out scuba/snorkeling gear. For non-beach entertainment, the **Museo de los Seris,** on Mar de Cortés at Progreso near the end of Kino Nuevo, offers air-conditioned refuge from shade-free Kino and teaches you more than you ever thought you'd learn about the Seris, a once-nomadic indigenous tribe whose specialty was fishing (open W-Su 9am-4pm; admission 2 pesos).

In Kino Nuevo about 300 yards past the Museo de los Seris, you'll see a giant image of the Virgin Mary painted on the face of a hill. The short pilgrimage up to her perch is worth the hike—it affords a breathtaking view of Bahia Kino.

Guaymas

Nestled by steep, rocky hills to the north and the Sea of Cortés to the east, Guaymas (pop. 130,000) is the principal port in Sonora and the proud home of an active shrimping fleet and busy seafood-processing plants. Nearby, beachy **San Carlos** is a popular tourist destination for many *norteamericanos* while **Miramar** (Guaymas's other neighboring beach town) draws a distinctly Mexican crowd. Guaymas itself, however, is no resort town. Its port area does offer a pleasant view of docked shrimping boats, the sea, and nearby mountains, and its charming cathedral and companion park do serve as havens for weary travelers. Still, Guaymas suffers from an acute lack of convenient beaches. Nevertheless, it's a nice place to rest on the trip south to the more alluring resorts at Mazatlán, San Blas, and Puerto Vallarta: its cool ocean breezes and civility give it a decided advantage over Hermosillo.

ORIENTATION

Guaymas is 407km south of Nogales on Rte. 15. Municipal buses (2.5 pesos) cruise its main strip, **Av. Serdán.** Running perpendicular to Av. Serdán are **Calle 1, Calle 2, Calle 3**...well, you get the idea. If you're walking along Av. Serdán and the numbers of the intersecting streets are increasing, you know you're headed east toward the waterfront. The center of the city lies around the crossings of Calles in the low 20s and Serdán, and buses arrive right in the thick of things at Calle 14, right off (surprise) Serdán. To get to Serdán from the bus station, turn left if you're coming out of the Transportes del Norte station and turn right if you're coming out of the Transportes del Pacífico or the Transportes Baldomero Corral stations. Women should not walk alone more than two blocks south of Serdán after dark. The waterfront begins around Calle 23 and Serdán; coming up to the water, the many public plazas and the cool ocean breeze will immediately provide relief from the heat.

Northbound vehicles, including buses, are often stopped by narcotics police. Have your identification ready and let them search whatever they want; it's better not to assert the right to privacy when dealing with humorless armed *federales.*

Along Serdán, you can also catch buses marked "Miramar" (2 pesos) and "San Carlos" (5 pesos) to reach the beaches north of the city; both buses run frequently between 6am and 8pm.

PRACTICAL INFORMATION

Transportation

Airport: To reach it, catch a bus marked "San José" along Serdán (2 pesos). **Aeroméxico** (tel. 2 01 23), Serdán at Calle 16, has daily flights to La Paz (50min., 4:45pm, 768 pesos one-way), Mexico City (4½hr., 4:45pm, 1364 pesos one-way), and Tucson (55min., 10:50am, US$203 one-way). Airport open M-F 8:30am-1pm and 2-6pm, Sa 8:30am-1:30pm.

Buses: The town's 3 bus terminals are on opposite sides of the street at Calle 14 and Rodríguez. **Transportes Norte de Sonora** (tel. 2 12 71) goes to Ciudad Juárez (13hr., 2:30pm, 303 pesos), Culiacán (9hr., every hr., 133 pesos), Guadalajara (23hr., every hr., 460 pesos), Hermosillo (1¾hr., every hr., 31 pesos), Los Mochis

(6hr., every hr., 85 pesos), Mazatlán (12hr., every hr., 258 pesos), Mexicali (12hr., every hr., 151 pesos), Mexico City (31hr., every 2hr., 678 pesos), Nogales (10hr., every hr., 97 pesos), Obregón (1¾hr., every hr., 31 pesos), Puerto Peñasco (9hr., 11am, 209 pesos), San Luis (6hr., every hr., 230 pesos), Tepic (18hr., every hr., 366 pesos), and Tijuana (15hr., every hr., 324 pesos). **Transportes del Pacífico** (tel. 4 05 76), offers fares to most of the above destinations for about 10% more than Transportes Norte del Sonora, while its 2nd-class service runs 3-5% less. **Transportes Baldomero Corral,** across the street, offers service to Nogales (5½hr., 4 per day, 104 pesos) and Navojoa (4hr., every hr. 7:45am-midnight, 48 pesos).

Ferries: Terminal (tel. 2 23 24) on Serdán, about 1km past Electricidad. The boat steams to Santa Rosalía Tu and F at 11am (arriving at 6pm); tickets may be bought on the day of departure from 6-8am or on M, W, or Th 8am-2pm (*salón* 111 pesos, *turista* 220 pesos). To get to the terminal, hop on a bus heading away from the Carretera Internacional and get off at the "Transbordador" sign, on your right (for more details, see **By Sea,** p. 133).

Tourist and Financial Services

Currency Exchange: Banks are located along Serdán. **Banamex** (tel. 4 01 23), Serdán at Calle 20, exchanges traveler's checks and greenbacks, and has two 24hr. **ATMs** that accept Visa, MC, Cirrus, and Plus. Open M-F 8:30am-4:30pm.

Luggage Storage: Lockers are available at the **Transportes Nortes de Sonora** bus terminal. 10 pesos for first 8hr., 4 pesos every extra hr. Open 24hr.

Local Services

Market: VH Supermarket (tel. 4 19 49), on Serdán between Calles 19 and 20. You can't miss it. Open M-Sa 8am-10pm, Su 8am-9pm.

Emergency and Communications

Police: (tel. 4 01 04 or 4 01 05), on Calle 11 at Av. 9, near the Villa School. Some English spoken. Open 24hr.

Pharmacy: Farmacia Sonora (tel. 2 11 00), Serdán at Calle 15. Open 24hr.

Hospital: Hospital Municipal (tel. 4 21 38), on Calle 12 between Av. 6 and 7. Some English spoken. Open 24hr.

Post Office: (tel. 2 07 57), Av. 10 between Calle 19 and 20, next to the pink Luis G. Davila School. Open M-F 8am-7pm, Sa 8am-noon. **Postal Code:** 85400.

Fax: Telecomm (tel. 2 02 92), next to post office. Open M-F 8am-5pm, Sa-Su 9am-noon.

Phone Code: 622.

ACCOMMODATIONS

Accommodations in Guaymas cluster around Av. Serdán, where tourists will find a handful of relatively inexpensive hotels and motels. A few *casas de huéspedes* can be found on streets off Serdán.

Casa de Huéspedes Lupita, Calle 15 #125 (tel. 2 84 09), 2 blocks south of Serdán and across from the castle-like *cárcel* (jail). This "house's" 30 rooms and 12 communal baths all open onto the tree-shaded courtyard. Birds in the trees will serenade you until the sun goes down. Fans in every room provide relief from the relentless heat outside; an ice-cold *agua purificada* dispenser awaits downstairs at the office. Singles 45 pesos, with bath 55 pesos, with A/C 65 pesos; doubles 55 pesos, with bath 65 pesos, with A/C 85 pesos. Towel deposit 10 pesos.

Motel del Puerto, Yañez 92 (tel. 4 34 08 or 2 24 91), 3 blocks south of Serdan on Calle 17. Reminiscent of a beachfront motel (without the beach), it offers superclean rooms with satellite TV and A/C at an affordable rate. LADATEL in lobby. Singles 100 pesos; doubles 150 pesos; triples 170 pesos.

Hotel Impala, Calle 21 #40 (tel. 4 09 22; fax 2 65 00), 1 block south of Serdán. The hotel revels in its antiquity through the photos of Guaymas's past gracing the walls. Rooms, however, have been modernized with polyester bedspreads and curtains, A/C, and TV. Singles 120 pesos; doubles 150 pesos; triples 190 pesos.

Hotel Rubi (tel. 4 01 69), Serdán between Calle 29 and 30. Although the hike from the bus station may seem daunting, the friendly atmosphere and the spacious rooms equipped with black-and-white cable TV and A/C will reward your efforts. Check out the funky iron spiral staircase from the 2nd to 3rd floor. Singles with 2 beds 120 pesos; doubles 130 pesos; triples 140 peso; quads 150 pesos.

FOOD

Seafood is the Guaymas specialty. Local favorites include frog's legs *(ancas de rana),* turtle steaks *(cahuna),* and oysters *(ostiones)* in a garlic and chile sauce. Unfortunately, if you want to sample these local delicacies, you're going to have to pay a fair sum for them. Otherwise, the **Mercado Municipal,** on Calle 20, one block from Serdán, sells fresh produce; there's an abundance of *comida corrida* joints along Serdán.

Restaurant Todos Comen (tel. 2 11 00), Serdán between Calles 15 and 16. Dark draperies extend outward from a central ceiling fan, creating a cool and cozy atmosphere. Try the *filete de pescado* (35 pesos) or the *especialidad de la casa* (20 pesos). Open daily 7am-midnight.

Los Barcos (tel. 2 76 50), Malecón at Calle 22. Gaze at the mural of the sea and nearby mountain peaks inside the restaurant or enjoy the sea breeze of its open air annex as you savor a seafood meal that won't bust your budget. Try a platter of *chimichangas de camarón* (shrimp), *pescado* (fish), *pulpo* (octopus), or *jaiba* (crab; 73 pesos), or the *machaca* (shredded beef; 46 pesos). Open daily.

Las 1000 Tortas, Serdán 188 (tel. 4 30 61), between Calles 17 and 18. The *torta* rules at this family-run joint (10-12 pesos each). Three types of delicious *comida corrida* (20 pesos) are prepared daily and served from noon-4pm. Energetic customers sit upright in orthopedic wooden chairs while tired neighbors slouch in brown vinyl booths, but everyone munches on enchiladas and *gorditas* (18 pesos). Tasty *burritos de machaca con frijoles* just 18 pesos. Open daily 7am-11pm.

S. E. Pizza Buffet (tel. 2 24 46), Serdán at Calle 20. Disney images and framed posters of American cars and athletes decorate the walls. Satisfy your appetite with the all-you-can-eat buffet of pizza, spaghetti, and salad (19 pesos). Open daily 11am-11pm.

SIGHTS AND ENTERTAINMENT

Guaymas's **beaches,** popular with tourists and locals alike, are located to the north in **San Carlos** (see p. 200) and **Miramar;** both are accessible by bus (15min.). The nicer (but smaller) beaches in Miramar are back along the bus route in front of the fancy villas. The beaches are safe, although camping in this area is not advisable; if you absolutely must, opt for San Carlos over Miramar.

Most of the scenic places in Guaymas lie on the east side of town near the waterfront. For the best view in town—of Guaymas, the mountains, the port, and the bay—seek out the shady benches of the **Plaza del Pescador,** just off Serdán toward the water, between Calles 24 and 25. Feel the soothing sea breeze and smile. While you're in the area, take a stroll in the **Plaza de los Tres Presidentes,** on Calle 23 at Serdán, in front of the **Palacio Municipal,** a classic Colonial-style structure built in 1899. The blue bay waters, the towering green-and-white **Catedral de San Fernando,** and three bronze statues of (rather obscure) Mexican presidents complete the scene. The small park directly in front of the cathedral has benches and many leafy trees which provide shade and cool respite for the hot and sweaty. **Cine Guaymas Plus** (tel. 2 40 00), Av. 11 (the Malecón) at Calle 20, two blocks off Serdán, shows U.S. films with Spanish subtitles daily between 3:40 and 11pm (admission 18 pesos, 10 pesos on Wednesday).

Travesty shows—transvestite acts imitating popular Mexican singers—are big in Guaymas. You can find them in clubs near the waterfront at **Charles Baby Disco Video** and **Zodiakos,** both on Serdán between Calle 25 and 26, or further down Serdán, between Calle 16 and 17, at **Cyrus**—the club with the wolf facade. Cover varies according to the popularity of the acts, but it's usually about 20 pesos for men and free for women. If you're just looking for a drink without the frills, head to the **Sahuaro Paino Bar,** next door to Zodiakos, where beers will run you about 8 pesos.

San Carlos

San Carlos is quickly becoming a major destination for Americans and Canadians. Condominiums, hotels, and malls are sprouting like wildflowers to accommodate the increasing influx of tourists. Just 12 miles outside Guaymas, San Carlos boasts a country club with an 18-hole golf course, the only 5-star hotel in Sonora, and the largest, shallowest shipwreck in the world. The unmistakable Tetakawi (*Las Tetas de Cabra*, literally "Teats of the Goat") overlook majestic cliffside homes and the Sea of Cortés. Although accommodations for the budget traveler are limited, a stop in San Carlos is worth it, if only for the views and a bath in warm waters.

ORIENTATION AND PRACTICAL INFORMATION The main (and basically only) road in San Carlos, **Blvd. Manlio F. Beltrones** runs east-west. Most of the shops, restaurants, and accommodations lie on Blvd. Beltrones between Hacienda Tetakawi Hotel and Trailer Park to the east and the San Carlos Country Club to the west. Green-and-white buses from Guaymas run the boulevard about every 10 minutes (6am-11pm) to the Marins and Plaza Las Glorias but don't go to the **Playa Algodones** (5 pesos to Guaymas, 2.5 within San Carlos).

The **tourist office** can be found in **Hacienda Tours** (tel. 6 02 97), at Luna and Beltrones (open M-F 9am-5pm, Sa-Su 9am-2pm). **Banamex** (tel. 6 12 40), on Beltrones next to the PEMEX station exchanges traveler's checks and has a convenient 24hr. **ATM** (open M-F 8:30am-4:30pm). Buy your groceries at **San Carlos Super Mercado** (tel. 6 00 43) in front of the Catholic Church at Plaza Comerical 2 (open 7am-9pm). **Lavandería San Carlos** (tel. 6 00 13), across the street from the post office and Ana Maria's Beauty Shop, offers full or self-service (open 9am-5pm). For **emergencies,** call **Rescate** (tel. 6 01 01 or 6 01 58). 24 hr. **Police** (tel. 6 14 00) are across the street from Plaza Las Glorias Hotel and Condos on Plaza Comercial. **Farmacia Bahia San Carlos** (tel. 6 00 97 or 6 02 42), across the street from Motel Creston, can satisfy your narcotic needs (open M-Sa 8am-7pm). The **post office** (tel. 6 05 06) is tucked in next to Ana Maria's Beauty Shop. **Copicentro** (tel. 6 11 80), next to Rosa's Cantina, sends and receives **faxes** (open M-F 9am-6pm, Sa 9am-1pm). The **phone code** is 622.

ACCOMMODATIONS AND FOOD The best way to stay in San Carlos cheaply is to bring a tent or RV. **Hacienda Tetakawi** (tel. 6 02 20; fax 6 02 48), on Beltrones, km 8.5, at the beginning of the main strip, offers full RV hookups (US$20 per day, US$126 per week) and rents tent spaces (US$10 for 1-2 people, US$5 each additional person). **Motel Creston** (tel. 6 00 20), across the street from Jax Snax, is the cheapest you'll find at 300 pesos for a room with two beds, A/C, bath, and a shower made for people 4 feet (1.3 meters) tall.

Many of the restaurants cater to tourists; it's evident from their prices. However, there are still a few places that appeal to the budget traveler. An eclectic collection of unframed paintings by local artists adorn the walls of **Banana's Restaurant,** just past El Mar Dining Center, which offers US$1 breakfasts (1 egg, toast, and hash browns) and happy hours from 10am to 11am and 4pm to 5pm. Or try **Cafeteria San Carlos** (tel. 6 05 72), just past the police station on Plaza Comercial, which serves up burritos (25 pesos) and *tortas* (20 pesos; open 8am-4pm.)

SIGHTS AND SAND Dining and sport fishing are the main attractions in San Carlos. The Sea of Cortés is home to a vast array of underwater wildlife. Nearby is **San Pedro Nolasco Island,** a popular dive site where sea lions and hundreds of marine birds coexist in harmony. The state of Sonora recently spent a large sum of money to sink a 120-foot tuna boat and 300-foot passenger liner, creating artificial reefs for scuba divers to explore. Dive shops along Beltrones rent scuba gear and sea kayaks and lead guided dives for a pretty penny. **El Mar Diving Center** (tel. 6 04 04), also rents bikes (US$10 for 8hr. on a cruiser; US$25 for 8hr. on a mountain bike; open 7am-6:30pm in summer, 7:30am-5:30pm in winter).

If fishing is your thing, pick up a license (47 pesos for the day) at the **Secretaria de Pesca** on Beltrones just before the turnoff to Plaza Las Glorias; it's illegal to fish without one (open 9am-3pm). In San Carlos, the beach gets better past the end of the bus route near Club Med and Howard Johnson's. There are two main beaches in this town: San Fransisco and Playa Los Algodones. **San Francisco,** beginning at Condominios Pilar and extending to about Hotel Fiesta, tends to be pretty rocky. The most beautiful beach, **Playa Los Algodones** (Cotton Beach), once used as a set for the U.S. movie *Catch 22*, is the most difficult to get to without a car; it lies west of Tetakawi.

Alamos

The sleepy town of Alamos (pop. 8000), in the scenic foothills of the Sierra Madre Occidental at the edge of the Sonoran desert, is a rambling collection of handsome colonial haciendas. Founded by Coronado in 1531, Alamos became the center of a rich mining district after the discovery of silver in the area in 1863. But when the silver veins ran dry at the turn of the century, Alamos shrank to ghost-town proportions. In the last 50 years, Alamos has experienced a return to its architectural glory days with the arrival of wealthy gringos in search of winter homes. The refurbished haciendas and cobblestone streets organized around the massive cathedral give Alamos an Old Mexico feel unlike anywhere in northwest Mexico. The city is safe and absolutely beautiful in its reclaimed authenticity.

ORIENTATION AND PRACTICAL INFORMATION Alamos is a comfortable size—you can explore the small and compact town on foot. As you come into town on **Calle Madero,** you'll reach a fork in the road at the bronzed statue of Benito Juárez and the PEMEX station; the left branch leads to **Plaza Alameda,** the commercial center (where the bus stops), and the right branch leads to **Plaza de Armas** in the historic district. A small alley known as the **Callejón del Beso** connects the Plaza de Armas with the market across from Plaza Alameda. The **cathedral** south of Plaza de Armas marks the northern edge of the **Barrio La Colorada,** where most of the *norteamericanos* have concentrated their hacienda-restoring efforts.

All **bus service** to Alamos passes through **Navojoa,** 53km southwest of Alamos. From the **Transportes Norte de Sonora** and **Elite** bus stations in Navojoa, stand at the corner of Allende and Ferrocarril, looking down Ferrocarril as you face the bus stations. Then, walk one block to the **Transportes del Pacífico** station, and turn left (toward the center of town) onto Guerrero. Six blocks along Guerrero (passing the **Transportes de Baja California** bus station after 3 blocks) is the **Los Mayitos** bus station at Rincón, where you can catch a bus to Alamos (1hr., every hr. 6am-6:30pm, 11 pesos). The return trip from Alamos starts from the bus station at Plaza Alameda (same times and price).

The **tourist office,** Calle Juárez 6 (tel. 8 04 50), is under the Hotel Los Portales on the west side of the Plaza de Armas (theoretically open M-F 9am-2pm and 4-7pm, Sa 9am-2pm), although it's anyone's guess when the eccentric shop owner will be around. Currency can be exchanged at **Bancrecer** (tel. 8 04 44), on Madero before the fork in the road (open M-F 9am-5pm, Sa 10am-2pm). A 24-hour **ATM** is right next door. Pick up some prescription drugs, a side of bacon, and a six-pack at **SuperTito's** (tel. 8 05 12), at the fork in Calle Maderos, which operates as a pharmacy, grocery store, and a liquor store (open daily 7:30am-10:30pm). Farther out of the center of town on Madero is the **Hospital Básico** (tel. 8 00 25 or 8 00 26). The **post office** (tel. 8 00 09) is also on Madero, between the Bancrecer and the hospital (open M-F 8am-3pm). The **postal code** is 85760. The **phone code** is 642.

ACCOMMODATIONS Unless you rediscover silver on your way into town, you'll probably have to turn away from the lush garden courtyards of the hacienda-hotels and head toward the outskirts for hotels whose courtyards look more like parking lots. For a hacienda hotel with prices that can't be beat, head for **Hotel Enrique,** next to the Hotel Los Portales on Juárez, on the west side of the Plaza de Armas. Traditional high-ceiling rooms off a courtyard take you back to Old Mexico. Fans keep you cool and the communal bathroom is irreproachable (singles 50 pesos; doubles 100 pesos).

Like Water for Chicharrones

In Mexico, there's no escaping the *chicharrones* (pork rinds), and in some towns the popular snack has become…an ice cream flavor! On sweltering hot days, vendors push long carts loaded with rows of metal casks and scoop out ice cold salvation in a crazy variety of flavors—*elote* (cornmeal), *cerveza* (beer), *aguacate* (avocado), and tequila. Hand a vendor 5 pesos and he'll cram a mammoth portion into a cone or plastic cup. Mexican ice cream is known to harbor more than a few nasty amoebas, so verify the product's hygienic integrity by looking at the cleanliness of the stand before placing that spoon in your mouth. Once you're assured of your food's safety, tuck a napkin into your shirt front, close your eyes, and lick away.

Motel Somar, Madero 110 (tel. 8 01 95), about 300m from Plaza Alameda, offers clean rooms with private showers and a chance to sit and chat with locals in the lobby. Loud fans cool the rooms. (Singles 100 pesos; doubles 120 pesos.)

FOOD True peso-pinchers patronize the taco stands, such as **Taquería Blanquero,** in the Mercado Municipal by Plaza Alameda (open daily 7am-10:30pm). You can choose from various delectable fruits sold within walking distance of where they were grown. **La Cita Cafe,** Madero 37, right before the fork, feels like a jungle lean-to with its brown wood walls, wire-wash windows, and the occasional birdcall in the distance. Enjoy a fish dish (38 pesos) or *antojitos* (about 25 pesos) while admiring how well the orange curtains, red-and-yellow tablecloths, brown chairs, and brown walls all match. (Open daily 7:30am-9:30pm.) For a good view of the Plaza de Armas, the distant foothills, and a hacienda or two, eat outside under the arches at **Restaurant Las Palmeras,** Cárdenas 9 (tel. 8 00 65), northeast of the Plaza de Armas. Here, you're likely to run into some transplanted U.S. tourists and any number of local officials. (Breakfasts 15-25 pesos, antojitos 20-35; open daily 7am-10pm.)

SIGHTS The main reason to visit Alamos is to get a glimpse of Old Mexico. Learn about the history of the town by strolling along the cobblestone streets and peeking into as many buildings as possible. Don't be hesitant to ask shop owners if you can look around their buildings and courtyards. If you're lucky, you'll run across a hacienda being renovated and be able to see the inner workings of the fabulous architecture. One of the grandest homes in town was constructed in 1720 and refinished in the 19th century, when it became the home of Don José María, owner of one of the world's richest silver mines. The **Hotel Las Portales** now occupies most of the building, including Don Alameda's foyer and overgrown courtyard. Several other impressive restored homes, many of which are now hotels, can be found around the cathedral, including Hotel **Casa de los Tesoros** (a former convent), the **Hotel La Mansión,** and the **Casa Encantada.**

Today, the town **jail** and the **Mirador** offer excellent views from the site Coronado chose for a fort in 1531. To get to the jail, walk along Madero west of the center of town and follow the signs. The current **cathedral** dates from 1805. A look inside at the height of the vault gives some dimension to Alamos's days of glory. In the mid-19th century, many Asians arrived in Alamos to work in the mines and to foster the growing silk industry. The only remainders of this period are a few mulberry trees and the **old silk factory** currently being restored as a private residence.

CHIHUAHUA

El Paso, Texas

The largest of the U.S. border towns, El Paso boomed in the 17th century as a passageway on an important east-west wagon route that followed the Río Grande through "the pass" *(el paso)* between the Rockies and the Sierra Madres. Today, modern El Paso (pop. 650,000) sits in the midst of sand and sagebrush, and it serves as a stop-over between the U.S. and Mexico. The exhaustive melding of American and Mexican cultures that makes this border town unique is evident in everything from the bilingual signs throughout the city to the eclectic mix of people in the streets. After dark, central El Paso becomes a ghost town: most activity leaves the center and heads to the University of Texas at El Paso (UTEP) or south of the border to El Paso's raucous sister city, Ciudad Juárez.

ORIENTATION

Before leaving the airport, be sure to pick up maps and information from the **visitor's center** at the bottom of the escalators descending from the arrival gates. To get to the city from the airport, take **Sun Metro** bus #33. The stop is located on a traffic island outside the air terminal building, across from the Delta ticket window (50min. to downtown. M-Sa every hr. 6:54am-8:54pm, Su every hr. 8:54am-7:54pm. US$1, students and children 6-13 US$0.50, seniors US$0.30, transfer tickets US$0.10; exact change only). Get off when the bus arrives at San Jacinto Plaza and you'll be right in the thick of things, near most of the hotels and restaurants.

When the bus stops running late at night, the only way to get to the city is to take a taxi (approximately US$20-25). Alternative approaches include **I-10** (running east-west) and **US 54** (north-south). El Paso is divided into east and west by **Santa Fe Ave.** and into north and south by **San Antonio Ave.** Tourists should be wary of the streets between San Antonio and the border late at night.

CROSSING THE BORDER

The best way to cross the border, unless you are traveling by car, is to walk. To reach the border from El Paso, take the north-south #8 green trolley operated by Sun Metro to the **Santa Fe Bridge,** its last stop before turning around (every 15min., weekdays 6:15am-8:15pm, Sa 7:45am-8:15pm, Su 8:45am-7:15pm, US$0.25). For information about **tourist cards,** see.

Do not confuse the inexpensive #8 trolley with the more costly trolley. Two pedestrian and motor roads cross the Río Grande: **El Paso Ave.,** a crowded one-way street, and **Santa Fe Ave.,** a parallel road lined with Western-wear stores, clothing shops, and decent restaurants. Entering Mexico costs US$0.25; the return trip costs US$0.45.

If entering Mexico by foot, walk to the right side of the Santa Fe Bridge and pay the quarter to cross. Daytrippers, including foreign travelers with multi-entry visas, should be prepared to flash their documents of citizenship in order to pass in and out of Mexico. You might get your bag searched by a guard, but usually you won't even have to show ID. After stepping off the bridge, you will be on the main strip, Av. Juárez. Two blocks down on the corner of Juárez and Azucenas, you'll find the air-conditioned Juárez **tourist office,** where friendly, English-speaking employees await with maps and info.

To enter the United States, cross over the Santa Fe Bridge near the large *"Feliz Viaje"* sign. Be ready to deal with U.S. border guards and to show a valid visa or proof of citizenship. You may be searched or asked to answer a few questions proving that you are who you say you are. Once in El Paso, wait at the bus stop on the right-hand sidewalk just across from the bridge. The north-south bus runs until 8:15pm to San Jacinto Plaza.

PRACTICAL INFORMATION

Transportation

Airport: Northeast of the city center; to reach it, take bus #33 from San Jacinto Square or any other central location. Daily flights to locations in Mexico, the U.S., and elsewhere, on a host of carriers, most with connections in Dallas/Ft. Worth or Houston.

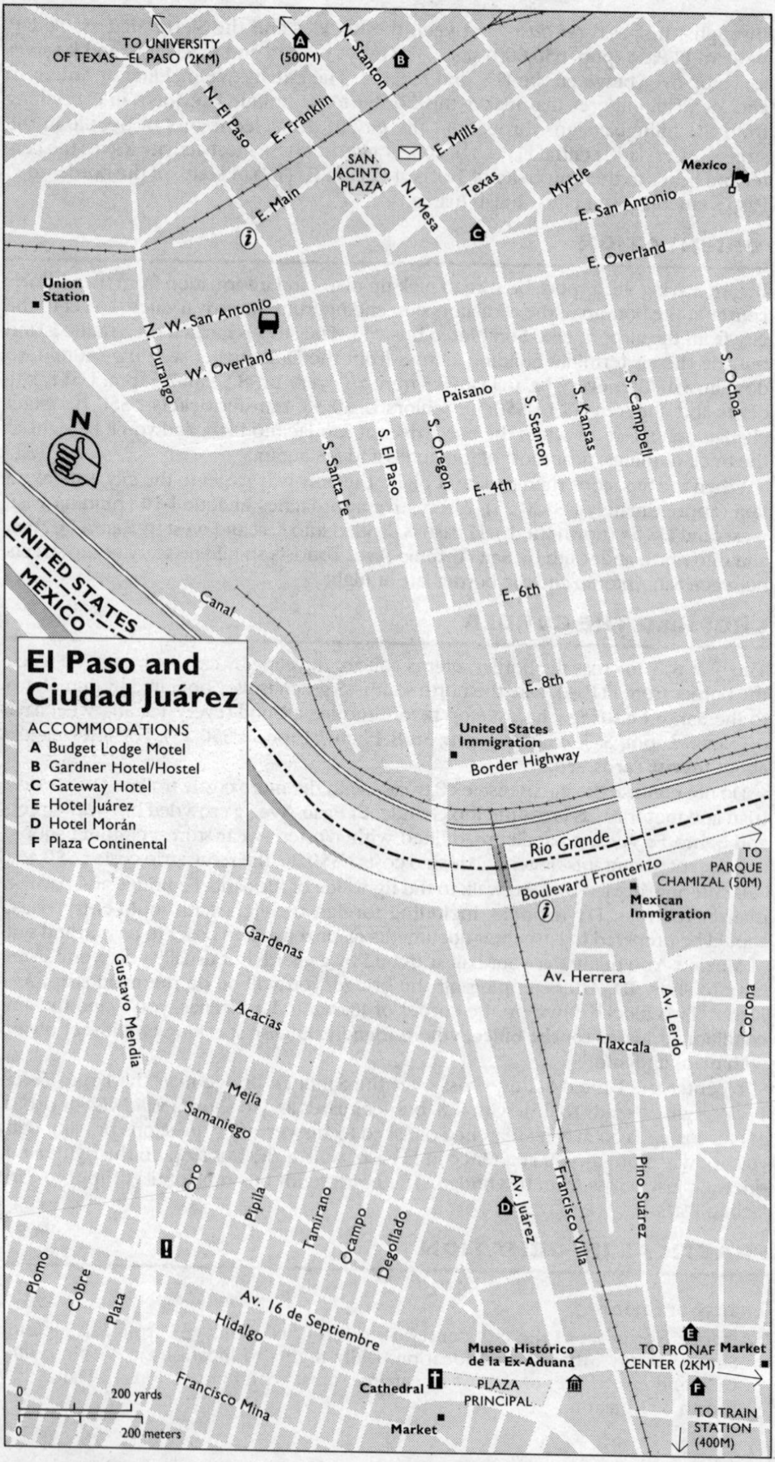
El Paso and Ciudad Juárez
ACCOMMODATIONS
A Budget Lodge Motel
B Gardner Hotel/Hostel
C Gateway Hotel
E Hotel Juárez
D Hotel Morán
F Plaza Continental
TO UNIVERSITY OF TEXAS—EL PASO (2KM)
(500M)
N. Stanton
N. El Paso
E. Franklin
E. Mills
SAN JACINTO PLAZA
E. Main
N. Mesa
Texas
Myrtle
E. San Antonio
Mexico
E. Overland
Union Station
N. W. San Antonio
N. Durango
W. Overland
Paisano
S. Ochoa
S. Campbell
S. Kansas
S. Stanton
S. Oregon
S. El Paso
S. Santa Fe
E. 4th
N
UNITED STATES
MEXICO
Canal
E. 6th
E. 8th
United States Immigration
Border Highway
Rio Grande
Boulevard Fronterizo
TO PARQUE CHAMIZAL (50M)
Mexican Immigration
Gardenas
Av. Herrera
Av. Lerdo
Corona
Gustavo Mendia
Acacias
Tlaxcala
Mejía
Samaniego
Oro
Pipila
Tamirano
Ocampo
Degollado
Av. Juárez
Francisco Villa
Pino Suárez
Plomo
Cobre
Plata
Av. 16 de Septiembre
Hidalgo
Francisco Mina
Museo Histórico de la Ex-Aduana
Cathedral
PLAZA PRINCIPAL
Market
TO PRONAF CENTER (2KM)
Market
TO TRAIN STATION (400M)
0 200 yards
0 200 meters

Buses: Greyhound, 200 W. San Antonio (tel. 532-2365 or 1-800-231-2222), across from the Civic Center between Santa Fe and Chihuahua. Daily service to and from Dallas (10hr., 7 per day, US$76), Los Angeles (16hr., 6 per day, US$39), New York (48hr., 7 per day, US$99), Phoenix, and other U.S. cities. **Storage lockers** US$2 per hr. Open 24hr.

Public Transportation: Sun Metro (tel. 533-3333), departing from San Jacinto Plaza, at the corner of Main and Oregon. US$1, students and children US$0.50, seniors US$0.30, transfer ticket US$0.10.

Car Rental: Alamo (tel. 774-9855), **Avis** (tel. 779-2700), **Budget** (tel. 778-5287), **Dollar** (tel. 778-5445), **Hertz** (tel. 772-4255), **Thrifty** (tel. 778-9236), and more, all at the airport.

Tourist and Financial Services

Tourist Office: 1 Civic Center Plaza (tel. 544-0062), a small round building next to the Chamber of Commerce at the intersection of Santa Fe and San Francisco. Be sure to pick up a map and brochures. Also sells **El Paso-Juárez Trolley Co.** tickets for day-long tours across the border leaving on the hour from the Convention Center. Tickets US$11, ages 4-12 US$8, under 4 free. Trolleys run 10am-5pm. Call for reservations, which are recommended, 544-0061 for recorded info.

Mexican Consulate: 910 E. San Antonio (tel. 533-3644), on the corner of Virginia. Dispenses **tourist cards** (see p. 7). Open M-F 9am-4:30pm.

Currency Exchange: Valuta, 301 E. Paisano (tel. 544-1152), at Mesa St. Conveniently near the border and open 24hr. **Melek,** 306 E. Paisano Dr. (tel. 532-4283), next to Valuta. Rates worse than those at the banks. Most banks change cash and **traveler's checks,** but for the best rates try **Bank of the West,** 500 N. Mesa St. (tel. 532-1000), on the corner of Missouri and Mesa. Open M-Th 9am-4pm, F 9am-5pm.

ATM: All of the banks in the downtown area around San Jacinto Plaza have them. Plan ahead because the banks close by 5pm and other ATMs are scarce.

American Express Office: 3100 N. Mesa (tel. 532-8900). Open M-F 8am-5pm.

Emergency and Communications

Hospital: Providence Memorial Hospital, 2001 N. Oregon (tel. 577-6011), at Hague near UTEP. Open 24hr. Immunizations recommended but not required to enter Mexico. Call the **immunization department** (tel. 591-2050) of the **El Paso City County Health District,** 222 S. Campbell (tel. 543-3560), at First St. When approaching the Mexican border, turn left on Paisano St. and walk 3 blocks.

Post Office: 219 E. Mills (tel. 532-2652), between Mesa and Stanton. Open M-F 9am-5pm, Sa 8am-noon. **Postal code:** 79901.

Internet Access: Cybersmith Internet Cafe (tel. 845-1440), located at Sunland Park Mall, offers connections to the Internet at a rate of US$0.20 per minute, US$5 per 30min., and US$9 per hr. Take Sun Metro Bus #12, 14, or 16, from San Jacinto Plaza to the Sunland Park Mall stop (approximately 20min.).

Phone Code: 915.

ACCOMMODATIONS

El Paso offers safer, more appealing places to stay than Juárez. Apart from the usual hotel chains (La Quinta, Days Inn, etc.) lining I-10 and some more upper-end establishments, several great budget hotels cluster around the center of town near Main St. and San Jacinto Square.

Gardner Hotel/Hostel (HI-AYH), 311 E. Franklin (tel. 532-3661), between Stanton and Kansas. From the airport, take bus #33 to San Jacinto Park, walk 2 blocks north to Franklin, turn right, and head east 1½ blocks. With a helpful staff, an authentically decorated lobby, and cozy rooms, the Gardner stands out as the ideal rest spot for the weary budget traveler. **Hotel:** All rooms have color TV with cable and a phone. Singles US$20, US$35 with bath; doubles and triples US$45 with bath. Rates may depend on occupancy. Check-out 1pm. **Hostel:** Small, 4-person dorm rooms and shared bathrooms. Spacious kitchen, common room with pool table and cable TV, and couches in the basement. US$13; non-HI members pay an extra

US$2.50. Locker rental US$0.75, US$0.50 for four or more days. Linen US$2. Laundry US$1.50 per load. Reception open 24hr. Check-out 10am.

Gateway Hotel, 104 S. Stanton (tel. 532-2611; fax 533-8100), at San Antonio Ave. A stone's throw from San Jacinto Square and a favorite stop for middle-class Mexicans. Clean and spacious rooms, large beds and closets, and thoroughly clean bathrooms, some with bathtubs. A/C upstairs; diner downstairs. Singles US$23, with TV US$30; doubles US$35, with TV US$37. Parking US$1.50 for 24hr. Reservations accepted up to 5 days in advance except during festivals and holidays.

Budget Lodge Motel, 1301 N. Mesa (tel. 533-6821), at California across from Cathedral H.S., a 10min. walk from San Jacinto Square up Mesa St. Even though it is more removed from downtown, it is only 6 blocks from UTEP. Rooms have A/C and cable TV. Small café, conveniently located on the first floor, serves breakfast and lunch at good rates. The swimming pool is a bonus. Singles US$27; doubles US$31.

FOOD

El Paso boasts a plethora of small mom-and-pop diners that prepare a wide variety of tasty, homemade Mexican and American dishes. Burritos are the undisputed local specialty, and the array of places that serve 'em up hot is almost dizzying. Unfortunately, many places close early, so your options may be more limited after 6pm.

La Malinche (tel. 544-8785), N. Stanton St., at the corner of Texas across from The Edge. The tiled, adobed decor lends authenticity to this cafe in the middle of downtown El Paso. Heaping portions of unique Mexican fare treats the tongue and the tummy just right. Burritos of all types US$1.75; full meals US$3.50-6. Open M-Sa 7:30am-4:30pm.

The Tap, 408 E. San Antonio (tel. 532-3304), at Stanton. The big lightbulb sign can't be missed. This bar/restaurant serves up authentic Tex-Mex to a local clientele in a fun atmosphere and has a major advantage: it's open late. Breakfast US$3, lunch specials US$4, and dinner plates US$4-7. Wash it all down with US$1 beer on tap. Open M-Sa 9am-2am, Su noon-2am.

Manolo's Café, 122 S. Mesa (tel. 532-7661), between Overland and San Antonio. Treat your stomach to the *menudo* (US$2), burritos (US$1), or the generous *comida corrida* (US$3.75) while digging the bullfighter posters covering the walls. Friendly service, free refills, and large portions make Manolo's a popular local hangout. Open M-Sa 7am-5pm, Su 8am-3pm.

SIGHTS AND ENTERTAINMENT

The majority of visitors to El Paso are either stopping off on the long drive through the desert or heading south to Ciudad Juárez and beyond. For a whirlwind tour of the city and its southern neighbor, hop aboard the **Border Jumper Trolleys** that depart every hour from El Paso (see **Tourist Office,** p. 205).

Historic **San Jacinto Plaza** is the heart of El Paso and swarms with daily activity. The plaza is the main bus stop for all San Metro buses, and throngs of locals gather there to sit under the shade of some of El Paso's only trees. South of the square, **El Paso St.** serves as a market for all kinds of goods, ranging from fruit to the latest fashions. A savvy negotiator can find tons of bargains along the bustling thoroughfare. To take in a complete picture of the Río Grande Valley, head northeast of downtown along Stanton and take a right on Rim Rd. (which becomes Scenic Drive); **Murchinson Park,** at the base of the ridge, offers a commanding vista of El Paso, Juárez, and the Sierra Madres. Bring your camera! The **Cielo Vista Mall** boasts a variety of shops, as well as a movie theater, **Cinema 6** (take Sun Metro bus #63 from San Jacinto Plaza). For museum enthusiasts, the area around the Civic Center on Santa Fe Ave. contains a renowned **Americana Museum,** as well as the **El Paso Museum of Art.**

For nightlife, try **The Palace,** 209 S. El Paso St. (tel. 532-6000), which pumps dance music to a packed house in a trendy, neon setting every Friday and Saturday night until 2am. (Second floor jazz lounge. 18+ admitted. US$5 cover.) **The Edge,** 201 N. Stanton (tel. 532-6644) at Texas, also offers a sophisticated nightclub in a safe part of town. Though the nightlife in El Paso isn't stellar, what little there is can still be dangerous. For more rowdiness, no minimum drinking age, and ubiquitous nightlife, many people head to Juárez by night.

During the spring and summer, the **El Paso Diablos** (tel. 755-2000), pride of the fabled Texas League, play the best minor league baseball around. (Games Apr.-May daily 6:45pm; June-Aug. M-Sa 7:15pm, Su 6:45pm. Call to confirm. General admission US$3, box seats US$4.75.) To reach **Cohen Stadium,** 9700 Gateway North, take Sun Metro bus #42 from San Jacinto Plaza as far north as it goes and walk the rest of the way. Ask the driver for directions.

Ciudad Juárez

Although Ciudad Juárez (pop. 1 million) is separated from El Paso only by the narrow Río Grande, the two cities are worlds apart. Visitors to Juárez are immediately bombarded with commotion on all sides and beset by a collage of bright paint and neon. Enterprising locals are eager to hawk their wares to anyone with a pulse. Near the border, the city is hectic, loud, dirty, and cheap. The incredibly high concentration of junkyards on the southern fringes of the city and the nearby dilapidated ghettoes provide a sharp contrast to the calm, ritzy, and pricey ProNaf area. Fleeing in the face of the American advance, Mexican culture can be found in the city's cathedral square and Parque Chamizal, pleasant respites from the sprawling industrial production centers and poor residential shantytowns that dot most of the cityscape.

ORIENTATION

Most of Old Juárez (the area immediately adjoining the Santa Fe and Stanton bridges) can be covered on foot. Street numbers start in the 600s near the two border bridges and descend to zero at **16 de Septiembre,** where **Av. Juárez** (the main street) ends. Both **Lerdo** and **Francisco Villa** run north/south, parallel to Juárez. To reach the **ProNaf center,** take public bus "Ruta 8A" (2.20 pesos), which leaves from the intersection of Presidencia and Juárez near the border. Most city buses leave from the intersection of **Insurgentes** and Francisco Villa or thereabouts; ask the driver whether your bus will take you to your destination. It's a good idea to grab a map from the **tourist office** (see below) because outside of Old Juárez the streets get convoluted and you don't want to be in the wrong part of town. Taxis are always downtown, but fees are steep; negotiate before getting in. To get from the bus station to downtown, walk out the left-most door (if you're facing the main station entrance) and up to the street. Don't be satisfied with just any bus that will take you to the *centro;* get on an old converted school bus labeled "Ruta 1A" or "Ruta 6," both of which go to Av. Juárez, or you'll be left a few blocks outside the real center.

During the day, Juárez is relatively safe for the alert traveler. As darkness increases, however, so does the ratio of drunk to sober people wandering the streets. Be wary of people loitering about late at night, which large numbers of men have a tendency to do. Juárez is not the safest of places, especially after dark, so be careful and avoid places that look at all suspicious. Don't go out unaccompanied. For information on entering and leaving Mexico, see **El Paso: Crossing the Border** (see p. 203) and **Entering and Leaving Mexico** (see p. 9). Women should not walk alone or in dark places; everyone should avoid the area more than 2 blocks west of Av. Juárez. The **police station** is on the corner of 16 de Septiembre and Juárez, so if you are in the downtown area, help is not far away.

PRACTICAL INFORMATION

Transportation

Airport: (tel. 33 09 34), about 17km out on Rte. 45 *(Carretera Panorámica)*. Catch the crowded "Ruta 4" bus and get off at the San Lorenzo Church; then board the "Ruta Aeropuerto" (1.80 pesos). **Aeroméxico** (tel. 13 80 89 or 13 87 19) flies to Chihuahua, Mexico City, Monterrey, and a few close U.S. locations.

Buses: Central Camionera, Blvd. Oscar Flores 4010, north of the ProNaf center and next to the Río Grande mall. To get there, take the Chihuahuenses bus from the El Paso terminal to Juárez (US$7), or cram into the "Ruta 1A" at Av. Insurgentes and Francisco Villa (2.20 pesos). Be sure to ask the driver of Ruta 1A whether it is going to the bus station, as not all do. **Chihuahuenses** (tel. 29 22 29), **Estrella Blanca** (tel. 13 83 02), **Ominbus de México** (tel. 10 64 45), and others offer service to Chihuahua (7hr., every 30min., 100 pesos), Guadalajara (24hr., 8:30am and 9pm, 550 pesos), Hermosillo (10hr., 290 pesos), Mazatlán (24hr., 440 pesos), Mexico City (26hr., 6 per day, 650 pesos), Nogales (8hr., 6pm, 250 pesos), and more. **Greyhound** serves the U.S., including Dallas (US$75), El Paso (50min., every hr., US$7), Los Angeles (US$45), San Antonio (US$79), and others.

Tourist and Financial Services

Tourist Office: The most conveniently located branch, the **Caseta de Información Turistica** (tel. 14 92 56), can be found on Av. Juárez Azucenas, 2 blocks from the border (main office, tel. 29 33 00, ext. 5160 or 5649; fax ext. 5648). Few helpful brochures, but an amiable English-speaking staff. Open M-F 8:30am-2pm, Sa 9am-1pm.

U.S. Consulate: López Mateos Nte. 924 (tel. 13 40 48 or 13 40 50), at Hermanos Escobar. From Av. Juárez, turn left on Malecón, right on López Mateos, and then walk for 15-20min. In an emergency, call the El Paso tourist office in the U.S. (tel. (915) 544-0062).

Currency Exchange: Banks congregate near the bus station, on Juárez and on 16 de Septiembre. Most are open M-F 9am-3pm. Traveler's checks cashed by **Comisiones San Luis** (tel. 14 20 33), on the corner of 16 de Septiembre and Juárez. Open M-Th 9am-7pm, F-Sa 9am-8pm, Su 9am-6:15pm. Also try **Chequerama** (tel. 12 35 99), at Unión and Juárez. Open M-Sa 10am-6pm. Any of the *cambios* lining Av. Juárez offer competitive exchange rates, although they charge for traveler's checks.

NORTHWEST MEXICO

Local Services

Supermarket: Smart, López Mateos and Carretera Casas Grandes, a 15min. ride from Av. Juárez. The **Río Grande Mall,** at Guerrero and López Mateos, sells groceries, clothes, furniture, and much, much more.

Laundromat: Lavasolas (tel. 12 54 61), Tlaxcala and 5 de Mayo. 12 other locations in town. Washers 9 pesos (large), 8 pesos (small); dryers 9 pesos. Open M-Sa 9am-9pm, Su 8am-5pm.

Emergency and Communications

Emergency: Dial 06.

Police: (tel. 15 15 51), Oro and 16 de Septiembre, near Juárez. English spoken.

Transit Police: (tel. 12 31 97 or 41 10 28), English spoken.

Red Cross: (tel. 16 58 06), in the ProNaf Center next to the OK Corral. English spoken. Open daily 24hr.

Pharmacy: El Félix Super Farmacia (tel. 14 43 31), 16 de Septiembre and Noche Triste, across from the cathedral. Turn right from Juárez. Open daily 8am-9pm.

Hospital: Hospital Latinoamericano, 250 N. López Mateos (tel. 16 14 67 or 16 14 15; fax 16 13 75), in the ProNaf area. English spoken. Open daily 24hr. Take Ruta 8A.

Post Office: Lerdo at Ignacio Peña. Open M-F 8am-5pm, Sa-Su 9am-1pm.

Postal Code: 32000.

Fax: Secrefax (tel. 15 15 10 or 15 20 49; fax 15 16 11), on Av. Juárez near the Santa Fe bridge, partially obscured under a white awning. Open daily 24hr.

Phone Code: 16.

ACCOMMODATIONS

In Juárez, a typical cheap hotel meets only minimal standards and charges some of the highest "budget" rates in Mexico. Relatively inexpensive lodging can be found along the main strip, Avenida Juárez; pricier places are located in ProNaf, around López Mateos and Avenida de las Américas.

Hotel Morán, Juárez 264 (tel. 15 08 12; fax 14 12 42), across from Mr. Fog Bar. Located in the heart of Juárez, patrons of this hotel don't have to venture far for excitement. Clean rooms with A/C, color TV, and private baths can't be beat in this part of town. Singles 106 pesos; doubles 160 pesos.

Hotel Juárez, Lerdo 143 Nte. (tel. 15 02 98 or 15 03 58), at 16 de Septiembre. Simple, small rooms in an old, yellow building, but one of the best deals you'll find in downtown Juárez—if you can deal without A/C. Room rates decrease as you move up the stairs. Third floor: singles 47 pesos; doubles 84 pesos; additional person 11 pesos.

Plaza Continental, S. Lerdo 112 (tel. 15 00 84, 15 03 18, or 15 02 59), at 16 de Septiembre. Centrally located, with all the makings of a luxury hotel: a spacious, elegant lobby with chandeliers, columns, and a wide staircase leading to large, comfortable, well-furnished rooms with A/C, color TV, and phones. An *Agua purificada* dispenser and—joy—a Tecate vending machine are in the hall. Singles 175 pesos; doubles 210 pesos; triples 220 pesos.

FOOD

Eateries vary from clean, air-conditioned restaurants catering to tourists to roadside shacks with picnic tables and TVs blasting *telenovelas* in Spanish. Weak-stomached travelers should avoid shacks. The quest for food that will not cause a bacteriological mutiny in gringo bellies is long; prudent travelers should beat a path to Av. Juárez and Lerdo or to the ProNaf center. In general, *mariscos* (shellfish) are overpriced and less than fresh.

Cafetería El Coyote Inválido, Juárez 615 (tel. 14 27 27), at Colón. We're still wondering about the name. A bustling, clean, American-style diner with heavenly A/C. Hamburgers (16 pesos), burritos (16 pesos), and an array of Mexican plates (16-32 pesos). Open daily 24hr.

Hotel Santa Fé Restaurante, Lerdo 675 Nte. (tel. 14 02 70) at Tlaxcala, in the Hotel Santa Fe. Roll from here to there on the wheeled chairs. Then roll back. Sample chicken enchiladas or club sandwiches (25 pesos) and wash 'em down with a beer (12 pesos). Open daily 24hr.

Restaurant/Bar Juárez de Noche, Juárez 222 Nte. (tel. 15 20 02), between Gonzáles and Carreño—the place with the open-air facade. Let the tunes of the *grupo norteño* lead you to their taco platter, which comes with salad, french fries, beans, and more (29 pesos). Irrigate it all with a nice, cold beer (11 pesos).

SIGHTS

The **Aduana Fronteriza** (tel. 12 47 07) stands in the *centro,* where Juárez and 16 de Septiembre cross. *(Open Tu-Su 10am-5pm; free.)* Built in 1889 as a trading outpost and later used for customs, it now houses the **Museo Histórico de la Ex-Aduana,** which chronicles the region's history during the Mexican Revolution. Peeking inside the antique wagons is not frowned upon. The **Museo de Arte e Historia** (tel. 16 74 14), at the ProNaf center, exhibits Mexican art of the past and present (open Tu-Su 11am-5pm; admission 8 pesos, students free.) Also at the ProNaf center, the **Centro Artesanal** sells handmade goods at sky-high prices; you'd be crazy not to haggle here. The "Ruta 8" bus will take you from the *centro* to ProNaf for 2.20 pesos; a taxi charges 20 times as much. Your call.

The deforested **Parque Chamizal,** near the Córdova Bridge, down Presidencia Av., is a good place to escape the noise of the city, if not the heat, and enjoy a picnic. Check out the newly inaugurated Mexican flag that's said to be as large as an American football field. The **Museo Arqueológico,** Av. Pellicer in Parque Chamizal, houses plastic facsimiles of pre-Hispanic sculptures as well as trilobite fossils, rocks, and bones (tel. 11 10 48 or 13 69 83; open Tu-F 11am-8pm, Sa-Su 10am-8pm.) The **Misión de Nuestra Señora de Guadalupe** (tel. 15 55 02), on 16 de Septiembre and Mariscal, is the oldest building on either side of the border for kilometers around. It features antique paintings and altars.

ENTERTAINMENT

Downtown Juárez was built for partying. It seems that every establishment along Av. Juárez that isn't selling booze or pulling teeth is a club or a bar; counting them could make you dizzy before you start drinking. Many establishments are unsavory, however, and even some of the better ones can become dangerous; stick to the glutted strip along Av. Juárez, or stay in the ProNaf area. On weekends, gringos swarm to Juárez in a 48-hour quest for fun, fights, and fiestas. **Mr. Fog Bar,** Juárez Nte. 140 (tel. 14 29 48), at González, is quite popular. A cartoon crocodile adorns the mirrored walls of this dark, reddish drinking establishment (beer 10 pesos, liquor 12 pesos). The dance floor is in the back. (Open Su-Th 11am-2am, F-Sa 11am-3am.)

However, despite its extensive partying reputation, Juárez does offer visitors activities beyond the club and bar scene. Enjoy the *toro* and the *matador* battle in traditional bullfights on occasional summer evenings at the **Plaza Monumental de Toros** (tel. 13 16 56), Paseo Triunfo de la República at López Mateos. General admission starts at 30 pesos, 60 pesos in the shade. Children 12 and under go free. The **Lienzo Charro** (tel. 27 05 55), on Av. Charro off República, also hosts bullfights and a *charreada* (rodeo) on Sunday afternoons during the summer. At the western edge of town, **Galgódromo** (also known as the **Juárez Racetrack;** tel. 25 53 94) rises from Vicente Guerrero. Dogs run Wednesday to Sunday at 7:30pm; there are also Sunday matinees at 2:30pm. Horse racing can be seen only on closed-circuit TV. Also during the summer, keep an eye out for the traveling carnival which periodically sets up on the soccer fields next to Parque Chamizal.

Nuevo Casas Grandes and Paquimé

Nuevo Casas Grandes belongs to a time when cowboys ruled the land. A quiet town (pop. 80,000) in the expansive Chihuahuan desert, this community arose at the beginning of this century after a group of pioneering families from (Viejo) Casas Grandes decided to move to the newly constructed railroad station. Nuevo Casas Grandes is cleaner than many of the neighboring towns and exudes a friendly, laid-back atmosphere. Instead of the gaudy nightclubs and cramped storefronts of Juárez, Nuevo Casas Grandes has shaded parks and an open-air market. Casas Grandes and the ruins of **Paquimé** (pah-kee-MEH)—one of the most important cities in pre-Hispanic northern Mexico—lie 8km to the southwest.

ORIENTATION AND PRACTICAL INFORMATION From the **Estrella Blanca** bus station on Obregón and 16 de Septiembre, walk one block down 16 de Septiembre to reach **Constitución,** which runs along the railroad tracks. One block further is **Juárez.** These are the two main streets in town; **5 de Mayo** and **16 de Septiembre** each run perpendicular to Juárez and Constitución and constitute the heart of the city. The main park in town, **Plaza Juárez,** is at the intersection of Juárez and 5 de Mayo. **Taxis** loiter on 16 de Septiembre at Constitución and on Minerva at Obregón. Everything listed below lies within the nine-block downtown area.

Estrella Blanca and **Caballero Azteca** (tel. 4 07 80) **buses** run to Chihuahua (5hr., 6 per day 2am-midnight, 105 pesos), Cd. Juárez (3½hr., 12 per day 5am-9pm, 80 pesos), and Cuauhtémoc (6½hr., 3 per day, 95 pesos). **Chihuahuenses** (tel. 4 14 75) runs buses all the way to Hermosillo (8hr., 6:30pm and midnight, 181 pesos), Monterrey (16 hr., 3 per day, 390 pesos), and Tijuana (16hr., 3 per day, 375 pesos). The **tourist office** (tel./fax 4 64 73), on the corner of Juárez and Domínguez, is on the second floor of the Cámara de Comercios office, across from La Mansión (open M-F 9am-4pm). Change money at **Casa de Cambio California,** Constitución 207 (tel. 4 32 32), at 5 de Mayo (open M-F 9am-2pm and 3:30-7pm, Sa 9am-2pm and 3:30-6pm). **Bancomer,** 16 de Septiembre (tel. 4 61 18), at Constitución has a 24-hour **ATM** (bank open M-F 9am-3pm, Sa 10am-2pm). Stock up on groceries at **Hiperama** (tel. 9 21 04), Juárez at Minerva (open daily 9am-9pm). The **police** (tel. 4 09 75) can be found on Blanco and Obregón. The **Red Cross** (tel. 4 20 20) is on Carranza at Constitución (open 24hr.). **Farmacia Benavides** (tel. 4 55 55) is on Obregón at 5 de Mayo (open daily 8am-10pm). The **post office** (tel. 4 20 16) is at 16 de Septiembre and Madero (open M-F 8am-6pm, Sa 8am-1pm). The **postal code** is 31700. **LADATELs** cluster around the central square. The **phone code** is 169.

ACCOMMODATIONS AND FOOD Despite its small size, Nuevo Casas Grandes has plenty of great hotel and restaurant options. Accommodations with modern conveniences cluster on Constitución and on Juárez between 5 de Mayo and Jesús Urueta. The **Hotel Paquimé,** Juárez 401 (tel. 4 13 20; fax 4 47 20; email npinon@paquinet.com.mx), a block from the plaza, offers rooms complete with everything but a butler. Courtyard views, extra large beds, cable TV, air-conditioning, and carpeting help to make Hotel Paquimé a great, though slightly pricey, option. (Singles 145 pesos; doubles 166 pesos.) At Constitución 209 next to 5 de Mayo, you'll be welcomed to live it up at the **Hotel California** (tel. 4 22 14), a first-class joint with spacious, clean, air-conditioned rooms and tiled bathrooms. Ask for the economical rooms—they are a bit smaller but still have a TV and phone and cost 30 pesos less. (Singles 160 pesos; doubles 190 pesos; triples 220 pesos.) At the **Hotel Juárez,** Obregón 110 (tel. 4 02 33), a block from the bus station, you can talk to the friendly, English-speaking owner Mario; his place is one of the cheapest in town. Clean rooms are small and have a fan and a comfy bed, but the plumbing can be an adventure. (Singles 55 pesos; doubles 65 pesos; triples 75 pesos.)

The low tourist count means that the food is cheap and the nightlife soporific. **Restaurante Constantino** (tel. 4 10 05), Juárez at Minerva, accompanies its *enchiladas de pollo* with fresh bread, chips, and salsa (31 pesos). The *comida corrida* is only 29 pesos (open daily 7:30am-midnight). The clean and icily air-conditioned **Dinno's Pizza** (tel. 4 02 40), Minerva and Constitución, has jalapeño, cherry, pineapple, and coconut pizzas (small 35 pesos, medium 40 pesos, large 50 pesos; open daily 8am-11:30pm).

SIGHTS The area around Nuevo Casas Grandes has a lot to offer the archaeology fan. Possible trips include the **Cueva de Olla** (75km southwest), the **Arroyo de los Monos** (35km southeast), and **Mata Ortiz** (35km south). About 254km southeast of Nuevo Casas Grandes is **Madera,** from which the **Cuarenta Casas** archaeological site can be reached (54km north). Ask at the tourist office for more info. The most accessible and significant site, however, is the pre-Conquest city of **Paquimé.**

Paquimé (Casas Grandes)

*Tel. 2 40 37. 8km southwest of Nuevo Casas Grandes. From Nuevo Casas Grandes, take the beige and blue **municipal bus** at the corner of Constitución and 16 de Septiembre in front of the furniture store (10min., 1 per hr., 3 pesos). Get off at the main plaza of Casas Grandes and turn left onto the road in front of you, Constitución. This road quickly turns into a dirt road which rounds a bend and goes straight to Paquimé (a 10min. walk). Almost any **taxi** driver will take you to the site from Nuevo Casas Grandes and walk around with you for about 70 pesos per hour. **Museum and site open** roughly 10am-5pm. **Admission** 10 pesos; free on Sundays.*

Paquimé lay hidden underground for 600 years. Its architecture suggests that it grew out of two different cultures: its many-storied pueblos resemble those in the southwestern U.S., but other structures show the influence of central and southern Mexico. From 1000-1200, Paquimé was the most important agricultural and trading center in northern Mexico. The inhabitants kept parrots and turkeys in adobe pens and built indoor aqueducts and hidden cisterns to supply the pueblos in times of siege. They earned their livelihoods by farming and trading sea shells brought from the Pacific coast. First exhumed in the early 1970s, Paquimé is now an archaeological zone administered by the Mexican government. When you go, be sure to visit the **museum** adjacent to the site. Designed to blend in with the ruins and to have a low impact on the environment, the museum displays artifacts that have been found at Casas Grandes, while explaining the history and layout of the labyrinth of ruins. After visiting the museum, feel free to walk among the ancient adobe walls and experience the city as its inhabitants did over 700 years ago.

On summer afternoons, the dry and shadeless ruins can become a blazing inferno, as temperatures approach or exceed 100°F (38°C). Be sure to bring sun protection, a broad-brimmed hat (cheap *sombreros* are available in town), and, most importantly, a gigantic bottle of water to quench your thirst.

Chihuahua

The capital of the Republic's largest state, Chihuahua (pop. 800,000) is the vibrant, historically rich mecca of Northern Mexico. Exposed to the sandstorms of Mexico's vast northern desert, the city may seem little more than a far-flung outpost of civilization. The seclusion of Chihuahua convinced Pancho Villa to establish the headquarters of his revolutionary *División del Norte* here. During the conflict, his feisty gang of *bandidos* and vagabonds staged attacks against the Porfiriato, using Chihuahua as

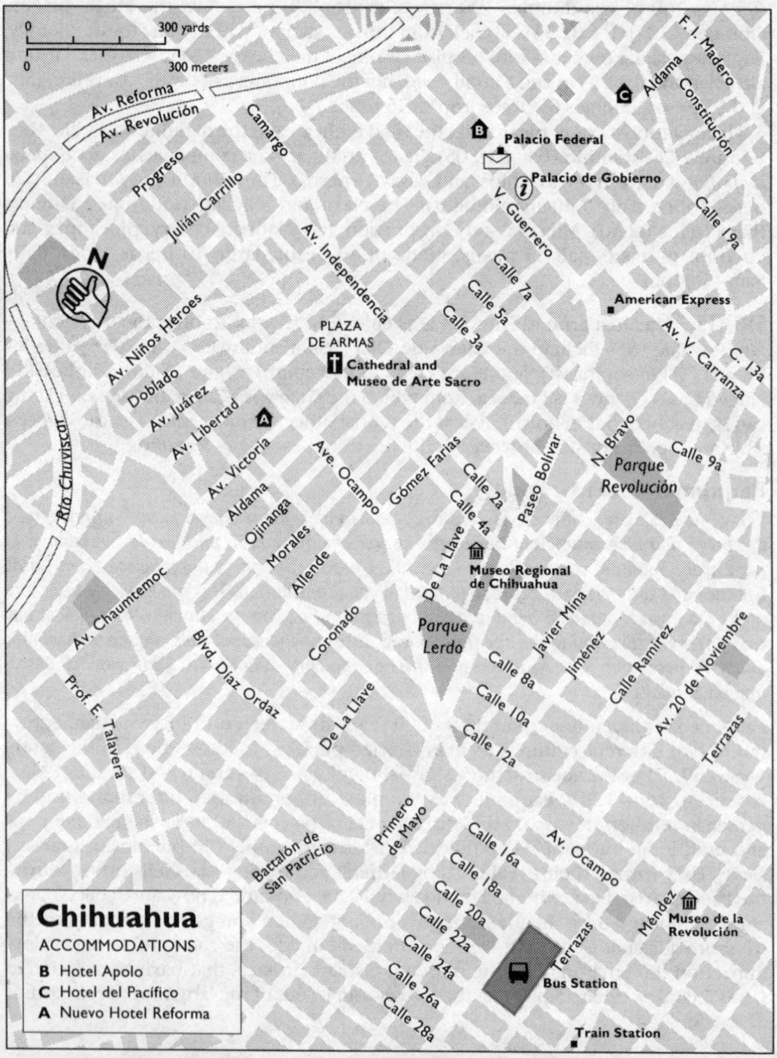

their base. Dilapidated shacks with crumbling adobe walls stretch as far as the eye can see, but then give way to a modern, bustling downtown and beautiful villas on the southern side of the city. As the cultural center of northern Mexico, Chihuahua attracts a wide array of people, from Mennonites to the *indígena* Tarahumara people living isolated in the nearby Sierra Madres, who venture into the city only on market day to sell handmade crafts. The plentiful plazas, *parques,* and vendors who line the downtown streets bring Chihuahua to life.

ORIENTATION

¡Ay! Chihuahua sprawls in every direction. Sliced in half by **Rte. 45** (the Pan-American Highway), the city serves as an important transportation hub for northern Mexico. Trains arrive at the **Estación Central de los FFNN,** just north of downtown. Trains headed for Los Mochis and Creel via the Barrancas del Cobre leave from the **Chihuahua al Pacífico** station, south of the city center off Ocampo, and two blocks from **20 de Noviembre.** To shorten the 20-minute walk to the *centro,* hop on one of the public buses (2.20 pesos) that run up and down Ocampo to Libertad, but be prepared for a ride—the old school buses can be an adventure. Alternatively, snag a cab (about 25 pesos), but set the price before you step in. From the bus station, a municipal bus (2.20 pesos) will take you to the cathedral. The kiosk near the main entrance to the bus station has a map indicating the various municipal bus routes and standard prices for cab rides to different zones.

Libertad is a pedestrian-only shopping arcade between **Independencia** and **Guerrero.** The two other main streets, **Victoria** and **Juárez,** run parallel to Libertad. **Av. Ocampo** crosses Juárez one block past the cathedral. Starting with Av. Independencia, parallel streets *(calles)* have ascending even numbers to the south and odd numbers to the north. *Avenidas* running north-south are named. Don't let Chihuahua's sheer size intimidate you; while the city is large, most sights are within walking distance from the **cathedral.** Budget hotels and restaurants cluster on the streets behind the cathedral. With the exception of Av. Victoria—the hub of Chihuahua's nightlife and replete with the flashing lights of bars and discos—the streets in Chihuahua are poorly lit. Women should avoid walking alone after dark.

PRACTICAL INFORMATION

Transportation

Airport: (tel. 20 51 04), 14km from town. **Aerolitoral,** Victoria 106 (tel. 20 06 16). **Aeroméxico,** Victoria 106 (tel. 15 63 03). **Aerovías de México,** Bolívar 405 (tel. 16 35 47). **Transportes Aéreos Ejecutivos,** Jiménez 1204 (tel. 16 02 37). All are open M-F 9am-6:30pm. "Aeropuerto" buses get you there from Ocampo. Buses heading downtown wait outside of the baggage area.

Buses: The main station (tel. 20 22 86) is a 20min. ride on the "Central Camionera" bus from Ocampo and Victoria. **Ómnibus de México** (tel. 20 15 80) sends its luxurious fleet to Aguascalientes (every 2hr., 352 pesos), Casas Grandes (6 per day, 105 pesos), Durango (7 per day, 217 pesos), Guadalajara (2:40am, 3, and 7:05pm, 440 pesos), Matamoros (2 per day, 415 pesos), Mexico City (7 per day, 539 pesos), Monterrey (4 per day, 293 pesos), Querétaro (1 per day, 457 pesos), and Saltillo (4 per day, 246 pesos). **Transportes Caballero Azteca** (tel. 29 02 42) sends buses to Hermosillo (14hr., 2, 7:30, and 10pm, 350 pesos), Tijuana (22hr., 6:30 and 10pm, 525 pesos), and Zacatecas (12hr., 14 per day 6am-11pm, 220 pesos). **Transportes Chihuahuenses** (tel. 29 02 42) sends buses daily to Cd. Juárez (5hr., every hr. until 9pm, 134 pesos), Mazatlán (18hr., 10:15am and 5:30pm, 328 pesos). **Turismos Rápidos Cuauhtémoc-Anáhuac** (tel. 10 44 33) has service to Cuauhtémoc (1½hr., every 30min. 5am-7:30pm, 27 pesos). **Estrella Blanca** has a slightly older fleet of buses that chugs to nearly all of the above cities for lower prices but requires more travel time.

Car Rental: Hertz, Av. Revolución 514 (tel. 16 64 73; fax 15 78 18), at José Nari Santos. VW Beetle with insurance and 300km per day costs 351 pesos per day.

Tourist and Financial Services

Tourist Office: (tel. 10 10 77; fax 16 00 32), on Aldama between Carranza and Guerrero, in the Palacio del Gobierno across from the Plaza Hidalgo. Helpful, English-speaking staff dispenses maps and brochures. Open daily 9am-7pm.

Currency Exchange: BanPaís, Victoria 104 (tel. 16 16 59 or 10 15 93), 1 block from the cathedral past Independencia. No exchange fee for traveler's checks. Open M-F 9am-2:30pm. **Hotel San Francisco** (tel. 10 73 30), across the street, has 24hr. exchange. **ATMs** near the lobbies of all the tall banks downtown near the *zócalo.*

American Express: Vicente Guerrero 1207 (tel. 10 10 77; fax 16 00 32), past Allendex where Guerrero curves to become Bolívar. Open M-F 9am-6pm, Sa 9am-noon.

Emergency and Communications

Police: Av. Homero 540 (tel. 81 28 88 or 21 35 75), across from the Ford plant, at the exit to Juárez.

Red Cross: (tel. 11 22 11 or 11 14 84), Calle 24 and Revolución. Open 24hr.

Pharmacy: Farmacia Mendoza, Calle Aldama 1901 (tel. 16 69 32 or 16 66 38), at Calle 19, away from the cathedral past Plaza de Hidalgo. Open 24hr. **Farmacia Hidalgo** (tel. 10 65 08), Guerrero and Aldama.

Hospital: Hospital General (tel. 16 00 22 or 15 60 84), Revolución and Colón, in Colonia Centro. **Clínica del Centro,** Ojinaga 816 (tel. 16 00 22).

Post Office: (tel. 37 12 00), on Libertad between Guerrero and Carranza, in the Palacio Federal. Open M-F 8am-7pm, Sa 9am-1pm. **Postal Code:** 31000.

Telephones: Silver **LADATELs** gleam in the sun all over the *zócalo.* Long distance service available in expensive hotels and at the plaza, in front of the cathedral.

Phone Code: 14.

ACCOMMODATIONS

Hotels in Chihuahua are like the city itself—charm smiling through the grit. Economical hotels lie in the area behind the cathedral between Victoria and Juárez. More luxurious accommodations are available, but for about 3 times the price of the perfectly comfortable economical set.

Hotel Apolo (tel. 16 11 00 or 16 11 01; fax 16 11 02), Juárez at Carranza, in the *centro.* A step up in price—and amenities. Dark but majestic lobby with sculptures, chandeliers, and paintings. All clean, bright rooms have A/C and nice, tiled bathrooms; those on the 3rd and 4th floors come with color TVs. Cafeteria, bar, and parking. Singles 150 pesos; doubles 165 pesos. Discounts for large groups.

Nuevo Hotel Reforma, Victoria 809 (tel. 10 68 48; fax 16 08 35). Unique and delightful architecture. The old courtyard is covered by a warehouse-like roof and is connected to the 2nd floor by an X-shaped staircase. The bug-free rooms have fans, soft beds, clean tile bathrooms, and incredibly tall ceilings. Singles 76 pesos; doubles 85 pesos; add 8 pesos for TV.

Hotel del Pacífico, Aldama 1911 (tel. 10 59 13), at Calle 21, a few blocks from the Palacio de Gobierno. A great bargain. Although the lobby is dark and musty, the clean rooms have A/C, large bathrooms, and decent foam mattresses with cement bases. Gregarious management and a restaurant. Parking available. Singles 70 pesos; doubles 80 pesos; triples 90 pesos; add 8 pesos for TV.

FOOD

Eateries in Chihuahua are not geared toward tourists. Some of the best meals can be found in small *cantinas,* where bands serenade drunken (and often rowdy) men. However, women should be careful in the *cantinas* alone. For a quick, cheap bite to eat, try the shopping arcade along Libertad between Independencia and Guerrero.

Rosticería Los Pollos, Aldama 702 (tel. 10 59 77), between Calle 7 and Guerrero. Cafeteria-style dining at its best and brightest. Plastic booths, mirrored walls, and A/C spice up your excellent *pollo en mole* with rice and tortillas (only 20 pesos). To finish it off, have some sweet *arroz con leche* (5 pesos). Open 9am-8pm.

Mi Café, Victoria 1000 (tel. 10 12 38), at Calle 10, across from Hotel San Juan. Put on your sunglasses to enter this bright, laid-back, 50s-style diner with melon-colored vinyl booths and an orange and white checkered ceiling. A 37-peso order of chicken comes with bread, soup, rice, potatoes, and dessert—a huge meal. Burritos 12-13 pesos. Breakfast platter 25-30 pesos. Open daily 9am-midnight.

Restaurant-Bar Degá (tel. 16 77 70), on Victoria at Hotel San Francisco near the *zócalo.* Oozing with class, this joint offers a rare (if pricey) chance at a vegetarian meal. The *plato vegetariano* (45 pesos) includes vegetarian soup, a soy steak, avocado, and white rice; the *ceviche vegetariano* (30 pesos) has mushrooms and olive oil. Fresh carrot, papaya, or grapefruit juice costs 15 pesos. Open daily 7am-10:30pm.

SIGHTS AND ENTERTAINMENT

The stately and regal 19th-century **Palacio de Gobierno** stands in the center of Chihuahua on Aldama. Inside, Aarón Piña Moratell's famous and beautiful **murals** tell the story of Chihuahua. Look for a **nude Emiliano Zapata,** whose modesty is maintained by another soldier's **conveniently placed rifle.** Behind the Palacio de Gobierno is the **Palacio Federal,** housing the post office and the jail of Miguel Hidalgo, where he was detained before being shot. A few blocks from the palace, on Victoria and Calle 2, is the giant **cathedral.** While construction began in 1725, the church was actually finished more than a century later in 1826. The unique stone facade is from the Baroque period. The area southwest of the *zócalo* offers an excellent, leafy retreat from downtown. At **Quinta Luz,** also called **Museo de la Revolución** (Pancho Villa's house; tel. 16 29 58), visitors can relive the turbulence of the revolution by looking through an extensive collection of documents and photographs, paintings of Señor Villa, the bullet-ridden Dodge in which he was assassinated, his household furnishings, and his vast collection of weapons. *(Open daily 9am-1pm and 3-7pm. Admission 10 pesos.)* Soldiers outside stand at attention. To reach Quinta Luz, hike 1.5km south on Ocampo, turn left on 20 de Noviembre, and go two blocks to Calle 10 and Méndez. Turn right, and Villa's house is two blocks down.

On the way to the Villa household is another, equally worthy museum: the **Quinta Gameros Centro Cultural Universitario,** also called the **Museo Regional de Chihuahua** (tel. 16 66 84), on the corner of Calle 4 and Paseo Bolívar. *(Open Tu-Su 10am-2pm and 4-7pm. Admission 10 pesos, children 5 pesos.)* This amazing architectural feat is one of the more stunning mansions in Mexico. Mining engineer Don Manuel Gameros, the aristocrat who had it built, never lived in it—the Revolution drove him to El Paso, Texas. The house was seized by revolutionaries and at one point served as Pancho Villa's barracks. Some astounding art-nouveau furniture and rooms now wow observers; look for the 3m-high toilet and the beautiful mahogany dining room woodwork. Upstairs, local painters exhibit their works.

Back in the *centro,* the basement of the cathedral hides the **Museo de Arte Sacro,** (tel. 10 38 77), Libertad and Calle 2. *(Open M-F 10am-2pm and 4-6pm. Admission 5 pesos, students and children 3 pesos.)* Pastoral religious paintings from the 18th century mingle with photos and portraits from the Pope's most recent visit to Chihuahua. For those craving more secular pleasures, the recently opened **Museo de Arte Contemporáneo** (tel. 29 33 00, ext. 3700), at Carranza and Aldama, across from the Palacio del Gobierno, has a formidable collection of modern art. *(Open Tu-Su 10am-8pm. Admission 5 pesos, students and teachers 3 pesos. Free Wednesdays.)* Sebastián's geometrical sculptures and Diego Rivera's sketch of a two-headed man/beast are among the highlights.

At night, catch a flick at **Cinépolis** (tel. 17 52 22), Vallarta at Zaragoza. *(Shows 3-9:30pm; 20 pesos, first show 15 pesos, Wednesdays 12 pesos.)* To get there, hop on a *"Cerro de la Cruz"* bus in front of the *Héroes de la Revolución* building, in the *centro* (15min., every 8min. until 9:30pm, 2.20 pesos). If the buses have stopped running, you'll have to take a 20-peso cab back. Afterward, you can discuss the film at one of the many cafes in the center of town. **Café Calicanto,** Aldama 411 (tel. 10 44 52), serves snacks and a wide selection of coffees and beers. *(Open Su-Th 4pm-midnight, F-Sa 5pm-3am.)* There is live music on weekends. **La Casa de Los Milagros,** on Victoria across from the Hotel Reforma, serves up an array of drinks in a classy courtyard setting. *(Open Su-W 3pm-midnight, F-Sa 3pm-2am.)* A *mariachi* band and occasional rock-and-roll bands serenade the many couples who flock to this romantic bar/cafe. Nightclubs tend to be far from the center, but taxis will get you there. **Quinto Sofia,** in front of Lerdo Park, brings out a twenty-something crowd to listen to live Spanish rock (beers 12 pesos; cover 15 pesos after 10:30pm). A somewhat older crowd flocks to **Old Town,** Juárez 3331 (tel. 10 32 71), between Colón and Calle 39 (cover F-Sa 30 pesos. Open Th 9pm-1am, F-Sa 9pm-2:30am.)

Hidalgo de Parral

Nestled in the foothills of the Sierra Madre, Hidalgo Parral (pop. 20,000) arose as the town surrounding the La Negrita mine, which was founded in 1631. The mine, now known as La Prieta, has been closed more than 10 years but still sits on the hills above town, keeping watch over the city to which it gave birth. With very little tourist activity, Parral (as it is affectionately known) is not only one of the cleanest cities in northwest Mexico, but also one of the most relaxed. The Río Parral, which hasn't seen water for five years, winds through downtown and "laps" up against the backsides of shops and hotels. The nine bridges that cross the river provide great vantage points to scan the downtown scene.

ORIENTATION AND PRACTICAL INFORMATION From the bus station, exit the main doors and go left down the entrance street. This runs into **Av. Independencia.** Turn left and you are on the main strip headed toward downtown, which is well within walking distance. The highways which intersect in Parral also empty onto Av. Independencia; from the junction, turn right to get to downtown. Parral's city center is compact and made for walking—this is a good thing, since there is no public transportation. The river runs through the center of downtown, and while streets zig-zag haphazardly, you're never far from the center if you stay near the river. Just after Av. Independencia crosses the river, it runs beside the **cathedral plaza,** where it intersects **Calle Benitez** and **Calle Hernandez,** the two other largest streets in town. There is no tourist office, but residents are happy to point you in the right direction. Buses leave from the Parral bus terminal off Av. Independencia near the Motel Comino Real. **Omnibus de Mexico** and **Estrella Blanca** run buses to Chihuahua (4hr., 5 per day, 95 pesos), Cuauhtémoc (3hr., 4 per day, 85 pesos), Juárez (7hr., 2 per day, 156 pesos), and Mexico City (20hr., 2 per day, 200 pesos). To **exchange currency,** the easiest place to go is **Banco Serfin** on Av. Independencia next to the old theater. The largest **grocery store** in town is **El Comino,** on Av. Independencia just outside of downtown, next to Hotel Margarita's. The **post office** is on Calle Maclovio Hernandez next to the museum, two blocks along the river from the cathedral plaza (open M-F 9am-4pm). The **postal code** is 33860. The **phone code** is 152.

ACCOMMODATIONS AND FOOD Parral has some very stately old hotels left over from its mining boomtown days. **Hotel Turista,** Independencia 12 (tel. 2 44 89), next to the old theater, has spacious rooms with commanding views of the city that come with air-conditioning, TV, and a phone (singles 120 pesos; doubles 160 pesos; triples 190 pesos). Food in Parral can be good even though restaurants are relatively scarce. For a sit-down meal indoors, the best bets are the restaurants attached to Hotels Turista and San José. **Restaurant Turista** serves up fantastic *comida corrida* (22 pesos; daily until 4pm). The true hidden culinary treasures, however, are the many family-run **taquerías** that dot the downtown area. Sit at the tables along the sidewalk and watch all of Parral stroll by, while chowing down on an order of tacos (10 pesos) or a burrito (6 pesos). Try the different homemade salsas at each stand. They'll light up your life—and set your mouth on fire. (Most stands open about 10am-10pm.)

SIGHTS AND ENTERTAINMENT Home to Pancho Villa during the last years of his life, Parral has many museums and sights dedicated to this hero of the Revolution. Chief among them is the **Museo de General Francisco Villa,** upstairs in the town library, near the post office (open M-F 9am-8pm; free). A bronze plaque marks the spot where Villa was assassinated when his car came to rest after being riddled by over 150 bullets. Although Villa's body rests in the **Cementerio Municipal,** on the outskirts of town, many of Parral's residents believe that, through a government conspiracy, his body has been robbed from the grave and moved to Mexico City. Other noteworthy sites in Parral include some of the magnificent buildings built with mining money. The interior of the **Catedral de San José** is decorated with ore from local mines and dazzles visitors with its sheer immensity. The **Templo de la Virgen de Fátima,** on a hill by the mine overlooking the city, even has pews made from local ore. The **Palacio Alvarado,** constructed by one of the mine owners, is an enormous mansion that rises up from among the ordinary houses on the city's northern side. Stop and gawk, but don't go in—part of the family still lives there.

If nightlife is what you're after, Parral has options besides the usual cinderblock *cantinas.* **J. Quísseme** is a lounge/dance club on Av. Independencia that starts hoppin' after 10pm (beer 10 pesos; cover 10 pesos; open Th-Sa 8pm-3am). The **Lone Star** club by the stadium is also a local favorite (open W-Sa 9pm-3am). If you are lucky enough to be in town at the right time, check out the **bullfights** two weekends each summer (usually in mid-July and late-August), complete with carnivals and day-long parties. Follow the noise to the stadium.

Cuauhtémoc Mennonite Colonies

Among the masses of Mexican businessfolk, street vendors, and families around Cuauhtémoc's *zócalo,* a blond-haired, blue-eyed Caucasian in overalls or a long dress will occasionally amble by—hardly a typical sight in northwest Mexico. It's not surprising in Cuauhtémoc; the town and surrounding communities are home to about 40,000 Mennonites. The Mennonites are a pacifist religious group founded in the 16th century in Germany. After being expelled from virtually every country in Europe due to their refusal to serve in the military and their steadfast determination to educate their children privately, a large number of Mennonites settled in the agricultural fields just outside Cuauhtémoc. The hard-working, almost compulsively clean group of Mennonites that now inhabits the area is renowned for the cheese that they produce. Most Cuauhtémoc Mennonites have abandoned most of the traditional tenants of their religion, such as the prohibition against the use of electricity or mechanization and the use of Lower German (everyone speaks Spanish here), but traditional dress is still standard: wide-brimmed, white hats and long, flowered dresses for women, tall hats and overalls for men.

ORIENTATION AND PRACTICAL INFORMATION Cuauhtémoc lies midway between Creel and Chihuahua and is a two- to three-hour bus ride from each. The highway into Cuauhtémoc from Chihuahua continues past the city and into the **Mennonite area,** organized in small communities called **campos.** Each *campo* has a number and is laid out in an orderly manner, with a main street, several farms, a creamery, a church, and a school. *Campos* are organized by number: on the left of the highway, numbers start at one and go up, on the right they start in the mid-20s and count down, and after a certain point, the field numbers switch to the 100s. The center of Cuauhtémoc is at the *zócalo,* with parallel odd-numbered streets increasing to the east and even-numbered streets increasing to the west. The cross-streets running east-west, Allende and Morelos, are the main streets in town. The **Estrella Blanca bus station** (tel. 2 10 18), Allende at Calle 9, runs buses to Basaseachi (5hr., 8am, 12:30pm, and 4:30pm, 70 pesos), Casas Grandes (5hr., 4 per day, 90 pesos), Chihuahua (1½hr., every 30min. 8:30am-9:40pm, 35 pesos), Cd. Juárez (9hr., 2 per day, 155 pesos), and Creel (3½hr., every 2hr. 7:30am-7:30pm, 64 pesos). **Public buses** (2 pesos) run all over the city and stop at blue bus stop signs—the main stop is on Calle 3 between Allende and Guerrero. **Banca Serfín** (tel. 2 63 33), Melgar (Calle 1) at Allende, has a 24-hour **ATM** and **changes money** at very good rates (open M-F 9am-5pm). The **Super Bonanza** (2 18 60), on Morelos between Calle 5 and 7, is a gigantic **supermar-**

ket (open M-Sa 8am-9pm, Su 8am-2pm). In case of an **emergency,** dial 06. The **police** (tel. 2 28 56) and the **Red Cross** (tel. 2 06 87) can be reached round the clock. **Farmacia Cuauhtémoc** is on Morelos 321 (tel. 1 48 77) between Calles 3 and 5 (open M-Sa 8am-midnight, Su 10am-6pm). The **post office** (tel. 2 03 14) is on Calle 4 at Guerrero, 1 block south of Allende (open M-F 8am-6pm). The **postal code** is 31500. The **phone code** is 158.

ACCOMMODATIONS AND FOOD Most hotels line Allende and cluster near the *zócalo*. **Hotel Princessa,** Allende 204 (tel. 2 07 83), one block west of the *zócalo,* boasts the cleanest rooms in town with carpeted floors, beautiful furniture, air-conditioning, TVs, and phones (singles 93 pesos; doubles 113 pesos; triples 120 pesos). **Nuevo Hotel Gran Visión,** on Allende between Calles 7 and 9, across from the bus station, offers tidy, smallish rooms with air-conditioning, TVs, and phones (singles 100 pesos; doubles 110 pesos; triples 130 pesos). If you're here to sample Mennonite culture, you might as well get out of the dirty city and into the ultra-clean kitchen of a Mennonite restaurant. Most have sinks with hand soap outside the bathrooms. A few restaurants line the main highway through the *campos*—try the **Travelers Restaurant** (tel. 2 64 70), between *Campo* 3B and *Campo* 19 near the Motel Gasthaus. Traditional Mennonite foods are very rich and very tasty: the *empanadas de requesón* (dough filled with cottage cheese and covered with cream sauce, 20 pesos) and *fideos con crema* (noodles with ham or sausage, also drowned in cream sauce, 19 pesos) are not exceptions. Eat here more than twice, however, and your cholesterol count may hit quadruple digits. (Open daily 9am-9pm.) **El Chalet,** Allende 544 (tel. 2 44 4 3), serves up traditional Mexican meals in a Spanish mission setting. Ask to sit in the courtyard and sample some of the best salsa and chips around. A full meal runs around 30 pesos. (Open M 8am-4pm, Tu-Sa 8am-10pm, Su 9am-9pm.)

SIGHTS AND ENTERTAINMENT There are a handful of ways to explore the Mennonite communities of Cuauhtémoc, but unless you have a car there are no easy ways. Public buses don't go into the Mennonite areas and can only give you a headstart on the 4km walk to the nearest colony. Hitchhikers report success on and off the main highway, but drivers are scarce on the desolate dirt roads between colonies removed from the highway. Another option is the Mennonite father-and-son team **Cumbres Friesen** (tel. 2 54 57 or 2 30 64; fax 2 40 60), at Calle 3 between Rayón and Guerrero, who provide tours tailored to your interests for around US$15 per person, depending on the sights you want to cover and the duration of the tour (open M-F 9am-7pm, Sa 9am-1pm). The owner of **Motel Gasthaus** also offers tours, but to get there you have to get the 13km down the highway somehow. Tours typically include a look inside an authentic Mennonite home, a tour of a cheese factory and a machinery plant, and a meal (at your expense) at a Mennonite restaurant. If you want to check out the Mennonite colony on your own, you'll need a car to get from place to place. To see a Mennonite cheese factory in action, take a left at the 2-B/22 sign and follow the road heading down into the village. After passing a school and church (only open Sunday) on your left, take a right into the **Quesería América,** one of the 20 to 25 cheese factories in the 80 or so Mennonite villages in the area. Make sure you visit in the morning, when the cheese is actually made. To see a genuine **Mennonite household,** take a left at the "Hotel La Estancia" sign at *Campo* 6A. Follow the road about 2km, then take a right down another road for a bit. You'll see a white house with a blue stripe around the bottom, surrounded by a white picket fence and tall trees; it's home to the **familia Guenther.** The friendly, Spanish-speaking family will show you their huge but stark kitchen with its jam-filled pantry, their living room, and their special guest room with a valuable wooden chair. Big families are standard among the Mennonites, and the Guenthers are no exception: Mrs. Guenther's 12 children all live nearby. After taking you on a tour of the house, Mrs. Guenther will offer her traditional Mennonite knitted crafts for sale. Outside, scope out the horizon for the **radio tower,** through which Mennonites communicated before they succumbed to that modern luxury, telephones. Before, they all had walkie-talkies. 10-4 *familia* Guenther.

Creel

High amid the stunning peaks and gorges of the Sierra Madres and lodged among pine forests, jagged rock formations, and rolling hills and valleys, the small village of Creel (pop. 5000; altitude 2340m) welcomes travelers with natural beauty, human warmth, and refreshing mountain air. Cabins dot the hillsides, the train rumbles through town two or three times a day, animals freely roam the streets, and the town's residents are friendly and rugged. Residents are used to life without modern conveniences, although with the influx of tourists, modern conveniences can now be found.

Creel is most popular as a base from which to explore the stunning **Copper Canyon** (see p. 222). Although tourism to Creel has increased lately, it hasn't damaged the unique ambience of the town nor has it substantially altered the lives of the 50,000 Tarahumara Indians living in the mountains surrounding Creel. Of Mexico's many *indígena* groups, the Tarahumara have best warded off modern Mexican culture, living in isolated caves and wooden houses and resisting all efforts to settle them in villages. They are famous for their non-stop long-distance sacred footraces, which last up to 72 hours. The countryside around Creel is also home to a number of other *indígena* groups, including the Pima to the northwest, the Northern Tepehuan to the south, and the Guarojio to the west.

ORIENTATION

You can use the railroad tracks as a rough compass: toward Chihuahua is north and toward Los Mochis is south. The *zócalo* is the center of town and the best place from which to get your bearings. With your back to the **bus station** and facing the **train station,** the *zócalo* is down a small hill in front of you and a bit to the right. The main street, **Mateos,** runs parallel to the trains on the opposite side of the *zócalo* and is the only street around the *zócalo* that extends any distance in one direction. Everything you need can be found on or near Mateos. Street numbers go up to the right and down to the left as you turn onto Mateos from the tracks. **Chapultepec,** farther north, runs parallel to Mateos and up to the tracks. **Avenidas Ferrocarril** and **Francisco Villa** run parallel to the train tracks on the opposite side of Mateos. Be sure to check out the map next to Banca Serfín.

PRACTICAL INFORMATION

Transportation

Trains: Av. Tarahumara 57 (tel. 6 00 15), right in town on the tracks—you can't miss it. Trains leave daily for Chihuahua (first-class 6hr., 3pm, 188 pesos; second-class 7hr., Tu, Th, Sa 4pm, 41 pesos) and Los Mochis (first-class 9hr., 11:30am, 225 pesos; second-class 10hr., M, W, F at 1pm, 50 pesos). You can get off anywhere along the way and avoid paying full price. Tickets in advance are no longer sold at the train station, so scramble on quickly when your train pulls up and elbow for a seat, then pay the conductor as he comes around. See **The Train Through the Canyons,** p. 223.

Buses: Estrella Blanca (tel. 6 00 73), in a small white and green building across the tracks from the *zócalo,* sends buses to Chihuahua (5hr., 7 per day, 90 pesos) and Cuauhtémoc (3hr., 5 per day, 64 pesos). From the Restaurant Herradero at Mateos 39, **Canyon buses** (tel. 6 02 79 or 6 02 30) leave for Batopilas (6hr., Tu, Th, and Sa 7:15am, 80 pesos; return trip leaves Batopilas M, W, and F 5:30am).

Bicycle Rental: Expediciones Umarie, south along the tracks next to the 2-story cabin. Rents bikes (65-80 pesos per day, 40-50 pesos per half-day, 12 pesos per hr.) as well as helmet and gloves (15 pesos); they also offer a half-day introductory **rock climbing** course (150 pesos per person, min. 2 people). Bikes can also be rented from **Complejo Turístico Arareko,** Mateos 33 (tel. 6 01 26), south of the *zócalo* for 15 pesos an hour.

Tourist and Financial Services

Tourist Information: Artesanías Misión (tel. 6 00 97), on the north side of the *zócalo.* Not an official tourist office, but the best source of information on Creel and the surrounding area. Sells books about the Tarahumara, crafts, and maps (12-40 pesos). English spoken. Open M-Sa 9:30am-1pm and 3-6pm, Su 9:30am-1pm.

Currency Exchange: Banca Serfín, Plaza 201 (tel. 6 02 50 or 6 00 60), next door to the Misión. Dollars exchanged 9am-4pm. Open M-F 9am-5pm. There is an **ATM.**

Local Services

Market: Abarrotes Pérez, on Mateos next to Cabañas Bertis. Fruit, vegetables, and purified water. Open daily 9am-9pm.

Laundromat: Lavandería Veno, Francisco Villa 112 (tel. 6 01 39). Across the tracks from the police. 20 pesos per load for wash and dry. Bring your load by 6pm if you want same-day service. Open daily 9am-8pm.

Emergency and Communications

Police: (tel. 6 04 50), in the Presidencia Seccional, on the south side of the *zócalo.*

Pharmacy: Farmacia Rodríguez, Mateos 43 (tel. 6 00 52). Open M-Sa 9am-2pm and 3:30-9pm, Su 10am-1pm.

Medical Services: Clínica Santa Teresita, on Calle Parroquia (tel. 6 01 05) at the end of the street, 2 blocks from Mateos. Little English spoken. Open M-F 10am-1pm and 3-5pm, Sa 10am-1pm. Open for emergencies 24hr.

Post Office: (tel. 6 02 58), in the Presidencia Seccional, on the south side of the *zócalo.* Open M-F 9am-3pm. **Postal Code:** 33200.

Fax: In the same building as the post office. Open M-F 9am-3pm.

Telephones: LADATELs have just been installed in town and tend to cluster around the *zócalo* and on Mateos and Francisco Villa.

Phone Code: 145.

ACCOMMODATIONS AND CAMPING

Due to Creel's flourishing popularity, the number of hotels here has multiplied and competition for tourists' pesos has become intense. Prices are often negotiable during low season, and budget rooms are never hard to find. Most budget rooms are a block or two from the *zócalo.*

Margarita's Casa de Huéspedes, Mateos 11 (tel. 6 00 45), across from the *zócalo.* An international backpacker's mecca. You'll have no trouble finding it—a young emissary meets almost every train and bus to lead you to the house, where you mingle with Margarita's family, friends, and guests, who come from every corner of the globe. Make it clear that you want to go to the *casa,* not the hotel. Freshly renovated rooms are spacious and beautifully furnished with floor tiles and pine furniture. Beds in shared rooms 30-40 pesos. If you must sleep alone, Margarita's has private rooms too. Singles 150 pesos; doubles 180 pesos. To top it all off, prices include two home-cooked meals and are negotiable—you may be able to work for room and board. English-speaking staff. Tours offered.

Cabañas Bertis, Mateos 31 (tel. 6 00 86). Log cabin feel with paneled walls, thick wool blankets, and a fireplace or wood stove in each abode. Rooms are spotless and much larger than any others in town. Parking, TVs available. A/C and heater. Singles 80 pesos; doubles 120 pesos; triples 150 pesos. Tours offered.

Pensión Creel, Mateos 61 (tel. 6 00 71; fax 6 00 82). Walk down Mateos away from the *zócalo.* Budget rooms available farther from downtown near the trails and woods. Boasts a fully equipped kitchen, a large common room with a roaring fireplace and magazine shelf, and shared bathrooms. Complimentary bus service transports you to the *pensión,* though it is within walking distance. Prices range from 50 pesos (if you have your own sleeping bag) to 100 pesos (with continental breakfast). French and English spoken.

Hotel Korachi, Francisco Villa (tel. 6 02 07), across the tracks from the train station. A wanna-be hunting lodge. Clean bedrooms with dark, wood-paneled walls and comfy beds, and wood and gas heaters in the bathroom. Singles 120 pesos; doubles

145 pesos. Strange but clean *cabañas* with animal skins on the walls sit under shady trees and include private bath and wood supply. Singles 150 pesos; doubles 180 pesos.

For those who would rather immerse themselves in nature, the campground and lodges around **Lago Arareko** are the way to go. The **campground** (10 pesos per person) is on the northwestern shore, on a hill overlooking the lake. The site sports 31 barbecue and fire pits, 12 latrines, hot showers, and picnic areas. You'll need a car to get there, though. Drive down Av. Mateos until you hit the highway and turn left towards Cusárare. The campground is 8km down on the left. The **Batosárachi Lodge** (tel. 6 01 26) on the southeast corner of this vast body of water, houses up to 50 in the three Tarahumara-style cabins (each has bunk beds, a common room, heaters, and hot water). At both places, guests can cook their own meals or let themselves be served. Both are located next to the campground. A new **KOA Campground** is just a few blocks down Mateos from Cusárare and welcomes campers and RVs for rock-bottom rates.

FOOD

Several inexpensive restaurants in town have friendly atmospheres and good, home-cooked fare, and most of them are on Av. Mateos. Everything is cheap, but not necessarily good. Picnicking spots lie on the quiet hillsides outside town.

Cafeteria "Gaby," Mateos 48, across from the grocery store, serves up any kind of home-cooked meal you desire. Sit in Gaby's kitchen and enjoy out-of-this-world food. Breakfast 20 pesos, lunch 25 pesos, dinner 25 pesos. Open daily 7am-10pm.

Restaurante Todo Rico (All-Rich), Mateos 37 (tel. 6 02 05) at Chapultepec. Lip-smacking good food served up in a bright, clean, and friendly atmosphere. *Comida corrida* is a mere 20 pesos. Try the *caldo de oso* (fish, not bear, soup) for 25 pesos or the tuna salad (19 pesos). Open daily 7:30am-11pm.

Restaurante Veronica, Mateos 34. This simple joint is a local favorite. Enjoy an order of eggs any style (15 pesos) or the *comida corrida* for 20 pesos. Open daily 7:30am-11pm.

SIGHTS AND ENTERTAINMENT

Creel's real draw, of course, is the canyon and surrounding countryside. If you pass Tarahumara cave dwellings, look at the caves from the road, but don't take their obvious accessibility as an invitation to approach more closely or to take a photograph. To explore the beautiful and wild surroundings, you'll need a car, a tour guide, or a brave heart to get there (see **Near Creel,** p. 222, and **Barrancas del Cobre (Copper Canyon),** p. 222).

The **Casa de las Artesanías del Estado de Chihuahua** (tel. 6 00 80) is on Av. Ferrocarril 178, in the old railroad station. *(Open Tu-Sa 9am-1pm and 3-7pm, Su 9am-1pm. Admission 5 pesos.)* There, local and Tarahumara arts, crafts, and a random assortment of historical relics are on display. But what steals the show is the mummy in the back room, which some Tarahumara claim as a relative and upon which local schoolchildren periodically sprinkle flowers.

Most of Creel's sights, interestingly enough, lie just outside of Creel. **Lago Arareko** is 8km down the highway toward Cusárare and has tons of trails with fabulous vistas— perfect for a day hike. Day tours leaving from the *zócalo* (hours can be arranged any time; about 60 pesos) venture into the nearby Barrancas del Cobre. Exploring the countryside with a **bike** is also a good option (see **Practical Information,** p. 219).

At night, a local *cantina* with a touch of class is **Laylo's Lounge and Bar,** inside **El Caballo Bayo** restaurant and hotel, López Mateos 25 (tel. 6 01 36). *(Open daily 3pm-1am.)* Its male-dominated crowd is classic *cantina*, but the shiny wood paneling and nice decor outdo most watering holes. **Tio Moleas,** Mateos 33 at Batiste Caro, also breaks *cantina* stereotypes and has a laid-back lounge atmosphere. *(Open daily 11am-1am.)* Satisfy a late night snack craving here—the place doubles as a restaurant during the day. Many local hotels, including the **Motel Parador** and the **Hotel Margarita's,** keep their guests entertained with night-time diversions at the bar, including *mariachis.* Hotels rock with live music and many all-too-willing dance partners—it is the job of the *animador* to get the women up and dancing with the male patrons. While most establishments in Creel close before 9pm, a few are open late, and the town usually has a few tourists roaming the streets or people strumming guitars until midnight. On Saturday nights, the **Casino de Creel** in front of the plaza offers outdoor and indoor dances, to which both locals and tourists are welcome (men 15 pesos, women 10 pesos; festivities run from 8pm-1am).

■ Near Creel

The best excursions are the ones that explore the surrounding Sierra Tarahumara/ Copper Canyon region. See **The Canyons: North of Creel to Basaseachi Falls** (p. 225), **The Canyons: South of Creel to Urique** (p. 226), **The Canyons: The Road to South to Batopilas** (p. 227), **Batopilas and Satevó** (p. 228).

Despite this, much of the immediate area is also very beautiful and worth exploring. Four kilometers down the road from Creel (and a left on a dirt road) lies the humble **San Ignacio Mission,** constructed in 1744 and still in use today—services are conducted Sundays at 11am in Rarámuri, the native language of the Tarahumara. The stone mission is dedicated to Saint Ignatius Loyola, the community's patron saint, and can easily be made into a daytrip along with the **Valle de los Hongos** (Valley of the Mushrooms, a.k.a. Valley of the Frogs or Ducks). The valley contains immense, oddly shaped stones formed by the San Ignacio River. To reach the valley and mission by foot, walk down Mateos past the Motel Parador. When the road forks, take the smaller branch to the left, beside the cemetery. A kilometer or so out of town you will pass through the gates of the Tarahumara's *ejidos* (communal lands), containing the caves in which they live. After the cultivated fields, the valley is to the right, and the mission is at the bottom of the hill. On the way you will pass through small dells and plains surrounded by rocky cliffs, pines, and oak trees characteristic of the Tarahumara highlands. Travelers can also hike to **Laguna Arareko,** an enormous lake 3km long and eight acres in area. Just bear right when the road forks past Mateos and follow the path 7km southeast. The water here is cold and contains dangerous weeds below the surface, so swimming is discouraged. From the small station next to the lake you can rent paddle boats. Nearby is **Recohuata Hot Springs,** where you can take a break from a long day of hiking in the soothing, warm waters (admission 10 pesos). A tour guide will take you for a one-and-a-half-hour ride and then send you on a 600m hike down into the canyon (around 60 pesos). The **Valle de las Monjas** (Valley of the Nuns), 9km away, makes a great daytrip on horseback.

■ Barrancas del Cobre (Copper Canyon)

Covering an area four times the size of Arizona's Grand Canyon, the **Copper Canyon region,** hidden deep within the Sierra Madres, is one of the most spectacular sights in all of Mexico. The Barrancas, comprised of five interlocking canyons in an area more generally known as the **Sierra Tarahumara,** hibernate under drifts of snow during the winter months and explode with color during the rainy season (July-Sept.) when the canyon's plants are in full bloom. The Copper Canyon, so-named for the minerals in the rock that give the canyon walls a copper color, is transversed on the western side by the tracks of the **Chihuahua-Pacífico Railroad;** trains careen along canyon walls at death-defying angles, plunge into tunnels (there are 96 of them), and briefly skim the rim of the *barrancas.* The railroad stretches from Chihuahua to Los Mochis, crossing the Continental Divide three times and soaring to a height of 2240m. Passengers peering from train windows can see a breathtaking series of landscapes—cactus-covered plateaus, mountains overgrown with pines, unusual rock formations, blue skies, and canyon floors teeming with tropical vegetation.

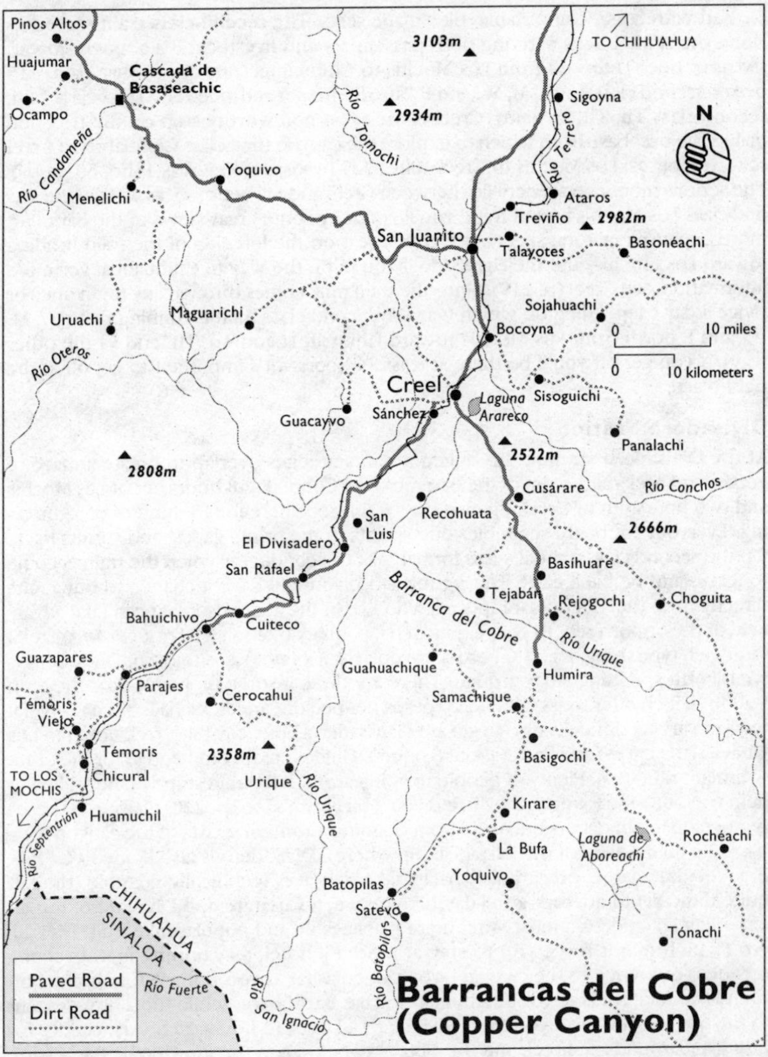

NORTHWEST MEXICO

Perhaps the most amazing feature of the expansive and magnificent Barrancas is what a well-kept secret they are. Few foreigners, even those familiar with Mexico, have ever heard of the Copper Canyon, and still fewer could place it. The immense area and singularity of the canyons means there is a wealth of breathtaking vistas, but with little infrastructure around the canyons, they are hard to explore, especially without a car. Dirt roads wind through remote corners of the canyons, but travelers without cars must rely on kind-hearted locals to give them a lift, or else they must really enjoy walking many miles. It almost doesn't matter where one goes—in this beautiful country, wilderness and adventure await everywhere.

■ The Train Through the Canyons

Two types of trains make the daily journey between Los Mochis and Chihuahua. The **first-class train** is for tourists: clean, air-conditioned, equipped with bathrooms, and blessed with large, comfortable, tilt-o-matic seats. The **second-class train** screeches along the same tracks carrying both passengers and livestock; it's a much slower, sweatier ride. Trains go from Los Mochis to Chihuahua (first-class 13hr., 6am, 415 pesos; second-class 16hr., M, W, and F 7am, 85 pesos) and vice-versa (first-class 7am; second-class Tu, Th, Sa 8am). Creel is the most noteworthy stop on the trip, and makes the best base from which to explore the canyon (first-class Chihuahua to Creel 6hr., 188 pesos; Los Mochis to Creel 10hr., 225 pesos; second-class 13hr., 50 pesos). The serious mountain scenery lies between Creel and El Fuerte, so if you take the second-class Los Mochis-bound train, you'll zoom by some great views in the dark. For more expansive natural spectacles, grab a seat on the **left side** of the train heading toward Los Mochis, and the **right side** if you're on the way to Chihuahua. For more information, see Creel (p. 219). Since the train only comes through any town once or twice a day (depending on which way the second class train is running that day; M, W, and F north from Los Mochis toward Chihuahua and Tu, Th, and Sa the other way), if you get off you'll be there at least 24 hours—it's important to get off at the right place.

Divisadero Station

At the **Divisadero station,** the jagged mountain edges overlap to create a maze of gorges and rocks at the rim of the Barrancas del Cobre. Eight hours out of Los Mochis and two hours out of Creel, the first-class train stops here for 15 minutes of sightseeing. Everyone on board scrambles out, sprints to the brink, gapes, and sprints back. On the second-class train, it's less formal. Ask the conductor when the train is going to leave, and be back early. During this stop, you will have a chance to buy crafts directly from the Tarahumara Indians who live in the area. Also, you can take advantage of the opportunity to grab a good, cheap, quick bite to eat. Try a *gordita* (fat li'l sandwich-type thing; about 6 pesos). If you've got a few pesos to burn, Divisadero is well worth spending a day around. There are three resort-type hotels near the train station, which offer tours (about 200 pesos per person) and horseback riding. Several trails of varying difficulty also begin at El Divisadero. For a day hike, trek down to **Las Cuevas** (the caves) and back (about 8 hours). Guides are recommended for the other overnight trail trips. Plenty of people roaming around the train stop will be willing to help you out. Don't worry, they'll find you. **Margarita's** (see p. 220) charges 70 pesos per person for an excursion. Aside from claiming an amazing vista of the canyon (perhaps the fullest view of the Barrancas anywhere), Divisadero is also home to **La Piedra Volada,** a large, precariously balanced stone. It is technically possible (though quite difficult) to attempt a full-day hike between Cusárare and Divisadero, but an experienced guide is a must. A far more manageable and popular hike from Divisadero (which might force you to stay at a pricey hotel, as camping is not recommended) is down into the canyon—you can go as far as you want. A four-hour, 4km round-trip hike leads to the Tarahumara village **Bacajipare,** while the 27km descent to the bottom of the canyon from Divisadero takes eight hours each way. Guides for hire hang around the hotel, and they'll take you down to the Río Urique, Bacajipare, or wherever your heart desires.

San Rafael

Just 7km down the tracks from **El Divisadero** lies the tiny, lovely village of **San Rafael.** The town sprung up on the hillsides around the saw mill outside of town and offers a rare peek into an older way of life. San Rafael has just a handful of phones and all cooking is still done on wood-burning stoves—running water is a luxury few people have. From San Rafael, continue down the tracks and marvel at the 300-year-old church at **Cuiteco,** but do it from the train because there is no place to stay in Cuiteco. **Bahuichivo** is the take-off point to go south into the canyons toward Urique (see p. 226), and it has several hotels and restaurants to offer the budget traveler.

Stroll down San Rafael's two main streets, Av. Centro and Av. Linda Vista, and enjoy the beautiful rose gardens in front of houses and the stone architecture that seems to be an extension of the hillside. Rather than the noise of automobiles and industry, the

Time Will Tell

You're wearing sandals from Ticul and a *huipil* from Valladolid; you sleep in a hammock from Mérida, sip *naranjadas* at lunch, and feign interest in the latest episode of "La Cente Bien" while downing an entire bowl of *chile habanero* (sans wincing). Slyly leaving your Tevas and *mochila* in storage, you could almost pass for one of the *indígenas.* So you blend in now, right? Not if you say "¡Buenos días!" when it's half past three, or "¡Buenas noches!" when it's only six. In Mexico, there are strictly adhered-to rules of greeting. *Buenos días* is for *good morning.* It's good until 11:59am. But come noon, sharp waiters and vendors alike won't bat an eyelash while correcting your greeting with a *Buenas tardes. Buenas noches* is only used when it's dark as *mole* outside. And for casual interactions, a muffled *Buenas* by itself is all it takes to get to business. So synchronize your watches, pay attention to the sun, and even if you roll out of bed at 1pm, remember to say *Buenas tardes.* Or they'll know. They'll see you're a *gabacho* (gringo) under that poncho, no matter how many tequila shots you can take standing.

air in San Rafael is filled only with the sounds of roosters crowing and horses neighing. Several great day hikes out of San Rafael won't disappoint nature-lovers or photographers. As you face Mochis at the railroad station, the best hikes are to your left up and over the ridge. Just follow Linda Vista Av. until it ends and then start heading up the ridge. The Tarahumara use several trails that lead in the right general direction. Because San Rafael is situated in the crook of two intersecting ridges, the views of the Copper Canyon are not that spectacular from the town itself; the surrounding high ground around the town offers much better vistas. There is no set path to hike into the hills, but if you plan on leaving the village, a compass is advisable.

Hotel de Los Magnolias, Linda Vista 18 just down from the plaza, has not only spotless rooms, real beds, and a patio and a deck that look out over the canyons, but flushing toilets and—be still, heart—hot water showers (singles 120 pesos; doubles 150 pesos; triples 200 pesos). Two hotels next to each other on Av. Centro have beds in the 40-50 peso price range, but lack running water or absolute cleanliness; they are much less attractive than the luxurious Magnolia. At **Restaurant Nalby,** Av. Centro across from Restaurant Doris, Nalby cooks up a huge Mexican meal for her family and some local single men, and you are welcome to eat all you want for just 12 pesos (meals served daily 8am, 1pm, and 7pm).

■ The Canyons: North to Basaseachi Falls

With water cascading from a height of 246m, the **Basaseachi Falls** are some of the world's most spectacular waterfalls. Basaseachi (Tarahumaran for "place of the cascade" or "place of the coyotes") is the highest waterfall in Mexico and the fourth highest in North America. Few waterfalls are blessed with such gorgeous surroundings. Tucked away back in the corner of Canyon Candameña, the falls are undisturbed and don't get many visitors because of their remoteness, but any person who makes the trip will be rewarded with scenery from a postcard photographer's wildest dream.

Getting to Basaseachi can be a little tricky unless you have a car. With a car, just pick up a map of the area and enjoy the drive on the newly paved road. Without one, there are a few options. **Margarita's** (150 pesos per person; see p. 220), **Cabañas Bertis** (140 pesos per person; see p. 220), and several tour guides operating out of the kiosk in the *zócalo* at Creel run tours to Basaseachi. Another option that is much cheaper and still fine (since trails are well marked and a guide isn't necessary) is to take an **Estrella Blanca** bus to Basaseachi from either Cuauhtémoc (2 per day, 80 pesos) or from Creel (5hr., 3 per day, 91 pesos). The bus from Creel stops at a pair of tiny crossroads called San Pedro where you'll have to change buses to get to Basaseachi.

Along the way to Basaseachi, you'll pass through some of the most sparsely populated areas of the Sierra Tarahumara area. **San Juanito** is the only town along the road with gasoline, reliable telephones, decent restaurants, and comfortable hotels (most of them near the bus station). Try **Hotel San Juanito** just two blocks down from the bus station; it has humble but clean rooms (singles 70 pesos; doubles 90 pesos; triples 110 pesos).

Once in Basaseachi, walk 3km down the paved road that runs through town to the trailhead to see the falls. The path is clearly marked and leads to the top of the falls after about a 30-minute walk. From the top of the falls where you won't actually be able to see much of the falls themselves, hike down the steep path to the natural *ventana* (window), which gives a breathtaking view of the falls and surrounding canyon. The hike is about 45 minutes each way. The stout-hearted can also trek to the bottom of the falls by following the path. The hike is difficult and takes about another hour from the "window," but you'll be alone at the bottom in a sub-tropical paradise.

Back in Basaseachi, there is one indoor accommodation—**Hotel Nena,** on the corner of the highway and the road to the falls. Don't believe the "hot water and TV" sign out in front, but the rooms do have private baths and comfy beds. (Singles 50 pesos; doubles 70 pesos; triples 100 pesos.) A **long distance telephone** can be found across the street at **Restaurant Betty,** which serves up quick and cheap burritos (7 pesos) and *chile rellenos* (8 pesos; open daily 7am-9pm). Restaurant Betty is also the place to **buy bus tickets** and wait for the bus.

■ The Canyons: South to Urique

It's a 154km jaunt from Creel to Urique. **Bahuichivo,** in a clearing in the forest, is 97km south of Creel. There's not much to see there, but it's often used as a departure point for spots deeper in the canyon or for Cerocahui and Urique, farther south. The beautiful mountain village of **Cerocahui** (pop. 600, elevation 1525m) is 17km southeast of Bahuichivo. You can grab a white "Transportes Cañón Urique" bus or van (50 pesos) which also goes to Urique, right at the Bahuichivo train station, but they leave only once a day down the twisting dirt road (ask the manager of the train station). The main attraction in Cerocahui is the **Jesuit Mission,** founded in 1681 by the priest Juan María de Salvatierra. **Sangre de Cristo** (gold and silver mines), the **Gallego Mountain** (38km away), the **Misión Churo,** and the **Yeparavo waterfall** (4km south) are among the possible excursions from Cerocahui. The **grocery store** at the fork in the road has all the information about excursions from Cerocahui. Several locals offer tours for steep prices, and unless you know the way yourself, they are your best bet.

The village of **Urique** sits in the **Barranca de Urique,** the deepest of the canyons. The three-hour, 54km, edge-of-your-seat dirt road ride from Bahuichivo to Urique takes you from a cool, frontier-like town in the forest to a warm, tropical village where the mango trees share the same humid air as the cacti beside them. About halfway down to Urique, the canyon opens up to reveal magnificent cliffs painted with lush, green vegetation, set against a pristine sky. Look down at what appears to be white spots along the Urique river—that's the village of Urique. A bus travels once a day from Bahuichivo to Urique, usually arriving after the second class train arrives at 4pm (50 pesos). Get your camera ready; the scenery rivals Divisadero and San Rafael as the most incredible in the Copper Canyons. Once in Urique, the minuscule town is almost entirely on Calle Principal, the main street running parallel to the river.

The limited services available in Urique are all along Calle Principal, including the **police** (at the pink building) and **caseta** (in the blue building; open M-Sa 8am-1pm and 2-7pm, Su 8am-noon). Accommodations in Urique are fairly cheap; options include the **campgrounds** on the main street, on the edge of town (15 pesos per person), and the only hotel in town, the **Hotel Cañon Urique,** on the main street, which offers clean and spacious rooms (singles 50 pesos; doubles 90 pesos; triples 120 pesos). If you're hungry, don't miss the **Restaurant Playa** on Calle Principal, which has a mango-tree-shaded patio where you can indulge—there is no menu; you simply tell the cook what you want (meals 15-25 pesos).

■ The Canyons: South to Batopilas

Heading south from Creel, a road winds through the more scenic parts of the Copper Canyon. Buses rumble past nail-biting hairpin turns along the edges of steep cliffs that will make your heart pound both from excitement (at the view) and nervousness (your life is in the hands of a stranger). The road has been called North America's most spectacular by many, but, unpaved most of the way, it is also one of the continent's most treacherous. The first 75km section of the road just south of Creel is happily two-laned and paved.

Margarita's and **Cabañas Bertis** in Creel (see p. 220) offer trips that cover **Cusárare** (mission and falls), Lake Arareko (see p. 222), a Tarahumara cave, and the **Elephant Rock.** It's a four-hour trip and runs about 60 pesos per person for at least five people. Bertis also runs trips to San Ignacio Mission, Lake Arareko, Valley of the Mushrooms, and Elephant Rock (2hr., 80 pesos per person). Tours that go as far as La Bufa run 170 pesos per person from Margarita's and 150 pesos from Cabañas Bertis (min. 6 people; 10hr. round-trip). On any trip, remember to bring plenty of water and food, adequate footwear, and protection from the sun. If you're averse to walking, you can arrange to navigate on bikes, horses, or even donkeys for a few extra pesos. **Pensión Creel,** Mateos 61 (tel. 6 00 71; fax 6 02 00), **Hotel Nuevo,** and **Motel Parador,** Mateos 44 (tel. 6 00 75; fax 6 00 85), offer somewhat more expensive tours, and locals hanging around the kiosk in the Creel *zócalo* will make cheaper offers than anyone. You can also catch the local bus from Creel to Batopilas (a red-and-white striped converted schoolbus), which leaves once a day sometime before 9am from in front of the train station (30 pesos); ask someone in the train station what time it leaves. Be warned that once in Cusárare, getting around is difficult—not having a car limits your options and your speed of travel.

On the right side heading south, still-inhabited **Tarahumara caves** are within view of the road. On tours, it's possible to go in and visit the homes for a small donation. Beds and other furniture, woodstoves with chimneys, and kerosene lamps adorn the insides of many of the dismal, stone-walled caves.

Twenty-two kilometers from Creel down the road to Batopilas is the town of **Cusárare,** which features its very own 18th-century Jesuit mission. Check out the mission's Tarahumara interior, with its crude wood floors and indigenous designs. There are no pews—people sit on the floor when it's used on Sundays. A boarding house for children and a small Tarahumara craft museum are nearby, but the most popular attraction in the town's vicinity is the **Cusárare Falls,** a 3km hike uphill through a pine forest. Although you can't swim in the falls, the view is spectacular.

Another 20km beyond Cusárare on the road to Batopilas, **Basíhuare** is an old overnight stop once frequented by silver carriers en route to Batopilas. Later, the road weaves around the narrowing canyon, offering spectacular vistas as it crawls up the **Cerro de Siete Pisos** (Seven-floor Hill), so named for the seven distinct layers of earth that lead up along the rocky inner walls of the canyon on the most frightening stretch of this incredible one-lane path. The seven steps can best be seen from **La Bufa,** 60km from Basíhuare and past the fork, a scenic lookout that has the most magnificent view of all. If you have good vision, you can make out the tiny thread that is the Río Urique far, far below and the yellow wooden bridge that runs across it. If you're driving, pull off onto the shoulder, and try not to look down. Get out and gape. Then gape some more. If you go left at the fork, you'll come to **Norogachi,** a Tarahumara mission center at the river with beautiful (but touristy) *Semana Santa* services, and **Guachochi,** a rocky, frontier-like village with both colonial and Tarahumara influences.

The right fork will take you to the more impressive town of **Batopilas** (see below). On the way you'll pass the bridge that spans the Urique; you can get out and walk down into the bushes for a smashing view of the waterfall down below. Keep your eyes peeled for **Tescalama trees,** which have yellow flowers and grow out of the sides of sheer rock. The last quarter of the ride to Batopilas has plenty of **piedra cobriza** (copper rock), which gives the canyon its copper tint.

■ The Canyons: Batopilas and Satevó

Batopilas (pop. 1200) is a tiny village nestled in the depths of the canyons, a mile below the rest of civilization. The village lies along the Río Urique, a rough 35km from La Bufa and a thrilling but scary 140km (6hr. by van, 8hr. by bus) from Creel. Batopilas was a silver-mining boom town founded in 1708. Its rich silver supply lasted until the late 1800s, which is why such a secluded place was the second city in all Mexico (after Mexico City) to receive electricity. Nowadays, phone service is limited to a single *caseta* in the center of town, a symbol of how little remains of the town's glory days. The wind whistles nostalgically through holes in once-proud hacienda walls, from which leafy vegetation has sprouted along Batopilas's steamy riverbank.

Take the local bus from Creel to Batopilas (see p. 219). The bus makes a couple of stops during the six-hour trip, allowing you to grab a bite to eat or simply to gape at spectacular scenery (the La Bufa stop is mind-blowing). **Estrella Blanca** does not go to Batopilas, so be sure to catch the local bus. Few places offer excursions to Batopilas. **Cabañas Bertis** (p. 220) offers a two-day trip for a minimum of six people that includes a one-night stay in the Hotel Mary (280 pesos per person). **Margarita's** (p. 220) does not organize formal trips to Batopilas, but if enough people are interested, a guide will travel with a group (min. 6 people) for 200 pesos per person.

Everything in Batopilas centers around the **old stone plaza,** referred to as the **parque.** Streets do have names, but locals don't use them. The main street (which connects Batopilas to Creel and the rest of the world) splits off into two streets, one of which encounters a dead end while the other becomes Juárez. At the main plaza, Juárez splits off into two more streets. At the end of the northernmost of these (farther from the river) is a second, **smaller plaza** dedicated to Don Manuel Gómez Marín, founder of the PAN political party. Across from the north side of the plaza is the Presidencia Municipal, headquarters of the Batopilas **police.** For medical attention, try the **Red Cross** on the main street. The **post office** is close to where the main street first forks (open M-F 9am-4pm). The **postal code** is 33400. The lonely **caseta** (tel. 6 06 32 or 6 06 33) is on the east side of the plaza. Calls cost 3 pesos per minute (open M-Sa 9am-1pm and 3-7pm, Su 3-7pm). The **phone code** is 145.

A good choice for lodging in town is the **Hotel Mary,** Juárez 15, next to the church near the plaza. Large, rustic adobe rooms with ceiling fans are naturally cool (50 pesos per person). During low season, restaurants' opening and closing times are left to the whims of visitors. Try **Restaurant Carolina** on the main street near the entrance to town. The menu includes *carne machaca* and *tacos dorados de machaca* for 30 pesos. Another eatery in town that's reliably open is the Hotel Mary's **Quinto Patio.** Enchiladas with fresh cheese (20 pesos), an order of tacos (20 pesos), and *bistek* (27 pesos) are on the menu, but you're limited to whatever happens to be in the refrigerator at the time. Check out the old lightbulbs converted into flowerpots. (Open daily 7am-6pm.)

The magnificent **haciendas** in ruins along the river are poignant reminders of the excesses of the owners in the silver-mining days of Batopilas. The brown, castle-like **Hacienda Shepard** belonged to an American, and its ruins now stand in contrast to the green of the surrounding trees and canyon. Look for the *tescalama* trees growing sideways out of the brown walls of the hacienda. Hikes from Batopilas leave daily for the **Porfirio Díaz mine** in town and for the more interesting **Peñasquito,** both an hour hike up a steep hill; for **Cerro Colorado,** a section of the old Camino Real during the mining boom, a 12-hour hike; and for the lost mission of **Satevó** (see below). The best source of information about departing tours is the **Riverside Lodge,** in town diagonally across from the plaza on the bench side (not the basketball-court side). A restored hacienda, the lodge is now an incredibly posh package-tour inn—stop by and check out the luxuriant piano room and the view from the rooftop. The historical photos on the walls may be the most interesting exhibits. Don't miss an 1899 shot of Pancho Villa at age 22, a photo of gold bars stacked to the ceiling, and another of the day the river ran as high as the hotel wall. **Artesanías Monse,** on the south side of the plaza, offers the opportunity to view and purchase handicrafts from Tarahumara gentiles—supposedly the least

Christianized of the Tarahumara. You might get a chance to meet the artists who often hang out in the garden in the back. If you've yet to find a place to stay, the owner of Artesanías Monse might be able to offer some suggestions.

The most fascinating excursion from Batopilas is to **Satevó,** a minuscule town with a spooky and beautiful mission. It's a 40-minute drive (you'll need 4WD or, better yet, pixie dust) or a two-hour walk. In the middle of a fertile valley straddled by the towering canyon rises a lonesome, round mission shrouded in mystery. Why was it built here, of all places? When was it built? (The 15th or 16th century are the best guesses, but no one knows.) And finally, how did the Tarahumara, barely able to find shelter for themselves, gather up the energy and desire to build such a thing? In any case, it's a sight to behold, especially at sunset, when the rays play off the red bricks of the roundhouse-like construction, combining with the clouds and valley to create a heavenly scene. In order to take a peek inside the mission, you'll have to tip the **family living next door;** they have the key. The inside of the mission is even eerier, with ancient tombs below and darkness above.

SINALOA

Los Mochis

Just 15 minutes from the ocean and linked to the Baja Peninsula (by a ferry departing from Topolobampo to La Paz) and the major cities of Mexico by rail and highway, Los Mochis is a relatively young town that has sprung up as a bustling center of trade and commerce. The strategic location and beautiful transportation options also make Los Mochis (or just "Mochis" to locals) an important stop-over for travelers. The open-air markets and trees lining the sidewalks make Mochis a pleasant place to wander and shop for a day. While not the bastion of Mexican culture or the showcase of cutting-edge entertainment, Los Mochis is a comfortable place to pass a few days on your way to a more exciting destination...say, **Las Barrancas del Cobre** (see p. 222).

TRANSPORTATION **Transportes Norte de Sonora** (tel. 12 17 57) and **Elite** (tel. 18 49 67) **buses** operate out of the modern terminal at the corner of Juárez and Degollado. **Transportes Norte de Sonora,** usually the cheapest carrier, runs buses to Guaymas (5hr., every hr., 80 pesos), Mazatlán (5½hr., every hr. 5am-5pm, 145 pesos), Mexicali (18hr., 7 and 8:15am, 380 pesos), Mexico City (24hr., 6pm, 528 pesos) via Culiacán (3hr., 60 pesos), and Tijuana (22hr., 4, 7, and 8:15pm, 423 pesos) via Hermosillo (7hr., 110 pesos) and Navajoa (2hr., every 2hr., 30 pesos). **Transportes del Pacífico,** on Morelos between Leyva and Zaragoza (tel. 12 03 47 and 12 03 41), sends *de paso* buses south to Mazatlán and north through Guaymas, Hermosillo, and Mexicali to Tijuana. These buses are relatively cheap, but often packed by the time they reach Los Mochis. Seats are easier to obtain on the slower local buses to Guadalajara, Mazatlán, and Tijuana (approximately 3 per day). Buses to El Fuerte and other destinations leave from Zaragoza, between Ordoñez and Cuauhtémoc. **Norte de Sinaloa** (tel. 18 03 57) sends a large fleet of rickety green buses every 15 minutes to Culiacán (3½hr., 45 pesos), Guamuchil (2hr., 25 pesos), and Guasave (1hr., 20 pesos).

The **ferry** to La Paz leaves from Topolobampo at 9pm and 2am every day and arrives at 7pm and midnight, respectively, the next day (*salón*-class tickets 140 pesos per person; 1500 pesos per car). Buy tickets at the **Sematur** office in Topolobampo on Rendón 519 (tel. 686 2 01 41; fax 686 2 00 35; open M-F 8am-1pm and 3-7pm, Su 9am-1pm; hours erratic). Tickets go on sale at 6pm every evening or can be puchased on the ferry at Topolobampo. To get to the office, walk nine blocks from Juárez on Flores, then turn left on Rendón. **Bus service** to Topolobampo begins every morning at 6am (every 20min., 7pesos). The bus leaves from a stop on Cuauhtémoc between Prieta and Zaragoza, one block north of Obregón. Buses to other parts of Los Mochis run throughout the city and cost 1.80 pesos. The main stop is on Zaragoza at Obregón. Ask the driver if he goes where you need to go. For **taxis,** call 2 02 83.

The **Chihuahua al Pacífico train** (tel. 12 08 47) runs back and forth from Los Mochis to Chihuahua, passing through the Copper Canyon. At the Divisadero stop, just south of Creel, tourists are allowed to get off the train and gape for 15 minutes. Unfortunately, the train can be unreliable due to frequent problems on the one set of tracks that carries trains in two directions simultaneously—if one train is late, they all are. The first-class train passes through daily at 6am (225 pesos to Creel; 400 pesos to Chihuahua). Tickets are sold on the train or from a travel agency in advance. The train arrives in Creel around 4pm. A second-class train, which departs from Los Mochis on Tuesdays, Thursdays, and Saturdays, supposedly leaves at 7am and arrives in Creel after dark. After dark, or early in the morning, those who rely on the train become the captives of cagey taxi drivers (30 pesos to downtown). Group rates can be much cheaper, so find a buddy and save some pesos. A free bus carries guests to and from the Hotel Santa Anita. No official documentation of guest status is generally required to get on board. To catch a public bus from the station back to town during the daylight hours (every 15min., 3 pesos), just walk away from the station down the road about 100m. If you miss the train and must get to Chihuahua or Creel, the best alternative (the coolest spot in hell) is to get a bus to Hermosillo (8hr., 10 pesos) and then catch the overnight Hermosillo-Chihuahua bus (14hr., 8pm, 217 pesos). From Chihuahua, buses run regularly to Creel (5hr., 80 pesos).

ORIENTATION AND PRACTICAL INFORMATION The city is laid out in a simple grid. The main streets running parallel to one another are **Constitución, Allende, Zaragoza,** and **Leyva.** Perpendicular to these streets are **Ordoñez, Castro, Obregón, Hidalgo, Independencia, Juárez, Morelos, Madero, Bravo, Carranza,** and **Serdán.**

Set office hours are the butt of town jokes. The **tourist office,** on Obregón and Allende (tel./fax 12 66 40), is in the Municipal Transit Building. As you walk into the main entrance on Ordoñez, follow the hallway on your left. After turning the first corner, the tourist office is the room at the end of the hall (open M-F 9am-3pm). Stop by and pick up a free map and billions of brochures. To purchase tickets in advance, try **Viajes Conelva,** Leyva 525 (tel. 15 60 90 or 15 80 90) at Valdez, inside Hotel El Dorado (open M-Sa 8am-7pm, Su 9am-2pm). For your banking needs, try the **Bancomer** (tel. 12 23 23) on Leyva and Juárez (open M-F 8:30am-2pm and 3:30-7pm, Sa 10am-2pm).

NORTHWEST MEXICO

Four 24-hour **ATMs** are at your disposal. If Bancomer doesn't suit your fancy, all its competitors cluster nearby on Calle Leyva. For fresh fish, fruit, and vegetables, check out the **market** in the area around Zaragoza, between Castro and Ordoñez; on weekends it bustles with activity (most stores close around 7pm). Los Mochis's hippest threads get washed and dried at **Lavamatic,** Allende 218 just before Juárez (20 pesos; open M-Sa 7am-7pm, Su 7am-1pm). The **Tourist Security** number is 91 800 90 392. In case of **emergency,** call 06. The **police** (tel. 12 00 33) are at Degollado at Cuauhtémoc in the Presidencia Municipal. No English is spoken. The **Red Cross** (tel. 15 08 08 or 12 02 92), at Tenochtitlán and Prieto, one block off Castro, has 24-hour ambulance service. **Super Farmacia San Jorge** (tel. 18 18 19), at Juárez and Degollado, is open 24 hours. Hit the **Hospital Fátima,** Blvd. Jiquilpán Pte. 639 (tel. 12 33 12), to check out the local medical scene. No English is spoken. The **Centro de Salud** can be reached at 12 07 74. The **post office** is at Ordoñez 226 (tel. 12 08 23), two blocks off Castro, between Prieta and Zaragoza (open M-F 8am-7pm). The **postal code** is 81200. **LADATELs** are scattered throughout downtown; when making local calls within the city, add "1" before any number with only five digits. Given the number of travel agencies in town, the residents of Los Mochis seem to be aware that their role in tourism is to help visitors get somewhere else. The **phone code** is 68.

ACCOMMODATIONS Budget hotels of variable quality are sprinkled throughout the downtown area demarcated by Castro, Juárez, Leyva, and Constitución. **Hotel Montecarlo,** Flores 322 Sur (tel. 12 18 18), a gracefully aging blue building at the corner of Independencia, has large rooms surrounding a quiet, palatial indoor courtyard. Air-conditioning, fans, and cable TV make life much easier. Take a room downstairs if you can—they're much cooler (one-person singles 130 pesos, two-person singles 145 pesos; doubles 160 pesos). The **Hotel Lorena** (tel. 12 02 83) on Calle Prieta, across from the market, has rooms furnished with everything but a butler. Huge windows give a great view of the city, air-conditioning keeps you from melting, and TVs and phones keep you entertained. (Singles 130 pesos; doubles 165 pesos; triples 195 pesos.) At **Hotel Hidalgo,** Hidalgo 260 Pte. (tel. 12 34 56), between Prieta and Zaragoza, ceiling fans and chilly colors (deep blue furniture and baby-blue walls) cool the small rooms. If there's a soccer game on the tube, the lobby becomes a local hangout. (Singles 90 pesos, with A/C 100 pesos; doubles 110 pesos; each additional person 10 pesos).

FOOD The crowning virtue of this farming region is the daily **public market** along Zaragoza, between Castro and Ordoñez, where prices are low and quality is high. Stores start to close around 7pm. The *taquerías* and *loncherías* in the market dish out cheap, home-brewed enigmas, many of which pack quite a wallop. Except for the *cantinas* (which women should avoid) and the corner *taquerías,* just about everything in town shuts down at 9pm; alcohol evaporates at 11pm. Good, cheap *tortas* can be found on Independencia and Hidalgo. Try **Tortas Moka,** Independencia 216 (tel. 12 39 41) at Prieto, where you can enjoy a *torta* (8 pesos) while you people-watch. At **El Taquito,** on Leyva between Hidalgo and Independencia (tel. 2 81 19), pink window shades provide shade from the offending sun, and air-conditioning dries your sweaty skin and prevents the vinyl booths from sticking to your thighs. Waiters in red jackets serve up *enchiladas suizas* (27 pesos), hamburgers and fries (20 pesos), and cheese-filled shrimp wrapped in bacon (42 pesos). "The Little Taco" offers group discounts. (Open 24hr.).

SIGHTS AND ENTERTAINMENT Los Mochis boasts a few modest amusements, but if you can, head to **Topolobampo.** Catch the bus at Prieto and Cuauhtémoc (every 20min., 7 pesos). One of Los Mochis's founders, the sugar baron Benjamin Johnston, assembled the extraordinary collection of trees and plants standing in **Sinaloa Park,** on Prolongación and Castro. Hundreds of species inhabit this outdoor forest-museum, where *indígena* performers strut their stuff every Sunday beginning at 11am. Check out the stump at the entrance to the park; a harem of wild animals and the insignia of the state of Sinaloa have been gouged into its roughened surface. The **Museo Regional del Valle del Fuerte** (tel. 2 46 92), on Pte. Municipal at Castro, was the home of an early settler whose guns and personal diary are now housed there. *(Open Tu-Su 9am-1pm and 4-7:30pm. Admission 5 pesos).* Photographs documenting the growth and development of Northern Mexico are also on display. Across the street is the **Plaza Solidaridad,** which hosts performances every Sunday at 6pm. For a schedule of upcoming festivals and musical events at the Pl. Solidaridad and the nearby **Plazuela 27 de Septiembre,** consult the **Secretaria de Cultura y Acción Social** (tel. 5 04 05, ext. 38 or 39). Adjoining the Plaza Solidaridad is the **Santuario del Sagrado Corazón de Jesús,** Los Mochis's oldest church, which was built after Johnston's wife donated the land to the people. Many locals find it ironic that she was not even Catholic. The **Cinema 70** is on Blvd. de la Plaza. If you spend the night in Mochis, head to the **Rodeo Bar,** on Obregón and Constitución, where you can down a few beers and take the mechanical horse for a ride (open 9pm-4am).

Mazatlán

Mazatlán (pop. 315,000) means "place of the deer" in Náhuatl. A less appropriate name can hardly be imagined, since there is nothing even remotely pastoral about this city. The only wildlife present roams the beaches in large herds.

Mazatlán is truly a city divided. The **old city** is traditionally Mexican, with a shady *zócalo,* busy streets, and bustling markets that lend it a genuine charm. Nearby on the shore is the **Olas Altas** (Tall Waves) neighborhood, with a peaceful, nearly empty beach, pleasant streets, and faded resorts of yesteryear that evoke Mazatlán's glory

Old Mazatlán
Ave. del Mar
México
Flores
16 de Septiembre
Bolivar
Quijano
Zúñiga
Carrasco
Zaragoza
Jabonería
Arribo
Domínguez
5 de Mayo
Guillermo Nelson
Juárez
Serdán
Azueta
Paseo Claussen
Paseo de las 3 Islas
Morelos
Hidalgo
Estrada
Ocampo
Cerro de la Nevería (Ice Box Hill)
Mercado
Canizales
High Divers of Mazatlán
21 de Marzo
Leandro Valle
Pederegoso
PLAZA REVOLUCIÓN
Escobedo
Angel Flores
Olas Altas/Claussen
Venus
Constitución
Carvajal
Osuna
Rojo
Niños Héroes
Carnaval
Guerrero
Galeana
Roosevelt
Avenida Miguel Alemán
N
Isla de los Pajaros
Estero del Sábalo
Calz. Camaron Sabalo
EL CID RESORT
ZONA DORADA
Av. de la Marina
Laguna
Av. Loaiza
Av. Lomas de Mazatlán
Bugambilia
Isla de los Venados
Isla de los Lobos
Calz. Rafael Buelna
Laguna del Camarón
Av. Insurgentes
Av. del Mar
Carretera Internacional
Universidad
Mazatlán
ACCOMMODATIONS
E Hotel Belmar
C Hotel Central
B Hotel del Centro
F Hotel Emperador
H Hotel Fiesta
D Hotel La Siesta
A Hotel Lerma
G Hotel Los Arcos
Bahía de Puerto Viejo
0 2 miles
0 2 kilometers
Tamazula
Pánuco
Beltrán
San Lorenzo
Av. Benemérito de las Américas
Estero del Infiernillo
OLD MAZATLÁN (See Inset)
Paseo Clausen
Fuerte
Baluarte
Piaxtla
Gavitas
Zaragoza
16 de Sept.
5 de Mayo
Juárez
Serdán
G. Nájera
Carrasco
Pesqueira
Bahía de Olas Altas
Olas Altas
Carnaval
Villa/Iturbide
Germán Evers
Av. Miguel Alemán
Azueta
A. Flores
Constitución
Potrero del Llano
Calz. Gabriel Leyva Solano
Playas del Sur
Serdán
Av. Emilio Barragán
Canal de Navegación
Mazatlán

days. The wide, breezy Malecón connects the old city with the more expensive and touristy northern part of town, and is a favorite destination of Mexicans and the few foreign tourists out for strolls along the beach.

Eight kilometers or so up the Avenida del Mar lies another city entirely—the **Zona Dorada** (Golden Zone), home to high-rise hotels, Disney-castle clubs and pleasure palaces, dollar-dishing Americans, time-share condos, trinket shops, and patronizingly friendly tourism agents. But the numerous honeymooners, spring-breakers, and just plain sun-seeking families that come each year to dip into the fine waters and lie on the pristine beaches of Mazatlán's ritz zone are greeted by lower prices and nicer beaches than its Floridian and Californian counterparts can offer, and those virtues go a long way. Budget travelers can save even more money by heading south and avoiding the swarms of tourists and fast-food franchises concentrated in this part of town.

Mazatlán offers little of historical or cultural interest to the traveler. The city's greatest assets are gifts of nature—glorious sunsets, a glittering ocean, and wide beaches. The *Zona Dorada* is the most popular, but not necessarily the best, way to appreciate those assets. It is the more senior **Old Mazatlán,** with its shore and its grand old hotels. that the *mariachis* evoke when they sing the classic bittersweet song of lost youth in Sinaloa.

ORIENTATION

Built on a rocky spur jutting southwest into the Pacific, Old Mazatlán's downtown area lies north of the *zócalo.* The main street running east-west is **Angel Flores,** the southern boundary of the *zócalo.* Farther south, the **Malecón** follows the shore line. It starts as **Olas Altas** on the south end near **Old Mazatlán,** then runs to the **Zona Dorada** 8km north, serving as the *Zona Dorada's* one main street; there it is called **Avenida del Mar.** In between the two areas, to the south of the fisherman's statue and north of Olas Altas, it is called **Paseo Clausen;** and to the far north, past Valentino's in the *Zona Dorada,* it's known as **Sábalo.** Since Mazatlán is very spread out, the easiest way to navigate the city is by bus (see **Practical Information,** below).

Mazatlán's **bus station** is three blocks behind the Sands Hotel, and about 2km north of Old Mazatlán, in Olas Altas. To head downtown from the bus station, catch the "Insurgentes" bus across the street (2.20 pesos). Most city buses are white with a green and yellow racing stripe—just look for the sign above the front window to figure out what bus it is. A cab will make the trip for 15 pesos. The area around the bus station, with several reasonably priced hotels and restaurants, along with a good beach and the vital "Sábalo" bus line nearby, makes a convenient home base. From the **train station,** on the far eastern edge of Mazatlán, the "Insurgentes" or the "Cerritos-Juárez" buses will take you downtown. From the **airport,** 18km south of the city, the "Central Camionera" bus makes the trip; the only way to get back to the airport from downtown is a 70-peso cab ride. It's a grueling 20-minute walk from the *centro* to the **ferry** docks; the blue "Playa Sur" school bus (1.80 pesos) makes the trip, and, for 10 pesos, so will a taxi.

Mazatlán's efficient **bus system** makes getting around the city a breeze. At some point, all municipal buses pass the public market on Juárez, 3 blocks north of the *zócalo.* The most useful bus line is the **"Sábalo-Centro,"** which runs from the downtown market with stops a few blocks from the Malecón in Olas Altas and at Playa Sábalo in the *Zona Dorada.* The **"Cerritos-Juárez"** bus continues up to Playa Bruja at Puerta Carritos. The **"Insurgentes"** route services the bus and train stations, and **"Playa Sur"** goes to the ferry dock and lighthouse (every 15min. 5am-midnight, 2.20 pesos). Feel free to wave down a bus at any point on its route—no official stops exist.

For late-night disco hopping, you'll have to take a cab or a *pulmonía* (pneumonia), an open vehicle that resembles a golf cart or a sawed-off Volkswagon and putters along blasting raucous music. Always set the price before you commit yourself to a ride; standard fare between Old Mazatlán and the *Zona Dorada* is 12 pesos. If you want to save the fare, it'll take you over an hour to walk the long path between the two sections. Olas Altas and the *centro* both make convenient home bases. The infinitely more pleasant Olas Altas is a 10-minute walk from the noisy *centro* (take a right on Angel Flores from the Malecón), and is also well connected by bus.

PRACTICAL INFORMATION

Transportation

Airport: Rafael Buelna International Airport (tel. 82 21 77), 18km south of the city.Served by **AeroCalifornia** (tel. 13 20 42), El Cid Resort; **Aeroméxico,** Sábalo 310A (tel. 14 11 11 or 91 800 36 202); **Alaska Airlines** (tel. 95 800 426 0333; fax 85 27 30); **Mexicana,** B. Domínguez and Av. del Mar (tel./fax 82 77 22). Call for schedules and fares. See **Orientation** above for info on getting to or from the airport.

Buses: Norte del Sonora sends buses north to Monterrey (17hr., 9pm, 322 pesos) and Tijuana (26hr., 11am, 2, and 6:30pm, 500 pesos). **Transpacífico** (tel. 81 38 01) serves Culiacán (2½hr., 5, 6, and 8:30pm, 60 pesos), Durango (7hr., 7:30pm, 100 pesos), Los Mochis (6½hr., every hr. 6am-4pm, 141 pesos), and Puerto Vallarta (7hr., 7:30am, 185 pesos). **Transportes del Pacífico** (tel. 81 51 56) has service to Guadalajara (7hr., almost every hr., 170 pesos) and Tepic (5hr., every hr., 90 pesos). The following 3 lines offer posher buses: **Elite** (81 38 11) has service to Aguascalientes (14hr., 4 per day, 300 pesos), HermTepic (4½hr., every hr., 108 pesos). **Transportes Chihuahuauses** (tel. 81 53 81) runs to Ciudad Juárez (24hr., 2pm and midnight, 450 pesos) and Monterrey (18hr., 7 per day, 360 pesos). **Transportes del Norte** (tel. 81 23 35) has 1st-class service to Durango (7hr., 5 per day, 140 pesos), Monterrey (18hr., 5 per day, 330 pesos), and Saltillo (16hr., noon, 5, 7, and 10pm, 279 pesos).

Ferry: Sematur (tel. 81 70 20 or 21), at the end of Carnaval, south of Angel Flores and the *centro.* Tickets are sold only on the day of departure. Arrive at the office at least 2hr. early to procure a spot, as capacity is very limited. You can buy tickets on the ferry, but you aren't guaranteed a spot, since they let ticketed passengers board first. Ticket office open daily Su-F 8am-3pm, Sa 9am-1pm. Purchase tickets in advance at a local travel agency. During the high season (Dec. and July-Aug.), make reservations at least 2 weeks ahead. Travels every day to La Paz, arriving around 8am (*salón* 17hr., 3pm, 163 pesos; *turista* 400 pesos; children 2-11 half-price).

Local Buses: The best and quickest way to get around the city. See **Orientation,** above.

Car Rental: Hertz, Sábalo 314 (tel. 13 60 60, airport office 85 05 48; fax 13 49 55). Starting around 300 pesos per day. Must be 21 years old.

NORTHWEST MEXICO

Tourist and Financial Services

Tourist Office: (tel. 16 51 62 or 16 51 65; fax 16 51 66 or 16 51 67) on Av. Camarón Sábalo at Tiburón, in the *Zona Dorada,* on the 4th floor of the pinkish Banrural building past El Cid resort on the "Sábalo Centro" bus line. Helpful staff doles out much-needed Mazatlán maps. English spoken. Open daily 8:30am-3pm. **Tourist Assistance:** (tel. 91 800 90 392).

Tourist Police: (tel. 14 84 44), on Gabriel Ruíz and Santa Mónica.

Consulates: Canada (tel. 13 44 55), Loaiza at Bugambiliain in Hotel Playa Mazatlán in the *Zona Dorada.* Open daily 9am-1pm. **U.S.** (tel. 16 58 89), Loaiza at Bugambilia in front of Hotel Playa Mazatlán. Open daily 9am-1pm.

Currency Exchange: Most banks open for exchange M-F 8:30-11am. *Casas de cambio* are open all day in the northern section of the downtown area, but tend to sport less than thrilling rates. Stick to banks in the *centro* to avoid getting ripped off. A good option is **Banca Serfin** (tel. 85 52 60), 21 de Marzo and Gillerman Nelson, across from the *zócalo.* Open M-F 8:30am-4pm, Sa 9am-1pm. 24hr. **ATM.**

American Express: (tel. 13 06 00; fax 16 59 08), in the Centro Comercial Plaza Balboa on Camarón Sábalo. Open daily 9am-5pm.

Local Services

Laundromat: Lavamatic del Centro, Serdán 2914 (tel. 81 35 56), on the Malecón. Will wash and dry 3kg in a few hr. for 24 pesos. Open M-Sa 8am-7:30pm.

Emergency and Communications

Emergency: (tel. 81 36 90), open 24hr. Or just dial 060.
Police: (tel. 83 45 10), on Rafael Buelna in Colonia Juárez.
Red Cross: (tel. 85 14 51), on Zaragoza and Corona.
Pharmacy: Farmacia Ibael (tel. 822 62 49), on Angel Flores and Campana. English spoken. Open daily 8:30am-10:30pm.
Hospital: Sharp Hospital (tel. 86 56 76), on Dr. Jesús Kumate and Rafael Buelna, near Zaragoza park. English spoken.
Post Office: (tel. 81 21 21), on 21 de Marzo and Juárez, across from the *zócalo.* Open M-F 8am-7pm, Sa 9am-1pm. **Postal Code:** 82000.
Fax: (tel. 81 22 20), in the same building as the post office. Open M-F 8am-7pm, Sa-Su 8-11am. Also at the *caseta* below.
Internet Access: Along with the *caseta* at Serdán 1510 and 21 de Marzo, you can surf the web at **Mail Boxes Etc.** (tel. 16 40 10), on Av. Camarón Sabado in the *Zona Dorada.* 30 pesos per 30min. Open M-Sa 9am-5pm. **Cyber Café Mazatlan** (tel. 14 00 08), across the street, can also hook you up. 25 pesos per 30min., 40 pesos per hr. Open daily 11am-9pm.
Phone Code: 69.

ACCOMMODATIONS AND CAMPING

High-quality cheap rooms do exist; simply avoid the *Zona Dorada,* where rates are exorbitant even at the shabbier joints. Budget hotels cluster in three areas: in Old Mazatlán along the three avenues east of the main square (Juárez, Serdán, and Azueta), in the noisy area around the bus station, and on the pleasant waterfront along Olas Altas, southwest of the center of Old Mazatlán. Large groups can even find cheap beds on Sábalo, near the beaches. The cheapest rooms are by the bus station, the most affordable nice rooms are in the *centro* and Olas Altas, and the posh resorts are in the *Zona Dorada.* The busiest seasons in Mazatlán are Christmas and the month following *Semana Santa*—check in early. There's a trailer park, **La Posta** (tel. 83 53 10), on Av. Rafael Buelna (full hook-up and tent space 85 pesos).

Olas Altas

Back in the 1950s, long before wily developers began constructing multi-million-dollar pleasure pits along the north shore, the focal point of Mazatlán's fledgling resort scene was Olas Altas, a winding, shore-hugging stretch southwest of town dotted with regal, colonial-style hotels. Although the majority of tourists now opt to stay in the flashy hotels to the north, Olas Altas is a calm oasis, only a 10-minute walk from the *centro,* and connected to the rest of Mazatlán by several buses.

Hotel Belmar, Olas Altas 166 (tel. 85 11 11), at Osuna. The second you get into Mazatlán, *run,* don't walk, to the Belmar, and plop down here; this absolute gem makes deciding where to stay in town a no-brainer. A resort of yesteryear, the Belmar glows with hazy marble floors, luxuriant dark wood paneling, and arches lined with colorful tiles. Cool, spotless rooms have gigantic bathrooms. Match other guests ping for pong at the table downstairs, take a dip in the pool, or crawl into an antique rocker with an English book in hand (they have a small collection). Singles with A/C and TV 130 pesos, with an ocean view (no A/C) 130 pesos; doubles with A/C and TV 160 pesos, with ocean view (no A/C) 160 pesos.

Hotel La Siesta, Olas Altas Sur 11 (tel. 81 26 40 or 81 23 34, toll-free 91 800 69 770; fax 13 74 76), at Escobedo. Next door to the Belmar, the Siesta is a newer, more modern clone. The beautiful courtyard and state-of-the-art amenities will cost you though. Singles 180 pesos; doubles 210 pesos. Make sure to get a room on the ocean.

Old Mazatlán

This is the noisier part of town ("downtown"), and the hotels here are farther from the beach—therefore rooms are on the cheap side. This area, especially the cathedral square, is well trafficked after sundown, and for that reason is somewhat safer than

NORTHWEST MEXICO

other parts of town. If you don't mind a little noise, and want to save some cash, you've come to the right spot.

Hotel Lerma, Simón Bolívar 622 (tel. 81 24 36), near Serdán. Riotously colored, centrally located, and clean. Fans make the heat bearable. Popular among backpackers who know a good deal when they see one. Singles 55 pesos; doubles 60 pesos.

Hotel del Centro, Canizales 705 (tel. 81 26 73), between Serdán and Juárez. Somewhat small, cool, turquoise rooms have A/C, purified water, and tiny bathrooms. Singles and doubles 100 pesos.

Hotel Central, Domínguez 2 Sur (tel. 82 18 88), at Escobedo. Spotless rooms decorated with funky wood carvings. Phone, TV, A/C, and sparkling bathrooms make this hotel a smart choice for larger groups. Singles, doubles, and triples 120 pesos.

Near the Bus Station

Hotels in this area are closer to the ritzy *Zona Dorada* in proximity, but not in quality. The places are a little more run-down and a little older. Be forewarned: buses do their noisy thing 24 hours a day.

Hotel Fiesta, Ferrosquila 306, in front of the bus station. Clean rooms have bathrooms, firm mattresses, and purified water. Aquamarine halls with fluorescent lights make you feel like you're in a fishbowl. Singles and doubles 70 pesos; 10 pesos extra for A/C or TV.

Hotel Emperador, Río Panoco 1000 (tel. 82 67 24), next to Hotel Los Arcos. The high-rise style hotel has a top-notch cleaning crew, tile floors, and fans. Singles 60 pesos; doubles 70 pesos; 10 pesos extra A/C or TV.

Hotel Los Arcos, Río Panoco 1006 (tel. 81 06 75), across from the bus station; you'll see it. Very basic rooms, but clean and cool (there is A/C) with a private bath. Singles 60 pesos, doubles 70 pesos.

FOOD

Mazatlán's restaurants serve up everything from *comida corrida* to charbroiled T-bone steak, a gringo favorite. Prices escalate as you get sucked toward the *Zona Dorada.* Mazatlán's *centro* is the place to be for quality budget meals. The busy **public market,** between Juárez and Serdán, three blocks north of the *zócalo,* serves the cheapest food in the area. If you need a **headless pig,** look no further. Jumbo shrimp, *antojito* platters, and steak are available for staggeringly low prices. Snacking opportunities exist outside in the **loncherías** and **taco stands.** For a more formal meal, try one of the *centro's* many inexpensive restaurants or, for the view, a joint along the Malecón in Olas Altas. Enjoy your meal with **Pacífico** beer, the pride of Mazatlán.

Cafe Machado, Constitución 515 (tel. 81 22 45), on the Plaza Machado. Funky artwork, cool tunes, and damn tasty food. *Comida corrida* 25 pesos. Impersonate Hemingway's Santiago by eating marlin tacos (28 pesos). Open M-Sa 8am-1am.

Restaurante Vegetariano (tel. 82 61 43), Angel Flores and Frías. Phenomenal veggie cuisine at unbeatable prices. Enjoy the enormous *comida corrida,* which includes salad, soup, a hearty main course, fresh wheat bread, juice, and dessert, all for only 30 pesos. A family joint. Open daily 8am-4:30pm.

Restaurant de Esther, Serdán 1605 at Canizales. Fans work furiously overhead to cool Mexican patrons feasting on Esther's home cooking. *Comida corrida* around 25 pesos. *Enchiladas suizas* 20 pesos. Open daily 7am-10pm.

Cafe Pacífico, Constitución 501 (tel. 81 39 72), across from the Plazuela Machado. This famous pub is a relic, with all the charm of grand Old Mazatlán shining through the big-screen cable TV and top-40 dance tunes. Try to tune out the "entertainment" and tune into the delicious tuna salad (20 pesos), platter of assorted cheeses (30 pesos), or Mexican style shrimp (35 pesos). Open daily 11am-1am.

El Mambo Lonchería, Espinoza Ferrusquilla 204 (tel. 8 04 73), across from the bus station. Mexican pottery, hanging seashells, eclectic art, a macaw, and a parrot that speaks more Spanish than most of the patrons. Tasty, large, and cheap meals. Shrimp *al mojo de ajo* (in garlic) 35 pesos. Open M-Sa 7am-7pm.

SAND AND SIGHTS

Mazatlán's greatest asset is its 16km of beach stretching from just north of Olas Altas to well north of the *Zona Dorada*. Just north of Old Mazatlán and along Av. del Mar is **Playa Norte,** a decent stretch of sand, if you don't mind small waves and the stares of local *machos* who play soccer here. Solo women should consider doing their swimming farther north. As you hone in on the *Zona Dorada,* the beach gets cleaner, the waves larger, and Playa Norte eases into **Playa Las Gaviotas.** Just past Punta Sábalo, in the lee of the islands, is **Playa Sábalo,** whose great waves and golden sand are enjoyed to the point of abuse by crowds of *norteamericanos.* Most area beaches are patrolled by lifeguards, who use color-coded flags to inform bathers of conditions: green, yellow, and red flags respectively indicate the level of undertow (green being little undertow, red meaning strong undertow); white flags mean *quemadores* (jellyfish) are around. "Sábalo-Centro" buses pass by all of these beaches.

As Playa Sábalo recedes to the north, crowds thin rapidly and you can frolic on the glorious beaches all by yourself. Take the yellow "Sábalo" bus to the last stop and walk left; you'll soon reach nearly deserted **Playa Bruja,** with tons of beautiful sand and 1 to 2m waves. Camping is permitted, but be cautious after dark, and camp in groups whenever possible. Solo women should be especially cautious. For a 360° view of Mazatlán, the sea, and the surrounding hills, climb to the top of **El Faro, the second-tallest lighthouse in the world.** The hike (about 30min.) is almost unbearable in the summer; avoid the heat by ascending in the early morning or late evening.

The **Acuario Mazatlán,** Av. de los Deportes 111 (tel. 81 78 15 or 81 78 16), off Av. Camarron Sabalo near the Bora Bora club, keeps piranhas and other feisty fish (up to 250 breeds in all) in a slew of cloudy tanks. *(Open daily 9:30am-6:30pm. Admission 25 pesos, children 3-13 10 pesos, students 15 pesos.)* The aquarium, supposedly the largest in Latin America, also hosts performing sea lions and birds. In the aviary, check out the hooded orioles, bar-vented wren, and social flycatchers in the trees. The Acuario is one block back from the beach and north of the Sands Hotel; the turn-off is marked by a shimmering blue sign.

Mazatlán's **tower divers** may not have their heads screwed on straight, but their acrobatic and dangerous plunges are nevertheless very entertaining. Performances take place during the day, but be forewarned that the divers will not perform unless they can pull in a sufficient number of "tips" beforehand. The best time to watch the divers is 10-11am and 4:30-6:30pm, when guided tour buses arrive and tourists fork over their pesos. The best viewing spots are located just south of the towers. On days when the water is too rough for diving, climb the tower to watch the waves break below. The diving platform is on Paseo Claussen, just south of Zaragoza and north of La Siesta Hotel.

William Blake saw the universe in a grain of sand and eternity in an hour. You too may get bored at the beach. When the throngs of tourists and street vendors hawking plastic sunglasses get on your nerves, hop on one of the boats to **Isla de la Piedra** (see p. 238), where locals go to escape the crowds. Boats leave from the wharf on Av. del Puerto at Gutiérrez Najera. Buses to the wharf depart from near the public market (2.20 pesos). To walk there, take 21 de Marzo from the cathedral past Serdán to the water, and then turn left on Av. del Puerto (7 pesos round-trip; last boat back leaves at 5pm). **Islas Venados** (Deer Island) is a relatively deserted scrap of land with fine diving; catamaran boats leave for the island from the Agua Sports Center in the **El Cid Resort** (tel. 13 33 33, ext. 341) in the *Zona Dorada* (daily 10am, noon, 2, and 4pm, 35 pesos). Waterpark mania has hit Mazatlán with the new **Mazagua** (tel. 88 00 41), located north of the *Zona Dorada* near Puerta Cerritos. *(Open Mar.-Oct. daily 10am-6pm. Admission 35 pesos, children under 4 free).* To get there, take a "Cerritos Juárez" bus (2.20 pesos). Go bonkers in the wave pool or shoot down slippery slides.

The newly restored and luxurious **Teatro Angela Peralta,** at Carnaval and Libertad near the Plaza Machado, hosts an impressive variety of cultural programs and has a fascinating history to boot.

NORTHWEST MEXICO

ENTERTAINMENT

Hordes of *norteamericano* high schoolers ditch the prom and hit Mazatlán yearly to twist, shout, and drink. Supply rises to meet demand, and more than a dozen discos and bars clamor for gringo dollars. Inside, only the occasional Mexican rock tune reminds you that you're in a foreign country. Most of the hot clubs are in the area known as **Fiesta Land,** in the *Zona Dorada,* a block from Paseo del Mar. If you address bartenders or bouncers in Spanish, they'll smile, pat you on the head, and answer in near-perfect English, never forgetting to address you as *amigo.* Cover charges can be hefty, especially during high season and holidays (such as *Semana Santa* and Christmas).

Bora-Bora (tel. 86 49 49), on Paseo del Mar at the southern end of the *Zona Dorada,* next to the beach. Always jam-packed with touring (and local) teenagers clad in neon (or nothing at all) and dancing on the bars. Those so inclined may dance in cages. Clubbers in search of more wholesome activities can head for the volleyball court and swimming pool. Drinks start at 18 pesos. Cover F-Su 20-40 pesos, including beer. Open daily 9pm-4am.

Valentino's (tel. 86 49 49), in the same complex as Bora-Bora, attracts a more sophisticated, late-20s crowd, which would rather lounge on leather couches and bob their heads to the music than get naked and procreate to it. Cover F-Su 30 pesos, beer 12 pesos, mixed drinks 20 pesos. Open daily 9pm-4am.

Cafe 808, Calle Laguna 13 (tel. 16 54 26), at Las Garzas. Acid jazz and techno are the house specialties. Long-haired locals clad in black sip drinks in the cool blue neon-lit interior. Open Tu-Su 6pm-2am. Cover 20 pesos (includes one drink) on high-season weekends.

Pepe Toro, Las Garzas 18 (tel. 16 54 26), at Loaiza. Caters to gay men and lesbians. The dance floor starts hoppin' after 11pm. Open daily 7pm-2am.

El Toro Bravo, Av. del Mar 550 (tel. 85 05 95). Watch twenty-something, would-be cowpokes drink their bladders full of beer (15 pesos) and then attempt to ride the bucking saddle—you put the rest together. Wednesday is Ladies' Night. Cover Th-Su 30 pesos. Open daily 9pm-4am.

Señor Frog's (tel. 85 11 10), on Paseo del Mar, a few blocks north of Bora-Bora. A chain establishment, but nonetheless a place to shake that booty. American pop and dance music blast from a wall of speakers as youngsters wriggle in a wall of flesh. Cover F-Su 25-45 pesos, open bar some nights. Open daily 9pm-4am.

■ Near Mazatlán: Isla de la Piedra

Just a five-minute boat ride from the mainland, Isla de la Piedra consists of 10km of glistening sand, crashing waves, and rustling palm trees. Imagine drinking out of a coconut while lying in a hammock and feeling like you're in a postcard—that's Isla de la Piedra. Less crowded and less shamelessly developed than mainland beaches, the island is an unspoiled haven of sunshine and ocean popular among Mexican families. Isla de Piedra's beaches don't have the intimidating undertow of the mainland, either.

The main attractions are, of course, the beautiful **beaches.** Wriggle your toes in the cool sand, duck the waves, or bask in the radiant sun. You won't have any trouble finding a place to spread your towel. Bring a frisbee or a kite or a surf board—you'd have to try to not have a good time at this beach. If you're into water sports, try a trip on a banana boat (40 pesos), rent snorkeling equipment (90 pesos per hr.), or borrow a boogie board (10 pesos per hr.). The restaurants will point you the right way. Aging horses may also be hired (60 pesos per hr.) farther up the beach.

Obtain **tourist information** at any of the restaurants near the beaches; most owners have been on the island for ages and are more than willing to help. The island's one **telephone** (tel. 85 44 50) is located across from the dock

The island is perfect for a daytrip or to camp out. **Carmelita's,** a few meters from the shore, offers space for tents, sturdy trees for hammock slinging, and use of the bathroom and grill free of charge. If you can't camp out, Carmelita also offers clean rooms with the basics: electricity and private bathrooms with running water (80 pesos for 1-3 people). **Lety's,** adjacent to Carmelita's, offers similar free lodging. It also has spacious rooms with modern bathrooms, desks, lighting, two beds, and a sofa-bed (85 pesos for 1-3 people). There's nothing nicer than camping out on a secluded beach and gazing at the stars, but be careful and don't stray too far from the center. Seafood rules on the island. **Carmelita's** serves shrimp platters and fish fillets, both with *frijoles,* tortillas, salad, and rice (25 pesos; open 9am-6pm). If you're tired of seafood, head to **Lety's** for a quarter-chicken (25 pesos) or quesadillas (20 pesos; open 9am-7pm). Listen to the cool tunes and watch folks play volleyball by the shore at **Restaurant Estebin,** a two-minute walk from Carmelita's. You'll find the same ol' grub: fish fillets (25 pesos) and chicken (22 pesos; open daily 9am-7pm).

Getting There: To get to the island, take a green "Independencia" **bus** (2 pesos) from the *mercado* to the **Embarcadero de la Isla de la Piedra.** From there, take a **boat** (5min., every 10min., 7 pesos round-trip) to the island. Remember that the last boat back to the mainland leaves at 5pm; **trucks** (2 pesos) and **taxis** (6 pesos) will be waiting to take passengers to the *playa.* Alternatively, walk straight away from the boat landing and follow the concrete path across the island for about 15 minutes. All the restaurants and stores (all three of them) are in a cluster on the beach.

DURANGO

Durango

State capital and commercial center, Durango (pop. 490,000) is a busy, heavily trafficked city caught up in Mexico's 20th-century push toward industrialization. The view of the impressive Baroque cathedral is partially obstructed by cars and buses busily cruising along the roads surrounding the central Plaza de Armas. Industrialization and commerce haven't completely taken over Durango, though, and Durango's residents revel in their city's Old-West flavor—cowboy boots and hats are the norm. The city's collection of colonial architecture and its handful of decent museums make it a deserving stopover on your way through the region, but it isn't likely to hold your interest for more than a day.

ORIENTATION AND PRACTICAL INFORMATION Durango's bus station is located on the eastern outskirts of town. To reach the *centro,* catch a "Centro" bus in front of the station (2 pesos); taxis are also available (10-12 pesos). After dark, a taxi is the only way to travel. The suburbs and outskirts of Durango are full of tractor-trailers and warehouses; to find fun, culture, and amenities, you'll have to head downtown. Most sites of interest lie within a few blocks of the cathedral and its **Plaza de Armas. 20 de Noviembre** is a major east-west thoroughfare passing in front of the cathedral; **Juárez** runs north-south. Navigating downtown is fairly simple; the streets are in a grid and rarely change names.

Estrella Blanca and **Rojo de los Altos** (tel. 18 30 61) send buses to Aguascalientes (6hr., 6 per day 5:30am-7pm, 102 pesos), Guadalajara (9½hr., 5 per day 7:15am-7pm, 190 pesos), and Mazatlán (7hr., 5 per day 10am-10pm, 100 pesos). **Transportes Chihuahuenses** has service to Mexico City (11hr., 4 per day 4-10pm, 276 pesos), Monterrey (8½hr., 9 per day, 195 pesos), Torreón (3hr., 18 per day, 75 pesos), and Zacatecas (4½hr., 6 per day 8am-11:15pm, 102 pesos). **Omnibus** (tel. 18 33 61) sends buses to Aguascalientes (7hr., 4 per day, 135 pesos), Ciudad Juárez (8hr., 3 per day 6-10pm, 315 pesos; non-direct 12hr., 5 per day 8am-11:05pm, 250 pesos), Matamoros (13hr., 7:35, 9:15pm, 310 pesos), Mexico City (direct 12hr., 4 per day 7-10pm, 317 pesos; nondirect 13hr., 7:30am, noon, 6:05 and 11:05pm, 317 pesos), San Luis Potosí (6hr., 7 per day 7:30am-11pm, 154 pesos), and Zacatecas (6hr., on the half hr. 7:30am-9:30pm, 102 pesos). **Turistar Ejecutivo** and **Futura** (tel. 18 37 84) serve Mazatlán (7hr., 9am, 5pm and midnight, 110 pesos), Monterrey (9hr., 6 per day 9am-10pm, 195 pesos), and Nuevo Laredo (12hr., 8 and 9:30pm, 300 pesos). **Transportes del**

Valle Poanas and **Transportes de Durango** send buses to points throughout the state of Durango, including Agua Vieja (2½hr., every hr. 7am-8pm, 28 pesos), Los Angeles (1¼hr., about every hr. 7am-8pm, 19 pesos), and Villa Unión (2hr., every half hr. 7am-8pm, 25 pesos). Tourist information can be found at the **Dirección Estatal de Turismo y Cinematografía,** Hidalgo 408. From the plaza, walk one block away from the cathedral to 5 de Febrero, which runs east-west parallel to 20 de Noviembre. Then turn right and walk about three blocks to Hidalgo, and turn left. The very helpful staff provides maps and brochures. **Banco Serfín** (tel. 12 80 33), on the plaza, is open 9am-5pm on weekdays and has great **exchange** rates, as well as a 24-hour **ATM.** In an **emergency,** dial 06. The **police** (tel. 17 54 06 or 17 55 50) are at Felipe Pescador and Independencia. **Hospital General** (tel. 11 91 15), on 5 de Febrero and Norman Fuentes, is open 24 hours. The **post office** (tel. 11 41 05) is at 20 de Noviembre and Roncal, 12 long blocks from the Plaza de Armas (open M-F 8am-7pm, Sa 9am-1pm). The **postal code** is 34000. **Telecomm,** at Felipe Pescada and Zaragoya, about eight blocks from the plaza, offers **fax** service (open M-F 8am-8pm, Sa 9am-4pm). There is a **caseta** at 5 de Febrero 106 Pte. (open daily 8am-10pm). The **phone code** is 118.

ACCOMMODATIONS Inexpensive accommodations abound near the market, a few blocks west of the Plaza de Armas. The **Casa de Huéspedes El Hotelito,** Progresso 102 Sur (tel. 12 31 81), near the market, has clean, basic rooms with TVs and bathrooms. The Casa is simple and gives you what you paid for. The elderly dueña also rents large furnished apartments with kitchens (singles 50 pesos; doubles 60 pesos; apartments 80 sweet pesos). For a step up in comfort (but also a step up in price), the **Hotel Plaza Catedral,** Constitución 216 Sur (tel. 13 26 60), right off 20 de Noviembre and next door to the cathedral, will fix you right up. The old convent that houses it is labyrinthine, rooms are carpeted and have phones and cable TVs, and bathrooms keep the hot water flowing (singles 110 pesos; doubles 130 pesos; triples 150 pesos). Adequate and affordable rooms can also be found at **Hotel Buenos Aires,** Constitución 126 Nte. (tel. 11 31 28), and **Hotel El Gallo,** 5 de Febrero 117 (tel. 11 52 90), near the market; come early because both places lock their doors around 11pm (singles around 80 pesos; doubles around 100 pesos).

FOOD Inexpensive meals aren't hard to find in Durango. Cheap comedores and taco stands cluster around the market, and most are open daily. The ones housed in their own buildings are generally better than the street-cart comedores. The tiny, plant-filled cafe and whole grain bakery **Al Grano,** Negrete and Zaragoza, a few blocks west of the cathedral, serves super breakfast specials (15 pesos) and tasty Mexican fare (burritos 5 pesos), including vegetarian dishes (open M-Sa 8am-8pm). Watch your food being prepared in the open kitchen at the family-run **Cafe de la Mancha,** 20 de Noviembre 807 Pte., at Zaragoza (*comida corrida* 22 pesos, *gorditas* 4 pesos, *tortas* 7 pesos; open daily 9am-8pm). **La Terraza,** 5 de Febrero 603 Pte., overlooks the Plaza de Armas from a spacious balcony. Garish stained glass and neon set the stage for well-prepared food and a popular after-hours nightspot (small pizzas around 30 pesos; breakfast 15 pesos; beer 10 pesos; nightly mariachi madness around 11pm; open daily 8am-1am).

SIGHTS AND ENTERTAINMENT The most imposing building in town is the enormous **cathedral** overlooking the Plaza de Armas. Its ornately carved Baroque facade rests under two enormous bell towers and includes figures of angels, an eagle, and a heavy iron cross. Its dim interior is filled with marble pillars, carved wood, and wrought iron. Just west of the cathedral on 20 de Noviembre waits the white brick **Teatro Ricardo Castro.** Construction of the building began in 1900; today it houses temporary exhibitions, and hosts theatrical productions and film screenings. The huge **Palacio de Gobierno,** on 5 de Febrero between Martinez and Zaragoza, was built by a Spanish mining tycoon and expropriated by the government after Mexico won independence. Inside, a bronze likeness of Benito Juárez glares amid colorful murals depicting the city's history.

Pick Up the Phone, Pick Up the Miles.

You earn frequent flyer miles when you travel internationally, why not when you call internationally? Callers can earn frequent flyer miles if they sign up with one of MCI's airline partners:

- American Airlines
- Continental Airlines
- Delta Airlines
- Hawaiian Airlines
- Midwest Express Airlines
- Northwest Airlines
- Southwest Airlines
- United Airlines
- USAirways

Please cut out and save this reference guide for convenient U.S. and worldwide calling with the MCI Card with WorldPhone Service.

Your MCI Worldphone Access Numbers

MCI

COUNTRY	WORLDPHONE TOLL-FREE ACCESS #
# Singapore	8000-112-112
# Slovak Republic (CC)	00421-00112
# Slovenia	080-8808
# South Africa (CC)	0800-99-0011
# Spain (CC)	900-99-0014
# Sri Lanka (Outside of Colombo, dial 01 first)	440100
# St. Lucia ✣	1-800-888-8000
# St. Vincent	1-800-888-8000
# Sweden (CC) ◆	020-795-922
# Switzerland (CC) ◆	0800-89-0222
# Syria	0800
# Taiwan (CC) ◆	0080-13-4567
# Thailand ★	001-999-1-2001
# Trinidad & Tobago ✣	1-800-888-8000
# Turkey (CC) ◆	00-8001-1177
# Turks and Caicos ✣	1-800-888-8000
# Ukraine (CC) ✣	8▼10-013
# United Arab Emirates ◆	800-111
# United Kingdom (CC) To call using BT ■	0800-89-0222
To call using C&W ■	0500-89-0222
# United States (CC)	1-800-888-8000
# Uruguay	000-412
# U.S. Virgin Islands (CC)	1-800-888-8000
# Vatican City (CC)	172-1022
# Venezuela (CC) ✣ ◆	800-1114-0
Vietnam ●	1201-1022
Yemen	008-00-102

#	Automation available from most locations.
(CC)	Country-to-country calling available to/from most international locations.
✣	Limited availability.
▼	Wait for second dial tone.
▲	When calling from public phones, use phones marked LADATEL.
■	International communications carrier.
★	Not available from public pay phones.
◆	Public phones may require deposit of coin or phone card for dial tone.
●	Local service fee in U.S. currency required to complete call.
▶	Regulation does not permit Intra-Japan calls.
❖	Available from most major cities

And, it's simple to call home.

1. Dial the WorldPhone toll-free access number of the country you're calling from (listed inside).
2. Follow the voice instructions in your language of choice or hold for a WorldPhone operator.
   - Enter or give the operator your MCI Card number or call collect.
3. Enter or give the WorldPhone operator your home number.
4. Share your adventures with your family!

The MCI Card with WorldPhone Service... The easy way to call when traveling worldwide.

COUNTRY		WORLDPHONE TOLL-FREE ACCESS #
American Samoa		633-2MCI (633-2624)
#Antigua		1-800-888-8000
	(available from public card phones only)	#2
#Argentina (CC)		0800-5-1002
#Aruba ✣		800-888-8
#Australia (CC) ◆	To call using OPTUS ■	1-800-551-111
	To call using TELSTRA ■	1-800-881-100
#Austria (CC) ◆		022-903-012
#Bahamas		1-800-888-8000
#Bahrain		800-002
#Barbados		1-800-888-8000
#Belarus (CC)	From Brest, Vitebsk, Grodno, Minsk	8-800-103
	From Gomel and Mogilev	8-10-800-103
#Belgium (CC) ◆		0800-10012
#Belize	From Hotels	557
	From Payphones	815
# Bermuda ✣		1-800-888-8000
#Bolivia (CC) ◆		0-800-2222
#Brazil (CC)		000-8012
#British Virgin Islands ✣		1-800-888-8000
#Brunei		800-011
#Bulgaria		00800-0001
#Canada (CC)		1-800-888-8000
#Cayman Islands		1-800-888-8000
#Chile (CC)	To call using CTC ■	800-207-300
	To call using ENTEL ■	800-360-180
#China ❖		108-12
	For a Mandarin-speaking Operator	108-17
#Colombia (CC) ◆		980-16-0001
	Collect Access in Spanish	980-16-1000
#Costa Rica ◆		0800-012-2222
#Cote D'Ivoire		1001
#Croatia (CC) ★		0800-22-0112
#Cyprus ◆		080-90000
#Czech Republic (CC) ◆		00-42-000112
#Denmark (CC) ◆		8001-0022
#Dominica		1-800-888-8000
#Dominican Republic	Collect Access	1-800-888-8000
	Collect Access in Spanish	1121
#Ecuador (CC) ✣		999-170
#Egypt (CC) ◆	(Outside of Cairo, dial 02 first)	355-5770
El Salvador		800-1767
#Federated States of Micronesia		624
#Fiji		004-890-1002
#Finland (CC) ◆		08001-102-80
#France (CC) ◆		0800-99-0019
#French Antilles (CC)	(includes Martinique, Guadeloupe)	0800-99-0019
French Guiana (CC)		0-800-99-0019
#Gabon		00-005
#Gambia ◆		00-1-99
#Germany (CC)		0-800-888-8000
#Greece (CC) ◆		00-800-1211
#Grenada ✣		1-800-888-8000
#Guam (CC)		1-800-888-8000
Guatemala (CC) ◆		99-99-189
Guyana		177
#Haiti ✣		193
	Collect Access in French/Creole	190
Honduras ✣		8000-122
#Hong Kong (CC)		800-96-1121
#Hungary (CC) ◆		00▼800-01411
#Iceland (CC) ◆		800-9002
#India (CC) ❖		000-127
	Collect Access	000-126
#Indonesia (CC) ◆		001-801-11
Iran ✣		(SPECIAL PHONES ONLY)
#Ireland (CC)		1-800-55-1001
#Israel (CC)		1-800-940-2727
#Italy (CC) ◆		172-1022
#Jamaica ✣	Collect Access	1-800-888-8000
	(From Special Hotels only)	873
	(From public phones)	*2
#Japan (CC) ◆	To call using KDD ■	00539-121▶
	To call using IDC ■	0066-55-121
	To call using ITJ ■	0044-11-121
#Jordan		18-800-001
#Kazakhstan (CC)		8-800-131-4321
#Kenya ❖		080011
#Korea (CC)	To call using KT ■	009-14
	To call using DACOM ■	00309-12
	To call using ONSE	00369-14
	Phone Booths✣ Press red button, 03, then ∗	
	Military Bases	550-2255
#Kuwait		800-MCI (800-624)
Lebanon	Collect Access	600-MCI (600-624)
#Liechtenstein (CC) ◆		0800-89-0222
#Luxembourg (CC)		0800-0112
#Macao		0800-131
Macedonia (CC) ◆		99800-4266
#Malaysia (CC) ◆		1-800-80-0012
#Malta		0800-89-0120
#Marshall Islands		1-800-888-8000
#Mexico (CC)	Avantel	01-800-021-8000
	Telmex ▲	001-800-674-7000
	Collect Access in Spanish	01-800-021-1000
#Monaco (CC) ◆		800-90-019
#Montserrat		1-800-888-8000
#Morocco		00-211-0012
#Netherlands (CC) ◆		0800-022-9122
#Netherlands Antilles (CC) ✣		001-800-888-8000
#New Zealand (CC)		000-912
Nicaragua (CC)	Collect Access in Spanish	166
	(Outside of Managua, dial 02 first)	
	From any public payphone	*2
#Norway (CC) ◆		800-19912
Pakistan		00-800-12-001
#Panama		108
	Military Bases	2810-108
#Papua New Guinea (CC)		05-07-19140
#Paraguay ✣		00-812-800
#Peru		0-800-500-10
#Philippines (CC) ◆	To call using PLDT ■	105-14
	To call using PHILCOM ■	1026-14
	Collect Access via PLDT in Filipino	105-15
	Collect Access via ICC in Filipino	1237-77
#Poland (CC) ✣		00-800-111-21-22
#Portugal (CC) ✣		05-017-1234
#Puerto Rico (CC)		1-800-888-8000
#Qatar ★		0800-012-77
#Romania (CC) ✣		01-800-1800
#Russia (CC) ◆ ✣	To call using ROSTELCOM ■	747-3322
	(For Russian speaking operator)	747-3320
	To call using SOVINTEL ■	960-2222
#Saipan (CC) ✣		950-1022
#San Marino (CC) ◆		172-1022
#Saudi Arabia (CC) ✣		1-800-11

For more information or to apply for a Card call: **1-800-955-0925**

Outside the U.S., call MCI collect (reverse charge) at: **1-916-567-5151**

Please cut out and save this reference guide for convenient U.S. and worldwide calling with the MCI Card with WorldPhone Service.

A few museums in town may be worth a visit. The **Museo de las Culturas Populares,** at Juárez and Barreda, displays ceramics and textiles and hosts talks, dances, and other events (open Tu-Su 10am-6pm; admission 5 pesos, free on Sundays). The **Museo Regional de Durango,** known as **El Aguacate** (the Avocado) for its unique shape and texture, at Madero Serdán and Negrete, houses some paintings by Miguel Cabrera, as well as exhibits on the state's history, indigenous groups, paleontology, and natural resources (open Tu-Su 9am-4pm; admission 1 peso, free on Sunday). The **Museo de Arte Contemporanea,** at Negrete and Pasteur, hosts temporary exhibits of local and national artists (open Tu-Su 10am-6pm; admission 3 pesos).

At night, live it up in the city's discos and bars. A popular disco is **La Covacha,** Pino Suárez 500 Pte. (tel. 12 39 69), at Madero, where locals dance to international and Latin hits (cover 25 pesos; open Th-Su 9pm-4am). **Excalibur,** at Mascareñas and Cárdenas, is a mellower hangout, with pool tables and live mariachi music on weekends (open daily 4pm-late).

On Sundays, city officials close off the streets in Durango's *centro* to celebrate **Domingo Familiar,** when vendors hawk kid-pleasing treats and street performers play to the crowds. For 10 days at the beginning of July, Durango celebrates the **Feria Nacional** in commemoration of the city's founding. Parades and fireworks liven things up and reservations become a must. Over 200 films have been shot in the desert around Durango. Some of the **sets** have been left standing and are now tourist attractions. The tourist office organizes trips to visit the sets. You can try a do-it-yourself version by taking an Estrella Blanca bus to **Chupaderos** (30min., every 25min., 8 pesos). Ask the driver to let you off on the highway near the sets.

Northeast Mexico

Dust-swept border towns, former colonial settlements, old mining hotspots, and congested urban centers dot the expansive deserts and occasional rich forests of Northeast Mexico. The incredible lack of tourists—one of the most constant features across the disparate towns and cities of the Northeast—creates a paradisiacal sense of calm among the proud, parched-white missions and wide streets. Eager for the industry and not (yet) inundated with tourists, Northeastern Mexicans welcome the few travelers who do trickle through with boundless hospitality, always open to share the culture of which they are so proud.

This description, though, does not apply to the border towns of **Tamaulipas** and **Nuevo León.** Not for the faint of heart, these towns are replete with money-dropping, booze-guzzling day tourists, lost souls, industrious young men and women from all over Mexico and Central America eager for access to the American Dream (or just a full day's work), and U.S. border police determined to keep them out.

Farther south, however, the gringo influence and grubbiness fade. In Monterrey, a metropolis of millions, lovely cathedrals and gorgeous parks peek out of a sea of gray skyscrapers; Monterrey has become a chic city without catering to tacky tourists and is one of the most gay-friendly cities outside the D.F. If it's beach you crave, the *noreste* offers little more than a taste. Fresh, salty Tampico has never been able to draw flocks of tourists: you can swim, tan on the sand, and munch on fresh seafood, but it's far from picturesque.

Perhaps the most wonderful part of the Northeast lies within the state of **San Luis Potosí.** Even the town of Real de Catorce, ridden with peyote-hungry backpackers, is largely untouched by modernity, with one phone, hundreds of burros, and mountain views. Xilitla offers the eco-warrior caves, waterfalls, rivers, wild parrots, semi-tropical rainforests, and ruins an hour or two from congested city centers. The city of San Luis Potosí is a quiet jewel—the capital of the state, it is a playground of regional culture, awesome architecture, and colonial appeal. The **Zacatecas** state was blessed with a location smack in the middle of Mexico's legendary silver store; as a result, its capital, now a university town, is far more classically colonial, commercial, and cosmopolitan than is customary for the Northeast. While the *noreste* might not feature prominently in the plans of most tourists, the quiet appeal and dry charm of its towns and cities might surprise you.

HIGHLIGHTS OF NORTHEAST MEXICO

- Despite incongruous architecture, the eclectic, fast-paced city of **Monterrey** (see p. 255) is still beautiful. Rage with the best of them in the one-of-a-kind **Barrio Antiguo** (see p. 260). Monterrey also has a **thriving gay scene** (see p. 260).
- The tiny, lush town of **Xilitla** (see p. 282) might very well be Eden. Be sure to check out **Las Pozas** (see p. 283), a gorgeous expanse of jungle "ruins" built early this century by a crazy Englishman.
- Dubbed "City of Plazas," **San Luis Potosí** (see p. 272) is one of the most beautiful and tourist-free cities in Mexico.
- **Real de Catorce** (see p. 280) is a tiny ex-mining town high in the Sierra Madres that now specializes in gorgeous mountain views and peyote.

Brownsville, Texas

"Bienvenidos Y'all" reads a sign in a store in Brownsville (pop. 135,000), capturing perfectly the bicultural spirit of the city. Lanky men sporting cowboy hats and driving late-model American cars are as likely to speak to you in Spanish as in English. A 90% Hispanic population and wholesale markets blaring Mexican top-40 hits will make you feel as though you've already entered Mexico. Few tourists come to Brownsville, and for good reason: despite its incredibly friendly and helpful residents, this border town offers little to comfort or interest tourists.

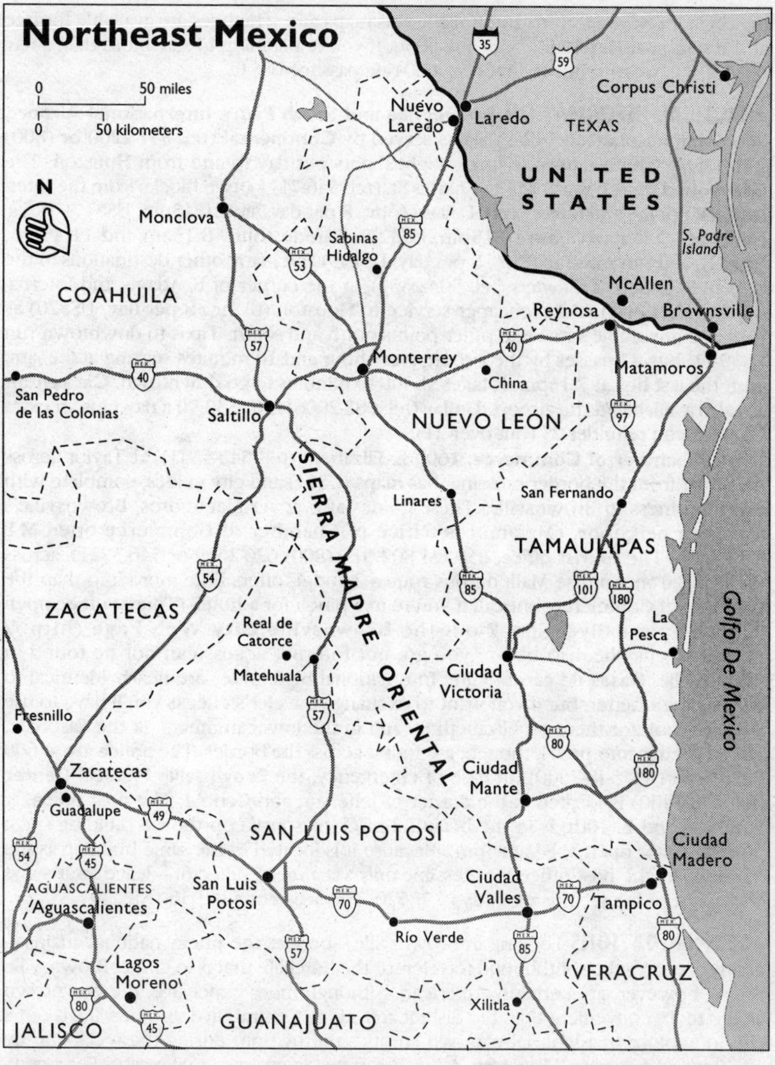

ORIENTATION Most points of interest lie northwest of **International Blvd.,** which traverses the city before turning into the **International Bridge** that leads into Matamoros, Mexico. Numbered streets run parallel to International Blvd., starting at **Palm Blvd.** Perpendicular streets are named after American presidents in order, and Washington and Adams hold the greatest touristic interest. **Elizabeth St.,** right near the border, is the city's main commercial thoroughfare and precedes the presidential streets. Street numbers correspond to location—770 Elizabeth is between 7th and 8th. The few tourists who do visit Brownsville are often drawn to the old city near the border and the swanky suburban hotel strip in the southeastern part of town. At night, the area around the border is desolate; women and solo travelers should probably avoid it. The cautious traveler should also think twice before entering **Southmost Rd.,** perpendicular to and east of International Blvd., late at night. **Local buses,** which travel long routes throughout Brownsville, run from 6am to 7pm and cost 75¢ (seniors 15¢); all buses leave on the hour or the half-hour from City Hall on E. Washington St. between E. 11th and E. 12th. Bus maps and schedules are available for free at the station at City Hall or call 548-6050. If you're planning to stay more than a day or two, it is worthwhile to invest in a 20-ride pass for US$12.

PRACTICAL INFORMATION **Brownsville and South Padre International Airport,** 700 S. Minnesota (tel. 542-4373), is served by **Continental** (tel. 541-2200 or (800) 231-0856), which currently offers eight flights per day to and from Houston. The **Greyhound** station is at 1134 E. Charles St. (tel. 546-7171), two blocks from the International Bridge, and **buses** serve Dallas (13hr., 8 per day 7am-10:15pm, US$49), Houston (8hr., 9 per day 7am-10:15pm, US$27), Laredo (6hr., 8:15am and 11:45pm, US$22), and San Antonio (7hr., 8 per day, US$33) and many other destinations in the U.S. and Mexico. **Trailways** (tel. 504-2351), at the corner of E. Adams and International, offers even faster, cheaper service to Houston (6½hr., 8 per day, US$20) as well as comparable service to other points north and south. **Taxis** to downtown run US$9-11. Bus #7 passes by the airport every hour and 10 minutes starting at 6:23am, with the last bus at 7:13pm. It takes about 40 minutes to go downtown. **Car rentals** are also available at the airport. **Dollar** (tel. 982-2006) is US$32.90 a day plus an extra US$15 if you're under 25 (but over 21).

The **Chamber of Commerce,** 1600 E. Elizabeth (tel. 542-4341), at Taylor across the street from the border crossing, has maps (US$1) and city guides, complete with every business in Brownsville. These guides also cover Matamoros, Brownsville's southern neighbor. (Matamoros Office of Chamber of Commerce open M-F 8am-5pm.) The **tourist office,** 650 FM 802 (tel. (800) 626-2639 or 546-3721), across the street from Sunrise Mall, on bus routes 2 and 4, offers little more info than the Chamber of Commerce, but call if you're in a pinch for a hotel. (Tourist office open 8:30am-5pm daily.) Check out the **Brownsville City Web Page** (http://www.brownsville.org) before you go, but Internet access can not be found in Brownsville. **Casas de cambio** line International Blvd.; rates are nearly identical to banks', if not better, but if you want to exchange traveler's checks you'll have to use a bank—look for them on Elizabeth St. and in the lower numbers on the East Side. The best rates into pesos, though, are found across the border. The **police** are at 600 E. Jackson (tel. 548-7000). In case of emergency, the **Brownsville Medical Center** (tel. 544-1400) is located at the corner of Jefferson and Central. The **post office,** at Elizabeth and E. 10th, is in the beautiful brick masonry courthouse building (post office counter open M-F 9am-5pm). Because it is located in the same building as the courthouse, the post office is accessible only via a metal detector—leave your swiss army knife at home. The **zip code** is: 78520. The **area code** is: 956.

ACCOMMODATIONS Lodging in Brownsville—besides the pricey national chains—gently prepares the southbound traveler for the hotel life that is to come. Brownsville prices, however, are certainly American. Although more expensive, the downtown area is more convenient than the distant area along Central Blvd. Brownsville is not a city to explore by night. Downtown empties out by 9pm during the week and by 10:30pm on Friday and Saturday. After that, travel in groups or take cabs. For a comfortable and reasonable place to stay downtown, head to **Hotel Colonial,** 1147 Levee St. (tel. 541-9176), the street next to Elizabeth, where bright rooms come with full amenities and a friendly staff awaits you in the quiet, cool lounge (singles $36; doubles $41). The **Cameron Motor Hotel,** 912 E. Washington (tel. 542-3551), also offers refuge from the interminable heat in a cool lobby. Rooms come with bath, cable TV (65 channels!), air-conditioning, and telephones—enough equipment to drown out the car alarms and thumping Mexican rap music from the vehicles on the street below. Call ahead because Hotel Cameron is often full. (Singles and doubles US$37 plus tax.) If you don't mind the trek, cheaper motels line Central Blvd. on the Los Ebanos and Jefferson and Central bus lines. But remember, you get what you pay for—rooms start at about US$29.

FOOD Catering primarily to local residents, Brownsville restaurants serve a combination of simple Mexican dishes and hamburgers. Downtown, cafes open and close early (most shut down by 5:30pm); all offer similar menus of burgers and burritos.

Late diners should seek out the friendly, red dining room of **Restaurant Nuevo Leon,** 1203 E. Adams St. (tel. 541-9522; open daily until 11pm). For a really late snack, **Lucio's Cafe,** 1041 E. Washington, is open 24 hours on Friday and Saturday. This is a comfortable place to hang out, but don't expect fast food. For the salsa-weary, **Artichoke Deli,** 108 E. Elizabeth (tel. 544-7636), a 10-minute walk from downtown (also on the #1 bus line), offers bright clean walls adorned with chile peppers, cartoons, and photos and paintings by local artists. Perhaps the closest thing in Brownsville to a vegetarian-friendly eatery, the deli offers fresh salads and sandwiches for about US$5, and the largest selection of beer south of San Antonio. On the weekends, the restaurant turns into one of the most happening places in town when local classic rock bands draw in lively, safe crowds. (Open M-Th for lunch 11am-4pm. Doors stay open Friday until midnight and Saturday until 1am.)

SIGHTS AND ENTERTAINMENT It may look like a non-descript border town, but Brownsville boasts one of the top zoos in the nation for rare and endangered species, as well as several museums honoring the city's role in American history. The **Gladys Porter Zoo,** 500 Ringgold St. (tel. 546-7187), off E. 6th on the #2 *(Los Ebanos)* bus line, offers a 31-acre tropical sanctuary where most animals live in open quarters surrounded only by waterways. *(Open daily 9am-sunset. Tickets sold until 5pm; extended to 6pm during summer weekends. Admission US$6, children US$3.)* The collection includes lowland gorillas, Sumatran orangutans, and white rhinos.

If a long, hot day of wholesale shopping and exchanging money leaves you longing for a yuppified evening, kick back at the **Artemis Sports Bar and Grille,** 1200 Central Blvd. (tel. 542-2361), a five-minute walk from the medical center. The Artemis is hip, clean, and relatively safe—even at night. TVs blare football games, and, on Fridays and Saturdays, live bands play everything from alterna-rock to Spanish pop. (Happy hour 11am-7pm. Open M-F 11am-2am, Sa-Su noon-2am; kitchen closes at midnight.)

Pump up the Volume

On the bus rides, in local bars, and on the street, you will hear three major types of Mexican music. **Corridas** are laments of love gone wrong, sung to a plaintive slow tune. Vincente Fernandez's "Volver, volver, volver a tus brazos otra vez" (roughly trans: "to return, to return, to return to you) is one of the most famous corridas. Sung by *gauchos,* the original cowboys, **rancheros,** always accompanied by accordion, celebrate the fruits of the earth or pray for God to bless or save crops and livestock. Young and old Mexicans alike belt out or quietly whistle corridas and rancheros on a regular basis. The black and red-clad men with bells and capes, the same ones that appear on tequila ads outside of Mexico, are **mariachis**. The most traditional Mexican music, mariachi is lively and light-hearted. Wandering *mariachis* will strike up in front of restaurants always play at traditional fiestas. When you feel moved by the spirit (or the tequila), feel free to stand with your legs shoulder-width apart, throw your head back, and cry "AY, ay ay ay..." along with any music.

TAMAULIPAS

Matamoros

While border-patrol jeeps line the Brownsville side of the Río Grande, cows quietly stare across the river from Matamoros. Calmer than its sister city to the north, Matamoros offers numerous tree-and-bench-lined squares for the weary traveler and store-lined walking streets for the exuberant shopper. But lest this sound too peaceful, don't worry: the town has enough booze and border brawls (especially at night) that you'll need to dream up your own reasons to stay out after dark.

ORIENTATION To reach Matamoros from Brownsville, walk or drive (bring along all documentation and check your insurance policy's validity in Mexico—see p. 9) across the International Bridge. Pedestrians pay a budget-busting 35¢ or 2 pesos to leave either country. Autos pay US$1. From the border crossing, the city extends out in a V-shape following the bend in the **Río Bravo;** the left (eastern) arm of the V is defined by **Calle 1,** which runs parallel to the river and leads directly to the **Central de Autobuses,** 2km down in the southeast corner of the city. As the city opens up to the right (west) toward **Calle Hidalgo,** the street numbers increase. Heading south of the border, the main area of activity and importance is the **centro,** focused in the area between Calles 5 and Calles 11, and between Bravo and Abasolo.

PRACTICAL INFORMATION To reach the center of town from the border area, take one of the yellow minibuses labeled "Centro" (3 pesos). "Central" minibuses go to the **bus station**, the **Central de Autobuses**. Returning to the border, catch a minibus marked "Puente." Minibuses really do make paradas continuas; just wave your index finger at them and they'll stop almost anywhere (local transport info tel. 17 88 80). **Bus** traffic flows through the **Central de Autobuses,** on Canales at Aguilar, off Calle 1 (station closed on Sunday). **ADO** (tel. 12 01 81) goes to Tampico (8hr., 6 per day 3:30-10pm, 140 pesos), Tuxpan (12hr., 4 per day 5:30-10pm, 216 pesos), and Veracruz (16 hrs., 3 per day 4-10pm, 343 pesos) with numerous stops in between. **Noreste** (tel. 13 27 68) services Monterrey (6hr., 12 per day, 104 pesos) and also travels to Reynosa (2hr., every 2hr., 31 pesos). **Transportes del Norte** (tel. 16 66 15 or 16 65 80) runs to Mexico City (14hr., 1 ejecutivo per day at 6:40pm, 517 pesos and 4 1st-class buses per day, 383 pesos), Saltillo (7hr., 4 per day, 145 pesos), and San Luis Potosí (10hr., 5 per day, 223 pesos). **Omnibus de Mexico** (tel. 13 76 93), sends buses to Reynosa (31 pesos), Saltillo (146 pesos), Monterrey (104 pesos) and Río Bravo (22 pesos) every hour on the hour or on the half-hour between 7am and midnight. Check your baggage at the bus station for as long as you want (1st hour 2 pesos, each additional hour 1 peso).

On your right, just past the turnstile marking entry into Mexico, lies the **tourist office** (tel. 12 36 30), which offers a few general pamphlets about all of Mexico, and lots of friendly advice. Get your Matamoros maps from the Brownsville **Chamber of Commerce. Casas de cambio** dot the centro, particularly along Calles 5 and 6, but the best exchange rates await in the bus station or from friendly **ATMs** like the one at **Bancomer** at Matamoros and Calle 6 (tel. 13 90 00). Bancomer, like all major banks, also exchanges traveler's checks (open M-F 9am-6pm, Sa 9am-5pm). **Police** (tel. 16 20 21, 17 22 05, or 17 01 35) are always stationed around International Bridge and the border. They can also be reached 24hr. The **post office** is in the bus station (office open M-Sa 9am-4pm). The **postal code** is 87361. The **phone code** is 891.

ACCOMMODATIONS AND FOOD Although prices in Matamoros are reasonable, expect the basics and little more. The market area, where most of the budget accommodations are located, quickly loses its bustling crowds after nightfall—be very careful. **Hotel Majestic** (tel. 13 36 80), on the pedestrian mall on Abasalo between Calles 8 and 9, offers simple, clean, bright rooms with private bath and promises an even greater selection when renovations are finished (singles 80 pesos for 1 person, 90 pesos for 2 people; doubles 110 pesos for 2 people, each additional person 25 pesos). **Hotel Sexta Avenida** (tel. 16 66 66 or 16 66 96), on Calle 6 between Zaragoza and Terán, is a bit more expensive and farther from the centro, but worth it for the rare quiet and comfort (singles 195 pesos; doubles 235 pesos).

The food in Matamoros is typically overpriced and border-town bland. If you choose to follow the crowds heading to delectable **outdoor stands,** try to avoid the generic nachos and look instead for **brisket.** Also be sure to check for proper cleanliness and hygiene. There are some great small **cafes** on the streets surrounding the pedestrian mall. **Café y Restaurant Frontera** (tel. 546 71 87), on Calle 6 between N. Bravo and Matamoros, is filled with locals soaking in the air-conditioning and enjoying the optical-illusion floor while digging into Mexican specialties (15-20 pesos). Look for the heart-shaped sign. (Open daily 7am-10pm.) Slip into an upstairs booth at **Cafeteria Deli,** 1307 Calle 7 (tel. 13 93 87), between Abasolo and Matamoros, to escape the bright sun and to enjoy a range of *antojitos* (15-25 pesos; open daily 6am-9pm).

SIGHTS AND ENTERTAINMENT Matamoros and Abasolo, pedestrian-only between Calles 6 and 11, are lined with shops and vendors; closer to Calle 6 is modern clothing, while crafts abound around Calle 9. Brash vendors pounce upon any sign of interest, so be wary and look weary. For even more condensed browsing, the old market, or **Pasaje Juárez,** has entrances on both Matamoros and Bravo between Calles 8 and 9. Bright piñatas and rows of glittering jewelry brighten the dim interior of **Mercado Juárez,** the new market on Abasolo between Calles 9 and 10. Remember, though—markets farther south offer higher quality and lower prices. For a cultured evening, stop by the **Teatro de la Reforma** (tel. 12 51 21), on Calle 6 between González and Abasolo. Renovated in 1992, this beautiful colonial brick building is home to everything from classical drama to contemporary Mexican theater (tickets 20-30 pesos). If you're in the mood to bar-hop, boogie, and booze, think twice. Most reasonably priced **bars and discos** near the border are very unsafe at night. More upscale drinking occurs in bars attached to fancy hotels.

Reynosa

Horse-drawn carts share the streets with 16-wheelers in Reynosa (pop. 600,000) as hand-pushed carts sell fruit cups outside American 7-11 mini-markets. Reynosa, which is just across the border from McAllen, Texas, still exudes the atmosphere of a small border town, despite its growing population. There isn't a lot to see or do in Reynosa, but with a walkable, well-planned center, wide clean streets, a shady plaza, and plenty of shopping, Reynosa is a tiny gem by border town standards.

ORIENTATION Reynosa is 150km from Monterrey and 645km from Mexico City; it can be reached from McAllen by taking 23rd St. 12km south into Hidalgo and then over the **International Bridge.** From Mexico, **Rte. 2** from Matamoros and **Rte. 40** from Monterrey both lead straight into town. The city forms a square with the **International Bridge** border crossing at the northeast corner. The city rises to the **central plaza**, one square block bounded by Zaragoza on the north, Hidalgo on the west, Morelos on the south, and Juárez on the east. The main city is a very walkable 10 blocks by 12 blocks, but if you get tired, peseros run in nearly all directions for about 1 peso; taxis will try to overcharge, so haggle.

PRACTICAL INFORMATION The **bus station** is on Colón in the southwest corner of town. To reach the center, turn left as you exit the station and walk until you hit Colón. Then take any city bus labeled "Centro" or turn left on Colón, walk five blocks to Juárez, and go right on Juárez; the plaza is six blocks down. Among the many companies servicing the Reynosa station, **ADO** (tel. 22 87 13) offers primarily evening service with routes to Tampico (7hr., 5 per day 4:30pm-11pm, 150 pesos), Veracruz (16hr., 2 per day 8:30pm and 11pm, 345 pesos), and Villahermosa (24hr., 11pm, 419 pesos). **Futurama** (tel. 22 17 19) offers ejecutivo service to Monterrey (4hr., 8pm, 102 pesos), Mexico City (16hr., 5:20pm, 519 pesos), and Guadalajara (15hr., 8pm, 482 pesos). **Omnibus de México** (tel. 22 33 07) runs to Monterrey (3hr., 16 per day, 77 pesos), Saltillo (5hr., 8 per day 3:30am-4:30pm, 108 pesos), and Chihuahua (18hr., 9am and 10:30 pm, 375 pesos). **Noreste** (tel. 22 02 06) offers the most extensive service; it will take you to San Luis Potosí (11½hr., 9 per day 4:20am-10:30pm, 210 pesos), Matamoros (2hr., every 45min. 6am-10:05pm, 29-31pesos), Monterrey (4hr., every 30min. 6am-8:45pm, 68-77 pesos), Nuevo Laredo (4hr., 7 per day, 80 pesos), and many other destinations.

The **tourist office,** Cámara de Comercio, on Chapa at Allende, one block north of Zaragoza and one block east of Juárez, has free pamphlets with maps and brochures (open M-F 9am-5pm). The friendly staff at the **Palacio Municipal** on the Morelos side of the plaza will also happily answer any questions. **Casas de cambio** are scattered all along Hidalgo and the plaza area, but none accept traveler's checks. **Banorte,** on Morelos at Hidalgo (open M-F 9am-2:30pm) and **Bancomer** (tel. 22 81 01), opposite Banorte on Zaragoza, have competitive rates, accept traveler's checks, and also offer 24hr. **ATMs.** The **exchange office** is open M-F 9am-6pm, Sa 9am-5pm. The **police** (tel. 22 00 88 or 22 00 08) are housed southwest across Canal Anzaldvas. The **post office** (tel. 22 01 10) is on the corner of Díaz and Colón (open M-F 8am-4pm, Sa 9am-1pm). The **postal code** is 88500. The **phone code** is 89.

ACCOMMODATIONS The many hotels around the plaza are pricey. The cheapest are around south Díaz and Hidalgo St. Although boisterous and congested during the day, this area becomes desolate and even a little scary at night. Cuídate. **Hotel Avenida,** Zaragoza 885 Ote. (tel. 22 05 92), sets its sparkling clean, carpeted rooms around a beautiful leafy patio complete with chirping birds. With its proximity to the main plaza, A/C-TV combo, and the occasional antique piece of furniture, you can't lose. You can receive calls in your room, but you have to go outside to make them. (1 person 150 pesos; 2 people 180 pesos; 3 people 220 pesos; 4 people 260 pesos.) If you are able to call three to four days in advance to reserve a room, **Hotel Nuevo Leon,** Díaz 580 (tel. 22 13 10), south of the plaza near the corner of Mendez, offers by far the best bargain in town. Although not air-conditioned, the small, clean rooms come with industrial-strength fans, fully functional bathrooms, and cable TV. (1 person 80 pesos; 2 people 90 pesos; 3 people 100 pesos; 4 people 110 pesos.)

FOOD For delicious, super-cheap fare, join locals at outdoor stands or at open-air family-run cafeterias. There are many near the bus station as well as near the plaza. To sit down and escape the heat, you don't need to go far, either. Despite the classy paintings by Frida Kahlo and Diego Rivera at the immaculate and cool **Café Sánchez** (tel. 22 16 65), on Morelos off Hidalgo at the southwest corner of the plaza, it's the food that lures in the diverse crowd of businessmen, bus drivers, and families of 10. Entrees (22-40 pesos) are riquisimos. (Open daily 7am-9pm.) **Cafe Paris,** Hidalgo 815 (tel. 22 55 35), just past Morelos, is as gorgeous inside as it is out, and, in addition, offers super-reasonable fixed-price meals (breakfast 14 pesos, lunch and dinner 17 pesos; open daily 6:30am-10pm).

SIGHTS AND ENTERTAINMENT At nightfall, the main plaza hosts congregating couples, young and old. The **Hidalgo marketplace** may not offer any substantial deals, but it is a great spot for people-watching. For an abridged history, check out the beautiful storefront mural on the corner of Zaragoza one block east of Canales, just a few blocks south of the border crossing. It was funded by Bacardi (their billboard forms the last scene of the mural). Doesn't it just make you want to sip a Cuba Libre?

Well...OK then, but be careful. Drinking in Reynosa is serious stuff. Most bars tend to be near the border. Most brawls and brain damage occur near the border. Coincidence? You decide. Clustered along Ocampo near the border, most nightspots have on- and off-seasons. For a month during spring breaks, Reynosa turns into a miniature Cancún; the off-season, on the other hand, is a mellow time. Young people head year-round to the **Alaska Grill,** on Ocampo between Allende and Zaragosa, a dark, cold discotheque with two levels, an enormous dance floor, and a fully-stocked bar. In summer, happy "hour" (1pm-1am) means no cover with all beers (US$1), and all shots and mixed drinks (US$1.50).

Check out Reynosa's community theater at one of **La Casa de la Cultura's** free productions (tel. 22 99 89), next door to the tourist bureau, or just drop in to find out about cultural events (open M-F 9am-7pm).

Laredo, Texas

Having served under seven flags in its history, Laredo is growing at a mad pace. The strip malls and interminable suburban sprawl of Laredo are offset somewhat by its beautiful central square and the highly wanderable surrounding historic districts. The

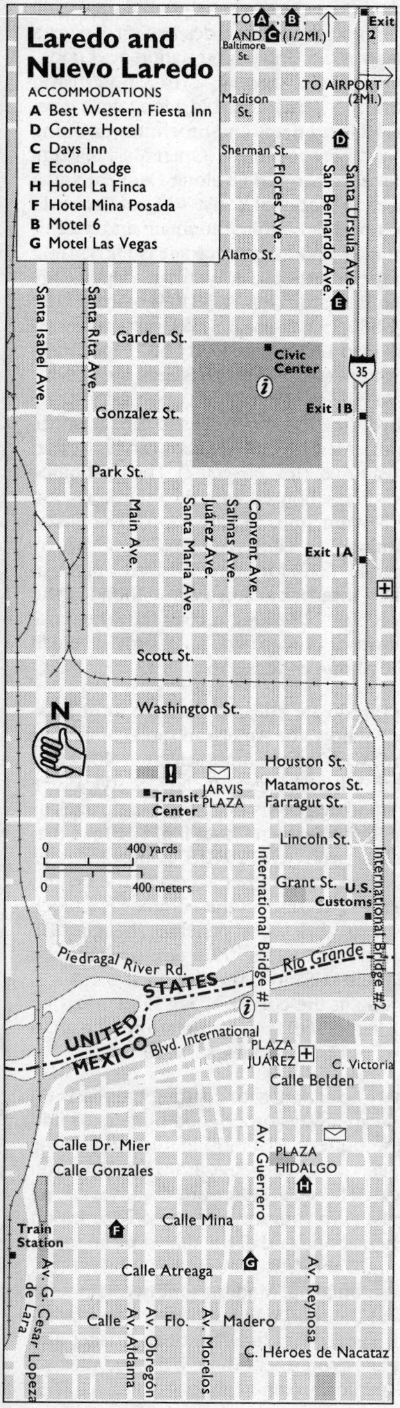

recent growth of this once-small town is exemplified by a modern bus station and the invasion of fast food chains.

ORIENTATION Laredo's downtown centers around **International Bridge #1,** which becomes **Convent St.** on the U.S. side and runs north. Seven blocks north of the border and one block west of Convent is **Jarvis Plaza,** surrounded by all the main government buildings and delimited by **Matamoros, Farragut, Salinas** and **Juárez.** The other main thoroughfare is **San Bernardo,** which originates near the border three blocks east of Convent and stretches north past the **Laredo Civic Center** and **Chamber of Commerce,** as well as most of the motels and restaurants. One block east lies **I-35,** which used to be the eastern border of town for most travelers. Many newer hotels and nightspots, however, now lie miles north and east of Jarvis Plaza and the border, accessible only by car and taxi. East-west streets are named after American and Mexican military and political figures.

PRACTICAL INFORMATION **The airport** (tel. 795-2000) is on Maher, northeast of town. **American Eagle** (tel. (800) 433-7300) serves Dallas (2hr., 6 per day); **Continental Express** (tel. (800) 525-0208 and 723-3402) covers Houston (1½hr., 10 per day); and **Taesa** (tel. (800) 328-2372 and (956) 725-1022) goes to Mexico City (2hr., M, Tu, Th, and F). The **bus station** (tel. 723-1321) is on San Bernardo and Matamoros. **Greyhound**-affiliated service runs to cities throughout the U.S., and sends daily buses to Aguascalientes and León (14hr., 5pm, US$55 or US$60), Monterrey (3hr., 7 per day, US$20), San Luis Potosí (11hr., 3 per day 7pm-2am, US$49), and Querétaro (13hr., 3 per day 3:30pm-2:30am, US$65). However, traveling south from Nuevo Laredo is much cheaper than leaving from Laredo and provides more destinations and departures as well as **luggage lockers** (first 6hr. US$2, next 6 hr., $US2, every additional 24hr. or portion US$5). Scoot around town on **El Metro city buses** (tel. 795-2280), which run from Matamoros and Farragut streets on Jarvis Plaza (every 30min. daily 6am-9pm, US$0.75, children US$0.25, seniors US$0.10). Get schedules from their office in the **Laredo Inter-**

modal Transit Center on the south side of the plaza, or sit in its air-conditioned waiting room and check the flashing board for the next bus to your destination. To get a look at the layout of the city, check out the map at the Greyhound station next door.

The **tourist office** is housed in the **Chamber of Commerce,** 2310 San Bernardo (tel. (800) 292-2122 or 722-9895). Take bus #2 San Bernal to avoid a long walk. Cordial staff offers colorful, informative, and easy-to-read maps and brochures directing you to a plethora of sights and eateries in the downtown area. (Open M-Sa 8:30am-5:30pm.) Currency can be exchanged at **Casas de cambio** all along Convent and a few are sprinkled throughout downtown. **Laredo National Bank,** 700 San Bernardo (tel. 723-1151), at the corner of Farragut, has both a bubbling fountain and a 24hr. **ATM** (bank open M-F 9am-4pm, Sa 9am-3pm). A good **supermarket** is **HEB,** 1002 Farragut (tel. 791-3571), two blocks south of the courthouse downtown. (Open daily 7am-10pm.) **Sunshine Laundromat,** 2900 San Bernardo (tel. 722-8403), north of the Chamber of Commerce, has do-it-yourself (US$0.75 per wash, US$1 per dry, detergent available) or same-day full service (small load US$5, large load US$7; open daily 8am-10pm). Although the main **police** department (tel. 795-2800) is near the airport, the foot and bike station is on Farragut next to HEB market (station open daily 10am-5pm). **J&A Pharmacy,** 201 West Del Mar Blvd. (tel. 717-3839), lies to the far northeast of town (open M-F 9am-8pm, Sa 9am-4pm). Medical emergencies can be treated at **Mercy Regional Medical Center,** 1515 Logan Ave. (tel. 718-6222). The **post office** is at 1300 Matamoros (tel. 723-3643), on Jarvis Plaza, housed with the courthouse, so be prepared for metal-detectors (open M-F 8:30am-5pm, Sa 9am-noon). The **postal code** is 78040. You can **fax** at the **Western Union,** 711 Salinas (tel./fax 722-08-50), by Jarvis Plaza. UPS and pool cues are also available. Look for more Western Unions in the bus station and in every HEB supermarket. **Internet access** can be found at the **Laredo Times,** 111 Esperanza Dr. (tel. 728-2505 or 728-2504), off San Dario, accessible by the San Bernardo bus, three miles north of downtown. They provide email accounts (US$17 per month, negotiable). The **phone code** is 956.

ACCOMMODATIONS Nice hotels in Nuevo Laredo are cheaper than the most inexpensive Laredo lodgings. Nevertheless, those who value American motel amenities (drinkable tap water, carpets, newer furniture) will find an ample selection along **San Bernardo** north of the Chamber of Commerce, where budget hotels (U.S. style) are a dime-a-dozen. Expect good deals and nice, standard rooms from such big names as **Days Inn,** 4820 San Bernardo (tel. 722-6321); **Best Western Fiesta Inn,** 5240 San Bernardo (tel. 723-3603); or **Motel 6,** 5310 San Bernardo (tel. 725-8187). Most lodgings are accessible by the #2 El Metro city bus. For relatively closer access to the center, try the **Cortez Hotel,** 3113 San Bernardo (tel. 727-1001), but the entrance is a block over on Santa Ursula. With jungle-print bedsheets, dark wood panelling, hanging Tiffany-style lamps, and wrought-iron decorated mini-patios, these are perhaps the kitschiest rooms around. (Singles US$35; doubles US$40.) Another great bargain is **EconoLodge,** 2620 Santa Ursula (tel. 722-6321) at the corner of San Bernardo, one block past the Chamber of Commerce. The friendly staff transforms it from a chain to a local joint: enjoy the ultra-clean rooms. (Singles US$35; doubles US$40.)

FOOD Head downtown for a copious culinary selection with a strong emphasis on Tex-Mex cuisine (who knew?). Salsa-phobes can always order good burgers or find salvation in seafood restaurants and Chinese buffets. Fast-food joints and yummy taquerías line San Bernardo. Great food awaits you at **Tacolare,** 1206 San Bernardo (tel. 727-5115), just north of the railroad tracks. The small storefront disguises a large and inviting restaurant, a favorite among locals. Turn your meal into a cooking lesson by watching the cooks in the glassed-in kitchen at one end of the dining room (great selection under US$5; open M-Sa 11am-10pm). **Danny's Restaurant,** 802 Juárez (tel. 724-3185), on Jarvis Plaza near the courthouse building. Modern southwest art adds local color to Danny's nondescript decor, and the food unquestionably sets it apart from the fast-food chains: it's good! Lunch specials include Mexican brisket and mushroom burgers (US$4-6). Danny encourages you to eat three balanced meals a day—heaping breakfast specials US$3.69. (Open daily 6am-11pm.)

SIGHTS AND ENTERTAINMENT The **Civic Center,** on **San Bernardo** next to the Chamber of Commerce, is the place to catch traveling performances or the **Laredo Philarmonic Orchestra** (tel. 727-8886; concerts some nights Oct.-May at 8pm). Every February, Laredo turns into one big **Washington's Birthday Celebration,** which includes a parade—led by the town princess dressed as Pocahontas—and the **Martha Washington Ball.** For something a bit more sinister, get a consultation, a palm-reading, or a cure at **Yerbería de San Judas,** 711 Salinas (tel. 725-8336), a witchcraft store selling herbs and religious charms.

"Entertainment" in Laredo (e.g. drinking yourself into a stupor and losing $150 to a pool shark) is complicated by the large distances between establishments and the relative scarcity of taxis—most people drive into Laredo from the highway. On top of this, police are cautious and alert, especially at night, frequently arresting people for public drunkenness and drunk driving.

Nuevo Laredo

Nuevo Laredo pulses with commerce, from small souvenir shops to enormous trailers passing through with NAFTA-spurred trade. Today, pesos and dollars pour through Nuevo Laredo (pop. 420,000) at a dizzying pace, leaving its residents to snatch the crumbs that fall through the cracks. Laredo's cheap liquor and abundant artisans attract over-the-border-for-an-afternoon tourists, but the city's many plazas and friendly inhabitants make it more desirable than most Mexican border towns.

ORIENTATION

International Bridge #1 is the main way for pedestrians to go into Mexico; simply plunk down the US$0.35 (for information on crossing the border, see p. 9). Travelers stick to the *centro.* **Av. Guerrero** emerges from **International Bridge #1** as the main thoroughfare running south from the border. Three plazas along Guerrero define the downtown. Small, inviting **Plaza Juárez** lies just two blocks from the border, large, central **Plaza Hidalgo** adjoins the **Palacio Federal** in the heart of the city, and **Plaza Mexico**, farthest south, is bordered on the southern end by Gonzales. The bus station lies to the far south of town. Areas of interest extend approximately seven blocks east and west of Guerrero.

PRACTICAL INFORMATION

Airplanes: (tel. 14 07 05), at the extreme southwest of the city, off Rte. 2. Purchase **Mexicana** tickets at **Viajes Furesa,** Guerrero 830 (tel. 12 96 68), open M-F 9am-7pm, for the flight to Mexico City (12:40am direct and 5:25pm M-Sa). Also purchase tickets here for U.S. destinations leaving from the Laredo airport.

Buses: Station is at Refugio Romo 3800, southwest of the city and quite a trek from the *centro.* To get to the border, take any blue-and-white or green-and-white bus marked *"Puente."* Hop off when you cross Gonzáles if you're going to the *centro.* To get to the station from the border, take the bus marked "Central." 24hr. **luggage storage** 22 pesos, but you have to drop off your bags before you exit the station: head toward the waiting room as if you were going to catch another bus rather than out the *salida.* **Ómnibus de México** (tel. 14 06 17) goes afternoons and evenings to Aguascalientes (10hr., 3 per day, 299 pesos), Leon (12hr., 3 per day, 350 pesos), Saltillo (3½hr., 121 pesos), and Zacatecas (8hr., 2 per day, 254 pesos). **Noreste** (tel. 14 21 00) travels to Matamoros (6hr., 8 per day 7am-midnight, 106 pesos) and Reynosa (4hr., 10 per day, 80 pesos). **Turistar, Futura,** and **Transportes del Norte** share an information line (tel. 14 06 70) and a counter, but they maintain separate routes and services. **Transportes del Norte** boasts a bus to Monterrey (3hr., every 30min., 85pesos).

Tourist Office: Delegación Turismo (tel. 12 01 04), at the Nuevo Laredo tip of the bridge before Mexican customs. Extensive supply of brochures in both Spanish and English. Open M-Sa 10am-3pm. If you miss the *delegación*, call the Consultario de Turismo (tel. 12 73 97), which is open M-F 9am-8pm.

Currency Exchange: As usual, **casas de cambio** (especially the one at the border) offer the best exchange rates. Major banks line Guerrero near Plaza Hidalgo. **Banamex** and **Serfin** (tel. 12 15 02), on Canales and Guerrero, each have a 24hr. **ATM.** Open M-F 9am-5pm.

Market: Gigante, Reforma 4243, on the southern extension of Guerrero. Take a bus toward the *centro* and get off when you see the enormous pink complex.

Emergency: Dial 06.

Police: (tel. 12 21 46).

Pharmacy: Farmacia Calderón (tel.12 55 63), on Guerrero west of Plaza Hidalgo. Open 24hr.

Hospital: ISSTE (tel. 12 34 91), on Victoria and Reynosa to the east of Plaza Juárez. Limited English spoken.

Post office: (tel. 12 21 00), in the back of the Palacio Federal, on the northeast corner of Dr. Mier and Camargo. **Fax** and **telegram** service. Open M-F 8am-6pm, Sa 9am-noon. **Mexpost** (tel. 13 47 17) is located on the opposite side of the *palacio.* Open M-F 9am-6pm, Sa 9am-1pm.

Telephones: LADATELs and **Telmexs** are throughout the downtown border area, particularly near Plaza Hidalgo and Plaza Juárez.

Phone code: 87.

ACCOMMODATIONS

Most hotels of all prices are found within a few blocks of the city's main plazas. There are some great bargains if you're willing to look around. A bed, a toilet, and a lightbulb are standard equipment, but don't expect much more.

Hotel Mina Posada, Mina 3521 (tel. 13 14 73), 6 blocks west of Guerrero. With just 6 rooms, this charming and quiet inn boasts better-than-U.S. lodgings at slightly less-than-U.S. prices. The individually decorated rooms have carpet, TV, A/C, telephones, lush flora, you name it. Two-person staff offers great service and conversation. Singles 209 pesos; doubles 256 pesos.

Hotel La Finca, Reynosa 811 (tel. 12 88 83), just off Gonzalez by the southeast corner of Plaza Hidalgo. On a quiet street smack in the *centro,* spacious, clean rooms rise above a cool, red-tile patio: great value with A/C, TV, phone. Singles 140 pesos; doubles 170 pesos; 30 pesos each additional person.

Motel Las Vegas, Arteaga 3017 (tel. 12 20 30), 1½ blocks west of Guerrero and 4 blocks south of Plaza Hidalgo. Spacious rooms boast folkloric wooden furniture and clean bathrooms. A/C, TV, and the stellar value make up for the slightly dank smell of some rooms. Singles 60 pesos; doubles 75 pesos.

FOOD

Home to the oft-imitated, never duplicated fajita, Nuevo Laredo's culinary fortes are meat and seafood. **Cabrito,** the roasted goat kid found throughout the northeast, and fajitas, often sold by the kilo, are well worth the extra money. Most of the good stuff is south of Herrera, around Guerrero 1700.

Playa Azul (tel. 14 55 35, ext. 735), around Guerrero 2001. Great place to kick back and relax as you enjoy your *ceviche* (marinated fish cocktail with lime juice) and *telenovelas* (soap operas). Homey dining room decorated with tasteful *campesino* furniture and a selection of seafood specialties (25-45 pesos) that will blow your mind. There's also a full traditional Mexican menu with lunch specials for 20-28 pesos. Open daily 8am-11pm.

Memo's Grill, Victoria 2803 (tel. 12 27 92), on Plaza Juárez, brings together good food, great decor, and a central location. Admire the ranch antiques covering the walls while you enjoy a lunch special, such as *guisados del día* (19 pesos) or anything else from the extensive $US5-and-under menu. Open 8am-8pm, every day except Wednesday.

Cafeteria los Pinos, on the east side of Plaza Juárez, is a hidden gem for travelers who find themselves getting hungry at an odd hour. The slow fan may leave you hotter than the delicious *salsa verde* at noon, but at 3am, it should be no problem. Open 24hr.

SIGHTS AND ENTERTAINMENT

What's a commercial center without a **market?** The largest (and most expensive) *mercados* are concentrated around **Guerrero** near the border. With an ample selection of sturdy wooden furniture, pottery, and practical goods, this may be just the place to load up on souvenirs for travelers exiting Mexico. Although better prices and higher-quality goods can be found further south, Nuevo Laredo has a tantalizing and terrific supply of liquor stores. Along Guerrero, for blocks south of the border, stores carrying lavish varieties of liquor all advertise the lowest prices in town. Pick up 750mL of Kahlua for US$7 or a liter of Cuervo Gold for US$4.50.

Those in search of cultural titillation can head to the **theater**, the **Teatro de la Ciudad** on Guatemala near Aguirre in the southeast corner of town, accessible via the "Viveros" buses. Strolling up and down Guerrero can be relaxing in the evenings when the three plazas fill with people gaily chatting and pleasantly passing time; the fountain on Nacatez and Guerrero is a favorite resting spot. If all this ambling about is not your style, then head to **Señor Frog's** (tel. 13 30 11), the self-proclaimed "Home of the Mother Margarita," just blocks south of the border on Belden at the corner of Ocampo. Although beers and tequila shooters are steeply priced (US$2 or 15 pesos), the lack of cover charge, the expert bartending, and the wonderfully hilarious cartoons and comics that adorn every inch of the restaurant/bar never cease to amaze. El Señor packs 'em in on weekends.

Tampico

If you've seen Humphrey Bogart in *The Treasure of the Sierra Madre,* you might think of contemporary Tampico (pop. 434,000) as the hot, dirty, unfriendly oil town that every gringo is itching to skip. Although it is somewhat dirty and crowded and incredibly hot, Tampico is anything but unfriendly. The pleasant nearby beach is often uncrowded on weekdays, and Tampico's two main plazas are full of fabulous architecture and much-needed greenery. Founded in the 16th century on the ruins of an Aztec village, Tampico was destroyed by pirates in 1623. Two hundred years later, though, Santa Anna ordered the city re-settled, and it soon grew into one of the most important oil ports in the world. Despite the ominous oil tankers and loads of litter, Tampico is trying to carve out a new identity: *tampiqueños* built the first beach resort in all of Tamaulipas, and their seafood is ridiculously fresh. Tampico may not be terrific yet, but it gets an "E" for "Effort."

ORIENTATION The town centers around the **Plaza de Armas** and the **Plaza de la Libertad.** To the north of the Plaza de Armas is **Calle Carranza,** to the east is **Olmos,** and to the south is **Díaz Mirón.** Juárez runs parallel to Olmos one block east and along the western side of Plaza de la Libertad. One block south of Olmos, **Madero** is the northern border of Plaza de la Libertad. Continuing east and parallel to Olmos, you'll find **Aduana** and **Lopez de Lara,** while **Colón, 20 de Noviembre,** and **Sor Juana Ines de la Cruz** run parallel to Olmos as you move westward. To get to the city center from the bus stop, take a yellow taxi (35 pesos), minibus (2.50 pesos), or *colectivo* (2.50 pesos, 5 pesos with luggage).

PRACTICAL INFORMATION The **bus station,** on Zapotal, north of the city, was under a mess of construction scheduled to be finished by September of 1998. **Omnibus de México** (tel. 13 43 49) serves Ciudad Valles (2½hr., 4 per day in the evenings only, 53 pesos), Monterrey (7hr.,11:30pm, 167 pesos), Saltillo (8½hr., 11:30pm, 167 pesos), and Tuxpan (3½hr., 4 per day, 69 pesos). **ADO** (tel. 13 55 02) serves Matamoros (7 hr., 6per day, 147 pesos), Puebla (10hr., 4 per day, 160 pesos), and Xalapa (9hr., 2 per day, 163 pesos). **Futura** (tel. 13 45 50) serves Monterrey (7½hr., 14 per day, 167 pesos). **Frontera** heads to Ciudad Mante (2½hr., every 2hr., 45 pesos), Guadalajara (12hr., 2 per day, 269 pesos), and Reynosa (7½hr., 9 per day, 150 pesos). **Estrella Blanca, Del Norte, Oriente,** and **Turistar** (tel. 13 42 35) unite to travel to Mexico City (9 or 12hr., every hr., 143 or 167 pesos), among other destinations.

The **tourist office,** 20 de Noviembre 218 Nte. (tel. 12 26 68 or 12 00 07), one block west and two blocks north of Pl. de Armas, has got the goods—maps 'n' guides to the city (open M-F 8am-7pm, Sa 9am-2pm). Exchange currency or traveler's checks at **Central de Divisa,** Juárez 215 Sur (tel. 12 90 00; open M-F 9am-6pm, Sa 9am-1:30pm). **Bancrecer** (tel. 12 20 32 or 14 26 21), on Díaz Mirón next door to Sixpack, also exchanges traveler's checks (open M-F 9am-5pm, Sa 10am-2pm) and has a 24-hour **ATM.** The **Sixpack,** Díaz Mirón 405 Ote. (tel. 12 24 15), three blocks east of the southeast corner of the Plaza de Armas, is a **supermarket** that sells more than just beer (open daily 8am-10pm).

In an **emergency,** dial 06. The **police** (tel. 12 10 32 or 12 11 57) are on Tamaulipas at Sor Juana de la Cruz. The **Red Cross** (tel. 12 13 33 or 12 19 46) offers 24-hour **ambulance service.** If you need a **pharmacy,** try **Farmacia el Fenix** (tel. 12 43 51), at the corner of Díaz Mirón and Olmos (open daily 8am-11pm). English-speaking doctors can be found at the **Hospital General de Tampico,** Ejército Nacional 1403 (tel. 15 22 20 or 13 20 35), near the bus station. Medical and legal aid for tourists is available toll-free (tel. 91 or 01 800 90 392). The **post office,** Madero 309 Ote. (tel. 12 19 27), in the yellow building on Plaza de la Libertad (open M-F 8am-7pm, Sa 9am-1pm), also has a **Mexpost** office (tel. 12 34 81) inside. **Internet access** can be found at the **video arcade** (tel. 12 44 43) at Juárez 102 Nte. for 20 pesos per hour (open M-Sa 9:30am-8:30pm, Su 10:30am-8pm). The **postal code** is 89000. **LADATELs** that work properly are clustered around the corners of the Pl. de Armas. The **phone code** is 12.

ACCOMMODATIONS AND FOOD Quality budget hotels are rare in Tampico, but for those willing to pay 170-250 pesos, many of the larger hotels on Madero and Díaz Mirón near the plazas provide excellent rooms. The cheapest of these, **Hotel Plaza,** 204 Madero (tel. 14 17 84 or 14 17 31), promises clean air-conditioned rooms with TVs, telephones, and a minimum of bugs. **Hotel Capri,** Juárez 202 Nte. (tel. 12 26 80), sits between Calles Altamira and Obregón. Clean, no-frills rooms with fans and free coffee are pleasant, except for the noise from the street below, but hey—at least you and a slew of fun-loving families are in the middle of things. (Singles 55 pesos; doubles 65 pesos; 10 pesos per additional person.)

Seafood is the standard fare in Tampico. Be sure to try delicious *jaiba* (blue crab). If you're feeling adventurous, try eating at a seaside stand or at the covered food court near the river (a few blocks from Plaza de la Libertad). As you walk upstairs, you will be accosted by small "restaurant" (read: moving countertop) owners pushing their fresh food and phat prices. Have fun—but investigate the kitchen before chowing down. **Naturaleza,** Aduana 107 Nte. (tel. 12 49 79), one of Tampico's vegetarian restaurants, offers excellent options and wonderful conversation with the owner, Catalina Durán Raigoza, in Spanish, English, or French (open daily 9am-8pm). Wait in line with locals at **Restaurant Lucy** to savor traditional dishes. This tiny place, on Altamira half a block past Lopez de Lara, is always packed for a reason. *Comida corrida* costs 12-15 pesos, and *antojitos* run 7-14 pesos. (Open daily 12:30pm-4pm and 6-11pm.)

SIGHTS AND ENTERTAINMENT For a seaside getaway, **Playa Miramar** is accessible by either the "Playa" or "Escollera" bus (2.50 pesos from López de Lara and Madero). By bus, the beach is about 30 minutes away. You can also hop into any taxi that is beeping and shouting "playa" to share the shortened ride for 15 pesos. Lay out on the sand or rent a palm-frond umbrella, chairs, and a table (30 pesos per day).

In the *centro,* join romantically minded young couples at **Boys and Girls,** 316 Olmos, as they make out and groove to dance music. Be there Saturday at midnight for a moment of lively *norteño* (cover 10 pesos; open W-Su 8pm-late). If you really want to rock out, catch a taxi to **Byblos** (cover 25 pesos; open F-Su). An *ambiente gay* welcomes you at **Obsession** and **Fiesta**; ask any taxi driver to take you there.

NUEVO LEÓN

Monterrey

Fast, frenetic, and fried (baking at an average summer temperature of 34°C), Monterrey has no tolerance for slackers. Three million people and growing, Mexico's third-largest city and industrial leader has expanded aggressively at the feet of Cerro de la Silla (Saddle Mountain). Although Monterrey is decked out with the unfortunate raiment of "progress" (traffic, pollution, and a sobering belt of factories and dingy, impoverished huts), the *centro* is a pleasantly cosmopolitan surprise. Gorgeous parks, chic, smoke-filled cafes, sun-drenched plazas, and modern art are all here—and all right next door to each other. Backed by some of the country's wealthiest corporations and families, modern development has given Monterrey a look that is bold, muscular, and at times incongruous: across the street from the old yellow cathedral, a 30-story red monolith that pays tribute to Monterrey's budding business sense shoots fluorescent blue laser beams into the semi-peaceful night.

ORIENTATION

As the largest city in northern Mexico, Monterrey serves as an important transportation hub. The bus and train stations are in the northern part of town, 3km north of the *centro.* All buses in and out of the city pass through Monterrey's huge **Central de Autobuses** at Colón and Villagrán. To reach the city center from the **bus station,** take any bus going south on Pino Suárez, the thoroughfare to the left as you exit the station (#18 lets you off at the central Gran Plaza), or walk 2 blocks east to the gray subway station at Cuauhtémoc and Colón, and take the **metro** (Line 2, 2.2 pesos) to Padre Mier or Zaragoza.

Downtown, **Av. Constitución** runs east-west along the Río Catarina, a 10km long dry river bed that has been converted into a series of athletic fields. From west to east, the most important streets running north-south across Constitución are **Gonzalitos, Pino Suárez, Cuauhtémoc, Av. Benito Juárez, Zaragoza, Zuazúa,** and **Dr. Coss.** From north to south, running east-west and parallel to Constitución are **Colón, Madero,** and farther south, **Washington, 5 de Mayo, 15 de Mayo, Matamoros, Padre Mier, Hidalgo,** and **Ocampo.** The **Zona Rosa** is bounded by Padre Mier to the north, Zaragoza to the east, Ocampo to the south, and Juárez to the west, with Morelos at its center, open only to foot traffic. The **Barrio Antiguo** is centered between Zaragoza and Constitución, east of Dr. Coss.

PRACTICAL INFORMATION

Transportation

Airport: Taxis charge 80-110 pesos for the 4km trip (20-30min.) to the center. Haggling for a lower price may work. The friendly staff at **Tourism Universo** (tel. 344 93 74), in the Plaza Dorado on Hidalgo just west of Pino Suárez, can help you with reservations. Some English spoken. Open M-F 9am-5pm, Sa 9am-2pm. You can also call **Aeromexico** (tel. 343 55 60) or **Mexicana** (tel. 340 55 11) directly. Make reservations at least 2-3 days in advance, more for weekend travel.

Buses: Colón at Villagrán to Amado Nervo. 24hr. **pharmacy** and **emergency** medical unit. **Luggage storage:** 24hr. Bag check 2 pesos per hr. for up to 2 days; 24hr. lockers 18 pesos. **Ómnibus de México** (tel. 374 07 16) to Aguascalientes (8hr., 5 per day, 202 pesos), Chihuahua (12hr., 3 per day, 293 pesos), Guadalajara (12hr., 2 per day, 338 pesos), Mexico City (12hr., 3 per day, 343 pesos), Querétaro (8hr., 10:30pm, 259 pesos), Zacatecas (6hr., 4 per day, 158 pesos), and more. **Sendor, Tamaulipas,** and **Noreste** share offices and computers (tel. 375 00 14). **Noreste** goes to Nuevo Laredo (3hr., 4 per day, 85 pesos) and Matehuala (4hr., every hr., 101 pesos), among other destinations. **Frontera** (tel. 375 09 87) goes to Saltillo (1½hr., every hr., 29 pesos), Leon (10 hr., 3 per day, 196 pesos), and other destina-

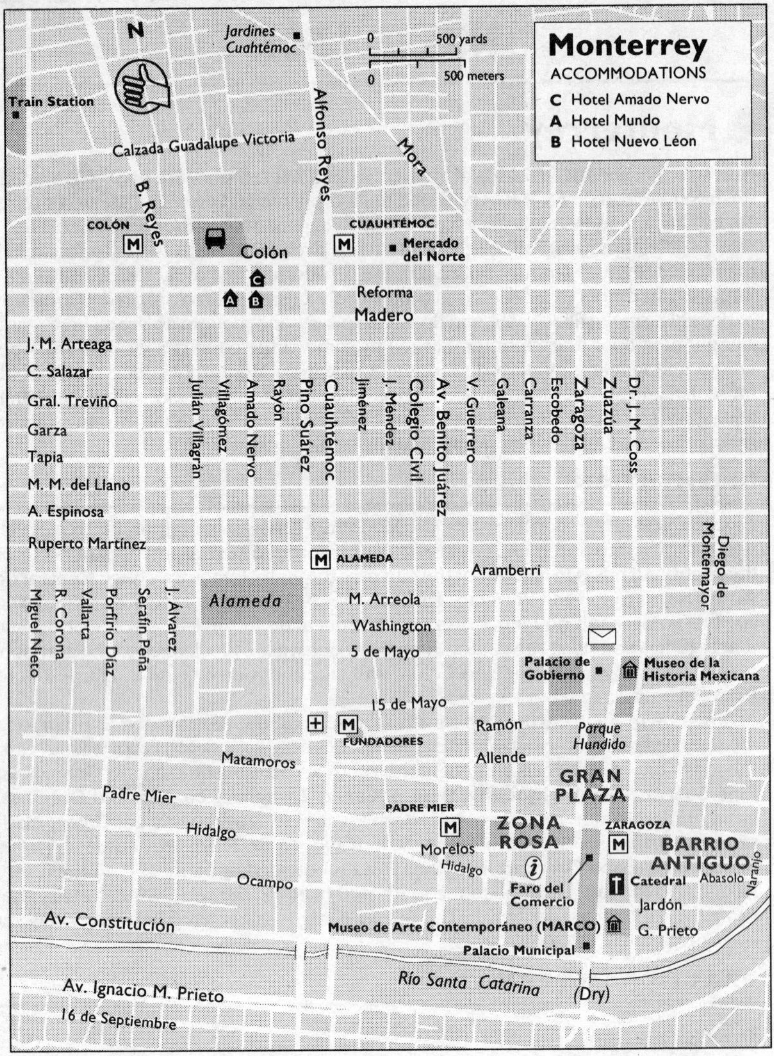

tions. Similar service provided by **Estrella Blanca** (tel. 318 37 37), **Líneas Americanas,** and luxurious **Futura** and **Turistar.**

Local Transportation: Monterrey's amazing **subway** system has all but replaced the large and confusing bus system. Although buses are useful in providing transportation to points far from the *centro* and near the city's periphery, the subway system is new, clean, and efficient—only 7min. from *el metro* near the bus stop to the Gran Plaza. Signs are clear and everywhere. Tickets are 2.2 pesos, 4 for 7.7 pesos, 9 for 16 pesos, 14 for 23 pesos (subway runs daily 6:30am-midnight). **Local buses** usually head in only one direction on any given street except for Constitución and Juárez (6am-midnight, 2.2 pesos). Popular routes include stops at the Gran Plaza (#18 or 42), points along Padre Mier and Hidalgo (#15) and along the perimeter of the downtown area (#69). To get from the budget hotel area to the city center, take the #1 Central or #17 Pío X bus, both of which run the lengths of Pino Suárez and Cuauhtémoc. For more detailed route information, ask locals or the outstanding bilingual staff at the tourist office.

Tourist and Financial Services

Tourist Office: Oficina de Turismo, Hidalgo 477 (tel. 345 08 70 or 345 09 02), just before Escobedo in the *Zona Rosa* 1 block down from Morelos. You can also check out the enlarged maps and miniature information booths at various points along Morelos. Helpful, with abundant maps and brochures in both English and Spanish. Open Tu-Su 10am-5pm.

Consulates: Canada (tel. 344 32 00). **U.K.,** Priv. Tamazunchale 104 (tel. 333 75 98), open M-F 8am-5pm. **U.S.,** Constitución Pte. 411 (tel. 345 21 20), downtown. Open M-F 8am-1pm for passports and citizen's concerns, 9am-5pm for telephone information; 24hr. guard and emergency answering service.

Currency Exchange: Banks dot Madero near the budget hotels and flood the *Zona Rosa,* lining Padre Mier in particular, but many refuse to cash traveler's checks and most of those who do charge high service fees (10%). All have 24hr. **ATMs.** Most open M-F 9am-1:30pm. **Mexdollar Internacional,** 1136 Nte. Pino Suárez (tel. 374 43 11), right by the bus station and Cuauhtémoc subway stop, offers 24hr. currency exchange at a great rate and without a service charge. They also exchange traveler's checks at a lower rate. **Banco del Bajío,** on Padre Mier between Zaragoza and Escobedo, exchanges traveler's checks. Open M-F 9am-1:30pm. Although their traveler's checks rates are lower than the bank's, the absence of commission leaves you with more pesos at **Eurodivisas** (tel. 340 16 83) in Plaza Mexico on Morelos and Padre Mier near Galeana. Open M-F 10:30am-8:30pm, Sa 10am-9pm, Su 11am-8pm.

American Express: San Pedro 215 Nte. (tel. 318 33 04). Catch bus #214 headed for "San Pedro" on Ave. Pino Suárez at the stop just past Ocampo with benches and an awning. Although it passes by, #214 will not pick you up at other nearby stops. Get off at the stop before Calzada de Valle and cross the street. Definitely your best bet for changing AmEx checks. Open M-F 9am-6pm, Sa 9am-1pm.

Local Services

Supermarket: Gigante, on Colón across from the bus station, offers clothes, food items, *panadería,* and an adjoining **pharmacy.** Open daily 8am-10pm. **Mercado del Norte,** also known as La Pulga, is an endless maze of vendor stalls covering Reforma, the street just south of Colón; enter on Colón, 2 blocks east of the bus station. Haggle. Open from morning to dusk.

Laundromat: Laundry services available at most hotels for about 40 pesos per load.

Emergency and Communications

Emergency: Dial 060.

Police: (tel. 11 11 77, 342 00 53, or 342 00 55), on the corner of Carranza and Espinosa or at the 24hr. stand on Morelos at Paraz in the *Zona Rosa*. For missing persons call **Locatel** (340 77 77). Little English spoken.

Medical Emergencies and Assistance: Red Cross, Alfonso Reyes 2503 Nte. (tel. 342 12 12), at Henry, is open 24hr. **Cruz Verde** (tel. 371 50 50 or 71 52 59), at Ciudad Madero and Ciudad Victoria, is also open 24hr. and English is spoken. Or try the **hospital** at subway stop "Hospital."

Pharmacy: In the bus station or **Benavides,** Pino Suárez at 15 de Mayo or on Morelos past Zaragoza. Open 24hr.

Post Office: (tel. 342 40 03) on Zaragoza at Washington, inside the Palacio Federal. Open M-F 8am-7pm, Sa 9am-1pm. Another option is the 2nd fl. of the bus station near Sala 3, open M-F 9am-4pm, Sa 9am-1pm. **Postal Code:** 64000.

Fax: Service in the bus station next to the post office upstairs. Open M-F 7am-11pm, Sa 9am-4pm, Su 9am-4pm.

Internet Access: Check out **Cybercafé El Alebrije,** Padre Mier 827 (tel. 333 88 43), inside La Tumba Cafe/Bar in the *Barrio Antiguo* (20 pesos per hour, students 15 pesos). Open M-Sa noon-9pm. Or a little outside of town, try **Cybercafé** (tel. 368 48 55) in Plaza Fiesta San Agustín.

Telephones: Most **LADATELs** are clustered in the *Zona Rosa*. There are also phones in every metro stop.

Phone Code: 8.

ACCOMMODATIONS

Hotels conveniently located near the *Zona Rosa* tend to be four-star or five-star hotels, and even the three-star ones inflate their rates to exploit tourists. Budget accommodations, catering more to local businessmen, are sprinkled throughout the underdeveloped area near the bus stations. Many rooms are full by early afternoon. Bugs are an ever-present reality in congested Monterrey; if they become a problem, ask the management to spray your room. Take precautions when walking in this area at night; the streets become deserted by 10pm.

Hotel Nuevo León, Amado Nervo 1007 (tel. 374 19 00). With something for everyone, fans and hallway phones accompany the cheap rooms, which also promise soft beds and warm water. The hotel planned a slew of improvements: carpeted rooms equipped with A/C, TV, and telephone were to be in place by late summer of 1998. Singles 80 pesos; doubles 130 pesos.

Hotel Mundo, Reforma 736 (tel. 374 68 50), just off Amado Nervo. Slightly more luxurious than other hotels near the bus station: the A/C works well, the TVs are newer, the floors shine a bit more brightly. Rooms for 1-2 people 164 pesos, with A/C 198 pesos; rooms for 3-4 people 187 pesos, with A/C 221 pesos.

Hotel Posada, Amado Nervo 1138 (tel. 372-3908), across from the bus station. Cross the overhead walkway on Colón. Expect wonderfully quiet rooms and a staff willing to do its best to combat the endless stream of bugs. 1-2 people 141 pesos, with A/C 164 pesos.

FOOD

Barbecued meats, especially *cabrito* (goat kid), are a specialty of northern Mexico; other popular dishes include *agujas* (collar bone), *frijoles a la charra* (beans cooked with pork skin, coriander, tomato, peppers, and onions), *machacado con huevos* (scrambled eggs mixed with dried, shredded beef), hot tamales, and for dessert, *piloncillo con nuez* (hardened brown sugar candy with pecans) or heavenly *glorias* (candy balls of goat's milk and nuts). Although the *Zona Rosa* is home to some of Monterrey's most expensive shopping (and some of northern Mexico's most expensive hotels), for food it can't be beat. Catering mainly to businesspeople on their lunch breaks or arduous shoppers, the service is good, the food *sabroso,* and the prices more than reasonable. *Buen Provecho.*

El Dicho, Naranjo 1003 (tel. 340 76 64), at the far end of the *Barrio Antiguo*, near Av. Constitución. This cafe/restaurant is the perfect place to sip an ice-cold soda and watch TV. The delicious *comidas* (19 pesos) change daily. Open M-Sa 8:30am-4pm.

Casa de Maíz, Abasolo 870b (tel. 40 43 32), in the *Barrio Antiguo*. Each table is a masterpiece painted by local artists; their work also covers the walls at this wonderful health food restaurant. Savor traditional Mexican dishes made with whole wheat flour, or try vegetarian versions (*P'a los herbívores*) such as tofu in red sauce (22 pesos). Open Tu-Th 1-10:30pm, F 1-11:30pm, Sa 2-11:30pm, Su 1-7:30pm.

Los Girasoles, on Padre Mier just down from Zaragoza in the *Zona Rosa*. This brand-new restaurant specializes in *gorditas* which are extra thick tortillas stuffed with your choice of meats (4 pesos each; it takes about four to make a meal). Tell the cook how delicious they are, and you'll have a friend for life. Open daily 8am-9pm.

SIGHTS

Monterrey's architects were kind to tourists. They jam-packed virtually all of Monterrey's sights, art, and historical relics (both new and old) into the 40-acre **Gran Plaza,** also known as the **Macroplaza.** The Gran Plaza is bounded by Washington on the north, Constitución on the south, Zaragoza on the west, and Dr. Coss on the east. The Gran Plaza is host to a slew of lovely government buildings, including the **Palacio Federal,** the **Palacio del Gobierno** (at the north end of the plaza), and the **Palacio Municipal** (at the southern end). Just east of the Palacio Federal lies the **Plaza 400 Años** with a man-made river on the lower level where you can rent pad-

Strange Brew

What do Mexican *beisból,* gardens, Monterrey's leading producer of beer, and modern art have to do with each other? If you said "nothing," you are 100% incorrect. Check out **The Cuauhtémoc,** 1½ blocks south of the General Anaya subway stop on Line 2. Featuring gardens, a **Hall of Fame** (tel. 528 57 96) that commemorates Mexican baseball legends, and the **Museo Deportivo** (a shrine to rodeos, boxing, soccer, etc.), the gardens also house a beer museum foaming over with beer-related artifacts (don't miss the mugs). Perhaps the most interesting part is the **Museo de Monterrey** (tel. 328 60 60; open Tu-Su 11am-8pm), covered wall to wall with the best in modern Mexican art. The museum cafe serves (what else?) Carta Blanca beer and many others. (*Let's Go* does not recommend sampling 30 different kinds of beer and then proceeding to observe and analyze modern art—you will look and sound foolish.) Every spring, Banamex, a large national bank, funds a competition including painting and sculpture. Each year thousands of top-notch artists compete for the honor of having their work judged by a bank and displayed in an old beer factory. Go figure.

dle boats. If the sun is too much for you, try dozing in the cool garden paradise of the **Parque Hundido** (Sunken Park), just south of the Palacio del Gobierno. One of Mexico's most notorious centers of public affection, the *parque* looks like Noah's Ark, with groups of two napping, nuzzling, and often just plain necking all over the place. Farther along the Gran Plaza lies the **Fuente de La Vida** (Fountain of Life), which douses an immense statue of Neptune surrounded by cavorting nymphs and naiads. The most striking construction, however, is the bright orange **Faro del Comercio** (Commerce Lighthouse), topped with a laser beacon that circles the skies at night. The lighthouse serves a purely symbolic purpose; it is a testament to the economic ambitions of Monterrey's leaders. The laser doesn't begin to pulse until after 10pm, when hundreds pack the adjoining *Barrio Antiguo* in search of some late-night fun. Just across Zuazúa from the Faro de Comercio is the resplendent, pale yellow **Catedral de Monterrey.**

If you're weary of planting yourself in front of *palacios* or watching couples go at it in the park, perhaps a good dose of culture is what you need. Don't worry—Monterrey's got plenty of that, too. At the far end of the Plaza 400 Años, the **Museo de Historia Mexicana,** Dr. Coss 445 Sur (tel. 345 98 98), offers a permanent collection that has something for everyone. *(Open Tu-Th 11am-7pm, F-Su 11am-8pm. Admission 10 pesos, students with ID 5 pesos. Tuesdays free, Sa 5 pesos, Su 1 peso.)* The exhibits include state-of-the-art audio/visual resources, intriguing artifacts, and informative exhibitions, as well as evening movies and many daytime shows, often free. To cool off and relax while you view, slip into the **Museo de Arte Contemporáneo (MARCO)** (tel. 342 48 20). *(Open Tu and Th-Sa 11am-7pm, W and Su 11am-9pm. Admission 5 pesos, students with ID 8 pesos, free Wednesdays.)* Avoid the pedantic placards in the museum and focus on some of the best exhibits of Mexico's truly great and innovative modern artists, or just recline by the enormous decorative pool in the center of the museum and watch for the periodic water shows. An immense bronze dove that looks like a huge phallus guards the entrance. The work of incredible as-yet-unknown artists as well as changing cultural exhibits can be enjoyed for no cost at the **Museo Estatal de Culturas Populares,** Abasolo 1024 (tel. 345 65 04), in the *Barrio Antiguo.*

The **Obispado** (tel. 346 04 04), former palace of the bishop of Monterrey, is now a state museum displaying artifacts from the colonial era. *(Open Tu-Sa 10am-6pm, Su 10am-5pm. Admission 10 pesos.)* The museum itself may not be worth the half-hour bus ride from the *centro,* but the view and cool breeze are nice. Bring a picnic and enjoy a break from the city on the wandering terraces. Take bus #1 from Dr. Coss along the Macroplaza, ask the driver to point out the stop, and hike up to the very top of the hill. Also worth a visit are the **Grutas de García** (Caves of García), 45km northwest of the city and accessible by car or bus. *(Open daily 9am-5pm; admission 26 pesos, children 16 pesos.)* The easiest way to get to the Grutas is on a three-hour Grayline **tour** (65 pesos) leaving from the Hotel Monterrey at 3pm on Thursdays, Saturdays, and Sundays (tel. 369 64 72 for reservations). A cheaper alternative is to take an **Estrella Blanca** bus from the central bus station (every 20min., 16 pesos). Once there, take the cable car railway to avoid the steep 700m uphill climb. The ticket for the cable car is included in the price of admission. The Grutas are a network of natural chambers; the dozens of sedimentary layers in their walls reveal that 50 or 60 million years ago, the caves lay on the ocean floor.

ENTERTAINMENT

The **Barrio Antiguo** is a beautiful and quiet place to wander away from the mobs in the *Zona Rosa* during the day, but if you want to party, head there at night for a totally different scene. After sundown, police cordon off the area to cars, and although the action doesn't get started until 10:30pm or so (9:30pm on weekends), many places have no cover if you come early enough. For something a bit mellow and Bohemian, try **El Infinito,** Raymundo Jardón 904 Ote. (tel. 340 36 34). This cafe-cum-used bookstore-cum-art-house movie theater promises radical politics and challenging conversation. Although no alcohol is served, if you donate a book, you get a free cup of coffee. On Thursdays and Saturdays, art-house international films are shown. (Open daily 5pm-midnight.) **Café Paraiso** on Morelos and Mina, with its huge 13-peso frappucinos, will reaffirm your caffeine addiction. This hip little place also serves French cuisine for 22-30 pesos. (Open daily 9am-midnight.) Things get a little louder at **Real de Catorce,** Padre Mier 1062, a club featuring live music—everything from hard rock to sweet ballads. The space is small, neat, and classy; the bar is a work of supreme godliness. (Drinks 7-8 pesos. Cover 20-25 pesos after 10pm. Open daily 9:30pm-3am.) Want something a little louder? No problem. **Hemispherio,** on Padre Mier, thumps with live rock, pop, and *manacos* (beer 15 pesos, cover 30 pesos; open Th-Sa 9pm-3am). Get your engines a-pumpin' and hearts a-thumpin' to go to **El Reloj,** one of the coolest clubs in town. With a young (read: pre-teen to 30-year-old) contingent, Reloj always has long lines and loud U.S. and Spanish rock playing. People-watching outside may be even better than groovin' inside—your call. (Cover 30 pesos. Open daily 9pm-late.) Playing everything from techno to modern folk, **La Tumba,** "musicantro cultubar" (tel. 345 68 60), draws the most varied crowd in the area with a mix of disco and live concerts.

After its first-ever Pride March in the summer of 1997, Monterrey is quickly becoming one of the most gay- and lesbian-friendly cities in Mexico. Young same-sex couples walk the streets of the *Zona Rosa* and the *Barrio Antiguo* day and night, and gay clubs are sprouting and overflowing daily. Although most nightspots cater primarily to men, women are more than welcome. **Club Vongole** on 300 Blvd. Pedreras east of *Barrio Antiguo*, is the most hip-hop, be-bop, and happening gay and lesbian night spot in town, with over 1000 people Wednesdays, Fridays, and Saturdays. Closer to the *centro*, **Chara'os,** at the corner of Garza and Zaragoza, is open every night to an exciting, young crowd. Ask for a copy of the free gay and lesbian monthly magazine *New Concept Gay* at any of these bars for more listings. There are lots more.

If you're looking for a calmer night out, try calling the **Teatro Municipal** (tel. 43 89 74), or stop by the immense theater on the **Gran Plaza** to see what is playing. Show types, times, and prices vary greatly, but there is always an early afternoon kids' show on Sundays.

COAHUILA

Saltillo

Only an hour and a half from Monterrey, Saltillo is a treat for the tired traveler. Once you get past the enormous dusty expansion that houses most of the 850,000 inhabitants as well as the industry (mostly foreign car companies), the *centro* is clean, relaxed, and easily walkable. Early to bed and early to rise, *saltillenses* are proud of their dry climate and pretty spot in the Sierra Madres. Although the limited sights and nightlife do not draw many tourists, excellent budget lodgings, food, and delicious cool afternoon breezes await those who do come.

ORIENTATION Saltillo, located in a valley between the jagged Sierra Madre mountains, lies 87km southwest of Monterrey, along desolate **Highway 40.** The **bus station** is about 3km southwest of the city center on Blvd. Echeverría Sur. To get to the *centro,* exit the terminal, cross the pedestrian overpass, and catch minibus #10 from the small street perpendicular to Echeverría, across the street from the Restaurant Jaslo. All local buses cost 2.10 pesos and run daily 6:30am to 11pm. Catch a return bus (#9) at the corner of Aldama and Hidalgo, a block down the street from the cathedral, in front of the entrance to the furniture store. The centro's streets form a slightly distorted grid not quite aligned with the four cardinal directions. The quiet **Plaza de Armas** is home to the cathedral and is bordered by **Juárez** to the south (or right, facing the cathedral) and **Hidalgo** to the east (between the plaza and cathedral). Walk one block to the west, past the **Palacio de Gobierno,** and one block north (or left, facing the cathedral) to arrive at **Plaza Acuña,** bordered on its west (far side) by the narrow **Padre Flores,** on the east by **Allende,** on the south by **Victoria,** and on the north by **Aldama.**

PRACTICAL INFORMATION The **Central de Autobuses,** at Echeverría Sur and Garza, is accessible by minibus #9. **Frontera** runs buses to Matamoros (7hr., 9 per day, 145 pesos) and other places; their special draw is a shuttle to Monterrey every 20 min. (second class, 29 pesos). **Omnibus de México** (tel. 17 03 15) serves Aguascalientes (7hr., 8 per day, 174 pesos) and Reynosa (5hr., every hr. 1am-noon, plus 4 evening buses, 101 pesos). **Transportes del Norte** (tel. 17 09 02) runs to Guadalajara (10hr., 6 per day, 275 pesos), Mexico City (10hr., 3 per day in the evenings, 310 pesos), San Luis Potosí (5hr., 9:35pm, 134 pesos), and Zacatecas (5hr., 5 per day, 130 pesos).

Wonderful maps of the city stand outside the bus station and dot the *centro*. They should be enough to orient you, but if you really want your very own map or brochure, you can trek out to the **Secretaría de Fomento Económico (tourist office),** Blvd. Luis Echeverría 1560 (tel. 15 17 14), on the 11th floor of the *über*-modern glass Edificio Torre Saltillo (not to be confused with the mushroom-shaped La Torre Hotel), on Saltillo's circular perimeter road; it's accessible by bus #9 from the *centro*. Ask to be let off at the Torre Saltillo and the driver will set you down near Gigante. Look for the tall glass building next to La Quinta Inn. (Tower open M-F 9am-3pm and 5pm-8pm.) For currency exchanges, **casas de cambio** offer the best rates. **Banamex,** at Allende and Ocampo, behind the Palacio de Gobierno, has a 24-hr. **ATM.** The **police** are at Treviño and Echeverría Ote. (tel. 14 45 50). The **post office** (tel. 14 90 97) is at Victoria 453 after Urdiñola (open M-F 8am-7pm, Sa 9am-1pm) with a Mex-Post office (tel. 14 18 90) in one corner (open M-F 9am-7pm, Sa 9am-1pm). The **postal code** is 25000. The **phone code** is 84.

ACCOMMODATIONS Blvd. Luis Echeverría, which runs along the bus station, teems with cheap places to rest your head, and the centro is full of lower-to-medium range, clean, comfortable spots. There are also a few higher-end hotels with accompanying quality. **Hotel Urdiñola,** on Victoria 207 (tel. 14 09 40), behind the Palacio del Gobierno, is very swank, with an exquisite marble staircase, beautiful stained-glass window, and charming courtyard. This elegant retreat is also equipped with *agua purificada,* cable TVs, and phones; unfortunately, such grandeur is reflected in the prices. (Singles 189 pesos; doubles 213 pesos.) At the modern **Hotel Saade,** Aldama Pte. 397 (tel. 12 91 20 or 12 91 21), a block west of Pl. Acuña, earth tones dominate the clean, well-furnished, and quiet rooms. Saade's location places you in the heart of it all. The rooftop restaurant offers a stunning panorama of the city and the Sierra and a full-service tourist office awaits you in the lobby. Rooms come in three styles, from económico (bed and bath) to ejecutivo (bed, bath, TV, phone, rug, etc.). (1 person 140-170 pesos; 2 people 170-190 pesos; 3 people 190-210 pesos. Reception M-F 9:30am-1:30pm and 3:30-7pm.)

FOOD Be sure to sample delicious *pan de pulque* (bread made with tequila-like fermented cactus juice), a Saltillo specialty. Restaurants on Allende and Carranza cater more to tourists, while the cafes on smaller streets remain local picks. **Café and Restaurant Arcasa,** Victoria 215 (tel. 12 64 24), is a family-run cafe that draws the locals in with delicious food and fast, solicitous service (breakfast 19-29 pesos, 3-course *menú del día* 22 pesos; open daily 7:30am-midnight). For more upscale dining and more adventuresome dishes, head out to the cheerful **Restaurant Principal,** Allende Nte. 702 (tel. 14 33 84), seven blocks north of the Palacio de Gobierno. Their cabecito (28 pesos) will leave you with that invigorating after-the-hunt feel, or splurge on grilled ram (69 pesos). (Open daily 8am-midnight.)

SIGHTS Weary travelers rest assured: Saltillo does not lend itself to much sight-seeing. Saltillo's streets burst with artistry and cultural pride (the town even host a series of rodeos and bullfights) during **Feria de Saltillo** from July 18 to August 3 in 1999. Otherwise, the most alluring site in town is probably the **Museo de las Aves** (tel. 14 01 68), on Hidalgo three blocks south (up) from the cathedral. The *museo* is home to an incredibly large number of bird species. If you're determined to find more, call Salvador Medina (tel. 17 42 55) who, for US$10 per hour, will take you around, proudly tell you in English or Spanish the history of Saltillo, and, if you're lucky, let you up into the cathedral's bell tower.

Plaza Acuña, two blocks northwest of the Plaza de Armas, is a good place to people-watch. Vendors spill out of the **Mercado Juárez** in the northwest corner of the plaza. Look here for reasonably priced *serapes*, for which Saltillo is famous, or drop in to the *serape* factory on Hidalgo just before the Museo de las Aves. Perched on a hill overlooking the city, **Plaza México** (or **El Mirador**) offers a smashing view of the whole area and the unconquerable mountains beyond. Follow Miguel Hidalgo uphill, take your first left after the Museo de las Aves, and continue for another four blocks, turning onto the winding Gustavo Espinoza and heading up to the small plaza with benches and old street lamps.

ZACATECAS

Zacatecas

At approximately 2400m above sea level, Zacatecas (pop. 1.3 million) is the second-highest city in Mexico (after Toluca)—don't be alarmed if the city's many hills leave you winded. The lifeblood of Zacatecas once flowed through rich veins of silver, and shop owners still cater to that legacy. A silver trinket, given to early Spanish colonists by an indigenous Cascane in the mid-1500s, triggered the mining frenzy that eventually stripped the surrounding hills of 6000 tons of silver. As far as mining towns go, Zacatecas was unusually fortunate: the arts flourished under the patronage of affluent silver barons, and the rows of grand colonial mansions downtown testify to an era of lavish consumption. As a result of silver money, Zacatecas is home to beautiful parks, elaborate cathedrals, cobblestone streets, and some of the most nationally renowned museums in all of Mexico When the mines ran dry, Zacatecas distinguished itself as a busy university town and center of commerce and tourism. The town's colonial beauty continues to attract a largely Mexican crowd of tourists.

ORIENTATION

Zacatecas is 347km north of Guadalajara, 135km south of Aguascalientes, and 832km south of Chihuahua. All buses arrive and depart from the **central bus terminal** on the outskirts of town. City buses (1.80 pesos; Ruta 8 to the *centro*) and taxis (12 pesos to the *centro*) wait outside. After dark, a taxi is the only option.

Zacatecas has no identifiable city center. Activity revolves around two streets, **Juárez** and **Hidalgo** (called **González Ortega** southwest of Juárez). Use the Juárez-

Hidalgo intersection, which falls one block northwest of **Plaza Independencia,** as your point of orientation. Many of the city's colonial monuments are on or near Hidalgo. Most museums are off Juárez as you head up the hill and west. Shops, restaurants, and clubs also cluster on Hidalgo. Zacatecas evenings can get chilly, so a sweater may come in handy.

PRACTICAL INFORMATION

Transportation

Airport: (tel. 498 03 38), accessible by *combis* (*combis* tel. 2 59 46) from the Mexicana office (20min., leave 1¼hr. before flight, 30 pesos). **Mexicana,** Hidalgo 406 (tel. 2 32 48). Open M-F 9am-7pm. **Taesa,** Hidalgo 306 (tel. 2 00 50 or 2 02 12). Open M-F 9am-7pm, Sa 10am-6pm.

Buses: Central de Autobuses (tel. 2 11 12), Lomas de la Isabélica, at Tránsito Pesado. From the *centro,* take the "Camionera Central" or Ruta 8 bus from González Ortega (1 block from Juárez). **Camiones de los Altos** (tel. 2 06 84) has service to Aguascalientes (2hr., every 30min. 6am-8:30pm, 41 pesos) and Nuevo Laredo (9hr., 7:30pm, 230 pesos). **Estrella Blanca** (tel. 2 06 84) serves Mexico City (8hr., 4 per day 3:20am-10:05pm, 175 pesos) and Torrean (6hr., about every hr. 6am-8:30pm, 111 pesos). **Futura** (tel. 2 00 42) sends buses to San Juan (4hr., 1:50am and noon, 70 pesos) and Reynosa (9½hr., 8:15 and 10:30pm, 216 pesos). **Omnibus de México** (tel. 2 54 95) has service to Durango (6hr., 11 per day, 102 pesos), Guadalajara (5hr., 16 per day, 140 pesos), Matamoros (11hr., 6 per day 4:30am-1am, 250 pesos), and Mexico City (8½hr., 11 per day 1am-10:50pm, 222

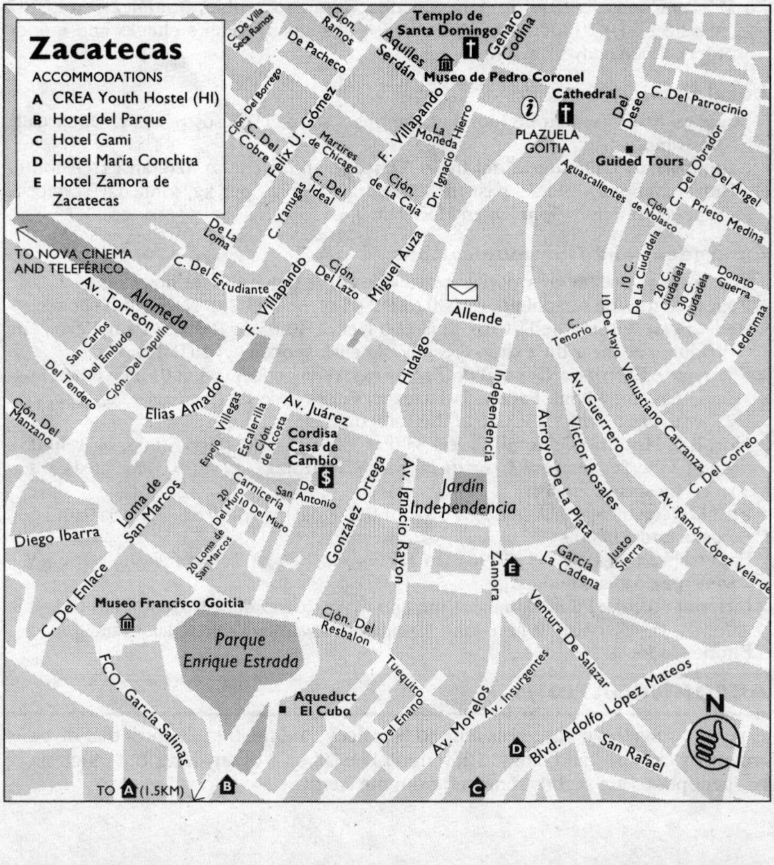

pesos). **Transportes Chihuahuenses** (tel. 2 00 42) has service to Chihuahua (12hr., about every 45min., 275 pesos), Irapuato (4½hr., 5 per day 1:15pm-12:30am, 90 pesos), and Puerto Vallarta (12hr., 1am, and 5pm, 273 pesos). **Turistar Ejecutivo** sends buses to Fresnillo (45min., 6:30am, 22 pesos), and León (4½hr., 10:30am, 120 pesos). **Transportes del Norte** (tel. 2 00 42) sends buses to Monterrey (6hr., 5 per day 11:30am-5pm, 152 pesos), Nuevo Laredo (11hr., 7:30, 9:30, and 10pm, 218 pesos), and Piedras Negras (11hr., 4:30am, 7:45, and 9:15pm, 259 pesos).

Car Rental: Budget, Mateos 104 (tel. 2 94 58). Minimum 320 pesos per day including insurance, taxes, and 200km daily. Must be age 25 with valid credit card and driver's license. Open M-F 9am-3pm and 5-8pm, Sa 9am-2pm.

Tourist and Financial Services

Tourist Office: Infotur, Av. Hidalgo (tel. 4 05 52), across from the cathedral. Young, helpful staff distributes useful maps and lists of museum schedules. No English spoken. Open daily 9am-8pm. For more in-depth info about the city and state, visit the tremendously informative **Dirección de Turismo** (tel. 4 03 93; fax 2 93 29), Esplanada del Ferrocarril, near the train station. Open M-F 9am-3:30pm and 5-8pm. **TIPS,** a Spanish-language weekly listing cultural events and tourist services, is available during high season at hotels and newsstands.

Guided Tours: Asociación de Guías Turistas, Calle del Angel 202 (tel. 4 18 17 or 2 85 09), behind the cathedral. Guided tours of the city 90 pesos, including admission to museums and transportation. Open daily 10am-8pm.

Currency Exchange: Cambios Zacatecas, González Ortega 136 (tel. 2 68 44), has excellent rates. Open M-F 9am-7pm, Sa 10am-2pm. **Banca Promex,** González Ortega 122 (tel. 2 22 40), also has good rates and a 24hr. **ATM.** Open for exchange M-F 8am-7pm., Sa 10am-2:30pm. **Cordisa Casa de Cambio,** González Ortega 142 (tel. 2 55 04), 1 block from Juárez, also changes traveler's checks and money orders. Open daily 9am-7pm.

Local Services

Luggage Storage: Can be found at the bus station, 15 pesos per day. Open daily 7am-10pm.

Laundromat: Lavandería del Indio Triste, Juan de Tolosa 826, an extension of Hidalgo, about 3 blocks past the cathedral. 7 pesos per kg; same-day service if dropped off before 5pm. Open M-Sa 9am-9pm.

Emergency and Communications

Emergency: Dial 06 for **ambulance service** to the rather distant hospitals.

Police: Héroes de Chapultepec 1000 (tel. 2 05 07 or 2 43 79). No English spoken.

Red Cross: Calzada de la Cruz Roja 100 (tel. 2 30 05 or 2 33 23), off Héroes de Chapultepec, near the exit to Fresnillo. English spoken. Open 24hr.

Pharmacy: Farmacia Central de Zacatecas, Hidalgo 318 (tel. 2 03 21). Open M-Sa 9am-3pm and 5-9pm. **Farmacia Isstezac,** Callejón de las Campanas 103 (tel. 4 37 25, ext. 19), on the right side of the cathedral. Open 24hr.

Hospital: Hospital General, García Salinas 707 (tel. 3 30 04, 3 30 05, or 3 30 06). Open 24hr. See **Dr. José Cruz de la Torre González** (tel. 4 07 03) for medical services; he speaks English.

Post Office: Allende 111 (tel. 2 01 96), off Hidalgo. Open M-F 8am-7pm, Sa 9am-1pm. **Postal code:** 98000.

Fax: (tel. 2 00 60; fax 2 17 96) On Hidalgo at Juárez. Telegrams too. Open M-F 8am-5pm, Sa 9am-noon.

Internet Access: Public library at the end of Av. Juárez across from Jardín Independencia. Free service (30min. limit if someone's waiting). Open daily 9am-9pm.

Phone Code: 492.

ACCOMMODATIONS

Hotels in downtown Zacatecas tend to be pricey, and the budget spots that do exist are rather cramped and dingy. They aren't like jail cells or anything, but much nicer budget options are slightly removed from the *centro.*

Hotel Zamora de Zacatecas, Plazuela de Zamora 303 (tel. 2 12 00). Within 1 block of the Plaza Independencia opposite Juárez. Zamora boasts a central location and prices that seem unbeatable for the area. Rooms are clean. Singles 50 pesos; doubles 60 pesos.

Hotel del Parque, González Ortega 302 (tel. 2 04 79), near the aqueduct. A tad out of the way, but in a nice area 3 blocks from Juárez, just past the beautiful Parque Enrique Estrada. Vanilla decor. Clean rooms are sort of dark, although the TVs brighten things up. Singles 70 pesos; doubles 80 pesos.

CREA Youth Hostel (HI; tel. 2 02 23, ext. 7), in the Parque La Encantada, southwest of the city. Take the Ruta 8 bus on Gonzales Ortega (1.25 pesos) from Pl. Independencia or the bus station, and get off after about 10min. at the sign for La Encantada. Walk down Calle 5 Señores for about 15min., turn left on Calle Ancha, and walk up the hill until you see the grounds of the youth camp. Veer right around the red building; the sherbet-green hostel is behind the pool to the left. Equipped with a soccer field and courts for basketball, volleyball, and racquetball. Small, sterile quads. Single-sex floors. Clean communal bathrooms. 20 pesos per person. Breakfast, lunch, and dinner 12 pesos each. Open daily 7am-11pm.

Hotel Gami, López Mateos 309 (tel. 2 80 05), about 3 blocks from the Plaza de Independencia. Yellow walls brighten carpeted rooms complete with firm mattresses, desks, purified water, and a view of the traffic on the street below. Singles 80 pesos; doubles with 1 bed 85 pesos, with 2 beds 125 pesos.

Hotel María Conchita, Av. López Mateos 401 (tel. 2 14 94 or 2 14 96), 3 blocks south of the Jardín Independencia on a busy street. Distinctive architecture and private bathrooms. Rooms have tiny TVs and phones. Singles 70 pesos; doubles 80 pesos.

FOOD

Zacatecas has some good eats that won't break the bank. As well as cheap tacos and *gorditas,* fantastic restaurants are tucked in between shops down Hidalgo near the cathedral. Get that sugar rush with a chunk of *dulce con leche, camote,* or *cocada,* sold by vendors throughout the *centro* (1 peso).

El Pueblito, Av. Hidalgo 403 (tel. 4 38 18), next door to Gorditas Doña Julia. Specializing in Zacatecan and regional food in an old renovated hacienda, El Pueblito won't disappoint. If you miss the *Peliquia Zacatecana* (35 pesos), you'll die a miserable, unfulfilled person. Well, maybe not, but the food is damn good. Open daily 11am-11pm.

Restaurant Parrilla Mexicana, C. Tacuba under La Terraza, serves up only a fixed menu every day, but portions are huge and delicious. Your taste buds will never want to leave (40 pesos). Open daily noon-2am.

Gorditas Doña Julia, Av. Hidalgo 409 (tel. 3 79 55), across the street about 1 block from the cathedral. Locals gorge themselves on delicious *gorditas* (3.80 pesos) of all types and varieties. If you can't find a table at the restaurant, ask for your *gorditas para llevar* (to go). Open daily 8am-9pm.

Mesón La Meña, Av. Juárez 15 (tel. 2 27 73), just off the Plaza de Independencia. This spacious local favorite serves up solid traditional Mexican fare. *Enchiladas verdes* 20 pesos. *Comida corrida* 35 pesos. Open daily 8am-11pm.

Cafe Zas, Av. Hidalgo 201 (tel. 2 70 89), about 3 blocks from the cathedral. Students giggle over milkshakes (10 pesos), and professionals munch on burgers (12 pesos) and *chilaquiles* (19 pesos) as they read the newspaper. Open daily 8am-9pm.

El Tragadero, Av. Juárez 132 (tel. 2 43 32), just after the intersection with Hidalgo. The open kitchen and light decor keep this family-run joint nice and cozy. Yummy vegetarian platter 18 pesos, enchiladas 14 pesos. Open daily 8am-10pm.

La Terraza (tel. 2 32 70), next to the cathedral. A lovely outdoor cafe. The menu is limited and servings are small, but it's still a great place to stop for coffee and a snack, or to finish off the day with a beer (8 pesos) as you watch the shadows get long and creep up the walls of the cathedral. Burgers 7 pesos. Ice cream 6 pesos. Open daily 10am-9:30pm.

SIGHTS

The 18th-century **cathedral,** four blocks northeast of Juárez, on Hidalgo, has an intricately sculpted facade representing the Eucharist. *(Open daily 7am-1pm and 3-9pm.)* Apostles, doctors, and angels jostle for space above the cathedral's main entrance. The Churrigueresque northern facade bears a representation of Christ on the cross, and the European Baroque southern facade pays homage to Nuestra Señora de las Zacatecas. The cathedral interior does not live up to the promise of its lavish exterior—it is surprisingly plain. Next to the cathedral, the **Palacio de Gobierno** is notable for the mural that surrounds its interior stairwell. *(Open M-F 8am-8pm.)* Painted in 1970 by Antonio Pintor Rodríguez, the work traces the history of Zacatecas from the pre-Hispanic era until the present. Much of the mural devotes itself to the mugs of Zacatecas's historical players.

Across Hidalgo and up the steep Callejón de Veyna is the **Templo de Santo Domingo.** *(Open daily 7am-1pm and 3:30-9pm. Quiet, respectful visitors are welcome during services.)* Built by the Jesuits in 1746, the church contains eight impressive Baroque gilded wood altars and an elaborate 18th-century German pipe organ. Next door is the **Museo de Pedro Coronel** (tel. 2 80 21), a building whose past incarnations include a monastery and a jail. *(Open M-W, F-Su 10am-2pm and 4-7pm. Admission 10 pesos, students and seniors 5 pesos, children under 10 free.)* Housing the tomb, sculptures, and paintings of the Zacatecan artist Pedro Coronel, the museum has one of the best modern art collections in Latin America, and is the pride of Zacatecas. The collection of Miró is especially impressive. Works by Picasso, Braque, Chagall, and Miró jostle for space; go in the afternoon to avoid crowds. Mesoamerican and African masks, as well as Japanese, Chinese, and Tibetan pieces break the Eurocentric spell.

The **Museo Rafael Coronel** (tel. 2 81 16) is housed in the dramatic **Ex-Convento de San Francisco,** an attraction in itself. *(Museum and ex-convent open M-Tu and Th-Sa 10am-2pm and 4-7pm, Su 10am-5pm. Museum admission 10 pesos, students, teachers, and seniors 5 pesos, kids free. Ex-convent free.)* To reach the museum from the cathedral, follow Hidalgo, bearing left at the first fork and right at the second. The museum is renowned for its fabulous collections of masks from around the world and of popular Mexican art. Southeast of the downtown area, 39 pink stone arches mark the end of Zacatecas's famous colonial aqueduct, **El Cubo.** Beside the aqueduct, the verdant **Parque Estrada's** winding stone pathways, rose bushes, and waterfalls border the former governor's mansion, now the **Museo de Francisco Goitia,** Enrique Estrada 101 (tel. 2 02 11). *(Open Tu-Sa 10am-1:30pm and 5-7:30pm, Su 10am-4:30pm. Admission 10 pesos, seniors and children 12 and under free.)* The museum displays historical artifacts of the region, and gives a good account of the history of Mexico.

The **Cerro de la Bufa,** named for its resemblance to a Spanish wineskin, peers down from the city's highest crag. La Bufa, as it is affectionately known, is lit by floodlights at night and is a favorite lookout point for the **spectacular view** it offers of Zacatecas and the surrounding area. The **Museo de la Toma de Zacatecas** (tel. 2 80 66) is adjacent to the Cerro. *(Open Tu-Su 10am-4:30pm. Admission 5 pesos, students, seniors, and teachers half-price, children under 11 free.)* Erected to commemorate Pancho Villa's decisive victory over federal troops in the summer of 1914, the museum lays claim to an array of revolutionary memorabilia, including photographs, cannons, and small arms. On one side of the museum lies the 18th-century **Capilla del Patrocinio,** whose graceful facade and cloistered courtyards are carved from deep-red stone. Nearby shops sell arts, crafts, and loads of geodes. A short, but steep walk up the hill leads to the ornate Moorish **Mausoleo de los Hombres Ilustres de Zacatecas** (Tomb of the Famous Men of Zacatecas), worth the hike if only for the view of the city (open daily 10am-6pm). There's an even better vista from the **Meteorological Observatory** behind the museum. Public buses run to La Bufa only on Sundays and holidays (take Ruta 9 from the Plaza de Armas). The most appealing way to make the trip if you aren't claustrophobic or afraid of heights is by **teleférico** (suspended cable car; tel. 2 56 94), which runs between the peak of El Grillo and La Bufa every 10 minutes. *(Runs daily 10am-6pm. 6 pesos each way.)* Follow García Rojas northwest to its end to reach the cable car stop.

The **Mina de Edén** (tel. 2 30 02) was one of the region's most productive silver mines until about 30 years ago, when continual flooding made mineral extraction futile. *(Open daily 11am-7:30pm. Admission 15 pesos.)* You may enter the mine from either the top or the side. The top entrance is 100m to the right as you leave the *teleférico.* From there, walk into the mountain, take the elevator down, and begin the tour. Otherwise, follow Juárez northwest along the **Alameda,** a tree-and-fountain-filled park lined by some of Zacatecas's grandest colonial mansions. Continue along Torreón until it ends, and then turn right and walk one block, veering to the left. From there, a mini-locomotive whisks tourists into the mountain to start a one-hour guided tour (in Spanish) of the cool subterranean tunnels. Tour groups cross rope bridges and learn about the haunting myths of the mine.

ENTERTAINMENT

Zacatecas's nightlife kicks off on Thursday and Friday nights, when university students slam the books shut and hit the bars and discos. Not surprisingly, the tourist favorite is **El Malacate** (tel. 2 30 02), which provides a rare opportunity to boogie in an old mine shaft. Solid rock walls are tastefully decorated with helmets, shovels, and plush green sectionals, and partiers quaff expensive drinks and dance to a mix of the latest U.S. top-40 hits and Latin rhythms. (Cover 40 pesos. Beer 10 pesos, mixed drinks 20 pesos. Open Th-Su 9pm-3am.) The newest and most popular club in town is **Casa de Sueños** on Av. Hidalgo, a block past the cathedral on the right—keep your eyes out for people socializing on the street because there's no sign. Everyone who's anyone in Zacatecas hangs out in the two-story converted mansion under the reddish lighting. The latest Mexican and American dance beats keep the crowd bouncing. (Cover 20-60 pesos, includes drinks some nights. Open Th-Su 9pm-3am.) The only club open every night is **Cactus,** Hidalgo 111 (tel. 2 05 09), at the Juárez intersection. The well-decorated interior is suitable for lounging with a beer (10 pesos), dancing on the faux-cathedral dance floor, or going upstairs to shoot some pool. (No cover. Open daily 9pm-3am.) As always, be careful walking around at night, as the streets can be deserted. Avoid walking alone and keep an eye out for danger.

If you're feeling a bit more mellow, check out **Nova Cinema,** Constituyentes 300 (tel. 2 54 04), for the latest in Mexican and American films. On Thursdays and Sundays at 7pm, take advantage of the free performance by the **Banda del Estado** in the Plazuela Goitia, next to the cathedral.

The yearly cultural highlight is **Zacatecas en la Cultura,** a festival during **Semana Santa** in which concerts and artistic activities are held in the elegant **Teatro Calderón,** on Hidalgo near the cathedral, and throughout the city. For two weeks near the beginning of September, the city celebrates the **Feria Nacional de Zacatecas** with musical and theatrical events, bullfights, agricultural and crafts shows, and sporting events.

AGUASCALIENTES

Aguascalientes

A charming city is the last thing a traveler expects to find in the prickly desert of Central Mexico—yet seemingly out of nowhere rises Aguascalientes (pop. 520,000). The marvelous Plaza de la Patria, numerous beautiful churches and palaces, a wealth of cultural sites, and a cosmopolitan feel are the last thing one would anticipate, and yet window shoppers, museum enthusiasts, and fun-seekers alike have found a home in Aguascalientes. The pride and joy of the city is the eagerly anticipated *Feria de San Marcos,* two weeks of festivities during the last two weeks of April and the first week of May. Aside from its yearly extravaganza, Aguascalientes offers a small range of attractions, including the impressive colonial architecture of its *centro histórico* and several worthwhile museums. Just wandering the tree-lined street is a pleasant way to spend a day—Aguascalientes is a thoroughly modern city with the laid-back attitude one would expect of a smaller Mexican town.

ORIENTATION Aguascalientes is 168km west of San Luis Potosí, 128km south of Zacatecas, and 252km northeast of Guadalajara. **Av. Circunvalación** encircles the city, while **Av. López Mateos** cuts through town east to west. The **bus station** is on Av. Convención, a few blocks west from **Av. José María Chávez.** All city buses are green and white, and "Centro" buses (2.20 pesos) run from outside the bus station to the Mercado Morelos, two blocks north of the **Plaza de la Patria,** the center of town. "Central Camionera" buses traverse the length of **Madero,** the main road downtown that runs along the north side of the *centro* and changes names to **Carranza** west of the plaza. These buses also will return you to the bus station. The drivers of Aguas are one of the city's miracles—due to strictly enforced city ordinance, everyone here wears a seatbelt. The strapped-in *taxistas* charge about 12 pesos from the bus terminal to the center of town. From the Plaza de la Patria, most sights are within walking distance either on **Montoro** (the street that runs east from the southeast corner of the plaza) or on Carranza, which begins to the west of the plaza, behind the basilica. When you plan your day in Aguas, keep in mind that the city takes its siestas quite seriously; most sights and businesses close from 2 to 4pm.

PRACTICAL INFORMATION The **bus station** is on Av. Circunvalación south of town at Blvd. Chávez. Take the "Central Commission" or a 12-peso cab to get there. **Estrella Blanca** (tel. 78 27 58) serves Durango (1st class 7hr., 4 per day 3:30pm-midnight, 150 pesos; 2nd class 8hr., 4 per day 9am-5:20pm, 123 pesos), Mexico City (6hr., direct every hr. 7am-4pm and 10pm-12:30am, 185 pesos), San Luis Potosí (3hr., 8 per day, 56 pesos), Torreon (6hr., 4 per day, 161 pesos), Zacatecas (2½hr., every 30min. 6am-8:30pm, 45 pesos), and nearby villages including San Juan and Xalapa (1hr., every hour, 25 pesos). **Flecha Amarilla** (tel. 78 26 61) has second-class service to Guanajuato (3½hr., 8:50, 9:40am, and 8:30pm, 60 pesos), Irapuato (3½hr., 14 per day, 60 pesos), Mexico City (8hr., 6 per day 2am-8:20pm, 155 pesos), and Uruapan (8½hr., 11:30am and 3pm, 120 pesos). **Futura** sends first-class buses to Mazatlán (12hr., 11pm, 262 pesos), Mexico City (6hr., every 2hr., 200 pesos), Monterrey (8hr., 4 per day, 269 pesos), Nuevo Laredo (13hr., 3 per day, 405 pesos), and San Luis Potosí (3hr., 12 per day 6am-11pm, 73 pesos). **Omnibus de México** (tel. 78 27 70) has first-class service to Acapulco (11hr., 11:30pm, 340 pesos), Ciudad Juárez (15hr., 3 per day, 488 pesos), Leon (2hr., 7 per day, 50 pesos), Cuernavaca (6½hr., 5 per day, 220 pesos), Durango (6hr., 5 per day, 148 pesos), Guadalajara (3hr., 15 per day, 95 pesos), Mexico City (6hr., every hr., 200 pesos), Monterrey (8hr., 6 per day, 202 pesos), and Zacatecas (2hr., 6 per day 6am-6pm, 45 pesos). **Primera Plus** (tel. 78 26 61) has first-class service to Durango (6hr., 3 per day, 123 pesos), Mexico City (6hr., 11 per day, 202 pesos) and Querétaro (4½hr., 6 per day 9am-11:30pm, 140 pesos), and Zacatecas (3hr., every hr. 8am-10pm, 45 pesos). **Roja de los Altos** can get you to Guadalajara (3hr., every 2hr., 95 pesos), Mexico City (6hr., every hr., 200 pesos), and Monterrey (8hr., 4 per day, 202 pesos). **Transportes Chihuahuenses** has first-class service to Chihuahua (10hr., 4 per day, 351 pesos), Ciudad Juárez (16hr., 2 per day, 888 pesos), Durango (6hr., 5 per day 2:30pm-midnight, 147 pesos), Fresnillo (2½hr., 8 per day, 65 pesos), Torreon (6hr., 3 per day, 189 pesos), and Zacatecas (2hr., 6 per day 10am-9:45pm, 46 pesos). **Transportes de Norte** (tel. 78 27 58) has first-class service to Matamoros (9hr., 2 per day, 320 pesos), Mazatlán (12hr., 2 per day, 300 pesos), Monterrey (8hr., 12 per day 9am-midnight, 202 pesos), and Saltillo (6hr., 11 per day 9am-midnight, 174 pesos).

The **tourist office** (tel. 15 11 55 or 16 03 47), on the Plaza de la Patria, is on the first floor of the Palacio de Gobierno, the first door to the right of the main entrance. Grab a decent map and as many brochures (some in English) as you want (open M-F 8:30am-3pm and 5-7pm, Sa 10am-1pm). **Moneytron** at Montoro 120 (tel. 15 79 79), one block from the *zócalo,* has excellent rates and charges no commission (open M-F 9am-5pm, Sa 9am-2pm). **Bancomer,** 5 de Mayo 112 (tel. 17 19 00 or 18 60 02), one block from the plaza, also offers good rates (open M-F 8:30am-5:30pm, Sa 10am-2pm). In an **emergency,** dial 06. The **police** (tel. 14 20 50 or 14 30 43) are at the corner of Libertad and Gómez Orozco. **Farmacia Sánchez,** Madero 213 (tel. 15 35 50),

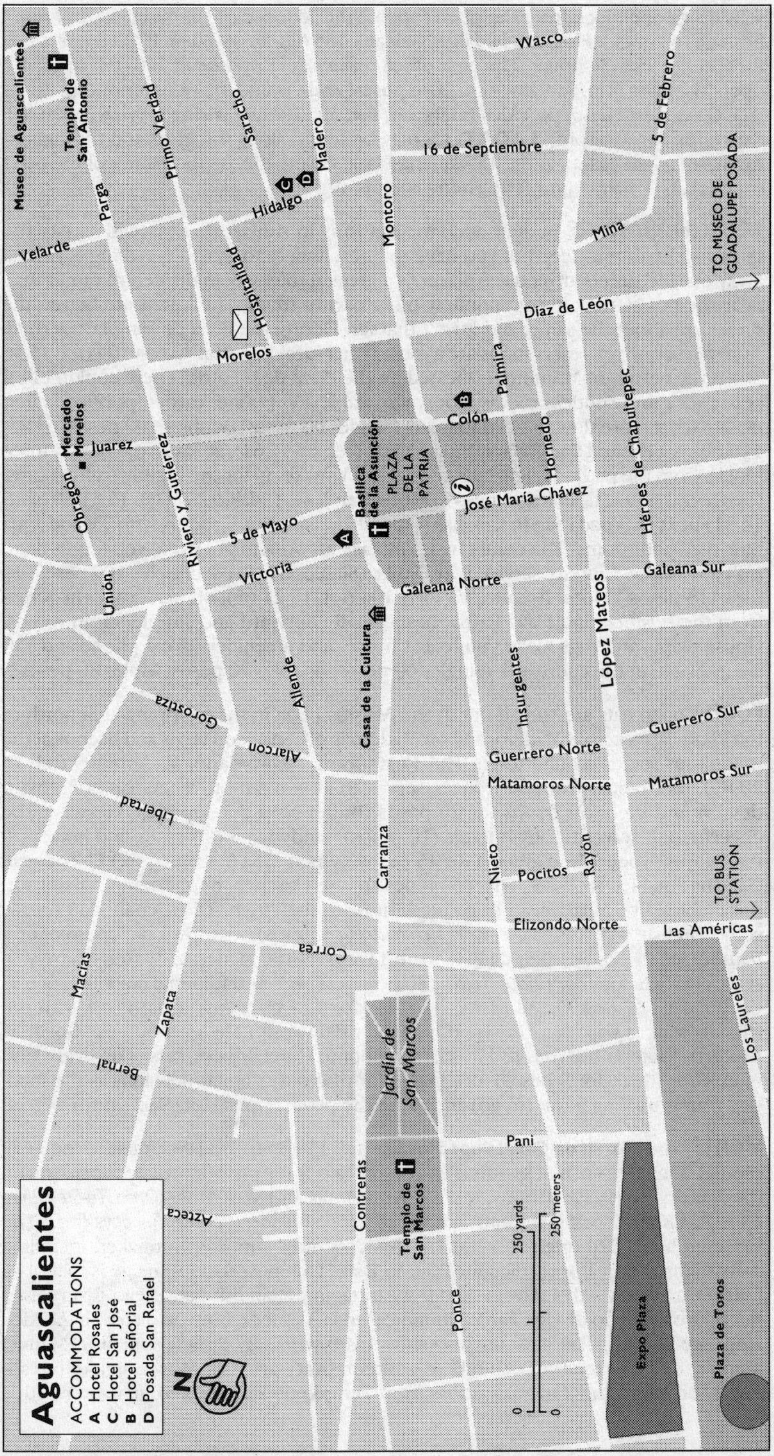
Aguascalientes
ACCOMMODATIONS
A Hotel Rosales
C Hotel San José
B Hotel Señorial
D Posada San Rafael
N
Museo de Aguascalientes
Templo de San Antonio
Velarde
Parga
Primo Verdad
Saracho
Madero
Hidalgo
Hospitalidad
Morelos
Montoro
Wasco
16 de Septiembre
5 de Febrero
Mina
TO MUSEO DE GUADALUPE POSADA
Díaz de León
Palmira
Colón
Mercado Morelos
Juarez
Obregón
Riviero Y Gutiérrez
Basílica de la Asunción
PLAZA DE LA PATRIA
José María Chávez
Hornedo
Héroes de Chapultepec
5 de Mayo
Victoria
Unión
Galeana Norte
Galeana Sur
Casa de la Cultura
López Mateos
Insurgentes
Allende
Gorostiza
Alarcon
Guerrero Norte
Guerrero Sur
Matamoros Norte
Matamoros Sur
Liberdad
Carranza
Nieto
Pocitos
Rayón
TO BUS STATION
Elizondo Norte
Las Américas
Correa
Macías
Zapata
Jardín de San Marcos
Los Laureles
Bernal
Pani
Contreras
Templo de San Marcos
Azteca
250 yards
250 meters
0
Ponce
Expo Plaza
Plaza de Toros

NORTHEAST MEXICO

sells drugs one block from the plaza (open 24hr., doors close at midnight, but don't hesitate to knock). **Hospital Hidalgo,** Galeana 465 (tel. 17 19 30 or 17 29 83), is open for emergencies 24 hours. The **post office** resides at Hospitalidad 108 (tel. 15 21 18; open M-F 8am-7pm, Sa 9am-5pm). The **postal code** is 20000. **Telecomm** (tel. 16 14 27), Galeana at Nieto, provides **telegram, fax,** and **money wiring service** (open M-F 8am-6pm, Sa 9am-1pm). **LADATELS** may be found along the plaza and throughout town; there is a **caseta** at the Tabaquería Plaza, Colón 102, on the corner of the plaza (open daily 8:30am-9pm). The **phone code** is 49.

ACCOMMODATIONS Budget accommodations in Aguascalientes will satisfy the most finicky of travelers, but you have to know where to look. Everything is tucked away on side streets around the plaza. As a general rule, stay in the centro rather than near the bus station; it's an infinitely nicer part of town. The hotels are better, the prices are about the same, and it isn't that far. During the Feria de San Marcos (mid-April to early May), reservations are a must. The **Hotel Señorial,** Colón 104 (tel. 15 16 30) at the corner of Montoro, is located on the Plaza de la Patria. There couldn't be a better location. Spotless rooms, hot water, cable TV, phone, carpet, purified water, desk—what more do you need to hear? (Singles 90 pesos; doubles 100 pesos; triples 110 pesos.) **Posada San Rafael,** Hidalgo 205 (tel. 15 77 61), at Madero, is about three blocks from the plaza. Ceiling fans and cable TV make up for the slightly stuffy rooms. (Singles 80 pesos; doubles 95 pesos.) **Hotel San Jose,** Hidalgo 207 (tel. 15 51 30 or 15 14 31) next to Posada San Rafael, has somewhat institutional rooms with TV and aqua blue-tiled bathrooms. The comfy beds and fake artwork might make you forget there isn't a window. Laundry service is available. (Singles 85 pesos; doubles 100 pesos; triples 115 pesos.) **Hotel Rosales,** Victoria 104 (tel. 15 21 65), off Madero, right across from the *basílica* and Plaza Patria, has a small courtyard and simple, clean rooms. House plants and rugs make you feel at home, and amenities (like a phone and TV) are available in the courtyard. (Singles 60 pesos; doubles 70 pesos; triples 80 pesos.)

FOOD Cheap eats are spread out in San Marcos Plaza in the shopping area north of the Plaza Patria across Madero, and on Madero itself. Snack on tacos and nachos at the ubiquitous stands around town. The **Restaurant Vegetariano,** Madero 409 (tel. 15 79 89), four blocks from the *zócalo,* serves an all-you-can-eat vegetarian buffet with dessert and *agua de frutas* for 25 pesos (buffet M-Sa 2-5:30pm). Otherwise, the cheerful staff serves up soy burgers (10 pesos), sandwiches (9 pesos), and huge platters of fruit, yogurt, and granola for 15 pesos. (Open M-Sa 8:30am-7pm.) **El Zodiaco,** Galeana Sur 113 (tel. 15 31 81), combines an open kitchen, bright orange chairs, formica tables, live canaries, and a painted shrine to the Virgin. The friendly staff speaks some English. Try the nice *comida corrida* (28 pesos), a sandwich (7 pesos), or a hamburger (8 pesos; open daily 8:30am-11pm). **Mitla,** Madero 220 (tel. 16 61 97), serves up delicious *comida corrida* (30 pesos) as well as traditional favorites such as enchiladas (24 pesos) and *bistec a la mexicana* (35 pesos). Chat it up with the friendly staff as you chow down. (Open daily 8am-9pm.) The ever-popular **Gorditas Victoria,** Victoria 108 (tel. 18 17 92), next door to Hotel Rosales, serves up every kind of *gordita* (three for 8 pesos) imaginable for prices that are as delicious as the food. Get your grub para llevar (to go) and eat in the plaza. (Open daily 9am-9pm.)

SIGHTS The **Museo de Guadalupe Posada** (tel. 15 45 56), on León, next to the Templo del Encino, four blocks south of López Mateos, displays morbidly witty turn-of-the-century political cartoons, replete with skulls and skeletons. *(Open Tu-Su 10am-6pm. Admission 5 pesos, students 2.50 pesos, children under 12 free, Sundays free.)* The museum holds 220 original works by Mexico's most famous printmaker, including many figures caricaturing dictator Porfirio Díaz. The most famous image is that of La Catrina, a society lady-calavera (skull) wearing an outlandish hat. Diego Rivera used her figure in Sueño de Una Tarde Dominical en la Alameda, now on display in Mexico City (see p. 103). The museum also shows 100 works by Posada's mentor, Manuel Manilla, and has rotating exhibits of contemporary art. The **Museo de Aguascalientes,** on Parga and Zaragoza across from Templo de San Antonio, may be worth a visit if just for the spectacular building in which it is housed. *(Open daily 8am-6pm. Admission 5 pesos, 2.50 pesos for students, senior citizens and children, free Sundays.)* Works by local artists adorn the rooms and courtyards.

The **Instituto Cultural de Aguascalientes,** popularly known as the **Casa de la Cultura,** Carranza 101 (tel. 15 34 43), at Galeana, hosts temporary sculpture, painting, and photography exhibits in another old hacienda that boggles the mind with its complexity and beauty. *(Open M-F 10am-2pm and 5-8pm, Sa-Su 10am-9pm; free.)* Walk through the sculpture garden and the many display rooms, while ogling the best art exhibits Mexico has to offer. Kiosks in the courtyard drip with listings for cultural events; you can also check the Casa's monthly bulletin or call 16 62 70. The **Centro Cultural Los Arquitos** (tel. 17 00 23), on the Alameda at Héroes de Nacozari, served as public bathrooms from 1821 until 1973. *(Center open daily 9am-2pm and 4-8pm.)* After a magnificent restoration process, the building became a beautiful cultural center in 1994 with a bookshop, a video room that shows children's movies (Friday 5pm), and a small **museum** (open M-F 9am-1pm and 3-8pm, Sa 9am-1pm and 3-6pm, Su 9am-2pm).

The soft grays and rose-colored Solomonic Baroque facade of the **Basílica de la Asunción de las Aguascalientes** make it the most remarkable structure in the city. *(Open daily 7am-2pm and 4-9pm.)* Located in the center of the Plaza de la Patria, the *basílica* is the most recognizable landmark in town and is the center of daily activity. Look for the sculptures of church patrons San Gregorio, San Jerónimo, and San Agustín. The cathedral's interior is graced with high ceilings, gold trimmings, and ornate icons, as well as paintings by José de Alcíbar, Andrés López, and Miguel Cabrera. Another beautiful church is the **Templo de San Antonio,** on Pedro Parga and Zaragoza; from the plaza walk three blocks down Madero, then three blocks left on Zaragoza. *(Open daily 7am-2pm and 4-9pm.)* Every inch of the interior is painstakingly decorated with a collage of soft blues, pinks, and gold leaf. The mix of patterns on the murals, frescoes, oil paintings, and delicate stained glass windows matches the eclectic exterior. The church was built by a local self-taught architect.

ENTERTAINMENT AND SEASONAL EVENTS Aguascalientes is not the mecca of wild nightlife, but the adventurous partier can still find fun. By city ordinance, *discotecas* in Aguascalientes aren't allowed in the *centro histórico* around the Plaza Patria and are only allowed to operate Thursday to Saturday; bars operate every night of the week. Cabs are your best bet to and from the relatively distant clubs; buses stop running around 10pm. **Bol Kristal,** inside the Centro Comercial Plaza Kristal, offers pool and dominos without the usual *cantina* atmosphere of a pool hall. (Open daily 9am-midnight; Sunday is the busiest day.) Shoot a few games and sit back in one of the cozy booths or at the super long bar. **Disco El Cabús** (tel. 73 04 32), Blvd. Zacatecas at Colosia in the Hotel Las Trojes, is a good place to shake your caboose amid the usual flashing lights and bass-heavy dance beats. (Cover Th-F 20 pesos, Sa 40 pesos. Open Th-Sa 9pm-3am.) Don't wear shorts, or the fashion police may apprehend you. **IOS,** Av. Miguel de la Madrid 1821 (tel. 12 65 76), is where the young crowd dances the night away. (Open Sa-Th 9pm-3am.) Jump on a table and grab a beer because the weekend is here. Thursday and Friday women pay no cover but men pay 30 pesos; Saturdays no one gets through the door without forking over the pesos. **Jubilee,** Calle Laureles 602-101 (tel. 17 05 07 or 18 04 94), is where to go if you value drinking over dancing. All drinks cost about half as much as those at other *discotecas*, and the lounging areas are more happening than the dance floor, which features live music and dancing Thursday through Saturday until 3am (no cover).

During the **Feria de San Marcos** (mid-April to early May), everything from cockfights to milking contests, take place in the **Jardín de San Marcos,** a 5- to 10-minute walk on Carranza from the **Plaza de la Patria.** The area around the *jardín* was originally an Indian pueblo, but around the year 1600, indígena labor erected the **Templo Evangelista San Marcos** at the site. The small church still has services today and is the center of a crowded pedestrian thoroughfare popular with Mexican families in the evenings (church open daily 7am-2pm and 4-9pm). Walk two blocks to the left down the pedestrian highway as you face the templo to reach the **Expo Plaza,** filled with shops and restaurants. The expansive Expo plaza has everything from a 10-screen **movie theater** to upscale dining and accommodations, to great shopping, to cheap eats, to a rose garden. If you can't stomach a real bullfight in the adjacent **Plaza de Toros** (most Sundays, Sept-Apr.), just watch the little gold matador and shiny black bull exit the clock of Fiesta America (just behind the statue of the horseman and running bulls)—they do their passes daily at noon, 3, 5, 7, and 9pm. Other seasonal events include the festival of the patron saint of Aguascalientes, **La Romería de la Asunción,** which takes place August 1-15. Festivities include dances, processions, and fireworks. The **Festival de las Calaveras,** a week toward the end of November, is another occasion for the city to cut loose and celebrate.

SAN LUIS POTOSÍ

San Luis Potosí

In San Luis Potosí, everyone smiles a lot. And there's a lot to smile about; *potosinos* are truly, madly, deeply in love with their city. With plazas galore, plenty of pedestrian walkways, and innumerable cathedrals gently and naturally dotting the landscapes as easily as overgrown trees, San Luis (pop. 820,000) is a crash course in urban planning. Founded in 1592 after Franciscan missionaries began to convert local Guachichil and nearby Tlaxcaltec and then discovered silver and gold, San Luis Potosí has twice served as the capital of Mexico. It also served as the site for many pivotal events of the Independence and Revolutionary wars, including the signing of Emperor Maximilian's death sentence and of the "Plan of San Luis" in October 1910. Of less national political importance now, the city is slipping quietly and gracefully into the 21st century. Its "downtown," with bright, squat buildings and wide median strips harboring pineapple palms, is downright inviting. Friendly and eager to embrace the surprisingly few tourists who arrive, it is the residents of San Luis who set the city apart. Bands, magicians, and soap-bubble blowers gather in the town plazas at dusk to entertain assembled crowds of young and old. Lanterns that dot the cathedrals and fountains are spectacularly lit. On a warm evening, it's hard not to feel that San Luis Potosí is the quiet capital of some magical world.

ORIENTATION

San Luis Potosí is at the center of a triangle formed by Mexico's three largest cities—Monterrey, Guadalajara, and Mexico City. Five main highways **(Rtes. 57, 85, 70, 49, and 80)** snake their way into the city. To get downtown from the **bus station,** catch an "Alameda" or "Centro" bus (5:30am-10:30pm, 1.80 pesos) and hop off at **Parque Alameda,** the first big stretch of green. Continue walking in the direction the bus was going, as straight as you can, past the **Plaza del Carmen** on your left, and you'll end up in the **Plaza de Armas.** A taxi costs 25 pesos.

San Luis's main drag is **Av. Carranza,** which runs east-west and passes the north side of the city's historic center, the Plaza de Armas (along which it is also known as **Jardín Hidalgo**). East of the plaza, Carranza is called **Los Bravos. Madero** runs parallel to Carranza one block south, touching the Plaza de Armas's south side. East of the plaza, Madero goes by **Othón.** Running parallel to Carranza one block north is **Av. Obregón. Zaragoza** forms the east side of Plaza de Armas; north of the plaza, it goes by **Hidalgo.** Parallel and one block east of Hidalgo is Morelos, which further north turns into **Moctezuma**—this is where most of the shopping in the *centro* is done. On the west side of the plaza is **5 de Mayo,** known as **Allende** farther north. **Aldama** is one block west of 5 de Mayo. The Plaza del Carmen is two blocks east of the plaza on Madero. A block farther east lies the Alameda, where the bus from the station drops off visitors. The **train station** is on Othón opposite the Alameda. Most city buses exiting the *centro* can be caught on **Ponciano Arriaga,** which runs north-south along the Alameda (back to the Central de Transportes Terrestres) or else on Othón in front of the train station.

PRACTICAL INFORMATION

Transportation

Airport: (tel. 2 22 29) 25min. north of the city. Tickets can be purchased at **2001 Viajes,** Obregón 604 (tel. 12 29 53). Open M-F 9am-2pm and 4-8pm, Sa 9:30am-2pm. Flights to Mexico City begin at 462 pesos with **Aerocalifornia** (tel. 11 80 50), and flights to Monterrey start at 1373 pesos with **AeroLiteral** (tel. 22 22 29). **Mexicana** (tel. 17 89 20) also flies to various destinations. Open M-F 9am-1:30pm and 4:30-7pm.

Trains: The station is on Othón near the north side of the Alameda. To Mexico City (6hr., W, F, Su 10:30am, 57 pesos) and Monterrey (8hr., M, W, F 5:30pm, 57 pesos). The ticket booth opens just before trains leave. Otherwise, the station is deserted except for an altar to the Virgin Mary.

Buses: Central de Transportes Terrestres is 2 blocks south of the chaotic convergence of highways that wrap around the Glorieta Benito Juárez, 4km east of the city center along Av. Universidad. Not to be confused with the old *central* which is now shut down. When going to the *central* from the *centro*, be sure to take only the *peseras* labeled Central TT or to ask the driver for the *central nuevo*. The *pesera* will let you off at the back side of the station. **24hr. luggage storage** in Sala 1 (3 pesos per hr. or 30 pesos per 24hr.). **Del Norte** (tel. 16 55 53) goes to Acapulco (12hr., 3 per day in the evenings, 308 pesos), Querétaro (2½hr., every hr., 75 pesos), and Uruapán (7hr., 2 per day in the nights, 184 pesos). **Estrella Blanca** (tel. 18 30 49) goes to Aguascalientes (3hr., 7 per day, 73 pesos), Chihuahua (14hr., 10 per day, 372 pesos), Cuernavaca (6hr., 3 per day in the evenings, 181 pesos), Monterrey (7hr., every hr., 142 pesos), Querétaro (2½hr., every hr., 2nd class 64 pesos, 1st class 75 pesos), and Zacatecas (3hr., every hr., 62 pesos). **Omnibus de México** (tel. 16 81 61), to Reynosa (9hr., 8pm only, 228 pesos), Saltillo (5hr., 2 per day in the evenings, 141 pesos), and Tampico (7hr., 3 per day in the evenings, 147 pesos). **Oriente** serves Río Verde (2-3hr., every hr., 51 pesos), and Tampico (7hr., 7 per day, 149 pesos). **Transportes Tamaulipas** and **Noreste** (tel. 16 69 64) jointly trek to Matehuala (2hr., 14 per day, 57 pesos), Monterrey (6hr., 12 per day, 158 pesos), and Reynosa via Linares or Monterrey (9hr., 6 per day, 210 pesos).

Car Rental: Hertz, Obregón 670 (tel. 12 95 00). Most small cars cost 280 pesos per day plus insurance and mileage. Must be 25 to rent. Open M-F 9am-2pm and 4-8pm, Sa 9am-2pm.

Tourist and Financial Services

Tourist Office: A city **tourist center** opens on the 1st floor of the Palacio Municipal, on the northeast corner of Pl. de Armas. Excellent city maps provided as well as a very friendly staff eager to help; some English spoken. Open M-F 8am-3pm. The **state tourist office,** Obregón 520 (tel. 12 99 39), 1 block west of the Pl. de los Fundadores, also has city maps with suggested walking tours and explanations in English, in addition to information about the rest of the state. Open M-Sa 8am-8pm.

Consulate: U.S., Mariel 103 (tel. 12 15 28); take the "Morales" bus. Open M-F 8:30am-1:30pm, but sometimes available in the afternoons. The police and the tourist office have consulate employees' home numbers in case of emergency.

Currency Exchange: Casas de Cambio can be found all along Morelos a few blocks north of the Plaza de Armas. **San Luis Divisas** (tel. 12 66 06), at the corner of Morelos and Bocanegra, usually accepts traveler's checks. Open M-Sa 9am-8pm. Many banks are around Pl. de Armas and are open M-F 9am-1:30pm. **Banamex,** at Allende and Obregón, 1 block east of Pl. de Armas, has a 24hr. **ATM** and exchanges traveler's checks with no commission. Get there early; by noon the lines are endless.

American Express: Grandes Viajes, Carranza 1077 (tel. 11 11 27), will help you out with lost or stolen checks or cards and will sell you checks; they do *not,* however, cash American Express traveler's checks. Open M-F 9am-2pm and 4-6pm.

Local Services

Supermarket: Gigante is an enormous supermarket. Cross the treacherous highway from the bus station, turn left, and follow the curve until you see the sign. Open M-F 9am-10pm, Sa-Su 9am-8pm. In the *centro,* the **Mercado Hidalgo,** on Morelos and Mier 3 blocks north of the Plaza de Armas, offers fruit, bread, and candy as well as an extensive selection of crafts. Open daily 8am-8pm.

Laundromat: Lavandería La Gotita, on 5 de Mayo, 7 blocks south of the Plaza de Armas. Full service only. Takes approximately 8hr. 14 pesos per job no matter the weight. Open M-Sa 10am-8pm, with brief breaks.

Emergency and Communications

Emergency: Dial 06.

Police: (tel. 12 10 37 or 12 54 23) can always be found in the Palacio Municipal.

Red Cross: (tel. 15 33 22 or 15 36 35), on Juárez at Díaz Gutiérrez.

Pharmacy: Botica Mexicana, Othón 180 (tel. 12 38 80), near the cathedral. 24hrs.

Hospital: Hospital Central, Carranza 2395 (tel. 13 03 43 or 13 05 95). 20 blocks west of the *centro*. Some English spoken. Open 24hr.

Post Office: Morelos 235 (tel. 2 27 40), 1 block east and 3 blocks north of the Plaza de Armas. Open M-F 8am-7pm, Sa 9am-1pm. Also contains a **MexPost** that is open M-F 9am-6pm, Sa 9am-1pm. **Postal Code:** 78000.

Internet Access: Escobedo 335 on Plaza del Carmen. To enter, walk past the green gates into what looks like a garage. Go up the marble stairs at the back. Computers with Internet 12 pesos per hr. Open M-Sa 10am-10pm.

Telephones: LADATELs are scattered throughout the numerous plazas, particularly on Av. Obregón and Carranza near the Plaza de las Armas and the Plaza de los Fundadores. **Computel,** Carranza 360 (tel.12 01 89 or 12 01 13), is opposite the Hotel Panorama. It allows international collect calls and has a **fax** (fax 12 01 86). Open M-Sa 7:30am-9pm.

Phone Code: 48.

ACCOMMODATIONS

Some good, cheap accommodations can be found near the bus station, but they fill up very quickly. Past-their-prime hotels close to the *centro* still boast somewhat commodious rooms, plaza views, and low prices. Alternatively, spring for a more expensive room in the centro and get a real treat.

Hotel Plaza, Jardín Hidalgo 22 (tel. 12 46 31), on the south side of the Plaza de Armas. This hotel, the first in San Luis Potosí, has seen better days, but the staff is wonderful and the rooms maintain a funny sort of charm and are kept quite clean. Ask for a room facing the plaza or with a balcony and you just may get it. Ask for some history of the hotel and you'll definitely get a tour replete with old photos and scrapbook clippings. 1-2 people 100 pesos, 3-4 people 130 pesos.

Hotel Alameda, Callejón La Perla 3 (tel. 18 06 06), next to the Pemex gas station on the northwest corner of the Alameda, is the cheapest option in San Luis Potosí. Rooms are small, dark, and in minor disrepair, but the plumbing is new, the water is hot, the manager is accommodating, and the price is right. 1 person 50 pesos, 2 people 60 pesos.

Hotel Filher, Universidad 335 (tel. 12 15 62 or 12 15 63), at the corner of Zaragoza 3 blocks south of the Plaza de Armas, boasts bright, clean rooms with beautiful wooden furniture, TV, phone, fan, and big bathrooms inside a renovated colonial building. Be sure to ask for a window to the outside and you'll get the extra quality you pay for. 1 person 166 pesos, 2 people 196 pesos.

Motel Potosí (tel. 18 26 88), next door to the bus station (the first building on your left as you exit), is shockingly affordable, considering the prices of nearby hotels. With a private garage for each room and little living rooms complete with lovable, mismatching desk and sofa, TV and telephone, you might just be lured away from the *centro* and live it up near the bus station. Get here early—this place fills up fast. Singles 115 pesos; doubles 150 pesos; triples 180 pesos.

FOOD

Although they are plentiful, restaurants in the *centro* often offer mediocre or bland dishes and poor service. The farther you stray, the better your chances of bumping into a gem. Both *tacos potosinos* and *enchiladas potosinas* are stuffed with cheese and vegetables, then fried. *Nopalitos* are tender and absolutely delicious pieces of cactus (spines removed) cooked in a salty green sauce of garlic, onion, and tomato. *Chongos coronados* (curdled milk in sweet maple water) is a popular dessert.

La Guëra, Tata Nacho 800 (tel. 11 87 28), near Parque Tangamanga. On the left as you approach the *parque,* in the block before the entrance. This traditionally decorated treasure offers some of the best meals in all of Northeast Mexico. Serving only breakfast specials (18-21 pesos, 8am-1:30pm) and *comida corrida* (28 pesos, 1:30-6pm), La Guëra assures you will groan with delight at every bite. From the pickled *nopalito* garnish served with your chips to the homemade *mole* (only one_main entree option among many), everything here is scrumptious. Open Tu-Su 8am-6pm.

Restaurant Cafeteria (tel. 12 29 57), with the bright orange doors on Madero just west of the Plaza de Armas. A bright hole-in-the-wall from which delicious odors waft. At 1 of just 3 tiny tables, you will be served breakfast, lunch, or dinner (*tortas* 9-20 pesos, meals 14-38 pesos), as well as rare and scrumptious desserts (5-10 pesos) and espresso. Open daily 8am-10:30pm.

Tokio, Zaragosa 305 (tel. 14 61 89). Only the jade-colored decor reflects the Japanese name. Tokio serves tasty Mexican dishes in a cool, modern atmosphere. *Comida corrida* (23 pesos) starts at 1:30pm. Open daily 7:30am-1am.

Yu Ne Nisa, Arista 360 (tel. 14 36 31). A Yucatec celebration of vegetarianism. Bright eating area is decorated with plants and matching green chairs. Veggie burgers are 20 pesos, and the quesadillas are a rock-bottom 12 pesos. Watch them squeeze juice and make luscious *licuados*—you'll howl in ecstasy. Adjoins an herbal/homeopathic/vegetarian store. Large variety of fruit juices, yogurt concoctions, and whole wheat breads. *Comida corrida* (30 pesos) starts at 1:30pm. Open M-Sa 9am-8pm.

SIGHTS

San Luis Potosí has so many beautiful buildings and lovely sights that it's almost appalling. The great majority have wonderful historical markers in front in both English and Spanish, for the edification of tourists.

Churches, Cathedrals, Parks, and Plazas

Dubbed the "City of Plazas," San Luis Potosí has three main town squares. The most central of these is the **Plaza de Armas,** replete with trees and peaceful *potosinos.* At the beginning of the 17th century, residents watched bullfights from the balconies of the surrounding buildings. Since 1848, a red sandstone gazebo bearing the names of famous Mexican musicians has graced the plaza; on Thursday and Sunday evenings, it hosts a local band that attracts crowds.

The west side of the Plaza de Armas is marked by the Neoclassical facade of the **Palacio del Gobierno.** *(Open M-F 9am-2:30pm; free.)* Constructed in 1798 and briefly serving as the capital of the country and the seat of the presidency in 1863, the structure was renovated in 1950 and continues to serve as San Luis Potosí's administrative seat. The building has interesting *salas* (living rooms; on the second floor) filled with murals, statues, plaques, and legends. Ask the guard to unlock the *salas* if the rooms are closed.

Opposite the Palacio de Gobierno stands the **cathedral,** with two bell towers that toll a different melody every 15 minutes. *(Cathedral open daily 8am-7pm; tourists should avoid visiting on Sunday or during Mass.)* Both magnificent and ominous, the cathedral was completed in 1710, but in 1855, when San Luis became a diocese, the building was "upgraded." Miners are said to have donated gold and silver to beautify the interior, and marble statues of the apostles (small copies of those at the Basilica of San Juan de Letrán in Rome) were placed in the niches between the Solomonic columns of the Baroque facade. Paintings are in the sacristy.

Not as high-profile as its counterpart, Armas, but still worth seeing, is the **Jardín de San Francisco.** The plaza is distinguished by its bronze fountain, quaint cobblestone streets, and red sandstone buildings. Elderly *potosinos* often congregate on the shady benches carrying grandkids and tossing crumbs to the pigeons. Book stalls line the east side of the plaza while artisan sellers extend down Universidad, off the west side. Soon after the city's founding, construction began on the **Iglesia de San Francisco,** on the plaza's west side. *(Open daily 6:30am-1:30pm and 4:30-9pm.)* Less ornate than its nearby counterparts, the orange stucco facade still boasts a highly Baroque interior beautifully accentuated by the flickering votives at each altar.

The bright, lively **Plaza de Carmen** with its Sunday festivals is host to the serene **Templo de Carmen** on its northeast corner, two blocks east of the Plaza de Armas. *(Open daily 7am-1:30pm and 4-9pm; avoid visiting during Mass.)* Many *potosinos* claim that the church is the most beautiful religious building in the city; it features hanging chandeliers, golden altars, and a huge mural of the crucifixion. During the day, the light filters in and the place really glows. Three blocks east along Manuel Othón from the Plaza de Armas is the expansive **Alameda Juan Sarabia** with artisans and trinket-vendors as well as game operators along the western side. Avoid the Alameda at night (when drunks and pickpockets roam). Finally, try **Parque Tangamanga,** with lakes for paddle-boating and fishing, a baseball field, electric cars, and bike paths. *(Open Tu-Su 9am-6pm.)* Bring a blanket and a picnic and spend the day lounging, or rent a bike (400m into the park on the main drag) for 17 pesos per hour and explore it all. To get to the park, catch a "Perimetral" bus (0.80 pesos) on Constitución across from the Alameda. Get off at the Monumento a la Revolución and walk south for three blocks.

Museums

Parque Tangamanga (see above) also houses the **Museo de las Culturas Populares** (tel. 12 29 76) with a great exhibit of indigenous handcrafts as well as rare photo exhibitions of indigenous communities and ceremonies (open Tu-Su 10am-5pm; 1 peso).

If you're wandering around a bit overwhelmed and clueless, perhaps a museum should be your guide. The pink sandstone **Museo Nacional de la Máscara,** Villerías 2 (tel. 12 30 25), in the Palacio Federal, half a block south of Pl. del Carmen along Villerías, displays hundreds of ancient and modern masks from every Mexican region, from *diablos* to dancing cows. *(Open Tu-F 10am-2pm and 4-6pm, Sa-Su 10am-2pm. Admission 2 pesos.)* This is a fascinating place; be sure to check out all of the oversized *mojigangas* in the hall—these enormous, eccentric representations are taken out of the museum and paraded around the streets during seasonal festivals.

The **Museo Regional Potosino** (tel. 12 51 85), on Independencia near the corner of Galeana, occupies the grounds of the former Franciscan convent. The government seized the land in 1950 and converted part of it into a museum. The first floor exhibits artifacts from all of Mexico, including a collection of artifacts of the Huasteca, natives of the region and contemporaries of the Maya. On the museum's second floor is the marvelous Baroque **Capilla a la Virgen de Aranzazu.** *(Open Tu-Su 10am-7pms. Admission 10 pesos, free on Sundays.)* A shepherd found the altar's image of the Virgin in a prickly thicket, hence the name (*aranzazu* means "from within the thorns").

ENTERTAINMENT AND SEASONAL EVENTS

Taxis are nearly impossible to catch on Saturday nights and few discos are in the *centro,* so if you plan on hitting the clubs, leave early. Both **Dulcinea** (tel. 18 13 12), Carretera Mexico km 5, inside the five-star Holiday Inn del Quixote, and **Oasis** (tel. 22 18 82), Carretera Mexico km 1, in the Hotel Maria Dolores, attract a young, styling crowd. Both are dark and grooving (cover 40 pesos; both open Th-Sa 10pm-late). A little closer to the *centro* is **Staff,** Carranza 423 (tel. 14 30 74), where a young, gay-friendly crowd grooves to Latin and dance music (cover 25 pesos; open F-Su).

For those itching for a bit of visual arts, check out **El Teatro de La Paz** (tel. 12 26 98), behind the Templo de Carmen. This theater is one of the four most famous and fabulously constructed in Mexico—many performers don't even need microphones. The salon holds a collection of modern art, the foyer has lovely sculptures and murals, and the theater plays everything from traditional Mexican fare to 101 Dalmatians. The best news? Prices tend to be below 30 pesos. Pick up a *guía* at the city tourist office to see what's playing, or look at the posters outside the *teatro.*

Sip an espresso with theater-going types for only 8 pesos at the **Café del Teatro** in the same building as the *teatro* (open Tu-Su 10am-10pm). If you'd rather spend money shopping and be totally hip, the area along Carranza west of the *centro* teems with trendy restaurants and clubs. Here, the swank **Jardín de Tequis** is a great place to relax and listen to the trickle of four beautiful fountains. This area is accessible via the "Morales" bus.

Finally, the last two weeks of August mark the **Fiesta Nacional Potosina.** Concerts, bullfights, fireworks, and a parade guarantee that a great time will be had by all.

Matehuala

Although Matehuala derives its name from a Huachichil phrase meaning "don't come," the town is anything but unfriendly. The few tourists who do trickle in are usually hallucinogen-hungry backpackers en route to Real de Catorce. They may be surprised to find that this town of 100,000, once a base for Spanish silver and gold mining, is relaxing, open, and beautiful—well worth a stay. Unlike some other Mexican cities, Matehuala has slid into the modern age with grace and good nature.

ORIENTATION Matehuala is 261km from Saltillo and 191km from San Luis Potosí. The **Central de Autobuses** is located on Calle 5 de Mayo, just south of the city and near the large, red **Arco de Bienvenida. Calle 5 de Mayo** runs north-south through the center of town. Across the street from the station, a pesera labeled "Centro" will take you to the downtown area for 1.60 pesos—ask the driver to let you off near the cathedral, or easier still, get off at Hidalgo, next to the Chalita market. Taxis charge 15 pesos for the trip.

Constantly forking or changing names, the streets of Matehuala are confusing, but they are so short and close together that you'll never be lost for long. Locals are eager to provide directions, and if they can't point you in the right one, they'll find someone who can. Maps can be obtained at the tourist office on Highway 57 or at the blue *Papeleteria Corias* on Morelos, next door to #510 (8 pesos; open M-F 8am-9pm), but if you speak any Spanish, asking directions is easier than reading the maps. **Miguel Hidalgo** runs north-south through most of the city; **Benito Juárez** runs parallel to it, one block west; and **Morelos** runs one block east. **Betancourt** forks off Morelos one block past Hotel del Valle. At the end of its 400 block, Morelos ends up perpendicular to Madero. **Constitución** runs up one side of the Templo, and **Reyes** runs perpendicular to Hidalgo starting directly in front of the Templo. Most points of interest lie somewhere on or between these streets.

PRACTICAL INFORMATION **Central de Autobuses** (tel. 2 26 50), on 5 de Mayo south of the downtown area, provides a consolidated service of **Transportes del Norte, Frontera, Estrella Blanca** and **El Aguila** to Mexico City (7hr., 5 per day, 1st class 223 pesos, 2nd class 192 pesos), Monterrey (4hr., 8 per day, 101 pesos), Nuevo Laredo (7hr., 8 per day, 205 pesos), Querétaro (6hr., 3 per day, 137 pesos), Saltillo (3hr., 5 per day, 80 pesos), and San Luis Potosí (2hr., 8 per day, 57 pesos). **Noreste** (tel. 2 09 97) serves Monterrey (4hr., 9 per day, 101 pesos) and Reynosa (7hr., 8 per day, 154 pesos). **Tamaulipas** (tel. 2 27 77) to Monterrey via Saltillo (9 per day, 101 pesos), Real de Catorce (5 per day, 19 pesos), Reynosa via Monterrey (7hr., 5 per day, 154 pesos), and San Luis Potosí (2 hr., 11 per day, 57 pesos).

For **tourist information,** head over to the **Cámara de Comercio,** Morelos 427 (tel. 2 01 10), one block east of Hidalgo. Low on maps, but high on knowledge, they also offer Internet connections for 10 pesos per hour. (Open M-F 9am-1:30pm and 4-7pm.) **Maps** are for sale (8 pesos) at the blue Papeleria Yrizar on Morelos next door to #510. There is a small-scale **tourist office** (tel. 2 12 81) next to the Padregal Motel on Highway 57, north of the city and accessible only by car or taxi (open M-F 10am-4pm). **Casas de cambio** dot the *centro,* all offering good rates. **Biotal,** 111 Reyes (tel. 2 48 18), exchanges cash and traveler's checks and has 24hr. **ATM** (bank open M-Sa 8am-9pm). **Banca Serfin** (tel. 2 12 82), at Reyes and Hidalgo, also has a 24hr. **ATM.** The **indoor market** next to the Templo de la Imaculada Concepción sells crafts and produce (open daily 9am-6pm). The **Lavandería Acuario** (tel. 2 70 88), Betancourt and Madero, offers self-service wash or dry of 5kg for 30 pesos (open daily 8:30am-2pm and 4-8pm).

In case of **emergency,** dial 06. The **police station** (tel. 2 06 47) is located next to the bus station. The **Red Cross** (tel. 2 07 26) is located at Ignacio y Ramírez and Betancourt about eight blocks east of Betancourt's original fork from Morelos. **Farmacia del Centro,** Morelos 623 (tel. 2 05 92), is open daily 9am to midnight, and English is spoken. The **Hospital General** (tel. 2 04 45), on Hidalgo a few blocks north of *el centro,* is open 24 hours. Little to no English is spoken. The **post office** (tel. 2 00 71) is located at Leandro Valle and Negrete. To get there, walk up Constitución, turn right on Independencia one block before the beautiful, quiet Iglesia Santo Niño, turn right again on Negrete and it's on your left at the corner. (Open M-F 8am-3pm, Sa 9am-1pm.) The **postal code** is 78700. **Faxes** can be sent from most papelerias or from **Telecomm,** 5 de Febrero at Juárez (tel. 2 00 08), a few blocks east of the *centro.* Telecomm also houses a **Western Union** office (open M-F 9am-7pm). **LADATELs** are not as common in Matehuela as in other cities but can still be found throughout the *centro.* If you don't run into one, try Hidalgo across the street from Hotel Matehuala or the corner of Juárez and Ocampo. The **phone code** is 488.

ACCOMMODATIONS Budget accommodations dot the *centro.* The *casas de huéspedes* on Calle Bocanegra are the cheapest options (singles 30 pesos; doubles 40 pesos with shared bathrooms), but spend more and get luxurious rooms and central location. This town's got some great hotels.

Hotel y Casino Del Valle (tel. 2 37 70), on Morelos right off the Plaza de Armas, offers its customers comfortable but fun doubles for reasonable prices. The lobby greets you with a counter of opaque glass and sandstone, black velour loveseats, and pink walls. TV, hyperactive ceiling fans in the rooms, and an attached dance hall (the good part is, you might get to watch a wedding from the balcony, the bad part is, you might get to listen to them dance the night away) make this hotel swank as a Vegas casino. Well, maybe not that swank, but worth the extra pesos. (All rooms are doubles, maximum 4 to a room. 1-2 people 160 pesos; 20 pesos for each additional person.) For less pricey though smaller rooms, check out **Hotel Blanca Estela,** Morelos 426 (tel. 2 23 00), next to the video store. Fans cool small, super-clean, colorful rooms with TVs. Beautiful wooden furnishings lend a classy feel to the rooms in this narrow, small hotel. Check in early; this may well be the most crowded shindig in town. (Singles 70 pesos; doubles 90 pesos.) **Hotel Matehuala,** Bustamante 134 (tel. 2 06 80), just north of the Plaza de Armas, has a distinct character in each of its single and double rooms. Spacious and airy, with a huge and empty tiled courtyard, this hotel is monastic in the best way. Though the rooms are dark as confessional booths, the 25 ft. ceilings with wooden rafters, white walls, and rust color bureaus and coat rack are not to be missed. Ask for a room with windows to the outside and a balcony. (Singles 80 pesos; doubles 100 pesos.)

FOOD The few restaurants in Matehuela are family-owned, family-prone cafeteria types with good food and low prices. Get ready to practice your hard-core menu-ordering Spanish. **Restaurant Fontella,** Morelos 618 (tel. 2 02 93) cooks up some of the best food in town. The murals of the city evoke a sense of yesteryear, while the food is the best of today. Charcoal-roasted specialties are 27 to 34 pesos. Comida corrida offers copious servings of fresh vegetable soup, rice, chicken or steak, and dessert for 23 pesos. (Open daily 7:30am-4am.) **Restaurant Video Bar House Rock** (tel. 2 20 08), on Hidalgo directly across from the Templo, offers exquisite simple fare in a cool family-style restaurant upstairs (*comida corrida* only 22 pesos; open daily 9am-11pm), while the hippest 20-30 year-olds hang out in the video bar downstairs where antique decorations mix with modern music (beer 10 pesos; open W-Sa 7pm-1am). **La Cava,** Callejón del Arte 1 (tel. 2 28 88), is just east of Hotel Matehuala in a little pedestrian walkway off Hidalgo. The elegant dining room is a pleasant escape from the merciless sun. A mix of Mexican, French, American, and Russian cuisine goes for 33 to 50 pesos. The cocktails are very smooth. (Open daily 1:30pm-10:30pm.)

SIGHTS While there are not a lot of big-name sights in Matehuala, every wide street and little park seems ripe for reclining. Standing solemnly at the center of Matehuala between Calles Juárez and Hidalgo is the almost completed **Templo de la Inmaculada Concepción,** a copy of Saint Joseph's cathedral in Lyon, France. Construction began in 1905, and although poor funding has slowed progress on the project, more than 90 years of Matehualans are proud of their all-but-finished cathedral. The large clock and seemingly impenetrable gray exterior of this Gothic-style edifice belie a beautiful interior flooded with light. Just in front of the main cathedral is the **Plaza Juárez,** now permanently occupied by vendor stalls and small, makeshift cafes. Sprawling out onto adjoining streets, the bazaar is collectively known as **Mercado Arista.** Leather and ceramic goods as well as the usual slew of cheap plastic toys and trinkets figure prominently here. The lovely **Alameda,** a few blocks south of the main plaza, offers lots of shade and jungle-like lushness.

Two other large parks stand at the northeast and southeast corners of the downtown area. Approximately three blocks east of Hidalgo, between Bocanegra and Altamirano, is the soothing and peaceful **Parque Vicente Guerrero** (also called the **Parque del Pueblo**). Vicente Guerrero's counterpart is the more lively **Parque Alvaro Obregón,** just south of Insurgentes. With basketball courts and benches aplenty, Álvaro Obregón draws entire families in the early evening hours.

Real de Catorce

Once a thriving mining town with 30,000 inhabitants, Real de Catorce now looms mysteriously on the side of a mountain, a veritable ghost town with a population of barely 1500 people. Still, backpackers come from all over to see this town's *burro*-trodden paths and brick ruins rising up from the Sierra Madre like desert flowers. The cobblestone streets and carts full of holy candles may not seem like much, but Real de Catorce is a Mexican miracle—the little town was left behind by time. Tourists from all over Mexico travel to Real de Catorce to investigate this dusty anachronism of a town, to explore hallucinogens, and to pray to Saint Francis. Its history and natural beauty may soon give Real de Catorce new life as wealthier Mexicans begin to invest in it as a vacation spot.

ORIENTATION AND PRACTICAL INFORMATION The town's main thoroughfare (read: rocky path) is **Calle Lanzagorta,** which runs from the **bus station** past the famed **cathedral** and a few hotels and restaurants to a little town square with a gazebo. **Calle Constitución** runs parallel to Lanzagorta up the hill, through the **Plaza Principal.** For transportation, **Autobuses Tamaulipas** (tel. 2 08 40) runs buses from Matehuala to Real de Catorce (1¼hr., during peak season every 2hr. 6am-6pm, round-trip 38 pesos; fewer buses during the rest of the year). Always check with the bus driver about the schedules, and always arrive 15-30 minutes early. Also, make sure to check which bus your return ticket is for. Although you'll always be let on a bus out of Real de Catorce, it may be standing-room only. Buses from Matehuala leave from a station at Guerrero and Méndez near the *centro* and always stop at the smaller station on Parque Vicente Guerrero. Although a little further, the second is easier to find. From the cathedral, walk down Reyes, turn left on Rayón, and follow it to the park. The station will be on your right. Buy tickets here also, or catch a shuttle bus from the **Central de Autobuses,** the central bus station on 5 de Mayo, for free. The ride to "Real de 14" is guaranteed to whiten the knuckles of the timid traveler: the bus rambles along a cobblestone road and a winding path chiseled into the mountainside, and riders change to a lower bus for the seven-minute tunnel at the end of the ride.

Self-appointed guides, offering **tourist information** and **peyote,** can be found as you get off the bus or in the back streets of the city. Most services (i.e. the civil registry, **police** station, and municipal government) are run out of the **Presidencia Municipal,** just by the Plaza Principal. The **post office** is on Calle Constitución to the right of the Presidencia as you are facing it, on the right side of the street (open M-F 9am-1pm and 3-6pm). The town's single **telephone** (tel. 2 37 33), on a side-street going up between the Presidencia and the post office, will put you in touch with the hotels.

ACCOMMODATIONS AND FOOD Real de Catorce has a conspicuous lack of decent budget accommodations (hotels cater almost exclusively to gringo tourists, mainly dazed backpackers, and journalists) as well as a strange penchant for expensive Italian food. For their prices, however, most of the hotels are beautiful and, if not equipped with the latest electronics, richly decorated. Many restaurants are open only during tourist season, which is late June, July, and August. Prices everywhere go down off-season. Your best option would be **El Mesón de la Abundancia,** Langazorta #11. The oldest edifice in town (it used to be the town treasury in the 1880s), this hotel is also an exercise in historical recreation. Most furniture is original, the blankets are made of superior wool, and the rooms are large and lovely enough to hold money. Some rooms have private terraces and sitting rooms. (1-2 people 190 pesos.) Adjoining restaurant/bar offers original artisanry, hanging plants, and more. A full meal runs 28 pesos and the menu includes vegetarian options. **El Real,** Morelos 20, has colorful, spic-and-span rooms with candlelight, wood furniture, and mosaics. Some rooms boast skylights and private balconies, and the roof terrace offers a smashing view. (Singles 170 pesos; doubles 190 pesos.) Italian dishes (50-100 pesos) are the *forte* of the hotel's restaurant. **Hotel Providencia,** Lanzagorta 29, offers a few bare-boned cheaper rooms (singles 60 pesos; doubles 130 pesos) and a few expensive ultra-modern rooms whose great attractions are bathtubs and soon-to-be-installed telephones (doubles only, 250 pesos, but prices may be negotiable). They also serve *comidas corridas* with delicious homemade tortillas in the restaurant downstairs for 25 pesos.

SIGHTS **Calle Lanzagorta** runs past most major sights. The **Templo de la Purísima Concepción** is down the road on the right; ascend the white walkway to reach the entrance. Inside, the floor seems to be composed of rectangular blocks of wood; the blocks are actually doors to subterranean **tombs,** each of which contains several bodies. The **cathedral** resembles a brightly colored Fabergé egg, with pastel decor and plastic figurines. It houses a lifelike image of St. Francis, whose miracles have created a devoted following; on October 4, the saint's feast day, the town attracts a flock of pious visitors hoping to pray at the cathedral. The most amazing part of the cathedral is a side room filled with **letters** of thanks and devotion to St. Francis for everything from visa waivers to cures from fatal diseases. Often hand-painted, stenciled, or filled with photographs, these thousands of letters spanning decades are full of hope and meticulously crafted. Uphill, on the right after the cathedral (a steep climb), is the **Plaza Principal,** where today only a crumbling fountain remains. Next to the plaza is the **Casa de Moneda,** formerly a mint, whose third floor houses a photography exhibit of Real de Catorce. Enter the museum by the plaza. *(Open daily 10am-4pm; free.)* You can also check out artifacts from Real de Catorce's past at the **Museo Parroquial** on Lanzagorta across from the cathedral. If you read Spanish, you can also buy a series of written guides on the area for 8-40 pesos. *(Open F-Su 9:30am-4:30pm. Admission 2 pesos, children 1 peso.)*

Turning right immediately after the *jardín,* continue two blocks uphill, then head one painfully uphill block to the left. There, the terraced steps of the **Palenque de Gallos** (cock-fight ring) replicate the layout of a classical Athenian theater (ask someone in the Casa de Moneda to unlock it for you). At the high end of Constitución lies **El Mirador,** a little area of ruins offering a view of the city. The surrounding cliff known as **El Voladero** offers breathtaking views of the nearby mountains and valleys. To reach it, walk downhill on Calle Constitución and you'll be rewarded with visions of 1000 ft. drops, dry riverbeds crackling with heat, and herds of cows on distant hilltops. At the top of Calle Zaragoza stands the stark white **Capilla de Guadalupe** (also called the Panteón), which overlooks a cemetery tightly paved with the graves of local saints. For a **guided horseback tour** of the region, ask at the first shop you come to or anywhere else in town for **Teofilo Aguayo Frías** (he's the only Teofilo in town). Having grown up in the city and worked in the mines, he will give you a wonderful tour for only 30 pesos per hour (per person). If you're feeling more adventurous, he can even take you on a two-day trip to a nearby *rancho* or down into the desert to collect your own peyote. Those who have a little more time and energy can try hiking on their own up toward the **Ciudad de las Fantasmas,** straight up off the end of Lanzagorta nearest the bus station. Beware of the mine shafts, which drop hundreds of feet into unknown tunnels—they are often unmarked.

Ciudad Valles

Ciudad Valles (pop. 350,000) is a major crossroads between the *noreste* and central Mexico. Valles (as it is commonly called) is a hot (the average summer temperature is 110°F/43°C) and dirty city, the second largest in the state after the capital; however, it lacks the charm, culture, and beauty of San Luis Potosí. With wide, bus-worn streets, the city evokes the U.S. midwest. Unfortunately it doesn't hint at the rich Huastecan culture surrounding the area—Valles feels more like Industrytown, Anywhere.

ORIENTATION AND PRACTICAL INFORMATION Ciudad Valles's main thoroughfare is **Calle Hidalgo. Carranza** runs perpendicular to Hidalgo and connects it to the city bus station, four blocks down Carranza from Hidalgo. **Juárez** runs parallel to Hidalgo one block south. Hidalgo and Juárez end at **Jardín Hidalgo,** Valle's only plaza, bordered on the west by the **Parque Colosio** and **Río Valles.** Most accommodations and points of interest lie along Hidalgo and Juárez.

The **Central de Autobuses,** on the outskirts of town, is accessible by bus from Calle Hidalgo (2 pesos) or taxi (20 pesos). **Oriente** (tel. 2 39 02) serves Guadalajara (10hr., 3 per day, 234-298 pesos), Matamoros (8hr., 4 per day, 162 pesos), Querétaro (8hr., 10:30pm, 155 pesos), San Luis Potosí (5hr., 9 per day, 102 pesos), Tampico (2½hr., every hr. in the morning and 3 in the afternoon, 53 pesos), and Xilitla (1½hr., 2 per day, 22 pesos). **Transpaís** (tel. 2 38 59) runs buses to Monterrey (7½hr., 10 per day, 165 pesos) and Reynosa (7½hr., 5 per day, 165 pesos).

Terrific maps of the town can be purchased for 8 pesos at the **Cámara de Comercio,** Carranza Sur 55 (tel. 2 01 44 or 2 45 11), half a block south of Hidalgo (open M-F 9am-1:30pm and 4-7:30pm, Sa 9am-1pm), or at the first two hotels listed below. Also find out about local and nearby sights from the friendly staff at the Cámara de Comercio. **Banamex** (tel. 2 02 12), on Hidalgo at Madero, exchanges traveler's checks (open M-F 9am-3pm) and has a 24-hour **ATM.** In case of an **emergency,** dial the **Red Cross** number (tel. 2 00 56) or call the **police** (tel. 2 53 53). The **post office** (tel. 2 01 04) with a **Mexpost** office inside is on Juárez 520 (open M-F 8am-7pm, Sa 9am-1pm). The **postal code** is 79000. The **phone code** is 138.

ACCOMMODATIONS AND FOOD Several hotels dot the *centro.* **Hotel Piña,** Juárez 210 (tel. 2 01 83), offers clean rooms with private bath. Enormous, empty closets with shelves may give the budget traveler (that's you) a clothes-shopping craving. Piña offers three different ranges of rooms—some have TVs or the much-needed air-conditioning (singles 92-143 pesos; doubles 111-173 pesos). **La Troje** (tel. 2 48 80), adjoining Hotel Piña, offers *comida corrida* for only 20 pesos as well as a tasty variety of *antojitos* (15-25 pesos) in brightly decorated and marvelously air-conditioned comfort.

Xilitla

A serpentine road winds through the rocky *huasteca* highlands to the tiny, lush hamlet of Xilitla, 90 minutes from and 1000m above Ciudad Valles. The town itself (pop. 10,000) consists of dozens of sidewalk stores and a tiny market offering food and basics to locals and crafts and trinkets to tourists. Xilitla's main attraction, however, is its incredible beauty; it rises to a picturesque central plaza with phenomenal views. The gorgeous greenery and surrounding hills scream "paradise," and the cultural legacy and natural gifts are rich indeed. The area has over 150 caves, including **El Sótano de las Golondrinas,** a spelunker's dream, over 450m deep with a cave floor covering approximately six acres. Xilitla's most fabulous and notable attraction is the beautiful and bizarre "ruins" built by Edward James early this century, known locally as **Las Pozas.** Dozens of waterfalls, rivers ripe for rafting, horseback trails, unofficial sanctuaries of wild orchids, and rare animals are accessible from Eden-like Xilitla.

ORIENTATION AND PRACTICAL INFORMATION The bus station sits just below town. It is served by **Vencedor,** with buses going to (and from) Ciudad Valles (1½hr., 8am-7pm, 21 pesos), Jalpan (45min., every hr., 28 pesos), San Luis Potosí (6½hr., 5 per day, 91 pesos), and Tampico (4½hr., 6 per day, 66 pesos). **Flecha Amarilla** (tel. 5 02 33) goes to Jalpan (2hr., 4 per day, 28 pesos), Mexico City (8hr., 3 per day, 116 pesos), and Querétaro (6½hr., 8 per day, 92 pesos). To get to the **Plaza Central,** officially named **Jardín Hidalgo,** go up the stairs to the right of the bus station and turn right on Zaragosa. Exchange currency or traveler's checks at the **Centro de Cambio** (tel. 5 02 81), on the right-hand side of Zaragosa as you go toward the plaza (open

8am-8pm daily). **Banorte** (tel. 5 00 29), on the Zaragosa side of the plaza, also exchanges currency and checks but does not have an ATM (open M-F 9am-2:30pm).

The Palacio Municipal, on the plaza, houses the **police.** The **Red Cross** (tel. 5 01 25) is on the road descending from Xilitla. **Farmacia San Augustín** (tel. 5 00 11) is on Hidalgo, at the northwest corner of the Plaza Principal (open daily 8:30am-9pm). Behind the *palacio* on Calle Zaragoza (south side of the plaza) is the **post office,** located on the second floor (open M-F 9am-3pm). The **postal code** is 79902. **Telecomm** (tel. 5 01 72) offers fax, telegram and Western Union service (open M-F 9am-2pm, Sa 9am-noon). There is a **long-distance public phone** at Hotel Ziyaquetzas on the Zaragosa side of the plaza. The **phone code** is 136.

ACCOMMODATIONS AND FOOD In mid-summer, Xilitla's few and wonderful hotels fill up fast. Make reservations. Right along Jardín Hidalgo, **Hotel Ziyaquetzas** (tel. 5 00 81 or 5 02 45) offers ultra-clean rooms with fans and astounding views. Room prices vary depending on bed size (singles 85-110 pesos; doubles 110-125 pesos). Nature-lovers will be happy to spend the extra pesos to **sleep in the forest** in **Las Pozas** (tel. 5 02 03; see description below). Rooms are as wild and varied as you can imagine. They range in price from 180 pesos for a room that holds two people to 400 pesos for a room that holds four. Las Pozas also has a little **restaurant** where you can eat to the sound of the waterfalls for 15-25 pesos (open daily 9am-5pm). In town, tiny restaurants line Escobedo just past the plaza, all offering delicious meals at rock-bottom prices (10-16 pesos; open from about 7am until no one is left on the streets).

SIGHTS Xilitla's main attraction is **Las Pozas** (the pools), formally called the **Enchanted Garden of Edward James.** *(Open daily 9am-8pm. Admission 8 pesos.)* To get there, walk down Ocampo, at the southwest corner of the plaza. Continue as it veers right and turns into a path. Ocampo lets you out onto the main road at a white bridge. Cross the bridge and take your first left, choosing the upward dirt path and follow it for about 2km. The breathtaking walk is about 30 minutes long. Las Pozas will be on your right. Those with sore feet can take a *combi* (4 pesos) from the top of the stairs near the bus station to the white bridge, or find a taxi to take you right to the gates (45 pesos).

The son of a wealthy English nobleman, James was a good, old-fashioned eccentric, obsessed with cleanliness and tissue paper and sometimes requiring his secretaries to work in the buff. After early experiments with poetry and art, James created a universe of concrete, steel, and stone in **wild colors** and even **wilder forms** throughout the jungle. James' melange of bridges, arches, and artistic relics recall *Alice in Wonderland,* with winding staircases that lead to nowhere, a library without books, and other touches of madness. Wander for hours through the forest to run into wild blue and pink flowers as well as crazily shaped houses now inhabited by older men who used to work for Señor Edward. James channeled the waterfall running through Las Pozas's 36 structures into the pools themselves (there are nine). They're safe for swimming—bring your bathing suit.

For more information about what else to do in the area, contact Avery and Lenore Danziger, owners of El Castillo, a resort down the hill from Xilitla's main plaza. This infinitely wise and fabulously friendly couple (tel. 5 00 38) is best contacted through email (junglegossip@compuserve.com), where they can direct you to their soon-to-be-finalized website. Besides running a lovely resort, these folks can provide information about nearby sites, Huastecan culture, hiking, rafting, and other outdoor opportunities. If they're not in, ask whoever answers the door for their pamphlets, which offer some guidance.

In town, Xilitla's historical claim to fame is the quietly graying **Ex-Convento Agostino,** on the western side of the plaza. Built between 1550 and 1557, the ex-convent is the oldest colonial building in the state. Although the exterior could use a good white-washing, the interior is beautifully preserved. A large, quiet courtyard is surrounded by little altars, childrens' creations, and, to one side, a never-empty church.

For the commercially inclined, shops and stands selling fruit, shoes, crafts, and trinkets line Zaragosa and Escobedo before and after the plaza. Enter the shop on the southeast corner of the plaza to find beautiful artisanry from all over Mexico at astoundingly low prices.

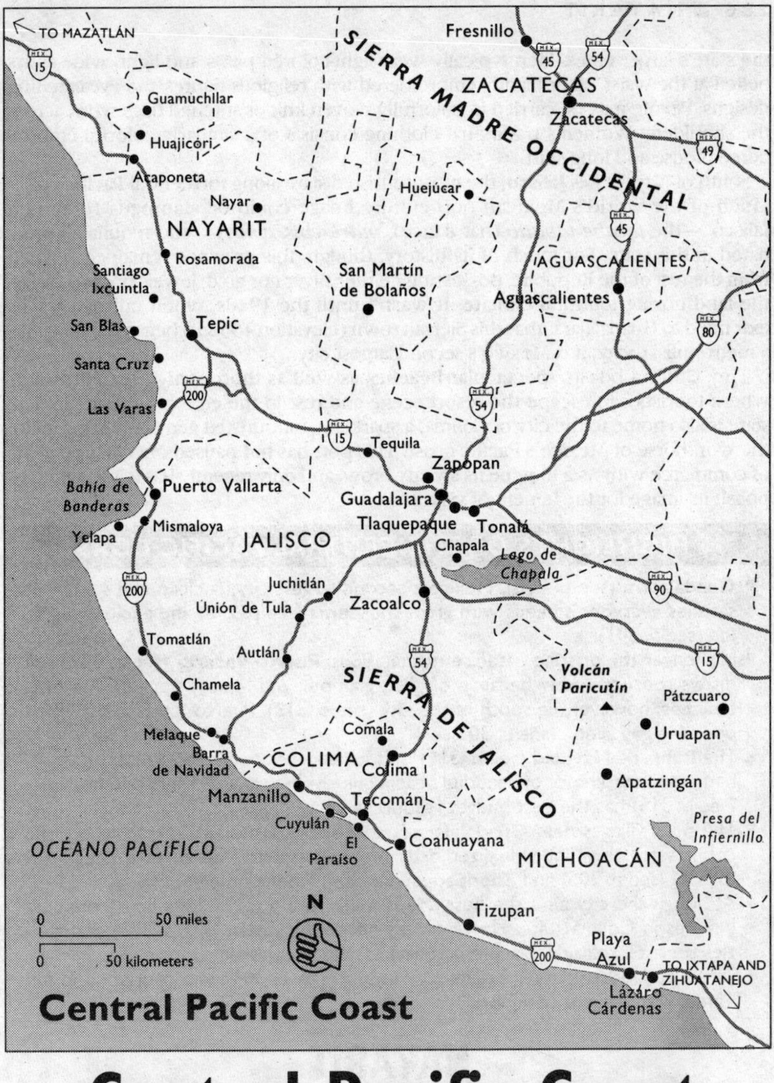

Central Pacific Coast

Stretching from the quiet fishing villages near San Blas to the busy port of Manzanillo, the Central Pacific Coast boasts kilometer after kilometer of smooth sand massaged by the ebb and flow of the tide. Hot but not overly humid, the region's climate leaves little room for dissatisfaction, and the sun never fails to illuminate the azure skies. The region prides itself on its diversity: its states range from the vibrant Jalisco, where *mariachis* and tequila were born, to the jungles and fertile land of Nayarit, to the quiet beachtowns in the state of Colima.

A state with diverse terrain, **Nayarit** is marked by volcanic highlands, tropical jungles, and a network of lakes and rivers. This verdant and fertile region grows the lion's share of the nation's marijuana and is home to the oldest native group in Mexico, the Huichol. It is not uncommon to see Huichols in colorful native dress, even in the state's larger cities. Men typically wear light-colored pants and light, wide shirts belted at the waist, all brilliantly embroidered with religious figures and eye-catching designs. Peyote may be carried in colorfully woven knit or stitched bags worn across the shoulders. Women's traditional clothing consists of a similarly colorful embroidered blouse and long skirt.

South of Nayarit lies **Jalisco,** the most touristed state along the central Pacific coast. Much of the world's Mexican pop culture image could be stamped "Hecho en Jalisco"—the *jarabe tapatío* (hat dance), *mariachis, charros,* and tequila all originated in this state. For much of its history, though, this province remained isolated from the rest of the Republic, possessing neither silver nor gold, jewels nor water, fertile land nor agricultural climate. It wasn't until the 1920s, when railroad tracks extended to Guadalajara, that this Sierran town (elevation 1552m) began to grow into a metropolis; today, it is Mexico's second-largest city.

Tiny **Colima** boasts spectacular beaches as well as thoroughly pleasant towns where tourists can escape the resort scene and rest in the cool mountain air. The state is also home to the city of Colima, a sparkling, untouristed gem, and Manzanillo, the workhorse of Mexico's Pacific coast. This port has not paused once in 700 years of commerce with Asia to wipe its sweaty brow, and only recently has it attempted to polish its image for the benefit of visitors.

HIGHLIGHTS OF THE CENTRAL PACIFIC COAST

- **Guadalajara** (see p. 290), Mexico's second-largest city, is clean and green—it satisfies everyone's needs with great **museums** (see p. 298) and exciting **nightlife** (see p. 301).
- No longer the pristine paradise of the 1960s, **Puerto Vallarta** (see p. 307) still draws tourists—now because of glitz, glamour and kitschy appeal. The **best beaches,** however, lie south of the city (see p. 313). Puerto Vallarta also has a booming **gay scene** (see p. 302).
- The **Bahía de Navidad** (see p. 316) isn't hyperdeveloped—yet. Swim, surf, sunbathe on your choice of beautiful beach, quickly, before word gets out. **Melaque** (see p. 316) has the best budget resources.
- The small villages **near Guadalajara** (see p. 303) are renowned throughout the country for their individualized artisanry and markets. Be sure to check out **Tonalá** (see p. 305) and **Zapopan** (see p. 304) among others.
- Although the city ain't the best, **Manzanillo** (see p. 319) does boast the best beaches in Colima state. However, it's nearby **Cuyutlán** (see p. 323) that dazzles tourists: solitude, black-sand beaches, and a wondrous lagoon.
- Tired of "authenticity"? Travel to **Tequila** (see p. 303), the touristy and fun home of your favorite liquor.

NAYARIT

San Blas

San Blas (pop. 19,000) is a mixture of shoe-worn buildings and crumbling relics from its glory days as a central port in Spain's colonial empire. Today, this tiny fishing village feeds off its ecological wealth: awesome beaches, over 300 species of birds (just listen as you exit the bus station), and the nearby jungle attract *norteamericano* expatriates, birdwatchers, and tourists en route to Puerto Vallarta. Bring plenty of bug repellent, though; ravenous mosquitoes are the downside of San Blas's ecological wealth. Also a mecca for surfers, San Blas's *zócalo* is a cool-dude sort of place; skate-rats, surfers, and video game junkies swagger about into the wee hours.

ORIENTATION AND PRACTICAL INFORMATION San Blas is 69km northeast of Tepic by Rte. 15 and 54. **Calle Juárez,** the town's main drag, runs parallel to the bus station on the south side of the *zócalo.* **Batallón** runs perpendicular to Juárez from the *zócalo*'s center and leads to the closest beach, **Playa Borrego.**

Transportes Norte de Sonora (tel. 5 00 43) has **buses** that run to Guadalajara (6hr., 7am, 118 pesos), Mazatlán (5hr., 7:30am and 5pm, 107 pesos), Puerto Vallarta (3hr., 7 and 10am, 70 pesos), Santiago Ixcuintla (1¾hr., 7:30am and 4pm, 27 pesos), and Tepic (1¾hr., every hr. 6am-7pm, 27 pesos). The **tourist office,** Juárez 83, across from Restaurant McDonalds, hands out maps and provides information about trips to La Tovara (see p. 288) and hikes to some of Nayarit's more beautiful waterfalls (office open daily 9am-2pm and 6-9pm). Change money at **Banamex** (tel. 5 00 30), on Juárez east of the *zócalo* (open M-F 8-2pm; also has a 24hr. **ATM**).

The **police** (tel. 5 00 28) are on Sinaloa opposite the bus station; theirs is the last door in the Palacio Municipal as you walk away from the *zócalo* (open 24hr.). **Farmacia Económica** is at Batallón 49 (tel./fax 5 01 11; open daily 8:30am-2pm and 4:30-9:30pm). The **Centro de Salud** (tel. 5 02 32) is on Batallón and Campeche, five blocks south of the *zócalo;* no English is spoken (open 24hr.). The **Clínica IMSS** (tel. 5 02 27), at Batallón and Guerrero, is open for consultation daily from 7am to 6pm; at other times, enter on Canalizo. The **post office** (tel. 5 02 95) is at Sonora and Echevería, one block north and one block east of the northeast corner of the *zócalo* (open M-F 8am-2pm, Sa 8am-noon). The **postal code** is 63740. Make long-distance **phone** calls from the *caseta de larga distancia* at Juárez 4. The **caseta** also has **fax** service. (Open daily 8am-10pm.) The **phone code** is 328.

ACCOMMODATIONS AND FOOD Finding a place to sleep in San Blas isn't difficult during the off-season, but autumn storms bring mile-long waves and bed-seeking surfers. During September, October, *Semana Santa,* and Christmas, make reservations and expect higher prices. The blood-sucking mosquitoes near the water make camping difficult; rooms inland are the best choice. **El Bucanero,** Juárez 75 (tel. 5 01 01), is reminiscent of a creaky pirate ship. It offers large, dim rooms with high ceilings, clean bathrooms, a swimming pool, and a huge, fading crocodile in the lobby. Hot water and fans make things comfy, but the adjoining disco is a little noisy on the weekends. (Singles 100 pesos; doubles 150 pesos.) To reach **Bungalows Portolá,** Paredes 118 (tel. 5 03 86), at Yucatán, walk up Juárez Ote. two blocks from the *zócalo,* and follow Paredes to your right for about four-and-a-half blocks. Clean, floral, furnished bungalows come complete with fans, baths, and kitchens for up to four people. The owner offers laundry services and rents bicycles. (Bungalos 150 pesos; singles 60 pesos, high season 120 pesos.) **Posada Azul,** Batallón 126 (tel. 5 01 29), about four blocks from the *zócalo,* offers clean, white-brick rooms with hard-working fans and blue floors (hence the name). Sunglasses may come in handy when looking for this place—its bright blue exterior is practically blinding. (Singles 90 pesos; doubles 120 pesos.)

La Isla (tel. 5 04 07), on Mercado and Paredes, lives up to its name—every space, crack, and crevice of "the island" is covered with shells. The food will knock you out (fried fish 30 pesos; open Tu-Su 2-10pm). **La Familia,** Batallón 18 (tel. 5 02 58), is a family joint, right down to the conversation-starting, wall-mounted shark's teeth, sea bottles, old drums, and provocative cow statue. A full breakfast goes for 10-22 pesos; enjoy fresh fish for 35-38 pesos. (Open daily 8am-10pm.)

SAND AND SIGHTS San Blas, known for its perfectly symmetric waves and safe, sandy bottom, has churned out many a surfing champ. To rent surfing equipment or take lessons, drop by **La Tumba de Yako,** Batallón 219 (tel. 5 04 62), about six blocks from the *zócalo,* which is run by Juan García, president of San Blas's surfing club and technical director of Mexico's surf team.

San Blas's main attractions are the smooth water, packed sand, and long waves of **Playa Las Islitas.** During the stormy months of September and October, surfers flock to San Blas in hopes of catching the famous, yearly mile-long wave that carries them from Las Islitas all the way to Playa Matanchén. To reach Las Islitas, you can take a bus from the bus station (every hr. 6am-5pm, 3 pesos; returning every hr. 7:30am-4pm) or from the corner of Sinaloa and Paredes in front of the green trim building (15min., 4 per day 8:30am-2:30pm, 3 pesos). The latter bus continues to other beaches, passing by Las Islitas on its way back to town about one hour later. A taxi to Las Islitas costs 40 pesos. Don't settle for the first few stretches of sand that greet you—seclusion and prettier coves await farther along the shore.

At the southern end of Batallón, **Playa Borrego** is easily accessible from town and offers a relaxing, though somewhat bland, view of the coast. Borrego's sand is gray, and mosquitoes feast on those who dare to venture outside around sunrise or sunset. Quiet and pretty **Playa del Rey,** off the coast of Borrego, has somewhat stronger currents. A *lancha* will take you there from the pier at the west end of Juárez (round-trip about 5 pesos; boats run daily about 7am-4pm).

Locals hype the springs of **La Tovara**—not the beaches—as San Blas's can't-miss attraction. While the winding jungle boat ride to La Tovara springs can be expensive, seeing a live crocodile just might make it worthwhile. Guides navigate the shallow, swampy waters, pointing out rare and interesting birds and the stilted huts left over from the set of the film *Cabeza de Vaca.* The path clears to reveal hordes of turtles and huge fish. Trips can be arranged through the tourist office or directly with a boat owner; they're found at the small docking area on Juárez's eastern end. Trips last one-and-a-half to two-and-a-half hours and can be made any day between 7am and 4pm, but it's best to journey to La Tovara early in the morning, when the water is still calm and the birds undisturbed by the *lanchas.* Expect to pay 130 to 220 pesos for a group of four, depending on the tour.

The short hike to the top of **La Contaduría,** the hill near town, affords a beautiful view of the city and coast. The splintering stone fortress that protected the city rests impressively above, while an 18th-century church stands farther downhill. To get there, head east on Juárez as if leaving town. Just before the bridge and the sign that reads "Cape Victoria 7," turn right onto the dirt road behind the houses and restaurants, and veer right off that road onto the stone path that winds uphill.

The **Comunidad Cultural Huichol** of San Blas, a non-profit organization, provides a non-exploitative forum of expression for Huichol artists—with the condition that the artists not partake of alcoholic beverages. The **Huichol** are considered Mexico's oldest native group, and more than 15,000 Huichol still live in rural mountain regions. For centuries, the Huichol have created unique crafts depicting mythological scenes. Agencies today purchase their work for paltry sums and sell it for 50 times the amount the artisan had been paid. Furthermore, Huichol artists are often coerced into producing identical designs and figures, a practice in conflict with traditional Huichol beliefs.

ENTERTAINMENT Except for bands of youths crowded in the *zócalo* on weekends, nights in San Blas are about as tranquilo as the days. Down a margarita (15 pesos) or two as you listen to an eclectic mix of American pop music at **Cocodrilos,** Juárez 1 (tel. 5 06 10), on the *zócalo* (open daily 10:30am-11pm). **Mike's CantaBar** (tel. 5 04 32), across from the tourist office, rarely gets wild or crazy, but it's an interesting place to pass the evening. Mike no longer performs vintage rock, but he sings live salsa in what looks like an antique airport lounge. (No cover. Open daily 6pm-1am. Live music Th-Su starting around 10pm.) If you are in the mood for something more upbeat and raucous, join the teen and pre-teen population of San Blas at **Disco Voga,** Juárez 75 (tel. 5 01 01), next to Hotel El Bucanero. Build up a sweat as the standard discoteca fare gets you into the groove (beer 6 pesos; cover 15-20 pesos; open F-Su 9pm-4am).

■ Near San Blas: El Custodio de las Tortugas

El Custodio de las Tortugas (The Guardian of the Turtles; tel. 329 2 29 54; email custodi@pvnet.com.mx; http://www.methow.com/~custodio) is an eco-resort in the tiny village of **Platanitos,** an hour-and-a-half south of San Blas and two hours north of Puerto Vallarta. *(Villa rental US$650-750 per week low season, US$800-900 per week high season; or US$15 per night to help out and bunk in the turtle camp; some meals and kayak trips to the lagoon included.)* The villa, run by owners Min and Mona, is perched on a precipice and overlooks 20km of virgin beach and the longest stretch of turtle camp in Nayarit. Between July and August, the Mexican government and several ecological organizations collect turtle eggs, protecting them from thieves and predators. Two elegant three-bedroom villas and one two-bedroom villa have TVs, air-conditioning, and huge breezy terraces for whale-watching and sunset-worshipping. The gorgeous pool perched on the overlook offers a respite from salty water. Don't miss going into town to try the local specialty, **pescado sarandeado** (mesquite grilled fish, 70 pesos per kilo—enough to feed 3-4 people).

Getting There: Transportes Norte de Sonora (tel. 5 00 43) gets you there from Puerto Vallarta (2hr., noon and 2:30pm, 55 pesos) or San Blas (1½hr., 6 per day 6am-2pm, 14 pesos). Ask the bus driver to let you off at Platanitos, then walk down the road and up the hill on your right.

Tepic

The steam-belching, tree-guzzling woodchip plant directly across from Tepic's bus station provides an appropriate introduction to this hard-working city. The state capital and an important crossroads for the entire region, hard-working Tepic (pop. 450,000) fits its name well—it comes from the Náhuatl words *tetl* (rock) and *pic* (hard). Although the breezy **Plaza Principal** is a perfect place to while away the afternoon, there is little of tourist interest here—just a few historical sites and La Loma Park. At best, the city can be used as a transportation hub and a base for exploring nearby towns. Tepic is 169km north of Puerto Vallarta, 228km northwest of Guadalajara, and 295km south of Mazatlán.

ORIENTATION AND PRACTICAL INFORMATION As you leave the bus station, the *centro* is down the highway **(Insurgentes)** to the left; cross the street and catch one of the yellow buses (6am-10pm, 1.50 pesos). Hustling *taxistas* charge 10-15 pesos for the short trip to the *centro.* **Av. México,** running north-south six blocks west of the bus station, is downtown Tepic's main drag. Addresses on Av. México change from *norte* to *sur* about four blocks north of Insurgentes, which is the largest east-west street. The yellow minivan *combis* (6am-midnight, 1.50-3 pesos) run back and forth daily along Av. México and Insurgentes. At its northern terminus, the many-fountained **Plaza Principal** (officially the **Centro Histórico**) is dominated on one end by the cathedral and on the other by the **Palacio Municipal.** Six blocks to the south, **Plaza Constituyente** appears to be shockingly desolate. Most tourist services lie on or near Av. México.

Buses leave Tepic from the newer long-distance station (the smaller one downtown, three blocks north of the plaza on Victoria, only serves local destinations). To get to the new station, take a 15-1 or "Mololoa Llanitos" bus from the corner of México Sur and Hidalgo (about a 20min. ride). **Estrella Blanca** (tel. 13 13 28) serves Aguascalientes (6hr., 4:30 and 7:45pm, 210 pesos), Monterrey (15hr., 4:30 and 7:45pm, 410 pesos), and Zacatecas (10hr., 4:30 and 7:45pm, 244 pesos). **Norte de Sonora** (tel. 13 23 15) speeds toward Culiacán (6hr., every hr., 197 pesos), Guadalajara (3hr., 10 per day 5:30am-5pm, 103 pesos), Mazatlán (5hr., 9:30am, 101 pesos), San Blas (1½hr., every hr. 5am-7pm, 27 pesos), Santiago (1½hr., every 45min. 5:30am-8pm, 27 pesos), and Tuxpan (1½hr., every hr. 6:15am-8:15pm, 27 pesos). **Transportes del Pacífico** (tel. 13 23 20) provides first-class service to Mexico City (10hr., every hr. 3pm-7am, 357 pesos) and Tijuana (29hr., every hr., 754 pesos), and second-class service to Puerto Vallarta (3½hr., 19 per day 1:30am-10pm, 78 pesos). At **Dirección de Turismo Municipal** (tel. 16 56 61), Av. Puebla at the corner of Amado Nervo, one block from the cathedral, students of *turismo* hand out maps and brochures (open daily 8am–8pm). **Banks** (most open M-F 8am-1:30pm) and **casas de**

cambio (commonly open M-Sa 9am-2pm and 4-7pm) clutter Av. México Nte. Both **Banamex** and **Bancomer,** on Av. México Nte., a few blocks south of the plaza, have **ATMs.** For faxes, try **Telecomm,** Av. México Nte. 50 (tel. 12 96 55), about one block from the cathedral (open M-F 8am-7pm, Sa-Su 8am-4pm). The station has **luggage storage** (1.50 pesos per hr.).

The **police station** is at Av. Tecnolópgica 3200 Ote. (tel. 11 58 51), but cabs are the only way to get there (8 pesos). **Farmacia CMQ,** on Insurgentes at Av. Mexico, is open 24 hours. The **Hospital General** (tel. 13 79 37) is on Paseo de la Loma next to La Loma Park. To walk there from the bus station (20min.), take a left as you leave the building and another left on Av. México. After three blocks, take the right-hand fork at the rotary; the hospital is two blocks down on your left (open 24hr.). Cabs to the hospital cost 10 pesos from the *centro.* The **post office** (tel. 12 01 30) is at Durango Nte. 33, between Allende and Morelos (open M-F 8am-7pm, Sa 8am-noon). The **postal code** is 63000. The **phone code** is 321.

ACCOMMODATIONS AND FOOD Budget hotels in Tepic provide the basics at a reasonable price. Hotels in the *centro* are closer to Tepic's few sights, but those near the bus station are more convenient for the traveler who is in Tepic for only a short stay. The best option in town may be the **Hotel Las Americas,** Puebla 317 (tel. 16 32 85), at Zaragoza. It is centrally located and has clean rooms with TVs, fans, and tiled bathrooms. Wooden furniture and sunny patchwork quilts make it feel like Grandma's house. (Singles 60 pesos; doubles 80 pesos.)

Tepic has tons of agricultural goodies. Mangos and *guanábanas* (soursops) make their way to the stalls at the **mercado,** on Mérida and Zaragoza, four blocks south and three blocks east of the Museo Regional (see below). For a more formal meal, head to **Restaurant Vegetariano Quetzalcóatl,** León Nte. 224 (tel. 12 99 66), at Lerdo, four blocks west of Plaza Principal. *Tranquilo* waiters serve yummy vegetarian food in a leafy courtyard decorated with local indigenous artwork and vibrant tablecloths. Sample the *comida corrida* (24 pesos) or stuff yourself with the buffet (Saturday only, 30 pesos; restaurant open M-Sa 8:30am-8:30pm).

SIGHTS In front of the Plaza Principal is the **Catedral de la Purísima Concepción de María,** a church marked by twin 40m-tall towers. South of the Plaza Principal, at México Nte. 91 and Zapata, is the **Museo Regional de Antropología e Historia** (tel. 12 19 00), which houses a small collection of Toltec and Aztec bones, pottery, and artifacts, as well as a stuffed 6m long crocodile and a collection of religious works from the 16th to 19th centuries (open M-F 9am-7pm, Sa 9am-3pm; free). The **Museo Casa de los Cuatro Pueblos,** Hidalgo Ote. 60 (tel. 12 17 05), displays the colorful artwork, embroidery, and beadwork of Nayarit's four indigenous groups: the Coras, Huichols, Náhuatls, and Tepehuanos (open M-F 9am-2pm and 4-7pm, Sa 9am-2pm; free). Also south of the plaza, at Av. México and Abasolo, is the **state capitol,** a gracefully domed structure dating from the 1870s. At Av. México's southern end, turn west (uphill) on Insurgentes and you'll come to **La Loma,** a huge and enchanting park. If in service, a miniature train will take you through the park's many playgrounds (3 pesos).

JALISCO

Guadalajara

More Mexican than Mexico itself, Guadalajara (pop. 5 million) is the crossroads of Mexico. The capital of the state of Jalisco and the second-largest city in the Republic, Guadalajara is where north meets south, colonial meets modern, and traditional meets cutting-edge; the result is a place you have to visit. This crowning achievement of Spanish colonial urbanity has spawned many of Mexico's most marketable icons: bittersweet mariachi music, the *jarabe tapatío* (the Mexican hat dance), and tequila. These icons, now important symbols of the entire Republic, grew out of the distinc-

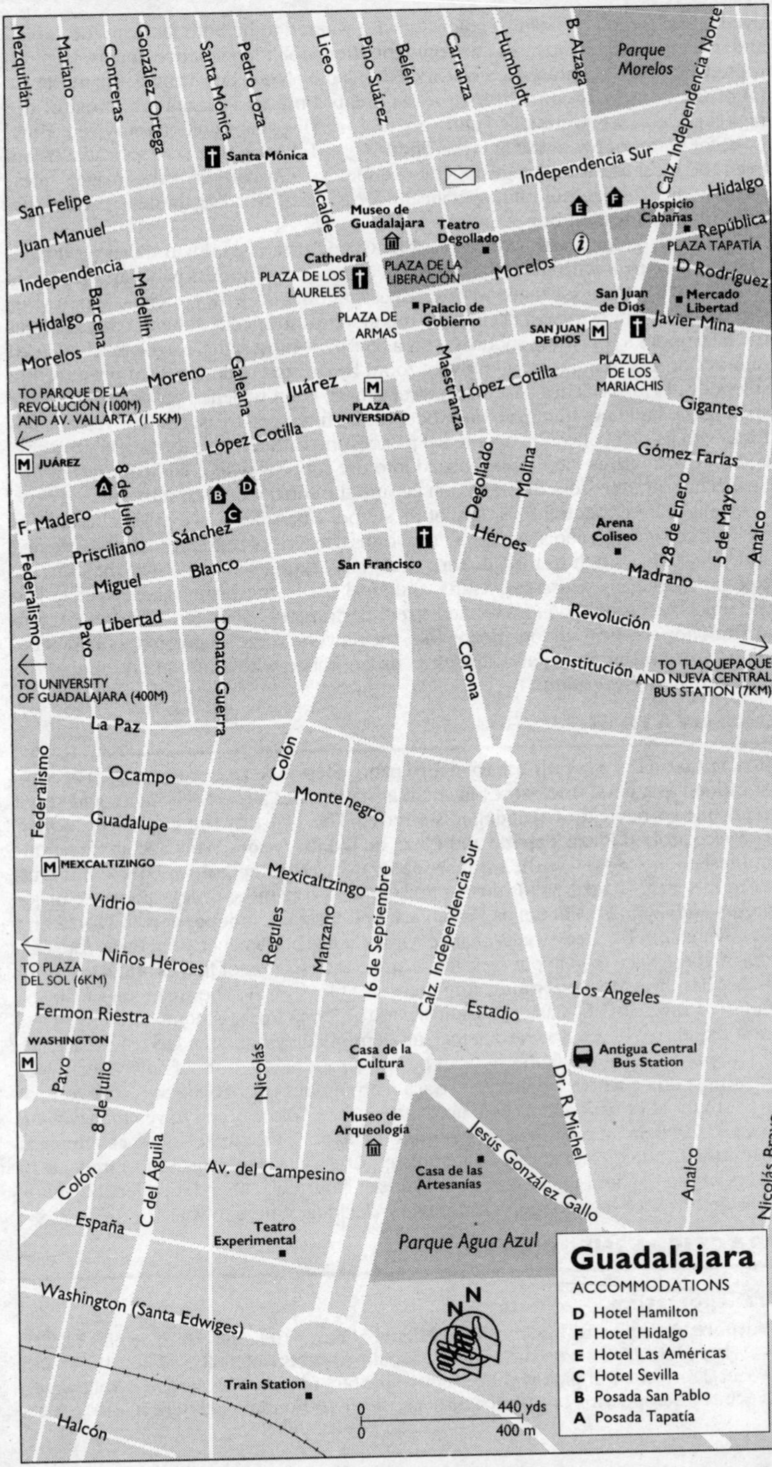
Guadalajara
ACCOMMODATIONS
D Hotel Hamilton
F Hotel Hidalgo
E Hotel Las Américas
C Hotel Sevilla
B Posada San Pablo
A Posada Tapatía
Parque Morelos
Santa Mónica
Museo de Guadalajara
Teatro Degollado
Hospicio Cabañas
PLAZA TAPATÍA
Cathedral
PLAZA DE LOS LAURELES
PLAZA DE LA LIBERACIÓN
PLAZA DE ARMAS
Palacio de Gobierno
San Juan de Dios
SAN JUAN DE DIOS
Mercado Libertad
PLAZUELA DE LOS MARIACHIS
PLAZA UNIVERSIDAD
TO PARQUE DE LA REVOLUCIÓN (100M) AND AV. VALLARTA (1.5KM)
JUÁREZ
San Francisco
Arena Coliseo
TO TLAQUEPAQUE AND NUEVA CENTRAL BUS STATION (7KM)
TO UNIVERSITY OF GUADALAJARA (400M)
MEXCALTIZINGO
TO PLAZA DEL SOL (6KM)
WASHINGTON
Antigua Central Bus Station
Casa de la Cultura
Museo de Arqueología
Casa de las Artesanías
Parque Agua Azul
Teatro Experimental
Train Station
Mezquitán
Mariano
Contreras
González Ortega
Santa Mónica
Pedro Loza
Liceo
Pino Suárez
Belén
Carranza
Humboldt
B. Alzaga
Calz. Independencia Norte
Independencia Sur
Hidalgo
República
D Rodríguez
Javier Mina
San Felipe
Juan Manuel
Independencia
Alcalde
Morelos
Hidalgo
Barcena
Medellín
Morelos
Moreno
Galeana
Juárez
Maestranza
López Cotilla
López Cotilla
Gigantes
Gómez Farías
Degollado
Molina
8 de Julio
F. Madero
Prisciliano
Sánchez
Héroes
28 de Enero
5 de Mayo
Analco
Madrano
Miguel
Blanco
Federalismo
Pavo
Libertad
Donato Guerra
Revolución
Corona
Constitución
La Paz
Colón
Ocampo
Federalismo
Montenegro
Guadalupe
Mexicaltzingo
Calz. Independencia Sur
Vidrio
Regules
Manzano
16 de Septiembre
Niños Héroes
Los Ángeles
Fermon Riestra
Estadio
Pavo
8 de Julio
Nicolás
Dr. R Michel
Jesús González Gallo
Analco
Nicolás Bravo
Colón
C del Águila
Av. del Campesino
España
Washington (Santa Edwiges)
Halcón
N
0
440 yds
0
400 m

CENTRAL PACIFIC COAST

tive culture forged by Spanish colonists who wanted to be both far from the capital and in a comfortably Spanish environment after pro-Independence convulsions disrupted life in 19th-century Mexico City. Founded by Nuño de Guzmán, the most brutal of the *conquistadores*, the city was created out of a bloodbath; most of the region's *indígenas* were killed and very few pre-Hispanic traditions survived. However, for better or for worse, it is this enduring and alluring *tapatío* legacy that colors even the most idealized images of colonial Mexico. Guadalajara is the image's finest incarnation. Though not built specifically for tourists, Guadalajara nevertheless succeeds in fulfilling their hopes entirely.

Shockingly green, clean, and accessible, Guadalajara is an urban traveler's dream. The city's *centro,* with its wide, tree-lined avenues and pocket parks and plazas, is wonderfully crafted for walking or just passing time on park benches. When your legs get tired, enjoy the excellent local bus system and speedy subways that connect the metropolis's sprawling suburbs with its *centro*—most sights can be reached in 20 minutes or less. Kamikaze bus drivers zoom by on streets designed to preserve the splendor of Guadalajara's past; many streets have been widened on one side, wisely sparing the buildings that have since become architectural treasures. The historic district, with its rich collection of colonial palaces and cathedrals, is the heart of the city, and industrial giants have been pushed into the suburbs where endless rows of flat, unspectacular, one-story houses reach far into the surrounding countryside.

As might be expected for a city of its scope, Guadalajara is a cultural mecca as well—a collage of colonial and modern worlds. Dozens of museums attest to Mexico and Guadalajara's rich history, culture, and glory. Markets in and out of the city provide no shortage of *jalisciense* crafts, and local artists, thespians, dancers (including the renowned *ballet folklórico*), and street performers continue to celebrate Guadalajara's fine artistic tradition. Meanwhile, the university, the second-oldest in Mexico, keeps Guadalajara young and shades its urban bustle with a measure of high-brow intellectual sophistication.

ORIENTATION

Step 1: Take a deep breath and try not to panic. Step 2: Get a detailed map. The tourist office has a good one, stores in the bus station and airport sell them, and you'll need one to navigate Guadalajara's sprawl. The heart of the city is the *centro histórico* around **Plaza Tapatía** and **Plaza de la Liberación.** Many accommodations and restaurants as well as the main **shopping district, cathedral,** and **museums** cluster in this area. Guadalajara is divided into four sectors more or less along the major streets **Hidalgo,** also known as **República,** and **Calzada Independencia Norte and Sur.** Watch out because streets change names at the borders between these four sectors. A good place to get your bearings is at the intersection of **Juárez** and **Alcalde/16 de Septiembre.** Most bus routes stop there or a block away. The area west of Tapatía and the University of Guadalajara, known as the **Zona Rosa,** is home to many of the most expensive hotels and restaurants, modern buildings, and the U.S. consulate.

The poorer *colonias* (suburbs) can be dangerous at any time of day. Check with the tourist office before blazing new trails. Throughout Guadalajara, it is wise to stick to lit streets after dark and to take taxis after 10pm. Solo women travelers may want to avoid **Calzada Independencia** after this hour as well; the street has a magnetic field that attracts raucous, drunken men and supports a thriving prostitution trade at all hours of the day and night. As you move east from Calzada Independencia, conditions deteriorate—use common sense when deciding where to walk.

PRACTICAL INFORMATION

Transportation

Airport: Aeropuerto Internacional Miguel Hidalgo (tel. 688 51 20 or 688 51 27), 17km south of town on the road to Chapala. *Combis* (tel. 688 59 25 or 812 43 08) run 24hr. and will pick you up from your hotel (40min., 60 pesos). A yellow and white "Aeropuerto" bus passes through the *centro* on Independencia at Los Angeles (every hr. 5:45am-8:45pm, 5 pesos). It makes the trip back from outside "Sala Nacional." Get off at 16 de Septiembre and Constituyentes. Don't pay more than 70 pesos for a cab. A major hub, served by **AeroCalifornia** (tel. 616 25 25), **Aeroméxico** (tel. 669 02 02), **American** (tel. 616 40 90), **Continental** (tel. 647 42 51), **Delta** (tel. 630 35 30), **Mexicana** (tel. 678 76 76), **Taesa** (tel. 679 09 00), and **United** (tel. 616 94 89).

Buses: Nueva Central Camionera, in nearby **Tlaquepaque.** Fixed-fare buses and taxis (15-40 pesos) head downtown frequently, as do "Centro" buses (2 pesos). From downtown, catch a #275, 275A, or "Nueva Central" bus on Av. Revolución or Av. 16 de Septiembre, across from the cathedral. In a taxi, be sure to specify the *new* bus station. Only partial listings provided; call for more info. **Terminal 1: Primera Plus** and **Flecha Amarilla** (tel. 600 07 70) provide first-class service to Aguascalientes (3hr., 4 and 8:15pm, 95 pesos), Guanajuato (4hr., 5 per day 11am-8pm, 115 pesos), Mexico City (10hr., every hr., 220 pesos), Morelia (6hr., 8 per day 4:30am-9:30pm, 120 pesos), Querétaro (8hr., every hr., 133 pesos), and San Miguel de Allende (5hr., 1 and 3pm, 157 pesos). **Terminal 2: Autobuses de Occidente** (tel. 600 00 55) to Manzanillo (4½hr., 14 per day 4am-11:45pm, 121 pesos) via Colima (3hr., 85 pesos), Pátzcuaro (7hr., 6 per day, 106 pesos), Toluca (11hr., 8 per day 3:30am-8pm, 172 pesos), and Uruapan (5hr., 7 per day 4:45am-5:15pm, 87 pesos). **Terminal 3: Transportes del Pacífico** (tel. 600 03 39) to Culiacán (10hr., 6 per day, 205 pesos), Mazatlán (8hr., 6 per day, 170 pesos), Mexico City (8hr., 7 per day 5am-1pm, 208 pesos), and Puerto Vallarta (6hr., 11 per day 4:30am-midnight, 165 pesos). **Terminal 4: Transportes de Sonora** (tel. 679 04 63) to Hermosillo (24hr., 14 per day, 428 pesos) via Mazatlán (8hr., every hr., 168 pesos) and points in between. **Terminal 5: Línea Azul** (tel. 600 62 31) to San Luis Potosí (first-class 5hr., 15 per day, 125 pesos; second-class 6hr., every 30min. 7am-11:30pm, 105 pesos). **Terminal 6: Ómnibus de México** (tel. 600 02 91 or 600 04 69) to Aguascalientes (3hr., every hr., 95 pesos), Ciudad Juárez (24hr., 5 per day 7am-10:30pm, 508 pesos), Durango (10hr., 7 per day 7:30am-midnight, 235 pesos), Guanajuato (4hr., 12 per day, 120 pesos), Hermosillo (24hr., 10 per day, 435 pesos), Mexico City (8hr., every 30min., 215 pesos), Oaxaca (10hr., 7 per day, 250 pesos), Querétaro (8hr., 12 per day, 135 pesos), Xalapa (10hr., 7 per day, 263 pesos), and Zacatecas (5hr., 14 per day 6:30am-midnight, 130 pesos). **Terminal 7: Estrella Blanca** (tel. 679 04 04) is the parent company of numerous smaller lines, including **Rojo de los Altos** and **Transportes del Norte.** This is the biggest terminal and it serves almost every major city in the Republic for cheaper or competitive prices.

Local Buses: Though usually crowded, always noisy, and sometimes uncomfortable, **minibuses** (2 pesos), **regular buses** (2 pesos), and the big blue **TUR** buses (4.50 pesos) are an excellent way to get just about anywhere in the city. Drivers all seem to dream of being on a racetrack, so trips can be short and exciting. Always be sure to check what letter (A, B, C, or D) the bus is—in general, the C and D buses have very different routes out into the residential neighborhoods. Buses **#60** and **#62** run the length of Calzada Independencia, from the train station past the zoo and Plaza de Toros. The electrically wired **"Par Vial"** bus runs west on Independencia, then Hidalgo, before turning onto Vallarta, just short of López Mateos. Coming back eastward, it cruises Hidalgo, 3 blocks north of Juárez. Bus **#258** from San Felipe, 3 blocks north of Hidalgo, runs from near the Plaza Tapatía down López Mateos to the Plaza del Sol—nightclub central. Bus **#52** is a direct link to downtown along 16 de Septiembre from exotic locations north and south of the city. Bus **#24A** runs the length of López Mateos, from Zapopan to beyond the Plaza del Sol, in both directions. TUR bus **#707A** circles from the *centro* on Juárez west to López Mateos, down to Mariano Otero at the Plaza del Sol, up to Niños Héroes, and north on 16 de Septiembre and Corona to the start of the route. The big red **Cardenal** bus runs west on Madero to Av. Chapultepec along which is the **Zona Rosa,** the upper class shopping district west of the *centro*. The **aqua** TUR bus and Route **#45** return east on Lopez Cotilla. Bus route **#51** runs up and down Av. La Paz. Buses run from 6:30am-10:30pm.

Subway: (tel. 853 75 70). Two lines run smoothly (every 5-10min. 6am-10:30pm, 2 pesos). It's a great alternative to the bus system if you're tired of breathing exhaust, but it's not so helpful if you don't know the stops. The tourist office hands out a good map. **Line 1** runs from the northern boundary of the city, Anillo Periférico Norte, more or less along Federalismo to Anillo Periférico Sur. There is a stop at Federalismo and Juárez. **Line 2** runs from Juárez and Av. Alcalde/16 de Septiembre to Av. Patria in the east. The limited coverage of the two lines doesn't make the subway as practical as the bus for most destinations, but if it goes where you want to, it's the better option.

Car Rental: Dollar, Av. Federalismo Sur 540-A (tel. 826 79 59, at the airport 688 56 89; fax 826 42 21) at Mexicalcinco. Renters need a driver's license, major credit card, and 21 years under their belts. Prices start at 325 pesos per day plus 8% tax, including insurance and 300km. Staff delivers cars free of charge. Open daily 7am-9pm. **Hertz** (tel. 688 54 83), at the airport (open 24hr.) and at Av. 16 de Septiembre and Niños Héroes, has similar rates for drivers over 25.

Tourist and Financial Services

Tourist Office: State Office, Morelos 102 (tel. 613 03 06, or toll-free within Mexico 91 800 363 22), in Pl. Tapatía. In addition to helpful information and maps, super friendly and helpful staff distributes *Guadalajara Weekly* (free tourist paper), *Tentaciones* (weekly listings of movies, exhibits, concerts, and theatrical events), and *Mexico Living and Travel Update* (detailed information for living in Mexico). English spoken. Ask about tours. Open M-F 9am-8pm, Sa-Su and holidays 9am-1pm.

Tours: Panoramex, Federalismo 944 (tel. 810 51 09 or 810 50 05), at España. Runs tours to Guadalajara and Tlaquepaque (5hr., M-Sa 9:30am, 85 pesos); Chapala and Ajijic (6½hr., Tu, Th, and Sa-Su 9:30am, 125 pesos). Tours (English available) leave from the Jardín de San Francisco at 9:30am and from the Arcos de Ballanca at 9:45am. Office open M-F 9am-2:30pm and 4:30-7pm, Sa 9am-1pm. Horse-drawn carriage tours of the *centro histórico* are also available from the Mercado Libertad (1hr., 120 pesos).

Consulates: Tons of 'em here. **Australia,** López Cotilla 2030 (tel. 615 74 18; fax 630 34 79), between López de Vega and Calserón de la Bara. Open M-F 8am-1:30pm and 3-6pm. **Canada,** Local 30 (tel. 615 62 70 or emergency 91 800 706 29; fax 615 86 65), at Hotel Fiesta Americana, on the Minerva traffic circle (catch a "Par Vial" bus). Open M-F 8:30am-5pm. **U.K.,** Quevedo 601 (tel. 616 06 29; fax 615 01 97) between Eulogio Parra and Manuel Acuña. Open M-F 9am-3pm, and 5-8pm. **U.S.,** Progreso 175 (tel. 825 27 00 or 825 29 98; fax 826 65 49). Open M-F 8am-4:30pm. The **Oficina de la Asociación Consular,** at the U.K. consulate, can provide listings for other consulates; most countries have one here.

Currency Exchange: The block of López Cotilla between Colón and Molina is a *mercado* with only one product: money. Rates don't vary much; most places open M-Sa 9am-7pm. **Banco Internacional,** Juárez 400 (tel. 614 88 00), at Galeana. Open M-Sa 8am-7pm. **Banamex** (tel. 679 32 52), Juárez at Corona. Open M-F 8:30am-5:30pm, Sa 10am-2pm.

American Express: Vallarta 2440 (tel. 615 89 10), at Plaza los Arcos. Take the "Par Vial" bus. Open M-F 9am-2:30pm and 4-6pm, Sa 9am-1pm.

Local Services

English Bookstores: Sandi Bookstore, Tepeyac 718 (tel. 121 08 63), near the corner of Av. de las Rosas in Colonia Chapalita. Take bus #50 from Garibaldi or the green "Plus" bus from Juárez. Extensive selection of new books and newspapers. Open M-F 9:30am-2:30pm and 3:30-7pm, Sa 9:30am-2pm. The **Hyatt** carries day-old copies of the *New York Times*. **Sanborn's** department store, at Juárez and Corona, carries a wide range of English-language magazines.

Cultural Information: Dirección de Educación y Cultura, 5 de Febrero and Analco (tel. 669 13 80 ext. 1487). **Instituto Cultural Cabañas,** Cabañas 8 in Pl. Tapatía (tel. 617 43 22). Open M-F 9am-3pm and 6-9pm. Blue and yellow Ayuntamiento stands in all the major plazas also field cultural and tourist queries. Open daily 8am-8pm.

Supermarket: Gigante, Juárez 573 (tel. 613 86 38) between Medellín and 8 de Julio. It has just about everything. Open M-Sa 8am-9pm, Su 8am-3pm.

Laundry: Lavandería Canadá, Patria 1123 (tel. 628 74 34) and Tepeyac. Open M-Sa 8am-8pm.

Emergency and Communications

Emergency: Dial 080.

Police: Independencia Nte. 840 (tel. 617 60 60 ext. 126 and 143) just before the *fuente olympica*.

Red Cross: (tel. 613 15 50 or 614 27 07), at Juan Manuel and San Felipe, on the 1st floor, behind Parque Morelos. Some English spoken. Open 24hr.

Pharmacy: Farmacia Guadalajara, Javier Mina 221 (tel. 617 85 55), at Cabañas. Minimal English spoken. Open 24hr.

Hospitals: México Americano (tel. 641 31 41 or 641 44 58), Colones and América. English spoken. **Green Cross Hospital** (tel. 614 52 52 or 643 71 90), Barcenas and Veracruz. English spoken.

Fax: Palacio Federal (tel. 614 26 64; fax 613 99 15), Alcalde and Juan Álvarez and at the airport. Open M-F 8am-7pm, Sa 9am-noon.

Internet Access: Cafe Arroba, Lázaro Cárdenas 3286 (tel. 121 36 50 or 122 49 88), at López Mateos in Col. Chapalita on bus route #258. Get off 1 block after the big traffic circle. The best option might be **PC Express,** 2077 López Mateos (tel. 647 69 20); take the #258 bus from the corner of Madero and 16 de Septiembre downtown and get off 3 blocks past Lázaro Cárdenas. Email 12 pesos per 30min. Open M-Sa 9am-9pm. Or try **Mailboxes Etc.,** Av. Chapultepec Sur 590 (tel. 616 26 81; fax 616 26 98) at Niños Héroes. Open M-F 9am-8pm, Sa 10am-2pm.

Post Office: (tel. 614 74 25), on Carranza between Juan Manuel and Calle de Independencia (not Independencia Sur). Open M-F 8am-8pm, Sa 9am-1pm.

Postal Code: 44100.

Telephones: LADATELs are all over the *centro*. **Caseta** in Nueva Central bus station is open 24hr.

Phone Code: 3.

ACCOMMODATIONS

Guadalajara is full of cheap places to stay. *Posadas* are an intriguing option—they're small, family-run establishments (often in beautiful, remodeled homes) that provide large, well-furnished rooms, good security, and (for a few extra pesos) meals. The drawbacks are curfews and less privacy. Check the tourist office for a list. Guadalajara also has an excellent hostel. Outside of the hostel and the *posadas,* reservations are only necessary in February and October, the festival seasons.

Near Plaza Tapatía and the Centro Histórico

The most variety of rooms, the best location, and the safest spots are all in this area. From *posadas* to standard hotel rooms, budget accommodations won't disappoint. But be cautious while here—even residents advise taking a taxi after dark.

Posada San Pablo, Madero 429 (tel. 614 28 11), between Ocampo and Donato Guerra. There isn't a sign and the door is always closed—ring the bell to enter this budget traveler's dream. Enormous rooms, a gorgeous courtyard, and balconies make Posada San Pablo a little slice of heaven. Singles 60 pesos; doubles 70 pesos; triples 80 pesos. Paperback books and laundry service available (30 pesos).

Hotel Hidalgo, Hidalgo 14 (tel. 613 15 67), a block from Hotel Las Americas, offers great rooms without fancy electronic equipment such as TVs and phones. Location can't be beat and the manager knows his stuff about attractions in the Big G. And it goes for a price you won't find anywhere else in the city. Singles and doubles 45 pesos; triples 65 pesos.

Posada Tapatía, López Cotilla 619 (tel. 614 91 46). A beautiful, old mansion with peachy walls and brightly colored trim, fuchsia sofas and spreads, and a leafy courtyard makes you feel like you're in a tropical paradise. Clean rooms with private baths and fans. Singles 90 pesos; doubles 140 pesos. Curfew 1am.

Hotel Las Américas, Hidalgo 76 (tel. 613 96 22), at Humboldt. A perfect location and very comfortable rooms make Las Americas an attractive option. Lots of hot water, a TV, phone, and ceiling fan will make you feel right at home. Singles 93 pesos; one-bed doubles 99 pesos, two-bed doubles 123 pesos; triples 130 pesos.

CODE Youth Hostel, Av. Prolongación Alcalde 1360 (tel. 624 65 15). Take bus #52 or #54 from the Jardín de San Francisco or anywhere on Alcalde. The CODE is just past the traffic circle, across from the Foro de Arte y Cultura in a blue fence encircled sports complex. Clean, single-sex rooms hold 20 metal bunks each. Water is hot and the management friendly. 30 pesos per person. 25% discount with HI membership. Bedding, pillows, and lockers provided, but bring your own lock. Reception M-F 8am-2pm and 4-9pm, Sa-Su 9am-3pm and 5-9pm. Curfew 11pm. Hostel closed during *Semana Santa* and Christmas.

Hotel Hamilton, Madero 381 (tel. 614 67 26), between Ocampo and Galeana. Stalactite ceiling makes the dim lobby feel like a cave. Rather small rooms are a reminder that you only paid 50 pesos for a single; 60 pesos for a double; 70 pesos for a triple. Discounts for longer stays. Add 15 pesos for a TV.

Hotel Sevilla, Sánchez 413 (tel. 614 91 72), between Ocampo and Donato Guerra. Rooms have TVs, phones, sky-blue bathrooms with 24hr. hot water, and oh-so-tasteful landscape photos. Old but very clean. Singles 90 pesos; 1-bed doubles 100 pesos, 2-bed doubles 120 pesos.

East on Javier Mina

Hotels in this area are generally cheaper than anywhere else, but Javier Mina and the dark side streets off it can be dangerous at night. If the establishments above don't work out (or if you just want to be closer to Plaza de los Mariachis), these hotels are basic, modern, and clean.

Hotel México 70, Javier Mina 230 (tel. 617 99 78), at Cabañas. White tile floors, red bedspreads, and aqua tile bathrooms are dizzying, delightful, and cheap. Singles 65 pesos; doubles 75 pesos. TV 10 pesos extra.

Hotel Ana Ísabel, Javier Mina 164 (tel. 617 79 20 or 617 48 59), at Cabañas. Clean, small, somewhat dark rooms with ceiling fans and TVs, all overlooking a green courtyard. Hot water in tiny bathrooms. Singles 70 pesos; doubles 85 pesos.

Hotel San Jorge, Javier Mina 284 (tel. 617 79 97). Plain but comfortable rooms with tile bathrooms and hot water. Dark hallways conserve energy. Singles 65 pesos; doubles 75 pesos. TV 10 pesos extra.

Zona Rosa

Hotels in the **Zona Rosa,** the wealthiest area of Guadalajara, are fancy but pricey. A pleasant option midway between the *centro* and the more expensive Av. Chapultepec is **Hotel La Paz,** La Paz 1091 (tel. 613 30 07), between Donato Guerra and 8 de Julio, on bus route #51 or #321. The clean, basic rooms are equipped with phones. It's tranquil, but peace has its price—it's in the boonies. (Singles 75 pesos; doubles 100 pesos; triples 125 pesos; TV 10 pesos extra.) If you have spare pesos and want a really classy, quiet lodging, the *Zona Rosa* has an abundance and is only a short bus ride from the heart of the action in the *centro.*

FOOD

Guadalajara has tons of budget eateries as well as many upscale restaurants with cuisine from around the world: French, Italian, Japanese, and more. *Birria* is a hearty local specialty made by stewing meat (typically pork) in tomato broth thickened with cornmeal and spiced with garlic, onions, and chiles. Guadalajara is also famous for its numerous *taquerías* and the astounding variety of morsels restaurateurs put between tortillas.

Near Plaza Tapatía

This is a great place to snack or fill up with a huge meal. Ice cream and fast-food are ubiquitous, sidewalk stands line the streets, and *panaderías* (bakeries) cluster around the area southwest of the plaza, primarily on the blocks enclosed by Pavo, Sánchez, Galeana, and Juárez.

Mercado Libertad, Calle Independencia right next to the plaza. The enormous market has an entire wing dedicated to family-run restaurants. Watch food be cooked before your eyes as you sit in the frenetic market atmosphere. You can find anything to eat here from *birria* to fried chicken at prices that'll leave you with plenty of pesos for shopping (huge meals average 25 pesos). Open daily 8am-9pm.

Hidalgo 112, at...Hidalgo 112 (tel. 614 54 47), across from Teatro Degollado. No sign, so look for the brownish red awning. A glorified juice bar with pine tables and traditional blue glasses. Squeeze in and chat with locals after the lunchtime rush. Fantastically cheap. Large fruit yogurt with granola in a glass 7 pesos. Whole wheat quesadillas (2.50 pesos) can't be beat. Open M-Sa 7am-10pm, Su 7am-5pm.

Restaurant Acuarius, Sánchez 416 (tel. 613 62 77), across from Hotel Sevilla. New Age, Mex-style. Don a peasant shirt and brandish your cosmic consciousness. *Jugo verde* 8.50 pesos. Soy burgers 15 pesos. Vegetarian *comida corrida* 32 pesos. Open M-Sa 9:30am-6pm, Su 10am-5:30pm.

Cafe Madrid, Juárez 264 (614 95 05), at 16 de Septiembre. A bit pricey, but fun: a 1950s diner flourishing in the *centro.* Waiters sporting white jackets and bow ties serve breakfast (22-32 pesos), enchiladas (28 pesos), and divine cappuccino (6.50 pesos) to patrons seated on stools along the formica counter or at tables beneath an enormous Alfredo Santos mural. Open daily 7:30am-10:30pm.

Restaurant Vegetariano Devachan, López Cotilla 570 and 8 de Juio, inside the mysterious Instituto Devachan. Bountiful and tasty vegetarian *comida corrida* (18 pesos) served in a plant-filled yellow courtyard. On Saturdays, devotees and mystics gather to gorge themselves on the buffet (22 pesos). Open M-Sa 2-6pm.

Taco Cabana, on the corner of Moreno and Maestranza in the pedestrian shopping district by the Plaza Tapatía. Cheap beer and tacos amid the mariachi-filled juke box and a panel of TVs tuned to *fútbol.* 2 beers 9 pesos, tacos 2 pesos. Open daily 9am-10:30pm.

El Farol, Moreno 466 (614 95 05), at Galeanax, 2nd fl. *Comida típica* at rock- bottom prices. Friendly owner makes a mean *chile relleno.* Complementary *buñuelos,* a fried dough dessert dripping with sugary syrup. Entrees 15-25 pesos, tacos 3 pesos, beer 8 pesos. Open daily 9:15am-11:30pm.

Jugui Torti Pollo, Corona 224 and Madero. What this tiny fast-food joint lacks in atmosphere it makes up for in taste. Burritos 6 pesos. *Tortas* 9 pesos. Juice 5 pesos. Open daily 6am-midnight.

East on Javier Mina

Restaurants near Javier Mina will fill your stomach but not with anything particularly thrilling. The exceptions are the restaurants in Plaza de los Mariachis, where *mariachis* will serenade you as you eat affordable enchiladas (20 pesos) and enjoy a beer (7 pesos). Don't go too late, because some real characters gravitate to the plaza later on.

Zona Rosa

Most places below cluster near the intersection of Vallarta and Chapultepec, on the "Par Vial" bus route. The #321 bus also does the trick. It's worth the trip—the extra pesos buy superior food and even a measure of elegance.

Naló Cafe, Justo Sierra 2046 (tel. 615 27 15), just off Chapultepec Nte. Sit outside under a big umbrella and sample the delicious breakfast and lunch specials (15-25 pesos). Menu changes daily but the friendly servers and relaxing atmosphere don't. Fettucine alfredo 20 pesos, salads 10 pesos, carrot cake 10 pesos. Open 8am-9pm.

Restaurant Samurai, Vidrio 1929 (tel. 826 35 54), the small street a block north of the Niños Héroes monument on Chapultepec. Japanese-Mexican food you ask? Don't knock it until you try it. Tasty creations served in a family's house. Very cozy, very quiet, very tasty. *Comida corrida* (Japanese style) with rice, soup, and main course 25 pesos. *Tonkatsu* 40 pesos. Open M-Sa noon-10pm, Su noon-7pm.

Café Don Luis, Chapultepec 215 (tel. 625 65 99), at Av. de la Paz at Libertad. Coffees and desserts. A great place to revive your sleepy bones after a *siesta;* Angel's Kiss (Kahlúa, coffee, and eggnog) is love at first sip (17 pesos). Open daily 9am-3pm and 5-11pm.

SIGHTS

A great city for walking, Guadalajara fills with families out for a stroll in the cool evening air. But don't limit your exploration to the *centro*—the city is huge, but its bus and subway systems make transportation into most areas a breeze. The sheer number of monuments testifies to the rich history and culture of Guadalajara. Statues commemorating everyone from the Niños Héroes to (who else?) Benito Juárez are ubiquitous. Guadalajara's plazas are clean, crowded, and often visited by party-hardy *mariachis.* The city's museums are the best introduction to Mexican culture and history outside of Mexico City.

Downtown

Downtown Guadalajara's four plazas punctuate the city's concrete sidewalks with splashes of greenery. Horse-drawn carriages wait at the Independencia side of the Mercado Libertad, offering one-hour tours for 120 pesos. The spacious **Plaza de la Liberación,** with its large, bubbling fountain and enormous Mexican flag that eclipses the sun, is surrounded by the cathedral, Museo Regional, Palacio de Gobierno, and Teatro Degollado. An enormous sculpture depicts Hidalgo breaking the chains of slavery in commemoration of his 1810 decree, signed in Guadalajara, to abolish the trade. Always bustling with activity, the Plaza de la Liberación is the effective center of historic Guadalajara.

The **Palacio de Gobierno,** on the plaza's south side, was built in 1774 and is a Churrigueresque building graced by a mural by José Clemente Orozco; check out Miguel Hidalgo's feverish eyes looking down from the wall. *(Open M-F 9am-8:45pm, Sa-Su 9am-3pm. Guided tours available for a few pesos.)* A second Orozco mural, covering the ceiling in the echoing **Sala de Congreso,** depicts enslaved *indígenas* and the heroism of Hidalgo and Juárez. Climb to the roof for a great view.

The imposing **cathedral** faces the Teatro Degollado across Plaza de la Liberación. *(Open daily 7:30am-7:30pm. To avoid Mass on Sunday, visit after 2pm.)* Begun in 1558 and completed 60 years later, the cathedral is a melange of architectural styles. After an 1848 earthquake destroyed its original towers, ambitious architects replaced them with much taller ones. Fernando VII of Spain donated the cathedral's 11 richly ornamented altars in appreciation of Guadalajara's help during the Napoleonic Wars. One of the remaining original altars is dedicated to Our Lady of the Roses; it is this altar, and not the flamboyant flowers, that gave Guadalajara its nickname "City of Roses." Inside the sacristy is the *Assumption of the Virgin,* painted by the showy 17th-century painter **Bartolomé Murillo.** The towers, known as the *cornucopías,* can be climbed with the permission of the cathedral's administrators, who hole up in the side of the building facing the Teatro Degollado. You can enter on this side or through the back of the church. The 60-meter jaunt to the top of the towers affords the best view in town. You may be able to take pictures of the church and sacristy, but be respectful. On the cathedral's west side is the arboreal **Plaza de los Laureles;** to the north, the **Plaza de los Mártires** commemorates *tapatíos* who have died in various wars.

On the north side of the Plaza de la Liberación, the **Museo Regional de Guadalajara,** Calle Liceo 60 (tel. 614 99 57 or 614 52 64), at Hidalgo, chronicles the history of western Mexico, beginning with the Big Bang. *(Open Tu-F 9am-7pm, Sa 9am-6pm, Su 9am-3pm. Admission 14 pesos; free for seniors, children under 12, and students with a Mexican ID, and for all on Sundays and Tuesdays.)* The most popular museum around, the *museo* is always crowded with fieldtripping students and tourists. The first floor spans the country's pre-Hispanic history. Collections of colonial art, modern paintings, and an exhibit on the history of the Revolution occupy the second floor. Artsy and educational movie screenings, plays, and lectures take place in the museum's auditorium.

Attend the *ballet folklórico* on Sunday mornings to get a good look at the breathtaking **Teatro Degollado,** a neoclassical structure on the Plaza de la Liberación's east end. The gold and red balconies, a sculpted allegory of the seven muses, and Gerardo Suárez's depiction of Dante's Divine Comedy on the ceiling may be more interesting to watch than the production; the theater plays host to amateur acts of sometimes dubious skill during the week. You can visit anytime, provided there is no performance scheduled. Tickets (tel. 614 47 73) are available at the theater box office.

The crowded **Plazuela de los Mariachis** is on the south side of **San Juan de Dios,** the church with the blue neon cross on Independencia at Javier Mina. Immediately after you sit down, roving musicians will pounce. Using every trick in their musical bag, the *mariachis* will try to separate you from your pesos. Prices for songs are completely variable; a good *mariachi* who likes you or a bad one without much choice may perform a song for only 20-25 pesos, post-haggling. The *mariachis* continue playing long into the night, but you don't want to be around to hear them—the Plazuela becomes the stage for roving unsavories who will also try to separate you from your pesos. And if they offer anything in return, it sure ain't music.

From the **Plaza Tapatía,** constructed in 1982, you can spy the glinting dome of the 190-year-old **Hospicio Cabañas** (or **Casa de Cultura Cabañas**), at the corner of Hospicio and Cabañas, three blocks east of Independencia. *(Open Tu-Sa 10am-6pm, Su 10am-3pm. Admission 8 pesos, with student ID 4 pesos, children under 12 free, free for all on Sundays. 10 pesos for camera rights—no flash.)* It was here that Hidalgo signed his proclamation against slavery in 1810; the building has since served as an orphanage and an art school. For its main chapel, Orozco painted a nightmarish and brilliant rendition of the **Four Riders of the Apocalypse;** some regard the work as Orozco's best. It demands that your eyes be riveted to every contorted, fiery shape. If you don't see anything else in Guadalajara, see Orozco's mural. *Espejos* (mirrors) are available free for those who don't want to strain their necks; alternatively, lie down on one of the many benches set up for reclined viewing. The *hospicio* also hosts photography and sculpture exhibits.

The cavernous **Mercado Libertad,** at Javier Mina and Independencia, is touted as the largest covered market in the Americas. *(Open daily roughly 9am-8pm, but some merchants don't open on Sundays.)* Although its size may be exaggerated, there are still oodles of sandals, *sarapes,* jewelry, guitars, dried iguanas, and other witchcraft supplies filling tier after tier of booths. Don't be afraid to get good and lost among all the merchandise or to bargain with savvy merchants. You can get a great deal on that purple sombrero you've always wanted if you're willing to get in the trenches and haggle. The weekly market **El Baratillo** on Javier Mina, approximately 15 blocks east of Mercado Libertad, offers bargain hunters even greater temptation. From Mercado Libertad, walk two blocks north to Hidalgo and catch bus #40 heading east or a "Par Vial" bus on Morelos. El Baratillo lasts all day Sunday and sometimes sprawls out over 30 or 40 blocks. If you thought the Mercado Libertad was huge, wait until you see its Daddy. Everything imaginable is peddled here, from hot *tamales* to houses.

South

If you're tired of the hustle and bustle of the streets, take a stroll in the sprawling **Parque Agua Azul,** a lavish green park with tropical bird aviaries, an orchid greenhouse, a sports complex, and a butterfly house. *(Open Tu-Su 10am-6pm. Admission 4 pesos, children 2 pesos.)* The park is south of the *centro* on Calzada Independencia; take bus #60 or #62 heading south along this main street. Almost everything is for sale inside the **Casa de las Artesanías de Jalisco** (tel. 619 46 64 or 619 51 79), on González Gallo, the street bisecting Parque Agua Azul. *(Open M-F 10am-6pm, Sa 10am-4pm, Su 10am-2pm.)* Prices can be 50% higher here than in the villages. Pottery, jewelry, clocks, hammocks, china, blankets, *equipales,* chessboards, shirts, and purses are all high-quality and have been carted over from Tlaquepaque and Tonalá (see p. 305).

Zona Rosa

Cultural activity in the city's wealthier areas focuses on the **Plaza del Arte,** on Chapultepec, one block south from its intersection with Niños Héroes. National artists bare their souls on a rotating basis in the plaza's **Galería de Arte Moderno** (tel. 616 32 66), on Mariano Otero and España. *(Open M-F 10am-7pm, Sa-Su 10am-4pm; free.)*

The cutting edge in Mexican art starts here. Although the exhibits vary in quality, the Galería is always a great place to get cultured. The **Teatro Jaime Torres Bodet** (tel. 615 12 69), also in the Plaza del Arte, has book expositions, concerts, and more. *(Open M-F 9am-9pm.)* Stand-up comedy and performance art enliven the premises with laughter and pretension.

North

To get to any of the sights listed below, take Ruta #60 or #62 north on Calzada Independencia. If you're missing your furry friends, head out to the **Zoológico Guadalajara** (tel. 674 44 88 or 674 43 60), way north on Calzada Independencia, near the Plaza de Toros. *(Open W-Su 10am-6pm. Admission 15 pesos, children 12 and under 7 pesos.)* The zoo also affords a spectacular view of the **Barranca de Huentitán,** a deep ravine. The **Centro de Ciencia y Tecnología** (tel. 674 41 06), a brief walk from the zoo, houses a planetarium and exhibits on astronomy, aeronautics, and rock formations. *(Open Tu-Sa 9am-7pm, Su 9am-6:30pm. Museum admission 2 pesos, children under 12 free; 4 pesos for the planetarium.)*

ENTERTAINMENT AND SEASONAL EVENTS

Guadalajara is known for its cultural sophistication and dizzying variety of entertainment options. To keep abreast of Guadalajara's goings-on, from avant-garde film festivals to bullfights, check listings of clubs and cultural events in *Tentaciones,* the Friday supplement to *Siglo 21; The Guadalajara Weekly; Vuelo Libre,* a monthly calendar of events; and the kiosks and bulletin boards of places like Hospicio Cabañas. Be prepared to take a taxi at night, as many of Guadalajara's streets become deserted and dangerous after dark.

Cultural Events

The **Ballet Folklórico** dazzles the world with amazingly precise rhythmic dance, regional garb, and amusing stage antics. There are two troupes in Guadalajara, one affiliated with the University of Guadalajara and the other with the state of Jalisco. The former, reputedly better, performs Sundays at 10am in the **Teatro Degollado** (tel. 614 47 73; box office open daily 10am-1pm and 4-7pm). Tickets (15-60 pesos) are sold one day in advance or on the day of the performance; spend the extra pesos for a seat up front—seats are reserved. The **Ballet Folklórico de Cabañas,** the state troupe, performs Wednesdays at 8:30pm in the Hospicio Cabañas (tickets 25 pesos); if you arrive before 8pm, you can take a tour of some of the murals of the Hospicio. The Hospicio also shows premieres of Mexican films to much fanfare (shows daily at noon, 3:50, 6:50, and 9pm daily, 8 pesos). The **Instituto Cultural Cabañas** presents live music on an open-air stage in the Hospicio Cabañas at least once a week. Drop by the Hospicio Cabañas ticket counter (see p. 299) or look for flyers with the Cabañas insignia (a building with pillars) for schedules.

University facilities, scattered throughout the city, have created a market for high culture on a low budget. The **Departamento de Bellas Artes,** García 720, coordinates activities at a large number of stages, auditoriums, and movie screens throughout the city. The best source of information on cultural events is the blackboard in the lobby, which lists each day's attractions.

For Luis Buñuel retrospectives and other vintage screenings, head to the cinema at Bellas Artes. The **Cinematógrafo,** Vallarta 1102 (tel. 825 05 14), just west of the university, is a film house that changes its show weekly (tickets 25 pesos). Guadalajara has dozens of other cinemas with admission around 15 pesos; check the newspapers for listings. **La Terraza,** 442 Juárez (tel. 658 36 91), at Ocampo, overlooks the *centro* and serves all-you-can-eat tacos (18 pesos; noon-5pm) and cheap beer (2 for 10 pesos; open daily noon-midnight). Otherwise try **La Hosta,** at México and Rubén Darío (open daily 1pm-1am).

Although they close earlier than bars, many **cafes** are still happenin' nighttime spots. **Cafe La Paloma,** López Cotilla 1855 (tel. 630 00 91), at Miguel de Cervantes, is definitely a hipster hangout. The cool patio filled with wicker chairs is a welcome respite from the hustle of downtown. Local artwork spanks the imagination while the body enjoys tasty dishes and desserts including *cafe de olla* (12 pesos), chocolate cheesecake (15 pesos), and quesadillas. (Open M-Sa 8:30am-11pm, Su 9am-10pm.)

Bars and Clubs

Guadalajara has a thriving nightlife; determined partiers can find something going on almost any night. For a more Mexican experience, skip the overpriced and generic *discotecas* and head instead to one of the city's many excellent bars. Live entertainment in these hot spots ranges from punk rock to mariachi.

Don Porfirio Cantina, Maestranza 70 (tel 658 10 80), a block down from Plaza Liberación. Students and twenty-somethings mingle and check each other out in an old massive government building. Balconies, classy furniture, and muraled walls make the Cantina a joy. Beer 10 pesos. No cover. Open 9pm-3am.

La Maestranza, Maestranza 179 (tel. 613 20 85), at López Cotilla, in the *centro*. Bullfight regalia and posters crowd the walls of this local hangout. Tasty and reasonably priced food, good music, and plenty of alcohol. Enchiladas 24 pesos. Beer 8 pesos. Live trio daily 3-5pm. No cover. Open daily 10am-3am.

La Cripta, Tepeyac 4038 (tel. 647 62 07), at Niño Obrero. Cool locals, mostly university types, down *cervezas* to live alternative tunes. Cover 20-40 pesos. Open daily 8pm-3am.

Babel, Av. Vallarta 1480 (tel. 615 63 61), at Chapultepec, is a typical (and fun) Mexican video bar. Flashing screens and loud rockin' music in English and Spanish. No cover. Open daily 8pm-2am.

Copenhagen, Marcos Castellanos 120-2 (tel. 825 28 03), between Juárez and López Cortilla. Enjoy mature company here. Live music M-Sa 8pm-12:30am. Open M-Sa 2:30pm-12:30am, Su 1-6pm.

Bananas Cafe, Chapultepec 330 (tel. 615 41 91), at Lerdo de Tejada, is slightly silly—donning pop-music posters under a thatched roof patio—but fun and worth a visit for the unusual drink offerings and music. Beer 10 pesos. Open daily noon-midnight.

Discotecas

Elegantly dressed partygoers line up to get into the classy joints along **Av. Vallarta** (taxi 15 pesos), while more classic discotheques with sophisticated track lighting and elevated dance floors cluster around **Plaza del Sol** (taxi 20-25 pesos). On Friday and Saturday nights, the crowds come out in droves; many bars and discos offer drink specials. In general, Guadalajara discos are fancy; most won't let you in with blue jeans or without leather shoes, so dress up and get ready to shake your goods.

Pasaje, Mariano Otero 1989 (tel. 121 13 63), by the Plaza de Sol. Thick smoke clouds a packed dance floor, while the crowd downs drinks amid flashing lights and big-screen TVs. The attached video bar, **Forever,** is very popular. Cover W-Th (open bar) men 70 pesos, women 40 pesos; Friday (open bar) pay your weight: 1 peso per kg; Saturday (no open bar) 45 pesos per person. Open 9pm-4am.

La Máquina, Vallarta 1920 (tel. 615 23 25), near Plaza Los Arcos. Housed in an 18th-century mansion with gold leaf, high ceilings, chandeliers, and dapper waiters in red jackets and frilly blouses. Thirsty patrons keep those waiters busy, and the latest hits blasting from the sound system make sure the patrons are gettin' busy too. Cover Wednesday (open bar) 80 pesos for men, women free; F-Sa (no open bar) 40 pesos for all. Open W-Sa 9pm-3am

La Marcha, Vallarta 2648 (tel. 615 89 99), at Los Arcos. Fancy artwork, fountains, and pretension, oh my. When you get tired of dancing (as most people quickly seem to), retreat to a secluded booth and do whatever it is you do. Cover Th-Sa men 80 pesos, women 40 pesos. Open W-Sa 10pm-3am.

Lado B, Vallarta 2451 (tel. 616 83 23), at Queredo, at Plaza Los Arcos. A blazing inferno full of creepy murals, images of the sphinx and phoenix, and metal and wire furniture. Cover Friday (no open bar) men 50 pesos, women 20 pesos; Saturday (open bar) men 90 pesos, women 40 pesos. Open W, F-Sa 9:30pm-3am

Praga (tel 658 10 80), on Maestranza, under Don Porfirio Cantina in the *centro*. Very popular with the university crowd; the top-40 tunes from Mexico and the U.S. pack parties in. Open bar every night makes for some choice drunken revelry. Cover men 50 pesos, women 30 pesos. Open Th-Su 9pm-3am.

Gay and Lesbian Nightlife

There is more gay nightlife here than anywhere other than Mexico City, mostly along Chapultepec, in the upscale *Zona Rosa,* and at the Plaza de los Mariachis.

Sahara, on Mariano Otero, two blocks from Pasaje in the Plaza del Sol, features the latest in lights and glitz as well as racy drag shows. Cover 40 pesos. Open W-Su 10pm-3am.

S.O.S., La Paz 1413 (tel. 826 41 79), at Federalismo and Tolsa, has incredibly vibrant drag shows W-Su at midnight. Cover 30 pesos. Bar open Th-Tu 9pm-3am. Disco open W-Su 10pm-3am.

Mastara's, Maestranza 238 (tel. 614 81 03), at Madero, is a popular gay bar with 2-for-1 beers (12 pesos). Open daily 9pm-1am.

Candillós, on Sanchez, across from Hotel Cervantes, and about 3 blocks from the *centro*, is a small bar and disco that draws loyal regulars who enjoy the 2-for-1 brew (13 pesos), non-existent cover charge, spirited dance floor, and occasional live "sensual performance." Open Th-Su 9am-3pm.

Open-air Activities

Finding a bench in the Plaza de Armas, across from the Palacio de Gobierno, on Thursday and Sunday nights is a tricky task—the **Jalisco State Band** draws crowds of locals for free performances of gusto-packed music. The music doesn't get going until about 6:30pm, but seat-seekers should arrive before 6pm (see next page), If you are looking for something to do, the **plazas** are a great bet. The **Plaza de los Fundadores,** behind the Teatro Degollado, serves as a stage every afternoon for the clown-mimes. Watch and give tips, but unless you like being the butt of jokes, keep out of the mime's eye. On any given day, the entire area around the *centro* is thronged with people and the artists, clowns, and actors who come to entertain them.

Every October, Guadalajara explodes with the traditional **Fiestas de Octubre,** a surreal, month-long bacchanal of parades, dancing, bullfights, fireworks, food, and fun. Each day of the month is dedicated to a different one of Mexico's 29 states or its two territories. Revelers are treated to regional dance performances, concerts, and cultural celebrations for 31 consecutive days. The small communities around Guadalajara also celebrate huge festivals during different parts of the year. Keep your eyes open for the copious advertisements that coat the city.

Sports

Bullfights take place almost every Sunday from October through April in the **Plaza de Toros** (tel. 637 99 82 or 651 85 06), on Nuevo Progreso at the northern end of Independencia (take Ruta #60 or 62 north). Tickets (25-180 pesos) can be purchased at the Plaza de Toros. (Open M-Sa 10am-2pm and 4-6pm.) More popular, colorful, and distinctly Mexican are the **charreadas** (rodeos) held every Sunday at noon at the **Lienzo Charro de Jalisco,** Dr. R. Michel 577 (tel. 619 32 32 or 619 03 15). Take the #60 or 62 bus to the stadium. Tickets are around 40 pesos.

Even by Mexican standards, *fútbol* is huge in Guadalajara. The Chivas, the local professional team, are perennial contenders for the national championship—conversations turn nasty, brutish, and short at the mention of the Pumas, the rival team for Mexico City. Matches are held September through May in **Jalisco Stadium** (tel. 637 05 63 or 637 02 99), at Calzada Independencia North in front of the Plaza de Toros (on the #60 or #62 bus route), and in **Estadio 3 de Marzo** (tel. 641 50 51), at the Universidad Autónoma (ticket office is at Colomos Pte. 2339).

Near Guadalajara

As if Guadalajara weren't overwhelming enough, its surrounding area is home to even more exciting activity. From evenings spent hiking around Mexico's second-largest lake to mornings spent slugging your favorite liquor out of a bullhorn, Guadalajara promises adventure even outside its city boundaries. The best part? Most of it is quickly and cheaply accessible by the local bus system. Take some time to unwind at some of these eclectic pleasure-promising places. **Tequila** is our favorite.

Near Guadalajara: Tequila

Surrounded by gentle mountains and prickly, blue-green *agave* plants stretching as far as the eye can see, Tequila is a typical Mexican *pueblo* with a difference: since the 17th century, Tequila has been dedicated solely to the production and sale of its namesake. The town is home to 11 tequila factories, and nearly every business in town is linked to the liquor in some way. Tourism sustains a slew of T-shirt and souvenir shops as well as numerous liquor stores in the *centro* and along the highway just outside of town. Although touristy (surprise!), this dusty town is lots of fun and makes a great daytrip from Guadalajara.

The town is organized around the main plaza; all roads lead to and from it. The tequila factories are all within easy walking distance on the outskirts of town. The José Cuervo and Sauza plants, the two biggest distilleries, are next door to each other two blocks north of the plaza. Tequila's **tourist office** is located on the town's main plaza in front of the Presidencia Municipal (office open daily 10am-5pm). The staff will arrange tours of the tequila factories and the tequila museum. **Banamex,** at Sixto Gorjón and Juárez, has an **ATM** and changes dollars. The **police** wait on the Plaza Principal at José Cuervo 33, next to the tourist office. Don't plan to spend the night in Tequila—it's wiser to head back to Guadalajara at dusk than to enjoy a Tequila sunrise. There's not a whole lot of choice in the dining department, either. One option is **Restaurant Bar El Sauzal,** Juárez 45, between Gorjón and Cuervo, home to a garish mural and beer-drinking locals (*bistec ranchero* 30 pesos; quesadillas 5 pesos; beer 8 pesos; open daily noon-11pm). True budget hunters will delight to find the *pollo* roaster **Aricola,** at Sixto Gorjón 20, where half a roasted chicken goes for about 25 pesos (open daily 7:30am-4pm). Tortillas are available at the *tortillería* next door.

There's not much to do here other than drink or take a **tequila factory tour**. But hey, why else did you come to a town called Tequila? The **government-sponsored tour** starts from the tourist office every hour (10am-5pm, 25 pesos), while the **Sauza** and **Jose Cuervo tours** kick off at the respective plants every hour (9am-6pm; 20 pesos). For the price of a few shots, you'll learn more than you ever wanted to know

Tequila Time

The best tequila, as the tour guides will tell you, bears a label boasting its content: 100% *agave.* Around 1600 varieties of this cactus exist in Mexico; only the blue *agave* is used to make tequila. Plants take eight to 12 years to mature, at which point their huge, dense centers (called *piñas*—pineapples—for their appearance) weigh 35-45kg. Although the *agave* plant's spiky leaves can tower above even tall *norteamericanos, agave* growers keep them trimmed short, as only the center is used to produce tequila. Once harvested, each plant provides around 5L of tequila. Not bad for a cactus. From the field, the *piñas* are taken to the factory where they are cooked for 36 hours in enormous traditional ovens, or for 12 hours in the modern and speedy autoclave. The *piñas* are then chopped and mixed with water. The mixture is poured into huge tubs where it ferments, attracting bees, flies, ants, and other bugs that inevitably join this not-so-appetizing concoction. But don't try to blame these critters for your tequila trauma—in the several months or more before this brew finds it way to anyone's mouth, it will be carefully sterilized and diluted.

about *agave* (the plant from which tequila is distilled), the distillation and aging processes, and the history of every *mariachi's* favorite liquor. The government tour includes a stop in a small **tequila museum** and **gift shop,** where you can sample the town's finest. The private tours end in the factories' very own bars, where the first three shots of assorted varieties of tequila are free; subsequent lip-puckering doses will run you 6-15 pesos. Those who can spare the pesos will find good deals on hard-to-find varieties and tequila-related knick-knacks for the folks back home.

For 12 days at the beginning of December, Tequila celebrates its **Feria Nacional del Tequila.** Each of the town's factories has its own day on which it holds rodeos, concerts, cockfights, fireworks, and other festivities. And of course, there are always plenty of drinks to go around.

Getting There: Buses to Tequila leave from Guadalajara's Antigua Central (2hr., about every 45min., 17 pesos) and return on the same schedule.

■ Near Guadalajara: Tlaquepaque

The "village" of Tlaquepaque is little more than the strip along Independencia and Av. Juárez, where upscale shops set in old colonial mansions sell silver, handicrafts, leather, ceramics, plastic toys, and junk. Although completely geared toward tourists, Tlaquepaque offers the best quality and prices for *artesanías* in the Guadalajara area (other than Tonalá). Just off its main square lies the *mercado,* where you can find cheaper goods of lesser quality.

Tlaquepaque was made for shopping, so bring your credit card and a big bag for carrying your loot. The **Museo Regional de las Cerámicas y los Artes Populares de Jalisco,** Independencia 237 (tel. 635 54 04), at Alfareros, sells an interesting collection of antique regional crafts as well as newer pieces (open Tu-Sa 10am-6pm, Su 10am-3pm; free). Another fun, if touristy, spot is **La Rosa de Cristal,** Independencia 232 (tel./fax 639 71 80), at Alfareros, where artisans blow glass by hand and then sell their work at inflated prices (glass-blowing M-F 10:30am-1:30pm, Sa 10:30am-noon; shop open M-Sa 10am-6pm, Su 10am-2pm). There is a small **tourist information** booth on Independencia at the **Parque Hidalgo** (tel. 635 57 56), where a cheerful employee will give you a photocopied map and a smile. Fancy restaurants dot Independencia and offer menus in English, outside seating, and delicious food. More affordable meals wait around the *mercado*. For accommodations, Tlaquepaque is a wasteland. The few places are either rented out on an hourly, not nightly, basis, or require collateral. Come to Tlaquepaque during the day; sleep in Guadalajara at night.

Getting There: Take the local #275 or 275A bus or the "Tlaquepaque" TUR bus (10min. from 16 de Septiembre). For the main markets, get off at Independencia, by the Pollo-Chicken joint on the left; if the driver turns left off Niños Héroes, you've gone too far. To get back to downtown Guadalajara, hop back on a #275 or TUR bus at the corner of Niños Héroes and Constitución, two blocks north of Independencia.

■ Near Guadalajara: Zapopan

Northwest of Guadalajara, the town of Zapopan is famous for the **Basílica de la Virgen de Zapopan,** a giant 16th-century edifice erected to commemorate a peasant's vision of the Virgin. The walls of the church are hung with many decades' worth of *ex votos,* small paintings on sheet metal recognizing the Virgin's aid in curing diseases. The image of the Virgin was made by natives from corn stalks in the 16th century. Pope John Paul II visited the shrine in 1979, and a statue of the pontiff holding hands with a beaming *campesino* boy now stands in the courtyard in front of the church. During the early fall, the figure of Our Lady of Zapopan is frequently exchanged from church to church throughout the state—each move occasions serious partying. Then, on October 12 (*Día de la Raza,* the day Columbus landed in America), the figure makes her way from Guadalajara's cathedral to Zapopan, in the midst of a large procession. The impressive cathedral and spectacular plaza are the only real attractions Z-town has to offer. The *mercado* adjacent to the fountain and tree-adorned plaza is the best place to take a break from lounging and grab a cheap taco or roasted chicken. Again, head back to Guadalajara to spend the night. The last bus leaves around 10pm.

Getting There: To reach Zapopan, catch the local #275A bus northbound on Av. 16 de Septiembre (25min., 2 pesos); hop off at the big church.

■ Near Guadalajara: Tonalá

So you want to go shopping, huh? Well, Tonalá is your place. A less accessible, mercifully less touristed version of Tlaquepaque, **Tonalá** is most fun on market days (Thursdays and Sundays) but is a hoot anytime. Activity centers around the **Plaza Principal** and spills out west to Av. Tonaltecas. Merchants, vendors, and restaurant owners sit around with their feet up and invite you in to scope their ornate metal or glass-ware. Women weave multi-colored rugs and sew dolls, while patient ceramics merchants paint personalized messages on their products. Here, the soft sell rules; merchants will take the time to talk with you, and you won't feel obliged to purchase anything. Tonalá specializes in inexpensive, conservatively decorated ceramics, good-quality, low-priced silver, and glass dishes; it has the best prices and **shopping** of anywhere in or near Guadalajara.

When you get tired of shopping, walk north of the city up the **Cerro de la Reina** to clown around in front of the camera with an astonishing view of Guadalajara behind you. The **tourist office** (tel. 683 17 40), on Zapata one block off the plaza, will be able to direct you to other worthy sights, such as the **Museo Nacional de la Cerámica,** where you can see how the beautiful pot you bought was made. The only hotel in town is **Hotel Tonalá** (tel 683 05 95), at Calle Madero a block away from the plaza. The water is hot, the rooms are airy and clean, and the TV reception is immaculate. Go early in the day or call ahead as the place tends to fill up. (Singles 110 pesos; doubles 120 pesos; triples 160 pesos.)

Getting There: Local bus #275 or TUR bus #706, which run along 16 de Septiembre, are the best way to reach Tonalá (30min., 2 pesos). Get off at the intersection of Av. Tonalá and Tonaltecas. The rows of furniture and pottery stores will indicate that you've arrived. Tonaltecas is a main drag; bear right (the only way you can go) to reach the plaza.

■ Near Guadalajara: Lago de Chapala and Chapala

Forty kilometers from the hustle and bustle of Guadalajara, the **Lago de Chapala,** Mexico's second-largest lake, rests against the mountains that haunt its shore. Although industrial waste has made swimming in the lake a bad idea, a visit to the small villages of **Chapala** and **Ajijic** (see p. 306) couldn't be a better one. Home to a peaceful mix of Mexican tourists, *norteamericano* retirees, local artists, and residents, these villages lie tucked between the lake's serene northern shore and surrounding mist-cloaked mountains. Hiking around the lake or in the hills, wandering through the markets, or sitting outside soaking up rays and fresh air are the main, soul-soothing activities to do around here. English speakers will feel at home: many of the signs and conversations are in English. But don't let the large number of gringos fool you—this is not a frenetic, hell-raising beach town but rather a beautiful and tranquil setting for a romantic get-away or intense relaxation.

Chapala is named after the Tecuexe Indian chief Capalac, who founded the village on the banks of the lagoon in 1510. The town's mix of history and geographic beauty has inspired artists for centuries; its charm shines through its growing size and modernity. Reeds thriving in the lake's now-polluted waters have caused the lake to shrink, but the beautiful walkways bordering the old water line are still perfect for a stroll. Nobody in Chapala is in a hurry to get anywhere, and cars on the main north-south drag, **Madero,** putter along, making the markets great places to wander.

The **bus station's** main entrance lies on Madero and Martinez. The lake is Chapala's southern and eastern boundary. **Hidalgo** (known as **Morelos** east of Madero) runs west to Ajijic from two blocks north of the lake. To exchange foreign bills, make a bee-line for **Banamex** (tel 376 5 22 71), on Madero and Hidalgo (open M-F 9am-

3:30pm). To get in touch with the real world, walk next door to the **caseta** to make a call or fax (open M-F 9am-5pm, Sa 9am-3pm). The **mercado de artesanías** is on the waterfront and extends four blocks east of Madero's terminus, on Ramón Corona. **D.H. Lawrence** lived in Chapala during the 1940s, and it was here that he began writing *The Plumed Serpent.* For a spectacular view of Chapala, Ajijic, and the surrounding countryside, walk up the stone stairway that winds up the hills from Madero, about four blocks from the lake.

If you plan on spending the night in Chapala, the **Hotel Nido,** Madero 202 (tel. (376) 5 21 16), which once played host to dictator Díaz's weekend soirées, offers the most comfortable rooms. The airy hotel has clean, simple rooms with floral stencils and hot water, a pretty courtyard, and a pool. (Singles 148 pesos; doubles 183 pesos; 15 pesos extra for TV.) The hotel also has a somewhat pricey restaurant. A much cheaper (and the only other) option is **Hotel Cardilejas** (tel. 376 5 22 79), on Lopez Cotilla one block off Madero near the bus station. Rooms are tiny but clean and some boast an awesome view of the lake. (Singles 75 pesos; doubles 85; triples 95 pesos.) There is no paucity of dining options in Chapala. Follow your nose down Madero or along the water/reed front and you can't miss. Drop in at **Restaurant Superior,** at Madero 415 (tel. (376) 5 21 80), near the lake. Expats are practically cemented to the sidewalk tables outside. Decent grub goes for excellent prices: *pollo con mole* is 28 pesos, and hamburgers are 10 pesos. (Open W-M 8am-10pm, Tu 8am-5pm.) More *típico* food is served at **Chabela's Fonda** (tel. (376) 5 43 80), at the far right corner of the plaza. Sunday swarms with locals brunching on the 15- to 20-peso *menú del día.* (Open daily 8am-7pm.)

Getting There: From the *antigua* bus station in Guadalajara, take a **Guadalajara-Chapala** (tel. (376) 617 56 75) bus (45min., every 10 min. 6am-9:30pm, 15 pesos). Buses back to Guadalajara leave from the station on roughly the same schedule. Otherwise, head to Guadalajara's new bus station (1¼hr., every hr. 7:45am-5:45pm, 12 pesos). From Ajijic, hop on any bus; all roads lead through Chapala (15min., every 20min., 2 pesos).

■ Near Guadalajara: Ajijic

Hugging the shore of Lake Chapala and commanding a beautiful view of the surrounding mountains, the sleepy, peaceful village of **Ajijic** is a charming blend of the old and the new. Cobblestone streets are dotted with old churches and buildings as well as high-tech telephone and fax services that are supported by the town's large expat community. The blending of cultures is also not new; it began years ago with the 1920s arrival of European intellectuals escaping political persecution.

The only paved street in Ajijic is the highway Carretera Chapala which divides the town into north and south. Buses down to Chapala or Guadalajara can be flagged anywhere along it. The town's north-south strip is **Colón. Constitución,** another useful street, changes its name to **Ocampo.** The plaza is one block inland. While Ajijic lacks an official tourist office, longtime resident **Beverly Hunt,** owner of **Laguna Axixic Realty,** Carretera 24 (tel. 376 6 11 74; fax 6 11 88), gets the job done, providing maps, brochures, English newsletters, tourist and realty tips, a friendly cup of coffee, and lots of tales. Exchange your greenbacks for more colorful bills at **Bancapromex** (tel. (376) 6 05 46), on Hidalgo at Morelos, which has a 24-hour **ATM** (open M-F 8am-7pm, Sa 10:30am-2:30pm). English is spoken at **Farmacia Jessica,** Parroquia 18 (tel. 376 6 11 91), on the plaza (open daily 9am-10pm). The **post office** is at Colón 23 (tel. (376) 6 18 88) at Constitución (open M-F 8am-3pm, Sa 9am-1pm).

Accommodations in Ajijic are geared more toward retirees than toward students; prices may be out of reach of the budget-conscious. More reasonably priced rooms and apartments are available for those planning a longer stay; check newspapers and bulletin boards for info. Any of the many realty offices will gladly help you out. Two neighboring bungalows on the Carretera near its intersection with Juárez compete for tourist dollars. **Las Casitas,** Carretera Chapala Pte. 20 (tel. 376 6 11 45), has the more charming interior: red tile floors, a dark wood dining set, a little kitchen, and a cozy living room with fold-out couch and chimney (bungalows for 2 people 180 pesos). Although the rooms next door at the **Posada Las Calandrías,** Carretera Chapala Pte. 8 (tel. 376 6 10 52), are a bit plainer, there is a flower-filled garden, barbecue space, and a great view of the *laguna* from the terraces (small bungalow with 2 single beds 160 pesos; large bungalow with 4 single beds 260 pesos). Both establishments have pools.

The best food in town can be found at **Restaurant El Serape,** one block from the lake on Colón, where *comida corrida* (25 pesos) is served hot and fast in the courtyard of an old house. (Open daily 9am-9pm.) For dinner, head upstairs to the newly opened **El Attic,** on the corner of Colón and the highway (open W-M 5-9pm).

On weekends, both young and old swing to the live Latin rhythms at the old **Posada Ajijic** on the laguna at Colón (live music F-Sa 9pm-1:30am; cover 15 pesos). Or if you just want to float your troubles away, look for the **Barcaza del Cuervo,** the **floating bar** on the *laguna* roughly in front of the Posada Nuevo.

Getting There: From the *antigua* bus station in Guadalajara, take a **Guadalajara-Chapala** (tel. 376 617 56 75) bus (45min., every 30min. 6am-9:40pm, 15pesos); ask to be dropped off at Ajijic. Buses back to Guadalajara can be caught along the highway (45min., every hr. 6am-9:30pm, 15 pesos). From Chapala, take the bus to Ajijic from the bus station on Madero and Martinez (15min., every 15min. 6:15am-8:30pm, 2 pesos). It first weaves through the village of San Antonio, then goes on to Ajijic. Catch a *camión* back to Chapala along the highway. The last buses to Chapala and Guadalajara pass by around 8:30pm.

Puerto Vallarta

In 1956, tabloid headlines had the world fantasizing about Puerto Vallarta (pop. 100,000). The torrid affair between Richard Burton and Elizabeth Taylor while Burton was on location shooting John Huston's *Night of the Iguana* helped paint the city as the world headquarters of sensuality. Back then, neither highway nor telephone wire linked the town to the outside world. Forty years and billions of dollars later, the city has become a world-class resort with carefully groomed beaches, luxurious hotels, and showy mansions. Puerto Vallarta, though, is not the place to practice your Spanish skills, nor to immerse yourself in Mexican culture.

The three most important industries in Vallarta are tourism, tourism, and tourism. Resort-mania here takes a variety of forms. The south end of town has virtually all the cheap hotels, best beaches, budget restaurants, and dance clubs. To the north, the hotels get more extravagant, and boutiques and restaurants cater almost exclusively to the thick-walleted. The artificiality of Vallarta's charm—white-stuccoed buildings, red-tiled roofs, and cobbled streets—doesn't bother the hordes of expats and retirees who call the ritzy resort condos home. Farther north, international resorts line the highway. On the outskirts, the mansions and property that are the fodder of glossy brochures sparkle in sensual luxuriance.

ORIENTATION

Running roughly east-west, **Río Cuale** bisects Puerto Vallarta before hitting the ocean. The main streets in the southern half of town are **Insurgentes** and **Vallarta,** which run north-south two blocks apart, and **Francisco Madero** and **Lázaro Cárdenas,** which run east-west one block apart. Most buses and *combis* pass along Insurgentes between Madero and Lázaro Cárdenas at some point on their route. Rte. 200 from Manzanillo runs into town south of the river, becoming Insurgentes. Insurgentes and Vallarta run north from Lázaro Cárdenas to the two bridges that link the south and north sections. The main streets in the northern section are **Morelos,** the continuation of Vallarta, and **Juárez,** one block east. Four blocks north of the river is the **Plaza Mayor;** its cathedral is an excellent landmark. The ritzy waterfront between Plaza Mayor and 31 de Octubre, called the **Malecón,** contains overpriced restaurants, clubs, and cheesy shirt shops. **Paseo Díaz Ordaz** runs parallel to the Malecón,

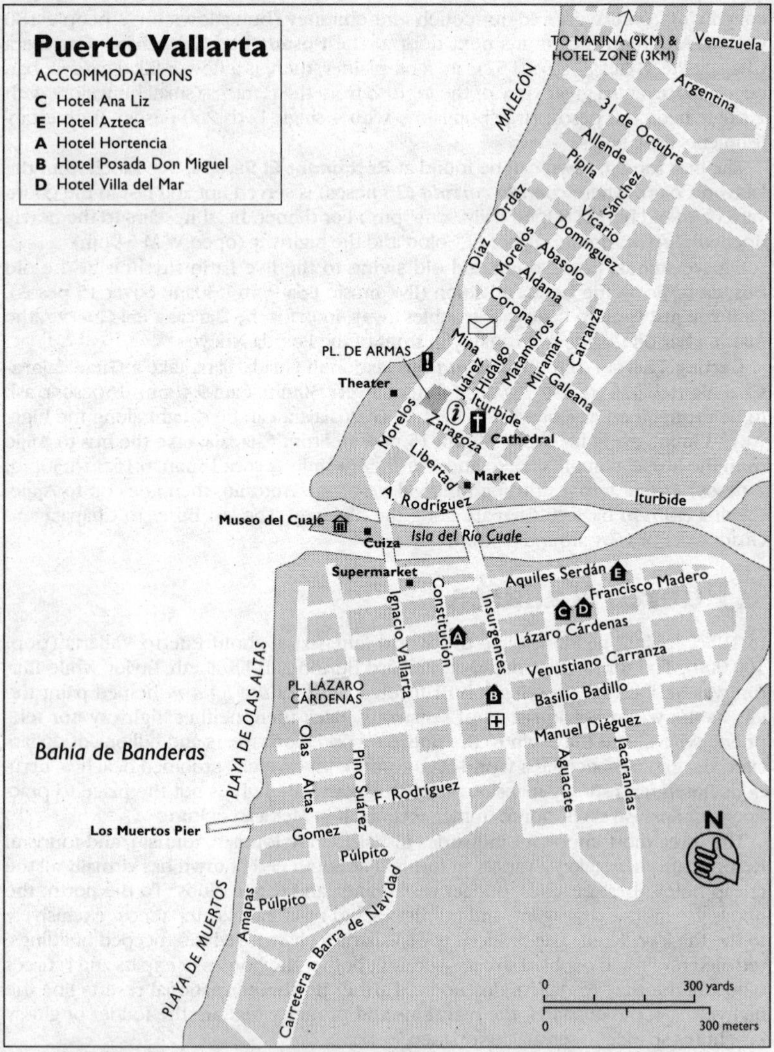

becoming **Av. México** to the north. North of the Malecón, Morelos becomes **Perú** and runs through a working-class neighborhood before joining the coastal highway. North along the highway lie the **airport,** the **marina,** and the **bus station.**

Taxis charge about 10 pesos to drive customers within the *centro* and about 32 pesos to go from the *centro* to the Marina Vallarta or to the airport in the north. Northbound **buses** and **combis** leave from the southern end of Insurgentes, run across the Insurgentes Bridge, head west on Libertad a few blocks, north on Juárez, and onto the highway. Buses enter the city on Av. México, which becomes Díaz Ordaz. Any municipal bus operating south of the Sheraton or labeled "Centro" and all *combis* pass the plaza. Buses and *combis* labeled "Hoteles" pass the hotel strip. For the most part, buses stop only at the clearly marked *parada* signs and at the covered benches (buses and *combis* operate daily 6am-10:30pm, 2.50 pesos).

To get downtown from the airport or the bus station, take a "Centro" or "Olas Altas" bus or a taxi. To get to the airport or the bus station from town, catch a "Novia Alta," "Marfil," or "Aeropuerto" bus on Lázaro Cárdenas, Insurgentes, or Juárez.

PRACTICAL INFORMATION

Transportation

Airport: 8km north of town via the highway. Served by **Alaska** (tel. 1 13 50 or toll-free 95 (800) 426-0333), **American** (tel. 1 17 99 or toll-free 01 (800) 904-6000), **Continental** (tel. 1 10 25), **Mexicana** (tel. 4 89 00), and **Taesa** (tel. 1 15 21 or toll-free 01 (800) 904-6300).

Buses: The modern, mammoth, air-conditioned bus station is located north of the *centro,* just beyond the airport. **Autocamiones Cihuatlán** (tel. 1 00 21) has service south to Manzanillo (5-6½hr., 12 per day 5am-11:30pm, 98-118 pesos). Second-class buses pass through Barra de Navidad (5hr., 78 pesos), Chamela (3½hr., 52 pesos), Melaque (5hr., 77 pesos), and Perula (3½hr., 50 pesos). First-class service to Manzanillo also stops in Barra de Navidad (3½hr., 92 pesos) and Melaque (3½hr., 91 pesos). **Elite/Estrella Bianca** (tel. 1 08 48 or 1 08 50) provides first-class service to Acapulco (18hr., 1am, 376 pesos), Aguascalientes (9hr., 5:30pm, 241 pesos), Ciudad Juárez (36hr.) and 21 points in-between (5pm, 790 pesos), Guadalajara (5½hr., every hr. 6am-1:30am, 184 pesos), Mexico City (13hr., 5 per day 5:15-9pm, 412-549 pesos), and San Blas (3hr., 12:15 and 2:30pm, 71 pesos). **ETN** (tel. 1 05 50) serves Guadalajara (5hr., 15 per day 8:30am-1am, 245 pesos) and Mexico City (12hr., 6:30 and 9pm, 555 pesos). **Primera Plus** (tel. 1 00 95) serves Aguascalientes (9hr., 2:30, 3:30, and 4:30pm, 260 pesos), Colima (7hr., 7:45am and 12:30pm, 172 pesos), León (9hr., 12:45am, 10pm, and midnight, 320 pesos), Manzanillo (5-7hr., 6 per day 7am-10pm, 98-118 pesos) via Melaque (4hr., 77-91 pesos), and Querétaro (12hr., 9pm, 340 pesos). **Transportes de Pacífico** (tel. 1 08 69), sends buses to Mexico City (13hr., 6 and 8pm, 412 pesos) and Tepic (3½hr., every 30min. 4:15am-8pm and 10:30pm, 78 pesos).

Car Rental: Almost all car rental companies have offices on Calle Francisco Medina Ascencio, the hotel strip. Prices are high. **National,** Medina Ascencio km 1.5 (tel. 2 27 42 or 1 12 26 at the airport), has the lowest rates—a VW with tax, insurance, and 200km goes for US$45. **Thrifty,** Medina Ascencio km 5.5 (tel. 4 07 75), rents VWs for US$50 per day, including tax, insurance, and unlimited mileage.

Tourist and Financial Services

Tourist Office: (tel. 2 02 4), in the Presidencia Municipal, on the north side of the Pl. Mayor (enter on Juárez), and at Av. Medina Ascencio 1712 (tel. 3 07 44 or 3 08 44; tel./fax 2 02 43); the street is also known as Av. Las Palmas. Free maps, brochures, and *Passport,* a publication that lists bars and restaurants and includes discount coupons. English spoken. Open M-F 9am-5pm.

Consulates: Canada (tel. 2 53 98 or 3 08 58; fax 2 35 17; open M-F 9am-5pm) and **U.S.** (tel. 2 00 69; fax 3 00 74; open M-F 10am-2pm) are both at Zaragoza 160 in the Vallarta Plaza, on the Pl. Mayor above "Subway."

Currency Exchange: Banamex (tel. 6 61 10), at Juárez and Zaragoza, in front of the Presidencia Municipal. Open M-F 9am-5pm, Sa 9am-2pm. **Bancrecer,** Olas Altas 246 (tel. 3 04 84), between Carranca and Badillo. Open M-F 9am-5pm, Sa 9am-2pm. Both banks have **ATMs.** *Casas de cambio* are everywhere, especially near the Malecón. Their rates are lower than the banks; better deals are generally found away from the beach. Usually open daily 9am-9pm.

American Express: Morelos 660 (tel. 3 29 55; fax 3 29 26), at Abasolo. English spoken. Open M-F 9am-6pm, Sa 9am-1pm.

Local Services

Laundromat: Laundry Aguamatic, Constitución 275 (tel. 2 59 78), between Lázaro Cárdenas and Carranza, charges 21 pesos to clean 3kg. Open M-Sa 9am-8pm.

Bookstore: Señor Book Café, Olas Altas 490 (tel. 2 03 24), at Rodolfo Gómez. Used English books sold and exchanged—two of your old ones get you either one of theirs or a beer (how they make pesos is beyond us). Open daily 7am-11pm.

Supermarket: Gutiérrez Rico (tel. 2 02 22), at Constitución and Serdán. Open daily 6:30am-11pm. **La Ley,** México and Uruguay, is even bigger. Open daily 24hr.

Emergency and Communications

Police: (tel. 3 25 00 or 2 01 23), on Iturbide at Morelos. On-call 24hr. Some English.

Red Cross: (tel. 2 15 33 or 2 49 73), on Río de la Plata at Río Balsas. Open 24hr. Some English spoken.

Pharmacy: Farmacia CMQ, Basilio Badillo 365 (tel. 2 13 30 or 2 29 41), half a block inland from Insurgentes, plus 4 other locations. All open 24hr.

Hospital: CMQ Hospital, Basilio Badillo 365 (tel. 3 19 19), at Insurgentes. English spoken. Open 24hr. Up the hill is **Hospital Medasist,** Manuel Diéguez 360 (tel. 3 04 44), at Aguacate. Some English spoken. Open 24hr.

Post Office: Mina 188 (tel. 2 18 88), left off Juárez past the Plaza Mayor. Open M-F 8am-7:30pm, Sa 9am-1pm. **Postal Code:** 48300.

Internet Access: The Net House, Ignacio Vallarta 232 (tel. 2 57 64), at Lázaro Cárdenas. Email 40 pesos per hr. Open 24hr. **Cyber Café,** Juárez 388 (tel. 2 02 04 or 2 02 35). Email 25 pesos per 30min., 40 pesos per hr. Open M-Sa 9am-11pm.

Phone Code: 322.

ACCOMMODATIONS AND CAMPING

The best budget hotels in Puerto Vallarta are south of Río Cuale, on or near Madero. Make sure the fan in your room works before whipping out your wallet. Prices vary with the season: June is the least expensive month of the year, December the most expensive. Reservations for November through January should be made two months in advance. Even in July, reservations should be made a few days ahead of time. Officially, Vallarta frowns on shiftless beach bums, but most travelers who choose to camp encounter few problems. Some beachfront clubs have night guards who may keep an eye on those who request their permission before bedding down. Many people sleep on the sand behind the Hotel Los Arcos or the Castle Pelícanos, or on the open space between the J. Newcombe tennis courts and the Sheraton. Exercise caution when selecting any camping site.

Hotel Azteca, Madero 473 (tel. 2 27 50), between Jacarandas and Naranjo. Clean and simple rooms at a great price. An abundance of long-term *huéspedes* lend to a friendly atmosphere. The brick and wrought-iron exterior and the giant leafy jungle plants set it apart. Fans and *agua purificada.* Long-distance phone for patrons. Singles 75 pesos; doubles 95 pesos; triples 115 pesos. Small suites with kitchen 150-200 pesos. 30 peso towel deposit.

Hotel Villa del Mar, Madero 440 (tel. 2 07 85 or 2 28 85), 2 blocks east of Insurgentes. Brick detailing, wooden doors, and lanterns hanging over brightly colored bedspreads give the well-scrubbed rooms a rustic feel. Modern tile bathrooms have plenty of hot water. Spiral staircases wind around Mexican and Cuban flags to a rooftop terrace with a fabulous view of the *centro.* Try for a room with a balcony. Singles 82 pesos; doubles 102 pesos. 15 peso towel deposit.

Hotel Ana Liz, Madero 429 (tel. 2 17 57), at Jacarandas, has basic, small, dim rooms with tiny bathrooms, but it's darn cheap. Oh-so-tasteful landscape photos do their best to brighten up the place. Singles high season 82 pesos, low season 75 pesos; doubles high season 105 pesos, low season 90 pesos. 25 peso towel deposit.

Hotel Hortencia, Madero 336 (tel. 2 24 84), at Insurgentes. Cheery bright blue walls are spruced up with a barrage of jungle plants. Ceiling fans, well-lit bathrooms, and exquisitely firm beds are all pluses. Singles 120 pesos, with TV or refrigerator 140 pesos; doubles 140 pesos, with TV or refrigerator 160 pesos.

Hotel Posada Don Miguel, Insurgentes 322 (tel. 2 45 40; fax 2 15 69), between Badillo and Carranza, may put a small dent in your wallet, but it offers amenities aplenty. Soak up the sun at the pool or retreat to massive air-conditioned rooms sporting a jungle theme and black-and-white checkered tile floors. Singles 130 pesos, 160 pesos with A/C; doubles 160 pesos, 260 pesos with A/C.

FOOD

Puerto Vallarta's Malecón specializes in tourist traps with *norteamericano* cuisine, but some excellent, decently priced restaurants can be found elsewhere on the north side. Near the beach on the south side, many upscale restaurants are built especially for gringos, particularly on the blocks enclosed by Basilio Badillo to the south, Olas Altas (the beachfront) to the east, Lázaro Cárdenas to the west, and Constitución to the south. Cheaper down-home eateries cluster along Madero, in the **market** (open M-Sa 8am-8pm) on the north side, where Insurgentes crosses Río Cuale and along Calle México to the north. Taco and quesadilla stands thrive south of the river.

La Casa de los Hot Cakes, Badillo 289 (tel. 2 62 72), at Constitución. A stupendously good breakfast. Indulge in the specialty pancake or waffle platters (26.50 pesos) or delectable cheese blintzes (30 pesos). Also serves lighter fare (scrambled egg whites 20 pesos) and traditional Mexican *desayunos* (*chilaquiles* 21 pesos). Memo, the friendly owner, offers Mexican cooking classes in high season (winter). Open daily 8am-2pm.

Café de Olla, Basilio Badillo 168 (tel. 3 16 26), 1 block from the beach. A tourist joint with attentive waiters, reasonable prices (for Vallarta, that is), and exceptional food. *Mariachis* weave between tables to serenade vacationers. Beautiful burgers 35 pesos; *chiles rellenos* 35 pesos. Open daily M and W-Su 10am-11pm.

Mi Casa Buffet II, Av. México 1121 (tel. 2 09 65), at Rep. de Chile, near the Malecón. Good all-you-can-eat buffet. The spread, which changes daily, features 9 salads and 6 entrees. Lunch buffet (25 pesos). All you can eat and drink in one hour (60 pesos). Feels so much like Mexico, you'll forget you're in Vallarta. Open M-Sa 9am-noon and 1-8pm during high season, otherwise M-Sa 1-8pm.

Una Página en el Sol, Olas Altas 399 at Diéguez. This coffee house and multi-language book exchange will percolate your brain cells with one shot of knock-your-socks-off coffee (5-12 pesos). Leaf through self-help books or chat with the throngs of new-agers between mouthfuls of banana splits (20 pesos) and veggie sandwiches (17 pesos). Bulletin board announces tarot card readings, rooms for rent, and language lessons. Open daily 7:30am-midnight.

Restaurant Buffet Vegetariano, Iturbide 270 (tel. 2 30 73), at Hidalgo, a few blocks inland from Plaza Mayor and up the steep steps of Iturbide. 100% vegetarian cuisine, with a strong Indian influence. Small, white-walled, and simple decor provides solace for hungry businesspeople and tourists. Buffet includes beans, rice, and soy patties (35 pesos). Open M-Sa noon-7pm.

La Fonda Dianita, Madero 243 and Vallarta. Find a table (if you can) in this teensy local favorite, and enjoy tasty and filling *comida corrida* (25 pesos). Clean and cheap. Open daily 8am-6pm.

La Fonda China Poblana Restaurante y Bar, Insurgentes 222 (tel. 2 31 70), between Cárdenas and Carranza. An open-air ground floor with wood and wicker tables to prop up the weary in the wee hours gives way to an airy second floor with a balcony. Breakfast 13-20 pesos, *enchiladas suizas* 30 pesos, beer 9-10 pesos. Open 7am-2am.

SAND AND SIGHTS

Although the veneer of tourism detracts somewhat from Puerto Vallarta's natural beauty, the panorama of the city's 40km of coastline and surrounding mountains is still enchanting. Some of the least crowded and most gorgeous beaches stretch along the coast south of town on the road to **Mismaloya** (see p. 313) and north into Nayarit. The most popular beach within the Puerto Vallarta city limits is **Playa de los Muertos** (Beach of the Dead), a strip in front of the south side's costliest hotels. It begins at its southern end with a rocky cliff spotted with small white homes, and runs north to a small dock that separates it from the **Playa de Olas Altas** (High Waves Beach). To get there, walk all the way west on Lázaro Cárdenas and then south along Playa de Olas Altas. Playa de Olas Altas continues to the Río Cuale, then becomes the rocky

Malecón (boardwalk). Near the southern end of Playa de los Muertos is a small section of the beach known as **Las Sillas Azules** (the blue chairs), one of Mexico's only **gay (male) beaches.**

Water sports are very popular, particularly during the morning hours. This is your chance to go **parasailing** (US$25 a shot, prices negotiable); parachutes are scattered on the Playa de Olas Altas and the beaches along the hotel strip, and owners will descend upon you like vultures if you look even remotely interested. Wave runners (doubles 250 pesos for 30min.), **banana boat** rides (50 pesos per person), **kayaks** (80 pesos per hr.), and **waterskiing** (500 pesos per hr.) are also there for the taking. **Bahía Deportes Aquaticos,** Olas Altas 477A (tel./fax 3 24 94), across from Señor Book Café, offers scuba certification classes (1 week, 8hr. per day, US$350), and introductory scuba diving classes (1½hr., US$15). Ask about renting scuba equipment, snorkeling equipment, and boats for excursions. (Open daily 7am-7pm.) **Chico's Dive Shop,** Díaz Ordaz 772 (tel. 2 18 95), on the Malecón, also offers scuba and snorkeling trips, as well as a diving certification program (open daily 8am-10pm; English spoken). Equestrian fanatics can boot the shore and take to the hills on **horseback;** rentals are available near Daiquiri Dick's on Olas Altas, at Carranza (horses 60 pesos per hr.; open daily around 7am-5:30pm).

Lots of new developments, condos, and resort facilities offer **freebies** to potential buyers. A common deal includes an invitation to eat a free meal at the resort, the opportunity to spend a few hours enjoying its facilities, half-price tickets to popular tours and cruises, and gift certificates to local stores and restaurants. The catch is that you have to spend about two hours listening to their ultra-high-pressure sales pitch, which can verge on coercion. Don't relinquish your credit card number, no matter what; remember, you are under no obligation to buy anything.

Isla Río Cuale lies between and underneath two bridges spanning the ponderous **Río Cuale.** A cool pathway runs the length of the verdant island among small stores selling postcards, jewelry, and souvenirs. The **Museo del Cuale,** at the seaward end of the island, houses interesting displays on Mesoamerican culture and the region's history (open Tu-Sa 10am-7pm, Su 10am-2pm; free). During the day, the walk along the river is pleasant, but do not try it alone after dark. The river can also be reached from the north via Zaragoza. Stairs, beginning behind the Church of Guadalupe, lead up the mini-mountain amid bougainvillea and hibiscus into the wealthy **Zaragoza** neighborhood, known locally as **Gringo Gulch.** The prominent bridge spanning the apex of the street connects Elizabeth Taylor's humble pad with Richard Burton's.

ENTERTAINMENT

After dark, Puerto Vallarta offers something for everyone, whether it's a cocktail in the moonlight or the chance to thrash across a crowded dance floor. The **Malecón** swarms with hundreds of U.S. and Mexican teeny-boppers batting eyelashes and showcasing their newly tanned bods. Most of the upscale action is along **Díaz Ordaz** on the northern waterfront, where clubs and restaurants cater to suntanned professionals quaffing pricey rum drinks and thrashing to U.S. top-40 tunes. Discos are aimed at those who don't mind dropping 40 to 50 pesos for cover and 15 to 20 pesos for a drink. For those clubs with covers, save a small fortune by obtaining free passes (which may not be honored during peak tourist season) from the condo-hawkers who lurk around the Malecón. Most discos aren't worth visiting until 11pm or midnight; the time before then is better spent tossing back drinks in cheap bars. Vallarta has sprouted a thriving **gay scene,** and boasts several clubs catering exclusively to gay men and, occasionally, to lesbians (see **Gay Nightlife** below).

Nightlife transportation is greatly aided by the "Marina Vallarta" bus, which goes to the marina, and the "Pitillal" bus, which will take you just past the hotel strip. After 11pm, you're stuck with a cab (about 35 pesos to the *centro*). For cheap fun, nothing beats the **pool hall,** Madero 279 (tel. 2 24 57). Pool is 10 pesos per hour and dominoes and backgammon are 6 pesos per hour, but the middle-aged men don't look too kindly upon female visitors (open daily 9am-1am). For some entertaining air-conditioning, take in a movie (20 pesos) at **Cine Bahía,** Insurgentes 189 (tel. 2 17 17), between Madero and Serdán.

Bars and Clubs

Carlos O'Brian's Bar & Grill & Clothesline (tel. 2 14 44), Díaz Ordaz at Pípila. The only things hanging out to dry here are totally trashed high-school students who've forgotten the names of their hotels. Teens bounce between here, **Kahlúa** (tel. 2 24 86), a few blocks south on the waterfront, and the **Zoo,** Díaz Ordaz 638 (tel. 2 49 45), next door (high-season weekend cover 50 pesos). It's the biggest party in town—block-long lines wrap around the building all night. Open daily 9am-4am.

Collage (tel. 1 08 61 62), next to Marina Vallarta, is big enough to house all of Vallarta. Bowling, pool tables, video games, a sushi bar (with cholera-free fish shipped from abroad), a sports bar in back, temporary tattoo parlors, an Internet cafe, and, of course, bars and a high-tech dance floor. Cover 50 pesos after 9pm. No cover Monday; no cover Wednesday for women; open bar Thursday. Cover 80 pesos for women, 120 pesos for men. Open daily 11am-6am.

J & B, Medina Ascencio km 2.5 (tel. 4 46 16), toward the hotel zone. An older crowd dances the night away to live salsa, merengue, and the occasional Michael Jackson tune. The raised dance floor makes it impossible to be shy. Those determined not to dance can play pool instead. Cover 50 pesos. Open daily 10pm-5am.

Club Roxy, Ingacio de Vallarta 217, between Madero and Carranza. A clientele of *extranjeros* jams to live reggae, blues, and rock and roll. Santana and Bob Marley covers are skillfully sung to a crowd of beer guzzlers (15 pesos) of all ages. No cover. Open M-Sa 8am-3am.

Cuiza (tel. 2 56 46), on Isla Río Cuale, at the foot of the *puente nuevo.* Doesn't get any mellower than this: find a table on the shady patio, order a margarita, and listen to the jazz. Mexican professionals and lots of new-waveish gringo couples. Live music daily 8pm-closing. Open daily 9am-1am; low season 5pm-midnight.

El Faro (tel. 1 05 41), in the Marina Vallarta. An elegant lighthouse bar 35m above ground provides a fantastic view of Puerto Vallarta, especially at sunset. Live music M-Sa after 10:30pm. 2-drink minimum. Open daily 5pm-2am.

Gay Nightlife

A **gay cruise,** departing daily at noon from the Los Muertos pier, takes partners Noah's ark-style to a private gay beach (includes drinks, snorkeling, and table dancing; around US$45). Tickets are available from travel agents or time-share hawkers; for more info, ask at Paco Paco (below). Also, a free boat to a private gay beach leaves daily at noon from Boca de Tomatlán.

Paco Paco, Ignacio Vallarta 578 at Lázaro Cárdenas, is Vallarta's hottest gay disco, with great music, lots of dance floor, mirrors, strobe lights, and aquariums. The friendly owner is a fount of information on Vallarta's gay scene. Transvestite show F-Su 1:30am, strip show daily 12:30am. Th-Su 30 peso cover for men, 60 pesos for women with one drink. Open daily noon-6am.

Porque No, Morelos 101 (tel. 3 62 19), on the Plaza Río next to the Vallarta Bridge. Art Deco coffee and video bar (with pool tables) sits above the vibrations of a rocking basement below. Wall-to-wall dancing—perhaps because there's no room at the bar. Almost exclusively gay men. Happy hour noon-8pm. Open daily noon-3am.

Los Balcones, Juárez 182 (tel. 2 46 71), at Libertad. International gay crowd practices looking languid on the balconies. Scantily dressed patrons sizzle on the neon-lit dance floor. Mixed drinks half-off on Fridays. Starts hopping at 11:30pm. Beer 10 pesos on M. Cover F-Sa 10-15 pesos. Open daily 9pm-4am.

■ Near Puerto Vallarta: Southern Coast

Vallarta's most popular beaches lie a few kilometers south of the city itself. The first few you'll come across are monopolized by resorts and condos, and though they're nicer and quieter than the ones back in town, access to them is usually only through the hotels. Farther down the coast lies **Los Arcos,** a group of pretty rock islands hollowed out in some spots by pounding waves. The coastline here lacks sand, but it still serves as a platform from which to start the 150m swim to the islands. Bring a mask or goggles, or risk missing the tropical fish that flit through the underwater reefscape. Flippers are useful against the heavy currents but mind your step—the coral is sharp enough to draw blood; use caution and swim with a friend. To get to Los Arcos, take the bus to Mismaloya and ask the driver to stop at Hotel de los Arcos. The beautiful crescent beach of **Mismaloya** lies just around the bend to the south. Best known as the setting of *Night of the Iguana* and Arnold Schwarzenegger's *cinéma vérité* classic, *Predator,* Mismaloya has recently been encircled by large hotels and is only slightly less crowded than the beaches in town. **Xanadu** is a gay club near this beach. Farther down, the road veers away from the coast just beyond the **Boca de Tomatlán;** this narrow cove contains only a small beach but offers a breather from the touristy hubbub of the northern coastline. The last place to check out on the southern road is **Chico's Paradise,** 5km inland from the Boca de Tomatlán. Wash down the view of the **Tomatlán Falls** with a drink at Chico's huge, airy *palapas.*

Farther south along the coast lie the beaches of Las Ánimas, Quimixto, and Yelapa, all of which are only accessible from the ocean. However, these lovely beaches are not deserted; they're inhabited by hordes of nacho-chomping tourists dropped off daily by cruise boats from Vallarta. **Las Ánimas** and **Quimixto** are twins, both boasting long stretches of unoccupied sand backed by small villages and a few *palapas.* Quimixto also offers a small waterfall as an alternative to the beach-weary. The trip can be made in an hour by foot from the beach or in 30 minutes by rented mule. **Scuba** trips (organized by Outcast—see p. 312—and others) also make their way from downtown Vallarta and Mismaloya to these beaches. **Yelapa,** destination of the popular boat ride and highly touted by locals, is a bit of a fake. Supposedly a secluded peasant fishing village, its seemingly simple *palapa* huts were designed by a *norteamericano* architect whose definition of "rustic" apparently included interior plumbing and hot water. Many of these *palapas* are occupied for only part of the year, and short- and long-term rentals can be arranged easily for varying and sometimes surprisingly low prices. The beach fills with hawkers and parasailers during the day, but the town, a 15-minute walk from the beach, remains *tranquilo,* with waterfalls and nude bathing upstream and poetry readings downstream. Don't miss the secluded swimming hole at the top of the stream that runs through town; follow the path along the stream uphill; just before the restaurant, duck under the water pipes to the right of the trail and head up the track. About 15m before it rejoins the stream bed, an inconspicuous trail leads off to the left to a deep pool that overlooks the bay.

Getting There: Buses run to Mismaloya from the corner of Constitución and Badillo in Puerto Vallarta (every 10min. 6:20am-10:30pm, 2.50 pesos; returning on the same schedule). Taxis to Mismaloya cost 50 pesos. Buses labeled "Tuito" run to Chico's Paradise from the corner of Carranza and Aguacate (every 30min. 5am-9pm, 6 pesos). **Taxis Acuáticos** are the cheapest way to get to the boats-only beaches. They leave from the Muelle de los Muertos and stop at Las Ánimas, Quimixto, and Yelapa (45min., departs at 11am, and returns at 4pm, 60 pesos each way). If you prefer something more organized, **cruises** to points south of Vallarta leave the marina every day starting at 9am and return around 4pm. The cheapest cruises to Yelapa are 180 pesos, including breakfast and music. The more expensive cruises include dinner and an open bar. Information about these ritzy tours can be found in the tourist office, at any large hotel, or at the marina.

■ Near Puerto Vallarta: Northern Coast

Bahía de Banderas (Bay of Flags), the bay that Puerto Vallarta calls home, owes its name to a blunder: when Nuño Beltrán de Guzmán sailed here in 1532, he mistook the colorful headdresses of the thousands of natives awaiting him for flags. The northern edge of the bay has some of the prettiest and least-exploited beaches on Mexico's central Pacific coast. Nuevo Vallarta, the largest and southernmost of nine small towns on the north bay, is 150km south of Tepic and 20km north of Puerto Vallarta.

Protected by a sandy cove, **Playa Piedra Blanca** has wonderfully calm waters. Farther north along the bay is **Playa las Destiladeras,** named for the freshwater pools formed by water trickling through the rocky cliff. Although the sandy bottom is colored with occasional rocks, the rougher waves make this strip of beach a haven for body-surfers and boogie-boarders. **Punta de Mita,** the northernmost point along the bay, is a lagoon sheltered by two rock islets. It is marked by the **Corral de Riscos,** a living reef. Freshwater showers (2 pesos) in Destiladeras make the bus ride home more comfortable. Bring a bag lunch to avoid inflated prices in beachside *palapas.*

Getting There: From Puerto Vallarta, flag down a Camiones del Pacífico "Punta de Mita" second-class bus on Lázaro Cárdenas, Insurgentes, Juárez, or Medino Ascencio (every 20min. 9am-5pm, returning until 5pm; to Piedra Blanca 40min., 8 pesos; to Destiladeras 1hr., 10 pesos; to Punta de Mita 1¼hr. plus a 4km walk, 12 pesos).

Bahía de Chamela

The tranquil and secluded **Bahía de Chamela,** 60km northwest of Melaque, marks the northern point of Jalisco's "Ecological Tourism Corridor." A chain of small rocky islands breaks the horizon, while 11km of golden-brown sand dotted with gnarled driftwood and the occasional *palapa* beckon to the pensive beachcomber. Although Chamela receives its share of tourism, especially in December and April, the Midas touch has yet to spoil the natural beauty and seclusion of the bay. This, however, presents other problems; lone travelers (particularly women) and small groups should use common sense in deciding which beaches to visit, particularly during the low season. Perula is the more populated of the two, but neither is completely protected.

Second-class buses from Puerto Vallarta to Manzanillo (3½hr., 40 pesos) pass through Perula, as do buses going from Melaque or Barra de Navidad to Puerto Vallarta (1½hr., 27 pesos) or Manzanillo (3hr., 49 pesos). Always tell the bus driver where you're going in advance so you don't miss the stop. To get to Playa Perula, get off by the big white "Playa Dorada" sign and walk 30 minutes down a winding dirt road—don't be surprised if friendly locals offer you a ride. To get to Playa Chamela, get off farther south at "El Súper," marked by the colorful figure directing passersby to the Villa Polinesia; walk 15 minutes down the country road until you hit the beach. Perula is a 30-minute walk along the shore. Hotels in Perula will also come pick you up or send a taxi. Unfortunately, there's only a **LATADEL** shell outside the Primera Plus Station, so your best bet for placing a long-distance call is cajoling one of the hotel or restaurant owners into letting you call collect. To get back, catch a **Primera Plus** bus from that station. They head to Guadalajara (3hr., 8, 10:30am, and 4pm, 50 pesos), Manzanillo (2½-5hr., every hr. 7:30am-10:30pm, 48-60 pesos), and Puerto Vallarta (every hr. 7:30am-10:30pm, 58 pesos) via Melaque (1½hr., 27-35 pesos).

Punta de Perula, the bay's northernmost point, shelters **Playa Perula,** making it perfect for swimming. A half-hour walk down the coast along completely virgin beach will bring you to the **Villa Polinesia Motel and Campsite,** marking **Playa Chamela.** Here, and farther south, the rougher waves invite body-surfing and boogie-boarding—though they have a strong undertow and can sometimes get rough. **Perula** is a tiny fishing *pueblo* whose main attraction is, well, the beach. The town lacks most services, but has a few hotels and seafood-serving *palapas.* Continuing south will bring you to **Playa Rosada** and even more secluded beaches. The occasional *palapa* refreshes the parched and weary bodysurfer. *Lanchas* from Playa Perula transport wannabe Crusoes to the nearby islands (round-trip about 200-250 pesos).

The **Hotel Punta Perula** (tel. 328 5 50 20) is at the corner of Juárez and Tiburón, two blocks from the beach. The Punta Perula features a massive courtyard laden with trees and overhanging hammocks that eclipse the comfortable, floral room. (Low season singles 100 pesos; doubles 155 pesos. High season singles 125 pesos; doubles 175 pesos.) In Perula, **Tejamar Restaurante y Cuartos** (tel. 328 5 53 61), on the corner of Independencia and the *carretera* (highway) on the *jardín,* one block south of

Hotel Punta Perula and less than a block from the beach, is a small, family-run taco restaurant and *posada.* Its basic rooms have ceiling fans and open onto a small courtyard. Friendly owners are eager to accommodate guests with bargain meals, trips to the nearby islands, and weekly discounts. (Singles and doubles with communal bath 80 pesos; private bath 100 pesos.) Feast on the catch of the day as you relax under palm frond umbrellas at **Mariscos La Sirena** (tel. 328 5 51 14), one of the several *palapas* along the shore. It serves shrimp (45 pesos) and fish (40 pesos). A cold one costs six well-spent pesos. (Open daily 7am-8pm, or until the last person leaves.)

Bahía de Navidad

Along with Guadalajara and Puerto Vallarta, Bahía de Navidad forms one vertex of Jalisco's "Tourist Triangle." Power is not shared equally within the triumvirate, however: with the exception of December and *Semana Santa,* few tourists are spotted on the placid shores of Bahía de Navidad. The *bahía,* a sheltered cove of talcum sand and shimmering water, is home to the towns of **Melaque** and **Barra de Navidad.** Both boast sparkling white sand beaches that frame spectacular crimson sunsets between two spits of a cove. Given their dearth of tourism and small size, both make excellent getaways. During high season, however, their growing pains are more evident, as the beach stretching between the towns is transformed into a river of bronzed bodies, and hotels in both towns overflow with tourists. Change is in the air: restaurants, hotels, and clubs are sprouting with great frequency; a Xanadu-esque hotel at the end of the bay opened in early 1997, and a 300-boat marina under construction threatens to overwhelm the bay with hordes of yachting foreigners.

Although Barra and Melaque lie only 5km apart, Melaque is worlds better than its counterpart: better beach, better hotels, better everything. While Barra offers few places to eat and sleep and a steep beach with powerful undertow (better for surfing or boogie-boarding than swimming), Melaque treats visitors to gentle, choppy waves—a swimmer's dream—and an abundance of quality budget accommodations. Visit Melaque quickly before its small-town cream is skimmed off by tourist dollars.

Melaque and Barra de Navidad are 55km northwest of Manzanillo on Rte. 200 and 240km southwest of Guadalajara on Rte. 54. Melaque is the northernmost of the two. They're well connected by road: **municipal buses** shuttle between the two towns (20min., every 15min. 6:20am-9:30pm, 1-1.50 pesos). Larger buses head to Manzanillo on the hour and are slightly more expensive (around 5 pesos) but faster and more comfortable. Of course, the 40-minute walk along the beach is the hard-core budget option. Don't walk after sunset; some incidents have been reported. **Taxis** cost 25 pesos.

Bahía de Navidad: Melaque

The placid town of Melaque offers little besides ambling through the *zócalo,* splashing around in the waves, and nibbling on fresh fish as you watch the sunset, but no one seems to complain. There's not much to do in beautiful Melaque. Savor it.

ORIENTATION AND PRACTICAL INFORMATION Melaque's bus station (tel. 5 50 03) is on **Gómez Farías,** the parallel-to-the-beach main drag. From the bus station, turn left on Gómez Farías and walk two blocks to reach **López Mateos.** Another left turn takes you to the plaza, a few blocks inland. López Mateos and **Hidalgo** are the main cross-streets toward the ocean.

Autocamiones Cihuatlán (tel. 5 50 03) sends **buses** to Guadalajara (6½ hr., 21 per day 12:15am-10:30pm, 110-132 pesos), Manzanillo (1½hr., every 30min. 5:30am-9:30pm, 22-27 pesos), and Puerto Vallarta (5hr., 14 per day 1:15-11:30pm, 77-91 pesos) via Chamela (1½hr., 22 pesos) and Perula (1½hr., 27 pesos). A few doors down, **Primera Plus,** Gomez Farías 34 (tel. 5 61 10), has service to Guadalajara (5hr., 10 per day 8am-8:30pm, 110-132 pesos), Manzanillo (1½hr., 15 per day 2am-10:30pm, 22-27 pesos), and Puerto Vallarta (5½hr., 8 per day 1:45am-9pm, 77-91 pesos); second-class service passes through Chamela (1½hr, 22 pesos) and Perula (1½hr, 27 pesos).

Banamex (tel. 5 52 77 or 5 53 52) is on Gómez Farías, across from the bus station and has a 24-hour **ATM**. (Open M-F 9am-3pm, Sa 9am-2pm; changes traveler's checks 9am-noon.) The **police** are upstairs at López Mateos 52 (tel. 5 50 80), north of the plaza. The **Red Cross** (tel. 5 23 00) is 15km away in Cihuatlán, accessible by buses that leave from the plaza (every 15min. 6am-8pm, 4 pesos) or by taxi (50 pesos). **Súper Farmacia Plaza,** López Mateos 48 (tel. 5 51 67), is on the south side of the plaza (open M-Sa 8am-3pm and 5-10pm, Su 8am-2:30pm and 6:30-10pm). **Clínica de Urgencias,** Carranza 22 (tel. 5 61 44), two blocks from the bus station, provides emergency service. The **post office,** José Clemente Orozco 13 (tel. 5 52 30), is two blocks left of the plaza as you face the beach, in the green building on your left (open M-F 8am-3pm, Sa 8am-noon). The **postal code** is 48980. **E-mail** and **Internet access** are available inside the *centro commercial,* Gómez Farías #27 A (tel. 5 59 19), next to the casa de cambio (open M-Sa noon-2:30pm, 4-6pm, and 8:30-10pm). Melaque is home to several **casetas;** convenient to the bus station is **"Yimmi's,"** Gómez Farías 34 (tel. 5 63 10; fax 5 54 52), next to the station (open M-Sa 8:30am-9pm, Su 8:30am-3pm; open until 10pm daily during high season). The public telephones by the bus station will let you make **long-distance collect calls.** The **phone code** is 335.

ACCOMMODATIONS AND FOOD Melaque boasts a crop of snazzy budget hotels, and bargains aplenty await the persistent and inquisitive. Most budget accommodations in Melaque are inland, near the *centro.* A bargain occasionally lurks among the beachside bungalows. Expect rates to rise, of course, during high season. If you don't mind a little innocent proselytizing, **Hotel Emanuel,** Bugambilias 89 (tel. 5 61 07), is half a block from the beach and two blocks south of Restaurant Kosonoy; look for the "Abarrotes Emanuel" sign. Spacious rooms have floral decor and clean, white-tile bathrooms, but no hot water. (Singles 50 pesos, 100 pesos with kitchen; doubles 80 pesos, 150 pesos with kitchen.) **La Sirenita** (tel. 5 55 99) is about two blocks toward the *zócalo* from Restaurant Kosonoy. Old but clean rooms are virtually on top of the water, but there is no hot water. (Low season 70 pesos for up to 4 people, high season 150 pesos.)

During the summer, restaurants ship in shrimp from the north, but come high season, local fishing boats catch everything that is served on the waterfront. More authentic (and less expensive) Mexican places can be found near the central plaza. Cheaper still are the sidewalk food stands that materialize after the sunset and the unnamed, dirt-floored eateries in the *mercado* and near the bus station. **La Flor Morena,** Juárez 21, on the *zócalo,* welcomes locals and expats alike with great, filling Mexican food at unbelievably low prices. Owner Ambita whips up cheap *tamales* (2.50 pesos) and enchiladas (10 pesos). Wash it down with a beer (4.50 pesos; open Tu-Su 6-11pm). **Restaurant Kosonoy** (tel. 5 62 81), at the end of the row of *palapas* on the beach, 200m beyond the huge Hotel Casa Grande, serves scrumptious avocado dip (12 pesos) and octopus salad (45 pesos; open daily 9am-8pm).

SAND, SURF, AND ENTERTAINMENT The main attraction in Melaque is, of course, the beach. Waves get smaller and the beach more crowded toward the western end of Melaque's sandy strip. Rent **jet-skis** at the Restaurant Moyo (tel. 7 11 04), on the far west end of the beach (200 pesos for 30min., 2 person maximum; available daily 10am-7pm). Be prepared to get wet if you go for a spin in a **banana boat** (20 pesos). Drivers regularly dump unsuspecting riders into the ocean. Although not many come to Melaque for the nightlife (for good reason), few refuse when it's thrust upon them. **Disco Tanga** (tel. 5 54 72 or 5 54 75), on Gómez Farías, is the after-hours oasis of Melaque's under-30 (but over-18, mind you) tourist crowd. Multicolored walls and stairs lined by strip lights create a game show effect. (Cover 20-30 pesos; open daily in high season, F-Sa off-season, 9pm-2am.) For something a bit more mellow and smoky, you can always twirl cues with the middle-aged men at **Billiard San Patricio,** Melaque's pool hall, on Orozco and Juárez, up the street from the post office, three blocks from the *zócalo* (pool and *carambola* 10 pesos per hr., dominoes 3 pesos per hr.; open daily 11am-11pm). Women will probably feel more comfortable elsewhere. Don't get your hopes up during the low season, though; nightlife just about dies for those months of the year.

■ Bahía de Navidad: Barra de Navidad

Though not nearly as alluring as Melaque, Barra de Navidad still boasts picture-book beaches ready for the taking. Facilities are lacking, but if you've come to sleep, sun, or sip cocktails—enjoy.

ORIENTATION AND PRACTICAL INFORMATION Barra de Navidad is a narrow peninsula flanked on its eastern shore by a salty, sleeping *laguna;* the restless waves tug at its western shore. Virtually everything closes during low season. **Veracruz,** the main street, runs towards the southeast, angling off at its end. There it meets **Legazpi,** another main street, which runs north-south, hugging the beach. Barra de Navidad's bus stop is at Veracruz 226, on the corner of Nayarit. Turn left on Veracruz from the bus station to get to the *centro.* **Buses** depart from **Autocamiones Cihuatlán,** Veracruz 228 (tel. 5 52 65), at Michoacán, to Guadalajara (6hr., 17 per day 3:15am-midnight, 111-133 pesos) and Puerto Vallarta (5½hr., 10 per day 7am-9:15pm, 78-93 pesos); second-class buses pass through Chanela (1½hr., 22 pesos) and Perula (1½hr., 27 pesos). **Primera Plus/Costa Alegre,** Veracruz 269 (tel. 5 61 11), at Filipinas, has service to Guadalajara (6½hr., 9 per day 7:45am-8:30pm, 111-133 pesos), and Manzanillo (1¼-5hr., 6 per day 11:45am-7:30pm, 26-78 pesos). Second-class buses stop at Chamela (1½hr., 22 pesos) and Perula (1½hr., 27 pesos).

The **tourist office** is at Jalisco 67 (tel. 5 51 00; open M-F 9am-5pm). The friendly Texans at **Crazy Cactus** (tel. 5 60 99), next to the church on Jalisco, between Legazpi and Veracruz, can help you out with insider's advice. The **travel agency,** Veracruz 204A (tel. 5 56 65, 66; fax 5 56 67), sells tickets for ETN buses departing from Manzanillo (open M-Sa 9am-8pm). Barra has no bank, but a **casa de cambio,** Veracruz 212C (tel. 5 61 77), exchanges money at a less-than-ideal rate(open M-Sa 9am-2pm and 4-7pm, Su 9am-2pm). For a better exchange rate, try the **Banamex** in Melaque. Barra de Navidad is without a *caseta,* so your best long-distance calling option is to use LADATEL calling cards (available in many of the convenience stores with the "old Venta" sign).

Police wait 'round-the-clock at Veracruz 179 (tel. 5 53 99). The **Centro de Salud** (tel. 5 62 20), on Puerto de la Navidad, is down Veracruz, just out of town. Make a right just after the signs for El Márquez, just before Veracruz becomes a highway; the Centro is the second building on the right, with the red and white gate. (Emergency service is available 24hr.) The **postal code** is 48987. The **phone code** is 335.

ACCOMMODATIONS AND CAMPING Budget accommodations in Barra are available only to the keen-eyed traveler, and they lack the charm and cleanliness of Melaque's hotels. Reasonable accommodations are sometimes available in private residences—ask around and look for signs in restaurants. All prices are subject to hikes during the *temporada alta.* It's no longer possible to camp in Barra de Navidad; try Melaque instead. **Casa de Huéspedes Caribe,** Sonora 15 (tel. 5 57 48; fax 5 52 37), has decent pastel rooms with fans and fluorescent-lit desks. The large lobby is enlivened by socializing elderly ladies. (Singles 90 pesos; doubles 125 pesos.) **Bungalows Karelia,** on Legazpi, on the beach between Hotel Bogavante and the Mexican armada, is a good deal for three or more people. Airy but worn suites house a refrigerator, table, stove, fan, and kitchen utensils. The romantic little loveseats aren't shabby either. (Suites for 2 people 220 pesos, 20 pesos each extra person.)

Try **Los Arcos,** Mazatlán 163 (tel. 5 58 76), across from the Posada Pacífico, for some of the best Mexican food in town. Enjoy *huevos al gusto,* juice, and coffee (15 pesos) in the outdoor patio. *Chiles rellenos* go for 20 pesos. (Open daily 9am-9pm.) For delicious, inexpensive Mexican food in a pleasant atmosphere, try **Restaurant Paty,** Jalisco 52 at Veracruz—dark red tablecloths lend to the semi-romantic atmosphere (grilled *pollo* 23 pesos, enchiladas 12 pesos; open daily 7am-11pm).

SIGHTS AND ENTERTAINMENT **Crazy Cactus** (tel. 5 60 99), at the corner of Jalisco and Veracruz, rents out **snorkeling** equipment and **boogie boards** (12 pesos per hr., 60 pesos per day), **surfboards** (20 pesos per hr., 100 pesos per day), and

Telenovela, Anyone?

Every evening, grown men and women across Mexico will be found glued to their TV sets, clutching boxes of Kleenex and seeming impervious to the outside world. Why? They are watching *telenovelas,* the strange hybrids between soap operas and mini-series that monopolize Mexico's airwaves from afternoon to late night. Mexico has made a name for itself internationally with these heart-wrenching and addictive shows. Each *telenovela* lasts between six months and one year and contains enough cliched love stories, tragedies, and cliff-hangers to put all other series to shame. In fact, characters and story lines are added and removed according to ratings; as a result, each show's plot is, in part, guided by audience response. This explains why the protagonist of a poorly watched show might suddenly get hit by a 4x4 truck and his younger, sexier brother will be called upon to assume the leading role. Having celebrated its 40th birthday in 1998, the *telenovela* looks like it's here to stay.

bikes (80 pesos per day). It also organizes bilingual **daytrips** to secluded **Tenacatita Bay,** where you can snorkel along a coral reef (boat trip, seafood, drinks, and gear 350 pesos per person). Serious fishers will want to call **Z Pesca,** Legazpi 213 (tel. 5 64 64; fax 5 64 65; http://www.zpesca.com), for a day-long **deep-sea fishing** expedition (1000 pesos per day; open daily 9am-7pm, high season 9am-9pm).

The short trip across the lagoon to the village of **Colimilla** is pleasant; a *lancha* will deposit up to 10 passengers at the far end of the lagoon or amid Colimilla's palms, pigs, cows, and open-air restaurants (60 pesos). Deserted **Playa de los Cocos,** 1km away, has larger breakers than those in Barra. If you don't want to swim back, remember to set a time to be picked up. Up to eight people can tour the lagoon behind Barra for 80 pesos. For 150 pesos per hour, up to four people can take a fully equipped *lancha* for tuna or marlin fishing. Operators formed a cooperative, so prices are fixed. Their office and docks lie at the end of Veracruz (office open daily 7am-7pm). Bibliophiles should not miss **Beer Bob's Book Exchange,** Mazatlán 61, a few blocks to the right as you face the Posada Pacífico. It's purely a book *exchange*—no cash involved. It's quite a collection. In the back room sit Bob and company, watching TV, playing cards, or engaging in "some serious beer-drinking." (Usually open M-F 1-4pm.)

Everyone out past midnight parties at **El Galeón Disco,** Morelos 24 (tel. 5 50 18), in Hotel Sand's. Sit on cushioned horseshoe-shaped benches as you quaff a beer for 8 pesos or a mixed drink for 16 pesos. (Cover 10-20 pesos; open F-Sa 9pm-3am, daily during high season.) Those who prefer singing to dancing may want to mellow out at the **Terraza Bar Jardín,** Jalisco 70 (tel. 5 61 35), a **karaoke** bar. Somebody will sing "New York, New York" all night if you won't. Beer goes for 8 pesos. (Open daily 6pm-2am.) If you just want to concentrate your efforts on drinking, make your way to **Piper Lovers,** Legazpi 138A (tel. 5 64 34), where drinks are cheap and **pool** and **ping-pong** are free for customers. (Beer 8-12 pesos, mixed drinks start at 10 pesos; open daily 9pm-2am.) If you tire of Piper Lovers, the many two-for-one happy hours along Legazpi make the giddy trip toward inebriation that much cheaper.

COLIMA

Manzanillo

Manzanillo (pop. 115,000) is home to the state's finest beaches, but you'd never know it from its dynamic, sweaty *centro* and the throngs of ships hugging the shore. Most tourists avoid central Manzanillo altogether and head to the glossy resorts on the city's two bays north and west of town. Thanks to a fortuitous combination of currents and latitude, Manzanillo is cooler in the summer than Puerto Vallarta and Acapulco. Reasonably priced hotels lie in the midst of the loud and brazen port action—those seeking only sand and surf would do better to retreat to some secluded village, such as Cuyutlán or Barra de Navidad, where there is no metropolis between the hotels and the Pacific. But for those excited by the prospect of beautiful, immensely popular beaches—and a real city—Manzanillo delivers.

ORIENTATION

Manzanillo lies 98km west of Colima and 355km south of Guadalajara. The **Jardín Obregón,** Manzanillo's *zócalo,* is the most useful orientation point in town. It faces north onto the harbor, but boxcars often obstruct the glorious view of oil tankers. **Morelos** runs east-west along the north (waterfront) edge of the plaza; **Dávalos,** which becomes **Juárez,** runs along the south. **Av. Mexico,** Manzanillo's main street, runs south from the plaza; most hotels and services are nearby. The "Centro" bus runs from the station to the corner of 21 de Marzo and Hidalgo (2 pesos). From the corner, a right turn on Allende and another on México will take you to the *zócalo.* A taxi from the bus station to the center of town costs 6 pesos. White and blue "Miramar" buses provide the main transportation to Manzanillo's beaches and the main strip, **Blvd. Costera Miguel de la Madrid;** they run along México, around the plaza, and turn on Morelos heading for the boulevard (about every 15min. 5am-11pm; price varies by destination).

PRACTICAL INFORMATION

Transportation

Airport: (tel. 3 11 19 or 3 25 25). In Playa de Oro, on the highway between Barra de Navidad and Manzanillo. Airlines include **Aerocalifornia** (tel. 4 12 90), **Aeromar** (tel. 3 01 51), and **Mexicana** (tel. 3 23 23). **Viajes Vamos a...,** Carrillo Puerto 259 (tel. 2 17 11), 1 block west of México and 3 blocks south of the *zócalo,* can facilitate ticket purchase. Open M-F 9am-2pm and 4-7pm, Sa 9am-2pm. **Colectivos** (60 pesos) transport passengers to the airport 2hr. before take-off (45min., daily 9am-1:30pm and 5-7pm); call the airport to make arrangements. **Taxis** from the airport to the *zócalo* cost 120 pesos. Taxis back to the airport cost 165 pesos.

Buses: On Hidalgo, on the outskirts of town between Laguna Cuyutlán and the ocean. Taxis to the *centro* 6 pesos. **Autobuses de Occidente** (tel. 2 01 23) serves Mexico City (16hr., 6 per day 2:45am-7:30pm, 269 pesos). **Autobuses de Jalisco** (tel. 2 01 23) provides first-class service to Colima (1hr., 8 per day 4:45am-9:30pm, 26 pesos), Guadalajara (4hr., 8 per day 1am-11:30pm, 103 pesos), Morelia (8hr., 10:45pm, 167 pesos), and Uruapan (8hr., 8:30pm, 130 pesos). **Autocamiones Cihuatlán** (tel. 2 05 15) provides second-class service to Guadalajara (6hr., 6 per day 9am-midnight, 125 pesos), and Puerto Vallarta (6½hr., 10 per day 7:30am-10pm, 98-118 pesos), stopping at Melaque and Barra de Navidad (1½hr., 22-27 pesos). **Autotransportes Sur de Jalisco** (tel. 2 10 03) serves Colima (1½hr., 2:45pm, 24 pesos). **Primera Plus** (tel. 2 02 10) sends buses to Puerto Vallarta (5hr., 12:30am, 118 pesos) and Querétaro (12hr., 6:15pm, 216 pesos). **Transportes Costalegre** (tel. 2 02 10) runs buses to Melaque and Barra de Navidad (1½hr., every hr. 4am-12:30am, 22 pesos). **Elite** (tel. 2 04 32) provides cushy service to Acapulco (12hr., 6am, 267 pesos), Mexico City (21hr., 7:30pm, 330 pesos), Zihuatanejo (8hr., 6am, 155 pesos), and Tijuana (36hr., 4 and 9pm, 896 pesos) via Hermosillo (24hr., 711 pesos), Mazatlán (12hr., 303 pesos), and Tepic (7hr., 186 pesos). There is a 24hr. **luggage storage** booth in the bus station (6 pesos per day).

Tourist and Financial Services

Tourist Office: Blvd. Costera Miguel de la Madrid 1033 (tel. 3 22 64 or 3 22 77; fax 3 14 26), 2 blocks past Fiesta Mexicana. Catch a "Miramar" bus (2.50 pesos) and tell the driver where you're headed. Open M-F 9am-3pm and 5-7:30pm. Helpful **tourist police** (tel. 2 10 02) reside in the Palacio Municipal on the *zócalo* and distribute maps and brochures about Manzanillo and other locations throughout the state of Colima. **Information booths** are in front of the *palacio,* around town, and along the beaches (open M-F 9am-7pm, daily in high season).

Currency Exchange: Bital, México 99 (tel. 2 21 50 or 2 09 50), at 10 de Mayo, has slightly better rates and longer hours than most banks. Open M-Sa 8am-7pm. **ATM** across the street at **Banamex.**

Local Services

Laundromat: Lavi-Matic, Hidalgo 1 (tel. 2 08 44), down Av. Mexico across the small plaza. Open M-Sa 8am-7pm. Wash and dry 3 kilos for 24 pesos.

Emergency and Communications

Police: (tel. 2 10 02 or 2 10 04), on Juárez in the Palacio Municipal, facing the *jardín.*

Red Cross: (tel. 6 57 70), on Av. Barotes. Open 24hr.

Pharmacy: Farmacia Manzanillo, Juárez 10 (tel. 2 01 85 or 3 24 11), on the south side of the *zócalo.* English spoken. Open daily 8:30am-midnight.

Hospital: (tel. 2 00 29), in Colonia San Pedrito Sector 7. Open 24hr. Some English spoken.

Post Office: Calle Miguel Galindo 30 (tel. 2 00 22), 3 blocks down Mexico from the *zócalo.* Open M-F 8am-7pm, Sa 9am-1pm. **Postal Code:** 28200.

Fax: Telecomm (tel. 2 30 30), in the Palacio Municipal, to the left of the stairs as you enter. Also sends **telegrams.** Open M-F 8am-6pm and Sa-Su 9am-12:30pm.

Internet Access: Juárez 115, 2nd floor (tel. 2 26 60), half a block down from the *zócalo*. Open M-F 10am-2pm and 5-9pm, Sa 5-9pm. 13 pesos for 30min.

Telephones: Computel, México 302 (tel. 2 39 26), at Galindo; another on Morelos, half a block east of the *zócalo,* next to Banca Serfín. Both open daily 7am-10pm.

Phone Code: 333.

ACCOMMODATIONS

Manzanillo's budget accommodations tend to be basic and plain, but you'll be on the beach the whole time anyway. Hotels near the *zócalo* are in a safer area than those near the bus station. **Camping** on Playa Miramar is feasible during *Semana Santa* and in December, when bathroom facilities are available and security is heightened.

Hotel Flamingo, Madero 72 (tel. 2 10 37), 1 block south of the *zócalo*. Old Spanish-style rooms with stucco walls and heavy wooden furniture. Try for a breezier corner room. Singles 55 pesos; doubles 80 pesos.

Hotel Emperador, Dávalos 69 (tel. 2 23 74), 1 block west of the plaza. Small rooms enlivened by rustic wooden furniture and ceiling fans. Singles 60 pesos; doubles 80-100 pesos.

Hotel Costa Manzanillo, Madero 333 (tel. 2 27 40), at Vicente Guerrero. Walk 2 blocks down México, take a left on Allende, your first right on Madero, and continue for 1½ blocks. Coral pink facade encloses spotless rooms with fan, TV, and well-scrubbed, spacious bathrooms. Purified water adds to the fun. Singles 100 pesos; doubles 120 pesos.

FOOD

Since tourists mostly stake their claims closer to the beach, food at the market and in downtown restaurants is simple and cheap. A few blocks from the plaza, at Cuauhtémoc and Madero, is a market with numerous family-run and inexpensive *fondas.*

Restaurante Chantilly (tel. 2 01 94), at Juárez and Moreno, on the plaza. Crowds of newspaper-reading professionals, flocks of families, and stragglers off the *zócalo* munch on fantastically good Mexican staples in a diner-like setting. Enchiladas 20 pesos. Mango *licuados* (8 pesos) are as good as it gets. Open Su-F 7:30am-10:30pm.

Restaurant Emperador, Dávalos 69 (tel. 2 23 74), below the eponymous hotel. The blank walls, white tablecloths, and fluorescent lights aren't nearly as pleasing to the eye as the food is to the palate. Gargantuan *comida corrida* for a mere 17 pesos. *Chiles rellenos* only 18 pesos; hotcakes 8 pesos. Open daily 8am-10pm.

Los Naranjos, México 366. Look hard: the white and red cafe is difficult to spot. When it rains, time stands still here; so do the flies and fans. Locals come here in droves to chow down on tasty entrees served with a mountain of tortillas, rice, and beans (20 pesos). Open M-Sa 7am-7pm.

SIGHTS

Manzanillo's beaches stretch from west to east along two bays, **Bahía de Manzanillo** and **Bahía de Santiago,** formed by the Santiago and Juluapan Peninsulas. The Bahía de Manzanillo has more expensive hotels and cleaner golden sand. Unfortunately, its beach slopes steeply, creating a strong and sometimes dangerous undertow. The beaches at Bahía Santiago, though twice as far from the *centro* and bordered by a noisy highway, are better protected by the Juluapan peninsula, providing a panoramic vista of the rugged terrain and more tranquil surf. The bay is ideal for swimming and water sports; it's very popular with sun worshippers.

The closest good beach on Bahía Manzanillo, **Playa Las Brisas,** has a few secluded spots, but for the most part is crowded with luxurious hotels and bungalows. To get to Las Brisas from downtown Manzanillo, take a taxi (25 pesos) or the "Las Brisas" bus (3 pesos). Catch the bus on Mexico or on the highway going toward the airport and Barra de Navidad. Alternatively, catch the "Miramar" bus and ask the driver to let you off at the *crucero* (crossroads), then turn left to populated shores or stake out a private piece of beach right at the junction.

The "Miramar" bus continues west of Peninsula Santiago, gear-grinding toward other excellent beaches on Bahía Santiago. Because this part of the bay is not used for shipping, the water is cleaner than at Las Brisas. Beyond **Olas Altas,** a beach popular with experienced (largely American) surfers but infamous for its powerful waves and dangerous undertow, is **Miramar Beach.** Get off where the footbridge crosses the highway. This is the most crowded section of the beach, but it boasts top-notch beachfront restaurants from which you can **rent body boards and surfboards** (15 pesos per hr.). Crowds thin out 20m to the east or west.

The calmer waters of the *palapa*-lined **Playa la Boquita,** the westernmost point on the Juluapan Peninsula, make this a popular spot for children and water sports. **Club Eureka** (tel. 6 57 02) is the last *palapa* on the shore. It offers **banana boat** rides (20 pesos, price negotiable), **water skiing** (US$20 per hr.), **snorkeling gear** (80 pesos for full day use), snorkeling excursions (2hr., 200 pesos), **sky riding** (2 people, US$50), **deep sea fishing** excursions (4hr., US$100), and deep sea fishing, sight-seeing and snorkeling all in one (2hr., 200 pesos; open daily 9am-5pm). If you're not much of a deep sea enthusiast, try taking a **horse,** available near Club Eureka, for a sandy spin (30 pesos per 30min.). To get to Playa La Boquita, take a "Miramar" bus to Club Santiago (4 pesos, 40min.). Walk through the white arches along the cobblestone and palm-lined street, which becomes a dirt road; you'll hit the road after 25 minutes (taxis 10 pesos). Also reveling in its tranquility is **Playa Audiencia,** a small but magnificent cove with calm waters, light brown sand, a few small boats, and a gorgeous, rocky vista. To reach the *playa,* take a "Las Hadas" bus from Niños Héroes or anywhere on Miramar Highway to the Sierra Radison (4 pesos), then follow the path to the beach. The bus ride back to town offers a spectacular view of the peninsula.

ENTERTAINMENT

Manzanillo doesn't sleep when the sun sets. "Miramar" buses run down the hotel strip. Taxis back to the *centro* cost 30-35pesos. After frolicking in the sun and splashing in the sea, those ready to rumble head over to **Tropigala,** Blvd. Miguel de la Madrid km 14.5 (tel. 3 24 74; fax 3 24 75) to get down to live tropical music. Work up an appetite showing off your moves to the mixed age crowd and then gorge on hot dogs, *frijoles*, chicken, and potatoes from the all-you-can eat buffet (included in cover). Ladies who have a special place in their hearts for the big and brawny should watch for the occasional Chippendale's night where oiled-up men strut their stuff. On Wednesdays and Thursdays, women drink for free. (Cover 30 pesos; open W-Su 9pm-4am.) Next door at the cavernesque **Baby Rock** (tel. 3 28 39), a young crowd gets down to popular Mexican and U.S. disco hits. As if the dancing weren't enough, a large-screen TV and extensive lights stimulate the senses. (Open bar on Wednesday and Thursday. 30 peso cover for men with 2 drinks Tuesday, F-Sa; 60 peso cover for men, 30 peso for women W-Th; Sunday 20 peso cover for all; open high season Tu-Sa; low season Th-Su.) Locals and tourists show off their **tans** and **cool threads** at **Vog,** Av. Miguel de la Madrid km 9.2 (tel. 3 18 75), on the hotel strip. At 11:30pm, sophisticated track lighting rhythmically sprays beams across prehistoric walls. Men, leave your tank tops, shorts, and sandals at the beach. (Cover 40 pesos; open W-Sa 10pm-4am, daily during high season.) Next door at the **Bar de Felix** (tel. 3 18 75), funky topiaries welcome an older crowd. Weary revelers recline in plush red chairs while the packed dance floor pulsates to a melange of disco and Latin rhythms. (Open Tu-Su 9pm-4am.) If your day at the beach has left you too drained for dancing, test your vocal cords at **Canta Bar Tetos,** Blvd. Miguel de la Madrid km 8.5 (tel. 3 19 90). Don't be afraid to sing along (just not too loudly) to the live romantic music. Heart-wrenching ballads coupled with dim lighting will make even the anti-Romeos reach for a loved one. (Open M-Th 9pm-5am, F-Sa 9pm-morning.)

■ Near Manzanillo: Cuyutlán

With its lush vegetation, breathtaking black-sand beach, and mysterious lagoon, quiet **Cuyutlán** (pop. 1650) offers the traveler a few days of solitude. Medium waves roll up on the shore, making for fairly safe and exciting swimming. In the off-season, closed buildings and silent streets give the place a ghost-town feel, and the huge golden head of Benito Juárez amid the palm trees of Cuyutlán's green and white *zócalo* is often the only face visible. Summer weekends are slightly busier, but it is only during the high tourist season (December and *Semana Santa*) that Cuyutlán truly comes to life. If you have to choose between Paraíso and Cuyutlán, the latter offers tourists a better beach, better hotels, and a greater variety of food.

There is no direct public transportation between Paraíso and Cuyutlán; the only way to get to Cuyutlán is from **Armería** (see **Getting there,** below). The road from Armería, 15km from Cuyutlán, runs parallel to the coast and becomes **Yavaros** as it enters town. It intersects **Hidalgo,** which runs along the east side of the town square; a left at this intersection takes you to the beach. **Veracruz,** Cuyutlán's other mighty boulevard, runs parallel to Yavaros, one block off the beach.

Most of Cuyutlán's municipal services are within one block of the *zócalo.* The bilingual owners of the **Hotel Fenix** will **change money** if they have the cash. Bring an adequate supply of *pesos* just in case. The only **caseta** is at Hidalgo 47 (tel. 6 40 00), one block inland from the *zócalo* (open M-Sa 9am-1pm and 4-8pm, Su 9am-1pm). uses going from Melaque or Barra de Navidad to Puerto Vallarta (1½hr., 27 pesos) or Manzanillo (3hr., 49 pesos) pass through Perula.The **phone code** is 332.

Waves lap at the doorsteps of most nearby budget hotels. Most are well maintained and very affordable. During high season (mainly in December and *Semana Santa*), expect rates to skyrocket to 130-150 pesos per person, with meals included to help justify the price. Make reservations a month in advance during this time. Most restaurants are on Yavaros. **Hotel Morelos,** Hidalgo 185 (tel. 6 40 13), at Veracruz, offers plush rooms with clean bathrooms and carved wooden furniture. Tiled floors, festive colors, and all the artificial flowers in Cuyutlán give the place pizazz. (50 pesos per person.) The rooms at **Hotel Fenix,** Hidalgo 201 (tel. 6 40 82), at Veracruz, may be taller than they are wide, but there's a fan in each one, and the bathrooms are tidy. The friendly English-speaking owners run a popular bar that serves as the town watering hole. (Rooms 35-60 pesos per person.) **Cabañas Rafles,** at López Mateos, a 10-minute walk east along the beach (or along Veracruz past the Hotel San Rafael), offers basic rooms, access to showers and toilets, and campsites. The super-friendly caretaker Rafles will treat you right. Unofficial camping sites lie 200m from Cuyutlán's hotels, in a private patch of black sand. Some travelers string up hammocks in one of the *palapas* near the hotels. For 5 pesos, campers and daytrippers can use the toilets and showers at Hotel Fenix. Almost all of the food in Cuyutlán is served up in the **hotel restaurants,** and seafood is the obvious specialty.

Aside from its gorgeous beach, Cuyutlán's biggest claim to fame is its **green wave,** a phenomenon that occurs regularly in April or May. Quirky currents and phosphorescent marine life combine to produce 10m swells that glow an unearthly green. The town itself reaches high tide during the **Festival de la Virgen de Guadalupe** (the first 12 days of December), when twice a day—at 6am and 6pm—men, women, and children clad in *traje de indios* walk 5km to the town's blue church. The celebrations peak on the twelfth day, when *mariachis* accompany the procession, and the marchers sing tributes to the Virgin. Cuyutlán's **Tortugario,** 3.5km east of town along Veracruz, is a combination of wildlife preserve and zoo. *(Open daily 10am-6pm. Admission 5 pesos; taxi to the camp 30 pesos.)* The Tortugario is home to hordes of turtles, iguanas, and crocodiles. The camp also has saltwater pools for (human) swimming.

Getting there: The only way to get to Cuyutlán is from Armería. Buses to Cuyutlán leave Armería from the Terminal Sub-Urbana (20min., every 30min. 7am-7:30pm, 4 pesos). Buses depart from Cuyutlán on the same schedule (sometimes early) from the plaza. **Autobuses Nuevos Horizonte y Rojos** (tel. 2 39 00) will take you to Armería from Manzanillo (45min., every 15min. 4:20am-10:30pm, 13 pesos). Get off at the blue "Paraíso" sign and cross the highway.

■ Near Manzanillo: Paraíso

Paraíso may soon be destroyed by the gods for its hubris, but for now it outclasses its unsightly sister city, nearby **Armería.** A well-paved road connects the two towns, cutting through 7km of banana and coconut plantations before it dead-ends at the lava-black sands that surround Paraíso's few hotels and thatched, beachfront restaurants. A shoreline strewn with endless lawn chairs and umbrellas backs the emerald green surf. Paraíso is popular among Mexicans for daytrips and weekend vacations; during the high season and on Sundays, the beachfront has a true family atmosphere, and the town's single dirt road is often crammed with buses and cars blaring music. But on lazy summer weekdays, the beach is almost deserted, and a few lucky swimmers have the water all to themselves. Long-distance **phone** calls can be made from **Abarrotes Valdovinos** (tel. 2 00 25), next to the bus stop (open daily M-Su 7am-10pm).

Just before the main road becomes the beach, you'll see Paraíso's only other street, the dirt road **Av. de la Juventud** (called **Calle Adán y Eva** by locals) which runs along the back of the beachfront restaurants. The first building on the beach to your left is **Hotel Equipales,** where you'll find no-frills rooms with a view of the shore. The cramped and dingy bathrooms leave much to be desired. (Singles and doubles 50 pesos.) Farther to the left lies **Hotel Paraíso** (tel. 7 18 25), a cut above Equipales, but pricier. Spacious beachfront rooms have yellow-tiled floors, ceiling fans, and cold showers. A jungle-theme mural adds a splash of color to the popular pool. (Singles and doubles 135 pesos.) At the opposite end of the strip lies **Posada Valencia,** where the beds are waist-high and the rooms are clean (singles 50 pesos; doubles 100 pesos). Paraíso's extensive **beach** makes a soft pillow for **campers,** and the Hotel Paraíso provides showers (5 pesos) and free access to bathrooms. Hotel Equipales also offers bathroom (1 peso) and shower (5 pesos) use. Some *enramada* owners may let you hang your **hammock** under their thatched roofs. During the high season (December and April), rooms may be available in **private houses;** ask in stores or at the town's *caseta.*

Restaurants run the slim gamut from rustic *enramadas* to cement-floored *comedores.* Locally caught seafood dominates menus. **Restaurant Paraíso,** in the Hotel Paraíso, is as popular as the hotel pool. Uniformed waiters provide snazzy service, and string quartets and *mariachis* sometimes appear in the afternoon. Breakfast goes for 15-20 pesos and tasty shrimp dishes cost 45 pesos. (Open daily 8am-6pm.) The restaurant at Hotel Equipales also offers a pleasant atmosphere and reasonable prices.

Getting There: Autobuses Nuevos Horizonte y Rojos (tel. 2 39 00) runs buses from Manzanillo to Armería (45min., every 15min. 4:20am-10:30pm, 13 pesos). Get off at the blue "Paraíso" sign and cross the highway. Buses to Paraíso leave from **Terminal Sub-Urbano,** which provides service to Paraíso (15min., every 30min. 6:30am-7:30pm, 3 pesos). Buses return from Paraíso to Armería on the same schedule and depart from where they leave passengers.

Colima

With 160,000 residents, the capital of the Colima state can hardly be called a *pueblo,* but it does manage to maintain a certain benevolence and informality. The streets and parks are magnificently groomed, the civic-minded inhabitants are remarkably friendly, and on Sundays, slews of stores close shop as families head off to church. Blessed with cool mountain air, pleasant budget lodging, a string of museums, theaters, and a university, under-touristed Colima provides relief from the sweaty, well-trodden coastal route; it's a great place to shake the sand from your shoes.

ORIENTATION

A string of plazas runs east to west across downtown Colima. The shady **Plaza Principal,** flanked by the cathedral and the Palacio de Gobierno on the east side, is the business center of town. The Plaza Principal is bordered by **Degollado** on the west, **16 de Septiembre** on the south, **Madero** on the north, and **Reforma** on the east. Just past the cathedral and *palacio* is the smaller, quieter **Jardín Quintero,** marked by the large fountain in its center. Three blocks farther east on Madero is the large, lush **Jardín Núñez,** the other significant reference point in town. Madero also forms the northern border of the Jardín Nuñez with Juárez on the west, **Morelos** on the south, and **Revolución** on the east. Many tourist services are on **Hidalgo,** which runs parallel to Madero one block to the south. The main **bus station** is 2km out of town, but mini-buses zip by every five minutes (6am-8:30pm, 2 pesos). **Taxis** charge 8.50 pesos to destinations within the *centro,* and 9 pesos to the outskirts.

PRACTICAL INFORMATION

Transportation

Buses: The bus station can be reached by "Bital" or "Ruta 5" on Bravo or "Ruta 4" on Zaragoza (2 pesos). **Autobuses de Occidente** (tel. 4 81 79) has service to Lázaro Cárdenas (6hr., 12:10am and 3:20am, 93-108 pesos) and Uruapan (6-8hr., 11am and 10:45pm, 94-100 pesos); and second-class service to Mexico City (13hr., 6 per day 5am-10pm, 240 pesos) via Morelia (8hr. 116 pesos). **Autotransportes Sur de Jalisco** (tel. 2 03 16) has second-class service to Manzanillo (1¾hr., 4 per day 6-11:40am, 24 pesos) via Armería (45min., 13 pesos). **Elite** (tel. 2 84 99) sends first-class buses to Hermosillo (27hr., 5pm, 698 pesos), Mazatlán (12hr., 5pm, 310 pesos), Mexico City (10hr., 9:30 and 11pm, 306 pesos), and Tijuana (36hr., 5pm, 897 pesos) via Tepic (6hr., 213 pesos). **ETN** (tel. 2 58 99; fax 4 10 60) sends plush buses to the Guadalajara airport (3hr., 3 and 9:30am, 132 pesos) and Morelia (6hr., 11:45pm, 195 pesos). **Flecha Amarilla** (tel. 2 11 35) has service to Guzman (2hr., 5 per day 7am-5:30pm, 32 pesos). **Omnibus de Mexico** (tel. 4 71 90) goes to Aguascalientes (6½hr., 3:20pm, 188 pesos), Mexico City (10hr., 7:45, 8:30, and 10pm, 306 pesos), and Monterrey (15hr., 6:50pm, 390 pesos). **Primera Plus** (tel. 4 80 67) send first-class buses to Aguascalientes (6hr., 12:30pm, 186 pesos), Guadalajara (3hr., 11 per day 5am-7:40pm, 87 pesos), Manzanillo (1¼hr., 11 per day 1:50am-11:30pm, 30 pesos), and Mexico City (10hr., 9 and 11:30pm, 326 pesos), and second-class buses to Querétaro (8hr., 3:30 and 8:30pm, 169 pesos).

Tourist and Financial Services

Tourist Office: Hidalgo 96 (tel. 2 43 60; fax 2 83 60), on the corner of Hidalgo and Ocampo, halfway between the Plaza Principal and Jardín Nuñez. Helpful staff doles out pamphlets and maps. Open M-F 8:30am-3pm and 6-9pm, Sa 10am-2pm.

Currency Exchange: Banamex, Hidalgo 90 (tel. 2 01 03), 1 block east of Pl. Principal, has an **ATM.** Open M-F 9am-5pm. **Majapara Casa de Cambio,** Morelos 200 (tel. 4 89 98; fax 4 89 66), on the corner of Juárez at Jardín Núñez, has slightly better rates. Open M-Sa 9am-2pm and 4:30-7pm.

Local Services

Luggage Storage: At the bus station. 2 pesos per bag for 6hr., 0.50 pesos each additional hour. Open daily 6am-10pm. 24hr. restaurant can assist after hours.

Laundromat: Lavandería Automática Amana, Dominguez 147, behind Hospedajes del Rey. 24 pesos to wash and dry 3kg. Open M-Sa 8am-9pm.

Emergency and Communications

Emergency: Dial 06.

Police: (tel. 2 09 67), Juárez at 20 de Noviembre.

Red Cross: (tel. 2 14 51), Aldama at Obregón. Open 24hr. Some English spoken.

Pharmacy: Sangre de Cristo (tel. 4 74 74), Obregón at Madero, 1 block northwest of Jardín Núñez. Open 24hr.

Hospitals: Hospital Civil (tel. 2 02 27 or 2 09 11), San Fernando at Ignacio Zandoval. **Centro de Salud** (tel. 2 00 64 or 2 32 38), Juárez at 20 de Noviembre. **Dr. Armando López** speaks English. Open M-F 7am-2:30pm, Sa 7am-1:30pm.

Fax: Madero 243 (tel. 2 60 64), next to the post office. **Telegrams** are also available. Open M-F 8am-6pm, Sa 9am-noon.

Post Office: Madero 247 (tel. 2 00 33), on the northeast corner of the Jardín Núñez. Open M-F 8am-7pm, Sa 8am-noon. **Postal Code:** 28000.

Telephones: LADATELs abound in the plazas. The **caseta** at **Comercializadora Sanvi,** Revolución 99 (tel. 3 50 80), on the southeast corner of the Jardín Núñez, is open daily 8am-10pm. Also has a **fax**.

Phone Code: 331.

ACCOMMODATIONS

Inexpensive, quality rooms can be difficult to find in Colima. If the options below don't work out, cheap lodging may be found near the Jardín Núñez. Higher-priced hotels tend to cluster around the university. Purified water is often not available.

Hospedajes del Rey, Rey Colimán 125 (tel. 3 36 83), half a block from the southeast of the Jardín Núñez. "Fit for a king" couldn't describe it better: Enormous, plush rooms sport fans, televisions, and wall-to-wall windows; hardwood floors and a beveled-glass dining table and chairs complete the royal ensemble. Bathroom floors are clean enough to eat from. Singles 100 pesos; doubles with 1 bed 120 pesos, with two beds 140 pesos.

Hotel Colonial, Medellín 142F (tel. 3 08 77), between Morelos and Nicolás Bravo, 1 block from the Plaza Principal. Rooms have fans, wicker chairs, wrought-iron beds, and enormous TVs (some with cable). Spotless, flower-tiled bathrooms make the hot water that much more enjoyable. Singles 70-100 pesos; doubles 80-110 pesos.

Casa de Huéspedes, Morelos 265 (tel. 2 34 67), off the southeast corner of Jardín Núñez. A friendly family-run *posada* with breezy but decaying rooms and billions of blooming plants. The bathrooms, however, could use a good scrub. Singles 40 pesos, with bath 60 pesos; doubles 50 pesos, with bath 70 pesos.

FOOD

Restaurant fare in Colima reflects the town's dearth of tourism; inexpensive and authentic Mexican meals consist of traditional faves like *pozole blanco* and *sopitos.* A few pricey joints cluster around the Plaza Principal, but a jaunt down the smaller sidestreets will lead to budget meals aplenty.

Samadhi, Medina 125 (tel. 3 24 98), 2½ blocks north of Jardín Núñez. Walk down Juárez (the western border of the *jardín*); Samadhi is next to the red and white church. Delicious, vegetarian-friendly cuisine served with new-age music in a leafy courtyard with soothing pastel walls. Breakfast buffet 28.50 pesos; soy burger with mushrooms and fries 14.50 pesos. Open daily F-W 8am-10pm, Th 8am-5pm.

Comedor Familiar El Trébol, 16 de Septiembre 59 (tel. 2 29 00), at Degollado, on the Pl. Principal. Colima at its best: popular and cheap. A family spot packed with kids laughing and stuffing their faces amid the festive decor. *Comida corrida* 15 pesos, breakfast 8-12 pesos, beer 7 pesos. Open Su-F 8am-11pm.

Los Naranjos, Barreda 34 (tel. 2 00 29), almost a block north of Madero, northeast of the Plaza Principal. Popular with those in the know. *Periódico*-perusing middle-aged men classily sip coffee over bright orange tablecloths while glass vases and wicker chairs add Euro-flair. Breakfast 7-20 pesos. *Pollo a la mexicana* 23 pesos. *Antojitos* 7-22 pesos. Open daily 8am-11:30pm.

Cenaduría Selecta de Colima, Morelos 299 (tel. 2 93 32), at Domínguez, 1 block off the southeast corner of Jardín Núñez. Tasty, cheap *pozole, tostadas, taquitos,* and the regional favorite, *enchiladas dulces* (sweet enchiladas) served with a mountain of diced onion and hot-ass sauce (entrees 10 pesos) in this light and airy establishment. Cool it off with a beer (5-6 pesos) or top it off with a sweet serving of flan (6 pesos). Open Tu-Sa 1:30-11pm.

SIGHTS

In Colima's **Plaza Principal,** the gazebo and fountains of the **Jardín Libertad** lure bureaucrats on their lunch breaks to the garden's ornate white wrought-iron benches. The double arcade around the plaza encompasses the **Museo Regional de Historia de Colima.** On the east side of the plaza, much of the state government is housed in the **Palacio de Gobierno,** an unremarkable beige and white building with a breezy courtyard and a four-wall mural, completed in 1954 by Jorge Chávez Carrillo in honor of the bicentennial of Hidalgo's birth. The intricate mural moves counterclockwise through Mexico's tumultuous history, beginning with a powerful depiction of the Conquest and ending at the Mexican Revolution with Pancho Villa's infamous bravado. Adjoining Colima's municipal complex is the colonial **Santa Iglesia Cathedral,** a pawn in the battle between humanity and nature—or, depending on your perspective, between Catholicism and the ghost of indigenous religions. *(Open daily 6am-2pm and 4:30-8:30pm.)* The Spanish first built a church on this spot in 1527, but an earthquake destroyed the original wood and palm structure; fire destroyed its replacement. Undeterred, the Spanish built yet another church. The cathedral's neoclassical interior sparkles with gilt paint, chandeliers, and polished marble decor and statues. A statue of San Felipe de Jesús, the city's patron saint, resides in the pulpit designed by Othón Bustos.

Colima's newest museum is the **Museo de Historia,** Portal Morelos 1 (tel. 2 92 28), at 16 de Septiembre and Reforma, on the south side of the Plaza Principal. *(Open Tu-Sa 9am-6pm, Su 5-8pm; free.)* The museum is home to a respectable collection of pre-Hispanic ceramics and includes a creepy replica of a western Mesoamerican burial site, complete with two real skeletons. In the same courtyard is an eclectic gallery of art. One block down Degollado, to your left as you face away from the Cathedral, stands **Teatro Hidalgo,** which was completed in 1883. Unmarred by the passage of time, the theater's four tiers of side-seating almost touch the high ceiling, and its swooping red curtains lend the stage a 19th-century ambience. Occasional performances enliven the majestic interior beyond those large wooden doors; inquire at the tourist office.

Colima is home to other stellar museums just a short bus ride away. The city's **Museo de Las Culturas de Occidente** (tel. 3 06 08), on Calle Calzada Galván at Ejército Nacional, is devoted to local pre-Hispanic art. *(Open Tu-Su 9am-7pm.)* To get to this excellent museum, take the yellow "Ruta #3 Sur" bus (2 pesos) on Av. Rey Colimán at Jardín Núñez. Taxis from the *centro* cost 5 pesos. Rarely seen outside the state, the Colima ceramic figurines displayed here, with their exaggerated, disproportionate bodies, are among the most playful and captivating artifacts in Mexico. The museum provides an excellent narrative of the artifacts' meaning and of their role in indigenous culture. The **Casa de la Cultura** (same tel.), the university's cultural center, is the best source of information on cultural events in Colima (open daily 8:30am-9pm).

Museo Universitario de Artes Populares (tel. 2 68 69), at Barreda and Gallardo, boasts a collection of traditional dresses and masks, figurines recovered from nearby tombs, and descriptions of the pre-Aztec western coast. *(Museum open Tu-Sa 9am-2pm and 5-8pm, Su 10am-1pm; free.)* A gift shop sells handmade reproductions of local ceramics. The *museo* is an easy 15-minute walk north on 27 de Septiembre from the Plaza Principal. Alternatively, catch the #7 bus (2 pesos) on Gabino Barreda between Zaragoza and Guerrero, and take it to the corner of Barreda and Gallardo.

The **Parque Regional Metropolitano,** on Degollado (tel. 4 16 76), four blocks south of the Plaza Principal, offers nature-lovers an afternoon stroll along a human-made duck pond, home to two absurdly large pelicans who pester young children for fish. A miniature **zoo** houses monkeys, crocodiles, and lions. *(Zoo open daily 7am-6:30pm. Admission 1 peso. Pool and waterslide open W-Su 10:30am-4:30pm. Admission 4.50 pesos, children 2.50 pesos. Waterslide and boat rides 6 pesos per hr., children 3.50 pesos.)* Children feed ice cream cones to deer through wire fences and frolic in the pool, zooming down the **waterslide.**

ENTERTAINMENT

Erupting volcanoes aren't the things shaking in Colima. Night spots are populated largely by students. **Bariloche,** Av. Rey de Colimán 440 (tel. 4 55 00), near the Monumento Rey Colimán, may be the hottest spot in town. Huge-screen videos, two pool tables, and wandering entertainers keep 'em coming. (Cover Wednesday 100 pesos for men, free for women; Friday 70 pesos for men, 30 pesos for women; Saturday 45 pesos including 2 drinks. Open W-Sa 10pm-3am.) **Splash**, Av. Benito Juárez 4 (tel. 3 65 07), is a dimly lit, ever-packed gay and lesbian bar where clientele get down on the dance floor in between transvestite lip-synching shows. (No cover Th; cover F 25 pesos, free beer 10pm-1am; 20 peso cover Sa; 20 peso cover Su with one free beer; open Th-Su 10pm-3:30am.) Work your way through the smoke at **Collash,** Zaragosa 521 (tel. 4 47 00), as you gyrate to popular Mexican dance music. If you're not up to dancing, play some pool as you sip a beer (10 pesos) or a mixed drink (18 pesos and up; cover 15 pesos Sa, open 11pm-3am; Su—under 18 night—cover 10 pesos; open 6-10pm). **Atrium,** Sevilla de Río 1574 (tel. 3 04 77), at Castellanos, features pool tables, peppy music, and a preppy crowd alongside cheesy 80s posters of dames with teased hair in ripped jeans (open daily 10am-2am). For some sappy tunes that'll make you cry in your beer, visit the Casa de la Cultura's cafe, **Dalí.** Prints by you-know-who drip from the walls under dim, smoky lights. The food isn't exactly cheap, but it's worth it just to drink *cervezas* or smoke cigars with conflicted intellectuals. Between 9 and 11pm, a *mariachi* stands on the cafe's small platform wailing love songs, a guitar cradled in his arms. (*Muy romántico.* Beer 9 pesos, *bebidas nacionales* 18 pesos and up. Open M-F 1:15pm-midnight, Sa-Su 5:30pm-midnight).

Near Colima

This is where the wild things are. If you want to commune with nature, or just check out the nearby indignant volcanoes, serene lakes, and quiet towns, Colima serves as an ideal base for daytrips to numerous sites. The soaring peaks of the **volcanoes** 25km away and the **large lakes** overflowing with wildlife send their siren calls to curious visitors and draw them in by the bus load. The neighboring town of **Comala** provides another outlet for travelers who want to escape the crowds of Colima, but are unwilling to march through flora and fauna to do it.

Near Colima: Volcanoes

In Náhuatl, Colima means "place where the old god is dominant." The old god is **El Volcán de Fuego** (3960m), 25km from Colima city. Puffs of white smoke continuously billow from the volcano; recorded eruptions date back to the pre-Conquest era. Lava was visible from the capital once again on June 24, 1994, when El Fuego reasserted its status as an active volcano (the tourist office assures visitors that the volcano is not a threat to the city). **El Nevado de Colima** (4335m) stands taller than its neighbor but is dormant and not much fun at parties. The soaring peak becomes snow-capped in the winter. The **Joya Cabin,** near the summit, lacks all amenities except a roof. The park is open sporadically; if you're planning a trip to the top, call the **police** ahead of time (tel. 2 18 01). As always, be cautious. The ascent should not be attempted by solo travelers or by those with little hiking experience.

Getting There: Guadalajara-bound *locales* (from the new bus station) pass through the town of **Atenquique,** 57km away. From here, a 27km dirt road runs to the summit of El Fuego. The trip is only recommended for 4-wheel-drive vehicles, though logging trucks based at the factory in Atenquique make trips to spots near the summit. You can get to El Nevado by car or by bus. **Flecha Amarilla** (tel. 4 80 67) runs buses from Colima to **Guzmán,** 83km away (2hr., 5 per day 7am-5:30pm, 32 pesos). Buses from Guzmán limp up to Joya, where you can make your epic assault on the summit.

■ Near Colima Lagunas Carrizalillo and La María

If you don't mind insects, frogs, and huge lizards, and just want to bask in peace, make a daytrip to **Laguna Carrizalillo,** 27km north of Colima. Larger, closer to the volcanoes, and more visited is **Laguna La María,** whose calm, green waters surrounded by a dense wall of plant life attract flocks of ornithologists in search of tiny yellow Singing Wilsons. If birds aren't your thing, try fishing at the shore or from a rented *lancha* (25 pesos per hr.). Five pesos buys access to either lagoon for a day.

Getting There: Green buses destined for San Antonio or Zapotitlán leave from the suburban bus station and chug up and down the mountain road to La María (1½hr., 7:10am, 2:40, and 5 pm, 6 pesos; buses return at 7:30am, 3, and 4pm). Survivors of the painfully bumpy ride are rewarded with a magnificent view of the mountains just before the lagoon. To get to the entrance from the bus stop, follow the wooden sign that says "La María" (a 15-minute hike). The bus back leaves from the same crossroads on the opposite side of the street. To reach Terminal Suburbano from the centro of Colima, catch a "Ruta 2" bus labeled "Los Rojos" on Morelos (2 pesos).

■ Near Colima: Comala

South of the lagoons and just 9km north of Colima is the picturesque *pueblo* of **Comala,** known as "El Pueblo Blanco de América" (The White Town of America). Originally, all the facades in town were white, with red-tiled roofs, huge porches, and windows filled with flowers. Comala's cozy *zócalo* is surrounded by cobblestone streets with white benches, fountains, and orange trees. The south side of the *zócalo* is lined by lively restaurants where *mariachis* perform and waiters supply patrons with a steady stream of free *botanas* (Mexican appetizers) to whet the appetite for *ponche* (warm rum and fruit punch), one of the region's traditional drinks.

Comala's main claim to fame is its colony of *indígena* artisans who craft wooden furniture and bamboo baskets. The **Cooperativa Artesenal Pueblo Blanco** (tel. 5 56 00), a small *tianguis* (market), stands just outside Comala's *centro,* 200m past the restaurants on Progreso; it's a 20-minute walk from the *zócalo* (open M-Sa 8am-4pm).

To the east of the *zócalo* lies the **Iglesia San Miguel del Espíritu Santo,** whose unfinished bare-bricked rear gives it character. Once inside, you are met not by ornate stained-glass windows but rather by a sky-blue ceiling. The nave of the church is occupied by still more birds, chirping in deafening cacophony. On the other side of the *zócalo* are the city offices, where a four-wall mural commemorates Comala's 130 years as a city and celebrates the "richness of its soil." Unfortunately, the birds who now control the church have also settled across the way; they have graciously added their own artistic expression to the mural. For more information, contact Ignacio Zamora, director of education, culture, and tourism (tel. 5 55 47), next door in the municipal building (available M-F 8:30am-2:30pm and 5-8pm).

Getting There: Green buses head to Comala from the far right end of Colima's suburban bus station (30min., every 15min. 6am-10pm, 2.50 pesos). Taxis charge about 30 pesos from Colima and, if you ask, the *taxista* may show you Colima's famous *magnético*—a segment of the road where cars can have their engines turned off but still appear to run uphill. Optical illusion or miracle of science, it's loads o' fun.

Southern Pacific Coast

Because many of the region's indigenous Purépecha lived by the rod and the net, the Aztecs dubbed the lands surrounding Lake Pátzcuaro **Michoacán** (Country of Fishermen). The distinctive Purépecha language (a variant of which is still widely spoken) and the terraced agricultural plots have convinced scholars that they were not originally indigenous to the area but were in fact immigrants from what is today Peru. Purépecha hegemony lasted from around 800, when they first settled Michoacán, to 1522, when the Spanish arrived. Michoacán's red, fertile soil, abundant rain, and mild weather make for bountiful crops, and agriculture swells the state's coffers. The gorgeous beaches and forest-covered mountain ranges serve as prime attractions to wildlife enthusiasts and tourists.

The state of **Guerrero** has been blessed by fortune. During the colonial period, the rich mining town of Taxco kept the state and most of New Spain swimming in silver. More recently, the state's precious commodities have not come from high upon the rocky Sierra de Guerrero, but rather from the rugged shores just past it on the Pacific coast. In the 1950s, Acapulco became the darling of the international resort scene; almost four decades later, wallflower Ixtapa and even quieter Zihuatanejo have managed to take their older sister's role. Today, most of the glitter has subsided, and Guerrero's beautiful colonial towns and Pacific beaches are popular with budget travelers.

Oaxaca is fractured into a crazy quilt by the rugged heights of the Sierra Madre del Sur. Despite its intimidating terrain, the land has inspired a violent possessiveness in the many people—Zapotecs, Mixtecs, Aztecs, and Spaniards—who have fought each other over the area. More than 200 indigenous tribes have occupied the valley over the past two millennia. Over one million *oaxaqueños* still speak an *indígena* language as a mother tongue, and more than 20% of the state's population speaks no Spanish whatsoever. This language barrier, and the cultural gap that it symbolizes and exacerbates, has long caused tensions between the Oaxacan government and its indigenous population. These tensions run through the veins of the enchanting highland colonial city of Oaxaca de Juárez, a perennial tourist favorite for its rich *indígena* culture, superb food, and sublime setting.

HIGHLIGHTS OF THE SOUTHERN PACIFIC COAST

- Despite 1997's devastating Hurricane Pauline, **Puerto Escondido** (see p. 392) and nearby **Zipolite** (see p. 391) still draw backpackers ready to sun, surf, and smoke on the beach.
- The site of **Monte Alban** (see p. 383) is home to the most important pre-Hispanic ruins in the region and some of the most well preserved in Mexico.
- **Oaxaca** (see p. 370) is a backpacker mecca—some say it's the most attractive city in the country. Its international student population, temperate weather, scenic location, and hot chocolate drive national and international visitors wild.
- **Taxco** (see p. 352) not only offers visitors silver, but also narrow streets, dazzling mountain views, and the beautiful **Catedral de Santa Prisca** (see p. 355).
- Aging, ultra-corny **Acapulco** (see p. 364) may be past its prime, but the **Guerrero coast** (**Costa Grande;** see p. 362) north of the city is home to some beautiful beaches, including **Barra de Potosí** (see p. 362).
- Despite over-development and the Western Hemisphere's largest Club Med, Ixtapa and Zihuatanejo still lure travelers to their sunny beaches. Skip **Ixtapa** (see p. 361); **Zihuatanejo** (see p. 360) is where it's at.
- The gorgeous beaches of the stormy **Michoacan coast** (see p. 349) boast powerful waves, privacy, and rugged terrain.
- The quiet mountain jewel of **Pátzcuaro** (see p. 337) and the **nearby area** (see p. 342) are home to an amazing variety of regional handicrafts.

MICHOACÁN DE OCAMPO

Uruapan

Surrounded by red soil, rolling hills, and rows upon rows of avocado trees, Uruapan (ur-WA-pan; pop. 300,000) sits amid a checkerboard of farmland wrested from the surrounding jungle and mountains. Farmers and their families come to Uruapan to sell their produce and buy bags of fried plantains, wristwatches, and other necessities of modern life. Cool mountain air and plenty of rain keep the city lush and green year-round. While Uruapan is developing into an important center of commerce, the surrounding countryside remains untainted—a nature lover's dream. In town, when residents aren't haggling over prices in the huge *mercado,* they are relaxing with a cup of strong *michoacano* coffee in the city's excellent cafes. Tourists come to the Uruapan in droves to explore the nearby waterfall, national park, and Paricutín Volcano.

ORIENTATION

Uruapan lies 120km west of Morelia and 320km southeast of Guadalajara. Everything in town is within easy walking distance of the *zócalo,* known as **Jardín de los Mártires** on its west side and **Jardín Morelos** on its east end. The statue in the center faces south, looking down **Cupatitzio. Emiliano Carranza** runs into the southwest corner of the square from the west, and **Obregón** is its continuation on the eastern

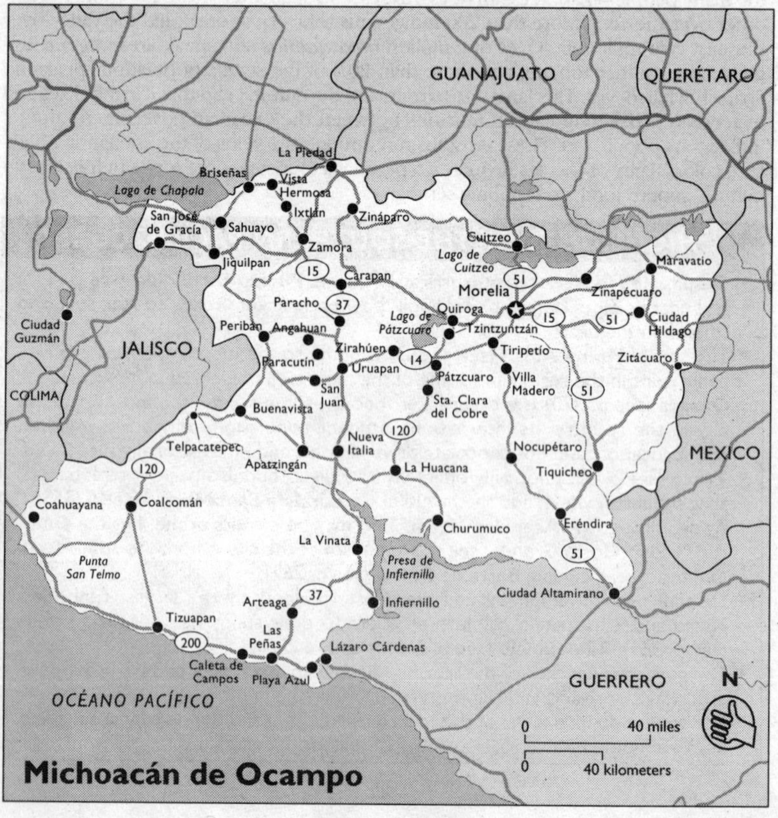

side of the plaza. **Venustiano Carranza** runs into the *zócalo*'s north side, and **Manuel Ocaranza** runs one block west of Cupatitzio into the plaza's south side. **Ocampo** runs along its western edge. To reach the center from the **bus station** on Benito Juárez in the northeast corner of town, hail a taxi (12 pesos) or hop aboard an "El Centro" bus (6am-9pm, 2 pesos).

PRACTICAL INFORMATION

Buses: Buses leave from Benito Juárez, in the northeast part of town, from the corner of Obregón and 5 de Febrero. To reach the station from the *zócalo,* take the "Central Camionera" or "Central" bus (2 pesos). A cab to the station costs 12 pesos. **Elite** (tel. 3 44 50 or 3 44 67) runs cushy first-class service to Mazatlán (5 and 7:30pm, 275 pesos), Mexico City (6hr., 11:30pm, 157 pesos), Monterrey (15hr., noon, 1, and 6:30pm, 355 pesos), and San Luis Potosí (8hr., noon, 1, and 6:30pm, 172 pesos). **Flecha Amarilla** (tel. 4 39 82) runs second-class buses to Aguascalientes (8½hr., 5:20, 7:40am, and 1pm, 130 pesos), Guadalajara (5hr., 5 per day, 95 pesos), Mexico City (10hr., 7:30am, 7, and 10pm, 160 pesos), Morelia (2hr., 6 per day, 43 pesos), Querétaro (6hr., 5 per day, 83 pesos), and San Luis Potosí (9hr., 5, 9am, 6:10pm, and midnight, 152 pesos). **ETN** (tel. 4 78 99) and **Primera Plus** (tel. 4 39 82) offer similar service. **La Línea** (tel. 3 18 71) is a good bet for Guadalajara (4½-6½hr., 16 per day, 95 pesos). **Transportes del Pacífico** (tel. 7 03 73) heads to points north.

Tourist office: Juan Ayala 16 (tel. 4 71 99), on the right, one block up Independencia from the *zócalo*. The friendly folks here provide a good map. Open M-Sa 9am-2pm and 4-7pm, Su 9am-2pm.

Currency Exchange: Bancomer, Carranza 7 (tel. 3 65 22), offers good exchange rates and an **ATM.** Open M-F 8:30am-5:30pm, Sa 10am-2pm. A veritable battalion of banks and the shotgun-toting guards that accompany them await a block south of the *zócalo* on Cupatitzio. Competitive exchange rates and ATMs are as common as mosquitoes.

Luggage Storage: At the bus station. 3 pesos per 3hr., 5 pesos per day. Open daily 7am-midnight.

Laundry: Autoservicio de Lavandería, Emiliano Carranza 47 (tel. 3 26 69), at García, four blocks west of the *zócalo,* will wash and dry 3kg for 30 pesos. Open M-Sa 9am-2pm and 4-8pm.

Police: (tel. 3 27 33), at Eucaliptos and Naranjo.

Pharmacies: Pharmacies rotate 24-hour shifts; call the Red Cross to find out which is on duty. **Farmacia Fénix,** Carranza 1 (tel. 4 16 40). Open daily 8am-9pm.

Medical Services: The **Red Cross,** Del Lago 1 (tel. 4 03 00), is a block down from the **Hospital Civil,** Calzada Fray Juan de San Miguel 6 (tel. 3 46 60), seven blocks west of the northern edge of the *zócalo.* Both open 24hr.

Internet Access: Logicentro, Juárez 57 (tel. 4 94 94 or 4 77 40). 35 pesos per hr. Open M-Sa 9am-2pm and 5-9pm.

Post Office: Reforma 13 (tel. 3 56 30), 3 blocks south of the *zócalo* on Cupatitzio and left one block. Open M-F 8am-7pm, Sa 9am-1pm. **Postal Code:** 60000.

Telephones: LADATELs line the plaza. Otherwise, make long-distance phone calls from **Computel,** Ocampo 3, on the plaza (open 7am-10pm).

Phone Code: 452.

ACCOMMODATIONS

The place to stay is on or near the *zócalo,* where the ritzy and affordable coexist side-by-side. Straying too far could be hazardous to your health; Uruapan's cheaper hotels, oozing from the eastern edge of the *zócalo,* tend to be sleazy, with tattered bedspreads, filthy bathrooms, prostitution, and a fraternity of jumbo *cucarachas* hosting 24-hour parties.

Hotel del Parque, Independencia 124 (tel. 4 38 45), 5½ blocks from the plaza, just half a block from the beautiful Parque Nacional. An exception to the aforementioned *zócalo* generalization. Clean rooms surrounding an airy patio and tree-filled *jardín* are popular with backpackers. Super-friendly *dueño,* 24hr. hot water and balconies overlooking the park add to the appeal. Singles 60 pesos; doubles 80 pesos; 10 pesos for each additional person.

Hotel Moderno, Portal Santos Degollado 4 (tel 4 02 20), next door to the Oseguera, has enough rooms for an army of tourists. Matching furniture, winding tile stairways, and spotless *habitaciones* are sure to please. Singles and doubles with 1 bed 40 pesos, with 2 beds 70 pesos.

Hotel Los Tres Caballeros, Constitución 50 (tel. 4 71 70). Go north up Portal Santo Degollado (the eastern border of the *zócalo*), then into the market for about 2 blocks; the hotel is on the right. Red tile floors and stone stairways lend a subtle charm. Small rooms are clean and loaded with furniture, but the bathrooms might cramp your style if you're larger than a 6-year-old. Singles 47 pesos; doubles 58 pesos.

Hotel Oseguera, Portal Santos Degollado 2 (tel. 3 98 56), right across from the *zócalo,* has a tile entryway and enough house plants to make you think you're in the jungle. Bounce on the heavenly beds, and look out the window at the town below. Singles 40 pesos; doubles 50 pesos; triples 70 pesos.

Hotel Regis, Portal Carillo 12 (tel. 3 58 44 or 3 59 66), on the south side of the *zócalo,* is the cheapest of the classier joints and offers spotless rooms, each with a TV, phone, and fan. Caged birds and sherbet-green walls covered with murals liven up the joint. Singles 150 pesos; doubles 180 pesos; triples 190 pesos; quads 150 pesos; prices increase during high season.

FOOD

Sticking near the *zócalo* is also your best bet with food. The bountiful farmland surrounding Uruapan means also that delicious avocado, tomato, and mango dishes are available at down to earth prices. Coffee is a local specialty, and most places serve it up strong and hot.

Mercado de Antojitos, between Constitución and Pátzcuaro y Quiroga, is an outdoor square where you can sample Michoacán specialties for a pittance. Dozens of eager restaurateurs vie to cook you their personal specialties. Large portions only cost about 18-25 pesos. Don't miss the green chile *tamales* (2 pesos). Open daily 7am-11pm.

Restaurant Fonda de la Villa, Carranza 15 (tel. 4 28 00), in Hotel Villa de Flores, is one of the many fine hotel restaurants. Great service and a relaxed atmosphere accompany the vegetarian platter (35 pesos) or *enchiladas verdes* (25 pesos). Open 8am-10pm.

Café Tradicional de Uruapan, Carranza 5B. Follow your nose to the "Tradicional," one of the many cafes on Carranza, where locals sit sipping their *café* so slowly that they might lose a race with a Mexican train. Dining here is like sitting inside a cigar box—the cafe's entire surface area is covered in richly stained wood, from the wood bannisters to the checkered ceilings and floors. Specialties are breakfast, snacks, and coffee. *Huevos rancheros* 18 pesos, cappucchino 6.50 pesos. Open daily 8:30am-10pm.

Café La Pergola, Portal Corillo 16, next to the Hotel Regis, is a great place to watch the crowds in the plaza as you sit at a table with clean linen and ask the bow-tie-clad waiters to bring you an avocado sandwich (12 pesos) and a beer (12 pesos). Open daily 8am-9pm.

SIGHTS AND ENTERTAINMENT

Most of the dazzling sights of Uruapan are outside the city rather than inside it. If you're going to be in Uruapan for more than a couple of hours, think about checking out the surrounding landscape (see **Near Uruapan,** below). For an idea of what those places are like, visit the stunning **Parque Nacional Barranca del Cupatitzio** (tel. 4 01 97) at the western end of Independencia. *(Open daily 8am-6pm. Admission 2 pesos.)* A bit of jungle right on the edge of town, the park boasts frothy waterfalls, dense vegetation, and seemingly endless cool, shaded, cobblestone walkways. The park makes for an excellent afternoon walk or picnic.

See Ya, Satan

At Uruapan's Parque Nacional Barranca del Cupatitzio, young children give tours of **La Rodilla del Diablo** (The Devil's Knee) for a small fee. Legend has it that the river once dried up, leaving the surrounding lands stark and bare. The village, left without food or water, prayed in their desperation. One day, the friar Juan de San Miguel led a procession to the river's parched mouth, carrying an image of the Virgin. The friar halted the procession to sprinkle some holy water on the Virgin's image and on the rocks at the river's mouth. Suddenly, Satan appeared, saw the Virgin, and with a tumultuous shaking of the earth, retreated into the rocks. The flow of water resumed, but one rock still bears the imprint of the knee of the *Príncipe de la Tinieblas* (Prince of Darkness).

The markets on Constitución and near the Mercado Antojitos are amusing to browse through. Also in that area is Uruapan's other attraction, the **Museo Regional de Arte Popular** (tel. 4 34 34), on the *zócalo,* which displays Michoacán crafts. *(Open Tu-Su 9:30am-1:30pm and 3:30-6pm; free.)* Although not likely to make your heart skip a beat, the Museo may be worth a peek if you're into clay pots and wooded masks.

Much of the after-hours scene is set in cafes, where locals spend hours chatting over strong and tasty coffee. The main *discoteca* in town is **La Scala Disco,** Madrid 12 (tel. 4 26 09), in Colonia Huerta del Cupatitzio, just outside of town on the road to Tzaráracua, and a 12-peso cab ride from the center of town. A young, local crowd dances to U.S. top-40 and Mexican dance tunes. (Cover Tu-Th 10 pesos, F-Sa 30 pesos. Open Tu-F 9pm-2am.) For a more low-key evening, saunter over to **Club 1710,** Cupatitzio 5 (tel. 3 20 25), less than a block from the *zócalo,* for some pool (12 pesos per hr.) or dominoes (6 pesos per hr.; open daily 10am-11pm). There is also a cinema in the mall on 5 de Febrero, one block south of the *zócalo,* which shows not-quite-current U.S. blockbusters (15 pesos, last show around 9pm).

Near Uruapan

Uruapan is a convenient place from which to explore the interior of beautiful Michoacán. The diverse landscape is home to everything from ill-tempered volcanoes to picture-perfect waterfalls. It's not just Mother Nature that colors the landscape; silly mortals do as well. If you're tired of feigning appreciation for natural things, check out the immensely revered image of Christ that was rescued by the whole village of **San Juan Nuevo** after a volcano. Elsewhere, a world-famous guitar competition turns into a full-fledged musical blowout for a week in the summer. Get out and explore.

Near Uruapan: Paricutín Volcano

A visit to the beautiful, black, still-active Paricutín Volcano makes a great daytrip from Uruapan. In 1943, the volcano began erupting. By the time it quit spewing lava eight years later, there was little dust left to settle—the land had been coated in a thick and hardening layer of porous lava. Along the way, entire towns had been consumed and a 700m dark-side-of-the-moon-type mountain had sprung up. In one area, the lava covered the entire village of San Juan except for the church steeple, which now sticks out of a field of cold, black stone. Getting to the volcano is no easy task: you are in store for either a major hike or a horseback ride. Numerous steaming hot-spots along the way serve as a reminder of the volcano's might.

At the Angahuán **Centro Turístico** (tel. (452) 5 03 83), you can rent **horses** (30 pesos per horse) and a **guide** (120 pesos) to ascend the volcano. Plan to get an early start to avoid afternoon thunderstorms, and bring along some warm clothing just in case. The trip is long but worth the time and pesos. Decathlon contenders may consider the six- to eight-hour **walking tours** (40-50 pesos). Save yourself the Centro's 8-peso entrance fee by arranging for your guide independently. The volcano is easy to spot, silhouetted against the sky, and the adventurous may opt to make a solo assault on the summit without the aid of a guide. **Cabins** are also available for rent from the Centro. (1-6 people 250 pesos; bunks 40 pesos in a communal cabin.)

Getting There: Paraíso Galeana buses (tel. 4 33 50), headed for Los Reyes, from the Central de Autobuses in Uruapan, run to Angahuán, the closest village to the volcano (40min., every 30min. 5am-8pm, 7 pesos).

■ Near Uruapan: San Juan Nuevo Parangaricutiro

Ten kilometers west of Uruapan is **San Juan Nuevo,** formed after the burial of the old village by the eruption of the Paricutín Volcano in 1943. Many devotees come to the village for only one reason—to see the **Lord of Miracles,** an image of Christ dating back to the late 16th century. The image is revered for answering countless prayers and performing miracles. When the volcano erupted, San Juan's 2000 inhabitants abandoned the village and began a three-day, 33km pilgrimage carrying their beloved Lord of Miracles. A beautiful rose brick **sanctuary** with blue and yellow tile *capillas* was eventually built to house the image. *(Open daily 6am-8pm.)* The interior's white walls and vaulted ceilings are adorned with gold leaf, delicate stained-glass windows, and sparkling chandeliers—altogether an impressive and fitting house for the revered *Señor de los Milagros*. Several colorful murals depict the figure's history. The **museum,** Av. 20 de Noviembre, around the corner from the sanctuary, exhibits photos depicting the volcano's eruption, as well as before-and-after shots of the village (open M-Sa 9:15am-7pm, Su 9:15-6:30pm; free).

Once you've seen the cathedral and museum, San Juan Nuevo quickly loses appeal. The two main streets, **20 de Noviembre** and **Cárdenas,** which run on either side of the cathedral, play host to several shops and a rather dirty market. The best **dining** option in San Juan is not to dine in San Juan. No matter how hungry you are, you can wait until you get back to Uruapan. The array of animal parts and "meat" products under heat lamps (a.k.a. 40-watt lightbulbs) in stands along the main streets will have your stomach doing more somersaults than an Olympic gymnast. If you get stranded in San Juan, the **Hotel Victoria,** Cárdenas 26 (tel. 4 00 10), across from the cathedral, will take care of you with clean, humble rooms and lots of hot water (singles and doubles 60 pesos).

Getting There: Take a **Galeana** (tel. 4 33 50) bus to San Juan Nuevo (45min., every 10min. 5am-9:30pm, 4 pesos) from the Central de Autobuses. Perhaps more importantly, to get back, wait for the same bus on the corner of Cárdenas and Iturbe two blocks up from the cathedral (45min., every 15 min. until 9:30pm, 4 pesos).

■ Near Uruapan: Tzaráracua and Tzararecuita

The waterfalls at **Tzaráracua** (sah-RA-ra-kwa), 10km from Uruapan, cascade 20m into a series of small pools, surrounded by dense, lush vegetation. The first waterfall, Tzaráracua, is about 1km from the small parking lot—walk or ride a horse through steep, tree-lined paths (horses and unnecessary guides await tourists at the lot). Expect to pay 35 pesos round-trip to the first waterfall. Jungle-like vegetation is an attraction in itself. Once there, you can also hoof it to the base of the waterfall on foot—the path descends a flight of cobbled stairs and culminates at the base of the falls after about 20 minutes. Look but don't swim; there's a dangerous undercurrent. Use the recently completed bridge (dig the view) or ask a worker to take you over the water in a suspended boxcar (2 pesos).

Tzararecuita, a privately owned waterfall with two smaller, pollution-free pools that are perfect for swimming, is another 1.5km beyond the large pool. Rumor has it that the owner doesn't mind visitors to the falls and that skinny-dipping is popular. Keep an eye on your clothes. The aid of a guide is necessary to find the falls; guides don't charge a set fee but do expect a generous tip. You'd better not "tip" fewer than 25 pesos, or risk hurting someone's feelings.

Getting There: "Tzaráracua" buses leave from the south side of the *zócalo* at the corner of Emiliano Carranza and Cupatitzio (every hr. 8am-5pm, 3pesos). During the week, the schedule is so imprecise that you could be stuck all day; Sundays are a bit more reliable. Taxis cost about 20 pesos.

■ Near Uruapan: Paracho

Thirty kilometers north of Uruapan, **Paracho** gives aspiring *guitarristas* a chance to strum their hearts out and unleash the *mariachi* within. Carefully crafted six-strings pack just about every store. Fantastic bargains are available for all varieties of guitar. In the first week of August, the town holds an internationally renowned **guitar festival.** Musicians and craftspeople partake in a **musical orgy** that includes classical concerts, fireworks, dancing, and guitar-strumming competitions. The main street in town is **20 de Noviembre,** which runs by the plaza and the market and is the street the bus stops on. Sights in Paracho are limited to the **Casa de Arte y Cultura** on the corner of the plaza, which displays (who could have guessed) guitars (open sporadically each day from 10am-8pm).

Getting There: Hop on a **Galeana** (tel. 4 33 50) bus bound for Zamora via Paracho (45min., every 15min. 4am-8:30pm, 6 pesos) from the Central Camionera.

Pátzcuaro

Michoacán's earthy jewel, Pátzcuaro (pop. 70,000), is slowly becoming a travelers' favorite. Set high in the mountaintops, the city is surrounded by rolling hills and forests (kept lush by daily showers) that extend to the shores of the expansive (and unfortunately polluted) Lake Pátzcuaro. The compact and quiet city center is nearly as striking as the surrounding landscape—the tolling of cathedral bells resonates through cobblestone streets and white stucco colonial-style buildings.

This is not even Pátzcuaro's biggest selling point; the town is best known for its crafts. In order to further economic development, the Spanish bishop Vasco de Quiroga encouraged residents of each Purépecha village around the lake to specialize in a different craft. Today Pátzcuaro's plazas overflow with stacks of locally produced woolen sweaters, meticulously carved wooden toys, and decorative masks.

ORIENTATION

Pátzcuaro lies 56km southwest of Morelia and 62km northeast of Uruapan. To reach the *centro* from the **bus station,** catch a *combi* (7am-9:30pm, 2 pesos) or city bus (6:30am-10pm, 2 pesos) from the lot to the right as you leave the station. A taxi costs 10 pesos. The city consists of two distinct areas: the small and easily navigated downtown and a residential part of town 2.5km to the north, on the lakefront. Downtown centers around Pátzcuaro's two main squares. The smaller **Plaza Bocanegra** is all bustle and thick crowds; it's also where many of the cheap accommodations and restaurants reside. It is bordered by **Padre Lloreda** to the north, **Dr. Bendito Mendoza** to the west, and **Iturbide** to the east. One block south on Dr. Benito Mendoza is the larger **Plaza Quiroga,** an elegant and quiet plaza with a fountain and well-shaded, rosebush-lined paths. For shops, pricey meals, and fancy accommodations, this is the place to be. Streets form a rough grid and change names at each plaza. Addresses on the plazas are not given with the street name, but with the name of the *portal* (arcade). For example, at Plaza Quiroga, Benito Mendoza, which borders the plaza's western side, becomes **Portal Hidalgo.** Summers in Pátzcuaro can be wet and cool, so bring along some rain gear and a light sweater.

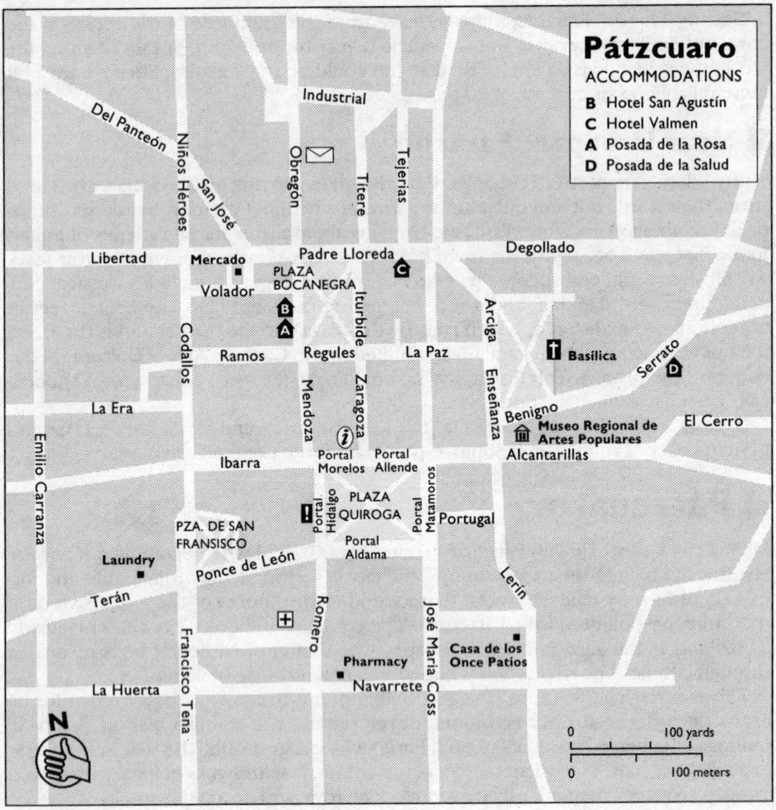

PRACTICAL INFORMATION

Buses: Off Circunvalación, 8 blocks south of the *centro*. **Autobuses de Occidente** (tel. 2 00 92) sends buses to Guadalajara (5hr., 12:15pm, 85 pesos) and many of the tiny villages around Pátzcuaro. **Elite** (tel. 2 14 60) goes to Nuevo Laredo (16hr., 1 and 7:45pm, 440 pesos) via Monterrey (14hr., 336 pesos). **Galeana** (tel. 2 08 08) goes to Lázaro Cárdenas (7hr., every 2hr. 5:30am-9pm, 70 pesos), Morelia (1hr., every 10min., 17 pesos), Uruapan (1½hr., every 10min., 20 pesos), and the small towns between them. **Herradura de Plata** (tel. 2 10 45) runs to Mexico City (first-class 5hr., 10 per day 8:15am-11pm, 130 pesos; second-class 7hr., 8 per day 7:35am-9:50pm, 112 pesos). **Primera Plus** (tel. 2 01 70) has cushy service to Guadalajara (5hr., 11:30pm, 90 pesos), Mexico City (7hr., 8 and 11:30am, 135 pesos), Querétaro (7hr., 11am and 1:40pm, 90 pesos), and San Luis Potosí (8hr., 10am, 140 pesos).

Tourist Office: Delegación Regional de Turismo, Plaza Quiroga 50A (tel. 2 12 14). Staff speaks English and hands out good maps. Open M-Sa 9am-2pm and 4-7pm, Su 9am-2pm. A smaller **information booth** is on the west side of Plaza Quiroga, in Portal Hidalgo. Booth open daily 10am-2pm and 5-8pm.

Currency Exchange: Banca Serfín, Portal Morelos 54 (tel. 2 15 16), on the north side of Plaza Quiroga. Also has an **ATM**. Open for exchange M-F 9am-3pm.

Luggage Storage: Available at bus station. 5 pesos per 1½hr., 10 pesos per day. Open 7am-10pm.

Emergency: Cuerpo de Rescate (tel. 2 21 65), open 24hr.

Police: (tel. 2 00 04), on the corner of Ibarra and Tangara, 4 blocks from Plaza Quiroga.

Pharmacy: Farmacia del Carmen (tel. 2 26 52), on the corner of Romero and Navarrete. Open 24hr. Doors open daily 8am-10pm; after hours, knock at the window on Navarrete.

Hospital: Hospital Civil, Romero 10 (tel. 2 02 85), next to San Juan de Dios church.

Post Office: Obregón 13 (tel. 2 01 28), half a block north of Plaza Bocanegra. Open M-F 8am-7pm, Sa 9am-1pm. **Postal Code:** 61600.

Fax: In the *caseta* in the bus station, or on the west side of Plaza Bocanegra. Open daily 7am-9pm.

Phone Code: 434.

ACCOMMODATIONS

Large numbers of hotels thrive on the burgeoning tourist population. Budget accommodations surround Plaza Bocanegra and feature very clean and comfy rooms. If you're lucky, you can score a balcony on the plaza and your very own bathroom. The three rooms for rent at the **Mandala** restaurant (see below) are the best bargain in town. If you're lucky enough to find one open, you can enjoy clean, beautiful rooms around a plant-filled courtyard and a complimentary breakfast, including homemade yogurt, all for 55 pesos.

Posada de la Salud, Serrato 9 (tel. 2 00 58), 3 blocks east of either plaza, a half block past the basilica. Beautiful courtyard draped in tropical scarlet flowers, rooms decked out with gorgeous carved furniture, cloud-soft mattresses, and clean bathrooms. Rooms can be cold and damp during the rainy season. Singles 100 pesos; doubles 140 pesos.

Hotel San Augustin, Portal Juárez 33, 2nd fl. (tel. 2 04 42), next door to Posada de la Rosa. Dark rooms off a green-tiled courtyard boast private baths, matching furniture, and an other-worldly cleanliness. Try to get a room overlooking the plaza. 50 pesos per person.

Posada de la Rosa, Portal Juárez 29, 2nd fl. (tel. 2 08 11), on the west side of Plaza Bocanegra. Red tiles and lots of sunlight. Simple rooms have a lone lightbulb hanging from the ceiling over clean hardwood floors and comfortable beds. Ask for a room overlooking the plaza. Singles 60 pesos; doubles 70 pesos; triples 80 pesos.

Hotel Valmen, Lloreda 34 (tel. 2 11 61), 1 block east of Plaza Bocanegra. Popular with international travelers. A great deal—if you don't mind the soft bed. Vibrant Aztec tile fills the lime-green courtyards. Well-lit rooms, some with balconies. 50 pesos per person. Strict lock-out 10pm.

FOOD

Food in Pátzcuaro ranges from pricey to dirt cheap, but it's all delicious. Economical restaurants ring Plaza Bocanegra and the accompanying market, while more fancy joints cluster in and around the hotels on Plaza Quiroga. *Pescado blanco* is the most popular dish in Pátzcuaro. *Charales* (smelts), served in the restaurants along the lakefront and on Janitzio, are fried, sardine-like fish that are eaten whole and by the fistful. *Caldos de pescado* (fish broths) bubble in large clay vats outside open-air restaurants on Janitzio; loaded with fish, shrimp, crab, or squid, these spicy soups are a meal-and-a-half in themselves.

Restaurant Yunuchen (tel. 2 08 94), Portal Juárez, on the east side of Plaza Bocanegra. This tiny gem, adorned with fascinating murals depicting local history and culture, serves amazing food. Friendly staff knows the area well and can give you information if you ever manage to tear yourself away from the food. Fantastic *comida corrida* 18 pesos. Open daily 9am-9pm.

Restaurant Posada la Basílica, Arciga 6 (tel. 2 11 08), in front of the basilica. A flower-filled courtyard leads to an elegant room with tiled floors, colorful tablecloths, and windows overlooking the town and nearby lakes. *Bistec a la Mexi-*

cana 30 pesos. Not the most inexpensive place in town, but the view is worth it. Open W-M 8am-5pm.

Mandala, Lerín 14 (tel. 2 41 76), just behind the Casa de los Once Patios. Scrumptious and filling vegetarian *menú del día* includes soup, salad, a tasty entree, and dessert (30 pesos). Homemade whole-wheat spaghetti (22 pesos) and organic veggies make for a new-age eating experience. Open Th-Tu 10am-8:30pm.

Restaurant Los Escudos, Portal Hidalgo 73 (tel. 2 12 90), on the west side of Plaza Quiroga, inside the Hotel Los Escudos. Bowtie-clad waiters, attractive wood furniture, and tasteful decorations create the perfect atmosphere for a huge meal. *Sopa tarasca* 15 pesos, most meals 32 pesos. Come Saturdays at 9pm to see the *danza de los viejitos,* a dance ridiculing the Spanish, while you dine. Open daily 8am-10:30pm.

Restaurant El Monje, Portal Aldama 12 (tel. 2 13 13), on Plaza Quiroga. Outdoor tables are perfect for people-watching. Breakfasts 15-30 pesos; *enchiladas suizas* 20 pesos; *bistec a la mexicana* 30 pesos. Open daily 8am-10pm.

SIGHTS

Some of the most notable sights around Pátzcuaro are just a short trip from the city center (see **Near Pátzcuaro,** p. 342). The **Museo Regional de Artes Populares** (tel. 2 10 29), at the corner of Lerín and Alcanterillas, one block south of the basilica, is housed within old fort-like walls, with stone floors and a flower-filled arcaded courtyard. *(Open Tu-Sa 9am-7pm, Su 9am-3pm. Admission 16 pesos, free on Sundays and for children under 13.)* It displays prize-winning regional crafts like pottery, copperware, and textiles, as well as an arresting collection of *maque* and *laca* ceramics.

Biblioteca Gertrudis Bocanegra, on the eponymous plaza, occupies the former site of an Augustine convent. *(Open M-F 9am-7pm.)* The library's multicolored mural illustrates the history of the Purépecha civilization from pre-Hispanic times to the 1910 Revolution. Once part of the Augustinian convent, the adjacent **Teatro Caltzontzín** (tel. 2 04 52) became a theater in 1936. *(Admission 7 pesos.)* An as-yet-unfulfilled prophecy was uttered upon the theater's erection: one Holy Thursday, the theater will crumble as punishment for the sin of projecting movies in a sacred place. Movies are still shown occasionally; keep an eye out for posters or ask at the library. Catch a Mexican or U.S. film, if you dare.

Statues of Pátzcuaro's two most honored citizens stand vigil over the town's principal plazas. The ceremonious, banner-bearing Vasco de Quiroga inhabits **Plaza Quiroga,** a vast and well-forested space that seems more like a humble city zoo than a *zócalo.* Famous throughout the state of Michoacán, Quiroga encouraged different indigenous peoples to make different crafts: hence, the specialization of each village into highly individualized forms of craft and artisanry. The massive, bare-breasted Gertrudis Bocanegra looks out from the center of **Plaza Gertrudis Bocanegra.** A martyr for Mexican independence, Bocanegra was executed by a Spanish squadron in the Plaza Quiroga in October of 1817. Locals claim that bullet holes still mark the ash tree to which she was tied.

When the Spanish bishop Vasco de Quiroga came to Pátzcuaro, he initiated not only social change but also bold architectural projects. Quiroga conceived the **Basílica de Nuestra Señora de la Salud,** at Lerín and Serrato, as a colossal structure with five naves arranged like the fingers of an extended hand. *(Open daily 8am-8pm.)* Each finger was to represent one of Michoacán's cultures and races; the hand's palm was to be the central altar representing the Catholic religion. Today, an enormous glass booth with gilded Corinthian columns and a dome protects the potentially edible statue of the *Virgen de la Salud.* When Vasco de Quiroga asked Tarascan artisans to design an image of the Virgin in 1546, they complied by shaping her out of *tatzingue* paste made from corn cobs and orchid honey, a typical 16th-century statue-making technique. The resulting statue is durable and incredibly light—only 5kg.

Three kilometers east of the city, at the end of Av. Benigno Serrato, is **El Humilladero** (Place of Humiliation), where the cowardly king Tangaxhuán II surrendered his crown and his daughters to Cristóbal de Olid and his Spanish troops. To reach it, take a *combi* marked "Panteón" or "El Cristo" (2.20 pesos). Two peculiar features distinguish this chapel: on its altar stands a rare monolithic cross, undoubtedly older than the date inscribed on its base (1553); and on the chapel's facade, images of gods represent the sun and the moon.

SHOPPING

Pátzcuaro's unique handcrafts—hairy Tócuaro masks, elegant Sierran dinnerware, and thick wool textiles—are sold in Plaza Bocanegra's **market** and in the small shops along the passage next to Biblioteca Gertrudis Bocanegra. Bargaining is easier in the market or when you buy more than one item, but don't expect much of a discount on the stunningly handsome wool articles. The thick sweaters, brilliantly colored *saltillos* and *ruanas* (stylized ponchos), rainbow-colored *sarapes,* and dark shawls are Pátzcuaro's specialty. Most shops are open daily from 8am to 8pm. For many of the same items at much cheaper prices, you may want to make the trek to some of the Pátzcuaro's surrounding villages.

Some higher quality (though pricier) items may also be found in the **Casa de Artesanías** (a.k.a. La Casa de los Once Patios, so named for the 18th-century building's 11 patios), down the street from the basilica, on Lerín near Navarette. *(Open daily 10am-2pm and 4-8pm.)* Originally a convent for Dominican nuns, the complex now houses craft shops, a small gallery of modern Mexican art, and a mural depicting Vasco de Quiroga's accomplishments. The *casa* sells cotton textiles, wooden and copper crafts, and superb musical instruments (guitars, flutes, and *güiros*) at decent prices (guitars 222-1200 pesos).

ENTERTAINMENT AND SEASONAL EVENTS

Unless there's an outdoor festival in the plazas, nightlife is confined mainly to restaurants and a few bars. At **Charanda's N,** Plaza Vasco de Quiroga 61B, local students and aging intellectuals match wits in chess tournaments amid wood carvings and potted plants. Live music stirs things up on weekends. (Cover Sa-Su 8-11pm 15 pesos. Open Tu-Su noon-1am.) The off-beat **El Viejo Gaucho,** Iturbe 10 (tel. 2 03 68), a colorful Argentinian bar and restaurant with art exhibits, features live Andean music, dramatic readings, and an open microphone (no cover; open Tu-Su 5pm-2am).

Pátzcuaro parties year-round. Its biggest celebration is without a doubt the spectacular **Noche de Muertos** (Nov. 1-2), which holds special importance for the Tarascans. Tourists from around the globe flock to Pátzcuaro and Janitzio to watch candle-lit fishing boats process to the tiny island. There, families and neighbors keep a two-night vigil in the haunting graveyard, feasting at the graves of their loved ones. The first night commemorates lost children; the second remembers deceased adults. Soon after Christmas celebrations come to a close, the town is electrified by **Pastorelas,** celebrated on January 6 to commemorate the Adoration of the Magi, and on January 17 to honor St. Anthony of Abad, the patron saint of animals. On both occasions, citizens dress their domestic animals in bizarre costumes, ribbons, and floral crowns. A few months later, Pátzcuaro's **Semana Santa** attracts devotees from all over the Republic. On Thursday, all the churches in town are visited, and on the night of Good Friday, the **Procesión de Imágenes de Cristo** is held, during which images of a crucified Christ are carried around town. The faithful flock from all over the state on Saturday for Pátzcuaro's **Procesión del Silencio,** celebrated elsewhere the day before. On this day, a crowd marches around town mourning Jesus's death in silence. Pátzcuaro and the surrounding regions party down with religious fervor on Sunday. If you aren't around for the bigger festivals and parties, don't fret. Most weekends still see bands playing in the plazas and young, attractive people getting down to the music.

Near Pátzcuaro

The area around Pátzcuaro is blessed with some of the most diverse landscapes in all of Mexico. Surrounding villages offer beautiful handicrafts, usually at cheaper prices than the cities, and the laid-back, low-key atmosphere is sure to gleefully infect even the most proud urbanites.

Near Pátzcuaro: Janitzio and Lago de Pátzcuaro

The tiny island of **Janitzio,** inhabited exclusively by Tarascan *indígenas* whose first language is Purépecha, subsists on its tourist trade—families, mostly Mexican, cast their lines into the lake for the tasty white fish that live there. There are basically two directions in Janitzio—up and down. The town's steep main street is lined with stores selling woolen goods, hand-carved wooden chess sets and masks. Among the shops, the bulk of which are quite pricey, numerous restaurants offer meals of fresh *pescado blanco* and *charales* (15 pesos).

Janitzio is best known for the enormous **statue of Morelos** that towers over the island. With his fist raised in the air in defiance of the Spanish, the awesome monument will make you want to lash out and fight the establishment, too. Inside the statue, a mural traces the principal events in Morelos's life and his struggle for independence. Endless steps lead you to the fantastic lookout point right around the height of Morelos' sleeve. There are two paths to the monument—one steep, and the other steeper (and more direct); both are to your left as you leave the ferry docks.

Getting There: First, hop on a "Lago" *combi* or bus (2 pesos) at the corner of Portal Regules and Portal Juárez, at Plaza Bocanegra in Pátzcuaro. At the docks, buy a ferry ticket (40min., ferries leave whenever they're full or on the hour, 8am-6pm, round-trip 18 pesos round-trip). Find out when the last boat leaves the island for Pátzcuaro; Janitzio does not accommodate the stranded.

Near Pátzcuaro: Tzintzuntzán

The most exciting thing about **Tzintzuntzán** (seen-soon-SAHN; Place of the Hummingbirds) may be saying the name—it is believed to be the phonetic sound of the many **hummingbirds** that flit through the sky. Tzintzuntzán was the last great city of the Tarascan empire. Before his death in the middle of the 15th century, the Purépecha lord Tariácori divided his empire among his three sons. When the empire was reunited years later, Tzintzuntzán was made the capital. Today, its claims to fame are the delicate, multicolored **ceramics** displayed on tables along Calle Principal.

Yácatas, a collection of peculiar pre-Hispanic temples, sits on a hill just outside the city on the road to Pátzcuaro. To reach the entrance, walk up the street in front of the market and convent. It's a bit of a hike—follow the road all the way around the hill until you reach the small museum/ticket booth. The bases of the structures, all that remain today, are standard rectangular pyramids. The missing parts, however, are what made them unique; each was originally crowned with an unusual elliptical pyramid constructed of shingles and volcanic rock. The pyramids are situated along the long edge of an artificial terrace. At the edge of the hill overlooking the lake is a sacrificial block from which victims were hurled; the bones of thousands of victims are said to lie at the base. The **Instituto Nacional de Anthropologia e Historia** at the entrance includes some Mesoamerican pottery, jewelry, and a narrative of Tarascan history (site open daily 9am-6pm; admission 10 pesos, free on Sundays). Also of interest is the 16th-century Franciscan **convent** closer to town. *(Open daily 10am-8pm).* The olive shrubs that now smother the extensive, tree-filled atrium were originally planted under Vasco de Quiroga's instructions over 450 years ago.

Getting There: Tzintzuntzán is perched on the northeastern edge of the Lago de Pátzcuaro, about 15km from Pátzcuaro, on the road to Quiroga and Morelia. Second-class **Galeana** buses (tel. 2 08 08) leave the Pátzcuaro bus station for Tzintzuntzán (30min., every 15min. 6am-8:30pm, 4 pesos) en route to Quiroga.

■ Near Pátzcuaro: Santa Clara del Cobre

Santa Clara del Cobre, 16km south of Pátzcuaro, truly shines when it comes to crafting copper. Long ago, rich copper mines filled the area, but they were hidden from the Spanish during the Conquest, never to be found again. The townspeople's passion for copperwork is unrivaled. When electricity was brought to the town, blackouts occurred when the artisans hammered the wires into pots and pans. Nearly every store in town sells highly individualized and decorative copper plates, pans, bowls, and bells. Prices here are only slightly better than elsewhere in Mexico, but Santa Clara is unbeatable for quality and variety. For a quick look at some highly imaginative pieces, step into the **Museo del Cobre,** near the plaza. Santa Clara celebrates the **Feria del Cobre** in early August. Like Quiroga, there is little to see in Santa Clara beyond *artesanías;* budget only a couple of hours for a trip here from Pátzcuaro. Unless you're a copper fiend, it is easy to get bored.

Getting There: Take a **Galeana** bus from Lago de Zirahuén (20min., every 30min. 7am-8pm, 3 pesos), or, from Pátzcuaro, catch a **Galeana** or **Occidente** bus to Santa Clara from the main station (every 30min. 7am-8pm).

■ Near Pátzcuaro: Lago de Zirahuén

The **Lago de Zirahuén** (Where Smoke Rose) makes for a fun trip from Pátzcuaro for those who like the pace of life slow—very slow. If you blink here, you won't miss anything; if you sleep for nine hours here, you won't miss anything. Smaller than Lake Pátzcuaro, Zirahuén is bordered by green farmland and gently sloping hills unobstructed by marshes and islands. On weekends, the lakefront fills with locals in search of a *tranquilo* place to relax. To **camp,** hike up one of the ridges that border the lake and set up in any one of the spots overlooking the water. Make sure to bring a tarp and wet-weather gear. If the land is privately owned (usually fenced off), you may have to pay a few pesos; ask before you pitch your tent. A choice spot is the sizeable piece of lakefront on the west end of town (left, as you face the lake). The strip, about 15m wide, is covered by grass cut short by grazing horses. The cabanas, a five-minute walk to the right along the dirt road bordering the lake, allow campers to use the bathrooms for 1 peso. Be forewarned: heavy afternoon rains during June and July can turn summer camping into a soggy experience.

After roughing it in the great outdoors, head to the *lancha* dock for a smooth one-hour ride around the lake (20 pesos in a collective boat; 150 pesos for a private ride, up to 10 people), and then sit down at one of informal lakefront restaurants, where a stack of tortillas, rice, salad, and fresh fish will run you a mere 15 pesos.

Getting There: From Pátzcuaro, catch one of the Zirahuén-bound cabs from Obregón and Industrial, past the post office, a block north of Plaza Bocanegra (about every 20min. 8am-6pm, 9 pesos). Taxis returning to Pátzcuaro leave a block inland from the church at "La Posta," by the "Marilu" sign (about 8 pesos). Or catch a **Galena** bus from the Pátzcuaro bus station (30min., every hr., 5 pesos).

Morelia

At 550,000 inhabitants and growing, Morelia is a city caught up in a dizzying whirl of growth and development. Sophisticated clothing stores and U.S. fast-food joints squeeze in among colonial houses and imposing stone facades along the main streets. Vendors hawk traditional textiles and wooden crafts alongside bootleg cassettes, Levi's knock-offs, and spare blender parts in the crowded *centro.* Nearby stand incongruous relics of Morelia's colonial magnificence—rose-colored stone arcades and grand, white-washed houses. Morelia is also the center of a proud tradition of Michoacán culture and history, and it has the museums, art exhibits, and performances to prove it. A sizeable student population spices up the cultural scene with theater, dance productions, and concerts. The residents are extremely friendly—they'll go out of their way to make you feel at home and are proud to help you maneuver

around their city. Blue exhaust clouds detract somewhat from the charm of Morelia's cobblestone side streets, but its bustling, eminently habitable spirit and sophisticated aura stimulate visitors without drawing crowds.

ORIENTATION

The streets in Morelia form a large grid, so navigating the city is relatively uncomplicated. Most sights are within walking distance of the *zócalo* and the adjacent cathedral on **Av. Madero,** Morelia's main thoroughfare. North-south streets change name at Madero, while east-west streets change name every other block. Getting downtown from the **bus station** is a quick 10-minute walk, a short cab ride (6 pesos), or a 10-minute bus ride (2.20 pesos). Walk to the left (east) as you exit the building, take the first right onto Valentín Gómez Farías, walk three blocks, then take a left on Av. Madero—the *zócalo* is three blocks ahead. The *centro* is the place to head if you're looking for food, lodging, or fun. Options abound in the three-block radius around the easily recognizable *zócalo.* Buses and *combis* serve the city (daily 6am-10pm, 2.20 pesos). Most routes can be picked up on Nigromante and Galeana, one block west of the *zócalo,* and on Allende, south of the *zócalo.* Taxis cluster in front of the bus station. Morelia's streets empty out after 10pm, especially on streets parallel to Madero. Although Morelia is a safe city, empty streets are never entirely safe—a taxi is often your best option.

PRACTICAL INFORMATION

Transportation

Airport: Aeropuerto Francisco J. Múgica (tel. 12 65 14), on the Carretera Morelia-Cinapécuaro at km 27. A special blue and white *Aeropuerto* bus will get you there for 7 pesos. Taxi (tel. 12 22 21) to the airport 85 pesos. **Aeromar** (tel. 12 85 45 and 13 05 55). **Mexicana,** Pirindas 435 (tel. 24 38 08 or 24 38 18). Open M-F 9am-6:30pm. **Taesa,** Av. Acueducto 60 (tel. 13 40 50). Open M-F 9am-2pm and 4-7pm, Sa 9am-1pm. All have offices at the airport.

Buses: Leave from the **Central** station (tel. 13 55 89) on Ruiz at V. Gómez Farías. **Autobuses de Occidente/La Linea** has second-class service to Manzanillo (10hr., 5 per day 6:45-1:15am, 139 pesos) and Mexico City (6hr., every 20min., 90 pesos). **Elite** (tel. 12 24 62) sends buses to Acapulco (second-class 12hr., 5 per day 7-2:30am, 217 pesos), Nuevo Laredo (16hr., 3, 6, and 9:30pm, 460 pesos) via Monterrey (13hr., 355 pesos), Reynosa (16hr., 5pm, 364 pesos) via San Luis Potosí (6hr., 143 pesos), and Tijuana (40hr., 1:15, 9, and 11:45pm, 787 pesos) via Mazatlán (16hr., 300 pesos). **ETN** (tel. 13 74 40) has executive service to Manzanillo (7¼hr., 10:30pm, 220 pesos) and Mexico City (4hr., 24 per day 2am-midnight, 165 pesos). **Flecha Amarilla** (tel. 13 55 89) goes to Colima (6½hr., 7:40am and noon, 130 pesos), Guanajuato (4hr., every hr. 5:30am-4:30pm, 65 pesos), Querétaro (4hr., 12 per day, 72 pesos), and San Luis Potosí (6hr., 8 per day 7:10am-8:30pm, 130 pesos). **Herradura de Plata** (tel. 12 29 88) goes to Mexico City (4½hr., 25 per day, 12:30am-11pm, 110-125 pesos). **Parhikuni** (tel. 13 99 10) sends first-class and *plus* buses to Lázaro Cárdenas (8hr., 10 per day 6:20am-1:30am, 125-135 pesos) and Uruapan (2hr., every 20min. 6am-8pm, 42-50 pesos). **Primera Plus** (tel. 13 55 89) runs first-class buses to Aguascalientes (6hr., 2:30am and 3 per day 8:05am-3:05pm, 145 pesos), Guadalajara (5hr., 9am, 1, 3:30pm, and midnight, 127 pesos), Mexico City (4½hr., 8 per day, 142 pesos), and San Luis Potosí (6hr., 8 per day, 142 pesos). **Ruta Paraíso/Galeana** (tel. 12 55 05) goes to Lázaro Cárdenas (8hr., every hr. 6:40am-7:50pm, 135 pesos), Pátzcuaro (1hr., every 10min. 6am-9pm, 18 pesos), and Uruapan (2¼hr., every 20min. 6am-9pm, 37 pesos). **Servicios Coordinados** (tel. 13 55 89) serves Aguascalientes (6hr., 10:15am and 2pm, 130 pesos), Guadalajara (5hr., 8 per day, 96 pesos), Querétaro (3½hr., 13 per day 5:20am-7:20pm, 70 pesos), and San Luis Potosì (6hr., 11 per day 2am-3:20pm, 132 pesos). **Transportes Fronteras** (tel. 12 24 62) serves Ciudad Juárez (24hr., 10:30am, 563 pesos) via Zacatecas (9hr., 184 pesos).

Tourist, Financial and Local Services

Tourist Office: State Tourist Office, Nigromante 79 (tel. 17 23 71), at Madero Pte., 2 blocks west of the *zócalo.* Staff distributes maps and a monthly list of cultural events. Free city tours on Sundays at 11am. Open M-F 8am-8pm, Sa-Su 9am-8pm.

Currency Exchange: Banks cluster on Av. Madero near the cathedral. **Bancomer,** Madero Ote. 21 (tel. 12 29 90). Open M-F 8am-7pm, Sa 9am-2pm. **BITAL,** Madero Ote. 24 (tel 13 98 00). Open M-F 8am-7pm, Sa 9am-2:30pm.

Laundromat: Lavandería Cuautla, Cuautla 152 (tel. 12 48 96), south of Madero. 16 pesos to wash/dry 3kg. Open M-F 9am-2pm and 4-8pm, Sa 9am-1:30pm.

Emergency and Communications

Emergency: Dial 06.

Police: (tel. 12 00 73 or 12 22 22), on 20 de Noviembre, 1 block northwest of the Fuente de las Tarascas, at the end of the aqueduct. Open 24hr.

Red Cross: Ventura 27 (tel. 14 51 51 or 14 50 25), next to Parque Cuauhtémoc. Some English spoken. Open 24hr.

Pharmacy: Farmacia Fénix, Allende 69 (tel. 12 84 92), behind the *zócalo.* Open M-Sa 9am-9pm, Su 9am-8:30pm.

Hospital: Hospital General Dr. Miguel Silva (tel. 12 01 02), Isidro Huarte and F. de Mogil. Open 24hr.

Post Office: Av. Madero Ote. 369 (tel. 12 05 17), in the Palacio Federal, 5 blocks east of the cathedral. Open M-F 8am-7pm. **Postal Code:** 58000.

Fax: Computel, Portal Galeana 157 (tel./fax 13 62 56), on the *zócalo.* Open daily 7am-10pm. Also, Av. Madero Ote. 371 (tel. 13 86 72), in the Palacio Federal next to the post office. Open M-F 8am-8pm.

Phone Code: 43.

ACCOMMODATIONS

Most budget hotels lie south of Madero and just west of the cathedral. The only time you may have trouble finding a room is during *Semana Santa,* though there is a small influx of summer school students during July and August. Hotels in Morelia are very comfortable, and even the budget ones tend to be extremely nice.

Mansión Posada Don Vasco, Vasco de Quiroga 232 (tel. 12 14 84), across from Hotel Mintzicuri. Spacious rooms come with cable TV, phones, wood furniture, and purified water. 1 person 90 pesos; 2 people 105 pesos; 3 people 120 pesos; 4 people 121 pesos. Ask the friendly staff about the availability of smaller rooms right off the courtyard; they come with all amenities for only 60 pesos.

IMJUDE Villa Juvenil Youth Hostel, Chiapas 180 (tel. 13 31 77), at Oaxaca. A 20min. walk from the *zócalo.* Walk west on Madero Pte., turn left on Cuautla, walk for 6 blocks, then turn right on Oaxaca and continue for 4 blocks to Chiapas. Very happening. Exceptionally well-maintained dormitories, bathrooms, and red-tiled lobby. Sports facilities and pool. 35 pesos per person. 25% discount for HI members. Breakfast 12.50 pesos, lunch and dinner 15 pesos. 50-peso linen deposit. Open daily 7am-11pm. Strict curfew 11pm.

Hotel Mintzicuri, Vasco de Quiroga 227 (tel. 12 06 64), 2 blocks east and 1½ blocks south of the cathedral. Wrought iron railings overflowing with flowers enclose sparkling clean, cozy, wood-paneled rooms equipped with phones, cable TV, and hot water. Very popular with Mexican tourist families, so come early or call ahead to make sure rooms are available. Singles 90 pesos; doubles 105 pesos; triples 120 pesos; quads 121 pesos.

Hotel Colonial, 20 de Noviembre 15 (tel. 12 18 97), at Morelos Nte. Cozy courtyard glows a deep yellow. Friendly staff. Rooms boast high ceilings, large windows, and private baths; some even have balconies. *Agua purificada.* Singles 65 pesos; doubles 80 pesos; add 15 pesos for TV.

Posada de Villa, Padre Lloreda 176 (tel. 12 72 90), 3 blocks south of the Museo de las Artesanías. Gigantic rooms have great views, house plants, and tasteful decor. Bathrooms are a bit run-down but very clean. Singles 95 pesos; doubles 115 pesos. Pastel apartments for 1-2 people 1500 pesos per month.

FOOD

Finding good, cheap food is a breeze in Morelia—almost every thoroughfare has at least one family-run restaurant that dishes out inexpensive *comida corrida* (usually around 15 pesos). The best deals cluster around the bus station. Restaurants on the *zócalo* tend to be pricier but are good places for breakfast, since other eateries tend to open late and close early.

Cocina de la Rosa, Tapía 270, right next to the rose garden. This family-run restaurant is where smart locals choose to while the day away. Saying "this family knows how to cook" will win you the 1999 Understatement Award. Great food (and lots of it) served fresh off the stove daily. *Huevos al gusto* 8 pesos, *comida corrida* 16 pesos. Open daily 8am-5pm.

Restaurante-Bar La Huacana, Aldama 116 (tel. 12 53 12), at Obeso. A gargantuan oil painting forms the backdrop for the large cafeteria-style dining area. Stone walls provide great acoustics for the *mariachis* who play on weekdays 3-5pm. The corner locale is perfect for people-watching. *Comida corrida* 16 pesos. Enchiladas 15 pesos. Open M-Sa 9am-8pm.

Restaurante Vegetariano Acuarias, Hidalgo 75, at the end of the walkway south of the *zócalo.* Set in a blue-tiled courtyard littered with plants, bikes, and an assortment of junk. Locals devour yummy vegetarian food as they listen to Mexican tunes in an extremely laid-back atmosphere. *Comida corrida* 19 pesos. Breakfast combos 15 pesos. Open daily 9am-6pm.

Restaurant Vegetariano, upstairs at Madero 549 (tel. 13 13 68), across from Salinas y Rocha store. Serves hearty, tasty vegetarian *comida corrida* (19 pesos), and veggie burgers (8 pesos), without any new-age frills. Open daily 8:30am-7pm.

El Tragadero, Hidalgo 63 (tel. 3 00 92). This open-front restaurant affords a great view of the marketplace area. Fans lazily whirl overhead. The food is not only tasty and cheap, but the restaurant is also open late (for Morelia). *Comida corrida* 24 pesos. Open daily 7:30am-11pm.

SIGHTS

Morelia is a history buff's dream come true. Still going strong at age 112, the **Museo Michoacano,** Allende 305 (tel. 12 04 07), one block west of the *zócalo* at Abasolo, has thorough exhibits divided into five categories: ecology, archaeology, the colonial period, the struggle for freedom, and independent Mexico. *(Open Tu-Sa 9am-7pm, Su 9am-2pm. Admission 16 pesos, free for children, seniors, and for all on Sundays.)* The most notable object on display is a huge, anonymous painting completed in 1738, *La Procesión del Traslado de las Monjas de una Universidad a su Convento Nuevo* (The Procession of the Nuns from the University to Their New Convent). A mural around the stairway by Alfredo Zalce will capture your attention—it portrays Hidalgo, Morelos, and others who have shaped Mexico's history. It also skewers those who blindly admire U.S. mass culture. The former residence of José María Morelos, the parish priest who led the Independence movement after Hidalgo's death, is now the **Museo de Morelos,** Morelos Sur 323 (tel. 13 26 51), one block east and two blocks south of the cathedral. *(Open M-Su 9am-7pm. Admission 5 pesos, free for children, seniors, and for all on Sundays.)* The museum displays Morelos's religious vestments, military ornaments, and uniforms, as well as other mementos of the surge for independence.

More of a civic building than a museum, the **Casa Natal de Morelos** (Birthplace of Morelos) is on Corregidora 113 (tel. 12 27 93), at García Obeso, one block south of the cathedral. *(Open M-Sa 9am-7pm; free.)* Glass cases preserve Morelos's wartime cartography, communiqués, and letters. Also notable are murals by Alfredo Zalce and a shady courtyard watched over by the martyr's bust. A few blocks away on Nigromante and Maderos is the **Colegio de San Nicolas de Hidalgo,** the oldest university in the Americas. Opened in the 16th century in Pátzcuaro, alma mater of such men as Hidalgo and Morelos, the school closed during the revolution and re-opened in 1847. The college is a great place to relax and people-watch.

Overlooking the *zócalo,* the massive **cathedral** has a stunning interior graced by vaulted ceilings, chandeliers, tapestries, and stained glass windows. *(Open daily 7am-9pm; free.)* The church's oldest treasure is the *Señor de la Sacristía,* an image of Christ sculpted by *indígenas* out of dry corn cobs and orchid nectar. In the 16th century, Felipe II of Spain donated a gold crown to top off the masterpiece. In the 19th century, a bishop tipped the careful balance that had existed between Neoclassical and Baroque elements by removing the elaborate Baroque filigree from the altarpieces and frescoes; he renovated the church's interior in a more conservative style.

The **Casa de Cultura,** Morelos Nte. 485 (tel. 12 41 51), is housed in the **Monasterio de los Carmelitas Descalzos,** four blocks north of Madero. *(Center and museum open M-F 9am-3pm and 5-8pm, Sa-Su and holidays 10am-6pm; free.)* A gathering place for artists, musicians, and backpackers, the *casa* houses a bookstore, art galleries, a theater, and a lovely cafe. Dance, voice, theater, guitar, piano, and sculpture classes are offered, and concerts, book presentations, art festivals, and literature workshops are held here (20-30 pesos). This is a great place to find out information on cultural events (tel. 13 12 15 or 13 13 20, ext. 233). The on-premises **Museo de la Máscara** exhibits a small collection of masks from all over the Republic.

The **Casa de las Artesanías** (tel. 12 12 48), Humboldt at Fray Juan de San Miguel, is a huge crafts museum and retail store, selling colorful macramé *huipiles,* straw airplanes, pottery, carved wood furniture, and guitars (open M-Sa 10am-3pm and 5-8pm, Su 10am-6pm). Better prices, however, await in Pátzcuaro.

When you get tired of being inside, head to the eastern end of Madero where you will find the statue of **Las Tarascas,** probably the most recognizable landmark in Morelia. The statue is of three indigenous women making an offering to the heavens. Continue walking down Acueducto and head up the hillside to **El Mirador** (the viewpoint) for a fabulous view of the city of Morelia and its surrounding area.

ENTERTAINMENT

Listings of events can be found at the Casa de Cultura and at the tourist office. Bright lights, musical celebrations, and thespian allure draw crowds to the **Teatro Morelos** (tel. 14 62 02), on Av. Camelina at Calzada Ventura Puente, and the **Conservatorio de las Rosas** (tel. 12 74 06), at the corner of Guillermo Prieto and Santiago Tapia. The **Casa Natal de Morelos** shows artsy films and holds cultural events on Fridays at 8pm (films screened the last Tu-Th of every month, noon and 7pm; admission 1 peso). **Multicinema Morelia** (tel. 12 12 88), on Santiago Tapia and Bernal Jiménez, behind the Palacio Clavijero, features Hollywood's latest (open daily 3-10pm; 17 pesos). If you find heavenly bodies more fascinating than scantily clad ones, head for the **Planetario** (tel. 14 24 65), on Ventura Puenta and Ticateme, in the Centro de Convenciones at Calzada (shows Tu-Sa 7pm, Su 6:30pm; 15 pesos). To get there, take the "Ruta Rojo #3" *combi* from Av. Allende/Valladolid, and watch for the *planetario* and convention center complex on the right.

La Casona del Teatro, Aquiles Serdán 35 (tel. 17 33 53), at Morelos, one block north of Madero, hosts comedies in Spanish (shows Tu-Sa 9pm, Su 7:30pm; 30 pesos). The coffee shop/theater is popular with students and bohemian types who play chess and drink coffee (6 pesos) until showtime (open M-Sa 9am-11pm). A similar hangout is the somewhat pricey bookstore and cafe **La Librería,** Calzada Fray Antonio de San Miguel 324 (tel. 12 02 87), at Av. Acuedicto and Madero, about three blocks east of the plaza de Villalongin; it sometimes has films and music.

Morelia has a thriving nightclub scene fueled by the hordes of local students. Twentysomethings bounce to the latest Spanish and English pop tunes at **Dalí's,** Av. Campestre 100 (tel. 15 55 14; beer 15 pesos; cover 25 pesos; open M-Sa 8pm-3am, Su 5pm-2am). Another hotspot with a similar crowd is **Siglo 18** (tel. 24 07 47), Blvd. García León and Turismo (cover 30-50 pesos; open Tu-Su 9:30pm-3:30am). To really get your money's worth, head for **Bar Intermedio,** where **beer costs 2 pesos** and patrons move chairs and tables to create a dance floor. Live music every third night really gets the place rockin'. (No cover. Open Tu-Su 8pm-3am.) The dark interior at **Badierna,** Lázaro Cárdenas 2225 (tel. 15 53 54), lures an older, slicker crowd to salsa the night away. Domestic drinks run about 13 pesos. (Cover 10-20 pesos. Open Th-Sa 9pm-3am.) **Freedom,** Av. Campestre 374 (tel. 15 66 61), hosts local teenage rebels out past their 10pm curfews (open daily 1pm-3am). For real multi-level, base-throbbing club madness, head to **Akbal** and **Balam** (the cab drivers know where they are). The jungle motif at each place won't fool you, but you'll be too busy gettin' down and boozing to notice. Partners dance on the bar, the tables, and every square inch of the terraced dance floor. Beers cost 9 pesos; domestic drinks cost 15 pesos. (Cover 30-40 pesos. Open W-Su 9am-3pm.)

Lázaro Cárdenas

Named after *michoacano* President Lázaro Cárdenas, whose ardent socialist measures included nationalizing oil in 1938, the hot, noisy city of Lázaro Cárdenas (pop. 135,000) is Mexico's most important port on the Pacific. It also houses the largest steel factory in Latin America. The city's size, services, and location make it a likely departure point or pit stop on an exploration of Michoacán's 260km of deserted, rugged, beautiful coast, but Cárdenas itself is a filthy pit: get in and get out.

ORIENTATION AND PRACTICAL INFORMATION Lázaro Cárdenas lies near the border of Michoacán and Guerrero states, 382km southwest of Morelia and 122km northwest of Ixtapa. Most services lie on the town's principal thoroughfare, **Av. Lázaro Cárdenas,** usually near its intersection with **Corregidora.** The main *zócalo*,

Plaza de la Reforma, is three blocks east of the *avenida*'s intersection with Guillermo Prieto. *Combis* and buses run up and down Av. Lázaro Cárdenas and whisk passengers to nearby beaches. **Buses** run out of independent stations on or close to the main drag. **Autotransportes Cuauhtémoc** and **Estrella Blanca**, Francisco Villa 65 (tel 2 11 17), four blocks west of Corregidora, sends buses to Acapulco (6-7hr., *directo* noon, 11 per day 11:15am-midnight, 73-91 pesos) and Tijuana (45 hr, 2:30pm, 988 pesos) via Mazatlán (25hr., 476 pesos) and points along the way. **Autotransportes Galeana,** Av. Lázaro Cárdenas 1810 (tel. 2 02 62) provides service to Manzanillo (6hr., 5 per day 4:15-11:30am, 80-93 pesos), Morelia (8hr., 13 per day 2am-7pm, 132 pesos) via Pátzcuaro (7hr., 109 pesos) and Uruapan (6hr, 88 pesos). **Estrella de Oro**, Corregidora 318 (tel 2 02 75) travels to Mexico City (13hr., 7 and 8pm, 230-290 pesos). **La Linea**, Av. Lázaro Cárdenas 171 (tel. 7 18 50) runs to Colima (7hr., 8pm, 108 pesos), Guadalajara (9hr., 8pm, 202 pesos), and Mexico City (14hr., 4 per day 3-11:30pm, 198 pesos).

Get the maps and info needed to attack the coast from the **Delegación Regional de Turismo,** Nicolás Bravo 475 (tel./fax 2 15 47), one block east of Av. Lázaro Cárdenas and two blocks north of Corregidora, in the big white Hotel Casa Blanca (open M-F. 9am-3pm and 5-7pm, Sa 10am-1pm). **Banamex,** Lázaro Cárdenas 1646 (tel 2 20 18) exchanges currency and has an **ATM** (open M-F 8:30am-4:30pm, Sa 10am-2pm), as does **BITAL,** Lázaro Cárdenas 1940 (tel. 2 26 33; open M-Sa 8am-7pm). Long-distance international **phone calls** can be made and **faxes** sent from **Caseta Goretti,** Corregidora 79 (tel. 7 31 55; open daily 7am-1am). The **airport** (tel. 2 19 20), named after you-know-who, hosts carriers **Aerosudpacífico** (tel. 7 11 78), **Transporte Aeromar** (tel. 7 10 84), and **Aerolínea Cuahonte** (tel. 2 36 35). The **Red Cross,** Aldama 327 (tel. 2 05 75), is open day or night. **Farmacia Paris** resides at Av. Lázaro Cárdenas 2002 (tel. 2 14 35; open 24hr.). Some English is spoken. The **Hospital General** (tel. 2 08 21) is also on Av. Lázaro Cárdenas. The **police** (tel. 2 18 55) await at the Palacio Municipal, on Av. Lázaro Cárdenas at Av. Río Balsas. The **post office** is at Nicolás Bravo 1307 (tel. 2 05 47; open M-F 8am-7pm, Sa 9am-1pm). The **phone code** is 753.

ACCOMMODATIONS AND FOOD The rent-by-the-hour atmosphere of most budget accommodations in town will make you happy to make your way to the reputable **Hotel Reyna Pio,** Corregidora 79 (tel. 2 06 20) at Lázaro Cárdenas. Clean rooms boast air-conditioning, telephone, mustard-yellow furniture, and 1970s TV sets. (Singles 100 pesos; doubles 130 pesos). Fill up that stomach at **El Chile Verde,** Francisco I. Madero 66 (tel. 2 10 85), across from Av. Lázaro Cárdenas. Hot chili peppers dance happily on the walls while waiters serve spicy *enchiladas verdes* (16 pesos) and *comida corrida* (15 pesos) in this casual, open-air cafe. (Open daily 7am-10pm.) The slightly pricier but air-conditioned **El Paraiso,** Lázaro Cárdenas 1862 (tel. 2 32 33), near the Galeana bus station, offers traditional Mexican food amid orange, green, and yellow decor straight out of the 70s. The *sopa de tortilla* (13 pesos) and fish (40 pesos) are both worth a try.

Michoacán Coast

Michoacán's temperamental, wildly beautiful coastline offers solace and tranquility one moment, then suddenly erupts into ripping, turbulent surf. Rte. 200, the solitary coastal highway, twists up, down, and around Michoacán's angry terrain. Hills are pushed up against each other; rocks are defaced by crashing white waves spraying against blue skies. Lush tropical vegetation lends a loving touch of green to the state's 260km of virgin beaches.

Michoacán's coast should be treated with cautious respect. Powerful waves make its beaches better suited for surfing than swimming, and the currents are strong even in the areas recommended for swimming. Since there are no lifeguards, exercise great caution. Rte. 200 tends to be deserted and dangerous at night; *Let's Go* does not recommend traveling there at night.

■ Michoacán Coast: Playa Azul

Playa Azul (pop. 5000), a small *pueblo* and nascent beach resort 26km west of Lázaro Cárdenas, is renowned for its long stretch of soft, golden sand and its majestic rose-golden sunsets. Here, the sea is temptress—the tide rises high to the shore, tracing the base of a line of *palapa* restaurants, then quickly recedes under crashing waves, good for surfing and boogie-boarding. Swimmers shouldn't stray too deep, as this open stretch of sea has a strong undercurrent. The beach is crowded with Mexican tourists during December and *Semana Santa,* but quiet the rest of the year.

ORIENTATION AND PRACTICAL INFORMATION Far from being a polished tourist town, Playa Azul is typically *michoacano.* Unmarked dirt roads are the main thoroughfares, lined with thatched roof houses, open-air markets, and the occasional pig. The village is so small that street names are seldom used (or known) by locals. The **Malecón** borders the beach; it is called **Aquiles Serdán** to the west of the plaza and **Emiliano Zapata** to the east. The other streets bordering the plaza are **Montes de Oca** to the west, and **Filomena Mata** to the east. **Av. Lázaro Cárdenas** runs into Playa Azul from the highway, runs perpendicular to the beach, and intersects **Carranza, Madero,** and **Independencia,** the three main streets parallel to the beach.

Though Playa Azul doesn't have a bank or *casa de cambio,* it does offer most other services. For long-distance **phone calls,** visit the town's **caseta** (tel. 6 01 22) on Independencia (open M-Sa 8am-9pm, Su 8am-1pm). The **market** is on Flores Magón, two blocks east of the plaza. The **police** (tel. 2 18 55 or 2 20 30) reside across from the PEMEX station. **Farmacia Eva Carmen,** Av. Lázaro Cárdenas at Madero, satisfies your drug needs (open daily 8am-9:30pm). The **Centro de Salud** is next door to the post office (open 24hr.). The **post office** (tel. 6 01 09) is on Madero at Montes de Oca, just behind Hotel María Teresa (open M-F 8am-3pm). The **phone code** is 753.

ACCOMMODATIONS AND FOOD Bucolic Playa Azul offers several adequate budget hotels from which to choose. Reservations are recommended in August, December, and during *Semana Santa.* **Hotel Costa de Oro,** on Madero three blocks away from Lázaro Cárdenas, is the best deal in town. White stucco walls and an elegantly scalloped bannister lead to clean, comfortable rooms with funky tile floors, fans, and mismatched bedspreads, but no hot water (singles 50 pesos; doubles or triples 80 pesos). **Bungalows de la Curva** (tel. 6 00 58 or 2 28 55), on Madero at Lázaro Cárdenas, offers a good deal for groups. Bungalows have kitchenettes, basic furniture, and hot water. A swimming pool is surrounded by a patio with tables for lazy days (2 beds 130 pesos; 4 beds 200 pesos).

Palapa restaurants are so close to the shore that the waves will come up and tickle your toes. The bubbly owners of **Coco's Pizza** will make you feel right at home. The *camarones al diablo* (shrimp with chile, 30 pesos) are a spicy taste of heaven. Cool off with a beer (5 pesos; open daily 8am-9pm). Inland, **Restaurante Familiar Martita** (tel. 6 01 11), on Flores Magón at Madero, is a cozy family-run restaurant with heavy, carved wooden chairs and fishnets on the walls. The *comida corrida* costs 25 pesos, while huge breakfast combos go for 20 pesos (open daily 7am-midnight).

Getting There: From Lázaro Cárdenas, take a "Playa Azul" *combi* on Av. Lázaro Cárdenas (45min., every 2min. 5am-9pm, 7pesos).

■ Michoacán Coast: Between Playa Azul and Caleta de Campos

Beautiful beaches cover the 43km of coast stretching from Playa Azul to Caleta de Campos. **Las Peñas,** 13km west of Playa Azul, is a beach that is better appreciated from the shore: its surf is terribly turbulent, and its waters are infested with sharks. **El Bejuco,** only 2km farther west, has a sandy cove with tamer waves and fewer rocks. Another 12km west, you'll find **Chuquiapan,** a long stretch of sandy beach with reasonable waves and a shore studded with tall green palms. **La Soledad,** enclosed by rocky formations 4km farther west, is more secluded and cozy, lying at the base of a hill covered with dense vegetation. Its gray sands are strewn with rocks and driftwood. As usual in Michoacán's Pacific coast, rough waters don't make for safe swimming. **Mexcalhuacán,** 2km west, offers a fantastic view from a bluff overlooking a rocky coast. Caleta de Campos comes 7km later. **Nexpa,** a sandy beach with powerful waves, is a surfer's heaven 5km west of Caleta. *Palapa* restaurants, known as *enramadas,* line most of the beaches. To be safe, bring bottled water and a snack.

Getting There: Buses and *combis* running from Lázaro Cárdenas to Caleta de Campos pass by each of the beaches listed above, except Nexpa (every 30min., 5am-7:30pm; Las Peñas 30min.; Chuquiapan 40min.; La Soledad 45min.). The beaches are a five- to 10-minute walk from the highway. To return to Playa Azul or Caleta, you'll have to wave a towel and flag down a *combi*—be sure to confirm when the last one is expected. To get to Nexpa, take a white *combi* from the bus depot at the beginning of Av. Principal in Caleta de Campos (10min., every 40min. 7am-7pm).

■ Michoacán Coast: Caleta de Campos

A tiny fishing village 47km west of Playa Azul, Caleta de Campos has a pleasant beach but little else for the fun-loving traveler. The entire town is laid out along its one main street; sneeze and you'll miss it. No one comes to Caleta for its urban thrills, though—its beach is the main act in town. The combination of green twisted terrain and brilliant blue surf massaging the shore is truly beautiful, and a dirt path climbs along the hills to the village above, offering a spectacular view of the coast. Because the water is somewhat sheltered, the surf is calmer than at Playa Azul, though the rolling waves make for good boogie boarding and body surfing. For most of the year, Caleta's two hotels are empty, but they fill up during *Semana Santa* and Christmas.

ORIENTATION AND PRACTICAL INFORMATION From Lázaro Cárdenas, **Rutas de Transportación Colectiva** (tel. 2 02 62) buses run from the Galeana bus station to Caleta (1½hr., every hr. 5:40am-8:10pm, 20 pesos). You can also board a "Caleta" *combi* anywhere along Av. Lázaro Cárdenas (1½hr., every 30min. 5:20-8pm, 20 pesos). To return to Lázaro Cárdenas from Caleta, pick up a bus or *combi* at the stop near the end of Av. Principal (5:30am-8pm). From Playa Azul, get on a "La Mira" *combi* across from the PEMEX gas station (5min., every 10min., 3 pesos). Get off at Acalpican (be sure to tell the driver where you want to go in advance) and catch a bus labeled "Caleta" at the intersection (every 30 min. 5:45am-8:45pm, 17 pesos).

Caleta de Campos has one paved main street, Melchor Ocampo, locally known as **Av. Principal.** The **police, post office** (open M-F 8am-3pm), and **bus stop** are all on Av. Principal. There are few private telephones in town; almost everybody just uses the **caseta** (tel. 6-01-92) located on the right-hand side of Av. Principal as you face away from the church at the far end of the street. Farther up the road is **Farmacia Morelia,** which will sometimes change dollars (open daily 7:30am-9pm). To get to the **Centro de Salud,** turn right on the side street before the paved road runs left and walk three blocks (open 24hr.). The **phone code** is 755.

ACCOMMODATIONS AND FOOD Caleta is home to only two hotels, both of which are nice and affordable. The **Hotel Los Arcos** (tel. (755) 6 01 92 or 6 01 93), next to the church as Av. Principal turns left, has very clean rooms with golden doors, tiled floors and bathrooms, fans, and hot water. Arch-shaped widows grace each room and provide a spectacular view of the coast. (Singles 70 pesos, 100 pesos with air conditioning; doubles 100 pesos, 140 with air conditioning.) It's always Christmas with the red and green bedspreads at **Hotel Yuritzi,** off Av. Principal after the church to the left. Yuritzi has spiffy rooms with hot water, fans, and TV. Restaurant downstairs open only in high season. (Singles 90 pesos; doubles 100 pesos; with A/C 170 and 220 pesos.) To get to the beach from the hotels, walk to the end of Av. Principal. Pass the church and the Lonchería Bahía, on your right, and follow the dirt road as it bends to the right; the beach lies at the bottom of the hill (a 10-minute walk).

Across the street from Hotel Yuritzi is one of Caleta's only restaurants, **Lonchería Bahía.** The classy and laid-back cafe serves hamburgers (10-13 pesos), *tortas* (10-13 pesos), and fruit drinks (6-8 pesos; open daily 8am-10pm). Also popular is **Enramada Omar,** the third *palapa* restaurant on the sandy cove. It specializes in seafood and serves shrimp any style for 35-40 pesos (open daily 7am-9pm).

GUERRERO

Taxco

With white homes surrounded by cascading waterfalls, Taxco seems to be a strange and unreal apparition. The whole beautiful town is built into the side of a preposterously steep hill. But this is no mirage—from the stunning Church of Santa Prisca to the glinting wares of silver shops, Taxco (pop. 110,000) is meant to be seen and savored from all angles. Cobblestone alleyways coil around *platerías* and churches. The two-way streets are so narrow that people have to flatten themselves along shop walls to let one VW bug pass. And, of course, beneath all the swarming confusion and old-fashioned beauty are the veins of silver that have shaped Taxco's history. When silver was discovered here in 1534, Taxco became the continent's first mining town, luring fortune seekers and artisans alike. Today, tourists buzz through the labyrinthine streets, drawn like bees to the sweet honey of countless jewelry shops.

ORIENTATION

Taxco lies 185km southwest of Mexico City. The city consists of a maze of twisting streets leading up a hill to the *zócalo,* **Plaza Borda,** and the town's centerpiece, the **Catedral de Santa Prisca.** The main artery is **Av. de los Plateros.** From Mexico City, visitors enter Taxco on Plateros through white arches. The road winds past the **Flecha Roja** bus station, becomes **Av. J.F. Kennedy,** and continues to the **Estrella de Oro** bus station before heading out of the city for Acapulco.

To reach the town center from the Flecha Roja bus station, walk uphill on Plateros and turn left on **Juan Ruiz de Alarcón,** which runs past some nice hotels and eventually feeds into the *zócalo.* From the Estrella de Oro station, cross the street and walk up the steep hill known as **Pilita.** When you reach the **Plazuela San Juan,** with a small fountain and a **Bancomer,** veer left and you will come out facing Santa Prisca. Keep in mind that the streets are narrow and uncomfortably steep. A *zócalo combi* will take you to the center from the bus station for 1.50 pesos. Taxis charge 8 pesos.

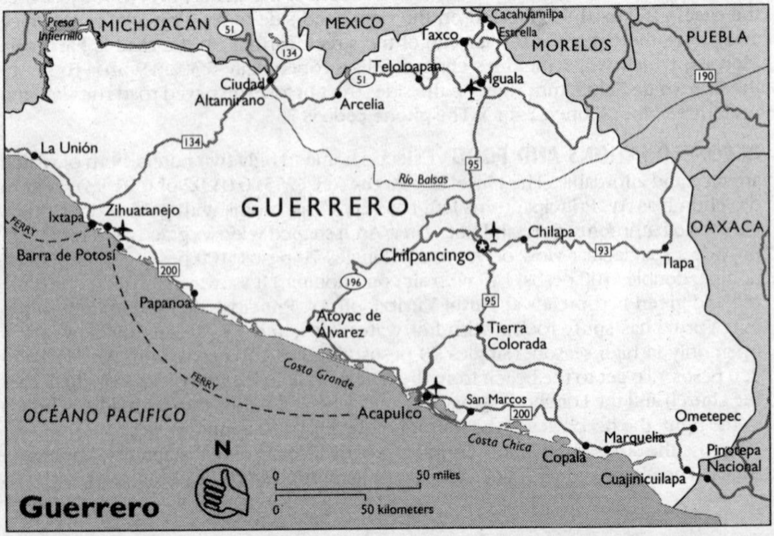

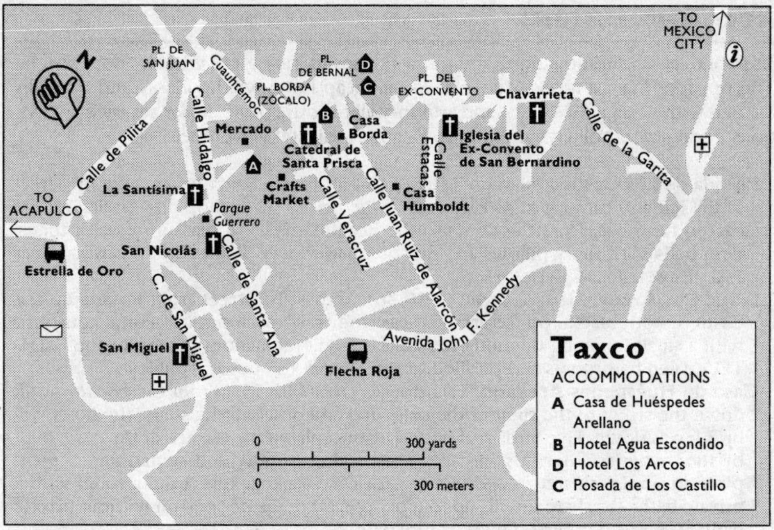

PRACTICAL INFORMATION

Buses: Estrella de Oro, Kennedy 126 (tel. 2 06 48), at the southern end of town. From the *zócalo,* head downhill and hang a right on Kennedy. First-class service to Acapulco (4hr., 9:10am, 1, and 3:30pm, 90 pesos), Cuernavaca (1¼hr., 9am, 2 and 4pm, 25 pesos), and Mexico City (3 hr., 6 per day 7am-6pm, 50-60 pesos). **Flecha Roja,** Plateros 104 (tel. 2 01 31), downhill from the cathedral. First-class to: Cuernavaca (1½hr., every hr. 6am-7pm, 25 pesos) and Mexico City (2½hr., 8 per day 6am-6pm, 62 pesos). Economic class to the Grutas de Cacahuamilpa (30min., every hr. 6:30am-3:30pm, 13 pesos), Mexico City (3hr., 7 per day 5am-8pm, 50 pesos), and Toluca (3hr., 1, 11:40am, and 2pm, 42 pesos).

Tourist Office: Subsecretaría de Fomento Turístico (tel. 2 22 74), at the entrance to town. "Los Arcos" *combis* end their route in front of the office on the 2nd fl. Open daily 9am-2pm and 5-8pm. Most hotels on the Plaza Borda also offer maps. **Procuraduría del Turista** (tel. 2 22 74 or 2 66 16) offers assistance in **emergencies.** Open M-F 9am-7pm.

Currency Exchange: Confía (tel. 2 02 37), on the *zócalo.* Has an **ATM.** Open M-F 9am-3pm. **Banco Santander Mexicano,** Cuauhtémoc 4 (tel. 2 35 35 or 2 32 70) off the *zócalo,* is another option. Open M-F 9am-5pm (only changes money until 4:30pm) and Sa 10am-2pm.

Market: Mercado Tetitlán, on the street to the right of Santa Prisca and down the stairs to the right. At the bottom level are several *fondas* for meals, bakeries, and fruit stands galore.

Police: (tel. 2 00 07). Always on duty. Some English spoken.

Red Cross: (tel. 2 32 32), on Plateros, next door to the tourist info *caseta.* Open daily 9am-8pm. 24hr. **ambulance service.** Little English spoken.

Pharmacy: Farmacia Guadalupana, Hidalgo 8 (tel. 2 03 95). Open daily 8:30am-10pm.

Hospital: IMSS (tel. 2 03 36), on Plateros. 24hr. emergency service.

Post Office: Plateros 382 (tel. 2 05 01), near the Estrella de Oro station. Open M-F 8am-7pm, Sa 9am-1pm. **Postal Code:** 40200.

Fax: Alarcón 1 (tel. 2 48 85; fax 2 00 01), by the *zócalo.* Open M-F 9am-3pm, Sa 9am-noon.

Internet Access: Azul, Hidalgo 7 (tel. 2 74 03). Minimum 25 pesos for 25min. Additional 1 peso per minute. Open daily 8am-10pm.

Telephones: LADATELs found around the main plazas (Plaza Borda and San Juan). **Farmacia Guadalupana,** Hidalgo 8 (tel. 2 03 95), near Plaza San Juan, has a long-distance *caseta.* Open daily 8:30am-10pm.

Phone Code: 762.

ACCOMMODATIONS

True budget accommodations and guest houses in Taxco are virtually nonexistent. The up side? Even a moderately priced or cheap hotel will be classy and centrally located with silver shops, bars, and artisanry all over the place. Make advance reservations during local holidays and during March, April, and November.

Posada de Los Castillo, Alarcón 7 (tel. 2 13 96). Facing Santa Prisca, take the street to the left and turn right. As exquisite as the pricey silver shop downstairs. All the carved furniture, from the doors to the headboards, is in reassuring earth tones. Firm beds with fluffy pillows and first-rate bathrooms. Singles 140 pesos; doubles 170 pesos; triples 240 pesos.

Hotel Los Arcos, Alarcón 4 (tel. 2 18 36), across the street from Posada de Los Castillo. With black iron fixtures and cavernous rooms around a central courtyard with a small fountain, the hotel feels like a medieval manor (except for the LADATEL). Tiled bathrooms and purified water. Singles 135 pesos; doubles 177 pesos.

Casa de Huéspedes Arellano, Pajaritos 23 (tel. 2 02 15). From the *zócalo,* walk down the street to the right of the cathedral and descend the stairs; the hotel will be 3 levels down. Live birds and potted plants enliven the terrace of the *casa,* built by the owner's father. A good space for drying laundry and sunbathing; a great place to smoke cigarettes and parlay with Euro-backpackers. Land a room with a private bath—or share it with up to 6 people. 60 pesos per person without private bath; 80 pesos per person with private bath.

Hotel Agua Escondida, Guillermo Spratling 4 (tel. 2 07 26 or 2 07 36), on the Plaza Borda. Although upscale and expensive, this stunning hotel offers rooms with balconies practically inside the lovely Santa Prisca Church. Wake up to pink sandstone, flowers, and breakfast. Lounge, ping-pong, swimming pool, and video arcade make the hotel worth every peso. Singles 200 pesos; doubles 250 pesos.

FOOD

The narrow cobblestone streets of Taxco lack the push-cart vendors and sidewalk cafes that are so common in other Mexican cities. *Taquerías* and *torterías* are virtually extinct around Plaza Borda, but as you descend into the swarming market areas, their numbers increase.

Restaurante Santa Fé, Hidalgo 2 (tel. 2 11 70), half a block down from Plaza San Juan. Figurines of Mexican *mariachis* brighten up this restaurant and its filling Mexican food. Delicious *tortas* (7-8 pesos), tacos (15 pesos), and enchiladas (17 pesos). Open daily 7:30am-10:30pm.

El Rincón del Abuelo, Callejón del Nogal 1 (tel. 2 30 77), at Cuauhtémoc, before Plaza San Juan. The name (Grandpa's Corner) belies the sleek hipness of the cafe. Gringos come in droves for the dance music and healthy entrees. *Tortas* run 14 pesos, *hamburguesas* 25 pesos, and *comida corrida* 35 pesos. Keep your eyes peeled for the daily specials. Sit upstairs for more private chats above the din of rock music. Open M-Th 8am-midnight, F-Su 8am-3am.

La Concha Nostra, Plaza de San Juan 7 (tel. 2 79 44), in the Hotel Casa Grande. A Bohemian hangout with a stage, old guitars hanging on the walls, and live music some Saturday nights. Slacker service to match the ambience. While you're waiting for your quesadillas (14 pesos), lasagna (26 pesos), or small pizza (15-20 pesos), watch the city's language students blow smoke through their noses and scribble tormented prose in their notebooks. On a good weekday afternoon, you can have this den o' angst to yourself. Open daily 8am-midnight. Bar open until 2am.

Bora Bora Pizza, Delicias 4 (tel. 2 17 21), on the unmarked street that slopes up to the right from Cuauhtémoc, just off the *zócalo.* Fishing nets and basket lamps dangle from the wooden ceiling. Dimly lit with low tables and stools. Pizzas start at 23 pesos, spaghetti at 20 pesos. Open daily 1pm-midnight.

SIGHTS

More than 300 shops cater to the busloads of tourists who are drawn to Taxco by the glint of silver. If you're dipping so deep into your pockets that you can feel your knees, head for **El Mercado de Artesanías,** off Veracruz just behind Santa Prisca. Merchants sell silver and peddle pomegranates and painted ashtrays. The market is open daily from 10am to 6pm, but is most crowded during siesta, when confused gringos hit Taxco's version of a mall instead of sleeping.

Even more impressive than the silver trinkets that shine from every shop window is the *zócalo*'s **Catedral de Santa Prisca,** with its beautiful Baroque facade of pink stone. Among the designs and figures on the facade, the standouts are the Churrigueresque *interestípite*—decorative inverted columns with a Corinthian flourish at the bottom. Despite its size, this gorgeous church looks other-worldly; at night, the sight of the pink monument is enough to bring even the least devout to their knees.

To the left of the church is **Casa Borda,** a stately 18th-century building that was José de la Borda's home; his family's coat of arms can still be seen beside the entrance. Enter through the bookstore on the *zócalo.* The interior gardens and several floors have been turned into the **Instituto Guerrerense de Cultura** (tel. 2 66 17). In addition to a library and dance studio, the center has ample gallery space for rotating exhibitions and photographs of daily life in Mexico (house and galleries open Tu-Su 10am-8pm).

The **Casa Humboldt,** Alarcón 12 (tel. 2 55 01), down the street past the Hotel Los Arcos, is one of the older colonial homes in town. *(Casa and museo open Tu-Sa 10am-5pm, Su 9am-3pm. Admission 10 pesos, students with ID 5 pesos.)* With its unusual bas-reliefs in Moorish *mudéjar* style, the *casa* served as a rest stop for explorer Alexander Von Humboldt for just one night, and it still bears his name. Nonetheless, this meticulously restored house now holds the collection of the **Museo de Arte Virreinal.** Exhibits provide a detailed look at 18th-century Catholic rituals and dress.

The **Ex-Convento de San Bernandino,** in the Plaza del Convento, was built in 1592 as a Franciscan monastery. *(Open daily 8am-1pm and 2-6:30pm; free.)* Destroyed by a fire two centuries later, the building was reconstructed in neoclassical style in 1823. The struggle for independence from the Spanish officially ended when the Plan de Iguala was signed within the walls of this ex-convent in 1821. Now a school convenes under its roof. To get to the ex-convent, follow Juárez past the city offices.

Perhaps the best sights in town are the **vistas** from surrounding hillsides. One of the more striking views of the city and the surrounding hills can be found from the **Church of Guadalupe.** The neoclassical church becomes the center of festivities during the celebration of the Virgin in December. From the *zócalo,* take Ojeda, the street to the right of Cuauhtémoc, to Guadalupe, and veer right until you reach the plaza in front of the church. For a more sweeping view, you can take a **teleférico,** or **cable**

All That Glitters Is Not Gold: It's Silver!

Although unscrupulous sellers and cheating craftspeople occasionally pass off *alpaca* (fool's silver) or *plateados* (silver-plated metals) as the real McCoy, buying silver in Taxco is usually a sure thing. Larger pieces, such as necklaces and bracelets, are consistently striking. Many proprietors speak English and accept U.S. currency, but if you stick with Spanish and talk in pesos while bargaining, you lower the risk of being charged tourist prices. While it's fun to ogle glamorous and expensive silver in the lovely shops around the Plaza Borda, sterling products become cheaper and the employees more amenable to bargaining the father you go from the *centro.* Bargain at stores with silver workshops by faking out the clerk and heading straight for the artisan. Most shops have two prices: *menudeo* (retail) and *mayoreo* (wholesale), the latter for those profit-oriented people who load their bags with silver in Taxco to resell at lofty prices back home. Remember that only the official ".925" stamp on the object's side guarantees that your shiny new charm is indeed silver; inspect merchandise carefully before purchasing anything.

car, to Hotel Monte Taxco. *(Runs daily 7:40am-7pm; call 2 14 68 for more info. Ride 26 pesos round-trip, 14 pesos for children; free for hotel guests.)* Take a "Los Arcos" *combi* to the white arches at the entrance of the city (2 pesos). Before passing through the arches, turn left up a hill and bear left into the parking lot for the cable cars. The ride is exhilarating, with waterfalls on one side and the city on the other.

ENTERTAINMENT AND SEASONAL EVENTS

Taxco's crowded streets somehow accommodate a tsunami of tourists during its two major festivals. The **Feria Nacional de la Plata,** a national contest designed to encourage silver artisanship, takes place the last week in November. **Semana Santa** festivities are even more popular in Taxco. On Good Friday, hooded *penitentes* carry logs made out of cactus trunks on their shoulders or subject themselves to flagellation in order to expiate their sins and those of the town, including the ill behavior of tourists. During the annual **Día del Jumil,** on the first Monday of November, Taxco residents make a pilgrimage to the *Huizteco* hill, where they collect insects known as *jumil* to eat live or add, along with chiles, to salsa. The 1.5cm-long brown insects contain more protein per gram than beef.

After silver shops close, much of Taxco gathers at the **Plaza Borda** in front of the illuminated facade of Santa Prisca. Those still up for dancing after a day of hiking up and down Taxco's relentless hills will have to wait until the weekend. **Windows,** in the Hotel Monte Taxco (tel. 2 13 00), has the area's hottest dancing. Although accessible only by cable car or taxi, this bar/dance club is beautifully done up in crystal and glass and offers an unparalleled view of the city combined with a ritzy party atmosphere (cover 30 pesos; open F-Su 10pm-late). For a more relaxed evening, move your way to La Concha Nostra in Hotel Casa Grande, Plaza de San Juan 7, for 8-peso beers and great conversation (open daily 8am-2am). Or try **Cine Alarcón,** near Plaza de San Juan. It shows American and "adult-interest" movies for about 15 pesos.

■ Near Taxco: Grutas De Cacahuamilpa

While the scenery around Taxco has an awe-inspiring, rugged grandeur, it is the beauty of an extensive network of *grutas* (caves) that compels tourists to forget about silver shopping and venture out of the city limits. According to lore, the **Grutas de Cacahuamilpa** were once a hideaway for runaway *indígenas.* *(Caves open daily 10am-5pm. Admission 15 pesos, children 10 pesos.)* Twenty huge *salones* (halls) are filled with stalactites, stalagmites, and rock formations in curious shapes, sizes, and colors. The columns and ceilings—some as high as 85m—are the work of the subterranean stream that developed into the **Río San Jerónimo.** Explorers hoping to traverse the caves have not always had great success—the makeshift grave of an English spelunker and his dog is the highlight of any tour of the *grutas.*

Two-hour tours leave on the hour from the visitor's center and afford little opportunity for traipsing about on your own. If your Spanish is good enough, the tour can be hilarious. You can only enter the caves with a tour guide: shoes with good traction are helpful.

Getting There: "Grutas" *combis* leave from Taxco's **Flecha Roja** bus station, dropping passengers off at the parking lot for the caves (13 pesos). "Grutas" *combis* also leave the caves every hour to return to Taxco (13 pesos). Flecha Roja buses also make the trip (30min., every hr. 6:30am-3:30am, 13 pesos), but will drop you off at an intersection a short jaunt from the caves. To get to the parking lot at the caves, take a right, then another right after the curve.

■ Near Taxco: Las Granadas and Ixcateopan

Twenty-six kilometers from Taxco, the ecological reserve of **Las Granadas** provides an Edenic respite from both Volkswagen-clogged streets and silver pushers. In addition to the flora and fauna, there are stunning natural waterfalls. There is no admission charge and no set hours.

Forty-two kilometers from Taxco, the town of **Ixcateopan** is known for both its beauty and its history. The marble and stone streets supply the former, while the

Museo de la Resistencia Indígena provides information on the latter. The remains of Cuauhtémoc, the last Aztec emperor, are said to be kept here in the **Templo de Santa María de la Asunción.**

Getting There: *Combis* leave Taxco from in front of the Seguro Social, on J.F. Kennedy. To get to Las Granadas, head to the town of **Acuitlapan,** 20km from Taxco (40min., every 25min. 7am-8pm, 13 pesos). There you can get transportation to the reserve. To get to Ixcateopan, just take the eponymous vehicle (1¼hr., every 30min. 6am-9pm, 13 pesos).

Zihuatanejo and Ixtapa

Six kilometers and a gargantuan rift in lifestyle separate the twin beach towns of Zihuatanejo (see-wah-tah-NAY-ho) and Ixtapa (ees-STOP-pah). Both thrive on tourism, offering the requisite stretches of sand, the whole range of water sports, and restaurants that frame the sunsets. Ixtapa has been meticulously constructed by Mexican

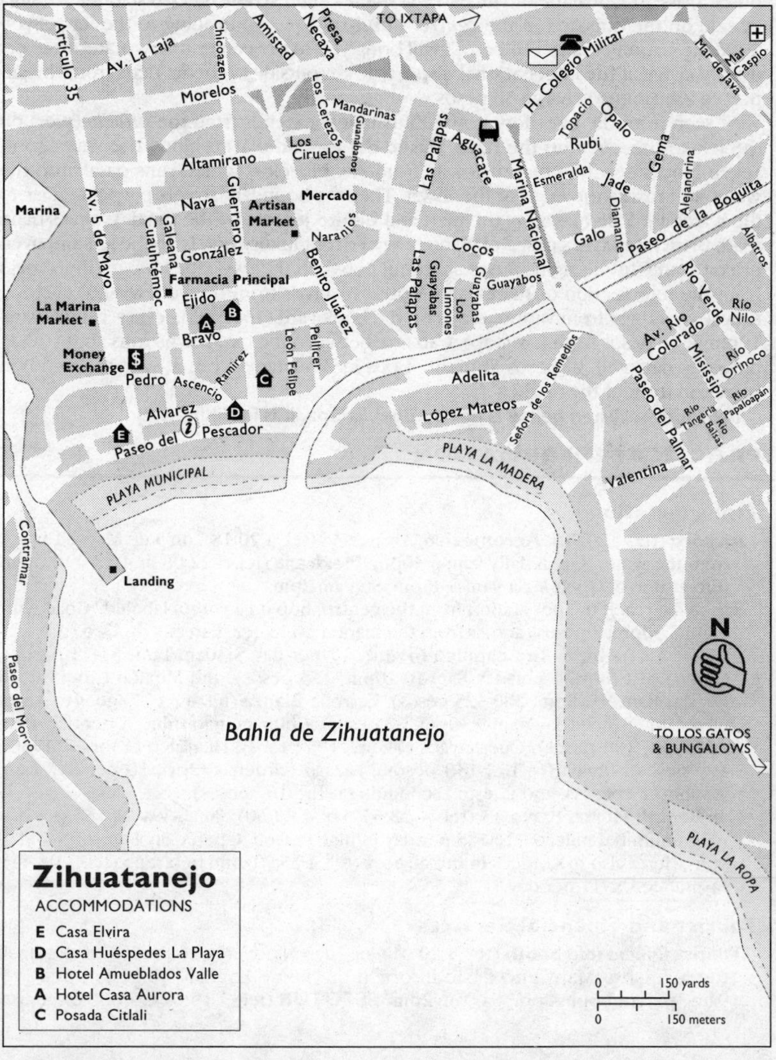

pleasure engineers to cater to moneyed foreign visitors; this glitzy resort has no downtown, no budget accommodations, and a surfeit of fancy restaurants. Meanwhile, Zihuatanejo, only a 15-minute bus ride away, hasn't shaken the grip of the net that marks it as a fishing town. There are budget hotels in its downtown, and they're all a few steps from excellent beaches. The tourist brochures aren't kidding when they promise two vacations in one.

As a budget traveler, you're likely to spend one-and-a-half of those vacations in Zihuatanejo. Ironically, the original plan designed the nascent resort paradise around Zihuatanejo Bay, but complications with land rights forced development north to Ixtapa. Although a visit to peaceful Zihuatanejo can be satisfying in and of itself, the glitzy Ixtapa, with its air-conditioned comfort and sophisticated nightlife, adds just the right amount of decadence. Together, the twin towns provide the complete escape that Mexico's other Pacific beaches hamper with pollution or lack of services.

ORIENTATION

Buses arrive in Zihuatanejo. The **Estrella Blanca** and **Estrella de Oro** stations are side-by-side on the outskirts of the *centro. Combis* (2 pesos) heading to the left as you leave the station or taxis (10 pesos) will bring you to the center of town. Resort-goers usually arrive at the **international airport,** 15km outside of town. Taxis from the airport to Zihuatanejo charge 50 pesos.

As seen from the bay, downtown Zihuatanejo extends from the *muelle* (pier) on the left to the canal on the right. **Paseo del Pescador** runs along the waterfront. Seven blocks separate that walkway from **Av. Morelos,** which runs parallel to the water and marks the edge of the town. The two boundary streets perpendicular to the water are **5 de Mayo,** by the pier, and **Benito Juárez,** by the canal. Ixtapa's main road, **Blvd. Ixtapa,** lies past a phalanx of waterfront luxury hotels on the left and overpriced stores to the right. Buses shuttling between the two cities leave Zihuatanejo from the intersection of Juárez and Morelos, across from the yellow Elektra store; they leave Ixtapa from various stops on the boulevard (15-25min., every 15min. 6am-10pm, 2.50 pesos from any stop). Cab fare between the two towns runs about 20-25 pesos by day, and 30 pesos at night. Taxis in Zihuatanejo can always be found on Juárez, in front of the market.

If an address listed below is not on Blvd. Ixtapa, it is in Zihuatanejo.

PRACTICAL INFORMATION

Transportation

Airport: (tel. 4 20 70). **Aeroméxico,** Álvarez 34 (tel. 4 20 18), on 5 de Mayo, 1 block from the water. Open daily 9am-6:30pm. **Mexicana** (tel. 4 22 08 or 4 22 09), Guerrero at Bravo. Open M-Sa 9am-6:45pm, Su 9am-2pm.

Buses: To reach the bus station from the centro, hop on a *combi*-labeled "Coacoyul" (7am-8:30pm, 2 pesos) across from the market on Juárez. **Estrella de Oro** (tel. 4 21 75) sends its buses to Acapulco (4½hr., 17 per day 5:30am-1am, 51-75 pesos), Cuernavaca (8hr., 4 per day 8am-10:10pm, 175 pesos), and Mexico City (9hr., 6 per day 8am-10:10pm, 200-325 pesos). **Estrella Blanca** (tel. 4 34 77) goes to Acapulco (4hr., 18 per day 4am-9:30pm, 62 pesos), Chilpancingo (6hr., 4 per day 4:20-midnight, 100 pesos), Cuernavaca (7½hr., 175 pesos), Huatulco (13hr., 7:45pm, 199 pesos), Iguala (6½hr., 130 pesos), Lázaro Cárdenas (2hr., 10 per day 1am-7:30pm, 29 pesos), and Puerto Escondido (12hr., 167 pesos).

Car Rental: Hertz, Bravo 13 (tel. 4 22 55; fax 4 30 50). Small VW US$35 per day with unlimited mileage, US$45 per day in high season. Open daily 8am-2pm and 4-8pm. Hertz also has offices in the **airport** (tel. 4 25 90) and in **Ixtapa** (tel. 3 04 44). Insurance US$11 per day.

Tourist and Financial Services

Tourist Office: Info booth (tel. 4 20 01), on Juan N. Álvarez, to the left of the small town square. Maps and basic information. Some English spoken. Open M-F 9am-3pm and 6pm-8pm, Sa 9am-2pm. **SEFOTUR** (tel. 3 19 67), on Blvd. Ixtapa, across from Hotel Presidente. Comprehensive *Guía Turística Urbana* to beaches and services. Some English spoken. Open M-F 9am-7pm, Sa 10am-2pm.

Currency Exchange: Banco Santander Mexicano (tel. 4 24 16), Los Mangoes at Juárez, and **Banca Serfín** (tel. 4 36 63), Juárez at Bravo. Both open M-F 9am-5pm, Sa-Su 10am-2pm. **Money Exchange,** Galeana #6 (tel. 4 28 00). From the beach, walk 1 block on Cuauhtémoc, take a right on Bravo, and make the first right onto Galeana. Worse rates than the banks, but no commission. Offers **fax** and **long distance** service as well. Open daily 8am-9pm.

Local Services

Bookstore: Byblos, Galeana 2 (tel. 4 38 11). English magazines, paperback novels, and the handy *Owen's English Language Guide to Ixtapa and Zihuatanejo* (written by a member of Cousteau's team). Open daily 9am-9pm.

Market: The **mercado** on Benito Juárez, 4 blocks from the water, sells fresh produce and has several small countertop eateries.

Laundromat: Súper Clean, Catalina Gonzalez 11 (tel. 4 23 47), at Galeana. 9 pesos per kilo, 27 peso minimum. Same day delivery. Open M-Sa 8am-8pm.

Emergency and Communications

Police: (tel. 4 20 40 or 4 23 66), in the Palacio Municipal in front of Playa Principal.

Red Cross: (tel. 4 20 09), on Av. de las Huertas as you leave Zihuatanejo. 24hr. emergency and ambulance service. No English spoken.

Pharmacy: Farmacia Principal (tel. 4 42 17), Cuauhtémoc at Ejido, 3 blocks from the water. English spoken. Open M-Sa 9am-9pm.

Medical Services: Centro de Salud (tel. 4 20 88), Paseo de la Boquita at Paseo del Palmar. Open for consultations M-F 8am-8pm, Sa 8am-3pm.

Post Office: (tel. 4 21 92) off Paseo del Palmar. Walking away from the beach, turn right on Morelos, walk a block past the blue wall, and turn right. Open M-F 8am-7pm. **Postal Code:** 40880.

Internet Access: Servinet, Cuauhtémoc 128 (tel. 4 43 87), at Gonzalez. 15min. for 15 pesos, discount for students with ID. Open daily 9am-8pm.

Phone Code: 753.

ACCOMMODATIONS AND CAMPING

Zihuatanejo has plenty of budget accommodations within a few blocks of the Playa Municipal. Prices rise substantially during the high season (Dec.-Apr.), as do the number of gringos per square foot. If you visit at an off-time, with a large group, or plan to stay several days, you will have excellent leverage for negotiating a discount. The tourist office discourages unofficial camping, partly for safety reasons. If you insist on pitching a tent, **Playa Barra de Potosí** (see p. 362) and **Playa Quieta,** near Club Med in Ixtapa, are the most sensible places to camp.

Hotel Casa Aurora, Bravo 27 (tel. 4 30 46), between Guerrero and Galeana. This budget mainstay features a friendly staff, clean, good-sized rooms, and 70s bedspreads. Rooms upstairs are pricier, but they come with hot water. With A/C 100 pesos per person, high season 150 pesos. Without A/C 70 pesos per person, high season 80-90 pesos. Ask the owners about their beachside bungalow which holds 2 people for 300 pesos, high season 400 pesos.

Hotel Amueblados Valle, Vicente Guerrero 14 (tel. 4 20 84; fax 14 32 20), between Ejido and Bravo. 8 fully-equipped apartments with large kitchens, ceiling fans, balconies, hot water, and daily towel service. 1 bedroom (up to 3 people) 180 pesos; 2 bedrooms (up to 5 people) 300 pesos. Monthly rates available. Expect prices to rise during high season.

Casa Elvira, Juan N. Álvarez 8 (tel. 4 26 61), 1 block from the Playa Municipal. The first guest house in Zihuatanejo remains a bargain. Excellent location. Rooms are clean, if dim and unspectacular, with portable fans, cold water, and small bathrooms. The treat is outside—an inviting courtyard filled with family members and proximity to the beach. Singles 50 pesos; doubles 60 pesos; triples 80 pesos.

Casa de Huéspedes La Playa, Alvarez 6 (tel. 4 22 47), at Guerrero. The best thing about this place is the location. The waves of the Pacific will lull you to sleep as will the soothing light of the moon shining on the sea. Basic and clean, with fans and no hot water. Rooms with 2 beds go for about 100 pesos.

Posada Citlali, Vicente Guerrero 3 (tel. 4 20 43), near Blvd. Álvarez. On the expensive side, but quite charming. Vines dangle lazily in the central courtyard; wooden rockers on the terrace encourage you to do the same. All rooms have overhead fans and hot water. Singles 150 pesos; doubles 200 pesos.

FOOD

Like the neighboring hotels, restaurants in Ixtapa are pricey. However, they are spotless and offer an array of authentic-tasting international cuisine—Italian food actually tastes Italian. The meal can be a reasonable splurge, especially if you eat at a cafe before they switch to the main menu (around 2pm). For consistent budget eats, restaurants in Zihuatanejo serve fish that were swimming in the bay the same morning. The farther you get from the beach, the cheaper and more desirable the restaurant.

Los Braseros, Ejido 64 (tel. 4 87 36). This exuberant open-air eatery specializes in heavenly stir-fried combinations of meat, veggies, and cheese (31-32 pesos). A sprinkling of veggie options. Large portions served with hot tortillas by an attentive staff. Open daily 10am-1am.

La Sirena Gorda (The Fat Mermaid), Paseo del Pescador 20A (tel. 4 26 87), next to the pier. Start your morning off with a stack of hotcakes (20-22 peso); dine on seafood tacos (22-45 pesos) when the sun goes down. The view of the fishing boats on the water and the painting of fat and happy mermaids make it all taste that much better. Open Th-Tu 7am-10pm.

Ruben's Hamburgers, Adelita 1 (tel. 4 46 17) on Playa Madera. Follow the Paseo del Pescador to the canal, turn left, and cross the bridge. Walk straight down the street for 2 blocks—it's on the right, up the stairs. A loud, fun family joint, a with booming jukebox and rolls of paper towels dangling overhead. Get your drinks from the fridge and add up your own check. Delicious *hamburguesas* (20-22 pesos) and sour cream-stuffed baked potatoes (16 pesos). Open daily 6pm-11pm.

Figaro's Restaurante (tel. 3 14 52), Plaza Ixpamar off Blvd. Ixtapa, in the Ixtapa mall. Ixtapa location without Ixtapa prices. Italian *comida del día* is a multi-course bargain at 21 pesos. Individual pizzas start at 20 pesos. Quesadillas 15 pesos. Open daily 8am-11pm.

SAND AND SIGHTS

Neither Zihuatanejo's self-conscious charm nor Ixtapa's resorts could ever eclipse the area's natural beauty. In Zihuatanejo, four stretches of sand line the water. They are, clockwise from the municipal pier, **Playa Principal, Playa La Madera, Playa la Ropa,** and **Playa Las Gatas.** Ixtapa overlooks the unbroken stretch of Playa del Palmar on the Bahía del Palmar, but the prettiest beaches lie beyond Laguna de Ixtapa: Playa Quieta, Playa Linda, and, at the bay's west edge, Isla Ixtapa.

Zihuatanejo

Downtown Zihuatanejo's beach, **Playa Municipal,** in front of the Paseo del Pescador, is more suited to seashell stores and fishing boats than to swimmers. The attractions here are the basketball court, the pier, and the fish that boats unload onto the dock. The beach ends at a canal that empties into the bay. Get your feet wet crossing over the rocks to **Playa Madera.** Its name refers to the local hardwood that used to be exported from the shore, but the fine sand and gentle waves bear no trace of its lumberyard past. Good for bodysurfing, the shallow beach hosts a number of restaurants and bungalows.

Zihuatanejo's two best beaches cannot be reached by walking along the bay's shores. Protected from the rough Pacific by the shape of the bay, **Playa La Ropa's** crescent of sumptuous white sand attracts tourists from the hotels on the surrounding cliffs. Because La Ropa is nearly 1km long, it never feels too crowded. Taxis are the easiest way to reach La Ropa (15 pesos). Follow Paseo de la Boquita along the canal to the bridge, cross over, and turn left, passing Playa Madera. The road curves to the right and passes Hotel Casa que Canta. Follow the stone road down to the left to the beach. At the opposite end of the beach, you can reward yourself with a meal at one of the waterfront seafood restaurants.

According to local lore, Tarascan King Calzontzin ordered the construction of the barrier reef in **Playa Las Gatas** as protection from the sharks that give the beach its name. Since then, coral and an abundance of marine life have taken over the stone barricade. The calm, transparent waters welcome snorkelers (equipment can be rented for 35 pesos per day). Escape the shops and restaurant tables by taking a path behind the last restaurant to the **Garrobo Lighthouse,** which offers a panoramic view. Since it's well hidden, ask any of the waiters for specific directions to *el faro.* To reach Las Gatas, take a *lancha* from the pier in downtown Zihuatanejo (10min., every 15min. 9am-4pm, last boat leaves Las Gatas 5pm, round-trip 20 pesos). It is possible, but not easy, to walk to Las Gatas from La Ropa over the rocks. Alternatively you may continue walking on the road that brought you to La Ropa for another 45 minutes or so until you reach the beach.

Ixtapa

Guarded by a row of hotels, **Playa del Palmar** is a people-watching, wave-hopping, massage-receiving paradise. Not only is it one of the more attractive beaches around, it is perhaps the most active. Without the protection of a bay, the beach is pummeled by sizeable waves, attracting parasailers, scuba divers, and jet skiers. All along the sand next to the swimming pools, people jog and play volleyball and soccer. Swimmers should obey the lifeguards and red/yellow/green flags). The beach can be reached from public access paths at its far ends, near the Sheraton hotel or near Carlos 'n' Charlie's. Otherwise, clutch your *Let's Go* confidently, wear your swimsuit proudly, and cut right through the hotel lobbies.

The less crowded and more stylish **Playa Cuatas, Playa Quieta,** and **Playa Linda** are northwest of Ixtapa. To drive to them from Ixtapa, follow the boulevard northwest beyond most of the hotels and turn right at the sign for Playa Linda. From Zihuatanejo, it is more convenient to use the access road from Rte. 200; go past the exit for Ixtapa in the direction of Puerto Vallarta and take the next left, marked Playa Linda. The road skirts **Laguna de Ixtapa** and hits the beach farther northwest. A taxi to Playa Linda or Playa Quieta costs about 30 pesos from Ixtapa or 50 pesos from Zihuatanejo. A "Playa Linda" bus begins in Zihuatanejo and passes through Ixtapa on its way to Playas Quieta and Linda. Crystal clear water and body-surfing waves await at Playa Cuatas, across the street from the tennis courts at Club Med on Playa Linda. Both Playa Linda and Playa Quieta are known for their tranquil waters and calm swimming conditions. At Playa Linda, it is possible to **rent horses** and ride all the way to the Ixtapa River.

Some claim that of all the area's beaches, the most picturesque are those on **Isla Ixtapa,** about 2km offshore from Playa Quieta. The island is a must for snorkeling enthusiasts. Activity picks up in a few shoreside restaurants by day, but the island's 10 acres remain uninhabited at night. The main beach is **Playa Cuachalalate,** frequented by fishermen and vacationers eager to water-ski. **Playa Varadero** is a small beach with calm waters and *palapa*-covered restaurants. On the ocean side of the island, **Playa Coral** is the least-visited beach of the three. It has no services and is not great for swimming, but the coral makes for excellent scuba diving. To get there, take a boat from the pier at Zihuatanejo (1hr., boats leave at noon, return at 5pm, 50 pesos round-trip). A cheaper alternative is to take a *microbús* from Zihuatanejo (3.50 pesos) or from Ixtapa (2.50 pesos) to the pier at Playa Linda and catch a *lancha* from there (every 15min. 9am-5pm, round-trip 20 pesos).

ENTERTAINMENT

The beaches of Ixtapa and Zihuatanejo may be similar, but by nightfall the contrast between the cities becomes clear. Ixtapa supports a varied collection of dance clubs and dress-up restaurants, all of them on Blvd. Ixtapa; Zihuatanejo does not.

Ixtapa

The premier place for dancing is **Christine** (tel. 3 04 56), in the Hotel Krystal. With its tiered seats, hanging vines, and light show, it is as artificially beautiful as Ixtapa itself. Beer costs 23 pesos, and *bebidas nacionales* go for 27 pesos; except during the open bar on Tuesdays and Sundays. (M and W no cover; Tu and Su 140 pesos for men, 100 pesos for women; Thursday 60 pesos for men, no cover for women; F-Sa 60 pesos cover for all.) A restaurant by day, **Los Mandiles** (tel. 3 17 10), in the commercial center, becomes a nightclub around 8pm. (Open bar F and Sa. No cover Su-Th; F-Sa 110 pesos men, 100 pesos for women. Open daily 8pm-4am.) **Carlos 'n' Charlie's** (tel. 3 00 85), at the end of the Playa Palmar next to Hotel Posada Road, attracts a crowd to its bar and specializes in beachfront dancing (no cover, but on weekend nights there is a 50-peso drink minimum; open daily 4pm-3am). **Señor Frog's** (tel. 3 22 82) is a restaurant until midnight; at that point, American dancers climb on the tables and the party begins. Spiral-designed fans whirl at top speed to keep the party cool. (Beer 23 pesos, *bebida nacional* 25 pesos. No cover. Open daily 6pm-3am.)

Zihuatanejo

Choices for nightlife in Zihuatanejo are limited. A recent addition to the scene is **D'Latino** (tel. 4 22 30), on the corner of Bravo and Guerrero. This spicy Latin dance club features salsa and reggae, with occasional live music. Those in the know get down on the dance floor illuminated with black lights as they sip drinks (18-22 pesos) from the fully stacked bar. (M-Th no cover, F-Su 30 pesos cover. Open daily 10pm-3am.) If you're in Zihuatanejo at night, dancing is probably not on your mind. Try your hand at singing at **Canta Bar Splash**, a **karaoke** bar on Guerrero between Ejido and Gonzalez. Sip a beer (12 pesos) or a mixed drink (18 pesos) as you croon away into the microphone. (Open daily 6pm-2am.)

Costa Grande

The Guerrero coast north of Acapulco is often called the Costa Grande in order to distinguish it from its smaller counterpart (Costa Chica) to the south. Although the stretch from Acapulco to Zihuatanejo/Ixtapa is marked by a dearth of friendly beaches, **Barra de Potosí,** 20km southeast of Zihuatanejo, and **Papanoa,** another 60km farther along Rte. 200, are two hidden treasures ideal for wasting the day away frolicking in the waves.

Costa Grande: Barra de Potosí

For the traveler whose head is spinning from ruins, cathedrals, and souvenirs, there is no better tonic than a spell at the seemingly infinite stretch of sand known as **Playa Barra de Potosí.** Life here just couldn't get any more *tranquila.* Tourists bask in the sun, their words rolling lazily off their tongues and their thoughts drifting effortlessly out to sea. *Camionetas* putter along the single sandy road, bouncing the inhabitants back and forth to their secluded homes. Now and then, someone stirs for a bit of fishing. The owners of the 12 or so open-air *enramadas* (informal *palapa* restaurants), just past the strip that constitutes "town," are proud of Playa Potosí's laid-back friendliness—and its reasonable prices.

Visitors to Barra de Potosí are expected to sleep in the hammocks that adorn each *enramada.* The owners don't care if you sack out in their hammocks forever—as long as you buy a meal from them every now and then. Toilets too, are free of charge. The *enramadas* farthest from the lagoon avoid flooding and tend to be the most magical in Barra de Potosí. Flex your travel savvy and sleep on the diagonal, so as to support your back. The mosquitoes are also free, so bring plenty of repellent.

Those still unskilled in the art of hammock-snoozing or traveling solo can indulge themselves at **Hotel Barra de Potosí** (tel. 4 82 90 or 4 34 45), an unfinished resort hotel that has nevertheless opened its doors for business. From the *enramadas,* walk away from the lagoon; you'll immediately see its name on the sidewalk. Rooms in the completed portion of the hotel have views of the beach, ceiling fans, washing machines, and kitchens. Not all rooms have the same amenities, but all have access to the beachside swimming pool and restaurant. (4-person rooms with ocean view and kitchen 300 pesos, without kitchen 250 pesos; doubles without either 150 pesos.)

In keeping with the casual spirit, restaurants do not have set menus; rather, they ask you what type of seafood you'd like to eat (expect to spend 20-30 pesos per person). **Enramada Bacanora,** the third restaurant from the right as you face the water, offers the friendliest atmosphere and cheapest prices. Show Estelle your copy of *Let's Go* and she'll discount your seafood feast. (Open daily 7am-6pm.)

If you insist on exerting yourself while in Barra de Potosí (something the locals may not understand), your only option is to hike up the dirt road to the lighthouse that sits atop **Cerro Guamiule** (2000m), the peak near the restaurants that guards the southern entrance to the bay. After a 30-minute walk, you will be rewarded with a view of the bay and its 20km of beaches. After gaping, walk north along the shore of Playa Potosí, the southernmost beach on the bay, to the aptly named **Playa Blanca** (3km). You will pass **Playa Coacoyul** (8km), **Playa Riscaliyo** (19km), and pebbly **Playa Manzanillo** (24km) before reaching another lighthouse (26km) that overlooks the northern edge of the bay. All beaches are free of tourists in the summer months but they fill up with hundreds of domestic visitors during Christmas.

Getting There: From Zihuatanejo, "Petatlán" buses for Potosí leave from a station on Las Palmas, around the corner from Restaurante La Jaiba on Juárez (30min., every 15min. 6am-9pm, 4 pesos). Ask to be let off at Achotes, an unmarked intersection. A pick-up truck will be waiting (or will be arriving soon) on the side road to collect passengers for the bumpy trip to the *enramadas* (30min., 5 pesos). Trucks return to the intersection from the same spot (every 30min., until 6pm); the bus to Zihuatanejo leaves from the other side of the highway.

■ Costa Grande: Papanoa

Much like Barra de Potosi, **Papanoa** offers small town charm alongside lolling waves. Pigs and roosters scuttle along the road that ends at multiple *enramadas* and the beach. **Cayaqutos,** 2km from town, is a bit more accessible (and less classy) than **Playa Vincente Guerrero,** 5 km from town. And while there's a scarcity of eateries on Cayaquitor, Vincente Guerrero is host to numerous restaurants that will tempt your taste buds with the ever-fresh catch of the day (20-30 pesos; open 7am-6pm).

Getting there: Buses from Acapulco to Zihuatanejo (2½hr., 34 pesos) and back (1½hr., 16 pesos) drop passengers off in Papanoa. In Papanoa, white pick-up trucks carry passengers to and from the beach (until 6pm, 3 pesos). Taxis run to **Cayaqutos** (10 pesos) and to **Vincente Guerrero** (20 pesos). If you plan to leave the beach later than 6pm, arrange for a taxi to pick you up ahead of time.

Miracle of Miracles

A source of pride for Barra is the **Iglesia de San Antonio,** on the corner of Jalisco and Veracruz, four blocks south of the bus station. (Open daily 7am-9:30pm. Masses daily 8am, noon, and 8pm.) The church is a modern structure famous for its miraculous icon, *el Cristo del Ciclón* (Christ of the Hurricane). Christ's arms, instead of extending out to form the traditional crucifix, are bent; they droop earthward as if he is shrugging. Local lore has it that when Hurricane Lilly furiously struck the bay on September 10, 1971, a young girl burst into the church begging the icon for help, causing Christ's arms to detach from the crucifix in order to hold the hurricane back and save the town from destruction.

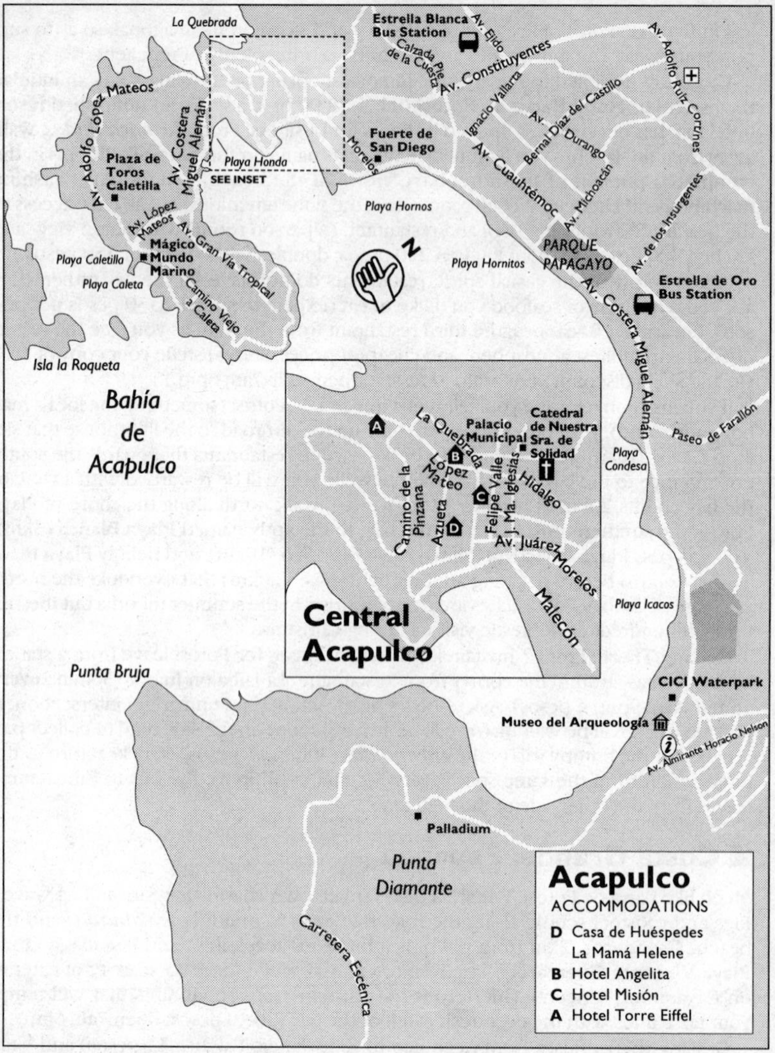

Acapulco

Once upon a time, Acapulco was the stunningly beautiful playground of the rich and famous. Hollywood legends once celebrated their silver-screen successes by dancing the Mexican nights away in its chic clubs, and politicians spent their honeymoons hopping between its attractive shores. But time passes and fairy tales fade. Today, Acapulco, a metropolis of 1.5 million, is two things—a slim, glitzy fingernail of a resort with its beaches to one side and its downtown to the other, and a slum that reaches up into the hills behind the resorts. This second, grimmer Acapulco was born when the heavily moneyed stopped vacationing on Acapulco's shores, and hotel jobs could no longer keep pace with the waves of immigration drawn seaward from the interior by the prospect of plentiful pesos. Now more than ever, everyone in Acapulco is driven by money—either the need to spend it or the need to earn it. Vendors crowd the streets and descend upon slow-moving or indecisive visitors as restaurant owners wave travelers inside with their menus. Peddlers of everything from bubble gum to "free information" run at tourists like eager bulls. But though the high-rise hotels crowding the waterfront have lost the first flush of youth, a roster full of festivals and city beautification projects promise a revamped Acapulco. Perhaps the best time to visit the city is at night, when darkness shrouds the grime and allows the glitter of the streetlamps to evoke Acapulco's fairytale past.

ORIENTATION

Acapulco Bay lies 400km south of Mexico City and 239km southeast of Ixtapa/Zihuatanejo. Rte. 200 feeds into **La Costera (Av. Costera Miguel Alemán),** the main drag. The traditional downtown area, with the *zócalo* and the cathedral, is in the western part of town (to the left as seen from the water). **Acapulco Dorado,** full of fast-food chains, malls, and luxury hotels, stretches from **Parque Papagayo** to the naval base. The ultra-chic resorts are found on **Acapulco Diamante,** farther east towards the airport. Most budget accommodations and restaurants lie between the *zócalo* and **La Quebrada,** the famous cliff-diving spot. In southwest Acapulco, a peninsula with **Playas Caleta** and **Caletilla** juts out into the bay.

"Hornos" or "Cici" buses run from Caleta along the Costera all the way to the naval base (2.50 pesos). "Cine Río-La Base" buses go from the *zócalo* to the base down Av. Cuauhtémoc. To get from the **Estrella de Oro** bus station to the *zócalo* (a 40min. walk), cross the street and flag down any bus heading southwest (2.50 pesos). A *"zócalo"* bus (2.50 pesos) will do the trick from the **Estrella Blanca** station. A **taxi** from the *zócalo* to the bus station costs 20 pesos, while one to the airport costs 75 pesos. **Shared taxis** (tel. 62 10 95) can take you to the airport for 45 pesos.

PRACTICAL INFORMATION

Transportation

Airport: on Rte. 200, 26km south of the city. Served by **Aerocaribe** (tel. 84 23 42), **Aerolines Internacionales** (tel. 86 56 30), **Aeroméxico** (tel. 66 91 90), **American** (tel. 66 92 27), **Continental** (tel. 66 90 40), **Delta** (tel. 66 94 84), **Mexicana** (tel. 66 91 38), and **Taesa** (tel. 86 56 00).

Buses: Estrella de Oro (tel. 85 87 05), on Cuauhtémoc at Massiu, sends buses to Cuernavaca (4hr., 4 per day 10:40am-8pm, 120-185 pesos), Mexico City (5hr., 20 per day 6:45am-1am, 170-250 pesos), Taxco (4hr., 5 per day 7am-6:40pm, 110 pesos), and Zihuatanejo (4hr., 13 per day 4:50am-4:50pm, 49-70 pesos). **Estrella Blanca,** Av. Ejido 47 (tel. 69 20 29), carts passengers to Chilpancingo (1½ hr., every 30min. 3:40am-11:30pm, 34 pesos), Cuernavaca (4hr., 9:35am and 2:20pm, 136 pesos), Mexico City (5hr., every hr. 6am-6pm, 167 pesos), Puebla (7hr., 5 per day 10am-midnight, 199 pesos), and Querétaro (9hr., 4:30pm, 264 pesos).

Car Rental: Hertz, Costera 1945 (tel. 85 68 89), past La Gran Plaza on the left. Small VW with insurance 431 pesos per day. Open M-Sa 8am-7pm, Su 9am-5pm.

Tourist and Financial Services

Tourist Offices: SEFOTUR, in the Centro Cultural de Acapulco, across from CICI waterpark. Amiable and helpful staff will happily overload you with brochures and maps. Some English spoken. Open M-F 9am-8pm, Sa 9am-2pm. In an **emergency,** contact the **Procuraduría del Turista,** Costera 4455 (tel. 84 45 83 or 84 44 16), in the Centro Internacional in front of CICI waterpark. Open daily 9am-9pm.

Tourist Police: (tel. 80 01 97 or 80 01 74). Officers clad in white wander around the *zócalo.* Office open daily 9am-1am.

Travel Agency: Agencia de Viajes Sol y Luna Excursiones, Costera 170 (tel. 84 51 40), in the Plaza Condes in front of Fiesta Americana. Open M-Sa 9am-9pm.

Consulates: Canada (tel. 86 50 45), Costera at Juan Pérez, in the Continental Hotel. Open daily 10am-2pm. **U.K.** (tel. 84 16 50), in the Hotel Las Brisas. Open M-F 1-3pm and 4-8pm. **U.S.,** Coster 121 Suite 14 (tel. 84 03 00), in the Continental Plaza Hotel. Open M-F 10am-2pm.

Currency Exchange: Banks on Costera have decent rates. All open M-F 9am-3pm. **Casas de cambio** are ubiquitous and often open until 8pm.

American Express, Costera 1628 (tel. 69 11 00 to 24; fax 69 11 88), on the bottom floor of the shopping center. Open M-Sa 10am-7pm.

Local Services

Bookstore: Sanborn's, Costera 209, 2 blocks from the *zócalo* toward the hotel zone. Selection of English paperbacks. Open daily 7:30am-11pm.

Markets: Mercado, Av. Constituyentes at Hurtado. Open daily 6am-6pm. **Supermarket Comercial Mexicana,** near the tourist office. Open daily 8am-10pm.

Laundromat: Super Lavandería, José Maria Iglesias #9 (tel. 80 01 46), 1 block from the cathedral. 4 kilos for 34 pesos. Open M-Sa 9am-2pm and 3-8pm, Su 10am-3pm.

Emergency and Communications

Police: LOCATEL (tel. 81 11 00 or 81 11 64). Open 24hr.

Red Cross: (tel. 85 41 01), on Ruiz Cortínez, north of the *zócalo.* Take a "Hospital" bus. 24hr. emergency service. Some English spoken. **Sociedad de Asistencia Médica Turística** (tel. 85 58 00 or 85 59 59) has a 24hr. doctor. English spoken.

Pharmacy: ISSTE Farmacias, Quebrada 1 (tel. 82 34 77), directly behind the cathedral on the *zócalo.* The storefront faces Independencia. Open daily 8am-8pm. **Farmacia Calleta,** Benito Juárez #21 (tel. 82 48 27). Open daily 8am-8:30pm.

Hospital: IMSS, Ruiz Cortínez 128 (tel. 86 36 08), north of the *zócalo* along Madero. Take a "Hospital" bus. 24hr. emergency service. No English spoken.

Post Office: Urdareta 1 (tel. 82 20 83), near Wantemóc. Open M-Sa 8am-8pm. **Postal Code:** 39300.

Telephones: LADATELs line the Costera. **Caseta Carranza,** Carranza 9, is 2 blocks from the *zócalo* toward the strip. Also has a **fax**. Open daily 8am-10pm.

Phone Code: 74.

ACCOMMODATIONS

Sleeping on the beaches of Acapulco Bay is unsafe. Fortunately, budget accommodations are easier to find here than anywhere else on Mexico's Pacific coast. Acapulco is a haggler's dream: be certain to inquire about discounts before paying for a room. However, during *Semana Santa* (March and April), rooms are nearly double the off-season prices, and it's hard to find lodgings without a previous reservation.

Hotel Misión, Prof. J. Felipe Valle 12 (tel. 82 36 43), at La Paz, 2 blocks left of the *zócalo.* The guests chatting over breakfast (15-30 pesos) in the courtyard, and the lazy cats sprawled out on the stairway give it a homey feel. Colonial architecture and well-tended plants make staying here as soothing as possible. All rooms have ceiling fans and private baths; some have desks and sofas. 80 pesos per person, 120 pesos per person during the high season.

Casa de Huéspedes Mama Hélène, Benito Juárez 12 (tel. 82 23 96; fax 83 86 97), at Felipe Valle. French owner holds court over a posse of ping-pong-playing, coffee-drinking, chain-smoking Euro-backpackers. Rooms assigned to match client's character. No hot water. Singles 80 pesos; doubles 150 pesos.

Hotel Angelita, Quebrada 37 (tel. 83 57 34). A cool night's sleep is guaranteed here—2 fans keep all rooms well ventilated. Welcoming proprietress, clean rooms, and hot water make Angelita popular among foreigners and Mexicans. 50 pesos per person, 70 pesos per person during the high season.

La Torre Eiffel, Inalámbrica 110 (tel. 82 16 63), at the top of La Quebrada. Turn left and walk up a very steep hill. All rooms have hot water, fans, TVs, and pretty pink bathrooms. Sit on the shady terrace to enjoy a clear view of the ocean, or take a quick dip in the swimming pool. 40-50 pesos per person.

FOOD

Acapulco's international restaurant scene conspicuously caters to tourists' palates. The many chic restaurants between Playa Condesa and the base are frequented mainly by tourists who don't fret much about money. If you insist on eating on the

Costera, try **El Fogón,** across from the Continental Plaza (sandwiches 12-28 pesos; open 24hr.) or **Jovito's** (tel. 84 84 33), across from the Fiesta Americana at Playa Condesa (*tacos de mariscos* 25 pesos; open daily 1pm-midnight). As usual, *típico* spots serve cheaper meals; try the hundreds of **fondas** (food stands) throughout the city or the Mercado Central.

Mariscos Nacho's, Azueta #7 (tel. 82 28 91), at Juárez, 1 block from the Costera. An open-air *marisquería* serving everything from red snapper seafood with rice (25 pesos) to delicious *camarones al mojo de ajo* (garlic shrimp, 50 pesos). Nacho's is always bustling; everyone from sunburned families straggling in from the beach to young hipsters dolled up for a night out come here. Open daily 8am-10pm.

100% Natural, Costera 248 (tel. 85 13 12 ext. 100), at the corner of Sebastián Vizcaíno, across from the tourist office. Several other branches line the Costera. Health food restaurant serving hearty sandwiches with sprouts and lettuce (30-35 pesos), fruit salad (19-30 pesos), and chilly, smooth *licuados* (15-16 pesos). Lots of options for vegetarians, like soy burgers (24-32 pesos). Open daily 8am-midnight. Other branches open 24hr.

The Fat Farm/La Granja del Pingui, Juárez 10, at La Paz, next door to Mama Hélène. Vegetable soup (8 pesos) is a specialty. Watch TV as you enjoy your poultry and meat (20-25 pesos) or fish (28-35 pesos) entree. Open daily 8am-9pm, 7am-11pm in the high season.

SAND AND SIGHTS

Unless you've won a game show, the reason you're in Acapulco is to enjoy the beach and booze. Acapulco's beaches aren't quiet and virginal; misanthropes might not like the noisy throngs of foreigners. However, those in the mood for a good dose of unadulterated people-watching will be satisfied.

Península de las Playas

At **La Quebrada,** Speedo-clad **clavadistas** (divers) perform death-defying dives that make Olympians look like wimps. *(Shows at 12:45, 7:30, 8:30, 9:30, and 10:30pm; 10 pesos.)* Although most spectators congregate at the bottom level, closest to the cliff, the view is better from the levels to the immediate right of the ticket booth. La Quebrada is a 15-minute walk from the *zócalo,* following the road that starts to the left of the cathedral's entrance. Continue until it ends at the parking lot of the hotel.

Each performance includes at least two 25m dives and one 35m dive. The divers all pray rather theatrically (who can blame them?) at a shrine at the top of the cliff before the plunge. The show is a quintessential part of the Acapulco tourist experience.

At the westernmost tip of Acapulco Bay, on the seaward side of the peninsula, lie **Playas Caleta** and **Caletilla.** Their gently rolling waves are ideal for swimming and attract hundreds of local families, making it hard to find an empty patch of sand anywhere. The narrow causeway that separates the two beaches leads to the island occupied by **Mágico Mundo Marino** (tel. 83 11 93), a water park with slides and pools (open daily 9am-7pm; admission 30 pesos, children under 12 15 pesos).

The **Plaza de Toros Caletilla** (tel. 83 95 61), Acapulco's main bull ring, sits beyond the abandoned yellow jai alai auditoriums 200m west of Caletilla beach. *Corridas* take place every Sunday at 5pm from December until Easter week, when the best-known *matadores* appear. Buy tickets at the **Centro Kennedy box office** (tel. 85 85 40), Costera at Álvaro Saavedra, or at the bull ring after 4:30pm on the day of the fight.

From the Comercial Mexicana to Parque Papagayo

The stretch of sand along the **Costera,** away from Old Acapulco, is blessed with fewer high-rises and smaller crowds than the beaches at Caleta or farther down the bay. **Playas Tamarindo, Hornos,** and **Hornitos,** between Las Hamacas Hotel and the Radisson, are called the "afternoon beaches." This is where the fishermen bring in their catches. The waves are moderate, and the sand is ideal for beach sports. The only drawback is that these beaches are unmistakably urban—you can hear the traffic on Costera as you sunbathe.

Mexican families who seek an alternative to the beach come to **Parque Papagayo** (tel. 85 24 90), which sprawls from Costera to Av. Cuauhtémoc. *(Open daily 6am-8pm.)* Entering on Costera by the Gigante supermarket, you'll find a **roller skating rink** (admission 10 pesos, 2 pesos to rent regular skates, 8 pesos for rollerblades; open daily 4pm-11pm). The rest of the park has shaded paths for bikes and walkers. There's an aviary in the center, surrounded by an artificial lake where you can rent **paddleboats** (10 pesos). Children will find a wading pool, exotic birds from Australia, and a zillion shady spots for hide and seek.

From La Diana to the Naval Base

A trip to **Playa Condesa,** at the center of the bay, is always exhilarating. Exercise caution: the waves are strong, and the sea floor drops without warning. The poor swimming conditions don't bother the throngs of sun worshippers who alternately lounge under their blue umbrellas and treat the beach as a runway for their minimal clothing fashion shows. Farther down the bay, between the golf course and naval base, is **Playa Icacos.** As you move toward the base, the waves become gentler.

CICI (tel. 84 80 33), Costera at Cristóbal Colón, is a fun-filled **water park.** *(Open daily 10am-6pm. Admission 40 pesos. Shows at noon, 2:30, and 5pm.)* Let artificial waves toss and hurl you head-first down the long, winding water slides, then rush to watch **trained dolphins** perform. To reach the park, follow Costera until you see the walls painted with bright blue waves and larger-than-life dolphins; otherwise take a "CICI" or "Base" bus (2.50 pesos).

Puerto Marqués

Lacking the prepackaged polish of the strip only a few kilometers away, the beach town of **Puerto Marqués** encompasses an unremarkable ribbon of sand lined wall-to-wall with restaurants so close to the water that the bay's waves lap at diners' feet. The bus ride to this bay is the real attraction, thanks to a magnificent vista from the top of the hill before the descent into town. Buses to Puerto Marqués depart across from La Diana or from Comercial Mexicana supermarket at Playa Hornitos, on the beach side of the street (45min., approximately every 30min. 5:30am-9pm, 2.50 pesos). As the bus rambles along, the Bahía de Puerto Marqués and the pounding surf of **Playa Revolcadero** come into full view. Beautiful **Playa Pichilingue,** a small, often-deserted patch of sand on the bay, is inaccessible by land. From Puerto Marqués, it's possible to get to nicer beaches that have fewer crowds. Catch a "Bonville" bus to get to **Playa Bonville;** it's a big improvement on the crowds and traffic of the downtown beaches.

ENTERTAINMENT

In Acapulco, every night is Saturday night: the nightlife busts out all the time, anywhere and everywhere. Most clubs pulsate with activity from 11pm to 5am and charge over 100 pesos for cover, which usually includes open bar. It's always easier and cheaper for women to get in; many clubs offer free admission (and open bar) to women on weeknights. The best clubs cluster in the area around the CICI, on the opposite side of the bay from the *zócalo.* Head and shoulders above the rest is **Palladium** (tel. 81 03 00), on the Carretera Escénica Las Brisas. A space-age structure perched on a cliff with a truly fabulous view of the downtown lights, this hot spot features a wall of glass; use it to enjoy the panoramic high-tech light and smoke effects. Watching the crowd is like attending a fashion show. The club reverberates with Mexican and American pop music until midnight when the light descends from the ceiling and the dance party begins. (Cover 200 pesos for men, 150 pesos for women, Tuesdays and Thursdays admission is free for women until 12:30pm. Open bar. Open daily 10:30am-5am.) Sporting a medieval castle theme, **Andrómedas,** on Costera, just past Planet Hollywood and the Hard Rock Café, is another happenin' place. Join scantily clad women and men in plaid dancing to the typical disco fare. (Cover 200 pesos for men, 150 pesos for women; free for women M, W, F, and Su before

12:30am. Open bar. Open daily 10:30pm-5am.) Across Costera from Andrómedas is **Sigono,** Costera 30 (tel. 81 18 87). Mirrored exterior, smoke, and laser lights keep the young crowd entertained. (Cover 160 pesos for men, 110 pesos for women. Open bar until 4am. Open Th-Su 10:30pm-5am.) Further down the Costera lies **Baby 'O,** Costera 22 (tel. 84 74 74). This club is slightly less frenetic and more sophisticated (read: older) than its rambunctious neighbors. (No cover weeknights; weekends 100 pesos for men, 50 pesos for women. No open bar; drinks 35 pesos. Open 10:30pm-late.) Alternatives to the hi-tech, exclusive discos include **Picante,** Privada Piedra Picuda #16, behind Carlos 'n' Charlie's, a spicy gay club. The predominantly male clientele is composed mainly of young, lithe bodies. There's some racy entertainment here, too. (No cover; 2 drink minimum, beer 15 pesos, *bebidas nacionales* 20 pesos. Open daily 10pm-4am.) **Disco Beach** (tel. 84 82 30), on Condesa beach, offers pool, video games, and thumping dance tunes. (Cover 150 pesos for men, 100 pesos for women, women free Su-Th. Open bar. Open 11pm-whenever the dancing stops.) **Nina's,** Costera 2909 (tel. 84 24 00), on the beach side near CICI, features tropical music and a more mature clientele (cover 120 pesos; open daily 10pm-5am).

Non-dancers flock to **Plaza Bahía,** a large shopping mall on Costera past La Gran Plaza on the water side, to satisfy the urge to acquire. Speed around a tiny race course at **Go-Karts** (tel. 86 71 47), on the third floor (1-seater 20 pesos for 5min., 2-seater 25 pesos for 5min; open daily 10am-11pm). There is **bowling** on the fourth floor at the **Boliche** (tel. 85 09 70; 130 pesos per hr., shoes 7 pesos; open daily 11am-2am) and a snazzy **movie theater** (tel. 86 42 55) on the second floor (admission 15-20 pesos).

Acapulco's tourist office organizes a variety of festivals designed to lighten the wallets of its tourists. **Festival Acapulco** in May is a celebration of music. In July, Acapulco hosts a **Black Film Festival** in which buff movie stars test their volleyball skills in front of gathering admirers. Men and women from around the globe journey to Acapulco in December to test their cliff diving skills during the **Torneo Internacional de Clavados en La Quebrada.**

■ Near Acapulco: Pie de la Cuesta

Pie de la Cuesta is known for its truly magnificent sunsets—the lazy sun lingers beautifully over the Pacific horizon just before dropping out of view. A single-lane highway runs through Acapulco's hills to Pie de la Cuesta, ending at the narrow road that separates the Pacific from the placid waters of **Laguna de Coyuca,** and the hustle and bustle of Acapulco from the serenity of a small beach community.

At Playa Pie de la Cuesta, pleasure-seekers can choose between salt and fresh water. Since the Pacific's rough waves preclude swimming, many head to the lagoon instead, the site of the area's best **water skiing. Sunset** (tel. 60 06 53 or 60 06 54), a ski club, near the air base offers **ski rental** (300 pesos per hr. for up to 3 people, lessons with tours of the lagoon 40 pesos per hr.). Rest and relaxation are all too often interrupted, unfortunately, by aggressive *lancha* agents who are more than happy to give passing tourists a tour of the lagoon, for a fee, of course (about 30 pesos per person in a *colectivo* boat). *Lancha* agents notwithstanding, the serenity of Pie de la Cuesta is worth at least a daytrip. The air is cleaner here, the water bluer, the surf stronger, the beach less crowded, and the scenery more stunning than in Acapulco. **Villa Nirvana** (tel. 60 16 31), a blue and white building a few blocks from the bus stop, carves out its own utopia complete with a restaurant, swimming pool, and rooms with fans and private baths (about 100 pesos per person; high season 125 pesos). Beyond the pharmacy toward the base is **Acapulco Trailer Park** (tel. 60 00 10), with campgrounds, trailer hook-up sites, bathrooms, ocean views, and a pet raccoon named "Charlie" (50 pesos per night, prices negotiable). If you work up an appetite, take the last road before you reach the base to **Chavelita,** Av. Fuerza Áerea Mexicana Ote. 14 (tel. 48 02 60; breakfast 18 pesos, *comida a la cana* 18 pesos, beer 5 pesos; open daily 8am-9pm).

Getting There: Buses leave from Costera, across from the post office in Acapulco. Buses marked "Pie de la Cuesta Playa" go directly to the road along the beach; those labeled "Pie de la Cuesta Centro" stop on a parallel street in a small marketplace (40min., 2.50 pesos). From there, turn left down a dirt road; you should be able to see the shimmering ocean in the distance. At the end of the road, turn right to head toward the base. Buses shuttle between the base and the town's *centro* (2.50 pesos). A *combi* will take you as far as **La Barra,** the enchanted spot where the water from the lagoon flows into the ocean (3.50 pesos). To return to Acapulco, go back to the market and hail a bus in the opposite direction.

OAXACA

Oaxaca de Juárez (Oaxaca)

Perched on a giant plateau that gracefully interrupts the Sierra Madre del Sur's descent into the Oaxaca valley, the city of Oaxaca de Juárez (wa-HAH-ka dey WA-rez; pop. 250,000) is a rare beauty. The city's surname was added in honor of native son Benito Juárez, a Oaxacan Zapotec and Mexico's only *indígena* president. It earned its older nickname, "City of Jade," after Hernán Cortés began to build his beloved (but unfinished) estate here in 1535. Cortés's deep green stone buildings have since aged to a dignified yellow, and throughout the streets this style has been lovingly preserved and imitated, giving Oaxaca the feel of a city that lives and breathes its own remarkable history. Especially in the early morning, the city is strikingly beautiful; at first light, the city's tall, green, gracefully aging silhouettes are spectacular.

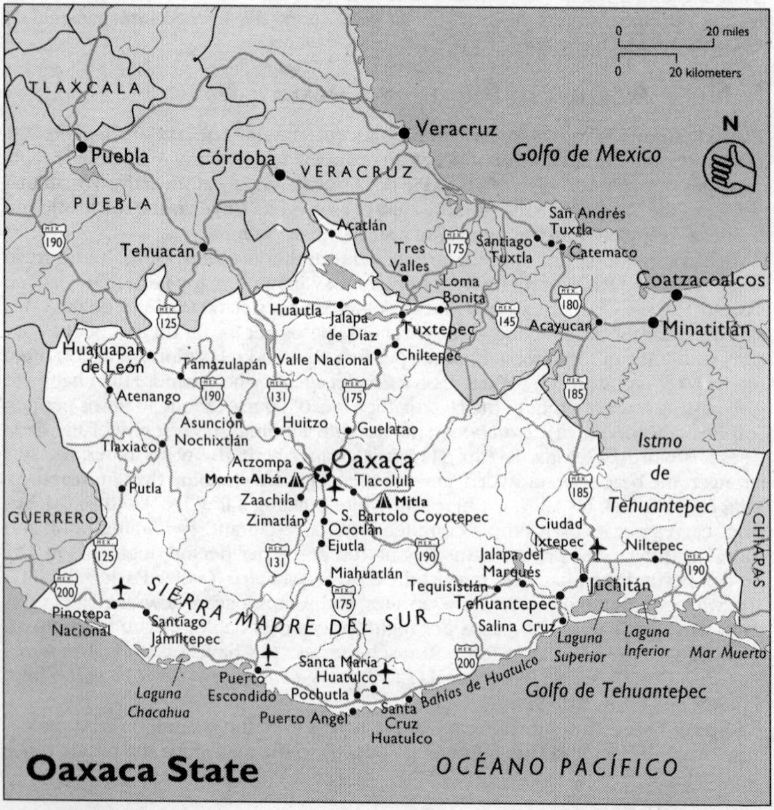

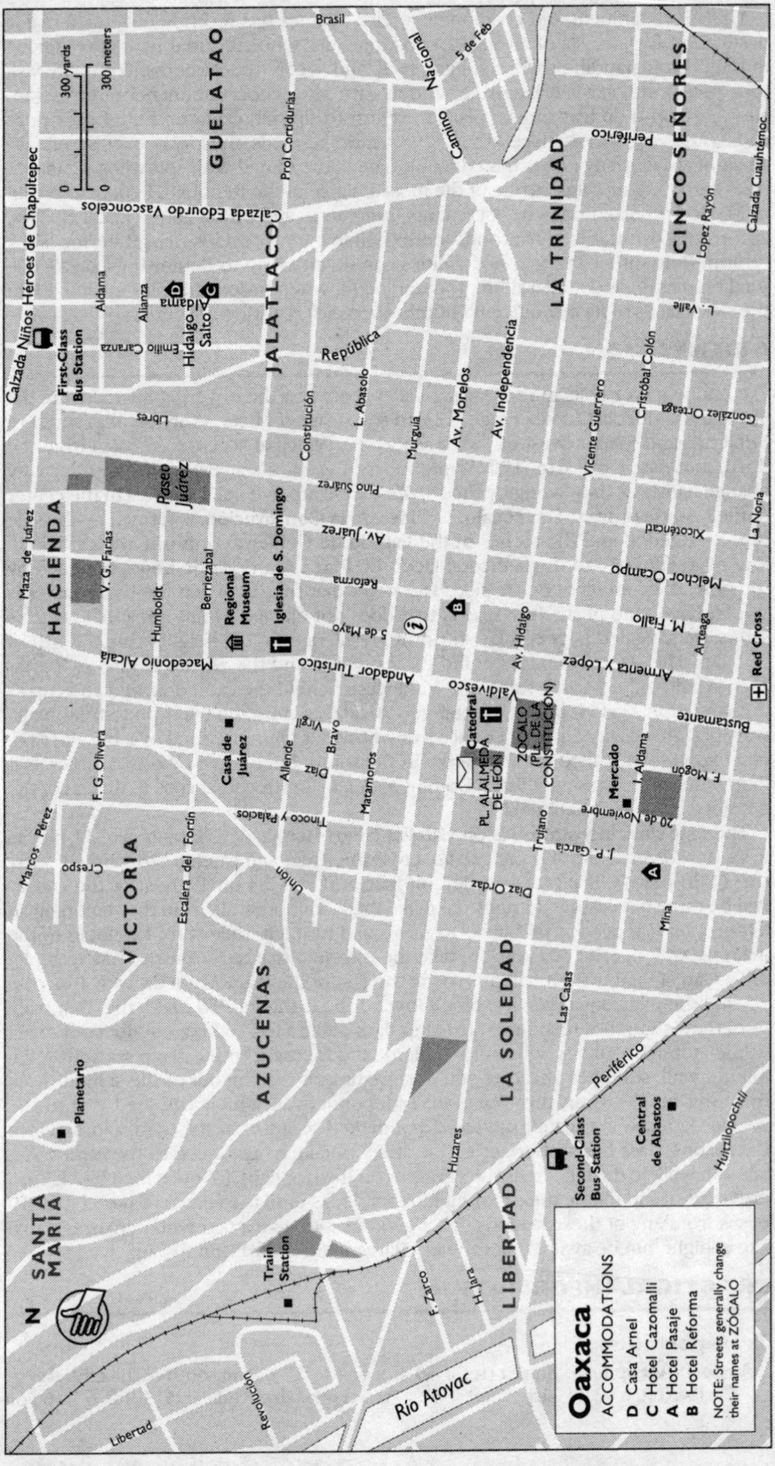
Oaxaca
ACCOMMODATIONS
D Casa Arnel
C Hotel Cazomalli
A Hotel Pasaje
B Hotel Reforma
NOTE: Streets generally change their names at ZÓCALO
N
0 300 yards
0 300 meters
SANTA MARÍA
VICTORIA
AZUCENAS
HACIENDA
GUELATAO
JALATLACO
LA TRINIDAD
CINCO SEÑORES
LA SOLEDAD
LIBERTAD
Planetario
Train Station
Second-Class Bus Station
Central de Abastos
First-Class Bus Station
Regional Museum
Iglesia de S. Domingo
Casa de Juárez
Catedral
PL. ALAMEDA DE LEÓN
ZÓCALO (PL. DE LA CONSTITUCIÓN)
Mercado
Red Cross
Paseo Juárez
Río Atoyac
Periférico
Calzada Niños Héroes de Chapultepec
Calzada Edourdo Vasconcelos
Prol Cortidurías
Brasil
5 de Feb
Camino Nacional
República
Av. Morelos
Av. Independencia
Av. Juárez
Pino Suárez
Reforma
5 de Mayo
Andador Turístico
Macedonio Alcalá
Valdivesco
Av. Hidalgo
Armenta y López
Bustamante
M. Fiallo
Melchor Ocampo
Xicoténcatl
Vicente Guerrero
Cristóbal Colón
González Ortega
L. Valle
Lopez Rayón
Calzada Cuauhtémoc
La Noria
Arteaga
F. Mogón
I. Aldama
20 de Noviembre
J. P. García
Mina
Díaz Ordaz
Trujano
Las Casas
Huzares
H. Jara
F. Zarco
Revolución
Libertad
Huitzilopochtli
Unión
Tinoco y Palacios
Matamoros
Bravo
Díaz
Allende
Virgil
Murguía
L. Abasolo
Constitución
Libres
Emilio Caranza
Aldama
Alianza
Hidalgo
Salto
Maza de Juárez
V. G. Farías
Humboldt
Berriozabal
F. G. Olivera
Marcos Pérez
Crespo
Escalera del Fortín

A relatively affluent and cosmopolitan city, Oaxaca has recently become a major destination for tourists of all ages and nationalities who are lured by its prestigious museums, outstanding archaeological sites, and sheer attractiveness. For many visitors, one-month stays at language schools turn into whole summers of immersion, and those who do leave make plans to return to sip rich Oaxacan hot chocolate as soon as they can. In the face of the Teva-wearing crowds, the city manages to retain an air of authenticity rather than dilution. The *zócalo,* lined with sprawling jacaranda trees and outdoor cafes, is one of the most amiable in the Republic. Expect to see all of Mexico represented here: merchants, *indígenas,* and professionals jostle elbows, and restless students tear around on expensive motorcycles or agitate for labor reform. But neither tourism nor politics can do anything to diminish Oaxaca's cultural richness—or colonial allure. Day and night, when streetlights play up and down the stone faces of its magnificent churches, Oaxaca is always a wonder.

ORIENTATION

Oaxaca de Juárez rests in the Oaxaca Valley, between the towering Sierra Madre del Sur and the Puebla-Oaxaca range, 523km southeast of Mexico City, 435km south of Veracruz, and 526km west of Tuxtla Gutiérrez. Principal access to Oaxaca from the north and east is via **Rte. 190.** While most of Oaxaca's streets form a grid, many change names as they swing by the *zócalo.* There are two main squares in the center of the historic district. The **zócalo,** or **Plaza de la Constitución,** is formed by the side of the cathedral and the arches of the Palacio de Gobierno opposite the cathedral. The main entrance to the cathedral faces the **Plaza Alameda de León,** bounded by the post office on its opposite side. The street that runs between the two squares is **Av. Hidalgo,** one of the few streets that does not change names. Most of Oaxaca's sights are snuggled between lavish private residences in the neighborhood north of Hidalgo. The street running behind the cathedral and the *zócalo* begins as **Bustamante** below the *zócalo,* turns into **Valdivieso** behind the cathedral, and ends up as the **Andador Turístico (Av. Macedonio Alcalá),** a museum-lined pedestrian walkway, past the Plaza Alameda. Oaxaca's **downtown** is circumscribed by a busy peripheral expressway, called the **Periférico** in the south, but known by other names as it loops above the Church of Santo Domingo. The main street that runs to the left of the entrance is **Av. Independencia.**

The **first-class bus station** is on Calzada Niños Héroes de Chapultepec, 11 blocks from the *zócalo.* To reach the *zócalo,* cross the street and catch a bus marked "Centro" (1.20 pesos). The bus turns left on Juárez. If you get off at Hidalgo, the *zócalo* will be three blocks to your right. To make the 20-minute walk from the station, head left on Chapultepec for six blocks to Alcalá and turn left; then walk 12 blocks to the main plaza. From the **AU station,** take the *colectivo* marked "Centro." Ask to be let off at García Vigil, which will put you at the end of the Plaza Alameda away from the *zócalo;* the main square is one block toward the cathedral. To make the 2km walk from the station (not recommended after dark), take a left coming out the door, walk to the stoplight, take a right onto Madero, and follow it to the **train station.** A 25-minute walk stretches ahead of you: turn right as if coming out of the station, walk five long blocks, then turn left onto Independencia, which will lead you to the *zócalo.* You can also catch the *colectivo* marked "Centro" at the train station. From the **second-class bus station,** cross the street to take a bus or taxi to the *centro.* Or, you can walk to the left, cross the Periférico at the stoplight, follow it for a block, turn on Trujano, and follow it east for eight long blocks until the *zócalo.* **Taxis** charge 10 pesos from any of these stations. It's a good idea to take a taxi when crossing town late at night, but be aware that cabbies charge extra from 11pm to 5am.

PRACTICAL INFORMATION

Transportation

Airport: Aeropuerto Juárez (tel. 1 50 40), on Rte. 175, 8km south of the city. **Aero-Caribe** (tel. 6 02 29, airport tel. 1 52 47). **Aeroméxico,** Hidalgo 513 (tel. 6 10 66 or

6 71 01, airport 1 50 44). **Mexicana** (tel. 4 72 53; fax 6 57 96), on Independencia at Fiallo. **Taxis** 40 pesos. **Transportes Aeropuerto** (tel. 4 43 50), next to the post office on the Plaza Alameda, will pick you up at your hotel. (*Colectivo* 12 pesos, *especial* 47 pesos; expect to pay more if you're not staying downtown.) Arrange a day in advance. Office open M-Sa 9am-2pm and 5-8pm.

Buses: From Oaxaca, it is possible to go almost anywhere in the Republic at any time. The **first-class station** is located at Niños Héroes de Chapultepec 1036. From this station, **ADO** (tel. 5 17 03) runs to Mexico City (9hr., 18 per day, 172 pesos), Puebla (7hr., 7 per day, 128 pesos), Tuxtepec (6hr., 3 and 11:30pm, 76 pesos), and Veracruz (9hr., 8:30am and 8:30pm, 170 pesos). **Autobuses Cuenca del Paloapan** (tel. 5 09 03) offers similar service; open M-Sa 9am-2pm and 4-7pm, Su 9am-3pm. **Cristóbal Colón** (tel. 5 12 14) goes to Puerto Escondido (12hr., 9:30am, 10:30pm, and midnight, 148 pesos), San Cristóbal (12hr., 7:30pm, 169 pesos), Tehuantepec (5hr., 12 per day, 70 pesos), and Tuxtla Gutiérrez (11hr., 7:30 and 10:15pm, 151 pesos). Tickets for ADO and Cristóbal Colón are also available at 20 de Noviembre 204. The **second-class station** is just past the Central de Abastos (big market), across the Periférico from the western end of Trujano. Small regional bus lines, many without signs or ticket windows, provide frequent service to every small town near Oaxaca, usually for under 3 pesos. **Estrella del Valle** (tel. 4 57 00 or 6 54 29) runs to Puerto Escondido (8hr., 8 per day 7am-11am, 49 pesos). The **Hotel Mesón del Angel,** Mina 518, between Mier y Terán and Díaz Ordaz, serves as a **bus stop** for **Autotransportes Turísticos** (tel. 6 53 27 or 4 31 61). Buses to Monte Albán (30min., peak season every 30min. 8am-3:30pm, off-season 5 per day, round-trip 12 pesos).

Car Rental: Budget, 5 de Mayo 305 (tel. 6 44 45). Also at the airport (tel. 1 52 52). VWs cost 320-350 pesos per day, depending on the season. Free mileage. Open daily 8am-1pm and 4-7pm. **Hertz** (tel. 6 24 34), on Valdivieso at Hidalgo, across from the American Express office, has similar rates. Slightly cheaper is **Arrendadora Express,** 20 de Noviembre 204-A (tel. 6 67 76), which **rents cars** (330 pesos per day), **motorcycles** (400 pesos per day), **mopeds** (180 pesos per day), and **bikes** (50 pesos).

Tourist and Financial Services

Tourist Offices: SEDETUR, 5 de Mayo 200 (tel. 6 48 28; email turinfo@oaxaca.gob.mx; http://oaxaca.gob.mx/sedetur), at Morelos, provides a lot of helpful information. English spoken. Smaller office at Independencia 607 (tel. 6 01 23), inside the Palacio Municipal. Both open daily 8am-8pm. **CEPROTUR,** Alcalá 407 (tel./fax 6 72 80), on the Andador Turístico at Allende and in the Plaza Santo Domingo, provides assistance to tourists. Open daily 9am-9pm. **Info booth** (tel. 1 50 40) at the airport. Also check *Oaxaca Times* (http://www.oaxacatimes.com), a monthly English newspaper, for up-to-the-minute tourist information.

Consulates: In an emergency, **CEPROTUR** (see above) will obtain consular assistance. **Canada,** Dr. Liceaga 119 #8 (tel. 3 37 77; fax 5 21 47). Open M-F 9am-2pm. **Italy,** Alcalá 400 (tel. 5 31 15 or 6 50 58). Open M-F 1pm-8pm. **France,** Portal Juárez 101 (tel. 6 35 22 or 6 35 20). Open M-F 9am-noon and 4-8pm. **Germany,** Hidalgo 817 #5 (tel. 3 08 65 or 6 72 80). Open M-F 9am-8pm. **Spain,** Díaz 340 (tel 8 00 31 or 8 01 00). Open M-F 4pm-8pm. **U.K.,** in the same building as the German consulate. **U.S.,** Alcalá 201 #204 (tel. 4 30 54), at Morelos. Hidden under an arched doorway. Open M-F 9am-2pm.

Currency Exchange: Banamex, Hidalgo 821 (tel. 6 59 00), at 3 de Mayo, 1 block from the *zócalo,* has an **ATM.** Open M-F 9am-5pm, Sa 9am-2pm. **Banco Serfín** (tel. 4 52 26), Independencia 705, to the left of the cathedral's entrance, also has an **ATM.** Open M-F 9am-5pm. **Cash Express,** Alcalá 201 (tel. 6 22 00), exchanges money at more flexible hours. Open M-Sa 8am-8pm, Su 9am-3pm. Also try **Internacional de Divisas** (tel. 6 33 99), next to the *zócalo* on Alcalá. Open M-Sa 8am-8pm, Su 9am-5pm.

American Express: Valdivieso 2 (tel. 6 27 00), at Hidalgo across from the *zócalo.* It also houses a **travel agency** that sells plane tickets and first-class bus tickets to Mexico City and Puebla. English spoken. Office open M-F 9am-2pm and 4-7pm, Sa 9am-2pm for travel services; closes one hour earlier for financial services.

Local Services

Foreign Bookstores: Librería Universitaria, Guerrero 104 (tel. 6 42 43), off the corner of the *zócalo.* Small selection of English-language used paperbacks (10 pesos) and books on Mexico. Open M-Sa 9:30am-2pm and 4-8pm. **Códice,** Alcalá 403 (tel. 6 03 39), on the Andador Turístico. Books about Mexico and Oaxaca in Italian, French, Japanese, German, English, and Spanish. Open daily 9am-9pm.

Libraries: Biblioteca Circulante, Alcalá 305. A haven for displaced U.S. tourists. Everything from the *New Yorker* to *Sports Illustrated.* Open M-F 10am-1pm and 4-7pm, Sa 10am-1pm. **Biblioteca Pública,** Alcalá 200 (tel. 6 47 14). Some English-language books on Oaxaca. Open M-F 9am-8:30pm. **Instituto Welte Para Estudios Oaxaqueños,** 5 de Mayo 412 (tel. 6 54 17). Large collection of English-language books and journals on Oaxacan history and anthropology. Open M-F 9:30am-1:30pm, plus Tu and Th 4-6pm. The **Instituto de Artes Gráficos de Oaxaca,** Alcalá 507 (tel. 6 69 80), across from Santo Domingo, has a library as well as changing art exhibits. Open daily 9:30am-8pm.

Cultural Centers: Instituto Oaxaqueño de las Culturas (tel. 6 24 83), Calzada Madero at Av. Técnica. Hosts plays, dance performances, and concerts. Listings are in the monthly *Guía Cultura* (5 pesos). **Casa de la Cultura,** González Ortega 403 (tel. 6 24 83), at Colón. Poetry readings and art galleries. Open M-F 8am-8pm, Sa 8am-2pm.

Markets: Mercado Benito Juárez, at the corner of 20 de Noviembre and Aldama, 2 blocks from the *zócalo* away from the cathedral, sells crafts, produce, flowers, and clothing. Its annex, **Mercado 20 de Noviembre,** on the next block over, has gastronomic goodies. Both markets open daily 6am-9pm. Saturday is the big day at **Central de Abastos,** at the end of Trujano, across from the second-class bus station, but vendors offer every type of product—including live animals—every day. Beware of pickpockets. **Mercado de Artesanías,** at the corner of J.P. García and Zaragoza, offers some artisan wares. Open daily 10am-8pm.

Laundromats: Súper Lavandería Hidalgo, J.P. García 200 (tel. 4 11 81), 2 blocks from the *zócalo.* Open M-Sa 8am-8pm. **Lavandería Clin,** 20 de Noviembre 606-B (tel. 6 23 42), charges 28 pesos for every 3.5kg. Open M-Sa 9am-8pm.

Emergency and Communications

Emergency: Dial 06.

Police: Aldama 108 (tel. 6 27 26 or 6 07 74), south of the *zócalo,* between Miguel Cabrera and Bustamante. Some English spoken. Open 24hr.

Red Cross: Armenta y López 700 (tel. 6 48 03 or 4 08 85), between Pardo and Burgoa. Ambulance service. English spoken. Open 24hr.

Pharmacies: Farmacia El Fénix, Flores Magón 104 (tel. 6 60 11), next to the *zócalo.* Open M-Sa 7am-10pm, Su 8am-9pm. **Farmacia Héroes de Chapultepec** (tel. 3 35 24), half a block east of the first-class bus station. Open 24hr.

Hospitals: Hospital Civil, Porfirio Díaz 400 (tel. 5 31 81 or 5 37 09), 1.5km out of town. Free medical service. **IMSS,** Chapultepec 621 (tel. 5 34 75), at Reforma. Open 24hr. **Sanatorio Reforma,** Reforma 613 (tel. 6 09 89 or 6 60 90), at Humboldt. Open 24hr. English spoken.

Post Office: (tel. 6 26 61), in the Plaza Alameda de León. Open M-F 8am-7pm, Sa 9am-1pm. **Postal Code:** 68000.

Fax: Telecomm (tel. 6 49 02), Independencia at 20 de Noviembre, around the corner from the post office. Open M-F 8am-6pm, Sa 9am-4pm.

Internet Access: Terra Nostra, Morelos 600, 2nd fl. (tel. 6 82 92; http://www.terranostra.com.mx), at Virgil. 20 pesos per 30min., 35 pesos per hr. Telnet, Netscape, IRC. Open M-F 9:15am-7pm, Sa 10am-2pm. **Milenium Café,** 5 de Mayo 412-3 (tel. 4 80 24; email milenium@infosel.net.mex), in the Plaza Gonzalo Lucero across from La Iglesia Santo Domingo. Offers speedy Netscape, Telnet, and IRC, but you'd better type fast—it's a peso per minute. 10% discount for students with ID. Open M-F 10am-8pm, Sa 10am-6pm.

Telephones: LADATELs are in front of the post office, at La Iglesia de Santo Domingo, and at the ADO station. *Casetas* available at **Computel,** Independencia 601 (tel. 4 80 84), across from the Telecomm office. Open daily 7am-10pm.

Phone Code: 951.

ACCOMMODATIONS AND CAMPING

As Oaxaca attracts more visitors, some old budget standbys have upgraded their rooms in an attempt to lure more upscale tourists. But bargains still await the penny-pinching soul, especially in the busy blocks south of the *zócalo,* which are within easy walking distance of the second-class bus station and all major sights and services. Reservations are a must on *fiesta* weekends, especially during the *Guelaguetza* in July, and during *Semana Santa* in late March or early April.

Outside the downtown area are a number of trailer parks. The **Trailer Park Oaxaca,** Violetas 900 (tel. 5 27 96), is near the *Zona Militar* in the northeast part of town. To get there, take the "Colonia Reforma" bus from the stop on J.P. García just north of Hidalgo. The **Trailer Park San Francisco,** Madero 705, in the northwest part of town, is accessible on the "Santa Rosa" bus from the same J.P. García stop.

For longer stays, many families rent rooms. (The Biblioteca Circulante, the tourist office, and all the *Oaxaca Times* post listings.) **Departmentos del Cuento,** Quintana Roo 107 (tel. 4 22 88), off Berriozabal past La Iglesia Santo Domingo, rents six one- or two-person rooms with kitchen and bath (1300 pesos per month, utilities included).

Near the First-Class Bus Station

This area is a residential neighborhood with cobblestone streets, about a 20-minute walk from the *zócalo* and the sights. **Parque Juárez** and the nearby movie theater lend a very laid-back feel to life here.

Casa Arnel, Aldama 404 (tel. 5 28 56; fax 3 62 85), at Hidalgo, a 20min. walk from the *zócalo.* Walk 7 blocks down Alcalá past La Iglesia Santo Domingo, turn right on Berriozabal, and cross to the other side of the park; it's 3 blocks down on Piño Suárez. The spotless, homey rooms offer beds and desks, but the real entertainment is provided by the social breakfasts and the talking parrots in the jungle-like courtyard. Laundry facilities, English-language books, a travel agency, and, for 40 pesos an hour, you can borrow Arnel's personal computer to check email or surf the web. Singles 70 pesos, 140 pesos with private bath; doubles 130 pesos, 160 pesos with private bath.

Hotel Cazomalli, El Salto 104 (tel. 5 35 13), on the corner of Aldama, just down the street from Casa Arnel. Cazomalli lives up to its name, which in Náhuatl means "peace and quiet." Large, luxuriously clean, tiled rooms have huge private baths. A jacuzzi, TV room, and dining room are also available. Singles 170; doubles 225.

North of the Zócalo

The northern part of town is more prosperous, residential, and tranquil. Hotels here offer desirable locations and are closer to the major sights.

Hostal Santa Isabel, Morelos 800 (tel. 5 20 49), at Alcalá, has one of the best locations in town, only a stone's throw away from the major sights. This recently renovated hostel offers over 60 beds, some in mixed rooms, and some in single-sex rooms. Hot water 24hr. Special prices available for large groups and extended stays. Marcel, the gregarious owner, speaks 5 languages. 40 pesos per night.

Hotel Reforma, Reforma 102 (tel. 6 09 39), between Independencia and Morelos, 4 blocks past the left side of the cathedral. Kick back on rustic, hand-carved wood furniture, and soak in the view of the city. Singles 85 pesos; doubles 95 pesos; triples 115 pesos; quads 135 pesos. Rooms are usually full; reservations help.

South of the Zócalo

South of the *zócalo,* there is a plethora of budget hotels; often four or five share the same block, particularly along **Díaz Ordaz.** Because of their proximity to the market and second-class bus terminal, many of these hotels face noisy, dirty streets; ask for a room in the back or on an upper level. Be cautious when walking in this area at night.

Hotel Mina, Mina 304 (tel. 6 49 66), is something of a favorite among international travelers. The plain rooms feature hard beds, but the communal baths are clean and convenient. Singles 50 pesos; doubles 60 pesos; triples 90 pesos.

Hotel Pasaje, Mina 302 (tel. 6 42 13), 3 blocks south of the *zócalo.* Well-scrubbed, tiled rooms open onto a plant-filled courtyard. Bathrooms are large and clean, but the fluorescent lighting makes everything look a bit withered. Rooms near the street are noisy, but you can smell the chocolate from the nearby sweet shops. Singles 80 pesos; doubles 100-120 pesos; triples 140 pesos.

Hotel Fortín, Díaz Ordaz 312 (tel. 6 27 15), is probably the best of the hotels that line this packed block. Freshly renovated rooms are fairly large and clean and feature strange "V" designs on the walls. The gray communal and private baths are rather clean. Singles 55 pesos, with bath 70 pesos; doubles 65 pesos, with bath 90 pesos; triples 120 pesos.

FOOD

The fine restaurants in Oaxaca offer food to please almost every palate and wallet. Oaxaca has seven versions of **mole,** a rich sauce made of over 30 ingredients including chiles and chocolate. Many restaurants also serve **tlayudas,** large, crisp tortillas topped with just about everything. If you're feeling adventurous, try **botanas oaxaqueñas**—plates full of regional goodies including chile, *quesillo* (boiled string cheese), *chorizo* (sausage), guacamole, and *chapulines* (tiny, cooked grasshoppers doused with chile; they're good, seriously).

Also a must is Oaxaca's cinnamon **chocolate caliente** (hot chocolate). The cafes in the *zócalo* are pricey, but you can find something on the cheaper side south of the *zócalo* on Mina. Another regional speciality is the **tamale,** now found in all parts of the Republic. Made of ground corn wrapped in banana leaves and then baked or boiled, tamales come stuffed with beans, chicken, or beef. And there's no better way to wrap up a *comida oaxaqueña* than with a large swig of **mezcal,** the potent cactus-based liquor that is only manufactured in the Oaxaca Valley.

The **markets** offer *chapulines* and spiced *jícama* (a crunchy beet-shaped fruit), as well as the usual inexpensive fare. Restaurants in the *zócalo* are tasty but pricey. On **20 de Noviembre,** you'll find row after row of eateries.

La Casa de la Abuela, Hidalgo 616, 2nd fl. (tel. 6 35 44), located at the corner of the *zócalo* and Plaza Alameda. The Casa offers only authentic Oaxacan dishes—including their delicious *mole* (50 pesos)—as well as stunning views of both plazas and the cathedral. It's expensive, but if you must eat in the *zócalo,* this is the place to do it. Open daily 1pm-9pm.

Antojitos Regionales Los Olmos, Morelos 403 at Crespo. Every night, the family that lives in this hedonist haven opens up their courtyard to share dinner with whoever is savvy enough to know about it. Almost always full of locals, with good reason. You won't find fresher, tastier food anywhere in Oaxaca. No menus, and you can watch the food being prepared. At 7 pesos, the *tamales de mole* are the most expensive item served. Open daily 7pm-midnight.

El Biche Pobre, Calzada de la República 600 (tel. 3 46 36), is quite a ways from the *centro,* but ideal if you are in Parque Juárez or staying at Casa Arnel. A local favorite, the restaurant fills on weekend afternoons. Serves up authentic *oaxaqueña* food as well as *antojitos* (10-20 pesos) and seafood. Open daily 1pm-9pm.

Mariscos Los Jorges, Pino Suárez 806 (tel. 3 43 08), across the street from Parque Juárez, toward the northern end of the park. This restaurant is definitely worth the short walk from downtown. Tables are scattered throughout a secluded and leafy courtyard, and the waitstaff is friendly and eager to please. Excellent seafood at reasonable prices (shrimp tacos 24 pesos). Open daily 8am-6:30pm.

Restorán Café Alex, Díaz Ordaz 218 (tel. 4 07 15). An extensive menu that runs the gamut of Mexican cuisine, with English explanations. Garden seating available. Generous breakfasts (starting at 15 pesos), *comida corrida* (21 pesos), and vegetarian specialties (21 pesos) are a cut above the grittier storefront fare in the neighborhood. Open M-Sa 7am-9pm, Su 7am-noon.

Flor de Loto, Morelos 509 (tel. 4 39 44), is one of Oaxaca's few restaurants with a predominantly vegetarian menu. Try the veggie soups (10 pesos), the *enchiladas de soya* (20 pesos), or the mushroom tacos (20 pesos). *Comida corrida* 25 pesos. Open daily 7am-10pm.

Coffee Beans, 5 de Mayo 114, specializes in coffee from the state of Oaxaca. Lattes, cappuccinos, and *chocolates calientes* can all be yours. Breakfast served 8am-noon. Open daily 8am-11pm.

SIGHTS

Oaxaca's museums, churches, and historical venues offer something for everyone, from pre-Hispanic to colonial to contemporary. Luckily for the weary traveler, the major sites are all located within walking distance of the pedestrian-only Andador Turístico. Don't leave without seeing the **Iglesia de Santo Domingo,** the **Museo de Arte Prehispánico de México Rufino Tamayo,** and the **Museo Regional de Oaxaca.**

The Zócalo

The **Catedral de Oaxaca** and the Palacio de Gobierno (not to be confused with the Palacio Municipal, which contains the tourist office) sit on opposite sides of the *zócalo*. *(Catedral open daily 7am-8pm.)* Originally constructed in 1535, the cathedral was damaged and finally destroyed by a series of earthquakes. Reconstructed from 1702 to 1733, the church now features a baroque facade with bas-relief work. The ornate bishop's seat, in the central altar, provides a structural focus. Inside the **Palacio de Gobierno,** a mural by Arturo García Bustos presents an informative historical collage. *(Palace open 24hr.)* A mural decorating the left staircase depicts a celebration of maize and water, the area's most important resources. In the central staircase, scenes of pre-Hispanic life with maize cultivation, weaving, and temples give way to the political and religious figures that dominate the other panels. The center panel celebrates the *oaxaqueño* Benito Juárez, his wife Margarita Masa, and one of his oft-repeated phrases, *"El respeto al derecho ajeno es la paz"* ("Respect for the rights of others is peace").

Along the Andador Turístico (Alcalá)

To the left of the cathedral, a cobbled pedestrian street leads to museums, restaurants, and stores. A block down the Andador (also known as Alcalá) is the **Museo de Arte Contemporáneo de Oaxaca (MACO),** Alcalá 202 (tel. 4 71 10), on the right. *(Open Su-M and W-Sa 10:30am-8pm; free on Sundays.)* This beautiful colonial building is known as the Casa de Cortés, although historians insist that it was not, in fact, Cortés's estate. Nevertheless, it is an example of vice-regal architecture, a style that was used by the *conquistadores* and their heirs. The museum features both rotating and permanent exhibitions, and shows free movies on its large-screen TV. The impressive permanent collection includes the works of *oaxaqueños* such as Rufino Tamayo, Francisco Toledo, and Rodolfo Morales. The bookstore carries a large number of art books and magazines, plus English guidebooks to the region (10 pesos).

Following the walkway for three more blocks, the imposing **Iglesia de Santo Domingo** looms on the right. *(Open daily 7am-1pm and 4-8pm.)* The church is the **tallest building in Oaxaca.** Upon entering, it takes a few seconds for the eyes to adjust to the dim interior. Further up, an explosion of gilt assaults the retina. Construction on the church began in 1575, and the structure was consecrated in 1611. Since then, the church, one of the best examples of Baroque style in Mexico, has functioned as a place of worship, a museum, and even as military barracks for both sides during the reform wars and the Revolution. The two-meter-thick walls have served the church well; it has stood for 400 years, despite Oaxaca's strong earthquakes. The interior is even more spectacular with waves of gilded stucco that cover the ceiling and walls. The real eye-catcher, though, is the massive gilded altar. Built in 1959 by Oaxacan artists and workers, the altar is one of the most elaborate (and expensive) of its kind. The **Capilla de la Virgen del Rosario,** off to the right as you walk in, also features relatively new altar works *(capilla open daily 7am-1pm and 4-8pm).*

The ex-convent next door was converted in 1972 into the city's prestigious **Museo Regional de Oaxaca** (tel. 6 29 91), and a year-long renovation has left the 16th century building in better condition than ever. The stellar museum houses a large collection of Mixtec and Zapotec pieces as well as displays on the history of the state of Oaxaca. The collection's prime attraction is the treasure extracted from Tomb 7 in Monte Albán. The exquisite collection of gold, silver, turquoise, bone, and obsidian is one of the best assortments of Zapotec artifacts ever found.

Near the Andador Turístico

The renowned **Museo de Arte Prehispánico de México Rufino Tamayo,** Morelos 503 (tel. 6 47 50), between Díaz and Tinoco y Palacios, shows off the Oaxacan artist's personal collection of pre-Hispanic objects. *(Open M, W-Sa 10am-2pm and 4-7pm, Su 10am-3pm. Admission 14 pesos.)* The figurines, ceramics, and masks that Tamayo collected are meant to be appreciated as works of art in their own right. Attractively displayed in pastel-schemed cases, the pieces are also chronologically ordered.

One block from Alcalá is the **Casa de Benito Juárez,** García Vigil 609 (tel. 6 18 60), once home to one of Mexico's most famous and beloved presidents. *(Open Tu-Sa 10am-7pm, Su 10am-5pm. Admission 10 pesos, free on Sundays.)* The house was owned by Antonio Salanuevo, who became a benefactor to the young Juárez when he moved to Oaxaca from the countryside in 1818. Juárez's subsequent education qualified him to marry the wealthy Margarita Masa, and to pursue a career in law and reform-minded politics. The house—living room, bedrooms, kitchen, well, and "bookbinding/weaving shop"—is a replica of a 19th-century, upper-class *oaxaqueño* home.

The **Teatro Macedonio Alcalá** (tel. 6 33 87), on 5 de Mayo at Independencia, two blocks behind the cathedral, is one of the most beautiful buildings in Oaxaca. *(Occasionally open for shows M-Sa 8pm, Su 6pm.)* It's also an example of the art and architecture fostered by dictator Porfirio Díaz, whose regime (1876-1911) had a taste for French art and intellectual formulas. Díaz's support was instrumental in the theater's construction. On the ceiling, scantily clad Muses float above the giant candelabra.

A minor but absorbing attraction is the funky museum of religious art at the **Basilica of Our Lady of Solitude,** Independencia 107 (tel. 6 75 66), three and a half blocks behind the post office. *(Open M-Sa 10am-2pm and 4-6pm, Su 11am-2pm. Admission 2 pesos.)* Located next to the church, the museum houses an astonishing array of objects—ranging from model ships to shell-and-pasta figurines—sent from around the world as gifts to the Virgin, who is said to have appeared here in 1620.

For a breathtaking view of the city, head to the **Cerro de Fortín. The Escalera de Fortín** begins on Crespo; these stairs will take you to the **Planetarium Nundehui** (tel. 6 69 84), past the Guelaquetza amphitheater. *(Planetarium open Th-Su 10am-1pm, 5pm-8pm. Admission 8 pesos.)* Enjoy a great vista of Oaxaca and the surrounding hills here. The stairs are a favorite destination for fitness fiends, so be prepared to be passed by joggers loping effortlessly uphill.

Also worth a visit is the **Centro Fotográfico Alvarez Bravo,** Murguía 302, between Reforma and Juárez. *(Open Su-M and W-Sa 9:30am-6pm; free.)* The center displays rotating photography exhibits.

ENTERTAINMENT

Keeping track of Oaxaca's cultural and music events requires some effort. The *Guía Cultural* and the *Oaxaca Times* are distributed free at the MACO and tourist offices; they list monthly activities, many of them free. During the summer, the streets fill with music: Sundays at 12:20pm, the Oaxacan Orchestra plays in the Plaza Alameda; Mondays and Saturdays, marimba performers hammer away after 7pm in the *zócalo* kiosk; Tuesdays and Thursdays, the state band stages concerts.

Discos and bars are packed—and dripping with sweat—on weekend nights. The two bars of the moment appear to be K-Os and La Costumbre, both located near the Iglesia Santo Domingo. **K-Os,** on Constitución right next to the church, is jam-packed with well-dressed *oaxaqueños* schmoozing under the psychedelic lighting (open Tu-Su 9am-1pm). **La Costumbre,** Alcalá 501, right across from the church, is older but still has people lined up out the door on summer weekends (open Tu-Su 9pm-1am).

Candela, Allende 211, two blocks over from La Iglesia Santo Domingo, is the place to go for salsa. Whether you are a beginner or an expert, the live band will keep you moving all evening long. (Cover 20 pesos. Restaurant open Tu-Sa 12-5pm; music and dancing 9pm-2am.) Currently the most popular club is **Snob,** at the intersection of Héroes de Chapultepec and Juárez, near the first-class bus station. The multi-colored exterior encloses an interior that is always packed and hopping. The crowd here seems to include a representative from nearly every nation in the western hemisphere as well as tons of people from the language school across the street. (Cover 20 pesos for men, 10 pesos for women; open W-Sa 10pm-3am.) **Tequila Rock,** Porfirio Díaz 102 (tel. 5 15 00), at Héroes de Chapultepec, is another popular destination. Around 11pm, the staff performs a short dance to encourage patrons onto the floor. (Cover F-Sa 35 pesos. Open W-Sa 9pm-3am.) Further down on Porfirio Díaz, you'll find the hip **L'Bouche** (tel. 3 81 22), on the corner of Dominguez. A set of international flags beckon you into this club. L'Bouche has the largest dance floor in the area. (Cover 25 pesos. Open Th-Sa 9:30pm-2:30am.) Back toward downtown is **Universo Discoteca,** Porfirio Díaz 219 (tel. 6 42 36), at Matamoros. A young crowd boogies under plastic-and-pipe palm trees and the grooviest mood lighting around. (Cover F 10 pesos, Sa 20 pesos. Open Th-Sa 9pm-2:30am.)

Watch a film at MACO or catch a recent flick in English with Spanish subtitles (15 pesos) at the **Plaza Alameda Cinema,** Independencia and Díaz (tel. 6 52 41). **Sala Versailles,** M. Ocampo 105 (tel. 6 23 35), three blocks behind the cathedral, hosts live shows as well as movies.

FESTIVALS AND SEASONAL EVENTS

On the two Mondays following July 16, representatives from every part of Oaxaca state converge on a hill overlooking the city for the **Guelaguetza.** The event grew out of an indigenous tradition of making offerings on the **Cerro del Fortín** (The Hill with the Beautiful View); the days of dancing in the theater on the hill are called *los lunes del cerro* (Hill Mondays). "Guelaguetza" refers to the Zapotec custom of reciprocal gift-giving. During the two public gatherings, groups from the seven regions of Oaxaca give audiences a taste of their heritage through dance, music, and dazzling costumes. In between the gatherings, food and handicraft exhibitions, art shows, and concerts take place. Tickets cost up to 250 pesos, but a handful of free seats open up hours before the show begins. If you miss the Guelaguetza, sample dances are performed year-round at the Hotel Camino Real and Hotel Monte Albán for a hefty fee.

The night of December 23, Oaxacans celebrate the unique **Noche de los Rábanos** (Night of the Radishes). Masterpieces of historic or biblical themes created with radishes fill the *zócalo,* where judges determine the best. Hundreds of people admire the artistic creations and eat sweet *buñuelos.* Upon finishing the treat, you're supposed to make a wish and throw the ceramic plate down on the ground; if the plate smashes into pieces, your wish will come true. We promise.

SOUTHERN PACIFIC COAST

■ Near Oaxaca

The villages surrounding Oaxaca are known both for their ancient Zapotec and Mixtec ruins and for their production of artisanry. As every organization from museums of folk art to the Nature Company took interest in the imaginative handicrafts made in these villages, many residents left farming work to devote themselves full-time to craft production. Villages often specialize in particular products: **Arrazola** and **San Martín Tilcajate** make wooden animals, **San Bartolo Coyotepec** black clay pottery, **Atzompa** green clay pottery, **Ocotlán** natural clay pottery, **Teotitlán del Valle** wool *sarapes,* and **Villa Díaz Ordaz** and **Santo Tomás Jalietza** textiles and weavings. Likewise, many villages hold *mercados* on specific days to attract visitors: Mahuatlán (Monday), Atzompa (Tuesday), San Pablo Etla (Wednesday), Zaachila (Thursday), Ocotlán (Friday), and Tlacolula (Sunday). All these villages can be reached by *taxi-colectivos* from the *Central de Autobuses.* For an adrenaline rush, rent a bike and transport yourself.

There is a lot to be said for getting out of the hustle and bustle of the city for at least part of the day. The surrounding countryside is lovely, and it's always fun to ride in a bus that has to stop for herds of cows. The tourist office in Oaxaca (**SECTUR,** tel. 6 01 23 or 6 48 28) rents out guest houses in the communities of Abasolo, Papalutla, Teotitlán del Valle, Benito Juárez, Tlacolula, Quialana, Tlapazola, Santa Ana del Valle, and Hierve el Agua. Accommodations include four beds, kitchen, and clean bedding; proceedings benefit the community. (Cabin 120 pesos; 1 person 35 pesos; students 25 pesos; campers in the garden 10 pesos.) Additionally, you can try one of the *paseos culturales,* which introduce visitors to the traditional medicinal, agricultural, and artistic practices of 15 villages in the area. The Zapotec ruins of **Mitla** lie 44km east of Oaxaca, making them an ideal destination for a daytrip from the city. Contact **Museos Comunitarios de Oaxaca,** Tinoco y Palacios 311, *interior* (room) 16, for more information.

■ Near Oaxaca: Atzompa, Arrazola, Cuilapan, and Zaachila

A culture and lifestyle different from the sophistication of Oaxaca de Juárez emerges in these small towns, all of which lie near Rte. 131. **Atzompa** (pop. 11,000) is where that magnificent blend of clay and sprouts, the **Chia Pet®,** was invented. Natural, green-glazed pottery, the town's specialty, can be found here at better prices than in the city. Atzompa's **Casa de Artesanías** is a publicly funded forum that brings together the work of the town's specialized artisans. The selection is good at the Casa, but bartering is easier with the artisans themselves.

Arrazola is the hometown of **Manuel Jiménez,** one of Mexico's most famous artisans. Jiménez is the originator of **alebrijes,** the brightly colored figurines of demons and zoo animals that rank among Mexico's most sought-after handicrafts. While success has made his pieces simply unaffordable for most (they start at about 1350 pesos), his workshop is worth visiting. Cheaper versions of Jiménez's work, as well as wooden animals, are sold everywhere in town. Nearly all the households around the center of town make figurines to supplement their incomes. Pick your way through yards full of goats and chickens to the workshop, or simply follow one of the 10-year-old guides; the owners will happily show you their wares and haggle for a fair price. A medium-sized iguana *alebrije* will cost you about 100 pesos.

Cuilapán de Guerrero (pop. 11,000) has an isolated but hauntingly lovely 17th-century Dominican monastery, once home to one of the most powerful and wealthy religious orders in Mexico. *(Gates open daily 10am-6pm. Admission to grounds free, 10 pesos to interior.)* Although it was never finished, the ruined monastery's stone arcades frame the fields of the surrounding valley and the sinews of the hills that embrace it. The highlight of the site—aside from the breathtaking views—is the cell that was once occupied by the Revolutionary hero Vicente Guerrero, before his untimely death by the firing squad on the patio outside. Today, all that remains to commemorate the hero is a portrait of him in his cell and a monument where he fell.

Zaachila (pop. 15,000), the last political capital of the Zapotecs before they fell to the Spanish in 1521, hosts a fascinating market each Thursday. *(Open daily 8am-6pm; admission 7 pesos.)* Drop your pesos on preserved bananas and squealing pigs. The fuchsia and yellow cathedral dominates the middle of town. Behind the church, a street heads uphill to a partially uncovered archaeological site. Until 1962, locals prohibited excavations to prevent outsiders from dissecting their Zapotec heritage. Exploration since has been limited, but two Mixtec tombs with well-preserved architecture and jewelry have been uncovered. The treasure of gold, turquoise, jade, and bone artifacts has been spirited away to museums in Oaxaca and Mexico City, but the tombs—the only decorated ones in Oaxaca—are easily accessible.

Getting There: Take a *taxi-colectivo* leaving from the parking lot on the side of the Central de Abastos in Oaxaca; destinations are labeled on the windshields (20min. to Cuilapán, 30min. to Aztompa, Arrazola, or Zaachila; 5 pesos). It's easy to hop from one town to the next; take a *colectivo* back to the main road and flag down another that's headed for your next destination. All four towns are ideally accessible in the course of a day, though your best bet is to start out in Arrazola or Atzompa and head back to Oaxaca via Cuilapan or Zaachila.

■ Near Oaxaca: San Bartolo Coyotepec and the Road South

The drive south from Oaxaca provides more spectacular scenery. Picturesque towns are nestled in the slopes of verdant hills, and, for the eager consumer, there are distinctive crafts and artisanry for sale. **San Bartolo Coyotepec,** 12km south of Oaxaca on Rte. 175, is the only place in Mexico that creates the ink-black pottery that populates souvenir shops throughout the state. Fine pieces are available here at fairly low prices. Valente Nieto, son of the creator of the craft, Doña Rosa, gives demonstrations for visitors. If you didn't pick up enough brightly colored animals in Arrazola, head to **San Martín Tilajete,** 21km south of Oaxaca and about 1km off the main road. Four kilometers farther south, **Santo Tomás Jalietza** has artisans who specialize in weaving on back-strap looms. The town also boasts a 17th-century church dedicated to its patron saint. **Ocotlán de Morelos,** 33km out of the city, offers visitors a brightly colored church, a spacious *zócalo,* and a lively market, where there is a highly eclectic set of offerings. Leather goods, wrap-type traditional clothing, and herbal remedies can be purchased for a song. Swashbuckle your way through Mexico with one of the swords produced here. Market day is Friday; most of the action takes place between 10am and 5pm.

Getting There: Take one of the *colectivos* (about 6 pesos) leaving from the end of the Central de Abastos opposite the second-class bus station. **Estrella del Valle** buses leave from their terminal on González Ortega for Ocotlán and will make stops at other villages (30min., every 8min. 5:45am-9:30pm, 4 pesos).

■ Near Oaxaca: Oaxaca to Mitla

The road from Oaxaca east to Mitla, the Pan-American Highway (Rte. 190), cuts through a valley full of artisanal towns, *mezcal* distilleries, and archaeological sites. The first point of interest is the town of **Santa María El Tule** (pop. 7000). This friendly little town, just 14km outside the city, houses one of Mexico's great roadside attractions: the **Tule Tree.** The 2000-year-old and 40-meter-tall tree has an astounding circumference of 52m—**the largest girth of any tree on earth.** Ask the bus driver to drop you off at El Tule; then ask for *el árbol* (the tree). There is a 2-peso fee to approach the fence closest to the tree, but the glory of this botanical behemoth can be appreciated from anywhere within a 100m radius. The **Dainzú** ruins, 22km from Oaxaca, just off the road branching to **Macuilxochitl,** date from Monte Albán's final pre-Hispanic epoch. *(Open daily 10am-6pm. Admission 7 pesos.)* A series of magnificently carved figures at the base of the tallest pyramidal monument represent ballplayers in poses similar to the "dancers" at Monte Albán (see p. 383). Two humans and two jaguars, gods of the sport, supervise the contest. Up the hill from the pyramid, another game scene is hewn in the living rock. Bring your walking shoes; the ruins are about 2km away from the main road.

The walls of the church in nearby **San Jerónimo Tlacochahuaya** (pop. 5300), 23km from Oaxaca, illustrate Zapotec decorative techniques as applied to Catholic motifs. *(Open daily 7am-noon.)* It was built at the end of the 16th century by Dominicans seeking to escape worldly temptations. **Teotitlán del Valle,** 28km from Oaxaca, is the oldest community in the state. The source of extremely beautiful woolen *sarapes* and rugs, Teotitlán is home to 200 to 300 families that earn their livelihood by spinning and weaving. Many allow tourists to visit their workshops and witness the process of natural-dye coloring and weaving. Unfortunately, Teotitlán is not as accessible as many of the other stops on the road; it's 4km from where the bus drops you off. There are *colectivo* taxis that run sporadically from the main road to the town. There are a few workshops scattered within walking distance of the main road; owners are happy to demonstrate the spinning process.

Tlacolula de Matamoros (pop. 12,700), 33km from Oaxaca, is one of the largest towns in the area and adds a slightly gritty underside to the rural charm of the region.

It hosts a lively market on Sunday mornings—the specialty is the potent liquor **mezcal.** The market is officially open until 6pm, but activity usually starts winding down around 2pm.

Yagul, 36km from Oaxaca, was a Zapotec city inhabited from 700 BC to AD 1521. *(Open daily 9am-5:30pm. Admission 10 pesos, free Su.)* Less impressive archaeologically than Mitla, the rarely visited Yagul is perhaps more aesthetically striking. A gorgeous 1km walk through cornfields and up a hill admirably preps the visitor for the commanding view that awaits at the top. If you go on a weekday, you'll be able to act out your fantasies of Zapotec kingship with lizards as your only audience members. The city is built into the skirts of a hill overlooking a spectacular mountain-ringed valley. Most of the more famous buildings and tombs are in the **Acrópolis,** the area closest to the parking lot, about 2km north of the highway. If you bring some friends, you can start a pick-up ball game in the restored ballcourt, the largest of its kind in the Oaxaca valley. The **Court of the Triple Tomb** is to the left of the ballcourt. Carved with an image that is probably a jaguar, the tomb is in three sections. Stone faces cover the largest section. Beyond the ballcourt rises the **Council Hall;** behind lies the **Palace of the Six Patios,** believed to have been the home of the city's ruler. Heading back to the parking lot, take the trail that climbs uphill to the rocky outcropping to catch a spectacular view of the cactus-covered hills. Look for the small stone bridge; it's behind the tomb on your right as you climb the hill. If you keep going up the rocky path up the hill, you will be rewarded by even more spectacular views, and ultimately, bathtubs. These two sink-looking bins on the right-hand side of the mountain top are believed to have served as bathtubs for the Zapotecs who inhabited Yagul. There is also a *palapa*-style restaurant on the way to the ruins where you can slake your thirst or grab a quick bite (*comida corrida* 18 pesos).

Beyond Mitla, **Hierve el Agua** (The Water Boils), 57km from Oaxaca, takes its name from two springs of carbonated water that look like boiling water. The waters are actually not hot and make for refreshing baths.

Getting There: All destinations listed above are accessible via a Mitla-bound bus, which leaves the second-class station in Oaxaca (every 15min. 8am-8pm, 5 pesos to Mitla). Ask the driver to let you off where you want to go. Most people visit these sites on daytrips, but the **tourist office** at Oaxaca (p. 373) can arrange for overnight stays in Teotitlán del Valle, Tlacolula, or Hierve el Agua.

■ Near Oaxaca: Mitla

Tucked away in a mostly Zapotec-speaking, dusty little village, the archaeological site of Mitla, 44km east of Oaxaca, is smaller and less popular with tourists than the immense Monte Albán. *(Site open daily 8am-5pm; admission 10 pesos, free on Sundays.)* Mitla was built in 800 by the Zapotecs; it was later appropriated by the Mixtecs and eventually became the largest and most important of the late Mixtec cities. When the Spaniards arrived in the valley, Mitla was the only ceremonial center of the Mesoamerican Classic period still in use. Ironically, the Catholic archbishop of Oaxaca built his home to echo the horizontal lines of the Zapotec priest's residence in Mitla, thus paying architectural tribute to an ancient indigenous religion virtually exterminated by Catholicism. On the 2km walk through town to the ruins, you may have to weave your way through the herds of goats and cows that occasionally fill the streets. The ticket booth to the archaeological site is on the far side of the red-domed church. To the left of it and behind the church are the three patios known as the **Group of the Church.** One of them has been almost completely buried by the church, and only a few of the original palace walls remain visible. The central patio is on the other side of the church; here, and in the surrounding rooms, you can see pieces of Mixtec decorative paintings glowing red against the stone, supposedly telling Mitla's history.

More impressive ruins are across the road in the **Group of the Columns.** Perhaps the most striking features of these structures are the intricate geometric designs that decorate both the exterior and the interior. Beyond the entrance are two patios joined at one corner. On the first one, the tombs of the pyramids form a cross; for years, Spaniards thought this proved that the Mixtecs somehow knew the story of Jesus. On the second patio, two temples have tombs that are open to visitors. The tomb in the east temple has large stones covered with mosaic patterns. The roof of the tomb in the north temple rests on a single huge column known as the **Column of Life.** Pilgrims travel here each year to embrace the column; in exchange for the hug, the column tells them how much longer they will live.

On the central plaza back in town, the unexciting **Frissell Museum** contains thousands of figurines from Mitla and other Mixtec sites, all arranged around a courtyard; some descriptions are in English (open daily 9am-5pm; admission 10 pesos).

Getting There: Take a bus from Oaxaca's second-class terminal (45min., every 15min. 8am-8pm, 5 pesos). The last Oaxaca-bound bus leaves Mitla at 8pm. The bus station is about 2km from the ruins. With your back to the station, walk to your left and turn left at the sign for "Las Ruinas." Make another left onto the main road, and follow it for several blocks through town. Cut through the small *zócalo* on your right, and walk uphill until you get to the church; the ruins will be on your right. **Autotransportes Turísticos Aragal** offers four-hour trips that leave from Oaxaca and visit Mitla, Yagul, and the Tule Tree (10am and 2pm, 25 pesos). Reservations (required) can be made at the **Hotel Trébol** (tel. 6 38 66), Las Casas at Flores Magón, across from the Benito Juárez market.

Monte Albán

The heart and soul of the Zapotec cosmos, the ancient mecca of the "Cloud People," regal **Monte Albán** now watches over its verdant mountaintop in utter calmness. *(Site open daily 8am-5pm. Admission 14 pesos, 30 pesos if you want to use a camcorder, free on Sundays and holidays.)* One of the most important and spectacular pre-Hispanic ruins in Mexico, Monte Albán is to Oaxaca what the Mona Lisa is to the Louvre—it's a travesty to leave without seeing it. The striking architecture of the monumental structures, the fascinating lay-out and organization of the city, and a stunning view of the surrounding area make Monte Albán memorable.

The best way to see Monte Albán is to use Oaxaca (see p. 370) as a base. Buses to Monte Albán leave from the Hotel Mesón del Angel, Mina 518 (tel. 6 53 27), between Mier y Terán and Díaz Ordaz, in Oaxaca. Monte Albán is only 10km from Oaxaca, but the ride through mountainous terrain takes 30 minutes. The normal procedure is to buy a round-trip ticket, with the return fixed two hours after arrival at the site (about the right amount of time for a full perusal); if you want to stay longer, you can pay an extra 6 pesos to come back on one of the later buses. During high season, buses from the hotel leave daily every 30 minutes between 8:30am and 5:30pm; during low season, buses leave five times per day during the week and six times per day on Sunday (round-trip 12 pesos). To avoid the tourist hordes, leave early. Travel agencies around the *zócalo* in Oaxaca arrange special excursions to the ruins, some with English-speaking guides (expect to pay around US$30 per person).

HISTORY

The monolithic, geometrically precise stone structures that constituted the ceremonial center of the city are the culmination of Zapotec efforts to engineer a world that fused the religious, political, and social realms. As Monte Albán grew to become the major Zapotec capital, daily life was carefully constructed to harmonize with supernatural elements: architecture adhered to the orientation of the four cardinal points and the proportions of the 260-day ritual calendar; residences were organized in families of five to 10 people in four-sided houses with open central courtyards. To emphasize the congruence between the household and the tripartite cosmos, families buried their ancestors underneath their houses—corresponding to the level of the underworld. Excavations of burials in Monte Albán have yielded not only dazzling artifacts, but also valuable information on social stratification.

Monte Albán flourished during the Classic Period (300-750), when it shared the spotlight with Teotihuacán and Tikal as a major cultural and ceremonial center of Mesoamerica. This was the greatest of Zapotec capitals—maize was cultivated, water was supplied through complex drainage systems, and the city engaged in extensive exchange networks in Mesoamerica, especially with Teotihuacán (see p. 124). Teotihuacán's influence is visible in the murals painted and pottery made in Monte Albán. Artists used representations of divinities to legitimize the kings' power, and many stones share the theme of portraying the sacrifice of defeated enemies.

The history of Monte Albán is divided into five parts, spanning the years from 500 BC until the arrival of the Spaniards in the 16th century. Periods I and II saw the rise of Monte Albán as the Zapotec capital. This time also witnessed a great deal of contact with the Maya culture; the Zapotecs adopted the Maya *juego de pelota* (ballgame) and steep pyramid structure, while the Maya appropriated the Zapotec calendar and writing system. The city reached its peak during the third period, which lasted from 300 to 750.

Almost all of the extant buildings and tombs, as well as several urns and murals of *colanijes* (richly adorned priests), come from this period. Burial arrangements of varying luxuriousness and size show the social divisions of the period: priests, clerks, and laborers lived apart and died apart. For reasons that remain unknown, Monte Albán began to fade around 750. Construction ceased, and control of the Zapotec empire shifted from Monte Albán to other cities such as Zaachila, Yagul, and, later, Mitla. Explanations for the abandonment of the city include drought, overexploitation of resources, and inability of the leaders to maintain stability. The subsequent periods IV and V saw the city taken over by the Mixtec people; this happened to many Zapotec cities. The Mixtecs used Monte Albán as a fortress and a sacred metropolis, taking over the tombs left by the Zapotecs. When the most noteworthy tomb, **Tomb 7,** was discovered in 1932 by Dr. Alfonso Caso, the treasure found within more than quadrupled the number of previously identified gold Mixtec objects. The treasures from Tomb 7 are now on display at the Museo Regional de Oaxaca (see p. 378).

THE RUINS

As you enter the **Central Plaza,** the most prominent building to the right is the **Northern Platform.** Bear left as you enter the site, and walk along the edge of the Central Plaza; the first structure on the left is the ball court. Although the steps of the court seem to conjure up echoes of rowdy cheering; the "bleachers" were actually covered with a layer of stucco and served as part of the playing area. After passing a series of related substructures, you'll reach two pyramids that dominate the center and southern end of the plaza. The inclined walls were originally flat and covered with stucco.

Building P, the first of the two pyramids, fascinates archaeologists because of an inner stairway feeding into a tunnel to the central structures. The tunnel apparently allowed priests to pass into the central temples unseen by the public. The second pyramid, the **Palace,** was once a wealthy Zapotec residence; it is graced by a patio-courtyard and a garden in which a cruciform grave was discovered, the walls separating the palace rooms are still standing. Outside the palace are the four central monuments of the plaza. **Buildings G, H,** and **I** together constitute what was likely the **principal altar** of Monte Albán. Directly to the east, between the central Building H and Building P, is the small, sunken **Adoratorio,** where archaeologists dug up an intricate jade bat mask. This is Monte Albán's oldest structure, dating from Monte Albán II. A sacred icon and the most famous piece from this period, the mask contains 25 pieces of polished, forest-green jade with slivers of white conch shell forming the teeth and eyes of the bat. In a **famous heist** in 1994, the mask was stolen from the Museo Nacional de Antropología in Mexico City. The fourth of the central structures, **Building J** is formed in the bizarre shape of an arrowhead on a platform and contains a labyrinth of tunnels and passageways. Unlike any other ancient edifice in Mexico, it is asymmetrical and built at a 45° angle to the other structures around the plaza. Its broad, carved slabs suggest that the building is one of the oldest on the site. Many of the glyphs depict an upside-down head below a stylized hill; the glyphs are thought to represent a place and a name. Archaeologists speculate that this image indicates a conquest, the head representing the defeated tribe and the name identifying the region conquered.

Behind Building J stands the highest structure at Monte Albán: the **Southern Platform.** If you climb only one pyramid in Monte Alban, make sure it's this one: the top affords a commanding view of the ruins, the valley, and the mountains beyond. On both sides of the staircase on the plaza level are a number of stelae carved with rain gods and tigers. The stela on the pyramid's right side contains a precise date, but archaeologists lack the point of reference needed to coordinate this date with the modern calendar. The neighboring stela is believed to depict the king of Monte Albán.

Along the border of the Central Plaza, to the left as you descend the pyramid, are the foundations of **Building M,** followed by the **Platform of the Dancers** at the foot of Building L. The low platforms in front of Building M were apparently designed to make the plaza—built around inconveniently located rock formations—more symmetrical. In front of Building M and to the left as you face it, are the haunting reliefs known as the **Dancers.** Among the most interesting examples of pre-Hispanic sculpture, the reliefs date from the 5th century BC and are nearly identical to contemporary Olmec sculptures along the Gulf Coast. Many depictions of the dancers show evidence of genital mutilation. There is much speculation whether these men were commoners or of high status. Beyond the Platform of the Dancers, the **Northern Platform,** which is almost as large as the Central Plaza itself, dominates the entire site. Steps rise to meet a sunken patio. **Building B,** to the left as you face north on top of the steps, is believed to be a Mixtec-influenced addition to the site.

The path exiting the site passes the gift shop and cafeteria on the way to **Tomb 104.** Duck underground, look above the entrance, and gaze at the urn. It is covered with a motif which interweaves images of the maize god and rain god. Near the parking lot is the entrance to **Tomb 7,** where the spectacular cache of Mixtec ornaments mentioned above was found. The **museum** at the site's entrance offers a chronological survey of Monte Albán's history and displays sculpted stones from the site's earlier periods. Unfortunately, the truly spectacular artifacts from the site have been hauled off to museums in Oaxaca and Mexico City.

A Night on the Town: a Spanish Lesson

You've spent endless hours conjugating verbs and rolling your "r"s, but you still don't fit in. What you need is something that no seventh grade Spanish teacher could (or would) teach—a brief review of all the slang necessary for a night out on the town. Luckily, *Let's Go,* with the help of the staff at **Los Mandiles** in Ixtapa (see p. 362), has compiled a list of the basics. Incorporate these into your vocab, and perhaps you'll lose your *gabacho* (gringo) status.

The night begins when you meet your friends and greet them, "*¿Qué onda?*" (What's up?). You guys head out *al antro* (to the disco). At the discoteca, grab a *chupe* (drink) or a *chela* (beer) and comment on how *chido* or *padre* (cool) the place is. *Fresas* (snobs) prefer the phrase *de pelos* to denote coolness. Of course, keep your eyes peeled for *papasitos* (studs) and women that are *buenísima* (very fine). Perhaps you'll flirt a bit, *ligar* (to hook up), and—if you are *cachondo* (horny)—maybe you'll *fajar* (to make out/get down) with a fellow discotechie. The next day be sure to review the events of the previous night with your friends, exclaiming "*¡Qué peda la de ayer!*" (I was soooo drunk yesterday!).

Isthmus of Tehuantepec

East of Oaxaca de Juárez, the North American continent narrows to a slender strip of land just 215km wide known as the Isthmus of Tehuantepec (TEY-wan-teh-PECK). The region, wedged between the Yucatán Peninsula and the highlands of south central Mexico, is home to a thriving Zapotec culture that is primarily matriarchal. The three main cities in the isthmus—**Tehuantepec, Juchitán,** and **Salina Cruz**—serve mainly as stop-over points for tourists to switch buses and refuel. Scorching temperatures ensure that life in the isthmus towns progresses at a lethargic pace.

Tehuantepec

Tehuantepec (pop. 60,000) is the oldest of the isthmus's principal cities. For tourist information, visit the **Casa de la Cultura** (tel. 5 01 14), Callejón Rey Cosijopi (open M-F 9am-2pm and 5-8pm, Sa 9am-2pm). From the **bus station** on the highway, **Cristóbal Colón** (tel. 5 01 08) travels to Mexico City (11hr., 5:30 and 9pm, 272 pesos), Oaxaca (4hr., 6 per day 5:30am-midnight, 70 pesos), and more; buses also go to nearby Juchitán (30min., every 30min., 5 pesos) and Salina Cruz (20min., every 30min., 4 pesos). To get to town, make an immediate left as you leave the station. Follow this street, which becomes **Av. Héroes,** as it veers to the right and eventually dead-ends. Turn right and walk a few more blocks; make a left on **Hidalgo** and follow it to the *zócalo.* Taxis will take you to the *centro* for 8-10 pesos.

Juchitán

Juchitán is characterized by the same Zapotec culture that distinguishes Tehuantepec, but sees little to no tourist traffic. An exuberant market and excellent cultural center round out this friendly isthmus town. **Local buses** connect Juchitán with the isthmus towns of Tehuantepec (30min.) and Salina Cruz (1hr.). **Cristóbal Colón** (tel. 5 01 08) sends **buses** to Mexico City (11½hr., 8:30am, 9, and 9:30pm, 239 pesos), Oaxaca (4½hr., 6 per day, 68 pesos), and other destinations. The bus station is on Prolongación 16 de Septiembre. To get to town from the station, follow that street to the right upon leaving the station. It soon splits into **5 de Septiembre** and **16 de Septiembre,** which run parallel and eventually form the sides of the *zócalo.* A taxi will bring you for 5 pesos.

Salina Cruz

Salina Cruz does not have much to offer the passing tourist aside from the huge mass of oil refineries that comes into view on the bus ride into town, but its central location makes it a common stop-over for buses. **Cristóbal Colón** runs **buses** to Huatulco (3hr., 6 per day 12:30am-9:15pm, 41 pesos), Mexico City (11½hr., 9:15pm, 278 pesos), Oaxaca (5hr., 5 per day, 66 pesos), and elsewhere. The bus station is far from the *zócalo.* To get there, walk right until you hit the main street and then catch one of the blue *microbuses* (1.50 pesos). A taxi will cost about 6 pesos. **Estrella Blanca** sends second-class buses to Acapulco and all stops in between, including Huatulco and Puerto Escondido (4 per day 6:15am-11pm). The bus station is three blocks to the right of the Cristóbal Colón station on the main street.

Bahías de Huatulco

With its wide, palm-lined streets, shiny electric lights, and sprawling resorts, Bahías de Huatulco is a paradise for those who like their vacations packaged, planned, and posh. If everything looks new here, that's because it is: Mexican government officials settled on the area as a prime candidate for resort development in the 1980s and began building from the bottom up in 1986. The recent economic recession seems to have temporarily set back government plans; buildings around Huatulco sit in mid-construction. Still, the entire city has the feel of something like a seaside country club; even the *zócalo* and the supposedly authentic downtown area smack of freshly poured concrete and professional landscaping. Visitors are primarily moneyed Mexicans, with a sprinkling of *norteamericanos* and Europeans, although U.S. tourists are starting to pour in by the busload. Huatulco has little to offer backpackers or budget travelers who might feel more at home—and more welcome—farther down the coast at Puertos Escondido and Angel. But for those who wish to see the next Cancún in the making, the place merits a visit. Huatulco's nine bays are breathtaking, filled with sapphire-blue waters and lined with lush vegetation. The days of Huatulco's virginal splendor are, however, dwindling rapidly.

ORIENTATION

Huatulco and its *bahías* (bays) occupy 35km of beaches and coves along the southern Oaxaca coast between the Coyula and Copalita rivers, about 295km south of Oaxaca de Juárez. The small downtown area, **La Crucecita,** is in the middle of a string of nine bays, which are, from east to west: Conejos, Tangolunda, Chahué, Santa Cruz, El Orégano, Maguey, Cacaluta, Chachacual, and San Agustín. La Crucecita houses the bus stations and most budget accommodations. The *zócalo,* four blocks from the bus stations on **Gardenia,** is bordered by **Bugambilias** on the other side. **Carrizal,** one more block from the *zócalo,* leads to the bays. **Santa Cruz,** the bay closest to downtown, is the least attractive of the lot. Hotels and an *artesanía* market clutter its main road, **Blvd. Santa Cruz.** From there, the bays of **Chahué, Tangolunda,** and **Conejos** lie to the east. Tangolunda Bay is also known as the **Zona Hotelera** because it houses seven resorts, including **the Western Hemisphere's largest Club Med.** Its main road is **Blvd. Benito Juárez.** From Santa Cruz, the bays to the north are **El Órgano, Maguey, Cacaclutla, Chachacual,** and **San Augustín.**

PRACTICAL INFORMATION

Airplanes: The airport (tel. 1 03 10) is 19km from Santa Cruz. Taxis charge 70 pesos for the 25min. trip; *microbuses* get you within a 200m walk of the terminal for 5 pesos. **Aerocaribe** (tel. 7 12 20) and **Mexicana** (tel. 7 02 43) serve the airport.

Buses: Cristóbal Colón (tel. 7 02 61), Gardenia at the corner of Ocotillo, has first-class service to Mexico City (12½hr., 8:30pm, 269 pesos), Oaxaca (*deluxe* 7hr., 10pm, 137 pesos; *ordinario* 7hr., 6pm, 97 pesos), Puebla (11hr., 6pm, 228 pesos), Puerto Escondido (2hr., 4 per day 4am-10am, 33 pesos), San Cristóbal (10hr., 10:45am and 8pm, 151 pesos), and Tuxtla Gutiérrez (9hr., 10:45am and 11:30pm, 128 pesos). **Estrella Blanca** (tel. 7 01 02), on Gardenia and Palma Rea, sends buses to Acapulco (9hr., 9 per day 5am-9pm, first-class 137 pesos, *ordinario* 110 pesos), Mexico City (13½hr., 6pm, 264 pesos), and Puerto Escondido (2hr., 10 per day 5am-9pm, 25 pesos). **Estrella del Valle** (tel. 7 01 93), on Jazmín at the corner of Sabali, provides service to Oaxaca (8hr., 8:45am, 12:45, and 10pm, 68 pesos; *ordinario* 8hr., 8:30 and 12:30pm, 55 pesos).

Car Rental: Budget (tel. 7 00 10), Ocotillo at Jazmín, 1 block from Cristóbal Colón station. Small cars 450 pesos per day, including mileage and insurance. Open M-F 9am-1pm and 4-7pm.

Tourist Office: SEDETUR (tel. 7 10 37 or 7 08 48), on Santa Cruz at Monte Albán in the Plaza San Miguel. Open daily 8am-3:30pm. **Módulo de Información,** Bugambilias 210 (tel. 7 13 09), on the side of the *zócalo* opposite the church. Open daily 9am-8:30pm during peak seasons.

Currency Exchange: In La Crucecita, **Bital** (7 03 24), Sabali at Bugambilia, is the only bank with a 24hr. **ATM.** Bank open M-F 8am-7pm. **Bancrecer,** Bugambilia 1104, exchanges currency. Open M-F 9am-5pm, Sa 10am-2pm. Large hotels also exchange money at slightly less favorable rates.

Market: 3 de Mayo, on Guamuchil off the *zócalo.*

Laundromat: La Estrella (tel. 7 05 85), Carrizal at Flamboyan, across from Hotel Busanvi. 3kg for 21 pesos, 25 pesos for same day service. Open M-Sa 8am-9pm.

Police: At Blvd. Chahué 100 (tel. 7 02 10), in the peach government building about 200m south of the intersection of Guamuchil and Chahué. Some English spoken.

Red Cross: (tel. 7 11 88), on Blvd. Chahué next door to the post office and police building. Ambulance service. Open 24hr. English spoken.

Pharmacy: Farmacia del Centro (tel. 7 02 32), Bugambilia at Framboyan. Open daily 8am-10pm.
Hospital: IMSS (tel. 7 02 64), on Blvd. Chahué past the government building. 24hr. service. No English spoken.
Post Office: Blvd. Chahué 100 (tel. 7 05 51), in the peach government building. Open M-F 8am-7pm, Sa 9am-1pm. **Postal Code:** 70989.
Fax: Telecomm (tel. 7 08 94), next to the post office. Also has **telegrams** and **Western Union.** Open M-F 8am-6pm, Sa 9am-12:30pm.
Phone Code: 958.

ACCOMMODATIONS AND CAMPING

Camping is a way to escape Huatulco's high-priced hotel scene, but it's allowed only on Chahué, Cacaluta, and Conejos. The other bays are off-limits because they lack security and are hard to reach. Under no circumstances should you try to camp on Santa Cruz or Tangolunda; hotel security will not be kind. If camping isn't your thing, be prepared for slim pickings. All affordable rooms are located in La Crucecita, and even they tend be overpriced, despite the fact that they are near the bus station instead of the ocean. Mid-range hotels are found with blocks south of the *zócalo.* Hot water is rare, but usually not too necessary. Rates rise by about 50% during the high season (July-Nov.); the listings below indicate low-high season ranges.

Hotel Posada San Agustín (tel. 7 03 68), on Macuil at the corner of Carriza. From the bus station on Gardenia, walk 1 block to the left, turn left on Macuil, and walk for 2 blocks. The futuristic-looking blue and white hotel is probably the cheapest around. Rooms are clean and bright; ask for one with a balcony. Rooms come with fans but not hot water. Singles or 1-bed doubles 70 pesos; 2-bed doubles 70-100 pesos.
Hotel Busanvi II (tel. 7 08 90), on Macuil between Carrizal and Bugambilias. This little sibling of the Hotel Busanvi on Carrizal offers decent rooms for decent prices. All have fans and hot water. Singles 100 pesos; doubles 130 pesos; triples 150 pesos.
Hotel Benimar, Bugambilias 1404 (tel. 7 04 47), at Pochote, 3 blocks from the bus station on Gardenia. Rooms come with ceiling fans and full bathrooms with hot water—if you tell management to turn it on. Homey common area with hammock and TV. Singles 100 pesos; doubles 130 pesos; triples 150 pesos.

FOOD

Huatulco's cuisine runs the financial gamut from pricey French food to cheap *típico* kitchens. As a general rule, the closer the restaurant is to the *zócalo,* the more expensive it will be. Carrizal is lined with small places that offer cheap food.

Comedor Gina, Guarumbo 201 at Carrizal, 1 block from the *zócalo.* Standard fare served on standard plastic tables. Refreshingly free of pretension and resort-goers; you'll feel at home with the warm service. Fish soup or *comida corrida* 20 pesos. Open daily 7am-9pm.
Restaurant-Bar La Tropicana (tel. 7 06 61), Guanacastle at Gardenia, across from Hotel Flamboyan. This restaurant may be the exception to the rule that all restaurants on the *zócalo* are overpriced. Sit outdoors and watch folks saunter by while tapping your foot in rhythm to Mexican and American pop. Breakfast 15-25 pesos; *tortas* 13 pesos. Open 24hr.
El Grillo Marinero, Carrizal at Macuhitl. This outdoor *palapa* catches cool breezes as well as seafood-loving locals. There is no official menu, but the woman behind the stove will be happy to help you decide what to order. Fish fillets 30 pesos. Open M-Sa 9am-9pm.

SAND, SUN, AND ENTERTAINMENT

Until some kind of efficient public transportation system is installed, Huatulco's nine bays and 36 beaches, spread across 35km, pose a transportation challenge; it's hard to get off the beaten track without shelling out for a taxi or boat. Santa Cruz, Tangolunda, and Chahué can all be reached by the blue and white *microbúses* (3 pesos) that leave from Carrizal, near the Hotel Busanvi, but they pass fairly infrequently. A taxi will take you to a beach at Santa Cruz, Chahué, Tangolunda, Conejos, Maguey, or San Agustín and retrieve you at a pre-set time for 60 pesos.

To get from the *zócalo* to **Santa Cruz,** walk on Guamuchil two blocks past the market, and turn right on the road in front of the government building across from the PEMEX station. Turn right on Blvd. Santa Cruz and then left on Mitla; the sands of **Playa Principal** are only a few meters away. This little strip of sand unfortunately gets crowded fast and is full of less-than-scenic *palapa* restaurants. A more spacious beach that is still conveniently accessible from downtown is **Tangolunda.** Hop on a *microbús* (3 pesos) or catch a *colectivo* taxi (3 pesos) and ask to be let off at the public beach entrance. Follow the dirt road to the gorgeous expanse of sand, home to many posh resorts. Swimming is less than ideal—unless you like getting tossed around like a rag doll—but visitors sometimes use the resorts' swimming pools and other facilities. The bus can also get you to within striking distance of the bay **Chahué;** its beaches, **Esperanza** and **Tejón,** are better for suntanning than for swimming because of a strong undertow.

To get to any of the other bays, you'll have to hire a taxi or catch an expensive *lancha* from Santa Cruz. Just 130 pesos will get you a seat on a *colectivo* whirlwind all-day tour of the *bahías.* A trip to a particular *bahía* or beach will cost you 80 pesos. The tourist office arranges boat trips for a bit more. **Playa Entrega,** in Santa Cruz, and **Playa Maguey** are best for snorkeling. Hurricane Pauline, which hit the area in 1997, wiped out some of the coral at these beaches, but snorkeling is still worth the 40-peso rental fee. Chahué and Tangolunda have slightly bigger waves and more surf. San Agustín has no hotels, only outdoor *palapas.* **Cacaluta** is known for lush plant life and cooling breezes. In terms of crowds, Entrega, Maguey, **San Agustín,** and **Tongolunda** are most popular; your best shots at solitude are at Cacaluta, **Conejos,** and **El Organo.**

The tourist office (tel. 7 10 37) organizes a variety of excursions, all with bilingual guides. Make reservations a day in advance to take a yacht to see **El Bufadero,** the **geyser** between Santa Cruz and El Órgano (200 pesos for up to 10 people), ride three-and-a-half hours on **horseback** (250 pesos), or go on a 15-minute hot-air-balloon ride (Wednesday nights, 75 pesos). The office also rents **snorkeling** equipment (35 pesos per day) and arrange scuba diving trips (US$50). The tourist office also has info about renting bicycles, motor scooters, and go-cart-type vehicles.

Huatulco's night scene is just getting off the ground, leaving travelers with few options after sunset. Most large hotels have their own bars, but the only full disco is **Magic Circus** (tel. 7 00 17), on Blvd. Santa Cruz next to the Hotel Marlin (cover Th-Su 50 pesos; open bar Th; open W-Su 10pm-late). Buses stop running at 8pm, so a taxi from La Crucecita (7-10 pesos) will be necessary both ways.

Pochutla

Pochutla serves as the gateway to Puerto Angel and Zipolite; if you're traveling by bus, you'll have to pass through. The lack of services in both beach towns makes Pochutla a good place to stock up on money, make any last phone calls, or buy stamps. Most banks, services, and shops—as well as the town's two bus stations—can be found on **Lázaro Cárdenas,** Pochutla's main street. To get to the *zócalo* from the bus station take a right on Juárez toward the church, and walk for about 10 minutes. From the **Cristóbal Colón bus station** on the left side of Lázaro Cárdenas just as you enter the city, **Cristóbal Colón** (tel. 4 02 74) sends first-class buses to Huatulco (1hr., 4 per day 9:15am-9pm, 13 pesos), Mexico City (15hr., 4, 5, and 7:30pm, 270 pesos), Oaxaca (8hr., 4, 5, and 7:30pm, 98 pesos), Puerto Escondido (1½hr., 9:30, 10, and 11pm, 20 pesos), and Tehuantepec (4½hr., 9:45am, 7, and 9pm, 59 pesos). **Estrella Blanca,** on Lázaro Cárdenas (tel. 4 03 80), a block down from Cristóbal

Colón, goes to Acapulco (semi-direct 8hr., 4 per day 6am-10pm, 125 pesos), Huatulco (1hr., 4 per day 9:15am-9pm, 13 pesos), and Mexico City (13hr., 7am, 270 pesos).

From the bus stations, follow Cárdenas to the left and uphill to get to **Bital** (tel. 4 00 97; open M-F 8am-7pm, Sa 8am-3pm) and **Bancomer** (open M-F 8:30am-5:30pm, Sa 10am-2pm), both of which have **ATMs.** To get to the **post office,** make a right on Juárez toward the church and the *zócalo;* it's to the left of the church and behind the Palacio Municipal (open M-F 8am-6pm, Sa 9am-1pm). The **postal code** is 70900. If the wait for your bus will be a long one, you can spend a pleasant night in the **Hotel Posada San José** (tel. 4 01 53), down the alleyway next to the Estrella del Valle station. Rooms are well kept and have generously sized bathrooms with hot water and small TVs. Take a dip in the swimming pool or hang out with the pet monkey named Pancho if you're looking for a little entertainment. (Singles 67pesos, with A/C 100 pesos; doubles 85 pesos, with A/C 120 pesos; prices rise 30-40 pesos during the high tourist season.)

Puerto Angel

Tucked away between the more glamorous towns of Huatulco and Puerto Escondido, Puerto Angel is a haven for urban escapists. The small fishing town is home to a moderately sized naval base, a few restaurants and hotels, and a scenic cove on the Pacific coast. The town is popular with Europeans, and most visitors are well-traveled, giving Puerto Angel a touch of a Bohemian flair. Unfortunately, Puerto Angel—and Zipolite further down the coast—bore the brunt of Hurricane Pauline's wrath in early October 1997. Debris, dead palms, and fallen walkways mark her violent passage, and the struggle to rebuild is still in progress, a struggle undertaken without much help from the Mexican government. Still, Puerto Angel merits a visit, especially for those looking to escape the commercialization of Huatulco or the juvenile beach-bum atmosphere of Puerto Escondido. Despite the recent tragedy, Puerto Angel still beckons to travelers—the food is good, the cove is beautiful, and the pace of life is slow.

ORIENTATION AND PRACTICAL INFORMATION Puerto Angel is 240km south of Oaxaca de Juárez and 68km east of Puerto Escondido. The road from Pochutla becomes Puerto Angel's main drag at the edge of town; **Av. Principal** descends a hill, then wraps around Playa Puerto Angel, becoming **Blvd. Virgilio Uribe.** The main road crosses a small creek next to the naval base and forks at a sign for Hotel Angel del Mar. The right-hand road rambles farther down the coast to Zipolite, while the left-hand road heads for Playa Panteón. The only significant side street climbs the hill near the entrance to town by Hotel Soraya. It starts out as **Vasconcelos,** curves to the left, becomes **Teniente Azuela,** and then arrives back at Uribe in front of the naval station. **Taxis** link Puerto Angel with nearby towns (to Pochutla, colectivo 5 pesos, especial 25 pesos; to Zipolite 6 pesos) and can be flagged down along Uribe. The **microbús** goes to Pochutla (every 45min. 6am-8pm, 2 pesos), returns to town, and leaves again for Zipolite (2 pesos) and Mazunte (3 pesos). Hop aboard anywhere along Uribe. Services in Puerto Angel are minimal; most must be begged, borrowed, or imported from nearby Pochutla. There is a supermarket, **Super Puerto,** on Uribe about 300m after the naval base. **Farmacia Villa Florencia** is attached to the restaurant of the same name, on the main street (open daily 8:30am-9pm). The **Agency of Public Ministry,** next to the base, will contact **police** in an **emergency.** The nearest **hospital** (tel. 4 02 16) is between Puerto Angel and Pochutla. Limited **medical services** are available at the **Centro de Salud,** at the top of Vasconcelos to the left on a dirt path (open 24hr. for emergencies). The **post office** is on the main street, at the beginning of town (open M-F 10am-3pm). The **postal code** is 70902. **Faxes** can be sent from the **Telecomm** office, next door to the post office (open M-F 9am-3pm). There is a **long-distance caseta** at Vasconcelos 3, around the corner from Hotel Soraya, which charges an astronomical 20 pesos per minute for international calls (open daily 8am-10:30pm). The **phone code** is 958.

ACCOMMODATIONS Budget lodgings dot the hills on the inland side of the main road that runs behind the two beaches, and prices for lodging have fallen in Pauline's aftermath. Ceiling fans are available in all of the following hotels, but hot water is not. Lie on the hammock in front of your room looking out over the cove at **Posada Rincón Sabroso** (tel. 4 30 95), on the high hill at the entrance to town. All rooms come with private baths and mosquito nets. Laundry facilities are in the hallway in front of the rooms. (Singles 80 pesos, high-season 100 pesos; doubles 100 pesos, high-season 120 pesos.) **Casa de Huéspedes Anahi,** on Uribe on the left-hand side immediately after the bridge, might be the only place where you can haggle over the price of a room. Rooms are plain, with private baths and mosquito screens. The terrace overlooking the cove has a kitchen for guests' use. (Singles 70 pesos; doubles 80 pesos; triples 100 pesos.) Seafood is the specialty of nearly every restaurant. Prices at the beachfront *palapas* aren't always in the budget range, but the tranquility is priceless.

FOOD Cheaper restaurants tend to be located inland, but these are often dim and hot. For some Italian fare, try the large, casual **Restaurant Villa Florencia** (tel. 4 30 44), in town on the landward side of Uribe, before the naval station (spaghetti 10-22 pesos; tortellini 30 pesos; pizzas 30-40 pesos). Villa Florencia also serves breakfast (5-10 pesos; restaurant and bar open daily 7am-11pm). **Beto's,** on your right as you walk uphill past the naval base and supermarket, has the cheapest seafood dinner in town, and the friendly service accompanying the 17-peso fish fillets just adds to the experience. (Open daily 4pm-midnight.)

SAND Of Puerto Angel's two beaches, the smaller **Playa Panteón,** on the far side of town, is the better. The water here is calm and warm, and the coves are great for exploring and snorkeling. You can reach it by taxi (about 5 pesos), by walking, or by car, driving uphill towards Zipolite and then turning left down a dirt road. Unfortunately, the cement walkway that once connected Playa Panteón to Playa Puerto Angel was torn apart by Pauline—no set schedule for reconstruction has been made. Many of the restaurants on the beach rent equipment for snorkeling.

Away from the polluted waters of Playa Puerto Angel and the restaurant-studded shores of Playa Panteón is the much less crowded **Playa Estacahuites** (pronounced "a stack o' Wheaties"). To get there, walk on the main road toward Pochutla and ascend the hill just past the post office until you find a yellow Corona sign. It takes 20 minutes to walk there from downtown. The three small bays have somewhat rocky sand and gentle water for swimming.

Zipolite

Zipolite is something of a paradise lost. Once a remote hippie beach that drew visitors in search of wind, surf, and marijuana, Zipolite is struggling to overcome its utter devastation by Hurricane Pauline, which also wreaked havoc upon Puerto Angel in 1997. But despite the destruction, those who love to lounge still flock to Zipolite. The lifestyle here is all about relaxation—eat when you're hungry, sleep as much as you want, and wear as little as you please. Come here to stroll naked down the long beach, check in with the international vagabond set, and generally partake of the fringe atmosphere. Pauline or no Pauline, Zipolite will continue to be a prime a destination for those who know how to chill.

ORIENTATION AND PRACTICAL INFORMATION Zipolite lies just 4km west of Puerto Angel; **microbuses** run back and forth between the two (every 20min., 2 pesos). Zipolite consists of one long stretch of beach. Get off the bus before it takes the curve right in front of a thick grove of palm trees. Cross the street and walk toward the shining sea. There is a **pharmacy,** small **general store,** and a place that **exchanges money** at pretty poor rates on the road near the entrance from Puerto Angel. A number of **stands** scattered around the beach also sell purified water and sodas. However, you're better off buying supplies and munchies in Puerto Angel or Pochutla.

ACCOMMODATIONS Lounge around long enough, and someone will eventually ask you if you want a cabana for the night. If you're the more active type, try **Shambhala,** at the very far end of the beach across some rocks and up the stairs, an international haven with a corresponding world-peace theme. Rooms have mosquito netting and lights. Unlike the other establishments it literally looks down on, Shambhala is drug- and alcohol-free. (Singles 40 pesos; doubles 50 pesos.) **San Cristóbal,** a cluster of *palapas* about 300m before the rocks that lead to Shambhala, has two floors of nicer-than-average wood and cement cabanas with lights and fans. Common bathrooms are conveniently located and clean. (1 or 2 people 60 pesos, with bath 100 pesos.) Also try the blue and white **Posada Brisa Marina,** one of the newer establishments along the beach. (1- or 2-person cabanas 40-60 pesos.)

FOOD For fish and seafood, the *palapas* are ready and waiting (most are open daily 8am-10pm and charge 20-30 pesos for their most expensive item). **Nuevo Sol** offers delicious pizzas prepared by the Italian owner. **3 de Diciembre,** 100m off the beach, offers vegetarian dishes and sweet desserts. **Lo Cósmico,** the last *palapa* before Shambhala, makes crepes that are out of this world.

SAND AND SIGHTS The only sights in Zipolite are the occasional **sunbathers in the buff,** who do little more than let the rays gleam off their naked curves. Waves come in from two directions, creating a series of channels that suck unsuspecting swimmers out to sea. Although ferocious, these channels are not very wide. If you find yourself being pulled away from shore, do not attempt to swim directly toward the beach; rather, swim parallel to the beach until you're clear of the seaward current.

Zipolite is unfortunately plagued by theft, so keep an eye on everything or leave it locked up. A final warning: **scorpions** frequent Zipolite, so either give your cut-offs a good shake before jumping into them or blend in by going about your business in the buff. If you *must* get out and do something, catch a bus to **Playa Mazunte,** which offers some beaches more suited to swimming than Zipolite's, as well as more *palapa* restaurants. **Playa Agustinillo** is on the eastern edge of town, before the Turtle Museum. Playa Mazunte is accessible from the area where the bus stops. Both beaches offer fewer crowds and gentler surf, though there are still significant currents; keep your wits about you. Manzunte's **Museo de la Tortuga** used to hold an impressive collection of turtles from all over the world, but Hurricane Pauline left the building in shambles and sent the turtles back home to the Pacific. It's unknown when the museum will be functioning, but if it's open, this important venue for turtle research and conservation is worth a look.

Puerto Escondido

Less than two decades ago, Puerto Escondido (pop. 20,000) was a quiet fishing village where only a handful of scantily clad *extranjeros* gleefully romped, wheedling overnight lodging from local families. Today, the "hidden port" no longer lives up to its name. The increasing volume of international visitors has given rise to a culture where hotels now outnumber hippies, nudity is uncommon, and excellent food, exotic drink, and kitschy trinkets compete for pedestrians' pesos. But even though Puerto Escondido is no longer a remote outpost, this coastal town still retains the natural beauty and spectacular surf conditions that attracted those first few *extranjeros* here in the first place.

ORIENTATION

Like any self-respecting seaside village, Puerto Escondido has its very own **airport.** It's also connected to the rest of the world by land. **Routes 175** (paved) and **131** (mostly unpaved) wind treacherously through the Sierra Madres toward the coast, while an expertly paved coastal road, **Rte. 200,** twists through ramshackle fishing towns and coastal forests on its way to Acapulco. Puerto Escondido is built on a hill. The **Carretera Costera** (Rte. 200) cuts across the hill, bisecting it into an uptown of well-marked, perpendicular residential streets and a touristy downtown maze of paths leading to the beach. At the *crucero,* Rte. 131 from Oaxaca crosses Rte. 200 and becomes **Pérez Gasga,** which twists downhill and turns into the **Adoquín,** a pedestrian walkway leading to the beach. The bus station is near the *crucero.* The airport, 3km away on Rte. 200, can be reached by taking a *colectivo* (15 pesos). Locals insist that Puerto Escondido is relatively safe, but recent assaults against tourists serve as a reminder that even the most seemingly secure places can be dangerous. Play it safe by staying in groups and avoiding isolated beaches, even during daylight hours. Taxis can be found by the tourist information booth and along the Carretera Costera; they are the safest way of getting around after nightfall.

PRACTICAL INFORMATION

Transportation

Airport: (tel. 2 04 92). Airlines include **AeroCaribe** (tel. 2 20 23) and **Mexicana** (tel. 2 00 98 or 2 03 020).

Bus Stations: Cristóbal Colón, Calle 1 Nte. 207 (tel. 2 10 73), 2 blocks uphill from the *crucero* and to the right. To: Huatulco (2hr., 6 per day 8:45am-9:30pm, 33 pesos), San Cristóbal (12hr., 8:45am and 9:30pm, 183 pesos), and Tuxtla Gutiérrez (10hr., 8:45am, 7, and 9:30pm, 160 pesos). **Estrella Blanca** (tel. 2 04 27), just uphill from the *crucero,* goes to Acapulco (semi-direct 7hr., 6 per day 7:30am-11:30pm, 106 pesos), Huatulco and Pochutla (30min., 7 per day 8am-6:30pm, 13 pesos), Mexico City (12hr., 7:30pm, 241 pesos; deluxe 12hr., 8pm, 185 pesos), and Zihuatanejo (11hr., 8:45pm, 123 pesos). **Oaxaca-Istmo** (tel. 2 03 92), behind Estrella Blanca, travels to Pochutla and Salina Cruz (1hr., 4 per day 6am-1pm, 10-39 pesos). **Estrella del Valle** (tel. 2 00 50), Hidalgo at 3 Ote., 3 blocks down, goes to Oaxaca (direct 6½hr., 8:15am and 10:15pm, 65 pesos; *ordinario* 8½hr., 6 per day 7:30am-10pm, 54 pesos).

Car Rental: Budget (tel. 2 03 12) has an office in Hotel Posada Real in Bacocho, 3km west of the *crucero* on Rte. 200. Small cars 390 pesos per day, including insurance and unlimited mileage. Open daily 9am-2pm and 4-8pm.

Tourist and Financial Services

Tourist Office: Módulo de Información Turística (tel. 2 01 75), a palm-shaded information booth just before the beginning of the pedestrian walkway. Advice and counsel given with good humor and the wisdom of insiders. Open M-F 9am-2pm and 5-8pm, Sa 9am-2pm.

Currency Exchange: Banamex (tel. 2 03 52), Pérez Gasga on the corner of the Adoquín. Exchanges traveler's checks and has an **ATM.** Open M-F 9am-noon. **Bancomer** (tel. 2 04 11), 1 Nte. at 2 Pte., near the bus station, also exchanges cash. Open M-F 8:30am-3pm. **Money Exchange** (tel. 2 05 92), on the Adoquín across from Farmacia Cortés, has bad rates but convenient hours. Open M-Sa 10am-3pm and 6-9pm.

Local Services

Market: Mercado Benito Juárez, 8 Nte. at 3 Pte., 1 block past the post office all the way up Av. Oaxaca. Open daily 7am-6pm, but most lively Wednesday and Saturday. **Raya Sol** (tel. 2 02 87), on Pérez Gasga, is a small grocery store near the beginning of the pedestrian mall. Open daily 8am-11pm.

Laundromat: Lavamática del Centro, Pérez Gasga 405, uphill from the pedestrian walkway on the right. 9 pesos per kg. Open M-Sa 8am-8pm, Su 8am-5pm.

Emergency and Communications

Emergency: In an extreme emergency, contact Minne Dahlberg (tel. 2 03 67), chair of **Friends of Pto. Escondido,** a neighborhood watchdog group of area expats. She will get you in contact with your embassy, the police, or medical help.

Police: (tel. 2 01 11 or 2 01 55), on the Agencia Municipal on the Carretera Costera, shortly past the *crucero* on the way to the airport. No English spoken.

Red Cross: (tel. 2 01 46), on Pérez Gasga across from Hotel Nayar. Open 24hr.

Pharmacy: Farmacia Cortés (tel. 2 01 12), on the Adoquín. Open daily 7:30am-11pm.

Hospital: IMSS (tel. 2 01 42), 5 de Febrero at Calle 7 Nte. Open 24hr. **Centro de Salud,** Pérez Gasga 409 (tel. 2 00 46), below and across from the Hotel Virginia. A small medical clinic open 24hr. for emergencies. No English spoken.

Post Office: (tel. 2 09 59), Calle 7 Nte. at Av. Oaxaca. A 20min. walk uphill from the *crucero* past the bus station. Open M-F 8am-7pm, Sa 9am-1pm. **Postal Code:** 71980.

Phone Code: 958.

ACCOMMODATIONS

The beach is not safe for camping, but a multitude of hotels cater to budget travelers, particularly during the off-season. During *Semana Santa,* Christmas, and the months of July and August, reservations are an absolute must, and the least expensive places are the rented rooms, trailer parks, and cabanas along the beach—there are lots of cabana places across the street from Plaza Zictela. Price ranges reflect seasonal variation.

Hotel Mayflower (tel. 2 03 67), on Andador Libertad. From the bus stations, cross the *crucero,* then take a left down a steep hill. The road ends, but stairs descend on the right to the hotel entrance. The Mayflower will make you want to sing. Clean, brightly tiled rooms with private baths surround a common area complete with hammocks and shelves full of magazines and books written in English, German, and French. An international crowd relaxes at the bar upstairs. The friendly, multilingual owner can provide valuable information about the area. Dorm beds 45 pesos.

Hotel Carrillo de Reyes (tel. 2 04 42), on the right-hand size of Pérez Gasga from the *crucero.* Rooms here are clean and spacious, with glossy wood furniture and fans. Courtyard bar is perfect for a round of drinks before dinner. Singles 65 pesos; doubles 82 pesos; triples 98 pesos.

Casas de Playa Acali (tel. 2 02 78 or 2 07 54), at the beginning of Zicatela Beach just past the rocks. Wooden cabins come complete with fans, mosquito netting, private hot-water bathrooms, a jug of purified water on the porch, and a swimming pool. If that's not enough, cross the road to the ocean. Singles 100 pesos; doubles 130 pesos; prices go up by 20 pesos during high season; 30 pesos extra for each additional person.

Casa de Huéspedes Naxhiely, Pérez Gasga 301. At the *crucero,* cross and follow Pérez Gasga to the aqua-blue hotel on the left. A bit removed from the beach action. Provides cold water, sheets, and large plain rooms. Singles 40-115 pesos; doubles 50-150 pesos.

FOOD

The restaurants on Pérez Gasga know their clientele: the ubiquitous "we accept dollars" signs should say it all. The pizza, pasta, and apple pie for sale on the pedestrian walkway are certainly prominent, but there are still some cheap seafood restaurants popular with locals.

Banana's (tel. 2 00 05), the last restaurant on the beach side of Pérez Gasga, at the end of the pedestrian mall. Catering to the cable TV set, this popular hangout has a program for every meal. Enjoy your breakfast (10-18 pesos) with CNN Headline News, and your mid-day crepes (25 pesos) lit up by MTV. Every night they show recent movies, with closed-captions for those who prefer to converse. Perfect with pizza (29-45 pesos). Happy hour 6-9pm. Open daily 7:30-12:30am.

La Gota de Vida (tel. 2 09 93), on Pérez Gasga, midway down Zicatela Beach. This vegetarian haven makes its own bread, pasta, yogurt, and tempeh, sterilizes all its vegetables, and prepares heavenly fruit *licuados* (12-14 pesos), tofu *tortas* (16-18 pesos), and salads (14-17 pesos). Watch surf acrobatics on Zicatela Beach as you eat. Open daily 8am-10pm.

Antojería Doña Claudia, at the end of the Adoquín, past Coco's bar on the left. This casual, open-air spot specializes in typical Oaxacan *antojitos.* Not yet discovered by most tourists, Doña Claudia's offers great food without pricey frills. Delicious *empanadas amarillas* are 6 pesos, enchiladas 15 pesos. Open daily 8am-10pm.

Carmen's Café (tel. 2 08 60), on Playa Marinero, across from Hotel Flor de María. Follow the sign left up the alley, then turn right after crossing the bridge. After you have one taste of the chocolate croissant (6 pesos), you'll never complain again about the gringo invasion of the beach. Fresh bread makes the peanut butter and banana sandwich (8 pesos) even more delicious. Open M-Sa 7am-6pm, Su 7am-midnight.

SAND AND SIGHTS

Beach, beach, and more beach. The main beach, **Playa Principal,** is just beyond the stores and restaurants that line the Andoquín. This beach, full of *lanchas* and *palapas,* can get awfully crowded. Past Banana's, you'll encounter fishing boats; the stretch of sand from there to the rocks is **Playa Marinero,** great for swimming or sunbathing. Stepping over the rocks will take you to **Playa Zicatela,** one of the world's best surfing beaches. Those dudes bobbing up and down in the water waiting to ride the next killer wave all have several years of experience. Watching them is exhilarating, but do not even think about trying to partake of their "fun"—you risk a fate worse than wiping out. Past Carmen's on the road facing the beach, **Acuario** (tel. 2 10 26) rents **snorkels** (20 pesos) and **scuba gear** (beginning at US$40 for a day's excursion). A few smaller beaches, suitable for snorkeling, lie on the other side of Playa Principal. The distance is short enough to walk, but you can also take a taxi (15 pesos) or a boat. From the tourist booth, walk to the right toward the lighthouse. A staircase will take you over the waves before climbing uphill to a road and an overlook. Follow the road and take the first left; stairs lead to **Playa Manzanillo.** On the other side of a rocky barrier is **Puerto Angelito.** Both tranquil beaches make for good swimming or languid lounging in the shaded hammocks or chairs (10 pesos per day). Even further removed from civilization is beautiful **Playa Carrizalillo,** offering fewer crowds. It's accessible by boat or taxi from Puerto Angelito, but you can also walk there; head uphill from the beach on Pérez Gasga. When it forks at the Banamex, follow the left-hand side. You will pass a turn-off for Puerto Angelito; continue straight on the dirt road until you come to the Rotary Club basketball courts. Make a left and keep walking downhill. For those rugged adventurers dying to explore secluded beaches, be sure to exercise proper caution. Because of crime, it's probably best to stick to the established beaches.

ENTERTAINMENT

When the sun goes down, sun worshippers turn into bar crawlers, making their way to the many pubs along the strip. In the early evening, every restaurant and bar has a happy hour, which oddly enough lasts three or four hours. Two-for-one drinks are one reason that everyone's happy. In addition to alcohol and TV, **Banana's** offers pool and foosball (20 pesos per hr.). Around 10pm, the music start

s. **Discoteque Bacocho,** in the Bacocho residential district, is the only full-fledged dance club; you'll have to shower and throw something nice over that thong bikini. Taxis will whisk you over there for 15 pesos. (Cover 25 pesos; open Sa-Su 10pm-3am.) More informal places line the pedestrian walkway. **El Tubo,** on the Playa Principal, plays reggae, salsa, and rock. The bacchanalian crowd spills out onto the beach by the end of the night. (No cover; open daily 11pm-4am.) **Montezuma's Revenge** and **The Wipeout Bar,** both on the Adoquín, feature live music every night. Keep your ears perked for Santana-esque tunes. (No cover; music usually runs 10:30pm-1am.)

Central Mexico

The states of **Guanajuato** and **Querétaro** form a vast, bowl-shaped plateau of fertile soil, rolling farms, and verdant hillsides, all home to some of Mexico's most exquisite colonial *pueblos* and cities. Since the 16th century, its silver-rich underground has brought the region prosperity and shaped its history. In the 18th century, the city of Guanajuato supplied most of Mexico's minting silver, and the area became one of the wealthier and more influential in the country. Guanajuato later became the commercial and banking center of this thriving region. Today, the region is home to a growing expat population in and around San Miguel de Allende, one of the most lively and culturally charged cities in Mexico. Nearby **Hidalgo,** one of the most mountainous states in Mexico and home to the pine-laden edge of the Sierra Madre Oriental, also lived on silver for much of its colonial history. Although best known for its archaeological sites, like Tula, Hidalgo is home to slow-paced colonial towns including the pleasant Pachuca.

Although Veracruz was the first part of Mexico to bear the colonial mark of Hernán Cortés, the Conquest did not really pick up steam until his group ventured inland to **Puebla** and **Tlaxcala,** where many local tribes joined the entourage. A glimpse into one of the region's 16th-century temples, where images from *indígena* mythology mingle with Catholic icons, indicates the pervasiveness of elements from indigenous cultures, despite missionaries and 'conquistadors' attempts at complete subjugation.

Contrary to popular belief, the **Estado de México** has more to offer than easy access to insanely populated Mexico City. In the area outside Mexico City's smog cloud, green plains creep up snowy volcanoes and swollen towns continue to grow, pushing against their natural barriers. The state is speckled with stellar archaeological sites, solemn convents, and vestiges of the colonial era. Forests seem to stretch forever, and small towns and villages within appear untouched by modernity.

After Emperor Maximilian built his summer home in Cuernavaca, thousands of Mexicans followed him and **Morelos** became a prime vacation spot. Once again, the state enjoyed the same interest that had first brought the Olmecs from the Gulf Coast nearly 3000 years earlier. These days, Mexicans and foreigners alike march to Morelos to take advantage of Cuernavaca's "eternal spring," Xochicalco's beautifully desolate ruins, and Tepoztlán's striking landscape. Unlike the overpopulated Federal District, parts of Morelos remain undeveloped, with plentiful tree-covered vistas and unspoiled streams. Morelos is just a short jaunt from the D.F.; you can easily spend a day in Cuernavaca or Tepoztlán and return to the capital in the evening.

HIGHLIGHTS OF CENTRAL MEXICO

- **Guanajuato** (see p. 399) and **San Miguel de Allende** (see p. 406) are two of Mexico's most perfect and picturesque colonial towns. They've got everything from cobblestone streets to mountain views to huge international student populations. Guanajuato is especially notable during its yearly festival in October, **el Cervantino** (see p. 406). You'll come for a day and stay for a month.
- The **great pyramid of Cholula** (see p. 460) is one of the largest in the world, rivaling those at Giza, Egypt.
- Learn to salsa with thousands of language-school students in **Cuernavaca** (see p. 433), a lively, posh city with an impressive array of **nightclubs** (see p. 438).
- Check out the **massive statues of warriors (the Atlantes;** see p. 425) at the archaeological site of **Tula** (see p. 424), once the capital of the Toltec Empire.
- Stuff your face with delicious **mole dishes** and **sweets** (p. 453) in the modern metropolis of **Puebla** (see p. 449).

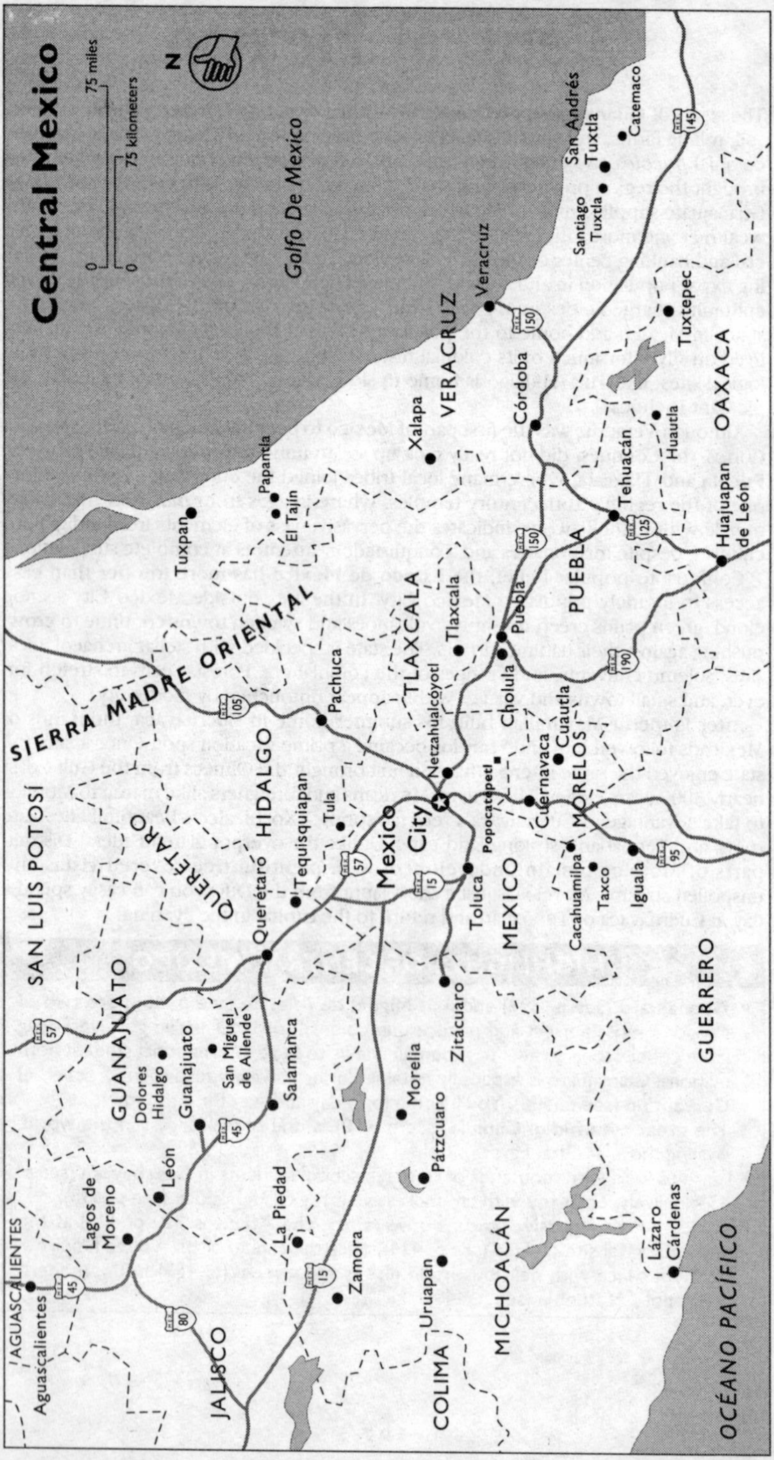
Central Mexico
0 75 miles
0 75 kilometers
N
Golfo De Mexico
OCÉANO PACÍFICO
SIERRA MADRE ORIENTAL
AGUASCALIENTES
JALISCO
COLIMA
MICHOACÁN
GUANAJUATO
SAN LUIS POTOSÍ
QUERÉTARO
HIDALGO
MEXICO
TLAXCALA
MORELOS
PUEBLA
VERACRUZ
GUERRERO
OAXACA
Aguascalientes
Lagos de Moreno
León
Guanajuato
Dolores Hidalgo
San Miguel de Allende
Salamanca
Querétaro
La Piedad
Zamora
Uruapan
Pátzcuaro
Morelia
Zitácuaro
Toluca
Tequisquiapan
Tula
Pachuca
Mexico City
Netzahualcóyotl
Popocatepetl
Cuernavaca
Cuautla
Cacahuamilpa
Taxco
Iguala
Cholula
Puebla
Tlaxcala
Tuxpan
El Tajín
Papantla
Xalapa
Córdoba
Veracruz
Tehuacán
Huautla
Tuxtepec
Huajuapan de León
Santiago Tuxtla
San Andrés Tuxtla
Catemaco
Lázaro Cárdenas
45
80
15
57
105
150
125
190
95
145

GUANAJUATO

Guanajuato

Guanajuato (Gwa-nah-WAH-toh) is simply beautiful. The former capital of the Republic under the presidency of Benito Juárez, it is now not only a bastion of cultural, historical, and natural wealth, but also a quintessential colonial town. The road into the city winds through lush mountains split at the base by winding streams and passes rows of *nopales* (prickly-pear cacti) that blend surreally into the landscape. The hills gradually give way to the city where the legacy of colonial days may be observed in the rich culture and fabulous architecture. Serpentine slate streets overflow with monuments to the silver barons who made Guanajuato one of the richest colonial mining towns in North America, while *callejones* (stone alleyways) sneak through Spanish archways and courtyards, leading to the city's myriad of museums, theaters, and cathedrals. Though the town's mining boom days are over, Guanajuato is now livelier than ever. Its university students and musicians promote an animated and youthful lifestyle, and Guanajuato continues to enjoy its status as a favorite destination among both Mexican and foreign tourists.

ORIENTATION

Guanajuato lies 380km northwest of Mexico City. Navigating the city's tangled maze of streets and *callejones* (alleyways) can be a teeth-gnashing experience even with the best of maps. The **Plaza de la Paz,** the **Basílica,** and the **Jardín Unión** mark the center of town. **Av. Juárez** climbs eastward past the *mercado* and Plaza de la Paz. Just past the basilica, the street becomes **Luis Obregón;** past Teatro Juárez, it turns into **Av. Sopeña.** The **Subterránea,** which roughly follows the path of Juárez/Sopeña, is an underground avenue built beneath the former riverbed, which now flows into an adjacent concrete channel. When you become lost (and you will), remember that the tunnel is always downhill from you.

Guanajuato's **bus station** is 3km west of town; from there, the "El Centro" bus takes you to the heart of the city, while the "Mercado" bus takes you to the market. Buses cross the city running westward above ground and eastward underground (every 5 min., daily 6am-10:30pm, 1.50 pesos). A taxi from the bus station to the *centro* costs 15 pesos. Taxis within the city cost about 10 pesos.

PRACTICAL INFORMATION

Buses: Central de Autobuses, west of the *centro.* Take the "Central de Autobuses" bus from Plaza de la Paz to the station (1.50 pesos). **Flecha Amarilla** (tel. 3 13 33), sends buses to Aguascalientes (3hr., 8:30 am, 4:40 pm, and 5:50 pm, 55 pesos), Celaya (2½hr, every 40 min. 6am-8:40 pm, 33 pesos), León (1hr., every 10 min. 5:40am-10:30pm, 15 pesos), San Luis Potosí (4hr., 7:20am and 1pm, 75 pesos), and San Miguel de Allende (1½hr., 8 per day 7am-6pm, 29 pesos). **Futura** (tel 3 13 44) sends first-class buses to Mexico City (5hr., 4 per day 10:20am-midnight, 135 pesos), and Monterrey (11hr., 6:30pm, 269 pesos). **ETN** (tel. 3 02 89) sends luxury buses to Guadalajara (3¾hr., 8am, 12:30, and 5:30pm, 160 pesos), Irapuato (45min., 5:30am, 8:30am, and 6:30pm, 22 pesos) and other destinations. **Servicios Coordinados** (3 13 33) and **Omnibus Mexico** (3 13 56) both sell tickets in Guanajuato and offer first-class bus service out of nearby León.

Tourist Office: Coordinación de Turismo, Plaza de la Paz 14 (tel. 2 15 74 or 2 19 82; fax 2 42 51; email turismo@quijote.ugto.mx.), on your right as you head up Juárez from the market to the *basílica.* Staff distributes *folletos* (brochures) and mediocre maps. Open M-W 9am-7pm, Th-F 9am-8pm, Sa 10am-4pm, Su 10am-2pm.

Currency Exchange: Banks line Juárez and Plaza de la Paz. **BITAL,** Plaza de la Paz 59 (tel. 2 00 18; fax 2 25 07), is open for exchange M-Sa 8am-7pm. **Banco Bilbao Vizcaya,** Plaza de la Paz 69 (tel. 2 94 78 or 2 94 79, is open for exchange M-F 9am-5pm. **ATM** inside same building as **Fax** (below).

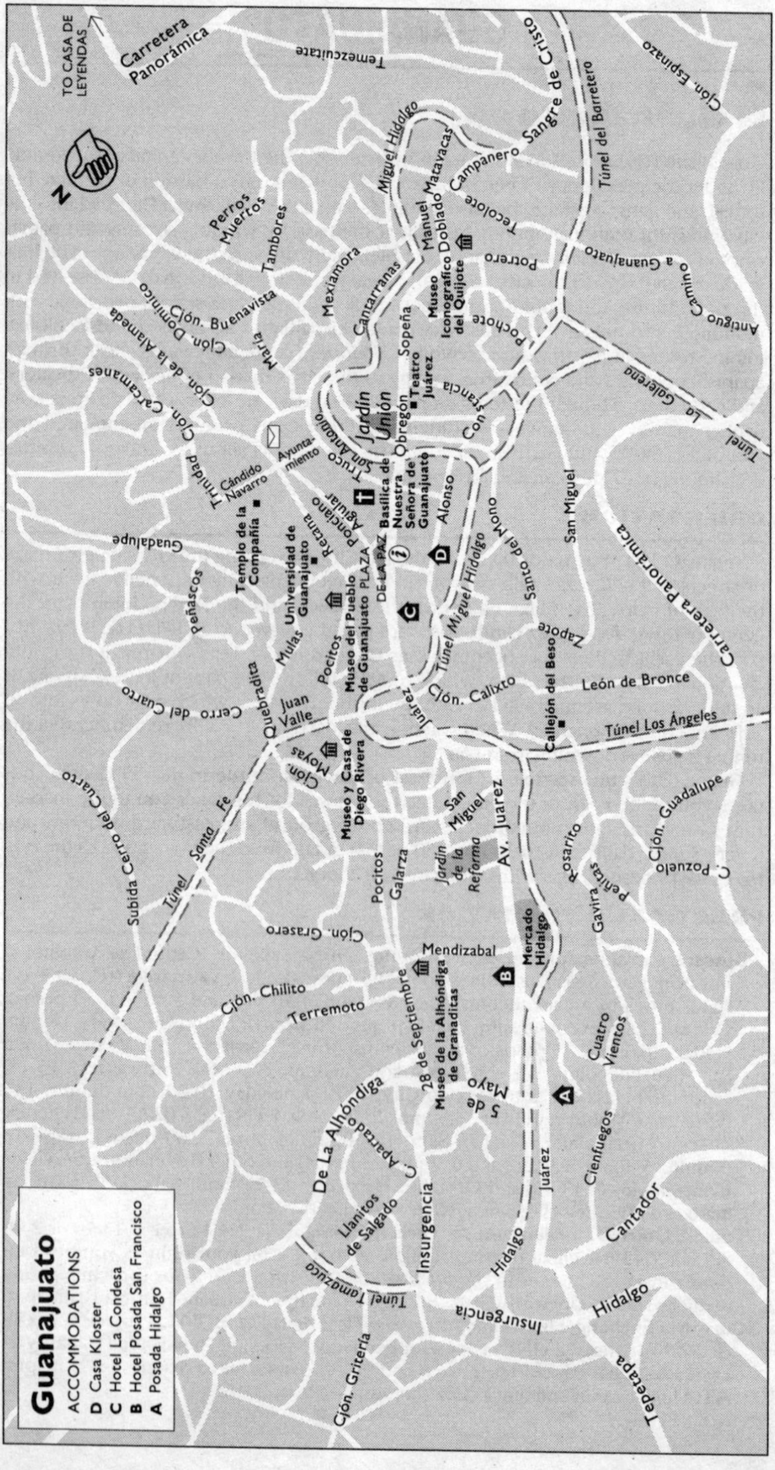
Guanajuato
ACCOMMODATIONS
D Casa Kloster
C Hotel La Condesa
B Hotel Posada San Francisco
A Posada Hidalgo
N
TO CASA DE LEYENDAS
Carretera Panorámica
Temezcuitate
Perros Muertos
Tambores
Miguel Hidalgo
Sangre de Cristo
Túnel del Barretero
Cjón. Espinazo
Campanero
Tecolote
Manuel Doblado
Matavacas
Potrero
Camino a Guanajuato
Antiguo
Mexiamora
Cantarranas
Museo Iconografico del Quijote
Sopeña
Pochote
Cjón. Buenavista
Cjón. Dominico
María
Cjón. de la Alameda
Carcamanes
Cjón.
Teatro Juárez
Jardín Unión
Obregón
Con stancia
La Galerena
Túnel
Trinidad
Cándido Navarro
Ayuntamiento
Truco
San Antonio
Basílica de Nuestra Señora de Guanajuato
Aguilar
Poncíano
Alonso
Templo de la Compañía
Guadalupe
Recana
Universidad de Guanajuato
PLAZA DE LA PAZ
Santo del Mono
San Miguel
Peñascos
Museo del Pueblo de Guanajuato
Túnel Miguel Hidalgo
Zapote
Carretera Panorámica
Mulas
Pocitos
Quebradita
Juan Valle
Cerro del Cuarto
Cjón. Calixto
Juarez
León de Bronce
Callejón del Beso
Túnel Los Ángeles
Cjón. Moyas
Museo y Casa de Diego Rivera
Cerro del Cuarto
Subida
San Miguel
Av. Juarez
Túnel Santa Fe
Jardín de la Reforma
Rosarito
Cjón. Guadalupe
C. Pozuelo
Pocitos
Galarza
Peñitas
Mercado Hidalgo
Gavira
Cjón. Grasero
Mendizabal
Cjón. Chilito
Terremoto
28 de Septiembre
Museo de la Alhóndiga de Granaditas
Cuatro Vientos
5 de Mayo
De La Alhóndiga
C. Aparado
Juárez
Cienfuegos
Llanitos de Salgado
Insurgencia
Hidalgo
Cantador
Túnel Tamazuca
Insurgencia
Hidalgo
Cjón. Gritería
Tepetapa

Laundromat: Lavandería Automática, Manuel Doblado 28 (tel. 2 67 18). Self- and full-service. Open M-Sa 9am-2pm and 4-8pm.

Emergency: Dial 060.

Police: At Alhóndiga 8 (tel. 2 02 66 or 2 27 17), 1 block from Juárez. Open 24hr.

Red Cross: (tel. 2 04 87), on Juárez, 2 blocks beyond the *mercado.* Open for emergencies 24hr. Some English spoken.

Pharmacy: San Francisco de Asis, Ponciano Aguilar 15 (tel. 2 89 16), just off the Plaza de la Paz. Open daily 7am-10:30pm.

Hospital: Clinica Hospital de Especialidades (tel. 2 23 05 or 2 13 38), Plaza de la Paz. English spoken by **Dr. Sanchez Leyva** and **Dr. López Márquez.** Open 24hr.

Post Office: Ayuntamiento 25 (tel. 2 03 85), across from the Templo de la Compañía. Follow Truco, the street running behind the *basílica,* for 1 block and turn left. Open M-F 8am-7pm, Sa 9am-1pm. **Postal Code:** 36000.

Fax: Sopeña 1 (tel. 2 69 91), to your left facing Teatro Juárez. Open M-F 8am-7pm, Sa-Su 9am-noon. Also in **Computel** (see below).

Internet Access: Redes Internet Guanajuato, Alonso 70 (tel. 2 06 11; email root@redes.int.com.mx). Email 25 pesos per 30min., 40 pesos per hr. MC, Visa, AmEx. Open M-F 9am-8pm and Sa 9am-2pm.

Telephones: LADATELs are around Plaza de la Paz and throughout the city. **Lonchería y Caseta de Larga Distancia Pípila,** Constancia 9 (tel. 2 00 75), behind the Templo de San Diego. Open M-Sa 10am-9pm, Su 11am-3pm. **Computel,** Ayuntamiento 20 (tel. 2 06 48; fax 2 06 00), 1 block from the post office. A bit expensive but discounts on calls to the U.S. after 7pm. Also fax service. Open M-Sa 8am-9pm, Su 8am-8pm.

Phone Code: 473.

ACCOMMODATIONS

The neighborhood around the *basílica* is home to some inexpensive hotels, often occupied by young people from every corner of the globe; Guanajuato frequently serves as a two-day getaway spot for students at language institutes in San Miguel de Allende or Mexico City. More economic lodgings cluster near the *mercado* and the Alhóndiga. Those visiting Guanajuato on weekends, during the *Festival Cervantino* in October, or during *Semana Santa* in April, should make hotel reservations far in advance and expect prices to rise dramatically. The tourist office keeps a list of families who rent out rooms during the festival.

Casa Kloster, Alonso 32 (tel. 2 00 88). As you leave the *basílica* and pass the Plaza de la Paz, turn left on Callejón de las Estrellas, and follow it to Alonso. A Garden of Eden right in the center of town. Clean, airy rooms overlook an open courtyard filled with flowers and chirping birds. Sparkling communal bathrooms with 24hr. hot water. Friendly guests and management. 50 pesos per person. Reservations recommended because the place tends to fill up quickly.

Hotel Posada San Francisco, Juárez 178 (tel. 2 24 67), at Plaza Gavira, the big green hotel next to the market. Clean, carpeted bedrooms with shiny, white bathrooms and an antechamber for entertaining guests. All rooms come with TV, but if you feel lonely you can watch in the 2nd floor lounge, with a suit of armor to keep you company. Singles 110 pesos; doubles 130 pesos. Rates increase during the high season.

Posada Hidalgo, Juárez 220 (tel. 2 31 45), 2 blocks past the market. The basic rooms have faux wood paneling, 24hr. hot water, and very small bathrooms (the shower head is above the toilet). Singles 40 pesos; doubles 80 pesos. Prices jump to 70 and 120 pesos respectively during the high season. The restaurant inside serves breakfast and lunch specials: all-you-can-eat for 20 pesos.

Hotel La Condesa, Plaza de la Paz 60 (tel. 2 14 62), nestled in the corner of the plaza, is a great base for exploring the attractions of Guanajuato. Neon signs and suits of armor brighten up the lobby. Each room's door is emblazoned with grim black-and-white scenes from around Guanajuato. Heavy wooden medieval chandeliers heighten the spooky but fun atmosphere. Never fear, rooms are old but clean and have bathrooms and 24hr. hot water—you may just have to wait a while for it to heat up. Expect noise from the *discoteca* downstairs. Singles 70 pesos; doubles 90 pesos (1 bed), or 120 pesos (2 beds).

FOOD

Inexpensive restaurants cluster around Guanajuato's plazas and near the *basílica.* Prices rise near the Jardín Unión, as does the gringos-per-square-inch ratio. **Juárez** and the **Mercado Hidalgo** have many affordable fruit and taco stands.

Truco No. 7, Truco 7 (tel. 2 83 74), the first left beyond the *basílica* as you head toward the Jardín. Artsy, funky, and immensely popular with both local and foreign students and families. International pop music fills the air of this dimly lit, soothing environment. Breakfast 11 pesos, *antojitos* 13-40 pesos. Open daily 8:30am-11:15pm.

La Loca Rana, Pocitos 32 (tel. 2 13 25), across the street from Diego Rivera's house. After you have worked up an appetite leering at the relics of Rivera's youth, catch a *fútbol* game on the tube with local students filling up on the tasty 3 course *menú del día* (15 pesos), *chilaquiles* (14 pesos), or *flautas* (5 pesos). Breakfast 12-15 pesos. Open M-F 8am-midnight, Sa 8am-5pm.

Cafetería y Restaurante Pinguis, on the Jardín Unión, sporting the burnt orange awning across from Posada Santa Fe. Great location and rockbottom prices. The bulletin board advertises local cultural events while Diego Rivera, Frida Kahlo, the Beatles, and Charlie Chaplin look on. The clientele is a bizarre combination of students, *señores* sipping coffee over the newspaper, and people wandering in off the *jardín.* Sip on juice (4-6 pesos) while you munch on enchiladas (17-25 pesos) or slurp on soup (10 pesos) in this light, airy establishment. Open daily 8am-10pm.

El Retiro, Sopeña 12 (tel. 2 06 22), across from the Teatro Juárez. Escape from the crowded *jardín* to join families and young couples feasting on breakfast (17-22 pesos), Mexican specialties (10-30 pesos), or the *menú del día* (26 pesos), while tapping to the beat of MTV. Top off your meal with a cold beer (14-16 pesos) or a drink (13-22 pesos) from the fully stocked bar. Some good vegetarian selections. Open daily 8am-11pm.

SIGHTS

The **Jardín Unión,** in the heart of the city and one block east of the *basílica,* is the town's social center. This triangular plaza boasts enough shops, cafes, and guitar-strumming locals to appease any tourist. During the afternoons and evenings, crowds gather to relax on the benches under the shade of the surrounding trees. The **Teatro Juárez** (tel. 2 01 83) faces one corner of Jardín Unión. *(Open Tu-Su 9am-1:45pm and 5-7:45pm, except on days of performances. Admission 5 pesos. Cameras 2 pesos, video cameras 5 pesos.)* Built in 1903 for dictator Porfirio Díaz, the theater has an unabashedly gaudy facade—try 12 columns, 12 lampposts, eight statues, and two bronze lions. The auditorium betrays its Moorish design: half-circles, arabesques, and endlessly weaving frescoed flowers in green, red, yellow, and brown make the interior seem overwhelmingly colorful. In addition to housing government offices, the Teatro Juárez still hosts plays, operas, ballets, classical music concerts, and the main events of the Festival Cervantino (tickets 30-50 pesos).

Churches

The elegant Baroque exterior of the **Basílica de Nuestra Señora de Guanajuato,** which took 25 years to construct, rises above the Plaza de la Paz. *(Open daily 8am-9pm.)* Inside, dozens of candelabra illuminate the Doric interior, including fine ornamental frescoes and paintings of the Madonna by Miguel Cabrera. The wooden image of the city's protectress, Nuestra Señora de Guanajuato, rests on a pure silver base and is believed to be the **oldest piece of Christian art** in Mexico.

The more interesting Jesuit **Templo de la Compañía** (tel. 2 18 27) is next to the university and one block north of the *basílica. (Church open M-Sa 7:30am-9pm, Su 7:30am-2:30pm and 6-9pm. Exhibit open daily 11am-2pm and 4-6pm. 5 peso donation requested to support the restoration process.)* Completed in 1765, the temple was shut down just two years later when the Jesuits were expelled from Spanish America. The ornate stone exterior is one of the most striking in the region, and it still has four of

Mummy Dearest

Museums in Guanajuato explore the historical, the artistic, the monumental, and the macabre. A museum of the latter variety is the **Museo de las Momias** (Mummy Museum; tel. 2 06 39), next to the city cemetery west of town. *(Open daily 9am-6pm. Admission 15 pesos, 9 pesos for students and seniors.)* To get to the museum, catch a "Las Momias" bus (1.50 pesos) in front of the *basílica* or the market. To catch the bus back, go up the hill to your right as you exit the museum and follow it as it goes downhill. At the bottom of the hill, take a left and walk to the end of the street. The minerals and salty water of Guanajuato's soil naturally mummified the 122 corpses now on display in the museum. Peruse the *Salon de Culto a la Muerte*, and behold morbid holograms, a mummified fetus, and weapons of torture from the colonial era (open daily 9am-6pm. Admission 5 pesos). Guides working for tips will point out the purplish, inflated body of a drowning victim; a woman buried alive, frozen in her attempt to scratch her way out of the coffin; two fashionable Frenchmen; a man who died by hanging; and another who was stabbed. Some buried babies still wear the colorful attire of saints to ensure divine intervention on their ride to heaven. The museum's oldest mummy has been around for 132 years, while its youngest has been on display for 12. The mummies are the most popular sight in Guanajuato, drawing a larger crowd than the less ghastly museums downtown. At the exit, vendors hawk candy figurines of the more memorable mummies, some wearing little sombreros (4 pesos).

the original five Churrigueresque facades. Soft light streams in from the delicate cupola, catching on the gold brocade and brightening the gray and rose stone interior. The ex-sacristy in the back of the church holds an art exhibit containing some of the church's original collection, including a 17th-century painting of San Ignacio de Loyola and an 18th-century representation of San Francisco de Asis. At the end of the exhibit is a spooky *relicario,* a wooden shelf enveloped in gold leaf, holding a collection of human bones.

Museums

In addition to beautiful colonial architecture, Guanajuato is home to a number of unique museums. One of the best is the **Museo Iconográfico del Quijote,** Manuel Doblado 1 (tel. 2 33 76 or 2 67 21; fax 2 61 17; http://www.guanajuato.gob.mx/mquijote), east of the Jardín Unión. *(Open Tu-Sa 10am-6:30pm, Su 10am-2:30pm; free.)* Housed in a gorgeous colonial mansion reminiscent of 18th-century Spanish architecture, its 10 large galleries contain over 600 works of art inspired by Cervantes's anti-hero Don Quijote, including paintings, sculptures, stained-glass windows, candlesticks, and clocks. Artists such as Dalí, Picasso, Daumier, Ocampo, and Coronel have all interpreted Quijote.

The **Museo del Pueblo de Guanajuato,** Pocitos 7 (tel. 2 29 90), next to the university, was inaugurated in 1979. *(Open Tu-Su 10am-6:30pm. Admission 8 pesos, students and teachers with ID 5 pesos, seniors and children free.)* The museum houses a permanent collection of 18th- and 19th- century works by Mexican artists and rotating exhibits of work by contemporary Mexican artists.

The **Museo y Casa de Diego Rivera,** Pocitos 47 (tel. 2 11 97), chronicles the life of Guanajuato's most famous native son. *(Open Tu-Sa 10am-6:30pm, Su 10am-2:30pm. Admission 8 pesos, students and teachers 5 pesos, seniors and children free.)* Works reveal the influence of Parisian friends Picasso from landscapes to Cubist sketches and elongated nudes. They also reveal Rivera's later fascination with Maya art. Visitors can ogle furniture from his childhood home and then move upstairs to admire works arranged chronologically and representative of his different artistic periods. Don't miss the outstanding watercolor illustrations for the *Popol Vuh* (the sacred book of the Maya), which imitate Maya iconography. Note also Rivera's sketch for a section of the mural commissioned in 1933 by New York's Rockefeller Center—the mural was destroyed after a portrait of Lenin was discovered in it. This sketch, which portrays a woman enslaved by a machine with the head of Adolf Hitler, was not incorporated into the final composition. The museum also holds several photos of Rivera and his wife of 22 years, fellow artist Frida Kahlo (see).

The **Museo de la Alhóndiga de Granaditas** (tel. 2 11 12), at the west end of Pocitos, is fairly conventional. *(Open Tu-Sa 10am-1:30pm and 4-5:30pm, Su 10am-2:30pm. Admission 14 pesos, free for students, seniors, children under 13, and on Sunday. Camera permit 1 peso, video camera permit 30 pesos.)* Constructed as a granary between 1797 and 1809, this building witnessed some of the more crucial and bloody battles of the fight for Mexican independence. Today, the Alhóndiga is an ethnographic, archaeological, and historical museum. A chamber on the first floor charts the course of Mexican nationhood. Other exhibits display the work of *indígena* artisans of the Bajío region—check out the masks, firecrackers, engraved machetes, tapestries, and candy horse skeletons designed for consumption on *El Día de los Muertos* (The Day of the Dead). Another gallery shows Romualdo García's photographs of Mexicans on the eve of the 1910 Revolution. While the hall, which contains huge busts of the heroes of 1910, is nothing short of stunning, the museum's finest exhibition traces the social history of Guanajuato from the Conquest through the Revolution.

The museum's most impressive pieces are the three murals gracing the building's stairwells. The works are often mistaken for those of José Clemente Orozco, Diego Rivera, or David Alfaro Siqueiros; the true painter, José Chávez Morado, was a contemporary of all three. *Abolición de Esclavitud* (1955), the earliest of these murals, follows Mexico's history from the Conquest, when Indians were oppressed slaves, to the Revolution, by which time native groups had regained some measure of power.

Other Sights in the Centro

Museums and churches, however, are not the only sites of interest in Guanajuato. Looking down on the *jardín* from the nearby hill is the **Monumento al Pípila,** which commemorates the miner who torched the Alhóndiga's front door. To reach the statue, follow Sopeña to the east and take the steep but manageable Callejón del Calvario to your right (a 5min. climb), or hop a bus marked "Pípila" from Plaza de la Paz (every 20min., 6am-10pm, 2 pesos). If you're planning to walk up at night, take a friend. The titanic Pípila looks most impressive at night, when he is illuminated by spotlights. While the view of Pípila from below is striking, the monument itself affords a magnificent panoramic vista of the city and the surrounding mountains. To ascend even higher, pay 1 peso to climb the narrow staircase inside the monument to a small platform behind the back of the infamous miner (8am-8pm).

The most famous alley in the city, the **Callejón del Beso** (Alley of the Kiss), is off Juárez, about two blocks down from the *basílica* off the Plaza de Los Angeles, just as Juárez curves right towards the market. Local lore has it that a Spanish aristocrat living on one side of the Callejón surprised his daughter one night while she was kissing her lover, a poor miner. Enraged by the lover's low breeding and occupation, the father cursed his daughter and forbade her to see her lover ever again. Ignoring her father, the young woman returned to her lover. When he discovered her insubordination, the Spaniard flew into a rage and stabbed his daughter to death. Another block farther down Juárez is the **Mercado Hidalgo.** *(Most stalls open daily noon-9pm.)* Constructed in 1910 in honor of the 100th anniversary of the struggle for national independence, the *mercado*'s entrance is a monumental Neoclassical arch. While Guanajuato's famed ceramic mugs have declined in quality, woolen items are still cheap, and the wide variety of *sombreros* will satisfy even the most discerning heads.

Sights Outside of the Centro

Guanajuato has many attractions that are just a short bus ride from the center of town. The **Casa de Leyendas** (tel. 2 13 57), at Súbida del Molino and Panorámica, is a museum aimed at conveying and preserving Guanajuatense legend. *(Open daily except W 10am-2pm and 4-7pm. Admission 25 pesos.)* To get there, catch a "La Presa" bus (1.50 pesos) in the *Subterránea* and ask the driver to let you off at the Escuela Normal.

From the Escuela, walk up the unmarked street to your left for two blocks, veering left at the fork. The museum will be directly in front of you. Dioramas complete with moving figures and loads of special effects recreate Guanajuato's many legends. Cringe as you watch the father of the famous lover from *Callejón del Beso* violently stab his daughter, then enter an elevator and "descend" into a mine filled with snakes, skeletons, and miners' unrealized dreams. Displays and guides in Spanish.

The **Ex-Hacienda de San Gabriel de Barrera** (tel. 2 06 19) is perhaps the most beautiful of Guanajuato's many natural attractions. (*Open daily 9am-6pm; closed Dec. 25-Jan. 1. Admission 10 pesos, students and seniors 5 pesos.*) Seventeen glorious gardens, each laid out in a different style, cover about three acres. Cobbled paths, well-groomed flora, and whistling birds make the gardens a stroller's dream. The ex-hacienda itself, a 16th-century structure, borders the gardens; its rooms contain furniture, silverware, and paintings from the era in which it was built. To get there, hop on a bus marked "Noria Alta/Marfil" across from the *mercado* (every 15min. 7am-9pm, 1.50 pesos), and tell the driver you're headed to San Gabriel de la Barrera.

About 20km from Guanajuato, atop a mountain and 2850m above sea level, is the **Monumento a Cristo Rey,** completed in 1956. Take the "Cristo Rey" bus from the bus station (1hr., 7 per day 6am-4pm, 7 pesos). Arrive 15 minutes early to be safe. The mountain, called the **Cerro del Cubilete,** is considered the **geographical center of Mexico.** The dark bronze statue of Jesus that lords over it is 16m tall and weighs more than 80 tons. Although the statue is striking, you may spend more time observing the surrounding landscape; long stretches of blue hills are visible from the summit.

ENTERTAINMENT

The core of Guanajuato's nightlife rests in the bar/cafe scene. The bars and cafes in the immediate vicinity of the Jardín Unión are friendly and comfortable, even for single women. A sophisticated crowd enjoys late night salsa and Latin rhythms at **Damas de las Camelias es él,** Sopeña 32. Decorated by Juan Ibañez, a student of the Spanish director Luis Buñuel (see p. 65), the bar's walls display cave-style paintings and pictures backed by tin foil. Chat with local professionals or dance to a wide selection of flamenco, jazz, salsa, Cuban, Peruvian, and Portuguese music. (Open daily 8pm-4am.) For a more mellow ambiance, try **Chez Santos,** at Juan Valle 19. Located off Juárez just before turning up into Plaza de la Paz, the bar is set in a former horse stable—its dark red carpet and stone walls make it feel like a strange, romantic dungeon. The dark and moody atmosphere calls for candlelight. Strangely enough, there is none, so it's a bit hard to see, which explains its reputation as a romantic rendezvous. The bar features beer for 10 pesos, and a bargain two beers for 15 pesos; mixed drinks run from 12-18 pesos. **Café Dada,** Baratillo 16, is a much more casual hangout. Follow Truco until it meets Calle Nueva, then head down Nuevo until Baratillo, a small avenue that extends upward to your left. Enjoy the work of local artists as you play chess or chat over an espresso for 5 pesos or capuchino for 6 pesos. (Open daily 8:30am-11pm.) If things slow down on the *jardín,* it's because they're picking up at the **Guanajuato Grill,** Alonso 20 (tel. 2 02 87), one block behind the Jardín Union. Neon palm trees, posters of sports heroes and scantily clad men and women, a nightly DJ with bass-booming speakers, and a *zócalo*-style gazebo in the center of the bar have the grill bursting at the seams with thirsty students when school's in session. The bouncers can be selective, and they may be more lenient toward women. (Beer costs 10 pesos. Open bar Tu and Th 9-10pm. No cover. Open Tu and Th-Sa 9pm-3am.) If you didn't get enough of Guanajuato Grill's loud music, try **El Capitolio,** Plaza de la Paz (tel. 2 08 10), next door to Hotel La Condesa. Find similar music (techno, dance, etc.) and clientele but in a larger and darker room. (Beer 10 pesos. Occasional cover charge. Open Tu-Sa 9pm-3am.)

FESTIVALS AND SEASONAL EVENTS

Each year, Guanajuato explodes during the **Festival Internacional Cervantino** for two or three weeks in early October. The city invites repertory groups from all over the world to make merry with the *estudiantinas* (strolling student minstrels). The festivities take place mostly at local theaters, but Guanajuato's many museums and churches are also transformed into stages for the events. Dramatic productions are always sold out. Tickets are sold by TicketMaster one month in advance and go really quickly. The **Office of the Festival Internacional Cervantino** (tel. 2 57 96; fax 2 67 75) can provide more information.

On June 24th of each year, Guanajuato celebrates the **Feria de San Juan,** at the Presa de la Olla, with dancing, cultural events, fireworks, and sports. Shorter celebrations occur on **Día de la Cueva** (July 31), when residents walk to a cave's entrance to honor San Ignacio de Loyola, first patron saint of Guanajuato and founder of the *Compañía de Jesús.* After the worshippers hold mass, they party. December religious celebrations include the famous *posadas,* which re-create Mary and Joseph's search for budget accommodations in Bethlehem. Other smaller festivals include **Viernes de Dolores,** which occurs a week before Good Friday, **Apertura de la Presa** on the first Monday of July, and **Las Iluminaciones** in November.

For the rest of the year, theater, dance, and music performances abound; check the tourist office for information or consult posters around town. On Thursday and Sunday nights in the Jardín Unión, the state band performs at about 7pm. *Callejonadas* (sing-alongs with the student minstrels down Guanajuato's winding alleys) are organized on Friday and Saturday nights at 8:30pm and depart from the Teatro Juárez. Student groups present films almost every day of the week. Call the **Teatro Principal,** Hidalgo 18 (tel. 2 15 26; admission 16 pesos, students and seniors 8 pesos) or the **Teatro Cervantes,** Plaza Cervantes (tel. 2 11 69; admission 14 pesos, students and seniors 12 pesos) for specifics.

San Miguel de Allende

The plethora of expatriates and long-term tourists who have settled in San Miguel de Allende (pop. 70,000) have made their presence evident. Shopkeepers humor customers who want to practice their Spanish, and young children of all backgrounds play together outside. Yuppies bring their children in for a painless injection of Spanish skills and cultural consciousness, and travelers come to relax among mostly welcoming locals in the city's shady plazas, colonial churches, and quiet green gardens. Throughout the year, tourists and inhabitants alike can enjoy outdoor concerts and other performances along the city's cobblestone streets.

San Miguel boasts impressive colonial architecture and a number of exquisite churches. The town was founded by the Franciscan friar Juan de San Miguel in 1542 and soon became an important stop on the route that connected the Zacatecas silver mines with Mexico City. San Miguel's character is shaped as much by its reign as a bustling commercial center in the 18th century as by its pivotal role in the struggle for Mexican independence in the following century. On September 16, 1810, when Hidalgo, the priest of nearby Dolores, led his rebel army into the city, the town rallied in opposition to Spanish rule under the leadership of the patriot Ignacio Allende. In 1826, the infant republic recognized Allende's role in the drive for independence by adding his name to San Miguel's.

Now known more for artisanry and academics than rebelliousness, San Miguel grows more crowded during the winter months when snowbirds follow the warmth south of the border to partake of San Miguel's mild year-round climate (the average annual temperature is 18°C, the altitude 6400 ft.). Beware the doldrums of June and July, when cold afternoon drizzle or day-long downpours from the rolling highlands can turn the cobblestone streets into gushing streams. The temperate climate, along with impressive colonial architecture (beautiful churches abound) and renowned foreign language institutes account for San Miguel's large expatriate resident population and booming tourist industry.

ORIENTATION

San Miguel is 94km southeast of Guanajuato and 428km northwest of Mexico City. To get from the **bus station** to the center (known as the **Jardín Allende** or **Plaza de Allende**), take a "Centro" bus to the corner of **Colegio** and **Mesones,** near the statue of Allende on horseback (every 15min. 7am-10pm, 1.80 pesos, exact change required). Walk two blocks down Mesones, then left one block on **Reloj** to the Plaza Allende. Alternatively, take a taxi (10 pesos). The **train station** lies 1km west of the bus station on the same road as the bus route.

Most attractions are within walking distance of the *jardín,* and the streets form a near-grid. **San Francisco, Reloj, Correo,** and **Hidalgo** border the *jardín.* West of the *jardín,* San Francisco becomes **Canal** and Correo becomes **Umarán.** East-west streets that run south of the *jardín* change their names every few blocks.

PRACTICAL INFORMATION

Transportation

Buses: On Calzada de la Estación, 1km west of the *centro.* Catch a "Central Estación" bus on Colegio at Mesones near the Plaza Cívica or on Insurgentes near the public library (1.80 pesos). **Ómnibus** (tel. 2 32 18) sends buses to Guanajuato (1¼ hr., 11:15am, 35 pesos). **Primera Plus** (tel. 2 73 23) runs first-class service to Guanajuato (1¼hr., 5 per day 7:30am-7:50pm, 40 pesos), León (2¼hr., 4 per day 7:30am-7:50pm, 64pesos), and Mexico City (3½hr., 9:40am and 4pm, 105 pesos). **Herradura de Plata** (tel. 2 07 25) runs to Dolores Hidalgo (1hr., every 40min. 6am-10:55pm, 13 pesos),

Mexico City (4hr., every 40min. 5am-7:40pm, 86 pesos), and Querétaro (1¼hr., every 40min. 5am-7:40pm, 20 pesos). Also has 1st-class service to Mexico City (3½hr., 6am and 1pm, 105 pesos). **Transportes del Norte** (tel. 2 22 37) serves Monterrey (10hr., 10:30am, 1:30pm, and 7pm, 253 pesos), and Nuevo Laredo (12hr., 7pm, 290 pesos), and also sells tickets to various destinations in Texas (call for more information). **Flecha Amarilla** (tel. 2 73 23) has service to Aguascalientes (3½hr., 12:35 and 2:35pm, 64 pesos), Celaya (1½hr., every 15 min. 5am-9:40pm, 14.5 pesos), and San Luis Potosí (4hr., 7 per day 7:40am-6:50pm, 62 pesos).

Car Rental: Gama Rent-a-Car, Hidalgo 3 #1 (tel. 2 08 15). Prices start at 180 pesos per day, 1 peso per km, plus 50 pesos insurance. Special weekly rates. Drivers must be 25 with a license, a major credit card, and another form of ID. In Jan., Feb., June, and Aug., make reservations at least 2 weeks in advance. May-June and Sept.-Dec. reservations can often be made as late as one day in advance. Open M-F 9am-2pm and 4-7pm, Sa 9am-2pm.

Tourist and Financial Services

Tourist Office: Delegación Regional de Turismo (tel./fax 2 65 65), on Pl. de Allende, to your left as you face the Parroquia. Knowledgeable and helpful staff speaks English and distributes maps. Also sells posters and the guidebook *The Insider's Guide to San Miguel de Allende* (130 pesos) is useful for an extended stay. Open M-F 10am-3pm and 5-7pm, Sa 10am-3pm, Su 10am-2pm.

Consulates: U.S., Macías 72 (tel. 2 23 57, after-hours emergencies only 2 00 68 or 2 06 53; fax 2 15 88), across the street from Bellas Artes. Open M and W 9am-1pm and 4-7pm, Tu and Th 4-7pm, or by appointment. **Canada,** Mesones 38 #15 (tel. 2 30 25, emergencies 01 800 706 2900; fax 2 68 56). Open M-F 11am-2pm. For other countries, or to extend visas or visitors' permits, contact the **Delegación Regional de Servicios Migratorios,** Pl. Real del Conde shopping center, 2nd Fl. (tel. 2 25 42 or 2 28 35). Catch the "Gigante" bus from the corner of Colegio and Mesons or from Juárez. Documents may be dropped off 9am-12:30pm and picked up 1:30-3pm. Allow at least 1 day for processing. Open M-F 9am-3pm.

Currency Exchange: Due to the huge foreign population in San Miguel, exchange spots abound. **Deal** (tel. 2 29 32, 2 17 06, or 2 34 22) at Correo 15, San Francisco 4, and Juárez 27, has good rates. All open M-F 9am-6pm, Sa 9am-2pm. **Helados Holanda** (tel. 2 05 67), Juárez 1 at San Francisco, not only serves tasty ice cream but also doubles as a *casa de cambio* with excellent rates. (Open M-F 10:30am-3:30pm, Sa-Su 11am-2pm.) **Banamex,** on the west side of the *jardín,* has two 24hr. **ATMs,** as does **Bancomer,** at Juárez 11.

American Express: Hidalgo 1 (tel. 2 18 56 or 2 16 95; fax 2 04 99). Full financial and travel services. Open M-F 9am-2pm and 4-6:30pm, Sa 10am-2pm.

Local Services

English Bookstore: El Colibrí, Sollano 30 (tel. 2 07 51), near Cuadrante. Paperback fiction and art supplies, some in French and German. Open M-Sa 10am-2pm and 4-7pm. **Lagundi** (tel. 2 08 30), Umarán 17 and Macías, has a large selection of English magazines and some in other languages, as well as books and art supplies. Open M-Sa 10am-2pm and 4-8pm, Su 11am-3pm.

Public Library: Insurgentes 25 (tel. 2 02 93), between Reloj and Hidalgo. Art-filled courtyard serves as a gathering place for expatriates and students. Wide selection in both English and Spanish. Sells old paperbacks (4-5 pesos), postcards, and posters. Computers available (see **Internet Access** below). Open M-F 10am-2pm and 4-7pm, Sa 10am-2pm. The building is also home to **Café Santa Ana,** which serves breakfast and lunch (19-25 pesos). Open M-F 9am-6pm, Sa 9am-2pm.

Market: Bonanza, Mesones 43A (tel. 2 12 60), has a good selection of Mexican and American groceries. Open M-Sa 8am-3pm and 4-9pm, Su 8am-5pm.

Laundromat: Lavandería El Reloj, Reloj 34, (tel. 2 38 43), in between Mesones and Insurgentes. Wash and dry 4kg for 25 pesos. Open M-F 8am-8pm, Sa 8am-5pm.

Public Toilets: Cuna de Allende, 1 peso.

Emergency and Communications

Emergency: (tel. 2 09 11), direct contact with Red Cross, fire department, police. A few dispatchers speak English.

Red Cross: (tel. 2 16 16) 1km on the Carretera Celaya. 24hr. emergency service.

Pharmacy: Botica Agundis (tel. 2 11 98), Canal 26 and Macías. Knowledgeable and helpful staff. Open daily 9am-11pm. Call police to find out which pharmacy is on call 24hr.

Hospital: Hospital de la Fe San Miguel (tel. 2 22 33 or 2 23 20; 24hr. emergency line 2 25 45; fax 2 29 00), Libramiento Hwy. 43 to Dolores Hidalgo, near the bus station. English spoken.

Post Office: Appropriately at Correo 16 (tel. 2 00 89), 1 block east of the *jardín*. Open M-F 8am-7pm, Sa 9am-1pm. **Postal Code:** 37700.

Fax: Telecomm, Correo 16-B (tel. 2 32 15; fax 2 00 81), adjacent to the post office. Open M-F 9am-5pm, Sa-Su 9am-noon. Also telegrams and money wiring.

Internet Access: Estación Internet, Recreo 11 2nd fl. (tel. 2 73 12), between Correo and Hospicio. 1 peso per min. for email and internet use; minimum charge of 10 pesos; 5hr. package 250 pesos. Open M-F 9am-2pm and 4-8pm, Sa 9am-2pm. **Unísono Net,** Macías 72 2nd Fl. (tel. 2 63 31; fax 2 49 58; email info@unisono.ciateq.mx; http://unisono.net.mx), across the street from Bellas Artes. 5 pesos per 10min. of email use, 30 pesos to surf the net for 30min. Open M-F 9am-2pm and 4-6pm, occasionally on Saturday. Unísono also runs a **San Miguel de Allende web page** (http://unisono.net.mx/sanmignew.html). **Mickler Computer Center** (email mickler@unisono.ciateq.mx), inside Biblioteca Pública, Insurgentes 25, charges 5 pesos per page to send or receive email and 15 pesos to surf the net for 15min. Less reliable than the two above. Open M-F 10am-2pm and 4-7pm, Sa 10am-2pm.

Telephones: LADATELs are scattered throughout town. **La Esquinita,** Correo at Recreo (tel. 2 36 21 or 2 39 39), charges 5 pesos for international collect calls. Open M-Sa 10am-2:30pm and 5-9pm, Su 10am-2:30pm. **El Toro Caseta,** Macías 58A (tel. 2 11 00), charges 4 pesos for international collect calls. Open M-Sa 8am-8:30pm, Su 8am-2pm.

Phone Code: 415.

ACCOMMODATIONS

As with many hot spots on the gringo trail, budget accommodations can be hard to find in San Miguel, particularly during the winter, *Semana Santa,* and the month of September, when San Miguel throws a huge fiesta in honor of Independence Day (Sept. 15-16) and the city's founding. Reservations (if possible) are strongly recommended during these times and might also be a good idea during the rest of the year. If you are planning an extended stay, check newspapers and bulletin boards in popular *norteamericano* cafes and restaurants for information on rooms for rent.

The San Miguel International Hostel, Los Órganos 34 (tel. 2 06 74). Walk 5 blocks down Calle Insurgentes from the Templo del Oratorio, turn right on Volanteros, then turn left onto Los Órganos. The hostel will be to your left. You'll come for a day and stay for a month. A communal effort: guests are expected to perform 10-minute morning chores. Everybody joins in the courtyard conversations. Well stocked with English books (including, of course, *Let's Go: Mexico*) and some in Hebrew, German, French, and Swedish. The hostel also has a sitting room and a piano. Clean single-sex dorm rooms for 6-10 people. 50 pesos per person, 40 pesos with HI membership or ISIC. Also has 2 private rooms. Continental breakfast included. Free kitchen use; food staples provided. Washing machine (10 pesos per load, including soap). 20 peso key deposit. Reservations not accepted. Open daily 7am-11pm; if you'll be arriving later, call ahead.

Hotel Parador San Sebastián, Mesones 7 (tel. 2 70 84), about 6 blocks from the *jardín.* Vibrant bougainvillea spill over arched stone walls enclosing the sunny courtyard of this friendly family-owned and operated establishment. Pleasant rooms with tiled bathrooms and 24hr. hot water. Common sitting room off the courtyard is filled with books and a television set. Try for a recently renovated room (117 pesos per person). Reservations not accepted.

Casa de Huéspedes, Mesones 27 (tel. 2 13 78) across from Juárez. More than just your generic "guest house." Serene, flower-filled patio and rooftop complete with ivy-covered arches, wooden lounge chairs, and back issues of *National Geo-*

graphic. Wonderfully friendly staff. Rooms offer private bath with 24hr. hot water. Some rooms have kitchens. Singles 120 pesos; doubles 160 pesos. Month-long stays available for 1950 pesos, with kitchen 2200 pesos.

Hotel La Huerta, Callejon de Atascarero #9 (tel. 2 05 34). Walk up Mesones, 3 blocks past Colegio; when you see a stream to your left, turn right onto Atascadero. Follow the stone path about 1 block uphill—the hotel is the large blue building on your left. After your spooky journey through the woods, you'll be wearied—and you'll thank your lucky stars for the respite this *tranquilo,* castle-like establishment offers. Personal bathrooms are kept clean. Some rooms have great views of the town and surrounding trees. 24 hr. hot water. Singles 100-120 pesos; doubles 120-140 pesos, depending on the size of bed. Discounts for students and for stays longer than 3 days.

FOOD

The sweet aroma of international cuisine wafts through the cobbled streets of San Miguel, and restaurants and cafes grace almost every corner. Unfortunately, their prices can be as *norteamericano* as their clienteles. For cheap eats, try **Calle Insurgentes** and the streets around the **mercado** on Colegio.

La Villa de Pancho, Quebrada 12 (tel. 2 12 47). From the corner of Hidalgo and Insurgentes, follow Insurgentes 3 blocks down to the west until it meets Quebrada. Continue to follow Quebrada for a half block to your left. Welcome to the kitchen of Cristina, the bubbly owner; she and her family will prepare tasty food while your hungry eyes follow each step of the process intimately. Enormously popular among backpackers. *Comida corrida* 25-40 pesos, breakfast 18 pesos. Open daily 9am-9pm. If you're feeling drowsy after your feast, let Cristina show you to a **rentable room** on the 2nd floor. 24hr. hot water and clean communal bathroom. 50 pesos per person. Continental breakfast provided.

Eclipse, Hidalgo 15 (tel. 2 80 93; email eclipse@unisono.net.mx), is a music store, furniture store, and sumptuous vegetarian restaurant rolled into one. Move your body to the beat of an amazing collection of Mexican, Cuban, Caribbean, and African music as you enjoy the *menú del día* (30 pesos) or such delicacies as a spinach hamburger on whole wheat bread and a salad (22 pesos). The clincher—Eclipse uses only purified water to wash vegetables and make juices, so you can eat everything without fear of gastrointestinal distress. Open daily 9:30am-7pm.

La Piñata, on the corner of Jesús and Umarán (tel. 2 20 60), 1 block from the *jardín.* A favorite among locals and travelers alike, this airy, vegetarian-friendly restaurant serves easily devourable food at prices that won't devour your wallet. Escape from the crowded *jardín* and join a mellow mix of artists, students, backpackers, and Mexican families feasting upon *tostadas* (4 pesos), *tacos de guisado* (3 pesos), and sandwiches (10-15 pesos). Fresh juice 6 pesos. Breakfast 14-20 pesos. Open daily except Tuesdays 9am-8pm.

Los Burritos, Mesones 69 (tel. 2 32 22) on Mesones between Hidalgo and Reloj. Watch while cooks prepare tasty and economical *"comida rápida"* that would make "los burritos" (whoever they are) proud. *Burritacos* (2 pesos) or *burriquesos* (3 pesos) make a meal. Open M-Sa 10:30am-6pm. Closed on Sundays.

La Grotta (tel. 2-41-19), Cuadrante 5 at Allende, 1 block behind the Parroquia. If you're a tortilla-weary traveler looking to splurge, you need only step a few feet below street level to enjoy a delectable small pizza (40 pesos) and join in the *extranjero* conversation at this tiny Italian restaurant. Pasta 40-49 pesos, beer 10 pesos. Open daily 1-11pm.

SIGHTS

The best way to experience San Miguel is on your own two feet. Nearly all sites of interest (and there are many) lie within walking distance of the *jardín,* and San Miguel's cobbled streets are easy to navigate.

La Parroquia (tel. 2 41 97 or 2 05 44), next to the *jardín,* is one of the most distinctive churches in central Mexico. *(Open daily 5:30am-9:30pm. Mass M-F 6-8am, noon-1pm, and 7-9pm; Sa 6-8am and 11am-1:30pm; all day Sunday.)* Its neo-Gothic facade and tower were designed by *indígena* mason Zeferino Gutiérrez, who is said to have learned the style from postcards of French cathedrals. The pointed arches and flute-like towers pull the eyes upward. Inside, the ceilings are graced by medieval-style banners, glittering chandeliers, and gold trim. At the front is a tremendous four piece, gold-leaf altar. Former President Bustamante is buried in the basement.

The **Museo Histórico de San Miguel de Allende,** Cuna de Allende 1 (tel. 2 24 99), at Umarán, is just across the street from La Parroquia and is built on Allende's birthplace. *(Open Tu-Su 10am-4pm; free.)* Although some exhibits have not been completed, the museum has a respectable collection of ancient ceramics, preclassical artifacts, exhibits on the history of the region, and, of course, a tribute to the man known everywhere.

Founded in 1712, the **Templo del Oratorio de San Felipe Neri** (tel. 2 05 21) lies at the corner of Insurgentes and Loreto, two blocks east of the library. *(Open daily 6:30am-1:00pm and 6:30-8:30pm.)* Rebuilt many times, the church is an amalgamation of styles—its interior is mainly Neoclassical, but its engraved Baroque facade shows syncretic *indígena* influences. The interior is incredibly ornate with pale pink walls, gold inlay, sparkling chandeliers, and a beautiful pink-and-mauve-toned dome. The altar holds a figure of Christ in red robes standing upon red carpets, surrounded by gold-leaf and marble pillars; it looks like a giant wedding cake. On the west side of the church, the towers and the dome belong to the **Santa Casa de Loreto,** a reproduction of the building of the same name in Italy; enter on the right side of the altar in San Felipe Neri. *(Open daily M-Su 8am-2pm.)* The floors and the lower wall are covered with glazed tiles from China, Spain, and faraway Puebla.

At the corner of Canal and Macías, one block west of the *jardín,* stands the enormous **Iglesia de la Concepción** (tel. 2 01 48) with its crumbling brick exterior and decaying grandeur. *(Open daily 7:30am-7pm. Mass M-F 7:30am and 7pm, Su 9:30, 11:30am, and 7pm.)* But the breathtaking interior has little to do with its weathered exterior. Graced by the representation of the Immaculate Conception crowning its two-story dome, the church was finished in 1891. Inside is an ornate gold altar with a likeness of a virgin in blue metallic robes.

Bellas Artes, at Macías 75 (tel. 2 49 46), is next door to the Iglesia de la Concepción. *(Open M-Sa 9am-8pm, Su 10am-2pm.)* Housed on an 18th-century former convent, this cultural center and art school all rolled into one has galleries with rotating exhibits and a concert hall. Great murals enliven the wall surrounding the peaceful, perfectly landscaped courtyard—look for *campesina* L. R. Santos lassoing a dreaded purple *chupacabras* (a monster that sucks the blood of goats). The school offers classes in ceramics, dance, art, guitar, and more, with a few in English.

Another worthwhile stop is the **Instituto de Allende,** Ancha de San Antonio 20 (tel. 2 01 90), about a 15-minute walk up Zacateros from Iglesia de la Concepción. *(Open M-F 8am-6pm, Sa 9am-1pm.)* The Instituto also houses several galleries with exhibits by local artists and offers art, Spanish, and social studies classes.

Not to be missed is San Miguel's spectacular **Jardín Botánico Cante,** home to a dazzling array of cacti and succulents. *(Open daily sunrise-sunset. Admission 7 pesos, children 2 for the price of 1.)* About 1,300 species grow along the *jardín's* 8km of walking paths. To reach the garden, walk past the Mercado Ignacio Ramirez, then turn right at Homobono, and continue on a steep uphill incline that flattens after about 10 minutes. Then walk straight for 20 minutes, following the signs; the *jardín* will be to your left (or take a taxi from Jardín Allende for 12 pesos). Proceeds benefit **Cante,** Mesones 71 (tel. 2 29 90; fax 2 40 15), a nonprofit conservation group.

Catch a breathtaking view of San Miguel and the surrounding mountains by visiting the **mirador** above the city. To get there from the *jardín,* walk two blocks up Correo to Recreo. Take a right and walk about 10 minutes. One block past the Plaza de Toros, take a left and walk uphill until you reach the main road, called "Salida a Querétaro." The *mirador* is a few minutes to your left. Or take the bus labeled "Gigante" from Colegio and Mesones or Juárez and ask to be let off at the *mirador* (1 peso there; 1.80 pesos back).

Every Tuesday, vendors from all around San Miguel converge upon the **Tianguis del Martes** (Tuesday market) near the municipal stadium to hawk their wares. Clothing, groceries, old doorknobs, and assorted odds and ends await the adventurous shopper. To get there, take a bus marked "Gigante" from Calle Juárez (1.80 pesos) or take a taxi (10 pesos). Most vendors set up around 7am and leave around 4pm.

Reverberating with the calls of tropical birds, **Parque Juárez** is the greenest park in San Miguel. To get there from the *jardín,* head down Luna de Allende until it meets Cuadrante. Follow Cuadrante for one short block to your left, and take your first right on Hermanos Aldama.

Hot springs fans will find their paradise at **La Gruta,** a 10-minute bus ride from San Miguel (4 pesos). *(Open daily 8am-5pm. Admission 35 pesos.)* Catch the Dolores Hidalgo bus and let the driver know that you want to go to La Gruta, but look out for the stop yourself. Ask to be let off at a hotel near a billboard that says "La Gruta". Walk in the direction of the billboard and take a left on the dirt road right in front of it. To reach the springs, veer to your left.

During high season, groups gather in front of the church in the *jardín* for 90-minute tours of the city (20 pesos per person). Tours are erratic, so call the tourist office for more information. The public library gives two-hour guided **home** and **garden bus tours** of the city in English (Sunday noon; around US$15; get there 30min. early). San Miguel boasts some beautiful orchid-filled courtyards, but some say the tours are something of a real estate pitch. **Centro de Crecimiento,** Zamora Ríos 6 (tel. 2 03 18), organizes trips to San Miguel's surroundings (Sat. 10:30am; 100pesos). The profits benefit children in need of health care.

ENTERTAINMENT

Did you think all these students came here just to learn? There are as many clubs as churches in San Miguel, and the arts pump through the city's veins daily. The magazine **Atención,** available every Monday in the tourist office and in local newsstands, is the best source of information on upcoming concerts, theatrical productions, and lectures by both locals and *extranjeros* (5 pesos). **Bellas Artes** and the **Instituto Allende** also have bulletin boards crammed with posters advertising art exhibits, openings, and other events.

Tourists permeate the nightlife scene, which centers around drinking and dancing. A warning—San Miguel is not cheap: don't expect bars to serve beer for under 15 pesos. Expect cover charges at clubs to skyrocket even more during fiesta times, especially *Semana Santa.* The listings below are for clubs; if you're not up for such a boisterous evening, there are *cantinas* all around town—though women may feel more comfortable elsewhere (*cerveza* about 7-8 pesos).

Mama Mía, Umarán 8 (tel. 2 20 63), just off the *jardín,* is a favorite destination of foreigners and friendly (especially *gringuita*-friendly) locals. Restaurant, bar, and *discoteca* in one, this enormous building is divided into several smaller establishments. **Mama Mía Bar,** to your right as you enter, attracts a twentysomething crowd and features jazz, soul, and rock music M-W, salsa Th-Su. Open M-Th 9pm-2am, F-Sa 9pm-3am. **Leonardo's,** across the entryway, scores points for its heavy bar stools and big-screen TV. Techno music blares as college-age customers crowd the bar. Open M-W 7pm-2am, Th-Sa 7pm-3am. Directly in front of the entrance is a rather pricey **restaurant** appealing mainly to tourists and hosting nightly *música folklorica,* traditional music performances. Open M-W 8am-midnight, Th-F 8am-1am. The **terrace** upstairs often pulses to the beat of live and loud rock performances Fridays and Saturdays. When there is no live music, a young crowd enjoys the great view of the city and makes conversation over a couple of beers (15 pesos). Open F-Sa 9pm-2am.

La Coronela, San Francisco 2 (tel. 2 27 46), on the corner of the *jardín,* has a decor that is as eclectic as its fabulous jukebox. A large-screen television, shotguns, and numerous posters of Mexican movie stars grace the walls while U.S. musicians such as Michael Jackson, the Gypsy Kings, and George Michael play on the jukebox. An older clientele frequents this place. The 16 peso beers are compensated for by the ultra-friendly staff. 2-for-1 Coronas on Monday and Tuesdays. Open M-Tu 2-9pm, W-Sa noon-1am.

Pancho and Lefty's, Mesones 99 (tel. 2 19 58), provides hours of entertainment for students and local youths returning home for boarding school vacation. Loud rock and cover bands or DJs spinning techno, disco, and Mexican pop songs thrill the young and tightly packed crowd every night. On Saturdays you'll pay 20 pesos for the right to pack yourself in. 2-for-1 beers Wednesday. Open W and F-Sa 8pm-3am.

El Ring, Hidalgo 25 (tel. 2 19 98 or 2 67 89), features standard *discoteca* fare and a late, lively, and very young Mexican crowd. Latin and U.S. dance hits will keep even the weariest club-hopper bouncing until the wee hours. Cover 30-50 pesos on F-Sa, free on W-Th. Open W 8pm-3am, Th-Sa 10pm-4:30am, Su 5:30-10:30pm.

100 Angeles, Mesones 97 (tel. 2 59 37), next door to Ponchos, is a private club that caters to a strictly gay (male or female) clientele. Disco balls illuminate the otherwise dark dance floor as the all-ages crowd gets down to tunes from the 70s and 90s. Cover 30 pesos on Saturday with one drink, Friday free. Open F-Sa 10pm-4am.

Char Rock, 2nd floor of Correo 7 (tel. 2 73 73) right off the *jardín,* hosts local bands playing to an eager college-age audience. The upstairs terrace offers a quiet escape and an opportunity for conversation as well as a view of the *jardín* from above. No cover. Open daily 10pm-2am.

FESTIVALS AND SEASONAL EVENTS

San Miguel is reputed to have more **fiestas** than any other town in Mexico. A celebration of some sort takes place nearly every weekend. In addition to national and religious holidays, San Miguel celebrates the **birthday of Ignacio Allende** on January 21 with parades and fireworks. The **Fiesta de la Candelaria,** which marks the start of spring, takes place each February 2. Nearly all of September is a party as San Miguel celebrates its **independence** and **founding.** On the third Saturday in September, the city emulates Spanish tradition and hosts **San Miguelada,** a running of the bulls in the *jardín.* The impressive **International Chamber Music Festival** is held in late July or early August at Bellas Artes, Macías 75 (tel./fax 2 02 89). Ticket packages start at 900 pesos and go on sale at the end of February.

Other festivals include the **Jazz Festival** in November and **El Día de San Antonio** and **El Festival de Locos** on June 13. Hotels tend to fill up during festivals, so tourists should plan accordingly.

■ Near San Miguel: Dolores Hidalgo

"Mexicanos, viva México!"

—Miguel Hidalgo, "Grito de Dolores"

Nearly 200 years later, Hidalgo's rousing words still echo through Mexico's dusty "Cradle of Independence." Best seen as a daytrip from San Miguel, the small town of Dolores Hidalgo (pop. 40,000) has little more to offer than hot, dirty streets, a thriving ceramics industry, and an amazing story. On Sunday, September 16, 1810, Don Miguel Hidalgo y Costilla, the town's priest, learned that the pro-independence conspiracy in which he had taken part had been discovered by the government. He decided to take decisive action and at 5am woke the entire town by tolling the parish church bell. The town's residents tumbled out of bed and gathered at the church; Hidalgo delivered a ringing speech proclaiming Mexico's independence from Spain—the *Grito de Dolores* (see). Then, calling his flock to arms, Hidalgo rallied an army to march on to Mexico City. Thus, the priest signed his own death warrant and paved the way for an independent Mexico years later. Today, Hidalgo is one of Mexico's most admired heroes, second only to Benito Juárez in the number of statues, streets, and plazas commemorating his heroism. However, coming to the actual locale of the *Grito* is worthwhile only for the most diehard history buffs.

ORIENTATION AND PRACTICAL INFORMATION Dolores Hidalgo sits 50km northeast of Guanajuato and north of San Miguel de Allende. To get downtown from the **Flecha Amarilla** bus station, walk straight out the door and take a left on **Hidalgo.** Three blocks down the street are the **Jardín,** the tourist office, **Plaza Principal,** and the **Parroquia.** To get to the Plaza Principal from the Herradura de Plata bus station, go out the door on your left as you face **Yucatán.** Go down Chiapas, which turns into Tabasco, take a left on Hidalgo and follow it into the plaza. A map is useful since streets have different names on opposite sides of the plaza. The town's points of interest all lie within a few blocks of the center.

Flecha Amarilla (tel. 2 06 39), sends buses from the station on Hidalgo at Chiapas to Guanajuato (1½hr., every 20min. 5:20am-9pm, 29 pesos) and San Miguel de Allende (40min., every 20min. 5am-8:45pm, 13 pesos). **Herradura de Plata** (tel. 2 29 37) has buses at the corner of Yucatán and Chiapas that go to Mexico City (5hr., every 40min. 5:20am-6:40pm, 96 pesos) and to San Miguel de Allende. Get a map from the **tourist office** (tel./fax 2 11 64), in the Presidencia Municipal, the large yellow building on the left side of the Plaza Principal as you face the Parroquia (open M-F 10am-3pm and 5-7pm, Sa-Su 10am-6pm). The **Casa de Cambio,** Plaza Principal 22 (tel. 4 15 86), has good exchange rates (open M-Sa 9am-6pm). The **post office** (tel. 2 08 07), is on Puebla 22 at Jalisco one block from the Plaza Principal (open M-F 9am-4pm, Sa 9am-1pm). The **postal code** is 37800. The **phone code** is 418.

ACCOMMODATIONS AND FOOD Quality budget rooms are rather scarce in Dolores Hidalgo. Expect prices to rise dramatically and rooms to fill up during the *Semana Santa* in March and April between September 8 and 17 when Dolores is overrun by Independence Day celebrants. Dolores is also crowded from Dec.15 to 31; reservations are advised. **Hotel Posada Cocomacán,** Plaza Principal 4 (tel. 2 00 18) on the *jardín,* has rooms with wooden floors, red brick walls with colored tiles, and tiled bathrooms. If it was good enough for Benito Juárez (on his way back south in 1867), it's good enough for you. Rooms have 24-hour hot water. (Singles 100 pesos; doubles 125 pesos. 10% discount with HI membership or ISIC card.) Around the *jardín,* most restaurants are reasonably priced, and those that aren't betray themselves by their touristy clienteles. **Torticlán,** Plaza Principal 28 (tel. 2 26 76), on the west end of the plaza, serves inexpensive and tasty food in a cafeteria-style setting. Join families and fellow tourists as you munch on *tortas* (7 pesos) with juice (3 pesos) or a beer (5-8 pesos). Vegetarians can get soyburgers for 10 pesos. (Open every day 7:30am-7pm.).

SIGHTS Most of Dolores's sights lie within four blocks of the bus station, and they revolve around the *Grito de Dolores.* The beautiful **Parroquia de Nuestra Señora de los Dolores,** where the *Grito* was sounded, still stands in the Plaza Principal, although the original bell now graces Mexico City's Palacio de Gobierno. *(Paroquia open daily 9am-2pm and 4-8pm.)* Constructed between 1712 and 1778, the church, with an intricate facade and towers of pink stone, is the most awe-inspiring structure in town. The lavish interior features a main altar surrounded by columns beautifully ornamented with gold leaf, and two side altars—one Churrigueresque and the other ultrabaroque. Dress appropriately—no shorts or tight dresses allowed. On the west side of the plaza is the **Casa de Visitas,** built in 1786 and now host to each president of the Republic during his last year in office, when he reissues the Grito. In the center of the plaza is a huge bronze statue of Hidalgo, the man who made Dolores Hidalgo *"la cuna de la independencia nacional"* (the cradle of national independence).

The **Museo de la Independencia,** Zacatecas 6, lies less than one block northwest of the Parroquia. *(Open daily except Thursday 9am-5pm. Admission 5 pesos, free for students, teachers with ID, seniors, and children under 13. Free for everyone on Sunday.)* Gory technicolor paintings detailing the material and spiritual conquest that characterized life under Spanish rule and the fight for independence add spice to Mexico's already exciting history. Relive Hidalgo's sounding of the *Grito* in an eerie life-sized diorama with wooden statues of an inspired Hidalgo and anxious *mexicanos.* The museum also includes Mexican *artesanía* and a shrine to Dolores Hidalgo's favorite musical son, mariachi legend José Alfredo Jiménez. Hidalgo's home from 1804 until 1810, the **Museo Casa Hidalgo** (tel. 2 01 71), at Morelos and Hidalgo one block from the Plaza Principal, is less than thrilling. *(Open Tu-Sa 10am-6pm, Su and holidays 10am-5pm. Admission 14 pesos, free Sunday and holidays, free for teachers and students with ID, children under 13, and seniors.)* The collection housed in it is comprised of contemporary religious paraphernalia, documents, and artwork relating to the independence movement.

QUERÉTARO

Querétaro

Situated between Mexico City and Guadalajara on the busiest stretch of highway in the Republic, Querétaro (pop. 870,000) lies at the crossroads of Mexico's geography and history. As the prosperous agricultural and industrial center of the Bajío, the outskirts of Querétaro assault the senses with whining grain elevators, monstrous warehouses, and truckloads of squealing pigs. Inside the commercial ring, however, the city center is a colonial wonder, with lantern-lit squares and an 18th-century aqueduct formed by 74 graceful arches. In Querétaro's heart, university students and entrepreneurs bustle past one another on centuries-old brick streets and *andares* (pedestrian walkways).

It was here that Emperor Maximilian, abandoned by Louis Napoleon and captured by Juárez's troops, ascended Cerro de las Campanas (Hill of the Bells) and uttered his

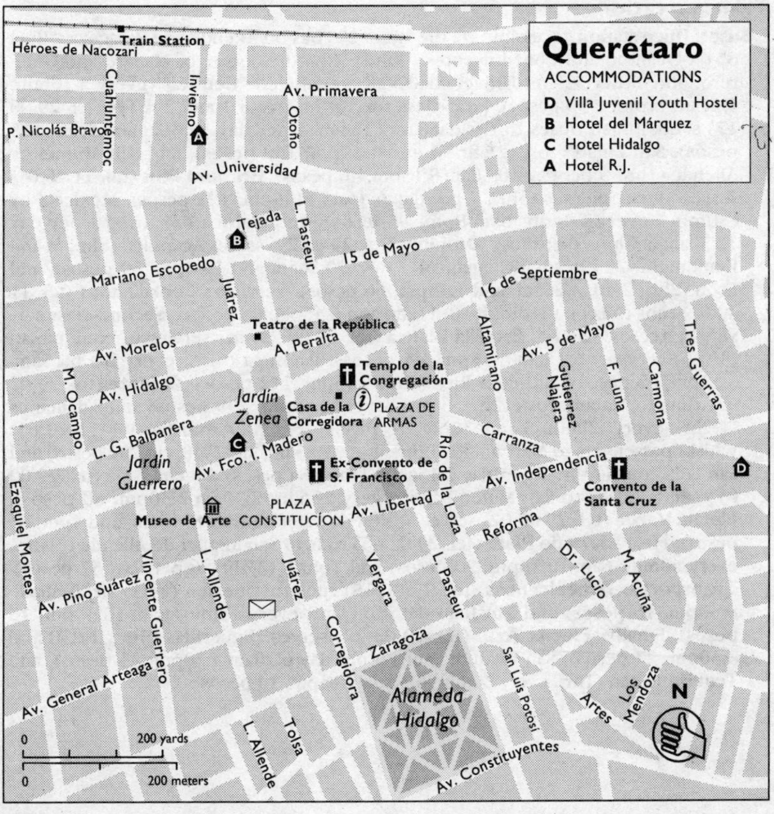

famous last words: "Mexicans, I am going to die for a just cause: the liberty and the independence of Mexico." In the subsequent 50 years, Mexico was plagued by violence. Perhaps hoping to inaugurate the peaceful era Maximilian had prematurely proclaimed, the victorious Carranza drafted the new constitution in Querétaro, now the capital of the eponymous state. While Mexico relinquished a great deal of its power and land in this city (the Treaty of Guadalupe Hidalgo, which compelled the Republic to cede its northern territories to the U.S., was signed in Querétaro) the many museums and monuments nevertheless indicate the city's pride in its history. Querétaro's historical and cultural offerings make this city a popular destination among Mexican tourists even though it is frequently overlooked by foreign travelers.

ORIENTATION

Querétaro's streets form a grid, and nearly all important sites are within walking distance of the **Jardín Zenea.** The *jardín* is bounded by **16 de Septiembre** (north), **Madero** (south), **Corregidora** (east), and **Juárez** (west). The **bus station,** with a modernity that puts most international airports to shame, is on the very south side of town. To catch a bus to the *centro,* follow the signs marked "Transporte Urbano" to *Salida A,* on the left-hand side of building "C" ("mercado") as you face it. A taxi will whisk you to your destination for 12 pesos—buy your ticket inside the station and give it to the driver. Blocks are really long in this city—they seem to stretch on for miles at a time—so remember to wear comfortable shoes and drink lots of water if you're planning to explore by foot.

PRACTICAL INFORMATION

Transportation

Buses: Huge station accessible via the "Ruta 25" bus on Allende and Zaragoza, "Ruta 8" on Ocampo and Constituyentes, "Ruta 19" at the corner of Madero and Guerrero, and "Ruta 72" on Universidad—all are labeled "Central" (every 5-10min. 5:30am-11pm, 2.50 pesos). **First-class service** in *Acesos* 1 and 2. **ETN** (tel. 29 00 17) sends plush buses to Guadalajara (4½hr., 5 per day 12:30am-6:45pm, 175 pesos), San Luis Potosí (2½hr., 1 and 1:30pm, 100 pesos), and San Miguel de Allende (1hr., 5 per day 10:30am-8:15pm, 40 pesos). **Primera Plus** (tel. 11 40 01) serves Aguascalientes (5hr., 7 per day 6:45am-1145pm, 121 pesos), Mexico City (30min., every 20min. 6am-8pm, 95pesos), and Toluca (2¾hr., 10 per day 12:30am-6:30pm, 68 pesos). **Ómnibus** (tel. 29 00 29) serves Acapulco (8hr., M and F midnight, 225 pesos), Guanajuato (3hr., 10:20am and 7:45pm, 59 pesos), and León (2hr., 2:40, 3:20am, and 1:15pm, 66 pesos). **Servicios Coordinados** (tel. 11 40 01) runs to León (2¾hr., 8:30, 11am, and 6:45pm, 66 pesos). **Second-class service** in Acesos 3 and 4. **Estrella Blanca** (tel. 29 00 22) has service to Ixmiquilpan (3hr., every hr. 6:15am-6:15pm, 44 pesos), Pachuca (5hr., every hr. 6:15am-6:15pm, 66 pesos), and Poza Rica (6hr., 9:15pm, 112 pesos). **Oriente** (tel. 29 02 02) runs to Matamoros (12hr., 6 per day 5-10:30pm, 299 pesos) and Salamanca (1½hr., every 20min. 5am-8:30pm, 26 pesos). **Flecha Amarilla** (tel. 11 40 01) whisks passengers to Manzanillo (12hr., 1:45, 7:45am, and 7:40pm, 202 pesos) and San Luis Potosí (3hr., 6 per day 2:15am-9:15am, 64 pesos). **Flecha Roja** (tel. 29 00 01) sends buses to San Mateo (4hr., every 20min. 2:30am-2:30pm, 60 pesos). **Flecha Verde** (tel. 29 00 02) serves Misión de Palmas (4hr., 8, 10am, and 4pm, 23 pesos). **Herradura de Plata** (tel. 29 02 45) runs to San Miguel de Allende (1¼hr., every 40min. 6am-10:10pm, 20 pesos) and Toluca (3½hr., 6 per day, 57 pesos). **Transportes Amealcences** (tel. 29 00 15) runs to Amealco (every hr. 6:30am-8:30pm, 15 pesos) and San Juan del Río (1hr., every 15min. 6am-10:30pm, 13 pesos). Finally, **Flecha Azul** (tel. 29 03 22) serves Higuerillas (3hr., 12:30 and 3:30pm, 27 pesos), San Joaquín (3hr., 6 per day 6:20am-4:20pm, 33 pesos), and Tequisquiapan (1hr., every 30min. 6:30am-8:15pm, 14 pesos).

Tourist and Financial Services

Tourist Office: State Tourist Office, Pasteur Nte. 4 (tel. 12 14 12 or 12 09 07; email turismo@ciateq.mx). From the *jardín,* take 5 de Mayo; the office is to your left at the end of the Plaza de Armas. Staff hands out maps and lists of local cultural events. City tours in English or Spanish depart at 9, 10, 11am, 4, 5, and 6pm (15 pesos). Open daily 8am-8pm.

Currency Exchange: There is a **casa de cambio,** Corregidora 108 (tel. 12 80 86), 2 long blocks south of the Jardín Zenea. Open M-Sa 9am-5pm. **ATM** next to the tourist office door on Pasteur Nte.; others by the *jardín* and elsewhere.

Local Services

Laundromat: Lavandería Veronica, Av. Hidalgo 153 (tel. 16 61 68), at Ignacio Pérez. From Teatro de la República, turn left onto Hidalgo and walk for about 20min. Leave 3kg of laundry and 32 pesos and return the next day—the friendly staff will have your clothes washed, dried, and waiting. Open M-F 9am-2:30pm and 4:30-8pm, Sa 9am-3pm.

Emergency and Communications

Emergency: Dial 080. **LOCATEL** will find lost people (tel. 14 33 11).

Police: Office at Pie de la Cuesta #107 (tel. 20 83 83 or 20 83 03), in Colonia Desarrollo San Pablo. **Angeles Verdes** (tel. 13 84 24) will rescue stranded motorists.

Red Cross: (tel. 29 06 65 or 29 07 29), at Balaustradas and Circuito Estadio, near the Estadio Corregidora.

Pharmacy: Súper Farmacia Querétaro, Av. Constituyentes Pte. 17 (tel. 12 44 23), 5 blocks south of the *jardín.* Open 24hr.

Hospitals: Sanatorio San José, Ezequiel Montes sur #34 (tel. 12 61 36 or 12 30 13); English spoken by **Dr. Encorrada** of **Grupo Médico Zaragoza,** Zaragoza Pte. 39-B (tel. 16 76 38 or 16 57 86), between N. Campa and E. Montes.

Post Office: Arteaga Pte. 5 (tel. 12 01 12), between Juárez and Allende, 2 blocks south of the *jardín.* Open M-F 8am-7pm, Sa 9am-1pm.

Postal Code: 76000.

Fax: Telecomm, Allende Nte. 4 (tel. 12 01 63; fax 14 39 48), 1 block west of the *jardín.* **Telegrams** and **Western Union,** too. Open M-F 8am-6pm, Sa-Su 9am-4pm.

Telephones: LADATELs abound. Also make long distance calls from the "Larga Distancia" *caseta* at 5 de Mayo 33 (tel. 12 11 67), half a block from the *jardín.* Open M-Sa 9am-7pm. Collect calls 10 pesos.

Phone Code: 42.

ACCOMMODATIONS

Due to the small-scale tourist industry, good and inexpensive accommodations can be difficult to find in Querétaro's *centro.*

Hotel Hidalgo, Madero Pte. 11 (tel. 12 00 81 or 12 81 02), half a block from the *jardín.* Comfortable rooms with small bathrooms and cable TV. Hot water 24hr. The attached restaurant serves inexpensive and tasty food (*menú del día* 19.50 pesos; open M-Sa 8am-10pm, Su 8am-8pm). Singles 85 pesos; doubles with 1 bed 100 pesos, with 2 beds 105 pesos.

Hotel del Márquez, Juárez Nte. 104 (tel. 12 04 14 or 12 05 54), 4 long blocks north of the *jardín.* An enormous stained-glass depiction of Querétaro's aqueduct welcomes guests to this hotel. *Agua purificada* in the lobby and from dispensers on each floor. Carpeted rooms have cable TV, telephones, sparkling clean tiled bathrooms, and 24hr. hot water. Singles 80 pesos; doubles 100 pesos.

Villa Juvenil Youth Hostel (tel. 23 43 50), Av. Ejército Republicano. From the *jardín,* walk 1 block south on Corregidora, then walk left on Independencia for 8 blocks. Veer right onto Ejército Republicano, just past the Convento de Santa Cruz. The hostel is inside the sports and recreation complex on the right side of the street. While a bit remote, it's a bargain—just beware of flocks of athletes taking up all the rooms (call ahead). No drinking or smoking. Single-sex dorms with 8 bunks per room. 20 pesos per person. 25% discount with HI card. 20-peso bedding deposit. Reception 7am-10:30pm; call if you will be arriving later.

Hotel R.J., Invierno 21 (tel. 12 04 88). Walk 5 long blocks north of the garden up Juárez to Universidad, cross the bridge onto Invierno and continue for half a block. While you certainly will not be living in the lap of luxury, this fairly clean hotel will go easy on your wallet. 24hr. hot water. 50 pesos per person.

FOOD

Inexpensive restaurants face the Jardín Zenea, pricier *loncherías* and outdoor cafes rim the nearby Plaza Corregidora, and taco, *torta,* and other fast-food stands line 5 de Mayo. Many restaurants stop serving their *menú del día* at 5 or 6pm.

La Mariposa, Angela Peralta 7 (tel. 12 11 66), at Juárez. This cafeteria and *pastelería* has been a local favorite for 57 years and counting. Enjoy *enchiladas verdes* (with green salsa; 21 pesos), fresh fruit juice (7 pesos), or a banana split (14 pesos) while you listen to patrons argue about *fútbol*. Open daily 8am-9:30pm.

Ibis Natura Vegetariana, Juárez Nte. 47 (tel. 14 22 12), half a block north of the *jardín.* Despite what you've heard, Mexican veggies can be delicious and nutritious. Try a lip-smacking veggie cheeseburger (8 pesos), or the hearty *menú del día* (18.50 pesos) with an energizing glass of freshly made fruit and vegetable juice (7 pesos). Catch your reflection in the stainless-steel ceiling and chat with the gregarious patrons and staff. Open daily 8am-9:30pm.

Café del Fondo, Av. Pino Suárez 9 (tel. 12 09 05), between Juárez and Allende 1 block south of the *jardín.* Good food and great prices make this local hangout an enticing stop for the budget traveler craving quesadillas (7.50 pesos) or sandwiches (6 pesos). Caffeine addicts, rejoice: this restaurant has a huge selection of exotic coffee drinks (from 6-19 pesos). Try the *Queretano*—coffee, brandy, vodka, chantilly cream, and cinnamon. Hearty breakfast specials 10.50-15 pesos. Open daily 7:30am-10pm.

Restaurante de la Rosa, Juárez Nte. 24 (tel. 12 87 84), at Peralta, across from the Teatro Republicano. Tasty Mexican cuisine seasoned to perfection. Red wooden chairs, plaid tablecloths, and brick floors are nice, but it's the food that gets rave reviews from locals and tourists. *Enchiladas queretanas* 15 pesos. *Menú del día* 18-20 pesos. Open M-Sa 9am-9pm, Su 9am-1pm (breakfast only on Sundays).

SIGHTS

Querétaro has more to see and to do than most colonial towns. For those tired of historical museums and Churrigueresque churches, Querétaro offers plazas and walkways perfect for a post-meal, pre-siesta stroll.

Convento de la Santa Cruz

Tel. 12 02 35. South of Jardín Zenea. Follow Corregidora to Independencia and turn left. After walking about five blocks, you'll reach the convent, which occupies a plaza dedicated to the founders of the city. ***Open*** *Tu-F 9am-2pm and 4-6pm, Sa, Su, and holidays 9am-4:30pm.* ***Free,*** *but a small donation is requested for the convent.* ***20min. guided tours*** *in Spanish, English, French, or Italian.*

The most intriguing sight in Querétaro is the *convento.* Nearly everything inside Santa Cruz (founded in 1683) is original—the clay pipes and water-catching system date from the city's aqueduct days. Maximilian devotees can make a pilgrimage to the cell in which the emperor spent his last minutes; it has been left exactly as it was on the day of his execution. In one courtyard, trees grow thorns in the form of crucifixes. According to legend, the thorns began growing into crosses after a friar stuck his cane into the ground near the trees. The tree is a mimosa and is known simply as the **Arbol de la Cruz** (Tree of the Cross). It is said that these are the only trees of their kind in the world; attempts to plant seedlings elsewhere have supposedly failed.

Other Sights

Querétaro's fascinating **Acueducto** stretches along Calzada de los Arcos west of the *centro.* This distinctive structure, with its 74 arches of pink sandstone, was constructed in 1735 as a gift to a perpetually parched community from the Marqués de Villas del Águila. A *mirador* overlooking all 1280m of the aqueduct is located on Av. Ejército Republicano, about three blocks past the Convento de la Santa Cruz. From the *mirador,* the arched aqueduct blends into the surroundings in contrast to the increasing modernization of the city that lies below. Up 5 de Mayo to the east of the *jardín* is the **Plaza de la Independencia (Plaza de Armas),** a monument to the aforementioned Marqués. Stone dogs hang around his statue, drooling respectfully into a fountain. The plaza is bordered by old square-rimmed trees, colorful cafés, shaded benches, and beautiful colonial buildings, including the **Casa de la Corregidora,** home of Doña Josefa Ortíz de Domínguez, heroine of the Independence movement. *(Open M-F 8am-9pm, Sa 9am-2pm.)* The *casa* is now the seat of the state government, so only the courtyard may be viewed; it's less than thrilling. One block north of the Casa de la Corregidora, at Pasteur and 16 de Septiembre, is the colorful **Templo de la Congregación** (tel. 12 07 32), with its two white towers and central dome that rise above all the other buildings in the area. *(Open daily 7am-9pm. Mass M-F at 8, 10am, and 8pm, and much more often Sa and Su.)* The stained glass windows toward the top of the church let in dim light, and delicate chandeliers are suspended against a backdrop of pillars and frescoes. The image of *La Guadalupana* is by Miguel Cabrera.

The **Museo de La Ciudad,** Vicente Guerrero 27 (tel. 24 37 56), is between Hidalgo and 16 de Septiembre. *(Open Tu-Su 11am-7pm. Admission 5 pesos, free for teachers, students, and seniors.)* To reach the museum, take a left on Hidalgo as you face the Teatro de la República and walk three blocks; turn left on Guerrero. The museum, which served as the final prison of Emperor Maximilian, contains a well-organized display of religious art and an ever-changing exhibit of contemporary art. Another quality museum is the **Museo de Arte de Querétaro,** Allende 14 (tel. 12 35 23), between Madero and Pino Suárez, about two blocks from the *jardín. (Open Tu-Su 11am-7pm. Admission 10 pesos, free for students with ID, seniors, children under 12, and for all on Tuesdays.)* The original edifice, an 18th-century Augustinian monastery, was rebuilt in 1889. An exhibition on local architecture supplements the bounty of Baroque paintings. European canvasses, 19th- and 20th-century Mexican art, and Cristóbal de Villal Pando's 19th-century depictions of the 12 apostles round out the formidable collection. The **Museo Regional** is housed in the **Ex-Convento de San Francisco** (tel. 12 20 31; fax 12 20 36), at Corregidora and Madero, east of the Jardín Zenea. *(Open Tu-Su 10am-7pm. Admission 16 pesos, free for seniors, children under 12, and for all on Sundays.)* Exhibits include various artifacts culled from the dustbin of history, such as the table upon which the 1848 Treaty of Guadalupe Hidalgo was signed with the U.S. The entire upper level is devoted to colonial-era religious paintings and artifacts relating to Querétaro's military and political history.

The **Cerro de las Campanas** (Hill of the Bells), named for the peculiar sound its rocks make when they collide, is where Emperor Maximilian first established his military headquarters and later surrendered his sword to General Escobedo in 1867. He was then taken to the cell in the Convento de la Santa Cruz. To reach the monument, walk a few blocks north of the Jardín Zenea on Corregidora and turn left onto General Escobedo. Proceed on Escobedo until the street ends at Tecnológico, then take a right and you will come to the monument (about a 30min. walk). Otherwise, catch the "Ruta 45" bus headed west on Zaragoza. To the left of the Cerro de las Campanas and up a low hill, Maximilian's family built a small **chapel** over the ground where the emperor and two of his generals were shot. *(Open Tu-Su 7am-6pm. Admission 1 peso.)* Three small white memorials inside designate the places where each took his last breath. Up the stairs to the left of the chapel stands a large stone sculpture of Benito Juárez, the man responsible for Maximilian's execution.

The newly remodeled **Teatro de la República** (tel. 24 00 40) stands at Angela Peralta and Juárez. *(Open Tu-Su 10am-3pm and 5-8pm; free.)* Many historic events have transpired here: in 1867, the final decision on Emperor Maximilian's fate; in 1917, the drafting of the constitution in the **Sala de Constituyentes** upstairs; and in 1929, the founding of the Partido Nacional de la Revolución (PNR), the precursor of today's Partido Revolucionario Institucional (PRI). The *sala,* however, is closed to the public, so the Teatro is best viewed in passing. For lazing around, nothing beats the shady trees of the **Alameda Hidalgo,** three long blocks down Corregidora. The Alameda, which was built in 1790, includes a duck pond, green lawns, tree-lined paths, a skating rink, two soda fountains, and a monument honoring Hidalgo. The **Andador Libertad,** two blocks from the *jardín* and connecting the Plaza de la Independencia and Av. Corregidora, is host to a slew of mellow vendors and *artesanía* shops (open daily from about 10:30am to 9:30pm). **Andador 5 de Mayo,** off the *jardín,* has several galleries with local artwork for sale.

Peel It, Slice It, Suck It, Dice It

Mangoes may be one of Mexico's more delicious offerings, but the fruit's sumptuous flavor is often passed over by foreigners who can't figure out how to eat it. There are many types of mangoes, but the two most popular are the *paraíso,* which is the larger of the two and red and green, and the yellow *manila.* Mexicans often eat mango seasoned with chile powder and fresh lime juice, but for those with less adventurous taste buds, they can also be consumed straight up. The easiest way to eat a mango is to pluck an end with your fingernail or fork, peel it like a banana, and suck away. But for hygiene's sake, consider a fancier option: cut along both sides of the seed, leaving yourself with two pieces and a seed with some fruit around the edges. Next, peel the skin around the seed and chomp away. Then take your two bowl-shaped pieces and cut down into the fruit, creating a grid in the pulp. Turn the skin inside-out and scrape your pieces onto a plate. Diced mango! Alternatively, cut the fruit into strips, shove them into your mouth, and use your teeth to scrape off the pulp. Mangoes are sometimes sold on a stick, and one can eat the fruit like ice cream by turning and sucking—be sure to lean over as you eat or you will soon be wearing your mango. No matter how you choose to eat your mango, remember the one vital rule of mango-eating: never, ever wear a white shirt.

ENTERTAINMENT AND SEASONAL EVENTS

Local entertainment, like almost everything else in Querétaro, revolves around the Jardín Zenea, with its spectacular people-watching each evening. Open-air brass-band concerts are given in the gazebo Sunday evenings from 6 to 8pm, and myriad jugglers, *mariachis,* and magicians perform there less regularly. Balloons in bunches big enough to fly you around the world and back are sold around the *jardín,* enlivening the already-festive plaza. **Jardín de los Platitos,** where Juárez meets Av. Universidad north of the *zócalo,* dances to mariachi music. Things start to heat up at about 11pm on Fridays and Saturdays. The *Cartelera de Eventos,* published monthly by the tourist office, is an excellent source of information about cultural events, concerts, performances, and festivals. Or call the **Academia de Bellas Artes** (tel. 12 05 70), Juárez Sur at Independencia, to find out what the students of the Universidad Autónoma de Querétaro have in store for the public. If you're lucky, you might catch a ballet recital, piano concert, theatrical event, or even a folk dance presentation. But call early; performances usually begin at 5pm. More fun than monster trucks, **Querétaro 2000** (tel. 20 68 10 or 20 68 13), on Blvd. Bernardo Quintana, is a huge stretch of parks and facilities, including a pool, football field, basketball court, amusement park, library, open theater, and camping area (open daily 7am-7:30pm).

The local twentysomething crowd hits the dance floor hard at **JBJ,** Blvd. Bernardo Quintana 109 (tel. 13 72 13 or 13 43 07). Booming rhythms and a merciless strobe light will keep you movin'. (Open W-Sa 10pm-2am; live music.) Next to the disco is the **JBJ Bar,** which has **karaoke** and **pool tables.** Live music is played to an eclectic audience while friendly waiters serve margaritas prepared with purified ice. (Open W-Sa 8pm-2am.) Another happening spot is the disco **Van Gogh,** Prolongación Pasteur Sur 285 (tel. 12 65 75; cover 20-25 pesos; open Th-Sa 9pm-2am).

A more relaxed atmosphere can be found at **Quadros,** Andador 5 de Mayo 16 (tel. 12 04 45), one block from the *jardín.* Everything from local artwork to pictures of Marilyn Monroe and replicas of the Mona Lisa cover the walls of this spacious but intimate cafe-bar, and each night from 8pm on, musicians play hour-long sets of anything from blues to *trova*. Friday and Saturday nights, twentyish would-be Selenas compete for drinks and prizes. (Cover 20 pesos after 8pm F-Sa. Open Tu-Su 6pm-2am.) **El Regio,** Jardín Corregidora 10 (tel. 14 12 75), is another spot to grab a beer, sit back, and relax. Busy waiters scurry about as people of all ages gather around patio tables and chat while a lounge singer belts out Mexican faves in the background. Beer costs 12 pesos. (Open M-F 8am-3am, Sa-Su 3pm-3am.)

The annual **Feria de Querétaro** usually takes place during the second week of December. The **Feria de Santa Ana,** complete with bulls running through congested streets, takes place every July 26th. The whole town dances during the **Celebración de la Santa Cruz de los Milagros** and the *Fiestas Patrias,* which take place during the second or third week of September. Other festivals include the **Feria Internacional del Queso y del Vino** in May or July, the festival commemorating the founding of the city on July 25, and, of course, **Semana Santa** in March and April.

HIDALGO

Pachuca

Hidalgo's capital city, Pachuca (pop. 220,000) offers much more than just *pulque,* the omnipresent alcoholic refreshment made from the maguey cactus. An important center for silver mining and processing since the 16th century, the city offers several lovely plazas, a few worthwhile museums, extremely friendly inhabitants, and invigoratingly crisp mountain air. Life moves at an orderly pace, but winding streets and hidden parks offer just the right degree of idiosyncratic charm. Pachuca exudes a sense of prosperity and contentment that is infectious, and the delightful streets are fairly tourist-free—Pachuca is a refreshing daytrip from the D.F.

ORIENTATION AND PRACTICAL INFORMATION Getting oriented is a bit difficult, as many streets curve and change names. The bus station is a fair distance from downtown. Frequent *combis* run from the bus station to the **Plaza de la Constitución** (6am-10pm, 2 pesos). To get from there to the *zócalo,* also known as **Plaza de la Independencia,** make a left on Hidalgo and a right on Ocampo. This will put you at the northeastern corner of the plaza. The street forming the eastern boundary of the square is **Matamoros;** it runs parallel to **Allende** (across the plaza) and **Guerrero** (one block west of the plaza). Matamoros and Allende converge a few blocks to the south at **Plaza Juárez. Juárez** and **Revolución** both begin at Plaza Juárez and run parallel to the south.

ADO runs first-class **buses** to Mexico City's North Station (1¼hr., every 15min. M-F 4:45am-10:15pm, Sa-Su 5:45am-10:15pm, 25 pesos), Poza Rica (5hr., 4 per day 8:30am-8:45pm, 53 pesos), and Tuxpan (7hr., 8:30am and 8:45pm, 69 pesos). **Flecha Roja** (tel. 3 27 94) has second-class buses to Mexico City (1½hr., every 10min. 4am-10pm, 23 pesos). **Estrella Blanca** (tel. 3 27 47) provides second-class service to Querétaro (4½hr., every hr. 5:15am-6:15pm, 66 pesos) and San Juan del Río (3½hr., every hr. 5:15am-6:15pm, 46 pesos). Pachuca's **tourist office** (tel. 5 14 11) lies in the bottom of the huge clock tower, on Plaza de la Independencia (open M-F 9am-3pm, Sa-Su and festivals 10am-6pm). **Bancomer** (tel. 3 06 00 and 3 06 09), on the west side of the plaza on Allende, changes money (open M-F 8:30am-5:30pm). There is a **mar-**

ket on the north side of Plaza de la Constitución. In case of an **emergency,** dial 060. The **police** (tel. 1 18 80) are in Plaza Juárez. The **Red Cross** provides 24-hour ambulance service (tel. 4 17 20 or 4 32 53). **Farmacia Rex Reloj,** Plaza de la Independencia 106 (tel. 5 00 52; fax 5 56 82), can help you with your pharmaceutical needs (open M-Sa 8am-10pm, Su 8am-8pm). For medical care, try **Clínica IMSS** (tel. 3 78 33), off Maderos, although it is a bit far from downtown. The **post office** (tel. 3 25 92), Juárez at Iglesias, is two blocks south of Plaza Juárez (open M-F 8am-7pm, Sa 9am-1pm). The **postal code** is 42070. The **phone code** is 771.

ACCOMMODATIONS AND FOOD There is a dearth of true budget establishments in the immediate area. **Hotel Los Baños,** Matamoros 205 (tel. 3 07 00), just south of the main square, is a good value. A spacious, tiled courtyard gives rise to good-sized rooms with carpets, bottled water, telephones, and color TVs. Bathrooms are small but clean, and the central location is to die for. (Singles 80 pesos; doubles 90 pesos.) A couple blocks farther south on Matamoros is **Hotel Hidalgo,** Matamoros 503 (tel. 5 48 18). Rooms feature carpet, a not-so-great view, TV, and flowered bedspreads. (Singles 95 pesos; doubles 135 pesos.)

In the 19th century there was an influx of Cornish miners to the Pachuca area. Their two lasting legacies are *fútbol* and *pastes.* Pastry shells filled with meat, potatoes, and onions, with a dash of chile to keep it all tasting Mexican, *pastes* make great, filling snacks; they are sold all over town for 2-4 pesos. Try the **market** on the north side of Plaza de la Constitución for other inexpensive bites. For a hearty, sit-down meal, make your way over to **Lisú Vegetariano,** Revolución 903 (tel. 4 78 73; owned by a fellow *Let's Go* aficionado), 8 blocks from Plaza Juárez. Feast on disinfected fruits and veggies before you dig into a hefty serving of eggplant lasagna (20 pesos; open M-Sa 8am-7pm). On the east side of the *zócalo* is **Restaurante La Blanca,** Matamoros 201 (tel. 5 18 96). This friendly spot, named in honor of the mine that furnished the stone for the Reloj Monumental, is popular with locals of all ages. The airy interior provides the perfect venue to enjoy breakfast (22-34 pesos) or *antojitos* (9-24 pesos). Tasty *pastes* (3 pesos) are available to go. (Open daily 8am-10pm.) A bit of a walk south from downtown is **Girasol Restaurant and Bar,** Revolución 1107 (tel. 8 70 93), about 10 blocks south of Plaza Juárez, across from the Revolución market. Brass fixtures, wood paneling, and forest-green walls are brightened by ubiquitous sunflower images. The lively ambience attracts a younger crowd, and the jazzy music keeps patrons happy while they munch on their *antojitos* (15-23 pesos; open M-Th and Sa 8am-11pm, F 8am-2am, Su 9am-9pm).

SIGHTS AND ENTERTAINMENT The Plaza de la Independencia is dominated by the impressive **Reloj Monumental,** built in celebration of 100 years of Mexican independence. This huge clock tower is a great example of the French architecture that was popular during the Porfirio Díaz regime. Four female statues represent Independence, Liberation, Constitution, and Reform. The clock and bell were made in England by the manufacturers of Big Ben. Funded by local mining companies, the Reloj was fashioned out of white stone brought from nearby Tezoantla de Mineral del Monte. To reach the **Archivo Histórico and Museo de Minería,** Mina 110 (tel. 5 09 72), walk down Matamoros one block past the Plaza de la Independencia, take your first left onto Mina and follow it up one-and-a-half blocks. *(Open Tu-Su 10am-2pm and 3-6pm. Admission 4 pesos, 2 pesos for students and teachers with ID. Video in English and Spanish shown at 11am, noon, 1, 4, and 5pm.)* The museum, a former mining company office, holds an impressive collection of rocks, minerals, mining tools, and heavy machinery. The **Centro Cultural Hidalgo** is in the **Ex-Convento de San Francisco.** *(Both museums open Tu-Su 9am-6pm; free.)* To get there from the *zócalo,* follow Matamoros south for two blocks. Make a left on Allende, which soon ends in a traffic circle. Follow Arista to the left for two blocks, then make a right on Hidalgo (not to be confused with Nuevo Viaducto Hidalgo); the Ex-Convento is on the left. The cultural center contains the **Museo Nacional de la Fotografía,** an impressive survey of the technological history of photography. The museum boasts a fascinating collection of Mexican photographs; gawk at Pancho Villa and Emiliano Zapata on their triumphal march into Mexico City in 1914. The center also contains the **Museo Regional de Hidalgo,** featuring exhibits on archaeology, history, crafts, and indigenous cultures. Adjoining the cultural center is the **Church of San Francisco.** One block past the Ex-Convento de San Francisco is **Parque Juárez**, perfect for relaxing with local teens.

■ Near Pachuca: Mineral del Chico

Forty minutes of breathtaking scenery separate Pachuca from the tiny town of **Mineral del Chico** (pop. 500). Nestled in the **Parque Nacional el Chico,** the town has only a couple of restaurants, a small church, and a few houses. The striking views of nearby rock formations and numerous hikes make it a great natural escape for those sick of urban congestion and noise. Follow the road that runs uphill to the right from the *combi* stop to reach the spectacular vista point at **Peña del Cuervo** (6km). Walking past the church and heading downhill to the left will take you through some old silver mines. That trail eventually leads up to the craggy rock formation dubbed **Tres Monjas** because of its resemblance to nuns bowed in prayer. Locals are very friendly and will happily suggest other trails to explore.

Getting there: *Combis* run from Pachuca to Mineral el Chico (40min., every 30min. 7am-8:30pm, 6 pesos). They leave from Galeana; to get there, follow Guerrero north of the *zócalo* and make a left on Galeana. Head uphill for about two blocks. If there isn't a *combi* waiting, there will be soon.

■ Near Pachuca: Real del Monte

Real del Monte, whose streets used to hum and reverberate with the sounds of nearby mines, is now a colorful idyllic little town located just 9km north of Pachuca. **Mina Acosta,** a 15-minute walk down Guerrero north of the Plaza Principal, stands as a testament to Real's rich mining history. This mine passed through the hands of Spanish, English (who built the edifice, on your right as you enter, in 1874), Mexican, and North American owners before finally coming under government control. The silver from Acosta was taken to Guerrero to be melted and molded. The building on the left housed the mine managers, and the obsidian shards that line the tops of the walls surrounding the mine served to keep silver-hungry intruders out. Real del Monte also offers hiking and climbing opportunities. *Combis* depart from "La Madre" in front of the Deportivo de la Ciudad for **Peñas Cargadas,** a massive rock formation 16km from town (every 30min. 6am-7pm, 5 pesos). Follow the sign for Peñas Cargadas (1km). *La cargada mayor* on your left stands 100m tall. Directly to its right is *cargada menor,* at a mere 80m. Next to the *menor* stands *el pilón,* just 70m tall. And on the far right is *cerrote,* 30m high. Multiple hiking paths surround *las peñas.* Climbers must come prepared with proper equipment (crosses at the bottom of *las peñas* mark the spots where unprepared climbers were also unlucky). Interested climbers should contact Lucio Ramirez, Club Alpino, Lerdo de Tejada #4, Mineral del Monte, Hidalgo 42130; or stop by the Club Alpino headquarters in the Deportivo de la Ciudad (headquarters open M-Sa 6am-8pm).

Getting there: To reach Real del Monte from Pachuca, hop in a shared taxi in front of the **Iglesia de la Asunción** on the corner of Carranza and Villigran (near the east side of the Plaza de la Constitución, 3 pesos).

Tula

Tula (pop. 90,000) is not much to look at, but she's got a great personality. Her **excellent ruins** (see **The Archaeological Site of Tula,** below) lure daytrippers from Mexico City (80km) and Pachuca (75km). Unfortunately, she herself is—well, to put it bluntly—unexciting at best.

Downtown Tula consists of a few commercial streets, a semi-central *zócalo* and a centrally located cathedral with an uncanny exterior resemblance to a prison. To reach the *centro* from the **bus station,** turn right down Xicoténcatl and then left at Ocampo. Take a left down Zaragoza, and then a right on Hidalgo. Thoroughly confused? Another option is to head toward the cathedral by whatever route pleases you—it's visible from anywhere and is near to everything. Juárez runs past the side of the cathedral to the *zócalo.* 5 de Mayo runs parallel to Juárez, one block from the *zócalo*. To get to Tula from Mexico City, take an **AVM** bus from the Central de Autobuses del Norte *Sala 8* (second-class 2hr., every 20min. 8am-8pm, 20 pesos; first-class 1½hr., every hr. 8am-8pm, 27 pesos).

Buses run out of the **AVM** terminal (tel. 2 02 25 or 2 02 64), on Xicoténcatl, to Mexico City (second-class 2hr., every 20min. 6am-8pm, 20 pesos; first-class 1½hr., every 40min. 6am-8pm), Pachuca (1½hr., every 30min., 23 pesos), and Querétaro (2hr., 9 per day 7am-7pm, 40 pesos). Currency and traveler's checks can be exchanged at **Banamex,** Leandro Valle 102 (tel. 2 37 72), down Juárez from the *zócalo* (open M-F 9am-5pm, Sa 10am-2pm). It also has a 24-hour **ATM.** The **police** (tel. 2 01 85) are at 5 de Mayo 408. Lovely **LADATELs** are found near the bus station and on Zaragoza and Hidalgo near the *centro.* The **phone code** is 773.

Because Tula is a small town and the few travelers that show up only come to see the ruins, budget rooms don't come easy. The best deal in town is the **Auto Hotel Cuéllar,** 5 de Mayo 23 (tel. 2 04 42). Here, your car will have a place to sleep, too. Cute rooms with phone and TV and slightly worn bathrooms surround a quiet courtyard full of flowering plants and singing birds. (Singles 90 pesos; doubles 110 pesos.) **Restaurante Casa Blanca,** Hidalgo 114 (tel. 2 22 74), serves up a cheap five-course *comida corrida* (35 pesos) in a bright, traditional atmosphere (open daily 8am-9pm). Some of the best and cheapest food in town is cooked at the **Restaurante El Ranchito,** on Zaragoza, half a block before Hidalgo, a family-owned, family-style restaurant. *Comida corrida* goes for 15 pesos. (Open daily 7am-2am.)

THE ARCHAEOLOGICAL SITE OF TULA

Tula is one of the most-studied sites in the Republic; archaeologists from all over the world have visited it. *(Site open daily 9am-5pm. Admission 14 pesos, free for children under 13, students and teachers with ID, seniors, and for all on Sundays and holidays. Museum free).* During the week, few people come, and it is possible to scale hills without seeing anyone. Taxis (tel. 2 05 65) will take you from the *sitio* stand on Zaragoza at Hidalgo in Tula (10 pesos). Taxis aren't available at the site for the return, but *peseros* stopping near the *central camionera* (bus station) and then the *centro* (2.50 pesos) pass frequently on the highway.

History

The first large settlement in northern Mesoamerican and once the Toltecs' greatest city, Tula was reputedly founded during the 9th century by the legendary **Ce Acatl Topiltzin** (a.k.a. **Quetzalcóatl**). Ce Acatl Topiltzin is the most venerated king in *indígena* history and mythology. Under his rule, Tula grew to hold thousands of inhabitants and developed an architecture that would serve as the prototype for Aztec cities. After many years at Tula, the story goes, strife arose with neighbors who took issue with his peaceful ways, and he abandoned the city in 884 and led many of his followers to the Gulf coast, supposedly heading out to sea off the coast of Veracruz and vowing to return in the year "1 Reed." In the following years, several kings expanded Tula into the center of the mighty Toltec empire. Hundreds of years later, Cortés arrived in Veracruz on the year "1 Reed." Legend had it that because of his skin color and this strange coincidence, the Aztecs believed the conquistador was the same light-skinned Quetzalcóatl who had fled to the east so many years before, causing Aztec Emperor Moctezuma to welcome Cortés with open arms.

The Toltecs (see p. 45), whose name means "builders" in Náhuatl, relied on irrigation for their agricultural success and modeled their architecture after the style of Teotihuacán. During the 200-year-long Toltec heyday, the kingdom abandoned its once-peaceful stance for violence and viciousness. When crop failures and droughts weakened the Toltec capital in 1165, the Chichimecs lashed out and destroyed Tula.

The ruins of the city (approx. 17 sq. km have been excavated) are eroded due to the poor quality of the materials (rock) found in this area, as well as to poor maintenance and the Toltecs' sporadic internal instability—at one point Quetzalcóatl urged the Toltecs to evacuate the city, prompting some residents to bury their belongings and move to the region called Tlapallan. Tula was eventually absorbed by the Aztec empire, and Aztec ceramics and pottery can be found scattered among the ruins.

Guide to the Ruins

From the entrance area, a 600m dirt path zigzags past super-prickly cacti through two sets of vendor stalls before arriving at the main plaza. Amid much junk, they sell some delicate and "authentic" reproductions at super-low (they get even lower if you bargain) prices. Illegal vendors inside the site will try to sell you the same pieces at much higher prices, claiming they are real Toltec pieces found in the fields—a highly unlikely story if they offer you anything other than tiny fragments or obsidian shards. The first structure you see to your right (north) as you reach the main plaza is **Ballcourt #1,** just north of the large **Edificio de los Atlantes.** This court, nearly 70m long, once held a depiction of a ball player in ritual dress, which is now located in the archaeological sponge that is the Museo Nacional de Antropología in Mexico City (see p. 106). To the left (south) is the monumental **Edificio de los Atlantes (Pyramid B).** Standing starkly against the horizon high above the rest of the site, **the Atlantes** emblemize Tula on covers of *National Geographic* and on posters hanging in tourist offices throughout the country. Close inspection of these statues (each a whopping 9.6m tall) reveals traces of red pigment, the only remnant of the many colors the statues once wore. Representing warriors, and originally standing inside a temple that had formerly held religious figures, the Atlantes are evidence of the change from theocratic to militaristic rule in Tula during the PostClassic period. Along the pyramid's northern side and currently covered by a tin roof is **El Coatepantli** (The Wall of Snakes). This wall, which depicts jaguars and serpents in procession, so impressed the Aztecs that they built copies of it around the plazas of their cities. Reliefs of serpents feasting on humans adorn the adjacent wall.

Immediately west of the Edifico de los Atlantes is the **Palacio Quemado** (Burnt Palace). It is thought to have been an administrative center in ancient Tula. A **chacmool** (messenger to the gods) was originally found in the central patio; now the black figure with a gaping mouth reclines near the steps to the Edifico de los Atlantes, under the awning. Like many other indigenous cultures, the Toltecs built their largest buildings on the eastern boundary of the plaza as witnesses to the sunrise. In this manner, Toltec leaders attempted to maintain sociopolitical control by inspiring awe and linking natural phenomena to the government. Tula's **Templo Principal** once towered over the others. The object of deliberate destruction by the Chicimecs and others following Tula's abandonment at the end of the 12th century, it now pales in comparison to the Edificio de los Atlantes. Not fully excavated and still overgrown with weeds, the Templo Principal can't be climbed from the front, but you can scramble up a steep rocky path in its southeast corner. It was most likely once adorned with a massive sculptural slab found nearby, covered with images of Quetzalcóatl in his manifestation as Tlahuizcaltec Uhtli, "the morning star." Adjoining the ballcourt on the interior of the plaza is **El Tzompantli,** a small platform built by the Aztecs. Tzompantli means "place of skulls" and was used to display the victims of sacrifice.

ESTADO DE MÉXICO

Valle de Bravo

Everything about this 16th-century town is perfect and picturesque, from the mountain views at the end of every cobblestone street to the luscious fruit sold at the market by traditionally clad *indígenas*. Wealthy Chilangos keep resplendent vacation homes on the edges of Valle, and although enough business is brought in to make this town feel newly wealthy, it still has a cozy, tiny, traditional feel. This is probably due in part to Valle de Bravo's having been declared a "typical town" in 1972; among other things, construction on new buildings is heavily restricted. Even the stray dogs look healthy and well-fed. You don't come to Valle to "do" anything but rather to wander and marvel at the beauty of it all. Relax in the leafy paradise of the plaza while you sip an *agua de fruta* or lick a *paleta* (frozen fruit bar). In the afternoons and on weekends, craftspeople from all over the country set up booths around the plaza. Quality and prices are both surprisingly good.

From the **Central de Autobuses Poniente** in Mexico City, Autobuses Mexico-Toluca-Zinacantepey sends buses to Valle de Bravo (3hr., every 20min., 46 pesos). They're almost all second-class, but mercifully they're rarely full. To return to the D.F., buses leave from the Central in Valle de Bravo twice every hour: on the hour and at 40 minutes past the hour.

To get to the *centro* from the bus station, turn right as you exit the station, walk downhill one block, and make a right on Zaragoza. Follow it two blocks until you see the Centro Comercial Isseymym, and turn left. You'll see the church at the end of the street. One block before the church, on the right, stretches the market. Just to the right of the cathedral as you face it, the **Plaza Independencia** overflows with well-trimmed greenery and the songs of tropical birds. Still facing the cathedral, the road running along the far side of the plaza is **Bocanegra.** On the far right corner, you will find **Joaquín A. Pagaza. Biotal,** Bocanegra 205 (tel. 2 44 04), has a 24-hour **ATM** and exchanges currency and traveler's checks during business hours (open M-Sa 8am-7pm). On the right-hand side of the plaza (facing the church), the **Farmacia Paty** is open daily from 9am to 3pm and 4pm to 9pm. The **post office** is on Joaquín A. Pagaza 200 (tel. 2 03 73; open M-F 9am-4pm, Sa 9am-1pm). **Telmex** phones are easy to find around the plaza.The **phone code** is 726.

A few expensive luxury hotels can be found on Bocanegra. **Hotel Mary,** Plaza Independencia 1 (tel. 2 29 67), however, offers a prime location and totally affordable prices. Clean and comfortable rooms are very simple with a random smattering of mismatched decorations. Try to get one of the two with a view of the plaza. (Singles 77 pesos; doubles 123 pesos, with shared bath 84 pesos; triples 184 pesos.) When you get hungry for something small, cheap, and quick, try any of the hole-in-the-walls between the bus station and the *centro.* Big, beautiful, expensive restaurants can be found on and around the *zócalo.* For something in between, duck into **La Parilla,** Bocanegra 104. This tiny, bright restaurant serves mouth-watering food in a sweet, homey atmosphere. *Comida corrida* is 25 pesos. (Open T, Th-Su 9am-9pm.) If you want to throw back a beer (or five) with the locals, check out **Restaurant Bar Los Torres,** across the street from the Centro Vocacional Isseymym, on the route from the bus station to the *centro. Comida corrida* costs only 15 pesos. See if you run into anyone who's brought a guitar along and after a few more beers, join in the singing. (Open daily 8am-11pm.)

Ixtapan de la Sal

Most people go to Ixtapan de la Sal for three reasons: the $200-per-day resorts, the upscale spas, and the water park. There is one reason why you should go: *everything else.* Ixtapan de la Sal (pop. 40,000) is the real thing—clean, quiet streets, rustic life, home-cooked meals. The gorgeous and refreshingly simple rust and whitewashed cathedral and *zócalo* are among the most scenic in Mexico. Only a quarter of a mile of road links Ixtapan's *centro* to the ritzy slew of resorts and natural spas that have made this sleepy little town famous, but in Ixtapan proper, *burros* still amble down the streets and people arrange flower offerings for the Virgin Mary and sleep outdoors. Come quickly, before resorts swallow the town itself, but once you're here, rest easy—life is slow, and good.

ORIENTATION AND PRACTICAL INFORMATION The **bus station** is on the main thoroughfare, **Juárez,** the same street that, almost 500m ahead, ends in the huge *balneario* (spa and waterpark) and chain of resorts. Running parallel to Juárez is **Allende.** Some main streets run perpendicular to Juárez (listed in order, from the bus station toward the resorts): **20 de Noviembre, Independencia, 16 de Septiembre, Ignacio Aldama, Constitución.** There is no tourist office, but an excellent **information booth** can be found at the end of Juárez, on the north side of the market in front of the water park. The **bus station** (tel. 3 05 12) sends first-class buses to Mexico City (2hr., every hr. M-Sa 6am-6pm, Su 6am-4pm, 40 pesos). It also runs second-class service to Acapulco (6hr., 10:45am, 1:15, and 5:45pm, 90 pesos), Cuernavaca (3hr., every 2hr. 5am-6pm, 21 pesos), and Mexico City (3hr., M-Sa every 15min. 3am-7:30pm, Su every 30min. 6am-7:30pm, 35 pesos). The **police** (tel. 3 02 44) can be reached 24 hours. The **Red Cross** (tel. 3 19 39), on the highway before the sports complex, has 24-hour emergency service (complex open from 9am-9pm). Buy shampoo at **Farmacia El Fénix,** Plaza de Mártires 1, on the *zócalo* (open M-F 8am-10pm, Sa-Su 9am-3pm and 5-9pm). The **post office** is located on 16 de Septiembre, two blocks from the cathedral (open M-F 9am-4pm). The **postal code** is 51900. The **phone code** is 714.

ACCOMMODATIONS AND FOOD If you stay away from the obscenely high-priced resorts and spas, some real deals await you in Ixtapan. **Casa de Huéspedes Sofia,** 20 de Noviembre 4 (tel. 3 18 51), is a short walk from the bus station. Go up Juárez three-quarters of a block, make your first right, and continue two blocks. Fluffy pink walls, floral bedspreads, and large bathrooms with purple fixtures make this place a winner. Rooms have TVs and 24-hour hot water. (50 pesos per person.) The pleasant **Casa de Huéspedes Francis,** Obregón 6 (tel. 3 04 03), near the cathedral, has a large, fern-filled lobby and a friendly dog. Rooms provide the basics, including 24-hour hot water. (80 pesos for 1-2 people.) The **Hotel Casa Sarita,** Obregón 1512 (tel. 3 01 72), is refreshingly posh. This 11-room hotel features soft beds and rocking chairs. Prices include three phenomenal home-cooked meals and excellent service. Watch and learn as the cook picks out melons and chicken carcasses. (175 pesos per person.)

For one of the best meals in town, eat at **Restaurante Yolis,** Juárez 33. The menu is posted every day. The huge *comida corrida* costs 30 pesos—breakfast (you tell 'em what you want and they'll make it) and *cena* (dinner) each go for 25 pesos. Watch *telenovelas* with the family and enjoy your home-cooked food. (Open daily 8am-7pm.) **Fonda Jardín,** Plaza 7 (tel. 3 02 74), offers both central location and cheap and yummy eats. The 12-peso enchiladas and ice-cold 5-peso beers (believe it) will make you want to wander around drunk and full for the rest of your days in Ixtapan. For the do-it-yourself traveler, **Panificadora Ixtapan,** Obregón 101 near Allende, offers freshly baked bread at 0.70 pesos per loaf. Or spring for the most expensive thing in the bakery—a 2.50 cream-filled *barkillo* (pastry; open daily 5am-9:30pm).

SIGHTS Most people come to Ixtapan to check out the massive water park/spa/thermal springs complex appropriately named **Ixtapan** (tel. 3 22 00), located at the end of Juárez (open daily 7am-7pm; admission 50 pesos, children 30 pesos). For a less expensive tryst in soothing thermal springs, check out the **balneario** (tel 3 02 97) back in town at the corner of Allende and 20 de Noviembre. *(Open daily 7am-6pm. Admission 10 pesos, children 2-10 7 pesos.)* Splurge on a massage (35 pesos, 25min.) or apply mud masks, courtesy of the management, as you soak. To get to the **Plaza de los Mártires,** make a right from Juárez (facing the water park) onto Independencia and continue straight for three or four blocks. This center of town life is surprisingly modern and clean, with plenty of recycling bins and a new obelisk-like monument dedicated to all the martyrs of the revolution. Adjoining the plaza is the **Santuario de la Asunción de Maria,** an astonishing white church with burgundy and rust trim. *(Open daily 7am-8pm.)* This cathedral with its little plaza-like "yard" is one of the reasons cameras were invented. Inlaid mosaic benches surround the garden, while gold ornamentation, stained glass windows, and intricate murals adorn the inside of the church. Completely open and airy, the church has a bulletin board filled with news of local weddings and a garden that sounds of buzzing bees and songbirds. Adjoining this Mediterranean-like cathedral is the **Capilla del Santísima y del Perdón,** in which a glass case holds a silver Christ. Sermons issue forth from the boombox-like speakers on either side of the altar.

Malinalco

Malinalco's Aztec ruins contain **one of four monolithic pyramids in the world**—the other three are in India, Jordan, and Egypt. *(Open Tu-Su 9am-6pm. Admission 16 pesos, free on Sundays.)* Malinalco is easily accessible from Cuernavaca, Mexico City, or Toluca. To get there, take a bus to **Chalma.** Once there, hail a taxi to Malinalco (20min., 30-35pesos for *taxi especial,* 5 pesos if shared). To get to the ruins from the *zócalo,* follow the blue pyramid signs along Guerrero and go straight. Take a left on Milgar, a right at the next blue arrow, and another right at the blue sign that appears to lead visitors into someone's driveway.

Malinalco was the sacred ground for the rituals that officially transformed an Aztec youth into a *guerrero tigre* or *guerrero águila* (tiger or eagle warrior). Because of the importance of these rituals and the ground they were performed on, the area was terraced and completely fortified from the outside. On the open circular stone platform—the first structure on the right as you enter—prisoners were bound to a pole with only their arms left free and made to wrestle the recently initiated warriors. If the prisoner won consecutive bouts with two *águila* and two *tigre* warriors, he was matched against a left-hander. If the prisoner defeated the lefty, he was granted freedom. Defeat, on the other hand, had more unpleasant consequences; the small rectangular basin in front of the entryway to the pyramid was used to hold the prisoner's blood after his ritual sacrifice. Behind the pyramid, the bodies of the sacrificed were burned to ashes on the oval bed of rock. The **Templo de la Iniciación** (Temple of the Initiation) for eagle and tiger warriors is a massive monolithic structure. All of its statues, rooms, and facades were carved from one giant slab of stone, and it was originally painted a brilliant crimson. To the right of the Templo de la Iniciación stand the remains of a **temascal,** the ancient predecessor to the sauna.

Although Malinalco has no tourist office, the **Casa de Cultura de Malinalco,** on one corner of the *zócalo,* can help you find the ruins and just about anything else you might need (open M-Sa 9am-2pm and 4-7pm).

Toluca

Capital of the Estado de México since 1846, Toluca (pop. 500,000) embodies many of the qualities that define the country as a whole. Industry is rapidly expanding on the outskirts of town, traffic congestion is becoming a serious problem, and the not-so-invisible hand of American economic imperialism has created huge ugly stores all over the place. But while these signs of the changing times may not always please tourists, they are indicators of a city eagerly moving forward. Toluca's downtown area remains truly striking for its beautifully preserved colonial architecture, complete with a traditionally elegant cathedral. Add a slew of great museums and a breathtaking botanical garden enclosed in an enormous stained-glass mural, and you have the makings of an escape from the sprawl of Mexico City, only an hour away.

ORIENTATION AND PRACTICAL INFORMATION Toluca is connected to Mexico City by the highway Paseo Tollocan. The *zócalo,* cathedral, and Portales shopping market constitute the *centro* and are bounded by **Av. Hidalgo** on the south, **Lerdo de Tejada** on the north, **Juárez** on the east, and **Bravo** on the west. **Independencia** runs parallel to Hidalgo one block to the north and forms the south side of the *zócalo.* The **Alameda** lies three blocks west of the *centro* on Av. Hidalgo. The amazing, stained-glass **Cosmovitral** (see **Sights,** below) is one block east of the *centro* on Lerdo de Tejada. Taxis (10 pesos) and buses (2.50 pesos) link the bus station to the *centro.*

The **bus terminal** in Toluca is tucked between Paseo Tollocan and Felipe Berriozabal, southeast of the *centro*. Tons of buses run to the *centro* from the terminal, and return trips can be caught on Juárez north of Independencia. **Flecha Roja** serves La Marquesa (30min., every 10min. 6am-10:30pm, 10 pesos), Mexico City (1hr., every 5min. 5am-8pm, 20 pesos), and Querétaro (3hr., every 1½hr. 4:40am-7:20pm, 56 pesos). **Naucalpan** goes straight to Mexico City's Metro stop "Toreo: Linea 2" (1½hr., every 5min. 5am-8:30pm, 20 pesos). **Herradura de Plata** (tel. 17 00 24) heads for Jilotepec (2½hr., every hr. 7am-5pm, 26 pesos) and Morelia (4hr., every hr. 6:15am-5:15pm and 6:30pm, 75 pesos). The **State Tourist Office,** Urawa 100, Room #110, (tel. 12 60 48, or toll free 01 800 8 49 13 33 00), is at Paseo Tollocan, about six blocks toward town from the bus station, in the large yellow municipal government building behind the Clínica IMSS and Wal-Mart. (Open M-F 9am-3pm and 5-8pm.) Change money at **Bancomer** (tel. 14 37 00), on the corner of Juárez and Hidalgo, which also has a 24-hour **ATM.** (Bank open M-F 8:30am-5:30pm, Sa 10am-2pm.) For a **market,** try **Mercado 16 de Septiembre** (tel. 14 52 47), Manuel Gómez Pedraza between Ignacio Rayón and Sor Juana Inés de la Cruz, two blocks north of the Cosmovitral (open M-Sa 8am-7:30pm, Su 8am-6:30pm).

For **emergencies,** dial 06 or call **LOCATEL** (tel. 13 31 83). The **police** are located at Morelos 1300 (tel. 14 93 51). The **Red Cross** (tel. 17 25 40) is on Jesús Carranza, one block south of Paseo Tollocan and one block west of Paseo Colón, southwest of the *centro* (open 24 hr.). There is a **pharmacy** (tel. 17 94 44) at the corner of Hidalgo and 5 de Febrero (open daily 7am-11pm.) For 24-hour **medical care,** go to **Clínica IMSS,** Paseo Tollocan #620 (tel. 17 07 33), about five blocks from the bus station. Some English is spoken. The **post office** is on Av. Hidalgo 300 (tel. 14 90 68), just east of Sor Juana Inés de la Cruz, two blocks east of Juárez (open M-F 8am-7pm, Sa 9am-1pm). A small branch in the bus station (tel. 17 08 85) has the same hours. The **postal code** is 50141. **Telecomm** (tel. 17 07 74), in the bus station, offers **fax, telegram,** and money wiring services (open M-F 9am-3pm, Sa-Su 9am-1pm). The **phone code** is 72.

ACCOMMODATIONS AND FOOD Although far from stellar, mid-range accommodations surround the *centro.* Avoid the noise and filth of rooms near the bus station. The centrally located **Hotel Don Primo,** Piño Suarez 507 (tel. 14 00 59), between Morelos and Instituto Literario, features a faux-marble lobby floor, chandeliers, carpeted hallways, and soothing peach walls. Enjoy your stay in a clean room with a slightly kinky fan-shaped mirror over the bed. Rooms have 24-hour hot water and black-and-white TVs. (1 or 2 persons with one bed 120 pesos, 10 pesos more for color TV; 2 twin beds 160 pesos; 2 double beds, 180 pesos.) **Hotel Maya,** Hidalgo 413 (tel. 14 48 00), a few blocks west of the *centro,* is small and homey. Quirky homespun quilts, clean communal bathrooms, and a flower-laden courtyard are welcome touches. (Singles 35 pesos; doubles 35 pesos, with 2 beds 70 pesos.)

Restaurants and cheap stalls clutter the storefronts of the Portales. *Chorizo* (sausage), the local specialty, makes an appearance in everything from *queso fundido* (melted cheese) to *tortas.* Also popular are traditional candies including *palanquetas* (peanut brittle), candied fruits, and *dulces de leche* (burnt milk candy). At **Yamin,** Leona Vicario 210 (tel. 15 83 39) at Independencia, the bright blue tablecloths and vibrant yellow walls will instantly put you in a good mood as you chomp on the hefty vegetarian *menú del día* (25 pesos). Breakfast will run you 9-18 pesos. (Open M-Sa 8am-8pm.) **Taquería Las Brisas del Sur,** on Morelos, one block south of Hidalgo, between Juárez and Aldama, is not for vegetarians. This carnivorous paradise specializes in *carnes al carbon* (24-28 pesos). Typical plastic tables and chairs may not excite you, but the mouth-watering smell wafting onto the sidewalk is a veritable temptation (tacos 12-16 pesos, drinks 4-7 pesos; open daily noon-midnight).

SIGHTS The bulk of Toluca's offerings are found in the *centro.* The **Cosmovitral** and **Jardín Botánico** (tel. 14 67 85) are housed one block east of the northeast corner of the *zócalo* in a building dating back to the turn of the century. *(Open daily 9am-5pm. Admission 5 pesos, children 2 pesos.)* The Cosmovitral, a stained glass mural designed by

Mexican artist Leopoldo Flores, occupies 3000 square meters and is made of half a million pieces of glass. It depicts the timeless struggle between universal binaries of good and evil, light and dark, etc. Its beauty enhances that of the many plants and pools of the *jardín.* A small plaque and friendship lantern commemorate Toluca's sister city, Saitama, in Japan.

Toluca is bursting at the seams with museums. Happily, they are universally well maintained and present their contents in easily digestible forms. The museum motherlode lies 8km out of town; the **Centro Cultural Mexiquense** is accessible by buses that say "C. Cultural" and run along Lerdo de Tejada (2.50 pesos). The complex houses **three museums.** *(All museums open Tu-Su 10:15am-5:45pm. Admission 5 pesos each, all three for 10 pesos, free W and Su; purchase tickets at the kiosk in the parking lot.)* The **Museo de Culturas Populares** is a beautifully restored hacienda with a large collection of folk art and colorful, traditional Mexican crafts, including an impressive Metepec Tree of Life (a large tree-like structure composed of clay figures incorporating Christian symbolism, baroque style, and fantastical elements). The **Museo de Antropología e Historia** offers a large and informative collection of assorted Mexican artifacts and exhibits. Don't miss the hair-raising collection of preserved animals, including cats, dogs, snakes, and **a pig with two snouts.** The **Museo de Arte Moderno,** housed in an edifice that's a far cry from colonial architecture, provides an eclectic potpourri of modern art.

The **Instituto Mexiquense de Cultura** sponsors five other museums in the *centro.* The **Museo José María Velasco,** Hidalgo 400 (tel. 13 28 14), and the **Museo Felipe S. Gutiérrez,** Bravo 303, are housed in adjoining restored colonial structures off the northwest corner of the *zócalo. (Both open Tu-Su 10am-6pm; free.)* Both artists were important 19th-century Mexican naturalists, and the museums house permanent collections of the two artists, as well as visiting exhibitions. The **Museo de la Acuarela,** Pedro Asencio #13 (tel. 14 73 04), two blocks west of the *portales,* displays all the watercolors you could possibly want to see. And finally, Toluca is home to a couple of museums only a specialized collector could love. The **Museo de Numismática,** Hidalgo 506 (tel. 13 19 27), another half block west on Hidalgo, is ripe with coins galore. *(Open Tu-Su 10am-6pm; free.)* Nine different rooms bear coins from eras in Mexican history. The **Museo de la Estampa** (tel. 14 44 25), on the south end of the Alameda, exhibits etchings, engravings, and graphic arts from all over the globe. *(Open M-Sa 10am-6pm, Su 10am-5pm; free.)*

Desierto de los Leones

Just outside of the city, this breathtaking park, **El Desierto de Los Leones (Desert of the Lions),** offers solace and clean air among zillions of pines. *(Park open daily 6am-5pm. Convent open for visits Tu-Su 10am-5pm. Convent admission 3 pesos. Guided tours Sa-Su 11am-3pm, around 10 pesos.)* Hundreds of paths wind through the woods for hiking, walking, or jogging; the longest is 30km. The beauty of the trails here, perched on the mountains above the urban sprawl, will take your breath away, and each inhalation will fill your chest with fresh, clean, pine-smelling air. This gorgeous park is one of Mexico City's main oxygen sources. At the heart of the park sit the pristine remains of the **Convento Santo Desierto,** for which the park is named. There was never a desert here; like all Barefoot Carmelite convents, this one was purposefully placed in a desolate area to facilitate the extreme self-abnegation practiced by its inhabitants. The woods may never have held lions, but they were home to hundreds of pumas.

Desierto de Los Leones makes a wonderful daytrip from Mexico City. From Metro: Observatorio in Mexico City, exit to your right; you will see tons of *autobuses urbanos*. Take any one going to San Angel. Get off in front of the Centro Cultural San Angel, just past the flower market to your left and the PEMEX station to your right. Whenever 10 people for Desierto de Leones gather, a bus (1hr., 5 pesos per person) will head off. The bus dispatcher, checking off sheets of paper and yelling out destinations, will be happy to help. If people are slow to gather, you can pay for the empty seats. The last stop is in front of the convent. To return to the city, *colectivos* to San

Angel or Tacubaya Metro stops leave from the entrance approximately every hour. The last bus leaves at 5pm.

The **convent** was originally built between 1606 and 1611. Exactly 100 years later, it was demolished by an earthquake. The re-building was completed in 1723. Between 1780 and 1801, however, the monks moved to another convent in the Nixcongo mountains due to harsh weather conditions. Wander through the immense corridors to catch a glimpse of a bedroom as it was left in 1801. Bring a flashlight or buy a candle (5 pesos) to descend into the basements. Winding in complete darkness under the entire structure, the basement passages are not for the claustrophobic.

On Saturdays and Sundays from noon until 3 pm, the church hosts free (with the entrance fee) **theater,** ranging from passion plays to the avant garde works of Federico García Lorca (shows change weekly). The **convent cafeteria** serves scrumptious savories. Another food option is at **Los Leones** restaurant, just outside the convent, where you can sit on the edge of the hillside looking out at the trees, trees, and more trees. Los Leones serves delicious *conejo* (rabbit) and *trucha* (trout) specialties (25-50 pesos), homemade *mezcal*, and Mexican traditionals (from 5 pesos). Alternatively, pack a lunch and take your pick of beautiful spots to spread out and enjoy.

Tepotzotlán

On the highway from Mexico City to Tula and Querétaro, the terrifically tiny town of Tepotzotlán (pop. 14,000) makes an easy and worthwhile daytrip from Mexico City. For those itching to escape the smog and bustle of the city, Tepotzotlán offers a beautifully masoned central plaza and an extensive church and monastery housing exquisite examples of religious art.

To get to Tepotzotlán from Mexico City, hop onto one of the AVMs' indirect second-class Tula buses (every 20min., 10 pesos) at the Central de Autobuses Norte and ask to be left off at the "*caseta* Tepotzotlán" (1hr.). Alternately, take the Metro to Cuatro Caminos (Line 2), then the yellow or blue bus from *salida H* (buses leave about every 30min. 6am-10pm, 7 pesos). Both will leave you at the *caseta*. The *zócalo* is half a mile up Insurgentes. A 10-peso cab ride will get you there, or follow the signs around the corner and just keep walking or flag any *pesero* (1.50 pesos). To get back to Mexico City, grab a bus across the street from Hotel Posada San José to "Toreos" which will let you off at the *Cuatro Caminos* metro station (1hr., every 15-20min., 7 pesos). From there you can walk or take a 10-peso cab ride to the *zócalo.*

Museo del Virreinato

Tel. 876 02 45 ext. 120. On the plaza. ***Museum open*** *Tu-Su 9am-5:45pm.* ***Admission*** *16 pesos, free for seniors, national students with ID, children, and for all on Sundays.*

In the 16th century, Jesuits established a convent in Tepotzotlán where *indígenas* could study language, art, theology, and mathematics. Martín Maldonado, an *indígena* convert, donated the land to the missionaries in 1582. Construction of the buildings continued until the end of the following century, and the huge bell in the tower was added in 1762. After the 1767 expulsion of the Jesuits, the church and buildings became a reform school for priests. Early this century, they were returned to the Jesuits, and the whole complex of buildings became the **Museo del Virreinato.** This church-turned-museum is a masterpiece of the Churrigueresque style; the craftsmanship is among the most well preserved in all of Mexico. Clerical vestments, murals lining the inner courtyard, and faded frescoes further enhance this divine religious collection. Look out for *El Crucifijo,* a 17th-century sculpture of Christ on the cross carved from a single piece of wood.

Exhibitions chronicle pre-Hispanic culture, colonial expansion, and missionary activities in the Republic. Jesuit imagery dominates the monastery's halls—St. Ignatius busts out all over the place, and St. Francis Xavier is only slightly less ubiquitous. Gregorian chants echo faintly throughout the halls, fitting the mood perfectly. Don't miss the concealed entrance to the upper floor near the exit; the hall contains more artifacts, and the balcony provides a great view of the surrounding area. Delight in the monastery's sweet-smelling orchard, criss-crossed by cobblestone paths. The high point of it all is the lavishly ornate Churrigueresque **Iglesia de San Francisco Javier** with the **Capilla de la Virgen de Loreto** as well as the astounding **Camarín de la Virgen** (altar room). Not a single millimeter is left unsculptured or uncolored here. The interplay between sunlight and gold leaf is perhaps the most wonderful relic of Baroque godliness and glitz.

Popocatépetl and Ixtaccíhuatl

Overlooking Morelos and Puebla are two snow-capped volcanoes veiled in Aztec mythology, **Popocatépetl** (5452m) and **Ixtaccíhuatl** (5282m), the second- and third-largest peaks in the country. These magnificent mountains are shrouded in indigenous mythology. Legend has it that the warrior Popocatépetl ("Smoking Mountain" in Náhuatl) loved Ixtaccíhuatl ("Sleeping Woman"), the emperor's daughter. Once, when Popocatépetl went off to battle, Ixtaccíhuatl came to believe that he had been killed; she subsequently died of grief. When Popo (as he was known to friends) learned of his lover's death, he built the two great mountains. On the northern one he placed her body (which you can see by looking at Ixtaccíhuatl from afar, with a little imagination), and on the southern one he stood vigil with a torch. Locals pay their respects to the supine, death-pale Ixtaccíhuatl on the mountain's snowy summit. The passage between the two is called *Paso de Cortés* because it is the route the Spanish conqueror took to the valley of Tenochtitlán.

From Mexico City's TAPO bus station, several bus lines go to **Amecameca,** the best jumping-off point for Ixta. **Volcanos** has the most frequent service (1½hr., every 30min. 5:30am-10pm, 12 pesos). **Taxis** located in front of Hotel San Carlos on the plaza can take you to the La Joya trailhead, and they'll charge you an arm and a leg for it. Expect to pay about 300 pesos for a round-trip fare including waiting time while you hike. A one-way trip runs 130 pesos, but no return taxi is guaranteed, and public transportation is not available. If you decide to visit Ixta via **San Rafael,** catch a *pesero* from **Tlalmanalco** (5am-7pm, 2 pesos) and get off in front of **La Fábrica,** a printing press. From there, another *pesero* (3 pesos) will take you to the San Rafael trailhead. To return to Mexico City, hop onto a **Volcano** bus or any bus labeled **Metro San Lázaro.** They stop along the plaza in Amecameca or on the road labeled "Mexico" in Tlalmanalco (daily every 30min. 6am-8pm).

From Cuernavaca, you'll want to take Estrella Roja to **Cuautla,** then walk to the Cristóbal Colón bus station (go right on Ing. Mongoy as you exit the station, walk one block and turn left on 5 de Mayo; the station is half a block ahead on your left), and catch a Volcanos bus to Amecameca (1hr., every 15min. 5am-7pm, 8 pesos). Buses return to Cuernavaca from Cuautla (1½hr., every 15min. 5am-7pm, 14 pesos).

Due to its increasingly active status, Popocatépetl has been closed to hikers since 1994. Be glad—in June 1997, it spat out enough volcanic ash to reach Mexico City. Parts of Ixtaccíhuatl can be explored on easy daytrips, but to reach the peak you'll need to be a seriously seasoned backpacker or else travel with a tour group. Signs pointing to *Rutas de Evacuación* (escape routes) in all nearby towns remind of the omnipresent danger.

The Federación Mexicana de Alpinismo, all Mexican officials, and *Let's Go* strongly recommend against making even a daytrip when the **Socorro Alpino (Alpine Assistance**; tel. 531 14 01) is not nearby. Popo is still active and let loose a belch of ashes as recently as July 1997; no season is free from rapid meteorological change. Always bring both warm clothes and raingear. By taking all the right precautions, you can have a superb adventure hiking the volcano. The Socorro Alpino is at the Paraje la Joya trailhead every weekend to provide guidance and ensure safety. Although Ixta is most easily reached from San Rafael via Tlalmanalco, a safe hike is well worth the extra pesos it takes to get to La Joya. You can make arrangements with Socorro Alpino from Mexico City or just show up Saturday or Sunday. If you are planning a longer or non-weekend trip, be certain to register with the Socorro Alpino before you go. Should you have an accident or **medical emergency** in the mountains, do your best to reach Danton Valle Negrete, Socorro Alpino's medical director in Mexico City (tel. 740 67 82; beeper 227 79 79, code 553 17 73).

MORELOS

Cuernavaca

No matter how you look at it, Cuernavaca is a blast. If you're heading into town, you'd better put on your party shoes and pool your pesos, because this once-mellow colonial town is now a chic weekend getaway and expat hotspot. The capital of Morelos, Cuernavaca (pop. 2 million) has long been seen as the quintessential colonial city, and it has earned the nickname "City of Eternal Spring" for its temperature, which hovers around 20°C year-round. Situated in an enviable place in the hills and strewn with classic colonial architecture and serpentine streets, Cuernavaca has more going for it than just climate. A victim of its own popularity, the city has become more noisy and industrialized in the past 10 years, and chaos, commotion, and construction dominate its ambience. For such a center of movement, however, Cuernavaca still has plenty of shady places to relax, grab a beer, and meditate.

Before there were gringos here, or even Mexicans, there were Aztecs. The valley was first populated by the Tlahuica, an Aztec tribe; the city that grew up in the valley was called Cuauhnahuac (Place on the Outskirts of the Grove). Mexico's *criollo* elite transformed the city into their private summer camp, and the name was corrupted into the Spanish quasi-homonym Cuernavaca. As word spread of the allure of Eternal Spring, Cuernavaca became a magnet for famous visitors like Cortés, García Marquez, Muhammad Ali, and the Shah of Iran; magnificent haciendas with vined fences too high for peeking began to radiate from the *zócalo.* Lately, the city's center of gravity has shifted away from the famous and toward the rich—wealthy Mexicans flock to Cuernavaca, and the city functions as a springtime playground for upper-class Mexico City residents fleeing bigger-city hassles. Unsurprisingly, this surge has been accompanied by equal, if not greater, swarms of foreigners (both tourists and residents), and innumerable foreign-language schools now draw them in by the bushel.

While penny-pinchers might snarl at Cuernavaca's cost of living, there's a reason people can't stay away—bars and clubs throb with nightly excitement, scores of fine restaurants pepper the streets, and an entire gringo scene has emerged. The city is hip, young, international, and full of art, culture, and Spanish instruction.

ORIENTATION

Route 95 from Mexico City intersects many of Cuernavaca's main avenues. To get to the city center, exit onto **Domingo Díaz** if coming from Mexico City, or **Emiliano Zapata,** which splits into the northbound **José María Morelos** and the southbound **Avenida Obregón.** Morelos serves as the principal access road, running straight through the center of town. **Benito Juárez** is the main north-south thoroughfare east of the *zócalo.* Near the *centro,* Domingo Diez merges with **Cuauhtémoc** off the México-Acapulco expressway to become **Plan de Ayala,** which turns east to become the principal east-west axis in town. Ayala later rejoins the expressway.

Two plazas together make up Cuernavaca's *zócalo.* **Plaza de la Constitución,** the main square, is a few blocks east of Morelos via Hidalgo, at the intersection of Guerrero, Salazar, Juárez, and Hidalgo. Diagonally opposite the *zócalo*'s northwest corner is the smaller **Jardín Juárez.** Several blocks east of the *zócalo* is the market area, municipal bus center, and gathering place for locals. Cuernavaca is not an easy city to navigate—expect irregularities, random turns, and sudden name changes, especially near the plaza. Even and odd numbers usually stay on different sides of the street but, because of two different numbering systems, buildings opposite each other may have addresses several hundred numbers apart. As if this isn't headache enough, by some strange governmental decree, the official address system was changed. On Morelos and nearby streets, it's not uncommon to see two addresses on each building. "400/antes 17" means that the old address was 17 and the new "official" one is 400.

To reach the *centro* from the **Flecha Roja bus station,** take a right at the exit and head south on Morelos. Turn left onto Rayón, Hidalgo, or any nearby cross-street. If

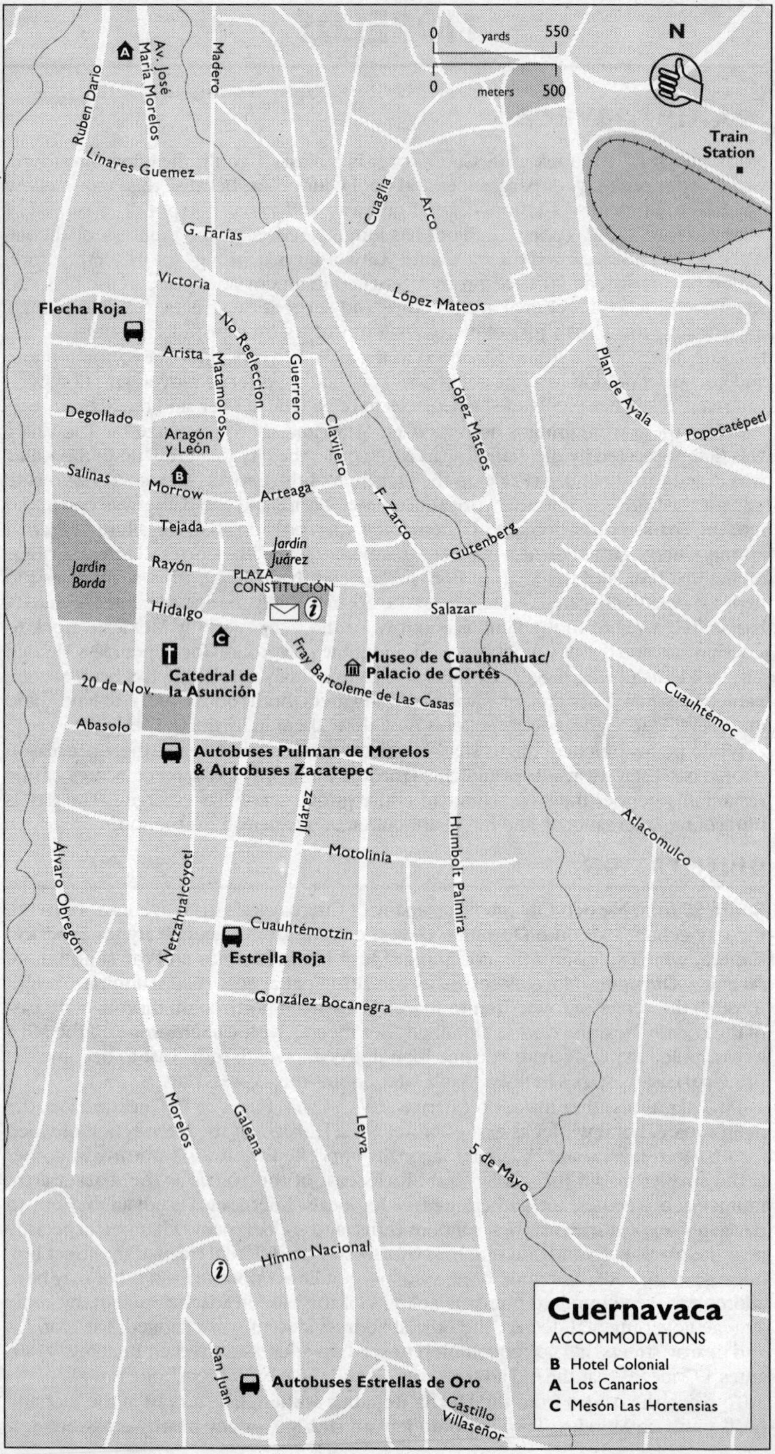

Cuernavaca
ACCOMMODATIONS
B Hotel Colonial
A Los Canarios
C Mesón Las Hortensias
0 yards 550
0 meters 500
N
Train Station
Ruben Dario
Av. José Maria Morelos
Madero
Linares Guemez
G. Farías
Cuaglia
Arco
Victoria
López Mateos
Flecha Roja
Arista
No Reeleccion
Matamoros y
Guerrero
Plan de Ayala
Popocatépetl
Degollado
Aragón y León
Clavijero
Salinas
Morrow
Arteaga
F. Zarco
Tejada
Jardín Juárez
Gutenberg
Jardín Borda
Rayón
PLAZA CONSTITUCIÓN
Hidalgo
Salazar
Fray Bartoleme de Las Casas
Museo de Cuauhnáhuac/ Palacio de Cortés
Catedral de la Asunción
20 de Nov.
Cuauhtémoc
Abasolo
Autobuses Pullman de Morelos & Autobuses Zacatepec
Juárez
Atlacomulco
Humbolt Palmira
Motolinía
Álvaro Obregón
Netzahualcóyotl
Cuauhtémotzin
Estrella Roja
González Bocanegra
Morelos
Galeana
Leyva
5 de Mayo
Himno Nacional
San Juan
Autobuses Estrellas de Oro
Castillo Villaseñor

you arrive via **Pullman de Morelos** (make sure it's **terminal #1, Terminal del Centro;** if it's not, ask the bus driver to take you there), head straight uphill on Netzahualcóyotl to Hidalgo; most major sights can be accessed from there. Those arriving via **Estrella de Oro** should cross the street and flag down any northbound minibus on Morelos (2.40 pesos)—they all run past the center of town.

Frequent local buses (2.40-3.50 pesos) called **rutas** run up and down Morelos; the *colonia* the bus is heading for is painted on the windshield. Taxis will go almost anywhere in the city for 12-20 pesos. After dark, because of Cuernavaca's active and spread-out nightlife, cabs charge 20-25% more. In any case, set prices before hopping in.

PRACTICAL INFORMATION

Transportation

Buses: Flecha Roja, Morelos 503 (tel. 12 81 90 or 12 26 26), 4 long blocks north of Jardín Borda. First-class service to Acapulco (4½hr., 8 and 10am, 121 pesos), Grutas de Cacahuamilpa (3½hr., every 2hr. 6am-4pm, 21 pesos), Guadalajara (9hr., 6 and 10pm, 299 pesos), Mexico City (1¼hr., every 30min. 5:30am-9pm, 29 pesos), and Taxco (1¾hr., every hr. 8am-8:30pm, 25 pesos). The **Tres Estrellas del Centro** desk in the same building offers local service to Chalma (2¼hr., 7:15am and 9:15am, 25 pesos), Santa Marta (1hr., every 30min. 5am-7:30am, 12 pesos), Santiago (1¾hr., every 30min. 5am-7:30pm, 18 pesos), and Toluca (2½hr., every 30min. 5am-8pm, 25 pesos). The station has 24hr. **luggage storage** (1.50-5 pesos per hr.; open 7am-10pm) and long-distance phones. Open daily 6:30am-10pm. **México-Zacatepec (LASSER)/Pullman de Morelos,** Netzahualcóyotl 106 (tel. 14 36 50) at Abasolo, 2 blocks south of the *zócalo.* To: Mexico City (1¼hr., every 15min. 5:45am-7pm and 7:30-9:30pm, 29 pesos), Zacatepec (1hr., every 30min. 6am-9:30pm, 10 pesos), and small cities throughout Morelos. **Estrella de Oro** (tel. 12 30 55), on Morelos Sur at Las Palmas Circle, 10 blocks south of the intersection of Reforma and Hidalgo. First-class service to Acapulco (4hr., 7 per day 7:15am-10:30pm, 120 pesos), Chilpancingo (2¾hr., 8:20pm, 60 pesos; luxury service 2½hr., 5 per day 9am-7:45pm, 70 pesos), Iguala (2hr., 2 and 3:45pm, 25 pesos), Ixtapa/Zihuatanejo (8hr., 8:20 and 10:10pm, 175 pesos), Mexico City (1½hr., 6 per day 7:30am-9pm, 28 pesos), and Taxco (1½hr., 9:10am and 9:10pm, 25 pesos). **Estrella Roja,** Galeana 401 (tel. 12 88 22), at Cuauhtémotzin, 7 blocks south of the *zócalo.* First-class service to Cuautla (1hr., every 10min. 5am-10pm, 10 pesos) and Puebla (3hr., every hr. 4am-7pm, 35 pesos). 2nd-class **Estrella Roja** and **Ometochtli** (tel. 5 07 44 or 18 09 60), on López Mateos at the south end of the *mercado.* Buses load in the parking lot across the highway and run to Tepoztlán (40min., every 15min. 5:45am-10pm, 8 pesos).

Tourist and Financial Services

Tourist Offices: State Office, Morelos Sur 187/antes 802 (tel. 14 38 72), a 15min. walk south from Hidalgo and Morelos. A moderately helpful staff doles out info about language schools and study options. Open M-F 9am-9pm, Sa-Su 10am-6pm. The informal white **info booth** on the north side of the cathedral also has brochures. Open daily 7am-7pm.

Currency Exchange: Try **Banca Serfín** (tel. 14 08 88), at the northwest corner of Jardín Juárez. **ATM.** Currency exchange M-F 9am-5pm. **Gold and Silver,** Morrow 9 (tel./fax 10 00 34) at Comonfort, is one of the many *casas de cambio* that line Morrow and offer good exchange rates. Open daily 9am-7pm.

American Express: Marín Agencia de Viajes (tel. 14 22 66), in Las Plazas Shopping mall on the *zócalo.* Holds mail and provides travel services. Open M-F 9am-2pm and 4-6pm, Sa 10am-1pm.

Local Services

Supermarket: Superama (tel. 12 81 20) at Morelos, just behind Helados Holanda, north of the cathedral and south of the Flecha Roja bus station. Huge grocery and **pharmacy.** Open daily 7am-midnight. The **market** on Blvd. Alfonso López Mateos sells excellent produce. Head east on Degollado, up the pedestrian bridge, and past the vendor stands.

Laundromat: Lavandería Obregón (tel. 12 94 98), on Obregón and Salinas. Head down Morelos past the *centro* and make a left on Salinas—the laundromat is at the bottom of the hill to your left. 6 pesos per kilo. Open M-F 9am-7pm, Sa 9am-2pm.

Emergency and Communications

Emergency: Dial 06.

Police: Emiliano Zapata 803 (tel. 17 11 15 or 17 10 00). Take Morelos north until it becomes Zapata; it's a bit farther up on the left. For something more heavy-duty, call the **Policía Judicial** (tel. 17 17 19).

Red Cross: (tel. 15 05 51 or 15 35 55), Ixtaccíhuatl at Río Panuco.

Pharmacy: Farmacia del Ahorro, Hidalgo 7 at Galeana, has English-speaking staff and a large selection. Open daily 7am-10:45pm.

Medical Assistance: Centro Quirúrgico, Juárez 507B (tel. 14 23 38). A pricey doctor for every ailment. No English spoken. Free help at **IMSS** (tel. 15 50 00).

Hospital: Hospital Civil Domingo Diez (tel. 11 22 10), in the Colonia de Empleado. Some English spoken.

Fax: Telecomm, Plaza de la Constitución 3 (tel. 14 31 81; fax 18 00 77), to the right of the post office. **Telegrams** and fax M-F 8am-7pm, Sa 9am-5pm, Su 9am-noon.

Internet Access: Sports and Internet Café, Morelos Sur 178 (tel. 12 16 56). From the Jardín Borda, turn left on Morelos and walk a few blocks—the cafe is on your left, across from a huge supermarket. 20 pesos per 30min. for email and the Web.

Post Office: Plaza de la Constitución 3 (tel. 12 43 79), on the southwest corner of the *zócalo*. Open M-F 8am-7pm, Sa 9am-1pm.

Postal Code: 62001.

Telephones: LADATELs are easy to find around the *zócalo*, along Morelos Sur, and in the bus stations. For a good, old-fashioned **caseta,** there's **Telcom,** Salazar 8, on the eastern edge of the *zócalo*. Open M-F 8am-8pm, Sa 9am-1pm.

Phone Code: 73.

ACCOMMODATIONS

Although Cuernavaca's status as an upper-class getaway does not necessarily affect one's peaceful meanderings through town, it does reveal itself in the hotel department. Simply put, rooms are chronically overpriced. The cloud has a silver lining, though—even the barest of hotels is often outfitted with a swimming pool or a lush courtyard. And if you don't mind some friendly old prostitutes standing in doorways and shady transactions, there are some extremely inexpensive *casas de huéspedes* on Aragón y León between Matamoros and Morelos. Just be sure they're clean.

For an extended stay (a couple of weeks or more), it's possible to lodge with a local family through one of the city's Spanish language schools. Students choose from a list of families willing to provide room, board, and language practice. **Cuauhnahuac,** Morelos Sur 123/antes 1414 (tel. 12 36 73), is especially willing to lend their family list to backpacking visitors who wish to spend time with *cuernavaquenses.* Sharing a room with a student costs US$18 per day for room and board; for a private single, you pay US$25 (contact José Camacho at Cuauhnahuac). Also try the bilingual language school, **Experiencia,** Leyva 200 (tel. 12 65 79), in Colonia Las Palmas.

Villa Calmecac, Zacatecas 114 (tel. 13 21 46; email meliton@mail.giga.com), in Col. Buenavista. From the *centro*, hop on a Ruta 1, 3 or 12 bus (2.40 pesos) and head north up Morelos/Zapata. Get off at the statue of Zapata (known as *Glorieta a Zapata*) and continue in the same direction, taking your first right on Zacatecas. Don't worry—it's worth the trip. Billing itself as an "ecotourist hostel," this unbelievable place offers lodging as well as numerous opportunities to bicycle, kayak, and generally participate in the great outdoors. With vegetable gardens, an art gallery, and ultra high-tech recycling and waste-management disposal, it's an earth-lover's dream. Facilities are new and well-maintained. Squeaky-clean communal baths. Dorms 100 pesos, 110 pesos with breakfast; private doubles, with breakfast 210 pesos. 10% discount with HI or ISIC. Reception open 8am-8pm; call before arrival.

Hotel Colonial, Aragón y León 19 (tel. 18 64 14), uphill and west of Matamoros. Despite the presence of nearby sketchy "hotels," this one is a gem. Pretty orange colonial home with a relaxing central courtyard and hospitable staff. Green-and-brown rooms enlivened by tiled floors and spotless bathrooms. Some of the singles even have cool bunk-bed-like fixtures. Singles 120 pesos, with TV 150 pesos; doubles 140 pesos, with TV 160 pesos.

Los Canarios, Morelos 369/antes 713 (tel. 13 00 00), 5 long blocks north of the *centro* (not to be confused with the restaurant "El Canario" a few doors before). Although some *cuernavaquenses* say this motor lodge is *de paso* (past its prime), it still groans merrily with groovy 50s decor and furnishings. Comfy, colorful rooms provide the basics, and 2 swimming pools and a restaurant complement your stay. All this, plus great prices, brings vacationing Mexican families in. Singles 75 pesos; doubles 145 pesos. 15% student discount, except during high season and festivals.

Mesón Las Hortensias, Hidalgo 13 Col. Centro (tel. 18 52 65), right near the Catedrál, across the street from the plaza. The key word is location. Step outside and you're in the middle of everything. One can't complain about the clean green rooms and gorgeous outdoor patio (also green). Charge your way into continual cleanliness but hurry—grab one of the 23 rooms before they're gone. Singles 128 pesos; 1-bed doubles 146 pesos; 2-bed doubles 167 pesos.

These Ain't the Sunday Funnies

As you are waiting for the bus, you notice that the teenage boys standing next to you are completely absorbed in the small comic books in their hands. Your curiosity wins out and you take a closer look—they're reading pocket-sized comic books with pictures of scantily clad couples doing things you thought couldn't be done by two-dimensional characters. Surprised, but amused, you shrug it off (after all, boys will be boys), and turn away. Suddenly you spot an elderly woman reading the comics. Now you're getting worried.

Don't worry, you haven't entered the twilight zone. These little comics (called *revistas*) are all the rage in Mexico. Each book graphically weaves tales of romance, passion, and lust, leaving little to the imagination. You'll find someone selling them and someone reading them on virtually every street corner and at every bus stop in Mexico. Although they may seem a little strange at first glance, the comics are harmless and often even amusing. Check one out—if nothing else, they're bound to teach you some new slang.

FOOD

Overflowing with tourists, Cuernavaca has more than its share of budget eateries (as well as all major U.S. fast food chains if you're truly desperate). For your main meal, take advantage of one of the excellent restaurants around the plaza. Head up the side streets (try Aragón y León) or larger thoroughfares Galeana and Juárez for lighter, less expensive fare. In the market, a *comida corrida* costs about 13-15 pesos *con refresco.* Along Guerrero, north of the plaza, street vendors sell mangoes, *piñas* (pineapples), and *elotes* (corn on the cob). The health drinks sold at the Eiffel kiosk in the Jardín Juárez include everything from the standard fruit and milk *licuados* to a spinach concoction not even Popeye could love (6-12 pesos).

Restaurante Los Arcos, Jardín de Los Héroes 4 (tel. 12 44 86), on the south side of the *zócalo.* Flanked by lush plants and a bubbling fountain, mosaic-inlaid outdoor tables are ideal for watching the day slip by. Musicians of varying ages and abilities serenade the clientele. *Comida corrida* 35 pesos, breakfast 18-28 pesos, *antojitos* 18-25 pesos. Open daily 7am-midnight.

Marco Polo Pizzería, Hidalgo 30 (tel. 12 34 84), on the 2nd floor. After he helped facilitate the Italy-China spaghetti trade, this robust young explorer rested his weary legs and smiled. He liked the view of the mountains and the cathedral. More importantly, he liked the delicious puffy pizzas that come in 4 sizes (starting at 24 pesos). *Cuernavaquenses* have followed in Marco's footsteps; everyone who's anyone eats here. Tempt your palate with the *tocino y cebolla* (bacon and onion) pizza (31 pesos). Open M-Th 1:30-10:30pm, F-Sa 1:30pm-midnight, Su 1:30-10pm.

Gin Gen, Rayón 13 (tel. 18 60 46), 2½ blocks west of the Jardín Borda at Morelos. Fans, lanterns, and pictures of Chinese pop stars adorn the walls. From 1-5pm, the super-filling *guisados del día* provide soup, rice, 2 entrees, and dessert for only 35 pesos. Great tofu and vegetarian options too (17-29 pesos). Open M-Sa 9am-9pm, Su 9am-6pm.

Serie de Taco, Rayón 28 (tel. 12 39 75). Not the most aesthetically pleasing of restaurants, but you can't beat the price. Gaze at cloth flowers as you devour the scrumptious *menú del día* (14 pesos). Breakfast 13 pesos. Open M-Sa 8am-8pm.

SIGHTS

Cuernavaca's popularity has little to do with scintillating sights, but there is a lot to see besides the city's sunglasses-clad elite sipping iced tea and speaking in newly acquired Spanish or English (although that too can be exciting).

For starters, the city's main square, the **Plaza de la Constitución,** is lovely (though it's often noisy as well). Extending east from the Palacio de Gobierno, the plaza is not content to just hold the entire Morelos state bureaucracy. It is truly the heart and soul of its own city as well, shaded by trees colored by fiery red *flamboyanes* (royal poinciana) and speckled with cafes and wrought-iron benches. Food vendors and *mariachis* engage in a Darwinian struggle for pesos. A kiosk designed by Gustave Eiffel (bearing no resemblance to its more famous Parisian sibling) and commissioned by Cuernavaca's Viennese community stands in the **Jardín Juárez,** at the northwest corner of the Pl. de la Constitución, north of the Palacio de Gobierno. Thursdays and Sundays at 6pm, a merry but mediocre local band commandeers the kiosk and belts out polkas, classical music, and Mexican country music. The kiosk houses a multitude of nutritionally sound fruit drink stands. Those with adventurous tastebuds should try "La Bomba," a concoction of various fruits, cereals, chocolate, and eggs (12 pesos).

Museo Cuauhnahuac (Palacio de Cortés)

Southeast corner of the Plaza de la Constitución, east of Benito Juárez. ***Museum open*** *Tu-Su 10am-5pm.* ***Admission*** *14 pesos; free on Sundays and for students with ID.*

The Palacio de Cortés stands as a stately reminder of the city's grim history—Cortés set Cuernavaca on fire in 1521, then built this two-story fortress from the remains of local buildings, situating the fortress atop a sacred pyramid. It was completed in 1524 when Cortés craved another conquest (and left to raise hell in Honduras); the building functioned as a prison in the 18th century and as the Palacio de Gobierno during the dictatorship of Porfirio Díaz.

A grant from the former British ambassador to Mexico (none other than Charles Lindbergh's father-in-law) transformed the Palacio de Cortés into the Museo Cuauhnahuac. On the first floor of the museum, archaeological and anthropological exhibits explore pre-Hispanic cultures. One of the more interesting displays is the collection of indigenous drawings and depictions of the Spanish arrival, in which valiant eagle and tiger warriors in full regalia battle the invaders. Second-floor exhibits on the Conquest and Mexican history include the **first public clock ever to toll in Mesoamerica.** The ubiquitous and astonishing Diego Rivera has yet another mural/masterpiece on the western balcony of the second floor. The mural, commissioned by then-U.S. ambassador to Mexico Dwight D. Morrow as a gift to the people of Cuernavaca, depicts Mexico's history from the Conquest until the Revolution of 1910, proceeding chronologically from right to left. If you're not up on your Mexican history, don't worry—a chart underneath the mural explains it all.

Other Sights

Black soot has darkened the tall walls and towers of the **Catedral de la Asunción,** three blocks down Hidalgo from the *zócalo,* at Morelos. *(Open daily 7am-2pm and 4-8pm.)* Although it's one of the oldest churches in the Americas (construction began in 1525), it was only 20 years ago that the removal of the aisle altars revealed some fabulous Japanese frescoes depicting the persecution and martyrdom of Christian missionaries in Sokori, Japan. Historians speculate that these startling frescoes were painted in the early 17th century by a converted Japanese artist who had settled in Cuernavaca. But ultimately, the simple altar makes this church special (and very unusual in a country of gold and gilded centerpieces). Here, seven plain baskets holding candles hang within a faceless box.

The **Jardín Borda** (tel. 12 92 37), once the site of glamorous soirees during the French occupation of Mexico, is now a Sunday gathering spot for young couples and families on picnics. *(Open Tu-Su 10am-5:30pm. Admission 10 pesos; students, teachers, and children 5 pesos; free on Sundays.)* The stone entrance is on Morelos, across from the cathedral. In 1783, the priest Manuel de la Borda built a garden of magnificent pools and fountains and, in 1864, Emperor Maximilian and his wife Carlota established a summer residence here. Today, it takes a vivid imagination to recognize the park's faded splendor amid the sometimes non-functional fountains and cracked sidewalks. Unlike the fountains and sidewalks, the flora—mango trees, tropical ferns, ornamental plants, and giant palm trees—have flourished through the years, accounting for the garden's heavy, overripe smell. Its modern amenities—an art collection near the entrance, a small theater, and a museum near Emperor Max's old summer home—make this more than just a garden past its prime. Patchwork **rowboats** are available for rent (10 pesos for 15min., 15 pesos for 30min., 20 pesos for 1hr.).

The **Pyramid of Teopanzolco** is on a glistening green lawn at the center of a public park near the southern end of Teopanzolco, southeast of the market on Guerrero. *(Open daily 9am-6pm. Admission 14 pesos, free Su and festivals.)* To get to the site from the marketplace or along Morelos, take a taxi (12 pesos) or hop on local bus #10 at the corner of Degollado and No Reelección (2.40 pesos) and ask the driver to let you off at the *pirámide.* If you're in the mood to break in walking shoes, head north along Morelos (the cathedral will be on your left), turn right on Pericón, and go right on Río Balsas to Teopanzolco. Strangely deserted and unkempt, the pyramid consists of two pyramids, one within the other. The first stairway leads to a ledge, at the bottom of which a second stairway, belonging to the second pyramid, begins. An eerie partial staircase suggests that the new pyramid was unfinished when Cortés arrived.

ENTERTAINMENT AND SEASONAL EVENTS

Cuernavaca's popularity as a vacation spot fuels a fairly glitzy nightlife, and the city's *norteamericano* expatriates, now over 20,000 strong, as well as its plethora of soon-to-be bilingual students from the U.S., lend a north-of-the-border feel to many festivities. Bars in Cuernavaca are modern and highly commercialized, and most clubgoers are dressed to the hilt and heedless of high cover charges. If you're up to it, a night on the town here promises a sleek, sophisticated time. Several of the clubs have live nightly entertainment. Around the *zócalo,* many of the clubs cater to tourists; some have no cover charge but expect patrons to buy drinks.

Discos are typically open from 9 or 10pm to 5am on Friday and Saturday. To deter the fistfights and *broncas* (brawls) that used to plague Cuernavaca's clubs, some now officially admit only male-female couples and require reservations; most, however, do not enforce these rules. The more popular discos in town are not on the *zócalo* but in different *colonias.* Most lie beyond walking distance (especially at night) and are best reached by *rutas* or a taxi after 9pm. Most *rutas* stop running around 10:30pm, and Cuernavaca is nationally notorious for nightly rains. During the wet season (May-Nov.), it rains at least an-hour-and-a-half during the late afternoon or evening; cabs are your best bet. All the spots listed are familiar to cab drivers. Only Angel Extermidar, La Strada, and Kaova are within walking distance of the *zócalo.* Sometimes lucky students from local language schools get free passes and avoid cover charges.

Zúmbale, Chapultepec 13A (tel. 22 53 43 or 22 53 44), next to Ta'izz. This 4-story salsa club is unbelievable—an indoor waterfall, amazing live music, and some of the best Latin dancing around (tropical, salsa, rumba, merengue)—watch practiced pelvises grind. Don't worry, though—the friendly atmosphere (and copious bar service) encourages gringos of all ages to give it a go. Great fun. No cover Thursday. Open bar 9-10pm. Cover 80 pesos F-Sa for men, women free. Beer 20 pesos, national drinks 30 pesos and up. Open Th 9pm-4:30am, F-Sa 9pm-5am.

Angel Extermidar, on the corner of Morelos and Rayón, 2nd fl. Join a 20- to 30-something crowd of regulars in this simply decorated yet classy establishment. Friendly staff serves beer (10 pesos) and cocktails (12-30 pesos) until everyone begins to dance. Open Tu-Su 6pm-2am.

La Casa del Dictador, Jacarandas 4 (tel. 17 31 86), on the corner of Zapata in Col. Buenavista. Raging dance music welcomes a strictly gay and lesbian clientele. Cover 30 pesos. Beer 15 pesos. Open F-Sa 10pm-4am.

La Strada, Salazar #38 (tel: 18 60 85). Pass right by the pricey Italian restaurant and head upstairs to relax and socialize with a more mature clientele as you listen to the live band play one jazz tune after another. Wine aficionados will delight in the super-stocked wine cellar (glasses 18 pesos and up). Beer 12 pesos, live music on Thursdays and Fridays. Open M-Sa 7pm-3am.

Barbazul, Prado 10 (tel. 13 19 76). This club with long lines out the door would make Bluebeard shake his "booty." Good lighting and continually hip. A staple of Cuernavacan nightlife, popular with the early-20s, hard-hitting techno crowd. Drinks 16 pesos and up. Cover on Saturday 50 pesos for men, women free. Open W and F-Sa 10pm-late.

Kaova, Av. Morelos Sur 241 (tel. 18 43 80), 3 blocks south of the cathedral. Rock-dance hybrid. Starts off mellow and turns into a full-fledged dance party later. Not many tourists here—senior citizens and college kids alike hit the small dance pit as waiters clad in bowties and suspenders run around busily. You, however, can come as bare as you dare. 50 peso cover F and Sa with bar tab up to 50 pesos on Friday only. 2 for 1 beers W 10-11pm. Beer 18 pesos. National drinks 25 pesos. Open W-Sa 9pm-late.

If you're in the mood for something more mellow, catch a flick for 10-12 pesos. Try **Cinema Las Plazas** (tel. 14 07 93), downtown, across from the Jardín Juárez, screening imports and high-quality Mexican films. On Saturday and Sunday, the **market** in the Jardín Juárez specializes in silver jewelry; don't be afraid to bargain. The **Feria de la Primavera** (Festival of Spring) brings parades and costumes for 10 days a year at the vernal equinox (March 21-22).

■ Near Cuernavaca: Xochicalco

Ceremonial center, fortress, and trading post rolled into one, **Xochicalco** (ho-chee-CAL-co; Place of the House of Flowers in Náhautl) is the most impressive archaeological site in the state of Morelos, worth the trip if only for the awesome vistas. *(Museum and site open daily 10am-5pm. Admission 20 pesos, free for children, students, and on Sunday.)* Although it was built around 200 BC and lasted to around AD 1100, Xochicalco had its peak between AD 60 and AD 900, just as the civilization at Teotihuacán was dwindling. Xochicalco's ruins and central location explain the similarities in ruins as far apart as Teotihuacán and Tula. Besides being a center of Toltec culture, it is also thought that Xochicalco was a Maya outpost, thus explaining its influence on architecture as far south as Central America. Archaeologists speculate that the site may even be the mythical city of **Tamoanchan,** the place where wise men of different cultures, including Maya and Zapotec sages, came to begin the cult of the new god Quetzalcóatl, as well as to synchronize civil and religious calendars.

ARCHAEOLOGICAL SITE OF XOCHICALCO

On the road right before the ruins, a stunning modern sight appears—the speckled green **Museo del Sitio de Xochicalco.** This museum was designed to mimic the ruins, greenery, and lush flora that pervades the area. It succeeds smashingly; inaugurated in April 1996, the museum's beautiful marble tiling and wall frescoes complement the site, and a gorgeous pyramidal motif is carried throughout the museum's skylights, tiling, and structure. Comprehensive exhibits on the site, invaluable brochures on the ruins (5 pesos), and the tickets allowing admission to the ruins make the museum a useful (and necessary) stop before climbing on to the site itself.

Guide to the Ruins

From the museum, a rocky path leads to the ruins. The ruins are best explored in a generally circular manner; start at the elevated plaza up to the left of the first patch of greenery. On the right side of the first plain, the **Pirámide de las Estelas** (Structure A) and the **Gran Pirámide** (Structure E) just south of it nearly dwarf the three smaller structures on the left. Remember, guards (when they're present) are strict about climbing in non-designated areas. Anyway, later on you can scale the back stairs and see the view. The Gran Pirámide forms the northern boundary of the **Plaza Central,** which can be reached by continuing straight (south) and taking the small slope down to the left. This area was most likely a trading center for the local and regional populations—many ancient roads converge here. Twin pyramids on the east and the west sides of the plaza, labeled **Structure C** and **Structure D,** were used in the worship of the sun, with one oriented toward the sunrise, the other toward the sunset. At the center of the plaza is a carved obelisk that bears two hieroglyphs related to the god Quetzalcóatl. Sadly, the coded inscriptions are faded and hard to see. Still, the lone obelisk is quite a sight—it looks like an alien outpost at the center of some old, obscene ritual. Apparently, priests plotted the sun's trajectory over the pyramids by tracing the obelisk's shadow.

The southwest corner of this plaza offers a great overhead view of the **Juego de Pelota** (ballcourt) below. To reach it, walk down the stone steps between Structures C and D. Straight ahead and off to the left lie unexcavated remnants of this sprawling city. Continue down the narrow rocky path directly to the right for the **ballcourt.** Many experts believe that this ballcourt was the earliest one built; ballcourts as far south as Guatemala show signs of the heavy influence (a.k.a. virtual plagiarism) of Xochicalco's. In fact, a statue found here bears a remarkable likeness to another found in Copán, Honduras, a remote Maya outpost. Xochicalco's widespread architectural influence is indicative of its once-great commercial and cultural exchange.

After heading back up the hill to the central plaza, make your way to the base of the **Gran Pirámide** (Structure E), atop which rest the remains of an even more ancient structure. Follow the path down to the left (west) and over to the stairway/portico section. This area was used to limit access to the main part of the city in case of invasion, a design ineffective in preventing Xochicalco from falling prey to a revolution.

Past the portico and up two sets of impressive stairways rebuilt in 1994, find the **Plaza Ceremonial,** which served as the main ceremonial center of the city. As you enter, the top of the Pirámide de las Estelas is accessible, enclosing a huge pit in the center that was the burial site for high priests and a place for ritual offerings. In the center of the plaza is the renowned **Pirámide de la Serpiente Emplumada** (Pyramid of the Plumed Serpent). Haphazardly reconstructed in 1910, it bears carved reliefs of Quetzalcóatl, the great feathered serpent who was a god-hero to a plethora of Indian groups, including the Toltecs and the Aztecs. QuetzalcóatlQuetzalcóatl's place in world myth and religion rivals that of Adam and Eve's salacious serpent.

On the rear (west) end of the plaza is the tremendous **Montículo 2,** the highest area of the site, and supposedly the spot where the rulers of Xochicalco lived. The eastern side was intended for daily activities, while the west end was exclusively ceremonial. Exit the Plaza Ceremonial on the north side and head west down the slope to the **Hall of the Polichrome Altar,** where a colored altar rests beneath an authentic reconstruction of the roofing used by the Toltecs. Farther down is a cistern used for water storage, a sauna used for pre-game initiation rites, and **Teotlachtli,** the northern ballcourt. Here, two massive rings of rock are attached in the middle, unlike most ballcourts in Mesoamerica, which have only one ring. Teams competed for the privilege of being sacrificed atop the Pyramid of Quetzalcóatl, a true honor and a sign of good sportsmanship. Nearby, the foundations of the **Calmecac,** the palace in which Toltec and Aztec priests underwent training and initiation, remain.

Continue west along the weed-ridden path, around the back of the base of Montículo 2 until you reach a large stone amalgamation. A small opening in the corner (with steps leading up) allows access to the stuccoed interior of the underground **Observatorio,** where ancient astronomers followed the cosmos. *(Observatory open 11am-4pm.)* On summer solstices, Aztec sages and stargazers peered through a shaft in the ceiling to trace the path of the sun; by doing so, they hoped to verify and adjust the Aztec calendar. A guide gives periodic presentations in Spanish as soon as a good-sized group has assembled.

Getting There: From Cuernavaca, **Flecha Roja** runs buses directly to Xochicalco (1 hr., every 2hr. 6am-4pm, 8 pesos). Alternatively, snag a bus to Miacatlán from the **Autos Pullman** station at Abasolo and Netzahualcóyotl, one block south of the cathedral (1 hr., 37 per day 5:30am-10pm, 11 pesos). Ask the driver to drop you off at the "Crucero de Xochicalco." **Taxis** wait at the *crucero* and, for 8 pesos, will take you to the site. Otherwise, the uphill walk to the site (4km) will take about an hour. Be prepared for the steep inclines and merciless sun. Bring a hat, a tank top, and some water. Catch a bus back at the *crucero* or hail a nearby taxi and ask to go to the *caseta* (4 pesos), a nearby bus stop. Buses go back to Cuernavaca every 30 minutes or so. Taxis sometimes sit at the site entrance, but it may be smart to ask a driver to pick you up at a specified time.

■ Near Cuernavaca: Tepoztlán

In northern Morelos, the quiet *pueblo* of Tepoztlán occupies one of the state's more scenic and impenetrable sites—towering cliffs form a natural fortress that allows entrance only from the south. Proceeding along Rte. 95D toward Tepoztlán, keep your eyes peeled for **Popocatépetl** and **Ixtaccíhuatl,** the two massive volcanoes that surge from the ground (seep. 432). The cobbled *indígena* village preserves a colonial feel despite the pool maintenance and satellite television stores. Some indigenous people still speak Náhuatl, and many of Tepoztlán's youth are learning to speak it, even in the town's schools. On Sundays, the *zócalo* comes alive with vibrant market activity. During the rest of the week, however, the town is quieter. Perched on a peak 360m above the village are the archaeological sites for which the town is famous. The thin air may leave you breathless and thirsty, so prepare accordingly.

The valley of Tepoztlán is charged with the myth, legend, and magic of ages gone by. It is thought that the god-hero of the Toltecs (and the Aztecs, and almost every other pre-Hispanic *indígena* group), Quetzalcóatl, was born here about 1200 years ago. Celebrations still take place every September 8, when the *pulque* flows and the dance floor fills in honor of Tepozécatl. *Los chinelos*—colorfully attired folk dancers—may invite you to join their traditional dance, *el salto.* Don't be shy; after pounding a couple of *pulques,* you'll be weeping cactus tears and dying to dance.

Tepoztlán's main draw is the **Pirámide del Tepozteco,** perched on the northern ridge of the cliffs that rise above one end of town, about 3km above the valley. *(Open daily 4am-5:30pm. Admission 14 pesos, free Su and for children under 13. Video cameras 30 pesos.)* Some say the pyramid was a Tlahuica observatory and defense post for the valley, while others swear it served as an Aztec sacrificial temple. The 10m structure has a porch inscribed with barely discernible Tlahuica glyphs. To reach the pyramid, follow Av. 5 de Mayo north out of town (passing the *zócalo* on your right) until you reach its end. The hour-long climb is steep and strenuous, but it's made bearable by the cooling shade of trees. If you intend to climb, equip yourself with appropriate footwear, water, and spirit. If you can't make it all the way up, don't worry—the view is spectacular from everywhere on the hill. Sunday excursions offer a fabulous people-watching experience; whole families, from newborns to great-grandfathers, don their Sunday best and hike up this holy hill. Don't be surprised to see an eight-year-old carrying an ice chest overtake you.

The **Museo de Arte Prehispánico** (more commonly known as the **Museo Carlos Pellicer;** tel. 5 10 98), at the rear of Capilla Asunción, holds a collection donated to the city by none other than the nationally renowned poet Carlos Pellicer. *(Open Tu-Su 10am-6pm. Admission 4 pesos.)* The impressive display includes masks, pottery pieces, and clay figures of Olmec, Zapotec, Maya, Totonac, and Aztec origin, as well as many objects from Teotihuacán.

Because of its natural beauty, vernal climate, and proximity to Mexico City, the area around Tepoztlán attracts an ever-growing population of wealthy *norteamericanos.*

While the town and surrounding area are still lovely, prices are incredibly steep. Tepoztlán lacks moderately priced anything—forget budget accommodations. Though expensive, your best bet is **Casa Iccemanyan,** Calle de Olvido 26 (tel. 5 08 99 or 5 00 96; fax 5 21 59), on the first cross street after the Pullman de Morelos station, all the way down the hill. This joint offers six bungalows for extended stays and gives travelers studying at neighboring language schools a chance to practice their skills with a welcoming Mexican family. Well-maintained and well-decorated rooms come with clean bathrooms and lots of privacy. Beautiful pool, lawn, and unlimited use of kitchen facilities offer additional perks. Call before you arrive. Tepozteco vistas are a plus. (Singles US$18, with 3 meals US$25; doubles US$25, with 3 meals US$35.) Budget restaurants are likewise a scarcity in popular Tepotzlan. If you are willing to splurge, grab a bite to eat in one of the many vegetarian-friendly international restaurants that line Av. 5 de Mayo. If not, head for the market or for **La Parilla de Tepotzlan,** Av. 5 de Mayo #6A (tel. 5 10 73). Don't be dissuaded by the tacky plastic tablecloths—the *menú del día* (24 pesos) is delicious. (Open daily 9am-8pm.)

Getting There: From Cuernavaca, **Ometochtli** buses leave from the market (40min., every 15min. 5:45am-10pm, 8 pesos). You can also take a *pesero* (5 pesos). If you arrive at the Ometochtli depot, follow the main road; it will curve to become Av. 5 de Mayo.

TLAXCALA

Tlaxcala

The approach to the capital of Mexico's smallest state is filled with vistas of cornfields, children riding on the backs of burros, and beautifully tiled churches. Although it might seem like things couldn't get any prettier, downtown Tlaxcala (tlax-KAH-la) exceeds all expectations. Carefully maintained buildings and well-tended flowerbeds make for a picture-perfect *zócalo.*

With a population of 50,000, Tlaxcala retains a small town charm and friendliness while drawing in weekenders looking to trade the noise and congestion of Puebla or Mexico City for the alluring cafes along Tlaxcala's *zócalo* and safe, tree-lined streets. Despite the fact that the city is ignored by most *norteamericanos,* the people of Tlaxcala have a long history of welcoming foreigners. Today, *tlaxcalteños* limit their violent urges to raising bulls for fights throughout Mexico. The city is also known for its magnificent colonial churches and its frequent regional fairs, which showcase artisans who weave *sarapes* or prepare dishes of maize. Also an ideal base from which to explore the archaeological sites of **Cacaxtla** and **Xochiténcatl,** Tlaxcala makes many other nearby colonial towns pale in comparison.

ORIENTATION

Most services can be found in and around **Plaza de la Constitución** (the *zócalo*), and **Plaza Xicoténcatl,** diagonally adjacent to it. You'll know you're there when you see the blue-and-white tiled dome of the orange **Parroquia de San José.** To get there from the bus station, exit through the glass doors to a swarm of idling *colectivos.* Those facing the right go to the downtown area, the market, and the hotel district on the northern edge of the city (2-3 pesos). To return to the bus station from the city center, take a "Central" *colectivo* from the market at 20 de Noviembre and Alonso Escalona, or flag one down behind San José at 20 de Noviembre and 1 de Mayo.

Facing the back of the church (the yellow side), the street behind you is **20 de Noviembre** and the street on the left is **Lardizábal.** Going around the church to the right will bring the entrance to the *zócalo* into view. The **Palacio de Gobierno** takes up the whole north side of the *zócalo* and will be on your left. At the end of the Palacio del Gobierno, at the corner of the *zócalo,* **Av. Benito Juárez** peels off to the left. After four blocks, Juárez veers right and becomes **Av. Guillermo Valle.** Several hotels

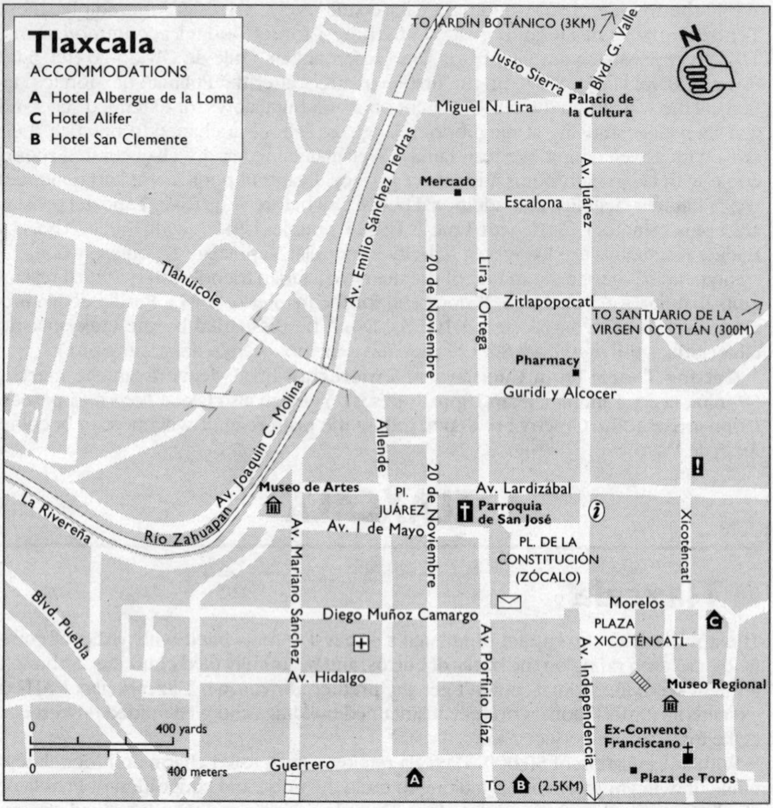

are on the northern edge of town, where Guillermo Valle angles to the right and becomes **Blvd. Revolución.** To get there, catch a "Santa Ana" *colectivo* at 20 de Noviembre, three blocks from the *zócalo,* behind San José (2-3 pesos); it's a 40-minute walk from the *zócalo.* It may be fairly safe to walk the streets at night in Tlaxcala, but as always, take precautions when walking along at night. If you do feel uncomfortable walking downtown after dark, hail one of the cabs at San José church.

PRACTICAL INFORMATION

Transportation

Buses: From the **Central Camionera, Autotransportes Tlaxcala** (tel. 2 02 17) runs to Mexico City (2hr., every 20min. 6am-8:30pm, 34 pesos) and Veracruz, stopping in Xalapa (6hr., 10:30am and 3:30pm, 37 and 58 pesos respectively). **Autotransportes México-Texcoco** has similar first-class service to Mexico City. **Flecha Azul** buses run to Puebla (45min., every 5min. 5:45am-10pm, 6 pesos).

Tourist and Financial Services

Tourist Office: Av. Benito Juárez 18 (tel. 2 00 27), at the intersection with Lardizábal, behind the Palacio de Gobierno. The office sponsors excellent and cheap tours of Tlaxcala and the surrounding area every Saturday and of Cacaxtla and Xochiténcatl every Sunday. The comprehensive tours leave at 10:30am from the Hotel Plaza San Francisco on the south side of the *zócalo* and are whirlwind adventures with a knowledgeable guide, all for 15 pesos. A gold mine of information from a friendly, English-speaking staff. Open M-F 9am-7pm, Sa-Su 10am-6pm.

Currency Exchange: Banamex, Plaza Xicoténcatl 8 (tel. 2 75 27 or 2 75 12) and **Banca Serfín,** Av. Independencia 4 (tel. 2 62 42), both in Plaza Xicoténcatl, have 24hr. **ATMs.** Open M-F 9am-2pm. There are also several banks on Av. Juárez past the tourist office. The **Centro de Cambio Tlaxcala** (tel. 290 85), Av. Independencia at the corner of Calle Guerrero, buys or sells dollars in cash, money orders, or traveler's checks. Open M-F 9am-4pm.

Local Services

Cultural Center: Palacio de la Cultura, Av. Benito Juárez 62 (tel. 2 60 69), 4 blocks from the *zócalo* at the corner of Av. Justo Sierra. Announces and sometimes stages concerts, exhibits, and performances all over town. Open daily 10am-6pm.

Markets: The entire street of **Alonso Escalona** teems with *mercado* activity. From San José, cross to Lira y Ortega and walk 3 blocks, keeping the church behind you. The vendors spill outside onto Sánchez Piedras on Saturdays. Open daily 8am-8pm. There are smaller markets beside the Parroquia de San Jose and on Saturdays in Plaza Xicoténcatl. **Gigante** is a behemoth of a supermarket on Blvd. Guillermo Valle, in the shopping center on the corner of Arévalo Vera. Open daily 8am-8pm.

Laundromat: Lavandería de Autoservicio Acuario, Alonso y Escalona No. 13-A (tel. 2 62 92). Go north from the *zócalo,* make an immediate left on Lardizábal, then take the first right on Lira y Ortega. Self-service 14 pesos, full service 15 pesos, 1hr. service with home delivery 30 pesos. Open M-Sa 9:30am-7:30pm.

Emergency and Communications

Police: (tel. 2 07 35) on Av. Lardizábal, 1 block past the tourist office, at the corner with Calle Xicoténcatl. Open daily 24hr.

Red Cross: Allende Nte. 48 (tel. 2 09 20 or 2 47 05). Go 2 blocks behind San José to Av. Ignacio Allende, then turn left and continue 1½ blocks past Muñoz Camargo. 24hr. walk-in emergency service. No English spoken.

Pharmacy: Farmacia Ocotlán, Av. Juárez No. 33 (tel. 2 04 50), on the corner of Guridi y Alcocer. Open daily 9am-7pm.

Hospital: Hospital General, Jardín de la Corregidora 1 (tel. 2 00 30 or 2 35 55), 4½ blocks from the *zócalo* down Av. Muñoz Camargo, past the post office. No English spoken. Open 24hr. **IMSS** (tel. 2 34 00 or 2 34 22), Blvd. Guillermo Valle across the street from the stadium. Take Av. Juárez from the *zócalo* until it turns into Blvd. G. Valle; the hospital is right after the Nestlé factory. Open 24hr.

Post Office: Plaza de la Constitución 20 (tel. 2 00 04), on the corner with Av. Muñoz Camargo. Open M-F 8am-8pm, Sa 9am-1pm.

Postal Code: 90000.

Fax: Telecomm, Porfirio Díaz 6 (tel. 2 55 87), behind the post office. Telegraph service as well. Open M-F 8am-6pm, Sa-Su 9am-noon.

Internet Access: Internet Café, Av. Independencia No. 21 (tel. 2 44 64), east of the Plaza Xicoténcatl, offers cheap services and a friendly staff, but no coffee. Programs include Microsoft Explorer and a temperamental version of telnet. 25 pesos per hour, 20 pesos per hour for students. Open M-Sa 9am-8:30pm.

Telephones: LADATELs under the arches along the *zócalo.* **Coin-operated phones** in front of and behind Parroquia de San José, northwest of the *zócalo.*

Phone Code: 246.

ACCOMMODATIONS

Finding budget accommodations in Tlaxcala can be disheartening at best and downright impossible at worst. As more urbanites from the D.F. and Puebla flock to Tlaxcala for weekend getaways, resort hotels spring up and prices rise across town. Most of the good budget hotels are now in the 100-150 peso range. Establishments are either downtown near most sights and services or in the hotel district on the city's northern edge and accessible via the "Santa Ana" *colectivo.* Be warned, however, that most hotels in the Santa Ana area are both more expensive and harder to get to.

Hotel Alifer, Morelos No. 11 (tel. 2 56 78; fax 2 30 62; email alifer@tlax.net.mx), is a pastel-colored hotel conveniently located about a 2min. walk from the *zócalo*. From the *zócalo,* take Av. Morelos past Plaza Xochiténcatl and up the hill until you reach the hotel on the right. The modern rooms are a tad expensive, but they feature wall-to-wall carpeting, 50+ channels of glorious cable TV, phone, and a full bath. The only drawback? The bells of the neighboring Ex-Convento Franciscano start ringing at a nightmarish 6am. Singles 130 pesos; doubles 150 pesos. Reservations recommended for weekend stays.

Hotel Albergue de la Loma, Calle Guerrero 58 (tel. 2 04 24), commands a breathtaking view of Tlaxcala from atop a hill on the city's southern side. To get there from the *zócalo,* walk past Parroquia de San Jose on Av. 1 de Mayo. Turn left on Av. Allende; the hotel is 3 blocks down on Calle Guerrero. The wooden stairs leading up to the hotel will be on your left. Rooms are large and comfortable with TV and phone. Ask for a room facing the city for an impressive view. A restaurant is next to the lobby. Singles 120 pesos; doubles 145 pesos. Reservations recommended for weekend stays.

Hotel San Clemente, Av Independencia 58 (tel. 2 19 89), is cheaper than most hotels in Tlaxcala but much farther away. To reach the hotel, take Av. Independencia next to Plaza Xicoténcatl and follow it down for about 2.5km. The hotel is on the left .8km after Av. Independencia starts to curve. Rooms differ in size and decor, and doubles seem prettier than singles. All rooms feature full baths and TVs. Use caution when walking back at night. Singles 100 pesos; doubles 130 pesos.

FOOD

Regional specialties include *pollo en xoma* (chicken stuffed with fruits and other meats), *barbacoa en mixiote* (meat cooked in *maguey* leaves), and *pulque,* an ancient, unrefined alcoholic drink made from the *maguey* cactus. You can either drink *pulque* straight, eat it with your chicken, or try *pulque verde,* a drink made with honeywater, *yerba buena* (spearmint), and lemon juice. The touristy restaurants on the *zócalo* are cheaper on weekday afternoons, when they cater to the lunch crowd rather than to tourists. Beware of *"comida típica"*—it is often a pricey journey into culinary mediocrity. There are good, inexpensive places along Av. Juárez, including the **market** on 20 de Noviembre at Alonso Escalona.

Los Portales Restaurant-Bar, Plaza Constitución 8 (tel. 2 54 19; fax 2 23 38), on the side of the *zócalo* under the arches. Dapper waiters serve food *al fresco. Antojitos* 10-15 pesos, spaghetti 18-22 pesos, sandwiches 10-16 pesos, but the main attraction is the Parisian-cafe ambience. After the sun goes down, *mariachis* prowl the arcade and music from live bands pours out into the *zócalo,* creating a lively atmosphere in the heart of Tlaxcala. Open M-F 7am-11pm, Sa-Su 24hr.

El Quinto Sol (tel. 2 49 28), on Av. Juárez diagonally across from the tourist office. A popular vegetarian joint full of tempting fruits that match the orange walls outside. Sprinkled with grains and smothered with fresh fruit, their yogurt will make your tastebuds sing praises to the gods of dairy food. Breakfasts include coffee, yogurt, eggs, and juice (16-21 pesos). Cheese or soybean *tortas* 7-9 pesos; specialty cure-all juices 7-10 pesos. Open M-Sa 8am-8pm.

Restaurant El Tirol, Av. Independencia No. 7-A (tel. 2 37 54), is one of the better restaurants along Plaza Xicoténcatl. With a bar downstairs, El Tirol is always full of loud music and television screens to entertain you while you munch on *antojitos* (15-25 pesos) or breakfast (18-20 pesos). For authentic Tlaxcalan food, try the *sopa Tlaxcalteca.* Also try the *gusanos de maguey,* but only if you're daring. Open M-F 8am-noon, Sa-Su 9am-6pm.

SIGHTS

A good place to start exploring the history and culture of Tlaxcala is in the *zócalo* itself. Known as the **Plaza de la Constitución,** it features not only carefully tended flower beds, but also a spectacular 14th-century kiosk in the center. Given as a gift to Tlaxcala by King Philip in 1646, it now serves as a fountain.

To the north side of the *zócalo* is the **Palacio de Gobierno.** *(Open daily 10am-6pm; free.)* Begun in 1545, the ancient building houses not only the Tlaxcalan bureaucracy but also vivid murals that illustrate the rich history of the area. In order to fully experience these 450 meters of painted Tlaxcalan history, start in the upper left corner through the arches and work your way clockwise around the room before going up the stairs. The artist, **Desiderio Hernández Xochitiotzin,** numbered the murals (visible in the text below each painting) and you can also consult one of the guides hanging out outside the door.

Next to the **Palacio de Gobierno** is the **Parroquia San Jose,** easily distinguishable thanks to its flame-colored exterior. The church was built during the 16th and 17th centuries in a baroque style featuring the *talavera* tiles of the area.

Cutting back through the *zócalo* and past the fountain is **Plaza Xicoténcatl.** The plaza is dedicated to the young Tlaxcalan warrior Xicoténcatl Axayacatzin, who was among the few Tlaxcalans who fought Cortés as the conquistador successfully seduced Tlaxcala into joining him against the Aztecs. Today Xicoténcatl is a hero, and his fierce-looking statue commands the center spot in the plaza. Normally a tranquil area, the plaza livens up on weekends as a carousel and small artisan markets occupy Xicoténcatl's grounds.

On the southeast side of Plaza Xicoténcatl, a cobblestone way leads about 200m up to the **Ex-Convento Franciscano de Nuestra Señora de la Asunción.** One of the first convents in North America, the ex-convent is also simply one of the most beautiful structures of 16th-century New Spain. Note the *mudéjar* woodwork and gilded 8-pointed stars that accent the wooden rafters of the choir loft and ceiling; they are among the best-preserved in the Americas. The ex-convent also played a prominent role in the beginning of the evangelization of the New World. The **Museo Regional de Tlaxcala** (tel. 2 02 62) is just next door to the church. *(Open Tu-Su 10am-5pm. Admission 7 pesos, free Sundays and holidays.)* The small museum presents artifacts from nearby archaeological zones as well as exhibitions of Spanish colonial art. The museum also has a library that specializes in Tlaxcalan history and anthropology. Take a peek through the fence across from the ex-convent to discover one of Tlaxcala's pride and joys, the **Plaza de Toros.** Named after the famous *toreo* Jorge "El Ranchero" Aguilar, the beautiful plaza has been in use since 1788 and comes to life during the last week of October and first week of November when Tlaxcala celebrates its annual fair.

About 1km away from the *zócalo* area is the **Basilica y Santuario de la Virgen Ocotlan,** a magnificent church in the late Baroque Mexican style known as Churrigueresque. To get there, take an "Ocotlán" *colectivo* (1.50 pesos). It stops right in front of the church, where it waits to go back into town. To hike there, take a right on Av. Benito Juárez, head one block past the tourist office, and hang another right on Guridi y Alcocer. When the road forks, follow it up the hill to the left. The road climbs to a small **Capilla del Pocito de Agua Santa,** where it becomes a cobblestone street with a staircase alongside; the stairs lead directly to the square of the church. Legend has it that the Virgin Mary appeared here in 1541 to cure a poor Indian of his terminal illness—*La Virgen de Ocotlán* has since become the patroness of Tlaxcala. The brilliant white stucco facade will dazzle you with its figures of militant archangels and its combination of brick and *argamasa* (mortar). In the interior, golden conch shells top the pilasters and another giant shell frames the end of the nave. Its lines lead the eye up to the presbyter, which explodes in Churrigueresque splendor. The star of the show, however, is the *camarín,* the small octagonal room off to the side where the Virgin is "dressed" for important festivals. Another attraction near the *centro* is the **Museo de Artes y Tradiciones Populares de Tlaxcala** (tel. 2 23 37) on the corner of Blvd. Sanchez and Av. 1 de Mayo. *(Open Tu-Su 10am-6pm. Admission 6 pesos, students 4 pesos.)* To get there, go west on Lardizábal until it ends at Blvd. Mariano Sanchez, about four blocks from the tourist office. The museum is across the street on the left. In nine exhibition halls, artisans demonstrate the technicalities of their crafts in real-life displays. Presentations include a tour of a traditional indigenous kitchen, an explanation of textile production, and perhaps most interestingly, a discourse on how *pulque*—an unrefined alcoholic drink—is made.

For more indigenous beauty without the tourist packaging, the **Jardín Botánico de Tizatlán** (tel. 2 65 46) delivers Mexican plants in an otherwordly setting. *(Open daily 6am-11pm; free.)* From the hotel district on Blvd. Revolución, turn left at Camino Real before the brick bridge passes over the road. No bikes, balls, radios, or beer are allowed in this pastoral paradise. The rocky paths meander across a stagnant creek to reveal a tucked-away greenhouse. Another sight also off the beaten track is **Tizatlán.** *(Site open Tu-Su 10am-5pm. Admission 7 pesos.)* Located about 4km outside of Tlaxcala, these tiny ruins compose all that is left of one of Tlaxcala's four *señoríos* (warrior city-states). To get to these ruins, take a *colectivo* from 20 de Noviembre labeled "Tizatlán." Get off in front of the golden-domed church and walk to the left until you reach the ruins which are located under a protective shelter near the back of a beautiful church that is also worth visiting.

ENTERTAINMENT

Tlaxcala has become something of a nightspot, at least on weekends. **Royal Adler's Disco,** Blvd. Revolución 4 (tel. 2 18 42), at the Hotel Jeroc, plays current hits (cover 15 pesos; open F-Sa 10pm-3am). Another local hotspot is **La Valentina,** 1 de Mayo 9 (tel. 2 64 57), a disco bar just two blocks west of the *zócalo* (cover 17 pesos; open M-W noon-7pm, Th-Sa 9pm-3am). Many of the restaurants and bars in the arcades feature live music on weekend nights as well. On weekdays, finding entertainment becomes a more difficult task, since much of the city shuts down by 10:30pm. Check the tourist office for concerts. **Cines 1 y 2,** at Guillermo Valle 113 and Calle de Bosque 1 (tel. 2 35 44), and **Cinema Tlaxcala** (tel. 2 19 62), on the south side of the *zócalo* across the street from the post office, show first-run American movies (15 pesos).

■ Near Tlaxcala: Cacaxtla and Xochiténcatl

Cacaxtla

One of the best-preserved and best-presented archaeological sites in the country is the hilltop ruin of **Cacaxtla** (kah-KASH-tla), 19km southwest of Tlaxcala. *(Open daily 9am-6pm. Admission 14 pesos; video camera 30 pesos; free Sunday.)* Guides are available for 30 pesos per person, with reduced rates for large groups, but few speak English.

The Olmecas-Xicalancas, who once dominated the southwest corner of Tlaxcala State and most of the Puebla Valley, built and expanded the city between 600 and 750. Cacaxtla was abandoned by 1000, and its inhabitants were finally driven from the area by Toltec-Chichimec invaders in 1168. Excavation began at Cacaxtla in 1975, and the area is now reconstructed as the ceremonial center it once was, complete with more modern additions such as a restaurant and gift shop.

Upon entering the site, visit the **museum** on the right. It contains artifacts and bones collected from the site and serves as a good intro to the area. From the small museum, a dirt path leads toward the pyramid by way of the **Gran Basamento,** the thick platform upon which the center was built. The pyramid is covered by the **world's second largest archaeological roof** in order to prevent the erosion of the adobe structures, and it makes for a refreshingly cool viewing experience. Once upstairs, visitors move clockwise around the excavations of ceremonial courtyards, temples, tombs, and what appears to have been a palace.

Two discoveries distinguish this site from others. One is a **latticework window** on the west side, opposite the entrance. The window, a free-standing fence, is the only one of its kind. It was produced by surrounding a latticework of twigs and branches with mud and stucco. Cacaxtla's other chief attraction is a series of murals scattered about the site, considered some of the best-preserved pre-Hispanic paintings in Mesoamerica. The largest of them, the **Battle Mural,** depicts a historical-mythological battle in which an army dressed in jaguar skins crushes the skulls of an army dressed as birds. The murals appear in all the glory of their original mineral-based colors, which are still amazingly bright and gruesome.

From the Battle Mural, the official circuit takes you to an area whose bland name, **Building A** (tel. 6 00 00), belies its beauty. Five of the site's murals stand together, united by color and imagery into a symbolic unit. The leftmost mural depicts the god Quetzalcóatl and a human figure in a jaguar skins, while the right-most one shows a bird-man surrounded by symbols of rain god Tlaloc.

Xochiténcatl

The civilization at **Xochiténcatl** (o-chee-TEN-cahtl) predates Cacaxtla by several hundred years, and its ruins are located on a hill just opposite Cacaxtla. Public transportation that runs between Cacaxtla and Xochiténcatl is difficult to find. Follow the signs around the Cacaxtla pyramid to the path that leads up the hill (about a 2km walk). In 300, the inhabitants of Xochiténcatl were conquered by the Olmecas-Xicalancas, who also took up residence at Cacaxtla. The site features four pyramids, the largest of which, **The Pyramid of Flowers,** is actually a pyramid on top of a pyramid. The **spiral pyramid,** the one farthest from the entrance, is also worth a look. Dedicated to the wind god Ehecatl, it is the only such spiral pyramid known to exist. Other interesting finds include a large snake sculpture and several large basalt founts. These founts are doubly impressive considering that they were made from a single large piece of stone without any steel tools. The site also offers a spectacular view of the surrounding volcanoes: **Popocatépetel, Ixtaccihuatl,** and **La Malinche.** One clear days the Puebla valley is also visible.

Getting There: From Tlaxcala, take one of the *colectivos* labeled "Texoloc-Tlaxcala" or buses marked "Nativitas" that leave from the bus plaza on 20 de Noviembre next to the market or along 20 de Noviembre behind San José. Ask whether the bus goes to Cacaxtla. Some go to the town of San Miguel del Milagro (San Miguelito) at the base of the site; others travel past the main entrance (40 min., 5 pesos). If you're dropped off in town, walk up the windy road, following the signs to the entrance. To return to Tlaxcala, walk downhill from the ticket booth and turn right to go down to San Martín. From Tlaxcala, *colectivos* go right go to Xochiténcatl; across the street, "Tlaxcala" *colectivos* return to the bus plaza next to the market (5 pesos). The tourist office offers guided trips to the two zones every Sunday for 15 pesos. The trips include transportation and usually an English-speaking guide. These tours are an excellent way to visit the sites.

PUEBLA

Puebla

Though it lies only two hours from Mexico City, Puebla keeps itself out of the capital's immense shadow by forging its own distinct culture based on its rich and unique history—Puebla has more to offer visitors than several hours of wandering through the *zócalo*. The capital and commercial center of the state of Puebla, the city is home to world-class museums, historical sites, and, of course, delicious *moles* and *dulces*.

According to legend, the angels in Puebla de los Angeles (the city's full name) came from the dreaming mind of Don Julian Garcés, the Bishop of Tlaxcala. In a vision, he saw a beautiful field next to a sparkling river. Angels descended from the sky, planted stakes, and stretched cords for the streets of a new city in a rectangular pattern that still characterizes Puebla's streets today. While hiking the next day, the Bishop recognized the land of his dreams and immediately erected the altar from which Fray Toribiode Benavente delivered Mexico's first Catholic mass in 1531. Puebla grew into a formidable fortress of Catholicism, commissioning more than 60 churches over the course of colonization.

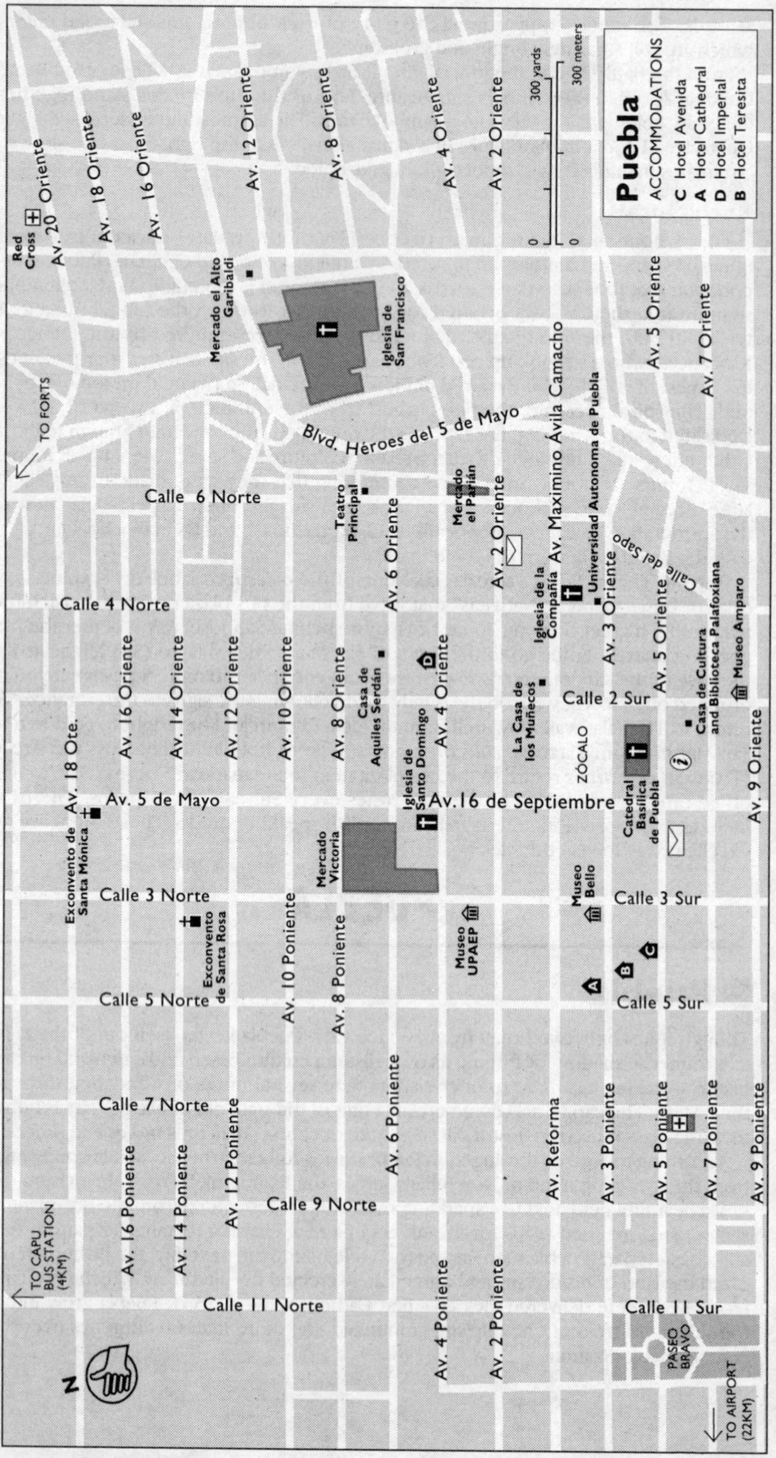
Puebla
ACCOMMODATIONS
C Hotel Avenida
A Hotel Cathedral
D Hotel Imperial
B Hotel Teresita
0 300 yards
0 300 meters
Red Cross
Av. 20 Oriente
Av. 18 Oriente
Av. 16 Oriente
Av. 12 Oriente
Av. 8 Oriente
Av. 4 Oriente
Av. 2 Oriente
Mercado el Alto Garibaldi
Iglesia de San Francisco
TO FORTS
Blvd. Héroes del 5 de Mayo
Av. Maximino Ávila Camacho
Universidad Autonoma de Puebla
Av. 5 Oriente
Av. 7 Oriente
Calle 6 Norte
Teatro Principal
Mercado el Parián
Av. 6 Oriente
Av. 2 Oriente
Calle del Sapo
Calle 4 Norte
Iglesia de la Compañía
Av. 3 Oriente
Av. 5 Oriente
Av. 16 Oriente
Av. 14 Oriente
Av. 12 Oriente
Av. 10 Oriente
Av. 8 Oriente
Casa de Aquiles Serdán
Av. 4 Oriente
La Casa de los Muñecos
Calle 2 Sur
Casa de Cultura and Biblioteca Palafoxiana
Museo Amparo
Av. 18 Ote.
Iglesia de Santo Domingo
ZÓCALO
Av. 9 Oriente
Av. 5 de Mayo
Av. 16 de Septiembre
Catedral Basílica de Puebla
Exconvento de Santa Mónica
Mercado Victoria
Calle 3 Norte
Museo Bello
Calle 3 Sur
Exconvento de Santa Rosa
Av. 10 Poniente
Av. 8 Poniente
Museo UPAEP
Calle 5 Norte
Calle 5 Sur
Av. 6 Poniente
Calle 7 Norte
Av. 16 Poniente
Av. 14 Poniente
Av. 12 Poniente
Av. Reforma
Av. 3 Poniente
Av. 5 Poniente
Av. 7 Poniente
Av. 9 Poniente
Calle 9 Norte
TO CAPU BUS STATION (4KM)
Calle 11 Norte
Calle 11 Sur
Av. 4 Poniente
Av. 2 Poniente
PASEO BRAVO
TO AIRPORT (22KM)
N

Over time, Puebla, with its ideal location between Mexico City and the Gulf of Mexico, became a formidable military location. Several historic battles were fought here, including the famous 5 de Mayo defeat of the French in 1862. On the battle fields that are occupied today by the *Centro Cívico de 5 de Mayo*, General Ignacio Zaragoza kept French troops from advancing on Mexico City in what is considered to be one of the most glorious moments for the Mexican Republic.

Today Puebla is home to more than two million inhabitants, making it one of the most important cities in the country. Despite its size, the city elegantly combines gilt churches and trendy clothing stores, while in the shady *zócalo* both teen hipsters and older locals relax together. And while the Bishop's angels may choke on the exhaust fumes or balk at the upsurge in fast food restaurants, they must still smile down on amorous couples in the *zócalo,* foreign students exercising their new-found language skills at the discos, and tourists soaking up a little history.

ORIENTATION

Puebla, capital of Puebla state, is connected through an extensive highway network to Mexico City (125km northwest along Rte. 150), Oaxaca (Rte. 190, 125, or 131), Tlaxcala (Rte. 119), Veracruz (Rte. 150), and countless other cities. All **bus** companies operate out of the **CAPU (Central de Autobuses Puebla)** on Blvd. Norte and Tlaxcala, in the northwest corner of the city.

The *avenidas* and *calles* of Puebla form a near-perfect grid, with the northwest corner of the *zócalo* in the center. Everything changes names at that point: the main north-south street is called **5 de Mayo** north of the *zócalo* and **16 de Septiembre** south of it; the main east-west drag is **Avenida Reforma** to the west, and **Avenida Máximo Ávila Camacho** to the east. *Avenidas* run east-west and are designated either *Poniente* (*Pte.,* west) or *Oriente* (*Ote.,* east), depending on where they lie with respect to that intersection. Similarly, *calles* run north-south and are labeled *Norte (Nte.)* or *Sur* with respect to the critical point. Numerical addresses correspond to the order of the block away from the city center. For example, 4 Ote. 212 is located on the second block of the street, in the section bounded by Calle 2 Norte and Calle 4 Norte. On the following block away from the center, addresses will be in the 400s.

Official yellow **taxis** labeled *taxis controlados* will take you to the *zócalo* from the bus station for about 15 pesos (about 17 pesos at night). If traveling with an independent *taxista,* set a price before getting in and don't be shy about haggling. Cabs from the train station to the *zócalo* run about 10 pesos. **Municipal buses** and *micros* (also known as *combis*), white Volkswagen vans that operate like buses, cost 2.50 pesos. Anything labeled "Centro" should take you close to the *zócalo.* On Calle 9 Nte.-Sur you can catch buses to the bus station (marked "CAPU"), or to the train station (marked *"Estación Nueva Popular"*). CAPU buses also run along Blvd. Héroes de 5 de Mayo. Be sure to stand up and alert your driver when your stop is near.

PRACTICAL INFORMATION

Transportation

Airport: In **Huejotzingo,** 22km away (tel. 32 00 32). Regional airlines fly to Guadalajara, Monterrey, and Tijuana.

Buses: CAPU (Central de Autobuses Puebla; tel. 49 72 11) at Blvd. Norte and Tlaxcala is one of the largest bus stations in the country, with buses regularly traveling to all parts of the republic. Prices and routes change frequently and vary from carrier to carrier, so the following is just a guideline. **ADO** (tel. 49 70 42), 1st class to Cancún (24hr., 11:45am, 480 pesos), Mérida (22hr., 7:55pm, 402 pesos), Mexico City (2hr., Tu-Th every 10min., F-M every 5min. 5am-midnight, 45 pesos), Oaxaca (14 hr., 7 per day, 119 pesos), Veracruz (4½hr., every 2 hours, 96 pesos), Xalapa (3hr., every 2hr. 6:45am-9:15pm, 55 pesos), and many other destinations. **Cristóbal Colón** (tel. 49 75 68), to Huatulco (9hr., 7:30pm and 9:55 pm, 196 pesos), Puerto Escondido (10hr., 7:30 pm and 9:55pm, 199 pesos), Tehuantepec (11hr., 8:15pm, 251 pesos), and other resort cities. **Estrella Roja** (tel. 40 76 96), first class to Mexico City (2hr., every 15min. 5am-9pm, 38-60 pesos). **Estrella Blanca** (tel. 49 75 61), 1st class to Acapulco (7hr., 5 per day, 144 pesos), Chilpancingo (6hr., 5 per day, 124 pesos), Taxco (5hr., 8am, 80 pesos), and others. **Flecha Azul** (tel. 49 73 55), to Tlaxcala (45min., every 10min. 4:40am-10pm, 7 pesos). Smaller bus lines also serve the CAPU bus station.

Tourist and Financial Services

Tourist Office: State Office, Av. 5 Ote. 3 (tel. 46 12 85 or 46 20 44), facing the cathedral's southern side, 1 block from the *zócalo.* Follow the blue signs with a white question mark to enjoy free maps and a monthly guide to cultural events in Puebla. The tourist office is currently undergoing renovations and a makeshift office has been set up next door. Open M-Sa 9am-8:30pm, Su 9am-2pm. There is also a **booth** at the bus station.

Currency Exchange: Banks line Av. Reforma and Av. 16 de Septiembre around the *centro.* **Bital,** Reforma 126 (tel. 46 40 44), is blessed with a 24hr. **ATM** and will change money from 9am-6:30pm. **Casas de cambio** offer slightly better rates and cluster in the Zona Esmeralda along Av. Juárez further from the *zócalo.* Try **Casa de Cambio Puebla,** Av. 29 Sur. 316-A at Juárez (tel. 48 01 99). Open M-F 9am-6pm.

American Express: Díaz Ordaz 6A Sur #2914, Suite 301 (tel. 40 30 18, 40 33 08, or 40 32 85), in the Plaza Dorada. Best bet for cashing and replacing AmEx checks; holds client mail for 10 days. Open M-F 9am-6pm.

Local Services

Markets: Mercados along 5 de Mayo, 1 block north of the *zócalo,* and along Av. 10 Pte. For hassle-free browsing, try **El Parián Market,** Calle 6 Norte 200. If you seek A/C and order, head for **Gigante,** at 4 Nte. and Blvd. Héroes del 5 de Mayo, to north of Templo de San Francisco. Open daily 9am-9pm. Also try **Comercial Mexicana,** Calle 5 Sur and Av. 19 Pte., by the large pelican sign. Open daily 8am-10pm.

Laundromat: Lavandería Roly, Calle 7 Nte. 404 (tel. 32 93 07). 18 pesos for 3kg self-service. Open M-Sa 8am-8pm, Su 8am-1pm.

Emergency and Communications

Emergency: tel. 06. Also try the **Policía Auxiliar** (tel. 88 18 63), open 24hr., or the Escuadrón S.O.S. (tel. 40 67 91).

Police: Dirección de Policía, 9 Ote. and 16 Sur. (tel. 32 22 23 or 32 22 22).

Red Cross: At 20 Ote. and 10 Nte. (tel. 35 80 40, 35 86 31, or 34 00 00). 24hr. ambulance service. Some English spoken.

Pharmacies: Farmacias del Ahorro, on the corner of Av. 2 Ote. and Calle 2 Nte. (tel. 31 33 83). Open daily 7am-11pm. **Sanborn's,** Av. 2 Ote. 6 (tel. 42 39 61), also has a pharmacy; some English is spoken. Open M-F 7am-11pm, Sa-Su 7am-1pm.

Hospital: Hospital UPAEP, Av. 5 Pte. 715 (tel. 46 60 99 and 32 91 51). **Hospital Universitario,** Calle 13 Sur at Av. 25 Pte. (tel. 46 64 64), 10 blocks south and 7 blocks west of the *zócalo.* 24hr. emergency service. Some English spoken.

Post Office: 16 de Septiembre at Av. 5 Ote. (tel. 42 64 48), 1 block south of the cathedral, just around the corner from the state tourist office. Open M-F 8am-8pm, Sa 9am-1pm. **Northern office,** Av. 2 Ote. 411, on the 2nd floor. Open M-F 8am-7pm, Sa 9am-noon. The 2 branches have separate *Lista de Correos,* so make sure you know where your mail waits. **Postal Code:** 72000.

Fax: Telecomm, 16 de Septiembre 504 (tel. 32 17 79), just south of the post office. Western Union, telegrams, fax. Open M-F 8am-6pm, Sa 9am-12pm.

Internet Access: The main post office (see above) offers access to the World Wide Web for 25 pesos and email accounts for a monthly rent of 25 pesos. For more comprehensive service, try **La Noria Café Internet,** 45 Poniente 1937 Local (tel. 43 09 26), which offers a myriad of services including telnet and FTP access. 15 pesos for ½ hour (20 if you need assistance). Open M-Sa 11am-2pm and 5pm-9pm. **RCP Electrónica,** Calle 4 sur 1922, south of Av. 21 Ote, upstairs in room 203. You can use an office member's computer, complete with telnet, for 30 pesos an hour. Open M-F 9am-2pm and 4pm-8pm.

Telephones: LADATELs are easy to find along 5 de Mayo and around the *zócalo.*

Phone code: 22.

ACCOMMODATIONS

Puebla is well stocked with budget hotels, and most are within a five- or six-block radius of the *zócalo.* When walking around the *zócalo*, be on the lookout for large signs with a red "H" jutting out of the packed buildings. These signs, friends of the weary traveler, indicate that a hotel—often a cheap one—is near. It's a good idea to ask to see your room first; same-priced rooms can vary widely in their size and decor. Hot water availability varies from hotel to hotel.

Hotel Imperial, Av. 4 Ote. 212 (tel. 42 49 80; fax 46 38 25). On the expensive side, but oh, the amenities! Telephone and TV in all rooms, 24hr. hot water supply, a mini-golf course, workout area, complete with weight and Stairmaster machines, laundry service, pool table, and a Hershey's kiss on your pillow every night. Rooms vary greatly in decor. Ask to see several before deciding. Singles 120 pesos; doubles 180 pesos. A 30% discount for proud *Let's Go* owners makes the Imperial's luxury more affordable. 15% discount for groups of over 10 people. Breakfast included.

Hotel Teresita, Av. 3 Pte. 309 (tel. 32 70 72), 2 blocks west of the Cathedral. All rooms have carpeting, TV, and refreshingly soft beds. There is 24hr. hot water in the sleek bathrooms, but not much space in the room to perform a dance celebrating the discovery of this budget-pleaser. Singles 90-110 pesos; doubles 150 pesos without windows, 170 pesos with windows, 170 pesos with amenities.

Hotel Cathedral, Av. 3 Pte. 310 (tel. 32 23 60), offers a sunny courtyard and friendly decor. If you don't mind the common baths, then the low price and good location might make this great hotel the place for you. Singles 60-70 pesos; doubles 80-90 pesos. Parking 10 pesos per night.

Hotel Avenida, Av. 5 Pte 336 (tel. 32 21 04) is arguably the cheapest hotel in Puebla. Shabby rooms feature cramped bathrooms and flaking plaster, while the green glass covering the skylight bathes the hotel in a strange green glow. Still, friendly staff and a good location, not to mention incredibly low prices, make Hotel Avenida a stellar bargain for the budget traveler. Singles from 35 pesos; doubles from 80 pesos; and triples from 100 pesos. Prices also rise with private baths.

FOOD

Mole is the word in Puebla. No, it's not the furry creature that inhabits your backyard. Not 6.02×10^{23} either. Think of a dark, rich sauce, ready to be eaten with beef, chicken or a plain tortilla. You haven't really visited Puebla unless you've tried one of the mole dishes. *Mole poblana* contains chiles and dark chocolate; *mole pipian* contains pumpkin seeds and chile; and finally, *mole adobo* is a spicier blend of cumin powder. Another famous dish from Puebla is *chile en nogada*, a green pepper stuffed with beef and then smothered in white walnut sauce.

Puebla is also known for its **dulces** (sweets), especially *dulces de leche*, which are sweets made out of milk, and *dulce de camote*, made out of candied sweet potatoes. Those with an incurable sweet tooth should head for 6 Oriente between Av. 5 de Mayo and Calle 2 Norte where they can find numerous shops that sell these famous Poblano sweets. As always, for truly cheap eats, the **mercados** are the way to go. A full meal at the **Mercado San Francisco del Alto Garibaldi,** at Av. 14 Ote, between Calles 12 and 14 Nte., goes for only 5-15 pesos (open daily 7am-10pm).

Restaurant Del Parián, 6 Norte 5 (tel. 46 47 98), near the **Mercado el Parián,** features specialities from the state of Puebla. Try the *mole poblano* for 24 pesos while enjoying the colorful decor of this small and friendly restaurant. You might even get to take a piece of Puebla home in the form of a free miniature ceramic *sombrero*. Open daily 9am-7pm.

Restaurant El Vegetariano, Av. 3 Pte. 525 (tel. 46 54 62). Popular in a city of carnivores for one very good reason—terrific food. Don't worry about the *chorizo* and *jamón* listed on the menu; soy-based substitutes are used. Try the always tasty *comida corrida* (22 pesos), or opt for meatless *antojitos* (17 pesos). Their *energética,* a plateful of tropical fruits topped with yogurt and their very own granola, is an unbridled breakfast joy (20 pesos). Open daily 7:30am-9pm. The same people operate **La Zanahoria,** Av. Juárez 2104, in the Zona Esmeralda.

Tepoznieves, Av. 3 Pts. 150 (tel. 46 14 63), serves the strangest ice cream and sherbet flavors imaginable. Do you like corn? Then you'll love their *nieve de elote* (corn ice cream). Tepoznieves also serves lettuce, beet, and celery ice cream. The more adventurous might want to try the spicy ice creams (such as *mango con chile*) or the alcoholic ice creams (popular flavors include tequila and pineapple rum). Those who don't feel daring enough to try the rice ice cream and other such flavors, have no fear. Tepoznieves also serves old favorites such as chocolate and vanilla, and all are delicious. Open daily 10am-9:30 pm.

Super Tortas Puebla, Av. 3 Pte. 317. Hordes of Mexicans come here to indulge in the country's favorite lunchtime tradition, the *torta* (8-9 pesos). For a nostalgic dining experience, savor yours in the back room near a pastel-colored shrine to Marilyn Monroe. Open daily 9am-10:30pm.

SIGHTS

Historic Puebla is a sightseer's paradise; this is, perhaps, the reason why bus loads of Mexican students and *norteamericanos* from nearby language schools file into the *zócalo* every weekend, cameras in hand. Most sights are within walking distance of the city center. If you have only a short time in Puebla, the **Museo Amparo, Capilla del Rosario,** and **Casa de Aquiles Serdán** should top your list. There are also a slew of museums in the nearby **Centro Cívico 5 de Mayo.** For those interested in churches, the **cathedral** and **Ex-Convento de Santa Mónica** should not be missed. Churches close between 2 and 4pm; shorts are usually acceptable. Museums often give 50% discounts to students with ID.

Near the Zócalo

In Puebla, modernity is tempered by many pre-18th-century architectural elements. The oldest buildings in town date from the 16th century and are notable for their Romanesque porches and smooth columns. While few original 16th-century edifices still stand, some later buildings on the west and north ends of the *zócalo* consciously attempt to imitate their style.

Puebla boasts over 100 churches with varied architectural styles, including Gothic, classical, and even Baroque. Many were built during the 17th century using oddly shaped red bricks and carefully painted *azulejos de talavera* (celebrated *mudéjar*-style Puebla tiles). For a prime example, head to the **Casa de los Muñecos** (House of the Dolls; tel. 46 28 99) on Calle 2 Nte. at the *zócalo*'s northeast corner. *(Open Tu-Su 10am-4:30pm. Admission 5 pesos, 2 pesos with student ID.)* Named for the *talavera* figures that populate the house, the building is a remarkable example of artistic spite: legend has it that the 16 so-called "dolls" on the outside of the building are actually caricatures of the architect's enemies. The museum inside the building showcases the architecture and history of the house.

The **Catedral Basílica de Puebla,** Av. 3 Ote. 302 at 5 de Mayo, stands adjacent to the *zócalo*. *(Open daily 10am-12:30pm and 4-6pm.)* It was entirely constructed by *indígena* laborers working under Spanish direction between 1575 and 1649. Music sometimes echoes from the cathedral's two organs (one is 400 years old) and from the 19 bells of the bell tower. The interior of the cathedral gets its zing from chandeliers, gold plating, and Pedro Muñoz's fine woodwork on the choir-stalls on the pulpit's periphery. A guided tour goes for about 30 pesos. The tourist office can arrange authorized English-speaking guides. At 72m, the cathedral is the **tallest in Mexico.** From 11am to noon, if the sexton is in the mood, visitors can climb the right tower of the cathedral for a panoramic view of Puebla (5 pesos). Two volcanoes, **Popocatépetl** and **Ixtaccíhuatl,** are visible to the northwest. To the northeast, you can see **La Malinche,** the volcano named in honor of Cortés's *indígena* lover and interpreter. Be sure to start your climb by 11:30am; the lower door is locked at noon.

The art collection of the late textile magnate José Luis Bello is housed in the **Museo Bello,** Av. 3 Pte. at Calle 3 Sur (tel. 32 94 75), one block west of the southeast corner of the *zócalo*. *(Open Tu-Su 10am-5pm. Admission until 4:30pm. 10 pesos, 5 pesos with student ID. Free Tu.)* The museum is crammed with ivory, iron, porcelain, earthenware, and *talavera* artifacts from different places and periods in world history; highlights include a collection of decorative keys and locks, a musical crystal door, and voluminous books of Gregorian chants from the 16th, 17th, and 18th centuries. A knowledgeable tour guide will spit out information about prominent pieces and answer questions in a spooky robot-like voice. Guided tours are offered in Spanish and English, but tours in English can be rather indecipherable.

Right down Calle 3 Sur from the Museo Bello is the **Museo UPAEP,** 3 Norte 3 (tel. 46 38 54) which features religious art from the state of Puebla. *(Open Tu-Su 10am-6pm. Admission 5 pesos, 2.50 with student ID. Free on Wednesdays from 10am-2pm.)* Although tiny, the collection has exhibits on the *Virgen de Dolores* and the *Sagrado Corazón de Jesus*.

Gohhhhhh-ohhhhhh!

Although *charretería* (horsemanship, rodeo, and bullfighting) may be the official national sport of Mexico, *fútbol* (soccer) is by far the most popular. If you want to check out the *fútbol* phenomenon, you're in luck—*fútbol* matches take place year-round. Mexico has two professional soccer leagues: the Winter League (season runs July-Dec.) and the Summer League (season runs Jan.-May). In addition, there are countless minor and amateur *fútbol* leagues throughout the nation. Each of the professional leagues has 17 regular games in its season, excluding the playoffs, semi-finals, and finals. In June, the World Cup takes Mexico by storm and soccer fans throughout the country pack bars and restaurants to watch the games. Whenever Mexico scores a goal, the entire country shakes from the shout of the word "GO!" that rings out from every bar, business, and bus.

When Mexico played in the World Cup in 1998, all of Mexico City shut down to watch the games; even gas and water delivery stopped. Enormous TV monitors were set up at the Monumento de la Revolución and the Angel de la Independencia so that all could see. After each of Mexico's three wins, great parties broke out in the streets. People paraded up and down the streets waving the Mexican flag, with their hair dyed the national colors of green, white, and red. When Mexico lost to Germany, the entire nation hung its head in sorrow. They did not, however, stop watching the games.

South of the Zócalo

The **Casa de la Cultura,** Av. 5 Ote. 5 (tel. 46 53 44), one block from the *zócalo* behind the Cathedral, in the same building as the tourist office, is a great place to start when visiting Puebla. Foreign students practice their Spanish in the courtyard while tourists view traveling art exhibits. Folk dances are performed every Saturday and Sunday; movies are shown Thursday through Sunday. Check the board on the right as you walk in from the street for the latest schedules. The same building houses the impressive **Biblioteca Palafoxiana** (tel. 46 56 13), a beautiful library holding 43,000 16th-century volumes. *(Open Tu-Su 10am-5pm. Admission 10 pesos.)* Belonging to no specific religious order himself, Don Juan de Palafox was a vocal critic of the Jesuits, condemning their aspirations to power, land, and money. His 6000-book library, which he donated to the city in 1646, includes an illuminated copy of the **Nuremberg Chronicle** from 1493.

Around the corner from the Casa de la Cultura, and two blocks away from the *zócalo*, is the **Museo Amparo,** Calle 2 Sur 708 (tel. 46 46 46.) *(Open W-M 10am-6pm. Admission 16 pesos, students 8 pesos. Free on Mondays. Guided tour Sundays at noon. Headphones 8 pesos with 8-peso deposit.)* The exhibit begins with a timeline comparing the development of Mesoamerican art with that of Oceania, Asia, Africa, and Europe from 2400 BC to AD 1500. From there, the rooms guide you through the techniques, uses, and trends in the art of dozens of Mesoamerican indigenous groups without losing the global perspective. Objects are presented in their contexts of use, in relation to other cultures, and finally as individual masterpieces. The last rooms of the museum jump to the colonial era, recreating the house as it once looked. As if Mexican pride hadn't been stroked enough, the exhibits open and close with two memorable paintings by Diego Rivera. Explanatory material is in both English and Spanish. Headphones provide visitors with more information on the pieces from the high-tech monitors in each room of the museum; explanations come in five languages.

Northeast of the Zócalo

The extravagant, gilded **Iglesia de Santo Domingo** was constructed between 1571 and 1611 on the foundation of a convent. *(Open daily 10am-noon and 4-8pm.)* It lies two blocks from the *zócalo*'s northwest corner; head away from the Cathedral along 5 de Mayo, and you will see it tower over you between Av. 4 and 6 Pte. Statues of saints and angels adorn the fantastic altar, but the church's real attraction is the exuberant **Capilla del Rosario,** laden with enough 23½-karat gold to make the King of Spain jealous. Masks depicting an *indígena,* a *conquistador* in armor, and a *mestizo* hang above each of the three doors along each side of the chapel. On the ceiling, three statues represent Faith, Hope, and Charity. The 12 pillars represent the 12 apostles; the six on the upper level are each made from a single onyx stone. Since there was no room for a real choir, designers painted a chorus of angels with guitars and woodwinds on the wall above the door

Casa de Aquiles Serdán, originally the home of the eponymous printer, patriot, and martyr of the 1910 *Revolución,* serves today as the **Museo Regional de la Revolución Mexicana** at Av. 6 Ote. 206 (tel. 32 10 76). *(Open Tu-Su 10am-4:30pm. Admission 10 pesos, children 5 pesos.)* Hundreds of bullet holes, both inside and out, bear witness to Serdán's assassination. The museum includes photos of Serdán, of the bloody battles of the Revolution, of the bedraggled battalions of Reyes and Obregón, and of the dead Zapata and Carranza. One room is dedicated to Carmen Serdán and other female revolutionaries *(las carabineras).*

When Benito Juárez's Reform Laws went into effect in 1857, they not only weakened the power of the Church but also forced the nuns at the **Convento de Santa Mónica,** on 5 de Mayo and 16 Pte., into hiding. *(Open Tu-Su 10am-5pm. Admission 7 pesos, free Sundays.)* The convent operated in stealth for 77 years before it was accidentally discovered. Now an *ex-convento,* the building serves as a museum for religious art. Regional clothing is sold at the **Mercado El Parián,** Av. 4 Ote. and Calle 6 Nte. (open daily 9am-7pm). The **Barrio del Artista,** on Av. 6 Ote. and Calle 6 Nte., is a pedestrian strip where local artists exhibit their work in small cubicles and paint the portraits of passersby. The best time to visit these markets is the weekend; they slow down considerably during the week.

The oldest church in Puebla, begun in 1535 and finished in 1575, is the **Templo de San Francisco,** Av. 14 Ote. and Calle 10 Nte. *(Open daily 10am-5pm, except when in use.)* The church's dark bell tower was added in 1672. Near the church is the **Teatro Principal,** on Av. 8 Ote. at Calle 6 Nte. (tel. 32 60 85). The *teatro* is a prime example of Puebla's distinctive 16th-century architecture.

In the Outskirts

A short trip from the *centro,* the **Centro Cívico 5 de Mayo** commemorates the Mexican army's victory over the French, which took place in these fields in 1862. To reach this historic site, walk to Blvd. Héroes del 5 de Mayo, about three blocks to the east of the *zócalo,* where you can catch a #72 bus or #8 *colectivo* (both 2.50 pesos). Get off by the large, multi-armed cement monument which sits alone on an empty-looking glorieta. (You know you're there when you look out the window and wonder out loud, "what's that?") Although some think the monument resembles an octopus, it is a dignified remembrance to Ignacio Zaragoza, the Mexican general who led the defeat of the French troops. Facing the monument, cross the street to the left and walk uphill. Past a now defunct information center, a large concrete representation of the Mexican flag marks a fork in the road. To the right is the **Fuerte de Loreto,** which now houses the **Museo de La No Intervención.** *(Both open Tu-Su 10am-4:30pm. Admission 10 pesos. Free on Sundays and major holidays.)* The oddly named museum houses artifacts, paintings, and documents dealing with the May 5th battle and, in particular, the actions of the courageous General Zaragoza. The museum also features a panoramic recreation of the battlefield as it might have looked in 1862 and more exhibits dealing with French rule in Mexico downstairs. The road to the left makes a loop; the first building is the **Museo de Historia Natural,** full of fossils, live snakes, and well-behaved school kids. *(Open Tu-Su 10am-5pm. Admission 10 pesos, children 5 pesos. Free on Tuesdays.)* Life-sized—but out of date—dinosaur models command a spot in the foyer while a spectacular butterfly collection lights up the left exhibition wing. The museum also boasts the largest collection of stuffed deer heads you'll ever see under one roof. **The Planetarium,** next to the Museum of Natural History, is hard to miss—it takes the shape of a giant, glittering, silver pyramid. The planetarium features the usual slew of space exhibits and an **Omnimax Theater**. *(Both open daily 10am-5pm. Admission including Omnimax 20 pesos.)* Shows vary and play approximately every hour. Across from the Museum of Natural History is the **Recinto Ferial,** an exposition center and fairgrounds. The **Parque Rafaela Padilla de Zaragoza** comes next, providing a large, nature-filled oasis. *(Open daily 9am-10pm. Videos cost 1 peso.)* Rambling trails descend to a theater, a playground, and benches that beckon to picnickers. The administration building near the entrance shows National Geographic-style videos, and the immersion in nature would be complete save for the oversized statues of animals and piped-in radio shows. At the tip of the loop, about a 10-minute walk from the rest of the museums, is the **Fuerte de Guadalupe** (Guadalupe's fort), "an altar to the patriotism of the heroes of the Fifth of May." This Fuerte offers a panorama of the city of Puebla. Finally, the **Museo Regional de Antropología** is on your right as you leave the fort and head back toward the flag. *(Open Tu-Su 10am-5pm. Admission 10 pesos. Sundays and holidays free).* The museum features clothing, artifacts, and information about the historic state of Puebla.

A somewhat longer trip from the *centro* takes you to **Africam Safari** (tel. 35 87 13 or 35 87 00), an ecological zoo dedicated to conservation and recreation. *(Open daily 10am-5pm. Admission varies; call for more information.)* Located about 16km (10 mi) southeast of Puebla, the easiest way to get to Africam Safari is by bus. *Estrella Roja* offers packages that include round-trip bus service from the CAPU and park admission for 45 pesos for adults and 40 pesos for children. Bus service alone is 20 pesos for adults and 16 pesos for children. Buses depart every two hours on weekdays and every 45 minutes on weekends and major holidays starting at 10:45am and continuing until 2:45pm. If driving, head to the south of the city and then go east, following the signs to **Valsequillo.** Once inside the park, you will be greeted by over 3000 animals representing approximately 250 species. Organized according to geographical area, the park encompasses areas such as Asia, America, and Antarctica, as well as specialized African areas such as Uganda, Kenya, Mombasa, and Botswana. But what makes the Africam Safari unique is that the animals roam freely. Visitors can drive through the park and get off at certain locations to take photos and to mingle with the animals.

ENTERTAINMENT

For evening entertainment, take a stroll along the **Zona Esmeralda,** on Av. Juárez, west of Calle 13 Sur. Enjoy the collection of movie theaters, shops, restaurants, and bars. A youngish Mexican crowd boogies to the beat of salsa and disco at **Pagaia,** Juárez 1906 (tel. 32 46 85), after Calle 19 (cover 30 pesos; open Su-Th 4pm-2am, F-Sa 4pm-3am). If you're feeling mellower, the **Italian Coffee Company** (tel. 46 28 26) is just across Av. Juárez from Charlie's. A sophisticated set sits on the patio enjoying espresso and pastries (open daily 9am-9:30pm).

For those who prefer to hear both sides of the conversation, bookstore/cafe **Teorema,** Reforma 540 (tel. 42 10 14), at Calle 7, is a hip hangout; lively banter and nightly live music pervade this literary lair (cover 11 pesos; open 9:30am-2:30pm and 4:30pm-2am; bookstore closes and music starts at 9:30pm).

If you're interested in nightlife, though, nearby **Cholula** (see p. 458) has some of the best in the area, especially along **Recta Cholula,** the highway that connects Puebla and Cholula. It's best to take a taxi there; ask to be let off by the clubs near UDLA.

Eighty kilometers north of Puebla lies **Tlachichuca,** the town closest to Mexico's highest peak. The **Pico de Orizaba** is a 5747m volcano, the **third-tallest mountain in North America.** To get to Tlachichuca, head to the CAPU.

Cholula

Visitors to Cholula are often overwhelmed by the large number of 17th-century churches that seem to dot every street corner. Legend holds that there are 365 churches in the city: one for each day of the year. Although the exact number may be in dispute, the prevalence of churches reminds the city's 69,000 residents (and the few foreign tourists) of the city's sacred place in history. Founded over 2500 years ago, Cholula ("water that falls in the place of escape") was inhabited by several pre-Hispanic cultures—Olmecs, Zapotecs, Teotihuacanos, Toltecs, Chichimecs, and Cholutecs. Each successive culture added a tier to the **Great Pyramid** (called the **Teneapa Pyramid**), and strengthened Cholula's reputation as a commercial and religious center. On top of the Great Pyramid and other religious ruins, the Spanish constructed Catholic churches, including the glittering **Santuario de los Remedios,** to outshine the pyramid. Together, the pyramid and its incongruous crown constitute Cholula's main attraction and are a tangible symbol of the Spanish conquest.

Cholula keeps resolutely to its own slow beat. Cafes and sidewalk restaurants are full of locals enjoying the usually beautiful weather. Nights are also lively, especially when students from nearby **UDLA (Universidad de las Américas)** come out to play. Cholula, with its archaeological zone, churches, and elite university, makes for a fine daytrip out of the larger cities nearby.

ORIENTATION

Cholula is on **Route 150,** 122km east of Mexico City and 8km west of Puebla. The Estrella Roja **bus station** is located on **Av. 12 Pte.** near the intersection with **Av. 3 Nte.** The bus station is tiny and poorly marked. Go down one block to the intersection of **12 Pte.** and **5 de Mayo.** To get to the *centro*, walk four blocks downhill toward the large yellow church of San Pedro on the right side of the street. With the church on the right, you are facing the edge of the **zócalo.** *Colectivos* to Puebla can be flagged down at a variety of locations in the city center, including the corner of **Av. 4 Pte.** and **Calle 3 Nte.,** as well as at **Morelos** and **Calle 4 Sur** (30 min. to Puebla's CAPU, 2 pesos). After the *colectivos* stop running at 8pm, you'll have to negotiate a price with a local taxi (20 pesos or more).

The numbered streets in Cholula form a grid with the *zócalo* roughly at the center. But beware: the municipality of Cholula encompasses two towns—**San Pedro Cholula** and **San Andrés Cholula.** The *zócalo,* tourist office, and the majority of the restaurants are located in San Pedro; everything on the other side of the Great Pyramid is in San Andrés. As is usual in Mexico, the same street may go by different names along different stretches. Streets change name at **Av. Miguel Aléman** (also **5 de Mayo**) and **Av. Hidalgo** (**Av. Morelos** or **Av. 14 Oriente** in San Andrés).

Though Cholultecos say that the little crime the city does have is more often directed at business establishments than at individuals, travelers should always exercise caution, especially when walking alone at night. The walk from San Andrés to Cholula past the pyramid can be uncomfortably lonely; cabs travel the distance for 10 pesos.

PRACTICAL INFORMATION

Buses: Estrella Roja, at Av. 12 Ote. and 3 Nte. To Mexico City (2hr., every 30 min. 5am-8:30pm, 15 pesos). Buses also run to Puebla (30 min., every 30 min. 5am-8:30pm, 2 pesos). More destinations through the Puebla bus station.

Tourist Office: Av. 4 Pte. 103 (tel. 47 33 93). Facing the *zócalo* with the yellow Church of San Pedro on the right, turn right and walk toward the red and yellow arches; the office is inside a white building on the left side of the street just past the public library. Books and pamphlets on Cholula and its history are available, as well as handy free maps. Open M-F 10am-6:30pm.

Currency Exchange: Casa de Cambio Azteca, Av. Morelos 605 at 2 Sur (tel. 47 08 19). Though they have more limited hours, the banks around the *zócalo* offer comparable rates. Open M-F 9am-7pm, Sa 9am-2pm. **Bancomer,** in the arcade on the side of the *zócalo* near the Church of San Pedro, is open for exchange M-F 8am-5:30pm, Sa 10am-2pm. **Banamex,** Morelos 8, on the side of the *zócalo* opposite the Church of San Pedro, has an **ATM.** Open M-F 9am-5pm.

Market: Cosmo del Razo, Av. Hidalgo and Av. 5 Norte, also in the *zócalo.* Cheap prices for meat, fruit, flowers, and clothing. Wednesdays and Sundays are *días de plaza* when the already crowded market swells with even more merchants.

Laundromat: Lavandería Burbujas, on Av. 14 Ote. (tel. 47 37 66), 1 block toward the *zócalo* from 5 de Mayo in San Andrés. 1kg for 5 pesos. Open M-Sa 9am-7pm. If it's closed, try **Lavandería Aqui Ahuac,** 14 Oriente No. 2, a few blocks down. Open M-Sa 9am-9pm.

Police: At the Presidencia Municipal, Portal Guerrero 1 (tel. 47 05 62), in the arcade under the arches on the side of the *zócalo.* The station itself is at the intersection of Av. Hidalgo and Calle 5 Sur.

Red Cross: Calle 7 Sur at Av. 3 Pte. (tel. 47 03 93), a bit of a hike from the *centro.* Walk-in service. Open 24hr. No English spoken.

Pharmacy: Farmacia San Juan Bautista, at the corner of Calle 3 Norte and Av. 6 Poniente (tel. 47 34 45) is open **24 hours.** Another option is **Farmacia Moderna,** Morelos 12 (tel. 47 11 99), on the *zócalo.* Open daily 8am-8pm.

Hospital: Clínica de IMSS (tel. 47 53 14), Calle 4 Nte. and Av. 10 Ote. Open 24hr. **Hospital San Gabriel,** Av. 4 Pte. 503 (tel. 47 00 14), 2 blocks west of the *zócalo.* No English spoken.

Post Office: At the intersection of Av. 7 and Av. 5 Pte. Open M-F 8am-7pm, Saturdays and holidays 8am-noon. **Postal Code:** 72760.

Fax: Telecomm, Av. 5 Pte. 102A (tel. 47 01 30). Telegrams, fax, Western Union. Open M-F 8am-6pm, Sa-Su 9am-noon. **Centro de Copiado Cholula,** Morelos 8B (tel./fax 47 14 72), on the south side of the *zócalo.* Open daily 8am-9pm.

Telephones: LADATELs line the west side of the *zócalo,* and phone cards are readily available in nearby stores. Or try the phone inside the **Casa de la Cultura,** which takes coins.

Phone Code: 22.

ACCOMMODATIONS

While there are several hotels beyond the bus station, there is a very limited choice of budget hotels near the *zócalo* and the ruins. Visitors have a larger choice half an hour away in Puebla.

Calli Quetzalcoatl Hotel, Portal Guerrero No. 11 (tel. 47 41 99), right on the *zócalo,* is far and away the best and most convenient hotel in Cholula. Although it is a bit pricey, the Calli Quetzalcoatl features fairly big rooms, telephones in every room (and TVs in most), a restaurant, and a great location. A swimming pool was being added in the summer of 1998. Reservations 5-6 days in advance are recommended, especially for weekend stays. Singles 140 pesos; doubles 170 pesos. Major credit cards accepted.

Hotel Reforma, Calle 4 Sur 101 (tel. 47 01 49), near the corner of Av. Morelos and Calle 4 Sur. From the *zócalo,* walk 2 blocks on Morelos towards the Great Pyramid, then turn right. Hotel Reforma offers spartan but reasonably priced accomodations. Rooms feature full baths with hot water and photographs of area churches, but they offer little protection against noise from the courtyard and from other rooms. Singles 80 pesos; doubles 125 pesos. The front gate is locked from 10:30pm-8am; ring to enter.

Hotel Las Américas, Av. 14 Ote. 6 (tel. 47 09 91), in San Andrés, is worth the 15min. walk from the *zócalo.* To reach the hotel from the *zócalo,* take Av. Morelos and walk past the pyramid approximately 4 blocks; the hotel is on the right after Av. 5 de Mayo (the one in San Andrés, not San Pedro). From the *Estrella Roja* bus station, catch the San Andrés *colectivo* in front of the bus station (2 pesos) and ask to be dropped off at Av. 14 Pte.; the hotel is half a block west. All rooms have TVs and phones, but rooms on the 2nd and 3rd floor have more light. Singles 60 pesos; doubles 80 pesos.

FOOD

Opportunities for the budget diner abound in the area around the *zócalo* and on Morelos and Hidalgo. For some of the cheapest eats in town, check out the food counters at the **mercado** on the north side of the *zócalo* and on Hidalgo and 5 Nte. Also, check out the **stalls in the zócalo,** which serve scrumptious quesadillas and *tortas* for stupefying prices.

Los Tulipanes, Portal Guerrero 13, on the side of the *zócalo* near the Church of San Pedro. You can watch the traffic of the *zócalo* go by as you munch on breakfast (starting at 13 pesos), *antojitos* (10-20 pesos), *comida corrida* (28 pesos), or meat and fish entrees (18-43 pesos). Open daily 8am-9:30pm.

La Lunita, Av. Morelos at 6 Norte (tel. 47 00 11), occupies a graffiti-laden spot next to the railroad tracks, diagonally across from the steps up the pyramid. The restaurant serves complete breakfasts in the morning (20 pesos). At night, the orange-and-purple interior fills mostly with locals. Open daily 8am-2am.

Restaurant Colonial, Morelos 605 (tel. 47 25 08), is across the street from the entrance to the pyramid, making it ideal for a pre-tunnel snack. Enjoy regional specialties (35-40 pesos) as a variety of exotic birds flutter in and out of cages, which are nestled around the secluded courtyard. The restaurant is a convenient stop on the way back to San Andrés. Open daily 9am-10pm.

SIGHTS

When visitors arrive in Cholula, their gaze invariably turns to two things: the city's churches and the huge hill near the *zócalo* called the **Great Pyramid.**

Great Pyramid

In the center of town. ***Ruins and tunnels open*** *daily 9am-7pm.* ***Admission*** *14 pesos, free for students with Mexican ID, seniors, and children under 13, and for all on Sundays. Video camera permit 30 pesos.*

When Cortés destroyed the Toltec temple atop the misshapen hill that dominates Cholula, he was unaware that the hump of earth was actually the giant pyramid of a culture that had dominated the area more than eight centuries before. This ancient civilization mysteriously collapsed in 700, and since then, the pyramid's outer layers of adobe brick have disintegrated and sprouted trees. When the Toltec-Chichimec groups settled in Cholula in the 12th century, they named the pyramid **Tlachiaualtepetl,** or "man-made hill," and are believed to have practiced human sacrifice atop it. Twentieth-century archaeologists tunneled into the "hill," discovering three other pyramids built one on top of the other, the oldest of which dates from roughly 200. Sophisticated drainage systems preserved the structure, which is volumetrically **the largest pyramid in the world.** Today, the archaeological tunnels and some excavations on the south and west sides of the pyramid are open to visitors. Due to a lack of funding, only 5% of Cholula's ruins have been uncovered. The entrance to the tunnel is on Morelos, at the base of the pyramid. To reach the ruined structure, walk from the *zócalo* on Morelos, away from the red and yellow arches, and cross the railroad tracks; 50m farther on the right is the ticket booth.

A pyramid ticket also buys admission to the **Museo del Sitio,** just across the street from the ticket booth. *(Museo open Tu-Su 10-5pm. Free with tickets to the pyramid.)* Enter the Museo first; it gives a general introduction to the archaeological site and is readily accessible when entering the pyramid. Fragments of the remarkable frescoes found on the second pyramid are exhibited in the back room. The fresco of the drinkers, as it was found on the pyramid, is 2.5m high and 65m long, making it one of the longest murals of pre-Hispanic Mexico.

If you're daring and don't mind walking through dimly lit and cramped spaces, enter the pyramid's tunnels. If you decide to brave it, guides will take you through the bewildering, unmarked excavation tunnels for 30-35 pesos. Look for the section of the main staircase that has been excavated from bottom to top to get an idea of the height of one of the smaller pyramids. Dioramas in illuminated sections of the tunnel demonstrate the evolution of the pyramid across the centuries.

Just south of the pyramid is the **Patio de los Altares,** a large grassy area with extraordinary acoustics surrounded by ruins and unearthed chunks of pyramid in various states of restoration. If you clap your hands while standing in the center of the courtyard, you will hear the extraordinary echo. Follow the path as it takes you back to the railroad tracks; make an immediate right outside the fence where it ends, and begin climbing. No ticket is required to reach the **Santuario de Nuestra Señora de los Remedios,** the church built atop the pyramid in 1594 and the highlight of the archaeological zone. Trekking up the pyramid demands as much effort as a Stairmaster workout, but you will be rewarded with a superb view of Cholula and its many churches. On a clear day, the snow-capped volcanoes **Popocatépetl** and **Ixtaccíhuatl** are visible in the distance. Although the church is small, it offers a stunning view on the inside as well: ornate gold decorations and fresh flowers for the daily mass.

Other Sights

There are three other churches worth visiting, all near the *zócalo*. **Parroquia de San Pedro** occupies a commanding place in front of the yellow-arched plaza at the corner of Av. 4 Pomente and Av. 5 de Mayo. *(Open daily 6:30am-1:30pm and 4-8pm.)* Despite undergoing some serious renovations, the church still delights visitors with its exquisitely painted ceilings and walls. Two other notable churches are the **Capilla Real** and the **Convento de San Gabriel,** on the side of the *zócalo* opposite the arches. *(Open M-Sa 9am-1pm and 4-7pm, Su 9am-7pm.)* The churches stand on the site of the **Templo de Quetzalcóatl,** yet another Spanish answer to pre-Hispanic temples. Unadorned but for its 49 domes, the Capilla Real exhibits remarkable structural elegance. The steps in front of San Gabriel's entrance are from the pyramid it replaced.

Aficionados of religious art and architecture should not miss the world-renowned church in the town of **Tonantzintla,** only 15 minutes away. Catch the bus marked "Chipilo" at Av. 6 Ote. and Av. 5 de Mayo (1.50 pesos). The bright saffron facade of **Santa María Tonantzintla** covers a startling interior, where over 450 stucco faces stare out from every spare inch of wall and ceiling. Saints, musicians, and chiefs congregate with animals and flowers in an explosion of spooky excess; it is the handiwork of the same indigenous artisan who executed the plans of European artists in Puebla's Capilla del Rosario (see p. 456). Here, the artisan reinterprets the colonial style with his own fascinating fusion of indigenous and rococo art. Only a 15-minute walk away (or an even shorter 1-peso minibus ride) lies the town, and 15th-century church, of **San Francisco Acatapec.**

A sight not included on most visitors' itineraries is **La Universidad de Las Americas (UDLA).** This elite—and expensive—university is nestled on the east side of Cholula, far away from the slow pace of *zócalo* life. To get to UDLA, catch a *colectivo* (any marked "UDLA" will do) for about 2-3 pesos, and get off about ten minutes later at the clearly marked UDLA gate. It's possible to walk to the UDLA campus by following Av. 14 Oriente, but the fence surrounding the campus is a significant deterrent to would-be walkers. Once at the gate, leave a form of ID with the guard (a student ID will do nicely) and enter the lush, flower-laden campus. Inside the gates, you'll find stereotypical brick university-style buildings with stylishly dressed students toting cellular phones and pagers. It's not one of the most expensive universities in Mexico for nothing. Maps are posted around campus. The **Admissions Office** (Office 112 in Bldg. 1) provides information on undergraduate and graduate programs, and the **bookstore** (in Bldg. 12; open M-F 8am-8pm and Sa 8am-2pm) has the usual college memorabilia as well as an **ATM.** Next to the bookstore is **Cafeteria Santa Catrina,** which offers typical snack-food fare (open M-F 7am-9:30pm, Sa-Su 7:30am-8:30pm). Other buildings on campus include the **William O. Jenkins Building for the Human-**

ities, the **Engineering Building,** and a modern **library**. There's not much to see inside the buildings (blackboards, desks, classrooms, etc.), but the campus itself is nice to explore. Those searching for a free way to check email will be disappointed; an ID is required to enter the university's computer labs.

ENTERTAINMENT

Thanks to its student population, it is not difficult to find distractions left and right in Cholula. Bulletin boards at the **Casa de la Cultura,** Av. 4 Pte. 103A (tel. 47 19 86), in the same white building as the tourist office, advertise special events, films, local arts programs, new book clubs in the area, and the schedules of local aerobics classes (open M-Sa 9am-5pm; Spanish bookstore upstairs). Cholula has plenty of bars and nightclubs for those in search of more alcoholic adventures. Many popular bars and discos line the streets of San Andrés, within a block or two of the Hotel Las Américas. Many others are located closer to the university itself, along **Recta Cholula** (see Puebla). While there is a high rate of turnover among nightclubs, one constant has been **Club Keops,** on the corner of Av. 14 Ote. and 5 de Mayo. Catering to both gay and straight patrons, Keops pulsates nightly with the beat of house and techno music. Keops is easy to spot; look for purple obelisks and fake Egyptian ruins on Av. 14 Ote. Don't miss Travesty, the drag show put on at midnight on Friday and Saturday. (Open W-Sa 9pm-2am, cover 25 pesos.) The video bar **La Tumba el Villa,** Av. Morelos 413, half a block away from the pyramid, features live music on weekend nights. Ignore the saccharine mural of cherubs on the back wall and enjoy the good music and exuberant local crowd. (Open daily 6pm-2am.) Back under the arches on the corner of the *zócalo,* **Bar Enamorada** features music (sometimes live) and a young, hip clientele Thursday through Saturday nights (open daily 10:30am-midnight).

Veracruz

The state of **Veracruz** is one of the hottest, poorest, and most mind-bogglingly diverse in the Republic. Stretching 300km along the Gulf of Mexico, Veracruz encompasses breathtaking beaches, burgeoning cities, and vast spaces filled only by roaming cattle and lush vegetation. Unlike most of Mexico's, its economy is not dependent only on farming. Although many local residents make their livings from tobacco and coffee farming and small-scale cattle ranching, the state's main income comes from oil and fishing. But the state that works hard also parties hard: *veracruzanos,* also known as *jarochos,* are renowned for their delightful senses of humor, their wonderful seafood and coffee, and their Afro-Caribbean inspired music that relies heavily on the marimba. The Afro-Caribbean influence dates back to the days when the city of Veracruz was the main slave trading port for the country—it pervades not only the state's music but also its cuisine and ethnic makeup. Local color is supplied by the over-hyped but still vital *curandero* culture. *Curanderos* (medicine men), called *brujos* (witches) by locals, practice a unique mixture of conjuring, devil-invocation, and natural healing.

Mexico's very first light-skinned visitors—Cortés and his ruthless band of *conquistadores*—reached land in Veracruz in 1519 and began the first European trek to the capital from these shores. Today, the state of Veracruz, especially the volcanic hills of La Sierra de los Tuxtlas, remains relatively untouristed; those who come are pleasantly surprised. Marimba rhythms and Caribbean colors flow through the steamy port city of Veracruz day and night, and the beautiful mountain city of Xalapa overflows with art and culture.

HIGHLIGHTS OF VERACRUZ

- **Veracruz** (see p. 476), the state capital, is a sweaty and alluring port city. Spend your days checking out the **Castillo de San Juan de Ulúa** (see p. 480) and your nights dancing to the sounds of marimba.
- The temperate, green, beautiful city of **Xalapa** (see p. 463) is also a cultural center—its **Museo Nacional de Antropología** (see p. 467) is considered the second-best museum in the country.
- Many movies have been filmed at the unearthly **Cascada de Texolo** (see p. 469). Check out these scenic falls and find out why.
- Many travelers ditch the beach resorts and instead choose to do their own exploration along the beautiful **Gulf coast** (see p. 485) south of Veracruz.
- **Papantla** (see p. 472) is not only a clean and friendly town, but also a bastion of Totonac culture—it's the best base from which to explore **El Tajín** (see p. 474), the most impressive ruins in the state.

Xalapa (Jalapa)

Perched high on a mountain slope, Xalapa (hah-LAH-pah) is many things: a home to a large and vibrant college community, a haven for talented artists, and a colonial town replete with old Spanish buildings and a fascinating history. Xalapa's rich, leafy landscapes and cooler climate lure visitors away from hotter Veracruz and surprise them with its cultural opportunities.

The capital of the state of Veracruz since 1885, Xalapa was first settled by Náhuatl speakers who dubbed the area "spring in the sand." After the Spanish conquest, Xalapa's annual fairs earned the city the economic importance it continues to enjoy today. Downtown Xalapa is the busy, giddy center from which the rest of the city ripples outward, merging gracefully with the raw beauty of the Veracruz landscape. Steep cobblestone streets provide a magnificent view of the verdant peaks surrounding Xalapa at every turn, while the bustling avenues give constant evidence of a city fairly bursting at the seams with artistic energy.

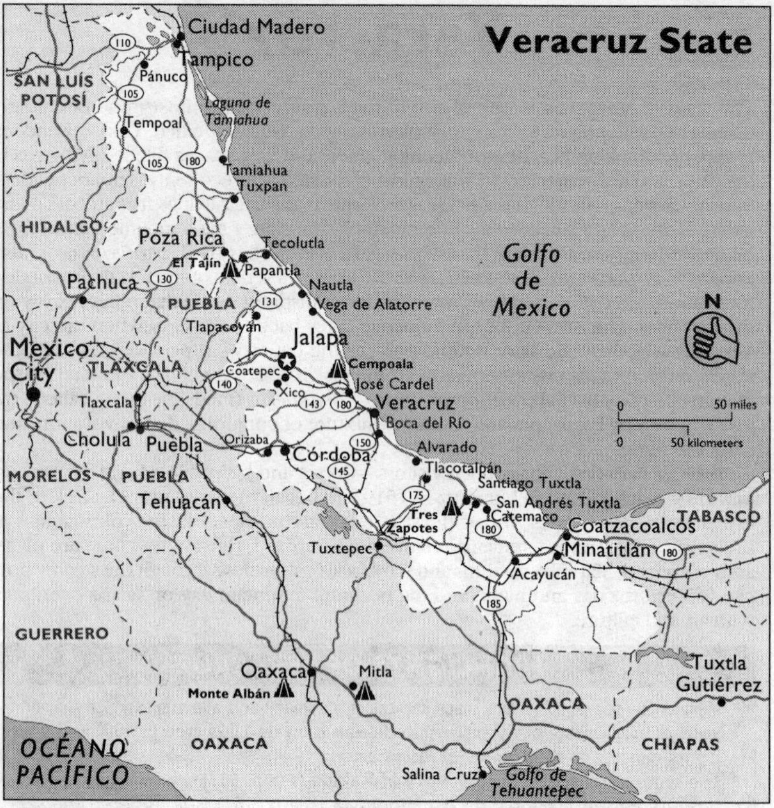

ORIENTATION

Xalapa lies 104km northwest of Veracruz along Route 140 and 302km east of Mexico City. The **train station** is at the extreme northeast edge of the city, a 40-minute walk or 8-peso taxi ride from the *centro.* To get from the **bus station** to the *centro,* catch buses marked "Centro" or "Terminal" (2.10 pesos); a taxi will cost 10 pesos. There are two bus stations. **CAXA** is the major one for service to distant cities. The **Terminal Excelsior** is a roundabout where you can catch buses to small neighboring towns. Make sure to clarify which bus station you want to go to.

Xalapa, like many other hilly towns, can be quite confusing. The **centro,** or downtown area, centers around the **cathedral** and **Palacio de Gobierno.** The street that separates them is **Enríquez,** which runs along **Parque Juárez.** Streets that branch from Enríquez toward the park and the Palacio de Gobierno run downhill; streets that split from Enríquez on the cathedral side run uphill. This uphill/downhill distinction works best for the streets near the *centro.* Going away from the park toward the cathedral, Enríquez becomes two streets: **Xalapeños Ilustres** to the left and **Zamora** to the right. In the opposite direction, Enríquez becomes **Av. Camacho.**

PRACTICAL INFORMATION

Transportation

Buses: CAXA, in a state-of-the-art building at 20 de Noviembre 571, east of the city center. The station has long-distance phones, telegraph service, a pharmacy, shopping, food, and drink. **ADO** (tel. 18 99 80) travels first-class to

LET'S GO Order Form

Last Name*	First Name*	Home and Day Phone Number* (very important)	
Street*	(Sorry, we cannot ship to Post Office Boxes)		
City*		State*	Zip Code*
Citizenship[‡§¤] (Country)	School/College[§]	Date of Birth[‡§]	Date of Travel*

Qty	Description	Color	Unit Price	Total Price

Shipping and Handling

2-3 Week Domestic Shipping	
Merchandise value under $30	$4
Merchandise value $30-$100	$6
Merchandise value over $100	$8
2-3 Day Domestic Shipping	
Merchandise value under $30	$14
Merchandise value $30-$100	$16
Merchandise value over $100	$18
Overnight Domestic Shipping	
Merchandise value under $30	$24
Merchandise value $30-$100	$26
Merchandise value over $100	$28
All International Shipping	$30

Total Purchase Price	
Shipping and Handling	+
MA Residents add 5% sales tax on gear and books	+
TOTAL	

☐ Mastercard ☐ Visa

Cardholder name:

Card number:

Expiration date:

When ordering an International ID Card, please include:

1. Proof of birthdate (copy of passport, birth certificate, or driver's license).
2. One picture (1.5" x 2") signed on the reverse side.
3. (ISIC/ITIC only) Proof of current student/teacher status (letter from registrar or administrator, proof of tuition, or copy of student/faculty ID card. FULL-TIME only).

* Required for all orders
‡ Required in addition for each Hostelling Membership
§ Required in addition for each International ID Card
¤ Required in addition for each railpass

Prices are in US dollars and subject to change.

Make check or money order payable to:
Let's Go Travel
17 Holyoke Street
Cambridge, MA 02138
(617) 495-9649

1-800-5LETSGO

Hours: Mon.-Fri., 10am-6pm ET

For your calling convenience tear off and take with you!

AT&T

Special Features

Just dial the AT&T Access Number for the country *you are in* and follow the instructions listed below.

- To call U.S. 800 numbers: Enter the 800 number you are calling. (Note: Based upon the 800 number dialed, calls may be toll-free or **AT&T Direct**℠ Service charges may apply for the duration of the call; some numbers may be restricted.)
- To set up conference calls: Dial AT&T TeleConference Services at 800 232-1234. (Note: One conferee must be in the U.S.)
- To access language interpreters: Dial AT&T **Language Line**® Services at 408 648-5871.
- To record and deliver messages: Dial #123 if you get a busy signal or no answer, or dial AT&T **True Messages**® Service at 800 562-6275.

Here's a time-saving tip for placing additional calls: When you finish your conversation, or if there is a busy signal or no answer, <u>don't hang up</u> – press # and wait for the voice prompt or an AT&T Operator.

To Call the U.S. and Other Countries Using Your AT&T Calling Card* or credit card,∞ Follow These Steps:

1. Make sure you have an outside line. (From a hotel room, follow the hotel's instructions to get an outside line, as if you were placing a local call.)
2. If you want to call a country other than the U.S., make sure the country *you are in* is highlighted in blue on the chart like this: ☐
3. Enter the AT&T Access Number listed in the chart for the country *you are in*.
4. When prompted, enter the telephone number you are calling as follows:
   - For calls to the U.S., dial the Area Code (no need to dial 1 before the Area Code) + 7-digit number.
   - For calls to other countries,† enter 01+ the Country Code, City Code, and Local Number.
5. After the tone, enter your AT&T Calling Card* or credit card number (not the international number). If you need help or wish to call the U.S. collect, hold for an AT&T Operator.

* You may also use your AT&T Corporate Card, AT&T Universal Card, or most U.S. local phone company cards.
† The cost of calls to countries other than the U.S. consists of basic connection rates plus an additional charge based on the country you are calling.
∞ Credit card billing subject to availability.

Calling From Specially Marked Telephones

Throughout the world, there are specially marked phones that connect you to **AT&T Direct**℠ Service. Simply look for the AT&T logo. In the following countries, access to **AT&T Direct** Service is *only* available from these phones: Ethiopia, Mongolia, Nigeria, Seychelles Islands.

Public phones in Europe displaying the red 3C symbol also give you quick and easy access to **AT&T Direct** Service. Just lift the handset and dial ✻60 (in France dial M60) and you'll be connected to AT&T.

Pay phones in the United Kingdom displaying the New World symbol provide easy access to AT&T. Simply lift the handset and press the pre-programmed button marked AT&T.

Customer Care

If you have any questions, call 800 331-1140, Ext. 707.

When outside the U.S., dial the AT&T Access Number for the country *you are in* and ask the AT&T Operator for Customer Care.

108-25 Printed in the U.S.A. on recycled paper.

AT&T

AT&T Direct℠ Service

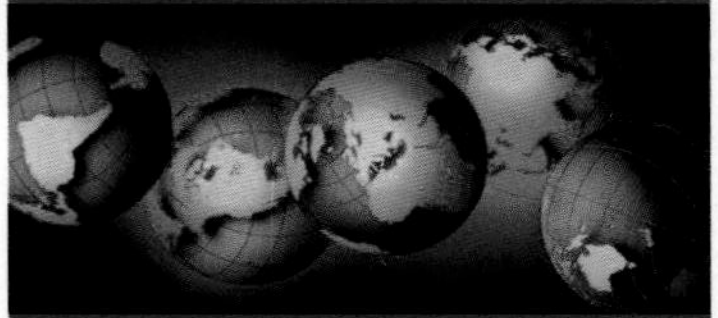

Wallet Guide

Inside you'll find simple instructions on how to use **AT&T Direct** Service to place calling card or collect calls from outside the U.S.

All you need are the AT&T Access Numbers when you travel outside the U.S., because you can access us quickly and easily from virtually anywhere in the world. And if you need any further help, there's always an AT&T English-speaking Operator available to assist you.

www.att.com/traveler

It's all within AT&T your reach.

AT&T Access Numbers (Refer to footnotes before dialing.) From the countries highlighted in blue below, like this ▭, you can make calls to virtually any location in the world; and from *all* the countries listed, you can make calls to the U.S.

Albania ●	00-800-0010
American Samoa	633 2-USA
Angola	0199
Anguilla ✚	1-800-872-2881
Antigua ✚	1-800-872-2881
(Public Card Phones)	#1
Argentina	0-800-54-288
Armenia ●,▲	8◆10111
Aruba	800-8000
Australia	1-800-881-011
Austria ○	022-903-011
Bahamas	1-800-872-2881
Bahrain	800-001
Bahrain ↑	800-000
Barbados ✚	1-800-872-2881
Belarus ✖,━	8◆800101
Belgium ●	0-800-100-10
Belize ▲	811
(From Hotels Only)	555
Benin ●	102
Bermuda ✚	1-800-872-2881
Bolivia ●	0-800-1112

Bosnia ▲	00-800-0010
Brazil	000-8010
British V.I. ✚	1-800-872-2881
Brunei ●	800-1111
Bulgaria ■,▲	00-800-0010
Cambodia ✻	1-800-881-001
Canada	1 800 CALL ATT
Cape Verde Islands	112
Cayman Islands ✚	1-800-872-2881
Chile	800-800-311 or 800-800-288
(Easter Island)	800-800-311
China, PRC ▲	10811
Colombia	980-11-0010
Cook Island	09-111
Costa Rica	0-800-0-114-114
Croatia ▲	99-385-0111
Cyprus ●	080-90010
Czech Rep. ▲	00-42-000-101
Denmark	8001-0010
Dominica ✚	1-800-872-2881

● Public phones require coin or card deposit. 2 Press red button. ◗ Additional charges apply when calling outside of Moscow. ■ **AT&T Direct**℠ calls cannot be placed to this country from outside the U.S. ✻ Available from pay phones in Phnom Penh and Siem Reap only. ✖ Not available from public phones. ⊛ From St. Maarten or phones at Bobby's Marina, use 1-800-872-2881.

Dom. Rep. ★,□	1-800-872-2881
Ecuador ▲	999-119
Egypt ● (Cairo)	510-0200
(Outside Cairo)	02-510-0200
El Salvador ○	800-1785
Estonia	8-00-8001001
Fiji	004-890-1001
Finland ●	9800-100-10
France	0800 99 00 11
French Antilles	0800 99 0011
French Guiana	0800 99 00 11
Gabon ●	00◆001
Gambia ●	00111
Georgia ▲	8◆0288
Germany	0130-0010
Ghana	0191
Gibraltar	8800
Greece ●	00-800-1311
Grenada ✚	1-800-872-2881
Guadeloupe ✚,✸ (Marie Galante)	0800 99 00 11

Guam	1 800 CALL ATT
Guantanamo Bay ↑ (Cuba)	935
Guatemala ○,✸	99-99-190
Guyana ★	165
Haiti	183
Honduras	800-0-123
Hong Kong	800-96-1111
Hungary ●	00◆800-01111
Iceland ●	800 9001
India ✖,➤	000-117
Indonesia ➙	001-801-10
Ireland ✓	1-800-550-000
Israel	1-800-94-94-949
Italy ●	172-1011
Ivory Coast ●	00-111-11
Jamaica ○	1-800-872-2881
Jamaica □	872
Japan KDD ●	005-39-111
Japan IDC ●,▲	0066-55-111
Kazakhstan ●	8◆800-121-4321
Korea ●2	0072-911 or 0030-911
Korea ↑	550-HOME or 550-2USA

◇ From this country, **AT&T Direct**℠ calls terminate to designated countries only. ↑ From U.S. Military Bases only. ━ Not yet available from all areas. ✸ Select hotels. ▲ May not be available from every phone/public phone. † Collect calling from public phones. ➤ Available from phones with international calling capabilities or from most Public Calling Centers. ✓ From Northern Ireland use U.K. access code.

Kuwait	800-288
Latvia (Riga)	7007007
(Outside Riga)	8◆27007007
Lebanon ○ (Beirut)	426-801
(Outside Beirut)	01-426-801
Liechtenstein ●	0-800-89-0011
Lithuania ✖,━	8◆196
Luxembourg †	0-800-0111
Macao	0800-111
Macedonia, F.Y.R. of ●,○	99-800-4288
Malaysia ○	1800-80-0011
Malta	0800-890-110
Marshall Isl.	1 800 CALL ATT
Mauritius	73120
Mexico ▽1	01-800-288-2872
Micronesia	288
Monaco ●	800-90-288
Montserrat	1-800-872-2881
Morocco	002-11-0011
Netherlands Antilles ⊛	001-800-872-2881

Netherlands ●	0800-022-9111
New Zealand	000-911
Nicaragua	174
Norway	800-190-11
Pakistan ▲	00-800-01001
Palau	02288
Panama	109
(Canal Zone)	281-0109
Papua New Guinea	0507-12880
Paraguay ■,▲ (Asuncion City)	008-11-800
Peru ▲	0-800-50000
Philippines ●	105-11
Poland	0◆0-800-111-1111
Portugal ▲	05017-1-288
Qatar	0800-011-77
Reunion Isl.	0800 99 0011
Romania ●	01-800-4288
Romania ↑	01-801-0151
Russia ●,◗,▲ (Moscow)	755-5042
(Outside Moscow)	8-095-755-5042

★ Collect calling only. ○ Public phones require local coin payment through the call duration. ◆ Await second dial tone. ▽ When calling from public phones, use phones marked "*Ladatel*." 1 If call does not complete, use 001-800-462-4240. △ Available from public phones only. ✚ Public phones and select hotels. ❮ When calling from public phones use phones marked Lenso.

Russia ●,◗,▲ (St. Petersburg)	325-5042
(Outside St. Petersburg)	8-812-325-5042
St. Kitts/Nevis & St. Lucia ✚	1-800-872-2881
St. Pierre & Miquelon	0800 99 0011
St. Vincent △,■	1-800-872-2881
Saipan ▲	1 800 CALL ATT
San Marino ●	172-1011
Saudi Arabia ◇	1-800-10
Senegal	3072
Sierra Leone	1100
Singapore ■	800-0111-111
Slovakia ▲	00-42-100-101
Solomon Isl.	0811
So. Africa	0-800-99-0123
Spain	900-99-00-11
Sri Lanka ■	430-430
Sudan	800-001
Suriname △	156

Sweden	020-795-611
Switzerland ●	0-800-890011
Syria	0-801
Taiwan	0080-10288-0
Thailand ❮	001-999-111-11
Trinidad/Tob.	0800-872-2881
Turkey ●	00-800-12277
Turks & Caicos ✚,■	01-800-872-2881
Uganda	800-001
Ukraine ▲	8◆100-11
U.A. Emirates ●	800-121
U.K. ▲,✜	0800-89-0011 or 0500-89-0011
U.S. ▼	1 800 CALL ATT
Uruguay ■	000-410
Uzbekistan	8◆641-7440010
Venezuela	800-11-120
Vietnam ●	1-201-0288
Yemen	00 800 101
Zambia	00-899
Zimbabwe ▲	110-98990

□ Calling Card calls available from select hotels. ➙ Use phones allowing international access. ▼ Including Puerto Rico and the U.S. Virgin Islands. ━ **AT&T Direct**℠ Service only from telephone calling centers in Hanoi and post offices in Da Nang, Ho Chi Minh City and Quang Ninh. ✜ If call does not complete, use 0800-013-0011.

Catemaco (4½hr., 7 per day, 78 pesos), Mexico City (5hr., 22 per day 1am-midnight, 95 pesos), Papantla (4hr., 7 per day, 74 pesos), Puebla (3hr., 9 per day, 55 pesos), San Andrés Tuxtla (3½hr., 11 per day, 74 pesos), Santiago Tuxtla (3½hr., 10:25am and 7:45pm, 71 pesos), Tuxtepec (5½hr., 6am and 3:35pm, 77 pesos), and Veracruz (2hr., 48 per day 5:30am-11:30pm, 32 pesos). Slightly slower, slightly cheaper second-class service to almost identical destinations provided by **Autobuses Unidos (AU).**

Tourist and Financial Services

Tourist Office: (tel. 18 01 96), a kiosk in the bus station, to the far left as you enter the terminal, is the best source of information. Open daily 8am-10pm. There is occasionally a makeshift kiosk run by the Palacio Municipal across from Parque Juárez on Enriquez that sells handy maps for 5 pesos.

Currency Exchange: Banamex, at the corner of Xalapeños Ilustres and Zamora (tel. 18 17 13), is open M-F 9am-5pm and has a 24hr. **ATM** across the street. Also try **Centro Cambio Jalapa** (tel. 8 68 60), further down on Zamora.

American Express: Carrillo 24 (tel. 17 41 14; fax 12 06 01), 3 blocks from Parque Juárez, past the cathedral off Enríquez. Cashier open M-F 9am-2pm and 4-7pm. **Viajes Xalapa,** a full-service **travel agency,** shares the office.

Local Services

Market: Jaúregui, Lucio at Altamirano, stationed on the left uphill from the right of the cathedral. Open daily 8am-6pm. **Chedraui** is a supermarket on the corner of Lucio and Callejón del Flores. Also has a **pharmacy.** Open daily 8am-9pm.

Laundromat: Lavandería Los Lagos, Dique 25 (tel. 17 93 38), around the corner from Casa de Artesanías. 3½kg for 15 pesos. Open M-Sa 9am-2pm and 4-7pm.

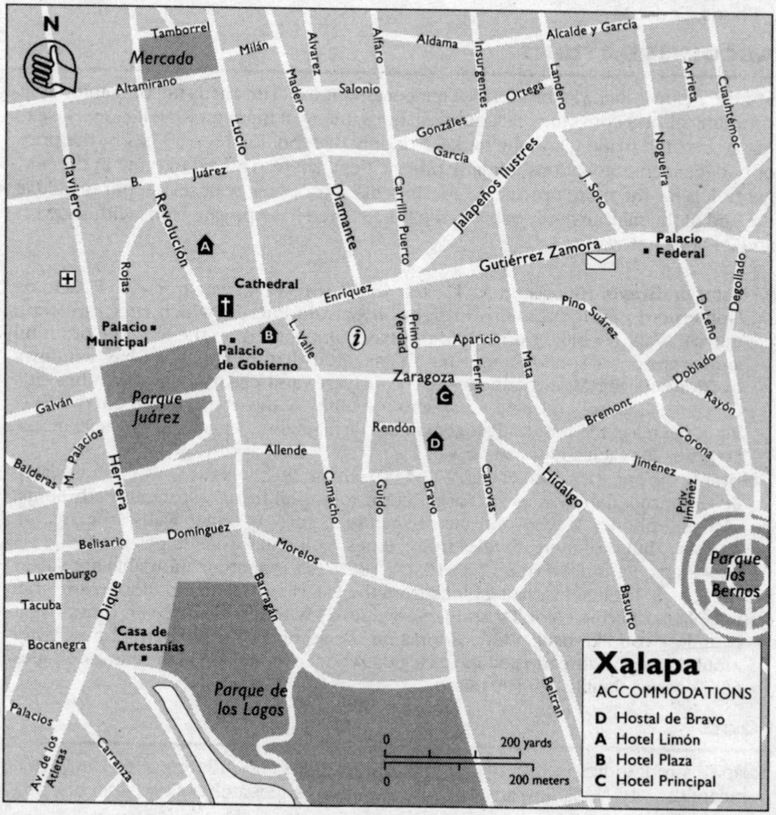

Emergency and Communications

Emergency: Dial 06.

Police: (tel. 18 18 10), helpfully sprinkled throughout the city, on the corner of Arteaga and Aldama and at the Cuartel San José.

Red Cross: Clavijero 13 (tel. 17 34 31 for emergencies or tel. 17 81 58 for administration), a block uphill from Parque Juárez. 24hr. ambulance service.

Pharmacy: Farmacia Benavides (tel. 18 92 01), Enríquez at Revolución next to the cathedral. Open daily 7am-10pm.

Hospitals: Hospital Civil, Pedro Rendón 1 (tel. 18 44 00), at Bravo. 24hr. emergency care. **IMSS,** Lomas del Estadio (tel. 18 55 55). No English spoken.

Post Office: (tel. 17 20 21), at Zamora and Diego Leño in the Palacio Federal. Open M-F 8am-8pm, Sa 9am-noon. **Postal Code:** 91001.

Fax: Telecomm, Zamora 70 (tel. 16 21 67), around the corner from the post office. Open M-F 9am-7pm, Sa 9am-5pm, Su 9am-noon. Also available at the bus station on the right-hand side.

Internet Access: Café Internet Xalapa, Pasaje Enrique Loc #1 (tel./fax 17 51 41; email cafexalapa@cafexalapa.com.mx; http://www.cafexalapa.com.mx), located in the commercial center of Enríquez. Offers basic Internet access (including telnet and Microsoft Explorer) as well as fax, scanning, copying, and virtual reality games. Access can be frustratingly slow, but staff is friendly and knowledgeable. 24 pesos per hour. Open M-Sa 9am-9pm. Also try **ServilExpress,** on Av. Zaragoza 14 (tel./fax 18 31 13). Offers Internet access (20 pesos per hour) but primarily concentrates on copying and printing services. Open M-F 9am-8pm, Sa 9am-2pm.

Telephones: LADATELs outside the Palacio de Gobierno on Enríquez and outside the post office. **Caseta** at Calle Guerro 9, off the southwest corner of the Parque Juárez. Open daily 9am-10pm. There are also plenty of phones at the bus station.

Phone Code: 28.

ACCOMMODATIONS

For the penny-pinching traveler, Xalapa is a gold mine. The city is full of comfortable, economical, and convenient accommodations, many of them on **Revolución,** close to the *centro,* the market, and the parks. Not only that, but for 100-150 pesos (the price of budget accommodations in many other cities), you can afford to trade in the budget hotels for the more upscale establishments. Ah, Xalapa really is the pot of gold at the end of the rainbow. All rooms in the hotels listed have private baths with showers and 24-hour hot water.

Hostal de Bravo, Nicolas Bravo 11 (tel. 18 90 38). Walk away from the Palacio de Gobierno on Enríquez and turn right on Carrillo Puerto (which later turns into Bravo). Walk 1½ blocks downhill; this oasis of a hotel is on the left. The beautiful and large rooms sparkle and offer TV, spacious bathrooms, huge bay windows overlooking the Mediterranean-style courtyard, and cedarwood wardrobes (it's true—smell them!). A friendly staff and proximity to the *centro* round out this little bit of paradise, the best budget gem in the city. Singles 75 pesos; doubles 90 pesos. 10 pesos for each additional person.

Hotel Principal, Zaragoza 28 (tel. 17 64 00), about 2½ blocks away from the Palacio de Gobierno along Zaragoza. Large, clean rooms all feature spacious bathrooms, TVs, and phones. Rooms with more amenities, such as wall-to-wall carpeting, are available, but cost more. Singles from 70 pesos; doubles from 80 pesos.

Hotel Plaza, Enríquez 4 (tel. 17 33 10; fax 18 27 14), is another affordable hotel near the *centro,* located just half a block from the Palacio de Gobierno. Rooms are large but plain, offering color TV and large windows with less than scenic views—that is, unless you like back alleys. Rooms on the second floor are better; most wrap around an open-air patio and have elegant wooden doors and high ceilings. Singles 60-70 pesos; doubles 70-100 pesos.

FOOD

Xalapa's strength lies in the myriad of sidewalk cafes and indoor coffee shops that populate the city. Walk into any one of these shops and watch college students, professors, and *norteamericanos* from language schools passionately argue and discuss subjects over their *café con leche*. Restaurants are somewhat harder to find than the omnipresent cafes, but some good ones surround the *centro*. As is typical of Mexican towns, particularly cheap cuisine can be found in the market.

Restaurante La Sopa, Callejón del Diamante 3A (tel. 17 80 69; fax 12 07 52), 2 blocks from the park along Enríquez on a narrow pedestrian street across from Banco Serfín. Ultra-hip waiters cater to a similar crowd in this ultra-hip joint, located on—you guessed it—an ultra-hip walkway. Fixed lunch menu 13-15 pesos, dinner from 10-20 pesos. And if you don't know what to do at night, ask the waiters; they'll be sure to know what's going on in town. Open 1-5:30pm and 8pm-midnight. Usually full after 9:30pm. Live music after about 9 Th-Sa.

Enrico's Restaurant, Enríquez 6 (tel. 17 64 47). About half a block down Enríquez from the Palacio de Gobierno. Ignore the cafeteria-style atmosphere of this place, and concentrate on the food. Delicious *enchiladas verdes* (with green sauce; 15 pesos) and *tacos de pollo* (with chicken; 10 pesos) are worthy of its excellent location. Open M-Sa 8am-9pm.

Café de la Parroquia, Zaragoza 18 (tel. 17 74 01), 1 block downhill from the Plaza de Gobierno. Like its famous cousin in Veracruz, the cafe is always full and lively and brimming with its well-known *café con leche* (8 pesos). Breakfast is a little steep, starting at 21 pesos, but *antojitos* are more reasonable (13-25 pesos). Also try the delicious fried plantains (10 pesos). Open daily 7:30am-10:30pm. Another branch, at Camacho 42 (tel. 17 71 57), is open daily 8am-midnight.

Café Chiquito, Zamora 35, directly across from the post office. Watch language students practice their skills or browse through a cultural newsletter while sipping coffee in this earth-toned nook. Breakfast 12-17 pesos, *antojitos* 11-19 pesos. Chocolate milkshakes 9.50 pesos. Open M-Th 8:30am-10pm, F-Sa 8:30am-11pm.

SIGHTS

Museo de Antropologia

To get there, catch a yellow "Tesorería" bus on Enríquez (2.10 pesos); take a taxi (8 pesos); or walk on Enríquez/Camacho away from the cathedral, then make a left on Av. Xalapa and continue on for several blocks until you see the museum on your left (45min.). ***Open*** *daily 9am-5pm.* ***Free tours in Spanish*** *are given daily at 11:30am (they last approximately 1½ hours), and English tours can be arranged at any time for 100 pesos.* ***Admission*** *15 pesos, students 8 pesos. Camera 10 pesos, video camera 40 pesos.*

This museum is probably the second best museum in all of Mexico, after Mexico City's Museo Nacional de Antropología (see p. 106). But while the Mexico City museum is a monster encompassing cultures from the entire county, Xalapa's museum focuses on just the cultures that inhabited what is today the state of Veracruz. The museum was finished in October of 1986, and today its shiny marble exhibits feature massive Olmec heads, smiling Totonac figurines, and Huastec skulls and artifacts, laid out in chronological order along the rectangular hallway that makes up the main part of the museum. Start your visit at the front, with the oldest and most elusive culture, the Olmecs. Displayed in spectacular marble galleries and outdoor gardens, the museum's 10 Olmec heads are perhaps the most impressive of its 3000 items (for more, see **The Beginnings of a History,** p. 44). With the decline of the Olmecs by 400 BC, power shifted north to the Totonac, whose rule stretched from El Tajín through Xalapa. The museum explores the Totonac rise and reign through a large panorama of the huge ceremonial city of El Tajín and through Totonac sculptures and jewels. Finally, the Huastec culture arose and remained powerful until the arrival of the Spanish, whose coming is noted in scrolls at the very end of the museum. A fascinating journey through the history of pre-Hispanic Veracruz, the museum is best viewed with the knowledgeable University of Veracruz students who work as guides at the museum. For more information, ask at the ticket booth. The bookstore in the lobby sells an assortment of anthropology books, and there is also a cafeteria.

Other Sights

Some of Xalapa's most popular sights are its **public parks and gardens,** the hallmarks of a vibrant and livable city. The **Parque Ecológico Macuitépetl** is primarily a preserve for the flora and fauna indigenous to the Xalapa area, but it also serves as one of the city's principal recreational areas. *(Park open daily 6am-6pm.)* To get there, take a "Mercado-Corona" *colectivo* (1.50 pesos) from Revolución and Altamirano (1.20 pesos), or hail a taxi (7 pesos). A brick path meanders past lip-locked lovers to the summit of an extinct volcano 186m above the city, where a spiral tower offers a commanding view of the city and mountains. Downhill from Parque Juárez, on Dique, lies the **Paseo de los Lagos,** where a bicycle path traces the perimeter of several urban lakes. On sunny afternoons, the park is full of children, chirping birds, panting joggers, and still more amorous young couples. Like any urban park, it can be dangerous at night. At the west end of the park, near Dique, is the **Casa de Artesanías** (tel. 17 08 04), an activity center that hosts different fairs, festivals, and exhibits (open M-F 8am-8pm, Sa-Su 10am-1pm). Check at the tourist office to see what's going on.

Through the east entrance of the **Palacio de Gobierno,** off Enríquez opposite Parque Juárez, lies a marble courtyard with a staircase marching upward into the bureaucratic chambers above. The banister is guarded by bronze *conquistadores,* their swords beaten into lamp-posts instead of ploughshares. The mural on the wall, by Mario Orozco Rivera, depicts a family overcoming ignorance and injustice. No shorts allowed. Nearby, the terraces of **Parque Juárez,** built in 1892, share their view of the city and mountains with a small cafe, located in the stairs behind the Agora de la Ciudad (open Tu-Su 8am-9:15pm). One place where you'll be sure to avoid public displays of affection is the 18th-century **cathedral** on the corner of Enríquez and Revolución (open daily 9am-1pm and 4-7pm).

If you're in the mood to satisfy your sweet tooth while getting a dose of religion, head to the convent of **Los Madres Capuchinas,** 20 de Noviembre Ote. 146. *(Open M-F 9am-6pm.)* The easiest way to get there is to take a cab (7 pesos). Don't let the deserted-looking grate deter you; ring the bell. These nuns have been making exquisite marzipan candy/art for over 20 years. Good-sized boxes of delicately colored and delicious fruits, vegetables, and birds go for 25-35 pesos. The store also sells religious art and trinkets.

ENTERTAINMENT

Xalapa is bursting with cultural opportunities. Ask at the bus station kiosk, or pick up a copy of a local newspaper for information about concerts, dance, and theater. The **Agora de la Ciudad** cultural center, located at the bottom of the stairs in the Parque Juárez (tel. 18 57 30), has a screening room, gallery space, and loads of information and schedules about local events. Open daily 9am-3pm; cafe open 9am-9pm. The **Teatro del Estado** (tel. 17 31 10), a 10-minute walk from Parque Juárez on Enríquez/Camacho, at the corner of Ignacio de la Llave, holds enticing performances—the excellent **Orquesta Sinfónica de Xalapa** and the **Ballet Folklórico de la Universidad Veracruzana** appear regularly. A city with more than 6000 students, Xalapa is also one of the major destinations in Mexico for aspiring artists. The **Festival de las Flores** drowns the town in petals every April.

On weeknights, the cafes along Enríquez and Zaragoza brim with activity. **Tierra Luna,** Diego Leño 28 (tel. 12 13 01), has frequent live music (open M-Th 8:30am-10pm, F-Sa 8:30am-11pm). As the weekend approaches, people migrate from cafe tables to bars and dance floors. **Bistro Cafe del Herrero,** Camacho 8 (tel. 17 02 68), is where a cool twenty-something crowd drinks to the sounds of a peppy 80s dance mix (open daily 1pm-2am). **Discotheque La Estación,** 20 de Noviembre 571 (tel. 17 31 55), just below the bus station, is the grande dame of Xalapa discos. With a crowd almost as diverse as your average college yearbook cover photo, 7a Estación caters to a wide array of people. Get your steady groove on the spacious dance floor. (*Barra libre* on Thursday. Cover Wednesday for men 30 pesos, Thursday 50 pesos, W-Th no cover for women, F-Sa 20 pesos for all after 10pm. Open W-Sa 9pm-2am.)

■ Near Xalapa: Xico and Cascada de Texolo

It's hard to believe that **Xico** (SHEE-koh) is located a mere 19km from Xalapa—here, there are almost as many mules on the road as there are automobiles. Xico is known for its cuisine (*mole xiqueño,* a slightly sweeter version of *mole poblano*) and its nine-day festival dedicated to Mary Magdalene, the town's patron saint. The festival begins on July 22 in 1999 and includes bullfights and a running of the bulls.

But if any tourists go to Xico, it's not for the culture or cuisine of the town. Most go for the spectacular **Cascada de Texolo,** located just 3km from the tiny town. The dramatic waterfall crashes into a gorge alive with vivid greenery, the songs of passing birds, and the constant drum of water as it spills into the river below. A restaurant and viewing area are across from the falls. From a bridge leading to the other side of the gorge, several paths yield stunning views of other waterfalls and dense vegetation. If it looks like it could almost be out of a movie, it is. Several American movies, including *Romancing the Stone* with Michael Douglas and *Clear and Present Danger* with Harrison Ford, have used the dramatic falls for key scenes. The falls are also used (somewhat less glamourously) for car and deodorant commercials. In any case, the filming crews have left no trace of their presence. The falls are clear and crisp and relatively free of tourists. The only signs of civilization are the restaurant and the few orange and blue buildings of the electric company that uses the falls to generate power.

The best viewing area is **Restaurante El Mirador.** The restaurant has a charming outdoor seating area and serves up regional specialties (10-15 pesos; open daily 9am-7pm). On the other side of the gorge, two gentle waterfalls are visible. The first appears as soon as you step off the bridge. Down a level by the white picket border, another waterfall plunges from the electricity plant to the river below. Only after returning across the bridge and turning right toward the white fence of the observation deck can you see the water whose rumble you've been hearing so loudly. To truly experience the falls in all their glory, head to the left and go down the cement steps with the orange railings. Go down until you reach a fork in the path (by the *"Peligro"*—"Danger"—signs). The path to the left leads to an electric company building while the path to the right leads to the most spectacular view of *la cascada.* Your persistence will pay off when you reach the base of the falls. The vista is like something out of a fantasy book. Surrounded by the rush of water and playful butterflies, take your time and explore—skip over to the other side of the river to rejoice in the mist generated by the waterfall. Don't forget that the path you came from is the rocky one directly across from the main waterfall.

The rocks are often slippery and deserted, so it is best to exercise extreme caution and to wear appropriate footwear. Also, the walk to the falls is a long and lonely one. Despite the friendliness of the people of Xico, try not to go by yourself and definitely don't try to hike to the falls at night. The insects are also silent and ferocious, so bring plenty of bug repellent.

Getting There: To get to Xico from Xalapa, take the "Terminal" bus from the stop in front of the 3 Hermanos shoe store on Enríquez (not the one on Lucio) and get off at the Excelsior bus roundabout (about 8min., 2.10 pesos). From there, cross the street to blue Excelsior where buses are lined up and take a "Xico" bus (45min., 5.30 pesos).

To reach the falls, alert the bus driver as soon as the blue "Entrada de la Ciudad" sign appears on the right side of the road. The bus will turn right onto a smaller street and let you off. Retrace the steps back to the main street and climb straight up the hill in front of you until you reach a fairly wide dirt T-intersection (about a 5-6 minute climb); head left. Descending the hill, you will reach another fork guarded by a makeshift shrine to the Virgin; bear right after paying respects. The road curves to the right and then downhill to the viewing area and Restaurante El Mirador. If you get lost, ask the (very) occasional passerby for directions to the *cascadas*. To return to Xalapa and develop that film, re-trace your steps, but be aware that the walk will take 40 minutes and is not a smooth one. Taxis sometimes make the trip to the waterfalls, but the ride is also neither smooth nor fast. As you go back downhill from the dirt road, stick to

Siempre Fidel

Mexico has a long tradition of close and friendly relations with Cuba. When Fidel Castro fled the island in the late 1950s, it was in Tuxpan that he organized the revolutionary forces that months later led the country in the fight against dictator Batista. The first hopeful years of the Cuban Revolution are celebrated in the **Casa de la Amistad México-Cuba.** *(Open daily 9am-2pm and 3-7pm. Admission free, but donations are always welcome.)* Photographs of a young, beardless Fidel line the walls, and a colorful mural depicts the valiant leader and his fellow boatsmen disembarking under the watchful gazes of Latin American heroes Benito Juárez, José Martí, and Simón Bolívar. The final room on the tour displays pictures of doctors and farmers, symbolizing Cuba's social progress, as well as a proud look back through the guestbook and the diverse crop of visitors expressing support for the Cuban Revolution. To get to the museum, take a blue ferry (1 peso) across the river. Walk right (west) along the sidewalk and continue straight up the dirt road, past the overgrowth to the paved sidewalk, turn left, and enter on the side of the two small, white buildings with the boat out front

the right of the street to hail one of the blue "Xalapa" buses, which will deposit you back at the Excelsior Terminal. Take a bus marked "Mercado" to head back into town, but make sure it refers to Xalapa and not elsewhere.

■ Tuxpan (Tuxpam)

The first thing you notice when you step into the heart of Tuxpan is the funky smell, something like seafood, sweat, and sulfur. Although this may sound unappetizing, almost everything about Tuxpan (pop. 120,000) is actually quite palatable. Despite the bustle of the fresh *marisco* markets, couples amble up and down the Río Tuxpan, and the humidity and mellow plaza make for lovely, lethargic lounging. Much like their Olmec, Huastec, and Totonac predecessors, boys stand on the shore flinging their nets repeatedly into the water and fruit vendors traverse the streets near the riverfront selling bananas and mangoes by the bag. If everything seems too loud and crowded elsewhere, fear not—Tuxpan makes for terrifically easy living. For a sandy, salty break, **Playa Azul** is just 12km away. On weekends, the beach overflows with families splashing about.

ORIENTATION AND PRACTICAL INFORMATION Tuxpan, 347km northwest of Veracruz, spreads along the northern bank of Río Tuxpan. Activity centers around two park-like plazas. **Blvd. Reyes Heroles** is Tuxpan's main street, running along the river. One block north lies the omnipresent **Benito Juárez** followed, moving north, by **Morelos. Parque Rodríguez Cano** is on the waterfront, just south of the busiest part of town, and **Parque Reforma** is between Juárez and Morelos a few blocks west of Rodriguez Cano. The bridge lies on the east edge of town. Streets perpendicular to the bridge and parallel to the water run roughly east-west. Each bus line has its own station. To get to the town center from any one, walk to the river. From the **Estrella Blanca** station, walk toward and past the bridge—from the other stations, walk away from the bridge. To get to the beach, catch a "Playa" bus from the bench along the boardwalk by the ferry docks (every 10min. 6am-9pm, 5 pesos).

Each **bus** line has its own station. **ADO,** Rodríguez 1 (tel. 4 01 02), three blocks east of Parque Cano down Reyes Heroles, has first-class service to Mexico City (5hr., 13 per day, 95 pesos), Papantla (1½hr., 7 per day, 21 pesos), Tampico (3½hr., every hr., 69 pesos), Veracruz (5hr., 11 per day, 93 pesos), and Xalapa (5hr., 5 per day, 94 pesos). **Estrella Blanca, Turistar,** and **Futura,** at Cuauhtémoc 18 (tel. 4 20 40), two blocks past the bridge and two blocks inland, offers first-class service to Matamoros (12hr., 2 per day in the evenings, 216 pesos), Mexico City (6hr., 8 per day, 95 pesos), and Monterrey (12 hr., 2 per day, 281 pesos) as well as second-class service to most nearby destinations. **Ómnibus de México,** Independencia 30 (tel. 4 11 47), at the bridge, has first-class service to Guadalajara (15 hr., 2 per day in the evenings, 302 pesos), Mexico City (6 hr., 6 per day, 95 pesos), and Querétaro (10 hr., 3 per day, 127 pesos).

The **tourist office,** Juárez 20 (tel. 4 01 77), is in the Palacio Municipal in Parque Rodríguez Cano. Enter on the Juárez side—it's a small office across from Hotel Florida. Try for maps. (Open M-F 8am-3pm and 6-8pm.) **Serfin** (tel. 4 09 25), on Juárez between the two parks, is open M-Sa 9am-5pm and exchanges traveler's checks M-F 9am-2:30pm. It also has a 24 hour **ATM. Banamex,** Juárez 21 (tel. 4 90 39), at Morelos, has a 24-hour **ATM** and exchanges traveler's checks (open M-F 9am-1pm).

There is a **laundromat, Lavandería Mejico,** Reyes Heroles 57 (tel. 4 27 08), 3 blocks west of the *centro* which will wash, dry, and iron your clothes in two hours flat (3 kg 24 -32 pesos; open M-Sa 8am-8pm). In an **emergency,** dial 06. The **police station,** Galeana 38 (tel. 4 37 22) is located next door to the Red Cross, west of the *centro* (open 24 hr.). The **Red Cross,** Galeana 40 (tel. 4 01 58), is eight blocks west of the *centro* along the river, then 4 blocks up Galeana, at the mini-bridge. Doctors speak English. For a **pharmacy,** try **Benavides,** Rodriguez 9 (tel. 4 12 41), at the bridge-side of the market one block in from the river (open daily 7am-10pm). To reach the **post office** with **MexPost,** Mina 16 (tel. 4 00 88), from the Parque Reforma, follow Morelos towards the bridge, and then take the second left onto Mina (open M-F 8am-6pm, Sa 9am-1pm). The **postal code** is 92800. **LADATELs** were last spotted in Parque Rodríguez Cano standing still. The **phone code** is 783.

ACCOMMODATIONS Budget accommodations in Tuxpan cluster around the two central parks, ensuring a reasonable measure of safety into the evening hours. **Hotel Parroquia,** Escuela Militar 4 (tel. 4 16 30), to the left of the cathedral on Parque Rodríguez Cano, offers rooms with spacious bathrooms, some with TV and balconies overlooking the park and river—all at rock-bottom prices. Full-length mirror, fan, and TV lounge provide all you need. (1 person 73 pesos; 2 people 91 pesos; 3 people 110 pesos; 4 people 200 pesos). **Hotel El Huasteco,** Morelos 41 (tel. 4 18 59), is half a block east from the northeast corner of Parque Reforma. While extreme claustrophobes may do well to skip the small, windowless rooms, museum lovers should not. Ask for a room with mosaiced walls, skylights, immaculate upkeep, and freezing A/C make this feel like the Guggenheim. (Singles 72 pesos, doubles 82-99 pesos.) Those in search of luxury at still lowish rates should head for **Hotel Plaza,** Juárez 39 (tel. 4 07 38 or 4 08 38). Smack dab between Tuxpan's two main plazas, the large rooms come with beautiful wooden furniture and are stocked with phones, TV and A/C. (1 person 150 pesos; 2 people 180 pesos; 3 people 200 pesos; 4 people 230 pesos.)

FOOD Balancing traditional Mexican decor (simple, elegant wooden furniture and colorful tiles) with modernity (TVs to track *telenovelas* or fútbol matches), **El Mejicano,** Morelos 49 (tel. 4 89 04), at the corner of Parque Reforma, serves up tasty regional cuisine. Sample *pescado a la mexicana* (32 pesos) or *antojitos* like *tacos de bistec* (22 pesos). Licuados (10 pesos) are simply orgasmic, made only with fresh, seasonal fruit. (Open daily 6am-1am.) The same owner operates **Cafetería El Mante,** Juárez 8 (tel. 4 57 36), one block west of Rodríguez. Enjoy your hotcakes (14 pesos) amidst a festive atmosphere—kiss-me-red tablecloths and hanging plants—and lots of locals. **Restaurant Don Carlos,** Escuela Amerigo Militar 12, near the Hotel Parroquia (above), is small and very clean. The resident familia will whip up delicious dishes of seafood and meat right in front of your face (5-22 pesos). The comida corrida is an unbelievable 10 pesos. (Open daily 7am-11pm.)

SIGHTS, SAND, AND ENTERTAINMENT Tuxpeños are justly proud of their river's relaxed beauty and scenic shores. Palm trees line the boardwalk, and goods are sold up and down the river; under the bridge, piles of pineapples, bananas, shrimp, and fish can be had for a bare minimum at the huge open-air market which flows from the indoor market on Calle Rodríguez. Located on the waterfront, **Parque Rodríguez Cano** comes alive every Monday at 5:30pm for the **Ceremonia Cívica,** when government officials make speeches and schoolchildren march in an orderly procession.

Twelve kilometers from the city center, Tuxpan's **beach** can be crowded and slightly dirty, especially during the high season and hot weekends, but the wide expanse of fine sand stretches far enough for you to stake a private claim somewhere down the line under the wild coconut palms. The beach is accessible by the "Playa" bus (every 15min. 6am-10pm, the last bus returns to Tuxpan at 8pm, 5 pesos).

There are a number of **bars** in Tuxpan's *centro,* and the town has had problems with brawls and rowdy nightgoers. Clubs and bars have short lifespans in Tuxpan, and places practically empty during the week are packed during the weekend. The best and safest nightlife in town can be found a few blocks down the river after the crowds in Parque Reforma thin out. At **Mantarraya** (tel. 4 00 51), Reyes Heroles at Guerrero, a young crowd grooves to American pop and techno hits. The enormous interior is the perfect place to chill, to dance, or to fall in love. Live music frequently includes elderly men crooning popular ballads while screaming teens drink and sing along (cover 20-40 pesos including 2 drinks; open Th-Sa 8:30pm-3am).

Papantla

Papantla is almost picture-perfect. Crawling up the green foothills of the Sierra Madre Oriental, the city (pop. 156,000) looks out onto the magnificent plains of Veracruz. Despite its poverty, the city's white stucco houses have gorgeous Mediterranean-tiled rooftops, and the white-tiled, always-swept plaza contains beautiful Indian stone carvings and wild yellow finches in the trees—even people climbing its insanely steep streets smile between huffs and puffs. Papantla is also one of the few remaining centers of Totonac culture. Conquered by the power-hungry Aztecs around 1450, the Totonac soon took their revenge, helping Cortés crush the Aztec Empire in the 16th century. In modern Papantla, barefoot white-clad *indígenas* share the plaza with tattooed teens. Totonac rituals persist in the flight of the *voladores,* a thrilling acrobatic ceremony once laden with religious meaning, now only performed on weekends for delighted tourists. Papantla makes also a good base for exploring **El Tajín,** the highly impressive ruins of the Totonac capital, 12km south of the city (see p. 474). So take a deep breath and start up that mile-high street; the view is worth the workout.

ORIENTATION Papantla lies 250km northwest of Veracruz and 21km southeast of Poza Rica along Rte. 180. Downtown activity centers around **Parque Téllez,** the central plaza. The perfectly white-washed cathedral on Nuñez y Dominguez rises on the plaza's southern side while **Enríquez** borders it on the north. Sloping downhill to the north are **Juárez** (on the east side) and **20 de Noviembre** (on the west side), both perpendicular to Enríquez. **Azueta** starts just past 20 de Noviembre, also running downhill at a slight angle. **16 de Septiembre** goes up along the right of the cathedral as you face it. To get from the **ADO bus station** to the *centro,* turn left on Juárez out of the station and veer left at the fork. Taxis (7 pesos to the *centro*) pass frequently along Juárez. The walk from the station to the *centro* is steep but not long. If you arrive at the **second class-bus station,** turn left outside the station and ascend 20 de Noviembre three blocks to the northwest corner of the plaza.

PRACTICAL INFORMATION Papantla has two **bus stations.** The first-class **ADO** station, Juárez 207 (tel. 2 02 18), serves Mexico City (5hr., 6 per day, 85 pesos), Tuxpan (1½hr., 4 per day, 21 pesos), Veracruz (4hr., 6 per day, 69 pesos), and Xalapa (4hr., 8 per day, 74 pesos). The second-class terminal, commonly called **Transportes Papantla,** 20 de Noviembre 200, heads to Poza Rica (40min., every 20min. 4am-10pm, 6.50 pesos). Pay after boarding. **Poza Rica** (21km northwest of Papantla) is a nearby transportation hub. Their **ADO** station (tel. 2 04 29 or 2 00 85) runs buses to Mexico City (4½hr., every hr., 79 pesos), Papantla (35min., 22 per day, 6 pesos), Puebla (5hr., 9 per day, 76 pesos), Tampico (4½hr., every hr., 85 pesos), Tuxpan (45min., 33 per day, 16 pesos), Veracruz (4hr., 17 per day, 76 pesos), and Xalapa (5hr., 13 per day, 80 pesos). The **Chamber of Commerce,** Ramón Castaneda 100 (tel. 2 00 25), sometimes has excellent maps and brochures about Papantla and rudimentary info about El Tajín and the Veracruz state. To get there, follow Lázaro Muñoz (the narrow street running east from the plaza) four blocks downhill and turn right. (Open M-F 9am-5pm, Sa 9am-2pm.) The staff of the **tourist office** (tel. 2 01 23), on 16 de Septiembre across from the side entrance to the cathedral, has maps and tons of information about the Voladores (open M-F 9am-3pm and 6-9pm). A slew of banks on the northern side of the plaza, including **Banamex,** Enríquez 102 (tel. 2 00 01), have 24-hour **ATMs** (open M-F 9am-5pm, Sa 9:30am-2pm; exchanges traveler's checks M-F 9am-2pm).

The **police** (tel. 2 00 75 or 2 01 50) are in the Palacio Municipal (open 24hr.). Back in Papantla, the **Red Cross** (tel. 2 01 26) is on Escobedo off Juárez. Some English is spoken. (Open 24hr.) **Farmacia Benavides,** Enríquez 103E (tel. 2 06 36), is at the northern end of the plaza (open daily 7:30am-10pm). **Clínica IMSS** (tel. 2 01 94), on 20 de Noviembre at Lázaro Cárdenas, provides emergency medical care. From the ADO station, take a right and walk two blocks to Cárdenas, then turn left; IMSS is half a block up on your right. Avoid walking straight down 20 de Noviembre from the plaza, as the road is extremely hilly. (Open 24hr.) Much more easily accessible, the **Clínica del Centro Medico** (tel. 2 00 82), on 16 de Septiembre just down from the tourist office, is also open 24hr. Little to no English is spoken. The **post office** with a **MexPost** attached is on Azueta 198 (tel. 2 00 73), second floor (open M-F 9am-4pm, Sa 9am-noon). The **postal code** is 93400. The **phone code** is 784.

ACCOMMODATIONS Few lodgings are available in tiny Papantla. A lovely, economical option is to stay at **Hotel Totancapán** (tel. 2 12 24 or 2 12 18), 20 de Noviembre at Olivo, four blocks down from the plaza. Here, hallway murals, crazy colors, funky re-tiling jobs, and large windows make things (unintentionally?) swank and totally cool. Furnishings are simple but complete, and a bedside TV and telephone will put you at ease. Enjoy the most affordable air-conditioning around. (Singles 90 pesos, with A/C 115 pesos; doubles 110 pesos, with A/C 140 pesos). For simpler and cheaper living, **Hotel Pulido,** Enriquez 205 (tel. 2 00 36), two-and-a-half blocks down from the plaza past Banamex, should be your pick. Set motel-style around a courtyard/parking lot full of happily chirping birds, simple rooms sport comfortable beds and fans. (Singles 70 pesos; doubles 80 pesos; twins 100 pesos; 3 people 130 pesos; 4 people 150 pesos.) A step up in ritz, **Hotel Tajín,** Núñez y Domínguez 104 (tel. 2 01 21), half a block to the left as you face the cathedral, displays a carved stone wall from El Tajín its lobby. Perched on a hill above the city, the balconies afford panoramic views. Amenities include purified water, TV, and phones. Guided horseback tours of the area are available (for a fee). Unfortunately, a luxury hotel means luxury prices. (Singles 160 pesos, with A/C 216 pesos; doubles 220 pesos, with A/C 280 pesos.) However, bargaining is an option, especially for large groups or in the off-season (Oct.-May). Ask for 10-30% off.

FOOD Papantla's few restaurants serve regional delicacies to tourists looking for authentic cuisine. Most eateries stick to beef and pork offerings with just a smattering of seafood. **Restaurant Plaza Pardo** (tel. 2 00 59), next door to Sorrento (below), serves up simply out-of-this-world food. Watch wise locals stuff their faces full of soft, delicious tamales (5 pesos) and *molotes* (12 pesos), or heavier meat dishes (16-30 pesos). There's a balcony, to boot, that catches a deliciously cool breeze and a superb view of the town: it's an ideal place to watch the *voladores* dance their way to earth. Large tacky murals and a view of the plaza enliven **Sorrento,** Enríquez 105 (tel. 2 00 67), a popular breakfast hangout. It's no wonder, with these kind of early-morning *menús económicos* (6-14 pesos). Lunchtime *comida corrida* is only 14 pesos, and *antojitos* hover around 10 pesos. (Open daily 7am-11pm.)

SIGHTS AND ENTERTAINMENT Papantla's biggest attractions are the relics of its Totonac heritage. South of the plaza is the **Catedral Señora de la Asunción,** remarkable not so much for its interior, but for the stone mural carved into its northern wall, which measures 50m long and 5m high. Called **Homenaje a la Cultura Totonaca,** the mural was created by Teodoro Cano to honor local Totonac heroes and folklore figures. Its focus is the plumed serpent Quetzalcóatl, whose image runs along the full length of the carving. Brimming with history, the mural depicts such wonders as the

Learning to Fly

Papantla's *voladores* are renowned for their graceful acrobatics. The performance begins with five elaborately costumed men climbing a stationary pole to a platform at least 28m above the ground. Having consumed courage-enhancing fluids, the *voladores* begin by saluting the four cardinal points: the sun, the wind, the moon, and the earth. Four of the hardy five then wind ropes around the pole, tie them around their waists, and start to "fly"—hanging from the ropes, spinning through the air, and slowly descending to earth. Meanwhile, the fifth man plays a flute and dances on the pole's pin-head. Once off the structure, the *voladores* become *los hombres pájaros* (the bird men). Slowly, they circle the pole 13 times head-down, as the pole turns to lengthen their ropes; this signifies the coming of the rains. Originally, each of the four fliers corresponded to one of the four cardinal directions; positions assumed during descent were related to requests for specific weather conditions. Now, however, the ritual has become more commercial: instead of performing once every 52 years, the *voladores* fly as often as tourists feed them pesos. You can watch the ceremony in Papantla during the festival of Corpus Christi in early June, at El Tajín whenever a crowd of tourists gathers, or in New York or Denmark when the *voladores* go on tour.

discovery of corn and eager ballplayers vying for the right of ritualistic death and deification. The mural is truly massive and is the most immediate and impressive structure in Papantla's *centro.*

The cathedral's spacious courtyard commands a view of the *zócalo.* Called the **Plaza de los Voladores,** the courtyard is the site of the ceremony in which *voladores* acrobatically entreat the rain god Tlaloc to water the year's crops. In early June, during the 10-day **Festival of Corpus Christi,** the *voladores* perform as often as three times a day. To get to the festival from the *centro,* take any *pesero* (1.60 pesos) from 16 de Septiembre behind the cathedral and ask for the *feria,* or flag a taxi (10 pesos). During the festival, Papantla itself remains quiet and calm as ever; only a trickle of tourists and small crowds of locals watch the *voladores.* The real action takes place at a fair just outside of town, with artistic expositions, fireworks, traditional dances, and cockfights. Once every 52 years, at the turning of the Totonac century, the festival takes on grandiose proportions.

Papantla's latest effort to enshrine its *voladores* is the **Monumento al Volador,** a gigantic flute-wielding *indígena* statue erected in 1988 atop a hill and visible from all over town. To get to the monument, where you can read explanatory plaques and see all of Papantla, walk up Reforma, the road to the right. Follow the road as it curves left, then make a sharp left before the road starts to slope down and continue uphill. Mountain-climbing picnickers be forewarned, there are no benches and little shade at the monument. There is, however, a small cafe.

The town's two markets are situated next to the central plaza. **Mercado Hidalgo,** on 20 de Noviembre off the *zócalo*'s northwest corner, beats **Mercado Juárez,** at Reforma and 16 de Septiembre off the southwest corner of the *zócalo,* hands down.

■ Near Papantla: El Tajín

The impressive **ruins of El Tajín** only hint at the thriving Totonac civilization that once spread across modern-day northern Veracruz. *(Admission on the same ticket to museum and ruins 16 pesos.)* Named for the Totonac god of thunder, El Tajín served as the political and religious center of the Totonac people. Marked similarities between buildings here and those at Teotihuacán reflect the influence of the Aztec and Maya civilizations. Next to the entrance stands a large pole, the apparatus of the **voladores** (see p. 473). June through August, the *voladores* perform almost hourly; the rest of the year, they descend through the air only on weekends. These daring acrobats—who typically request a 10-peso donation when they are finished—generally perform after a large group has finished touring the ruins. A tiny but useful brochure and map (5 pesos) about El Tajín in English or Spanish can be purchased at the **information desk.** In addition to overpriced plastic carvings, the **store** adjoining the information desk carries maps and excellent tour guides of Veracruz state, Tuxpan, and Papantla—often better information than is frequently available in the cities themselves.

As you enter the ruins, you will pass the **Museo del Sitio del Tajín.** The museum features original fragments of murals and an eerie, fascinating display filled with sand and ancient skeletons, some with cracked skulls and visible bone injuries—a must-see for the secretly morbid maniac in you. The meager explanations are in English and Spanish; guards will be happy to expand on them, mostly in Spanish.

From the museum, a straight path leads to the ruins. They are not labeled or explained in any way. Besides a good guidebook, the best information sources are the blue uniformed "rangers" stationed throughout El Tajín. Totonacs themselves, the rangers may offer to give you an ad hoc tour of a certain area; they will eagerly answer any questions, although their English proficiency may be limited. You can also hire a guide from the information desk or tag along with a school or big tour group.

The **Plaza del Arroyo,** the central rectangular plaza formed by four tiered pyramids, lies just to the left of the gravel road. Each pyramid points toward the northeast at a 20° angle, in a feat of architectural planning maintained in all of the early buildings at this site. The heart of El Tajín is just past the pyramids. Two identical, low-lying, slanted constructions to the left of the observation area form a central ballcourt in which the famous one-on-one game called **pok-ta-pok** (see **Hoop Dreams,** p. 564) was played. Every 52 years, a contest was held between the most valiant ballplayers. The winner gained the honor of being decapitated and sacrificed. Puts the World Cup to shame, no? Approximately 17 such courts grace the ruins of Tajín.

Across from the plaza stands an elevated central altar surrounded by two climbable temples. Just left of the altar is a split-level temple that displays a statue of Tajín. This area was known as the **Central Zone** and is notable because the styles and functions of the buildings here vary considerably. To the northwest stands **La Pirámide de los Nichos,** a fascinating structure with seven levels and a total of 365 niches corresponding to the days of the year. Each niche was once painted in red, crimson, and blue. The Totonacs marked time in 52-year epochs, during which a single flame was kept continuously burning. At the end of each epoch, the carefully nurtured flame was used to ritually torch many of the settlement's buildings. Each new epoch of rebuilding and regeneration was inaugurated by the lighting of a new flame. Ritual ceremonies are now held annually at the pyramid during the vernal equinox; farmers place seeds in the pyramid's niches and later retrieve them for planting.

Farther north and atop a hill is **Tajín Chico,** accessible either by a series of large stepping stones or an easy-to-ascend staircase off to the west. Whereas Tajín was a public religious and social center, archaeologists hypothesize that Tajín Chico was where the ruling class and political elite actually lived. This is one of the less-excavated areas and is bordered by "no access" signs where more structures may be hidden. However, park officials don't mind if visitors scamper up the higher buildings to get a view of the site and surrounding hills or climb through the tunnel at the back end of the structures. East of Tajín Chico, down the hill and around the curve in the gravel road, is the **Great Xicalcoliuhqui,** a tremendous recreational and/or religious area that is still being unearthed.

Getting There: El Tajín is accessible via *pesera* from the bus stop in Papantla behind the cathedral on Calle 16 de Septiembre. Buses (every 15min. 5am-8pm, 4.50 pesos) going to Poza Rica pull into Tajín. Ask the man with the clipboard recording the buses for "Tajín", and he'll make sure you get on the right one. Your bus will first pass through El Chote and stop at the entrance to El Tajín, marked by a stone mural. To return to Papantla, catch a "Papantla" bus just outside the museum (last bus leaves at 5pm, 4.50 pesos), or walk down the access road to the main highway and cross the road to the bus stop to catch a *pesera* running back to El Chote (2.50 pesos). From El Chote, you can catch one of the many buses leaving for nearby Papantla (2 pesos).

Veracruz

The oldest port city in the Americas, Veracruz possesses the nearly untranslatable qualities of *sabor,* rich and alluring flavor, and *ambiente,* unique and enchanting atmosphere. Amid a slew of new construction projects, the sounds of bamba and marimba music play into the warm Gulf nights as tourists and citizens alike sip the city's delicious *café con leche* by day and fall sway to a seductive marimba beat by night. Since Cortés landed in "La Rica Villa de la Vera Cruz" in 1519, Veracruz has been Mexico's port to the outside world. Pirates long frequented the steamy port; after colonial contact, the city prospered as the only port in New Spain officially permitted to trade with the mother country. It was here that Juárez proclaimed the laws of the Reforma and here that he staged the reconquest of Mexico from the Hapsburg Emperor Maximilian. Twice the city was occupied by American troops.

Today, Veracuz's streets continue to fill with sailors—as well as tourists—from around the world. Modern Veracruz (pop. 327,500) sprawls along Mexico's Gulf coast, merging gracefully with **Boca del Río** (pop. 143,800), the prosperous home of the area's best beaches, most chic discos, and most expensive hotels. Touristy beach glitz is undercut by the numerous oil rigs and barges that fill the harbor. A hot, humid urban sprawl that drips with sweat into the night, the twin cities are buffeted by strong winds called *nortes,* a display of nature's force that some people find disagreeable and others spectacular.

ORIENTATION

Veracruz lies on the southwestern shore of the Gulf of Mexico, 104km south of Xalapa, 424km west of Mexico City, and 376km north of Oaxaca. To get to the *zócalo* from the **bus station,** take a "Díaz Mirón" bus (2.10 pesos) to Parque Zamora and walk away from the park on Independencia for 7 blocks. To get back to the bus station from downtown, catch a Díaz Mirón bus heading toward Parque Zamora on 5 de Mayo. A taxi will cost you 10 pesos. From the **train station,** turn right at the exit and walk toward the opposite end of the plaza in front of you. The plaza ends at Lerdo; take a right and follow it into the *zócalo.*

Downtown Veracruz is laid out grid-style; streets run either parallel or perpendicular to the coast. **Díaz Mirón** runs north-south and converges with **Av. 20 de Noviembre** at **Parque Zamora,** south of downtown. Here, the two streets become **Independencia,** the main drag. Independencia forms the boundary of the *zócalo* farthest from the water. **Miguel Lerdo,** to your left as you face the Palacio Municipal, has a string of hotels and restaurants. It runs toward the water and the **Plaza de la República,** home of the train station and the post office, as well as the drop-off point for many municipal bus routes. To your right is **Zamora;** across **Zaragoza** toward the Gulf, it becomes **Malecón,** the boardwalk. At the edge of the water, Malecón makes a 90° turn to the right and becomes **Avila Camacho,** which follows the Gulf to **Boca del Río,** a suburb housing some posh discos and restaurants.

The *centro* is generally safe, but visitors should be careful. As always, never give the name of your hotel to somebody you just met—thieves have been known to chum up to tourists in the *zócalo* and then rob them at their hotel. Do not walk far from the downtown area after dark. Women may find themselves the object of more male attention than they would receive in smaller towns, typically in the form of invitations from random men. A firm and polite refusal will be grudgingly accepted during the day, but at night it may well be taken as a challenge to overcome.

PRACTICAL INFORMATION

Transportation

Airport: (tel. 34 00 08). 8km south of downtown Veracruz on Rte. 150. **Aeroméxico** (tel. 35 01 42) and **Mexicana** (tel. 32 22 42, at airport 38 00 08) are both represented by **Viajes Carmi,** Independencia 837 (tel. 31 27 23), north of the *zócalo.* Open M-F 9am-1:30pm and 3:30-7:30pm, Sa 9am-1pm.

Buses: Central de Autobuses, Díaz Mirón 1698. **ADO** (tel. 37 57 88), with first-class service to Cancún (21hr., 10:35pm, 380 pesos), Catemaco (3hr., 5 per day 9:30am-5:15pm 46 pesos), Mexico City (5½hr., 19 per day, 130-168 pesos), and Xalapa (1¾hr., every 30min. 2:30am-11pm, 32 pesos). **Cristóbal Colón** (tel. 37 57 88) has first-class service direct to Oaxaca (6½hr., 11pm, 145 pesos) and Tuxtla Gutiérrez (12hr., 6 and 7pm, 151 pesos). **Cuenca** (tel. 34 54 05) sends second-class buses to Oaxaca (6½hr., 6:30am and 8pm, 87 pesos) and Tuxtepec (3hr., every hr. 5am-8pm, 37 pesos). **AU** (tel. 37 57 32; buses leave from La Fragua, 1 block behind ADO station) offers second-class service to Córdoba (1½hr., 3:40, 5, and 6:20pm, 40 pesos), Mexico City (6½hr., every hr. 6am-1am, 110 pesos), Orizaba (2½hr., 3:40, 5, and 6:20pm, 40 pesos), Puebla (4½hr., every hr. 6am-7pm, 11pm, and midnight, 83 pesos), and Xalapa (1¾hr., 12 per day 1am-4pm, 32 pesos). **Líneas Interunidas** (tel. 37 28 78) operates from the AU terminal to Catemaco (3½hr., every 30min. 2am-midnight, 40 pesos), San Andrés Tuxtla (3hr., every 10min. 2am-midnight, 37 pesos), and Santiago Tuxtla (2½hr., every 10min. 2am-midnight, 35 pesos).

Tourist and Financial Services

Tourist Office: (tel. 32 19 99), in the Palacio Municipal on the right side as you face it in the *zócalo.* Helpful staff speaks some English and hands out maps and brochures. Open M-Sa 9am-9pm, Su 9am-3pm. Try to go earlier in the day when there is more staff on hand.

Currency Exchange: There are a slew of banks on the corner of Juárez and Independencia, 1 block from the *zócalo*. **Banamex** (tel. 32 68 93) has 4 24hr. **ATMs.** Open M-F 9am-5pm. **Bital** (tel. 32 50 36) also has a 24hr. ATM. Open M-Sa 8am-7pm. Nearby is **Casa de Cambio Puebla,** Juárez 112 (tel. 24 50 52). Open M-F

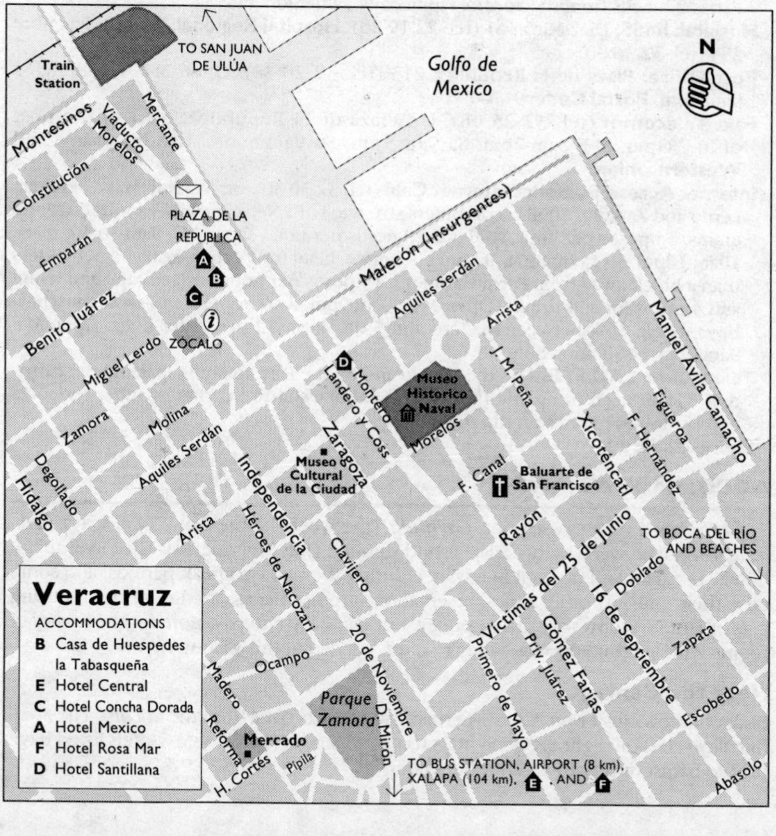

9am-6pm. Virtually the only place open for exchange on the weekends is **Mini Súper Pete's,** Aquiles Serdán 797 (tel. 32 09 18), 2 blocks from the *zócalo* (open daily 8am-noon).

American Express: Camacho 221 (tel. 31 46 36), inside "Viajes Olymar," across from Villa del Mar beach. "Villa del Mar" bus stops behind the tourist office on Zaragoza. Won't cash traveler's checks. Open M-F 9am-1:30pm and 4-6pm, Sa 9am-noon.

Local Services

Markets: Mercado Hidalgo, on the corner of Cortés and Madero, 1 block from Parque Zamora away from the Gulf. Fruit, vegetables, *piñatas,* seafood, flowers, meat, you name it. Open daily 8am-6pm. Touristy **artisan markets** and stalls found at the corner of Landero y Cross and Malecón and along the boardwalk along Malecón.

Supermarket: El Alba (tel. 32 24 34), M. Lerdo between Independencia and 5 de Mayo, just 1 block from the *zócalo.* Open M-Sa 9am-2:30pm and 5-9pm. The **ATM** at Banco Serfin next door will help you fund those purchases.

Laundromat: Lavandería Ultra-Clean, Serdán 789 (tel. 32 94 23), between Madero and 5 de Mayo. Same day service, 5 pesos per kg. Open M-Sa 9am-7pm.

Emergency and Communications

Emergency: Dial 060.

Police: (tel. 38 06 64 or 38 06 93) in the Palacio Municipal.

Red Cross: (tel. 37 55 00) on Díaz Mirón between Orizaba and Pérez Abascal, 1 block south of the Central de Autobuses. No English spoken. 24hr. emergency service and ambulance on call.

Pharmacy: Farmacia del Ahorro (tel. 37 35 25) on Paseo del Malecón at Gómez Farías 2 blocks from the *zócalo.* Open daily 7am-midnight.

Hospital: IMSS, Díaz Mirón 61 (tel. 22 19 20). **Hospital Regional,** 20 de Noviembre 284 (tel. 32 36 90).

Post Office: Plaza de la República 213 (tel. 32 20 38). Open M-F 8am-8pm, Sa 9am-1pm. **Postal Code:** 91700.

Fax: Telecomm (tel. 32 25 08). On Plaza de la República, next to the post office. Open M-F 8am-7pm, Sa 9am-5pm, Su 9am-noon. Also **telegrams** and **Western Union.**

Internet Access: Stationet Internet Café (tel. 32 30 36), on Av. 5 de Mayo between Lerdo and Zamora. 80mHz computers struggle with Netscape and various chat programs. 14 pesos per hour, students 10 pesos per hour. Open M-F 9am-10:30pm, Sa 10am-10pm, Su 11am-8pm. If telnet is a must, head for **Webcafé,** Rayón 579-A, less than a block away from Parque Zamora. 15 pesos per hour for Netscape and telnet and 4 pesos for soft drinks. Open M-Sa 9am-9pm. Another place to try is **Netchatboys,** Lerdo 369, between Madero and 5 de Mayo. 12 pesos per hour. Open M-F 9am-9pm, Sa-Su noon-8pm.

Telephones: LADATELs on the *zócalo* and by the Palacio Municipal and the cathedral. If you need to escape the noise, **Sanborn's** at the corner of Independencia and Lerdo has phones on the second floor.

Phone Code: 29.

ACCOMMODATIONS

Veracruz has three peak seasons: *Carnaval* (the weeks before Ash Wednesday), *Semana Santa* (the week before Easter), and summer (July and August). The city is full of hotels, but many fill up well in advance during the first two peak periods, and some raise their rates. At other times, reservations are not necessary. Rooms with ceiling fans or large windows are not so pricey, but you'll have to pay more for the luxury of rooms with air conditioning—they're often needed in this steamy city.

Near the Centro

Budget hotels cluster on Aquilés Serdán, two blocks over from the *zócalo.* The area, full of revelers all night every night, is fun, loud, and relatively safe. Hotels listed have private bathrooms with 24-hour hot water.

Hotel México, Morelos 343 (tel. 32 43 60), across the street from the Aduanos building. Beautiful red-tiled rooms surround a courtyard that looks like a ski lodge. Wooden supports and furniture complete the down-home look. Perks include fan, TV, and phone in every room as well as a great location. Singles 90-110 pesos; doubles 130-150 pesos.

Hotel Concha Dorada, M. Lerdo 77 (tel. 31 29 96 or 31 32 46), on the *zócalo* to the left of the Palacio Municipal. Despite its premier location, the hotel's entrance is obscured by the labyrinth of cafe tables under the *zócalo's* arches. Rooms are remarkably insulated from the hubbub outside, but prices keep rising. Singles 115 pesos, with A/C and TV 140; doubles 140 pesos.

Hotel Santillana, Landero y Coss 208 (tel. 32 31 16), at Dehesa. Rooms surround a purple and green courtyard that emanates a certain garish charm. Fans, TV, phone, and wall-to-wall carpeting. Bathrooms are small. Singles 70 pesos; doubles 80 pesos.

Casa de Huespedes La Tabasqueña, on Morelos next to Hotel Mexico, is for those who like their hotels cheap and without frills. Rooms are spartan but functional, with only a noisy fan to ward off the heat and a *cantina*-style door to keep the outside world at bay. Singles 40 pesos; doubles 80 pesos.

On Díaz Mirón and Near the Bus Station

Not as central, but less likely to be full. Hotels close to the bus station tend to be very noisy, for obvious reasons. At night, take a cab back.

Hotel Central, Díaz Mirón 1612 (tel. 32 22 22), next to the ADO station. When the architects of Tomorrowland were done in Orlando and Anaheim, they designed this modern-looking hotel, complete with faux-marble lobby. Large rooms have TV, phone, and large bathrooms; some even have balconies. Singles 120 pesos, with A/C 140 pesos; doubles 150 pesos, with A/C 190 pesos.

Hotel Rosa Mar, La Fragua 1100 (tel. 37 07 47), behind the ADO station. On a forgettable strip of aging storefronts, it valiantly tries to remain a clean, wholesome establishment. Convenient for catching early-morning buses. Singles 70 pesos; doubles 110 pesos, with 2 beds 150 pesos; add 15 pesos for A/C, 5 pesos for color TV.

FOOD

Red snapper, shrimp, octopus, and a host of other sea beasts are hauled in daily from the Gulf. **Huachinango a la veracruzana** (red snapper decked out in olives, capers, onions, and olive oil) is the city's most brilliantly shining seafood star. The **fish market** on Landero y Coss, between Arista and Zaragoza, sells fine seafood at incredibly cheap prices. The risk of cholera means that raw or partially cooked fish, including *ceviche* and sushi, should be avoided. Ice cream shops sell delicious flavored ices made with mango, coconut, and strawberry (4 pesos)—great for fighting the heat. And don't leave without trying what's arguably the best coffee in the country.

Gran Café de la Parroquia, Gómez Farías 34 (tel. 32 35 84), at the corner of the Malecón. One of Veracruz's greatest traditions—the entire town always seems to be here and every president since 1810 has joined the diners for the famous *café con leche.* Sit back to people-watch, eavesdrop, and enjoy one yourself. After your glass is half filled with syrupy coffee, clink your spoon against your glass to have it completed with steaming milk (8 pesos). Food 13-30 pesos. Open daily 6am-1am.

El Cochinito de Oro, Zaragoza 190 (tel. 32 36 77), on the corner of Serdán. Serves not only seafood specials (25-32 pesos), but also *comida corrida* (23 pesos) and *antojitos* (8-14 pesos). Eating at this welcoming, roomy restaurant, you'll appreciate not only the locals' food but also their friendliness. Open daily 7am-5pm.

Alaska (tel. 31 78 73), in the Parque Zamora. Alaska's got the jukebox and the soda fountain plus the lackadaisical ice cream lickers. Frozen treats 10-15 pesos, *antojitos* 14 pesos; the view of the peachy-keen park is free. Open daily 8am-midnight.

La Gaviota, C. Triqueros 11 (tel. 32 39 50), between Molina and Serdán. Sparkling linens and wood paneling give this restaurant and bar a touch of elegance. Fish specialties 23-39 pesos. Don't miss the *huachinango a la veracruzana* (40 pesos). Open daily 8am-3pm.

SIGHTS

In the evening, the hymns of the cathedral spilling out into the *zócalo* yield to the sexy rhythms of marimbas. Crowds gather on benches and outside bars to drink in music that doesn't relent until daybreak.

Castillo de San Juan de Ulúa

Tel. 38 51 51. To reach the fort, take a "San Juan de Ulúa" bus (2.10 pesos) in front of the Aduana building in the Plaza de la República. Taxis should charge around 25 pesos. ***Open*** *Tu-Su 9am-4:30pm.* ***Admission*** *14 pesos. Free Sundays and holidays.* ***Guides*** *in Spanish 30 pesos. Video camera 30 pesos.*

The Castillo, Veracruz's most important historic site, rests on a fingertip of land that juts into the harbor. Spaniards first arrived at this point on the saint's day of San Juan; "Ulúa" was the greeting the native Totonacs offered the sailors as they disembarked. Construction, using coral as bricks, began in 1582 as part of the system of fortifications built around the Spanish Caribbean to protect the trade fleet and treasure from pirates. In the 400 years that the fort has stood, it has served many purposes, including that of a high-security prison for illustrious and exiled political prisoners—big-name prisoners include Mexican presidents Benito Juárez and Porfirio Díaz. Despite these famous names, San Juan's best-known prisoner was the hero **Chucho el Roto,** a Robin Hoodesque character who stole from the rich and gave to the poor. Chucho's legend has grown to mythic proportions, as he was believed to have escaped from San Juan not once, but twice.

Enter the site through the arched entrance and head for the last room on the right. As you enter, there are two openings in the wall to the left. The hole closer to the grass leads to some stairs and a dim, dank room that was known as *El Purgatorio* (Purgatory). The other room contains *El Inferno* (Hell), the cell without windows, surrounded by walls 9m thick, where men lost their sense of time and their sanity. Another set of stairs leads to *La Gloria* (Heaven), so named because it was one of the few cells in the Castillo with a window. To maintain your sanity, walk toward the row of 14 arches that hold a small museum. Through the arches, you can take in a panoramic view of the city and of the hungry angelfish nibbling for crackers.

Most of the other rooms in the Castillo are *bodegas,* or storage rooms, but are notable for their stalagmite formations which were 400 years in the making. Also interesting is the yellow house-like building in the center of the courtyard. This **Presidential Palace** served as Porfirio Díaz's home when he was in exile here.

Other Sights

A museum not often visited by tourists is the **Museo Histórico Naval,** which celebrates Mexico's rich maritime past, from the times of Columbus to the modern Mexican Navy. *(Open Tu-Su 9am-5pm; free.)* Located on the old grounds of the *Escuela Militar* (Naval School), the museum is a short walk from the *zócalo.* To get there, walk three blocks down Independencia and then turn left on Arista for another two blocks until you see the Naval School on your right; it's hard to miss since it occupies the entire block bordered by 16 de Septiembre, Arista, Montero, and Morales. Once inside, leave packages at the door and sign in. You'll be immediately sucked into gallery after gallery of air-conditioned comfort showcasing panoramas, pictures, and, of course, tons of model ships acquired by the Naval School.

Upstairs is the *Sala de las Intervenciones,* displaying information about French and American invasions, as well as the auditorium that is temporarily housing the **Museo Venustiano Carranza.** This small museum displays some of Carranza's belongings and lovingly details the revolutionary's life through pictures and artifacts. It remains unknown when the Carranza collection will return to its home, the yellow lighthouse on Malecón between Xicoténcatl and Hernández. Your best bet is to head for the Naval School first and inquire with one of the cadets.

The **Baluarte de San Francisco** (tel. 31 10 59), on Canal between 16 de Septiembre and Gómez Farías one block down from the Naval School, is a 17th-century bulwark that protected inhabitants from swashbuckling pirates like Sir Francis Drake. *(Open Tu-Sa 10am-4:30pm. Admission 14 pesos. Sundays and holidays free.)* It is all that remains of the old city wall that once enclosed the area between the train station and Parque Zamora. The museum inside displays a beautiful collection of pre-Hispanic gold ornaments called *Las Joyas del Pescador* since they were rescued from the ocean by a lucky octopus fisherman. Farther down Canal away from the water, turn right on Zaragoza to see the **Museo Cultural de la Ciudad,** Zaragoza 397 (tel. 31 84 10), where paintings, models, dioramas, and Spanish explanations tell the history of the city from pre-Hispanic times to the present. *(Open Tu-Su 9am-4pm; free.)* The museum's most interesting attraction is a relic from its days as an orphanage. In the back stairwell, a stained-glass window depicts the legend of Talinmasca, an orphan whose transgressions brought thunder, lighting, and the fierce autumn winds called *nortes* to the area.

On Zaragoza, between Morelos and Arista, you'll find the **Casa de Salvador Díaz Mirón** (tel. 32 31 31, ext. 146), the famous *veracruzano* poet. *(Open M-Sa 9am-8pm; free.)* Díaz Mirón occupied the house during the last seven years of his life (from 1921-1928), and the people here swear that they have heard his ghost pacing in the upper chambers of the house. Today the house serves as a literary center for Veracruz. Recently renovated, the foyer holds a cafe and the rear houses a literary forum. Upstairs you'll find a small museum that replicates what the house looked like while Mirón lived in it.

SAND AND SUNSHINE

The beaches in Veracruz are far from world-class. The general rule is that the farther from the city, the nicer the beach, although it's practically impossible to escape the oil barges and tugboats in the distance. **Playa Villa del Mar** is a fairly pleasant hour-long walk from the *zócalo* along the waterfront on Camache; it is also accessible via one of the frequent "Villa del Mar" or "Boca del Río" buses (2.10 pesos) that stop on Zaragoza behind the tourist office.

Few people swim at Villa del Mar. Restaurants in huts have set up camp along the boardwalk, and their tables are only meters from the surf, making beachside frolicking almost impossible. But the restaurant huts and bars create a lively atmosphere and, at night, when Camacho is lit up, the Playa Villa del Mar area is even more festive. The **Acuario de Veracruz** (tel. 32 79 84) is a popular beachside attraction for local families. Located in the Centro Commercial Plaza Acuario, a shopping mall on the left when facing the ocean at Villa del Mar, the aquarium features fish, sharks, and turtles native to the Gulf. *(Aquarium open Su-Th 10am-7pm, F-Sa 10am-7:30pm. Admission 15 pesos, seniors 10 pesos, children 5 pesos. Mall open daily 10am-10pm.)* Try to dodge the bird droppings that descend from the toucans that freely fly above your head near the entrance. Farther on Blvd. Camacho away from downtown Veracruz, luxury homes and pricey resorts hog the waterfront. A peaceful stretch of sand is **Costa de Oro** (Gold Coast), between the orange-pinkish hotels Fiesta Americana and Torremar.

The best beach in the Veracruz area (although that's not saying much) is **Playa Mocambo,** next to the Hotel Torremar, in the neighboring city of Boca del Río. Take a "Boca del Río" bus from Zaragoza and Serdán (30min., 2.10 pesos) and get off at Plaza de Las Americas. From there, cross the pedestrian-unfriendly streets to the Hotel Torremar; the beach is on the other side. At the bottom, veer left to head for the beach or go straight into the **Balneario Mocambo** (tel. 21 02 88), which has a clean, Olympic-sized public pool surrounded by artificial palm trees, changing rooms, and a poolside bar-restaurant (open daily 9am-5pm; admission 16 pesos, children 8 pesos). Catch the bus back to Veracruz at the top of the drive, on the right hand side, or head into Plaza de Las Americas to do some post-beach cooling down. The mall features restaurants, banks, arcades, an Internet cafe, and, of course, tons of chic shops.

ENTERTAINMENT AND SEASONAL EVENTS

Neither rain nor darkness will prevent the nightly release of tension on the streets and in the clubs of Veracruz. A great place to partake of the nightly festivities is the *zócalo,* which changes dramatically once night falls. Vendors spread out their wares on the paths, and the bars and restaurants are jam-packed with merry drinkers and traveling mariachi bands. The *zócalo* area tends to attract older and less affluent crowds than the discos and clubs in Boca del Río, but the location and lower price make it an excellent nighttime hang-out.

Apart from the spontaneous singing in the *zócalo,* most action takes place along **Av. Camacho,** the stretch of road along the coast that connects Veracruz and Boca del Río. **Café Andrade** (tel. 32 82 24) is on Blvd. Camacho at the corner of Callejón and 12 de Octubre, across the street from the Plaza Acuario and the Playa Villa del Mar. Beautiful people of all ages flock to the cool outdoor patio. The cafe sells beans from nearby Coatepec for grinding at home, and the pungent smell permeates the place. (Open daily 8am-2pm and 4pm-midnight.) The other hopping night spots are about three miles farther down Blvd. Camacho away from Veracruz. A good landmark is the purple high-rise Hotel Lois. Just before the violet beacon, Ruiz Cortínes branches off Camacho. This is a good point to get off the bus. One block up Ruiz Cortínes is **Ocean,** Ruiz Cortínes 8 (tel. 22 03 55). A slick aluminum facade and its status as one of the older clubs in town make it a popular destination. (Cover 30 pesos. Open Th-Sa 11pm-6am. No jeans, shorts, or tennis shoes.)

Head down Blvd. Camacho for about 200m and you'll hit **Master Club Billar,** Blvd. Camacho 4 (tel. 37 67 48), one of the friendliest, safest poolhouses you've ever seen, with TV, music, bar, air-conditioning, and tables for dominoes or cards (open daily 1pm-2am; pool 28 pesos per hr.). Keep walking down Camacho and you'll hit **Blue Ocean,** Blvd. Camacho 9 (tel. 22 03 55), the offspring of Ocean. Outside, green lasers beckon dancers; inside, a waterfall and a mix of English and Spanish tunes keep the crowd moving. (Cover 20 pesos for women, 80 pesos for men. Same hours and dress code as Ocean.) Señor Frog's, the touristy restaurant chain that just keeps on giving, has bestowed **Carlos 'n' Charlie's,** Blvd. Camacho 26 (tel. 22 29 10), on Veracruz. The restaurant regularly fills to the point of immobility—but that's okay, since everyone sits, drinks, and sings along merrily with the salsa music. (Restaurant open Su-Th 9am-midnight, F-Sa 9am-2am; bar open Su-Th 1pm-midnight, F-Sa 1pm-2am.)

If two hours of air conditioning appeal to you, catch a movie—who cares what's showing? For English-language films, check out **Plaza Cinema,** Arista 708 (tel. 31 37 87), or **Cinema Gemelos Veracruz,** Díaz Mirón 941 (tel. 32 59 70), between Iturbide and Mina (17-20 pesos).

Every December 31 at midnight, *veracruzano* families dress in their Sunday best and fill Blvd. Camacho, looking east to the Gulf to witness the first sunrise of the year. With that auspicious start, a year of celebrations begins. The climax comes early, in late February or early March, just before Ash Wednesday. **Carnaval** literally invades the *zócalo* and usurps the streets with parades, expositions, dance performances, and music. With the requisite ceremonies and parades, a king and queen are crowned. There's an entire office devoted to organizing the week-and-a-half-long event, the **Consejo Directivo del Carnaval** (tel. 32 31 31 ext. 149 172; fax 32 75 93). If you are able to, by all means come—but make hotel reservations early.

■ Near Veracruz: Zempoala Ruins

The ruins at **Zempoala** (sometimes spelled **Cempoala**), one of the most impressive archaeological sites in the state, lie 40km north of Veracruz, off Rte. 180. *(Open daily 9am-4:30pm. Admission 12 pesos, free on Sundays and holidays.)* Zempoala was one of the larger southern Totonac cities, part of a federation that covered much of Veracruz in pre-Hispanic times. In 1469, the Aztecs subdued Zempoala and forced the Totonacs to join their federation. Cortés arrived in 1519, attracted to the glitter of the seashells in the stucco used to build the structures (thinking, of course, that they were gold). The Totonacs were happy to lend Cortés soldiers for his campaign against Moctezuma at Tenochtitlán in 1521.

If It's Good Enough for Ike...

Even if he's sitting at the right cafe, a guy can't claim to really know Veracruz until he's worn the traditional white shirt called a *guayabera.* The name comes from the word *guayaba,* Spanish for "guava." Cuban guava collectors got tired of shimmying up and down the tree countless times, so they designed a shirt with four pockets to expedite the task. From there, the *guayabera* shirt passed to Panama and then Mexico, where Carlos Cab Arrazate added the thin pleats that form vertical stripes connecting the pockets. His grandson continues the family business, **Guayaberas Finas,** Zaragoza 233 (tel. 31 84 27; fax 31 33 43), between Arista and Serdán, in Veracruz city. Everyone who's anyone has bought one of their high-quality, hot-weather shirts—check out Dwight Eisenhower's note of appreciation on the store's wall. Fashion tip: shirts are not meant to be tucked in (*guayaberas* 150-1400 pesos, women's clothing also sold; open M-F 9:30am-8pm, Sa 9:30am-7pm, Su 10am-4pm).

Once a city of 30,000 people, the site now consists of stone structures surrounding a grassy field next to present-day Zempoala. A museum to your left as you enter displays a small collection of pottery and figurines unearthed here. The structure closest to the entrance is the **Temple of Death.** Continuing to the left, you will see three **pyramids.** Climbing the narrow stairs is forbidden, just like in the old days, when only priests and sacrificial victims were allowed to enter the altars that topped the temples. The pyramid on the left is dedicated to Tlaloc (god of rain), the one on the right to the moon, and the one in the center, decorated with circular stone receptacles for the hearts of people sacrificed in religious offerings, to the sun. Turning to the right, you will encounter the largest structure on the site, the **Templo Mayor.** When Cortés arrived, the Spaniards erected an altar to the Virgin on top of the temple, literally imposing Catholicism on the Totonacs. In front of the Templo Mayor is the **throne** where the king sat to observe the sacrifices that took place on the platform next to him. The throne also faces the temple known as **Las Chimeneas.** Moving toward the entrance of the site, you will see a fenced-in structure. For the Totonacs, this piece played a central role in the "New Five Ceremony," a five-day fast that took place when a "century" of the ritual calendar ended every 52 years. Every spring equinox, people still come to the circle to expel negative energy and absorb positive energy.

Getting There: From the second-class bus station on La Fragua, in Veracruz, **Autobuses TRV** sends buses to **Cardel** (45min., 10 pesos), where you can take a bus to Zempoala (15min., 5 pesos). Ask the driver to let you out at **las ruinas,** at the intersection of Av. Prof. José Ruíz and Av. Fcodel Paso y Troncoso Norte. If driving from Veracruz, follow Rte. 180 past Cardel, take the Zempoala city turn-off, and proceed until an obscured "Zona Arqueológica" sign appears on the right (about 1km before town). To get back, stand across the street from where you were dropped off and hail a passing "Cardel" bus (5 pesos). From Cardel, you can catch a bus to Veracruz (45min., every 10min. midnight-8pm; every 15min. 8-10pm, 10 pesos).

Catemaco

Catemaco is really two cities in one. During *Semana Santa* (the week before Easter) and around July 16 (the day of its patron, Saint Carmen), the town goes wild. Hotels are filled to capacity, restaurants and bars are hopping, and the lakes and beaches are overflowing with gringos and urbanites from the D.F. But the rest of the year sees a different Catemaco, one with empty hotels and beaches. The town slows to a crawl as some touristy businesses shut down and practically everything closes for the afternoon siesta. Catemaco is sometimes a tourist mecca and, at other times, a hot and sleepy little town. Whichever the case, Catemaco is today the most popular tourist destination in the Tuxtlas area but fortunately retains some of the charm that attracted visitors in the first place.

The **Laguna Catemaco** and its islands are often compared to Switzerland, and the intense green of the surrounding foliage does suggest a degree of alpine seclusion.

Another distinguishing characteristic is Catemaco's status as a center for *brujería,* or witchcraft. *Curandero* culture is usually a hodge-podge of pre-Hispanic myth and New Age kitsch, but Catemaco's friendly residents provide a glimpse of a more traditional way of life.

ORIENTATION AND PRACTICAL INFORMATION Catemaco lies along Rte. 180 and is a frequent stop for both first- and second-class buses. Streets are poorly marked, but the *basílica* on the *zócalo* is usually visible. From the **Autotransportes Los Tuxtlas** (second class), turn right and follow the curve of the road, past the "Bienvenidos a Catemaco" arches. Follow a straight path for 10 to 15 minutes until you arrive at the spires of the *basílica,* which awaits at the corner of **Boettinger** and Madero. To the left, **Carranza** runs past the Palacio Municipal. Straight ahead, the road becomes **Aldama.** One block downhill to the right is **Playa** and then **Malecón,** which follows the curves of the beach. The **ADO** (1st-class) station is on the Malecón, along the waterfront. To get to the church from this station, take a right onto the street and follow it until you reach Hotel Julita several blocks down and then take a right.

First-class **ADO buses** (tel. 3 08 42) leave for Mexico City (9hr., 10 and 11pm, 158 pesos), Puebla (6hr., 9am and 10pm, 123 pesos), Villahermosa (5hr., 12:30pm, 74 pesos), and Xalapa (3hr., 4 per day 6:15am-5pm, 67 pesos). **AU** (tel. 3 07 77) goes to Mexico City (9hr., 11:30am, 163 pesos), San Andrés (20min., 11:30am, 3 pesos), and Veracruz (3½hr., 11:30am, 41 pesos). **Autotransportes Los Tuxtlas** goes to San Andrés (20min., every 10min., 3 pesos) and Santiago (40min., every 10min., 5 pesos). **Currency exchange** is available at **Bancomer** (tel. 3 03 17), across Aldama from the *basílica.* Unfortunately, it operates on a very limited schedule. (Open Tu-Th 9am-1:30pm.) The **market** is on Madero before the *zócalo* (open daily 6am-8pm). The **police** (tel. 3 00 55) are in the Palacio Municipal on the *zócalo.* **Farmacia Nuestra Señora del Carmen** (tel. 3 00 91) is at the corner of Carranza and Boettinger (open daily 7am-9pm). The **Centro de Salud** (tel. 3 02 47), on Carranza, is in a white building with a blue roof, three blocks south of the *zócalo,* on the left. Some English is spoken. Medical services are available 24 hours. The **post office** is on Mantilla, between the lake and Hotel Los Arcos (open M-F 9am-4pm). The **postal code** is 95870. **LADATELs** line the *zócalo,* and phone cards are available at Farmacia Nuestra Señora del Carmen next to the *palacio municipal.* Long-distance **casetas** can be found on the right-hand side of the entrance to the Palacio. The **phone code** is 294.

ACCOMMODATIONS AND FOOD Most hotels cluster around the *zócalo* and the waterfront. Hotels fill up during Christmas, *Semana Santa,* and most of July. During these times, prices usually go up by about 10 pesos. But you'll practically have the town to yourself during the *temporada baja* (the off-season). It is not safe to camp on the beaches, since crime has become a problem in the area. The **Hotel Julita,** Playa 10 (tel. 3 00 08), on the waterfront, one block downhill from the *zócalo,* is a very good deal, boasting an unbeatable location and large rooms with fans (singles 40 pesos, peak season 50 pesos; doubles 60 pesos). **Hotel Acuario** (tel. 3 04 18), at Boettinger and Carranza, next to the Palacio Municipal, provides large, relatively clean rooms with 70s curtains, some with balconies (singles 50 pesos; doubles 80 pesos).

When choosing a waterfront restaurant, pay attention primarily to the view of the lake, as menus vary little. *Mojarra* and *topote,* two types of local fishes, will hop right from the lake onto your plate, but be sure to have them well cooked, since the waters can be polluted. *Mojarra* is prepared in a variety of ways, while the bite-sized *topote* is fried up whole and heaped with *tamales.* Shrimp, much of it from surrounding rivers, is also a local specialty. **Restaurant La Casona del Recuerdo,** Aldama 6 (tel. 3 01 20), just off the *zócalo,* is a haven from the busy waterfront. The terrace out back overlooks a peaceful wooded garden. Locals flock here for the excellent *comida corrida* (15 pesos; open daily 8am-8pm). On the waterfront across from the Hotel Julita, **7 Brujas** (tel. 3 01 57) serves the standard seafood dishes (20-35 pesos). While it's not your mom's kitchen, what the idiosyncratic wooden structure lacks in soothing furnishings it makes up for in funky ambience. (Open daily 8am-10pm.) **Restaurant/Bar El Pescador,** just a few doors to the right of 7 Brujas as you face it, serves up good food with a nice view on the side (seafood 25-35 pesos; open daily 9am-11pm).

SIGHTS The rocky beaches of **Laguna Catemaco** don't resemble Cancún, but a dip in the lake can be a refreshing break from the hot Veracruz sun. The water immediately in front of town is not safe for swimming, but a hiking path runs along the edge of the lake—walk down from the *zócalo* to the waterfront and turn left. The trail, bordered by trees knotted with character, will guide you the 1.5km to **Playa Expagoya** and then another 0.5km down the road to the more secluded and sandy **Playa Hermosa,** the first swimmable beach on the trail. The path is not safe at night. It's also possible to swim off a *lancha* in the deeper and sometimes clearer waters in the middle of the lake.

The lake is nearly circular and about 15km across. Several small islands dot its smooth surface. The waterfront is lined with long, flat-bottomed, brightly colored *lanchas* equipped with chairs and canopies. These boats lie ready to take you on an hour-long trip to the best-known island of the lot, **Isla de Changos.** *(Standard tour of the lake, including the Isla de Changos and the shrine of the Virgin, 180 pesos per boat, 30 pesos per person on a colectivo.)* A group of semi-wild, red-cheeked *changos* (mandrills, a kind of baboon) was brought from Thailand for a scientific experiment by the University of Veracruz in 1979, and the scientists wanted to see if the animals could survive in their new environment. Lo and behold, 18 years later the *changos* are alive, well, and posing for snapshots. Despite strict orders from the scientists not to feed the monkeys, tourists and *lanchistas* cannot seem to withhold chunks of bananas and coconuts from the already **grossly overweight monkeys.** En route to the island, you'll pass a cave-shrine that stands on the spot where Juan Catemasco, a local fisherman, had a vision of the Virgin Mary over a century ago. It is for him that the town is named and his statue, poised elegantly at the tip of the lagoon, overlooks the calm waters. Negotiate with the *lanchistas* for longer trips, including an exploration of the rivers that feed the lake or a trip to the tropical forests of the nearby national park. The *lanchas* leave from the docking area below the *zócalo.* Go in the morning or on the weekend if you want to share the boat and save money.

ENTERTAINMENT AND SEASONAL EVENTS Catemaco's **bars** and **discos** are the best in the Tuxtlas area, although that's not saying much. Nightlife only really heats up during the high tourist season—Semana Santa, July, and August. Many bars and clubs shut down or operate irregularly during the off-season. **Chanequa's** (tel. 3 00 42 or 3 00 01), in the Hotel Playa Azul, some distance from Catemaco, caters to the chic crowd that frequents this posh hotel. Walking there at night is difficult and dangerous; a boat will take you for 20 pesos. The road along the beach dominates nightlife in Catemaco. Four blocks from the Hotel Julita, one block away from the water on Madero, is **Jahac 45** (tel. 3 08 50), a video bar and disco that sometimes sponsors concerts by bands from the area (cover 12 pesos; open F-Sa after 9pm). It's the only club that remains faithfully open during the off-season. Just past Hotel Julita is the bar portion of the restaurant **7 Brujas,** offering a more mellow atmosphere (open daily until 10:30pm). A few doors down is **Pescado Loco,** which plays a potpourri of music from salsa and rancheras to English pop (cover 15 pesos; open F-Sa 9pm-3am).

In addition to *Semana Santa* and Christmas festivities, the town goes crazy on July 16, the day of its patron saint Carmen. May 30 is the Day of the Fisherman.

■ Near Catemaco: The Gulf Coast

Some say that the only reason to go to Catemaco is for its proximity to secluded beaches on the Gulf Coast. Waves, they will tell you, crash more crisply in the absence of Corona bars and souvenir shops. These beaches are off the beaten track—cattle roam the spaces between fishing villages that have no telephone lines and only the most basic services. The state of Veracruz wants to pave the road to the coast and develop the region for tourism. When this will happen is anyone's guess, but the sage traveler will visit the area before it does.

Getting to the Gulf Coast near Catemaco is an adventure. Public transportation to the area is limited to **Transportes Rurales's** pick-up trucks, dubbed **piratas** by locals. A four-door vehicle with wooden benches built into its caged-in bed, a *pirata* can carry the entire population of a small town. From Catemaco, *piratas* depart from the intersection of two unmarked streets on the eastern edge of town. To get to them, follow the lakefront past 7 Brujas for several blocks until you pass the last restaurant before foliage takes over the street. Turn left and walk until the intersection of a paved road. From the second-class bus station, a taxi will take you for 7 pesos. There are two main routes: one ends at **Montepío** on the Gulf Coast and one goes to **Coyame** on the other side of Lake Catemaco. Although traveling by *pirata* sounds exciting and adventuresome, it can actually be quite frustrating. *Piratas* are scheduled to depart every 50 minutes from 6am to 6:30pm, but they only do so when enough passengers have gathered to make the trip, making waits of up to two hours not uncommon. Also, the rough, unpaved road translates into frequent flat tires, slowing the *piratas* down even more.

The Road to Montepío

The first point of interest on the way to Montepío (besides the jaw-dropping views) is **Sontecomapán,** 20km from Catemaco (6 pesos). This is also the end of the paved road. Hold on tight for the points beyond. Sontecomapán is a small town beside an eponymous saltwater lake that empties into the Gulf of Mexico. *Lanchas* are available for excursions on the lake, and farther down the coast. They are expensive, though, at 180 pesos per boat and 30 pesos per person on a *colectivo.* An interesting spot just to the left of the swarms of *lanchas* is the **Pozo de los Enanos** (Pond of the Midgets). This small, fresh-water pond looks right out of a fairy tale, with its crystal-clear water and huge shady trees. In fact, the pond is supposed to be so clear that upon stepping into it, the water creates an optical illusion that makes you appear half your size, thus giving the *pozo* its name. **La Barra** is a fishing community where Laguna Sontecomapán empties into the Gulf of Mexico. To get there, ride a *pirata* 8km beyond Sontecomapán until the road forks. Your *pirata* will normally follow the left fork; you can either negotiate with the driver to take the right fork instead, or you can hop off, take a right, and hike the 5-6km to La Barra yourself. Once there, locals will show you a modicum of hospitality if you introduce yourself politely; a friendly *viajero* will be allowed to camp near someone's home.

The *pirata* route comes closer to the coast near Playa Jicacal and Playa Escondida; ask the driver to let you off (50min., 15 pesos). A half-hour walk through a lush and remote rural area leads to **Playa Jicacal,** a true gem. The long, slightly stony beach is almost completely empty; the only footprints lead to a few modest fisherman's shacks and—inevitably—a *refresco* stand and snack bar. The pink cabanas of **Hotel Icacos** (tel. 2 05 56; fax 2 00 39), located right near the entrance to the beach, do little to take away from the natural beauty. Its spartan rooms contain two large beds and a fan, but not much else. But hey, who needs hot water when the Gulf of Mexico is just a stone's throw away? (100 pesos per cabana per night.) The beach is said to be safe for camping, and hammock-hanging sites may be available. Safety goes hand and hand with good manners, and campers who wish to crash on the beach would do well to ingratiate themselves with the *jicacaleños.*

Instead of turning right to Playa Jicacal, you can walk uphill 30 minutes to the left to get to **Playa Escondida** (Hidden Beach), a beach that lives up to its name. The simple white **Hotel Playa Escondida** (tel. 2 16 14 or 2 20 01 in San Andrés) appears like a mirage. The hotel provides not only access to the small rocky beach below, but also the chance to explore the surrounding jungle. Rooms have fans. (Singles 100 pesos; doubles 120 pesos.) This beach offers the safest camping in the area, as access is available only through the hotel. Be prepared to pay 25 pesos for this security. Swimming is possible at both beaches, but an undertow and big waves make for less than ideal swimming conditions. Access to the beach for non-guests is 5 pesos. Visitors who want a secluded beach without the 30-minute walk through the jungle have the *pirata* drop them off at **Balzapote** (1¾hr., 14 pesos). A handful of houses and a small restaurant-store are all that separates this empty beach from the dirt road.

At the end of the 40km *pirata* route is the tiny village of **Montepío** (2hr., 17 pesos). The town consists of a handful of buildings, including a little light-blue church whose facade is barely big enough to accommodate the door. Montepío is less spectacular than Playa Escondida, but it does offer a long, narrow beach framed by a tall bluff and volcanic rocks on one end and the green hills of the Sierra on the other. Locals rent **horses** for 15 pesos per hour. *Piratas* (every hr., 6am-6pm) take travelers to a nearby **biological research station,** where young scientists may tell you about the flora and fauna of the area and show you the snakes and monkeys they're studying. The new **Hotel Posada San José** (tel. 2 10 10 or 2 20 20 in San Andrés) stands on the bank of the small river leading to the beach. Colorfully painted rooms are clean and spacious. (Singles 120 pesos; doubles 150 pesos; add 30 pesos for each additional person.) The *posada* also features a restaurant with a commanding view of the water; the *a la carte* menu offers most dishes for around 10 pesos. If your wanderlust urges you to go even farther afield, check out **Playa Hermosa,** another 8km down the beach from Montepío. It's an hour's walk to get there, or a *lancha* will take you for 50 pesos. This beach features waterfalls and even more secluded sand.

Coyame

Alternatively, you can take a *pirata* headed for Coyame, 12km from Catemaco, where you can watch the cool waters that are bottled to make the soft drink of the same name bubble up from underground springs. Seven kilometers toward Coyame, the **Proyecto Ecológico Educacional Nanciyaga,** or simply **Nanciyaga** (tel. 3 01 99; 3 pesos in *pirata*), has lured Hollywood producers, beauty queens, and uptight Americans to its cleansing fountain of pre-Hispanic therapy. From the highway, turn right and walk in front of the "Nanciyaga" sign on a dirt path that leads towards the shore of the lake. All of the vegetation in the area is part of a preserve. The regulations protecting the area forced the makers of the U.S. movie *Medicine Man* (with Sean Connery) to alter the landscape with styrofoam trees. Remains from the movie shoot as well as a facial mask of local mud and sips of natural spring water are part of the tour of the site (10 pesos; consultation with a real medicine man, who is a cross between a chiropractor and a faith healer, 50 pesos more). Guests can stay overnight in mosquito-netted bungalows and enjoy the Olmec *temazacal* sweat lodge, full-body mud baths, open-air concerts, and boat tours of the lake that sparkles through the trees (180 pesos; full-body mud baths 45 pesos; activities like massages and vegetarian meals require advance reservations). *Lanchas* or taxis will also take you to Nanciyaga (20 pesos). To return to Catemaco, walk back to the highway, cross the street, and flag down any *pirata* headed back to town.

San Lorenzo

Along with Tres Zapotes and La Venta, San Lorenzo is one of the three best-known Olmec ceremonial sites. Flourishing from 1200-900 BC, San Lorenzo is thought to have been the largest and most important center as well as the oldest. While it must have truly been splendid in its day, San Lorenzo now retains little of what made it spectacular; most of what has been uncovered has been removed and relocated to museums elsewhere, particularly to the famous anthropology museums in Xalapa and Mexico City. Nevertheless, for the true anthropology buffs, San Lorenzo is worth a look, albeit a brief one.

The ruins—or what the museums have left behind—are spread out over two sites: one in the small town of Tenochtitlán and the other a few kilometers southeast in the even smaller town of San Lorenzo. The collection at Tenochtitlán, under a protective shelter near the town's main dirt road, features an assortment of artifacts including one of the famous giant **Olmec stone heads,** easily distinguishable by the thick lips, slightly crossed eyes, and helmet. Of the 10 heads found at San Lorenzo, this is the only one that hasn't been shipped off to a museum.

About 4km farther down the main dirt road and past the microscopic town of San Lorenzo lies the second archaeological zone. Named **Zona Azuzul,** this site is located on the original ceremonial territory occupied by the Olmecs. *(Site open daily 7am-6pm.)* Two small shelters atop the hill house the modest but remarkably well-preserved collection. The first hut holds four stone statues, two depicting kneeling human forms and the other two depicting jaguar forms. The second hut houses another jaguar statue, this one even larger than the first two. These remarkably old statues hint at the origins of the pre-Hispanic obsession with the jaguar, an obsession that began with the Olmecs but later spread to the Maya and other Mesoamerican civilizations.

San Lorenzo appears to be a work in progress. Much of the area is unexcavated and unexplored and will likely remain that way until more money is allocated. Fortunately, thanks to new regulations, artifacts that are found here in the future will not be sent off to museums, but will be displayed in their original locations.

In order to get to San Lorenzo, you have to go through the hot, smelly, dirty town of **Acayucan.** The **bus station** is on the eastern side of town, near a market and a supermarket. Four bus lines share the **bus station. Autobuses Golfo Pacífico Sur** (tel. 5 12 46) has service to nearby towns, and you can get to Acayucan from Puebla (6hr., 151 pesos), Mexico City (8hr., 188 pesos), and Villahermosa (4hr., 5:45 and 7:35am, 57 pesos). **Cristóbal Colón** (tel. 5 00 46) provides service to and from Tuxtla Gutierrez (8hr., 114 pesos), Veracruz (5hr., 57 pesos), and other destinations. Acuyucan also has quite a few affordable budget hotels, including **Hotel Joalicia** (tel. 5 08 77) and **Hotel Jesymar** (tel. 5 05 55 or 5 02 61) as well as most major facilities.

Getting there: From Acayucan take a "Texistepec" (sometimes labeled just "Texi") *colectivo* at the corner of Victoria and Zaragoza right in front of the Hotel Joalicia. 5 pesos and about 35 minutes later, the *colectivo* will deposit you in Texistepec, a small town 10km from the ruins. On this narrow street alongside the town's main church, catch a blue bus marked "San Lorenzo" or "Teno" (short for "Tenochtitlán") for 11 pesos. These buses leave every two hours starting at 8am, so plan accordingly. The ride from Texistepec to San Lorenzo/Tenochtitlán lasts about an hour and is anything but smooth. To visit the Tenochtitlán site, get off at the town stop. The site is easily visible under a shelter on the left side. To visit the Azuzul site, hop off at the fork about 10 to 15 minutes later. The hut immediately on the right of the fork serves as a welcoming booth, and the statues themselves are up the dirt path on the hill. To get back to Texistepec, wait by the main dirt road until one of the blue buses comes rumbling along.

San Andrés Tuxtla

Lodged between the lush lakeside resorts of Catemaco and the Olmec artifacts of Santiago, San Andrés Tuxtla (usually just San Andrés) is the relatively untouristed anchor of 125,000 inhabitants that keeps the Sierra de los Tuxtlas peacefully down to earth. A quiet little town, San Andrés serves mainly as a center for the tobacco and cattle industries of the surrounding countryside, and it offers a cache of budget hotels, an entertaining *zócalo* and some nearby natural attractions. As the transportation hub of the region, San Andrés serves as a good base from which to stage daytrips to most locations in Los Dos Tuxtlas.

ORIENTATION AND PRACTICAL INFORMATION Located midway between Catemaco and Santiago Tuxtla on Rte. 180, San Andrés is built on and around a volcanic range that hugs the Gulf Coast. The downtown area lies in the slightly raised center of a valley. To get there from the bus station, walk down **Juárez,** the city's main street. Branching to the right off Rte. 180, Juárez descends a steep hill, crosses a small stream, and gradually ascends to meet the cathedral at the north corner of the *zócalo.* Right before reaching the cathedral, Juárez passes by the **Palacio Municipal** on the right and intersects **Constitución** to the left and **Madero** to the right, in front of the Palacio Municipal. Following Constitución to the left, you will come to the intersection of **Pino Suárez,** where some hotels are located. The walk takes 10 minutes from the bus station; a taxi costs 7 pesos.

Autotransportes Los Tuxtlas (tel. 2 14 62), on the right hand side of Rte. 180 about 300m beyond the ADO station, sends **buses** to Catemaco (15min., every 10min. 4am-10pm, 2.50 pesos), Coatzacoalcos (3½hr., every 10min. 4am-10pm, 28 pesos), Santiago Tuxtla (20min., every 10min. 4:30am-9:30pm, 3 pesos), and Veracruz (3½hr., every 15min. 2am-10pm, 30.50 pesos). **ADO** (tel. 2 08 71), at the intersection of Juárez and Route 180 (also called **Blvd. 5 de Febrero**), serves Mexico City (7½hr., 9, 10:30, and 11:10pm, 179 pesos; comfy deluxe service 7½hr., 11pm, 280 pesos), Veracruz (2½hr., 25 per day 12:20am-9:25pm, 38 pesos), and Villahermosa (5hr., 12 per day 12:20am-9:25pm, 87 pesos). **AU** (tel. 2 09 84) goes to Puebla (6hr., 9:50pm, 112 pesos), Veracruz (2½hr., noon and 9:50pm, 34 pesos), and Xalapa (4hr., noon and 9:50pm, 60 pesos). **Cuenca** covers Tuxtepec (3hr., 10 per day 4am-6pm, 43 pesos).

The often-deserted **tourist office** is on the first floor of the Palacio Municipal, on your right as you walk in. (Officially open M-F 9am-1pm and 4-6pm, but your best bet is from 11am-1pm.) Exchange your money at **Bancomer** (tel. 2 27 92), about half a block south of the *zócalo* on Madero (open M-F 8:30am-5pm, Sa 9am-1pm). Also try **Serfín** (tel. 2 11 00) at Carranza as it curves to intersect 16 de Septiembre (open M-F 9am-5pm). Both have 24-hour **ATMs.** The **market, Mercado 5 de Febrero,** spills onto the streets several blocks from the *zócalo.* To get there, walk on Madero, turn right on Carranza and walk uphill. (Open daily 6am-10pm; food stands close at 6pm.) **Lavandería Lava Maac** (tel. 2 09 26), at Hernández and Hernández No. 75, intersection Revolución, will wash 1kg of your dirtiest duds for 6 pesos (open M-Sa 8am-8pm). The **police** (tel. 2 14 99) are located on Pasaje Rascón, in the Palacio Municipal (open 24hr.). The **Red Cross** is at Boca Negra 25 (tel. 2 05 00), north of the *zócalo* (open 24hr.). No English is spoken in **Farmacia Garysa,** Madero 3 (tel. 2 44 34; fax 2 15 06), in the "Canada" building to the left of the Palacio Municipal (open 24hr.). The **Hospital Regional** (tel. 2 31 99), at the edge of town, has an **ambulance service.** The **post office** (tel. 2 01 89) is at La Fragua and 20 de Noviembre, one block from the *zócalo* (open M-F 8am-8pm, Sa 9am-noon). The **postal code** is 95701. **Internet access** can be found at **SAT Internet** (tel. 2 38 05) at the corner of Pino Suárez and Argudín. SAT Internet offers speedy computers, Netscape, telnet, and a soft drink or two. (18 pesos per hour; open daily 8am-midnight.) Three or four blocks down Pino Suárez past the hotels, you can find SAT Internet's rival, **Internepolis** (tel. 2 41 60), which offers the same services but is more expensive (25 pesos per hour; open daily 8am-2am). The recently installed **LADATELs** have made their debut around the *zócalo* and across the street from the Hotel de los Pérez. Phone cards are also available in the stores around the *zócalo.* The **phone code** is 294.

ACCOMMODATIONS AND FOOD Although San Andrés remains almost tourist-free, budget accommodations with private bath and hot water are abundant. Two of the best bargains are within spitting distance of each other, just to the left of the cathedral. Follow the street in front of the church to the left on Constitución and turn right onto Pino Suárez at the orange supermarket. The **Hotel Colonial,** Pino Suárez 7 (tel. 2 05 52), has a spacious lobby and more modestly sized rooms cooled vigorously by a ceiling fan. Mural-sized map behind the check-in desk gives a comprehensive overview of the area. (Singles 35-40 pesos; doubles 60 pesos.) **Hotel Figueroa,** Pino Suárez 2 (tel. 2 02 57), is across the street. The Colonial and the Figueroa have almost identical rooms; the only notable distinction is that Colonial has ceiling fans whereas Figueroa has portable fans. (Figueroa singles 35 pesos; doubles 50 pesos.) The most affordable rooms with all-important air conditioning are in **Hotel Isabel,** Madero 13 (tel. 2 16 17), to the left of the Hotel Parque next to the *zócalo* (singles 90 pesos, with A/C 120 pesos; doubles 120 pesos, with A/C 150 pesos).

Several sidewalk cafes on the *zócalo* serve breakfast and coffee and also afford a pleasant view of simple small-town life. **Winni's Restaurant,** located south of the *zócalo* next to the Banamex on Madero, is a local favorite. Even after a long day, Winni's cheerily serves up *antojitos* (10-15 pesos) and cakes for dessert. (Open daily 8am-midnight.) The older and more affluent huddle at **Restaurant del Parque** (tel. 2 01 98), on the ground floor of the Hotel Parque on the *zócalo.* Food (breakfast 6-14 pesos, *antojitos* 9-15 pesos, *tortas* 10-17 pesos) is secondary to the socializing (open daily 7am-midnight). The folks at **El Pequeño Archie,** on Pino Suárez just downhill from the hotels and across the street from the movies, serve a delicious *comida corrida* (12 pesos) and *antojitos* (6-10 pesos; open M-Sa 8am-9pm, Su 8am-2pm).

SIGHTS, ENTERTAINMENT, AND SEASONAL EVENTS Even nonsmokers will be impressed by the **Tabacos San Andrés Factory** (tel. 2 12 00), where Santa Clara cigars are made. *(Open M-Sa 7am-7pm, but the workers, the real stars of the show, leave around 5pm.)* From the *zócalo,* walk up Juárez to the ADO terminal and turn right at the fork in the road—it's about 200m down Rte. 180 (here called Blvd. 5 de Febrero) on the right. An open door and the smell of tobacco leaves invite you in. Be polite and someone from the amiable staff will gladly walk you through the entire process, from selecting the leaves to rolling the stogies to putting on the company seal. You can buy some near the entrance: the bottom of the line starts at 150 pesos, while a box of 25 of their finest *puros* goes for 750 pesos. Customs regulations may limit the number of cigars you can take back into your country (see p. 9).

The sheer number of video rental stores just about says it all: San Andrés is not exactly a town that parties until dawn. Unless you brought your VCR along, it might be hard to find nighttime entertainment. Most of the action centers on the *zócalo,* where folks in San Andrés gather to meet, gossip, see, and be seen. **Cafe de la Cathedral,** to the right of the Singer store on the north side of the *zócalo,* used to be a real coffee shop but now functions as one of the most popular bars in San Andrés. It begins to fill up around 11pm. On Sunday nights, families bring their children, and the square becomes a little kiddie carnival with balloons and small electric cars for hire. **Cinemas San Andrés** (tel. 2 42 50), on Pino Suárez across from El Pequeño Archie, brings English-language movies to the big screen for 12 to 15 pesos.

On Independence Day, September 16, giant balloons of colorful paper are flown over the *zócalo.* The town's patron saint is celebrated on November 30. December 12 is the day of Guadalupe, Mexico's patron virgin. As part of the celebrations, young people playfully hit each other with wooden figures called *mojigangas.*

Santiago Tuxtla

Of the three cities that constitute Los Tuxtlas, Santiago (pop. 50,000) has the least to offer visitors in terms of sights and recreational activities. Its main attraction stems from its close connection to the ancient Olmec ceremonial center of Tres Zapotes. Virtually untouristed save the few archaeologists and doctoral students that pass through, Santiago is nevertheless known in the Tuxtlas area for its superstitions and elaborate festivals.

ORIENTATION AND PRACTICAL INFORMATION The **ADO bus station,** like everything else in Santiago, is just a few blocks from the *zócalo.* To reach the town center, walk downhill from Rte. 180 where the bus drops you. The first right is **Ayuntamiento,** which leads to the **Palacio Municipal** with its clock tower on the right and the **zócalo** in front of it. From the ADO bus station, walking downhill and then following **Morelos** will bring you to the **Autotransportes Los Tuxtlas** station on the left and **Calle Obregón** on the right.

ADO (tel. 7 04 38) sends buses to Mexico City (7hr., 9:20am, 10:45, and 11:30pm, 175 pesos) and Xalapa (4½hr., 7:05, 7:50, and 9:20am, 71 pesos). **Cuenca** sends buses to Tuxtepec (4hr., every hr. 4:35am-6:35pm, 34 pesos). **Autotransportes Los Tuxtlas** buses leave from next to the ADO station for Catemaco (40min., every 10min. 8am-10pm, 7 pesos) and San Andrés (20min., 3 pesos). The archaeology museum offers **tourist information. Currency exchange** is available at **Bancrecer** (tel. 7 08 02), located to the left of the circular Hotel Castellanos. (Open M-F 9am-4pm.) The **market, Mercado Municipal Morelos,** begins to the left of the *zócalo* as you face it from the Palacio Municipal and continues one street over to the left (open daily 5am-8pm). Find the **police** (tel. 7 00 92) downstairs in the Palacio Municipal (open daily 24hr.). The nearest **Red Cross** is in San Andrés; for **24-hour ambulance service,** dial 2 05 00. **Super Farmacia Roma** (tel. 7 09 99), 5 de Mayo just off the *zócalo,* is open daily from 8:30am to 9pm. The **Clínica Doctores Castellanos,** across from the Hotel Castellanos (tel. 7 02 60), provides medical assistance daily from 8am to 8pm. **LADATELs** are found along the perimeter of the *zócalo,* and phone cards are available inside the Super Farmacia Roma on the *zócalo.*

ACCOMMODATIONS The **Hotel Castellanos** (tel. 7 03 00), on the corner of 5 de Mayo and Comonfort, at the far corner of the *zócalo,* is not only a place to stay but also Santiago's most interesting attraction. The rooms fit together like slices of a pie; each offers A/C, telephones, color TV, and a balcony with a panoramic view. If you can stop admiring the scenery, there is also a pool and restaurant. Too bad it's so expensive. (Singles 138 pesos; doubles 161 pesos.) Both less expensive and less stimulating, **Casa de Huéspedes Morelos,** Obregón 15 (tel. 7 04 74), downhill from the bus stations, has basic small rooms with fans and bathrooms with hot water (singles 50 pesos; doubles 70-80 pesos; triples 80 pesos).

SIGHTS AND SEASONAL EVENTS The **largest Olmec head** ever discovered (45 tons) sits complacently at the far end of Santiago's *zócalo,* shaded from the sun by a large cupola. The head is distinctive not only for its size but also because its eyes are closed. The **Museo Regional Tuxteco,** to the left of the head along the *zócalo,* displays terra-cotta masks of the Totonacs and another Olmec head, along with other artifacts from around the region (open M-Sa 9am-5pm; admission 14 pesos). Celebrations for the **fair** in honor of Santiago, the town's patron saint, take place July 20-29 and include a choreographed fight between Christians and Moors and a *torneo de cintas* in which men dress in medieval gear and ride horses.

■ Near Santiago Tuxtla: Tres Zapotes

Tres Zapotes, one of the three main Olmec ceremonial centers, reached its peak between 300 BC and AD 300, but there is evidence that the site was occupied as early as 900 BC. *(Open daily 9am-5pm. Admission 10 pesos, free Su.)* Today, calling the artifacts on display a "museum" would be either optimistic or an exaggeration; there are barely enough artifacts to fill a room, nor are the items displayed at their original sites. The lack of written explanations can be frustrating, but the attendants at the ticket booth are friendly and knowledgeable. If you have at least a cursory knowledge of Spanish, solicit explanations.

The most imposing figure at Tres Zapotes is one of the trademark Olmec stone heads that always seems to carry the label "colossal." The first of the dozen or so Olmec heads to be found, it was discovered in 1862 by a *campesino* who first thought it was an overturned cooking pot. To the left of the head is the **Stela C,** which, together with its more famous upper half (now at the Museo Nacional de Antropología in Mexico City, see p. 106), bears the oldest written date in the Americas—31 BC, inscribed in late Olmec, or Spi-Olmec glyphs similar to those later used by the Maya. The date is visible on the back of the stela as a bar (representing "5") and two dots, giving a total of seven on the Olmec calendar. **Stela A** lies in the transept to the left. Decorations on the stela include the figure of a man, a serpent coiling upon itself (on the right side), and a man holding an axe (on the left side). **Stela D,** to the right of the head, resembles a tablet. Within the mouth of a jaguar are renderings of three people whose relative heights symbolize their power and importance. The tallest figure, on the far right, is most likely a ruler; the central, skirted figure is perhaps an emissary; the kneeling figure on the left is probably a prisoner of war or someone making an offering. On the left side of the piece, the broad mouth of what is possibly a toad is visible; on the right side it's possible to discern a skeletal face.

Getting There: Exiting the Museo Regional Tuxteco in Santiago, head right and turn right on Zaragoza. Cross the street about a block later and pass through the market and cross the bridge to Morelos, where you can take a *taxi-colectivo* to Tres Zapotes (30min., 8 pesos). You will be let off in the town of Tres Zapotes. From the stop, turn left and walk to the first cross-street. Turn left and walk around the chain-link fence until you see the entrance on your right. Buses (marked "Tres Zapotes") also pass through this stop, but while they're cheaper (3 pesos), they're also slower.

Chiapas and Tabasco

For centuries, **Chiapas** has been known for its environmental diversity—its cloud-enveloped heights provide a stark contrast to its basins of dense, lowland rainforest. Chiapas's climate is unique for southern Mexico—the chilly nights and crisp fresh air give the highlands a distinct flavor. Cortés must have had the Sierra de Chiapas in mind when he crumpled a piece of parchment and dropped it on a table to demonstrate what Mexico looked like. In these rugged green mountains, buses careen around hairpin turns above deep valleys before hurtling into jungles on rutted roads. One of Mexico's most beautiful cities, San Cristóbal de las Casas, known for its cobblestone streets and surrounding *indígena* villages, rests high amid these peaks.

Throughout the state, you will hear diverse Mayan dialects and find markets and other public places filled with *indígenas.* Indeed, the state is part of the Maya heartland; the Lacandón Rainforest shields the remote ruins of Bonampak and Yaxchilán and is still home to the Lacandón Maya, whose isolation has kept them from both the Spanish Conquest and tourist invasion. Chiapas's *indígenas* remain fiercely traditional—in many communities, schools teach in the local dialect as well as in Spanish, and regional dress, while it varies across communities, is almost always maintained. The EZLN rebellion of 1994 (see p. 57) succeeded in drawing the world's attention to the central Mexican government's lack of attention to the needs and rights of the highland region's poor indigenous villages.

Tabasco, Chiapas's neighbor to the north, is often overlooked in favor of its more glamorous neighbors. But while Tabasco lacks the party attitude of Veracruz and the turquoise beaches of the Yucatán Peninsula, the state has plenty to offer its visitors. Dotted with lakes and swamps, criss-crossed by rivers, and swathed in dense jungle, Tabasco (which literally means "damp earth") is something of a natural beauty. Beaches, most of them untouristed, line its northern side, and the southern and eastern sides are dotted with parks and natural sanctuaries. In the center of it all is the capital city of Villahermosa, struggling to retain its colonial identity in the midst of a modern growth spurt. But perhaps what Tabasco is best known for is its intense heat, humidity, and wetness. The weather behaves like clockwork—be prepared for showers every afternoon during the rainy season (June-Sept.). Happy (and dry) is the well-prepared tourist.

HIGHLIGHTS OF CHIAPAS AND TABASCO

- The mountaintop city of **San Cristóbal de las Casas** (see p. 504) is the reason many people come to Mexico—inevitably a good visit.
- The jungle ruins of **Palenque** (see p. 518) are startling. Skip the town and head straight to the gleaming **archaeological site** (see p. 524), set amidst a dense backdrop of beautiful falls, foliage, and wildlife.
- Be sure not to miss the indigenous villages near **San Cristóbal** (see p. 511), especially the community of **San Juan Chamula** (see p. 511) and its famous **church,** host to a fascinating syncretic religious ritual involving burping.
- The adjacent archaeological sites of **Yaxchilán** (see p. 523) and **Bonampak** (see p. 526) are worth the jungle trek—they house some of the most well-preserved Maya remnants in the country.

TABASCO

Villahermosa

Contrary to its name, Villahermosa (pop. 1.6 million) is neither a *villa* (small village) nor *hermosa* (beautiful). The capital of Tabasco is actually a sprawling metropolis whose recent growth has been driven by rich oil discoveries and its strategic location

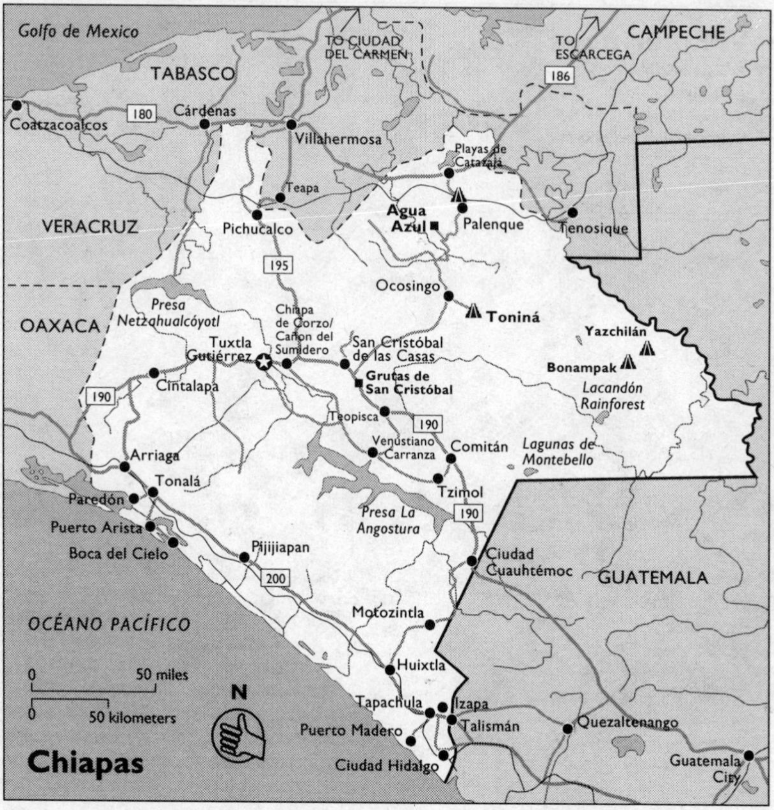

along the Río Grijalva, one of the few navigable rivers in the Republic. Founded in 1519 as Santa María de la Victoria by Hernán Cortés, the city was an agricultural center of minor importance and was accessible only by river. In the past 50 years, oil-spurred growth has given the ailing city a shot in the arm, transforming Villahermosa from boondock to boomtown and creating a dense urban forest of satellite antennae, luxury hotels, and apartment complexes. It is Villahermosa's proximity to the **Palenque** ruins and its position as a crossroads between Chiapas and the Yucatán that make it a common stopover for travelers, but the city does offer museums and sights (particularly the terrific **Museo-Parque La Venta**) that make longer stays worthwhile.

ORIENTATION

Tabasco's state capital lies 20km from the border with Chiapas and 298km west of Escárcega, the major crossroads for Yucatán-bound travelers. The spine of the downtown area is **27 de Febrero.** The **Zona Luz,** the city's pedestrian-only downtown area, is bordered by **5 de Mayo, Zaragoza, Madero,** and 27 de Febrero. **Paseo Tabasco** runs north-south and connects the **Tabasco 2000** complex to the *centro,* intersecting 27 de Febrero in front of the cathedral. *Saetas* **(public buses)** and *combis* (each 1.50 pesos) run from 6am to 10:30pm. First- and second-class **buses** depart from the eastern part of town. An **airport** lies northwest of the city, 14km from the downtown area; taxis shuttle between the airport and the *centro* (40 pesos *especial,* 15 pesos *colectivo*).

To reach downtown from the **first-class ADO station,** walk two-and-a-half blocks to your right on Mina to Méndez. From there, take a *combi* labeled "Tierra Colorada Centro-Juárez" and get off a few minutes later at **Parque Juárez.** Most hotels are south

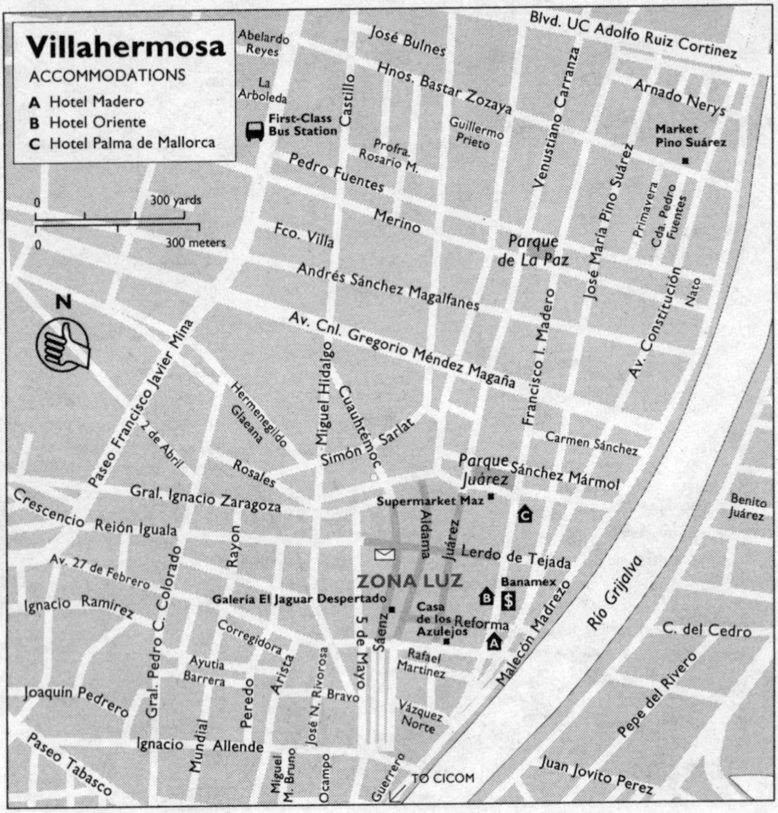

of the park on either **Madero** or its parallel cousin **Constitución.** Walking from the station to Parque Juárez takes 15 to 20 minutes; upon exiting the terminal, head right down Mina for eight blocks, then turn left onto 27 de Febrero. Eight more blocks take you to the intersection with Madero. To get downtown from the **second-class bus terminal,** cross Grijalva on the pedestrian bridge to the left of the station exit, then jump on a bus labeled "Indeco Centro" (1 peso) and disembark at Parque Juárez on Madero. To make the 25-minute walk from the station, cross the bridge and continue south on Mina for three blocks until you reach the ADO station (see above). A cab ride to the center of town costs about 10 pesos.

PRACTICAL INFORMATION

Transportation

Airport: (tel. 56 01 57; fax 56 01 58), on the Villahermosa-Macupana highway. **Aeroméxico,** Cámara 511, Locale 2 (tel. 12 15 28). **Aviacsa,** Via 3, #120 Locale 10 (tel. 16 57 00). **Aerocaribe,** Via 3 #120, Locale 5 and 6 (tel. 16 50 46). **Mexicana,** Via 3 #120 (tel. 16 31 31 or 16 31 38).

Buses: The first-class terminal is on Mina 297 at Merino, a few blocks east of Juárez. **ADO** (tel. 12 89 00) runs to Acayucan (4hr., 13 per day 9:30am-9:40pm, 64 pesos), Agua Dulce (2hr., 6:15 and 8:15pm, 38 pesos), Balancan (3hr., 6 per day 6:45am-6pm, 58 pesos), Campeche (5hr., 15 per day 9:10am-10:50pm, 121 pesos), Cancún (11hr., 8 per day 8-11:45pm, 249 pesos), Chetumal (8hr., 9:20pm, 152 pesos), Mérida (8hr., 5 per day 9:10am-midnight, 171 pesos), Mexico City (11hr., 5 per day 6:30-10pm, 272 pesos), Oaxaca (11hr., 6 and 9:25pm, 197 pesos), Palenque (2hr., 8 per day 6:15am-9:15pm, 36 pesos), Playa del Carmen (8hr., 8 and 10pm, 233 pesos), Puebla (8hr., 8:40 and 11:15pm, 231 pesos), and Veracruz (7hr., 9 per day 8:35am-11pm, 131 pesos). **UNO** (tel. 14 22 40) has *servicio de lujo* (luxury service); tickets must be purchased 5 days in advance.

Radio Taxi: (tel. 15 82 33 or 15 23 39). On call 24hr.

Car Rental: There's no such thing as budget. **Renta de Autos Tabasco,** Paseo Tabasco 600 (tel. 15 48 30), next to the cathedral, offers one of the lowest prices in town: 391 pesos per day. Open M-F 8am-7pm, Sa-Su 8am-2pm and 4-6pm.

Tourist and Financial Services

Tourist Offices: Instituto de Turismo, Av. de los Ríos 113 (tel. 16 36 33 or 16 28 89), located in a red building diagonally behind the Palacio Municipal. 1 block behind the planetarium. Offers plenty of information, but every brochure has a price. Open M-F 9am-3pm and 6-9pm. **Tourist Information Booths** can be found at the airport (tel. 56 03 93; open daily 7am-8pm) and at **Museo La Venta** (tel. 12 89 10; open daily 8am-4pm).

Currency Exchange: Banks are plentiful in the *Zona Luz* and along Paseo Tabasco. Try **Banamex** (tel. 12 00 11), on Madero at Reforma. Open for exchange M-F 9am-5pm with 24hr. **ATM.** Another option is **BITAL** (tel. 10 25 37), at the corner of Lerdo and Juárez. Open M-F 8am-7pm, Sa 8am-1:30pm. It has 3 24hr. **ATMs.**

American Express: Patriotismo 605 (tel. 91 800 5 00 44). Open M-Sa 9am-6pm.

Local Services

Luggage storage: At the bus station from 7am-11pm (1 peso per piece per hr.).

Market: Pino Suárez, encompassed by Pino Suárez, Constitución, Hermanos Zozaya, and Grijalva, in the northeast corner of town. Open daily 6am-6pm.

Supermarket: Maz (tel. 12 10 06), on Madero at Zaragoza. Open daily 7am-10pm.

Laundromat: Lavandería Rex, Madero 705, just past Méndez. High per-piece rates; try to swing a per-kg deal. Open M-F 9am-6:30pm, Sa 9am-1pm.

Emergency and Communications

Emergency: Dial 06.

Police: Aldama 101 (tel. 15 26 33 or 15 26 30), in the *Zona Luz,* is a module open 24hr. The actual office is farther away, on 16 de Septiembre at Periférico (tel. 15 25 17). No English spoken. Office open 24hr.

Red Cross: (tel. 15 55 55 or 15 56 00), on General Sandino in Col. 1 de Mayo. Take the "1 de Mayo" bus from Madero. No English spoken.

Pharmacy: Farmacia del Ahorro, right in the Zona Luz at the corner of Reforma and Aldama, across from the Howard Johnson. Open 7am-10pm. Also has an **ATM** and **fax** service.

Medical Services: Clínica 39, Zaragoza 1202 (tel. 12 20 49), at Carmen Buen Día. English-speaking staff. Small charge for services rendered. Open daily 7am-8pm.

Post Office: Sáenz 131 (tel. 12 10 40), at Lerdo near the stairs leading up the hill. Open M-F 8am-7pm, Sa 9am-1pm. **Postal Code:** 86000.

Fax: Telecomm, Lerdo 601 (tel. 14 28 33) at Sáenz around the corner from the post office. Open M-F 8am-8pm. Also has **Western Union** and **telegraph** services.

Internet Access: C@fé Internet Zona Luz (tel. 14 46 45, ext. 521), right beneath the huge Howard Johnson Hotel along 27 de Febrero and Juárez in the Zona Luz. The computers have groovy names (like "Zip" and "Disk"), but they are limited to Netscape and IRC. No telnet. 24 pesos per hour. Open M-F 9:30am-10pm, Sa 8am-7pm.

Telephones: LADATELs are abundant all over town. For some peace and quiet, try the ones that line Sáenz.

Phone Code: 93.

ACCOMMODATIONS AND CAMPING

Hotels in Villahermosa range from the dirt-cheap budget accommodations clustered around the intersection of 27 de Febrero and Madero to the five-star glamor of the *Zona Hotelera* near Tabasco 2000. **Camping** and **trailer parking** are allowed in **La Choca Park** in Tabasco 2000, but the site lacks facilities.

Hotel Oriente, Madero 425 (tel. 12 01 21), across the street from a VIPS restaurant, is probably the best deal in town. Rooms are quiet and clean, and all have windows, fans, and private baths. Singles 50 pesos; doubles 60 pesos. TV extra.

Hotel Madero, Madero 301 (tel. 12 05 16), near 27 de Febrero. Great central location, but try to get a room that's not on the street. Rooms of varying quality; shop around. Most are clean and equipped with fans. Singles 70 pesos; doubles 90 pesos; triples 100 pesos; cable TV an additional 50 pesos.

Hotel Palma de Mallorca, Madero 510 (tel. 12 01 44 or 12 01 45), offers the most affordable rooms with A/C. Located near the intersection of Zaragosa and Madero; rooms are spartan, cheap, and clean—they offer a welcome escape from Villahermosa's heat. Singles 70 pesos, with A/C 100; doubles 90 pesos, with A/C 120 pesos.

FOOD

Villahermosa, like the rest of Tabasco, specializes in *mariscos* (seafood). A typical *tabasqueño* dish not for the faint of heart is *pejelagarto* (tortoise sautéed in green sauce and blood and then mixed with pickled armadillo). Other specialities include ingredients like *chipilín, chaya* leaves, and *amashito* chile.

Restaurant Los Tulipanes (tel. 12 92 17 or 12 92 09), in the CICOM complex, specializes in *comida tabasqueña*. Enjoy fresh seafood right on the banks of the Río Grijalva in this sophisticated joint, a local favorite. Unfortunately, it's a tad on the expensive side; seafood dishes start at 40 pesos. Open Sa-Tu noon-9pm, Th-F noon-11pm.

Cocktelería Rock and Roll, Reforma 307 (tel. 12 05 93), right across from the Hotel Miraflores, serves up seafood and local specialties for some of the lowest prices around and provides a swinging, rowdy atmosphere to boot. *Antojitos* around 10 pesos. Open daily 9am-11pm.

Café Bar Impala, Madero 421 (tel. 12 04 93). A cluttered hole in the wall with superb *tamalitos de chipilín, panuchos* (fried tortilla shells stuffed with meat and beans), and tacos (each a mere 1.50 pesos). Open daily 9am–8pm.

SIGHTS

For a city that seems unconcerned with tourism, Villahermosa has a surprising number of fine museums, many of them within walking distance of the downtown area known as the Zona Luz or the Zona Remodelada. The downtown area is comprised of a series of pedestrian streets lined with specialty *tiendas, licuado* stands, gurgling fountains, shaded benches, and more hair salons than should be legal.

The best place to begin exploring Villahermosa's sights is at the **Museo de Historia de Tabasco,** at the corner of Juárez and 27 de Febrero in the Zona Luz. *(Open Tu-Sa 9am-8pm, Su 10am-5pm. Admission 5 pesos.)* Located in the famous **Casa de los Azulejos** (House of the Tiles), the museum houses artifacts and pictures detailing the history of the state of Tabasco. The real show-stealer, though, is the tiled house itself. Built between 1889-1915 by a wealthy merchant, the bright blue edifice is decorated with Italian and Spanish baroque tiles with a different style adorning each room. Eleven classic sculptures sit atop the roof; the seated female figures are said to be members of the merchant's family. Also note the Egyptian tiles decorating the ledge on the outside walls.

Also in the Zona Luz is the **Casa Museo Carlos Pellicer,** Saenz 203 (tel. 10 01 57), slightly past the post office. *(Open Tu-Su 10am-7pm; free.)* This tiny four-room museum pays homage to Carlos Pellicer Cámara, the great Mexican poet and philanthropist born in this very house. Written manuscripts, pictures, and artifacts commemorate the man and his work. Free guided tours are often available in the mornings. An even smaller museum is the **Museo de Cultura Popular,** Zaragosa 810 (tel. 12 11 17), located to the left of the Zona Luz and uphill. *(Open Tu-Su 10am-7pm; free.)* This museum displays authentic *tabasqueña* dance costumes and examples of pottery and jars used by indigenous families. A shop to the side peddles artisan wares.

Parqu e-Museo La Venta

Tel. 14 16 52. *To get to La Venta, take the "Tabasco 2000," "Carrisal," "Petrolera," or "Palacio"* **bus** *(1.50 pesos) from Madero in the center to the intersection of Tabasco and Ruiz Cortínez. Walk northeast on Ruiz for 10 minutes or cut through the Parque Canabal until you reach the entrance. From the Tabasco 2000 complex, you can reach the museum by following the Paseo Tabasco down to the intersection of Ruiz Cortinez; it is about a 10- to 15- minute walk.* **Site open** *daily 8am-5pm;* **tickets** *only sold until 4pm.* **Admission** *15 pesos.* **2hr. tours** *in Spanish or English cost 150 pesos.*

Villahermosa's most stellar attraction is perhaps this archaeological park in northern Villahermosa. The site features artifacts discovered in La Venta, one of the major known Olmec ceremonial centers. Included in the stellar collection are three of the famous massive stone heads and several impressive altars, all of which are on display along a pathway that winds through a verdant jungle and mimics the setting in which these monuments might have been found—down to the insects and trees that surround them. Doubling as an archaeological park and zoo, the site is enchanting. At the park's northern edge, birds flit through the aviary, grand felines bask in the sun, and cheeky monkeys toy with iguanas foolish enough to enter their pit. You can get a good look at the jaguars that roam around their enclosure in the south of the park, halfway around the archaeological walk near the gift shop.

Surrounding the Museo is the **Parque Tomás Garrido Canabal,** which lies on the Laguna de las Ilusiones and surrounds the Parque-Museo La Venta. The main entrance is at the corner of Tabasco and Grijalva. Landscaped alcoves hide benches and fountains. While the *mirador* claims to offer a panoramic view of Villahermosa, all you get in reward for your 40m climb is a good look at a few treetops. You can, however, get a spectacular view of the *lagunas* below.

CHIAPAS & TABASCO

Other Sights

Northwest on Paseo Tabasco, away from the city center and Río Grijalva, is **Tabasco 2000,** a complex containing futuristically bland buildings and pedestrian- unfriendly streets that is light years away from the cozy, car-free Zona Luz. Take the "Tabasco 2000" bus from the city center and get off by the Liverpool store, right smack in the middle of the complex. The long strip of sparkling new buildings includes the city's **Palacio Municipal,** a convention center, several fountains, a shopping mall, and a **planetarium** (tel. 16 36 41) with **OmniMax** shows dubbed in Spanish (shows Tu-F 6 and 7pm, Sa-Su 6, 7, and 8pm; admission 15 pesos).

Carlos Pellicer's name graces yet another museum—the **Museo Regional de Antropología Carlos Pellicer Cámara,** the main attraction at Villahermosa's new **Center for the Investigation of Olmec and Maya Cultures (CICOM;** *Museum open daily 9am-8pm; free.)* From the Zona Luz, the museum is best reached with a 15-minute walk south along the Río Grijalva. The #1 and "CICOM" buses pass often. The collection focuses mainly on the Olmec and Maya, with a scant selection of artifacts from other cultures. Most of the items and pictures on display are from the nearby archaeological sites of La Venta and Comalcalco. The center also houses a public library, an arts school, a theater, and traveling exhibits.

Elephants and zebras run free at the ecological reserve known as **Yumká** (Elf Who Tends the Jungle), just 14km from the hustle and bustle of Villahermosa. *(Open daily 9am-5pm; ticket counter closes at 4pm. Admission 15 pesos, children 10 pesos.)* A multitude of animals from around the world roam the three *tabasqueño* ecosystems: jungle, savannah, and wetlands. A *colectivo especial* is the fastest way to get there (60 pesos). Otherwise, go to the PEMEX station at Ruíz Cortinez in La Colonia; at the corner of Sierra and Cortinex, snag a five-peso bus to the zoo.

ENTERTAINMENT

Villahermosa presents two basic nightlife options: the discos in the luxury hotels or a myriad of cultural activities. For those wishing to take the mellower road, the **Instituto de Cultura Tabasco** (tel. 12 90 24), on Magallanes in the Edificio Portal del

Agua, publishes a monthly calendar of musical, theatrical, and other cultural events; look for it in museums and major hotels. Another place to try is the **Galería El Jaguar Despertado,** Sáenz 117 (tel. 14 12 44) near Reforma in the Zona Luz. The cafe in the back sometimes features live classical music or jazz. Even without the tunes, though, fountains, original Mexican art, and the gallery upstairs attract an interesting mix of intellectuals and romantics. A weekly program of cultural events is posted outside the door. (Open M-Sa 9am-9pm, Su 3pm-8pm.) Across the street, **Galería de Arte Tabasco,** Sáenz 122, features a slew of contemporary *tabasqueño* artwork, much of it for sale (open M-F 9am-9pm, Sa 10am-2pm).

For those itching to hit the discos and nightclubs, head to the *Zona Hotelera* in and around Tabasco 2000. Here, Villahermosa's young and sophisticated boogie down to the hottest mix of salsa, tropical music, and visual stimuli. Villahermosa's granddaddy of discos, **Disco Ku,** Av. Sandino 548 (tel. 15 94 31 or 15 84 33), is one of the few not found in the *Zona Hotelera*. The club features live music on Thursday nights and caters primarily to an older crowd except on Sundays, when it accepts 18 and under. (Cover around 40 pesos for men and 30 pesos for women. Open W-Su 9pm-3am.) Another local favorite is **Disco Etherea** (tel. 16 53 73 or 16 53 74), located next to the Camino Real Hotel behind the Galerias Tabasco 2000. The sleek purple-and-black club is decorated with groovy Greek letters and yin-yangs and features standard house mixes. Ladies may enter the land of Etherea for free. (Open bar on Fridays. No cover W-Th; 80 pesos on Friday; 40 pesos Saturday. Open W-Sa 7pm-3am.) Etherea's fierce rival is its newly opened neighbor **Disco Dasha** (tel. 16 21 74 or 16 62 85), in front of the Galerías Tabasco 2000 behind the anonymous government buildings. (Saturday is "crazy bar." Cover 40-100 pesos for men and 30-60 pesos for women. Students with ID get in free on Thursday. Open W-Sa 9pm-3am.) Taxi drivers are well-acquainted with disco hot spots, and their vehicles are the only efficient means of reaching them.

CHIAPAS & TABASCO

Less raucous nightlife awaits you at **Flambouyan** (tel. 15 12 34), a sophisticated, elegant bar-and-club found in the lobby of the five-star Hyatt Hotel. The bar features live music every night, and rotating bands keep the music fresh. (Open daily 9pm-2am.) For something a bit less ordinary, there's the **Rodeo Nocturno Cowboy Palace** (tel. 54 00 60) on Carretera Villahermosa-Cárdenas. *Música grupera* (country music) has found its home here, among wannabe *vaqueros* and a rodeo setting. (Cover 25 pesos. Open F-Sa.) For entertainment that's less exotic, **Cinema Superior** on Madero, one block south of 27 de Febrero, has daily showings of English-language movies at 5pm and 7pm (17 pesos).

■ Near Villahermosa: Comalcalco

Whereas La Venta documents Tabasco's Olmec past, **Comalcalco** demonstrates the Maya's dominance over the area in the later Classic period (200-700). *(Site open daily 10am-5pm. Admission 10 pesos.)* One of the northernmost Maya settlements, Comalcalco has yielded evidence of contact with other Yucatec Maya societies, as well as with the Toltecs, Mexica, and Totonacs. The site's most distinctive feature is its architecture: unlike those of other Maya cities, the pyramids and buildings of Comalcalco were constructed from packed earth and clay and later covered with stucco oven-fired bricks. Eroded but still imperial, the ruins contrast dramatically with the jungle behind them.

With 10 levels, the hulking 25m **pyramid** to the left of the entrance to the site is Comalcalco's best-known landmark. The north face bears traces of the elaborate stucco carvings that once completely covered the structure's sides. Behind the pyramid lies the north plaza, surrounded by a series of ruined minor temples and mounds. If you look closely at the dilapidated walls, you'll be able to see the insides of Comalcalco's brickwork and oyster-shell mortar.

From the plaza, a well-worn path leads up the side of the acropolis area and passes a group of three temples on the way. As with the main pyramid, vestiges of elaborate decorative carvings can be seen on each of these temples. Farther up the acropolis, turn right to reach the **Tomb of the Nine Knights of the Night,** named after the nine bas-relief figures on the walls of the tomb. Visible from the acropolis, three sides of Comalcalco's **ballcourt** (to the left) remain unexcavated and covered with tropical vegetation. Several temples, including one known as **The Palace,** stand in pieces atop the acropolis against a backdrop of tall, square brick columns and several roofless rooms.

Getting There: The site lies 34km northwest of Villahermosa, 2km from the town of Comalcalco, and is best reached by one of the taxi *colectivos* that leave frequently from Abelardo Reyes and Mina, on the other side of the supermarket from the first class bus station. The taxis wait until five people are gathered to go your direction (about 10-15min.) and deposit you about 50 minutes and 15 pesos later in Comalcalcos's market. From where the taxi stops, turn onto the corner of Reforma and Escobedo and hop on a bus labeled "Ruinas." It will take you directly to the entrance of the ruins or let you off at the access road (3 pesos). From here, the walk to the site is a pleasant 1km.

Teapa

An hour's drive south of Villahermosa along roads flanked by banana groves, Teapa's sulfuric spa and splendiferous caverns lure daytrippers from the state capital. The town itself (pop. 35,000) is slow-moving; its dilapidated, leafy *zócalo* and quiet streets make for peaceful strolling.

ORIENTATION AND PRACTICAL INFORMATION The bus station (served by Transportes Villahermosa-Teapa and Cristóbal Colón) is on **Méndez,** Teapas's main drag. To get to the *zócalo,* exit the bus station, turn right on Méndez, and walk five minutes to the *zócalo.* Most hotels and services are around Méndez and the *zócalo.* **Cristóbal Colón** sends **buses** (tel. 2 03 52) to Tuxtla Gutiérrez (5hr., 8:20am, 4 and 8:20pm, 57 pesos) and Villahermosa (1hr., 38 pesos). **Transportes Villahermosa-Teapa** runs second-class buses to Villahermosa (every hr. 4:45am-7:45pm, 17 pesos; Teapa station open daily 7am-10pm). Villahermosa is much more easily reached by hopping into one of the red **taxi-colectivos** right in front of the bus station on Méndez. Serving both Villahermosa and Pichucalco, they leave as soon as they have five people (45min., approximately every 20min., 20 pesos). **Banamex,** Méndez 102 (tel. 2 02 84) next door to the church, offers a 24-hour **ATM** (bank open M-F 9am-5pm). The **police** (tel. 2 01 10) are in the Palacio Municipal on Méndez (open 24hr.). **Nueva Farmacia del Pueblo** (tel. 2 00 23 or 2 01 70) is right across the street from the cathedral on Méndez (open daily 8am-9pm). The **post office** is at Calle Manuel Buelta 109 near the *zócalo* (open M-F 9am-3pm). The **postal code** is 86800. The **phone code** is 932.

ACCOMMODATIONS AND FOOD Teapas's small size translates into few accommodations. Your best bet is **Casa de Huéspedes Miye,** Méndez 211 (tel. 2 00 11), diagonally across from the bus station. Each bright room has its own color scheme and fan. Birds and flowers make the outside as cheerful as the inside. (Singles 40 pesos; doubles 50 pesos; add 10 pesos for private bath.) Across the park from the church on Av. Plaza de la Independencia, **Hotel Jardín** (tel. 2 00 27) is another possibility. Lime-green rooms have small windows and even smaller bathrooms. (Singles 60 pesos; doubles 80 pesos; triples 100 pesos). A place somewhat off the beaten budget track is Teapas's famous **Balneario El Azufre,** Méndez 720 (tel. 12 05 22 or 12 67 52). The *balneario* is located quite a way out of town; to get there, take a taxi-*colectivo* headed for Pichucalco and ask to be let off at "El Azufre" (15min., 5 pesos). Getting back is a bigger problem, as hailing unwilling cabs near the hotel can be problematic. There is always the second-class bus that rumbles through about every 30 minutes on its way back to Teapa (2.5 pesos). The *balneario* (dubiously called "spa" in its brochures) is known for the thermal mineral springs that flow nearby, and nature's beauty has been converted into the hotel's two pools. Although they look like two uninteresting dirty pools, they supposedly possess mythical cleansing and rejuvenating properties, and they make the skin tingle after a prolonged soak. Cabanas at the hotel go for about 60 pesos, and a day-pass will cost you 10 pesos. As for yummy food, **fruit stands** and **panaderías** line Av. Méndez. **Josegay,** Méndez 125, half a block west of the church, makes a divine *pollo en mole* (15 pesos; open daily 8am-midnight).

■ Near Teapa: Las Grutas Coconá

Just a few kilometers from town, **Las Grutas Coconá** were discovered in the late 1800s by two adventurous brothers who were out in the woods hunting. *(Caves open daily 9am-4pm. Admission 10 pesos. Guides cost about 10-15 pesos.)* The caves (or *grutas*) contain a path that winds for 500m into the hillside, passing impressive caverns and underground lagoons along the way. Twelve-year-old guides offer their services at the entrance, giving details on rock formations and pointing out where the natural formations resemble something else (the Virgin Mary, the head of a moose, etc.). Once you are inside the cave system, shine your light into the roof—sometimes you can catch bats during their *siestas.* Farther on, you'll enter a breathtaking, acoustically funky, domed cavern replete with mighty stalactites. Beyond, a wooden walkway leads over a pool into a dripping cave. Locals say the pool, although dark, is safe for swimming. On the way back from the final, largest cave, look for a left-hand turn-off where the path diverges below some rocks. Here you can limbo beneath a 1m ledge to reach a secluded emerald pool called *Pozo de los Peces Ciegos* (Pond of the Blind Fish) because...well, because the pond is inhabited by tiny blind fish. If you're feeling truly adventurous, you can negotiate with the guides to take you to the unexplored, unnamed *gruta* about 200m away. This *gruta* lacks the wooden path and artificial lights of the first one, so descending into its damp, muddy caverns is truly an adventure. Leave your shoes at the entrance and be prepared to leave covered in grime. Tours of this *gruta* last anywhere from one-and-a-half to three hours and are not recommended for anyone who is claustrophobic or afraid of the dark.

Getting There: *Combis* for the *grutas* leave from Calle Bastar on the right-hand side of the church (every 30min., 3 pesos). Taxis charge 10-15 pesos.

CHIAPAS

■ Tuxtla Gutiérrez

An energetic young city, Tuxtla Gutiérrez (pop. 350,000) is the capital of Chiapas and the focal point of commerce and transportation for most of southern Mexico. The city was named for a progressive *chiapaneco* governor who, rather than succumb to imperialist right-wing forces, wrapped himself in the Mexican flag and dramatically leapt to his death from a church spire. In some ways, the city has adopted the indomitable spirit of its namesake. Rather than bow to the pressures of rapid industrialization, Tuxtla has flourished with the help of vibrant citizens, pretty parks, and the vivacious, colorful animals that reside in one of the best zoos in Latin America.

ORIENTATION

Tuxtla Gutiérrez lies 85km west of San Cristóbal and 293km south of Villahermosa. *Avenidas* run east-west and *calles* north-south. The central axis of the city, upon which the *zócalo* rests, is formed by **Av. Central** (sometimes called **Av. 14 de Septiembre**) and **Calle Central.** Streets are numbered according to their distance from and geographical relation to the central axis. For example, Calle 2 Oriente Sur lies south of Av. Central and two blocks east of Calle Central. Fifteen blocks west of the town center, Calle Central becomes **Blvd. Dr. Belisario Domínguez;** 11 blocks east it turns into **Blvd. Angel Albino Corzo.**

To get to the *centro* from the **ADO/Cristóbal Colón bus station,** walk left on 2 Nte. Pte. (away from the buses) for two blocks. The *zócalo* is two blocks to the left on Av. Central. The **Autotransportes Tuxtla Gutiérrez station** is in a cul-de-sac near Av. 3 Sur and Calle 7 Ote. From the station, turn right and then make another right onto the walled-in alley that doubles as a market. Make the first left onto Av. 2 Sur and continue west to Calle Central—the *zócalo* is two blocks to the right. Travelers from Chiapa de Corzo often disembark at a small station on 3 Ote. between 2 and 3 Sur. Facing the street from the bus stop, head left to Av. Central, then left again for the *zócalo.*

Major **bus** lines run west on 2 Sur, east on 1 Sur, north on 11 Ote., and south on 12 Ote. (daily 5am-11pm, 2 pesos). **Colectivos** run frequently through the city (6am-10pm, 3 pesos). As locals often crowd the *colectivos* in the *centro,* it may be more efficient to walk to your destination outside the *centro* and then catch a (less full) *colectivo* running back into town.

PRACTICAL INFORMATION

Transportation

Airport: Aeropuerto Francisco Sarabia (tel. 5 01 11), 15km southwest of town. **Taxtel** (tel. 5 31 95) runs to the airport and charges 40 pesos; a cheaper option is to grab a cab off the street (12 pesos). **Aerocaribe,** Av. Central Pte. 206 (tel. 2 00 20, at airport tel. 5 15 30). **Aviacsa,** Av. Centra l Pte. 1144 (tel. 2 80 81, at the airport tel. 5 02 58).

Buses: Cristóbal Colón, 2 Nte. Pte. 268 (tel. 2 16 39), at 2 Pte. First-class buses run to Campeche (12hr., 3:30pm, 176 pesos), Cancún (18hr., 12:30pm, 329 pesos), Chetumal (13hr., 12:30pm, 227 pesos), Comitán (3½hr., 8 per day 5am-11:30pm, 43 pesos), Escárcega (9½hr., 12:30pm, 145 pesos), Huatulco (9½hr., 9:45am and 10:15pm, 128 pesos), Mérida (14hr., 3:30pm, 221 pesos), Mexico City (15hr., 4 per day 2:30-11:30pm, 345 pesos), Oaxaca (10hr., 11:30am and 7:15pm, 154 pesos), Ocosingo (4hr., 6 per day 5am-midnight, 42 pesos), Palenque (6hr., 6 per day 5am-midnight, 73 pesos), Playa del Carmen (17hr., 12:30pm, 314 pesos), Puebla (13hr., 4 per day 2:30-11:30pm, 304 pesos), Puerto Escondido (11hr., 9:45am and 10:15pm, 160 pesos), San Cristóbal (2hr., every hr. 5am-midnight, 21 pesos), Tapachula (6hr., 14 per day 6am-midnight, 114 pesos), Tonalá (3½hr., every hr. 6am-11pm, 50 pesos), Tulum (16½hr., 12:30pm, 296 pesos), Veracruz (12hr., 7:30 and 8:45pm, 208 pesos), and Villahermosa (6hr., 4 per day 1-11:45pm, 85 pesos). **Autotransportes Tuxtla Gutiérrez,** 3 Sur 712 (tel. 2 03 22 and 2 02 88), between 5 and 6 Ote., has less frequent buses to the same destinations at cheaper fares.

Local Transportation: Combis leave from their stand on 2 Sur Ote., next to Hotel San Antonio, for San Cristóbal (1½hr., every 20min., 20 pesos). To reach Chiapa de Corzo, hop on a **Transportes Chiapa-Tuxtla** *microbús* at the station at 2 Sur and 2 Ote. (25min., every 10min., 8 pesos). You can also try hailing the bus as it leaves town on Blvd. Corzo.

Car Rental: Gabríel Rent-A-Car, Blvd. Dr. Belisario Dominquez 780 (tel. 2 24 52), across from the Pepsi-Cola factory. As cheap as they come in the big city; be ready to bargain for lower prices. VW bus 450 pesos per day. Open daily 7am-9pm.

Tourist and Financial Services

Tourist Office: Dirección Municipal de Turismo (tel. 2 55 11, ext. 214), 2 Nte. Ote. at Calle Central, on the northwest corner of the *zócalo.* You'll need their city map. Open M-F 8am-4pm, Sa 8am-1pm.

Currency Exchange: Banamex, 1 Sur Pte. 141 (tel. 2 87 44), at Calle Central. Credit card cash advances. 24hr. **ATM.** Open for exchange M-F 9am-3:30pm.

American Express: (tel. 2 69 98), on Blvd. Dr. Belisario Domínguez, across from the tourist office, near Plaza Bonampak. Doubles as a **travel agency.** English spoken. Open M-F 9am-2pm and 4-6:30pm, Sa 9am-1pm.

Local Services

Laundromat: Lavandería Automática Burbuja, 1 Nte. 413A (tel. 1 05 95), at 3 Pte. 8 pesos per kilo. Open M-Sa 8am-8pm, Su 9am-1pm.

Emergency and Communications

Emergency: Dial 06 or call **Policía de Seguridad Pública** (tel. 2 05 30 or 3 78 05).

Police: (tel. 2 11 06), in the Palacio Municipal, at the north end of the *zócalo.* Go left upon entering the building. No English spoken. Open 24hr.

Pharmacy: Farmacia 24 Horas, 1 Sur 716, between 6 and 7 Pte. Open 24hr.

Red Cross: 5 Nte. Pte. 1480 (tel. 2 00 96 or 2 95 14), on the west side of town. Open 24hr.

Hospital: Sanatorio Rojas, 2 Av. Sur Pte. 1487 (tel. 2 54 14 or 2 54 66). 24hr. emergency service. English spoken.

Post Office: (tel. 2 04 16), on 1 Nte. at 2 Ote., on the northeast corner of the *zócalo.* Open M-F 9am-2pm and 4-6pm, Sa 9am-noon. **Postal Code:** 29000.

Fax: (tel. 3 65 47; fax 2 42 96), on 1 Nte. at 2 Ote., next to the post office. Open for **telegrams** and fax M-F 8am-6pm, Sa 9am-1pm.

Internet Access: Corporacíon Electrónica y Computacional, 1 Av. Nte., Pte. # 675-A, 2nd fl. (tel. 3 54 92; email celcom@chis1.telmex.net.mx). Expensive, but several new computers get the job done. 40 pesos per hr. Open M-F 9am-noon and 3-7pm.

Phone Code: 961.

ACCOMMODATIONS AND CAMPING

Budget accommodations are as they should be in a capital city: affordable, decent, and convenient. Cheap hotels line the sides of and back streets around the *zócalo, and* a quick *colectivo* ride will take you to the stellar youth hostel.

Villas Deportivas Juvenil, Angel Albino Corzo 1800 (tel. 3 34 05), next to the yellow footbridge over the road. Take a *colectivo* east on Av. Central (1 peso) and tell the driver it's next to the Angel Corzo statue on Blvd. Corzo. Clean, single-sex, 4-person rooms have comfortable beds and good cooling fans. Communal bathrooms and showers are well maintained. Free soccer fields and basketball courts. Beds 25 pesos per person. Breakfast 8.50 pesos; lunch and dinner 13 pesos.

Hotel Avenida, Av. Central 244 (tel. 2 08 07), between 1 and 2 Pte., 1½ blocks west of the *zócalo.* Authentic 70s decor isn't a gimmick; it's just that this oddly tasteful centrally located hotel with big, well-kept rooms hasn't changed much. The satellite TV in the lobby sure is new, though. Singles 70 pesos; doubles 80 pesos; triples 110 pesos; quads 130 pesos.

Hotel Oasis, 11 Ote. Sur 122 (tel. 3 72 52), off Av. Central. 11 blocks east of the *zócalo,* but no harder to get to by *colectivo* than the hostel. Modern rooms have TV, phone, and nice private bath. Singles 82 pesos; doubles 94 pesos; triples 117 pesos; each additional person 20 pesos.

Hotel San Antonio, 2 Sur 540 (tel. 2 27 13), between 4 and 5 Ote. Cavernous rooms have fans and adequate baths. Singles 40 pesos; doubles with A/C 70 pesos; triples 80 pesos; 10 pesos per extra person.

FOOD

Culinary miracles don't happen in Tuxtla, but the city is speckled with inexpensive eateries. *Licuados* come in every flavor imaginable, from mango to spinach.

Restaurante Imperial, Calle Central Nte. 263 (tel. 2 06 48), 1 block from the *zócalo.* Surprisingly classy joint serves delicious *comida corrida* for only 18 pesos. Popular with local businesspeople on lengthy lunch breaks. Open daily 7am-7pm.

La Antigua Fogata, 4 Ote. Sur 115, just off Av. Central. Although the restaurant may look like a tin-roofed shack, they've got 23 years of experience behind their scrumptious chicken *al carbón.* (¼ chicken 20 pesos). Open daily 7:30am-midnight.

Restaurante Vegetariano Nah-Yaxal, 6 Pte. 124 (tel. 3 96 48), north of Av. Central. Peruse books on yoga theory and parenting as you enjoy the veggie *comida del día* (27 pesos). Smooth *licuados* 7-10 pesos. Open M-Sa 7am-9:30pm, Su 8am-4pm.

SIGHTS

The shady forest foliage of the **Miguel Alvarez del Toro Zoo** offers a refreshing change of scenery from Tuxtla's gritty urban landscape. *(Open Tu-Su 9am-5:30pm; free.)* To get to the zoo, take the "Cerro Hueco" or "Zoológico" bus, which leaves from 1

Ote. between 6 and 7 Sur (every 30min., 1.50 pesos). The bus traces an indirect and sometimes unbearably slow route to the zoo's front gate. Renowned throughout Latin America, the zoo houses only animals native to Chiapas, including playful monkeys, stealthy jaguars, bright green parrots, and rare quetzals. Many of the enclosed forest's inhabitants roam freely throughout the park. To return to the center, catch the same bus at the zoo's entrance as it goes up the mountain.

The **Conviviencia Infantil** (though many signs still read **"Parque Madero"**) unfurls in the northeast part of town at the intersection of 11 Ote. and 5 Nte. Its focal point is a large and modern theater, the **Teatro de la Ciudad Emilio Rabasa.** Films by Latin American directors and performances of *ballet folklórico* dominate the schedule (check the tourist information center for details). A children's amusement park is on the pleasant *paseo* east of the theater (open Tu-Su 9am-10pm). Past the amusement park is the open-air **Teatro Bonampak,** where free folk dance performances are held (Su 5-8pm). The eastern extremity of Parque Madero is demarcated by a light aircraft next to the open-air theater, upon which several eight-year-old fighter-pilots-in-the-making usually clamber. A broad concourse, lined with fountains and bronze busts of famous Mexicans, leads west of the theater past the **Museo Regional de Chiapas,** which displays the region's archaeological finds (open Tu-Su 9am-4pm; admission 20 pesos, free on Sundays). Farther down the concourse, at the **Jardín Botánico Dr. Faustino Miranda,** you can amble under towering *ceibas* (silk-cotton trees) and admire the colorful grandeur of Chiapanecan flora (open Tu-Su 9am-6pm). Across the concourse is the **Museo Botánico** (open M-F 9am-3pm, Sa 9am-1pm). Back in the center, the air-conditioned **Cinema Vistarama Tuxtla** (tel. 2 18 31), at 1 Sur and 5 Ote., shows mostly American films with Spanish subtitles (admission 15 pesos).

Chiapa de Corzo

Friendly and quiet **Chiapa de Corzo** has a rich history behind it, as reflected by the small Maya temple by the road into town. Also behind the town and its fascinating *zócalo* is the **Cañón del Sumidero** (see p. 504), an impressive vegetation-clad canyon that stretches 32km to the north of the city. Carved out by the industrious Río Grijalva, the mist-enshrouded slopes of the gorge peal at 1200m above the water. According to local lore, nearly 15,000 Chiapan *indígenas* threw themselves into the canyon in 1528 after their chief, Sanguiem, was burned alive by the Spaniards.

ORIENTATION AND PRACTICAL INFORMATION Chiapa de Corzo overlooks the Río Grijalva, 15km east of Tuxtla and 68km west of San Cristóbal. Most sights lie near the *zócalo* **(Plaza Angel Albino Corzo),** which is bounded on the north by 21 de Octubre (the Tuxtla-San Cristóbal highway), on the east by La Mexicanidad, on the south by Julián Grajales, and on the west by 5 de Febrero. **Boats** leave for **El Sumidero** from the riverbank, two blocks southwest of the *zócalo,* on 5 de Febrero.

Transportes Chiapa-Tuxtla *microbuses,* heading back to Tuxtla, stop on 21 de Octubre opposite the police station (25min., every 10min., 6 pesos). Contact the **tourist office** in **Tuxtla** for detailed tourist information. **Bancomer** (tel. 6 03 20) is on the eastern side of the *zócalo;* it also has a 24-hour **ATM** (bank open M-F 8am-3:30pm, Sa 10am-2pm). The **police station** (tel. 6 02 26) is in the Palacio Municipal, on the northeast side of the *zócalo* (open 24hr.). **Farmacia Esperanza** (tel. 6 04 54) is on 21 de Octubre, one block east of the *zócalo* (open M-Sa 7am-11pm, Su 7am-2pm). The **post office,** Calle Cenullo Aguilar 244, is a block-and-a-half north of the *zócalo* (open M-F 8am-6pm). The **postal code** is 29160. The **phone code** is 968.

ACCOMMODATIONS AND FOOD Most people visit Chiapa de Corzo as a daytrip from Tuxtla. Yet the **Hotel Los Angeles,** Julián Grajales 2 (tel. 6 00 48), at La Mexicanidad, on the southeast corner of the *zócalo,* makes a good case for staying the night. Tall-ceilinged rooms have wooden bed frames and firm mattresses facing a large, pleasant courtyard. (Singles 70 pesos; doubles 85 pesos; triples 100 pesos; quads 115 pesos.) Since you've come to Chiapa to see the river, you may as well head to the waterfront for mid-range, filling food. Cheaper food can be found at the **market** to the left of the church (open dawn to dusk). **Restaurant Comitán,** to the left as you hit the dock, offers a 25-peso breakfast special, occasional live marimba performances, and a view of the river partly obscured by the lush banks (open daily 8am-7pm). **Restaurant Nancy,** around the corner to the right as you hit the dock, is shorter on atmosphere but long on selection—come here if you crave a wide variety of seafood (30-40 pesos; open daily 6am-6pm).

SIGHTS *Chiapañecos* are very proud of their immense **Cañon del Samidero;** the landmark adorns the state seal. A two-hour *lancha* journey begins with humble views of cornfields, but shortly after the Belisario Domínguez bridge, the hills jump to form near-vertical cliffs that rise over 1000m above water level. Protected as a natural park, these steep walls are home to troupes of monkeys, hummingbirds, and soaring falcons, while the murky waters harbor crocodiles and turtles. Along the meandering river lies a dripping cave and the park's most famous waterfall, the **Arbol de Navidad.** This spectacular *cascada* plummets from the sky, rambling over a series of scalloped rock formations before disintegrating into a fine mist that envelops passing boats. El Sumidero's northernmost extremity is marked by the 200m-high hydroelectric dam **Netzahualcóyotl,** which, with the Río Grijalva's three other dams, provides 25% of Mexico's electricity.

Boats leave as soon as they're full from Chiapa's *embarcadero* (dock) at the end of 5 de Febrero, two blocks from the southwest corner of the *zócalo* (departing daily 7am-4:30pm; 60 pesos per person). Boats can also be taken up the canyon from **Cahuaré,** where the highway to Tuxtla Gutiérrez crosses the river near the Cahuaré Island Resort. The trip down the river is best made during the month of August, at the height of the rainy season, when up to 42 waterfalls can be seen.

Back in Chiapa de Corzo, most architectural gems date from the city's colonial period. The *zócalo* contains two colonial structures: a small **clock tower** and a fountain shaped like the crown of Queen Isabel of Spain. Often called **La Pila,** this famous Moorish fountain taps underground waterways 5km long and provided the town with fresh drinking water during a 1562 epidemic. Inside the fountain, tile plaques tell the story of Chiapa's colonial-era history. The red and white **Catedral de Santo Domingo** is one block south of the *zócalo* near Río Grijalva. The most famous of the four bells dangling in its tower, Teresa de Jesús, is named after a mystical Spanish saint (open daily 6am-2pm and 4-6:30pm). Alongside the cathedral, a 16th-century ex-convent houses the **Museo de la Laca,** which displays fine examples of Mexican lacquerwork, a handicraft practiced only in Chiapa de Corzo and four other cities (open Tu-Su 10am-4pm; free). You can also join one of the ongoing lacquering lessons during the summer months (check posted schedules in the museum).

During Chiapa's **Fiesta de San Sebastián** (Jan. 16-22), *los parachicos,* men in heavy costumes and stifling masks, dance from dawn to dusk. The fiesta's grand finale is a mock **Combate Naval** between *"españoles"* and *"indios."* More a beauty pageant than a battle, the event features decorated boats, costumed sailors, and fireworks.

San Cristóbal de las Casas

San Cristóbal de Las Casas (pop. 75,000) is nestled in the pine-filled Valley of Hueyzacatlán at an elevation of 2100m. The city derives its immense popularity from its picturesque, unsullied, red-tile-roofed, narrow-street colonial coziness; its courtyard and gardens; its invigorating highland climate; and its infusion by a remarkable diversity of Chiapan indigenous culture. Top off this combination with a 360° view of the lush green mountains, where clouds form spectacular formations as they tumble down the steep slopes into San Cristóbal's outskirts, and you'll understand why hordes of Mexican and foreign tourists have flocked here for years. A large resident contingent of North Americans and northern Europeans rounds out the populace and is primarily responsible for everything from clothing boutiques and English movies to yuppified but heartfelt campaigns to save the Lacandón jungle.

Although San Cristóbal is a much-touristed, aesthetic wonder, its life has long been animated by the age-old conflict between *mestizos* and *indígenas.* Founded in 1528 by the invading Spaniards and their Aztec allies, San Cristóbal de Las Casas was once the colonial capital of the region, a *mestizo* enclave in the midst of Maya territory.

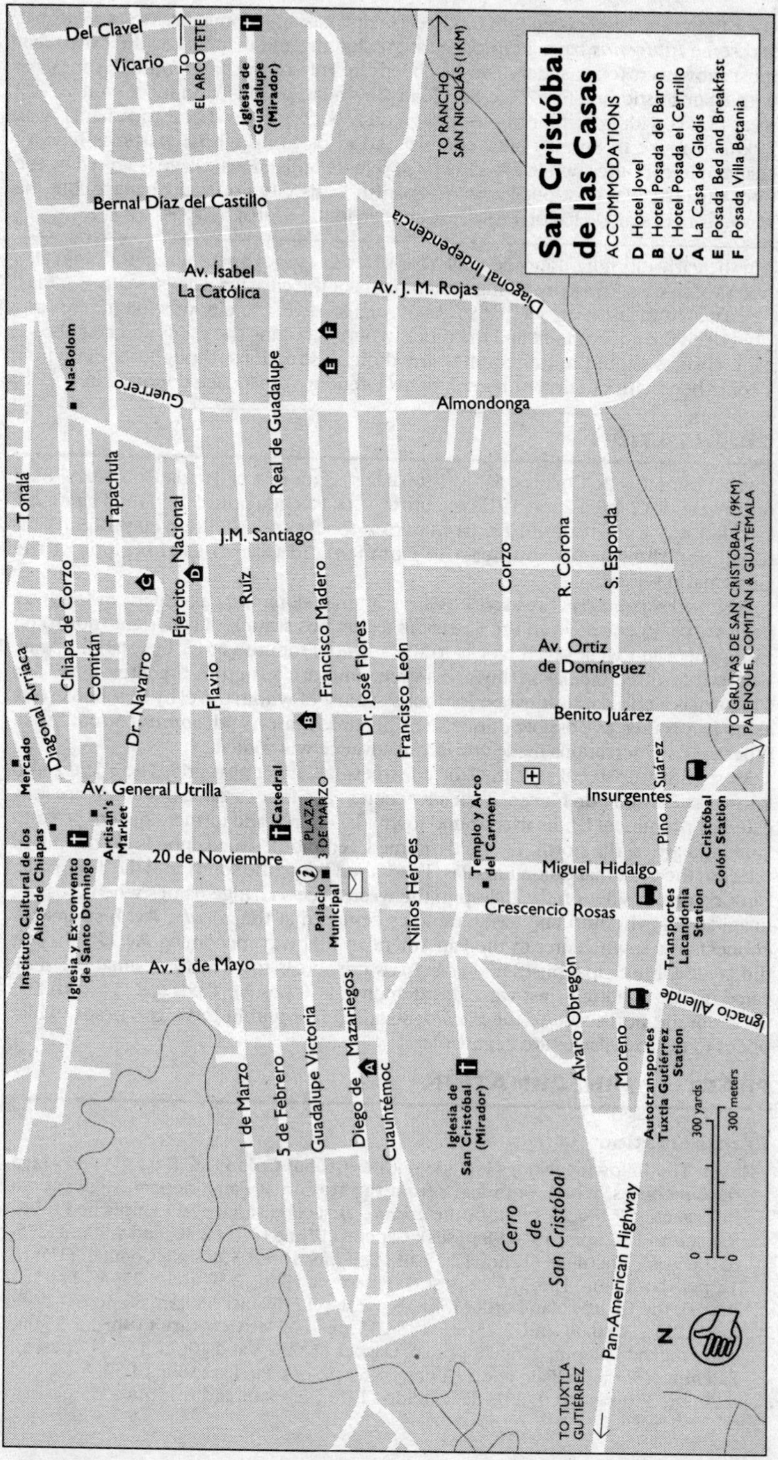
San Cristóbal de las Casas
ACCOMMODATIONS
D Hotel Jovel
B Hotel Posada del Baron
C Hotel Posada el Cerrillo
A La Casa de Gladis
E Posada Bed and Breakfast
F Posada Villa Betania
Del Clavel
Vicario
TO EL ARCOTETE
Iglesia de Guadalupe (Mirador)
TO RANCHO SAN NICOLÁS (1KM)
Bernal Díaz del Castillo
Diagonal Independencia
Av. Ísabel La Católica
Av. J. M. Rojas
Na-Bolom
Guerrero
Almondonga
Real de Guadalupe
Tonalá
Tapachula
Nacional
J.M. Santiago
Ruiz
Corzo
R. Corona
S. Esponda
Ejército
Chiapa de Corzo
Francisco Madero
Comitán
Dr. Navarro
Flavio
José Flores
Dr.
Francisco León
Av. Ortiz de Domínguez
Diagonal Arriaga
Benito Juárez
TO GRUTAS DE SAN CRISTÓBAL (9KM) PALENQUE, COMITÁN & GUATEMALA
Mercado
Av. General Utrilla
Catedral
PLAZA 31 DE MARZO
Templo y Arco del Carmen
Insurgentes
Suárez
Pino
Instituto Cultural de los Altos de Chiapas
Artisan's Market
Iglesia y Ex-convento de Santo Domingo
20 de Noviembre
Palacio Municipal
Niños Héroes
Miguel Hidalgo
Cristóbal Colón Station
Crescencio Rosas
Transportes Lacandonia Station
Av. 5 de Mayo
Alvaro Obregón
Ignacio Allende
Moreno
Autotransportes Tuxtla Gutiérrez Station
1 de Marzo
5 de Febrero
Guadalupe Victoria
Diego de Mazariegos
Cuauhtémoc
Iglesia de San Cristóbal (Mirador)
Cerro de San Cristóbal
300 yards
300 meters
0
0
Pan-American Highway
N
TO TUXTLA GUTIÉRREZ

CHIAPAS & TABASCO

Over the years, *mestizo* culture has become increasingly dominant in San Cristóbal, and some *indígenas* have adopted Western clothing and manners as their own. For most, however, tense syncretism has been the rule of the day. Catholicism mixes with shamanistic practices (see **San Juan Chamula,** p. 511), and most women still wear braids with colorful ribbons and grand *rebozo* scarves. Local merchants walk 20km or more to Sunday markets, dressed in clothing whose patterns haven't changed in centuries, while even the most remote indigenous village is served by the Coca-Cola truck at least once a week. Spanish is the city's official language, but the Mayan tongues of Tzeltal or Tzotzil are spoken in the nearby villages.

> In the early morning hours of New Year's Day in 1994, Zapatista rebels caught all of Mexico by surprise by taking hold of parts of the city (for details, see p. 57; for updates from last year, see p. 59). As of August 1998, the city was full of tension between the government and the rebels. Tourists visiting the sights and neighboring villages should not encounter any difficult situations, though people who come here with political or human rights intentions could face deportation.

ORIENTATION

High in the Altos de Chiapas, San Cristóbal lies 83km east of Tuxtla Gutiérrez, 78km northwest of Comitán, and 191km southwest of Palenque. Rte. 190, the Pan-American Highway, cuts east from Tuxtla Gutiérrez, touches the southern edge of San Cristóbal, and then heads southeast to Comitán and Ciudad Cuauhtémoc at the Guatemalan border.

First- and second-class **bus stations** are scattered along the Pan-American Highway near Av. Insurgentes. From the **Cristóbal Colón bus station**, take a right (north) on Insurgentes and walk seven blocks to the *zócalo.* From the other bus stations, walk east two or three blocks on any cross-street and turn left on Insurgentes. Since San Cristóbal is a popular destination for tourists, most of whom travel by bus, book seats as far in advance as possible during the Christmas season and *Semana Santa.* At all other times, reservations made one day in advance will suffice.

Most of San Cristóbal's clearly labeled streets fall into a neat grid. The *zócalo,* also known as **Plaza 31 de Marzo,** is the city center. The four cardinal directions are indicated by prominent landmarks around town: the church and former convent of Santo Domingo are to the north, the gold-trimmed Templo de Guadalupe is on the hill to the east, the Cristóbal Colón first-class bus station lies to the south, and the Templo de San Cristóbal resides on the hilltop to the west. Streets change names when crossing imaginary north-south and east-west axes centered at the *zócalo.* **Av. Insurgentes** connects the town center to the Pan-American Highway, becoming **Av. Utrilla** past the *zócalo.* Municipal buses and *colectivos* criss-cross town with destinations indicated on the window—just wave to catch one (1.50 pesos). **Taxis** (tel. 8 03 96) line up along the north side of the *zócalo.* Standard fare within town is 8 pesos, while prices to nearby villages are negotiable.

PRACTICAL INFORMATION

Transportation

Buses: The following listings include both **Cristóbal Colón** (tel. 8 02 91) and **Maya de Oro** buses, which both leave from the **station** at Pan-American Highway on Insurgentes, 7 blocks south of the *zócalo.* First-class service to Campeche (10hr., 9:30am and 5:25pm, 154-198 pesos), Cancún (17hr., 12:15, 2:30, and 4:30pm, 275-350 pesos), Chetumal (12hr., 12:15 and 2:30pm, 186-203 pesos), Comitán (1½hr., 12 per day 10am-11pm, 25-29 pesos), Escárcega (8hr., 2:30 and 5:25pm, 111-121 pesos), the Guatemalan border (3hr., 6 per day 12:30am-11:30pm, 88 pesos), Mérida (12hr., 9:30am and 5:25pm, 198-255 pesos), Mexico City (18hr., 2:25am, 3:30pm, and 6:20pm, 375-572 pesos), Oaxaca (12hr., 5 and 10pm, 175-214 pesos), Palenque (5hr., 11:25am and 2:30pm, 53-60 pesos), Puebla (16hr., 3:30, 5:30, and 6:20pm, 330 pesos), Puerto Escondido (12hr., 7:45am and 6:15pm, 183 pesos),

Tulum (13hr., 12:15 and 2:30pm, 249-271 pesos), and Tuxtla Gutiérrez (2hr., 9 per day 7:45am-11:30pm, 21-28 pesos).

Car Rental: Budget, Mazariegos 36 (tel. 8 18 71 or 8 31 00), 2 blocks west of the *zócalo.* With prices starting at 365 pesos per day, it's time they changed their name. Open M-Sa 8am-2pm and 4-8pm, Su 8-11am.

Bike Rental: Bicirent, Belisario Domínguez 5B (tel. 8 63 68), between Real de Guadalupe and Madero. 25 pesos per 3hr. or 55 pesos per day. Guided tours available.

Tourist and Financial Services

Travel Agencies: Viajes Pakal, Cuauhtémoc 6A (tel. 8 42 93; fax 8 28 19), between Insurgentes and Hidalgo, 1 block south of the *zócalo.* Daytrips to Agua Azul, Grutas de San Cristóbal, Palenque, and nearby villages. Trips to Bonampak, Yaxchilán, and Guatemala by special arrangement. Open M-F 9am-2pm and 4-8pm, Sa 9am-1pm. **Viajes Lacantún,** Madero 16 (tel. 8 25 88), a half block east of the *zócalo,* for flights within Mexico and abroad. Open M-F 9am-2pm and 4-7pm, Sa 9am-1pm.

Tourist Office: Main branch located on Hidalgo 2, a half block south of the *zócalo.* Open M-F 9am-9pm, Sa 9am-8pm, Su 9am-2pm. The branch office (tel. 8 06 65), at the northwest end of the Palacio Municipal, has even more info. Open M-Sa 9am-8pm, Su 9am-2pm. **Information Booth** at the Cristóbal Colón terminal, has maps and brochures. Some English spoken. Open 24hr.

Currency Exchange: Bancomer (tel. 8 01 37; fax 8 40 34), on the southern side of the *zócalo*. 24hr. ATM. Open M-F 9am-5:30pm, Sa 10am-2pm.

CHIAPAS & TABASCO

Local Services

English Bookstore: **La Pared,** Hidalgo 2 (tel. 8 63 67), half a block south of the *zócalo.* Buys, trades, sells, and, uh, lends used books. Open M-Sa 10am-2pm and 4-8pm, Sunday only during high season.

Markets: Between Utrilla and Domínguez, 7 blocks north of the *zócalo.* Best selection on Saturdays. Open daily 6am-2pm. Huge artisan's market forms around the Santo Domingo Church, 5 blocks north of the *zócalo* on Utrilla. Open daily 8am-5pm.

Laundromat: Orve, Domínguez 5 (tel. 8 18 02), between Real de Guadalupe and Madero. 28 pesos for 1-3kg, 8 pesos per additional kg. Promises to wash loads separately and to separate colors, just like Mom. Open M-Sa 8am-8pm.

Emergency and Communications

Police: (tel. 8 05 54), in the Palacio Municipal, on the west side of the *zócalo.*

Red Cross: Ignacio Allende 57 (tel. 8 07 72), 3 blocks south of the Pan-American Highway. No English spoken. 24hr. emergency service.

Pharmacy: Farmacia Regina (tel. 8 02 41), Mazariegos at Crescencio Rosas. No English spoken. Open 24hr.

Hospital: Hospital Regional, Insurgentes 24 (tel. 8 07 70), 4 blocks south of the *zócalo,* across from Santa Lucía, in Parque Fray Bartolomé. Open 24hr.

Post Office: (tel. 8 07 65), on Cuauhtémoc at Crescencio Rosas, 1 block southwest of the *zócalo.* Open M-F 8am-7pm, Sa and holidays 9am-1pm. **MexPost,** in the same office. Open M-F 8am-7pm. **Postal Code:** 29200.

Fax: Mazariegos 29 (tel. 8 42 71), 2½ blocks from the *zócalo.* Open M-F 8am-6pm, Sa 9am-noon.

Internet Access: Cybercafe (tel. 8 74 88), in Pasaje Mezariegos, off Real de Guadalupe, 1 block east of the *zócalo.* Trendy and expensive, charging 10 pesos per 15min. Open M-Sa 9am-10pm, Su 11am-9pm. **La Llamada,** Real de Guadalupe 55, a few blocks west of the *zócalo,* has a handful of computers. 40 pesos per hr. Open M-Sa 8am-2pm and 4-9pm.

Phone Code: 967.

ACCOMMODATIONS AND CAMPING

There are two more reasons to stay in San Cristóbal: the accommodations are cheap and comfortable. Most of them lie on **Real de Guadalupe, Madero, Insurgentes,** and **Juárez,** with prices decreasing relative to their distance from the *zócalo.* Camping is only available outside of town (see below). Due to the altitude, the temperature often drops below 10°C (50°F, 283 K), making hot water and blankets indispensable.

Posada Villa Betania, Madero 87 (tel. 8 44 67), 5 blocks east of the *zócalo.* Huge, quiet rooms with big, firm beds, a table for two, private bath, and fireplace (30 pesos per fire). Small gardens and intimate kitchen complete the relaxed, familiar atmosphere. Clothesline and unforgettable vista on the spacious roof. Singles 50 pesos; doubles 80 pesos; triples 90 pesos.

Hotel Jovel, Paniagua 28 (tel. 8 17 34), 2½ blocks east and 2 blocks north of the *zócalo.* Great natural lighting illuminates small rooms with colorful *sarape* bedspreads. Multi-level terraces offer a great view of the city and cozy reading areas. Hot water. Staff will watch luggage for a few days. Singles 60 pesos; doubles 70 pesos; triples 80 pesos; add 40 pesos for private bath.

Hotel Posada el Cerrillo, Domínguez 27 (tel. 8 12 83), 2 blocks east and 2½ blocks north of the *zócalo.* Freshly painted rooms match the freshly painted courtyard adorned with fresh plants. This place is fresh. Good communal bathrooms; 100 extra pesos for privacy. Singles 50 pesos; doubles 100 pesos.

La Casa de Gladis, Diego de Mazariegos #65, (tel. 8 57 75), 4 blocks west of the *zócalo.* Murals, hammocks, and a fountain decorate the colorful courtyard, while dorms come with animal throws and firm beds. Small, well-decorated private rooms and more sparse cabanas (25 pesos per person). Communal bathrooms are exceptional. Hot water. Singles 50 pesos, with bath 70 pesos; doubles and triples, 60 pesos, with bath 80 pesos; dormitory beds 35 pesos (make sure to keep dorms doors locked); camping 20 pesos per person.

Hotel Posada del Barón, Belisario Domínguez 2 (tel. 8 08 81), 1 block east of the *zócalo.* If you feel like splurging, this is the place. Colonial architecture gives way to classy rooms and modern bathrooms. Singles 120 pesos; doubles 150 pesos; triples 180 pesos.

Posada Bed and Breakfast, Madero 83 (tel. 8 04 40), 5 blocks east of the *zócalo.* The second bed and breakfast on Madero, just before the Villa Betania. Small, dim rooms open to brighter dining area. Tiny, communal bathrooms. Singles 30 pesos, with bath 70 pesos; doubles 50 pesos, with bath 70 pesos. Dorm beds 25 pesos.

Rancho San Nicolás (tel. 8 00 57), on the extension of Francisco León, 1km east of town. If no one is around, ring the bell for the hacienda across the road. Rooms, camping, and trailer park in a pastoral setting complete with whispering trees and hot water. During high season (Dec.-Feb.), rooms are often full, so call in advance. RVs 40 pesos; camping 20 pesos; rooms 35 pesos; each additional person 20 pesos. **Horse rental** 20 pesos per hr., 60 pesos per day.

FOOD

Inexpensive, high quality *comida corrida* joints abound in San Cristóbal. Rev up your afternoon with *sopa de pan* (bread soup) and grainy wheat breads from the Barrio San Ramón. Vegetarian restaurants are as plentiful as *churro* stands. End your meal with exquisite *cerveza dulce* or a cup of Mexico's best coffee.

Restaurante Madre Tierra, Insurgentes 19 (tel. 8 42 97), opposite the Iglesia de San Francisco, 2½ blocks south of the *zócalo.* Everything a *panadería* could be and more. The delicious pastries and excellent coffee attract the local foreign crowd. Breakfasts are good—and good for you (13-20 pesos). Open daily 8am-9:30pm.

Cafetería del Centro, Real de Guadalupe 15B (tel. 8 63 68), 2 blocks east of the *zócalo. Comida corrida* (soup, entree, rice, bread, *postre,* and coffee) and 15-peso breakfasts satisfy even the hungriest of heavyweight rowers. Open daily 7am-9:30pm.

Café Altura, 20 Noviembre 9 (tel./fax 8 40 38). The only organic vegetarian restaurant in town (entrees 30-40 pesos); brews some of the best coffee. At night, poets and musicians come to serenade well-caffeinated patrons. Open daily 7am-11pm.

La Salsa Verde, 20 de Noviembre 7 and 11, 1 block north of the *zócalo.* Two *taquerías.* Same name. Same street. Different owners, who both swear they were first.

CHIAPAS & TABASCO

The one at #7 is bigger and boasts great service. The one at #11 is smaller and cozier, offering similar choices. Tacos 3 pesos each. Both open daily 8am-11pm.

Restaurante París México, Madero 20 (tel. 8 06 95), 2½ blocks east of the *zócalo.* Offers French and Italian fare to the tortilla-tired tourist. Local dishes available. Extensive *menú del día* comes with a margarita and goes for 25 pesos. Open daily 8am-10pm.

Centro Cultural El Puente, Real de Guadalupe 55 (tel. 8 22 50), 3 blocks from the *zócalo.* Cafe/language-school/cinema mixes in local art and jazz as well, all with a distinct leftist flavor. Vegetarians can feast on the cheese, tomato, and avocado omelette (13 pesos). Sandwiches 9-12 pesos. Hot breakfast croissants with cheese (6 pesos). Open M-Sa 8am-11pm.

El Oasis, 1 de Marzo 6C, 1 block north of the cathedral. Veggie cuisine. 4-course *comida corrida* 26 pesos. Excellent breakfasts. Open M-Sa 7am-9pm.

Emiliano's Mustache, Crescencio Rosas 7, 1 block west and 1 block south of the *zócalo.* Elegantly tiled *taquería* serves all kinds of tacos (3 pesos) and some local specialties (25-30 pesos). Open daily 8am-1am. Taco stand open daily 6pm-1am.

Las Estrellas, Ecuadrón 201, across from the artisan market. Batik decor complements healthy vegetarian entrees. Hearty pesto pasta 16 pesos. Open daily 8am-10pm.

CHIAPAS & TABASCO

SIGHTS

Na-Bolom

Guerrero 33. In the northeastern section of the city, at the end of Chiapa de Corzo. ***Museum open*** *with the guided tour at 11:30am and 4:30pm in Spanish and 4:30pm in English, followed by a 15-minute film.* ***Admission*** *15 pesos. Museum shop open Tu-Su 10am-2pm and 4-7pm. Library open M-F 10am-1:30pm.*

San Cristóbal's most famous attraction is **Na-Bolom** (House of the Jaguar), a private house that turns into a museum twice daily. Guided tours will lead you through the estate of Franz and Trudy Blom, who worked and studied for many decades among the dwindling communities of the **Lacandón Rainforest** along the Guatemala border. After the death of her husband in 1963, Trudy Blom continued their work, winning acclaim as an ecologist, ethnologist, and photographer before her death in the winter of 1993. Many volunteers live at Na-Bolom, carrying out the jungle reforestation project begun by Mrs. Blom and conducting tours of the Fray Bartolomé de Las Casas library, the gardens, and the Bloms' personal museum. Travelers interested in **volunteering** at Na-Bolom should contact the main office (tel. 8 14 18) or email nabolom@scic.ecosur.mx at least two months prior to arrival. Positions last two to three months and include free housing and discounts on Na-Bolom meals. The library's manuscripts concentrate on Maya culture, with numerous periodicals, news clippings, and rare papers dealing with rainforest ecology and the plight of *indígena* refugees. The small, ornate chapel (the building was originally intended as a seminary) now serves as a gallery of colonial *chiapañeco* religious art created by *ladinos* and *indígenas* alike. Other rooms are devoted to archaeological finds from the nearby site of **Moxviquil,** religious artifacts from the Lacandón Rainforest, and the work of artists in residence. You can also stay in one of Na-Bolom's 14 fabulously decorated rooms.

Other Sights

Since its construction by the Spanish in the 16th century, San Cristóbal's *zócalo* has been the physical and spiritual center of town. The colonial **Palacio Municipal** and the yellow-orange **cathedral,** with its white Corinthian columns and patterned wooden roof, dominate the heart of the city. *(Cathedral open daily 7am-7pm.)* Consecrated in 1528, the cathedral pews are filled with a bevy of devout followers, and its rafters with a flock of chirping birds

North on Utrilla and beyond the **Iglesia de la Caridad** is the **Iglesia y Ex-convento de Santo Domingo,** whose grounds make up the artisan market. *(Santo Domingo church open daily 7am-8pm.)* While dirty and gigantic on the outside, Santo Domingo's inner walls are delicately covered in restless gold leaf that slithers in elaborate patterns up walls, around portraits, and over the left nave's exquisite pulpit. Tucked into the Ex-convento is **Sna Jolobil** (tel./fax 8 26 46), which means "House of Weaving" in Tzeltal. *(Open M-Sa 9am-2pm and 4-6pm.)* It is a cooperative of 800 weavers from 10 Tzotzil and Tzeltal villages in the *chiapañeco* highlands whose objective is to preserve and revitalize their ancestral weaving techniques. While many of the extremely high-quality, intricately embroidered *huipiles* will cost more than your plane ticket home, Sna Jolobil is a great place to window-shop and view the area's traditional garments. Another cooperative, **J'pas Joloviletic,** General Utrilla 43 (tel. 8 28 48), is on the opposite side of Santo Domingo (open M-Sa 9am-2pm and 4-7pm, Su 9am-1pm).

Next door to Sna Jolobil, the **Centro Cultural de Los Altos de Chiapas** houses an excellent multimedia exhibit on the history of San Cristóbal and Chiapas. *(Open Tu-Su 10am-5pm. Admission 10 pesos, free on Sundays. Free group tours in Spanish.)* On display are colonial artifacts, photographs, and a collection of Chiapanecan textiles, some of which are hundreds of years old. During the summer, visitors bring along pen-knives to leave their mark on the avocado tree in the courtyard.

San Cristóbal's daily morning **market** overflows with fruit, veggies, and an assortment of cheap goods. *(Market open daily 7am-3pm or until the afternoon rain.)* There aren't really any *artesanías* on sale though—look to the market around Iglesia de Santo Domingo for souvenirs. Try coming on Sunday, when *indígenas* from nearby villages turn out in droves or go to the villages themselves (see **Near San Cristóbal,** below). Utrilla and Real de Guadalupe, the two streets radiating from the northeastern corner of the *zócalo,* are dotted with colorful shops that sell *típico* attire for less than the market stands or neighboring villages. Locals do their shopping on Saturday mornings. Watch, listen, and learn—these experts wrote the book on bargaining.

ENTERTAINMENT AND SEASONAL EVENTS

While the *zócalo* empties around 11pm, coffeeshops and restaurants host live music into the wee hours. A stroll down Madero or Guadalupe will uncover any number of places to sip a cool *licuado,* kick back, and enjoy some Latin strumming. Try the **Restaurante Margarita,** on Madero next door to the Hotel Margarita, two blocks east of the *zócalo,* for a trio offering Flamenco and classical selections (music daily 9:30pm-midnight). **La Galería,** Hidalgo 3 (tel. 8 15 47), is a chic courtyard restaurant with live music during the high season (open nightly until 2am; cocktails around 10 pesos). **Café Altura** (see p. 508) serves great coffee, hot poetry, and live music as well (daily, starting at 9pm).

Not to be outdone by the Yucatán, San Cristóbal has its own Maya route—here, the temples are smoke-filled discos with throbbing bodies and flowing taps. Locals start around 11pm, gathering at Margarita's before heading to La Galería, then on to **Latinos** and **Las Velas,** two discos off the *zócalo* on Madero. Hard-core throbbers twitching for more can try **Disco Palace,** Av. Crescendio Rosas 59 (tel. 8 26 00), on weekends, and **Disco Pop-Rock** (tel. 8 11 81), in the Hotel Maya Quetzal on the Pan-American Highway, 300m west of the Cristóbal Colón bus station, on Saturday nights (open Sa only after 10pm).

For those with aching feet, technophobia, or lack of disco wear, **Cinemas Santa Clara** (tel. 8 23 45), on 16 de Septiembre between Escuadrón and 28 de Agosto, screens U.S. movies.

In San Cristóbal and the nearby villages, hardly a week goes by without some kind of religious festival. Although the city's *Semana Santa* celebration is rather *tranquila.* Many business establishments close their doors, and the processions and cultural events that take place are decidedly reverent and low-key. On Easter Sunday, however, *Semana Santa* gives way to the week-long **Feria de la Primavera y de la Paz.** Before the riotous revelry really gets going, a local beauty queen is selected to preside over the festivities, which include concerts, dances, bullfights, cock fights, and baseball games. Hotel rooms for either week must be reserved several months in advance. The *fiesta* of the city's patron, San Cristóbal, is celebrated from July 18 to 25 with elaborate religious ceremonies and numerous concerts.

Near San Cristóbal de Las Casas

Sunday morning is the best and often the only time to visit the markets of nearby villages. However, because service is always routed through San Cristóbal, visiting more than one village in a single morning is almost impossible. Buses and *combis* leave from the lot one block past the market at Utrilla and Honduras. Destination signs next to the buses are only occasionally accurate; always ask drivers where they're going. Drivers don't leave until the *combi* is completely full, so be prepared to squeeze in.

Visiting the villages on your own can give you a greater sense of freedom and a lesser sense of being a herd animal, but it can also be like watching a chess game blindfolded without knowing the rules; there's a lot in each *pueblo* that happens behind closed doors. Sometimes joining a tour group is a good idea, especially if the group leader is the energetic and knowledgeable **Mercedes Hernández Gómez.** Something of an expert on local *indígena* culture and a splendid storyteller, Mercedes's five-hour tour includes political, domestic, and spiritual teachings; she takes tourists into a private home, a saint's house, and the *pueblo* church (70 pesos for Chamula and Zinacantán tours). Look for Mercedes and her huge golf umbrella at the *zócalo* every day at 9am. An equally viable option is the intelligent and gregarious **Raúl López** (tel. 8 37 41), a thirtysomething local who happily divulges a wealth of information on everything from regional customs to the Zapatista uprising to religion and back again, with refreshing frankness. Raúl, who only speaks Spanish (his *compañero* Manuel gives the same tour in English), meets interested travelers outside the cathedral. Look for the blue *combi* daily at 9:30am (tour covers Chamula and Zinacantán; 60 pesos; van returns around 2pm).

CHIAPAS & TABASCO

Near San Cristóbal: San Juan Chamula

The community of San Juan Chamula (96 villages, 60,000 inhabitants) is the largest and most touristed of the communities around San Cristóbal. Located 10km northwest of San Cristóbal in a lush valley, Chamula's dirt roads, single-story houses, and wandering children are used to visitors. Chamula is known for its colors (black and blue), its *carnaval,* and its shamanic-Catholic church. Visitors come to Chamula to check out the spectacular traditional clothing and to witness a civic and religious structure quite unlike any other in Mexico. Older Chamulan men wear traditional black wool *sarapes* tied with thick leather belts (black signifying *carga,* or duty), while the young men, still unburdened, sport either blue or white *sarapes.* Designs on the sleeves of the tunics indicate the wearer's *pueblito* or *colonia.* Village officials (elected by a hand-count) and elders drape ribbons over their large sombreros. If you should see officials in their official dress, stifle the urge to snap a shot—the men refuse to be turned into a tourist attraction while they are performing their *cargas.*

Chamulans, who expelled their last Catholic priest in 1867, are famous for their fierce resistance to Mexico's religious and secular authority. Villagers have far more faith in the powers of the village shamans, and Catholic bishops are allowed into the church solely for baptisms. Similarly, the government medical clinic is used only as a last resort, after incantations with eggs, bubbly *refrescos,* and chickens have failed.

Before entering the brightly painted **church** (open 24hr.), you must obtain a permit (3 pesos) from the tourist office on the *zócalo* and show the permit to the guards outside the church. **Under no circumstances should you take pictures**—the church functions as a hospital, and it is disrespectful to the sick and to the shaman doctor to try to capture a very personal ceremony on film. The church's predominant color is green; it is meant to recall the ancient Maya practice of praying in caves—hence the pine needles on the floor, the branches, and the flowers. Inside the church, families, candles, and chickens fill the pewless hall as shamans chant petitions to the Catholic saints on a conversational level. Different colored candles signify different levels of prayer-severity, and other Maya rituals are aided by the ubiquitous Pepsi bottles. The importance of carbonated beverages cannot be overstated; Chamulans believe that **burping** helps to purify the self by expelling evil spirits. Prior to the discovery of fizzy drinks, locals had to drink gallons of water to achieve the same cathartic effect.

To the left of the church stands a cluster of distinctive, green foliated Maya crosses. The crosses' origin is in the crucifix-shaped **Tree of Life,** featured on the sarcophagus of King Pacal at Palenque. When Fray Bartolomé de Las Casas showed up bearing the Christian cross, he waltzed right into Chamula, where he was believed to be a messenger from the gods. Chamula's small but diverse artisans' **market** is behind the tourist office; here the hungry tourist can find roasted corn (5 pesos) among the scattered taco stands and avoid the overpriced cafes at the *zócalo.*

Private homes usually have brick-mud walls, thatched roofs, and dirt floors, with beds on one end and open fires on the other. No walls divide up the different sections, and most homes have little in terms of furniture. The village has a private house or chapel for each saint—just look for the leaf arches outside signaling the house's holy function. Inside the chapel are ceramic incense bowls, animal-shaped candleholders, and a leaf curtain separating the holy altar from the seating area, which has little more than a few low benches lining the mud-caked walls and pine needles cushioning the floor. Homes and chapels are generally not open to the public—join Mercedes and her tour for a peek into private Chamulan life (see p. 511).

The best time to visit Chamula is one week before Ash Wednesday, during **Carnaval,** which draws 40,000 *indígenas* and countless tourists. While they coincide with Lent, the festivities have their origins in the ancient Maya ritual concerning the five "lost" days at the end of the 360-day agricultural cycle. Expect to see religious leaders dashing through fire in order to purify themselves, as well as men decked out in monkey skins singing and dancing. In addition to Chamula's *carnaval* and the assumption of the *cargo* (Dec. 3-Jan. 1), the **fiestas** of **San Sebastián** (Jan. 20), **San Mateo** (Sept. 21-22), and **San Juan Bautista** (June 22-24) warrant a trip to the village.

Getting There: *Combis* to Chamula leave from San Cristóbal, on Utrilla one block west and one block north of the market (30min., every 15min. 6am-5pm, 5 pesos). To reach Chamula by car from San Cristóbal, drive west from the *zócalo* on Guadalupe Victoria, and bear right after crossing the small bridge on Diagonal Ramón Larraínzar. At the fork, go right; Chamula is at the end of the 8km stretch of paved road.

■ Near San Cristóbal: Zinacantán

Just beyond Chamula lies the smaller community of Zinacantán (pop. 35,000), comprised of 36 villages. If you have the time, ask to be let off at the dirt road near the head of the valley, and make the 3km descent into town; you'll pass women washing their hair upon stones and men wearing dazzlingly red *sarapes,* decorated with colorful stitched flowers and dangling tassels of deep red and purple. During **fiestas,** residents wear heel-guards on their *huaraches* (sandals) in accordance with ancient Maya custom. Many of the women walk about barefoot. This is not an indication of poverty but rather a reflection of the Maya emphasis on the importance of female fertility—they believe that women can draw fertility from the ground. Thus, as girls approach puberty, they begin to go without shoes. The unfortunate few women who are sterile are cast out of the village and must move, usually to San Cristóbal.

Somewhat exceptional for a *chiapañeco* village is the fact that Zinacantán has accepted the Catholic clergy. The village's handsome, whitewashed **church** dates back to the 16th century and features standard Roman columns and Corinthian arches. It is used exclusively for Catholic worship, while the small white convent has been set aside for ritual healing and pre-Conquest forms of worship. You won't find confessionals in the church, though—confession here is a public act, directed at the effigies on the altar. The Catholic priest, independent of the village church, merely busies himself with confirmations, baptisms, and wedding ceremonies. To enter the church you must pay a 3-peso visitor's fee at the tourist booth in front. Tourists who step inside the convent are expected to drop a small donation into the *limosna* box. As with all traditional communities, Zinacantán does not tolerate picture-taking, note-taking, or hat-wearing.

Of late, the village's flower industry has flourished, and Zinacantán has gained a considerable economic edge over neighboring San Juan Chamula. Every Friday morning, town residents inaugurate what they hope will be a profitable weekend by marching down Av. Insurgentes in San Cristóbal. Today, many houses in Zinacantán contain stereos, TVs, and gas stoves, although these serve principally as status symbols—many women prefer to cook directly on the ground. The children who bother tourists for pesos or pens will be severely scolded by their parents if caught. If you wander around town long enough, you'll stumble upon a backyard full of women **weaving,** and may well be invited in to browse the selection of clothes—you won't find souvenirs any more homemade than these.

Zinacantán's festivals include **Fiesta de San Sebastián** (Jan. 18-20), **Semana Santa, Fiesta del Patron San Juan** (July 24-29), and the **Fiesta de San Lorenzo** (Aug. 10-20).

Getting There: *Combis* to Zinacantán (7 pesos) leave San Cristóbal from the lot near the market as they fill up (daily 6am-8pm). If driving, follow Guadalupe Victoria west from the *zócalo* and turn right after crossing the small bridge on Diagonal Ramón Larraínzar. At the fork, turn left toward the "Bienvenido a Zinacantán" sign.

■ Near San Cristóbal: San Andrés Larraínzar

The site of the Zapatista negotiations during the summers of 1995 and 1996, San Andrés Larraínzar lies 26km northwest of San Cristóbal and 16km from Chamula. Because there are no convenient tours to the village, its 5000 citizens are better disposed toward the outsiders who do make the trip. The village colors are red, black, and white, appearing on most clothing and market items. Mexicans refer to the village as Larraínzar, but local Tzotziles prefer San Andrés. Since many of the villagers are reluctant to carry their produce all the way to San Cristóbal, San Andres's **market** (open F-Su until 1pm) is better stocked than the ones at Chamula or Zinacantán. For a panoramic view of the beautiful green valleys and patches of cornfields that surround the city, walk up the hill from the main church to La Iglesia de Guadalupe.

Getting There: Starting at 6am, *combis* (50min., 15 pesos) make several trips to San Andrés from the small terminal behind the San Cristóbal market—continue on the dirt road for about a block; the stop will be on your right. It's best to return before 2pm, soon after the market begins to shut down and before the *combis* stop running. To reach San Andrés by car, take the road northwest from San Cristóbal to Chamula and continue past the village. On a curve some 10km later, a prominent sign announcing "S.A. Larraínzar" points left to a road climbing the steep side of the valley; the village lies approximately 6km beyond the fork.

■ Near San Cristóbal: Chenalhó

Chenalhó (pop. 6000) seems even more remote from San Cristóbal than 32km would suggest. Foreigners are rare birds here. In Chenalhó, typical dress for men varies from white or black ponchos worn over pants and bound with heavy belts to short, light, white tunics. Women who have not adopted more current fashions dress uniformly in dark blue *nalgas* (skirts) and white *tocas* (shawls) embroidered with bright orange flowers. A small **store** behind the enclosed market supplies the town with nearly all of its clothing. The **market** spreads out into the plaza in front of the church on Sunday and sells mostly foodstuffs, including *chiche,* a potent drink made from fermented cane. Villagers enthusiastically wave visitors into San Pedro, the church in the town's center, which serves as both a secular and a religious meeting place. Inside, the main aisle often shimmers with the light rising from candles. Chenalhó residents celebrate the **Fiesta de San Sebastián** (Jan. 20) and the **Fiesta de San Pedro** (July 29) in style.

Getting There: Autotransportes Fray Bartolomé de Las Casas usually operates buses to Chenalhó and the even more remote town of **Pantelhó.** The bus leaves San Cristóbal from the station on Utrilla north of the market at about 2pm. The bus sometimes does not return until the next day, so make sure you have a ride back to San Cristóbal before you go. Bus trips take two hours. If you get stranded, Chenalhó does have some beds available—just ask nicely to be shown the way. Driving to Chenalhó can cut transit time in half, but the cost to your car's suspension system will be high—the dirt road northwest of Chamula is guaranteed to chatter some teeth.

■ San Cristóbal: Huítepec Ecological Reserve

While the villages around San Cristóbal are home to rare textiles, the mountains that rise above harbor their own rare attractions. The **Huítepec Ecological Reserve,** situated on the east face of the Huítepec Volcano, offers the chance to explore an **evergreen cloud forest** ecosystem, not found in many other places on the planet. *(Open Tu and Th-Su 9am-4pm. Admission to the reserve 10 pesos. Guided tours of groups of 8 or more people 150 pesos.)* Two trails wind around the park, which is home to some 60 species of birds and 40 other North American avian species during the winter migrations, as well as more than 300 plant species. Those with medicinal properties or religious importance to *indígena* villagers are marked with small signs. The shorter of the two trails makes for a self-led, invigorating 2km hike, rising to a height of 2390m, while the longer 8km hike is headed by a guide. The owner of Restaurant el Oasis, along with his three dogs, also leads a daily hike from 8am to 3pm to the park, with explanations of flora and fauna along the way (120 pesos).

Getting There: The Reserve rests just off the road to San Juan Chamula, 3½km from San Cristóbal, and can be reached by any *combi* headed in that direction; ask the driver to let you off at the "Reserva Huítepec" (15min., every 15min., 5 pesos).

■ Near San Cristóbal: Grutas de San Cristóbal

The Grutas de San Cristóbal lie just off the Pan-American Highway, 10km southeast of San Cristóbal. From the small entrance at the base of a steep wooded hillside, a tall, narrow fissure, incorporating a chain of countless **caves,** leads almost 3km into the heart of the rock. *(Caves open daily 9am-5pm. Admission 3 pesos.)* Because of the caves' unusual shape, their floors are not particularly friendly to the feet. Instead, a modern concrete walkway, at times 10m above the boulder-strewn cave floor, navigates 750m into the system. The dimly lit caves boast a spectacular array of stalactites and columns. Stamping on the boardwalk at certain points generates a rumbling echo throughout the caves. Consider soliciting the help of one of the local youths who hang around outside to help uncover the natural light and shadow formations (a small tip is appropriate). Or bring your own flashlight and let your imagination run wild.

Getting There: Almost any east-bound *combi* passing across the road from the Iglesia de San Diego in San Cristóbal passes the *grutas* (15min., every 15min., 4 pesos). From the highway, a five-minute walk through the park brings you to the entrance. Miguel Angel, through the Café Tuluc, Av. Insurgentes 5 (1½ blocks south from the *zócalo*), organizes horseback rides to the caves. For 70 pesos you get an energetic horse for four hours and a sore bum for days.

■ Comitán

Eighty-six kilometers southeast of San Cristóbal, Comitán is the last major town on the Pan-American Highway before the Guatemalan border (85km away). While rapid growth has transformed Comitán (pop. 85,000) into a dreary maze of tangled streets, the city can be active and genial; its verdant multi-terraced *zócalo,* filled with incessant marimba music, breeds raucous, youthful fun—in striking contrast to the quiet lakes nearby. Residents of Comitán know they've got a good thing going and enthusiastically welcome the tourists who decide to stay and explore the area on their way to and from Guatemala.

ORIENTATION AND PRACTICAL INFORMATION Streets increase numerically in both directions away from the *zócalo* and are named according to the geographical quadrant in which they fall. To reach the *zócalo* from the Cristóbal Colón bus station, cross the **Pan-American Highway** and turn left. After 200m, take the first right onto

Things that Go Bump in the Night

Everything only seems normal in Comitán. Little do visitors know that they are about to enter a zone where the supernatural has not yet lost its grip on the modern age. Ask around discreetly; a good majority of residents will be able to tell you where to find the **Calle de Llorona** (Street of Tears). Many are soundly convinced that you can still hear the shrill cries late at night of a mother who murdered her children in a fit of rage. And that door that just closed behind you? Well, it could have been the wind....or it could have been the mischievous spirit of a playful *huérfano* (an orphan children who died before being baptized).

On a more material plane, odd stories circle about, or rather *under*, Comitán's busy daily life. Several of the city's richest inhabitants came into their wealth not by traditional means (like timber and ranching) but by unearthing buried gold on their property. Less than a century ago, the main currency in more remote towns in Mexico was gold, and banks were never really secure from bandits. Consequently, much of Comitán's early wealth wound up underground. Combine these accounts with local stories of even older colonial treasures, and it amounts to buried treasure galore. Skip the expensive hotel. Buy a pick and shovel instead.

Calle 4 Pte. Sur. Walk five blocks east, turn left, and walk three blocks north, past the post office, to the *zócalo* on **Av. Central.**

Autotransportes Tuxtla Gutiérrez (tel. 2 10 44), on the highway between Calles Sur Pte. 1 and 2, has first-class service to San Cristóbal (2hr., 9 per day, 23 pesos), continuing to Tuxtla (3hr., 34 pesos). Nine second-class buses also make the run to San Cristóbal and Tuxtla daily. You can shorten the walk to these stations by catching a *microbús* on the highway (2 pesos). **Cristóbal Colón** (tel. 2 09 80), on the Pan-American Highway between Calles Sur Pte. 8 and 4, runs to Mexico City (16hr., 4 per day 6:15am-3:30pm, 401 pesos), Ocosingo (4hr., 10am and 2pm, 35 pesos), Palenque (6hr., 10am, 4, and 11pm, 62 pesos), Puebla (14hr., 4 per day 6:15am-3:30pm, 360 pesos), San Cristóbal (1½hr., 12 per day, 29 pesos), Tapachula (6hr., 7 per day, 66 pesos), Tuxtla Gutiérrez (3½hr., 12 per day, 43 pesos), and Villahermosa (9hr., 4pm, 150 pesos). **Taxis** (tel. 2 56 30) cost 12 pesos from the bus station to the *zócalo* and can be found in the *zócalo* or along the highway.

The **tourist office** (tel. 2 40 47), on the first floor of the Palacio Municipal, overflows with brochures and maps (open M-F 9am-3pm and 5-9pm). Guatemalan visas (see p. 529) can be obtained from the **Guatemalan Consulate,** Av. 1 Sur Pte. (tel. 2 04 91), at Av. 2 Sur Pte.; look for the blue-and-white flag (open M-F 8am-4:30pm). **Banca Serfin** (tel. 2 12 96 or 2 15 70), at Av. 1 Sur Pte. 1, just off the southwest corner of the *zócalo,* changes U.S. dollars only. It also has a 24-hour **ATM** (bank open M-F 9am-3pm). Comitán's indoor **market** is on Central Benito Juárez, just before Av. 2 Ote. Sur, one block east of the *zócalo* (open daily dawn-dusk). The **police** (tel. 2 00 25) are on the ground floor of the Palacio Municipal. The **Red Cross** (tel. 2 18 89) is on Calle 5 Nte. Pte., two-and-a-half blocks west of the highway. **Farmacia Regina,** Calle 1 Sur Ote. 1 (tel. 2 11 96 or 2 07 54), is on the south side of the *zócalo* (open daily 7am-10pm). In case of a **medical emergency** contact the **Hospital Civil** (tel. 2 01 35 or 2 20 51), on Calle 2 Ote. Sur 13 and Av. 9 Sur Ote. The **post office,** Central Dr. Belisario Domínguez 45 (tel. 2 04 27), is one-and-a-half blocks south of the *zócalo* (open M-F 9am-4pm, Sa 9am-1pm). Get on the Internet at **Café Internet,** Pasaje Morales 12 (email sinco@comitan.podernet.cm.mx; 25 pesos per hr.), to the right of the Palacio Municipal (open M-F 9am-2pm and 4-8pm, Sa 9am-2pm).

ACCOMMODATIONS AND FOOD Comitán's various new and expensive hotels would likely crowd out the cheaper accommodations if the two best budget accommodations didn't occupy choice spots right near the *zócalo.* **Pensión Delfín,** Central Belisario Domínguez 21 (tel. 2 00 13), on the west side of the *zócalo,* offers an authentic tile courtyard surrounded by rooms with firm beds. The green-tiled floors may be a subliminal reminder to visit the lakes. (Singles 80 pesos; doubles 120 pesos; triples 150 pesos; quads 180 pesos; for TV 40 pesos extra.) **Hospedaje Montebello,**

Calle 1 Nte. Pte. 10 (tel. 2 35 72), near Av. Central Nte., has brown, dark rooms with decent beds and small windows that open to a concrete courtyard (40 pesos per person, with private bath 55 pesos). Finding a cheap meal in Comitán is easier than downing *flan,* the universal Mexican *postre.* Several *taquerías,* clustered around the northwest corner of the *zócalo* and on Calle Central Nte., have *comida corrida* for 15 to 20 pesos and tacos (3 pesos).

■ Near Comitán: Parque Nacional Lagunas de Montebello

A hop, skip, and a 52km bus ride from Comitán lie the pine-covered hills of the **Parque Nacional Lagunas de Montebello.** Some 59 lakes peacefully await exploration in this scenic playground, each sporting distinctive shades of green and blue. The main paths and even the roadside parking provide spectacular views of these natural wonders. Unfortunately, only 16 have trails leading from the main road, and some are notorious for bandit attacks. Be sure to inquire ahead at the Comitán tourist office or with guides at the lakes before undertaking any off-the-beaten-path hikes. Women traveling alone or in small groups should not try to hike the trails. Buses unload passengers anywhere along the road to **Laguna Bosque Azul** or **Laguna Tziscao.** Camping is available at both of these sites, and Tziscao offers cabanas (30 pesos per person).

Getting There: From Comitán, the blue "Montebello" bus leaves the station on Av. 2 Pte. Sur, between Calles Sur Pte. 2 and 3 (1hr., every 15min. 5:30am-4:30pm, 12 pesos). The bus swings by the Cristóbal Colón bus station for those who want to head straight to the lakes.

■ Near Comitán: Other Sights

Just 22km south of the city, the recently unearthed ruins of **Tenam Puente** include a ballcourt and a handful of smaller pyramids. *(Site open daily 8am-5pm; free.)* To reach the site, take the "Francisco Sarabia" bus from the Transportes Comitán-La Trinitaria station on Calle Sur Pte. 1, between Calles Pte. Sur 3 and 4 (30min., M-F 8am and 2pm, 5 pesos); it will drop you off at the access road, a few kilometers from the entrance. Check with drivers for the return schedule.

Thirty-two kilometers from the Comitán-Cuauhtémoc (Pan-American) highway, on the way to Lagunas Montebello, **Chinkultic** is home to another set of Maya ruins. *(Site open daily 9am-4pm; 12 pesos.)* The "Montebello" bus can drop you off at the access road, an easy 2km from the ruins. Perhaps more interesting than the 7th-century pyramid and ballcourt are the diminutive *cenote* (freshwater sinkhole) and the striking view of the lake region from the hilltop.

Popular with locals but more obscure than Montebello is the **Cascada de Chiflón,** a 250m waterfall, 45km west of Comitán. To get to Chiflón, take a *combi* to Tzimol from the Tuxtla Gutiérrez bus station on the highway (45min., every 30min. 5:45am-10am, 10 pesos). The waterfall is a 5km walk from the roadside. The lake is relatively safe (albeit cold) for swimming, but don't venture too close to the waterfall. There are some nice places to camp in this area but no facilities.

Contrasting with the cold, mineral-colored water of the Montebello lakes are the warm, crystal-clear waters of the **Lagunas de Colón.** The lakes lie in a valley 39km south of Comitán. Take any bus or *colectivo* headed to Comalapa (40min., every 30min. 7am-5pm, 20 pesos), and ask to be let off at the *crucero* with the 12km road to the Lagunas, right before the bridge into the small village of Chamic. From the intersection take a *colectivo* to the Lagunas (15min., 8 pesos); leave early, since these *colectivos* stop running around 4pm. Smaller and less well known than those at Montebello, the Lagunas de Colón are rarely visited and provide many secluded swimming spots. This group of 44 lakes is near the small, nearby Maya site of **Lagartero.**

Ocosingo

More rural than the bustling *zócalo* first lets on, tourist-free Ocosingo (pop. 24,000) straddles the head of a valley in central Chiapas. As the nearest large settlement to the Lacandón rainforest—the fringes of which harbor the majority of Zapatista rebels, the strategic importance of Ocosingo's location is as obvious as the Mexican *ejército*—presence. Ocosingo's residents still bear painful memories of the January 1994 uprising, when a shootout in the market between the army and Zapatista-allied locals claimed dozens of lives. Despite the military backdrop, dusty streets, and ramshackle buildings, Ocosingo is a relatively safe and quiet base from which to explore the nearby ruins of **Toniná** (see below) Furthermore, it is the home of **quesillo,** huge balls of cheese that are sold from every window and doorway.

Ocosingo lies 72km northeast of San Cristóbal de las Casas and 119km south of Palenque. To get to the *zócalo* from either the **Cristóbal Colón bus station** or the **Autotransportes Tuxtla station,** walk uphill two blocks and take a left at the "centro" sign. The *zócalo* is three blocks uphill. The town is laid out in the customary compass grid, but it's small enough that street names can be ignored almost entirely. From the *zócalo,* cardinal directions are marked by the Hotel Central to the north, the Iglesia de San Jacinto to the east, and the Palacio Municipal to the west.

Autotransportes Tuxtla Gutiérrez (tel. 3 04 31), on the highway, offers first-class service to Campeche (7hr., 7:30am, 116 pesos), Cancún (14hr., 2:30 and 4:30pm, 241 pesos), Mérida (10hr., 8am, 161 pesos), Palenque (2hr., 8 per day 6:30am-10pm, 30 pesos), and Villahermosa (5hr., 4 per day, 72 pesos). **Cristóbal Colón** (tel. 3 04 31) runs buses to Escárcega (6hr., 2:15 and 4:30pm, 75-96 pesos), Mexico City (18hr., 4:15pm, 394 pesos) via Puebla (16hr., 4:15pm, 353 pesos), and Tuxtla Gutiérrez (3½hr., 5 per day 6:15am-10:55pm, 42-49 pesos). **Luggage storage** will cost you 5 pesos per day. **Banamex** (tel. 3 00 34), in the northwest corner of the *zócalo,* does not change U.S. dollars, but a lengthy procedure will get you cash advances on major credit cards (open M-F 9am-3:30pm). For any kind of **emergency,** contact the staff at the Palacio Municipal (tel. 3 00 15) or the **police** (tel. 3 05 06), who roost on Calle Central between 1 Pte. and 2 Pte. (open 24hr.). In case of a **medical emergency,** contact **IMSS** (tel. 3 01 52), 1.2km south of the *zócalo* on 1 Ote. Sur (open 24hr.). A **pharmacy, Cruz Blanca** (tel. 3 02 33), 1 Ote. and 2 Sur, is one block south of the church (open daily 7am-10pm). The **post office** is at 2 Sur Ote. 12, one block south of the *zócalo* (open M-F 9am-1pm and 3-6pm, Sa 9am-1pm). The **postal code** is 29950. The **phone code** is 967.

Two hotels are a world apart from the seedy, cave-like, slightly cheaper *posadas* found within a couple of blocks of the *zócalo.* **Hotel Central,** Av. Central 1 (tel. 3 00 24), on the north side of the *zócalo,* is an oasis of clean, well-ventilated rooms with comfortable beds and spacious bathrooms. Each room comes with *agua purificada* and cable TV. (Singles 90 pesos; doubles 110 pesos; triples 120 pesos.) **Hotel Margarita,** Calle Central Nte. 16 (tel. 3 02 80), half a block north of Hotel Central, is old but features nice, firm beds and a sofa-laden lobby with cable TV (singles 90 pesos; doubles 100 pesos; triples 110 pesos; TV and A/C 20 pesos extra). **Restaurant La Montura,** Av. Central 5 (tel. 3 05 50), in the Hotel Central on the north side of the *zócalo,* is somewhat overpriced, but the outdoor tables under the arcade are the most pleasant in town. Entrees are 35-40 pesos. Delicious *tortas* stuffed with *frijoles* and avocado go for 12 pesos. (Open daily 7am-11pm.) **Restaurante Las Cazuelas,** 1 Ote. 127, secluded in the Hotel Agua Azul, serves up tasty food in a tiny log cabin with tree-trunk tables. The menu changes at the whim of the chef and with the seasons. Meals cost 15-20 pesos. (Open daily 8am-9pm.)

Near Ocosingo: Toniná Ruins

While the **ruins of Toniná** rarely surface on lists of Mexico's can't-miss sights, the unique tiered-city architecture of the enormous acropolis is certainly hard to find anywhere else. *(Site open daily 9am-4pm. Admission 10 pesos, free on Sundays.)* After a brief, conflict-imposed absence, archaeologists and their builders are back at the site, carefully reconstructing the main pyramid. As these ruins don't have the user-friendly plaques present elsewhere, a guide can be very helpful.

The Toniná complex, encompassing 15 acres of ruins, was a religious and administrative capital for the Maya city-state that flourished from 300 to 1000. Structures at Toniná do not share the orthodox symmetry or precise floorplan of Monte Albán or Chichén Itzá. Many statues have lost pieces to decay and neglect. The governor of Ocosingo took stones from the site to build roads around the turn of the century; because of this, the pyramids will never be fully restored.

The entrance path, which leads across the river east of the ruins and up a small gully, emerges at the **main ballcourt,** beyond which lies a **sacrificial altar.** This altar is situated on the first artificially terraced level of the site, the **Plaza of War.** The ruins of a smaller ballcourt lie near the steps of the acropolis, next to chunks of stelae scattered by the fence. Extensive glyphs on the backs of these relate to the scenes on the front, often giving the *fechas fatales* (birth and death dates) of prominent characters. Three animals—snake, bat, and jaguar—appear together repeatedly. The three stelae at the foot of the first level commemorate the inauguration of new governments.

Toniná's chief attraction is a massive **acropolis,** which towers 60m over the plaza. Its seven tiers corresponded to the city's various social strata, from the general populace to the high priests, whose temples are perched on the seventh level. Well-preserved panels and sculptures survive from almost all the levels, but most have been moved to the on-site museum or hauled off to Mexico City. At the center of the pyramid's fifth level is a royal grave. Here, archaeologists discovered a stone sarcophagus, made of a single piece of limestone, which held a king's body and two unidentified corpses. To the left of the grave, on the same level, is a shrine to Chac, the Maya rain god. The **Altar de Monstruo de la Tierra** is on the right-hand side of the sixth level. The seventh level of the pyramid was Toniná's religious focal point, and it supports four large pyramids dedicated to a curious mix of cosmic and civic forces. The lowest and least impressive is the **Temple of Agriculture,** on the far right of the terrace. This crumbling building contained private rooms for ranking priests and governors. To the left rises the **Temple of the Prisoners.** Despite the name, which comes from the reliefs of tied prisoners at the base, archaeologists believe that this mound once housed the king and the royal family. Behind it loom Toniná's two most important temples. The higher **Pyramid of War,** on the right, served as an observatory; from the top of the structure, guards scanned the countryside for foreign heavies. Nearby is the symmetrical **Pyramid of Finances.** From the peak of either pyramid, you can enjoy a brilliant view and a cool breeze. Below the Pyramid of War is a newly excavated statue of **King Zotz-Choj** (the jaguar-bat king), whose giant headdress is adorned with an eagle and serpents, as well as symbols for wind, smoke, and fire.

Getting There: The ruins are located 15 bumpy kilometers from Ocosingo (a 20min. drive). By car, follow Calle 1 Ote. south out of town, past the clinic on the right. Bear right past the radio station on the left. Follow the signs for "Toniná ruins" to the Rancho Toniná; the road to the left of the gate leads to the ruins and museum. Inquire at the ranch about camping. Travelers without a car can catch a morning **colectivo,** dole out a steep **taxi** fare (80-100 pesos one way), or walk for days. You can catch a *colectivo* VW bus from the market (every 15min., 10 pesos).

Palenque

You've seen Uxmal. You made it to Chichén Itzá. Still, nothing can prepare you for Palenque, where time-defying temples, grand palaces, and gigantic pyramids gleam like white diamonds against an emerald backdrop. In all of Mesoamerica, three sites are world-renowned for the degree to which they reflect the beauty, power, and fascinating glory of the Maya Classic period. Honduras has Copán, Guatemala has Tikal, and Mexico has Palenque. These impressive ruins straddle a magnificent 300m high *palenque* (natural palisade) in the foothills of the Altos de Chiapas. Dense *selva* (jungle) reaches down to the bases of Palenque's breathtaking pyramids, and the sounds of birds, monkeys, and nearby waterfalls still echo off the walls of the grand palace and numerous courtyards.

Yet while Palenque's temples stand solidly after the centuries, they no longer tower over the idyllic rainforest described in romantic journals kept by the many explorers who began trekking here in the 18th century. A steady number of visitors add their own sounds to the site, and stark traces of many farming fires are evident from the valley-wide views.

One of those views is of the grimy town of Palenque (pop. 17,000), 8km away. Tourism has kept life here rather hectic even along some of the more run-down streets; the town is an important crossroads for travelers arriving from all directions to visit the ruins, sample the water at the famous cascades of Agua Azul, Agua Clara, and Misol-Ha, and make forays into the heart of the Lacandón jungle.

ORIENTATION

Palenque is in the northeastern corner of Chiapas, 274km from Tuxtla Gutiérrez. Streets running east-west are labeled *avenidas,* while those running north-south are *calles.* **Av. Juárez** runs west, away from the **parque** (town square) toward the ruins and highway. Parallel to Juárez to the south are **Avs. 5 de Mayo** and **20 de Noviembre.** To the north lie **Miguel Hidalgo, Nicolás Bravo, Reforma,** and **Domínguez.** From west to east, the *calles* are **Allende, Aldama, Abasolo, Independencia, Jiménez,** and **Guerrero.** The *parque* is bounded by Hidalgo, 20 de Noviembre, Independencia, and Jiménez. To get to the *parque* from the bus station, walk five blocks uphill (east) on Juárez.

PRACTICAL INFORMATION

Buses: All stations are located 5 blocks west of the *parque* on Juárez. **ADO** runs first-class buses to Campeche (6hr., 8am and 9pm, 106 pesos); Cancún (12hr., 8pm, 244 pesos); Chetumal (7½hr., 8pm, 139 pesos), Escárcega (3hr., 8am, 61 pesos), Mérida (8hr., 10:15pm, 133 pesos), Mexico City (12hr., 6pm, 335 pesos), Oaxaca (13hr., 5:30pm, 245 pesos), Playa del Carmen (11hr., 8pm, 194 pesos), Puebla (10½hr., 7pm, 291 pesos), and Villahermosa (2hr., 11 per day, 43 pesos). **Cristóbal Colón** sails for Campeche (6hr., 9:30am, 6, and 10:15pm, 90 pesos), Escárcega (3hr., 5:30

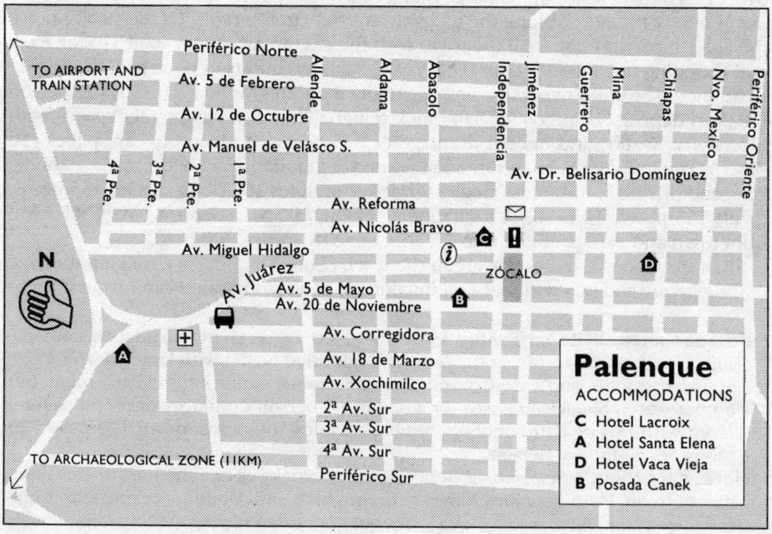

and 10:15pm, 53 pesos), Mérida (8hr., noon, 6:30, and 10:30pm, 133 pesos), Ocosingo (2hr., 9:30am, 6, and 8pm, 33 pesos), San Cristóbal (4½hr., 9:30am, 6, and 8pm, 53 pesos), and Tuxtla Gutiérrez (6hr., 4 per day, 73 pesos). **Autobuses de Tuxtla Gutiérrez** (tel. 5 12 33) has first- and second-class service and **luggage storage** for 13 pesos a day (half a block toward town from ADO station).

Taxis: (tel. 5 01 12 or 5 03 79). 25 pesos to the ruins; 8 pesos in town.

Tourist Office: In the **Casa de las Artesanías,** at the corner of Juárez and Abasolo. Helpful staff speaks some English and can provide excellent maps of the town and ruins for 2 pesos. Open M-Sa 8am-8:30pm, Su 9am-1pm.

Travel Agencies: Yax-Ha, Av. Juárez 123 (tel. 5 07 98; fax 5 07 67), next door to Bancomer. Trips to Misol-Ha, Agua Azul, Yaxchilán, and Bonampak. Reasonable exchange rate for U.S. dollars. Open daily 8am-9pm.

Currency Exchange: Bancomer, Av. Juárez 40 (tel. 5 01 98), 2 blocks west of the *parque.* 24hr. **ATM.** Open for exchange M-F 8:30am-3pm. **Viajes Yax-Ha** (see **Travel Agencies,** above) has a *casa de cambio.*

Laundromat: Lavandería "Ela," 5 de Mayo at Allende, opposite the Hotel Kashlan. 30 pesos for 3kg. Same-day service. Open M-Sa 8am-1pm and 4-7pm.

Police: (tel. 5 08 28), on Calle Independencia, in the Palacio Municipal. Open 24hr.

Pharmacy: Farmacia Central, Av. Juárez near Independencia. Also changes dollars at slightly unfavorable rates. Open daily 8:30am-10pm.

Medical Services: Centro de Salud y Hospital General (tel. 5 07 33), on Av. Juárez near the bus station, at the western end of town. Open 24hr. No English spoken.

Post Office: Independencia at Bravo, north of the *parque.* Open M-F 8am-3pm, Sa 9am-3pm. **Postal Code:** 29960.

Fax: (tel. 5 03 68) on Hidalgo, 1½ blocks east of the *parque* in the Chaka-max building, next to the post office. Open M-F 9am-3pm, Sa 9am-1pm.

Internet Access: Cibernet (tel. 5 17 10; email cibernet@mail.ciberpal.com.mx), Calle Independencia between 5 de Mayo and 20 de Noviembre, across from the park. Offers Netscape and Eudora for a hefty sum—20 pesos for 30min, 40 pesos per hour. Open daily 9am-2pm and 5-9pm.

Telephones: Caseta California, Av. Juárez 4 (tel. 5 11 50 or 5 12 12; fax 5 09 97), half a block from the *parque.* Open daily 8am-3pm and 6-11pm.

Phone Code: 934.

ACCOMMODATIONS AND CAMPING

The town of Palenque has none of the aesthetic appeal of its ruins; this is especially true of its budget accommodations. Budget travelers can either stay in town or sack out at one of the hotels along the highway en route to the ruins. Of the two options, the latter tends to be more expensive, with the exception of **Mayabell Trailer Park and Camping** (tel. 8 06 19; fax 5 07 67), which allows guests to pitch a tent, string up a hammock, or put down a sleeping bag under a *palapa* for just 20 pesos per person (10-peso deposit, 10 pesos for hammock rental). They also have trailer spaces with electricity, water, and decent drainage (15-25 pesos) and simple car spaces (10 pesos). The few rooms boast terra cotta honeycomb tiles, plaid bedspreads, standing fans, and private bathrooms. (Singles 95 pesos; doubles 105 pesos; triples 135 pesos; quads 155 pesos; 10 pesos per additional person; 100-peso deposit.) Mayabell, 6km from town and 2km from the ruins, is accessible by *combi* (5 pesos).

All of the hotels listed below are in the town center, within easy walking distance of the *parque* and bus station. Camping outside of a campground can be unsafe.

Posada Canek, 20 de Noviembre 43 (tel. 5 01 50), between Independencia and Abasolo, a half block west from the *parque.* A glorified hostel with large, clean rooms, good bathrooms, and a view of the mountains to the south. Fans in each room, but no hot water. Singles 30 pesos for a bed in a 5-person dormitory or 60 pesos for a room with private bath; doubles 70 pesos; triples 100 pesos; quads 120 pesos; 20 pesos per additional person.

Hotel Vaca Vieja, 5 de Mayo 42 (tel. 5 03 88), 3 blocks east of the *parque* in a quiet part of town. Plain, spacious rooms with firm beds and dauntless ceiling fans. Comfortable second-floor reading area looks out over town to surrounding hills. Singles

70 pesos; doubles 90 pesos; triples 120 pesos. Prices increase 10 pesos during the high season.

Hotel Santa Elena (tel. 5 10 29), on Jorge de la Vega Domínguez, around the corner from the ADO bus station. This hotel's blue-green tile interior comes with wood paneling, fans, and hot water. Convenient location makes it worth the 60 pesos for singles; 80 pesos for doubles; 100 pesos for triples. Ask for less noisy rooms opposite the bus station.

Hotel Lacroix, Hidalgo 10 (tel. 5 00 14), just off the *parque* and opposite the church. A large, gaudy Maya mural leads the way to cozy, cool, blue rooms and bluer bathrooms. No hot water. Singles 80 pesos; doubles 100 pesos; triples 120 pesos; quads 140 pesos.

FOOD

Finding a cheap restaurant in Palenque that serves full meals is like striking gold. For cheap produce, try the **market** on Velasco Suárez, about four blocks northwest of the *parque*. The travel agency on the corner of Av. Hidalgo and Calle Independencia doubles as one of the best bargain joints for eating and hanging out. There is also a surprisingly good restaurant at the ruins.

Restaurant Yunuen, 5 de Mayo 42 (tel. 5 01 77), at Chiapas 3 blocks east of the *parque*, annexed to the Hotel Vaca Vieja. Small, friendly, and very inexpensive. Feast on the *comida del día*—soup, meat dish, rice, tortillas, fruit, and coffee—for just 22 pesos. Open daily 7am-11pm.

Restaurant Maya (tel. 5 00 42), Independencia at Hidalgo, right on the *parque*. This classy, spotless dining establishment offers excellent service and *menús del día* for 30-35 pesos, sandwiches for 20 pesos. Open daily 7am-11pm.

Restaurante Las Tinajas, 20 de Noviembre 41, at Abasolo. Popularity may have nudged up prices, but the quality local dishes keep the tourists coming back—even the ones who aren't staying across the street at the Posada Conek. Entrees 35 pesos; *licuados* 10 pesos. Open daily 7am-11pm.

Restaurant Rocamar, 20 de Noviembre at Independencia, near the *parque*. Small seafood joint with lively spreads for the plastic tables, the better on which to serve *filete empanizado* (entrees 25-35 pesos). Open daily 8am-8pm.

THE ARCHAEOLOGICAL SITE OF PALENQUE

During the Maya Classic Period (300-900), Palenque was of central importance to the Maya. Though impressive, the **ruins of Palenque** only hint at the former majesty of the city, as only a small fraction of the structures have been shorn of their dense jungle blanket; excavation is ongoing. *(Archaeological site and museum open daily 8am-4:45pm; crypt open daily 8am-4pm. Admission 24 pesos, free Su. Map 6 pesos.)*

Palenque owes much of its finery, including its unparalleled stucco bas-relief sculptures, to an early ruler, the club-footed god-man **King Pacal** (Pak-AL; 615-683). According to inscriptions made at the time of his death, Pacal lived into his fifth *katun* (20-year period) and was then succeeded by his elderly son **Chan-Bahlum.** Chan-Bahlum celebrated his ascension by building a great pyramid-crypt (Temple of the Inscriptions) for his father. After Chan-Bahlum died, Palenque slipped into oblivion; when Cortés arrived in the 16th century, he marched past the abandoned city without noting its existence. An excellent **museum** can be found 2km before the site near Mayabell.

Combis to the site run daily from 6am-6pm (7 pesos); catch them off Juárez on Allende. Visiting the ruins at night is prohibited and extremely unsafe. Do not take shortcuts to the back entrance of the ruins from the campgrounds or the road—the dense jungle will isolate you from any other tourists who may be nearby.

Guide to the Ruins

On entering the site, you pass the tomb of Alberto Ruz, one of Mexico's most famous archaeologists, who was so devoted to restoring Palenque that he insisted on being buried there. To the right rises the steep **Temple of the Inscriptions.** Named for its

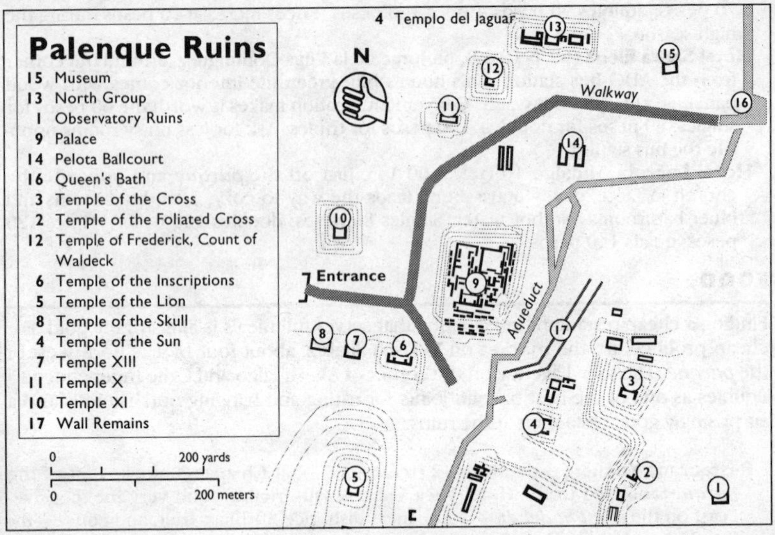

magnificent tablets, the temple was the burial place of King Pacal and the first substantial burial place discovered in the Americas. After his disappointing discovery of six unimpressive skeletons, Ruz bore into the interior of the crypt. There, he discovered the perfectly preserved, elaborately carved sarcophagus of the king. The figure in the lower center of the tablet is Pacal himself, shown descending into the underworld with the tree of life directly over him. Ruz and his men had to remove more than 400 tons of rock fill by hand to reach the burial chamber. Visitors must scramble the long way down slippery stone steps in a steep and stuffy tunnel to view the royal crypt. The **hollow duct,** which allowed Pacal's spirit to exit the underworld and communicate with Palenque's priests, is located on the right after the staircase.

A trail leads up the mountainside to the east of the Temple of the Inscriptions. About 100m along this trail, on the right, is the **Temple of the Lion.** Descend the pitch-black stairwell inside the structure, and you'll come upon the site of the ancient well. There, a few faint traces of paint are slowly surrendering to the green slime of the jungle. Bring a flashlight—the steps are wet, and there's no light. The trail continues up the hill for 7km before reaching the tiny *indígena* village of Naranjo. Guides can be found for this difficult hike through beautiful terrain. Next to the Temple is a trapezoidal **palace** complex, consisting of four patios and a four-story tower. This immense complex is replete with religious tributes, such as the relief on the north side depicting the nine gods of the underworld. Other carvings laud the godlike priests and royal families that inhabited its many chambers. The palace's T-shaped air tunnels cooled the air and doubled as representations of Ik, the god of the breezes. Clamber down the staircase from the top of the platform to explore the extensive, dimly-lit network of underground passageways. Flat-nosed masks of the rain-god Chac glare accusingly off to the north end's stuccoed walls. An exclusively female steam bath and latrines have also been excavated.

The path between the palace and the Temple of Inscriptions fords the recently reconstructed aqueduct before leading up to the **Sun Plaza,** another landscaped platform comprised of the **Temple of the Sun,** the **Temple of the Cross,** the **Temple of the Foliated Cross,** and the smaller **Temple 14.** The Temple of the Cross was named for a stucco relief of a cross discovered inside, which inspired a flurry of hopeful religious theories among the *conquistadores.* For the Maya, the cross represents the *ceiba* tree, the tree of life, with a snake as its horizontal branch and a bird perched atop it. The outer layer of stucco has worn away, but the inner sanctum protects a large, sculpted tablet and reliefs on either side of the doors.

About to be swallowed again by the jealous jungle, the **Temple of the Foliated Cross** lies across the plaza from the Temple of the Sun. Despite the overgrown path, the inner sanctum here contains a surprisingly clear carved tablet. To the south, through the wall of trees, several unreconstructed temples surround the uncleared **Plaza Maudslay.** Downhill from Temple 14 and past the palace lie the vestiges of a **ballcourt.** Palenque is full of small paths leading to unrestored ruins and cascades; bring bug spray and a buddy if you intend to explore on your own.

To the left of the ballcourt is the **Temple of Frederick, Count of Waldeck,** who lived here for three years while studying the ruins in the 1830s. The four other temples that share the platform with the Temple of the Count comprise the **North Group.** Waterfall enthusiasts may catch a glimpse of the **Queen's Bath** (so named for its exclusively female clientele), a small set of falls down the wide dirt path that leads right, away from the North Group. A second set of falls, **Cascada Montiepa,** is hidden in the jungle, 600m down the road from the ruins. At the right-hand bend, follow the path into the woods. Unfortunately, overgrown banks and shallow water make swimming impractical.

■ Near Palenque: Cascadas de Agua Azul and Misol-Ha

Both of these large **cascadas** (waterfalls) have overflowed with tourists of late, and for good reason. **Agua Azul,** 62km south of Palenque, is a breathtaking spectacle: the Río Yax jumps down 500 individual falls, then slips into rapids, whirlpools, and calm swimming areas in between. *(Admission to each of the falls 3 pesos, 8 pesos per carload.)* The rainy season, however, brings rivers of mud down from the highlands into the once-azure falls. There is a tiny beach and swimming area 20 minutes upstream from the falls—if you swim, stay close to the bank and swim with a friend; more than 100 people have met their watery end here. The falls are best visited as a daytrip. If, however, the muddy, buggy, 4km walk from the *crucero* has you all tuckered out and you simply must spend the night, **cabanas** are available on site (doubles 140 pesos; quads 240 pesos), and space for tents or hammocks can be arranged. The falls at **Misol-Ha,** higher and less-visited than Agua Azul, are 24km from Palenque and only 2km from the highway crossing. There's a large cataract here, and the swimming area is clean and relatively safe. Bring a flashlight if you want to explore the small cave behind the falls. There is also a small **restaurant** here.

Getting There: The most painless way to visit Agua Azul and Misol-Ha is aboard a **Transportes Chambalu** *combi* (70 pesos round-trip). **Combis** leave daily from the Palenque station at Hidalgo and Allende (9, 10am, and noon) and proceed to Agua Azul, after a 30-minute photo stop at Misol-Ha. Passengers are dropped off by the falls for a three-hour swimming session. **Buses** between Palenque and Ocosingo or San Cristóbal will also stop at the crossroads for either Agua Azul or Misol-Ha (3 pesos). Since few buses pass after 4pm, you should leave the falls in the early afternoon. Hitchhikers report that steady pick-up truck traffic makes catching a ride fairly easy.

■ Yaxchilán

Rising from the banks of the Usumacinta River, deep within the Lacandón jungle, is a city that neither time nor tourists have touched. Covering eight square kilometers and extending across the river into Guatemala, only a fourth of the site has been fully excavated. Yet the vast number of stelae and other carvings understood have revealed a very personal and fascinating history behind the silent temples. The heavy jungle that still hides many of the structures is far from quiet, though—families of toucans, spiders, and howler monkeys, as well as other wildlife, are more frequent visitors to the ruins than humans. The political trouble of the mid-1990s postponed plans for a museum and a general expansion of tourism at the site, so a journey to Yaxchilán is still like the archaeological expeditions of old. This ancient city is so remote, its carvings so clear, and the enveloping jungle so wild that visitors may later think back and wonder if Yaxchilán was anything but a fascinating dream.

The nearest town to Yaxchilán, **Frontera Corozal,** is 197km southeast of Palenque. The site is a 45-minute boat ride downstream on the Río Usumacinta, but the strong currents make it a two-hour trip back. The brand-new road is a very smooth ride, and constant patrolling by all sorts of Mexican security have made it very safe. Make sure to bring your **passport** and **visa** because of various army roadblocks. The **Lacondonia** bus line makes one morning and one afternoon trip to Frontera Corozal (25 pesos) from its terminal next to the Autotransportes Tuxtla Gutiérrez station in Palenque; inquire ahead, since schedules are subject to frequent changes. The launches charge a staggering 270 pesos for a round-trip ticket to Yaxchilán; the more people, the cheaper per person. Only those who are willing to splurge can even begin to think about chartering a plane directly to the ruins (930-1000 pesos). Consider joining a tour group put together by the countless travel agencies in Palenque; prices range from 300 pesos for one-day trips to 600 pesos for two days and vary according to demand; prices include meals, boat fare, lodging, and often a visit to **Bonampak** (see p. 526). Make sure to get any chores done before leaving—the nearest services of any kind can be found in Palenque. The handful of permanent residents at the entrance to the site have so recently begun to offer **camping** space that prices have not yet been set. Try the new, self-proclaimed **Centro Ecoturístico Escudo Jaguar** (tel. 5 03 56) in Frontera Corozal. It offers colorful cabanas with firm beds, fans, and hot water (100 pesos for singles and doubles; triples and quads 200 pesos), as well as a *palapa* with 12 hammock spaces and a common bathroom (30 pesos per hammock) and camping (15 pesos per tent). **Food** can be found in the *centro.*

THE ARCHAEOLOGICAL SITE OF YAXCHILÁN

History

Yaxchilán ("Green rocks" in Maya) is famous for its thousands of glyphs, which is why an almost-complete story of the city can be told. It had its humble beginnings around 350 as just another Maya fishing and farming village along the Usumacinta. Yaxchilán's emblem glyph (a glyph representing a particular polity) began to appear at other sites such as El Cayo, Piedras Negras, and Bonampak after 526, suggesting that it played a role at those sites and may have been a regional capital. Years of bloody conquest and expansion during the reign of Shield-Jaguar (726-742) made Yaxchilán one of the most important cities of the Maya Late Classical Period. Shield's Jaguar's son, **Bird-Jaguar,** took the throne in 752. When questions arose over the validity of his ascension, Bird-Jaguar undertook the greatest construction projects Yaxchilán had ever seen to reinforce his legitimacy. Most of the buildings and stelae in the city date to the period of his rule, and it was during these years that Yaxchilán rose to the peak of its power, through new acropoles, royal intermarriages, and alliances with neighboring regions. Evidence of trade and symbolic influence with cities as far away as Teotihuacán can also be found dating to this period. In 770, a man called Shield-Jaguar II, most likely a son of one of the other wives of Shield-Jaguar I, took power and ruled until 808. During his reign, Shield-Jaguar II took several governors of other cities prisoner; one such event is chillingly portrayed on a lintel in Bonampak's **Temple of the Paintings** (see p. 526). By 900, lesser nobles were flouting whatever ruling authority was left and began constructing their houses in the midst of old royal ceremonial centers. Along with many other Maya cities of this time, Yaxchilán was depopulated and eventually abandoned.

Guide To The Ruins

While **Yaxchilán** is no longer a lost city, the path winding from the airstrip into the jungle past a large unexcavated temple makes it still seem hidden. *(Site open daily 10am-4:45pm. Admission 18 pesos, free on Sundays, enthusiastic caretakers will give "free" tours—a tip is expected.)* Visitors actually enter Yaxchilán through a door: the rear entrance to Building 19. Better known as the **Labyrinth,** its pitch-black underground passageways, which have not yet been fully explored, probably symbolized the underworld during initiation rites for priests. Bring a flashlight to wander the false-arch halls and admire the original stucco work. At the end of the labyrinth, the front door opens onto the vast **Grand Plaza.** Running west to east, the plaza (500m long and 60m wide) was the monumental heart of the city, lined by temples and palaces on both sides. Thankfully, enough structures remain to give a good sense of Yaxchilán's past glory. The first significant structure on the north side of the plaza, to the left of the Labyrinth, is **Building 16.** Three doorways are all that remain of the building, each with carved lintels. The middle one depicts a scene with Bird-Jaguar's holding a ceremonial bar dated 743 (see **Hoop Dreams** p. 564). Further down the Grand Plaza is the **ballcourt,** built for two players during Shield-Jaguar's rule. Five markers were placed in the court, one of which still shows a figure adorned with quetzal and feathers holding a serpent. To the right of the ball court lie the remains of a palace. Building 12 is one of the most ruined of the cluster, yet it still has glyphs that tell of the early history of the Jaguar dynasty, dating back to 360.

Continuing east past the palace, visitors arrive at **Stela 1,** which, except for a missing triangular portion, looks as though it was just chiseled. One of Bird-Jaguar's many monuments, it shows the king and his wife undergoing a ritual self-sacrifice. Glyphs on the stela give the date of 762, and on either side of the stela are statues representing a jaguar and a crocodile. Still on the north side of the plaza, past Stela 1, stands **Building 6,** also called the **Red Temple.** The original stucco still retains some of its bright color. Lying in a very unmajestic position east of Building 6 is Yaxchilán's most elaborate and important carving—**Stela 11.** Engraved on four of its six sides, this monolith was originally found towering in front of Building 40. After numerous efforts to send it to the Museo Nacional de Antropología in Mexico City, it was unceremoniously dropped here. This key stela depicts the all-important transfer of power from Shield-Jaguar to Bird-Jaguar, although such an event never really took place. The taller figure, of course, is Bird-Jaguar, shown with eagle wings on his back, holding a ceremonial scepter, and wearing a sun-god chest plate and a Chac headdress. Bird-Jaguar's emblem glyph is the second from the right along the thin bottom side of the stela (between 743 and 754). Across from Stela 11 on the south side of the plaza, past some circular altars and another stela dedicated to Bird-Jaguar, is **Building 20.** Next door to the west is, believe it or not, **Building 21.** The engraved lintels over the doorways are impressive enough, but inside is a stunning stela of Shield-Jaguar's wife, Lady Ik-Skull. The side facing out of the building shows her holding a bowl of self-sacrificial tools under a figure of the rain god Tláloc, an indication of cultural influence from Central Mexican civilizations. A nifty mirror allows visitors to view the other side of the stela, which clearly shows Lady Ik-Skul's passing an obsidian-studded rope through her tongue; glyphs give the date 743. Along the back wall are stucco reliefs that still have some original red and blue colors.

Some minor buildings line the rest of the southern side of the plaza. Before them is a long, steep slope with lintels describing the rise of power of Shield-Jaguar and his first wife, Lady Fist-Fish, that climbs past Buildings 25 and 26 on the left, reaching the immense **Building 33** at the top. The best-preserved of Yaxchilán's buildings, it was the result of yet another of Bird-Jaguar's projects and is called the **House of Music.** It is said that as storms blow in from the north over Guatemala, the wind creates musical harmonies as it is forced through the many openings of different shapes and sizes of the building's facade. Outside the building is a rare stalactite stela and a sharp stucco work showing a ball game in progress. Inside sits the ominous, decapitated statue of Bird-Jaguar himself. No one knows how, when, or why his head came to rest in the next room, but when archaeologists attempted to replace it, they were stopped by the Lacandón Maya, who still regularly hold religious ceremonies at Yaxchilán. One of their central religious beliefs is that the moment the head is rejoined, the end of the world will begin; supernatural jaguars will descend from the heavens and destroy all living beings. **Archaeologists have not moved the head.** The trail behind and to the right of Building 33 leads to the main **acropolis,** composed of Buildings 39, 40, and 41. The unimpeded 360° view of the Mexican jungle and Guatemalan highland is well worth the arduous 10-minute hike. It was from here that kings ruled over the lives of approximately 10,000 families.

The True People

Travelers visiting the ruins of Yaxchilán or Bonampak may have the fortune to meet a member of a particularly intriguing indigenous group. The Lacandón Maya, or **Winik** (True People) as they call themselves, have succeeded for centuries longer than any other Maya people in maintaining strictly traditional religious practices and beliefs. While the rest intermixed Christianity with their indigenous religions within the first two centuries of Spanish colonialism, the Lacandón accepted no facets of Christianity until the 1950s. At that time, the town of Lacanha Chan Sayab converted to Protestantism; in the 1970s, their neighbors in Mansabak converted to Seventh Day Adventism. Today, the Lacandón in the town of Naja continue to live entirely outside the influence of Christianity.

Although they are Mexico's only jungle-dwelling people, the Lacandón themselves are not native to the Lacandón jungle; their ancestors emigrated from the Yucatán peninsula in the 13th century. Today, only a few hundred people identify themselves as Lacandón (largely defined by speaking Lacandón Mayan); the settlement near Crucero Bonampak known as **San Javier** is home to a number of Lacandóns. While in Mexico's only rainforest, ask around to find residents who will take you to the pristine **Cascadas de Lacanha** (15 pesos) or to one of Na Bolom's **Casas de Cultura** (see p. 509).

■ Near Yaxchilán: Bonampak

Practically every book, pamphlet, or other published material in the world having to do with Maya archaeology has a reproduction of the murals of **Bonampak.** *(Site is open daily 8am-4:45pm. Admission 16 pesos.)* The murals have single-handedly changed scholars' conceptions of Maya civilization since their discovery in 1946. These images put to rest forever the theory that the Maya were a peaceful people who never engaged in violence. Just to see these clear murals with your own eyes is more than enough reason to make the short 8km detour from the road to Yaxchilán. The ceremonial center open to the public is much smaller than Yaxchilán's, though, consisting of a near-empty plaza and a hillside that was made into one long, wide series of steps. Since Bonampak does not nearly have the number of engraved glyphs of Yaxchilán, its history is also less detailed.

THE MURALS OF BONAMPAK

The **murals of Bonampak** have certainly aged after 12 centuries and an ill-advised dousing with kerosene by an early restoration team, but these one-of-a-kind paintings still have the power to leave visitors gaping in awe. The colors of these murals, painted al fresco, are a vivid array of bright and dark reds, blues, greens, yellows, browns, and various combinations of these colors.

Much of what is known about Bonampak pertains to a ruler known as **Chaan Muan II,** who is depicted on the enormous *Stela* 1. This 6m high slab is the first major sight to greet visitors as they enter the Great Plaza, but it is only carved on its south side, aligned directly with the central floor of the House of Paintings. The uppermost portion is in total disrepair, but enough remains to present the whole figure of the glowering king holding a spear and shield (787). Two other important stelae are situated close to the plaza on the wide steps: Stela 2, to the east and Stela 3, to the right of Stela 2, which shows a richly attired Chaan Maun II standing over a prisoner. Try to make out the prisoner's beard—facial hair is rarely depicted in Maya art.

The **House of Paintings** is a three-room building found just above the Great Plaza to the right. Over the three doorways, from left to right, are lintels of Knotted-Eye Jaguar, an ancestor of Chaan Muan II (743); Shield-Jaguar II of Yaxchilán (788); and Chaan Muan II (787)—all about to execute a groveling prisoner. Inside, the murals of the three rooms combine to form a narrative that reads from left to right. In chamber 1, the murals depict a procession and the presentation of a heir to the throne, on the right side of the room. Note the musicians and lobster-costumed figure on the lower level to the left. Chamber 2 shows a fierce battle in a forest—over the doorway is a blood-curdling display of tortured prisoners with fingers dripping blood, vainly pleading for mercy from the jaguar-skin robed royalty of Bonampak. The third chamber is a portrait of a victory celebration with more dancers and musicians, as well as of the royal family undergoing more self-sacrificial rituals.

Behind and above the House of Paintings, or Building 1, are a set of buildings numbered four to eight from right to left. Climb up behind Building 4 to get a look at roofless Building 9. If the caretaker is in a good mood, he won't mind your exploring the pair of unexcavated temples at the very top of the hill.

Getting There: Any **Lacandonia** bus or *colectivo* will make the stop at **Crucero Bonampak,** which is on the way to Frontera Corozal, 18km east. Follow the right fork of the road 8km south through the jungle, which is a manageable hike along the new road. There is a tiny Lacandón settlement at the *crucero,99* which now has a small *cantina* and open-air restaurant, as well as plenty of space for **camping.** Guides can easily be found to take you to the site for a small fee.

Tonalá

Most people don't visit Chiapas for the beaches, but hey, if you've got to go, you've got to go. Tonalá is one of the best, if not the only, major coastal town the state has to offer, and while the beaches nearby don't compare to Oaxaca's golden stretches of sand, **Puerto Arista** and (especially) **Boca del Cielo** are pleasant enough spots to spend a few hours. During *Semana Santa,* Christmas, and weekends in July and August, these seaside stretches fill with Chiapanecan families. During the rest of the year, however, their only guests are the *zancudos blancos*—vicious biting insects that exploit the holey nature of hammocks. Tonalá proper, though lively, is very hot and humid and offers little in the way of cooling refreshment. Stop for lunch and head for the sand further afield.

ORIENTATION Tonalá lies 223km northwest of Tapachula and 172km southwest of Tuxtla Gutiérrez. All **bus stations** are on **Av. Hidalgo,** Tonalá's main street. To get to the *zócalo* from the **Cristóbal Colón** bus station, take a left and head six blocks south. Both the **Autotransportes Tuxtla Gutiérrez** and **Fletes y Pasajes** bus stations are south of the centro, so turn right and walk five blocks north. As the coastal highway, Av. Hidalgo runs roughly north-south through town. To the east, **Av. Rayón** parallels Hidalgo, while to the west run **Avs. Matamoros, Juárez,** and **Allende.** Listed from north to south, **Calles Madero, 16 de Septiembre, 5 de Febrero, Independencia,** and **5 de Mayo** run east-west, completing the grid that compose the city center.

PRACTICAL INFORMATION **Autotransportes Tuxtla Gutiérrez,** Hidalgo 56, five blocks south of the zócalo, has first-class **bus service** to Mexico City (13hr., 6:30pm, 217 pesos) via Puebla (11hr., 176 pesos). First-class buses, including **Maya de Oro** (tel. 3 05 40), leave from the **Cristóbal Colón** station, six blocks north of the zócalo, for Mexico City (13hr., 8pm, 313 pesos), Oaxaca (6½hr., 10pm, 125 pesos), Puebla (10hr., 8pm, 269 pesos), Tapachula (3hr., every hr. 3am-7pm, 68 pesos), Tuxtla Gutiérrez (3hr., every hr. 3am-7:30pm, 65 pesos), and Villahermosa (12hr., 10:30pm, 174 pesos). **Fletes y Pasajes,** Hidalgo 52 (tel. 3 25 94), 50m south of the bridge and three-and-a-half blocks south of the zócalo, sends second-class buses to Mexico City (13hr., 4 per day, 204 pesos), Puebla (11hr., 4 per day, 170 pesos), and Tapachula (3½hr., 6 per day, 56 pesos). From the same building, **TRF** (tel. 3 12 61) has first-class service to Tapachula (3hr., 4 per day 6am-5:30pm, 59 pesos) and Tuxtla Gutiérrez (3hr., 10 per day, 58 pesos). **Taxis** (tel. 3 06 20) cruise up and down Hidalgo and hang out in the zócalo (40 pesos to Puerto Arista). If you're getting up early, the 24-hour **radio-taxis** (tel. 3 10 41 or 3 26 08), opposite the Colón bus station, will rouse you at your hotel. **Luggage storage** is 5 pesos per day.

The **tourist office** (tel. 3 27 87) is at Hidalgo and 5 de Mayo, two blocks south of the bus station, on the second floor of the Esmeralda building (no city maps; open M-F

9am-3pm and 6-9pm, Sa 10am-1pm). **Banamex,** Hidalgo 137 (tel. 3 0 0 37), at 5 de Febrero, half a block south of the *zócalo,* will **exchange currency** (open M-F 9am-3:30pm). It has a 24-hour **ATM.** The **police** station (tel. 3 01 03) is on Calle Libertad, two blocks north of Cristóbal Colón and to the right. **Hospital General** (tel. 3 06 87), Av. 27 de Septiembre at Mina, is six blocks south of the *zócalo* and three blocks east before the gas station (open 24hr.). The **Red Cross** (tel. 3 02 76) is on Av. Joaquín Miguel Gutiérrez (open 24hr.). **Clínica de Especialidades,** Hidalgo 127 (tel. 3 12 90), at Independencia south of the *zócalo,* is a hospital and pharmacy; one doctor speaks English (open daily 9am-1pm and 5-7pm; open 24hr. for emergency medical service). The **post office** is at Zambrano 27 (tel. 3 06 83), two blocks north and half a block east of the *zócalo* (open M-F 8am-7pm, Sa 9am-1pm). The **postal code** is 30500. The **phone code** is 966.

ACCOMMODATIONS AND FOOD Leaving Tonalá with a good impression of the town often means not spending the night, as lodgings are over-priced and under-cleaned. The **Hotel Tonalá** (tel. 3 04 80), a few blocks south of the Cristóbal Colón station, charges high rates for little space in its plain rooms. There is *agua purificada* in the lobby. (Singles 80 pesos; doubles 130 pesos; triples with TV and A/C 150 pesos.) Cheaper accommodations come at a price at **Hotel Thomás** (tel. 13 00 80), on Hidalgo before the bridge, two blocks south of the *zócalo.* Small, blue rooms are equipped with ceiling fans, and the barely flushing toilets are the best feature of the bathrooms. (Singles 65 pesos; doubles 75 pesos; triples 100 pesos.) **Restaurant Sambors** (tel. 3 06 80), Madero and Hidalgo, on the *zócalo,* has good food, a great *marisco* salad, and an excellent, wide-angle view of the *zócalo.* Enjoy *tortas* for 12 pesos and *licuados* for 8 pesos. (Open daily 8am-1am.) The **Restaurante Nora,** Independencia 10 (tel. 3 02 43), less than a block east of Hidalgo, and a block from the *zócalo,* is a calm refuge from the heat and sun. The congenial owner will make you feel right at home with a tasty three-course *comida corrida.* (24 pesos; open M-Sa 7am-6pm.)

SAND AND SIGHTS Eighteen kilometers southwest of Tonalá, **Puerto Arista** offers 32km of gray, sandy beach and the pounding waves of the Pacific. For calmer waters, head to the sheltered, saltwater estuary of **Boca del Cielo,** 15km farther down the coast. The estuary is about 400m wide, but you can wade across more than half of it and swim the rest to the beachfront restaurants and open ocean. To get there with a dry wallet, hop in a *lancha* (40 pesos). There are no hotels in Boca del Cielo, so you'll want to base yourself in Puerto Arista or Tonalá. Every 20 minutes, *colectivos* run to both Puerto Arista (10 pesos) and Boca del Cielo (12 pesos) from their stand on 5 de Mayo, in Tonalá, one-and-a-half blocks west of Hidalgo.

Tapachula

Must be something about those border towns. Tapachula (pop. 300,000) is loud and dirty, crowded and crass, enormous and smelly...and let's not forget hot. But the all-out assault on the senses—completed by marimba music echoing through the hazy air from practically every street corner—can actually be quite fun. If you're not finding it so, escape to the *zócalo,* where topiary trees, their leafy crowns trimmed square and joined to one another, form a green canopy over two square blocks and relaxing outdoor cafes provide sanctuary. During the rainy season, hundreds of Guatemalan immigrants crowd under these trees, reading newspapers or socializing. For tourists, Tapachula is primarily a point of entry into Guatemala.

ORIENTATION Tapachula is 18km from Talismán at the Guatemalan border on Rte. 200 and 303km west of Guatemala City. Tonalá lies 220km to the northwest, along the Pacific coast. Avenidas run north-south, and calles run east-west. Calles north of **Calle Central** are odd-numbered, while those south are even-numbered. Similarly, avenidas east of **Av. Central** are odd-numbered, while those west of it have even numbers. Tapachula's main plaza is at **3 Calle Pte.** between **6** and **8 Av. Nte.,** northwest of the center. To get to the zócalo from the **bus station,** take an immediate left upon exiting onto 17 Av. Ote, another left on Av. Central, and then walk south six blocks. If you take a right on 5 Av. Pte and continue four blocks west, you will arrive at the plaza's northeast corner.

CROSSING THE BORDER TO GUATEMALA New policies have made crossing the border easier. Almost no one needs a visa (see p. 8), and you'll get 30 days in Guatemala on your tourist card. If you plan to stay longer, be sure to visit a consulate in Guatemala to ask for more time. Otherwise, be prepared to pay a fee when you leave Guatemala. Cross the border early in the day to avoid bureaucratic delay and early, unofficial closings. It's best to buy your mandatory **tourist card** (US$5) or get a visa from the Guatemalan consulate in Tapachula; the Talismán office has erratic hours.

From Tapachula, **Unión y Progreso buses** leave their station on 5 Calle Pte., half a block west of 12 Av. Nte., for Talismán (30min., every 5min., 8 pesos). For those who don't want to spend any time in Tapachula, the bus swings by the Cristóbal Colón bus station on 17 Calle Ote. on its way to the border. Buses from Tapachula drop off passengers at the entrance to the Mexican emigration office. Forget about a Guatemalan daytrip; once you leave Mexico, you cannot return for three days. Enter the building and present your **passport** and Mexican **tourist card** to officials behind the desk, then follow the crowd across the bridge, where you'll need to pay a toll of approximately 3 pesos. Proceed to a small building on the left to have your passport stamped by Guatemalan authorities; there is a charge of 5 quetzales. A **taxi** from the *zócalo* to Talismán costs 50 pesos. Those crossing the border **on foot** will be besieged by money changers and self-appointed "guides."

The **money changers** on the Guatemalan side of the border generally give better rates for pesos than those on the Mexican side, but your best bet is to avoid small money changers and head for the **Banco de Quetzal,** on the Guatemalan side.

From Talismán, you can take a **bus** to Guatemala City (6 per day, 4am-midnight). Don't travel at night, since this route has recently been plagued by assaults. Should you have to spend the night in Tapachula, the **Hotel José Ricardo,** just past the official buildings on the right, offers nice, clean rooms with bathrooms and hot water. The various eateries in Talismán can turn seedy when the drunks come out of the woodwork. Women traveling alone should exercise extreme caution. The Tapachulan tourist office recommends that tourists not cross the border at Ciudad Hidalgo, as the bridge there is long and deserted, leaving travelers particularly vulnerable to assault. For more information about Guatemalan border crossings, check out *Let's Go: Central America 1999.*

PRACTICAL INFORMATION The **airport** is on the road to Puerto Madero, about 17km south of town. It's served by **Aeroméxico,** 2 Av. Nte. 6 (tel. 6 20 50) and **Aviacsa** (tel. 6 31 47 or 6 14 39), Av. Central and Calle 1 Pte. **Autotransportes Tuxtla Gutiérrez,** 11 Calle Ote. 14 (tel. 6 95 13), between 3 and 4 Av. Nte., provides second-class service to Mexico City (16hr., 12:30 and 7pm, 296 pesos) and Tuxtla Gutiérrez (7hr., 7 per day, 101 pesos). **Cristóbal Colón** (tel. 6 43 75 or 6 28 80), is at 17 Calle Ote. at 3 Av. Nte. It sends buses to Brownsville, TX (24hr., 10pm, 622 pesos), Comitán (6hr., 5 per day, 66 pesos), Mexico City (16hr., 5 per day, 356 pesos), Oaxaca (11hr., 6:30 and 8pm, 208 pesos), Puebla (14hr., 4:30, 5:30, and 8:15pm, 311 pesos), Puerto Escondido (7hr., 10:45pm, 195 pesos), San Cristóbal (7hr., 5 per day, 88 pesos), Tampico (16hr., 10pm, 425 pesos), Tonalá (3hr., 12:30, 9am, and 5pm, 68 pesos), Tuxtla Gutiérrez (6hr., every hr. 5am-11pm, 117 pesos), Veracruz (12hr., 10pm, 192 pesos), and Villahermosa (12hr., 9pm, 180 pesos). **Fletes y Pasajes** (tel. 6 76 03), 3 Av. Norte and 9 Calle Ote., has second-class service to Mexico City (17hr., 1:45 and 5pm, 260 pesos) and Oaxaca (13hr., 12:30 and 6pm, 138 pesos). **Luggage storage** costs 5 pesos per day.

The **tourist office** (tel. 5 54 09) is in the Antiguo Palacio Municipal, south of the Iglesia de San Agustín, on the west side of the *zócalo* (open M-F 9am-3pm and 6-9pm, Sa-Su 9am-2pm). The **Guatemalan consulate** is on 2 Calle Ote. 33 (tel. 6 12 52), between 7 and 9 Av. Sur. Citizens of the U.S., Canada, and European Union countries don't need a visa. Your passport will get you across the border hassle-free. Citizens from other countries (Switzerland, South Africa, etc.) will need a visa (see p. 8). Make sure to photocopy the first page of your passport and obtain a visa application. Visas usually take less than 30 minutes.; arrive early, though, in case of crowds. (Open M-F 9am-1:30pm and 3-5pm.) **Exchange currency** at **Banamex** (tel. 6 29 24), on Av. Central Nte. 9; it has 24-hour **ATM.** The **police** (tel. 5 28 51) are on 8 Av. Nte. and 3 Calle Pte., in the Palacio Municipal (open 24hr.) Buy drugs at **Farmacia 24 Horas,** 8 Av. Nte. 25 (tel. 6 24 80), at 7 Calle Pte. No English is spoken, but they promise free delivery to anywhere within the city daily from 7am to 11pm. The **hospital** (tel. 6 80 80) is on the highway to the airport (open 24hr.). The **post office** is at 1 Calle Ote. 32 (tel. 6 24 92), between 7 and 9 Av. Nte. (open M-F 8am-6pm, Sa 9am-1pm.) The **postal code** is 30700. The **phone code** is 962.

ACCOMMODATIONS AND FOOD Due to the huge influx of Guatemalan refugees, budget accommodations are a dime a dozen in Tapachula, especially near the market. Unfortunately, many hotel rooms are as noisy and dirty as the rest of the city. The two spots listed provide clean, pleasant accommodations at reasonable prices. Your best option is **Hotel San Agustín,** 12 Av. Nte. 14 (tel. 6 14 53), between 1 and 3 Calle Pte., two blocks west of the *zócalo.* Rooms are like nice, new garages: gigantic, empty, and made of white cement. Two-room suites have a bed in one room and nothing in the other. The floors and walls *radiate* heat; you won't need hot water from your clean private bath. (1 big bed 60 pesos; 2 beds 80 pesos; 3 beds 120 pesos; A/C 50 pesos extra.) **Hotel La Amistad,** 7 Calle Pte. 34 (tel. 6 22 93), between Av. 10 and 10 Nte, is a quiet, cool retreat from Tapachula's sweltering bustle. Watch out for the clothesline in the courtyard/owner's residence as you make your way to the small room lit just well enough to bring out the peach walls. (Singles 55 pesos; doubles 80 pesos; triples 115 pesos; quads 150 pesos; quints 180 pesos.) Lots of cheap Chinese restaurants await on 1 Calle Pte., one block southeast of the *zócalo,* but portions are often small. For cheap eats, head to the **San Juan food market** on 17 Calle Pte., north of the *centro* (open daily 6am-5pm). **Mercado Sebastián Escobar,** 10 Av. Nte. between 5 and 3 Calles Pte., sells produce and baked goods. Though Tapachula boasts a rich ethnic mix due to German and Chinese immigrants from World War II, it hasn't helped the food—prices are high and fare is sub-par.

Yucatán Peninsula

Hernández de Córdoba mistakenly ran aground here in 1517; when the freshly disembarked sailors asked the locals where they were, the Maya replied something to the effect of, "We haven't a clue what you're talking about." Unfamiliar with the Mayan language, Córdoba only caught the last few syllables of their reply, "Tectetán," and erroneously dubbed the region Yucatán. This encounter established a paradigm that would hold throughout Yucatán's history; misunderstood and continually abused by outsiders, it would always retain an element of its heritage. Today, the peninsula's culture remains essentially Maya and thrives in the small towns, where the evidence of Western influence arrives in the form of the weekly Coca-Cola truck. Mayan is still the first language of most inhabitants, and indigenous religious traditions persist within the practices of Catholicism that were instilled in the peninsula almost 500 years ago. Yucatec women still carry bowls of corn flour on their heads and wear embroidered *huipiles* (woven shirts), and fishing, farming, and hammock-making out-produce big industry and commerce. But foreign influence fights on: more workers are drawn by the dubious allure of the tourism industry and flood the big cities and resorts to work in gringo-friendly restaurants, weave hammocks for tourists, or act as multilingual guides at archaeological sites. The engineering of the pristine pleasure-world of Cancún has brought tourists in by the droves. Developers seized similar areas stretching farther and farther along the Yucatán coast in an effort to emulate Cancún; much of the virgin Caribbean beach land is currently under massive construction. However, the surging popularity of ecotourism in the past few years has shown dollar-seekers that some kinds of conservation can be lucrative as well.

The peninsula's inter-state borders form a "Y" down its center. Yucatán state sits in the crest of the "Y," Quintana Roo sees the Caribbean sun rise on the eastern coast, and Campeche faces the Gulf Coast to the west. Flat limestone scrubland and tropical forest dotted with *cenotes* (freshwater sinkholes) dominates the landscape. Because of the highly porous limestone subsoil, there are no above-ground rivers in the Yucatán. Poor soil and the lack of water make farming difficult, so maize remains the staple crop. The prominence of the rain god Chac at most Maya ruins testifies to the eternal importance of the seasonal rains, which fall from May to late summer.

"The Yucatán" refers to the peninsula, not the state, whereas "Yucatán" without the article can refer to either entity. **Yucatán** state's rich history draws thousands of visitors each year, who come to scramble up and down the incomparable Chichén Itzá and other majestic Maya ruins, marvel at old colonial towns, explore the area's many dark caves, and take a dip in the *cenotes*. **Quintana Roo**'s luscious jungle, fantastic coastline, and magnificent Maya ruins were

HIGHLIGHTS OF THE YUCATÁN PENINSULA

- No visit to the Yucatán is complete without a visit to the Maya ruins of **Chichén Itzá** (see p. 559). You've got to see 'em to believe 'em.
- Despite its artificiality and the presence of better nearby beaches, visitors from all over the world flock to **Cancún** (see p. 573), Mexico's biggest resort.
- Some of Mexico's best shopping waits in the bustling city of **Mérida** (see p. 547).
- Cruise through the **La Ruta Puuc (The Puuc Route;** see p. 539), checking out the eclectic assortment of Maya ruins that don't draw Chichén's crowds.
- Ruins on a beach? The stunning backdrop to the ruins of **Tulum** (see p. 591) is no joke—just look at our cover.
- Not as touristy as Cancún, the laid-back island of **Isla Mujeres** (see p. 581) draws a hip, international crew of backpackers who come to soak up sun and party.
- Some of the best snorkeling and scuba-diving in the world can be found around the oft-touristed isle of **Cozumel** (see p. 587).

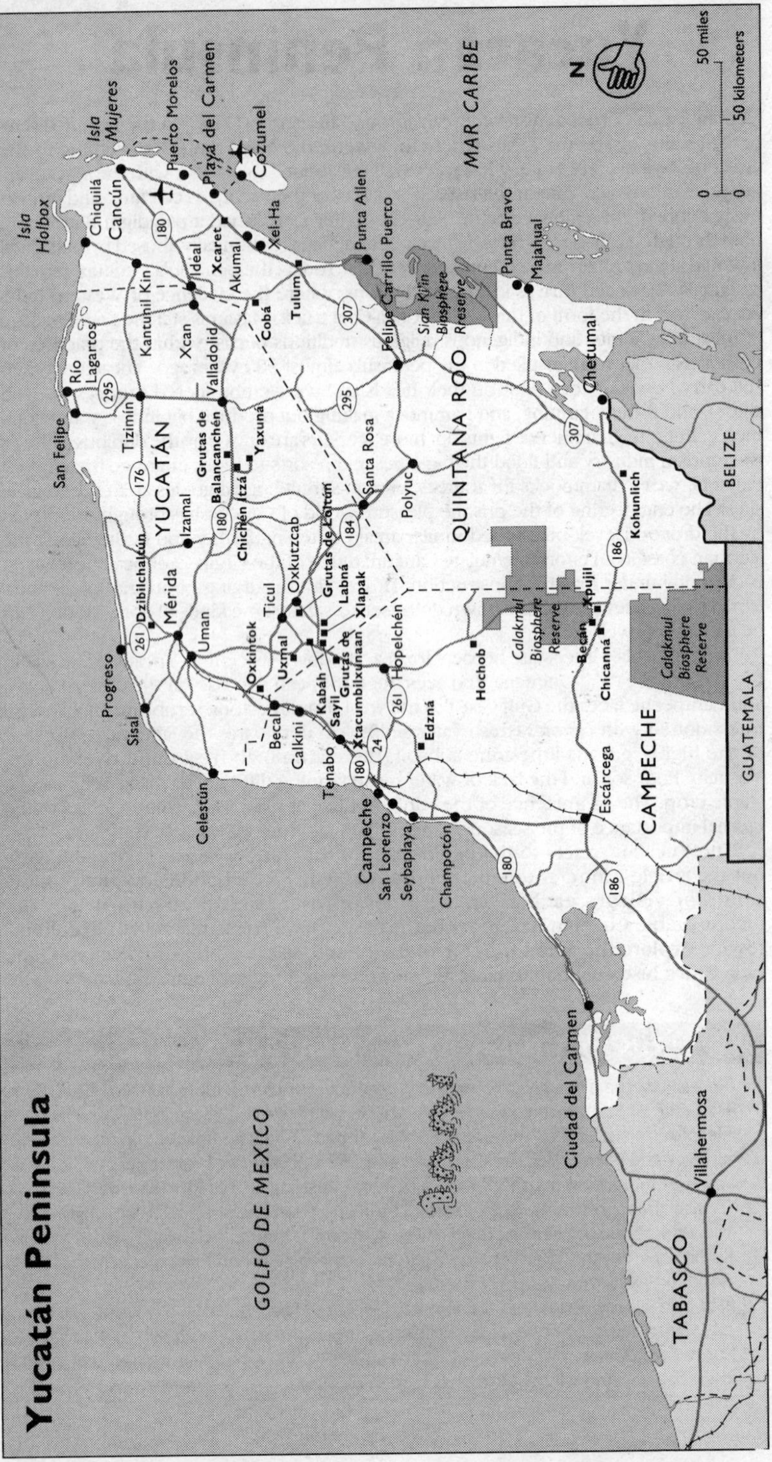
Yucatán Peninsula
GOLFO DE MEXICO
MAR CARIBE
N
0
50 miles
0
50 kilometers
Isla Holbox
Isla Mujeres
Chiquilá
Cancún
Puerto Morelos
Playa del Carmen
Cozumel
Xcaret
Xel-Ha
Akumal
Ideal
Tulum
Cobá
Punta Allen
Felipe Carrillo Puerto
Sian Ka'an Biosphere Reserve
Punta Bravo
Majahual
Chetumal
BELIZE
GUATEMALA
Kohunlich
Xpujil
Becán
Chicanná
Calakmul Biosphere Reserve
Calakmul Biosphere Reserve
Hochob
QUINTANA ROO
Polyuc
Santa Rosa
YUCATÁN
Valladolid
Xcan
Kantunil Kin
Río Lagartos
San Felipe
Tizimín
Grutas de Balancanchén
Yaxuná
Chichén Itzá
Izamal
Mérida
Dzibilchaltún
Progreso
Sisal
Celestún
Uman
Oxkintok
Uxmal
Ticul
Oxkutzcab
Grutas de Loltún
Labná
Xlapak
Kabáh
Sayil
Grutas de Xtacumbilxunaan
Hopelchén
Edzná
Becal
Calkini
Tenabo
Campeche
San Lorenzo
Seybaplaya
Champotón
Escárcega
CAMPECHE
Ciudad del Carmen
Villahermosa
TABASCO
180
295
176
261
307
184
24
186

idylls beneath the Caribbean sun until the government transformed the area from tropical paradise to tourist factory. Cancún rapidly became the beachhead for what some wryly call "the Second *Conquista,*" and the nearby beaches and ruins are following in suit. Although its countryside is dotted with Maya ruins, its coastline is over 200km long, and its colonial history predates Veracruz's, **Campeche** pulls in fewer visitors than Yucatán to the north or Quintana Roo to the east, perhaps because it lacks a kind of swaggering grandeur—ruins are modest and relatively inaccessible, while the beaches are kept humble by wind and rock

CAMPECHE

Escárcega

This town has about as much character as its original name, E47. Then an important railroad junction, the town grew into an unattractive example of centrally planned architecture. It's still an important junction; today, Routes 261 and 186 meet directly in front of the **first-class ADO station**. The station serves the cities of Campeche (2hr., 5 per day 11:30am-11:30pm, 145 pesos), Chetumal (5hr., 8:30, 10:30am and 12:30pm, 78 pesos), Cancún (8hr., 4 per day 7am-10:30pm, 83 pesos), Mérida (5hr., 2:30 and 9pm, 78 pesos), Mexico City (19hr., 6 per day 2-8:30pm, 378 pesos); Palenque (3½hr., 1 and 4pm, 61 pesos), Playa del Carmen (7hr., 7, 10:30am and 9pm, 82 pesos), Puebla (17hr., 12:30am, 334 pesos), Veracruz (11½hr., 9:15 and 10:30pm, 225 pesos), and Villahermosa (4hr., 10 per day 11:45am-11pm, 85 pesos). One kilometer down Av. Hector Martínez, the **second-class station** runs buses to similar locations and in between; it sells cheaper wine.

As buses leave around the clock for most destinations, it is unlikely you'll be stranded for very long in Escárcega. However, if you're too tired to continue, head into town on **Av. Héctor Martínez.** A good many blocks (about 1.5km), one railway crossing, and two stoplights later, make a right to reach Escárcega's small *zócalo.* The 50s clock tower tells you that you've made it. Escárcega and the long road leading to it are not the safest of places after dark, so take a taxi if it's late. For lodging, try the **Hotel Las Tres Hermanas** (tel. 981 4 01 10), right on the *zócalo,* which provides comfortable rooms with fans and cable TV (singles 50 pesos; doubles with 1 bed 60 pesos, with 2 beds 70 pesos; triples 100 pesos).

YUCATÁN PENINSULA

Campeche

Once called "Ah Kin Pech"—Mayan for "Place of the Serpents and Ticks"—Campeche is, thankfully, much more hospitable and pleasant than its original name suggests. When Francisco Hernández de Córdoba arrived, he transliterated the name to Campeche and, by 1540, had begun transforming the small city into a trading port. As it grew, Campeche battled buccaneers and pirates, erecting stunning *baluartes* (bulwarks), fortified churches, and forts, all of which still stand but are now fragmented and crumbling. As if to underscore the immutability of the city's spirit, the historic center, with its light, pastel facades and sidewalks raised over the flood-prone cobblestone streets, is an inner sanctum of colonial architecture. With a number of city-sponsored entertainments, beaches, and nearby haciendas and Maya ruins, Campeche is becoming less a stopover and more a destination for appreciating old Spanish beauty.

ORIENTATION

Campeche lies 252km southwest of Mérida and 444km northeast of Villahermosa via Rte. 180. All major routes into the city intersect the peripheral highway that encircles it. A smaller road, **Circuito Baluartes,** circumscribes the old city. All main roads con-

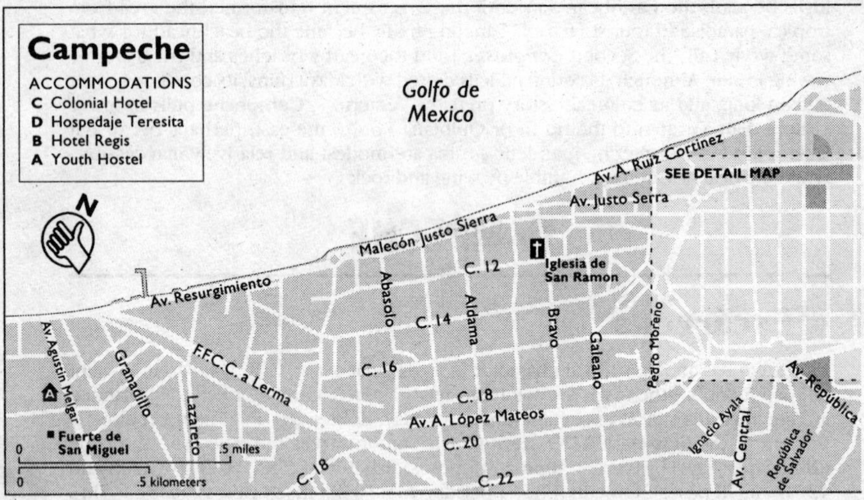

verge on the Circuito in the city center. **Avenida Gobernadores** comes in from the Mérida highway northeast of the city, crosses the peripheral highway, and passes the airport, train station, and bus terminals on its way to the Circuito.

To reach the *zócalo* from the **bus terminals,** catch the "Gobernadores" bus (2 pesos) across the street from the station, and ask the driver to let you off at the **Baluarte de San Francisco.** Turn right into the old city and walk four blocks on **Calle 57** to the *zócalo.* Front-door hotel escorts by **taxi** from the *zócalo* cost only 20 pesos, but if you'd rather walk (15min.), head left on Gobernadores and veer left when you reach the Circuito. Three blocks later, turn right on Calle 57 through the stone arch and walk four blocks to the *zócalo.*

The *centro*'s east-west streets have odd numbers that increase to the south. **Calle 8** runs north-south between the *zócalo* and the western city wall. Parallel to Calle 8 to the east lie Calles 10 to 16. The *zócalo* lies near the sea, bordered by Calles 8, 10, 55, and 57. To the west, outside the city wall, **Av. 16 de Septiembre** and **Av. Ruiz Cortínez** also run parallel to Calle 8. North of the *centro,* Calle 8 becomes **Malecón Miguel Alemán,** running past the Iglesia de San Francisco uphill to Fuerte de San José El Alto. **Av. Resurgimiento,** the main coastal drag south of the city, runs past the youth hostel and the Fuerte San Miguel on its way to San Lorenzo and Seybaplaya.

A confusing network of **buses** links Campeche's more distant sectors to the old city (1.50-2 pesos; daily 6am-11pm). The **market,** where Gobernadores becomes the Circuito, serves as the hub for local routes. Buses have no established stops, but they can be flagged down at the **post office** and at **Jardín Botánico** at Calle 51. You'll have to get around the city center on foot, since buses only come in as far as the Circuito.

PRACTICAL INFORMATION

Transportation

Airplanes: (tel. 6 31 09) on Porfirio, 13km from the city center. **Aeroméxico** (tel. 6 56 78), at the airport. Taxis to the *centro* cost 30 pesos.

Buses: From the **second-class station** (tel. 6 28 02), Calle Chile just off Av. Gobernadores. **Camioneros de Campeche** goes to Dzibalchén (2hr., 6 per day, 17 pesos), Escárcega (2½hr., 5 per day, 24 pesos), Holpechén (1½hr., 11 per day, 15 pesos), Iturbide (2hr., 5 per day, 40 pesos), Muna (4½hr., 5 per day, 28 pesos), and Uxmal

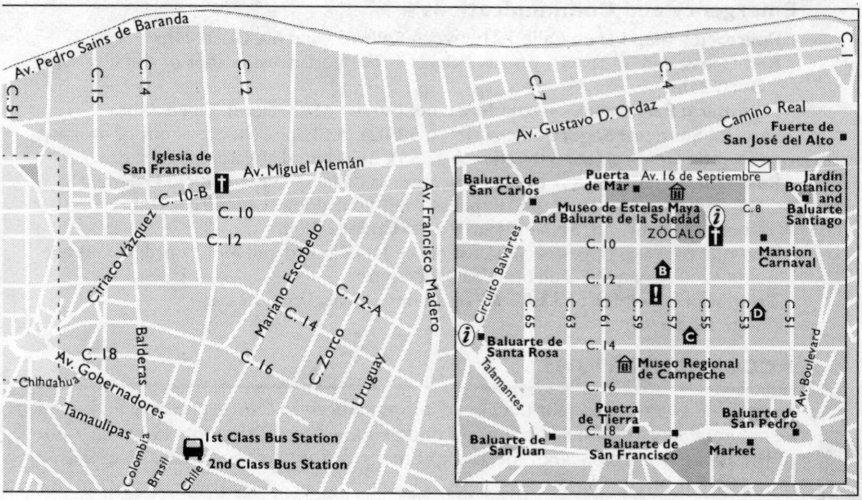

(4hr., 5 per day, 26 pesos). **Autobuses del Sur,** to Mérida (2½hr., 6 per day, 32 pesos), Palenque (5½hr., 10:30pm, 88 pesos), San Cristóbal (12hr., 11pm, 115 pesos), and Villahermosa (9hr., 4 per day, 78 pesos). The **first-class station** is on Av. Gobernadores #289, 4 blocks north of Circuito Baluartes at Baluarte San Pedro. **Autotransportes de Oriente (ADO),** to Cancún (6hr., 10 and 11:30pm, 130 pesos), Chetumal (7hr., noon, 114 pesos), Escárcega (2½hr., 7 per day 9:30am-11:30pm, 42 pesos), Mérida (2½hr., 12 per day 5:45am-10pm, 51 pesos), Mexico City (16hr., 2:50 and 7pm, 392 pesos), Palenque (5hr., 12:30am, 2am, and 10:45am, 100 pesos), Valladolid (4hr., 11:30pm, 97 pesos), Veracruz (12hr., 10pm, 251 pesos), and Villahermosa (7hr., 6 per day 2:15am-11pm, 121 pesos). **Cristóbal Colón,** to Ocosingo (8hr., 10pm, 118 pesos), San Cristóbal (10hr., 10pm, 139 pesos), and Tuxtla Gutiérrez (12hr., 10pm, 159 pesos). **Maya de Oro** offers service to Palenque (midnight, 114 pesos) and San Cristóbal (midnight, 181 pesos).

Taxis: (tel. 6 23 63). Three stands: Calle 8 at 55, to left of the cathedral; Calle 55 at Circuito, near the market; and Gobernadores at Chile, near the bus terminal. Intra-city travel 7-10 pesos.

Car Rental: Hotel Baluartes (tel. 1 18 84), at Av. Cortínez, a block from the *zócalo.*

Tourist and Financial Services

Tourist Office: Calle 55 #3 (tel. 1 39 89), next door to the cathedral at the *zócalo.* Open M-F 8am-10pm.

Travel Agency: Prof. Augustín Zavala y Lozano, Calle 16 #348 (tel. 6 44 26), gives 4hr. tours of Edzná (9am and 2pm, 90 pesos).

Currency Exchange: Banamex (tel. 6 52 51), at the corner of Calles 53 and 10. Open M-F 9am-5pm. 24hr. Visa, MC **ATM.**

American Express: (tel. 1 10 00) Calle 59 between 16 Septiembre and shore. Open M-F 9am-2pm and 5-8pm, Sa 9am-1:30pm.

Local Services

Market: On Circuito Baluartes between Calles 53 and 55. Unexceptional handicrafts and cheap food. Open M-Sa sunrise-sunset, Su until 3pm.

Supermarket: Súper Diez (tel. 6 79 76), in the Pl. Comercial A-Kin-Pech on 16 de Septiembre, across the street from the post office. Open daily 7am-9:30pm.

Laundromat: Lavandería y Tintorería Campeche, Calle 55 #22 (tel. 6 51 42), between Calles 12 and 14. Same-day service 8 pesos per kg. Open M-Sa 8am-4pm.

Emergency and Communications

Police: (tel. 6 21 11) on Calle 12 between Calles 57 and 59. Open 24hr.
Red Cross: (tel. 6 21 11), on Las Palmas at the northwest corner of the city wall. Open 24hr.
Pharmacy: Farmacia Gobernadores, next to the ADO station. Open 24hr.
Medical Services: Seguro Social (tel. 6 52 02), on López Mateos south of the city. **Hospital General** (tel. 6 09 20 or 6 42 33), Av. Central at Circuito Baluartes.
Post Office: (tel. 6 21 34) 16 de Septiembre at Calle 53 in the Edificio Federal. Open M-F 8am-8pm, Sa 8am-1pm. **Express mail** next door at **MexPost** (tel. 1 17 30). Open M-F 9am-6pm, Sa 9am-1pm. **Postal Code:** 24000.
Fax: (tel. 6 43 90) opposite MexPost in the Edificio Federal. Money orders and telegrams too. Open M-F 8am-6pm, Sa 9am-noon.
Telephones: TelMex and **LADATEL** phones throughout the city.
Phone Code: 981.

ACCOMMODATIONS

Budget travelers looking for decent accommodations in Campeche may be forced to pay indecent prices. Several good middle-range establishments hover just out of the range of backpackers' pesos, and many of the cheaper places overcharge for just what offer.

Colonial Hotel, Calle 14 #122 (tel. 6 22 22 or 6 26 30), between Calles 55 and 57, 2½ blocks from the *zócalo.* The retro lime-and-peach layout makes for tall ceilings and tiny bathrooms. The genuinely hot water and cold *agua purificada,* though, will soothe any objections to showering with the sink. Singles 81 pesos; doubles 110 pesos; triples 140 pesos; 23 pesos per additional person; 40 pesos for A/C.

Hotel Regis, Calle 12 #148 (tel. 6 31 75), at Calle 57, 1½ blocks from the *zócalo.* The extensive, modern renovations to this colonial mansion must have cost a mint, cause that's what they're charging for immaculate, spacious rooms with TVs, fans, and new bathrooms. Singles and doubles 135 pesos; triples 175 pesos; extra person or A/C add 40 pesos.

Hospedaje Teresita, Calle 53 #31 (tel. 6 45 34) between Calles 12 and 14. In a residential part of the old city, 3 blocks northeast of the *zócalo.* The cheapest place in the *centro,* and for good reason. Large, bare, concrete-walled rooms have fans. Communal bathrooms lack privacy. Singles or doubles 40 pesos, with decent private bath 50 pesos.

Youth Hostel Villa Deportiva Juvenil Campeche (tel. 6 18 02), on Agustín Melgar several blocks east of the water and the coastal highway. From the eastern section of the Circuito Baluartes, take the "Lerma" bus south along the coastal highway to the intersection with Melgar, then walk half a block toward the ocean. A black iron gate on the left marks the spot. Single-sex college dorm rooms won't get too stuffy with just two bunks and well-kept bathrooms. No hot water. Often full July-Aug. and Dec.; call to reserve. Bunks 25 pesos plus 20 peso deposit. Breakfast, lunch, and dinner, 14 pesos each.

FOOD

Campeche has developed some culinary experiences that are just as colorful as its streets. No visitor should leave without sampling *pande cazón* (stacked tortillas filled with baby shark and refried beans and covered with an onion, tomato, and chile sauce). Other local specialties include *pámpano en escabeche* (pompano broiled in olive oil and flavored with onion, garlic, chile, peppers, and a dash of orange juice).

Restaurant Del Parque, Calle 57 #8 (tel. 6 02 40) at Calle 8. Clean, white, pressed tablecloths and dark red, cushioned chairs make it the height of budget elegance, serving equally tasteful dishes. *Tortas al pastor* 11 pesos, *pande cazón* 28 pesos. Open daily 7am-10:30pm.

Cenaduría Portales (tel. 1 14 91), also known as **San Pancho** for its proximity to Iglesia de San Francisco. Take any bus headed north on Malecón Miguel Alemán to the church. Cross the plaza in front of the church and head left to another smaller square. The restaurant huddles beneath the arches straight ahead. An assembly line of highly trained sandwich makers jumps into action at your order and nearly instantly produces not just a sandwich but a work of art. Sandwiches 8-10 pesos. Exceptional *horchata* (sweetened rice water, 4 pesos). Open daily 7pm-midnight. This area is not safe after dark, and the last bus back passes around 10pm.

Restaurant La Parroquia, Calle 55 #9 (tel. 6 80 86) between Calles 10 and 12. A cavernous all-night local eatery with good, cheap food, and TV around the clock. Fat, steaming stacks of hot cakes with honey, 18 pesos. Open daily 24hr.

Nutrivida (tel. 6 12 21), on Calle 12 between 57 and 59. Not much larger than a snack stand, Nutrivida serves small portions of meatless burgers (7-13 pesos), homemade yogurt, flaky bread, and fresh juice in a pleasant courtyard. Open M-F 8am-2pm and 5:30-8pm, Sa 8am-2pm.

SIGHTS AND SAND

Campeche's historical treasures are best seen at night, when spotlights warm up cold stone and the moonlight spills over the ocean. The most convenient way to see Campeche is by "Tranvia," the comfortable **trolley** that gives a historical tour of the major sights. Catch it at the *zócalo* in front of Los 3 Hermanos shoe store (1hr., M-F 9:30am, 6, and 8pm, Sa-Su 9:30am, 6, 7, and 8pm, 7 pesos). Walking tours of the city leave from the corner of Calles 18 and 59 daily at 4:30pm (1hr., 18 pesos).

The **Fuerte de San Miguel** houses well-documented exhibits describing nearby ruins and displays Maya jewelry, pottery, and several magnificent jade masks. *(Open Tu-Su 8am-8pm. Admission 4 pesos, free Sunday.)* On the top level, cannons still project protectively over the sea and Campeche to the north. To reach the fort, take the "Lerma" bus from the eastern end of the Circuito Baluartes, and head south until the bus turns onto the coastal highway near the "Maxi" *tienda.* The road leading up to the fort is about a block ahead on the left.

San Miguel's counterpart to the north, the **Fuerte de San José El Alto,** is a few kilometers from the *centro. (Open Tu-Su 8am-8pm. Admission 4 pesos, free on Sundays.)* The "Bellavista" or "San José El Alto" bus from the market will drop you halfway up the hill; a five-minute walk will get you to the fort at the top. If you decide to walk, head north on Gobernadores, turn left on Cuauhtémoc, left on Calle 101, and right on Calle 7. Built in 1792, San José was amazingly defensible when in use. The path leading to the portcullis winds deliberately so that battering rams could not be used on the gate. The fort's moat was supposedly rife with vicious spikes; the water was obscured with chalk so as to hide these spikes from anyone thinking about jumping in. Today, the ships and armaments have moved inside the fort for a small exhibit. The view from San José is spectacular: kilometers of green shoreline give way to the urban waterfront.

In the **Baluarte de la Soledad,** off Calle 8 near Calle 57 across from the *zócalo,* the **Museo de Estelas Maya** houses a small collection of well-preserved Maya stelae and reliefs taken from sites in Campeche state. *(Museum open Tu-Sa 8am-8pm, Su 8am-1pm. Admission 4 pesos.)* Informative Spanish texts and remaining pictographs elaborate on sculpted figures' occupations. Visitors may also climb the walls of the fort, which is surrounded by a park. A showroom across from the museum occasionally features free exhibitions.

Enclosed by the walls of the **Fuerte Santiago** at the northwest corner of the small city, the **Jardín Botánico Xmuch'altún** (tel. 6 68 29), on Calles 8 and 51, makes an inviting stop. *(Open M-F 8am-1pm and 4-8:30pm, Sa 8am-1pm and 4-8pm, Su 9am-1pm. Guided tours M-F 9am-3pm.)* Over 250 species of plant thrive in a tiny open-air courtyard shaded by trees and marked by benches, fountains, and frogs.

Campeche's **cathedral** looms above the *zócalo. (Open daily 7am-noon and 5-8pm; free.)* Don Francisco de Montejo first ordered the construction of the cathedral in

1540, but builders did not complete the massive structure until 1705. The cathedral's main attraction is its facade. Inside, you'll find the *Santo Entierro* (Holy Burial), a sculpture of Christ in a carved mahogany sarcophagus replete with gold ornaments inside a glass case with silver trim.

A little farther from the center of town on Av. Gustavo Díaz, the **Iglesia de San Francisco,** built in 1518, claims to be the oldest church on the American mainland. *(Open daily 8am-noon and 5-8pm.)* Inside, yellow Corinthian arches project toward an ornate altar. A few blocks south of the *centro,* the **Iglesia de San Román** houses El Cristo Negro, greatly venerated by *campechanos* in Mexico (open daily 6am-noon and 4-8pm; free).

Locals usually head south for **sand** and **sunbathing. San Lorenzo** is ideal for swimming, although the beach is pebbly. The closest half-decent stretch of sand is at **Playa Payucán.** The beach is great for snorkeling, but rentals are not available. Buses (4 pesos) for **Seybaplaya,** 2km from the beach, leave from behind the market.

ENTERTAINMENT AND SEASONAL EVENTS

Campeche sponsors various free outdoor musical events, including the **Ballet Folklórico** in the *zócalo.* Every Tuesday, Friday, and Saturday night at 8:30pm, an impressive **sound and light show** at Puerta de Tierra, Calles 59 and 18, recounts in Spanish the dramatic story of residents repelling pirates. The performers' awful acting is as entertaining as the historical account. Weather permitting, a Ballet Folklórico performance follows the conclusion of the show. (Sound and light show 15 pesos, 50% discount with student ID; translated text in three other languages is projected onto the wall.) The wildly popular **Noche de Trova,** including music and performances by the Ballet Folklórico, is celebrated in the *zócalo* on Wednesdays and Thursdays at 8pm, but usually only during the high months of July, August, and December. On Sundays at 8pm, the state band strikes up *campecho* music from the kiosk in the *zócalo.* For a schedule of events, ask for the *programa de actividades* at the tourist information center. **San Román** is Campeche's patron, and two weeks of both religious and secular festivities, starting September 15, celebrate his feast.

Atlantis (tel. 6 22 33), at the Ramada Inn on Av. Ruiz Cortínez, lords over Campeche's nightlife. (Cover 75 pesos for men, 35 pesos for women. Thursday is singles night and free. Friday is ladies' night. Open Th-Sa 10pm-3am.) **La Cueva de Las Ranas,** near the university on López Mateos, attracts aspiring rock stars and a hip student crowd (open 9pm-3am). The swinging local crowd gets down at **Disco Dragon,** on Av. Resurgimiento 87 (tel. 6 42 89 or 1 18 10). Ask the tourist office for more info.

■ Near Campeche: Edzná

If you're already in Campeche, visit the nearby ruins of **Edzná** (House of the Grimaces). *(Site open daily 8am-5pm. Admission 16 pesos, half-price with student ID, free Su.)* Despite its lack of elaborately sculpted detail, the **Edificio de Cinco Pisos** (Building of the Five Floors) towers over the surrounding valley atop the elegant **Gran Acrópolis.** Sixty-five stairs, some adorned with hieroglyphics over 1300 years old, lead up to tiers of columns crowned by a magnificent five-room temple. During its Maya heyday, the perch atop the monument afforded a view of the network of irrigation canals criss-crossing the valley close to the Río Champotón, 20km to the west. The canals were built without the use of wheels, metal tools, or domesticated animals. Nearby, among the many thistle bushes, are the remains of a ballcourt and several other temples on a central plaza which are presently being excavated. Also on display are some of the 19 stelae found at Edzná—one crafted as early as 672, others made during the 10th-century evacuation of the ceremonial center.

Getting There: One bus makes three daily round-trips from the market in Campeche to Alfredo Bonfil (1½hr., 7, 10, and 11am, 6 pesos), leaving you off at the Edzná access road. From there, a sign points the way and gives a distance 1500m too long. To avoid being stranded, be sure to ask the driver when he will return. A canteen of water and plenty of insect repellent are a must in Edzna's jungle terrain.

Near Campeche: Grutas de Xtacumbilxunaan

The **Grutas de Xtacumbilxunaan** (shta-koom-bill-shu-NAN, "Caves of the Sleeping Girl") lie 27km from the Yucatán-Campeche border. *(Open daily 9am-6pm. Free, but guide expects a tip. Tours in Spanish only.)* A custodian leads a tour past seven deep *cenotes* and points out barely discernible shapes on the cavern's walls and ceilings. These caves are poorly lit, a far cry from the high-roofed galleries of Loltún or the clean-cut passageways of Balankanché, but you can still have fun poking around. Hard-core cave lovers who bring their own rock climbing equipment can take a two-day trip underground with the guides to visit the seven connected *cenotes* 150m below ground. Bring camping gear.

Getting There: The *grutas* lie 1km down the road that crosses Rte. 261 2km south of Bolonchén. Second-class buses drop passengers at the access road.

YUCATÁN

La Ruta Puuc (The Puuc Route)

La Ruta Puuc is a long stretch between Campeche and Mérida that traverses the Puuc Hills. This area was home to about 22,000 people during the Classic period of Maya civilization (4th to 10th centuries). Decimated by diseases introduced by the Spanish, the Maya slowly surrendered most of their cities and ceremonial centers to the jungle. Beginning in the 18th century, the Maya population began a slow recovery. While today's Puuc Maya live in towns with paved roads and plumbing, women continue to wear traditional embroidered *huipiles,* and Mayan remains the dominant language.

The easiest way to see the ruins is by **renting a car** in Mérida (see p. 549). The drive along the Ruta Puuc is one of the most liberating and enjoyable on-the-road experiences, as small Maya villages and green jungle line the winding road.

Recently, more and more travel agencies in Mérida or Campeche are offering organized tours through this and other new tourist routes (the **Convent Route,** for example). The tourist offices in both cities will be more than happy to provide information on arrangements. Public transportation is more difficult. Second-class **buses** traverse Rte. 261 frequently, and will stop when requested, but none travel the Sayil-Oxkutzkub road with the exception of the **Autotransportes del Sur "Ruta Puuc" bus** that leaves Mérida at 8am and visits Kabah, Sayil, Labná, and Uxmal, returning to Mérida at about 2:30pm. If you don't mind a whirlwind tour through the sites, this bus is an incredible bargain (48 pesos; admission to sites not included). But be on the bus promptly when it leaves each site; it only spends about half an hour at each site, and drivers have been known to leave tourists stranded at smaller sites. **Combis** are abundant in the morning and make frequent trips between Oxkutzkab, Ticul, Santa Elena, and Muna (it is easiest to get a *combi* to Uxmal from Muna), and they will make any trip if paid enough. Unfortunately, with both *combis* and buses, return trips are not always guaranteed. If you can only make it to one or two sights, don't miss Uxmal, and try to see Sayil—they have the best ruins of all.

Most travelers who make the Ruta Puuc more than a daytrip use **Ticul** (see p. 545) as a base; the town offers cheap accommodations and restaurants. Yet, **Santa Elena** (see p. 546) is an even more central location and boasts two superb budget dining and sleeping establishments on its outskirts. From either of these places, two to three days should be ample time for exhaustive exploration. Most sites sell *refrescos,* but the only one with accommodations is Uxmal. And at those prices, there ought to be a light-and-sound show for each room.

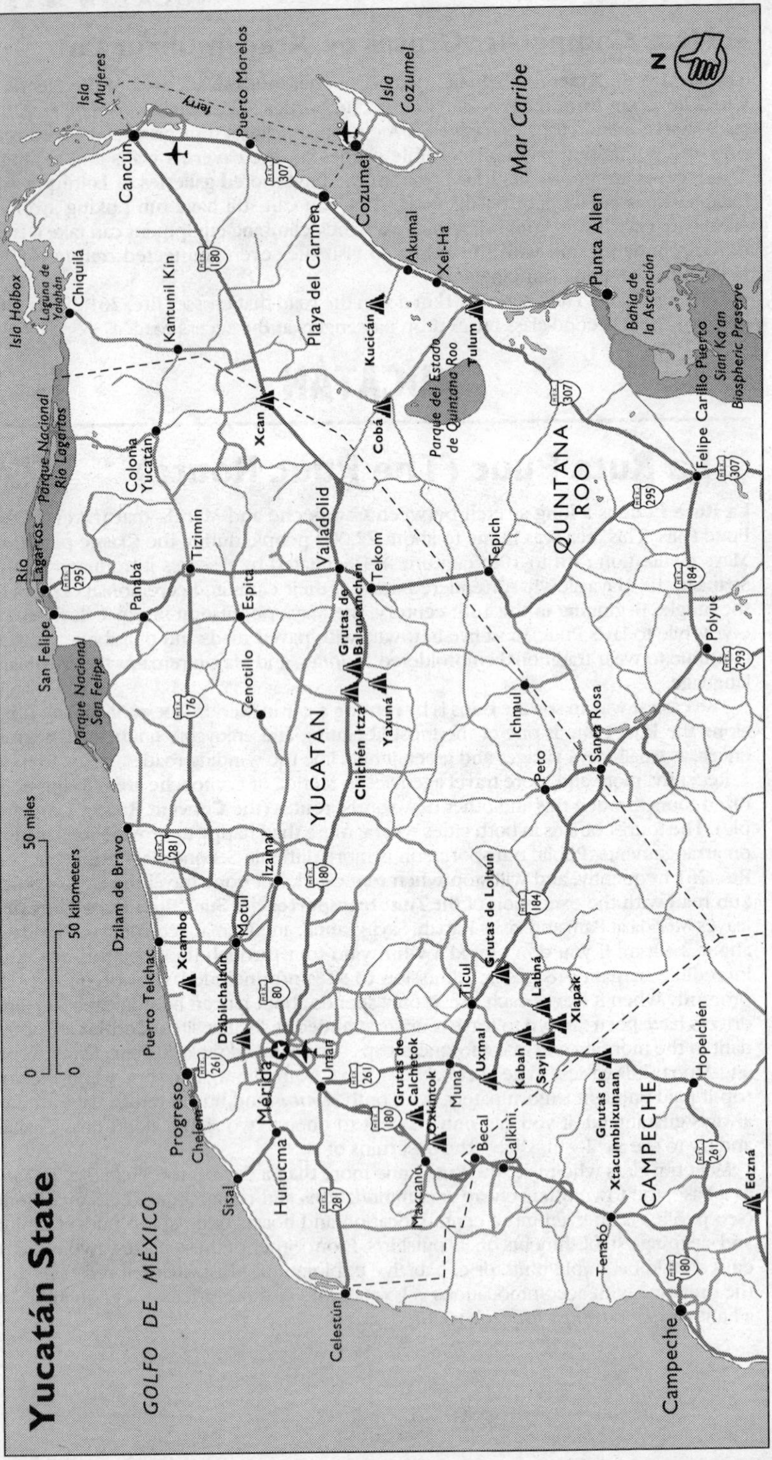
Yucatán State
GOLFO DE MÉXICO
Mar Caribe
YUCATÁN
QUINTANA ROO
CAMPECHE
0 50 miles
0 50 kilometers
N
Isla Mujeres
ferry
Puerto Morelos
Isla Cozumel
Cancún
Cozumel
Playa del Carmen
Akumal
Xel-Ha
Tulum
Punta Allen
Bahía de la Ascención
Sian Ka'an Biospheric Preserve
Felipe Carillo Puerto
Isla Holbox
Laguna de Yalahán
Chiquilá
Kantunil Kín
Parque Nacional Río Lagartos
Río Lagartos
Colonia Yucatán
Tizimín
Xcan
Kucicán
Cobá
Parque del Estado de Quintana Roo
Valladolid
Tekom
Tepich
Panabá
San Felipe
Parque Nacional San Felipe
Espita
Cenotillo
Grutas de Balancanchén
Chichén Itzá
Yaxuná
Ichmul
Peto
Santa Rosa
Polyuc
Dzilam de Bravo
Izamal
Grutas de Loltún
Puerto Telchac
Xcambó
Motul
Dzibilchaltún
Progreso
Chelem
Mérida
Umán
Ticul
Labná
Xlapak
Sayil
Kabah
Uxmal
Muna
Grutas de Calchetok
Oxkintok
Grutas de Xtacumbilxunaan
Hopelchén
Becal
Calkiní
Maxcanú
Hunucmá
Sisal
Celestún
Tenabó
Edzná
Campeche
180
307
295
176
281
80
261
184
293

La Ruta Puuc: The Ruins

The Ruta Puuc refers specifically to the 254km on Rte. 261 between Campeche and Mérida and the Sayil-Oxkutzkub road which branches off just meters after the Campeche-Yucatán border. Taking this turnoff, **Sayil** is the first archaeological site to materialize (after 5km), followed by **Xlapak** (10km), **Labná** (13km), **Loltún** (25km), **Oxkutzkab** (45km), and **Ticul** (62km). Alternatively, if the turnoff is not taken, the road winds through **Kabah** (right after the border) and the stunning site of **Uxmal** (23km); 16km from Uxmal lies the junction at **Muna.**

Ground Zero

Although the theory that *chile relleno* indigestion exterminated the dinosaurs has not gained much ground with scientists, their extinction may still be connected to Mexico. A link has been made between the dinosaur-wiped-out-by- meteor theory and the explanation for why much of the Yucatán lacks above-ground water and topsoil. It turns out that the peninsula may have been ground zero for the catastrophic impact of a meteor that hit earth 65 million years ago.

Just wild speculation? Maybe. But archaeologists have identified a large piece of meteor rock that slammed through the roof of the **Grutas de Loltún.** Whatever soil didn't fly into space from this alleged crash solidified into the porous limestone rock (a nightmare for farmers) that dominates the landscape today. If you stand on the end of the long wooden dock at the end of Calle 20, you can survey what is believed to be the center of the 180km-wide impact zone of the meteor.

Grutas de Loltún

The **Grutas de Loltún** are 58km east of Uxmal on the Sayil-Oxkutzcab road. *(Entrance only with tours. Tours daily 9:30, 11am, 12:30, 2, 3, and 4pm. Admission 34 pesos, Sundays 16 pesos. Restaurant open only M-Sa 10am-8pm.)* To get to Loltún, catch a bus as far as Muna or Ticul, hop in a *combi* headed for Oxkutzcab, then follow signs to *centro.* Passing the market on your left, walk two blocks, turn right at the sign for Ruta Puuc, then pray for deliverance—Las Grutas are 7km down the road. A pick-up truck in Oxkutzcab's *zócalo* may be willing to make the trip, but it will cost you at least 20 pesos.

Below a dense jungle of mahogany and *ceiba* trees kilometers of enormous caverns wind through the rock. Guides can be enticed to lengthen their tours (the caves go on forever) with the promise of a nice, fat tip. The ancient Maya first settled this area in order to take advantage of the *grutas'* water and clay. Hundreds of years later, Maya *campesinos* returned to the caves seeking refuge from the Caste War (1847-1848). Important caverns include the **Room of the 37 Inscriptions,** which dons many still-visible markings (i.e. handprints), and the **Na Cab** (House of the Bees), where you can see the *ka'ob* (grindstones) left by the Maya. Ancient inhabitants broke off the stalactite tips in the **Gallery of Fallen Rocks** to use as spears and arrows. In the **Gallery of the Five Chultunes,** a sculpted jaguar head drips water into cisterns while a huge warrior and eagle look on. The **Cathedral** is a palatial room that once hosted Maya feasts and assemblies. The shadowy silhouette above the entrance is popularly believed to represent the Virgin of Guadalupe. Several caves contain partially hollow stalactites and columns—thump one with the heel of your hand and listen to the soft booming sound *("loltún...loltún...")* reverberate throughout the cave system. Archaeologists speculate that the Maya used these formations as a means of musical underground communication.

Guides will lead English tours, but Spanish ones tend to be more comprehensive. Bear in mind the exorbitant rates charged by above-ground guides when leaving a tip for the free guide service. As you exit the caves (0.5km from the entrance), you'll stumble on the conveniently located **Restaurant El Huinoc de Loltún,** which prepares a good range of local dishes for about 40-50 pesos. Get ready to wait—service is slow as molasses, and the restaurant can be packed with people from tour buses.

■ Labná

The final destination on the "Ruta Puuc" bus, **Labná** lies 42km east of Uxmal, 22km before Las Grutas (see below), and 4km beyond Xlapak. *(Site open daily 8am-5pm. Admission 14 pesos, free on Sundays.)* Almost no *combis* come and go on this branch of the Ruta Puuc; hitching is reportedly tough.

Labná's buildings were constructed toward the end of the Late Classic period (700-1000), when the Puuc cities were connected by *sacbeob* (paved, elevated white roads). Today, a short reconstructed section of the *sacbe* runs between Labná's two most impressive sights: the palace and the stone arch. To deal with parched conditions, the Maya constructed huge **chultunes** (plastered catch basins), 70 of which are found at Labná. The *chultunes* collected both water (up to 8000 gallons in each) and the bodies of peasants who couldn't afford to be buried. Only a few of the narrow openings can be seen. Many of Labná's buildings are too far gone to climb, giving rest to the tired and weak-kneed tourist.

Labná's **palace** is on the northern side of the site, to the left as you enter. While the construction of this building occupied the Maya for several centuries, the edifice was never actually completed. Labná's palace is reminiscent of the one at Sayil; they both boast exceptionally ornate second-floor facades. Nearby mosaics depict figures in palm huts, reminding present-day visitors that the stone palaces once housed only the privileged few. Now, they house scores of chipper birds.

Labná is famed for its picturesque **stone arch,** 3m wide and 6m high. Its western facade is intricately decorated in a trellis pattern, while the eastern side is carved in a Grecian style. Archaeologists now believe that the arch previously thought to have been the entrance to another temple served as a ceremonial point of entry for victorious warriors returning from the battlefield.

Beyond the arch, on the unrestored base of a pyramid, stands the **observatory,** also known as **El Mirador** (the lookout). Its notable facade rises over the box-like structure and bears tenons, spikes, and dowels that used to support bas-relief sculptures. The top of the observatory affords a view of the entire site; keep your eyes peeled for falcons' nests. As you head back toward the palace, the **Edificio de las Columnas** is off the *sacbe* to the right. This "Building of the Columns" is one of the best examples of the Puuc style of 800 to 1000. One of the openings to the *chultunes* that were vital to Labná's 2500 ancient residents can be seen in front of the *edificio.*

■ Sayil

Sayil lies 9km past Kabah off Rte. 261 on the Sayil-Oxkutzcab road and 5km past Xlapak. *(Site open daily 8am-5pm. Admission 14 pesos, free Su and holidays.)* The only public transportation to the site is provided by the **Autotransportes del Sur "Ruta Puuc" bus** (see p. 548). Buses do run, however, from Mérida to Kabah, 10km away on the main highway. Some travelers hitch from Kabah to Sayil.

The **Palace of Sayil** is an architectural standout among the region's ruins. While time, weather, and the jungle have taken down most of its buildings since its construction between 800 and 1000, the palace is still breathtaking. Between its three terraced levels, the building's 50 rooms exhibit unparalleled ornamental diversity. Walls are carved with rows of slender columns, the second-story frieze depicts the descending serpent-god's body. Elegant second-floor chambers open onto pleasant porticos, each graced by bulging columns. Climb to the top for a gorgeous and panoramic view of the rolling Puuc hills.

The path continues past the palace to **El Mirador,** a lofty temple with once-grandiose columns. Left of El Mirador, the path leads deeper into the jungle, where the extremely graphic **Estela del Falo** (Stela of the Phallus) was a tribute to Yum Keep, a Maya god of fertility. A few other temples are barely visible through the dense jungle undergrowth.

■ Kabah

Once the second largest city in the northern Yucatán, **Kabah** was built with the blood and sweat of many slaves; their effort has mostly succumbed to the ravages of time, with a few notable exceptions. *(Kabah site open daily 8am-5pm. Admission 14 pesos, free on Sundays and holidays.)* Kabah is bisected by Rte. 261, and lies 23km southeast of its Ruta Puuc cousin, Uxmal. Because of its location on the Campeche-Mérida highway (*vía ruinas*), it can easily be reached by any second-class bus running between Mérida and Campeche, although the noon bus does not pass (see p. 548 and p. 534). Buses will stop at Kabah only if a passenger notifies the driver beforehand or if the driver sees a person wildly gesticulating on the shoulder of the highway. Things are easier with the **ATS "Ruta Puuc" bus** (see p. 548). Since almost all the tourists who come to Kabah have cars, those who do not sometimes try to hitch.

The striking **Codz Pop Temple** ("rolled mat" in Mayan), immediately to the right of the entrance, is famous for the steps carved as noses Chac, who is depicted on the doorways. The temple's broad facade displays nearly 300 masks of Chac, each comprised of 30 carved pieces. The elaborate **Chenes style** of the temple is unique to the Codz Pop—its neighbors to the east, **El Palacio** (a 25m pyramid) and **Las Columnas,** were executed in plainer fashion. The site is thought to have served as a court where justices settled disputes, with gods comprising the jury. Across the street by the parking lot, the short dirt road leads to rubble (right), more rubble (left), and the famous **Kabah Arch** (straight ahead). The arch marks the beginning of the ancient *sacbe* that culminated in a twin arch at Uxmal. The perfect alignment of the archway with the north-south line is testimony to Maya astronomical understanding.

■ Uxmal

If you've spent the day doing all the ruins of the Ruta Puuc in the order in which they have been listed, then you'll be arriving in Uxmal just as the larger crowds are clearing out and as the sun is starting to set, bathing the striking ruins in a flame-yellow light. Meaning "thrice built or occupied," it's not hard to see why Uxmal, once a capital with 25,000 inhabitants, keeps drawing more and more visitors.

ORIENTATION AND PRACTICAL INFORMATION **Autotransportes del Sur (ATS)** sends six buses per day from Mérida to Uxmal (1½hr., 13 pesos), as well as a "Ruta Puuc" bus which visits Kabah, Labná Sayil, Uxmal, and Xlapak all in one day for just 45 pesos (see p. 548). From Campeche you'll have to take the **Camioneros de Campeche** bus to Mérida (3hr., 5 per day, 25 pesos). Ask the driver to stop at the access road to the ruinas. To return, grab a passing bus at the crucero just outside the entrance to the ruins. The last buses to Mérida and Campeche pass at 8pm and 7pm, respectively. A modern **tourist center** with a small but interesting museum, restaurant, gift shop, photographic supply shop, and bathroom greets you at the entrance to the ruins. The **Kit Bolon Tun auditorium,** also in the tourist center, screens documentaries on the Ruta Puuc and gives 15-minute presentations on Chichén Itzá, Uxmal, and the Yucatán (6 shows per day in Spanish and 4 in English; free).

ACCOMMODATIONS AND FOOD Even the bravest of ruins crumble under the huge prices of Uxmal's lodging and food. Consider staying 30 minutes away in Ticul, where hotel rooms cost half as much (see p. 546). In Uxmal, the cheapest option is **Rancho Uxmal** (tel. 49 05 29), 4km north of the ruins on Rte. 261. From the highway near Uxmal, you can reach Rancho Uxmal by hopping aboard a passing bus or combi (3 pesos). Rooms have inviting bedspreads, hand-painted murals, and adequate bathrooms. The Rancho also features a pool. (Singles 170 pesos; doubles 250 pesos.) The Ranch's restaurant serves *típico* dishes for 35-45 pesos and breakfast for 25 pesos (restaurant open daily 7am-10pm).

THE ARCHAEOLOGICAL SITE OF UXMAL

According to the **Books of Chilam Balam** (see p. 62), a group of Maya historical accounts written in Yucatec Mayan, Yucatán was invaded at the end of the 10th century by Ah Suytok Xiu and his warriors from the Valley of Mexico. Xiu and his successors dominated Uxmal until the city's strength was sapped by civil warfare in the 12th century. Because their priests foretold the coming of white, bearded men, the Xiu did not resist the attacks of Spanish conquistadors on Uxmal. The last Xiu ruler of the city was Ah Suytok Tutul Xiu, whose descendants still live in the region.

Guide to the Ruins

The 40m-tall near-pyramid visible upon entering Uxmal is the **Temple of the Magician.** As legend goes, the pyramid was built by a dwarf-magician who hatched from a witch's egg and grew to maturity in one year. The legend of the dwarf-magician's birth struck terror into the heart of the governing lord of Uxmal, who, it was prophesied, would be replaced by a man "not born of woman." He challenged the dwarf to a contest of building skills. The dwarf's pyramid, built overnight, easily outclassed the governor's **Great Pyramid,** still visible to the right of the **Governor's Palace.** Grasping at straws, the spiteful ruler complained that the base of the dwarf's pyramid was neither square nor rectangular but elliptical. Having undermined the legitimacy of the dwarf-magician's triumph, the governor proposed that he and his adversary compete to see who could break a *cocoyol* (a small, hard-shelled fruit) on his head. The dwarf-magician, in whose skull a turtle shell had been placed, easily cracked open the *cocoyol.* The governor crushed his own unaltered skull.

Continuing to the west is a large quadrangle—Uxmal's famed **Nunnery.** It was misnamed for the same reason as the one at Chichén Itzá; the Spanish thought its many rooms resembled that of a convent. The four long buildings of this quad were each built on a different level, and each has a distinctive decor. The building to the north is adorned with Chac masks; the eastern building boasts intricate lattice work and Venus symbols; the southern building has a series of hut sculptures; and the western building shows kings and bound prisoners in high relief. The sizeable entryways of the southern building lead to the **ballcourt.** Only one of the glyph-engraved stone signs remains, through which well-padded players tried to knock a hardened rubber ball (see **Hoop Dreams,** p. 564).

Emerging from the ballcourt, head right along a narrow path to the **Cemetery Group,** a small, leafy plaza bounded by a modestly sized pyramid to the north and a temple to the west. Stones that once formed platforms bear haunting reliefs of skulls and crossbones. Returning to the ballcourt, head south to the well-restored **Great Pyramid,** built by the governor in his contest with the dwarf-magician. On top of the pyramid sits the **Macaw Temple,** named for its many engravings of that bird on its facade, inside of which sits a Chac-motif throne. To the west the pyramid looks down on the fretworks of the **Pigeon House.** Behind this structure lie the jungle-shrouded remains of the **Chenes Temple.**

The **House of Turtles** and the **Palace of the Governor** top a man-made escarpment east of the Great Pyramid. The two-story house is on the northwest corner of the escarpment and is adorned along its upper frieze with a series of sculpted turtles (turtles symbolized rain and were venerated by the Maya). The larger building is the palace, replete with engravings and arches.

From the Palace of the Governor, try to spot the overgrown, pyramidal **House of the Old Woman,** which lies to the east and can be reached by following the path directly to your left as you emerge from the entrance. About 400m south of the house is the **Temple of the Phalli.** Phallic sculptures hang from the cornices of this ruined building and spurt rain runoff from the roof. Experienced guides are available to give more detailed tours of the site (about 45 pesos per person as part of a group).

Nightlife

Uxmal's entire **nightlife** consists of a light-and-sound show celebrating Maya history and culture. The Spanish version (25 pesos) begins at 8pm and ends after the last of the Campeche-bound buses passes. Although it requires language fluency, it is usually more fun than the English version (which is 1 hour later; 35 pesos).

La Ruta Puuc: Practical Information

The Ruta Puuc is a well-marked, *tope*-ridden road that can be driven without purchasing a road map. Simply follow signs to Uman from Mérida, then head toward Muna. From there on, just follow "Ruta Puuc" in Ticul.

Without a car, you'll be faced with relay races. Public transportation in Ticul is not geared toward ruin-happy tourists. While Uxmal and Kabah are fairly accessible if you have luck with *combi* transfers, the lack of traffic on the Sayil-Oxkutzcab road will leave the car-less traveler frustrated and stranded. In general, you should reconcile yourself to changing buses. To reach the ruins around Uxmal, take a Mérida-bound bus from the Ticul bus station (tel. 2 01 62), on Calle 24 behind the main church, and get off at Muna (every 45min., 5 pesos). *Combis* for Muna leave from Parque de la Madre, at Calle 23 between Calles 28 and 30. From Muna, board a southbound bus or *combi* for Uxmal, Kabah, or other sites from the *zócalo* (7 per day, 5 pesos). You can also reach the ruins by catching a *combi* on Calle 30, between Calles 25 and 25A, to Santa Elena (30min., about 4 pesos). Change *combis* at Santa Elena for Uxmal, 16km from Mérida, or at Kabah, south of Campeche. *Combis* are most plentiful in the morning. Considering the amount of time it will take to make connections, you might want to reconsider the rush tour bus from Mérida (see p. 548).

To reach the Grutas de Loltún, snag a *combi* to Oxkutzcab at Parque de la Madre; you'll be let off at the intersection of Calles 23 and 26 (15min., 3 pesos). *Combis* and pick-up truck *colectivos* leave for Loltún from the lot across from Oxkutzcab's market, "20 de Noviembre." Tell the driver to let you off at the *grutas* (10min., 3 pesos), as everyone else is probably headed for the agricultural cooperative 3km farther down the road. Because the road is more crowded with *combis*, it's easier to reach the Grutas than Uxmal or Kabah. Hitchhikers rarely find rides on any of these roads.

Ticul

A bustling provincial town off the Campeche-Mérida highway, **Ticul** (pop. 20,000) is known for its excellent ceramics and cheap, durable shoes. It also enjoys a status as a convenient and inexpensive base from which to explore the Puuc sites of Labná, Kabah, Sayil, Uxmal, and Xlapak as well as the Grutas de Loltún. Aside from obvious differences in size and population, a stay in Ticul is a far cry from one in Mérida. For those with wheels, a number of *cenotes* and colonial buildings await exploration in the nearby towns of **Teabo,** 30km southeast of Ticul, and **Holcá,** 105km to the northeast. **Mayapán,** which lies only 45km to the northeast, was once one of the capitals (along with Chichén Itzá and Uxmal) of an ancient Maya united kingdom. **Maní,** 15km east of Ticul, features a colonial monastery; **Tekax,** 35km to the southeast, a hermitage; and **Tipikal,** an impressive colonial church. Ticul itself is home to an 18th-century church (open 8am-6pm) and pulls out all the stops for the week of its **Tobacco Fair** starting on April 3, 1999.

ORIENTATION AND PRACTICAL INFORMATION Ticul's streets form a grid with the main drag, Calle 23, which passes east-west through the center. Even-numbered streets run north-south. Most commercial activity transpires between the *zócalo* (at Calle 24) and Calle 30, four blocks to the west.

From Muna, five **buses** run daily to Campeche (20 pesos) via Uxmal and Kabah, from the **Terminal** at the *zócalo.* Hourly buses head north to Mérida (7 pesos). The town's pedal-powered **taxis** transport passengers for a couple of pesos. **Combis** leave from Parque de la Madre, Calle 23 between Calles 28 and 30, for Muna (7 per day, 5 pesos); from Calle 30 between Calles 25 and 25A, for Santa Elena, Uxmal, and Kabah (6 pesos); and from Calle 25 between Calles 26 and 28, for Oxkutzkub (every 15min., 5 pesos).

Banco del Atlántico, Calle 23 #195 (tel. 2 09 79), off the *zócalo,* changes U.S. dollars and traveler's checks (open M-F 9am-2pm). **Farmacia San Jose,** Calle 23 #214J (tel. 2 03 93), is between Calles 28 and 30 (open daily 8am-1pm and 4-10pm; no English spoken). **Dr. Estela Sanabria** can be reached at the same number for 24-hour **medical assistance. Police** headquarters (tel. 2 00 10 or 2 02 10) are on Calle 23 at the northeast corner of the *zócalo* (open 24hr.). Ticul's **post office** (tel. 2 00 40) is in the Palacio Municipal on the *zócalo* (open M-F 8am-2:30pm). The **postal code** is 97860. The **telegram office,** Calle 21 #192-C (tel. 2 01 46), is in the blue and white building behind the post office (open M-F 9am-3pm). There is a **LATADEL** across the street from the Hotel Sierra in the *zócalo.* The **phone code** is 997.

ACCOMMODATIONS AND FOOD Ticul has several hotels and good restaurants. One option is **Hotel San Miguel** (tel. 2 03 82), on Calle 28, opposite Parque de la Madre. The bargain prices mean you get what you pay for. (Singles 35 pesos; doubles 60 pesos; triples 90 pesos.) **Hotel Sierra Sosa** (tel. 2 00 08; fax 2 02 82) on Calle 24, on the northwest corner of the *zócalo,* has practical rooms with firm beds, strong fans, and TVs loud enough to drown out the sound of hot-rod mopeds outside. *Agua purificada* is in the lobby. (Singles 61 pesos; doubles 74 pesos; triples 85 pesos; add 20 pesos for A/C.)

After a hot day on the Ruta Puuc, you can refuel and rehydrate yourself in Ticul. **Los Almendros,** Calle 23 #207 (tel. 2 00 21) between Calles 28 and 30, is known world-wide for its *poc-chuc;* the chain of restaurants started here in little ol' Ticul. The restaurant also makes a mean *pollo pibil* (chicken with herbs baked in banana leaves, 24 pesos; open daily 9am-9pm). **Restaurant Los Delfines** (tel. 2 04 01), Calle 27 between Calles 28 and 30, serves shrimp dishes, *chile relleno* (38 pesos), and jars of lemonade under an airy *palapa* (open daily 11am-7pm). The menu is on the wall at **Pizzeria la Gondola** (tel. 2 01 12), but whatever the order, it'll be big, and they deliver (spaghetti 20 pesos, pizza 30 pesos; open daily 8am-1pm and 5:30pm-midnight). Ticul's **market** is off Calle 23 between Calles 28 and 30 (open daily sunrise-sunset).

■ Santa Elena (Saint Elena)

This tiny town of 2500 residents has a *zócalo,* soda shops, and an 18th-century church like most other Yucatec towns, but Santa Elena wins for location. The town lies 8km north of Kabah and 15km east of Uxmal on the Ruta Puuc. It even has its very own archaeological site of **Mul-Chic,** a small collection of platforms and substructures. The main draws for budget travelers are not actually in the town, but they can be found along Rte. 261 where it dips south 1km of St. Elena. The **Sacbe Camping-Bungalows** offers weary travelers pristine campgrounds with new shower and toilet facilities, outdoor grills and tables, and even a mosquito-netted thatched hut where the owners serve meals for 17-20 pesos. (Campsite 20 pesos per person; bungalows with hot water, fans, and private bathroom 110 pesos, with common bathroom 75 pesos.) Only 150m north (toward Uxmal), on the opposite side of the road, lies the **Restaurant El Chac-Mool** (tel. 1 01 91). Large helpings of eggs, tacos, and sandwiches (20-25 pesos) are served under a friendly *palapa* roof (beer 10-12 pesos; open daily 11am-8pm).

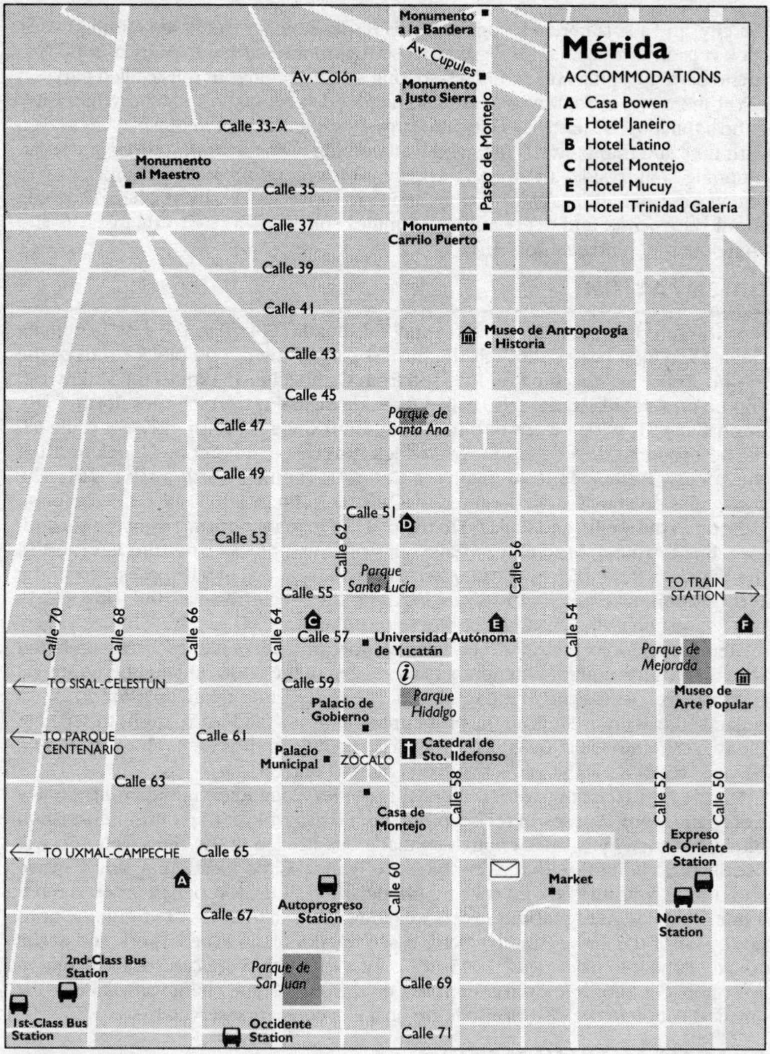

Mérida

Built atop the ruins of the Maya capital of T'hó, modern Mérida is haunted by its pre-Hispanic history—the stones of the city's fortress-like cathedral even bear traces of the Maya temples from which they were stripped. The Maya called this site "Place of the Fifth Point," to indicate that it was the center of the universe, the spot between the four points of north, south, east, and west. As the state's capital and key commercial center, Mérida (pop. 1.5 million) is at least the center of Yucatán. Panama hats, made from the leaves of the *jipijapa* plant and the *guano* palm, come from Becal in the neighboring state of Campeche, hammocks arrive from nearby Tixcocób, and *henequén* is trucked to Mérida from all over Yucatán before being exported as hemp.

Mérida has been a magnet for international immigrants since its Spanish colonial days. Recently *merideños* of Lebanese and Syrian descent have made their home in the city, and a small French community is responsible for the Paseo Montejo, Mérida's version of the Champs-Elysées. Jet-setting tourists arrive in Mérida in bulk to spend days shopping and nights whispering sweet nothings in music-filled parks.

Yet more and more travelers are finding Mérida's reputation as "the White City" to be a thing of the past. This city, the largest on the Yucatán Peninsula, has grayed with time and traffic. Residents, who lead nothing of the *tranquilo* lives of the surrounding countryside, are not fazed. Recent restoration projects are under way to renew some of Mérida's elegant glory. Intimate conversations are still heard swirling about the *zócalo,* and every Sunday, families still enjoy a day to themselves and come out for Mérida *en domingo.*

ORIENTATION

Rte. 180 runs from Cancún (322km) and Valladolid (168km) to the east, becoming **Calle 65,** which passes through the busiest part of town, one block south of the *zócalo.* Those approaching on Rte. 180 from Campeche, 153km to the southwest, end up on **Avenida Itzáes** (also called **Avenida de la Paz**), which runs north-south, or on **Calle 81,** which feeds into the north-south **Calle 70.** Both intersect **Calle 59,** the best route to the center of town, which runs east to a point one block north of the *zócalo.* **Paseo Montejo** begins at **Calle 47,** running north as **Rte. 261.** The *zócalo* fills one city block, bordered by Calle 61 to the north, Calle 62 to the west, Calle 63 to the south, and Calle 60 to the east. To reach the *zócalo* from the **second-class bus terminal,** head east to Calle 62, walk three blocks, and turn left (north); the *zócalo* is three blocks ahead. Alternatively, take a taxi (15-18 pesos). From the **train station,** take a taxi (15-18 pesos), catch the "Seguro Social" bus, or walk six blocks west on Calle 55 and three blocks south on Calle 60.

Mérida's gridded one-way streets have numbers instead of names. Even-numbered streets run north-south, with numbers increasing to the west; odd-numbered streets run east-west, increasing to the south. Addresses in Mérida are given using an "x" to separate the main street from the cross streets and "y" ("and" in Spanish) to separate the two cross streets if the address falls in the middle of the block. Thus "54 #509 x 61 y 63" reads "Calle 54 #509, between Calles 61 and 63."

Mérida's **municipal buses (camiones)** meander along idiosyncratic routes (daily from 5am-11pm, 2 pesos.) Precise information is available at the tourist information office, but the city is small enough so that a bus headed in the right direction will usually drop you off within a few blocks of your desired location. A simple wave won't work with the bus drivers here, though; find a bus stop sign in order to catch a ride. **Taxis** do not roam the streets soliciting riders; it is necessary to phone or to go to one of the *sitios* (stands) along Paseo de Montejo, at the airport, and at the *zócalo.* Expect to pay at least 12-15 pesos for a trip within the *centro.* **Taxi-colectivos** (more commonly known as **combis**), on the other hand, charge only 2 pesos for any destination in the city; **dropoffs** are on a first-come, first-served basis.

PRACTICAL INFORMATION

Transportation

Airport: 7km southwest on Rte. 180. A taxi charges 45 pesos for the trip. Post office, telegrams, long-distance telephone, and car rental are at the airport. **Aerocaribe,** Paseo Montejo 500B x 47 (tel. 28 77 90, at airport 28 67 90). **Aeroméxico,** Paseo Montejo 460 x 35 y 37 (tel. 20 12 99, at airport 25 57 10). **Aviateca** (tel. 25 80 54, at airport 46 12 96), Calle 58 x 45 y 43. Also at Calle 58 x 49 y 51. **Mexicana,** Calle 58 #500 (tel. 24 66 33).

Buses: Most bus lines operate out of the main **second-class** terminal, **Unión de Camioneros,** Calle 69 #544 x 68 y 70, 3 blocks west and 3 blocks south of the *zócalo.* **ADO** (tel. 23 22 87) sends buses to Cancún (6hr., every hr. 10am-midnight, 59 pesos), Chichén Itzá (2hr., every hr. 4am-midnight, 24 pesos), Chiquilá (6hr., 11:30pm, 61 pesos), Playa del Carmen (7hr., 4 and 11am, 11pm, 75 pesos), Tizimín (3½hr., 4pm, 39 pesos), and Valladolid (3hr., every hr. 4am-midnight, 30 pesos). **Autotransportes del Sur (ATS)** goes to Campeche (3hr., every 30min. 4am-7pm, 38 pesos), Escárcega (5½hr., 4 per day 5:45am-10:30pm, 66 pesos), and Uxmal (1½hr., every hr. 5:45am-7pm, 13 pesos). **ATS** provides a special **Ruta Puuc** bus (8am-2:30pm, 48 pesos, admission to sites not included) which visits the archaeological sites of Labná, Kabah, Sayil, Uxmal, Xlapak returning around 2:30pm (see p. 539). **Línea Dorada** serves Chetumal (6hr., 8:30am, 12:30 and 9pm, 80 pesos) and Ticul (every hr., 17 pesos). **Premier** goes to Chichén Itzá (2hr., 10 per day, 32 pesos), Cobá (3hr., 6:30am and 11, and 1pm, 57 pesos), Playa del Carmen (5hr., 10 per day, 77 pesos), Tulum (6hr. 6:30 and 11am, 4:30pm, 69 pesos), and Valladolid (2½hr., 10 per day, 40 pesos). Some buses leave from the **first-class terminal,** called **CAME,** located around the corner on Calle 70 between Calles 69 and 71. **Autobuses de Occidente** runs to almost anywhere on the peninsula as well as to Córdoba (17hr., 4 per day, 343 pesos), Mexico City (19hr., 5 per day, 443 pesos), Palenque 8hr., 8am, 10 and 11:30pm, 149 pesos), Puebla (20hr., 5:45pm, 402 pesos), Veracruz (15hr., 10:45am and 9pm, 301 pesos), and Villahermosa (9hr., 7:30 and 10am, 12:05pm, 171 pesos). **Expreso** goes to Cancún (4hr., 15 per day, 65 pesos). The 9:15pm **Maya de Oro** or **Cristóbal** bus can take you to Campeche (2½hr., 42 pesos), Palenque (6½hr., 127 pesos), Ocosingo (8½hr., 160 pesos), San Cristóbal de las Casas (12½hr., 173 pesos), and Tuxtla Gutiérrez (16hr., 205 pesos).

Taxis: Found at **Palacio Municipal** (tel. 23 09 60), on the northwest corner of the *zócalo.* **Mercado Municipal** (tel. 23 11 35), at Calles 56 and 65, in **Parque de la Maternidad** (tel. 28 53 22) at Teatro Peón Contreras, and dozens of other *sitios.* All are on call 24hr. It's much cheaper to use the *camiones.*

Car Rentals: México Rent-a-Car, Calle 57A Dept. 12 x 58 y 60 or Calle 62 #483A x 57 y 59 (tel. 27 49 16 or 23 36 37). VW Beetles, including insurance and unlimited *kilometraje,* 270 pesos per day. Open M-Sa 8am-12:30pm and 6-8pm, Su 8am-12:30pm.

Tourist and Financial Services

Tourist Information: Central Office (tel. 24 92 90), Calles 60 x 57 y 59, in the Teatro Peón Contreras. Distributes *Yucatán Today,* a free monthly guide listing practical info and local events. Additional office at the airport (tel. 46 13 00). Both open daily 8am-10pm.

Travel Agencies: Yucatán Trails, Calle 62 #482 x 57 y 59 (tel. 28 25 82 or 28 59 13; fax 24 19 28; email denis@finred.com.mx). Canadian owner Denis Lafoy is a genial source of info on Mérida and the Yucatán. Arranges cheap Saturday daytrips to Ruta Puuc sites (100-250 pesos). Open M-F 8am-2pm and 4-7pm, Sa 8am-1pm.

Consulates: U.K., Calle 58 #498 x 53 (tel. 28 61 52; fax 28 39 62). Open M-F 9am-1pm. **U.S.**, Paseo de Montejo 453 (tel. 25 50 11), at Av. Colón. Unless you have an emergency, try to go on Th or F. Bring your passport. Open M-F 7am-1pm.

Currency Exchange: Banamex (tel. 23 06 33 or 28 33 50), in Casa de Montejo on the *zócalo.* 24hr. **ATM.** Open M-F 9am-5pm.

American Express: Paseo de Montejo 494 #106 x 43 y 45 (tel. 42 82 00 or 42 82 10; fax 24 42 57). English spoken. Open M-F 9am-2pm and 4-6pm, Sa 9am-1pm. Money exchange desk closes 1hr. early.

Local Services

Bookstore: Dante (tel. 24 95 22), Calle 60 x 57, in Teatro Peón Contreras. Guidebooks, maps, and magazines in English, French, and Spanish. Open M-Sa 8am-9:30pm, Su 10am-6pm.

Laundromat: La Fe, Calle 61 #518 x 62 y 64 (tel. 24 45 31), near the *zócalo.* 24 pesos per 3kg. Open M-F 8am-7pm, Sa 8am-4pm.

Market: Four square blocks of covered stalls and street vendors extend south of Calle 65 and east of Calle 58. Open dawn to dusk. **Supermarket: San Francisco de Asís,** Calles 65 x 50 y 52, across from the market in a huge gray building. Open daily 7am-9pm.

Emergency and Communications

Police: (tel. 25 25 55 or 25 73 98) on Av. Reforma (Calle 72) x 39 y 41, accessible with the "Reforma" bus. Some English spoken.

Red Cross: Calle 68 #533 x 65 y 67 (tel. 24 98 13 or 28 53 91). 24hr. emergency and ambulance services (tel. 24 77 74). Some English spoken.

Pharmacy: Farmacia Canto, Calle 60 #513 x 63 y 65 (tel. 28 50 27). Open 24hr.

Hospital: Centro Médico de las Américas, Calle 54 #365 (tel. 26 21 11 or 26 26 19), at Calle 33A. 24hr. service, including ambulances. **Clínica de Mérida,** Calle 32 #242 x 27 y 25 (tel. 25 41 00). English spoken in both.

Post Office: (tel. 24 35 90), on Calles 65 x 56 y 56A, 3 blocks from the *zócalo* in the Palacio Federal. Open M-F 9am-6pm. Branches at Calle 58 x 49 y 51, at the airport, and at the main bus station. **MexPost** at Calle 58 x 53 y 55.

Postal Code: 97000.

Internet Access: The Instituto Tecnológico de Hotelería, Calle 57 #492 x 56 y 58 (tel. 24 03 87; email dccmid@minter.cieamer.conacyt.mx) has installed a comfortable and social computer lab offering Netscape and Eudora. Better yet, they're only charging 10 pesos per hr. Open M-F 8am-8pm, Sa 9am-2pm.

Fax: (tel. 28 23 69; fax 24 26 19), in the same building as the main post office. Entrance around the corner on Calle 56A. Telegrams as well. Open M-F 8am-7pm.

Telephones: LADATELs are around the *zócalo.* Phone cards sold at a stand in the Palacio del Gobierno on the *zócalo.* Otherwise, you'll be left at the *casetas'* mercy.

Phone Code: 99.

YUCATÁN PENINSULA

ACCOMMODATIONS

Choosing from among Mérida's budget accommodations is like deciding in which bygone era to stay. What were once elaborate, private 19th- and turn of the century mansions are now often affordable hotels. While they may have lost some of the spotless sheen given by armies of servants, they have not lost any of the character now evident in the small courtyards, columned porticos, or stained glass.

Casa Bowen, Calle 66 #521B x 65 y 67 (tel. 24 07 28 or 28 61 09), halfway between the main bus station and the *zócalo*. Grecian columns line the hallway from the wicker-chaired lobby with a LATADEL to the dining room and portico with TV and full bookshelf. The large rooms upstairs have fans, hot water, and firm beds facing the lush courtyard. A backpacker mecca. Singles 70 pesos; doubles 92 pesos. Rooms with kitchenette and fridge 130 pesos, with A/C 150 pesos; extra person 25 pesos. 1-week reservations recommended in Aug. and Dec.

Hotel Montejo, Calle 57 #507 x 62 y 64 (tel. 28 02 77; fax 24 62 92), 2 blocks north and 1 block east of the *zócalo.* Rooms are guarded by large iron-studded wooden doors. Inside are wood ceiling beams and clean, woodless bathrooms. Singles 117 pesos; doubles 137 pesos, with A/C 167 pesos; 25 pesos per extra person.

Hotel Trinidad Galería, Calle 60 #456 x 51 (tel. 23 24 63; fax 24 23 19). Every nook in the winding halls of this creative colonial mansion is filled with works of art, making for an interesting stay, no matter which room you stay in. Head past the modern art gallery and the fish-filled fountain to find a masterpiece of a pool. Singles 130 pesos; doubles 140 pesos; triples 170 pesos. Rooms with A/C 180 pesos.

Hotel Mucuy, Calle 57 #481 x 56 y 58 (tel. 28 51 93; fax 23 78 01), 2 blocks north and 2 blocks east of the *zócalo.* The expansive courtyard and peaceful, sky-blue rooms mask the hotel's central location. Elegant glass doors enclose the reading room and piano room in the lobby. Laundromat next door and internet access across the street. Singles 100 pesos; doubles 110 pesos; triples 120 pesos.

Hotel Latino, Calle 66 #505 x 63 (tel. 23 50 87). Few amenities aside from the funky wind-driven sign out front. Singles 45 pesos; doubles 55 pesos; triples 70 pesos. Discounts for longer stays.

Hotel Janeiro, Calle 57 #435 x 48 y 50 (tel. 23 36 02 or 23 83 73), a hike from the bus station. For those sick of colonial mansions, this hotel provides typical modern relief. Shallow pool and sun deck outside, practical rooms and dim hallways inside. Parking available. Singles and doubles with fans 100 pesos, with A/C 120 pesos; add 30 pesos per extra person.

FOOD

Mérida's inventive specialties make good use of the fruits and grains that flourish in the Yucatán's hot, humid climate. Try *sopa de lima* (frothy lime soup with chicken and tortilla bits), *pollo pibil* (chicken with herbs baked in banana leaves), *poc-chuc* (pork steak with onions doused in sour orange juice), *papadzules* (chopped hard-boiled eggs wrapped in corn tortillas served with pumpkin sauce), and the most important dish of the most important meal of the day, *huevos motuleños* (refried beans, fried egg, chopped ham, and cheese on a tortilla garnished with tomato sauce, peas, and fried banana). Given all these options, it's not surprising that there are as many places to eat as there are to shop. Quality varies widely from cook to cook, but some of the best meals in Mérida can be found in the hundreds of plastic-chair-and-table joints. The cheapest food in town awaits at the **market,** particularly on the second floor of the restaurant complex on Calle 56 at Calle 67. *Yucateco* dishes go for five to ten pesos. (Most stalls open M-Sa 8am-8pm, Su 8am-5pm.)

Restaurante Amaro, Calle 59 #507 x 60 y 62 (tel. 28 24 51). Affordable, classy fare makes this place worth coming back to again and again. Excellent meals are healthy and delicious, offering lean meat and vegetarian options. At night, the well-lit courtyard sets the mood. Refreshing *horchata* (rice milk and almond shake) 10 pesos. Avocado and cheese sandwich 18 pesos. Huge, invigorating fruit salads 12-20 pesos. Meat entrees 35-40 pesos. Open M-Sa 9am-11pm.

Restaurante y Cafe Express (tel. 28 16 91), Calle 60 x 59 y 61, across the street from Parque Hidalgo. Small tables face the busy street or the large canvases along the walls at this modern cafe. Although a tad touristy, the service makes the cafe live up to its ambitious name. Breakfast and sandwiches 15-20 pesos, main entrees 35-45 pesos. Open daily 7am-11pm.

El Rincón (tel. 24 90 22), Calle 60 x 59 y 61 situated right in Parque Hidalgo. The restaurant for the Hotel Caribe, it has tables both in the tiny, quiet interior and the bustling park. Serves fantastic *sopa de lima* (16 pesos). Try *arroz con plátanos* (9 pesos) or *pollo pibil* (35 pesos). Open daily 7am-11pm.

Los Almendros and **Los Gran Almendros,** Calle 50 #493 x 57 y 59 (tel. 28 54 59) on Parquet Mejorada, and at Calle 57 #468 x 50 y 52 (tel. 23 81 35). The world-famous food has made this a tourist-oriented restaurant, but the picture menu will be the first hint that you can't argue with the *poc-chuc* (48 pesos) or *pollo pibil* (25 pesos). Los Almendros is open daily 10:30am-11pm with music trio 2-5pm and 7:30-11pm. Less touristy Gran Almendros is open daily noon-6pm.

El Louvre, Calle 62 #499-D, on the northwest corner of the *zócalo.* Any disappointment with the lack of art will vanish once you bite into the Super Club or Super Louvre sandwiches (16-18 pesos). Popular with locals and tourists alike due to the super location and super hours. Open daily 24hr.

El Tucho, Calle 60 #482 x 55 y 57 (tel. 24 23 23). A loud and popular restaurant, El Tucho draws families, predominantly male crowds, or predominantly female crowds, depending on the afternoon cabaret act. While performers entertain you, troupes of waiters ferry trays of free *botanas* (hors d'œuvres) between customers. As long as you keep on drinkin', the food keeps on comin'. Real meals 35 pesos. Open daily 11:30am-9:30pm.

SIGHTS

In a peninsula of impressive *zócalos,* Mérida's stands alone as a living testament to the fascinating history of the Yucatán. Even though it is surrounded on all sides by historic palaces and a towering cathedral, the *zócalo* is renowned as a social center. The *zócalo* is busiest on Sundays, when street vendors cram in dozens of stalls, Yucatec folk dancers perform in front of the Palacio Municipal, and crowds of people come from all over to see the crowds already there.

Just over 400 years old, the **Catedral de Saint Idelfonso** has stood watch over Mérida's often convoluted history since 1598, making it the **oldest cathedral in North America.** *(Open daily 6am-6pm.)* The sturdy stone blocks from which the cathedral was built were stolen from the Maya temples of T'hó. Built in the austere Herrericano style, the cathedral features rose-colored arched domes and an immense 20m wooden Christ and cross, the **second-largest crucifix in the world.** On the northern edge of the *zócalo* stands the **Palacio de Gobierno.** *(Open daily 8am-10pm.)* Built from 1883 to 1892, it fuses two architectural styles—Tuscan (main floor) and Dorian (upper floor). Inside, gigantic murals narrate the strife-filled history of the Yucatán peninsula. The stairway painting illustrates the Maya belief that their ancestors were made from maize. An image from the *Popol Vuh,* an account of Maya creation written in 16th-century Guatemala, dominates the next layout. Concerts and classes in *jarana,* the Yucatecan colonial dance, take place under the sheltering balcony of the **Palacio Municipal,** across the *zócalo* from the cathedral. *(Open M-Sa 8am-8pm.)* A jail until the 1700s, the building was rebuilt in 1735 with two stories of arches. The Yucatán declared its independence from Spain and joined with Mexico here.

On the southern side of the *zócalo,* the **Casa de Montejo,** the oldest colonial structure in Mérida, was constructed in 1549 as the residence of city founder Francisco de Montejo. *(Open M-F 9am-5pm.)* Built with stones from the Maya temple T'hó, the carved facade is a boastful depiction of Spanish conquest. The carving follows the Toltec tradition of representing warriors standing on their conquests' heads.

Mérida's most impressive museum, the **Museo de Antropología e Historia** (tel. 23 05 57), is housed in a magnificent Italian Renaissance-style building called the Palacio Canton on the corner of Paseo Montejo and Calle 43. *(Museum and shop open Tu-Sa 8am-8pm, Su 8am-2pm. Admission 16 pesos, free Sundays.)* Most notable of the collections inside are the ancient Maya head-flattening devices for infants and the enamel teeth inserts of jade and silver. The shop downstairs sells comprehensive English-language guidebooks cheaper than they're sold at the ruins themselves.

Celebrating the indigenous crafts and artisans of the Yucatán, **Museo de Arte Popular** is located six blocks east of the *zócalo* on Calle 59 x 48 y 50, behind the Convento de la Mejorada. *(Open Tu-Sa 9am-8pm, Su 8am-2pm; free.)* The small museum shares the building with a school of design, and there is a student lounge where you can rest after the long walk. The displays feature exhibits on modern-day Maya customs and handicrafts.

On the corner of Calle 59 and Av. Itzáes (Calle 86) lies the **Centenary Park and Zoo.** *(Park open Tu-Su 6am-6pm. Zoo open Tu-Su 8am-5pm. Both free.)* Snag a bus at Calle 65 x 56 (2 pesos) and ask to be let off at "el Centenario," a favorite destination for local schools. The zoo is at the end of the park and is home to lions, tigers, preening peacocks, flamingos, antelope, Aztec dogs, and jaguars. A miniature train makes regular circuits of the park, but don't expect a quiet ride or a glimpse of many of the dozing creatures. The **Museo de Historia Natural,** with its main entrance on Calle 59 x 84, one block east of Itzáes, also has a back entrance accessible from the park. *(Open Tu-Su 9am-4pm. Admission 10 pesos; free Sundays.)* Housed in a 19th-century hacienda, this small but ambitious collection is concerned with the history of life from the origin of the universe through the emergence of species.

Aging French-style mansions and local and international boutiques line the **Paseo Montejo;** promenades along the Paseo's broad pink sidewalks culminate in the **Monumento a la Patria.** In faux-Maya style, the stone monument, built in 1956, depicts major figures of Mexican history. For a tantalizing detour from the Paseo, veer left (southwest) onto **Av. Colón,** a street flanked by closely grouped historic mansions in varying stages of decay.

Mérida takes special pride in the **Teatro Peón Contreras,** on the corner of Calles 60 and 57. The beautiful Italian Renaissance-style building is notable for its marble Rococo interior and for its history—starting in 1624, it served as a university for nearly two centuries. The **Universidad Autónoma de Yucatán,** on Calle 57 x 60 y 62, is a Hispano-Moorish complex built in 1938. *(Galería and video room open M-F 9am-*

1pm and 4-8pm, Sa 4-9pm, Su 10am-2pm; free.) The ground floor contains a gallery exhibiting works by local artists and a screening room for a variety of films.

The many churches, statues, and pocket-sized parks scattered throughout Mérida's *centro* also invite exploration. Among the most noteworthy are the Franciscan **Convento de la Mejorada,** on Calle 59 x 48 y 50; the old **Arco** behind the park; the **Iglesia Santiago,** on Calles 59 x 72, one of the oldest churches in Mexico; and the **Iglesia de San Juan de Dios,** located on Calle 64 x 67 y 71, marking the *centro*'s southern limit.

SHOPPING

The fact that Mérida offers the best shopping in the Yucatán is both a boon and a curse. Nowhere is there such a variety of goods, and nowhere are there such nagging vendors and such high-pressure salespeople as in Mérida. If all those pesos you saved by cramming two into a hammock at night, riding dirty second-class buses, and eating *tortas* and *comidas corridas* are starting to weigh you down, then this is the place to find relief. The main **mercado** occupies the block southwest of the Palacio Federal, spreading outward from the corner of Calles 65 and 58. Behind the *palacio,* shops, awnings, and tin-roofed shacks ramble for many blocks both east and west. The only border is the busy Calle 65 to the north, but even there, stands spill onto the other side of the street and around the small square across from the Palacio Federal.

The pricier second-floor **artisans' market,** part of a modern building behind and to the right of the Palacio Federal, sells mainly regional clothing: white *huipiles* with colorful embroidery skirting the neckline and hem go for 90-110 pesos, *rebozos* (woven shawls) cost around 180 pesos, and *guayaberas* (Yucatec men's short-sleeve shirts with distinctive vertical columns of double stitching) are between 100 and 120 pesos. Bargaining is expected, but those who get carried away are considered rude. Cheaper goods such as *huaraches* (hand-made leather sandals) are sold on the first floor of the market. Be sure to give them a try for good measure, as the sandals are sometimes hastily made. Although jewelry stores line the streets, the best prices are at the smaller *prestas* on the streets, in the market, or at the *zócalo* every Sunday.

YUCATÁN PENINSULA

ENTERTAINMENT

Mérida's municipal government provides a never-ending series of free music and dance events organized by day. **Mondays** bring outdoor concerts with traditional Yucatec dancing and dress (9pm at Palacio Municipal). **Tuesdays** offer either a 1940s big-band concert (9pm at Santiago Park, Calles 59 x 72) or the University's wonderful **Ballet Folklórico** (9pm at Teatro Peón Contreras, Calles 60 x 57; 25 pesos). **Wednesdays** take you through a musical journey from the 18th century to the present (8pm at Ermita Park, Calles 66 x 77). **Thursdays** host **"The Serenade,"** the most traditional event in Mérida, with music, poetry, and folklore (9pm at Calles 60 x 55). **Sundays** bring **Mérida en Domingo,** when the *zócalo* and surrounding streets are crowded with vendors, strollers, food stalls, and live music (9am-8pm). Movie buffs can flock to **Cinema Fantasio,** at Parque Hidalgo, or **Plaza Internacional,** on Calle 58 x 57 y 59—both offer American movies with Spanish subtitles for only 14 pesos (evening showings daily around 7 and 9:30pm).

When in Mérida, do as *merideños* do—keep your eyes peeled for announcements of upcoming events glued to walls all over town. The **Teatro Peón Contreras** (tel. 23 73 54) hosts special events and frequent concerts. Just around the corner on the Parque de la Modernidad, an excellent acoustic guitar trio plays mellow tunes at the **Café Peón Contreras.** Avoid the cafe's pricey food—enjoy the music for free from one of the park benches (every night, 8pm-midnight). **Parque Hidalgo** has free **marimba concerts** each night; locals and tourists grab margaritas and some **botanas** (hors d'œuvres) at one of the many outdoor cafes and enjoy the cool evening breeze.

For a less high-brow evening, settle in for a **beer.** Mérida has many good local beers, such as the distinctive **Montejo León** and the darker **Negra Leon,** both tough to find in other parts of the country. At local establishments, buy a few and you'll get free *botanas.* Enjoy comedians and dance at **Pancho's** (tel. 23 09 42), Calle 59 x 60 y 62 (open M-Sa 9pm-2am), or **El Tucho** (see p. 551). Another option is **Tulipanes,** Calle 42 #462A x 45 y 47; get ready for non-stop music, *yucateco* dance, and a chilling re-enactment of a Maya sacrifice (62 pesos). Air-conditioned, panchromatic discos are far from the center; a taxi ride will cost 40 pesos. **Kalia,** Calle 22 #282 by Calle 37 (tel. 44 42 35), is where the young and sophisticated dance (open W-Sa 10pm-3am).

■ Near Mérida: Dzibilchaltún

Saying the name is half the fun. Situated 20km north of Mérida en route to the Gulf coast, Dzibilchaltún (dzib-ill-shahl-TOON; Place Where There Is Writing on Flat Stones) sprawls over 60 sq. km of jungle brush. The site flourished as a ceremonial and administrative center from approximately 300 BC until the Conquest. While its influence on Maya culture is of great interest to archaeologists and historians, the excavated site now open to tourists is neither as impressive nor as accessible as the other ruins near Mérida.

While the site may not offer any majestic pyramids, it is home to a magnificent **museum.** *(Site open daily 8am-5pm. Museum open daily 8am-4pm. Admission 30 pesos, free Sunday and for children under 13. Parking 5 pesos. Wheelchair-accessible.)* The pathway to the museum, to the left of the entrance just beyond the cactus garden, is lined with an all-star gallery of Maya stelae. Inside, the precious air-conditioning invites lengthy stays in front of the attractive and informative displays. All lingering questions about the Maya calendar and pantheon will be answered in the first main room, devoted to Maya history and artifacts; the second describes the arrival of the Spanish and the turbulent colonial era, complete with a glass floor that reveals an under-the-sea display.

From the museum, follow the path to **Sacbe No. 1,** the central axis of the site, and turn left. Farther along this road, Dzibilchaltún's showpiece, the fully restored **Temple of the Seven Dolls,** possesses a rare harmony of proportion and style. The seven clay "dolls" discovered here are now in the museum (they are the small, mangled figures that look like some toddler really went at them). The temple also furnishes further proof of the craftsmanship of the Maya. Shortly after sunrise, a huge shadow mask of the rain god Chac is said to appear as the sun's rays pierce the temple (too bad the site opens at 8am). The temple is so carefully aligned that it can be used to verify the winter and summer solstices. At 5:30pm each summer solstice, the sun threads the tiny space between the doorjambs on the north side; at 7:30am each winter solstice, the phenomenon is repeated on the south side.

The other end of Sacbe No. 1 leads to a quadrangle containing a symbol of hundreds of years of history: a Maya temple converted into a chapel. Just beyond the eastern edge of the quadrangle is the **Cenote Xlacah,** reminiscent of Quintana Roo's oval, saltwater *lagunas.* Xlacah served as a sacrificial well similar to those at Chichén Itzá and as a source of water. Divers have recovered ceremonial artifacts and human bones from the depths of the 44m-deep *cenote.* While the *cenote* is not the most striking of its sort, the water invites a non-sacrificial dip among the water lilies and fish. A path to the south leads past a handful of smaller structures to the site's exit.

Getting There: Getting to the ruins is a breeze, and the return trip should pose *poco problemas.* Conkal-bound *combis* leave the Parque de San Juan in Mérida as soon as they fill up (about every 20min., 3 pesos). The *combi* will drop you off at the access road to the ruins, a five-minute walk from the entrance. To get back, you'll need to walk back to the Conkal road and wait a short while for one of the many *combis* that run between Mérida and the string of villages past Conkal. Some travelers hitch the 5km to the highway. **Autoprogreso buses** and Mérida-bound *combis* abound on Rte. 261, passing by in both directions every 15 minutes.

■ Near Mérida: Celestún

The combination of beach, breeze, and biosphere reserve has recently brought some well-deserved attention to Celestún, but it will be years before the *tranquilo* atmosphere of this small beach town alters. Many people come for the warm Gulf waters and refreshing breeze, but the main draw is the **Río Celestún Biosphere Reserve,** home to 230 species of bird, including pelicans, cormorants, the occasional stork, and hot pink flamingos. Mexican tourists and biologists flock here in July and August; call your hotel ahead to make sure there's room.

Calle 11 in Celestún, on the western shore of the Yucatán, runs into Rte. 281 about 155 kilometers from Mérida. Calle 11 passes the *zócalo,* passes **Calle 12** one block later, and hits the **shore** one block after that (as do all odd-numbered streets). Odd numbers increase to the south, while even numbers decrease moving away from the sand and run parallel to the waves. The **zócalo** is bounded by Calles 11, 13, 10, and 8.

Autobuses de Occidente sends **buses** from a small booth at the corner of Calles 8 and 11, at the *zócalo,* to Mérida (30min.-2hr., 20 per day 5am-8:30pm, first-class 22 pesos, second-class 12 pesos). The **police** (tel. 6 20 15) stand guard at the Calle 13 side of the *zócalo.* **Farmacia Don San Luis,** Calle 10 #108 (tel. 6 20 02), between Calles 13 and 15, is open daily from 8am to 11pm. The **health center** (tel. 6 20 46) is on Calle 5 between Calles 8 and 10 (open daily 8am-8pm). The **post office** is on Calle 11 at the *zócalo* and shares a building with the **telegram** service (both open M-F 9am-2pm). Long-distance **phone** calls can be made from **Hotel Gutiérrez,** but be prepared for staggering rates. The **phone code** is 991.

Budget accommodations in Celestún are few but at least not far between. All are on Calle 12. At the **Hotel San Julio,** Calle 12 #93A (tel. 6 20 62), fairly cheap means fairly adequate rooms with fans and hot water (singles 75 pesos; doubles 95 pesos; triples 100 pesos). **Hotel María del Carmen,** Calle 12 #11 (tel. 6 20 51), has rooms with sea views, balconies, billowing curtains, and immaculate bathrooms (singles 125 pesos; doubles 160 pesos; triples 190 pesos; 10% student discount). **Hotel Gutiérrez,** Calle 12 #127 (tel. 6 20 41 or 6 20 42), between Calles 13 and 15, offers bulk lodging; fit as many as you like in the dull blue rooms (150 pesos; ask for a room with a view). Restaurants line Calle 12, both on and off the beach, and a few *loncherías* cluster in the *zócalo.* At **Restaurant La Playita,** Calle 12 #99 (tel. 6 20 52), between Calles 9 and 11, pack away a huge steaming plate of *jaiba frita* (fried blue crab) with rice and tortillas for just 28 pesos (open daily 9am-10pm). Don't expect to see any pelicans (or much else) from the view at **Pelicano's,** Calle 12 #90 between Calles 9 and 11, but you will get to enjoy gulpfuls of good, cheap seafood. Twenty pesos will get you fried fish, and for 50 pesos, a heaping plate of crab claws will appear. At **Restaurant Celestún,** Calle 12 #101 (tel. 6 20 32), you can enjoy fantastic fish *al mojo de ajo* (with garlic butter; 42 pesos) amid larger-and pinker-than-life painted flamingos (open daily 10am-10pm).

While the larger flocks of **flamingos** hang out at Río Lagartos, you can nevertheless spot some clusters along the breathtaking coastline by taking one of two tours offered. The first heads north to **Isla de Pájaros** (Island of Birds), an avian playground where the name says it all. A stop along the way at a freshwater spring provides welcome relief. The second tour heads south through petrified forests and a river tunnel of intertwined tree branches and vines before winding through the abandoned fishing village of **Real de Salinas.** Both tours can be arranged with *lancheros* at the bridge right before the entrance to the town (one tour 1½-2hr., 300 pesos). Depending on the tide, a tour will accommodate five to eight people. If you want to combine both tours or explore other areas, fishermen will give tours (3½hr., 400 to 450 pesos). Hang out on the beach by the *lanchas* to find a ride and a group to go with, as most guides won't leave with fewer than five people.

Mérida to Chichén Itzá

The route from Mérida to Chichén Itzá harbors small villages that are quintessential Yucatán. Churches are oversized and blackened by time, unexcavated ruins abound, *benequén* is still harvested, and for many inhabitants, Spanish is a second language.

As Rte. 180 heads east from Mérida to Chichén Itzá, it passes the five private *benequén* haciendas of San Pedro, Teya, Ticopó, San Bernardino, and Holactún. Next come the villages of **Tahmek** and **Hoctún** (47km from Mérida). **Izamal** (see p. 558) is only 24km northeast of Hoctún, but buses don't make the detour—catch a direct bus from Mérida (see p. 548). The ancient *cenote* of **Ixcolasc** is only 1km away.

Back on Rte. 180, you will find **Kantunil** (68km from Mérida). **Xocchel** (The Place Where the Chels Read) is an attractive town along Rte. 180 before Kantunil. Next is **Holcá,** and finally, **Libre Unión,** with a sizeable *cenote.* During squabbles between the territories of Yucatán and Quintana Roo, Libre Unión found itself smack on the border. The town voted to stick together and become part of the state of Yucatán—thus earning its name, Free Union.

Some travelers hitch or hop buses from one Maya village to another along the busy road between Mérida and Chichén Itzá. Those who choose to hitch should bring water—the waits can be long, and shade is sparse. Second-class bus drivers stop anywhere if requested, but a new fare is charged for each trip, and slow and irregular bus service limits the number of places you can visit in one day. If dusk arrives, be sure to take the next bus to Pisté or Mérida—you don't want to get stranded. If no buses are in sight, there are *palapas* for sleeping in Xocchel and most other towns; ask in the town store in the *zócalo.* Tourists planning to drive a car through the mesmerizing countryside will have an easier time and just as much of a chance to see small, rural villages, with their characteristic thatched huts, dirt roads, and Coca-Cola stands. The real destination, however, is always the incomparable **Chichén Itzá** (see p. 559).

Progreso

Progreso (pop. 40,000) holds the distinction of being the only non-sleepy fishing town on the Yucatán coast. Although the paved streets don't run far in any direction before turning into sand, that hasn't kept the residents from making a small fortune hauling in shrimp, red snapper, octopus, and tuna from the wind-swept waves. A different type of hauling brings in cars and other large goods while *benequén* (hemp) is exported from Progreso's one long, oversized pier. On the weekends, Progreso's proximity to the capital makes it a popular retreat for *merideños,* many of whom make the 33km jaunt northward to enjoy the big, clean, sandy beaches of the Gulf coast, and to help keep the town wide awake at night. During the week, Progreso does reach a measure of tranquility and is remarkably tourist-free.

ORIENTATION AND PRACTICAL INFORMATION Calle 19, Progreso's **Malecón** (coastal avenue), runs east-west along the beach. Odd-numbered roads run parallel to Malecón, increasing to the south. North-south streets have even numbers and increase to the west. Progreso's *zócalo* is bounded by Calles 78, 80, 31, and 33. To reach the *zócalo* from the **bus station** (tel. 5 30 24), on Calle 29 between Calles 80 and 82; head east on Calle 29 to the end of the block, turn right, and walk two blocks on Calle 80. To reach the beach, follow Calle 80 in the opposite direction.

Autoprogreso buses, Calle 62 between Calle 65 and 67, run to Mérida's Autoprogreso station (40min., every 10min. 5am-9:45pm, 7 pesos assumed). *Combis* make a slightly quicker trip for the same price and leave from Calle 31 on the *zócalo.* The often-bored but helpful staff of the **tourist office,** Calle 80 #176 (tel. 5 01 04), between Calles 37 and 39, can provide you with a tourist booklet and map (open M-F 9am-2pm and 4-7pm, Sa 9am-noon; some English spoken). **Banamex,** Calle 80 #126 (tel. 5 08 31), stands between Calles 27 and 29 (open M-F 9am-5pm with 24hr. **ATM**).

Lavamática Progreso, Calle 74 #150A (tel. 5 05 86), between Calles 29 and 31, provides next-day service (5 pesos per kg; open M-Sa 8am-1:30pm and 4:30-7:30pm). The **Supermarket San Francisco de Asís** is at Calle 80 #144 between Calles 29 and 31 (open daily 7am-9pm). The **police station** (tel. 5 00 26) is in the Palacio Municipal on the *zócalo* at Calle 80, between Calles 31 and 33 (open 24hr.). **Farmacia YZA** (tel. 5 06 84) is on Calle 78 at Calle 29 #143 (open 24hr.). Emergency medical service is provided by the **Centro Médico Americano** (tel. 5 01 18), at Calles 33 and 82 (open 24hr.; some English spoken). The **post office** is at Calle 31 #150 (tel. 5 05 65), between Calles 78 and 76 just off the *zócalo* (open M-F 7am-7pm). The **postal code** is 97320. **Long-distance phone calls** can be made from any one of the many TelMex *casetas* found throughout town. The **phone code** is 993.

ACCOMMODATIONS AND FOOD The frequently fluctuating number of vacationing urbanites from the south has made finding budget accommodations as hit or miss as the catch of the day. It's hard to go wrong at the **Hotel Miramar,** Calle 27 #124 (tel. 5 05 52), between Calles 72 and 74. The hotel offers spacious, classy rooms with neat bath and skylight or cool, fiberglass Apollo spacecraft rooms with capsule-sized bathrooms. Either way, the friendly owner will be happy to bring up some ice-cold *agua purificada* in a pitcher. (Moonshot singles 80 pesos, with TV 100 pesos; doubles 120 pesos, with TV 140 pesos; triples 150 pesos; long-term stays cheaper.) The **Hotel Progreso,** in the center of town, Calle 78 #142 (tel. 5 00 39), near Calle 29, has designer rooms and bathrooms with TVs and a breeze (singles 110 pesos; doubles 120 pesos; with A/C add 30 pesos; extra person 35 pesos). The **Hotel Real del Mar** (tel. 5 07 98), Calle 19 at Av. Malecón #144, is more touristy but right on the beach. Simple but ample rooms come with firm beds, fans, and hammock space. (Singles 100 pesos; doubles 120 pesos; 25 pesos per extra person.)

One fish. Two fish. Red fish. Blue fish. It's all about fish. And it's pretty darn cheap, too. Try the beach end of Calle 80. Fish with a view? Try Avenida Malecón, the main drag along the coast. Unfortunately, some restaurants only open during the summer. At **Carabela** (tel. 5 33 07), just east of Calle 72 on Av. Malecón, the handwriting is on the wall; you can leave some too if you finish dishes like the Super Taco Carabela (21 pesos) or the *filete empanizado* (28 pesos; open daily 7am-1am, dancing on weekends). Watch your fish come in from the dock at **Restaurant Los Cocos,** on Malecón between Calles 76 and 78, where you can enjoy a fish served whole and practically still flopping around, for just 18 pesos (open daily 7am-7pm). At **El Cordobés,** Calle 80 #150 (tel. 5 26 21), right on the *zócalo,* you can treat yourself to *pescado en tikinxic,* a slow-cooked fish specialty with chiles (35 pesos). Most fish entrees go for 30-35 pesos. (Open daily 6:30am-midnight.)

SIGHTS Progreso's kilometers of clean beach and shallow water attract hordes in August but remain calm in other months. For a more placid spot, head for the beach at **Chelém,** 8km west of town, or for the wind-sheltered beach at **Yaculpatén,** just before Chelém. *Combis* leave for Chelém every 30 minutes from the parking lot outside Supermarket San Francisco on Calle 80 (5 pesos). If he's not too busy, the custodian of **El Faro** (the lighthouse), at Calle 80 near Calle 25, might let you climb the 120 bright red steps to the top. Step out on the balcony, where you can view the ocean and the kilometers of marshy river that give the city its distinctive briny scent. The 2km *muelle* (pier) clings tenuously to the sandy beach; in the early morning it's a great spot from which to reel in fish.

If all that sunbathing and fishing has you ready for some adventure, head out to the largely unexplored Maya site of **Xtambo,** at the end of a 2km access road that intersects with the road to Telchac Puerto 25km east of Progreso. *(Site open daily 9am-4pm; free.)* The small area that has just been restored includes two pyramids—

one of which supports two large, unidentified stucco masks and offers a panoramic view of the coast—and several smaller structures. There is also the peculiar sight of a functional church built into the side of a pyramid. Many small paths branch out from the site to unexcavated ruins and small villages; the caretaker may be coaxed into acting as a guide. *Combis* headed to Telchac Puerto from Progreso leave the Supermarket San Francisco about every 30 minutes and will drop you off at the access road (15 pesos).

Izamal

This town (pop. 13,500) is called by several names, which reflects why a visit here is like a physical summary of the past millennia of Yucatán's history. Izamal, or "City of the Hills" in Mayan, is referred to today as the *Ciudad Amarilla* (the Yellow City) because almost all of its buildings are painted in colonial yellow with white trim. Yet another name, the City of the Three Cultures, begins to fully describe what there is to be seen and learned in Izamal. Word is spreading about this place as enthusiastic residents show off their historical treasure of a town, but the growing number of tour groups can only stay for a few hours. The midday and evening quiet is broken only by the occasional school-produced *ballet folklórico* and the clattering of the horse-drawn carriages on the broad streets.

ORIENTATION AND PRACTICAL INFORMATION The road from Hoctún, 24km to the southwest, turns into Calle 31, which runs east-west as do all odd-numbered streets, increasing to the south. This street runs past the **Convent** (on the right going east), passing north-south streets with increasing even numbers. Calles 28, 31, 32, and 33 frame the town's *zócalo,* municipal palace, and market. The **bus station** is halfway between Calles 31 and 33 on Calle 32, right behind the municipal palace. **ADO** buses (tel. 4 01 07) leave from the terminal for Cancún (5½hr., 7 per day 4:30am-5pm, 46 pesos), Mérida (1½hr., 7 per day 1:30am-8pm, 11 pesos), and Valladolid (2½hr., 7 per day, 17 pesos). Next door, the **Autobuses de Centro del Estado** sends a bus to Cancún (5½hr., every 2hr., 46 pesos), Mérida (1½hr., every 30min., 11 pesos), and Valladolid (2½hr., every 2hr., 17 pesos).

The singularly staffed **tourist office** (tel. 4 00 32), on the corner of Calles 32 and 33, will go out of its way to provide maps, pamphlets, and anything and everything there is to know about the Convent across the street (office open M-Sa 9am-1pm). **Banterers** is on Calle 31 between Calles 26 and 28 (open M-F 9am-5pm). The **police** are directly across from the bus station in the Palacio Municipal (open 24hr.). The **mercado** on the corner of Calles 30 and 33 offers all sorts of food; it also has decent enough **public restrooms.** Knock on the door of the **24hr. Farmacia Itzalam** (tel. 4 00 32), on the corner of Calles 31 and 32, if it looks closed. The **IMSS** (tel. 4 00 57) provides 24-hour medical attention, two blocks south and three blocks east of the *zócalo* on the corner of Calles 37 and 24. The small **post office** is on Calle 31 between Calles 30 and 32 (open M-F 9am-1:30pm); **telegram and fax** services are available on the corner of Calles 31 and 32. **LADATELs** can be found outside the bus station and the post office. The **phone code** is 995.

ACCOMMODATIONS AND FOOD Izamal bucks the overall lodging price-to-location trend; the cheapest places to stay are on the *zócalo,* while the nicer and more expensive hotels are farther away. The **Hotel Canto,** on Calle 31 between Calles 30 and 32, has old but large blue rooms and a pleasant courtyard, but the price is great (singles 50 pesos; doubles 60 pesos; fit 4-5 to a room at no extra charge). The **Hotel Kabul** next door nestles right up to the Kabul pyramid and has fans and hammock hooks but no hot water; the smaller rooms haven't aged as well (singles 50 pesos; doubles 60 pesos; fit as many as you like).

Don't plan on too much late-night wining and dining in the Yellow City, as most restaurants close in the early evening, but at least a plentiful meal in Izamal won't cost much. The **Restaurant Kinich Kakmó,** Calle 27 #299 (tel. 27 31 62) between Calles 28 and 30, serves up regional dishes under a plant-ensconced *palapa* for 25-35 pesos and is an excellent conclusion to an exhaustive search of the pyramid 50m away (open daily 11:30am-6pm). The **Restaurant Portales,** on the corner of Calles 30 and 31A next door to the market, has the best view of the *zócalo* but the cheap, filling meals and friendly service are more likely to hold your attention (full breakfasts, lunches 13-20 pesos; open Th-Tu 7am-8:30pm).

SIGHTS Upon entering the *zócalo,* the **Convent of Saint Anthony de Padua** seems to be the most dominating feature of Izamal. This ecclesiastical complex, dedicated to San Antonio, is actually made up of three parts: the **church,** built in 1554; the **convent,** built in 1561; and the immense **atrium,** built in 1618 with 75 arches and **second in size only to the Vatican.** When entering the church through the atrium, several original 16th-century frescoes can be seen; the one dedicated to Santa Barbara is today the most colorful and complete. Inside the Baroque-style church is an ornate altar with a doorway at the top. Izamal's famed statue of the Immaculate Conception is wheeled out for every Mass. To see the statue and some interesting rooms, head out the left side doors of the church; a flight of stairs to the right will bring you to a room exhibiting pictures and mementos of the Pope's August 1993 visit to Izamal, including the chair he used in the ceremony to officially crown the statue. There is also a showcase of pre-Hispanic artifacts and curious knobs on the wall, used when this room was Izamal's electrical plant. Continue up the stairs to arrive at Mexico's oldest *camarin,* where the statue of the Immaculate Conception rests when not in use. Fray Diego de Landa commissioned this statue in 1558 in Guatemala. There were originally two statues, one of which was sent to Mérida and the other to Izamal. They were called *Las Dos Hermanas,* but in 1829 Izamal's statue was burned in a fire, so Mérida's copy was brought here. It is said, though, that Izamal's original was saved and taken to the nearby pyramid of Kinish Kakmó and every December 8th, at the climax of the town's week-long fiesta, the two switch places in *el paso de las Dos Hermanas.* Dozens of other legends surround Izamal, more of which can be learned in Izamal's small **museum,** located on the northeast corner of the convent and still inhabited by four monks (note the original sundial above the courtyard). *(Open M-F 9am-3pm; free.)* The guides at the foot of the convent will also be more than happy to regale you with stories. The museum details Izamal's three phases of history and has a model of the ancient Maya city as it stood in 500 BC.

It is not until after ascending the **pyramid of Kinich Kakmó** that visitors can appreciate what truly is Izamal's most dominating structure. This massive pyramid, measuring 200m by 180m, is the fifth-tallest and ranks third in volume of all of Yucatán's pyramids, yet even it was outclassed by the **Popolchac,** the largest pyramid in ancient Izamal, whose remains lie under the convent. Kinich Kakmó (Temple of the Fire Macaw) was built during the Early Classic period from 400 to 600 and is only one of the remaining pyramids that dot Izamal, along with **Kabul, Itzamaltul,** and **Habuc.** Kinich Kakmó is the most fully restored, though, and offers an awe-inspiring view of Izamal's churches and pyramids as well as the flat Yucatec countryside.

Chichén Itzá

The faultless architecture and sheer size of the structures of this former Maya capital allow Chichén Itzá (chee-CHEN eet-SAH) to serve as a window to the past on a grand scale. Unrivaled as the Yucatán's premier cultural attraction, the site attracts thousands of visitors hoping to unveil the mysteries of this ancient city. Complete with a peculiar mix of Maya and Toltec styles of architecture, the structures here inspire endless questions while evoking awed responses to the skill and creativity apparent in the construction.

Unfortunately, for two hours each day, Chichén becomes a writhing mass of foreign invaders; tour buses bombard the site, and camera-toting travelers overrun the crumbling barricades. Parroting the ideas of tour-guide-impersonating vendors, they often videotape every last *chacmool* while chasing errant sunhats across the central plaza. For the other 22 hours, these magnificent ruins are peaceful.

Despite the hype, the camera crews, and the trash cans, Chichén rightly deserves its status as one of Mexico's most powerful tourist magnets. **El Castillo** is breathtaking from the bottom and harrowing from the top; the ballcourt features elaborate carvings and wholly intact rings left from original games; the sacrificial *cenote* has yielded enough bones and artifacts to reconstruct the fates of hundreds of human victims; and the observatory attests to a level of astronomical understanding far beyond that of Old World contemporaries. During the solstices, busloads of phenomenon-aholics arrive to watch serpentine shadows dance across El Castillo. A visit to Chichén might just be the pinnacle of your Yucatán experience—don't miss it for the world.

ORIENTATION AND PRACTICAL INFORMATION The ruins of Chichén Itzá lie 1.5km from **Route 180,** the highway running from Mérida (121km west) through Valladolid (43km east) to Cancún (213km east). As nearly every travel agency in Mexico pushes a Chichén Itzá package, the ruins tend to get overpopulated around noon. In order to avoid the stampede (and hot sun), use nearby **Pisté** (2.5km west of the ruins) as a base and get an early start, or visit late in the afternoon and head back to Pisté at nightfall.

Getting to the ruins is easy. If you would rather skip the 20 minute walk from Pisté, catch a taxi (18 pesos) or flag down any eastbound bus (approximately every 30min., 2-3 pesos). As with all Mexican buses, a vigorous, supplicatory wave to the driver gets you on the road. To get to Chichén Itzá from other towns, see bus listings for Mérida (see p. 534), Cancún (see p. 574), and Valladolid (see p. 567). To head back to Pisté after a day at the ruins, hang out in the bus parking lot until a taxi or bus swings by (every hr.). From Pisté you can get to almost any city in the state (see listings below). Pisté's **bus station** (tel. 1 00 52) is near the Stardust Inn on the eastern side of town. To Cancún (1st class 2½hr., 5:30pm, 44 pesos; 2nd class 4hr., 8 per day, 40 pesos), Mérida (1st class 1½hr., 3pm, 32 pesos; 2nd class 2hr., 11 per day, 19 pesos), Playa del Carmen (5hr., 1:30 and 3:30pm, 53 pesos), and Valladolid (1hr., 8 per day, 9 pesos). Services at the site are located in the dominant stone edifice at the site's western entrance. Across from the ticket counter is a small **information booth.** Refer specific questions about the ruins to official guides. The booth often provides free **luggage storage** (open daily 8am-5pm). The **Centro Telefónico** (tel. 1 00 89; fax 1 00 88) also exchanges currency (which you'll need plenty of if you plan to spend any time at the ruins). There are also restrooms, a restaurant, an ice cream parlor, a gift shop (which changes U.S. dollars), a bookstore with guidebooks, an air-conditioned auditorium showing documentaries about Maya ruins, and a small museum. **Parking** is available right at the site (parking 8 pesos; open daily 8am-10pm).

A single **police** officer sits at a desk in the *comisario* on the eastern side of the *zócalo*. **Farmacia Isis,** Calle 15 #53, lies a short way past the *zócalo* toward the ruins (open daily 7am-10pm). For medical emergencies, the **Clínica Promesa,** Calle 14 #50 (tel. 6 31 98, ext. 198), is in the blue-green building past the *zócalo* and 100m off Rte. 180 (open 24hr.). The **post office** is in a small gray building near the *zócalo* across from Abarrotes "El Alba" (open M-F 9am-3pm). There is a **caseta** (tel. 1 01 24) right around the corner from the ticket counter. Pisté provides a few additional services. Across from the bus station, both **Centro Telefónico** and **Teléfonos de México** (tel. 1 00 58 or 1 00 59) let you phone home (open daily 9am-9pm). **LATADELs** can be found along Rte. 180. The **phone code** is 985.

ACCOMMODATIONS Even though some luxury hotels have taken a corner of Chichén Itzá, they haven't cornered the market. Plenty of economical lodging awaits in Pisté. All of the places listed below can be found either on or just off Rte. 180, which doubles as the town's main road. Some line and a tarp will do at the **RV trailer park** right next to the bus station. Spaces have light and power outlets. There are also communal bathrooms and a pool. (30 pesos per person.) The trailer park is administered by the Stardust Inn (tel. 1 01 22), on the other side of the bus station. At the other end of the spectrum is the friendly **Posada Olalde** (tel. 1 00 86). To find it, take a left off Rte. 180 directly across from the Carrousel Restaurant and continue to walk two blocks down the unmarked dirt road. The large, exquisitely decorated rooms in the main house and the four spotless rooms with *palapa* roofs off the intimate courtyard make the Posada a honeymooner's dream. During the low season, you can try asking for something *más económico.* (Singles 120 pesos; doubles 160 pesos; triples 210 pesos; 30 pesos per extra person.) Nearby **Hotel El Paso,** Calle 15 #48, offers similar rooms. Bouncy beds make for good jumping games and small windows ensure that no one falls out (singles and doubles 100 pesos; 30 pesos per extra person). Its restaurant offers a well-priced *menú del día* (25 pesos).

FOOD Those that are too engrossed with the ruins to think about a meal while on a daytrip to Chichén Itzá are lucky, 'cause few are the options. The air-conditioning at the on-site **restaurant** isn't free; it's paid for through a combination of high prices and small servings (dishes 35-45 pesos with a regional dance or two). Picnickers can save a few pesos by packing a lunch from one of the **small grocers** that line Calle 15 in Pisté. Quick tip: eat the heavier mangoes and melons before climbing El Castillo, and be prepared for your picnic to be as hot and wet as the inner Temple of the Jaguar. For those determined to save *dinero,* Pisté's main road is lined with small restaurants offering cheap and savory *comida yucateca.* **El Carrousel** (tel. 1 00 78) serves three simple meals a day. Start a long, hot day right with eggs any style (13-15 pesos) or enchiladas (18 pesos; open daily 7am-10:30pm). **Restaurant Sayil,** between El Carrousel and the Stardust Inn, has a quiet corner where you can refuel on *pollo pibil* (15 pesos; open daily 7am-10pm). **Restaurant Poxil** (tel. 1 01 16), on the right just past the *zócalo,* is a bigger joint for bigger crowds with bigger dishes of *comida típica* for just 35 pesos (open daily 8am-9pm).

THE ARCHAEOLOGICAL SITE OF CHICHÉN ITZÁ

History

As the Mayan name Chichén Itzá (Mouth of the Well of the Itzás) implies, the area's earliest inhabitants were drawn here by the two nearby freshwater *cenotes* (freshwater sinkholes). The ritual offerings that were thrown into three *cenotes,* including pottery, jade, and gold, have provided the basis for archaeologists' theories on the lives of Chichén's previous residents. Later periods in Chichén Itzá's history are illuminated by the **Books of Chilam Balam,** written shortly after initial contact with the Europeans in the 15th and 16th centuries, which describe the construction of many buildings visible today, focusing on the period between 500 and 800, when construction was purely Maya.

For reasons that are still unclear, Chichén lost many of its residents and its political power after its height in the 7th century. There is still much contention on what happened next. One group of experts adheres to the traditional view (found on most markers) that sometime before 1000, the Toltec tribes of Tula (see) infiltrated the Yucatán and overcame peaceful Maya settlements, bringing with them the cult of the plumed serpent Quetzalcóatl (Kukulcán in Mayan). The Toltecs fortified Chichén and built the structures found in the main plaza that made Chichén the most important city on the peninsula. Toltec influence is visible in Chichén's buildings, which became more rounded, as well as in its iconography. They also introduced *chac mools,* reclining figures who, by holding forth a plate between their hands, seem to be awaiting an offering or a sacrifice. A growing number of archaeologists argue that although Chichén had been abandoned by the Itza, it was revitalized by this contact with other pre-Hispanic societies and only grew stronger. In 1461, Chichén Itzá was abandoned for the last time, this time due to a tumultuous war, but religious pilgrimages to the site continued well after Spanish conquest. Today, the relentless flow of tourists ensures that Chichén will never again stand in solitude.

For an even more comprehensive (not to mention air-conditioned) understanding of Chichén and its people, visit the **Centro Cultural Cecijema,** Calle 15 #45 (tel. 1 00 04; email Aluxes@DF.telmex.net.mx), in Pisté. *(Open daily 8am-5pm; free.)* The modern gray building houses a small selection of Maya ceramic replicas as well as attractive rotating exhibits. The real draw, however, is a magnificent little library with books, magazines, and other information in English and Spanish on practically every major Maya site. A helpful staff can answer any questions you may have and can also convert your birthdate into colorful, handmade Maya date glyphs for a small fee.

Information about the Ruins

From the main parking lot and visitor's center, the first group of **ruins** is up the gravel path and to the left. *(The entire site of Chichén Itzá is open daily 8am-5pm. Admission 48 pesos; free on Sunday and for children under 14.)* A small **museum** in the **visitor's complex** at the entrance to the site recaps the history of Chichén Itzá and displays some sculptures and objects removed from the **Sacred Cenote.** Its **auditorium**

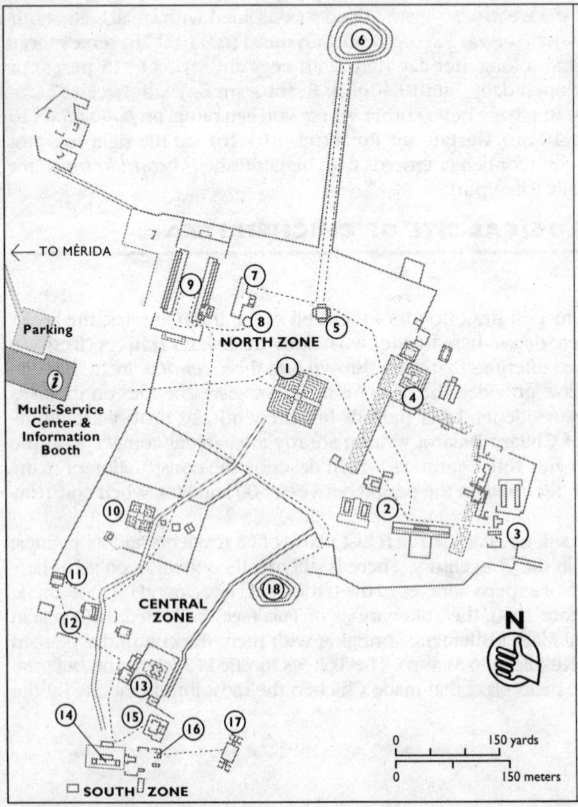

Chichén Itzá

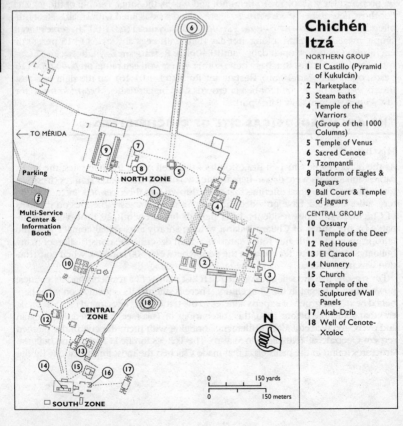

NORTHERN GROUP
1 El Castillo (Pyramid of Kukulcán)
2 Marketplace
3 Steam baths
4 Temple of the Warriors (Group of the 1000 Columns)
5 Temple of Venus
6 Sacred Cenote
7 Tzompantli
8 Platform of Eagles & Jaguars
9 Ball Court & Temple of Jaguars

CENTRAL GROUP
10 Ossuary
11 Temple of the Deer
12 Red House
13 El Caracol
14 Nunnery
15 Church
16 Temple of the Sculptured Wall Panels
17 Akab-Dzib
18 Well of Cenote-Xtoloc

screens documentaries about the ruins in both Spanish and in English (showtimes vary; museum and auditorium open daily 10am-5pm; free).

If you are mainly interested in the architecture of the ruins, hiring a guide at the entrance is unnecessary. A guidebook (or even just a map) and the multilingual explanatory captions on plaques at each major structure are all you need to appreciate the ruins. Free maps are available at the telephone desk around the corner from the ticket counter. You'll need a guide, though, to decipher some of the symbolism of the ruins or to hear some of the more intriguing, if not totally substantiated, interpretations of the site. Join one of the guided tours that begin at the entrance (Spanish, English, or other languages 1½hr., 6-8 people, 260-360 pesos per person depending on the language and duration), or get your own group together and hire a private guide (2hr., up to 20 people, 300 pesos). Of course, eavesdropping on any of the tours is always free. If you do choose to hire a guide, ask to see identification, which guarantees certification and foreign language ability.

Guide to the Ruins

The first sight to meet your eyes is **El Castillo,** Chichén's hallmark. This pyramid, built in honor of Kukulcán, rises in perfect symmetry from the neatly cropped lawn, culminating in a temple supported by pillars in the form of serpents. El Castillo stands as tangible evidence of the astounding astral understanding of the ancient Maya: the 91 steps on each of the four faces, plus the upper platform, total 365 (one for each day of a non-leap year); the 52 panels on the nine terraced levels equal the number of years in a Maya calendar cycle; and each face of the nine terraces is divided by a staircase, yielding 18 sections representing the 18 Maya months. Even more impressive is the precise alignment of El Castillo's axes, which, in coordination with the sun and the moon, produce a bi-annual optical illusion. At sunrise during the spring and fall equinoxes, the rounded terraces cast a **serpentine shadow** on the side of the northern staircase. The sculpted serpent head at the bottom of the staircase completes the illusion. In March, the serpent appears to be sliding down the stairs straight toward the Sacred Cenote, while in September the motion is reversed. A light-and-shadow lunar serpent-god, identical to that of the equinoxes, creeps up and down the pyramid at the dawn of the full moon following each of the equinoxes. People from all over the world converge on Chichén to see this incredible phenomenon.

Climbing El Castillo is easier than coming down; many tourists do the entire descent on their behinds. That sight might elicit a chuckle, but the ambulance blatantly parked at El Castillo each day will sober you a bit. Nestled within El Castillo is an early Toltec **temple** that can be entered at the bottom of the north staircase on the western side. *(Open daily 11am-3pm and 4-5pm; free.)* After climbing up steps whose walls sweat as much as you do, you'll be grimacing like the *chacmool* located in the ceremonial chamber. Behind the chamber is a fanged, molding jaguar throne with jade eyes. West of El Castillo, or to the left of the entrance, lies the **ballcourt.** The enormous "I"-shaped playing field is bounded by two high, parallel walls with a temple at each end. The **largest ballcourt in Mesoamerica,** it also has an amazing side-to-side echo that repeats seven times in the center. The game played here was called **pok-ta-pok.** The elaborate game fascinated the Spanish so much that Cortés took two entire teams back to Europe in 1528 to perform before the royal court. After that, European ball games replaced their unwieldy wooden balls with rubber ones.

A short distance from the ballcourt toward the grassy open area is the **Tzompantli,** Náhuatl for "Platform of the Skulls." When the Spaniards conquered the Aztecs, they were shocked to find ritualized human sacrifice and horrified by the racks in Tenochtitlán designed to display the skulls of the sacrificed. Chichén's Toltec-designed structure served a similar macabre purpose. Today, eerie columns of bas-relief skulls decorate the low platform's walls. Next to the Tzompantli stands the **Platform of Jaguars and Eagles,** named after the military men bearing the names of these ferocious animals who were charged with obtaining prisoners from other tribes for human sacrifice. To either side of the feathered serpent heads on the bal-

Hoop Dreams

The great ballcourts found at Chichén Itzá and other Maya cities once witnessed an impressive game called **pok-ta-pok,** in which two contending teams endeavored to keep a heavy rubber ball in constant motion by using only their hips, knees, and elbows. Players scored by knocking the ball through stone rings placed high on the court's side walls. The ballgame was much more than a cultural pastime for the Maya; it was symbolic of both a battle between good and evil and a way to keep the celestial bodies in motion (the ball represented the sun; its constant movement through the game symbolized the constant movement of the sun through the heavens). According to the *Popol Vuh* (a 16th-century account of creation by the Quiché Maya), the god of corn (Hun Hunahpu) was decapitated; his head was planted in the ground and became the seed of all corn plants. Magically impregnating a woman by spitting in her pocket, he bore twin sons, Xbalanque and Hunahpú, who became avid ball players. Infuriated by the noise of the ball bouncing above them, the lords of Xibalba (the underworld) coerced the two into descending to Xilbalba for a ballgame, using the contest as a pretense to kill the brothers. Through their own trickery, however, the twins prevailed, defeating and decapitating the gods—showing the conquest of good over evil. Because of this myth, the Maya that believed they were made from corn and continued to play the game in homage to their creators. Some players were decapitated as offerings to the gods.

ustrades, reliefs of jaguars and eagles vividly clutch human hearts in their claws. East of the platform is the **Temple of Venus,** decorated with a feathered serpent holding a human head in its mouth. The temple's reliefs symbolize stars and give information on their motion.

The dirt path leading directly north from El Castillo, over the ancient Maya roadway, links the ceremonial plaza to Chichén Itzá's most important religious center, the **Sacred Cenote,** 300m away. The roughly circular, 60m-wide sink-hole induced vertigo in the sacrificial victims perched on the platform before their 25m plunge into the murky depths. The rain god Chac was believed to dwell beneath the water's surface and to require frequent gifts to grant good rains. Human remains recovered by divers suggest that children and young men were the victims of choice. If they could keep afloat until noon, they were fished out and forced to tell what they had witnessed during the ordeal.

On the eastern edge of the central plaza, the **Temple of the Warriors** and **Group of the Thousand Columns** present an impressive array of elaborately carved columns that at one time supported a roof of some perishable material. On the temple itself (not open to the public), in front of two great feathered serpents and several sculpted animal gods, reclines one of Chichén's best-preserved *chacmools.* The ornamentation of this building has much Toltec influence; a nearly identical structure stands at Tula, the Toltec capital far to the west. The Temple of the Warriors marks the end of Chichén's restored monuments and the beginning of an overgrown area extending to the southeast of El Castillo. This corner houses the **Palace of the Sculptured Columns,** the back of which hides a couple of beady-eyed masks of Chac. The rest of the quadrangle is comprised of the **Southeastern Colonnade,** the **market** and its courtyard, and the expansive **Western Colonnade.**

A red dirt path on the south side of El Castillo leads to the less photogenic **South Group** of ruins. Beyond the cafeteria and bathrooms, the first pyramid on the right is the **Ossuary,** or **High Priest's Grave.** Its distinctive serpent heads mimic El Castillo. A natural cave extends from within the pyramid 15m into the earth. The human bones and votive offerings found in this cavern are thought to have belonged to an ancient high priest. Past the Ossuary, the road forks, presenting two routes to the second set of ruins in the South Group, often missed by tourists but well worth the visit. The most interesting structure in this group is the **Observatory,** the large circular building on the left-hand side. This ancient planetarium consists of two rectangular platforms with large, west-facing staircases and two circular towers. Because of the tower's interior spiral staircase (not open to the public), this structure is often called **El Caracol** (The Snail). The slits in the dome of the Observatory can be aligned with the important celestial bodies and cardinal directions. El Caracol was built in several stages and layers by Maya builders. Notice the small red handprints on the wall of the building just as you come up the stairs. These were supposedly the hands of the sun god Kinich Ahau. Walking south from El Caracol toward the Nunnery at the other end of the clearing, you will pass a tiny, ruined **sauna** and the **Temple of the Sculptured Wall Panels** behind it. Though difficult to decipher, the panels on the exterior walls contain emblems of warriors—jaguars, eagles, and serpents—in three rows.

The largest structure in this part of Chichén is the misnamed **Nunnery,** located on the south side of the quadrangle. Although it was probably a Maya royal palace, its stone rooms reminded Spaniards of a European convent. After several superimpositions and some decay, the building is now almost 20m high on a base 65m long and 35m wide. Above the entrance on the eastern side of the building, you can still see Maya hieroglyphs. Also on the eastern side is yet another misnamed building. This **Annex** actually predates the rest of the nunnery. Above the doorway facing the small eastern courtyard is a spectacular bas-relief of a seated royal-divine figure. Grab a flashlight and go exploring—many rooms in the nunnery have doorways that lead to dark corridors that are home to bats and frogs.

The Spaniards again got it wrong and named the elaborate building diagonally across from the nunnery and annex the **Church.** Its upper, almost top-heavy walls are encrusted with intricate masks of the hook-nosed Chac. The church is remarkable for its fusion of cultural styles: over the doorway are Maya stone **lintels,** while the use of wood and inclined edges is evidence of Toltec influence. Above the door are representations of the four **bacabs** that hold up the sky.

A rocky path runs about 60m east from the nunnery group, past the church to the 17-room **Akab-Dzib.** The oldest parts of this structure are believed to be Chichén's most ancient constructions. The two central rooms date to the 2nd or 3rd century, while the annexes on either side and to the east were added later. Inside the rooms, it is possible to make out the small, rose-red handprints of Kinich Ahau on the ceiling. The overgrown **Cenote Xtoloc** hides in a dip behind the South Group ticket office. To reach it from the office, take the first left 20m into the site. The *cenote* is in the hollow, beyond the small, ruined temple of Xtoloc, dedicated to the eponymous lizard god. There is no path down the steep slope through the undergrowth, and swimming is prohibited because of the dangerous underwater currents. A counterpart to the holy waters of the Sacred Cenote, this pool at one time provided all of Chichén with secular drinking water. Follow **Sacbe No. 5,** which becomes a narrow, winding trail, to get to the back of the observatory.

As if Chichén Itzá couldn't muster enough daytime spectacle, those green panels (whose purpose you've been contemplating all day) pop open for the evening **light** and **sound show.** The buildings are splashed in red, blue, green, and yellow lights while booming voices detail the history of the site (Spanish version daily at 7pm, 12 pesos; English version daily at 9pm, 30 pesos). If you trust your bug repellent, the nighttime stroll from Pisté is quiet and well-lit; otherwise grab a cab for 20 pesos each way.

Chichén Viejo

Not too many visitors to Chichén Itzá know that another whole site exists, and even fewer bother to visit. That's not necessarily bad—those who do go can enjoy the solitude in which these ruins rise out of the jungle, punctuated only by the calls of colorful birds. Beginning about 1km south of the Nunnery and spreading out southwest of the main site, Chichén Viejo is so named because it was originally thought to be the minor ruins of the first inhabitants of Chichén Itzá. Recent work done at the site suggests, though, that it was probably inhabited around the same time as the rest of the city. Most of the ruins are unrestored, and all are scattered throughout the jungle. The **Group of the Initial Series** and the **Phallic Cluster,** the first set of ruins in Chichén Viejo, are easy enough to find on your own. Follow the dirt road (simply marked with arrows) to the right of the Nunnery past the intersection of other dirt paths to a deep well. Shortly beyond the well, a right at the T-junction brings you to the cluster, set in a clearing. Chichén Viejo carries the only dated inscriptions at Chichén Itzá, one of which can be clearly seen on the only remaining lintel of the **Temple of the Initial Series.** This **block,** upheld by two columns, features a hieroglyphic inscription corresponding to July 30, 878. The rest of the temple stands in ruin. The main features of the appropriately named Phallic Cluster jut out from the interior walls of the temple, while nine warriors stand watch in the courtyard.

The remaining ruins at Chichén Viejo, reached by taking the path to the right of the **House of the Phalli,** following the rusted cart tracks, and then cutting through the bushes, are best located with the help of a guide. Though official guides will charge you almost as much to get to Viejo as they would for a tour of the main site, you can ask some of the merchants at Chichén if they know of someone who would be willing to serve as guide for a cheaper flat fee. Unlicensed guides can be very knowledgeable, although few speak English. Fifteen minutes beyond the Phallic Cluster and shrouded by dense jungle, lie the remains of the **House of the Four Lintels,** carrying another inscription dating to 881. In the **Principal Group of the Southwest,** hieroglyphs depict the Maya practice of compressing children's foreheads with stone plates—conically shaped heads were considered beautiful, as were crossed eyes and precious stones embedded in the flesh of the face. The Principal Group contains a magnificent **ruined pyramid,** the restored **Temple of the Three Lintels** (dating to 879; watch out for the wasps which now live there), and the **Jaguar Temple,** where a handful of columns salute the ancient military order of the Jaguars.

■ Near Chichén Itzá: Grutas de Balancanchén

The inner caves of the **Grutas de Balancanchén** were only re-discovered in 1959 when a local amateur speleologist noticed a passageway blocked with stones. *(Tours in Spanish daily 9am, noon, 2, and 4pm; in English 11am, 1, and 3pm; in French 10am. 22 pesos on Sundays and 7 pesos on holidays, children under 13 free.)* Further exploration opened 300m of caves filled with stalactites carved to resemble leaves on the ceiling and a huge tree-like column, which came to represent the sacred *ceiba* tree, surrounded by dozens of votive vessels with ghoulish masks. Archaeologists have come to believe that the cave was a center for Maya-Toltec worship of the gods Chac, Tlaloc (the Toltec rain god), and Kukulcán (Quetzalcóatl) during the 10th and 11th centuries. For unknown reasons, subterranean worship in Balancanchén stopped at the end of this period, and the offerings of ceramic vessels and stone sculptures rested undisturbed for nine centuries. The impressive **stalactites** and the plethora of **ceramic offerings** definitely merit a visit, but be prepared for an almost incomprehensible Disney-esque tour which dramatizes the cave's history through a series of hidden speakers. A guide, available for questions, paces the group through the chambers along the 1km path. Self-guided tours are not permitted, and you'll need at least two people to start a tour.

Getting There: Located 6km east of Chichén Itzá and 2km past the Dolores Alba Hotel, the caves are easily reached from Chichén or Pisté by hopping on any bus traveling east on Rte. 180 (3 pesos). When you board, be sure to ask the driver to stop there. To get back, catch any westbound vehicle, but be prepared to wait a while for one.

■ Near Chichén Itzá: Yaxuná

Yaxuná, 30km southeast of Chichén Itzá, is home to the ruins of yet another ancient Maya city. The temple was built by the Maya of Cobá, who were planning to declare war on the people of Chichén. A 100km *sacbe,* the **longest in the peninsula,** linked

Yaxuná and Cobá. To keep a close eye on their enemy, the Maya of Cobá aligned their temple with El Castillo.

Getting There: There is no public transportation to Yaxuná, but it's possible to hire a truck in Pisté (about 180 pesos round-trip; arrange for your driver to wait for you and ask to stop at the *cenotes* and caves between Chichén and Yaxuná). Road conditions are incredibly poor; the trip is only possible during the dry season. The easiest route is take Rte. 180 to Libre Unión and then left to **Yaxcaba,** a small town with a fascinating history of its own; the Caste war started here in 1847, and the remains of some of those killed lie in the three-towered church, the only one of its kind. The town is 17km down the road from Chichén and 8km from Yaxuná.

Valladolid

The hard work of Valladolid's 100,000 residents has paid off; their city works. Sharply uniformed police officers direct heavy but unclogged traffic, modern facilities complement newly restored historical buildings, and each spout on the colorful *zócalo* fountain dutifully casts its water in graceful shallow arcs. The buzz of mopeds and loud cries from the market will remind any visitor that this is a city on the move, but the relaxed *indígena* women selling *huipiles* in the *zócalo,* the quiet cathedrals, and the cool freshwater *cenotes* will keep one from wanting to move on.

ORIENTATION AND PRACTICAL INFORMATION Traversed by Rte. 180, Valladolid lies midway between Mérida and Cancún. Even-numbered streets run north-south, increasing westward. Odd-numbered streets run east-west, increasing to the south. The *centro* is bordered by Calles 27, 53, 28, and 60. Except for **Cenote X-kekén,** in the nearby village of Dazitnup, everything lies within comfortable walking distance from the *zócalo* (circumscribed by Calles 39, 40, 41, and 42). To get to the *zócalo* from the bus station, take a taxi (10 pesos) or walk one block south on Calle 54 to Calle 39. Turn left (east) and follow Calle 39 for six blocks. Or better yet, get off before the bus station at the *zócalo* (look for a big twin-towered cathedral; you can't miss it).

The **ayuntamiento** (city hall), on the corner of Calles 40 and 41 provides **tourist information.** There are also some interesting murals upstairs (open M-Sa 9am-1pm and 6-9pm). For total relief, **Bancomer** (tel. 6 21 50), on the Calle 40 side of the *zócalo,* has air-conditioning, good exchange rates, and a 24-hour **ATM** next door (bank open M-F 9am-2pm). **Buses** leave from the station on Calle 54 at 37. **ADO** (tel. 6 34 49), on Calle 37 at Calle 54 sends buses to Cancún (2 hr., 7 per day, 32 pesos), Chichén Itzá (1hr., 8 per day, 12 pesos), Mérida (2hr., 9 per day, 30 pesos), Playa del Carmen (2½hr., noon, 2, and 7pm, 44 pesos), and Tizimín (1hr., every hr., 11 pesos). To reach Tinum, buy a ticket on a Mérida-bound bus and ask the driver to drop you off (30min., 8 pesos). **Luggage storage** costs 2 pesos per piece per day (open 8am-7pm). The freshest, cheapest fruits and vegetables can be found in the **market** five blocks northeast of the *zócalo,* bordered by Calles 30, 32, 35, and 37. Get there early for the best picks. (Open daily 5am-noon.) **Lavandería Teresita** (tel. 6 23 93), Calle 33 at 42, takes care of your dirty laundry (self-service 7 pesos for 3kg, full service 5 pesos per kg; open daily 7am-7pm). The **police** (tel. 6 21 00) are on Calle 41, 10 blocks east of the *zócalo.* **El Descuento** (tel. 6 26 44), Calle 42 at 39 on the northwest corner of the *zócalo,* is a **24-hour pharmacy.** In a medical emergency look for **Hospital S.S.A.** (tel. 6 28 83), on Calle 41, two blocks west of the *zócalo,* then five blocks southwest on Calle 41A. The **post office** (tel. 6 26 23) is on the Calle 40 side of the *zócalo* (open M-F 8am-3pm). The **postal code** is 97780. **Telecomm** (tel. 6 21 70), on the corner of Calles 38 and 39 has **fax** service (open M-F 8am-6pm, Sa-Su 9am-noon). You can access the **internet** at **Internet del Oriente** (tel. 6 12 92 or 6 12 95; email orinet@orinet.valladolid.net.mx; http://www.valladolid.net.mx), located four blocks west of the *zócalo* in the Super Maz Bazar on Calle 39. Rates are

20 pesos for 30 minutes. (Open M-F 9am-1pm and 5-9:30pm, Sa-Su9am-1pm.) The **phone code** is 985.

ACCOMMODATIONS AND FOOD The priciest hotels in town are on the *zócalo.* Head one block west for better bargains. A stay at the **Hotel Zací,** Calle 44 #191 (tel. 6 21 67), between Calles 37 and 39, can be a vacation from your vacation. Stepping into its courtyard is like finding an oasis, complete with a restaurant fountain and glittering pool. Colonially furnished rooms with fans, cable TV, and large bathrooms are worth the extra pesos. (Singles 120 pesos; doubles 150 pesos; triples 193 pesos; quads 217 pesos; add 20 pesos for A/C.) At the **Hotel María Guadalupe,** Calle 44 #198 (tel. 6 20 68), between Calles 39 and 41, the colorful bedcovers and new ceiling fans liven up the somber dark wood furniture (singles and doubles 70 pesos; triples 80 pesos). **Hotel Mendoza,** Calle 39 #204 (tel. 6 20 02), is one-and-a-half blocks west of the *zócalo.* The prices haven't changed for the older rooms because neither have the rooms (singles 50 pesos; doubles 70 pesos; triples 90 pesos). Newer, larger suites have better baths and come with extra fans, cable TV, and a refrigerator (singles and doubles 120 pesos; doubles 140 pesos; triples 170 pesos).

Valladolid's crossroad location makes it a veritable showcase of Yucatec food. Try the *poc-chuc, panuchos* (small tortillas filled with various combinations of chicken, pork, beans, lettuce, tomato, and chile), or *escabeche oriental de pavo* (a hearty turkey soup). **El Bazaar,** Calle 39 at 40, is a narrow, *mercado*-like courtyard crowded with several cafes and juice bars right off the *zócalo* (open daily 6am-midnight). They all serve pretty decent *comida típica;* the primary deciding factor is where you want to sit. **La Rancherita,** with its 5-peso tacos and 15-peso *yucateca* entrees, along with **Sergio's,** a self-styled pizzeria (*chile relleno* 25 pesos, pizza 25-35 pesos) are closer to the street. **Amigo Casiano** specializes in *comida yucateca* and does quite a job of it. Overlooking its namesake is the **Restaurante Cenote Zací** (tel. 6 21 07), on Calle 36 between Calles 37 and 39. This neatly kept restaurant plays background music as patrons gaze out over the *cenote*; it also serves great food (sandwiches 15-20 pesos, entrees 35 pesos). The excellent liquor selection includes locally produced *xtabentún,* a delectable concoction of rum, anise, and honey (6 pesos; open daily 8am-6pm).

SIGHTS AND ENTERTAINMENT Seekers of *cenotes* and cathedrals are in the right place. Valladolid has two fantastic examples of each. **Cenote Zací** (sah-KEY) is only three blocks east of the *zócalo,* on Calle 36 between Calles 37 and 39. *(Open daily 8am-6pm. Admission 5 pesos, children 2 pesos. Free view from the palapa restaurant on the edge. Free parking.)* Well-worn stone stairs lead down into a cavernous hollow studded with plunging stalactites. **Daredevil divers** do their best to imitate those of Acapulco while the **weaving bats** put on the real show. Though it is farther from the center of town, **Cenote X'kekén** (chay-keh-KEN) is something you definitely shouldn't miss. *(Open daily 7am-5pm. Admission 8 pesos, children 4 pesos.)* To get there by car or bike (20min.), take Calle 39 to the highway and ride toward Mérida. Make a left at the sign for Dzitnup and continue to the entrance plaza on your left. Without your own wheels, take a taxi (15 pesos) or ask the driver of a second-class Mérida bus to drop you off. Visit before noon, as plunging schoolkids disrupt the deliciously cool, turquoise, glassy surface of the covered *cenote*'s water in the afternoon. At midday, a beam of light slices through the narrow hole in the roof, reflecting off the dripping stalactites and tree roots, bathing the room in a soft grayish-blue hue; bring a camera.

The most famous church in town is **San Bernardino de Siena,** affiliated with the **Ex-Convento de Sisal,** Calle 41A, four blocks southwest off Calle 46. *(Church open M, W-Su 8am-noon and 5-8pm. Admission 5 pesos.)* The walk along Calle 41A is fascinating. Built in 1552, the church and convent are the oldest ecclesiastical buildings in the Yucatán. On the altar at the rear of the church is a large image of the Virgin of Guadalupe. Original frescoes are visible behind two side altars. The **Catedral de San Ger-**

vasio, with its colonial-style twin towers, stands protectress over the *zócalo* on Calle 41. *(Open daily 5am-noon and 3-9pm.)* It would rival San Bernardino de Siena for the title of oldest church in the state had residents not violated the sacred right to sanctuary. According to legend, two alleged criminals who took sanctuary in the church were discovered and brutally murdered by an angry mob. When the bishop learned of the mob's sinful actions, he closed the church and had it destroyed. It was later rebuilt facing north instead of east.

Tizimín

Though Tizimín (pop. 50,000) dominates a prime location in the middle of one of the finest colonial, archaeological, and nature reserve routes on the peninsula, it only attracts a handful of tourists. Both Valladolid to the south and Río Lagarto to the north lie about an hour's drive away on Rte. 295, and along the way are archaeological sites such as Kulubá, Kikil, and Ek Balam, where tourists are stumbling over ruins faster than archeologists can research them.

Taking its cue from Valladolid, Tizimín is capitalizing on its colonial history with ambitious restorations of many buildings around its beautifully manicured *zócalo,* while maintaining the traditional way life characteristic of Yucatec cattle country. Tizimín's mornings have the big-city bustle of uniformed schoolchildren rushing to class, old wives on their way to market, and trucks clattering down narrow streets loaded with the best pigs from outlying ranches. Things quiet down in the sultry afternoons, as swinging hammocks in the shade wait for cooling rains. Sometimes it rains, sometimes it doesn't—life goes on in Tizimín.

ORIENTATION AND PRACTICAL INFORMATION Tizimín lies 75km south of Río Lagartos by Rte. 295, and 120km west of Kantunil Kin by Rte. 175. Even-numbered streets run north-south, increasing to the west. Odd-numbered streets run west-east, increasing to the south. Almost everything in Tizimín is centered around its *zócalo*. To get there from the main, blue-colored entrance of the bus station on Calle 47, walk west (to your right) on Calle 47 down the hill for two blocks. There will be a market on the left and a bakery on the right after the first intersection. Turn left on Calle 50 and walk south two blocks toward the large stone church (La Iglesia de los Tres Santos Reyes). **Buses** leave from the terminal at Calles 46 and 47. **ADO** (tel. 3 24 24) goes to Cancún (3½hr., 7 and 9am, 38 pesos), Chetumal (5hr., 3:30am and 1pm, 68 pesos), and Valladolid (1hr., every hr., 9 pesos). **Autotransportes del Noreste** (tel. 3 20 34) has first-class service to Kantunil Kin (1½hr., 10 per day, 13 pesos), Mérida (2hr., 7 per day, 44 pesos), and Río Lagartos (1hr., 5 per day, 11 pesos). **Bancomer** (tel. 3 23 81), on Calle 51 at 48, exchanges currency across from a little park behind the church. It also has a 24-hour **ATM.** (Open M-F 8:30am-3pm, Sa 10am-2pm.) There is a **LADATEL** on Calle 50, one block north of the ex-convento, on the right. It's hard to miss the three kings atop the **Lavandería de los Tres Reyes** (tel. 3 38 83), three blocks south of the *zócalo* on Calle 57 between 52 and 54. (15 pesos for 3kg. Open daily 8:30am-1:30pm and 4:30-7:30pm.) **Farmacia Centro de Drogas** (tel. 3 37 26), is on Calle 51, behind the ex-convento, next to Bancomer (open M-Sa 7:30am-9:30pm). The **Centro Médico de Oriente San Carlos,** Calle 46 #461 (tel. 3 21 57), has a 24-hour pharmacy and **ambulance service.** The **post office** is at Calles 48 and 55 (open M-F 8am-3pm, Sa 9am-1pm). The **postal code** is 97700. The **phone code** is 986.

ACCOMMODATIONS Only a block from the *zócalo,* **Hotel San Carlos,** Calle 54 #407 (tel. 3 20 94), is very quiet and clean. From the southwest corner of the *zócalo* (by Tres Reyes restaurant) walk west one block and make your first right. Each spotless room has two beds and a private bathroom, and faces a very green, very well-kept garden. There's also free bottled water. (Singles 110 pesos, with A/C 130 pesos; doubles 130 pesos, with A/C 150 pesos.) **Hotel San Jorge** (tel. 3 20 37) is the big square building across from the south side of the *zócalo.* The rooms take advantage of the space, but besides the TVs and fans, they are as austere as the hotel's exterior. Beds and bathrooms are unimpressive but adequate, and chilled *agua purificada* lends the halls some character. (Singles and doubles 130 pesos, with A/C 150 pesos.) What you see is what you get with the **Posada Marian** (tel. 3 28 57), in the *zócalo* on the southern side of the church. A small, aging purple facade leads to small, aging purple rooms, each with two beds, hot water, a fan, and a TV. (Singles and doubles 95 pesos; each additional person 10 pesos; add 15 pesos for A/C.)

FOOD For the cheapest meal, buy some fruits, vegetables, and bread at the **market** and **bakery** (bread 1 peso, donuts 2 pesos) on Calle 47 and picnic in the beautiful zócalo. The people at the popular **Restaurante Tres Reyes** know how to have a good time; during the holiday months, this festively decorated eatery hosts house-packing ranchero parties. Huge meals come with a generous stack of tortillas (pollo frito con arroz 32 pesos; open daily 7:30am-11pm). **Restaurante Portales** (tel. 3 35 05), on the corner of Calle 50 and 51, provides sweet shade and cheap food under its awning facing the zócalo. You can eat eggs however you desire them for 20 pesos. Sandwiches and tacos cost 12 pesos. (Open M-Sa 7:30am-12:30pm and 6-11:30pm, Su 6-11:30pm.) For a change of zócalo scenery, head out to the **Restaurante Las Palmas,** Calle 51 #331A (tel. 3 24 51), between Calles 38 and 40. Regional dishes are served under a big palapa roof (25-35 pesos), which also shades live bands and dancing on Sunday afternoons. (Open daily 10am-10pm.)

SIGHTS, ENTERTAINMENT, AND SEASONAL EVENTS Dominating its central square, Tizimín's church was built in 1563 with distinctive castle-like ramparts. Facing the northern side of **La Venerada Iglesia de los Tres Santos Reyes** is the crumbling ex-convent, beside which begin many of the town's religious processions. The most important of these is the **Festival of the Three Kings** (Dec.30-Jan.12), when pilgrims and partiers pour into Tizimín from surrounding towns and the countryside. While the parades, dancing, bullfights, and banquets of *comida típica* last for two weeks, the most important day of the festival is January 6, when the pilgrims file through the church to touch the patrons with palm branches. On Sundays around 7:30pm during the academic year, local schools perform **ballet folklóricas** that are free to the public.

Those who do make the out-of-the-way trip to Tizimín can find out anything they want to know about the region from one man—**Julio Caesar** (tel. 3 38 86 or 87 14 55, code 9157), who knows more about the region's famous Maya ruins than just about anyone else. Having **discovered the archeological site of Kulubá,** Caesar can make entering the private ranch on which the site lies much easier. If you can't reach him by phone, try tracking him down at his photography studio on Calle 47 #405, between Calle 50 and 52 (studio open M-Sa 8am-1pm and 5-8:30pm).

Since it's somewhat hard to reach, **Kulubá** is virtually untouristed, and worth visiting. The ruins date from the Late Classical period (800-1000) and are the easternmost point of Puuc architectural influence. The style here resembles to the buildings at Chichén Itzá. Although neither building has survived the years intact, the details that remain are impressive. **El Edificio de Las Ues,** a structure about 40m long, 8m high, and 7m wide, is carved with "U"s all along its facade. The original red stucco with which the whole building was once painted can still be seen on the carved portions of the stone. The second partially restored building, the more impressive of the two, features two surprisingly well-preserved pairs of masks of the rain god Chac, as well as other carved ornamentation. To get to the ruins, take the Tixcanal-bound bus a half-block from the *zócalo* and ask the driver to drop you off at Kulubá. **Taxis** from Tizimín charge 100 pesos for a round-trip jaunt with a wait. Traveling to the site during the rainy season is especially difficult.

The tiny town of **Kikil** (pop. 3000), 5km from Tizimín, has the enormous jungle-encroached remains of a colonial church and ex-convent as well as the fresh waters of a stunning *cenote.* A taxi to Kikil will run you 70-80 pesos round-trip with a wait. Alternatively, you can get dropped off by one of the Río Lagartos-bound buses. The church, known to locals simply as **Iglesia Kikil,** is just to the right of the highway as you enter Kikil from Tizimín. The church was burned during the Caste War (1847-48) and is now utterly abandoned. Legend has it that years ago, some residents of the town threw a stone at a passing Catholic *sacerdote* (priest), who then predicted that the church would be laid to ruin and that Kikil would remain small forever. Just inside the gate of the little courtyard to your left as you face the church stands an elaborately carved stone baptismal font that rings like a bell when you strike it with your hand. A beautiful *cenote* hides just across the road from the church. In May and June, visitors to Kikil can enjoy the enactment of several traditional Maya ceremonies such as the **Kaash Paach Bi,** a ritual to cleanse the land, and the **Ch-Chac,** a rain petition.

Río Lagartos

Known affectionately as "*la ría*," this long inlet of ocean water is much the same today as it was when Hernán Cortés chanced upon it and mistook it for a river. The head of this inlet is now commanded by the small arcadian fishing village Río Lagartos (pop. 3500), which is slowly but steadily adapting to its role as an ecotourist hotspot. Bordering the town is the reason for the recent interest—the 47,000-hectare Río Lagartos National Park, home to some 30,000 pink flamingos, 211 other bird species, spider monkeys, white-tailed deer, jaguars, and crocodiles. A secluded and pristine beach, sumptuous seafood restaurants, and hospitable locals often turn day-trips to the park into weekend stays.

ORIENTATION AND PRACTICAL INFORMATION Río Lagartos is easily accessed from Tizimín (48km), Valladolid (104km), and Mérida (156km). The main road, **Calle 10,** runs north-south and ends at the waterfront on the north end. There is neither a post office nor a bank in the village; the town's services are limited to the long-distance **caseta** in the *zócalo* (tel. 3 26 68 or 3 26 65). **Autotransportes de Oriente (ADO)** has frequent buses to Tizimín (1hr., 6 per day, 9 pesos). If you're lucky, the cheerful owner of La Cueva de Macumba (see **Accommodations and Food** below) might arrange for someone to take you on his boat to **Isla Holbox** (see p. 579) which is infinitely more convenient than traveling by land via Chiquilá, though the stunning journey along the coast may be a bit pricey. The **phone code** is 986.

ACCOMMODATIONS AND FOOD Helping solve what was a critical shortage of bedspace, the sparkling new **Posada Ceyli** (tel. 2 00 05) is one block south of the restaurant La Cueva de Macumba and the beach. All but two rooms have their own large, private bathrooms, and all rooms have still-firm beds and ceiling fans. (Singles 90 pesos; doubles 120 pesos.) **Cabañas Los Dos Hermanos** (tel. 2 00 83) is on the same street as the bus station, three blocks to the east and almost on the waterfront. The buildings, like most in Río Lagartos, are lockless—a reflection of the town's relative safety (although the gates surrounding the houses do have locks on them). Each of the sizable *cabañas* has a double bed, cable TV, fans, and a clean bathroom with hot water. (One room 80 pesos and you can fit as many people as you like. Hammock hooks provided. Reservations highly recommended.)

Restaurante Isla Contoy (tel. 3 26 68, ext. 100) is right on the shore, two blocks west of the *zócalo;* from the bus station walk five blocks west and a few meters north. Sup on delectable *fillete relleno* (breaded fish stuffed with shrimp and salsa, 36 pesos) as you enjoy the beach view and gregarious owner. (Open daily 6am-11pm.) The restaurant also owns four **lanchas** that can be hired for a tour of the

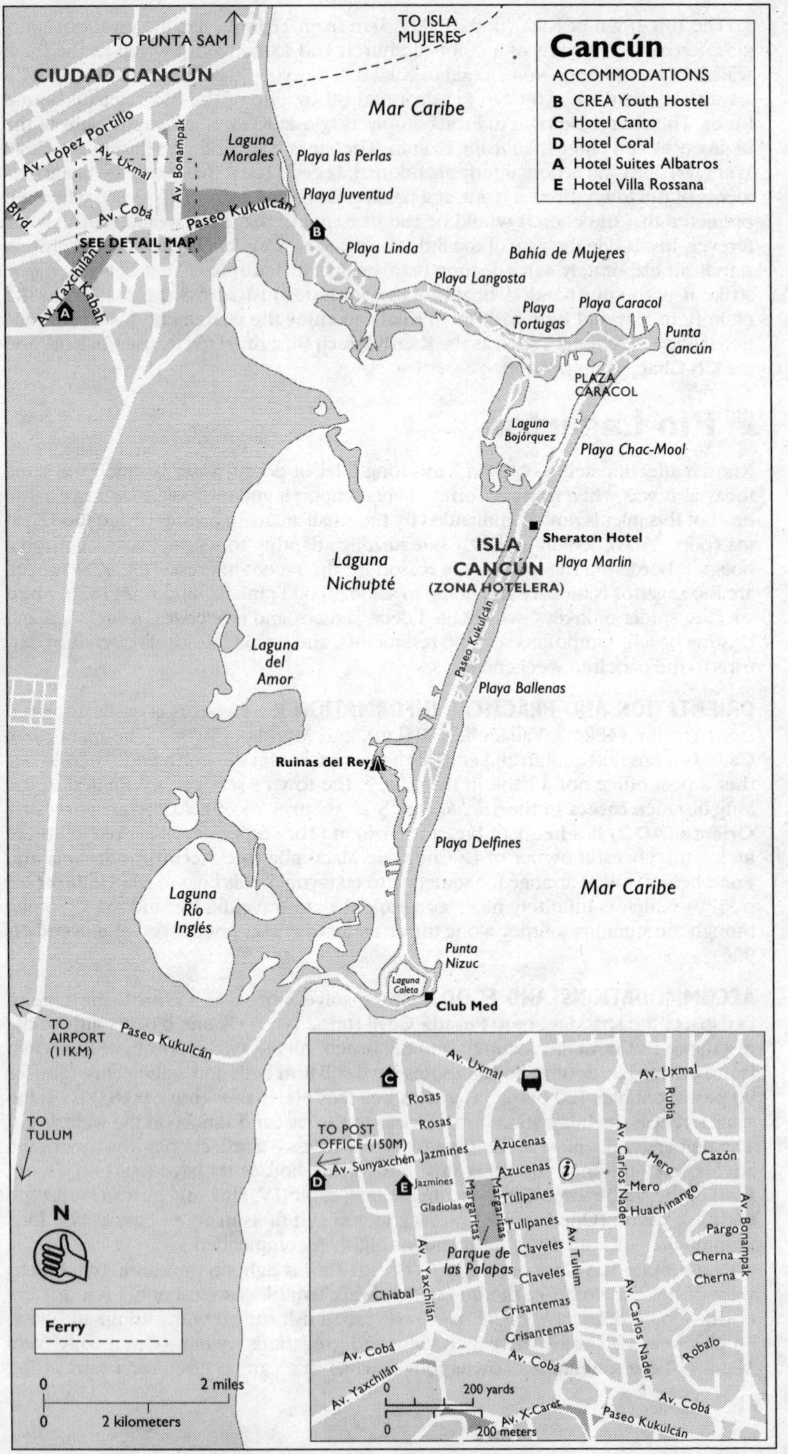
Cancún
ACCOMMODATIONS
B CREA Youth Hostel
C Hotel Canto
D Hotel Coral
A Hotel Suites Albatros
E Hotel Villa Rossana
TO PUNTA SAM
TO ISLA MUJERES
CIUDAD CANCÚN
Mar Caribe
Av. López Portillo
Av. Uxmal
Av. Bonampak
Laguna Morales
Playa las Perlas
Playa Juventud
Blvd.
Av. Cobá
Paseo Kukulcán
SEE DETAIL MAP
Playa Linda
Bahía de Mujeres
Av. Yaxchilán
Kabah
Playa Langosta
Playa Tortugas
Playa Caracol
Punta Cancún
PLAZA CARACOL
Laguna Bojórquez
Playa Chac-Mool
Sheraton Hotel
ISLA CANCÚN
(ZONA HOTELERA)
Playa Marlin
Laguna Nichupté
Paseo Kukulcán
Laguna del Amor
Playa Ballenas
Ruinas del Rey
Playa Delfines
Mar Caribe
Laguna Río Inglés
Punta Nizuc
Laguna Caleta
Club Med
TO AIRPORT (11KM)
Paseo Kukulcán
TO TULUM
N
Ferry
0
2 miles
0
2 kilometers
Av. Uxmal
Av. Uxmal
Rubia
Rosas
Rosas
TO POST OFFICE (150M)
Av. Sunyaxchén
Jazmines
Azucenas
Azucenas
Av. Carlos Nader
Mero
Mero
Cazón
Jazmines
Gladiolas
Margaritas
Margaritas
Tulipanes
Tulipanes
Huachinango
Av. Bonampak
Pargo
Av. Tulum
Parque de las Palapas
Claveles
Claveles
Cherna
Cherna
Chiabal
Av. Yaxchilán
Av. Carlos Nader
Crisantemas
Crisantemas
Robalo
Av. Cobá
Av. Cobá
Av. Yaxchilán
0
200 yards
0
200 meters
Av. X-Caret
Paseo Kukulcán
Av. Cobá

park (300-400 pesos depending on the season). Unfortunately, the owner of **La Cueva de Macumba,** well-known for his artistic flourish with seashell, feather, and floral arrangements, fell on bad luck when his thatch roof burned down. The restaurant may not have the same eclectic decor as before, but the doves still coo and the food is still quite a bargain (seafood entrees 25-35 pesos; open daily in the evening.)

SIGHTS AND ENTERTAINMENT There are several groups of guides offering their services for tours of **Río Lagartos National Park;** those that are qualified in ecotourism work out of the Restaurante Isla Contoy. With maps, enthusiasm, and a great love of their *Ría*, the guides will do their best to ensure flamingo sightings and will take you to lesser-known treasures, such as the Maya ruins deep within the park, the colorful salt banks at **Los Colorados,** and the several waterways hidden under mangrove trees. To see flamingos, early mornings are best, and May through June is their courtship period (from which the flamenco derives) and nesting time. When hiring a guide, always look for a badge verifying training in ecotourism; their enthusiasm is contagious.

Not much happens during the day in this town except a whole lot of fishing: it's not surprising, then, that even less is going on at night. Cool down with some of the local beers, listen to the playful sounds emanating from the *zócalo*, and watch the lighthouse's beacon glance off the rolling waves of the Río. On Saturday nights, **Titanic,** on Principal by the bus station, cranks up the disco. The town fiesta runs from July 20 to July 30, as parades and a circus are put on to honor Santiago Aposto (the little brother of Spain's patron saint).

QUINTANA ROO

Cancún

Visitors do not come to Cancún to see Mexico. Most visitors do not even come to Cancún to see Cancún. For many who plan extended stays in Cancún (pop. 450,000), it comes down to beaches and bodies. The name Cancún means "snake nest" in Mayan, and it has come to be oddly prophetic—sunburned, scantily-clad U.S. vacationers come here to stare and be stared at. Much has been said of Cancún, Mexico's biggest resort and one of the world's most notorious places to party. The island was built up in the 1960s by Mexican entrepreneurs striving to match the enormous success of the resort cities of Puerto Vallarta and Acapulco. Cancún was deemed (by a computer) as having the most desirable climate and setting for a tourist haven in the country. The L-shaped island is bordered on one side by 22km of world-class white beaches with tame, crystal-clear water and on the other by a mangrove-lined blue lagoon on the other. It is just wide enough to accommodate a continuous stretch of hotels and an adjacent row of strategically placed, glam shopping malls and flashy restaurants. Proximity to renowned Maya ruins and a stable Caribbean climate add to the resort's splendor. Over two million visitors a year seek out this overwhelming convenience and fork over the requisite cash.

First opened in 1974, the *Zona Hotelera* (Hotel Zone) was built in its gilded high-rise splendor on Isla Cancún with the goal of avoiding the chaos of third-world urban growth that could scare tourists away. This complacent bubble encompasses every conceivable tourist need: there is a water purification system to provide safe tap water, an enforced ban on panhandling, and strict zoning laws to prevent a scourge of skyscrapers. Here, in the middle of the *norteamericano* winter, you can parasail and scuba dive, shop in chic boutiques, snack at McDonald's and slam tequila at anything-goes Tex-Mex bars—all while speaking English, spending greenbacks, and being shuttled from hotel to beach to bar and back.

The renowned hotel zone, however, is not all that Cancún has to offer. Budget travelers use the international airport as an important starting point for trips across the Yucatán Peninsula, and those willing to forego the precise, profit-driven calculation of the *Zona Hotelera*, are often surprised by the bargains that are to be had in Ciudad Cancún. Older, cheaper, and farther from the beaches, the city has none of the appeal, aesthetic or otherwise, of the secluded beaches and tropical savannah of the surrounding Yucatán countryside. Nevertheless it can be affordable, helping budget travelers defeat the popular myth that credit cards are required to enjoy Cancún.

ORIENTATION

On the northeastern tip of the Yucatán Peninsula, Cancún lies 285km east of Mérida via Rte. 180 and 382km north of Chetumal and the Belizean border via Rte. 307. There are two main areas to the resort: Ciudad Cancún, where you'll find more bargains but no beaches, and Isla Cancún (or the *Zona Hotelera)*, with fewer bargains but all the beaches. The main drag in Ciudad Cancún, **Av. Tulum,** runs north-south and parallel to **Av. Yaxchilán** (Yash-chee-LAN), three blocks west. These two streets form a rough parallelogram with **Avenidas Cobá** and **Uxmal** framing the **Parque de las Palapas** in the center of town. Facing the bus station (south), Av. Tulum is the busy throroughfare to the left (east) and Av. Uxmal is to the right (west). Downtown, the *centro* lies south of the bus station. On the island, the *Zona Hotelera*'s main drag is **Paseo Kukulcán,** conveniently marked off in 1km segments.

To reach either section of town from the airport, buy a ticket for the shuttle bus **TTC** (60 pesos). Tickets are sold in the baggage claim and buses leave from outside. A private taxi (white with green stripes) will charge around 90 pesos for that trip; it'll take at least 30 pesos to go from the beach to the stores, depending on how far into the *Zona Hotelera* you are. Always settle the price before getting into a cab. White buses marked "Hoteles" run the long stretch between the city's bus station and the island's tip at Punta Nizuc around the clock. Buses can be caught at any blue sign along Av. Tulum and Paseo Kukulcán (4 pesos). To get off the bus in the *Zona Hotelera,* push one of the little square red buttons on the ceiling when in sight of your stop—if you don't know where you need to get off, mention the name to the bus driver as you board, with a *por favor.* While many places rent mopeds (useful for exploring the 18km of beaches that stretch from the Youth Hostel to Punta Nizuc), buses are much cheaper and just as convenient.

PRACTICAL INFORMATION

Transportation

Airport: (tel. 86 00 28), south of the city on Rte. 307. *Colectivos* 60 pesos, taxis 90 pesos (fixed rates to downtown; buy a ticket at the desk). Airlines include **Aerocaribe** (tel. 84 20 00); **American** (tel. 86 00 55 or 86 00 86); **Continental** (tel. 86 00 06); **LACSA** (tel. 87 41 01); **Mexicana** (tel. 87 44 44); **Northwest** (tel. 86 00 44); and **United** (tel. 86 01 58 or 86 00 25).

Buses: (tel. 84 13 78). The **bus station** is located on the corner of Av. Uxmal and Av. Tulum. **ADO** travels to Campeche (6hr., 11:30am, 1:30 and 10:30pm, 150 pesos), Valladolid (2hr., 11:30am, 1:30, and 10:30pm, 40 pesos), and Palenque (16hr., 3:45 pm, 222 pesos). **Premier** sends a bus to Chichén Itzá (2½hr., 9am, 44 pesos), and one to Playa del Carmen every 15min. (45min., 8:45am-10:45pm, 15 pesos). You can save about 25% by hopping on the second-class buses that leave from the curbside and go to Mérida, Tulum, and Chetumal.

Ferries: To get to **Isla Mujeres,** take a bus marked "Pto. Juárez" for the 15min. ride to the 2 ferry depots north of town (Punta Sam for car ferries, Puerto Juárez for passenger ferries). Express service *(servicio express)* passenger ferries shuttle across in 15min. (every 30min., 6am-8:30pm, 22 pesos). Normal service (40min., every 2hr. 8am-6pm, 10 pesos) is cheaper than express but takes almost 3 times as long. You can also get to **Cozumel** from Playa del Carmen, south of Cancún—Cozumel is also accessible by bus from the terminal in town (15 pesos).

Taxis: (tel. 88 69 90). The minimum fare within the *Zona* is 25 pesos; a ride into town can cost as much as 60 pesos. Within the *centro,* a taxi ride should run around 20 pesos. Prices are negotiable; be sure to settle the deal before getting in.

Moped Rental: Look for vendors in between Hotel Aquamarine and Hotel Costa Real. Mopeds go for 80 or 100 pesos per hour and 400 or 500 pesos for the day, depending on the vendor. **Bicycles** and **rollerblades** are also rented, both at 60 pesos per hour and 150 pesos all day. Open daily 9:30am-6:30pm. License needed for moped rental; deposits negotiable.

Tourist and Financial Services

Tourist Offices: Av. Tulum 5 (tel. 8 73 11, ext. 114; email hbjvp@cancun.com.mx), inside the *Ayuntamiento Benito Juárez* (tel. 85 05 69 for information in English). Open daily 8:30am-4pm. For national tourist assistance, call toll-free 91 800 9 03 92. **Visitor office,** located right next door in the little red building at Av. Tulum 26 (tel. 84 80 73), offers similar paraphernalia and help. Open daily 9am-9pm. Ask for **Cancún Tips,** a free magazine full of useful information and maps (in English). Can also be found at Av. Tulum 29 (tel. 84 40 44), at Plaza Caracol in the *Zona Hotelera,* and at the airport.

Consulates: Canada (tel. 83 33 60 or 83 33 61; fax 83 32 32), 3rd fl. of Plaza Caracol at km 8.5. Open M-F 10am-2pm. For emergencies outside of office hours, call the embassy in Mexico City (tel. 91 57 24 79 00). **U.K.** (tel. 81 01 00), in the Hotel Royal Caribbean. Open M-F 8am-5pm. **U.S.** (tel. 83 13 73 or 83 22 96), Plaza Caracol, 3rd fl. at km 8.5. Open M-F 9am-1pm.

Currency Exchange: Bancomer, Av. Tulum 20 (tel. 84 44 00), across from the intersection of Av. Tulum and **Calle Claveles,** has the best rate of all banks on Av. Tulum. Open M-F 9am-7pm, Sa 10am-7pm, Su 11am-4pm. The bank also has Visa and Mastercard **ATMs.** Both **Banamex,** Tulum 19 (tel. 84 54 11; open M-F 9am-4pm), and **Banca Serfín** (tel. 81 48 50), Av. Tulum at Cobá, give cash advances on Visa and MasterCard. They also have Cirrus, Visa, and Mastercard **ATMs.** Equally competitive but more convenient is **CUNEX Exchange** (tel. 87 09 01), next to Banca Serfín on the corner of Tulum and Cobá. Open daily 8am-11pm.

American Express: Tulum 208 (tel. 81 40 00 or 81 40 43), 3 blocks south of Cobá away from the city. Open M-F 9am-6pm, Sa 9am-1pm.

Local Services

Luggage storage: At the bus station. 7 pesos for 24hr.

English Bookstore: Fama, Av. Tulum 105 (tel. 84 65 86), between Calles Claveles and Tulipanes. Newspapers, magazines, guidebooks, maps, and the latest in U.S. mass-market paperbacks. Open daily 8am-10pm.

Supermarket: Across the street from the bus station on Av. Tulum is the **Comercial Mexicana** (tel. 84 33 30); you can't miss the big orange-and-white pelican out in front. Department store meets grocery store here with bakery and pharmacy included. Open daily 7am-noon. Smaller but more centrally located is **Super San Francisco** (tel. 84 11 55), Av. Tulum next door to Banamex. Open M-Sa 7:30am-10pm, Su 7am-9pm.

Laundry: Lavandería Automática "Alborada," Av. Náder 5 (tel. 84 15 84), behind the Ayuntamiento Benito Juárez. Self-service 8 pesos. Open M-Sa 9am-8pm. **Tintorería Banderia** (tel. 84 26 69) has dry cleaning. Open M-Sa 9am-8pm.

Emergency and Communications

Emergency: Dial 060.

Police: (tel. 84 19 13) at Av. Tulum next to Ayuntamiento Benito Juárez.

Red Cross: Av. Yaxchilán 2 (tel. 84 16 16). English spoken. Open 24hr.

Pharmacies: Several along Av. Tulum and Av. Yaxchilán. **Farmacia Paris,** Av. Yaxchilán 32 (tel. 84 01 64), at the intersection with Calle Rosas, is open 24hr.

Medical Assistance: Hospital Americano, Calle Viento 15 (tel. 84 61 33, after-hours 84 63 19), 5 blocks south on Av. Tulum after its intersection with Av. Cobá.

For an ambulance, call **Total Assist** (tel. 84 10 92 or 84 81 16), at Claveles 5 near Av. Tulum. English spoken.

Post Office: (tel. 84 15 24), at Av. Xel-Ha at Av. Sunyaxchén. From Av. Tulum, cut through any side street to Av. Yaxchilán and head up Av. Sunyaxchén. The post office is 4 blocks farther. Open daily 8am-1pm and 4-8:30pm. **Postal Code:** 77500.

Fax: (tel. 84 15 24) at the post office. Open M-F 9am-8:30pm, Sa 9am-4:30pm. Telegram service available as well.

Internet Access: CaribeNet (tel. 84 90 05; http://caribe.net.mx), in Local 9-A on Av. Bonampak and Av. Coba, provides Internet access for US$10 per hour. Open M-F 9am-2pm and 4-7pm, Sa 9am-1pm. **Camhel Computation** (tel. 84 11 91), Local B-02 on Av. Coba 5, opened in May 1998 and provides access to the World Wide Web (18 pesos for 30min; M-Sa 9am-2pm and 4-8pm).

Telephones: LADATELs and 30-, 50-, and 100-peso phone cards make for easy and cheap long-distance calls. The **public phone** in Plaza Nautilus near the youth hostel is another option, provided you have a big pile of coins. **Casetas** throughout the city tend to charge hefty fees.

Phone Code: 98.

ACCOMMODATIONS AND CAMPING

YUCATÁN PENINSULA

A drive through *La Zona* on Paseo Kukulcán is like a highway to the danger zone for your funds. Budget travelers often stay or camp at the **CREA Youth Hostel,** at the end of the *Zona Hotelera.* Even in Ciudad Cancún, some hotels will charge you upwards of US$20 for a room that'll leave you stuck to your bed staring at a poor, overworked, and ineffective ceiling fan. Some daredevils sleep on the beach in the *Zona* where they must evade robbers and the police. With the exception of the CREA, all hotels listed are within a 10- to 15-minute walk from Av. Tulum in the city. Prices can fluctuate as much as 40 to 50% throughout the year. During high season, phone reservations are a good idea.

Hotel Coral, Sunyaxchén 30 (tel. 84 20 97). Heading west from Av. Yaxchilán, the hotel is 2 blocks down on the left; look for the big, blue building. The ceiling fans in each room more than make up for the sparse furnishings; their two speeds are fast and superfast. The attentive staff keep the bathrooms clean and the *agua purificada* in the halls well stocked and cold. Singles 100 pesos, with A/C 130 pesos; doubles 150 pesos, with A/C 200 pesos; triples 180 pesos, with A/C 250 pesos; 20 pesos for each additional person. Check-out 1:30pm. To make reservations, wire payment 10 days in advance.

Suites Albatros, Av. Yaxchilán 154 (tel. 84 22 42), 2 blocks south of Av. Cobá and across the street from the Red Cross. It's easy to forget the extra bit of effort it takes to get here while walking through the shady courtyard and into one of the apartment-like rooms. The classy decor only adds to the full kitchens, large beds, hot water, and A/C. Each of the upstairs rooms has a balcony with laundry lines and sink. All rooms are 200 pesos. Pepe's place is in demand, so reservations are suggested.

CREA Youth Hostel (HI), Paseo Kukulcán at km 3 (tel. 83 13 37). For those who plan to beach or club it, CREA is the closest and cheapest place to the *Zona Hotelera.* Just catch any *Hotelera* bus from the bus station or Av. Tulum and asked to be let off at "CREA." CREA's best asset is its location. 200 single-sex dorm rooms with 8 bunk beds apiece. Sheets and towels provided. No A/C; ask for a room with a working ceiling fan. Use the personal lockers when you leave the room, even to shower. No hot water. Beach volleyball, basketball court, and table-tennis. Bunks 77 pesos, and you can pitch a tent on the front lawn for 40 pesos per person. 10% discount with HI card. Locker not included, but place your stuff with hostel security. 50-peso deposit. 15-night max. stay. Check-out 1pm. No curfew.

Hotel Canto (tel. 84 12 67), on Av. Yaxchilán. As you turn off Av. Uxmal onto Av. Yaxchilán, look for the fading pink building 2 blocks down on your right. Travelers who like to keep informed will appreciate the color TV and telephone in each room, and while some of the lumpy beds may not help you sleep, the A/C will.

Spotless, groovy-blue bathrooms with monogrammed soap with hot water. *Agua purificada* in the lobby. Singles, doubles, and triples 200 pesos; quads 250 pesos.

Hotel Villa Rossana, Av. Yaxchilán 68 (tel. 84 19 43). On the right past Av. Sunyaxchén across from Calle Jazmines. The spacious rooms of this aging building have ceiling and floor fans, hot water, and ample beds. Balconies look out over Av. Yaxchilán (light sleepers, take note). Singles and doubles 160 pesos; triples 220 pesos; quads 260 pesos. Check-out 1pm.

FOOD

Two simple rules will help the hungry traveler find affordable cuisine for all tastes in Cancún: avoid restaurants with their own clotheslines (in fact, stay away from the *Zona Hotelera* altogether), and steer clear of the roadside booths, which serve meats of dubious origin. For good, inexpensive food, try the many joints between Avenidas Tulum and Yaxchilán. **Mercado 28,** behind the post office and circumscribed by Av. Xel-Ha, is a unique option for budget fare. Numerous *loncherías* are located in its western courtyard; a hearty *comida corrida* at **Restaurants Margely, Acapulco,** or **La Chaya** costs well under 25 pesos. La Chaya offers vegetarian meals. (All open daily 8am-6pm.) Almost all restaurants listed below are in Ciudad Cancún.

100% Natural, Av. Sunyaxchén 6 (tel. 84 36 17), near the corner of Av. Yaxchilán; another 24hr. location in Plaza Caracol. Fresh and savory fruit drinks and vegetable dishes are served in the hacienda-style courtyard by a welcoming, excellent staff. Choice meat and scrumptious vegetable entrees 25-45 pesos, refreshing tropical shakes 10-15 pesos. Open daily 7am-11pm.

El Tacolote, Av. Cobá 19 (tel. 87 30 45), 2 blocks east of Av. Yaxchilán toward the *Zona Hotelera*. Look for the sombrero-sporting, taco-gobbling, yellow chicken out front. Delicious grilled meat and tortillas start at 18 pesos. The *alambre* can clear the sinuses for 30 pesos; for those without *habano*-hardened tongues, there is *la gringa* (25 pesos). Open daily 11am-2am.

Restaurante Río Nizuc, Paseo Kukulcán at km 22. Get on the "Hoteles" bus (4 pesos) and ask to be let off at Río Nizuc after passing most of the hotels. Take a left after crossing the bridge, then walk 3min. along a path on the right bank. Those who make the effort will be rewarded with a breathtaking view (and jealous stares from passing jetskiers). Watch the cook prepare enormous servings of fresh, barbequed *tikin xic* (50 pesos). Other entrees 40-50 pesos. Open daily 11am-6pm.

Restaurante Pop, Av. Tulum 25 (tel. 84 19 91), near the corner with Av. Uxmal. Located just about a block from the bus station, the air-conditioned interior and huge helpings provide the perfect recovery from a long bumpy bus ride. Any traveler will enjoy starting the day on 3-course breakfasts like *el Yucateco* (32 pesos). Lunch and dinners 20-40 pesos. Open daily 8am-11pm.

SIGHTS

Seeking out unique sights and local culture in Cancún is a little harder than stumbling upon the glimmering, multi-hued ocean, but those who didn't check their brains at the airport will appreciate what the lively inhabitants of this city really have to offer. Even if you stay inland in Ciudad Cancún, you can take advantage of the well-groomed beaches in front of the luxury hotels in the *Zona Hotelera.* Remember, all beaches in Mexico are public property, and travelers often discreetly use hotel restrooms, fresh-water showers, and lounge chairs. If you wisely choose to avoid the resort beach scene, head for the peaceful **Playa Langosta,** west of the CREA, or for the shores south of the **Sheraton Hotel,** some of the safest and the most pleasant in Cancún. Organized beach activities include volleyball, scuba classes, and Mexican-style painting lessons; become a visitor of the hotel for the day to join in. Boogie boards can be rented at the small marina on the beach (35 pesos for 2hr.), but Cancún's surf is a whimper to the roar of the rest of the *costa* *turquesa.* **Playa Chac-Mool,** where waves are about 1m high, is as exciting as it gets. For some free, no-frills encounters with a surprising variety of tropical fish and coral, make your way over near the rocks on the east side of **Playa Tortugas.**

For the not-so-aquatically inclined, **Scuba Cancún** (tel. 83 10 11) offers diving lessons (US$80), snorkeling (US$28), and other services at comparatively reasonable prices. Certified divers will get the better deals: a one-tank dive with **Mundo Marino** (tel. 83 05 54), at around km 5.5, goes for US$45. The dock to the right of the CREA hostel supports a dive shop that offers two hours of snorkeling, equipment included, for about US$25.

ENTERTAINMENT AND SEASONAL EVENTS

The **Parque de las Palapas,** between Avenidas Tulum and Yaxchilán in the very center of town, hosts free regional music and dance performances on Sunday evenings. Admirable foresight or lucky timing could mean enjoying Cancún's celebrated jazz festival (mid- to late-May) or the refreshingly native Caribbean festival (November). Check with the tourist office for info. For slightly more intense entertainment, death in the afternoon occurs every Wednesday at 3:30pm, in the **Plaza de Toros** (tel. 84 83 72; fax 84 82 48), on Av. Bonampak at Av. Sayil. Tickets for the bullfights are available at travel agencies on Av. Tulum for 250 pesos per person (less if you're in a large group; children free, if they're up for it) or at the bullring on a bullfight day. Show includes a cockfight and a performance by the **Ballet Folklórico.**

If you have burning greenbacks and you want frenetic, laser-lit partying, you are the reason why Cancún was erected. **Discos and bars** are both downtown (at the south end of Av. Tulum near Av. Cobá) and in the *Zona Hotelera* at Plaza Caracol (km 9 on Paseo Kukulkán). Most establishments open at 9pm and close when the crowds leave, around 5 or 6am. Crowds differ according to time and season—April is for college spring-breakers, June is for high school graduates, and late night year-round belongs to the *Latinos*. Dress code for the discos is simple; less is more, and tight is just right. Bikini tops often get women in for free, but use your better judgement for the more laid-back dives. Discos in the *Zona* prefer U.S. dollars.

Roots, Tulipanes 26 (tel. 84 24 37; fax 84 55 47), between Palapas Park and Av. Tulum. Cool Caribbean-colored walls and understated artwork with a music motif set the stage for this upstart jazz-n'-blues joint. Watch and listen as the best regional musicians play their digs from the bar or the intimate and cushioned listening area, or get a table a little farther back to converse with the mostly European and expat crowd. Live music 3-6 nights a week; shows start around 10pm. 25 peso cover on Friday and Saturday (most of the money goes to the local arts association). Open Tu-Su 7pm-2am.

La Boom and **Tequila Boom** (tel. 83 11 52), near the youth hostel (a 10min. walk toward the *Zona*). Two nightclubs, a bar, and a pizzeria under the same roof, Boom offers the least artificial atmosphere to young crowds. Serious dancers, get ready to boogie with lasers and (yes) phone booths on stage. Ladies night and open bar vary week to week. Tequila Boom's huge video screens are always accessible free of cover; US$10 to get inside La Boom.

Dady'O (tel. 83 33 33), at km 9, and the premier attraction on Plaza Caracol. Its cave-like entrance makes you feel like you're heading for a disco inferno ("burn, baby, burn"). The cave-scape continues through to a stage and dance floor, surrounded by winding, layered walkways whose crevices sport tables, stools, and passed-out partiers. A cafeteria in the club serves snacks (20-35 pesos). Laser show nightly at 11:30pm. Cover 80 pesos (US$10). Numerous wristband-hawking staff members outside will fill you in on the nightly special. Open daily 10pm-late.

Dady Rock (tel. 83 16 26), next door to Dady'O. Provides the headbanging to complement Dady'Os hip-hopping. Hosts 2 live bands every night and has open bar deals (US$15) several nights per week (open daily 6pm-late). Behind Dady'O, **Tequila Rock** (tel. 83 13 02) keeps the same hours and has the same slant; hard-hitting techno bludgeoning your eardrums on several different green stages. Male eardrums US$15, female eardrums US$5. Open bar on Mondays.

Christine (tel. 83 11 33), next to the Hotel Krystal and across the street from the Convention Center. The staff that introduce themselves at the door, but won't take you in a tank top. A 21+ limit is enforced along with the dress code. The results make for a pounding, fog-ensconced dance floor with a mature twist. A younger crowd still frequents the ladies' nights (W, F), while the second honeymooners come out for 70s and 80s night (Th). There is also a laser light show set to famous classical music at 11:30pm. Cover US$10. Open daily 10pm.

Karamba, on Calle Tulipanes just off Av. Tulum, in Ciudad Cancún. Gay disco with a spacious multi-level floor, funky pop-art murals, and a colorful variety of dance music to complement the wild lights. Tu-F 2-for-1 beers. Cover on Saturday 20 pesos. Open Tu-Su 10pm-4am.

La Candela, Av. Tulum 37 across from Bancomer; keep your eye out for a black door with a candle flame painted on it. The place to go to hear and dance salsa, this club is a local favorite. Live music each night. Sunday is ladies' night and 2-for-1 cocktails are offered Thursday. Cover 25 pesos. Open daily except for Tuesdays 9pm-3am.

Isla Holbox

It becomes apparent that hidden treasure still exists when mention of Isla Holbox (EES-la ohl-BOSH) draws puzzled looks from experienced Yucatán travelers. Aside from the Mexican tourists who storm the island in April and December, this 33km long finger-shaped island is still a mystery to almost all foreign tourists, and you'll want it to stay that way. Just off the northeastern tip of the Yucatán Peninsula, it is home to a handful of *holboxeños* and their fishing. The pace of life here is unbelievably *tranquila,* the beaches and surrounding tiny *islas* inspiring, and the people welcoming. If you think you've never seen such a beautiful sunset, stay another night. **Chiquilá** is the embarkation point for passengers ferrying to the secluded beaches of Isla Holbox. The small settlement will not delay in-transit tourists, but after the last ferry chugs out, late arrivals usually prefer to head back to civilization for a meal and a bed for two simple reasons: there's no place to stay in Chiquilá, and the mosquitoes suck. Literally.

ORIENTATION AND PRACTICAL INFORMATION Getting to Isla Holbox requires previous planning, but it's well worth it. The easiest way to go is to take the 8:30am bus from Cancún (26 pesos), which reaches Chiquilá at 11:30am, and hop on the **lancha** of "Los 9 Hermanos" (boats run every 2hr. 6am-5pm, 20 pesos; they return to Chiquilá every 2hr. 5am-4pm). There are more options when it comes to returning from Isla Holbox, since both Valladolid-bound and Cancún-bound buses and vans (35 pesos) meet the early boat from the *isla.* Most options mean a 5am ferry ride, though, so be sure to prepare for the mosquitos. Be ready to leap off when the boat strikes the dock, because the buses wait for no one. If the Cancún bus doesn't show, take the Valladolid-Mérida bus to Kantunil Kin; the Cancún bus swings by there at 6:30am. You can always flag down a Valladolid-Cancún bus at Ideal, though waiting in the sun will be torturous.

There are no options when it comes to staying the night or eating in Chiquilá. The swamp that surrounds the town doesn't make for much sightseeing either. If you miss the last ferry to Holbox, call a *lanchero* (tel. 5 20 21) and beg them to come get you; otherwise return to **Kantunil Kin,** a town 43km south of Chiquilá on the Chiquilá access road. In Kantunil Kin, beds are available at the red-and-white **Casa de Huéspedes "Del Parque"** (tel. 5 00 17), on the other side of the basketball court next to the church (singles 65 pesos; doubles 75 pesos; triples 95 pesos).

On the Isla, the palm tree median and packed sand of Av. Juárez begins at the dock, runs past the *zócalo* and ends up on the beach. There is no bank on the island, and locals may not have enough cash on hand to cover your newly planned extended stay. The one-man **police** force lounges in the station at the *zócalo* on the corner of Juárez and Díaz (open daily 9am-2pm and 4-8pm, but don't count on it). The **Centro de Salud,** on the right side of Juárez in the blue-and-white building, houses a doctor who may be awakened in case of a serious emergency. There is a new place with **fax** and **telegram** on the corner of Juárez and Díaz, which also has **Western Union** service (tel. 5 20 53; open M-F 9am-3pm). Holbox's **public telephone** *caseta* is a half-block east of the *zócalo* on Igualdad (open M-Sa 8am-1pm and 4-8pm; 2-3 pesos).

ACCOMMODATIONS AND FOOD Two words: simple and fish. And parrots too (though that makes three words). There's one to whistle with at the **Posada D'Ingrid** (tel. 5 20 70) two blocks from the northwestern corner of the *zócalo;* veer left. Gleaming salmon-colored rooms with hot water, clean bathrooms, and ceiling fans open up to a *palapa*-roofed patio with lights, speakers, and card tables. (Doubles 100 pesos; brand-new quads 150 pesos.) Señora Dinora is the friendly owner of **Tienda Dinora** on the west side of the *zócalo*. She also owns the **Posada Los Arcos** next door. Rooms with fans and hot water surround a large courtyard. (Singles 90 pesos; doubles 100 pesos; triples 110 pesos.) Sra. Dinora also rents out **bikes** at 15 pesos an hour, which are useful for exploring the many kilometers of beach. The cheapest rooms are found on the other side of the island at the **Hotel Flamingo,** which stands near the dock. Featuring a view of the mainland shaded by coconut palms, it has four small rooms with fans and hot water. (70 pesos per person, less for longer stays.)

Restaurants in Holbox follow the pace of island life, meandering through time without a fixed schedule. Among them is **Zarabanda,** one block south of the *zócalo* and two blocks east of Juárez. Colorful tissue paper cut-outs strung up along the thatched roof sway with the breeze as the cooks prepare excellent fish and meat dishes (25-40 pesos). Fruit and vegetable fans land at **La Isla del Colibrí,** Av. Juárez and Díaz, and find refreshment in huge 10-15 peso fruit drinks and 25 peso entrees (open M-Sa 8am-1:30pm and 7-11pm, Su 7-11pm). The family at **Lonchería El Parque,** on Juárez, two doors down from Dinora's, cooks up fresh and inexpensive seafood. A chicken or beef dish with a frosty beer will cost about 30 pesos. (Open daily 9am-10pm.)

SIGHTS AND ENTERTAINMENT Shell-lined North Beach, on the island's north shore, is pleasant enough. For more, head about 8km west from North Beach to Punta Francisca, where a 25km stretch of raw, unspoiled beach begins. The main draws, aside from sunning and sleeping, are the boat trips provided by local fishermen (4hr. cruise 400 pesos; try to get a group together). East of the island is **Isla de Pájaros,** called **Isla Morena** by locals and home to nearly 40 species of birds including flamingos and pelicans. Next stop is **Ojo de Agua,** an inlet on the mainland fed by a subterranean freshwater spring. Jump in and splash around in the shallow pools. Finally, you'll head across the lagoon that separates Isla Holbox from the mainland (look out for the many dolphins) to **Isla de la Pasión,** at the western end, so named for the couples of birds and *isleños* that relax there during the off-season. During the high season, Isla Holbox caters to daytrippers with its restaurant-bar, live music, and volleyball court. To see *holboxeños* at their liveliest, cruise the brightly lit *zócalo* at dusk, when old friends and families gather to socialize, enjoy the playground, and watch the refereed basketball games. Be sure to head down to the north shore sometime during the night. There, if conditions are right, you can witness *ardentía*, a rare and completely natural phosphorescent phenomenon. Microorganisms respond to movement in the water by turning bright green; just kick the water a bit to see the eerie glow. Open Friday and Saturday, **Cariocas Restaurant and Disco,** on Igualdad two blocks off the *zócalo*, is the place to be when the music starts up.

Isla Mujeres

When the Spaniard Francisco Hernández de Córdoba blew into this tiny island (7km by 1km, 11km northeast of the coast of Quintana Roo) in 1517 looking for slaves to work the Cuban mines, he instead found hundreds of small, wooden female statuettes scattered among the beaches. When he named the island "Isla Mujeres" (Island of Women), he did not seem to realize that he had stumbled upon a Maya sanctuary for Ixchel, the goddess of fertility. The island was uninhabited until it became the favorite hideout for pirates who, for the 200 years after Córdoba's arrival, marauded the "Spanish Lake." However, Caribbean fishermen began to regain control of the island as fewer and fewer bullion-laden Spanish galleons sailed up from South America.

Some present-day inhabitants of the island (pop. 13,500) still fish, but many now sell souvenirs and cater to the daytrippers who arrive each morning from Cancún. Popular among British, German, and Australian travelers, the island is free from the American culture and young crowds that characterize Cancún, and it offers its treasures at much cheaper prices. A different, welcomed worry sometimes afflicts visitors to the island—it's easy to lose track of time as siestas come and go under the shade of the tree-lined beaches. Here, time just slips away.

ORIENTATION

Just as beach lovers will dream of Isla Mujeres, so will walkers enjoy getting around the island's small but lively *centro,* although crowds pack the streets from December through April. The town is laid out in a rough grid. Right in front and perpendicular to the dock is **Av. Rueda Medina,** which runs the length of the island along the coastline, past Makax Lagoon, Playas Paraíso, Lancheros, and Indios, and the Garrafón National Park. Perpendicular to Medina are the six major east-west streets of the *centro:* **Avenidas**
Mateos, Matamoros, Abasolo, Madero, Morelos, and Nicolás Bravo, from north to south. Avenidas Juárez, Hidalgo, Guerrero, and Carlos Lazo run parallel to Rueda Medina. Turning left on any of these streets will quickly lead you to **Playa Norte.** Finally, on the southern tip of the island beyond an abandoned lighthouse, are the remains of a Maya temple, **Ixchel.** A good source of general information is *Islander,* a local publication available at travel agency shops, the ferry dock at Puerto Juárez, and the tourist office in the *zócalo.* Maps are available both on the ferry and in the many tourist offices. The best way to explore the island for yourself is by moped (which can be caught every 15min. on R. Medina)—the whole trip won't take more than three hours, even with a few stops for a swim. Public buses go only as far as Playa Lancheros (3 pesos). Taxis, on the other hand, roam the length of Isla Mujeres; you should have no problem catching one unless you're mesmerized by the crashing waves on the southern tip until well after dark.

PRACTICAL INFORMATION

Ferries: To get to the island, catch a boat from **Puerto Juárez,** 2km north of Ciudad Cancún and accessible by a "Puerto Juárez" bus (15min., 3 pesos) or by taxi (30 pesos). Normal service boats take much longer but sometimes have live music to pass the time (45min., every hr. 8am-8pm, 9 pesos). Express service cruisers leave for the island every 30min. (15min., 5:30am-8:30pm, 22 pesos). Arrive early—ferries are notorious for leaving ahead of schedule if they're full. A car ferry runs to Mujeres from Punta Sam, 5km north of Puerto Juárez (8 and 11am, 2:45, 5:30 and 8:15 pm; 9 pesos per person, 40 pesos per car).

Taxis: (tel. 7 00 66). Unmistakable bright red cabs line up at the stand directly to the right as you come off the passenger dock. Rides from town to Playas Paraíso and Lancheros, to Garrafón, and to the ruins cost 8 pesos, 26 pesos, and 33 pesos, respectively.

Moped Rental: You may be hard pressed to find mopeds for less than 40 pesos per hour, but certainly try. At **El Zorro,** on Guerrero between Abasolo and Matamoros, they go for 150 pesos (gas included) per day. Open daily 8am-6pm.

Tourist Office: Hidalgo 7, 2nd. fl. at Plaza Isla Mujeres, between Mateos and Matamoros. Most information, including a map of the town, is also available in Islander, Cancún Tips, and Isla Mujeres Tips.

Currency Exchange: Bank **Bital** (tel. 7 00 05), on Rueda Medina to the right when coming off the passenger dock. Open M-Sa 8am-7pm. Also has a 24hr. ATM which takes Visa, Mastercard, and Cirrus.

Markets: Súper Betino, Morelos 3 (tel. 7 01 27), on the *zócalo.* Deli and bakery inside. Open daily 7am-11pm. For fruit on the run, try the **fruit stalls** just outside or the mini-market **Isla Mujeres,** on Hidalgo between Abasolo and Madero.

Laundry Service: Lavandería Tim Phó, Av. Juárez 94 at Abasolo. 4kg for 25 pesos, 2hr. turnaround. Open M-Sa 7am-9pm, Su 8am-2pm.

Police: (tel. 7 00 98) on Hidalgo at Morelos, in the Palacio Municipal. Open 24hr.

Red Cross: Dial 7 02 80.

Pharmacy: La Mejor, Madero 18 (tel. 7 01 16) between Hidalgo and Juárez. Open daily 9am-10pm.

Medical Assistance: Centro de Salud, Guerrero 5 (tel. 7 01 17) at Morelos. The white building at the northwest corner of the *zócalo.* Open 24hr. Some doctors speak English, such as **Dr. Antonio E. Salas** (tel. 7 04 77 or beeper 91 98 88 78 68 code 1465), at Hidalgo near Madero. Will make house calls. Open 24hr.

Post Office: (tel. 7 00 85) Guerrero and López Mateos, at the northwest corner of town, 1 block from the Playa Norte. Open M-F 8am-4pm, Sa 9am-1pm. **Postal Code:** 70085.

Fax: Guerrero 13 (tel. 7 02 45), next to the post office. Open M-F 9am-3pm. They also have a **telegram** service.

Telephones: Call home from one of the numerous LADATELS, or try the long-distance *caseta* in the lobby of **Hotel María Jose** (tel. 7 01 30), on Madero by Rueda Medina. Open daily 9am-2pm and 4-7pm.

Phone Code: 987.

ACCOMMODATIONS AND CAMPING

One may wonder how the price of lodgings can decrease after crossing Mujeres Bay while the quality of the surroundings is absolutely superior. After about two seconds, however, far more pressing concerns (like which beach to hit first) distract visitors from this quandary. Prices can fluctuate by as much as 80 pesos depending on the season, less so over the length of stay; inquire ahead. Camping on the beach is not strictly regulated; most people find **Playa Indios** (500m past Playa Paraíso on Rueda Medina) the most hospitable and unobtrusive spot to sack out. However, it's always wise to sample local opinion before settling in for the night. All hotels listed below are in town, north of the *zócalo.*

Hotel Marcianito, centrally located at Abasolo 10 (tel. 7 01 11), between Juárez and Hidalgo. Pesa the cocker spaniel tries to be the first to greet visitors at the gate, and the service gets even friendlier from there. Great central location, yet the secluded rooms keep out any late-night noise. Well-furnished rooms have ceiling fans and hot water. Singles and doubles 130 pesos; triples 160 pesos; quads 180 pesos.

Poc-Na Youth Hostel, Matamoros 15 (tel. 7 00 90) on the eastern beach. Whether people are sacking out on a bed (25 pesos; 8-14 to a room), in one of the quiet hammock rooms (29 pesos) or in a tent on the side lawn (40 pesos for 2-person tent), it all comes together under the lazy fans of the *palapa* dining hall. More socializing and less eating goes on here among the largely European crowd. 3 private rooms available (60-80 pesos). Small additional fees for sheets, towels, and lock. Check-out 1pm, 13 pesos more to stay later. Cafeteria open 7am-10pm.

Hotel Xul-Ha, Hidalgo 23 (tel. 7 00 75), between Matamoros and López Mateos. Sporting large rooms, colorful beds, and ceiling fans, the hotel also offers a color

TV, coffee machines, refrigerator, and English paperbacks in its lobby. Doubles 170 pesos; triples 200 pesos. 80 pesos more during peak season. Check-out noon. Discounts for longer stays.

Hotel Carmelina, Guerrero 4 (tel. 7 00 06), between Abasolo and Madero. Bright yellow bathrooms liven up the rooms and both are well-kept. Fans don't get much help from the windows, though. Hot water. Singles 120 pesos; doubles 140 pesos; triples 180 pesos. A/C 40 pesos extra.

FOOD

Seafood gets a lot of exposure here, Isla Mujeres being an island and all. Go with the flow and try some *pulpo* (octopus, no ink) or give your jaws a workout with some *caracol* (conch, a tender meat). Either one of these, along with several types of seafood, can be ordered as *ceviche* (seafood marinated in lime juice, cilantro, and other herbs). For cheap grub, visit the *loncherías* on Guerrero between Matamoros and López Mateos, or look for roaming vendors selling seafood from gigantic pots. Plan ahead since many restaurants close between lunch and dinner.

Café Cito, Matamoros 42 (tel. 7 04 38; email cafe-cito@sybcom.com), at Juárez. Patrons can pretend they haven't left the beach with the sand and shells under the see-through tabletops of this newly redecorated cafe. A visit here can replenish both body and soul; crepes and sandwiches take care of the body and Sabina can take care of the rest. Open M-W and F-Sa 8am-noon and 6-10pm, Th-Su 8am-noon.

Chen Huaye ("only here" in Mayan), just off the *zócalo* across from the playground on Av. Bravo. Unlike the wagon wheels out in front, the service inside keeps those local dishes rolling. Entrees 15-25 pesos. Try the zesty *pescado a la veracruzana* (29 pesos). Open daily except Wednesday 9am-11pm.

Red Eye Cafe, Av. Hidalgo between Mateos and Matamoros. For a bite to eat on the way to the beach, sample the heavily German-influenced trilingual menu. Stuff yourself on sandwiches (15-20 pesos), breakfast (20 pesos), bratwurst or *wiener schnitzel* (30 pesos). Open daily except Tuesday 6am-3pm.

SIGHTS AND SAND

Many of Isla Mujeres' characteristics, like soft white beaches, rocky promontories overlooking stormy seas, lighthouses, fishing boats, and mangroves, make it a slice of the West Indies a quick ferry ride from Mexico. Starting with the beaches, this unique opportunity should be fully enjoyed. The most popular and accessible beach is **Playa Norte. Playas Lanchero** and **Paraíso** (km 3 on Rueda Martínez) are similar, but they open up onto Mujeres Bay. Snorkeling connoisseurs should head to **Garrafón National Park,** 1km past Lanchero and Paraíso, whose net-enclosed waters ensure the presence of shy marine life (park open daily 9am-5pm; 15 pesos). **Bahía Dive Shop** (tel./fax 7 03 40), on Rueda Medina across from the car ferry dock, rents quality snorkeling equipment; the staff can direct you to the best spots (open M-Sa 8:30am-7pm). Or join them year-round for organized reef snorkeling (120 pesos), diving (360 pesos), and fishing trips (80 pesos).

La Isleña travel agency (tel. 7 05 78), on Morelos a half block from the dock, offers snorkeling gear (30 pesos) and mopeds (50 pesos) and organizes trips to nearby **Isla Contoy,** a wildlife sanctuary rife with pelicans, cormorants, and about 5000 other bird species. *(Tour lasts 8:30am-4pm. Equipment and 2 meals included. 250 pesos or US$32. Deposit of at least 50% required the previous day. Agency open daily 7:30am-9:30pm.)* The tours include reef snorkeling at **Isla-Che.**

To see and support a group of dedicated individuals helping to save the planet and to have an unforgettable time while doing so, head over to **PESCA,** km 5 on Carretera Sac Bajo, across the Laguna de Makax from the populated northern half of the island. *(Open daily 9am-5pm.)* This biological research station is engaged in a breeding program for three species of sea turtles. Female turtles, captured by PESCA in May, lay their eggs in the safety of the station's beach throughout the summer and are returned to the wild in October. The young are reared for a year before they, too, are released. For a mere 10 pesos, a guide will take you on a stroll through the center to see the turtles and their offspring.

In the case of the Maya ruins of **Ixchel,** getting there truly makes the trip. The temple was reduced to rubble by Hurricane Gilbert in 1988, yet there is still a partially reconstructed one-room building to be seen as well as an immense panorama of the Yucatán and the Caribbean Sea.

ENTERTAINMENT

Isla Mujeres' nightlife is commensurate with its small size and laid-back demeanor. Nevertheless, a handful of *locales* blast the music and hawk two-for-one nights in order to keep at least some of the visitors awake at night. **Kokonuts** (tel. 7 01 55), on Av. Hidalgo behind the North Beach, has live music each night and an even livelier bar. **Chimbo's,** on Playa Norte to the right of Av. Hidalgo, just about accounts for the rest of Mujeres's nightlife. With a temporary dance floor laid out on the sand and decked out in holiday lights and UV artwork, this place makes up in energy what it lacks in decor. You may expect Pancho Villa himself to come stumbling out of the swinging wooden doors of Pancho Tequila. On Matamoros between Hidalgo and Guerrero, the small dance floor and lively mix of Mexican and international dance music are as refreshing as the air-conditioning. **Restaurant La Peña,** Guerrero 5 (tel. 7 03 09), at the *zócalo,* becomes a disco after 11pm. The thatched roof and stone archway house dancing in front and waterfront dining in back. Things usually start up at the bars after 10pm, but as schedules are erratic, it's best to ask around. For less alcohol-driven fun, families can head over to the eastern end of the *zócalo* and go nuts on the trampoline or at the foosball tables. During rainy season, plan for nighttime showers to flood the streets.

Playa del Carmen

Smack in the middle of Quintana Roo's legendary *costa turquesa* (turquoise coast), Playa del Carmen (pop. 15,000) is a crossroads for archaeologically inclined travelers en route to inland ruins and beach hunters heading for Cozumel and Cancún. Although Playa (as locals call it) used to be a fishing village, its silky white sand and startlingly blue waters made it a tourist paradise. Focusing on the present rather than the past, the town's *palapas* and moderately priced seafood restaurants look out onto the breezy pedestrian walkway, where spray-paint artists and hammock vendors hawk their wares.

ORIENTATION

Playa is centered around its main transportation centers, the ferry dock and the bus stations. The bus drops you off on the main drag, **Av. Principal** (Juárez), which runs west from the beach to the Cancún-Chetumal Highway 1.5km away. Most services lie along this road. At the **bus station/plaza,** perpendicular to Av. Principal, runs **Av. Quinta,** which is parallel to the shore and encompasses most of the *tiendas* and restaurants. East-west *calles* increase by two in either direction; north-south *avenidas* increase by five. Playa's *playa* lies one block east of Quinta.

PRACTICAL INFORMATION

Buses: (tel. 3 01 09), at corner of Quinta and Principal. **ADO** runs first-class buses to Chetumal (4½hr., 6 per day 7:30am-midnight, 100 pesos), Coatzacoalcos (12hr., 7am, 4:30, and 9pm, 299 pesos), Córdoba (22hr., 7am, 435 pesos), Escárcega (6hr., 7am, 8, and 9pm, 165 pesos), Mexico City (25hr., 7am, noon, and 7pm, 518 pesos), Orizaba (14hr., noon and 7pm, 442 pesos), Puebla (23hr., 6pm, 498 pesos), San Andrés (9½hr., 3:30pm, 393 pesos), Veracruz (12hr., 3:30pm,

389 pesos), and Villahermosa (12hr., 7 per day noon-9pm, 249 pesos). **Cristóbal Colón** goes to Ocosingo (13hr., 4:15pm, 259 pesos), Palenque (11hr., 4:15pm, 201 pesos), San Cristóbal (15hr., 4:15pm, 272 pesos), and Tuxtla Gutiérrez (16hr., 4:15pm, 294 pesos). **ATS** has second-class service to Tulum (1hr., 11 per day, 18 pesos). **Premier** goes to Mérida (5hr., 8 per day, 89 pesos) via Ticul (3½hr., 56 pesos).

Tourist Office: A wooden booth on the northwest corner of the plaza, diagonally across Av. Quinta from the bus station. Self-service pamphlets only. Open daily 7am-11pm.

Currency Exchange: Bital (tel. 3 02 72), on Av. Principal, one block west of the plaza. Changes U.S. dollars only. Has a 24hr. **ATM.** Bank open M-F 8am-3:30pm.

Laundromat: Maya Laundry (tel. 3 02 61), on Quinta, 1 block north of the plaza, on the right. Wash and dry 8 pesos per kg. Dry cleaning too. Open daily 8am-8pm.

Supermarket: El Súper del Ahorro (tel. 3 03 06), on Principal, 3½ blocks west of Quinta. Open daily 6:30am-10:30pm.

Police: (tel. 3 02 21), on Av. Principal, 2 blocks west of the plaza. Open 24hr.

Pharmacy: Farmacia París (tel. 3 07 44), on Av. Principal, opposite the bus station. Open daily 7am-midnight.

Medical Assistance: Centro de Salud (tel. 3 03 14), on the corner of Av. Principal, across from the post office. Some English spoken. Open 24hr.

Post Office: On Av. Principal (tel. 3 03 00), 3 blocks from the plaza. Open M-F 8am-7pm, Sa 9am-1pm. **MexPost** in the same building. Open 9am-5:30pm. **Postal Code:** 77710.

Phone Code: 987.

ACCOMMODATIONS AND CAMPING

As Playa's accommodations begin to test the tempting waters of tourist-gouging prices, bargains become more and more scarce. Fortunately, as prices rise, so does quality. Most establishments lie along either Quinta or Principal, close to the beach.

Hotel Lilly, on Av. Principal, the flaming pink building 1 block west of the plaza. Convenient but noisy location near the bus stop. Small, cushy beds in ordinary, but clean rooms with fans. Singles 120 pesos; doubles 150 pesos; triples 180 pesos.

La Copacabana (tel. 3 02 18), on Av. Quinta, 4 blocks north of the plaza. Colorful and classy rooms have spotless bathrooms and space to spare. Recently renovated courtyard and strong new hammocks are a great place to relax after a meal at the restaurant next door. Singles and doubles 180 pesos; triples 220 pesos.

Campamento La Ruina (tel. 3 04 05), on the beach, 200m north of the ferry dock. Popular with Europeans. Hostel-style, with communal bathrooms and cooking facilities. Ceiling fans cool cabanas *rústicas* with tiny, stiff military-style beds. Bring a lock. Singles and doubles 72 pesos; triples 165 pesos (prices vary with season and room). Hammock-space under the *palapa* 45 pesos, plus 5 pesos for a plastic hammock rental. Pitch a tent in the sand for 45 pesos; 15 pesos per extra camper. Lockers 5 pesos.

CREA Youth Hostel (HI; tel. 3 15 08), a 1km trek from the plaza. Walk 4 blocks on Principal, and turn right before Farmacia La Salud. Walk another 4 blocks, passing the big concrete IMSS building; the hostel is a block-and-a-half farther on the left. Bleak and deserted during the low season. Bring a lock for your locker. Single-sex dorms with quaking bunk beds 30 pesos with a 30-peso deposit. Cabanas with private bathrooms and A/C 150 pesos plus an 80-peso deposit. 10% discount with HI card. No curfew or max. stay.

FOOD

It's hard to find a bargain in the glare of Quinta's flashy restaurants, although the occasional all-you-can-eat deal does come along. Take the time to shop around—

high prices and quality don't necessarily go hand in hand. Cheaper fruit and *torta* experiences are found along breezy Principal.

Sabor, 1½ blocks north on Quinta. Easily missed if you're scurrying for shade on a hot day; look for the crowded, flowery, turquoise *parasoles* next to Pez Vela. Scrumptious sandwiches made with whole-wheat bread (14 pesos) and top-notch coffee. Bean and cheese burritos (18 pesos) are fit for the fussiest of culinary critics. Open daily 8am-10pm.

Antojitos El Correo (tel. 3 03 99). Walk up Principal 2 blocks to the clinic, then go left 1 block. Can't be beat for the all-important amount-of-food-for-money measurement. A *palapa*-roofed setting for the *comida corrida* (25 pesos) and *desayunos* (17 pesos) served to locals. Cheap and classy. Open daily 7am-midnight.

Media Luna (tel. 3 00 56), on Quinta, 3 blocks north of the plaza. Whether you're devouring one of their healthy breakfasts or simply sipping coffee, you'll want to linger in the padded wooden corners. Unusual and delicious mango crepes (40 pesos). Open daily 7am-11pm.

Playa Caribe, just north of the bus station on Quinta. Très chic. Enjoy your soup, fish fillet, and beer (42 pesos) to the sound of happily sunburned foot traffic. Food tends to be on the *picante* (spicy) side. Open daily 7am-11pm.

SAND, SIGHTS, AND ENTERTAINMENT

Decorated with an occasional palm tree and fringed by the turquoise waters of the Caribbean, Playa del Carmen's **beaches** are simply beautiful. They are relatively free of seaweed and coral, and covered with scantily clad sunbathing tourists; the wave

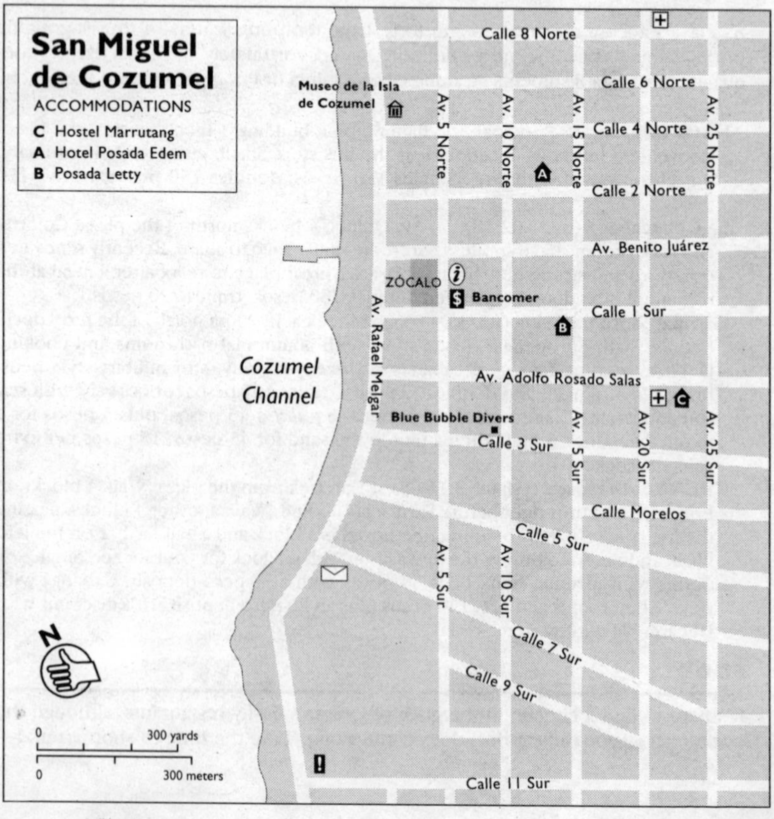

that began in Cancún has officially splashed down on Playa. One kilometer north of town, the beach goes **nude.** If you want a water-escape, 80-120 pesos (depending on the place and your bargaining ability) will buy you an hour's worth of **windsurfing.** Windsurfing equipment and other gear can be rented from some of the fancier hotels just south of the pier, or from shacks a few hundred meters north. **Albatros** offers windsurfing lessons; just look for the pink sign. Although Playa has no snorkel-friendly reefs nearby, there's a decent reef 200m past the Shangri-La Caribe Hotel; the high surf, however, often hinders visibility.

While the pace of life here is gentle and relaxed, there is one thing the locals do promptly: close shop. After dark, sun-lovers recuperate from the hot rays, relaxing in swaying hammocks with cold beers or enjoying mellow guitar-strumming that can soothe even the meanest burn. Come nightfall, many move on to **Karen's Grill,** on La Quinta one-and-a-half blocks north of the plaza, which is often embellished with popular local bands (happy hour 7-9pm). Quinta teems with late-night **bars** and local **bands**—just follow the music and the crowds to find the hottest places. If you're looking for a smaller place, hop onto a barside saddle at **La Bamba,** where you can drink and watch music videos until 11pm (or until you fall off the saddle, whichever happens first). Only the **Calypso Bar Caribeño,** two blocks north of the plaza on the beach, its small dance floor lit an iridescent blue, stays open late, pumping out salsa until the first signs of dawn brighten the sea (open daily 10pm-4am). For those with a hankering for Hollywood, **Cinema Playa del Carmen,** four blocks west of the *zócalo* and one block north of Av. Principal, has evening showings of U.S. flicks (12 pesos).

Isla Cozumel

Cozumel (pop. 60,000) originally drew attention to itself as a key trading center for the Maya and later as a pirate refuge for Sir Francis Drake and Jean Lafitte. It took Jacques Cousteau in the 1950s to call worldwide attention to the natural wonders of the nearby Palancar Reef and the sea life it sustains. The reefs were too good to be left to idealistic research, however. Cozumel has been marketed lately as an "ecological getaway" for tourists wishing to "leave" Cancún's confines and "explore" Mexico (without saying goodbye to luxury, dollars, or sycophantic service). There is more to Cozumel, however, than over-priced dive shops and snorkeling tours; while the red and white diving banner has become the island's unofficial flag, much of the island is undeveloped. Miles upon miles of empty white beach greet the tourist who musters the energy to leave Cozumel the city and explore Cozumel the island. Isolated beachfront cafes and by-the-sea roads offer splendid views of gorgeous water and plenty of opportunities to explore the famous reefs that lie below.

ORIENTATION

The island of Cozumel lies 18km east of the northern Quintana Roo coast and 85km south of Isla Mujeres. The island is most commonly accessed via ferry from Playa del Carmen (to the west) or **Puerto Morelos** (to the north). **Ferries** from Puerto Morelos (tel. 2 09 50) transport cars to and from Cozumel twice daily, docking in the island's only town, **Cozumel,** on the west shore (2½hr., 9am and 1pm, US$30 per car, US$4.50 per person). Tourist vehicles supposedly have priority, but the **car ferry** is inconvenient and unpredictable. The tourist office recommends that you secure a spot in line 12 hours in advance. **Water Jet Service** (tel. 2 15 08) sends three boats back and forth between Playa del Carmen and Cozumel. Tickets can be bought at the dock in Cozumel and from the booth on the Playa's plaza (40min., 12 trips daily from each shore 4am-8pm, round-trip 80 pesos). If you are coming from Cancún, an alternative to the bus-ferry ordeal is the 20-minute **air shuttle** operated by Aerocaribe.

At 53km long and 14km wide, Cozumel is Mexico's largest Caribbean island. Although public transportation is literally nonexistent, downtown streets are clearly labeled and numbered with stubborn logic. If you don't mind occasionally spine-wrenching road conditions, the rest of the island is easily explored by bike or moped. Taxis are everywhere.

As you step off the ferry into Cozumel, **Av. Rafael Melgar** runs along the shore, circling the entire island. **Av. Juárez,** a pedestrian walkway for the first two blocks, is directly in front of you, running perpendicular to the shore and crossing the town. Juárez continues on to cross the island as **Carretera Transversal,** and joins Av. Melgar on the other side. *Calles* run parallel to Juárez and are labeled *Sur* and *Norte* (Nte.) with respect to Juárez. North of Juárez, *calles* increase in even numbers; south of Juárez, they increase in odd numbers. *Avenidas* run north-south, are numbered in multiples of five, and are designated *Norte* or *Sur* with respect to Juárez. **Av. Adolfo Rosada Salas** is between Calles 1 and 3 Sur. Av. Melgar leads south to the main points of interest: the national park at **Laguna Chankanaab** and the popular beach at **San Francisco** are south of town on the western shore; **Palancar Reef** lies off the island's southern tip. The nearly deserted eastern coast is dotted by Maya ruins and supports only a few restaurants and camping spots.

PRACTICAL INFORMATION

While there are no consulates on Cozumel, Mr. Bryan Wilson (tel. 2 06 54), who works closely with the Mérida U.S. consulate, provides unofficial, free assistance to English-speaking travelers. In an **emergency,** knock on the door of the white house at Av. 15 and Calle 13 Sur.

Transportation

Airport: (tel. 2 04 85), 2km north of town. **Aerocaribe** (tel. 2 05 03), **Aerocozumel** (tel. 2 09 28), **Continental** (tel. 2 08 47), and **Mexicana** (tel. 2 00 05) serve Cozumel.

Ferries: Passenger ferries leave for Cozumel every hr. starting at 5am from the dock at the end of Av. Juárez (40 pesos). Arrive early, as ferries sell out several minutes before departure. Buy tickets at the corner of Melgar and the dock. **Car ferries** leave from the dock south of main dock.

Taxis: (tel. 2 02 36). From the plaza, 30 pesos to the airport; 56 pesos to Chankanaab; 88 pesos to Punta Morena. Expect to pay more for more people.

Car Rental: Less Pay (tel. 2 47 44), on Av. Melgar, about 1km south of town. VW Safaries for US$25 per day, less for multiple-day rentals. Open daily 8am-8pm. Bring driver's license and major credit card.

Moped Rental: Pretty expensive. Get one outside Hotel Posada Edem (see below) for about 160 pesos. Haggle for all you're worth.

Bike Rental: Rentadora Cozumel (tel. 2 11 20 or 2 15 03), on Av. 10 at Calle 1 Sur. 40 pesos per day. Return by 6pm. US$20 deposit required. Open daily 8am-8pm.

Tourist and Financial Services

Tourist Office: (tel. 2 09 72), on the second floor of "Plaza del Sol," the building to the left of Bancomer, on the plaza. *Cozumel Today* has a decent map. The *Blue Guide to Cozumel* is quite helpful. Open M-F 8am-2:30pm.

Currency Exchange: BanNorte (tel. 2 16 82), right off the dock, charges a 1% commission for exchanging traveler's checks. Bank open M-F 9am-12:30pm. **Bancomer** (tel. 2 05 50), on the plaza, has the same rates but charges a flat fee of US$0.50 per check. Open M-F 9am-4:30pm, Sa 10am-2pm. **BITAL** (tel. 2 01 42), on the plaza, has a 24hr. **ATM.** Open M-F 9am-2:30pm, Sa 10am-1pm.

Local Services

Bookstore: Agencia de Publicaciones Gracia (tel. 2 00 31), on the plaza. Last week's *Newsweek* for the price of a meal (25-35 pesos). Open daily 8am-10pm.

Laundromat: Margarita, Av. 20 Sur 285 (tel. 2 28 65), near Calle 3 Sur. Self-service 19 pesos per machine for wash and dry, soap 4 pesos. Open M-Sa 7am-9pm, Su 9am-5pm.

Emergency and Communications

Police: (tel. 2 00 92; English tel. 2 04 09 and ask for a bilingual officer), on Calle 11 Sur near Rafael Melgar, in the Palacio Municipal.

Red Cross: (tel. 2 10 57 or 2 10 58), on Av. 20 Sur at Av. Adolfo Salas. Open 24hr.

Pharmacy: Farmacia Kiosco (tel. 2 24 85), on the *zócalo* near Hotel López. Everything for the sun-happy or sun-sick tourist. Open daily 8am-10pm.

Medical Services: There are several English-speaking private physicians in Cozumel. Try **Dr. M. F. Lewis** (tel. 2 09 12), on Av. 50 at Calle 11, for consultations or 24hr. tourist medical service. **Medical Center (CEM),** Av. 20 Nte. 425 (tel. 2 29 19 or 2 14 19), between Calles 10 and 8 Nte. For an **ambulance,** call 2 14 19.

Post Office: (tel. 2 01 06), off Rafael Melgar, just south of Calle 7 Sur, along the sea. Open M-F 8am-7:30pm, Sa 9am-1pm. **Postal Code:** 77600.

Fax: (tel. 2 00 56), next to the post office.

Internet Access: Internet Cozumel (tel. 2 13 17), Local 1, 3 blocks east of the waterfront on Calle 11 Sur. New computers, new office, reasonable prices. 30 pesos per hr. Open M-F 9am-6:30pm, Sa 10am-2:30pm.

Phone Code: 987.

ACCOMMODATIONS AND CAMPING

Although hotels in Cozumel are more expensive than in Playa, your extra pesos buy higher-quality rooms. Peak-season travelers should expect slightly higher prices and should hunt down a room before noon. Clean, reasonably cheap accommodations lie within blocks of the plaza—resist being roped into a pricey package deal when you step off the ferry. Secluded camping spots are at **Punta Morena** and **Punta Chiqueros,** on the island's Caribbean coast. Short-term campers should encounter no problems with the authorities, but for longer stays, you might want to consult the tourist office to find out the best camping options.

Hotel Posada Edem, Calle 2 Nte. 12 (tel. 2 11 66), between Calles 10 and 15. Upon docking, go left 1 block, turn right, and walk up 2 blocks. Astoundingly clean rooms with fresh linen, 2 beds, fans, fluffy towels, and hot water. *Agua purificada* in lobby. Singles 105 pesos; doubles 125 pesos; extra person 30 pesos.

Hotel Marruang (tel. 2 16 78), on Av. Adolfo Salas, just past Av. 20. Look for the dentist sign on the big blue building. This hotel shines like freshly cleaned teeth—too bad it costs about as much. Spotless floors lead to comfy beds, ceiling fans, and fantastic bathrooms with hot water. Singles and doubles 140 pesos; triples 170 pesos.

Cabañas Punta Morena, Carretera Transversal km 17. For those who have their own transportation. Next to a beachfront seafood restaurant, these cabanas have the view around. Rooms lack furniture, but you'll be so mesmerized by the view, you won't even notice. At night during summer, turtles come to lay their eggs on the nearby shore. Volleyball court on the beach. All rooms 100 pesos. Surfboards (120 pesos) and boogie boards (55 pesos) for rent.

Posada Letty (tel. 2 02 57), on Calle 1 Sur past Av. 10. Their business card promises "Cleanliness-Order-Morality." We can only vouch for the first. Big green rooms have big windows, big beds, and little else. Feels more like a house than a hotel. Singles 120 pesos; doubles 140 pesos; extra person 30 pesos.

FOOD

Food in Cozumel tends to be expensive, especially if you buy it near the beach or the plaza. Avoiding places that advertise in English will keep pesos in your pockets. There are several moderately priced restaurants a few blocks from the center, as well as some small *típico* cafes hiding on side streets. The **market,** on Av. Adolfo Salas, between Av. 20 and 25 Sur, offers the standard items: meat, fish, and fruits. The five small restaurants outside the market offer generous portions of regional dishes. For a quick treat, stop by at the **Panificadora Cozumel,** on Calle 2 Nte., between Quinta and Melger, where pastries and baked goods can be yours for pocket change (open daily 6am-9:30pm).

Restaurant Casa Denis (tel. 2 00 67), across from the flea market on the *zócalo.* Ancient sketches and the 116-year-old *mamey* tree glorify this cheerful and sunny spot. Wide choice of breakfast (18 pesos). Sandwiches 15 pesos. Good view of pricey restaurants across the plaza. *Comida regional,* including seafood plates, 30-40 pesos. Open daily 7am-10:30pm.

El Paso del Cedral, opposite the road to the El Cedral ruins. on the southwestern tip of the island. A bit far, but worth it. The seafood arrives on shore mere seconds before you do. Accompany Don Carlos, the chef, to choose the very fish you want. Get a few people together and go in for the house specialty, a monstrous red snapper (about 120 pesos—haggle). String up a hammock on the serene public beach for a post-feast siesta before you snorkel in the nearby reef. Open daily 10am-6pm.

Alfalfa's, on Calle 1 Sur, between Av. 10 and 15, across from Posada Letty. Chic vegetarian restaurant serves a huge *comida del día* (55 pesos) and lemonade to match. Some meat dishes. Open daily 11am-11pm.

El Abuelo Gerardo (tel. 2 10 12), on Av. 10, between Juárez and Calle 2 Nte. A mellow place to grab an ice-cold afternoon beer. *Antojitos* 10-30 pesos. For something more substantial, try a fish fillet (28-35 pesos). Good breakfasts (12-24 pesos) with some of the best toast in Mexico. Open daily 7:30am-10:30pm.

Cocina Económica Mi Chabelita (tel. 2 08 96), on Av. 10 Sur near Adolfo Salas. Budget dining in a bright, coral-colored garage. Great *comida corrida* (22 pesos). Fried bananas (8 pesos) are a specialty. Open M-Sa 8am-9pm.

YUCATÁN PENINSULA

CORAL, SAND, AND SIGHTS

Most visitors to Cozumel have one sight in mind: the beautiful coral reefs around the island. Mopeds are the best way of getting to your favorite snorkeling spot or finding a new one. Be nice to yourself and get some wheels. Otherwise, expensive taxis will be your only option. Although hitchhiking is possible, it's uncertain and dehydrating.

As you head south out of town on a counter-clockwise circuit of the island, **Hotel La Ceiba** makes a good stop-off point for snorkeling. The hotel has a beach perfect for swimming and a reef and plane wreck offshore waiting to be explored. The **Del Mar Aquatics** dive shop (tel. 2 08 44), 200m north of La Ceiba, rents out snorkeling gear (US$6 per day) and scuba equipment (US$38 per day), as well as offering deep-sea fishing, night/day dives, and snorkeling trips (open daily 7:30am-7:30pm).

Chankanaab National Park, a few more kilometers down the coastal highway, is comprised of a small *laguna,* a botanical garden, museum, restaurant, snorklel area, and a few gift shops. *(Open daily 7am-6pm. Admission 52 pesos.)* A stroll through the endemic forest in the botanical garden, past the meter-long, beady-eyed, sunbathing iguanas, brings you to some ruins. The perfectly oval natural lagoon, once brimming with reef fish, is now home to the hardy survivors of years of gringo sunscreen attrition. Never mind; the real attraction is the abundant tropical fish and coral in the Caribbean a few meters away. Matching the capacity crowds on land, the reef teems with eels, anemones, and gorgeous fish. The small museum focuses on the park's natural resources and houses incredible photographs of the underwater caves in the lagoon. For more info, contact the **Fundación de Parques** (tel. 2 09 14) in town.

The best underwater sightseeing in Cozumel is likely to be on the offshore reefs, accessible by boat. You can rent snorkeling equipment anywhere, including at Laguna Chankanaab and Playa de San Francisco. The standard rate is US$5-10 per day, plus deposit. Most of the numerous **dive shops** in town are on the waterfront or on Calle 3 Sur, between Av. Melgar and Av. 10. Always consider safety before price; look for shops with **CADO** (Cozumel Association of Dive Operators) insignias on their doors. **Blue Bubble Divers** (tel. 2 18 65; http:///www.bluebubble.com), on Av. 5 at Calle 3 Sur, has a mellow, English-speaking staff and a choice of 20 reefs to visit (1½hr. single-tank dive US$45, snorkeling equipment US$6 per day; open daily

7am-9pm). Another option is **Aqua Safari,** Melgar at Calle 5 Sur (single-tank dive US$30, 2hr. snorkeling boat trip US$15; open daily 7am-1pm and 4-6:30pm).

The route along the eastern coast passes many secluded beaches that make for good camping spots. Always ask before pitching a tent. While the beaches boast magnificent turquoise waters and few tourists, the water is turbulent and somewhat dangerous; it should be treated with cautious respect. Midway along the coast, Carretera Transversal branches west and loops back through the jungle to town.

Between beach hops and reef drops, you may want to hunt down one of several small ruins in Cozumel's overgrown interior. You can visit **El Cedral** and the **Tumba de Caracol** ruins on a bumpy trek to the **Celarain Lighthouse,** on the island's southernmost point. The top of the lighthouse offers a thrilling view of the northern shores of the island. To get to the crumbled stone structures of **San Gervasio,** the only extensively excavated and partially reconstructed ruin on the island, take Juárez out of town. *(Open daily 8am-4pm. Admission 26 pesos; 10 pesos on Sundays.)* After 8km, a "San Gervasio" sign marks a gravel road branching to the left. The ruins are another 8km down this road. The small, air-conditioned **Museo de la Isla de Cozumel** (tel. 2 14 75 or 2 14 74), on the waterfront between Calles 4 and 6, is filled with photographs and artifacts (open daily 9am-5pm; admission US$3). Check for other cultural events in the **Centro de Convenciones,** between the Plaza del Sol and Bancomer, or in the plaza itself, where locals gather on Sunday nights for that irresistible rumba beat.

YUCATÁN PENINSULA

ENTERTAINMENT

Although not as expensive as Cancún, Cozumel's nightlife is targeted toward the spendthrift gringos who jaunt into town from their cruise ships. Obnoxiously boisterous all night long, **Carlos 'n' Charlie's** (tel. 2 01 91), on Rafael Melgar, just one block north of the dock, entertains *norteamericanos* with crazy drinks, slammer contests, and arm-wrestling matches. Occasional awards of free tequila are given to those willing to make fools of themselves. (Cover US$5 on live music nights. Open daily 10am-2:30am.) A mellow, more native crowd enjoys reggae music and relives the swinging 70s at **Joe's Lobster Bar** (tel. 2 32 75), on Av. 10, between Calles 1 and 3 Sur. A live band starts up the action at 10:30pm and the place keeps kicking until 2 or 3am (beers 16 pesos). For the best in live Mexican music (rock, reggae, salsa) under a hip groovy-colored *palapa,* head to **Raga,** on Salas, between Calles 10 and 15. Live music begins and attractive *cozumeleños* converge nightly around 9pm. (Open daily 5pm-12:30am.) The full-fledged disco **Neptuno** (tel. 2 15 37), five blocks south of the plaza, has multi-level dance floors bombarded with lasers and throbbing bass (cover 45 pesos; open daily 9pm-early morning).

For action and romance with happy endings and no alcohol, try **Cinema Cozumel,** on Av. Rafael Melgar between Calles 2 and 4, or **Cine Cecillo Borques,** on Juárez between Av. 30 and 35. Borques is cheaper (12 pesos) but more remote.

Tulum

On the eastern edge of the age-old Etaib (Black Bees) jungle, halfway down the Caribbean coast of the Yucatán, lies the walled Maya "City of the Dawn." Although the architecture of the ruins here may be less impressive than that of Uxmal and Chichén Itzá, the backdrop is stunning. Tulum's graying temples and nearly intact watchtowers rise above tall, wind-bent palm trees, clinging to a cliff above white sand pummeled by the candy-blue Caribbean Sea, forming one of Mexico's most photogenic scenes (see the cover of this book). Tulum brings together two of the best aspects of the Yucatán: archaeological wonders and Caribbean waters. First settled in the fourth century, Tulum was the oldest continuously inhabited city in the New World when the Spanish arrived. Today, sun worshippers of a different kind tramp through the ancient city, complementing their sightseeing with healthy doses of swimming.

Under the Sea

The **Palancar Reef** of Cozumel, the **second-largest in the world,** continually draws legions of scuba fanatics eager to explore its dramatic underwater formations. While the aesthetics are unmistakable, few visitors realize the biological importance of those majestic coral pillars. Coral is to a reef as topsoil is to a rainforest—without it, the basis of all life disappears. If the coral is destroyed, the entire reef's ecosystem disintegrates. International law prohibits the harvesting of coral, but it does not forbid the purchase or exportation of coral-derived jewelry and crafts. Several shops in Cozumel sell goods made from black coral, and, by patronizing these establishments, tourists heighten the demand for coral and adversely affect the splendorous reefs they have come to see.

ORIENTATION

Located 42km southeast of Cobá, 63km south of Playa del Carmen, and 127km south of Cancún, Tulum (pop. 12,000) is the southernmost link in the chain of tourist attractions on the Caribbean coast of Quintana Roo, and the eastern extreme of the major Maya archaeological sites. Although few people live here, Tulum sprawls out over three separate areas: the **crucero** (the crossroads), the beach **cabanas,** and **Pueblo Tulum.** Arriving in Tulum from Cancún on Rte. 307, buses first stop at the *crucero,* a few kilometers before town. Here, a couple of restaurants, hotels, and overpriced minimarts huddle together 800m west of the ruins. The access road turns south at the ruins, leading to food and lodging at cabanas 2km farther down the road. Pueblo Tulum, 4km south of the *crucero,* offers travelers a handful of roadside restaurants, minimarts, and some services.

Second-class **buses** provide cheap transportation from Tulum to nearby cities and to the sights and beaches that lie to the north on Rte. 307. Some travelers hitchhike from sight to sight along the highway. Taxis congregate at the *crucero* and at the bus stop at Pueblo Tulum.

PRACTICAL INFORMATION

The few services available in Pueblo Tulum are along Rte. 307, which serves as the tiny town's main street. There is no tourist office, though a few stands at the ruins can provide sketchy maps. Those desperate to **exchange money** can do so at the *crucero* or next to the bus office in Pueblo Tulum.

Buses: A small waiting room sandwiched between 2 currency exchange booths opposite the Hotel Maya. **ADO** to Córdoba (12hr., 8am, 396 pesos), Escárcega (4hr., 8am and 5pm, 144 pesos), Mexico City (22hr., 8am, 495 pesos), Veracruz (12hr., 4:30pm, 352 pesos), and Villahermosa (9hr., 4:30pm, 227 pesos). Various **second-class buses** with shifting schedules run to Cancún (2hr., 10 per day, 25 pesos), Chetumal (4hr., 8 per day, 48 pesos), Chichén Itzá (3½hr., 4 per day, 50 pesos), Cobá (30min., 4 per day, 12 pesos), Escárcega (8hr., 2:30 and 7:30pm, 138 pesos), Mérida (5hr., 4 per day, 68 pesos), Ocosingo (15hr., 2:30 and 7:30pm, 192 pesos), Palenque (14hr., 2:30 and 7:30pm, 175 pesos), Playa del Carmen (1hr., 10 per day, 16 pesos), San Cristóbal (16hr., 2:30 and 7:30pm, 220 pesos), and Valladolid (2½hr., 6 per day, 34 pesos).

Taxis: Available at the *crucero,* in Pueblo Tulum, along Rte. 307, and at various cabanas. From the *crucero* to Pueblo Tulum 12 pesos, to cabanas 26 pesos.

Police: (tel. 1 20 55), in the Delegación Municipal, 2 blocks past the post office.

Pharmacy: Súper Farmacia, just past the post office. Open daily 8am-9pm. English-speaking **Dr. Arturo F. Ventre** available daily 8am-noon and 6-9pm.

Post Office: A few hundred meters into town on Rte. 307. Open M-F 9am-1pm and 3-6pm. **Postal Code:** 77780.

Phone Code: 987.

ACCOMMODATIONS AND CAMPING

Tulum offers two lodging options: hotels at the *crucero* in town, or beachside cabanas. If you plan to stay only one night to visit the ruins, the road hotels can't be beat for sheer convenience. However, your inner beach bum will be much happier in the cabanas—there's an endless stream from which to choose. There you can chill with mellow international travelers and perfect your tan on the spectacular beach.

Cabañas Santa Fe, just off the paved road, 1km south of the ruins. Follow the signs to Don Armando's and turn left. If you don't mind the perpetual sand, you can shack up here with backpackers from all over the world. Several sticks 'n' *palapa* combos to choose from: bare cabana with sand floor and small hammock 40 pesos; 1-bed cabana with cement floor 75 pesos; 2-bed cabana 150 pesos; hammock rental 20 pesos per night.

Don Armando Cabañas (tel. 4 76 72 or 1 13 54), on the access road 1km south of the ruins. A humble paradise with a volleyball court. The cabanas are generally solid and secure, and the communal facilities are spotless. Cabana with 1 bed and 1 hammock 90 pesos, with 2 beds 120 pesos; 2 double beds 220 pesos. Deposit 50 pesos. Camp or hang a hammock for 20 pesos per person.

Hotel Maya (tel. 1 20 34), on Rte. 307, across from the bus station in Pueblo Tulum. Small, stuffy singles—bigger rooms have more air, and more charm. Singles 100 pesos; doubles 120 pesos, with bath 160 pesos; additional 10 pesos per person.

FOOD

Although the points of interest in Tulum tend to be rather spread out, a hearty and inexpensive bite of *típico* food is never too far away. Both the Pueblo and the *crucero* have satisfying and authentic restaurants as well as *mini-súpers;* the former are slightly cheaper and provide filling sustenance for daytrips.

La Chica Poblana, a block south of Hotel Maya in Pueblo Tulum. The place to be for some delicious family cooking; *comida corrida* (18 pesos) and the best *huevos moluteños* (12 pesos) in the pueblo. Fifteen pesos gets you the day's entree, served, of course, with beans and tortillas. Open daily 8am-midnight.

Restaurante El Crucero, in Hotel El Crucero. Comfortable and shady interior provides respite from all that Maya sun. Get intimate with that old standby, *pescado al mojo de ajo* (38 pesos). Breakfast (fruit salad, orange juice, toast, and coffee) 22-30 pesos. Open daily 7am-9pm.

Restaurante Santa Fe, at the campground on the beach. Mellow reggae tunes and the cabana-like sand floor are the perfect compliment to the fresh fish (30-40 pesos), and quesadillas (18 pesos). Restaurant and bar open daily 7am-11pm.

SIGHTS

Tulum has a rare and exquisite combination of ruins and beaches. In fact, it's got ruins on its beaches (see our cover).

The Ruins

While a sharp increase in tourists necessitated the cordoning off of most of **Tulum's ruins,** you can still admire the architecture and murals from a short distance away and the beach and inviting waves first-hand. *(Open daily 8am-5pm. Admission 20 pesos; free on Sundays. Guided tours about 160 pesos for 1-5 people, 220 pesos for groups up to 25 people.)* Tulum's ruins lie a brisk eight-minute walk east of Rte. 307 from the *crucero.* For the Homeresque, a dinky **train** (7 pesos) covers the distance in slightly less time. Admission tickets are sold at a booth to the left of the parking lot.

The first thing visitors see in Tulum is the still-impressive **dry-laid wall** that surrounded the city center's three landlocked sides. The wall, made of small rocks wedged together, was originally 3.6m thick and 3m high. It shielded the city from the aggression of neighboring Maya city-states and prevented all but the 150 or so priests and governors of Tulum from entering the city for most of the year. After Tulum's defeat at the hands of the Spanish in 1544, the wall fended off English, Dutch, and French pirates and, in 1847, gave rebel Mayas refuge from government forces during the Caste War. Magnificent representations of a **figure diving into the water** cover the western walls. The images depicting the Maya sunset god are illuminated every evening by the rays of the setting sun.

Just inside and to the left of the west gate stand the remains of platforms that once supported huts. Behind these platforms are the **House of the Halach Uinik** (the House of the Ruler), characterized by a traditional Maya four-column entrance; the **Palacio,** the largest residential building in Tulum; and the **Temple of the Paintings,** a stellar example of PostClassic Maya architecture. Well preserved 600-year-old murals inside the temple depict deities intertwined with serpents, as well as fruit, flower, and corn offerings. Masks of Itzamná, the Maya Creator, occupy the northwest and southwest corners of the building.

El Castillo, the most prominent structure in Tulum, looms behind the smaller buildings and over the rocky seaside cliff. Serving as a pyramid and temple, it commands a view of the entire walled city. It also served as a lighthouse, allowing returning fishermen to find the only gap in the barrier reef just offshore. Its walls, like those of many buildings in Tulum, slope outward, but its doorposts slope inward. The castle's architectural and structural eccentricities are due to its numerous rebuildings.

In front of the temple is the **sacrificial stone** where the Maya held battle ceremonies. Once the stars had been consulted and a propitious day determined, a warrior-prisoner was selected for sacrifice. At the climax of the celebration, attendants painted the warrior's body blue—the sacred color of the Maya—and the chief priest cut his heart out and poured the blood over the idols in the temple. The body was given to the soldiers below, who were thought to acquire the strength to overcome their enemies through cannibalism.

To the right of El Castillo on the same plaza is the **Temple of the Initial Series.** Named after a stela found here, the temple bears a date that corresponded to the beginning of the Maya religious calendar in the year 761. The **Temple of the Descending God,** with a fading relief of a feathered, armed deity diving from the sky, stands on the other side of El Castillo's plaza. Perched on its own precipice on the other side of the beach, the **Temple of the Winds** was acoustically designed to act as a storm-warning system. Sure enough, before Hurricane Gilbert struck the site in 1988, the temple's airways dutifully whistled their alarm.

The Beach

Hanging out on the beach in cabanas is a popular way to end a day at the ruins. While cigarette butts are starting to mar the idyllic scene, the waves near the beach can still take your mind off anything. Nude bathing is tolerated, and it usually takes one uninhibited soul to start the ball rolling. Offshore, you can see the waves mysteriously breaking on Tulum's **barrier reef,** the largest in the Americas; it runs the full length of the Yucatán peninsula, including Belize. Although the water here is not as clear as at Xel-Ha or Akumal (see below), the fish are just as plentiful. To enjoy them, you can rent **scuba and snorkeling equipment** from the **dive shop** (tel. 1 20 96) at **Cabañas Santa Fe** (35 pesos per day for snorkeling; open daily 8am-3:30pm). The shop plans trips to the reef and a nearby *cenote* (US$15, including rental, *antojitos,* and *refrescos*). You can also get certified for scuba here (US$30) or go diving in the Cenote Dos Ojos (you must be an experienced diver; US$50; see p. 595). Get fins if you snorkel; the 500m swim to the reef is often a struggle against a north-south current.

To escape the beaches, waves, and salty water, rent a bike from Cabañas Santa Fe (24 pesos per hr.) and visit one of the *cenotes* in the woods near Pueblo Tulum.

Look for a small patch of gravel, large enough for two cars, on the right side of the road as you head toward Chetumal. Follow a rugged path to the serene **Cenote Escondido** or the smaller **Cenote Cristal** 100m farther down the road.

■ Near Tulum: Sian Ka'an Biosphere Reserve

Seven kilometers south of Tulum on the coast road lies the 1.5-million-acre **Sian Ka'an Biosphere Reserve.** Sanctuary to over 345 species of bird as well as every endangered cat species of southern Mexico, the reserve also guards a wide range of wetland and marine habitats, as well as 27 Maya sites. Entrance is free but limited, and *lancha* tours are given exclusively by Sian Ka'an biologists. For more info, contact **Amigos de Sian Ka'an** in Cancún, Av. Cobá 5 (tel. (98) 84 95 83; fax 87 30 80; email sian@cancun.rce.com.mx), in Plaza América.

■ Near Tulum: Xel-Ha And Akumal

Although swimming is not permitted in the lagoon for which **Xel-Ha** (SHELL-ha) is famous, its natural aquarium, almost 2m deep, is a fun (and expensive) place for snorkeling. *(Open daily 8am-5pm. Admission 12 pesos.)* You can splash around all you want in the *caleta* (inlet) nearby. Don't bet on seeing any unusual fish life, but you can find parrot fishes and meter-long barracudas toward the rope that marks the open sea. For relative peace during busy times, cross the inlet and explore the underwater caves, where an altar was once discovered. Be careful and don't go duck-diving under overhangs on your own. The steep 150-peso entrance fee to the caves includes visits to two *cenotes,* a natural river, underground sea caves, and a hammock siesta. You still have to pay for rental of snorkel equipment, which is available near the inlet for 60 more precious pesos (no discounts this time). Visit before noon, when busloads of tourists from the resorts overrun the place. Lockers (7 pesos plus a 3-peso deposit) and towels (10 pesos plus a 30-peso deposit) are available at the shower area (shower area open daily 8:30am-6pm).

YUCATÁN PENINSULA

Xel-Ha also maintains a small archaeological site on the highway, 100m south of the entrance to the inlet. **El Templo de Los Pájaros** and **El Palacio,** small Classic and PostClassic ruins, were only recently opened to the public. The former (the ruin farthest into the jungle) overlooks a peaceful, shady *cenote* where swimming is permitted. A strategically hung rope-swing makes the experience all the more Tarzanesque. The jungle at Xel-Ha is rife with mosquitoes, so bring insect repellent.

A few kilometers north of Xel-Ha toward Playa del Carmen lies the bay of **Akumal.** An older, wealthier crowd is drawn to its older, wealthier underwater attractions. The **Akumal Dive Shop** (tel. 987 4 12 59) rents **snorkeling equipment** (US$6 per day), organizes **snorkeling** and **scuba trips** (US$20 per person; US$25 per one-tank dive), and offers **cavern-diving courses** (US$350; open daily 8am-1pm and 2-5pm).

Getting There: Xel-Ha lies 15km north of Tulum; Akumal is 10km farther north. Get on any northbound **bus** and ask to be let off at the site of your choice (5 pesos). Taxis charge exorbitant rates. Hitchhiking here is tough because the traffic is fast and the wait can be unnerving. Getting back to Tulum at the end of the day, when buses begin to come less and less frequently, can be challenging. Vigorously wave down a bus on its way to Tulum or Cancún. Locals will usually be able to tell you when the next one is due to pass.

■ Near Tulum: Cenote Dos Ojos

Cenote Dos Ojos, 1km south of Xel-Ha, is the **second-largest underwater cavern in the world**, stretching for 33,855m. It was originally a dry cave system with beautiful rock formations in shades of amber as well as massive calcic stalactites, stalagmites, and natural wind-etchings. The whole system was flooded long, long ago, preserving the caves in their new underwater condition. It is now possible to **snorkel** and

dive in the *cenote,* along with tetras, mollies, and swordfish. You must be an experienced diver with a minimum of 40 dives under your belt, including night dives.

The trip begins with a bumpy 20-minute ride in an open truck. Monstrous bugs whiz by as you zip through the pristine jungle. A complete underwater circuit of the caves, at a depth of 10m, takes about 45 minutes. Meanwhile, snorkelers can explore the larger of the two cave entrances. For divers and snorkelers alike, this is a unique opportunity to explore a spectacular unspoiled cave system that has only been open to the public since 1993. The dive costs US$50 (plus US$15 equipment rental). Snorkelers pay US$25. Three trips depart daily from **Dos Ojos Dive Center** (tel. 987 4 12 71), several hundred meters south of the park entrance, at 10am and 2pm. Trips also leave from the **Cabañas Santa Fe** (see p. 593).

Cobá

Deep within the Yucatán jungle, Cobá receives less attention than her big sisters, Chichén Itzá and Tulum. The government has poured less money into the site, leaving an estimated 6500 buildings unexcavated. The site's isolation only heightens the impressiveness of its towering **Nohoch Múl,** the tallest Maya structure (42m) in the northern Yucatán. The town of Cobá itself, unfortunately, is little more than a glorified tourist trap.

THE ARCHAEOLOGICAL SITE OF COBÁ

To get to the **ruins of Cobá,** walk south on the main street in town as far as the T-junction at the lake. *(Ruins open daily 8am-5pm. Admission 18 pesos; free on Sundays.)* Here, take a left onto the Av. Voz Suave (Soft Voice); the ruins are a five-minute walk down the road. It's a good idea to find a guide at the entrance, as this will make the visit much more enlightening. Regardless of when you arrive at the site, bring a water bottle and wear a hat. And unless you feel like being sacrificed to the mosquito god, bring plenty of repellent as well. During the high season, 11am to 2pm are peak tourist hours

Guide to the Ruins

Once through the gate, the site's six attractions are laid out before you in a "Y"-shaped formation, with the entrance at the base of the "Y." Take an immediate right to the **Grupo Cobá.** To the left looms the impressive **Temple of the Churches,** built over seven 52-year periods, each one associated with a new chief priest. Only the front face of the temple has been excavated, revealing a corbel-vaulted passageway (to the left) that you can explore. Rising out of the jungle to the northeast are the gray steps of the ancient city's centerpiece, **El Castillo.** In front of the structure is a stone sacrificial table, upon which animal offerings were made to Chac, the rain god. The stela depicts Chac; another nearby features a kneeling Maya. Follow a second passageway farther south to the **Plaza del Templo,** where assemblies were once held. The red plant dye still visible on the walls of the passageway dates from the 5th century. A mortar here hints at the staple food of the ancient (and contemporary) Maya—maize. Return to the main path for a look at the **ballcourt.**

A 1km walk up the "trunk" of the "Y" takes you to four other sites. Follow the right branch for another kilometer to reach a collection of eight stelae in the **Grupo Macanxoc.** On the way, you cross over a well-engineered Maya *sacbe.* This particular road is 20m wide and raised 4m from the jungle floor. The ornate stone slabs of the Grupo Macanxoc were erected as memorials above the tombs of Maya royals. Especially impressive and well preserved is the first, the **Retrato del Rey.** The king is shown standing on the heads of two slaves, bow and arrow in hand, wearing a *quetzal*-feather headdress.

Continue north to the left-hand branch of the "Y." After 200m, follow an unmarked trail on the right to the three stelae of **Chumuc Múl.** The first stela depicts a kneeling Maya ballplayer. Sure enough, this is the tomb of a victorious captain. You can make out the *chicle* ball in the upper-left-hand corner. The second stela depicts a princess, while the third portrays a *sacerdote* (priest). His seal is stamped on top of the slab, along with a jaguar's head, a common Maya symbol of worship. Two hundred meters farther up this branch of the "Y," you'll run into **Sacbe No. 1.** This thoroughfare ran from Chichén Itzá, 101km to the west; runners were posted every 5km so messages could be sent between settlements via a series of quick dashes. During the city's height (900-1200), Cobá is believed to have been the major crossroads in a commercial region of 17 cities. Images of the honeybee god around the site are a reminder of this ancient economic hub—the Maya used honey (along with coconuts and jade) as a medium of exchange.

The tour climaxes with the breathtaking sight of the **Nohoch Múl,** the highest structure in the Yucatán. While the view may not quicken your pulse, the 120-step climb surely will. The pyramid's nine levels, where Maya priests once led processions, display carvings of the "diving god." Just before the pyramid is **Stela No. 20.** The stela depicts a dignitary of high rank (note the plumed crest and rich clothing) standing on a board.

Chetumal

Residents of Quintana Roo are very proud of their state, the youngest in Mexico, as well as its relatively new capital, which straddles the border with Belize. Although Chetumal (pop. 200,000) was founded in 1898 to intercept shipments of arms to Maya rebels and to prevent illegal timber harvesting, it was leveled in 1955 after a hurricane. The complete reconstruction explains the wide avenues and modern architecture. While the city has no beaches to attract the sun-loving tourist, it is home to an extensive market.

ORIENTATION

Tucked into the Yucatán's southeastern corner, Chetumal is just north of the Río Hondo, the natural border between Mexico and Belize. There are three principal approaches to the city: on Rte. 186 from Escárcega (273km), along the Caribbean coast from Cancún (379km), and from Mérida via Valladolid (458km). The **bus terminal** at Av. de los Insurgentes and Av. Belice is Chetumal's ground transportation hub.

Take a taxi (8 pesos) into town, or walk 4km through shadeless streets. Chetumal's thriving shopping district lines **Av. de los Héroes,** starting at **Av. Efraín Aguilar** at the city's market and extending 1km south to the bay. This compact commercial area encompasses most of Chetumal's hotels and restaurants. At the southern terminus of Héroes lies **Blvd. Bahía,** a wide avenue flanked by statues and small plazas that follows the bay for several kilometers. From here you can see part of Belize, the long spit of land stretching out to the right as you face the sea.

PRACTICAL INFORMATION

Airport: (tel. 2 04 65), 5km south of the city on Aguilar. **Aerocaribe,** Héroes 125 (tel. 2 66 75). **Aviacsa** (tel. 2 76 76). **Bonanza** (tel. 2 83 06). Offices open M-Sa 8am-1pm and 5-8pm.

Buses: (tel. 2 98 77), on Insurgentes at Belice. **ADO** (tel. 2 51 10) offers first-class service to Campeche (7hr., noon, 122 pesos), Cancún (5hr., 7 per day 12:30-11pm, 105 pesos), Escárcega (4hr., 7 per day 9am-9pm, 78 pesos), Mexico City (22hr., 11:30am, 4:30, and 9pm, 455 pesos), Palenque (8½hr., 8pm, 121 pesos), Playa del Carmen (4hr., 7 per day 12:30-11pm, 105 pesos), Veracruz (15hr., 6:30pm, 302 pesos), and Villahermosa (9hr., 6 per day 9am-9pm, 163 pesos). **Línea Dorada** goes to Mérida (6hr., 7:30am, 1:30, 5, and 11:30pm, 116 pesos). **Cristóbal Colón** trucks to Ocosingo (9hr., 9:15pm, 178 pesos), San Cristóbal

(10hr., 9:15pm, 203 pesos), and Tuxtla Gutiérrez (12hr., 9:15pm, 227 pesos). **Batty's Bus** goes south to Belize (3hr., 6am, 3:15, 5:15, and 7:15pm, 40 pesos). **TRP** goes to Tulum (4hr., 6 per day, 52 pesos). **Lockers** 2 pesos per hr.

Tourist Office: Information booth (tel. 2 36 63), on Héroes at Aguilar. Pick up a map of the city. Open M-Sa 8:30am-1:30pm and 6-9pm.

Currency Exchange: Bancomer (tel. 2 53 00), on Juárez at Obregón, has good rates, short lines, and a 24hr. **ATM.** Open M-F 9am-4:30pm, Sa 10am-2pm.

Consulates: Belize (tel. 2 01 00), on Obregón, west of Juárez, next to Bancomer. To enter Belize for 30 days, all that is needed for U.S., Canadian, and EU citizens is a valid passport and a bus ticket. Open M-F 9am-2pm and 5-8pm, Sa 9am-2pm. **Guatemala,** Chapultepec 356 (tel. 2 30 45), at Cecilio Chi. Again, U.S., Canadian, and EU citizens don't need a visa. For those who do, the process is quick and almost painless (US$10, see p. 8). Open M-F 8am-2pm.

Market: Corner of Aguilar and Héroes. Vendors peddle everything from a what's-this-for to a damned-if-I-know. Open daily 6am-3pm. **Súper San Francisco de Asis,** next to the bus station.

Police: (tel. 2 15 00), on Insurgentes at Belice, next to the bus station. Open 24hr. **Tourist Safety Line:** (tel. 91 800 90 392).

Red Cross: (tel. 2 05 71), on Chapultepec at Independencia, 2 blocks west of Héroes, in the back of Hospital Civil Morelos. Open 24hr.

Pharmacy: Farmacia Canto, Av. Héroes 99 (tel. 2 04 83), conveniently located at the northern end of the market. Open M-Sa 7am-11pm, Su 7am-5pm.

Hospital: Hospital General (tel. 2 19 99), on Quintana Roo at Juan José Sordio.

Post Office: Plutarco Elías Calles 2A (tel. 2 25 78), 1 block east of the *mercado*. Open M-F 8am-7pm, Sa 9am-1pm. **Postal Code:** 77000.

Phone Code: 983.

ACCOMMODATIONS

Chetumal's budget accommodations aren't an extraordinary bunch, but they do score points for location. All are within easy walking distance of the *mercado.* A scenic **trailer park** in Calderitas, 9km northeast of Chetumal, offers electricity, water hookups, and clean bathrooms (vehicles 40 pesos; tent or hammock space 10 pesos per person; big bungalows with kitchen 70 pesos for 1-2 people).

Hotel María Dolores, Obregón 206 (tel. 2 05 08), half a block west of Héroes. Look for the Donald Duck image pointing the way to the comfortable, sea breeze-cooled hotel. Lime-colored rooms come with strong fans and spacious bathrooms. Singles 65 pesos; doubles 72 pesos; triples 90 pesos. U.S. dollars accepted.

CREA Youth Hostel (HI; tel. 2 05 25 or 3 00 19), on Heroica Escuela Naval at Calzada Veracruz, at the eastern terminus of Obregón. For once, a youth hostel within manageable walking distance. Small but clean single-sex rooms with 2 bunk beds each. Bed with sheets, towel, and locker 30 pesos. Lawn for camping 15 pesos. Breakfast 14 pesos; lunch and dinner 14 pesos. Front desk open daily 7am-11pm, but you can make arrangements to return later. 30-peso deposit. Fills during July and August, so call to reserve.

Hotel Brasilia, Aguilar 186 (tel. 2 09 64), at Héroes, across from the market. Rooms are hit-or-miss; all are clean but some are cramped—ask to see one first. Friendly management will store backpacks. Singles 50 pesos; doubles 70 pesos; triples 90 pesos; quads 110 pesos. Add 70 pesos for TV and A/C.

FOOD

Aside from a dish or two flavored with coconut (it's the *belizeño* influence), Chetumal offers standard Mexican fare. For cheap eats, try the cafe/restaurants at the end of Héroes, on 22 de Enero near the bay, or the eateries on Obregón, west of Héroes.

Restaurante Pantoja, M. Gandhi 181 (tel. 2 39 57), past Hotel Ucum, just north of the market. An extremely popular family restaurant, and with good reason: the food is *muy rica* and piping hot. Enchiladas (18 pesos) are *sabrosa.* Gigantic lemonades 6 pesos. Open M-Sa 7am-9pm.

El Taquito, Plutarco Elías Calles 220, near Juárez, 1 block west of Héroes. Groove with the locals as you savor *antojito* after *antojito.* Tacos 3.50 pesos. *Queso fundido* 20 pesos. Open M-Sa 9am-midnight.

SIGHTS AND SAND

People come from far and wide to visit **El Mercado.** If you think having your name written on a grain of rice is a pretty neat idea, you'll love this market. Across from the northern end of the market is the **Museo de la Cultura Maya,** complete with full-scale temples and indoor waterfalls. *(Open Tu-Sa 9am-7pm. Admission 16 pesos; free on Sundays.)* The brand-new museum is part educational lesson and part Disneyworld. It's also one of the best museums devoted to Maya culture. The nearest beach is the *balneario* at **Calderitas,** a 10-minute bus ride from Chetumal. Buses leave from Av. Colón, between Héroes and Belice (every 30min. 5am-10pm, 3 pesos). Although the water is turbid and the shores rocky, the beach packs crowds in during summer and school holidays. Much nicer, both for atmosphere and for swimming, are the three watering holes near the town of **Bacalar,** 38km away. The local bus to Bacalar leaves from Chetumal's bus station (every 7hr. 5:30am-10:30pm); *combis* leave from the corner of Hidalgo and Primo de Verdad in front of the public library (30min., every 15min., 8 pesos). The route passes **Laguna Milagros** and **Cenote Azul** before reaching Bacalar. Quieter than the Bacalar, both have bathing areas, dressing rooms, and lakeside restaurants. The huge dining room by Cenote Azul, though expensive, is right on the water.

Past the Fuerte de San Felipe in Bacalar lie the docks of the **Laguna de Siete Colores,** named for the hues reflected in its depths. The fresh water is warm, perfectly clear, devoid of plant or animal life, and carpeted by powdery limestone, making it excellent for swimming (although don't expect a beach). Nearby are bathrooms, dressing rooms, fruit vendors, expensive dockside restaurants, and a campground.

Much farther afield from Chetumal, the small seaside town of **Xcalac** (200km, 3hr.), the southernmost center of population on the spit of land extending south from the Sian Ka'an reserve, provides super-mellow bungalows, restaurants, snorkeling, and boat rentals. Nearby off the coast lies the enticing **Banco Chinchorro,** the **second largest shipwreck site in the world,** making for a funky deep-sea treasure-hunting dive. **Buses** (25-35 pesos) to Xcalac and the closer, less service-laden **Mahahval** (150km from Chetumal) depart daily at 7am from Av. 16 de Septiembre at M. Gandhi, 20m from the Restaurante Pantoja.

Appendix

International Telephone Codes

Once you are in Mexico, getting lines to foreign countries can be very difficult. Many public phones don't access international lines. Dial 09 for an English-speaking international long-distance operator. You then need to dial the international calling code (a few listed below) of the country you are trying to reach before dialing the phone number. If you speak Spanish fluently and can't reach the international operator, dial 07 for the national operator, who will connect you (sometimes even a local operator can help). The term for a collect call is a *llamada por cobrar* or *llamada con cobro revertido.* Calling from hotels is usually faster. For specifics, refer to p. 42.

Australia	61	**New Zealand**	64	**U.K.**	44
Ireland	353	**South Africa**	27	**U.S./ Canada**	1

Weights and Measurements

Mexico, like most of the rational world, uses the metric system. Check out the inside back cover for handy conversions.

1 inch = 25 millimeters (mm)	1mm = 0.04 inch (in.)
1 foot (ft.) = 0.30 meter (m)	1m = 3.33 feet (ft.)
1 mile = 1.61 kilometers (km)	1km = 0.62 mile (mi.)
1 pound (lb.) = 0.45 kilogram (kg)	1kg = 2.22 pounds (lb.)
1 gallon = 4 quarts = 3.76 liters (L)	1 liter = 1.06 quarts (qt.)=0.27 gallon

Language and Pronunciation

Pronunciation in Spanish is straightforward. Vowels are each pronounced only one way: a ("ah" in father); e ("eh" in ethical); i ("ee" in eat); o ("oh" in oat); u ("oo" in boot); y, by itself, is pronounced like the Spanish i. Most consonants are pronounced the same as in English. Important exceptions are: j, pronounced like the English "h" in "hello"; ll, pronounced like the English "y" in "yes"; ñ, pronounced like the "gn" in "cognac"; rr, the trilled "r"; h is always silent; x has a bewildering variety of pronunciations: sometimes it sounds like the "h" in "hello," sometimes like the "cz" in "czar." Stress in Spanish words falls on the second to last syllable, except for words ending in "r," "l" and "z," in which it falls on the last syllable. All exceptions to these rules require a written accent on the stressed syllable. The Spanish language also has masculine and feminine nouns and gives a gender to all adjectives that end in "o." When describing a man, the adjective ends with an o: *él es tonto* (he is a fool). When describing a woman, it ends with an a: *ella es tonta* (she is a fool).

Phrasebook

See the inside back cover for a quick, condensed list of useful phrases.

English	Spanish	English	Spanish
THE BARE MINIMUM			
Church	Iglesia	**I would like...**	Quisiera.../Me gustaría
Closed	Cerrado	**In Spanish, how do you say...?**	¿Cómo se dice... en español?

English	Spanish	English	Spanish
Could you speak more slowly, please?	¿Podría hablar más despacio, por favor?	Man	Hombre
Could you tell me...?	¿Podría decirme...?	Mr./Mrs./Miss	Señor/Señora/Señorita
Do you speak English?	¿Habla inglés?	My name is...	Me llamo...
Excuse me	Con permiso/Perdón	No	No
(Very) Expensive	(Muy) Caro	Open	Abierto
Good morning!	¡Buenos días!	Please	Por favor
Good afternoon!	¡Buenos tardes!	Thank you very much!	¡Muchas gracias!
Good evening/night!	¡Buenas noches!	What?	¿Qué?
Goodbye!	¡Adiós! or ¡Hasta luego!	What did you say?	¿Qué dijo?/¿Mande?
Hello	Hola	What is your name?	¿Como se llama? (form.)
	Bueno (phone)		¿Como te llamas? (inf.)
How are you?	¿Cómo está? (formal)	What time is it?	¿Qué hora es?
	¿Cómo estás? (informal)		
How do you say...?	¿Cómo se dice...?	When?	¿Cuándo?
I'm fine, thanks	Estoy bien, gracias	When is it open?	¿A qué horas está abierto?
I'm sorry	Lo siento/Perdón	Where is the bathroom?	¿Dónde está el baño?
I don't know	No sé	Woman	Mujer
I don't speak Spanish	No hablo español	Yes	Sí
I don't understand	No entiendo	You're welcome!	¡De nada!

CROSSING THE BORDER

Age	Edad	Customs	Aduana
Backpack	Mochila	Border	Frontera
Baggage	Equipaje	Passport	Pasaporte

GETTING AROUND

Airplane	Avión	Road	Camino
Airport	Aeropuerto	Round-trip	Ida y vuelta
Arrivals & Departures	Llegadas y salidas	Second class	Segunda clase
Avenue	Avenida	South	Sur
Bus	Autobús/Camión	Stop!	¡Alto!
Bus depot	Estación de Autobuses/ Central Camionera	Straight ahead	(Siempre) Derecho
Bus stop	Parada	Street	Calle
Caution!	¡Atención!/¡Cuidado!	Subway	Metro
Daily	Diario/diariamente	Taxi depot	Sitio
Danger!	¡Peligro!	Ticket	Boleto
Driver	Chofer	Ticket window	Taquilla
East	Este or Oriente (Ote.)	Toll	Cuota
Every half hour	Cada media hora	Train	Ferrocarril/Tren

English	Spanish	English	Spanish
Every hour	Cada hora	**West**	Oeste or Poniente (Pte.)
First class	Primera clase	**All the way to the end**	Al fondo
(To) get aboard	Subir	**Does thi s bus go to...?**	¿Se va este autobús a...?
(To) get off	Bajar	**How long does it take?**	¿Cuánto tarda?
Highway	Autopista/Carretera	**How much is a ticket to...?**	¿Cuánto cuesta un boleto a....?
Hitchhike	Pedir aventón/ Pedir ride	**I lost my baggage.**	Se me perdió mi equipaje.
Map	Mapa	**I want a ticket to...**	Quiero un boleto a...
North	Norte	**To the left/right**	A la izquierda/derecha
One-way	Ida	**What bus line goes to...?**	¿Qué linea tiene servicio a...?
(I'm going) On foot	(Me voy) A pie	**What time does the bus leave to...?**	¿A qué hora sale el camión a...?
Passenger	Pasajero	**Will you give me a ride to...?**	¿Me da un aventón a...?
Reserved seat	Asiento reservado	**Where is ... Street?**	¿Dónde está la calle...?
Reservation	Reservación	**Where is the road to...?**	¿Dónde está el camino a...?
Train station	Estación de ferrocarril/ Estación de trenes		

ACCOMMODATIONS

Air conditioning	Aire acondicionado	**Manager**	Gerente
Bath or Bathroom	Baño/Servicio/W.C.	**Motel**	Motel
Bed/Double bed	Cama/Cama matrimonial	**Pillow**	Almohada
Blanket	Cobija	**Private Bathroom**	Baño privado
Boarding house/ Guest house	Casa de huéspedes	**Room**	Cuarto/Recámara/ Habitación
Cold/Hot water	Agua fría/caliente	**Sheets**	Sábanas
Dining room	Comedor	**Shower**	Regadera/Ducha
Fan	Ventilador/Abanica	**Swimming pool**	Alberga/Piscina
Hotel	Hotel	**Do you have a room for two people?**	¿Tiene un cuarto para dos personas?
Inn	Posada	**Do you have any rooms available?**	¿Tiene cuartos libres?
Key	Llave	**Do you know of a cheap hotel...?**	¿Sabe de algún hotel barato?

EATING AND DRINKING

Apple	Manzana	**Meal**	Comida
Beer	Cerveza/Chela/Cheve	**Meat**	Carne
Bakery	Panadería	**Menu**	Menú/Carta
Bottle	Botella	**Milk**	Leche
Bread/Sweet bread	Pan/Pan dulce	**Napkin**	Servilleta

English	Spanish	English	Spanish
Breakfast	Desayuno	**Orange**	Naranja
Coffee	Café	**Purified water**	Agua purificada
Dessert	Postre	**Rice**	Arroz
Dinner	Cena	**Salt**	Sal
Drink	Bebida	**Seltzer Water**	Agua mineral (con gas)
Eggs	Huevos	**Snack**	Antojito/Botana
Fixed menu	Comida corrida	**Soda**	Refresco
Fish	Pescado	**Spoon**	Cuchara
French fries	Papas Fritas	**Spring Water**	Agua mineral (sin gas)
Fork	Tenedor	**Steak**	Bistec
Glass	Vaso	**Strawberry**	Fresa
Ice cream	Helado	**Supermarket**	Supermercado
Juice	Jugo	**Tea**	Té
Knife	Cuchillo	**Vegetarian**	Vegetariano
Lime	Limón	**Wine**	Vino
Liquor	Licor	**I am hungry**	Tengo hambre
Lunch	Almuerzo/Comida	**Check, please**	La cuenta, por favor

BANK, POST OFFICE, AND TELEPHONE

Address	Dirección	**Money**	Dinero
Air mail	Correo aereo/Por avión	**Number**	Número
Bank	Banco	**Operator**	Operador
A call	Una llamada	**Package**	Paquete
To call	Llamar	**Postcard**	Postal/Tarjeta postal
To cash	Cambiar	**Post office**	Correo/ Oficina de correos
Certified	Certificado	**Signature**	Firma
Change	Cambio	**Stamp**	Estampilla
Check	Cheque	**Telephone**	Teléfono
Collect	Por cobrar/ Cobro revertido	**Traveler's check**	Cheque de viajero
Dollar	Dólar	**Weight**	Peso
Envelope	Sobre	**Do you accept traveler's checks?**	¿Acepta cheques de viajero?
Letter	Carta	**I would like to make a call to the U.S....**	Quiero llamar a los Estados Unidos...
Long distance	Larga distancia	**The number is...**	El número es...

HEALTH AND MEDICINE

Allergy	Alergia	**It itches**	Me pica
Antibiotic	Antibiótico	**Medicine**	Medicina
Aspirin	Aspirina	**Pain**	Dolor
Bandage	Venda	**Pill**	Pastilla
Birth control pills	Anticonceptivos	**Prescription**	Receta
Blood	Sangre	**Shot**	Inyección

APPENDIX

English	Spanish	English	Spanish
Burn	Quemadura/Quemada	**Sick**	Enfermo/Enferma
Condom	Condón/Preservativo	**Stomachache**	Dolor de estómago
Cough	Tos	**Sunburn**	Quemadura de sol
Dentist	Dentista	**Toothache**	Dolor de muelas
Doctor	Doctor/Médico	**I need aspirin, please.**	Necesito aspirina, por favor.
Drugstore	Farmacia	**Where is there a doctor?**	¿Dónde hay un médico?
Fever	Fiebre	**I am sick.**	Estoy enfermo(a)
Flu	Gripe	**I have a stomachache/ headache**	Me duele el estómago/ la cabeza
Hospital	Hospital	**I have a cough/a cold**	Tengo tos/gripe
Headache	Dolor de cabeza	**Help!**	¡Ayuda! or ¡Socorro!

DAYS AND NUMBERS

Sunday	Domingo	**Today**	Hoy
Monday	Lunes	**Tomorrow**	Mañana
Tuesday	Martes	**Day after tomorrow**	Pasado mañana
Wednesday	Miércoles	**Yesterday**	Ayer
Thursday	Jueves	**Day before yesterday**	Antes de ayer/Anteayer
Friday	Viernes	**Week**	Semana
Saturday	Sábado	**Weekend**	Fin de semana
0	cero	**21**	veintiuno
1	uno	**22**	veintidos
2	dos	**30**	treinta
3	tres	**40**	cuarenta
4	cuatro	**50**	cincuenta
5	cinco	**60**	sesenta
6	seis	**70**	setenta
7	siete	**80**	ochenta
8	ocho	**90**	noventa
9	nueve	**100**	cien
10	diez	**101**	ciento uno
11	once	**200**	doscientos
12	doce	**300**	trescientos
13	trece	**400**	cuatrocientos
14	catorce	**500**	quinientos
15	quince	**600**	seiscientos
16	dieciseis	**700**	setecientos
17	diecisiete	**800**	ochocientos
18	dieciocho	**900**	novecientos
19	diecinueve	**1000**	mil
20	veinte	**1 million**	un millón

Glossary of Terms

agua (purificada): water (purified)
ajo: garlic
amigo: friend
andador: pedestrian walkway
antiguo: old
antojitos: appetizers
arroz: rice
artesanía: artisanry
avenida: avenue
bahía: bay
balneario: spa; bathing place
bandidos: bandits
baños: bathrooms
barra libre: open bar
barrancas: canyons
batido: milkshake
basílica: basilica (type of church)
bodega: winery
botanas: appetizers
buena suerte: good luck
buen provecho: bon appetit
calle: street
callejón: little street; alley
cascadas: waterfalls
cama: bed
camarones: shrimp
camión: bus
campesino: farmer
cantina: saloon-type bar (mostly-male clientele)
capilla: chapel
casa: house
casa de cambio: currency exchange booth
caseta: phone stall
castillo: castle
catedral: cathedral
cenote: freshwater sinkhole
centro: center (of town)
cerro: hill
cerveza: beer
ciudad: city
colectivo: shared taxi
colonia: neighborhood
combi: small local bus
comida: food
comida corrida: fixed menu
consulado: consulate
correo: post office
costa: coast
crucero: crossroads
cuarto: room
cuevas: caves
cucaracha: cockroach
de paso: bus that picks up passengers by roadsides
diablo: devil
dinero: money
Dios: God
dulces: sweets
embarcadero: dock
extranjero: foreigner
farmacia: pharmacy
faro: lighthouse
fiesta: party; holiday
fonda: inn
frijoles: beans
frutas: fruits
fútbol: soccer
gabacho: gringo, whitey
glorieta: traffic circle
gobierno: government
gratis: free
gringo: whitey
grutas: caves
güera: blond
iglesia: church
indígena: indigenous person
isla: island
jardín: garden
lago: lake
laguna: lagoon
lancha: a launch (boat)
lavandería: laundromat
libre: free
licuado: milkshake
limosna: alms
lonchería: li'l lunch place
maquiladora: a large, foreign-owned factory
malecón: promenade
mar: ocean; sea
mariscos: seafood
menú del día: pre-set meal
mercado: market (often outdoor)
microbús: minibus
mirador: viewpoint
monte: mountain/peak
mucho/muy: a lot
museo: museum
norte (Nte.): north
nuevo: new
oriente (Ote.): east
palacio: palace
palapa: palm-thatched beach bungalow
panadería: bread shop
parque: park
paseo: promenade
pescado: fish
pesero: local bus
pico: peak
pirámides: pyramids
plátano: banana
playa: beach
pollo: chicken
poniente (Pte.): west
posada: inn
postre: sweet; dessert
poza: well; pool
primera clase: first-class
pueblo: village; community
queso: cheese
refrescos: refreshments
río: river
ruinas: ruins
sacbe (Mayan): upraised, paved road
sacerdote: priest
sala: waiting room
salida: exit
salúd: health
sarape: woven, colored shawl
segunda clase: second-class
selva: jungle
servicio de lujo: luxury service
simpático: friendly/nice
sol: sun
sopa: soup
stela: upright stone monument
supermercado: supermarket
sur: south
taquería: li'l taco stand
tejano: Texan
telenovela: soap opera
templo: church; temple
tienda: store
típico: typical, traditional
torta: sandwich
turismo: tourism
turista: tourist; diarrhea
tranquilo: peaceful
vaquero: cowboy
valle: valley
zócalo: central square
zona: zone; region

Distances (km) and Travel Times (by Bus)

	Acapulco	Chihuahua	Cancún	El Paso	Guadalajara	La Paz	Mazatlán	Mérida	Mexico City	Monterrey	Oaxaca	Puebla	San Cristóbal	San Luis P.	Tijuana	Veracruz
Acapulco		2440	1938	2815	1028	4917	1429	1779	415	1402	700	544	1036	828	3228	847
Chihuahua	24hr.		3262	375	1552	3237	1031	2945	1496	834	2154	1625	2785	1195	1548	1841
Cancún	33hr.	47hr.		3637	2442	6499	2963	319	1766	2506	1693	1895	902	2267	4810	1421
El Paso	29hr.	5hr.	54hr.		1549	3009	1406	3320	1871	1209	2529	2000	3127	1569	1320	2216
Guadalajara	15hr.	17hr.	45hr.	25hr.		4159	521	2125	676	885	1222	805	1853	348	2340	1021
La Paz	60hr.	46hr.	96hr.	41hr.	60hr.		3508	6180	4733	4071	5279	4862	5883	4283	1689	5050
Mazatlán	21hr.	15½hr.	53hr.	25hr.	8hr.	50hr.		2646	1197	940	1743	1326	2374	799	1819	1542
Mérida	29hr.	42hr.	4hr.	47hr.	40½hr.	92hr.	40hr.		1449	2189	1374	1791	743	799	4491	1104
Mexico City	6hr.	20hr.	26hr.	25hr.	10hr.	68hr.	18hr.	22hr..		950	546	129	1177	413	3044	345
Monterrey	18hr.	12hr.	38hr.	17hr.	11hr.	60hr.	17hr.	32hr.	12hr.		1533	1116	1918	537	2382	1085
Oaxaca	9hr.	29hr.	29hr.	34hr.	17hr.	77hr.	27hr.	24½hr.	9hr.	21hr.		417	631	959	3590	450
Puebla	7hr.	22hr.	24hr.	27hr.	12hr.	71hr.	20hr.	20hr.	2hr.	14hr.	4hr.		1048	542	3285	303
San Cristóbal	16hr.	39hr.	17hr.	44hr.	28hr.	88hr.	19hr.	12½hr.	18hr.	30hr.	12hr.	16hr.		1590	4193	833
San Luis P.	10hr.	14hr.	31hr.	18hr.	6hr.	60hr.	12hr.	27hr.	5hr.	7hr.	20hr.	16hr.	23hr.		2743	846
Tijuana	46hr.	22hr.	72hr.	17hr.	36hr.	24hr.	26hr.	66hr.	44hr.	36hr.	53hr.	46hr.	62hr.	36hr.		3361
Veracruz	13hr.	28hr.	21hr.	33hr.	17hr.	76hr.	26hr.	13hr.	8hr.	17hr.	8hr.	4½hr.	13hr.	13hr.	52hr.	

Index

INDEX

INDEX

D

M

INDEX

INDEX

Researcher-Writers

Jennifer Gootman *Central and Southern Pacific Coasts, Central Mexico*
Jenny had a blast. Our ultra-friendly R-W chatted with everyone from club owners to expats to bus drivers—she met anyone and everyone. Jenny flashed her disarming smile all along the Pacific coast and gained a tremendous amount of cultural savvy. From Cuernavaca to Acapulco, Jenny wrote and wrote well, expanding our nightlife coverage to gargantuan proportions. Unperturbed by the scores of men who fawned over her, Jenny managed to score a free Sunday on a yacht and a free Snickers bar from a famous Mexican *telenovela* hunk. Mexico loved Jenny. No wonder.

Art "Arturo" Koski-Karell *Yucatán Peninsula, Chiapas*
Arturo worked his butt off, and we can't thank him enough for it. His lightweight crew thighs carried him from tourist office to tourist office, where he charmed female employees into giving him more information than we could ever need. This archaeology buff's research was unbelievably thorough, and his masterful marginalia included everything from a brilliant journalistic investigation of the current Chiapas situation to Paul Simon lyrics. Arturo's love of and respect for Mexico shone through in his copy—his new coverage of Yaxchilán and Bonampak left us begging for more.

Maya Sen *Oaxaca, Central Mexico, Veracruz, Tabasco*
Who knew that a small town in Central Mexico without phone service could have three Internet cafes? Maya not only had time to find them all...she also sent us adventure-packed emails from each one. Maya's jam-packed itinerary kept her hard at work, but she still found time to do exhaustive write-ups of the sights in Veracruz state and add stellar new coverage of San Lorenzo. Fighting illness at the end of her trip, Maya kept going and going and...you get the picture. Even bad weather and waiters with amorous intentions couldn't stop Ms. Sen. Thanks for the comics, Maya.

Jim Stewart *Northwest Mexico, Guadalajara, Michoacán de Campo*
Despite a grueling itinerary that took him thousands of miles, from El Paso, Texas to Central Mexico, Jim found time to make us laugh. Jimmy Stewart had no trouble adjusting to Mexico—he blew through the harsh *noroeste* desert, communed with Mennonites, and even found time to don a tuxedo and dance 'til dawn at a Mexican wedding. Jim's sense of humor earned him a from us—his write-up of "alternative accommodations" had us rolling on the floor. Jim would definitely not like to thank the Zacatecan men in black.

Keja Lys Valens *Northeast Mexico, Northern Veracruz, Mexico City*
When we grow up, we want to be just like Keja. Her research was impeccable, and she managed to infuse her love of Mexican culture and literature with her funny, beautifully written and organized copy. Her knack for finding new budget gems still left her with enough time time to reflect on her fascination with Barefoot Carmelite nuns. Only the perenially smiling Keja could do justice to the biggest city in the world—her exhaustive coverage of Mexico City put that of last year's R-W to shame. Keja would like to thank Blanca Alcaraz for making Mexico romantic.

Paul Torres *Northwest Mexico, Baja California*
Cruising down Route 1 in a little white rented Chevy, laid-back Paul breezed through Baja. In his own words, it was a "long, great, bizarre, and refreshing trip." Equally refreshing was Paul's bionic handwriting and his wide-eyed appreciation of Baja. Paul gazed upon pristine landscapes fit only for the gods—from the secluded beaches of Bahía de la Concepcíon to the desert oasis of San Ignacio—and lived to write about it. Straight outta Jersey, Paul brought sensitivity to his coverage, and his calm, relaxed attitude managed to infect even his stressed-out editors—thousands of miles away.

Acknowledgments

All the thanks in the world to our incredibly hardcore RW's and to the salsa room.

Many thanks to: my AEs—the amazing Anne, who will never be fired, and Lara, for details and gettin' things done; the salsa room for music and madness; my office-mates and roomies (John, Ethan, and Saadi), for putting up with me; Bob and Pants, for support; "home slice" Christian, partner in crime; A & J Branch for a happy home and good times; Carrie, my BFF; Erin, *mi mucha mujer,* for everything; Vern, Adam S., the Artist, disco, the Mach 3, the broken server, and anyone or anything I forgot. Special thanks to my family: Mom, Dad, Soman, and Sanjeev—I love you all so much. This book is for my grandparents: Grandma, Grandpa, and Dada in Bombay.—**SLC**

Much grooviness to: Sonesh, who got me to kick back and learn to love this amazing country; Lara for being an amazing co-*unión* member; the salsa room for a wicked good time and the Immaculate Collection; Kristy, whose groovy phone calls and letters kept me sane; my amazing roommate Sarah for tolerating my crazy hours; Allison and Tracy for looking out for me; Matthew for being an incredibly groovy friend; Larissa for being my kindred spirit; Peggy for being an endlessly supportive friend and sister; Susan, who's always been better to me than I deserve; Mom for the emails, love, and support; and Daddy for being the cutest twerd around.—**ACK**

My thanks to: all my grandparents (Sid in my heart); Mom, Dad, Danny; Jennifer, Trisha, Franklin, Shaheen, Jana, Alex B; Alex (cuz), Hayden, Jenny, Meredith, Emily, Catie, Gen, Becky (both), Ann, Lisa, Kellin, Misasha; Esti (associate, twin sis, friend!) & teams Ecuador and Mexico (Anne and Sonesh *especially*); and the beloved salsa room (y'all rock my world). Read LG Ecuador to see your names in print again. —**JLF**

Editor	Sonesh S. Chainani
Associate Editor	Anne C. Krendl
Associate Editor	J. Lara Fox
Managing Editor	M. Allison Arwady
Publishing Director	Caroline R. Sherman
Publishing Director	Anna C. Portnoy
Production Manager	Dan Visel
Associate Production Manager	Maryanthe Elizabeth Malliaris
Cartography Manager	Derek McKee
Design Manager	Bentsion Harder
Editorial Manager	M. Allison Arwady
Editorial Manager	Lisa M. Nosal
Financial Manager	Monica Eileen Eav
Personnel Manager	Nicolas R. Rapold
Publicity Manager	Alexander Z. Speier
New Media Manager	Måns O. Larsson
Map Editors	Matthew R. Daniels, Dan Luskin
Production Associate	Heath Ritchie
Office Coordinators	Tom Moore, Eliza Harrington, Jodie Kirschner
Director of Advertising Sales	Gene Plotkin
Associate Sales Executives	Colleen Gaard, Mateo Jaramillo, Alexandra Price
President	Catherine J. Turco
General Manager	Richard Olken
Assistant General Manager	Anne E. Chisholm

Thanks to Our Readers...

Mano Aaron, CA; **Jean-Marc Abela,** CAN; **George Adams,** NH; **Bob & Susan Adams,** GA; **Deborah Adeyanju,** NY; **Rita Alexander,** MI; **Shani Amory-Claxton,** NY; **Kate Anderson,** AUS; **Lindsey Anderson,** ENG; **Viki Anderson,** NY; **Ray Andrews,** JPN; **Robin J. Andrus,** NJ; **L. Asurmendi,** CA; **Anthony Atkinson,** ENG; **Deborah Bacek,** GA; **Jeffrey Bagdade,** MI; **Mark Baker,** UK; **Mary Baker,** TN; **Jeff Barkoff,** PA; **Regina Barsanti,** NY; **Ethan Beeler,** MA; **Damao Bell,** CA; **Rya Ben-Shir,** IL; **Susan Bennerstrom,** WA; **Marla Benton,** CAN; **Matthew Berenson,** OR; **Walter Bergstrom,** OR; **Caryl Bird,** ENG; **Charlotte Blanc,** NY; **Jeremy Boley,** EL SAL; **Oliver Bradley,** GER; **A.Braurstein,** CO; **Philip R. Brazil,** WA; **Henrik Brockdorff,** DMK; **Tony Bronco,** NJ; **Eileen Brouillard,** SC; **Mary Brown,** ENG; **Tom Brown,** CA; **Elizabeth Buckius,** CO; **Sue Buckley,** UK; **Christine Burer,** SWITZ; **Norman Butler,** MO; **Brett Carroll,** WA; **Susan Caswell,** ISR; **Carlos Cersosimo,** ITA; **Barbara Crary Chase,** WA; **Stella Cherry Carbost,** SCOT; **Oi Ling Cheung,** HK; **Simon Chinn,** ENG; **Charles Cho,** AUS; **Carolyn R. Christie,** AUS; **Emma Church,** ENG; **Kelley Coblentz,** IN; **Cathy Cohan,** PA; **Phyllis Cole,** TX; **Karina Collins,** SWITZ; **Michael Cox,** CA; **Mike Craig,** MD; **Rene Crusto,** LA; **Claudine D'Anjou,** CAN; **Lizz Daniels,** CAN; **Simon Davies,** SCOT; **Samantha Davis,** AUS; **Leah Davis,** TX; **Stephanie Dickman,** MN; **Philipp Dittrich,**GER; **Tim Donovan,** NH; **Reed Drew,** OR; **Wendy Duncan,** SCOT; **Melissa Dunlap,** VA; **P.A. Emery,** UK; **GCL Emery,** SAF; **Louise Evans,** AUS; **Christine Farr,** AUS; **David Fattel,** NJ; **Vivian Feen,** MD; **David Ferraro,** SPN; **Sue Ferrick,** CO; **Philip Fielden,** UK; **Nancy Fintel,** FL; **Jody Finver,** FL; **D. Ross Fisher,** CAN; **Abigail Flack,** IL; **Elizabeth Foster,** NY; **Bonnie Fritz,** CAN; **J. Fuson,** OR; **Michael K. Gasuad,** NV; **Raad German,** TX; **Mark Gilbert,** NY; **Betsy Gilliland,** CA; **Ana Goshko,** NY; **Patrick Goyenneche,** CAN; **David Greene,** NY; **Jennifer Griffin,** ENG; **Janet & Jeremy Griffith,** ENG; **Nanci Guartofierro,** NY; **Denise Guillemette,** MA; **Ilona Haayer,** HON; **Joseph Habboushe,** PA; **John Haddon,** CA; **Ladislav Hanka,** MI; **Michael Hanke,** CA; **Avital Harari,** TX; **Channing Hardy,** KY; **Patrick Harris,** CA; **Denise Hasher,** PA; **Jackie Hattori,** UK; **Guthrie Hebenstreit,** ROM; **Therase Hill,** AUS; **Denise Hines,** NJ; **Cheryl Horne,** ENG; **Julie Howell,** IL; **Naomi Hsu,** NJ; **Mark Hudgkinson,** ENG; **Brenda Humphrey,** NC; **Kelly Hunt,** NY; **Daman Irby,** AUT; **Bill Irwin,** NY; **Andrea B. Jackson,** PA; **John Jacobsen,** FL; **Pat Johanson,** MD; **Russell Jones,** FL; **J. Jones,** AUS; **Sharon Jones,** MI; **Craig Jones,** CA; **Wayne Jones,** ENG; **Jamie Kagan,** NJ; **Mirko Kaiser,** GER; **Scott Kauffman,** NY; **John Keanie,** NIRE; **Barbara Keary,** FL; **Jamie Kehoe,** AUS; **Alistair Kernick,** SAF; **Daihi Kielle,** SWITZ; **John Knutsen,** CA; **Rebecca Koepke,** NY; **Jeannine Kolb,** ME; **Elze Kollen,** NETH; **Lorne Korman,** CAN; **Robin Kortright,** CAN; **Isel Krinsky,** CAN; **George Landers,** ENG; **Jodie Lanthois,** AUS; **Roger Latzgo,** PA; **A. Lavery,** AZ; **Joan Lea,** ENG; **Lorraine Lee,** NY; **Phoebe Leed,** MA; **Tammy Leeper,** CA; **Paul Lejeune,** ENG; **Yee-Leng Leong,** CA; **Sam Levene,** CAN; **Robin Levin,** PA; **Christianna Lewis,** PA; **Ernesto Licata,** ITA; **Wolfgang Lischtansky,** AUT; **Michelle Little,** CAN; **Dee Littrell,** CA; **Maria Lobosco,** UK; **Netii Ross,** ITA; **Didier Look,** CAN; **Alice Lorenzotti,** MA; **David Love,** PA; **Briege Mac Donagh,** IRE; **Brooke Madigan,** NY; **Helen Maltby,** FL; **Shyama Marchesi,** ITA; **Domenico Maria,** ITA; **Natasha Markovic,** AUS; **Edward Marshall,** ECU; **Rachel Marshall,** TX; **Kate Maynard,** UK; **Agnes McCann,** IRE; **Susan McGowan,** NY; **Brandi McGunigal,** CAN; **Neville McLean,** NZ; **Marty McLendon,** MS; **Matthew Melko,** OH; **Barry Mendelson,** CA; **Eric Middendorf,** OH; **Nancy Mike,** AZ; **Coren Milbury,** NH; **Margaret Mill,** NY; **David H. Miller,** TX; **Ralph Miller,** NV; **Susan Miller,** CO; **Larry Moeller,** MI; **Richard Moore,** ENG; **Anne & Andrea Mosher,** MA; **J. L. Mourne,** TX; **Athanassios Moustakas,** GER; **Laurel Naversen,** ENG; **Suzanne Neil,** IA; **Deborah Nickles,** PA; **Pieter & Agnes Noels,** BEL; **Werner Norr,** GER; **Ruth J. Nye,** ENG; **Heidi O'Brien,** WA; **Sherry O'Cain,** SC; **Aibhan O'Connor,** IRE; **Kevin O'Connor,** CA; **Margaret O'Rielly,** IRE; **Daniel O'Rourke,** CA; **Krissy Oechslin,** OH; **Johan Oelofse,** SAF; **Quinn Okamoto,** CA; **Juan Ramon Olaizola,** SPN; **Laura Onorato,** NM; **Bill Orkin,** IL; **K. Owusu-Agyenang,** UK; **Anne Paananen,** SWD; **Jenine Padget,** AUS; **Frank Pado,** TX; **G. Pajkich,** Washington, DC; **J. Parker,** CA; **Marian Parnat,** AUS; **Sandra Swift Parrino,** NY; **Iris Patten,** NY; **M. Pavini,** CT; **David Pawielski,** MN; **Jenny Pawson,** ENG; **Colin Peak,** AUS; **Marius Penderis,** ENG; **Jo-an Peters,** AZ; **Barbara Phillips,** NY; **Romain Picard**, Washington, DC; **Pati Pike,** ENG; **Mark Pollock,** SWITZ; **Minnie Adele Potter,** FL; **Martin Potter,** ENG; **Claudia Praetel,** ENG; **Bill Press,** Washington, DC; **David Prince,** NC; **Andrea Pronko,** OH; **C. Robert Pryor,** OH; **Phu Quy,** VTNM; **Adrian Rainbow,** ENG; **John Raven,** AUS; **Lynn Reddringer,** VA; **John Rennie,** NZ; **Ruth B.Robinson,** FL; **John & Adelaida Romagnoli,** CA; **Eva Romano,** FRA; **Mark A. Roscoe,** NETH; **Yolanda & Jason Ross,** CAN; **Sharee Rowe,** ENG; **W. Suzanne Rowell,** NY; **Vic Roych,** AZ; **John Russell,** ENG; **Jennifer Ruth,** OK; **William Sabino,** NJ; **Hideki Saito,** JPN; **Frank Schaer,** HUN; **Jeff Schultz,** WI; **Floretta Seeland-Connally,** IL; **Colette Shoulders,** FRA; **Shireen Sills,** ITA; **Virginia Simon,** AUS; **Beth Simon,** NY; **Gary Simpson,** AUS; **Barbara & Allen Sisarsky,** GA; **Alon Siton,** ISR; **Kathy Skeie,** CA; **Robyn Skillecorn,** AUS; **Erik & Kathy Skon,** MN; **Stine Skorpen,** NOR; **Philip Smart,** CAN; **Colin Smit,** ENG; **Kenneth Smith,** DE; **Caleb Smith,** CA; **Geoffrey Smith,** TX; **John Snyder,** NC; **Kathrin Speidel,** GER; **Lani Steele,** PHIL; **Julie Stelbracht,** PA; **Margaret Stires,** TN; **Donald Stumpf,** NY; **Samuel Suffern,** TN; **Michael Swerdlow,** ENG; **Brian Talley,** TX; **Serene-Marie Terrell,** NY; **B. Larry Thilson,** CAN; **J. Pelham Thomas,** NC; **Wright Thompson,** ITA; **Christine Timm,** NY; **Melinda Tong,** HK; **M. Tritica,** AUS; **Melanie Tritz,** CAN; **Mark Trop,** FL; **Chris Troxel,** AZ; **Rozana Tsiknaki,** GRC; **Lois Turner,** NZ; **Nicole Virgil,** IL; **Blondie Vucich,** CO; **Wendy Wan,** SAF; **Carrie & Simon Wedgwood,** ENG; **Frederick Weibgen,** NJ; **Richard Weil,** MN; **Alan Weissberg,** OH; **Ryan Wells,** OH; **Jill Wester,** GER; **Clinton White,** AL; **Gael White,** CAN; **Melanie Whitfield,** SCOT; **Bryn Williams,** CAN; **Amanda Williams,** CAN; **Wendy Willis,** CAN; **Sasha Wilson,** NY; **Kendra Wilson,** CA; **Olivia Wiseman,** ENG; **Gerry Wood,** CAN; **Kelly Wooten,** ENG; **Robert Worsley,** ENG; **C.A.Wright,** ENG; **Caroline Wright,** ENG; **Mary H. Yuhasz,** CO; **Margaret Zimmerman,** WA.

★Let's Go 1999 Reader Questionnaire★

Please fill this out and return it to **Let's Go, St. Martin's Press,** 175 Fifth Ave., New York, NY 10010-7848. All respondents will receive a free subscription to ***The Yellowjacket***, the Let's Go Newsletter. You can find a more extensive version of this survey on the web at http://www.letsgo.com.

Name: ______________________________

Address: ______________________________

City: __________________ **State:** _____ **Zip/Postal Code:** ________

Email: __________________ **Which book(s) did you use?** ____________

How old are you? under 19 19-24 25-34 35-44 45-54 55 or over

Are you (circle one) in high school in college in graduate school employed retired between jobs

Have you used Let's Go before? yes no **Would you use it again?** yes no

How did you first hear about Let's Go? friend store clerk television bookstore display advertisement/promotion review other

Why did you choose Let's Go (circle up to two)? reputation budget focus price writing style annual updating other: ____________

Which other guides have you used, if any? Fodor's Footprint Handbooks Frommer's $-a-day Lonely Planet Moon Guides Rick Steve's Rough Guides UpClose other: ______________

Which guide do you prefer? ______________________________

Please rank each of the following parts of Let's Go 1 to 5 (1=needs improvement, 5=perfect). packaging/cover practical information accommodations food cultural introduction sights practical introduction ("Essentials") directions entertainment gay/lesbian information maps other: ____________

How would you like to see the books improved? (continue on separate page, if necessary) ______________________________

____

How long was your trip? one week two weeks three weeks one month two months or more

Which countries did you visit? ______________________________

What was your average daily budget, not including flights? ____________

Have you traveled extensively before? yes no

Do you buy a separate map when you visit a foreign city? yes no

Have you used a Let's Go Map Guide? yes no

If you have, would you recommend them to others? yes no

Have you visited Let's Go's website? yes no

What would you like to see included on Let's Go's website? ____________

____

What percentage of your trip planning did you do on the Web? __________

Would you use a Let's Go: recreational (e.g. skiing) guide gay/lesbian guide adventure/trekking guide phrasebook general travel information guide

Which of the following destinations do you hope to visit in the next three to five years (circle one)? Canada Argentina Perú Kenya Middle East Caribbean Scandinavia other: ______________

Where did you buy your guidebook? Internet independent bookstore chain bookstore college bookstore travel store other: ________

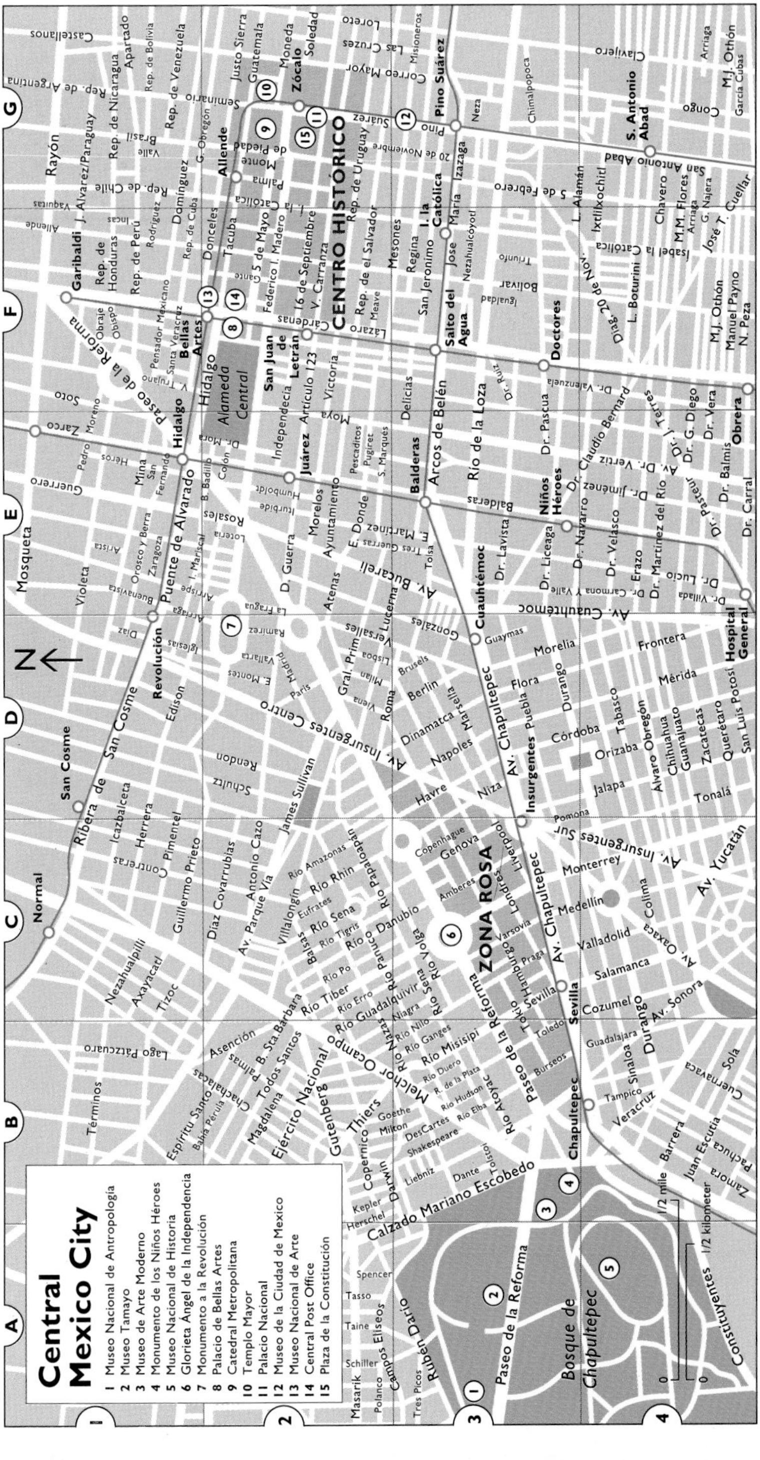
Central Mexico City
1 Museo Nacional de Antropología
2 Museo Tamayo
3 Museo de Arte Moderno
4 Monumento de los Niños Héroes
5 Museo Nacional de Historia
6 Glorieta Ángel de la Independencia
7 Monumento a la Revolución
8 Palacio de Bellas Artes
9 Catedral Metropolitana
10 Templo Mayor
11 Palacio Nacional
12 Museo de la Ciudad de Mexico
13 Museo Nacional de Arte
14 Central Post Office
15 Plaza de la Constitución
A
B
C
D
E
F
G
1
2
3
4
N
0
1/2 mile
0
1/2 kilometer
CENTRO HISTÓRICO
ZONA ROSA
Bosque de Chapultepec
Alameda Central
Zócalo
Paseo de la Reforma
Av. Insurgentes Centro
Av. Insurgentes Sur
Av. Chapultepec
Av. Cuauhtémoc
Av. Bucareli
Puente de Alvarado
Ribera de San Cosme
Arcos de Belén
Calzado Mariano Escobedo
Melchor Ocampo
Ejército Nacional
Av. Yucatán
Av. Oaxaca
Av. Sonora
Normal
San Cosme
Revolución
Hidalgo
Bellas Artes
Allende
Pino Suárez
I. la Católica
Salto del Agua
Doctores
Niños Héroes
Balderas
Juárez
San Juan de Letrán
Cuauhtémoc
Hospital General
Obrera
S. Antonio Abad
Insurgentes
Sevilla
Chapultepec
Garibaldi

Mexico City Metro

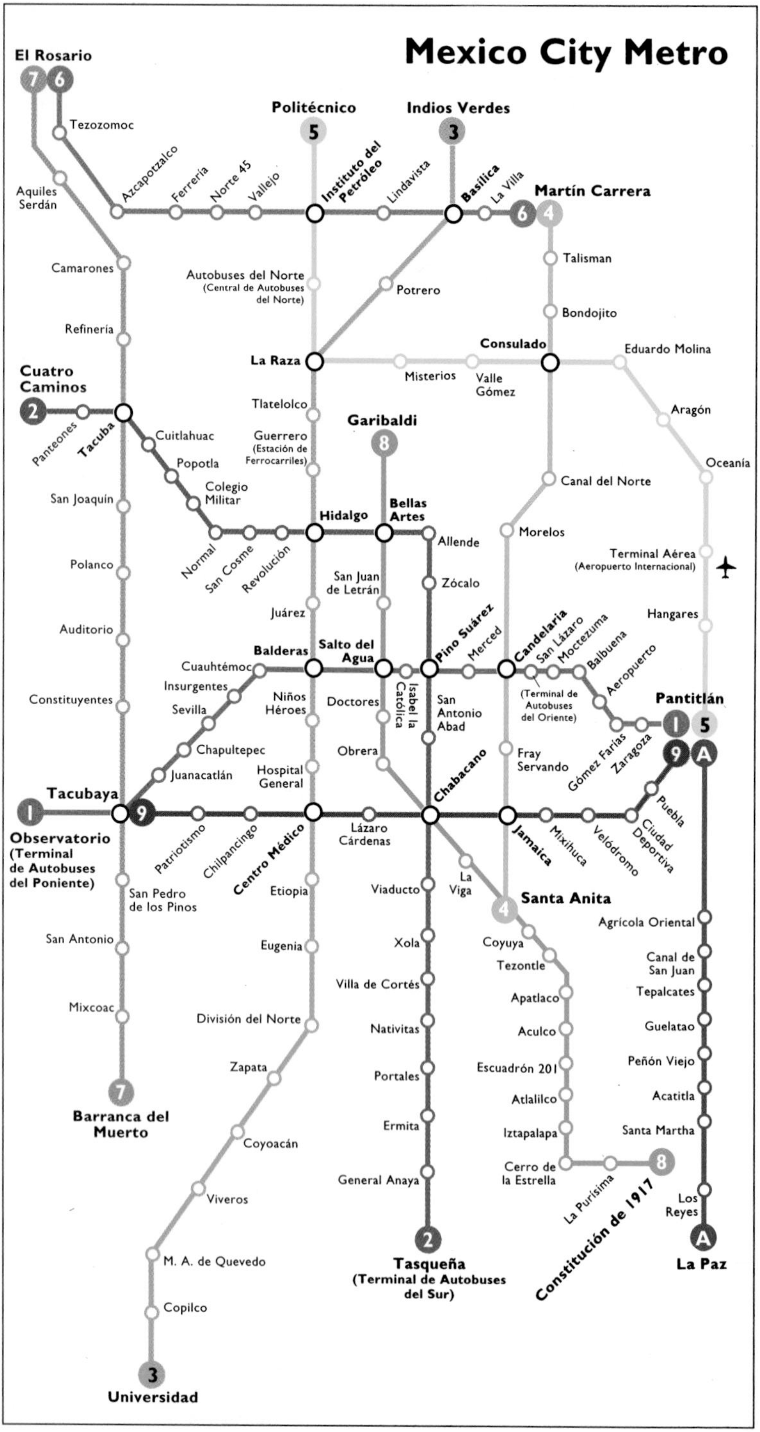
Mexico City Metro
El Rosario
Tezozomoc
Azcapotzalco
Ferrería
Norte 45
Vallejo
Politécnico
Instituto del Petróleo
Lindavista
Indios Verdes
Basílica
La Villa
Martín Carrera
Aquiles Serdán
Camarones
Autobuses del Norte
(Central de Autobuses del Norte)
Potrero
Talisman
Bondojito
Refinería
La Raza
Misterios
Valle Gómez
Consulado
Eduardo Molina
Aragón
Cuatro Caminos
Panteones
Tacuba
Cuitlahuac
Popotla
Colegio Militar
Tlatelolco
Guerrero
(Estación de Ferrocarriles)
Garibaldi
Oceanía
Canal del Norte
San Joaquín
Normal
San Cosme
Revolución
Hidalgo
Bellas Artes
Allende
Morelos
Terminal Aérea
(Aeropuerto Internacional)
Polanco
San Juan de Letrán
Zócalo
Juárez
Hangares
Auditorio
Cuauhtémoc
Balderas
Salto del Agua
Isabel la Católica
Pino Suárez
Merced
Candelaria
San Lázaro
Moctezuma
Balbuena
Aeropuerto
(Terminal de Autobuses del Oriente)
Pantitlán
Insurgentes
Sevilla
Niños Héroes
Doctores
San Antonio Abad
Constituyentes
Chapultepec
Juanacatlán
Hospital General
Obrera
Fray Servando
Gómez Farías
Zaragoza
Tacubaya
Observatorio
(Terminal de Autobuses del Poniente)
Patriotismo
Chilpancingo
Centro Médico
Lázaro Cárdenas
Chabacano
Jamaica
Mixihuca
Velódromo
Ciudad Deportiva
Puebla
San Pedro de los Pinos
Etiopia
Viaducto
La Viga
Santa Anita
Agrícola Oriental
San Antonio
Eugenia
Xola
Coyuya
Tezontle
Canal de San Juan
Tepalcates
Villa de Cortés
Apatlaco
Mixcoac
División del Norte
Nativitas
Aculco
Guelatao
Peñón Viejo
Zapata
Portales
Escuadrón 201
Atlalilco
Acatitla
Barranca del Muerto
Ermita
Iztapalapa
Santa Martha
Coyoacán
General Anaya
Cerro de la Estrella
La Purísima
Viveros
Los Reyes
Constitución de 1917
M. A. de Quevedo
Tasqueña
(Terminal de Autobuses del Sur)
La Paz
Copilco
Universidad